THE ROMAN MISSAL

RENEWED BY DECREE OF
THE MOST HOLY SECOND ECUMENICAL COUNCIL OF THE VATICAN,
PROMULGATED BY AUTHORITY OF POPE PAUL VI
AND REVISED AT THE DIRECTION OF POPE JOHN PAUL II

ENGLISH TRANSLATION ACCORDING
TO THE THIRD TYPICAL EDITION

For Use in the Dioceses of the United States of America

Approved by the
United States Conference of Catholic Bishops
and Confirmed by the Apostolic See

2011

Concordat cum originali:
✠ Most Reverend Gregory M. Aymond
Chairman, USCCB Committee on Divine Worship
after review by Reverend Richard B. Hilgartner
Executive Director, USCCB Secretariat of Divine Worship

Latin text © Libreria Editrice Vaticana, Vatican City State, 2008.

The English translation and chants of *The Roman Missal* © 2010 International Commission on English in the Liturgy Corporation. All rights reserved.

The English translations of the Gospel Readings for the Palm Sunday Procession, the Gospel Readings for Pentecost, the Second Reading for the First Sunday of Advent (Year A), and the First Reading for the First Sunday of Advent (Year B) are taken from the *Lectionary for Mass for Use in the Dioceses of the United States of America*, second typical edition © 2001, 1998, 1997, 1986, 1970 Confraternity of Christian Doctrine, Inc., Washington, DC. Used with permission. All rights reserved. No portion of this text may be reproduced by any means without permission in writing from the copyright owner.

The English translation of Psalms 24[23], 47[46], and 116[115] from *The Revised Grail Psalms* © 2010 Conception Abbey/The Grail, admin. by GIA Publications, Inc., www.giamusic.com. All rights reserved.

Particular adaptations and proper texts for the Dioceses of the United States of America © 2010 United States Conference of Catholic Bishops, Washington, DC. All rights reserved. No part of this work may be reproduced or transmitted in any form or by any means, electronic or mechanical, including photocopying, recording, or by any information storage and retrieval system, without permission in writing from the copyright holders.

Musical setting of the Lord's Prayer by Robert Snow, 1964.

Latin Typical Edition, 1970.
Amended Latin Typical Edition, 1971.
Second Latin Typical Edition, 1975.
Third Latin Typical Edition, 2002.
Amended Third Latin Typical Edition, 2008.

Copyright © 2011, United States Conference of Catholic Bishops, Washington, DC. All rights reserved. No part of this work may be reproduced or transmitted in any form or by any means, electronic or mechanical, including photocopying, recording, or by any information storage and retrieval system, without permission in writing from the copyright holder.

SACRED CONGREGATION FOR DIVINE WORSHIP

Prot. n. 166/70

DECREE

The Order of the Eucharistic celebration having been established, and the texts belonging to the Roman Missal having been approved by the Supreme Pontiff PAUL VI by means of the Apostolic Constitution *Missale Romanum*, dated 3 April 1969, this Sacred Congregation for Divine Worship, by mandate of the same Supreme Pontiff, now promulgates this new edition of the Roman Missal prepared in accordance with the decrees of the Second Vatican Council and declares it to be typical.

As to use of the new Roman Missal, it is permitted for the Latin edition to be put into use as soon as it is published, with the necessary adjustments concerning the celebrations of the Saints, until the revised calendar is brought definitively into effect. To the Conferences of Bishops is entrusted the responsibility for preparing editions in the vernacular and for setting the date for them to come into force, after due confirmation by the Apostolic See.

All things to the contrary notwithstanding.

From the offices of the Sacred Congregation for Divine Worship, 26 March 1970, Thursday of the Lord's Supper.

BENNO Card. GUT
Prefect

A. BUGNINI
Secretary

SACRED CONGREGATION FOR DIVINE WORSHIP

Prot. N. 1970/74

DECREE
CONCERNING THE SECOND TYPICAL EDITION

Since the *Missale Romanum* must be printed once more, variations and additions have been introduced so that this new edition may accord with documents published subsequent to the appearance of the first edition of 1970.

In the *Institutio Generalis*, whose marginal numbers are unchanged, a description of the functions of acolyte and lector has been inserted instead of those that the subdeacon used to carry out (nos. 142-152).

There is another change of some importance in the part of the Missal that contains the Ritual Masses and the Masses for Various Needs. Certain formularies have been completed by the insertion of Entrance and Communion Antiphons. In addition, texts have been added for the Ritual Mass of Dedication of a Church and Altar and for the Mass for Reconciliation and, among Votive Masses, the texts that were widely requested for the Masses of the Blessed Virgin Mary, Mother of the Church, and of the Most Holy Name of Mary.

Some other variations of lesser importance have been introduced in headings and rubrics, so that they might correspond better to the words and expressions that occur in the new liturgical books.

The Supreme Pontiff PAUL VI has approved by his authority this second edition of the *Missale Romanum* and the Sacred Congregation for Divine Worship now issues it and declares it to be typical.

It will be the responsibility of Conferences of Bishops to introduce the variations contained in this second edition of the *Missale Romanum* into editions to be prepared in the vernacular languages.

All things to the contrary notwithstanding.

From the offices of the Sacred Congregation for Divine Worship, 27 March 1975, Thursday of the Lord's Supper.

JAMES ROBERT Card. KNOX
Prefect

✠ A. BUGNINI
Titular Archbishop of Diocletiana
Secretary

CONGREGATION FOR DIVINE WORSHIP
AND DISCIPLINE OF THE SACRAMENTS

Prot. N. 143/00/L

DECREE
CONCERNING THE THIRD TYPICAL EDITION

At the outset of the third millennium after the Incarnation of the Lord, it has been decided to prepare a new edition of the *Missale Romanum*, to take account of the more recent documents of the Apostolic See and especially of the new Code of Canon Law, and to meet the various needs for emendation and augmentation.

Regarding the *Institutio Generalis Missalis Romani*, some variations have been introduced consistent with the manner of expression and prescriptions of other liturgical books and also recommended by pastoral experience. The permitted cases regarding the faculty to distribute Holy Communion under both kinds are set out more clearly; a newly-composed Chapter 9 has been added, in which a way is outlined of adapting the Roman Missal in an appropriate way to pastoral needs.

Other formulas have been added for celebrations recently inserted into the General Roman Calendar. With the aim of fostering devotion to the Mother of God, the Common of the Blessed Virgin Mary has been endowed with new Mass formularies. Likewise, in other Commons, in Masses for Various Needs and Occasions and in the Masses for the Dead, the order of prayers has from time to time been changed for the sake of greater consistency in the texts. In the Masses of Lent, in accord with ancient liturgical practice, a Prayer over the People has been inserted for each day.

In an appendix to the Order of Mass are also to be found the Eucharistic Prayer for Reconciliation and a special Eucharistic Prayer, which may be used for various needs.

The Supreme Pontiff JOHN PAUL II approved by his authority this third edition of the Roman Missal on 10 April 2000, and the Congregation for Divine Worship and Discipline of the Sacraments now publishes it and declares it to be typical.

Conferences of Bishops shall ensure that, within an appropriate period of time, new vernacular versions of the *Missale Romanum* are faithfully and accurately prepared from this third typical edition for the *recognitio* of the Apostolic See in accordance with the norm of law, with the preceding versions in use up till now being emended accurately in fidelity to the original Latin text.

Furthermore, this third typical Latin edition of the *Missale Romanum* may be used in the celebration of the Most Holy Eucharist from the day on which it is published, but it will come into force on the Solemnity of the Body and Blood of the Lord in the year 2000.

All things to the contrary notwithstanding.

From the offices of the Congregation for Divine Worship and Discipline of the Sacraments, 20 April, Thursday of the Lord's Supper, in the year of the Great Jubilee 2000.

JORGE A. Card. MEDINA ESTÉVEZ
Prefect

✠ FRANCESCO PIO TAMBURRINO
Archbishop Secretary

CONGREGATION FOR DIVINE WORSHIP AND DISCIPLINE OF THE SACRAMENTS

Prot. N. 1464/06/L

UNITED STATES OF AMERICA

At the request of His Eminence Francis Eugene Cardinal George, Archbishop of Chicago, President of the Conference of Bishops of the United States of America, in a letter dated December 9, 2009, and by virtue of the faculty granted to this Congregation by the Supreme Pontiff BENEDICT XVI, we gladly approve and confirm the text of the English-language translation of the Roman Missal, according to the third typical edition, as found in the attached copy.

In printed editions, mention must be made of the approval and confirmation which this Congregation has conceded. Moreover, two copies of the printed text should be forwarded to this Congregation.

All things to the contrary notwithstanding.

From the offices of the Congregation for Divine Worship and Discipline of the Sacraments, March 26, 2010.

ANTONIO Card. CAÑIZARES LLOVERA
Prefect

✠ JOSEPH AUGUSTINE DI NOIA, O.P.
Archbishop Secretary

UNITED STATES CONFERENCE OF CATHOLIC BISHOPS

DECREE OF PUBLICATION

In accord with the norms established by decree of the Sacred Congregation of Rites in *Cum, nostra ætate* (January 27, 1966) and of the Congregation for Divine Worship and the Discipline of the Sacraments in *Liturgiam authenticam* (March 28, 2001), this third edition of the *Roman Missal* is declared to be the vernacular typical edition of the *Missale Romanum, editio typica tertia*, and is published by authority of the United States Conference of Catholic Bishops.

The various sections of the third edition of the *Roman Missal* were canonically approved for use by the United States Conference of Catholic Bishops on June 15, 2006, November 11, 2008, July 17, 2009, and November 17, 2009, and were subsequently confirmed by the Apostolic See by decree of the Congregation for Divine Worship and the Discipline of the Sacraments on March 26, 2010 (Prot. n. 1464/06/L). The proper calendar, texts, and adaptations for the dioceses of the United States of America were confirmed by the Apostolic See by decrees of the same Congregation on July 24, 2010 (Prot. n. 577/10/L, 578/10/L, and 579/10/L).

The third edition of the *Roman Missal* enters into use in the dioceses of the United States of America as of the First Sunday of Advent, November 27, 2011. From that date forward, no other English edition of the *Roman Missal* may be used in the dioceses of the United States of America.

Given at the General Secretariat of the United States Conference of Catholic Bishops, Washington, DC, on August 15, 2010, the Solemnity of the Assumption of the Blessed Virgin Mary.

FRANCIS Card. GEORGE, O.M.I.
Archbishop of Chicago
President
United States Conference of Catholic Bishops

Reverend Monsignor DAVID J. MALLOY
General Secretary

APOSTOLIC CONSTITUTION
MISSALE ROMANUM

APOSTOLIC CONSTITUTION

PROMULGATION OF THE *MISSALE ROMANUM* RENEWED BY DECREE OF THE SECOND ECUMENICAL COUNCIL OF THE VATICAN

PAUL, BISHOP

SERVANT OF THE SERVANTS OF GOD
FOR AN EVERLASTING MEMORIAL

The *Missale Romanum*, promulgated in accordance with the decree of the Council of Trent by Our Predecessor Saint Pius V in the year 1570,[1] is recognized by all as being numbered among the many wonderful fruits that issued from that same Sacred Synod to the benefit of the whole Church of Christ. For throughout four centuries not only have Priests of the Latin Rite had it as their norm for celebrating the Eucharistic Sacrifice, but messengers of the holy Gospel have also carried it into almost every land. Moreover, innumerable men of great holiness have abundantly nourished their devotion to God by drawing from it both readings taken from the Sacred Scripture and prayers, the chief part of which Saint Gregory the Great had arranged in a certain order.

Yet since the time when there began to grow and gain strength among the Christian people a concern for promoting the Sacred Liturgy which, in the opinion of Our Predecessor of venerable memory Pius XII, manifested both an indication of the very great favor of God's providence towards the men of this age, and the salvific movement of the Holy Spirit through his Church, it has similarly become clear that the formulas of the Roman Missal need both to be somewhat revised and also to be enriched with additions.[2] This task Our same Predecessor inaugurated with the restoration of the Easter Vigil and of the Rite of Holy Week,[3] and thus took, as it were, a first step towards the adaptation of the Roman Missal to the sensitivities of this new age.

The recent Second Ecumenical Council of the Vatican, in the Constitution *Sacrosanctum Concilium*, laid the foundations for the general renewal of the Roman Missal, laying down that "texts and rites should be ordered in such a way that they express more clearly the holy things they signify,"[4] and later that "the Order of Mass should be revised in such a way that the purpose proper to its individual parts, as also the connection between them, may be more clearly evident, and that devout and active participation by the faithful may be facilitated,"[5] then that "the treasures of the Bible be opened up more abundantly so that richer fare may be spread before the faithful at the table of God's Word,"[6] and finally that "a new rite for concelebration is to be drawn up and inserted into the Roman Pontifical and the Roman Missal."[7]

---

1 Cf. Apostolic Constitution, *Quo primum*, 14 July 1570.
2 Cf. Pius XII, *Discourse to the Participants in the First International Congress of Pastoral Liturgy at Assisi*, 22 September 1956: *Acta Apostolicae Sedis* 48 (1956), p. 712.
3 Cf. Sacred Congregation of Rites, Decree, *Dominicae Resurrectionis*, 9 February 1951: *Acta Apostolicae Sedis* 43 (1951), pp. 128ff.; General Decree, *Maxima redemptionis nostrae mysteria*, 16 November 1955: *Acta Apostolicae Sedis* 47 (1955), pp. 838ff.
4 Second Vatican Council, Constitution on the Sacred Liturgy, *Sacrosanctum Concilium*, no. 21.
5 Cf. *ibidem*, no. 50.
6 Cf. *ibidem*, no. 51.
7 Cf. *ibidem*, no. 58.

However, it should in no way be thought that this revision of the Roman Missal has been introduced without preparation, since without any doubt the way was prepared by progress in liturgical disciplines these last four centuries. For if, after the Council of Trent, the reading and examination of "ancient manuscripts, both those in the Vatican library and others discovered elsewhere" helped not a little in the revision of the Roman Missal, as is confirmed by the Apostolic Constitution *Quo primum* issued by Our Predecessor Saint Pius V, subsequently on the one hand very ancient liturgical sources have of course been discovered and published, and on the other hand the liturgical formularies of the Eastern Church have been studied more deeply. As a result, it has been the desire of many that not only these doctrinal and spiritual riches not lie in the darkness of archives, but rather be brought out into the light to enlighten and nourish the minds and spirits of Christians.

Now, however, in order to set out, at least in broad outline, the new arrangement of the Roman Missal, We first point out that in the *Institutio Generalis*, which We have used as a proemium to the book, new norms are given for the celebration of the Eucharistic Sacrifice, regarding both the rites to be carried out and the functions proper to each person present and participating and to the furnishings and the places necessary for the conduct of divine worship.

The principal innovation is to be considered to lie in the restoration concerning the Eucharistic Prayer, as it is called. For although in the Roman Rite the first part of this Prayer, that is, the Preface, acquired various formulas over the passage of centuries, the second part, which was called the *Canon Actionis*, took on a fixed form between the fourth and fifth centuries; whereas, by contrast, the Oriental Liturgies admitted a certain variety among the Anaphoras themselves. Regarding this matter, besides the endowment of the Eucharistic Prayer with a number of Prefaces, either taken from the earlier tradition of the Roman Church or now newly composed, so that through them particular parts of the mystery of salvation may become more clearly evident and more numerous and richer motives for thanksgiving, We have also ordered that three new Canons be provided, added alongside this same Prayer. However, both for what are called pastoral reasons and to facilitate concelebration, We have ordered that the words of the Lord be one and the same in each formula of the Canon. Hence in each Eucharistic Prayer We wish those words to be proclaimed as follows: over the bread, *Accipite et manducate ex hoc omnes: Hoc est enim Corpus meum, quod pro vobis tradetur*; and over the chalice: *Accipite et bibite ex eo omnes: Hic est enim calix Sanguinis mei novi et aeterni testamenti, qui pro vobis et pro multis effundetur in remissionem peccatorum. Hoc facite in meam commemorationem*. As to the words *Mysterium fidei*, removed from the context of the words of Christ our Lord and spoken by the Priest, these open the way, as it were, to the acclamation of the faithful.

Regarding the Order of Mass, "the rites have been simplified, due care being taken to preserve their substance."[8] For those things "that, with the passage of time, came to be duplicated or were added to little advantage"[9] have been omitted, especially with regard to the rites for the offering of the bread and wine and with regard to the rites of the breaking of the bread and of Communion.

Furthermore, "there have been restored . . . in accordance with the ancient norm of the holy Fathers, various elements which have suffered injury through accidents of history."[10] Among such are the Homily,[11] the Universal Prayer or Prayer of the Faithful,[12] and the Penitential Rite or rite of reconciliation with God and with the brethren, to be enacted at the beginning of Mass: to which due importance has been restored, as was opportune.

In addition, according to the prescription of the Second Vatican Council that "over the course of a prescribed number of years a more representative portion of the Holy Scriptures be read to the people,"[13] the entire body of readings to be read on Sundays has been arranged over three years. Moreover, on days that are in any way festive, the readings of the Epistle and Gospel are preceded by another

---

8 Cf. *ibidem*, no. 50.
9 Cf. *ibidem*, no. 50.
10 Cf. *ibidem*, no. 50.
11 Cf. *ibidem*, no. 52.
12 Cf. *ibidem*, no. 53.
13 Cf. *ibidem*, no. 51.

reading taken from the Old Testament, or during Easter Time from the Acts of the Apostles. For by this means, the continuous process of the mystery of salvation is illustrated, as set forth in the revealed words of God. This great abundance of biblical readings, which sets before the faithful on feast days the most precious part of the Sacred Scriptures, is completed by the addition of other parts of the sacred books, which are read on days that are not festive.

All these things have been arranged in this way so as to arouse more and more among Christ's faithful that hunger for the Word of God[14] by which, under the guidance of the Holy Spirit, the people of the New Covenant can be seen, as it were, to be impelled towards the perfect unity of the Church. We trust that given this arrangement both Priests and faithful may make more devout spiritual preparation for the Lord's Supper and that, meditating more deeply on Sacred Scripture, they will be nourished more abundantly each day by the words of the Lord. In consequence, in accord with the teachings of the Second Vatican Council, Sacred Scripture will be regarded by all as an abiding fountain of spiritual life, as the principal basis for the handing on of Christian doctrine, and finally as the core of all theological formation.

In this restoration of the *Missale Romanum*, not only have the three parts We have already mentioned been changed, namely the Eucharistic Prayer, the Order of Mass, and the Order of Readings, but the others in which it consists have been revised and notably modified, that is: the Temporal, the Sanctoral, the Common of Saints, the Ritual Masses, and the Votive Masses, as they are called. Among these, particular care has been taken with the orations, which have not only been increased in number, so that new prayers respond to the new needs of these times, but also the most ancient prayers have been revised to accord with the ancient texts. As a result, to each weekday of the principal liturgical times, namely, Advent, Christmas, Lent, and Easter, has now been assigned its own distinct oration.

Moreover, although the text of the *Graduale Romanum*, at least as regards the music, has been left unchanged, for the sake of easier understanding, the Responsorial Psalm, which Saint Augustine and Saint Leo the Great often mention, and the Entrance and Communion Antiphons for use where appropriate in Masses without singing, have been restored.

Finally, from the matters that We have explained so far concerning the new *Missale Romanum*, there is something that We are now pleased to insist upon and to effect. When Our Predecessor Saint Pius V promulgated the *editio princeps* of the *Missale Romanum*, he presented it to the Christian people as an instrument, as it were, of liturgical unity and as a monument of true and reverent worship in the Church. We, too, no less, even though We have accepted into the new Roman Missal "lawful variations and adaptations"[15] in virtue of what the Second Vatican Council prescribed, We are no less confident that it will be received by the Christian faithful as a help in witnessing to and strengthening the unity of all, by means of which, in the variety of so many languages, one and the same prayer of all will rise up, more fragrant than any incense, to the heavenly Father, through our High Priest Jesus Christ, in the Holy Spirit.

What We have prescribed in this Our Constitution shall enter into force on the thirtieth day of the month of November this year, that is, the First Sunday of Advent.

We decree that these Our laws and prescriptions be firm and effective now and in the future, notwithstanding, to the extent necessary, the Apostolic Constitutions and Ordinances issued by Our Predecessors nor other prescriptions, even those worthy of particular mention and derogation.

Given at Rome, at Saint Peter's, on the third day of the month of April, the day of the Supper of Our Lord Jesus Christ, in the year 1969, the sixth of Our Pontificate.

PAUL VI, POPE

---

14   Cf. Amos 8:11.
15   Cf. Second Vatican Council, Constitution on the Sacred Liturgy, *Sacrosanctum Concilium*, nos. 38-40.

THE GENERAL INSTRUCTION OF THE ROMAN MISSAL

INTRODUCTION

1. As Christ the Lord was about to celebrate with the disciples the paschal supper in which he instituted the Sacrifice of his Body and Blood, he commanded that a large, furnished upper room be prepared (Lk 22:12). Indeed, the Church has always judged that this command also applied to herself whenever she decided about things related to the disposition of people's minds, and of places, rites and texts for the Celebration of the Most Holy Eucharist. The present norms, too, prescribed in keeping with the will of the Second Vatican Council, together with the new Missal with which the Church of the Roman Rite will henceforth celebrate the Mass, are again a demonstration of this same solicitude of the Church, of her faith and her unaltered love for the supreme mystery of the Eucharist, and also attest to her continuous and consistent tradition, even though certain new elements have been introduced.

Testimony of an Unaltered Faith

2. The sacrificial nature of the Mass, solemnly defended by the Council of Trent, because it accords with the universal tradition of the Church,[1] was once more stated by the Second Vatican Council, which pronounced these clear words about the Mass: "At the Last Supper, Our Savior instituted the Eucharistic Sacrifice of his Body and Blood, by which the Sacrifice of his Cross is perpetuated until he comes again; and till then he entrusts the memorial of his Death and Resurrection to his beloved spouse, the Church."[2]

What is taught in this way by the Council is consistently expressed in the formulas of the Mass. Moreover, the doctrine which stands out in the following sentence, already notable and concisely expressed in the ancient Sacramentary commonly called the Leonine—"for whenever the memorial of this sacrifice is celebrated the work of our redemption is accomplished"[3]—is aptly and exactly expounded in the Eucharistic Prayers; for as in these the Priest enacts the anamnesis, while turned towards God likewise in the name of all the people, he renders thanks and offers the living and holy sacrifice, that is, the Church's oblation and the sacrificial Victim by whose death God himself willed to reconcile us to himself;[4] and the Priest also prays that the Body and Blood of Christ may be a sacrifice which is acceptable to the Father and which brings salvation to the whole world.[5]

So, in the new Missal the rule of prayer (*lex orandi*) of the Church corresponds to her perennial rule of faith (*lex credendi*), by which we are truly taught that the sacrifice of his Cross and its sacramental renewal in the Mass, which Christ the Lord instituted at the Last Supper and commanded his Apostles to do in his memory, are one and the same, differing only in the manner of their offering; and as a result, that the Mass is at one and the same time a sacrifice of praise, thanksgiving, propitiation, and satisfaction.

3. Moreover, the wondrous mystery of the real presence of the Lord under the Eucharistic species, confirmed by the Second Vatican Council[6] and other teachings of the Church's Magisterium[7] in the same sense and with the same doctrine as the Council of Trent proposed that it must be believed,[8]

---

1 Ecumenical Council of Trent, Session XXII, September 17, 1562: Denzinger-Schönmetzer, nos. 1738-1759.
2 Second Ecumenical Council of the Vatican, Constitution on the Sacred Liturgy, *Sacrosanctum Concilium*, no. 47; cf. Dogmatic Constitution on the Church, *Lumen gentium*, nos. 3, 28; Decree on the Ministry and Life of Priests, *Presbyterorum ordinis*, nos. 2, 4, 5.
3 Evening Mass of the Lord's Supper, Prayer over the Offerings. Cf. *Sacramentarium Veronense*, L.C. Mohlberg editor, no. 93.
4 Cf. Eucharistic Prayer III.
5 Cf. Eucharistic Prayer IV.
6 Second Ecumenical Council of the Vatican, Constitution on the Sacred Liturgy, *Sacrosanctum Concilium*, nos. 7, 47; Decree on the Ministry and Life of Priests, *Presbyterorum ordinis*, nos. 5, 18.
7 Cf. Pius XII, Encyclical Letter, *Humani generis*, August 12, 1950: *Acta Apostolicae Sedis* 42 (1950), pp. 570-571; Paul VI, Encyclical Letter, *Mysterium fidei*, September 3, 1965: *Acta Apostolicae Sedis* 57 (1965), pp. 762-769; Paul VI, Solemn Profession of Faith, June 30, 1968, nos. 24-26: *Acta Apostolicae Sedis* 60 (1968), pp. 442-443; Sacred Congregation of Rites, Instruction, *Eucharisticum mysterium*, May 25, 1967, nos. 3f, 9: *Acta Apostolicae Sedis* 59 (1967), pp. 543, 547.
8 Cf. Ecumenical Council of Trent, Session XIII, October 11, 1551: Denzinger-Schönmetzer, nos. 1635-1661.

is proclaimed in the celebration of the Mass, not only by the very words of consecration by which Christ is rendered present through transubstantiation, but also with a sense and a demonstration of the greatest reverence and adoration which strives for realization in the Eucharistic liturgy. For the same reason, the Christian people are led to worship this wondrous Sacrament through adoration in a special way on Thursday of the Lord's Supper in Holy Week and on the Solemnity of the Most Holy Body and Blood of Christ.

4. In truth, the nature of the ministerial Priesthood proper to the Bishop and the Priest, who offer the Sacrifice in the person of Christ and who preside over the gathering of the holy people, shines forth in the form of the rite itself, on account of the more prominent place and function given to the Priest. The essential elements of this function are set out and explained clearly and extensively in the Preface for the Chrism Mass on Thursday of Holy Week, the day, namely, when the institution of the Priesthood is commemorated. For in the Preface is made clear how the conferral of Priestly power is accomplished through the laying on of hands; and, by the listing one by one of its duties, that power is described which is the continuation of the power of Christ, the High Priest of the New Testament.

5. Moreover, by this nature of the ministerial Priesthood, something else is put in its proper light, something certainly to be held in great esteem, namely, the royal Priesthood of the faithful, whose spiritual sacrifice is brought to completion through the ministry of the Bishop and the Priests, in union with the Sacrifice of Christ, the sole Mediator.[9] For the celebration of the Eucharist is the action of the whole Church, and in it each one should carry out solely but totally that which pertains to him, in virtue of the place of each within the People of God. The result of this is that greater consideration is also given to some aspects of the celebration that have sometimes been accorded less attention in the course of the centuries. For this people is the People of God, purchased by Christ's Blood, gathered together by the Lord, nourished by his word, the people called to present to God the prayers of the entire human family, a people that gives thanks in Christ for the mystery of salvation by offering his Sacrifice, a people, finally, that is brought together in unity by Communion in the Body and Blood of Christ. This people, though holy in its origin, nevertheless grows constantly in holiness by conscious, active, and fruitful participation in the mystery of the Eucharist.[10]

Uninterrupted Tradition

6. When it set out its instructions for the renewal of the Order of Mass, the Second Vatican Council, using, namely, the same words as did St. Pius V in the Apostolic Constitution *Quo primum*, by which the Missal of Trent was promulgated in 1570, also ordered, among other things, that a number of rites be restored "to the original norm of the holy Fathers."[11] From the fact that the same words are used, it can be noted how the two *Roman Missals*, although four centuries have intervened, embrace one and the same tradition. Furthermore, if the inner elements of this tradition are reflected upon, it is also understood how outstandingly and felicitously the older *Roman Missal* is brought to fulfillment in the later one.

7. In truly difficult times, when the Catholic faith in the sacrificial nature of the Mass, the ministerial Priesthood, and the real and perpetual presence of Christ under the Eucharistic species were called into question, St. Pius V was first of all concerned with preserving the more recent tradition, then unjustly assailed, introducing only very slight changes into the sacred rite. In fact, the Missal of 1570 differs very little from the very first printed edition of 1474, which in turn faithfully takes up again the Missal used in the time of Pope Innocent III. Moreover, manuscript books in the Vatican Library, even though they provided material for several textual emendations, by no means made it possible to

---

9 Cf. Second Ecumenical Council of the Vatican, Decree on the Ministry and Life of Priests, *Presbyterorum ordinis*, no. 2.
10 Cf. Second Ecumenical Council of the Vatican, Constitution on the Sacred Liturgy, *Sacrosanctum Concilium*, no. 11.
11 *Ibidem*, no. 50

INTRODUCTION

pursue inquiry into "ancient and approved authors" further back than the liturgical commentaries of the Middle Ages.

8. Today, however, innumerable writings of scholars have shed light on the "norm of the holy Fathers," which the revisers of the Missal of St. Pius V assiduously followed. For following the first publication in 1571 of the Sacramentary called the Gregorian, critical editions of other ancient Roman and Ambrosian Sacramentaries were disseminated, often in printed form, as were ancient Hispanic and Gallican liturgical books; these editions brought to light numerous prayers of no slight spiritual value but previously unknown.

In the same way, traditions of the first centuries, before the rites of East and West were formed, are now better known because of the discovery of so many liturgical documents.

Furthermore, continuing progress in the study of the holy Fathers has also shed upon the theology of the mystery of the Eucharist the light brought by the doctrine of such illustrious Fathers of Christian antiquity as St. Irenaeus, St. Ambrose, St. Cyril of Jerusalem, and St. John Chrysostom.

9. Hence, the "norm of the holy Fathers" requires not only the preservation of what our immediate forebears have handed on to us, but also an understanding and a more profound pondering of the Church's entire past ages and of all the ways in which her one faith has been expressed in forms of human and social culture so greatly differing among themselves, indeed, as those prevailing in the Semitic, Greek, and Latin regions. Moreover, this broader view allows us to see how the Holy Spirit endows the People of God with a marvelous fidelity in preserving the unalterable deposit of faith, even though there is a very great variety of prayers and rites.

Accommodation to New Conditions

10. Hence, the new Missal, while bearing witness to the Roman Church's rule of prayer (*lex orandi*), also safeguards the deposit of faith handed down by the more recent Councils and marks in its turn a step of great importance in liturgical tradition.

For, when the Fathers of the Second Vatican Council reaffirmed the dogmatic pronouncements of the Council of Trent, they spoke at a far different time in world history, and, for that reason, were able to bring forward proposals and measures regarding pastoral life that could not have even been foreseen four centuries earlier.

11. The Council of Trent had already recognized the great catechetical usefulness contained in the celebration of Mass but was unable to bring out all its consequences in regard to actual practice. In fact, many at that time requested that permission be given to use the vernacular in celebrating the Eucharistic Sacrifice. To such a request, the Council, by reason of the circumstances of that age, judged it a matter of duty to answer by insisting once more on the teaching of the Church as had been handed on, according to which the Eucharistic Sacrifice is in the first place the action of Christ himself, whose inherent efficacy is therefore unaffected by the manner in which the faithful participate in it. The Council for this reason stated in these firm and likewise measured words: "Although the Mass contains much instruction for the faithful people, it did not seem to the Fathers expedient, however, that it be celebrated indiscriminately in the vernacular."[12] And the Council declared worthy of censure anyone maintaining that "the rite of the Roman Church, in which part of the Canon and the words of consecration are pronounced in a low voice, is to be condemned, or that the Mass must be celebrated only in the vernacular."[13] Nevertheless, at the same time as it prohibited the use of the vernacular in the Mass, it ordered, on the other hand, pastors of souls to put appropriate catechesis in its place: "Lest Christ's flock go hungry . . . the Holy Synod commands pastors and each and all of those others having the care of souls that frequently during the celebration of Mass, either personally or through

---

12   Ecumenical Council of Trent, Session XXII, *Doctrina de ss. Missae sacrificio*, chapter 8, September 17, 1562: Denzinger-Schönmetzer, no.1749.

13   *Ibidem,* chapter 9: Denzinger-Schönmetzer, no. 1759.

others, they should explain what is read at Mass; and expound, among other things, something of the mystery of this most holy Sacrifice, especially on Sundays and feast days."[14]

12. Hence, the Second Vatican Council, having come together in order to accommodate the Church to the requirements of her proper apostolic office precisely in these times, considered thoroughly, as had the Council of Trent, the catechetical and pastoral character of the Sacred Liturgy.[15] And since no Catholic would now deny a sacred rite celebrated in Latin to be legitimate and efficacious, the Council was also able to concede that "not rarely adopting the vernacular language may be of great usefulness for the people" and gave permission for it to be used.[16] The eagerness with which this measure was everywhere received has certainly been so great that it has led, under the guidance of the Bishops and the Apostolic See itself, to permission for all liturgical celebrations in which the people participate to be in the vernacular, so that the people may more fully understand the mystery which is celebrated.

13. In this regard, although the use of the vernacular in the Sacred Liturgy is a means, admittedly of great importance, for expressing more clearly catechesis on the mystery, a catechesis inherent in the celebration itself, the Second Vatican Council ordered additionally that certain prescriptions of the Council of Trent that had not been followed everywhere be brought to fruition, such as the Homily to be given on Sundays and feast days[17] and the faculty to interject certain explanations during the sacred rites themselves.[18]

Above all, the Second Vatican Council, which recommended "that more perfect form of participation in the Mass by which the faithful, after the Priest's Communion, receive the Lord's Body from the same Sacrifice,"[19] called for another desire of the Fathers of Trent to be put into effect, namely, that for the sake of a fuller participation in the Holy Eucharist "at each Mass the faithful present should communicate not only by spiritual desire but also by sacramental reception of the Eucharist."[20]

14. Prompted by the same intention and pastoral zeal, the Second Vatican Council was able to give renewed consideration to what was established by Trent on Communion under both kinds. And indeed, since nowadays the doctrinal principles on the complete efficacy of Eucharistic Communion received under the species of bread alone are not in any way called into question, the Council gave permission for the reception on occasion of Communion under both kinds, because this clearer form of the sacramental sign offers a particular opportunity for understanding more deeply the mystery in which the faithful participate.[21]

15. In this manner the Church, while remaining faithful to her office as teacher of truth, safeguarding "things old," that is, the deposit of tradition, fulfills at the same time the duty of examining and prudently adopting "things new" (cf. Mt 13:52).

For part of the new Missal orders the prayers of the Church in a way more open to the needs of our times. Of this kind are above all the Ritual Masses and Masses for Various Needs, in which tradition and new elements are appropriately brought together. Thus, while a great number of expressions, drawn from the Church's most ancient tradition and familiar through the many editions of the *Roman Missal*, have remained unchanged, numerous others have been accommodated to the needs and conditions proper to our own age, and still others, such as the prayers for the Church, for the laity, for the sanctification of human labor, for the community of all nations, and certain needs proper to our

---

14 *Ibidem*, chapter 8: Denzinger-Schönmetzer, no. 1749.
15 Cf. Second Ecumenical Council of the Vatican, Constitution on the Sacred Liturgy, *Sacrosanctum Concilium*, no. 33.
16 *Ibidem*, no. 36.
17 *Ibidem*, no. 52.
18 *Ibidem*, no. 35, 3.
19 *Ibidem*, no. 55.
20 Ecumenical Council of Trent, Session XXII, *Doctrina de ss. Missae sacrificio*, chapter 6: Denzinger-Schönmetzer, no. 1747.
21 Cf. Second Ecumenical Council of the Vatican, Constitution on the Sacred Liturgy, *Sacrosanctum Concilium*, no. 55.

era, have been newly composed, drawing on the thoughts and often the very phrasing of the recent documents of the Council.

On account, moreover, of the same attitude toward the new state of the world as it now is, it seemed to cause no harm at all to so revered a treasure if some phrases were changed so that the language would be in accord with that of modern theology and would truly reflect the current state of the Church's discipline. Hence, several expressions regarding the evaluation and use of earthly goods have been changed, as have several which alluded to a certain form of outward penance which was proper to other periods of the Church's past.

In this way, finally, the liturgical norms of the Council of Trent have certainly been completed and perfected in many particulars by those of the Second Vatican Council, which has carried into effect the efforts to bring the faithful closer to the Sacred Liturgy that have been taken up these last four centuries and especially those of recent times, and above all the attention to the Liturgy promoted by St. Pius X and his Successors.

CHAPTER I
THE IMPORTANCE AND DIGNITY OF THE CELEBRATION OF THE EUCHARIST

16. The celebration of Mass, as the action of Christ and of the People of God arrayed hierarchically, is the center of the whole of Christian life for the Church both universal and local, as well as for each of the faithful individually.[22] For in it is found the high point both of the action by which God sanctifies the world in Christ and of the worship that the human race offers to the Father, adoring him through Christ, the Son of God, in the Holy Spirit.[23] In it, moreover, during the course of the year, the mysteries of redemption are celebrated so as to be in some way made present.[24] As to the other sacred actions and all the activities of the Christian life, these are bound up with it, flow from it, and are ordered to it.[25]

17. It is, therefore, of the greatest importance that the celebration of the Mass or the Lord's Supper be so ordered that the sacred ministers and the faithful taking part in it, according to the state proper to each, may draw from it more abundantly[26] those fruits, to obtain which, Christ the Lord instituted the Eucharistic Sacrifice of his Body and Blood and entrusted it as the memorial of his Passion and Resurrection to the Church, his beloved Bride.[27]

18. This will fittingly come about if, with due regard for the nature and other circumstances of each liturgical assembly, the entire celebration is arranged in such a way that it leads to a conscious, active, and full participation of the faithful, namely in body and in mind, a participation fervent with faith, hope, and charity, of the sort which is desired by the Church and which is required by the very nature of the celebration and to which the Christian people have a right and duty in virtue of their Baptism.[28]

19. Even though it is on occasion not possible to have the presence and active participation of the faithful, which manifest more clearly the ecclesial nature of the celebration,[29] the celebration of the Eucharist is always endowed with its own efficacy and dignity, since it is the act of Christ and of the Church, in which the Priest fulfills his own principal function and always acts for the sake of the people's salvation.

Hence the Priest is recommended to celebrate the Eucharistic Sacrifice, in so far as he can, even daily.[30]

20. Since, however, the celebration of the Eucharist, like the entire Liturgy, is carried out by means of perceptible signs by which the faith is nourished, strengthened, and expressed,[31] the greatest care is to be taken that those forms and elements proposed by the Church are chosen and arranged, which,

---

22 Cf. Second Ecumenical Council of the Vatican, Constitution on the Sacred Liturgy, *Sacrosanctum Concilium*, no. 41; Dogmatic Constitution on the Church, *Lumen gentium*, no. 11; Decree on the Ministry and Life of Priests, *Presbyterorum ordinis*, nos. 2, 5, 6; Decree on the Pastoral Office of Bishops, *Christus Dominus*, no. 30; Decree on Ecumenism, *Unitatis redintegratio*, no. 15; Sacred Congregation of Rites, Instruction, *Eucharisticum mysterium*, May 25, 1967, nos. 3e, 6: *Acta Apostolicae Sedis* 59 (1967), pp. 542, 544-545.
23 Cf. Second Ecumenical Council of the Vatican, Constitution on the Sacred Liturgy, *Sacrosanctum Concilium*, no. 10.
24 Cf. *ibidem*, no. 102.
25 Cf. Second Ecumenical Council of the Vatican, Constitution on the Sacred Liturgy, *Sacrosanctum Concilium*, no. 10; cf. Decree on the Ministry and Life of Priests, *Presbyterorum ordinis*, no. 5.
26 Cf. Second Ecumenical Council of the Vatican, Constitution on the Sacred Liturgy, *Sacrosanctum Concilium*, nos. 14, 19, 26, 28, 30.
27 Cf. *ibidem*, no. 47.
28 Cf. *ibidem*, no. 14.
29 Cf. *ibidem*, no. 41.
30 Cf. Second Ecumenical Council of the Vatican, Decree on the Ministry and Life of Priests, *Presbyterorum ordinis*, no. 13; *Code of Canon Law*, can. 904.
31 Cf. Second Ecumenical Council of the Vatican, Constitution on the Sacred Liturgy, *Sacrosanctum Concilium*, no. 59.

given the circumstances of persons and places, more effectively foster active and full participation and more aptly respond to the spiritual needs of the faithful.

21. Hence this Instruction aims both to offer general lines for a suitable ordering of the celebration of the Eucharist and to explain the rules by which individual forms of celebration may be arranged.[32]

22. The celebration of the Eucharist in a particular Church is of the utmost importance.

For the Diocesan Bishop, the prime steward of the mysteries of God in the particular Church entrusted to his care, is the moderator, promoter, and guardian of the whole of liturgical life.[33] In celebrations that take place with the Bishop presiding, and especially in the celebration of the Eucharist by the Bishop himself with the Presbyterate, the Deacons, and the people taking part, the mystery of the Church is manifest. Hence, solemn celebrations of Mass of this sort must be exemplary for the entire diocese.

The Bishop should therefore be determined that the Priests, the Deacons, and the lay Christian faithful grasp ever more deeply the genuine significance of the rites and liturgical texts, and thereby be led to the active and fruitful celebration of the Eucharist. To that end, he should also be vigilant in ensuring that the dignity of these celebrations be enhanced and, in promoting such dignity, the beauty of the sacred place, of the music, and of art should contribute as greatly as possible.

23. Moreover, in order that such a celebration may correspond more fully to the prescriptions and spirit of the Sacred Liturgy, and also in order that its pastoral effectiveness be enhanced, certain accommodations and adaptations are set out in this *General Instruction* and in the Order of Mass.

24. These adaptations consist, for the most part, in the choice of certain rites or texts, that is, of the chants, readings, prayers, explanatory interventions, and gestures capable of responding better to the needs, the preparation, and the culture of the participants and which are entrusted to the Priest Celebrant. However, the Priest will remember that he is the servant of the Sacred Liturgy and that he himself is not permitted, on his own initiative, to add, to remove, or to change anything in the celebration of Mass.[34]

25. In addition, at the proper place in the Missal are indicated certain adaptations which in accordance with the Constitution on the Sacred Liturgy pertain respectively to the Diocesan Bishop or to the Conference of Bishops[35] (cf. below nos. 387, 388-393).

26. As for variations and the more profound adaptations which give consideration to the traditions and culture of peoples and regions, to be introduced in accordance with article 40 of the Constitution on the Sacred Liturgy, for reasons of usefulness or necessity, those norms set out in the *Instruction on the Roman Liturgy and Inculturation*[36] and below in nos. 395-399 are to be observed.

---

32 Special celebrations of Mass should observe the guidelines established for them: For Masses with particular groups, cf. Sacred Congregation for Divine Worship, Instruction, *Actio pastoralis*, May 15, 1969: *Acta Apostolicae Sedis* 61 (1969), pp. 806-811; for Masses with children, cf. Sacred Congregation for Divine Worship, *Directory for Masses with Children*, November 1, 1973: *Acta Apostolicae Sedis* 66 (1974), pp. 30-46; for the manner of joining the Hours of the Office with the Mass, cf. Sacred Congregation for Divine Worship, *General Instruction of the Liturgy of the Hours*, nos. 93-98; for the manner of joining certain blessings and the crowning of an image of the Blessed Virgin Mary with the Mass, cf. Rituale Romanum, *De Benedictionibus*, editio typica, 1984, Praenotanda, no. 28; *Ordo coronandi imaginem beatae Mariae Virginis*, editio typica, 1981, nos. 10 and 14.
33 Cf. Second Ecumenical Council of the Vatican, Decree on the Pastoral Office of Bishops, *Christus Dominus*, no. 15; cf. also Constitution on the Sacred Liturgy, *Sacrosanctum Concilium*, no. 41.
34 Cf. Second Ecumenical Council of the Vatican, Constitution on the Sacred Liturgy, *Sacrosanctum Concilium*, no. 22.
35 Cf. Second Ecumenical Council of the Vatican, Constitution on the Sacred Liturgy. *Sacrosanctum Concilium*, nos. 38, 40; Paul VI, Apostolic Constitution, *Missale Romanum*, above.
36 Congregation for Divine Worship and the Discipline of the Sacraments, Instruction, *Varietates legitimae*, January 25, 1994: *Acta Apostolicae Sedis* 87 (1995), pp. 288-314.

CHAPTER II
THE STRUCTURE OF THE MASS, ITS ELEMENTS, AND ITS PARTS

I. THE GENERAL STRUCTURE OF THE MASS

27. At Mass or the Lord's Supper the People of God is called together, with a Priest presiding and acting in the person of Christ, to celebrate the memorial of the Lord or Eucharistic Sacrifice.[37] In an outstanding way there applies to such a local gathering of the holy Church the promise of Christ: "Where two or three are gathered in my name, there am I in their midst" (Mt 18:20). For in the celebration of Mass, in which the Sacrifice of the Cross is perpetuated,[38] Christ is really present in the very assembly gathered in his name, in the person of the minister, in his word, and indeed substantially and uninterruptedly under the Eucharistic species.[39]

28. The Mass consists in some sense of two parts, namely the Liturgy of the Word and the Liturgy of the Eucharist, these being so closely interconnected that they form but one single act of worship.[40] For in the Mass is spread the table both of God's Word and of the Body of Christ, and from it the faithful are to be instructed and refreshed.[41] There are also certain rites that open and conclude the celebration.

II. THE DIFFERENT ELEMENTS OF THE MASS

Reading and Explaining the Word of God

29. When the Sacred Scriptures are read in the Church, God himself speaks to his people, and Christ, present in his word, proclaims the Gospel.

Therefore, the readings from the Word of God are to be listened to reverently by everyone, for they are an element of the greatest importance in the Liturgy. Although in the readings from Sacred Scripture the Word of God is addressed to all people of whatever era and is understandable to them, a fuller understanding and a greater efficaciousness of the word is nevertheless fostered by a living commentary on the word, that is, by the Homily, as part of the liturgical action.[42]

The Prayers and Other Parts Pertaining to the Priest

30. Among those things assigned to the Priest, the prime place is occupied by the Eucharistic Prayer, which is the high point of the whole celebration. Next are the orations, that is to say, the Collect, the Prayer over the Offerings, and the Prayer after Communion. These prayers are addressed to God by

---

37 Cf. Second Ecumenical Council of the Vatican, Decree on the Ministry and Life of Priests, *Presbyterorum ordinis*, no. 5; Constitution on the Sacred Liturgy, *Sacrosanctum Concilium*, no. 33.
38 Cf. Ecumenical Council of Trent, Session XXII, *Doctrina de ss. Missae sacrificio*, chapter 1: Denzinger-Schönmetzer, no. 1740; Paul VI, Solemn Profession of Faith, June 30, 1968, no. 24: *Acta Apostolicae Sedis* 60 (1968), p. 442.
39 Cf. Second Ecumenical Council of the Vatican, Constitution on the Sacred Liturgy, *Sacrosanctum Concilium*, no. 7; Paul VI, Encyclical Letter, *Mysterium fidei*, September 3, 1965: *Acta Apostolicae Sedis* 57 (1965), p. 764; Sacred Congregation of Rites, Instruction, *Eucharisticum mysterium*, May 25, 1967, no. 9: *Acta Apostolicae Sedis* 59 (1967), p. 547.
40 Cf. Second Ecumenical Council of the Vatican, Constitution on the Sacred Liturgy, *Sacrosanctum Concilium*, no. 56; Sacred Congregation of Rites, Instruction, *Eucharisticum mysterium*, May 25, 1967, no. 3: *Acta Apostolicae Sedis* 59 (1967), p. 542.
41 Cf. Second Ecumenical Council of the Vatican, Constitution on the Sacred Liturgy, *Sacrosanctum Concilium*, nos. 48, 51; Dogmatic Constitution on Divine Revelation, *Dei Verbum*, no. 21; Decree on the Ministry and Life of Priests, *Presbyterorum ordinis*, no. 4.
42 Cf. Second Ecumenical Council of the Vatican, Constitution on the Sacred Liturgy, *Sacrosanctum Concilium*, nos. 7, 33, 52.

the Priest who presides over the assembly in the person of Christ, in the name of the entire holy people and of all present.[43] Hence they are rightly called the "presidential prayers."

31. Likewise it is also for the Priest, in the exercise of his office of presiding over the gathered assembly, to offer certain explanations that are foreseen in the rite itself. Where this is laid down by the rubrics, the celebrant is permitted to adapt them somewhat so that they correspond to the capacity for understanding of those participating. However, the Priest should always take care to keep to the sense of the explanatory text given in the Missal and to express it in just a few words. It is also for the presiding Priest to regulate the Word of God and to impart the final blessing. He is permitted, furthermore, in a very few words, to give the faithful an introduction to the Mass of the day (after the initial Greeting and before the Penitential Act), to the Liturgy of the Word (before the readings), and to the Eucharistic Prayer (before the Preface), though never during the Eucharistic Prayer itself; he may also make concluding comments regarding the entire sacred action before the Dismissal.

32. The nature of the "presidential" parts requires that they be spoken in a loud and clear voice and that everyone listen to them attentively.[44] Therefore, while the Priest is pronouncing them, there should be no other prayers or singing, and the organ or other musical instruments should be silent.

33. For the Priest, as the one who presides, expresses prayers in the name of the Church and of the assembled community; but at times he prays only in his own name, asking that he may exercise his ministry with greater attention and devotion. Prayers of this kind, which occur before the reading of the Gospel, at the Preparation of the Gifts, and also before and after the Communion of the Priest, are said quietly.

Other Formulas Occurring during the Celebration

34. Since the celebration of Mass by its nature has a "communitarian" character,[45] both the dialogues between the Priest and the assembled faithful, and the acclamations are of great significance;[46] for they are not simply outward signs of communal celebration but foster and bring about communion between Priest and people.

35. The acclamations and the responses of the faithful to the Priest's greetings and prayers constitute that level of active participation that is to be made by the assembled faithful in every form of the Mass, so that the action of the whole community may be clearly expressed and fostered.[47]

36. Other parts, most useful for expressing and fostering the active participation of the faithful, and which are assigned to the whole gathering, include especially the Penitential Act, the Profession of Faith, the Universal Prayer, and the Lord's Prayer.

---

43 Cf. *ibidem*, no. 33.
44 Cf. Sacred Congregation of Rites, Instruction, *Musicam sacram*, March 5, 1967, no. 14: *Acta Apostolicae Sedis* 59 (1967), p. 304.
45 Cf. Second Ecumenical Council of the Vatican, Constitution on the Sacred Liturgy, *Sacrosanctum Concilium*, nos. 26-27; Sacred Congregation of Rites, Instruction, *Eucharisticum mysterium*, May 25, 1967, no. 3d: *Acta Apostolicae Sedis* 59 (1967), p. 542.
46 Cf. Second Ecumenical Council of the Vatican, Constitution on the Sacred Liturgy, *Sacrosanctum Concilium*, no. 30.
47 Cf. Sacred Congregation of Rites, Instruction, *Musicam sacram*, March 5, 1967, no. 16a: *Acta Apostolicae Sedis* 59 (1967), p. 305.

37. Finally, among other formulas:

a) Some constitute an independent rite or act, such as the *Gloria in excelsis* (Glory to God in the highest), the Responsorial Psalm, the *Alleluia* and Verse before the Gospel, the *Sanctus* (Holy, Holy, Holy), the Memorial Acclamation, and the *chant* after Communion;
b) Others, on the other hand, accompany some other rite, such as the chants at the Entrance, at the Offertory, at the fraction (*Agnus Dei*, Lamb of God) and at Communion.

The Manner of Pronouncing the Different Texts

38. In texts that are to be pronounced in a loud and clear voice, whether by the Priest or the Deacon, or by a reader, or by everyone, the voice should correspond to the genre of the text itself, that is, depending upon whether it is a reading, a prayer, an explanatory comment, an acclamation, or a sung text; it should also be suited to the form of celebration and to the solemnity of the gathering. Consideration should also be given to the characteristics of different languages and of the culture of different peoples.

Therefore, in the rubrics and in the norms that follow, words such as "say" and "proclaim" are to be understood either of singing or of reciting, with due regard for the principles stated here above.

The Importance of Singing

39. The Christian faithful who come together as one in expectation of the Lord's coming are instructed by the Apostle Paul to sing together Psalms, hymns, and spiritual canticles (cf. Col 3:16). Singing is the sign of the heart's joy (cf. Acts 2:46). Thus St. Augustine says rightly, "Singing is for one who loves,"[48] and there is also an ancient proverb: "Whoever sings well prays twice over."

40. Great importance should therefore be attached to the use of singing in the celebration of the Mass, with due consideration for the culture of peoples and abilities of each liturgical assembly. Although it is not always necessary (e.g., in weekday Masses) to sing all the texts that are in principle meant to be sung, every care should be taken that singing by the ministers and the people not be absent in celebrations that occur on Sundays and on Holydays of Obligation.

However, in the choosing of the parts actually to be sung, preference is to be given to those that are of greater importance and especially to those which are to be sung by the Priest or the Deacon or a reader, with the people replying, or by the Priest and people together.[49]

41. The main place should be given, all things being equal, to Gregorian chant, as being proper to the Roman Liturgy. Other kinds of sacred music, in particular polyphony, are in no way excluded, provided that they correspond to the spirit of the liturgical action and that they foster the participation of all the faithful.[50]

Since the faithful from different countries come together ever more frequently, it is desirable that they know how to sing together at least some parts of the Ordinary of the Mass in Latin, especially the Profession of Faith and the Lord's Prayer, according to the simpler settings.[51]

Gestures and Bodily Posture

42. The gestures and bodily posture of both the Priest, the Deacon, and the ministers, and also of the people, must be conducive to making the entire celebration resplendent with beauty and noble

---

48 St. Augustine of Hippo, *Sermo* 336, 1: PL 38: 1472.
49 Cf. Sacred Congregation of Rites, Instruction, *Musicam sacram*, March 5, 1967, nos. 7, 16: *Acta Apostolicae Sedis* 59 (1967), pp. 302, 305.
50 Cf. Second Ecumenical Council of the Vatican, Constitution on the Sacred Liturgy, *Sacrosanctum Concilium*, no. 116; cf. also no. 30.
51 Cf. Second Ecumenical Council of the Vatican, Constitution on the Sacred Liturgy, *Sacrosanctum Concilium*, no. 54; Sacred Congregation of Rites, Instruction, *Inter Oecumenici*, September 26, 1964, no. 59: *Acta Apostolicae Sedis* 56 (1964), p. 891; Instruction, *Musicam sacram*, March 5, 1967, no. 47: *Acta Apostolicae Sedis* 59 (1967), p. 314.

simplicity, to making clear the true and full meaning of its different parts, and to fostering the participation of all.[52] Attention must therefore be paid to what is determined by this *General Instruction* and by the traditional practice of the Roman Rite and to what serves the common spiritual good of the People of God, rather than private inclination or arbitrary choice.

A common bodily posture, to be observed by all those taking part, is a sign of the unity of the members of the Christian community gathered together for the Sacred Liturgy, for it expresses the intentions and spiritual attitude of the participants and also fosters them.

43. The faithful should stand from the beginning of the Entrance Chant, or while the Priest approaches the altar, until the end of the Collect; for the *Alleluia* Chant before the Gospel; while the Gospel itself is proclaimed; during the Profession of Faith and the Universal Prayer; and from the invitation, *Orate, fratres* (*Pray, brethren*), before the Prayer over the Offerings until the end of Mass, except at the places indicated here below.

The faithful should sit, on the other hand, during the readings before the Gospel and the Responsorial Psalm and for the Homily and during the Preparation of the Gifts at the Offertory; and, if appropriate, they may sit or kneel during the period of sacred silence after Communion.

In the dioceses of the United States of America, they should kneel beginning after the singing or recitation of the *Sanctus* (*Holy, Holy, Holy*) until after the *Amen* of the Eucharistic Prayer, except when prevented on occasion by ill health, or for reasons of lack of space, of the large number of people present, or for another reasonable cause. However, those who do not kneel ought to make a profound bow when the Priest genuflects after the Consecration. The faithful kneel after the *Agnus Dei* (*Lamb of God*) unless the Diocesan Bishop determines otherwise.[53]

For the sake of uniformity in gestures and bodily postures during one and the same celebration, the faithful should follow the instructions which the Deacon, a lay minister, or the Priest gives, according to what is laid down in the Missal.

44. Among gestures are included also actions and processions, by which the Priest, with the Deacon and ministers, goes to the altar; the Deacon carries the Evangeliary or *Book of the Gospels* to the ambo before the proclamation of the Gospel; the faithful bring up the gifts and come forward to receive Communion. It is appropriate that actions and processions of this sort be carried out with decorum while the chants proper to them are sung, in accordance with the norms laid down for each.

Silence

45. Sacred silence also, as part of the celebration, is to be observed at the designated times.[54] Its nature, however, depends on the moment when it occurs in the different parts of the celebration. For in the Penitential Act and again after the invitation to pray, individuals recollect themselves; whereas after a reading or after the Homily, all meditate briefly on what they have heard; then after Communion, they praise God in their hearts and pray to him.

Even before the celebration itself, it is a praiseworthy practice for silence to be observed in the church, in the sacristy, in the vesting room, and in adjacent areas, so that all may dispose themselves to carry out the sacred celebration in a devout and fitting manner.

---

52   Cf. Second Ecumenical Council of the Vatican, Constitution on the Sacred Liturgy, *Sacrosanctum Concilium*, nos. 30, 34; cf. also no. 21.
53   Cf. *ibidem*, no. 40; Congregation for Divine Worship and the Discipline of the Sacraments, Instruction, *Varietates legitimae*, January 25, 1994, no. 41: *Acta Apostolicae Sedis* 87 (1995), p. 304.
54   Cf. Second Ecumenical Council of the Vatican, Constitution on the Sacred Liturgy, *Sacrosanctum Concilium*, no. 30; Sacred Congregation of Rites, Instruction, *Musicam sacram*, March 5, 1967, no. 17: *Acta Apostolicae Sedis* 59 (1967), p. 305.

III. THE INDIVIDUAL PARTS OF THE MASS

A) THE INTRODUCTORY RITES

46. The rites that precede the Liturgy of the Word, namely, the Entrance, the Greeting, the Penitential Act, the *Kyrie*, the *Gloria in excelsis (Glory to God in the highest)* and Collect, have the character of a beginning, an introduction, and a preparation.

Their purpose is to ensure that the faithful, who come together as one, establish communion and dispose themselves properly to listen to the Word of God and to celebrate the Eucharist worthily.

In certain celebrations that are combined with Mass according to the norms of the liturgical books, the Introductory Rites are omitted or take place in a particular way.

The Entrance

47. When the people are gathered, and as the Priest enters with the Deacon and ministers, the Entrance Chant begins. Its purpose is to open the celebration, foster the unity of those who have been gathered, introduce their thoughts to the mystery of the liturgical time or festivity, and accompany the procession of the Priest and ministers.

48. This chant is sung alternately by the choir and the people or similarly by a cantor and the people, or entirely by the people, or by the choir alone. In the Dioceses of the United States of America there are four options for the Entrance Chant: (1) the antiphon from the Missal or the antiphon with its Psalm from the *Graduale Romanum* as set to music there or in another setting; (2) the antiphon and Psalm of the *Graduale Simplex* for the liturgical time; (3) a chant from another collection of Psalms and antiphons, approved by the Conference of Bishops or the Diocesan Bishop, including Psalms arranged in responsorial or metrical forms; (4) another liturgical chant that is suited to the sacred action, the day, or the time of year, similarly approved by the Conference of Bishops or the Diocesan Bishop.

If there is no singing at the Entrance, the antiphon given in the Missal is recited either by the faithful, or by some of them, or by a reader; otherwise, it is recited by the Priest himself, who may even adapt it as an introductory explanation (cf. no. 31).

Reverence to the Altar and Greeting of the Assembled People

49. When they have arrived at the sanctuary, the Priest, the Deacon, and the ministers reverence the altar with a profound bow.

Moreover, as an expression of veneration, the Priest and Deacon then kiss the altar itself; the Priest, if appropriate, also incenses the cross and the altar.

50. When the Entrance Chant is concluded, the Priest stands at the chair and, together with the whole gathering, signs himself with the Sign of the Cross. Then by means of the Greeting he signifies the presence of the Lord to the assembled community. By this greeting and the people's response, the mystery of the Church gathered together is made manifest.

After the greeting of the people, the Priest, or the Deacon, or a lay minister may very briefly introduce the faithful to the Mass of the day.

The Penitential Act

51. After this, the Priest calls upon the whole community to take part in the Penitential Act, which, after a brief pause for silence, it does by means of a formula of general confession. The rite concludes with the Priest's absolution, which, however, lacks the efficacy of the Sacrament of Penance.

From time to time on Sundays, especially in Easter Time, instead of the customary Penitential Act, the blessing and sprinkling of water may take place as a reminder of Baptism.[55]

---

55   Cf. below, pp. 1453-1456.

The Kyrie, Eleison

52. After the Penitential Act, the *Kyrie, eleison* (*Lord, have mercy*), is always begun, unless it has already been part of the Penitential Act. Since it is a chant by which the faithful acclaim the Lord and implore his mercy, it is usually executed by everyone, that is to say, with the people and the choir or cantor taking part in it.

Each acclamation is usually pronounced twice, though it is not to be excluded that it be repeated several times, by reason of the character of the various languages, as well as of the artistry of the music or of other circumstances. When the *Kyrie* is sung as a part of the Penitential Act, a "trope" precedes each acclamation.

The Gloria in Excelsis

53. The *Gloria in excelsis* (*Glory to God in the highest*) is a most ancient and venerable hymn by which the Church, gathered in the Holy Spirit, glorifies and entreats God the Father and the Lamb. The text of this hymn may not be replaced by any other. It is intoned by the Priest or, if appropriate, by a cantor or by the choir; but it is sung either by everyone together, or by the people alternately with the choir, or by the choir alone. If not sung, it is to be recited either by everybody together or by two choirs responding one to the other.

It is sung or said on Sundays outside Advent and Lent, and also on Solemnities and Feasts, and at particular celebrations of a more solemn character.

The Collect

54. Next the Priest calls upon the people to pray and everybody, together with the Priest, observes a brief silence so that they may become aware of being in God's presence and may call to mind their intentions. Then the Priest pronounces the prayer usually called the "Collect" and through which the character of the celebration finds expression. By an ancient tradition of the Church, the Collect prayer is usually addressed to God the Father, through Christ, in the Holy Spirit,[56] and is concluded with a Trinitarian ending, or longer ending, in the following manner:

- If the prayer is directed to the Father: *Through our Lord Jesus Christ, your Son, who lives and reigns with you in the unity of the Holy Spirit, one God, for ever and ever;*
- If it is directed to the Father, but the Son is mentioned at the end: *Who lives and reigns with you in the unity of the Holy Spirit, one God, for ever and ever;*
- If it is directed to the Son: *Who live and reign with God the Father in the unity of the Holy Spirit, one God, for ever and ever.*

The people, joining in this petition, make the prayer their own by means of the acclamation *Amen*.

At Mass only a single Collect is ever said.

B) THE LITURGY OF THE WORD

55. The main part of the Liturgy of the Word is made up of the readings from Sacred Scripture together with the chants occurring between them. As for the Homily, the Profession of Faith, and the Universal Prayer, they develop and conclude it. For in the readings, as explained by the Homily, God speaks to his people,[57] opening up to them the mystery of redemption and salvation, and offering spiritual nourishment; and Christ himself is present through his word in the midst of the faithful.[58]

---

56   Cf. Tertullian, *Adversus Marcionem*, IV, 9: *Corpus Christianorum, Series Latina* 1, p. 560; Origen, *Disputatio cum Heracleida*, no. 4, 24: *Sources chrétiennes* 67, p. 62; *Statuta Concilii Hipponensis Breviata*, no. 21: *Corpus Christianorum, Series latina* 149, p. 39.
57   Cf. Second Ecumenical Council of the Vatican, Constitution on the Sacred Liturgy, *Sacrosanctum Concilium*, no. 33.
58   Cf. *ibidem*, no. 7.

By silence and by singing, the people make this divine word their own, and affirm their adherence to it by means of the Profession of Faith; finally, having been nourished by the divine word, the people pour out their petitions by means of the Universal Prayer for the needs of the whole Church and for the salvation of the whole world.

Silence

56. The Liturgy of the Word is to be celebrated in such a way as to favor meditation, and so any kind of haste such as hinders recollection is clearly to be avoided. In the course of it, brief periods of silence are also appropriate, accommodated to the assembled congregation; by means of these, under the action of the Holy Spirit, the Word of God may be grasped by the heart and a response through prayer may be prepared. It may be appropriate to observe such periods of silence, for example, before the Liturgy of the Word itself begins, after the First and Second Reading, and lastly at the conclusion of the Homily.[59]

The Biblical Readings

57. In the readings, the table of God's Word is spread before the faithful, and the treasures of the Bible are opened to them.[60] Hence, it is preferable that the arrangement of the biblical readings be maintained, for by them the unity of both Testaments and of salvation history is brought out. Nor is it lawful to replace the readings and Responsorial Psalm, which contain the Word of God, with other, non-biblical texts.[61]

58. In the celebration of the Mass with the people, the readings are always read from the ambo.

59. The function of proclaiming the readings is by tradition not presidential but ministerial. Therefore the readings are to be read by a reader, but the Gospel by the Deacon or, in his absence, by another Priest. If, however, a Deacon or another Priest is not present, the Priest Celebrant himself should read the Gospel, and moreover, if no other suitable reader is present, the Priest Celebrant should also proclaim the other readings as well.

After each reading, whoever reads it pronounces the acclamation, and by means of the reply the assembled people give honor to the Word of God that they have received in faith and with gratitude.

60. The reading of the Gospel constitutes the high point of the Liturgy of the Word. The Liturgy itself teaches the great reverence that is to be shown to this reading by setting it off from the other readings with special marks of honor, by the fact of which minister is appointed to proclaim it and by the blessing or prayer with which he prepares himself; and also by the fact that through their acclamations the faithful acknowledge and confess that Christ is present and is speaking to them and stand as they listen to the reading; and by the mere fact of the marks of reverence that are given to the *Book of the Gospels*.

The Responsorial Psalm

61. After the First Reading follows the Responsorial Psalm, which is an integral part of the Liturgy of the Word and which has great liturgical and pastoral importance, since it fosters meditation on the Word of God.

The Responsorial Psalm should correspond to each reading and should usually be taken from the Lectionary.

---

59 Cf. Missale Romanum, *Ordo lectionum Missae*, editio typica altera, 1981, no. 28.
60 Cf. Second Ecumenical Council of the Vatican, Constitution on the Sacred Liturgy, *Sacrosanctum Concilium*, no. 51.
61 Cf. John Paul II, Apostolic Letter, *Vicesimus quintus annus*, December 4, 1988, no. 13: *Acta Apostolicae Sedis* 81 (1989), p. 910.

It is preferable for the Responsorial Psalm to be sung, at least as far as the people's response is concerned. Hence the psalmist, or cantor of the Psalm, sings the Psalm verses at the ambo or another suitable place, while the whole congregation sits and listens, normally taking part by means of the response, except when the Psalm is sung straight through, that is, without a response. However, in order that the people may be able to sing the Psalm response more easily, texts of some responses and Psalms have been chosen for the different times of the year or for the different categories of Saints. These may be used instead of the text corresponding to the reading whenever the Psalm is sung. If the Psalm cannot be sung, then it should be recited in a way that is particularly suited to fostering meditation on the Word of God.

In the Dioceses of the United States of America, instead of the Psalm assigned in the Lectionary, there may be sung either the Responsorial Gradual from the *Graduale Romanum*, or the Responsorial Psalm or the *Alleluia* Psalm from the *Graduale Simplex*, as described in these books, or an antiphon and Psalm from another collection of Psalms and antiphons, including Psalms arranged in metrical form, providing that they have been approved by the Conference of Bishops or the Diocesan Bishop. Songs or hymns may not be used in place of the Responsorial Psalm.

The Acclamation before the Gospel

62. After the reading that immediately precedes the Gospel, the *Alleluia* or another chant laid down by the rubrics is sung, as the liturgical time requires. An acclamation of this kind constitutes a rite or act in itself, by which the gathering of the faithful welcomes and greets the Lord who is about to speak to them in the Gospel and profess their faith by means of the chant. It is sung by everybody, standing, and is led by the choir or a cantor, being repeated as the case requires. The verse, on the other hand, is sung either by the choir or by a cantor.

   a) The *Alleluia* is sung in every time of year other than Lent. The verses are taken from the Lectionary or the *Graduale*.

   b) During Lent, instead of the *Alleluia*, the Verse before the Gospel as given in the Lectionary is sung. It is also possible to sing another Psalm or Tract, as found in the *Graduale*.

63. When there is only one reading before the Gospel:

   a) during a time of year when the *Alleluia* is prescribed, either an *Alleluia* Psalm or the Responsorial Psalm followed by the *Alleluia* with its verse may be used;

   b) during a time of year when the *Alleluia* is not foreseen, either the Psalm and the Verse before the Gospel or the Psalm alone may be used;

   c) the *Alleluia* or the Verse before the Gospel, if not sung, may be omitted.

64. The Sequence which, except on Easter Sunday and on Pentecost Day, is optional, is sung before the *Alleluia*.

The Homily

65. The Homily is part of the Liturgy and is highly recommended,[62] for it is necessary for the nurturing of the Christian life. It should be an explanation of some aspect of the readings from Sacred Scripture or of another text from the Ordinary or the Proper of the Mass of the day and should take into account both the mystery being celebrated and the particular needs of the listeners.[63]

---

62   Cf. Second Ecumenical Council of the Vatican, Constitution on the Sacred Liturgy, *Sacrosanctum Concilium*, no. 52; *Code of Canon Law*, can. 767 §1.

63   Cf. Sacred Congregation of Rites, Instruction, *Inter Oecumenici*, September 26, 1964, no. 54: *Acta Apostolicae Sedis* 56 (1964), p. 890.

66. The Homily should ordinarily be given by the Priest Celebrant himself or be entrusted by him to a concelebrating Priest, or from time to time and, if appropriate, to the Deacon, but never to a lay person.[64] In particular cases and for a just cause, the Homily may even be given by a Bishop or a Priest who is present at the celebration but cannot concelebrate.

On Sundays and Holydays of Obligation there is to be a Homily at every Mass that is celebrated with the people attending, and it may not be omitted without a grave reason. On other days it is recommended, especially on the weekdays of Advent, Lent, and Easter Time, as well as on other festive days and occasions when the people come to church in greater numbers.[65]

It is appropriate for a brief period of silence to be observed after the Homily.

The Profession of Faith

67. The purpose of the Creed or Profession of Faith is that the whole gathered people may respond to the Word of God proclaimed in the readings taken from Sacred Scripture and explained in the Homily and that they may also honor and confess the great mysteries of the faith by pronouncing the rule of faith in a formula approved for liturgical use and before the celebration of these mysteries in the Eucharist begins.

68. The Creed is to be sung or said by the Priest together with the people on Sundays and Solemnities. It may be said also at particular celebrations of a more solemn character.

If it is sung, it is intoned by the Priest or, if appropriate, by a cantor or by the choir. It is then sung either by everybody together or by the people alternating with the choir.

If it is not sung, it is to be recited by everybody together or by two choirs responding one to the other.

The Universal Prayer

69. In the Universal Prayer or Prayer of the Faithful, the people respond in some sense to the Word of God which they have received in faith and, exercising the office of their baptismal Priesthood, offer prayers to God for the salvation of all. It is desirable that there usually be such a form of prayer in Masses celebrated with the people, so that petitions may be offered for holy Church, for those who govern with authority over us, for those weighed down by various needs, for all humanity, and for the salvation of the whole world.[66]

70. The series of intentions is usually to be:

   a) for the needs of the Church;
   b) for public authorities and the salvation of the whole world;
   c) for those burdened by any kind of difficulty;
   d) for the local community.

Nevertheless, in any particular celebration, such as a Confirmation, a Marriage, or at a Funeral, the series of intentions may be concerned more closely with the particular occasion.

71. It is for the Priest Celebrant to regulate this prayer from the chair. He himself begins it with a brief introduction, by which he calls upon the faithful to pray, and likewise he concludes it with

---

64 Cf. *Code of Canon Law*, can. 767 §1; Pontifical Commission for the Authentic Interpretation of the *Code of Canon Law*, response to *dubium* regarding can. 767 §1: *Acta Apostolicae Sedis* 79 (1987), p. 1249; Interdicasterial Instruction on certain questions regarding the collaboration of the non-ordained faithful in the sacred ministry of Priests, *Ecclesiae de mysterio*, August 15, 1997, art. 3: *Acta Apostolicae Sedis* 89 (1997), p. 864.

65 Cf. Sacred Congregation of Rites, Instruction, *Inter Oecumenici*, September 26, 1964, no. 53: *Acta Apostolicae Sedis* 56 (1964), p. 890.

66 Cf. Second Ecumenical Council of the Vatican, Constitution on the Sacred Liturgy, *Sacrosanctum Concilium*, no. 53.

an oration. The intentions announced should be sober, be composed with a wise liberty and in few words, and they should be expressive of the prayer of the entire community.

They are announced from the ambo or from another suitable place, by the Deacon or by a cantor, a reader, or one of the lay faithful.[67]

The people, for their part, stand and give expression to their prayer either by an invocation said in common after each intention or by praying in silence.

C) The Liturgy of the Eucharist

72. At the Last Supper Christ instituted the Paschal Sacrifice and banquet, by which the Sacrifice of the Cross is continuously made present in the Church whenever the Priest, representing Christ the Lord, carries out what the Lord himself did and handed over to his disciples to be done in his memory.[68]

For Christ took the bread and the chalice, gave thanks, broke the bread and gave it to his disciples, saying: Take, eat and drink: this is my Body; this is the chalice of my Blood. Do this in memory of me. Hence, the Church has arranged the entire celebration of the Liturgy of the Eucharist in parts corresponding to precisely these words and actions of Christ, namely:

   a) At the Preparation of the Gifts, bread and wine with water are brought to the altar, the same elements, that is to say, which Christ took into his hands.
   b) In the Eucharistic Prayer, thanks is given to God for the whole work of salvation, and the offerings become the Body and Blood of Christ.
   c) Through the fraction and through Communion, the faithful, though many, receive from the one bread the Lord's Body and from the one chalice the Lord's Blood in the same way that the Apostles received them from the hands of Christ himself.

The Preparation of the Gifts

73. At the beginning of the Liturgy of the Eucharist the gifts which will become Christ's Body and Blood are brought to the altar.

First of all, the altar or Lord's table, which is the center of the whole Liturgy of the Eucharist,[69] is made ready when on it are placed the corporal, purificator, Missal, and chalice (unless this last is prepared at the credence table).

The offerings are then brought forward. It is a praiseworthy practice for the bread and wine to be presented by the faithful. They are then accepted at an appropriate place by the Priest or the Deacon to be carried to the altar. Even though the faithful no longer bring from their own possessions the bread and wine intended for the liturgy as was once the case, nevertheless the rite of carrying up the offerings still keeps its spiritual efficacy and significance.

Even money or other gifts for the poor or for the Church, brought by the faithful or collected in the church, are acceptable; given their purpose, they are to be put in a suitable place away from the Eucharistic table.

74. The procession bringing the gifts is accompanied by the Offertory Chant (cf. no. 37 b), which continues at least until the gifts have been placed on the altar. The norms on the manner of singing are the same as for the Entrance Chant (cf. no. 48). Singing may always accompany the rite at the Offertory, even when there is no procession with the gifts.

---

[67] Cf. Sacred Congregation of Rites, Instruction, *Inter Oecumenici*, September 26, 1964, no. 56: *Acta Apostolicae Sedis* 56 (1964), p. 890.
[68] Cf. Second Ecumenical Council of the Vatican, Constitution on the Sacred Liturgy, *Sacrosanctum Concilium*, no. 47; Sacred Congregation of Rites, Instruction, *Eucharisticum mysterium*, May 25, 1967, no. 3a, b: *Acta Apostolicae Sedis* 59 (1967), pp. 540-541.
[69] Cf. Sacred Congregation of Rites, Instruction, *Inter Oecumenici*, September 26, 1964, no. 91: *Acta Apostolicae Sedis* 56 (1964), p. 898; Instruction, *Eucharisticum mysterium*, May 25, 1967, no. 24: *Acta Apostolicae Sedis* 59 (1967), p. 554.

75. The bread and wine are placed on the altar by the Priest to the accompaniment of the prescribed formulas; the Priest may incense the gifts placed on the altar and then incense the cross and the altar itself, so as to signify the Church's offering and prayer rising like incense in the sight of God. Next, the Priest, because of his sacred ministry, and the people, by reason of their baptismal dignity, may be incensed by the Deacon or by another minister.

76. Then the Priest washes his hands at the side of the altar, a rite in which the desire for interior purification finds expression.

The Prayer over the Offerings

77. Once the offerings have been placed on the altar and the accompanying rites completed, by means of the invitation to pray with the Priest and by means of the Prayer over the Offerings, the Preparation of the Gifts is concluded and preparation made for the Eucharistic Prayer.

At Mass, a single Prayer over the Offerings is said, and it ends with the shorter conclusion, that is: *Through Christ our Lord*. If, however, the Son is mentioned at the end of this prayer, the conclusion is: *Who lives and reigns for ever and ever*.

The people, joining in this petition, make the prayer their own by means of the acclamation *Amen*.

The Eucharistic Prayer

78. Now the center and high point of the entire celebration begins, namely, the Eucharistic Prayer itself, that is, the prayer of thanksgiving and sanctification. The Priest calls upon the people to lift up their hearts towards the Lord in prayer and thanksgiving; he associates the people with himself in the Prayer that he addresses in the name of the entire community to God the Father through Jesus Christ in the Holy Spirit. Furthermore, the meaning of this Prayer is that the whole congregation of the faithful joins with Christ in confessing the great deeds of God and in the offering of Sacrifice. The Eucharistic Prayer requires that everybody listens to it with reverence and in silence.

79. The main elements of which the Eucharistic Prayer consists may be distinguished from one another in this way:

   a) The *thanksgiving* (expressed especially in the Preface), in which the Priest, in the name of the whole of the holy people, glorifies God the Father and gives thanks to him for the whole work of salvation or for some particular aspect of it, according to the varying day, festivity, or time of year.
   b) The *acclamation,* by which the whole congregation, joining with the heavenly powers, sings the *Sanctus* (Holy, Holy, Holy). This acclamation, which constitutes part of the Eucharistic Prayer itself, is pronounced by all the people with the Priest.
   c) The *epiclesis,* in which, by means of particular invocations, the Church implores the power of the Holy Spirit that the gifts offered by human hands be consecrated, that is, become Christ's Body and Blood, and that the unblemished sacrificial Victim to be consumed in Communion may be for the salvation of those who will partake of it.
   d) The *Institution narrative and Consecration,* by which, by means of the words and actions of Christ, that Sacrifice is effected which Christ himself instituted during the Last Supper, when he offered his Body and Blood under the species of bread and wine, gave them to the Apostles to eat and drink, and leaving with the latter the command to perpetuate this same mystery.
   e) The *anamnesis,* by which the Church, fulfilling the command that she received from Christ the Lord through the Apostles, celebrates the memorial of Christ, recalling especially his blessed Passion, glorious Resurrection, and Ascension into heaven.
   f) The *oblation,* by which, in this very memorial, the Church, in particular that gathered here and now, offers the unblemished sacrificial Victim in the Holy Spirit to the Father. The Church's intention, indeed, is that the faithful not only offer this unblemished sacrificial

Victim but also learn to offer their very selves,[70] and so day by day to be brought, through the mediation of Christ, into unity with God and with each other, so that God may at last be all in all.[71]

g) The *intercessions*, by which expression is given to the fact that the Eucharist is celebrated in communion with the whole Church, of both heaven and of earth, and that the oblation is made for her and for all her members, living and dead, who are called to participate in the redemption and salvation purchased by the Body and Blood of Christ.

h) The *concluding doxology*, by which the glorification of God is expressed and which is affirmed and concluded by the people's acclamation *Amen*.

The Communion Rite

80. Since the celebration of the Eucharist is the Paschal Banquet, it is desirable that in accordance with the Lord's command his Body and Blood should be received as spiritual food by those of the faithful who are properly disposed. This is the sense of the fraction and the other preparatory rites by which the faithful are led more immediately to Communion.

The Lord's Prayer

81. In the Lord's Prayer a petition is made for daily bread, which for Christians means principally the Eucharistic Bread, and entreating also purification from sin, so that what is holy may in truth be given to the holy. The Priest pronounces the invitation to the prayer, and all the faithful say the prayer with him; then the Priest alone adds the embolism, which the people conclude by means of the doxology. The embolism, developing the last petition of the Lord's Prayer itself, asks for deliverance from the power of evil for the whole community of the faithful.

The invitation, the Prayer itself, the embolism, and the doxology by which the people conclude these things are sung or are said aloud.

The Rite of Peace

82. There follows the Rite of Peace, by which the Church entreats peace and unity for herself and for the whole human family, and the faithful express to each other their ecclesial communion and mutual charity before communicating in the Sacrament.

As for the actual sign of peace to be given, the manner is to be established by the Conferences of Bishops in accordance with the culture and customs of the peoples. However, it is appropriate that each person, in a sober manner, offer the sign of peace only to those who are nearest.

The Fraction of the Bread

83. The Priest breaks the Eucharistic Bread, with the assistance, if the case requires, of the Deacon or a concelebrant. The gesture of breaking bread done by Christ at the Last Supper, which in apostolic times gave the entire Eucharistic Action its name, signifies that the many faithful are made one body (1 Cor 10:17) by receiving Communion from the one Bread of Life, which is Christ, who for the salvation of the world died and rose again. The fraction or breaking of bread is begun after the sign of peace and is carried out with proper reverence, and should not be unnecessarily prolonged or accorded exaggerated importance. This rite is reserved to the Priest and the Deacon.

---

70 Cf. Second Ecumenical Council of the Vatican, Constitution on the Sacred Liturgy, *Sacrosanctum Concilium*, no. 48; Sacred Congregation of Rites, Instruction, *Eucharisticum mysterium*, May 25,1967, no. 12: *Acta Apostolicae Sedis* 59 (1967), pp. 548-549.

71 Cf. Second Ecumenical Council of the Vatican, Constitution on the Sacred Liturgy, *Sacrosanctum Concilium*, no. 48; Decree on the Ministry and Life of Priests, *Presbyterorum ordinis*, no. 5; Sacred Congregation of Rites, Instruction, *Eucharisticum mysterium*, 25 May 1967, no. 12: *Acta Apostolicae Sedis* 59 (1967), pp. 548-549.

The Priest breaks the Bread and puts a piece of the host into the chalice to signify the unity of the Body and Blood of the Lord in the work of salvation, namely, of the Body of Jesus Christ, living and glorious. The supplication *Agnus Dei (Lamb of God)* is usually sung by the choir or cantor with the congregation replying; or at least recited aloud. This invocation accompanies the fraction of the bread and, for this reason, may be repeated as many times as necessary until the rite has been completed. The final time it concludes with the words *grant us peace*.

Communion

84. The Priest prepares himself by a prayer, said quietly, so that he may fruitfully receive the Body and Blood of Christ. The faithful do the same, praying silently.

Then the Priest shows the faithful the Eucharistic Bread, holding it over the paten or over the chalice, and invites them to the banquet of Christ; and along with the faithful, he then makes an act of humility, using the prescribed words from the Gospels.

85. It is most desirable that the faithful, just as the Priest himself is bound to do, receive the Lord's Body from hosts consecrated at the same Mass and that, in the cases where this is foreseen, they partake of the chalice (cf. no. 283), so that even by means of the signs Communion may stand out more clearly as a participation in the sacrifice actually being celebrated.[72]

86. While the Priest is receiving the Sacrament, the Communion Chant is begun, its purpose being to express the spiritual union of the communicants by means of the unity of their voices, to show gladness of heart, and to bring out more clearly the "communitarian" character of the procession to receive the Eucharist. The singing is prolonged for as long as the Sacrament is being administered to the faithful.[73] However, if there is to be a hymn after Communion, the Communion Chant should be ended in a timely manner.

Care should be taken that singers, too, can receive Communion with ease.

87. In the Dioceses of the United States of America, there are four options for singing at Communion: (1) the antiphon from the Missal or the antiphon with its Psalm from the *Graduale Romanum*, as set to music there or in another musical setting; (2) the antiphon with Psalm from the *Graduale Simplex* of the liturgical time; (3) a chant from another collection of Psalms and antiphons, approved by the Conference of Bishops or the Diocesan Bishop, including Psalms arranged in responsorial or metrical forms; (4) some other suitable liturgical chant (cf. no. 86) approved by the Conference of Bishops or the Diocesan Bishop. This is sung either by the choir alone or by the choir or a cantor with the people.

However, if there is no singing, the antiphon given in the Missal may be recited either by the faithful, or by some of them, or by a reader; otherwise, it is recited by the Priest himself after he has received Communion and before he distributes Communion to the faithful.

88. When the distribution of Communion is over, if appropriate, the Priest and faithful pray quietly for some time. If desired, a Psalm or other canticle of praise or a hymn may also be sung by the whole congregation.

89. To bring to completion the prayer of the People of God, and also to conclude the whole Communion Rite, the Priest pronounces the Prayer after Communion, in which he prays for the fruits of the mystery just celebrated.

---

72 Cf. Sacred Congregation of Rites, Instruction, *Eucharisticum mysterium*, May 25, 1967, nos. 31, 32: *Acta Apostolicae Sedis* 59 (1969), pp. 558-559; Sacred Congregation for the Discipline of the Sacraments, Instruction, *Immensae caritatis*, January 29, 1973, no. 2: *Acta Apostolicae Sedis* 65 (1973), pp. 267-268.

73 Cf. Sacred Congregation for the Sacraments and Divine Worship, Instruction, *Inestimabile donum*, April 3, 1980, no. 17: *Acta Apostolicae Sedis* 72 (1980), p. 338.

At Mass a single Prayer after Communion is said, and it ends with the shorter conclusion; that is:
- if the prayer is directed to the Father: *Through Christ our Lord;*
- if it is directed to the Father, but the Son is mentioned at the end: *Who lives and reigns for ever and ever;*
- if it is directed to the Son: *Who live and reign for ever and ever.*

The people make the prayer their own by means of the acclamation *Amen*.

D) THE CONCLUDING RITES

90. To the Concluding Rites belong the following:
   a) brief announcements, should they be necessary;
   b) the Priest's Greeting and Blessing, which on certain days and occasions is expanded and expressed by the Prayer over the People or another more solemn formula;
   c) the Dismissal of the people by the Deacon or the Priest, so that each may go back to doing good works, praising and blessing God;
   d) the kissing of the altar by the Priest and the Deacon, followed by a profound bow to the altar by the Priest, the Deacon, and the other ministers.

CHAPTER III
DUTIES AND MINISTRIES IN THE MASS

91. The celebration of the Eucharist is the action of Christ and of the Church, namely, of the holy people united and ordered under the Bishop. It therefore pertains to the whole Body of the Church, manifests it, and has its effect upon it. Indeed, it also affects the individual members of the Church in a different way, according to their different orders, functions, and actual participation.[74] In this way, the Christian people, "a chosen race, a royal Priesthood, a holy nation, a people for his own possession," expresses its cohesion and its hierarchical ordering.[75] All, therefore, whether ordained ministers or lay Christian faithful, in fulfilling their function or their duty, should carry out solely but totally that which pertains to them.[76]

I. THE DUTIES OF THOSE IN HOLY ORDERS

92. Every legitimate celebration of the Eucharist is directed by the Bishop, either in person or through Priests who are his helpers.[77]

When the Bishop is present at a Mass where the people are gathered, it is most fitting that he himself celebrate the Eucharist and associate Priests with himself in the sacred action as concelebrants. This is done not for the sake of adding outward solemnity to the rite, but to signify more vividly the mystery of the Church, "the sacrament of unity."[78]

If, on the other hand, the Bishop does not celebrate the Eucharist but has assigned it to someone else to do this, then it is appropriate that he should preside over the Liturgy of the Word, wearing the pectoral cross, stole, and cope over an alb, and that he should give the blessing at the end of Mass.[79]

93. A Priest, also, who possesses within the Church the sacred power of Orders to offer sacrifice in the person of Christ,[80] presides by this fact over the faithful people gathered here and now, presides over their prayer, proclaims to them the message of salvation, associates the people with himself in the offering of sacrifice through Christ in the Holy Spirit to God the Father, and gives his brothers and sisters the Bread of eternal life and partakes of it with them. Therefore, when he celebrates the Eucharist, he must serve God and the people with dignity and humility, and by his bearing and by the way he pronounces the divine words he must convey to the faithful the living presence of Christ.

94. After the Priest, the Deacon, in virtue of the sacred Ordination he has received, holds first place among those who minister in the celebration of the Eucharist. For the sacred Order of the Diaconate has been held in high honor in the Church even from the early time of the Apostles.[81] At Mass the Deacon has his own part in proclaiming the Gospel, from time to time in preaching God's Word, in announcing the intentions of the Universal Prayer, in ministering to the Priest, in preparing the altar and in serving the celebration of the Sacrifice, in distributing the Eucharist to the faithful, especially

---

74　Cf. Second Ecumenical Council of the Vatican, Constitution on the Sacred Liturgy, *Sacrosanctum Concilium*, no. 26.
75　Cf. *ibidem*, no. 14.
76　Cf. *ibidem*, no. 28.
77　Cf. Second Ecumenical Council of the Vatican, Dogmatic Constitution on the Church, *Lumen gentium*, nos. 26, 28; Constitution on the Sacred Liturgy, *Sacrosanctum Concilium*, no. 42.
78　Cf. Second Ecumenical Council of the Vatican, Constitution on the Sacred Liturgy, *Sacrosanctum Concilium*, no. 26.
79　Cf. *Caeremoniale Episcoporum*, editio typica, 1984, nos. 175-186.
80　Cf. Second Ecumenical Council of the Vatican, Dogmatic Constitution on the Church, *Lumen gentium*, no. 28; Decree on the Ministry and Life of Priests, *Presbyterorum ordinis*, no. 2.
81　Cf. Paul VI, Apostolic Letter, *Sacrum Diaconatus Ordinem*, June 18, 1967: *Acta Apostolicae Sedis* 59 (1967), pp. 697-704; Pontificale Romanum, *De Ordinatione Episcopi, presbyterorum et diaconorum*, editio typica altera, 1989, no. 173.

under the species of wine, and from time to time in giving instructions regarding the people's gestures and posture.

II. THE FUNCTIONS OF THE PEOPLE OF GOD

95. In the celebration of Mass the faithful form a holy people, a people of God's own possession and a royal Priesthood, so that they may give thanks to God and offer the unblemished sacrificial Victim not only by means of the hands of the Priest but also together with him and so that they may learn to offer their very selves.[82] They should, moreover, take care to show this by their deep religious sense and their charity toward brothers and sisters who participate with them in the same celebration.

They are consequently to avoid any appearance of singularity or division, keeping in mind that they have only one Father in heaven and that hence are all brothers or sisters one to the other.

96. Moreover, they are to form one body, whether in hearing the Word of God, or in taking part in the prayers and in the singing, or above all by the common offering of the Sacrifice and by participating together at the Lord's table. This unity is beautifully apparent from the gestures and bodily postures observed together by the faithful.

97. The faithful, moreover, should not refuse to serve the People of God in gladness whenever they are asked to perform some particular service or function in the celebration.

III. PARTICULAR MINISTRIES

The Ministry of the Instituted Acolyte and Lector

98. The acolyte is instituted for service at the altar and to assist the Priest and Deacon. It is his place principally to prepare the altar and the sacred vessels and, if necessary, to distribute the Eucharist to the faithful as an extraordinary minister.[83]

In the ministry of the altar, the acolyte has his own proper functions (cf. nos. 187-193), which he must carry out in person.

99. The lector is instituted to proclaim the readings from Sacred Scripture, with the exception of the Gospel. He may also announce the intentions for the Universal Prayer and, in the absence of a psalmist, recite the Psalm between the readings.

In the celebration of the Eucharist, the lector has his own proper function (cf. nos. 194-198), which he himself must carry out.

Other Functions

100. In the absence of an instituted acolyte, there may be deputed lay ministers to serve at the altar and assist the Priest and the Deacon; these carry the cross, the candles, the thurible, the bread, the wine, and the water, or who are even deputed to distribute Holy Communion as extraordinary ministers.[84]

---

82 Cf. Second Ecumenical Council of the Vatican, Constitution on the Sacred Liturgy, *Sacrosanctum Concilium*, no. 48; Sacred Congregation of Rites, Instruction, *Eucharisticum mysterium*, May 25, 1967, no. 12: *Acta Apostolicae Sedis* 59 (1967), pp. 548-549.
83 Cf. *Code of Canon Law*, can. 910 §2; cf. also the Interdicasterial Instruction on certain questions regarding the collaboration of the non-ordained faithful in the sacred ministry of Priests, *Ecclesiae de mysterio*, August 15, 1997, art. 8: *Acta Apostolicae Sedis* 89 (1997), p. 871.
84 Cf. Sacred Congregation for the Discipline of the Sacraments, Instruction, *Immensae caritatis*, January 29, 1973, no. 1: *Acta Apostolicae Sedis* 65 (1973), pp. 265-266; *Code of Canon Law*, can. 230 §3.

101. In the absence of an instituted lector, other lay people may be deputed to proclaim the readings from Sacred Scripture, people who are truly suited to carrying out this function and carefully prepared, so that by their hearing the readings from the sacred texts the faithful may conceive in their hearts a sweet and living affection for Sacred Scripture.[85]

102. It is the psalmist's place to sing the Psalm or other biblical canticle to be found between the readings. To carry out this function correctly, it is necessary for the psalmist to be accomplished in the art of singing Psalms and have a facility in public speaking and elocution.

103. Among the faithful, the *schola cantorum* or choir exercises its own liturgical function, its place being to take care that the parts proper to it, in keeping with the different genres of chant, are properly carried out and to foster the active participation of the faithful by means of the singing.[86] What is said about the *schola cantorum* also applies, with due regard for the relevant norms, to other musicians, and especially the organist.

104. It is fitting that there be a cantor or a choir director to direct and support the people's singing. Indeed, when there is no choir, it is up to the cantor to direct the different chants, with the people taking the part proper to them.[87]

105. A liturgical function is also exercised by:
   a) The sacristan, who diligently arranges the liturgical books, the vestments, and other things that are necessary for the celebration of Mass.
   b) The commentator, who, if appropriate, provides the faithful briefly with explanations and exhortations so as to direct their attention to the celebration and ensure that they are better disposed for understanding it. The commentator's remarks should be thoroughly prepared and notable for their restraint. In performing this function the commentator stands in a suitable place within sight of the faithful, but not at the ambo.
   c) Those who take up the collections in the church.
   d) Those who, in some regions, welcome the faithful at the church doors, seat them appropriately, and marshal them in processions.

106. It is desirable, at least in cathedrals and in larger churches, to have some competent minister or master of ceremonies, to see to the appropriate arrangement of sacred actions and to their being carried out by the sacred ministers and lay faithful with decorum, order, and devotion.

107. Liturgical functions that are not proper to the Priest or the Deacon and are mentioned above (nos. 100-106) may even be entrusted by means of a liturgical blessing or a temporary deputation to suitable lay persons chosen by the pastor or the rector of the church.[88] As to the function of serving the Priest at the altar, the norms established by the Bishop for his diocese should be observed.

---

85   Cf. Second Ecumenical Council of the Vatican, Constitution on the Sacred Liturgy, *Sacrosanctum Concilium*, no. 24.
86   Cf. Sacred Congregation of Rites, Instruction, *Musicam sacram*, March 5, 1967, no. 19: *Acta Apostolicae Sedis* 59 (1967), p. 306.
87   Cf. *ibidem*, no. 21: pp. 306-307.
88   Cf. Pontifical Commission for the Interpretation of Legal Texts, response to *dubium* regarding can. 230 §2: *Acta Apostolicae Sedis* 86 (1994), p. 541.

IV. THE DISTRIBUTION OF FUNCTIONS AND THE PREPARATION OF THE CELEBRATION

108. One and the same Priest must always exercise the presidential function in all of its parts, except for those parts which are proper to a Mass at which the Bishop is present (cf. above no. 92).

109. If there are several present who are able to exercise the same ministry, nothing forbids their distributing among themselves and performing different parts of the same ministry or duty. For example, one Deacon may be assigned to execute the sung parts, another to serve at the altar; if there are several readings, it is well to distribute them among a number of readers, and the same applies for other matters. However, it is not at all appropriate that several persons divide a single element of the celebration among themselves, e.g., that the same reading be proclaimed by two readers, one after the other, with the exception of the Passion of the Lord.

110. If at a Mass with the people only one minister is present, that minister may exercise several different functions.

111. There should be harmony and diligence among all those involved in the effective preparation of each liturgical celebration in accordance with the Missal and other liturgical books, both as regards the rites and as regards the pastoral and musical aspects. This should take place under the direction of the rector of the church and after consultation with the faithful in things that directly pertain to them. However, the Priest who presides at the celebration always retains the right of arranging those things that pertain to him.[89]

---

89 Cf. Second Ecumenical Council of the Vatican, Constitution on the Sacred Liturgy, *Sacrosanctum Concilium*, no. 22.

CHAPTER IV
THE DIFFERENT FORMS OF CELEBRATING MASS

112. In the local Church, first place should certainly be given, because of its significance, to the Mass at which the Bishop presides, surrounded by his Presbyterate, Deacons, and lay ministers,[90] and in which the holy People of God participate fully and actively, for it is there that the principal manifestation of the Church is found.

At a Mass celebrated by the Bishop or at which he presides without celebrating the Eucharist, the norms found in the *Caeremoniale Episcoporum (Ceremonial of Bishops)* should be observed.[91]

113. Great importance should also be given to a Mass celebrated with any community, but especially with the parish community, inasmuch as it represents the universal Church at a given time and place, and chiefly in the common Sunday celebration.[92]

114. Moreover, among those Masses celebrated by some communities, a particular place belongs to the Conventual Mass, which is a part of the daily Office, or the "community" Mass. Although such Masses do not involve any special form of celebration, it is nevertheless most fitting that they be celebrated with singing, especially with the full participation of all members of the community, whether of religious or of canons. Therefore, in these Masses all should exercise their function according to the Order or ministry they have received. Hence, it is desirable that all the Priests who are not obliged to celebrate individually for the pastoral benefit of the faithful concelebrate in so far as possible at the conventual or community Mass. In addition, all Priests belonging to the community who are obliged, as a matter of duty, to celebrate individually for the pastoral benefit of the faithful may also on the same day concelebrate at the conventual or community Mass.[93] For it is preferable that Priests who are present at a celebration of the Eucharist, unless excused for a just reason, should usually exercise the function proper to their Order and hence take part as concelebrants, wearing sacred vestments. Otherwise, they wear their proper choir dress or a surplice over a cassock.

I. MASS WITH THE PEOPLE

115. By Mass with the people is meant a Mass celebrated with the participation of the faithful. Moreover, it is appropriate, in so far as possible, and especially on Sundays and Holydays of Obligation, that the celebration take place with singing and with a suitable number of ministers.[94] It may, however, take place even without singing and with only one minister.

116. If at any celebration of Mass a Deacon is present, he should exercise his function. Furthermore, it is desirable that an acolyte, a reader, and a cantor should usually be there to assist the Priest Celebrant. Indeed, the rite described below foresees an even greater number of ministers.

---

90   Cf. Second Ecumenical Council of the Vatican, Constitution on the Sacred Liturgy, *Sacrosanctum Concilium*, no. 41.
91   Cf. *Caeremoniale Episcoporum*, editio typica, 1984, nos. 119-186.
92   Cf. Second Ecumenical Council of the Vatican, Constitution on the Sacred Liturgy, *Sacrosanctum Concilium*, no. 42; Dogmatic Constitution on the Church, *Lumen gentium*, no. 28; Decree on the Ministry and Life of Priests, *Presbyterorum ordinis*, no. 5; Sacred Congregation of Rites, Instruction, *Eucharisticum mysterium*, May 25, 1967, no. 26: *Acta Apostolicae Sedis* 59 (1967), p. 555.
93   Cf. Sacred Congregation of Rites, Instruction, *Eucharisticum, mysterium*, May 25, 1967, no. 47: *Acta Apostolicae Sedis* 59 (1967), p. 565.
94   Cf. Sacred Congregation of Rites, Instruction, *Eucharisticum mysterium*, May 25, 1967, no. 26: *Acta Apostolicae Sedis* 59 (1967), p. 555; Instruction, *Musicam sacram*, March 5, 1967, nos. 16, 27: *Acta Apostolicae Sedis* 59 (1967), pp. 305, 308.

THE DIFFERENT FORMS OF CELEBRATING MASS

Things to Be Prepared

117. The altar is to be covered with at least one white cloth. In addition, on or next to the altar are to be placed candlesticks with lighted candles: at least two in any celebration, or even four or six, especially for a Sunday Mass or a Holyday of Obligation, or if the Diocesan Bishop celebrates, then seven candlesticks with lighted candles. Likewise, on the altar or close to it, there is to be a cross adorned with a figure of Christ crucified. The candles and the cross with the figure of Christ crucified may also be carried in the procession at the Entrance. On the altar itself may be placed a *Book of the Gospels* distinct from the book of other readings, unless it is carried in the Entrance Procession.

118. Likewise these should be prepared:
   a) next to the Priest's chair: the Missal and, if appropriate, a hymnal;
   b) at the ambo: the Lectionary;
   c) on the credence table: the chalice, corporal, purificator, and, if appropriate, the pall; the paten and, if needed, ciboria; bread for the Communion of the Priest who presides, the Deacon, the ministers, and the people; cruets containing the wine and the water, unless all of these are presented by the faithful in the procession at the Offertory; the vessel of water to be blessed, if the sprinkling of holy water takes place; the Communion-plate for the Communion of the faithful; and whatever is needed for the washing of hands.

It is a praiseworthy practice for the chalice to be covered with a veil, which may be either of the color of the day or white.

119. In the sacristy, according to the various forms of celebration, there should be prepared the sacred vestments (cf. nos. 337-341) for the Priest, the Deacon, and other ministers:
   a) for the Priest: the alb, the stole, and the chasuble;
   b) for the Deacon: the alb, the stole, and the dalmatic; the latter may be omitted, however, either out of necessity or on account of a lesser degree of solemnity;
   c) for the other ministers: albs or other lawfully approved attire.[95]

All who wear an alb should use a cincture and an amice unless, due to the form of the alb, they are not needed.

When the Entrance takes place with a procession, the following are also to be prepared: a *Book of the Gospels*; on Sundays and festive days, a thurible and incense boat, if incense is being used; the cross to be carried in procession; and candlesticks with lighted candles.

A) MASS WITHOUT A DEACON

The Introductory Rites

120. When the people are gathered, the Priest and ministers, wearing the sacred vestments, go in procession to the altar in this order:
   a) the thurifer carrying a smoking thurible, if incense is being used;
   b) ministers who carry lighted candles, and between them an acolyte or other minister with the cross;
   c) the acolytes and the other ministers;
   d) a reader, who may carry a *Book of the Gospels* (though not a Lectionary), slightly elevated;
   e) the Priest who is to celebrate the Mass.

---

95 Cf. the Interdicasterial Instruction on certain questions regarding the collaboration of the non-ordained faithful in the sacred ministry of Priests, *Ecclesiae de mysterio*, August 15, 1997, art. 6: *Acta Apostolicae Sedis* 89 (1997), p. 869.

If incense is being used, before the procession begins, the Priest puts some into the thurible and blesses it with the Sign of the Cross without saying anything.

121. During the procession to the altar, the Entrance Chant takes place (cf. nos. 47-48).

122. When they reach the altar, the Priest and ministers make a profound bow.
The cross adorned with a figure of Christ crucified, and carried in procession, may be placed next to the altar to serve as the altar cross, in which case it must be the only cross used; otherwise it is put away in a dignified place. As for the candlesticks, these are placed on the altar or near it. It is a praiseworthy practice for the *Book of the Gospels* to be placed on the altar.

123. The Priest goes up to the altar and venerates it with a kiss. Then, if appropriate, he incenses the cross and the altar, walking around the latter.

124. Once all this has been done, the Priest goes to the chair. When the Entrance Chant is concluded, with everybody standing, the Priest and faithful sign themselves with the Sign of the Cross. The Priest says: *In the name of the Father, and of the Son, and of the Holy Spirit*. The people reply, *Amen*.
Then, facing the people and extending his hands, the Priest greets the people, using one of the formulas indicated. The Priest himself or some other minister may also very briefly introduce the faithful to the Mass of the day.

125. The Penitential Act follows. After this, the *Kyrie* is sung or said, in accordance with the rubrics (cf. no. 52).

126. For celebrations where it is prescribed, the *Gloria in excelsis (Glory to God in the highest)* is either sung or said (cf. no. 53).

127. The Priest then calls upon the people to pray, saying, with hands joined, *Let us pray*. All pray silently with the Priest for a brief time. Then the Priest, with hands extended, says the Collect, at the end of which the people acclaim, *Amen*.

The Liturgy of the Word

128. After the Collect, all sit. The Priest may, very briefly, introduce the faithful to the Liturgy of the Word. Then the reader goes to the ambo and, from the Lectionary already placed there before Mass, proclaims the First Reading, to which all listen. At the end, the reader pronounces the acclamation *The word of the Lord*, and all reply, *Thanks be to God*.
Then a few moments of silence may be observed, if appropriate, so that all may meditate on what they have heard.

129. Then the psalmist or the reader proclaims the verses of the Psalm and the people make the response as usual.

130. If there is to be a Second Reading before the Gospel, the reader proclaims it from the ambo. All listen and at the end reply to the acclamation, as noted above (no. 128). Then, if appropriate, a few moments of silence may be observed.

131. After this, all rise, and the *Alleluia* or other chant is sung as the liturgical time requires (cf. nos. 62-64).

132. During the singing of the *Alleluia* or other chant, if incense is being used, the Priest puts some into the thurible and blesses it. Then, with hands joined, he bows profoundly before the altar and quietly says the prayer *Munda cor meum* (Cleanse my heart).

133. If the *Book of the Gospels* is on the altar, the Priest then takes it and approaches the ambo, carrying the *Book of the Gospels* slightly elevated. He is preceded by the lay ministers, who may carry the thurible and the candles. Those present turn towards the ambo as a sign of special reverence for the Gospel of Christ.

134. At the ambo, the Priest opens the book and, with hands joined, says, *The Lord be with you*, to which the people reply, *And with your spirit*. Then he says, *A reading from the holy Gospel*, making the Sign of the Cross with his thumb on the book and on his forehead, mouth, and breast, which everyone else does as well. The people acclaim, *Glory to you, O Lord*. The Priest incenses the book, if incense is being used (cf. nos. 276-277). Then he proclaims the Gospel and at the end pronounces the acclamation *The Gospel of the Lord*, to which all reply, *Praise to you, Lord Jesus Christ*. The Priest kisses the book, saying quietly the formula *Per evangelica dicta* (Through the words of the Gospel).

135. If no reader is present, the Priest himself proclaims all the readings and the Psalm, standing at the ambo. If incense is being used, he puts some incense into the thurible at the ambo, blesses it, and, bowing profoundly, says the prayer *Munda cor meum* (Cleanse my heart).

136. The Priest, standing at the chair or at the ambo itself or, if appropriate, in another worthy place, gives the Homily. When the Homily is over, a period of silence may be observed.

137. The Symbol or Creed is sung or recited by the Priest together with the people (cf. no. 68) with everyone standing. At the words *et incarnatus est*, etc. *(and by the Holy Spirit . . . and became man)* all make a profound bow; but on the Solemnities of the Annunciation and of the Nativity of the Lord, all genuflect.

138. After the recitation of the Symbol or Creed, the Priest, standing at the chair with his hands joined, by means of a brief address calls upon the faithful to participate in the Universal Prayer. Then the cantor, the reader, or another person announces the intentions from the ambo or from some other suitable place while facing the people. The latter take their part by replying in supplication. At the very end, the Priest, with hands extended, concludes the petitions with a prayer.

The Liturgy of the Eucharist

139. When the Universal Prayer is over, all sit, and the Offertory Chant begins (cf. no. 74).
An acolyte or other lay minister places the corporal, the purificator, the chalice, the pall, and the Missal on the altar.

140. It is desirable that the participation of the faithful be expressed by an offering, whether of bread and wine for the celebration of the Eucharist or of other gifts to relieve the needs of the Church and of the poor.
The offerings of the faithful are received by the Priest, assisted by the acolyte or other minister. The bread and wine for the Eucharist are carried to the Celebrant, who places them on the altar, while other gifts are put in another suitable place (cf. no. 73).

141. The Priest accepts the paten with the bread at the altar, holds it slightly raised above the altar with both hands and says quietly, *Benedictus es, Domine* (Blessed are you, Lord God). Then he places the paten with the bread on the corporal.

142. After this, as the minister presents the cruets, the Priest stands at the side of the altar and pours wine and a little water into the chalice, saying quietly, *Per huius aquae* (*By the mystery of this water*). He returns to the middle of the altar and with both hands raises the chalice a little, and says quietly, *Benedictus es, Domine* (*Blessed are you, Lord God*). Then he places the chalice on the corporal and, if appropriate, covers it with a pall.

If, however, there is no Offertory Chant and the organ is not played, in the presentation of the bread and wine the Priest may say the formulas of blessing aloud and the people acclaim, *Blessed be God for ever*.

143. After placing the chalice on the altar, the Priest bows profoundly and says quietly, *In spiritu humilitatis* (*With humble spirit*).

144. If incense is being used, the Priest then puts some in the thurible, blesses it without saying anything, and incenses the offerings, the cross, and the altar. While standing at the side of the altar, a minister incenses the Priest and then the people.

145. After the prayer *In spiritu humilitatis* (*With humble spirit*) or after the incensation, the Priest washes his hands standing at the side of the altar and, as the minister pours the water, says quietly, *Lava me, Domine* (*Wash me, O Lord*).

146. Returning to the middle of the altar, and standing facing the people, the Priest extends and then joins his hands, and calls upon the people to pray, saying, *Orate, fratres* (*Pray, brethren*). The people rise and make the response *May the Lord accept the sacrifice*, etc. Then the Priest, with hands extended, says the Prayer over the Offerings. At the end the people acclaim, *Amen*.

147. Then the Priest begins the Eucharistic Prayer. In accordance with the rubrics (cf. no. 365), he selects a Eucharistic Prayer from those found in the *Roman Missal* or approved by the Apostolic See. By its very nature, the Eucharistic Prayer requires that only the Priest say it, in virtue of his Ordination. The people, for their part, should associate themselves with the Priest in faith and in silence, as well as by means of their interventions as prescribed in the course of the Eucharistic Prayer: namely, the responses in the Preface dialogue, the *Sanctus* (*Holy, Holy, Holy*), the acclamation after the Consecration, the acclamation *Amen* after the concluding doxology, as well as other acclamations approved by the Conference of Bishops with the *recognitio* of the Holy See.

It is most appropriate that the Priest sing those parts of the Eucharistic Prayer for which musical notation is provided.

148. As he begins the Eucharistic Prayer, the Priest extends his hands and sings or says, *The Lord be with you*. The people reply, *And with your spirit*. As he continues, saying, *Lift up your hearts*, he raises his hands. The people reply, *We lift them up to the Lord*. Then the Priest, with hands extended, adds, *Let us give thanks to the Lord our God*, and the people reply, *It is right and just*. After this, the Priest, with hands extended, continues the Preface. At its conclusion, he joins his hands and, together with all those present, sings or says aloud the *Sanctus* (*Holy, Holy, Holy*) (cf. no. 79 b).

149. The Priest continues the Eucharistic Prayer in accordance with the rubrics that are set out in each of the Prayers.

If the celebrant is a Bishop, in the Prayers, after the words *N., our Pope*, he adds, *and me, your unworthy servant*. If, however, the Bishop is celebrating outside his own diocese, after the words *with . . . N., our Pope*, he adds, *my brother N., the Bishop of this Church, and me, your unworthy servant*; or after the words *especially . . . N., our Pope*, he adds, *my brother N., the Bishop of this Church, and me, your unworthy servant*.

THE DIFFERENT FORMS OF CELEBRATING MASS 49

The Diocesan Bishop, or one who is equivalent to the Diocesan Bishop in law, must be mentioned by means of this formula: *together with your servant N., our Pope, and N., our Bishop (or Vicar, Prelate, Prefect, Abbot)*.

It is permitted to mention Coadjutor Bishop and Auxiliary Bishops in the Eucharistic Prayer, but not other Bishops who happen to be present. When several are to be mentioned, this is done with the collective formula: *N., our Bishop and his assistant Bishops*.

In each of the Eucharistic Prayers, these formulas are to be adapted according to the requirements of grammar.

150. A little before the Consecration, if appropriate, a minister rings a small bell as a signal to the faithful. The minister also rings the small bell at each elevation by the Priest, according to local custom.

If incense is being used, when the host and the chalice are shown to the people after the Consecration, a minister incenses them.

151. After the Consecration when the Priest has said, *The mystery of faith*, the people pronounce the acclamation, using one of the prescribed formulas.

At the end of the Eucharistic Prayer, the Priest takes the paten with the host and the chalice and elevates them both while pronouncing alone the doxology *Through him*. At the end the people acclaim, *Amen*. After this, the Priest places the paten and the chalice on the corporal.

152. After the Eucharistic Prayer is concluded, the Priest, with hands joined, says alone the introduction to the Lord's Prayer, and then with hands extended, he pronounces the prayer together with the people.

153. After the Lord's Prayer is concluded, the Priest, with hands extended, says alone the embolism *Libera nos (Deliver us, Lord)*. At the end, the people acclaim, *For the kingdom*.

154. Then the Priest, with hands extended, says aloud the prayer *Domine Iesu Christe, qui dixisti (Lord Jesus Christ, who said to your Apostles)* and when it is concluded, extending and then joining his hands, he announces the greeting of peace, facing the people and saying, *The peace of the Lord be with you always*. The people reply, *And with your spirit*. After this, if appropriate, the Priest adds, *Let us offer each other the sign of peace*.

The Priest may give the Sign of Peace to the ministers but always remains within the sanctuary, so that the celebration is not disrupted. In the Dioceses of the United States of America, for a good reason, on special occasions (for example, in the case of a funeral, a wedding, or when civic leaders are present), the Priest may offer the Sign of Peace to a small number of the faithful near the sanctuary. According to what is decided by the Conference of Bishops, all express to one another peace, communion, and charity. While the Sign of Peace is being given, it is permissible to say, *The peace of the Lord be with you always*, to which the reply is *Amen*.

155. After this, the Priest takes the host, breaks it over the paten, and places a small piece in the chalice, saying quietly, *Haec commixtio (May this mingling)*. Meanwhile the *Agnus Dei (Lamb of God)* is sung or said by the choir and by the people (cf. no. 83).

156. Then the Priest, with hands joined, says quietly the prayer for Communion, either *Domine Iesu Christe, Fili Dei vivi (Lord Jesus Christ, Son of the living God)* or *Perceptio Corporis et Sanguinis tui (May the receiving of your Body and Blood)*.

157. When the prayer is concluded, the Priest genuflects, takes a host consecrated at the same Mass, and, holding it slightly raised above the paten or above the chalice, facing the people, says, *Ecce Agnus Dei (Behold the Lamb of God)* and together with the people he adds, *Lord, I am not worthy*.

158. After this, standing facing the altar, the Priest says quietly, *Corpus Christi custodiat me in vitam aeternam* (*May the Body of Christ keep me safe for eternal life*), and reverently consumes the Body of Christ. Then he takes the chalice, saying quietly, *Sanguis Christi custodiat me in vitam aeternam* (*May the Blood of Christ keep me safe for eternal life*), and reverently partakes of the Blood of Christ.

159. While the Priest is receiving the Sacrament, the Communion Chant begins (cf. no. 86).

160. The Priest then takes the paten or ciborium and approaches the communicants, who usually come up in procession.

It is not permitted for the faithful to take the consecrated Bread or the sacred chalice by themselves and, still less, to hand them on from one to another among themselves. The norm established for the Dioceses of the United States of America is that Holy Communion is to be received standing, unless an individual member of the faithful wishes to receive Communion while kneeling (Congregation for Divine Worship and the Discipline of the Sacraments, Instruction *Redemptionis Sacramentum*, March 25, 2004, no. 91).

When receiving Holy Communion, the communicant bows his or her head before the Sacrament as a gesture of reverence and receives the Body of the Lord from the minister. The consecrated host may be received either on the tongue or in the hand, at the discretion of each communicant. When Holy Communion is received under both kinds, the sign of reverence is also made before receiving the Precious Blood.

161. If Communion is given only under the species of bread, the Priest raises the host slightly and shows it to each, saying, *The Body of Christ*. The communicant replies, *Amen*, and receives the Sacrament either on the tongue or, where this is allowed, in the hand, the choice lying with the communicant. As soon as the communicant receives the host, he or she consumes the whole of it.

If, however, Communion is given under both kinds, the rite prescribed in nos. 284-287 is to be followed.

162. In the distribution of Communion the Priest may be assisted by other Priests who happen to be present. If such Priests are not present and there is a truly large number of communicants, the Priest may call upon extraordinary ministers to assist him, that is, duly instituted acolytes or even other faithful who have been duly deputed for this purpose.[96] In case of necessity, the Priest may depute suitable faithful for this single occasion.[97]

These ministers should not approach the altar before the Priest has received Communion, and they are always to receive from the hands of the Priest Celebrant the vessel containing the species of the Most Holy Eucharist for distribution to the faithful.

163. When the distribution of Communion is over, the Priest himself immediately and completely consumes at the altar any consecrated wine that happens to remain; as for any consecrated hosts that are left, he either consumes them at the altar or carries them to the place designated for the reservation of the Eucharist.

Upon returning to the altar, the Priest collects the fragments, should any remain, and he stands at the altar or at the credence table and purifies the paten or ciborium over the chalice, and after this purifies the chalice, saying quietly the formula *Quod ore sumpsimus, Domine* (*What has passed our lips*), and dries the chalice with a purificator. If the vessels are purified at the altar, they are carried to the credence table by a minister. Nevertheless, it is also permitted to leave vessels needing to be purified,

---

[96] Cf. Sacred Congregation for the Sacraments and Divine Worship, Instruction, *Inaestimabile donum*, April 3, 1980, no. 10: *Acta Apostolicae Sedis* 72 (1980), p. 336; Interdicasterial Instruction on certain questions regarding the collaboration of the non-ordained faithful in the sacred ministry of Priests, *Ecclesiae de mysterio*, August 15, 1997, art. 8: *Acta Apostolicae Sedis* 89 (1997), p. 871.

[97] Cf. Roman Missal, Appendix III, Rite of Deputing a Minister to Distribute Holy Communion on a Single Occasion.

especially if there are several, on a corporal, suitably covered, either on the altar or on the credence table, and to purify them immediately after Mass, after the Dismissal of the people.

164. After this, the Priest may return to the chair. A sacred silence may now be observed for some time, or a Psalm or other canticle of praise or a hymn may be sung (cf. no. 88).

165. Then, standing at the chair or at the altar, and facing the people with hands joined, the Priest says, *Let us pray*; then, with hands extended, he recites the Prayer after Communion. A brief period of silence may precede the prayer, unless this has been already observed immediately after Communion. At the end of the prayer the people acclaim, *Amen*.

The Concluding Rites

166. When the Prayer after Communion is concluded, brief announcements should be made to the people, if there are any.

167. Then the Priest, extending his hands, greets the people, saying, *The Lord be with you*. They reply, *And with your spirit*. The Priest, joining his hands again and then immediately placing his left hand on his breast, raises his right hand and adds, *May almighty God bless you* and, as he makes the Sign of the Cross over the people, he continues, *the Father, and the Son, and the Holy Spirit*. All reply, *Amen*.

On certain days and occasions this blessing, in accordance with the rubrics, is expanded and expressed by a Prayer over the People or another more solemn formula.

A Bishop blesses the people with the appropriate formula, making the Sign of the Cross three times over the people.[98]

168. Immediately after the Blessing, with hands joined, the Priest adds, *Ite, missa est* (*Go forth, the Mass is ended*) and all reply, *Thanks be to God*.

169. Then the Priest venerates the altar as usual with a kiss and, after making a profound bow with the lay ministers, he withdraws with them.

170. If, however, another liturgical action follows the Mass, the Concluding Rites, that is, the Greeting, the Blessing, and the Dismissal, are omitted.

B) Mass with a Deacon

171. When he is present at the celebration of the Eucharist, a Deacon should exercise his ministry, wearing sacred vestments. In fact, the Deacon:
   a) assists the Priest and walks at his side;
   b) ministers at the altar, both as regards the chalice and the book;
   c) proclaims the Gospel and may, at the direction of the Priest Celebrant, give the Homily (cf. no. 66);
   d) guides the faithful people by giving appropriate instructions, and announces the intentions of the Universal Prayer;
   e) assists the Priest Celebrant in distributing Communion, and purifies and arranges the sacred vessels;
   f) carries out the duties of other ministers himself, if necessary, when none of them is present.

---

98 Cf. *Caeremoniale Episcoporum, editio typica*, 1984, nos. 1118-1121.

The Introductory Rites

172. Carrying the *Book of the Gospels* slightly elevated, the Deacon precedes the Priest as he approaches the altar or else walks at the Priest's side.

173. When he reaches the altar, if he is carrying the *Book of the Gospels*, he omits the sign of reverence and goes up to the altar. It is a praiseworthy practice for him to place the *Book of the Gospels* on the altar, after which, together with the Priest, he venerates the altar with a kiss.

If, however, he is not carrying the *Book of the Gospels*, he makes a profound bow to the altar with the Priest in the customary way and with him venerates the altar with a kiss.

Lastly, if incense is being used, he assists the Priest in putting some into the thurible and in incensing the cross and the altar.

174. Once the altar has been incensed, the Deacon goes to the chair together with the Priest and there stands at the Priest's side and assists him as necessary.

The Liturgy of the Word

175. During the singing of the *Alleluia* or other chant, if incense is being used, the Deacon ministers to the Priest as he puts incense into the thurible. Then, bowing profoundly before the Priest, he asks for the blessing, saying in a low voice, *Your blessing, Father*. The Priest blesses him, saying, *May the Lord be in your heart*. The Deacon signs himself with the Sign of the Cross and replies, *Amen*. Having bowed to the altar, he then takes up the *Book of the Gospels* which was placed on it and proceeds to the ambo, carrying the book slightly elevated. He is preceded by a thurifer carrying a smoking thurible and by ministers with lighted candles. At the ambo the Deacon greets the people, with hands joined, saying, *The Lord be with you*. After this, at the words *A reading from the holy Gospel*, he signs with his thumb the book and then himself on his forehead, mouth, and breast. He incenses the book and proclaims the Gospel reading. When this is done, he acclaims, *The Gospel of the Lord*, and all reply, *Praise to you, Lord Jesus Christ*. He then venerates the book with a kiss, saying quietly the formula *Per evangelica dicta* (*Through the words of the Gospel*), and returns to the Priest's side.

When the Deacon is assisting the Bishop, he carries the book to him to be kissed, or else kisses it himself, saying quietly the formula *Per evangelica dicta* (*Through the words of the Gospel*). In more solemn celebrations, if appropriate, the Bishop may impart a blessing to the people with the *Book of the Gospels*.

Lastly, the Deacon may carry the *Book of the Gospels* to the credence table or to another suitable and dignified place.

176. Moreover, if there is no other suitable reader present, the Deacon should proclaim the other readings as well.

177. After the introduction by the Priest, it is the Deacon himself who announces the intentions of the Universal Prayer, usually from the ambo.

The Liturgy of the Eucharist

178. After the Universal Prayer, while the Priest remains at the chair, the Deacon prepares the altar, assisted by the acolyte, but it is the Deacon's place to take care of the sacred vessels himself. He also assists the Priest in receiving the people's gifts. After this, he hands the Priest the paten with the bread to be consecrated, pours wine and a little water into the chalice, saying quietly, *By the mystery of this water*, etc., and after this presents the chalice to the Priest. He may also carry out the preparation of the chalice at the credence table. If incense is being used, the Deacon assists the Priest during the incensation of the offerings, the cross, and the altar; and after this the Deacon himself or the acolyte incenses the Priest and the people.

179. During the Eucharistic Prayer, the Deacon stands near the Priest, but slightly behind him, so that when necessary he may assist the Priest with the chalice or the Missal.

From the epiclesis until the Priest shows the chalice, the Deacon usually remains kneeling. If several Deacons are present, one of them may place incense in the thurible for the Consecration and incense the host and the chalice at the elevation.

180. At the concluding doxology of the Eucharistic Prayer, the Deacon stands next to the Priest, and holds the chalice elevated while the Priest elevates the paten with the host, until the people have acclaimed, *Amen*.

181. After the Priest has said the prayer for the Rite of Peace and the greeting *The peace of the Lord be with you always* and the people have replied, *And with your spirit*, the Deacon, if appropriate, says the invitation to the Sign of Peace. With hands joined, he faces the people and says, *Let us offer each other the sign of peace*. Then he himself receives the Sign of Peace from the Priest and may offer it to those other ministers who are nearest to him.

182. After the Priest's Communion, the Deacon receives Communion under both kinds from the Priest himself and then assists the Priest in distributing Communion to the people. If Communion is given under both kinds, the Deacon himself administers the chalice to the communicants; and, when the distribution is over, standing at the altar, he immediately and reverently consumes all of the Blood of Christ that remains, assisted, if the case requires, by other Deacons and Priests.

183. When the distribution of Communion is over, the Deacon returns to the altar with the Priest, collects the fragments, should any remain, and then carries the chalice and other sacred vessels to the credence table, where he purifies them and arranges them as usual, while the Priest returns to the chair. Nevertheless, it is also permitted to leave vessels needing to be purified on a corporal, suitably covered, on the credence table, and to purify them immediately after Mass, following the Dismissal of the people.

The Concluding Rites

184. Once the Prayer after Communion has been said, the Deacon makes brief announcements to the people, if indeed any need to be made, unless the Priest prefers to do this himself.

185. If a Prayer over the People or a formula of Solemn Blessing is used, the Deacon says, *Bow down for the blessing*. After the Priest's blessing, the Deacon, with hands joined and facing the people, dismisses the people, saying, *Ite, missa est* (*Go forth, the Mass is ended*).

186. Then, together with the Priest, the Deacon venerates the altar with a kiss, makes a profound bow, and withdraws in a manner similar to the Entrance Procession.

C) THE FUNCTIONS OF THE ACOLYTE

187. The functions that the acolyte may carry out are of various kinds and several may occur at the same moment. Hence, it is desirable that these duties be suitably distributed among several acolytes. If, in fact, only one acolyte is present, he should perform the more important duties while the rest are to be distributed among several ministers.

The Introductory Rites

188. In the procession to the altar, the acolyte may carry the cross, walking between two ministers with lighted candles. Upon reaching the altar, however, the acolyte places the cross upright near the

altar so that it may serve as the altar cross; otherwise, he puts it away in a dignified place. Then he takes his place in the sanctuary.

189. Through the entire celebration, it is for the acolyte to approach the Priest or the Deacon, whenever necessary, in order to present the book to them and to assist them in any other way required. Thus it is appropriate that, in so far as possible, the acolyte should occupy a place from which he can easily carry out his ministry either at the chair or at the altar.

The Liturgy of the Eucharist

190. In the absence of a Deacon, after the Universal Prayer and while the Priest remains at the chair, the acolyte places the corporal, the purificator, the chalice, the pall, and the Missal on the altar. Then, if necessary, the acolyte assists the Priest in receiving the gifts of the people and, if appropriate, brings the bread and wine to the altar and hands them to the Priest. If incense is being used, the acolyte presents the thurible to the Priest and assists him while he incenses the offerings, the cross, and the altar. Then the acolyte incenses the Priest and the people.

191. A duly instituted acolyte, as an extraordinary minister, may, if necessary, assist the Priest in distributing Communion to the people.[99] If Communion is given under both kinds, in the absence of a Deacon, the acolyte administers the chalice to the communicants or holds the chalice if Communion is given by intinction.

192. Likewise, after the distribution of Communion is complete, a duly instituted acolyte helps the Priest or Deacon to purify and arrange the sacred vessels. In the absence of a Deacon, a duly instituted acolyte carries the sacred vessels to the credence table and there purifies them, wipes them, and arranges them as usual.

193. After the celebration of Mass, the acolyte and other ministers return together with the Deacon and the Priest in procession to the sacristy, in the same manner and in the same order in which they entered.

D) THE FUNCTIONS OF THE READER

Introductory Rites

194. In the procession to the altar, in the absence of a Deacon, the reader, wearing approved attire, may carry the *Book of the Gospels*, slightly elevated. In that case, the reader walks in front of the Priest but otherwise walks along with the other ministers.

195. Upon reaching the altar, the reader makes a profound bow with the others. If he is carrying the *Book of the Gospels*, he approaches the altar and places the *Book of the Gospels* upon it. Then the reader takes his own place in the sanctuary with the other ministers.

The Liturgy of the Word

196. The reader reads from the ambo the readings that precede the Gospel. In the absence of a psalmist, the reader may also proclaim the Responsorial Psalm after the First Reading.

---

99   Paul VI, Apostolic Letter, *Ministeria quaedam*, August 15, 1972: *Acta Apostolicae Sedis* 64 (1972), p. 532.

197. In the absence of a Deacon, the reader, after the introduction by the Priest, may announce the intentions of the Universal Prayer from the ambo.

198. If there is no singing at the Entrance or at Communion and the antiphons given in the Missal are not recited by the faithful, the reader may read them at an appropriate time (cf. nos. 48, 87).

II. CONCELEBRATED MASS

199. Concelebration, by which the unity of the Priesthood, of the Sacrifice, and also of the whole People of God is appropriately expressed, is prescribed by the rite itself for the Ordination of a Bishop and of Priests, at the Blessing of an Abbot, and at the Chrism Mass.

It is recommended, moreover, unless the good of the Christian faithful requires or suggests otherwise, at:

a) the Evening Mass of the Lord's Supper;
b) the Mass during Councils, gatherings of Bishops, and Synods;
c) the Conventual Mass and the principal Mass in churches and oratories;
d) Masses at any kind of gathering of Priests, either secular or religious.[100]

Every Priest, however, is allowed to celebrate the Eucharist individually, though not at the same time as a concelebration is taking place in the same church or oratory. However, on Holy Thursday, and for the Mass of the Easter Vigil, it is not permitted to celebrate Mass individually.

200. Visiting Priests should be gladly admitted to concelebration of the Eucharist, provided their Priestly standing has been ascertained.

201. When there is a large number of Priests, concelebration may take place even several times on the same day, where necessity or pastoral advantage commend it. However, this must be done at different times or in distinct sacred places.[101]

202. It is for the Bishop, in accordance with the norm of law, to regulate the discipline for concelebration in all churches and oratories of his diocese.

203. To be held in particularly high regard is that concelebration in which the Priests of any given diocese concelebrate with their own Bishop at a stational Mass, especially on the more solemn days of the liturgical year, at the Ordination Mass of a new Bishop of the diocese or of his Coadjutor or Auxiliary, at the Chrism Mass, at the Evening Mass of the Lord's Supper, at celebrations of the Founder Saint of a local Church or the Patron of the diocese, on anniversaries of the Bishop, and, lastly, on the occasion of a Synod or a pastoral visitation.

In the same way, concelebration is recommended whenever Priests gather together with their own Bishop whether on the occasion of a retreat or at any other gathering. In these cases the sign of the unity of the Priesthood and also of the Church inherent in every concelebration is made more clearly manifest.[102]

---

100 Cf. Second Ecumenical Council of the Vatican, Constitution on the Sacred Liturgy, *Sacrosanctum Concilium*, no. 57; *Code of Canon Law*, can. 902.
101 Cf. Sacred Congregation of Rites, Instruction, *Eucharisticum mysterium*, May 25, 1967, no. 47: *Acta Apostolicae Sedis* 59 (1967), p. 566.
102 Cf. *ibidem*, no. 47: p. 565.

204. For a particular reason, having to do either with the significance of the rite or of the festivity, the faculty is given to celebrate or concelebrate more than once on the same day in the following cases:

   a) a Priest who has celebrated or concelebrated the Chrism Mass on Thursday of Holy Week may also celebrate or concelebrate the Evening Mass of the Lord's Supper;
   b) a Priest who has celebrated or concelebrated the Mass of the Easter Vigil may celebrate or concelebrate Mass during the day on Easter Sunday;
   c) on the Nativity of the Lord (Christmas Day), all Priests may celebrate or concelebrate three Masses, provided the Masses are celebrated at their proper times of day;
   d) on the Commemoration of All the Faithful Departed (All Souls' Day), all Priests may celebrate or concelebrate three Masses, provided that the celebrations take place at different times, and with due regard for what has been laid down regarding the application of second and third Masses;[103]
   e) a Priest who concelebrates with the Bishop or his delegate at a Synod or pastoral visitation, or concelebrates on the occasion of a gathering of Priests, may celebrate Mass again for the benefit of the faithful. This holds also, with due regard for the prescriptions of law, for groups of religious.

205. A concelebrated Mass, whatever its form, is arranged in accordance with the norms commonly in force (cf. nos. 112-198), observing or adapting however what is set out below.

206. No one is ever to join a concelebration or to be admitted as a concelebrant once the Mass has already begun.

207. In the sanctuary there should be prepared:

   a) seats and texts for the concelebrating Priests;
   b) on the credence table: a chalice of sufficient size or else several chalices.

208. If a Deacon is not present, the functions proper to him are to be carried out by some of the concelebrants.

   If other ministers are also absent, their proper parts may be entrusted to other suitable faithful laypeople; otherwise, they are carried out by some of the concelebrants.

209. The concelebrants put on in the vesting room, or other suitable place, the sacred vestments they customarily wear when celebrating Mass individually. However, should a just cause arise (e.g., a more considerable number of concelebrants or a lack of vestments), concelebrants other than the principal celebrant may omit the chasuble and simply wear the stole over the alb.

The Introductory Rites

210. When everything has been properly arranged, the procession moves as usual through the church to the altar. The concelebrating Priests walk ahead of the principal celebrant.

211. On arriving at the altar, the concelebrants and the principal celebrant, after making a profound bow, venerate the altar with a kiss, then go to their designated seats. As for the principal celebrant, if appropriate, he incenses the cross and the altar and then goes to the chair.

---

103   Cf. Benedict XV, Apostolic Constitution, *Incruentum altaris sacrificium*, August 10, 1915: *Acta Apostolicae Sedis* 7 (1915), pp. 401-404.

The Liturgy of the Word

212. During the Liturgy of the Word, the concelebrants remain at their places, sitting or standing whenever the principal celebrant does.

When the *Alleluia* is begun, all rise, except for a Bishop, who puts incense into the thurible without saying anything and blesses the Deacon or, in the absence of a Deacon, the concelebrant who is to proclaim the Gospel. However, in a concelebration where a Priest presides, the concelebrant who in the absence of a Deacon proclaims the Gospel neither requests nor receives the blessing of the principal celebrant.

213. The Homily is usually given by the principal celebrant or by one of the concelebrants.

The Liturgy of the Eucharist

214. The Preparation of the Gifts (cf. nos. 139-146) is carried out by the principal celebrant, while the other concelebrants remain at their places.

215. After the Prayer over the Offerings has been said by the principal celebrant, the concelebrants approach the altar and stand around it, but in such a way that they do not obstruct the execution of the rites and that the sacred action may be seen clearly by the faithful. Nor should they obstruct the Deacon whenever he needs to approach the altar by reason of his ministry.

The Deacon exercises his ministry near the altar, assisting whenever necessary with the chalice and the Missal. However, in so far as possible, he stands back slightly, behind the concelebrating Priests standing around the principal celebrant.

The Manner of Pronouncing the Eucharistic Prayer

216. The Preface is sung or said by the principal Priest Celebrant alone; but the *Sanctus* (Holy, Holy, Holy) is sung or recited by all the concelebrants, together with the people and the choir.

217. After the *Sanctus* (Holy, Holy, Holy), the concelebrating Priests continue the Eucharistic Prayer in the way described below. Only the principal celebrant makes the gestures, unless other indications are given.

218. The parts pronounced by all the concelebrants together and especially the words of Consecration, which all are obliged to say, are to be recited in such a manner that the concelebrants speak them in a low voice and that the principal celebrant's voice is heard clearly. In this way the words can be more easily understood by the people.

It is a praiseworthy practice for the parts that are to be said by all the concelebrants together and for which musical notation is provided in the Missal to be sung.

Eucharistic Prayer I, or the Roman Canon

219. In Eucharistic Prayer I, or the Roman Canon, the *Te igitur* (*To you, therefore, most merciful Father*) is said by the principal celebrant alone, with hands extended.

220. It is appropriate that the commemoration (*Memento*) of the living and the *Communicantes* (*In communion with those*) be assigned to one or other of the concelebrating Priests, who then pronounces these prayers alone, with hands extended, and in a loud voice.

221. The *Hanc igitur* (*Therefore, Lord, we pray*) is said once again by the principal celebrant alone, with hands extended.

222. From the *Quam oblationem* (Be pleased, O God, we pray) up to and including the *Supplices* (In humble prayer we ask you, almighty God), the principal celebrant alone makes the gestures, while all the concelebrants pronounce everything together, in this manner:

   a) the *Quam oblationem* (Be pleased, O God, we pray) with hands extended toward the offerings;
   b) the *Qui pridie* (On the day before he was to suffer) and the *Simili modo* (In a similar way) with hands joined;
   c) the words of the Lord, with each extending his right hand toward the bread and toward the chalice, if this seems appropriate; and at the elevation looking toward them and after this bowing profoundly;
   d) the *Unde et memores* (Therefore, O Lord, as we celebrate the memorial) and the *Supra quae* (Be pleased to look upon) with hands extended;
   e) for the *Supplices* (In humble prayer we ask you, almighty God) up to and including the words *through this participation at the altar*, bowing with hands joined; then standing upright and crossing themselves at the words *may be filled with every grace and heavenly blessing*.

223. It is appropriate that the commemoration *(Memento)* of the dead and the *Nobis quoque peccatoribus* (To us, also, your servants) be assigned to one or other of the concelebrants, who pronounces them alone, with hands extended, and in a loud voice.

224. At the words *To us, also, your servants, who though sinners*, of the *Nobis quoque peccatoribus*, all the concelebrants strike their breast.

225. The *Per quem haec omnia* (Through whom you continue) is said by the principal celebrant alone.

Eucharistic Prayer II

226. In Eucharistic Prayer II, the part *You are indeed Holy, O Lord* is pronounced by the principal celebrant alone, with hands extended.

227. In the parts from *Make holy, therefore, these gifts* to the end of *Humbly we pray*, all the concelebrants pronounce everything together as follows:

   a) the part *Make holy, therefore, these gifts,* with hands extended toward the offerings;
   b) the parts *At the time he was betrayed* and *In a similar way* with hands joined;
   c) the words of the Lord, with each extending his right hand toward the bread and toward the chalice, if this seems appropriate; and at the elevation looking toward them and after this bowing profoundly;
   d) the parts *Therefore, as we celebrate* and *Humbly we pray* with hands extended.

228. It is appropriate that the intercessions for the living, *Remember, Lord, your Church*, and for the dead, *Remember also our brothers and sisters*, be assigned to one or other of the concelebrants, who pronounces them alone, with hands extended, and in a loud voice.

Eucharistic Prayer III

229. In Eucharistic Prayer III, the part *You are indeed Holy, O Lord* is pronounced by the principal celebrant alone, with hands extended.

230. In the parts from *Therefore, O Lord, we humbly implore you* to the end of *Look, we pray upon the oblation*, all the concelebrants pronounce everything together as follows:

   a) the part *Therefore, O Lord, we humbly implore you* with hands extended toward the offerings;
   b) the parts *For on the night he was betrayed* and *In a similar way* with hands joined;

c) the words of the Lord, with each extending his right hand toward the bread and toward the chalice, if this seems appropriate; and at the elevation looking toward them and after this bowing profoundly;
d) the parts *Therefore, O Lord, as we celebrate the memorial* and *Look, we pray, upon the oblation* with hands extended.

231. It is appropriate that the intercessions *May he make of us an eternal offering to you*, and *May this Sacrifice of our reconciliation*, and *To our departed brothers and sisters* be assigned to one or other of the concelebrants, who pronounces them alone, with hands extended, and in a loud voice.

Eucharistic Prayer IV

232. In Eucharistic Prayer IV, the part *We give you praise, Father most holy* up to and including the words *he might sanctify creation to the full* is pronounced by the principal celebrant alone, with hands extended.

233. In the parts from *Therefore, O Lord, we pray* to the end of *Look, O Lord, upon the Sacrifice*, all the concelebrants pronounce everything together as follows:

a) the part *Therefore, O Lord, we pray* with hands extended toward the offerings;
b) the parts *For when the hour had come* and *In a similar way* with hands joined;
c) the words of the Lord, with each extending his right hand toward the bread and toward the chalice, if this seems appropriate; and at the elevation looking toward them and after this bowing profoundly;
d) the parts *Therefore, O Lord, as we now celebrate* and *Look, O Lord, upon the Sacrifice* with hands extended.

234. It is appropriate that the intercessions *Therefore, Lord, remember now* and *To all of us, your children* be assigned to one or other of the concelebrants, who pronounces them alone, with hands extended, and in a loud voice.

235. As for other Eucharistic Prayers approved by the Apostolic See, the norms laid down for each one are to be observed.

236. The concluding doxology of the Eucharistic Prayer is pronounced solely by the principal Priest Celebrant or together, if this is desired, with the other concelebrants, but not by the faithful.

The Communion Rite

237. Then the principal celebrant, with hands joined, says the introduction to the Lord's Prayer. Next, with hands extended, he says the Lord's Prayer itself together with the other concelebrants, who also pray with hands extended, and together with the people.

238. The *Libera nos (Deliver us)* is said by the principal celebrant alone, with hands extended. All the concelebrants, together with the people, pronounce the concluding acclamation *For the kingdom*.

239. After the Deacon or, in the absence of a Deacon, one of the concelebrants, has given the instruction *Let us offer each other the sign of peace*, all give one another the Sign of Peace. Those concelebrants nearer the principal celebrant receive the Sign of Peace from him before the Deacon does.

240. During the *Agnus Dei (Lamb of God)*, the Deacons or some of the concelebrants may help the principal celebrant to break the hosts for the Communion of both the concelebrants and the people.

241. After the commingling, the principal celebrant alone, with hands joined, quietly says either the prayer *Domine Iesu Christe, Fili Dei vivi* (*Lord Jesus Christ, Son of the living God*) or the prayer *Perceptio Corporis et Sanguinis tui* (*May the receiving of your Body and Blood*).

242. Once the prayer for Communion has been said, the principal celebrant genuflects and steps back a little. Then one after another the concelebrants come to the middle of the altar, genuflect, and reverently take the Body of Christ from the altar. Then holding it in their right hand, with the left hand placed underneath, they return to their places. However, the concelebrants may remain in their places and take the Body of Christ from the paten held for them by the principal celebrant or held by one or more of the concelebrants passing in front of them, or they may do so by handing the paten one to another, and so to the last of them.

243. Then the principal celebrant takes a host consecrated in the same Mass, holds it slightly raised above the paten or the chalice, and, facing the people, says the *Ecce Agnus Dei* (*Behold the Lamb of God*). With the concelebrants and the people he continues, saying the *Domine, non sum dignus* (*Lord, I am not worthy*).

244. Then the principal celebrant, facing the altar, says quietly, *Corpus Christi custodiat me in vitam aeternam* (*May the Body of Christ keep me safe for eternal life*), and reverently receives the Body of Christ. The concelebrants do likewise, giving themselves Communion. After them the Deacon receives the Body and Blood of the Lord from the principal celebrant.

245. The Blood of the Lord may be consumed either by drinking from the chalice directly, or by intinction, or by means of a tube or a spoon.

246. If Communion is consumed by drinking directly from the chalice, one of these procedures may be followed:

a) The principal celebrant, standing at the middle of the altar, takes the chalice and says quietly, *Sanguis Christi custodiat me in vitam aeternam* (*May the Blood of Christ keep me safe for eternal life*). He consumes a little of the Blood of Christ and hands the chalice to the Deacon or a concelebrant. He then distributes Communion to the faithful (cf. nos. 160-162).
   The concelebrants approach the altar one after another or, if two chalices are used, two by two. They genuflect, partake of the Blood of Christ, wipe the rim of the chalice, and return to their seats.
b) The principal celebrant consumes the Blood of the Lord standing as usual at the middle of the altar.
   The concelebrants, however, may partake of the Blood of the Lord while remaining in their places and drinking from the chalice presented to them by the Deacon or by one of the concelebrants, or even passed from one to the other. The chalice is always wiped either by the one who drinks from it or by the one who presents it. After each has communicated, he returns to his seat.

247. The Deacon reverently drinks at the altar all of the Blood of Christ that remains, assisted, if the case requires, by some of the concelebrants. He then carries the chalice to the credence table and there he or a duly instituted acolyte purifies it, wipes it, and arranges it as usual (cf. no. 183).

248. The Communion of the concelebrants may also be arranged in such a way that each communicates from the Body of the Lord at the altar and, immediately afterwards, from the Blood of the Lord.
   In this case the principal celebrant receives Communion under both kinds in the usual way (cf. no. 158), observing, however, the rite chosen in each particular instance for Communion from the chalice; and the other concelebrants should do the same.

After the principal celebrant's Communion, the chalice is placed at the side of the altar on another corporal. The concelebrants approach the middle of the altar one by one, genuflect, and communicate from the Body of the Lord; then they move to the side of the altar and partake of the Blood of the Lord, following the rite chosen for Communion from the chalice, as has been remarked above.

The Communion of the Deacon and the purification of the chalice take place as described above.

249. If the concelebrants' Communion is by intinction, the principal celebrant partakes of the Body and Blood of the Lord in the usual way, but making sure that enough of the precious Blood remains in the chalice for the Communion of the concelebrants. Then the Deacon, or one of the concelebrants, arranges the chalice together with the paten containing particles of the host, if appropriate, either in the center of the altar or at the side on another corporal.

The concelebrants approach the altar one by one, genuflect, and take a particle, intinct it partly into the chalice, and, holding a purificator under their mouth, consume the intincted particle. They then return to their places as at the beginning of Mass.

The Deacon also receives Communion by intinction and to the concelebrant's words, *Corpus et Sanguis Christi* (*The Body and Blood of Christ*) replies, *Amen*. Moreover, the Deacon consumes at the altar all that remains of the Precious Blood, assisted, if the case requires, by some of the concelebrants. He carries the chalice to the credence table and there he or a duly instituted acolyte purifies it, wipes it, and arranges it as usual.

The Concluding Rites

250. Everything else until the end of Mass is done by the principal celebrant in the usual way (cf. nos. 166-168), with the other concelebrants remaining at their seats.

251. Before leaving the altar, the concelebrants make a profound bow to the altar. For his part the principal celebrant, along with the Deacon, venerates the altar as usual with a kiss.

III. MASS AT WHICH ONLY ONE MINISTER PARTICIPATES

252. At a Mass celebrated by a Priest with only one minister to assist him and to make the responses, the rite of Mass with the people is followed (cf. nos. 120-169), the minister saying the people's parts if appropriate.

253. If, however, the minister is a Deacon, he performs his proper functions (cf. nos. 171-186) and likewise carries out the other parts, that is, those of the people.

254. Mass should not be celebrated without a minister, or at least one of the faithful, except for a just and reasonable cause. In this case, the greetings, the instructions, and the blessing at the end of Mass are omitted.

255. Before Mass, the necessary vessels are prepared either at the credence table or on the right hand side of the altar.

The Introductory Rites

256. The Priest approaches the altar and, after making a profound bow along with the minister, venerates the altar with a kiss and goes to the chair. If he wishes, the Priest may remain at the altar; in which case, the Missal is also prepared there. Then the minister or the Priest says the Entrance Antiphon.

257. Then the Priest, standing, makes with the minister the Sign of the Cross as the Priest says, *In the name of the Father,* etc. Facing the minister, he greets him, choosing one of the formulas provided.

258. Then the Penitential Act takes place, and, in accordance with the rubrics, the *Kyrie* and the *Gloria in excelsis (Glory to God in the highest)* are said.

259. Then, with hands joined, the Priest pronounces, *Let us pray*, and after a suitable pause, with hands extended, he pronounces the Collect. At the end the minister acclaims, *Amen*.

The Liturgy of the Word

260. The readings should, in so far as possible, be proclaimed from the ambo or a lectern.

261. After the Collect, the minister reads the First Reading and Psalm, the Second Reading, when it is to be said, and the verse of the *Alleluia* or other chant.

262. Then the Priest, bowing profoundly, says the prayer *Munda cor meum (Cleanse my heart)* and after this reads the Gospel. At the end he says, *The Gospel of the Lord*, to which the minister replies, *Praise to you, Lord Jesus Christ*. The Priest then venerates the book with a kiss, saying quietly the formula *Per evangelica dicta (Through the words of the Gospel)*.

263. After this, the Priest says the Symbol or Creed, in accordance with the rubrics, together with the minister.

264. The Universal Prayer follows, which may be said even in this form of Mass. The Priest introduces and concludes it, with the minister announcing the intentions.

The Liturgy of the Eucharist

265. In the Liturgy of the Eucharist, everything is done as at Mass with the people, except for the following.

266. After the acclamation at the end of the embolism that follows the Lord's Prayer, the Priest says the prayer *Domine Iesu Christe, qui dixisti (Lord Jesus Christ, who said to your Apostles)*. He then adds, *The peace of the Lord be with you always*, to which the minister replies, *And with your spirit*. If appropriate, the Priest gives the Sign of Peace to the minister.

267. Then, while he says the *Agnus Dei (Lamb of God)* with the minister, the Priest breaks the host over the paten. After the *Agnus Dei (Lamb of God)*, he performs the commingling, saying quietly the prayer *Haec commixtio (May this mingling)*.

268. After the commingling, the Priest quietly says either the prayer *Domine Iesu Christe, Fili Dei vivi (Lord Jesus Christ, Son of the living God)* or the prayer *Perceptio Corporis et Sanguinis tui (May the receiving of your Body and Blood)*. Then he genuflects, takes the host, and, if the minister is to receive Communion, turns to the minister and, holding the host a little above the paten or the chalice, says the *Ecce Agnus Dei (Behold the Lamb of God)*, adding with the minister, *Lord, I am not worthy*. Then facing the altar, the Priest partakes of the Body of Christ. If, however, the minister does not receive Communion, the Priest, after genuflecting, takes the host and, facing the altar, says quietly, *Lord, I am not worthy*, etc., and the *Corpus Christi custodiat me in vitam aeternam (May the Body of Christ keep me safe for eternal life)*, and consumes the Body of Christ. Then he takes the chalice and says quietly, *Sanguis Christi custodiat me in vitam aeternam (May the Blood of Christ keep me safe for eternal life)*, and consumes the Blood of Christ.

269. Before Communion is given to the minister, the Communion Antiphon is said by the minister or by the Priest himself.

270. The Priest purifies the chalice at the credence table or at the altar. If the chalice is purified at the altar, it may be carried to the credence table by the minister or may be arranged once again on the altar, at the side.

271. After the purification of the chalice, the Priest should observe a brief pause for silence, and after this he says the Prayer after Communion.

The Concluding Rites

272. The Concluding Rites are carried out as at a Mass with the people, but the *Ite, missa est* (*Go forth, the Mass is ended*) is omitted. The Priest venerates the altar as usual with a kiss and, after making a profound bow with the minister, withdraws.

IV. SOME GENERAL NORMS FOR ALL FORMS OF MASS

Veneration of the Altar and the Book of the Gospels

273. According to traditional practice, the veneration of the altar and of the *Book of the Gospels* is done by means of a kiss. However, where a sign of this kind is not in harmony with the traditions or the culture of some region, it is for the Conference of Bishops to establish some other sign in its place, with the consent of the Apostolic See.

Genuflections and Bows

274. A genuflection, made by bending the right knee to the ground, signifies adoration, and therefore it is reserved for the Most Blessed Sacrament, as well as for the Holy Cross from the solemn adoration during the liturgical celebration on Good Friday until the beginning of the Easter Vigil.

During Mass, three genuflections are made by the Priest Celebrant: namely, after the elevation of the host, after the elevation of the chalice, and before Communion. Certain specific features to be observed in a concelebrated Mass are noted in their proper place (cf. nos. 210-251).

If, however, the tabernacle with the Most Blessed Sacrament is situated in the sanctuary, the Priest, the Deacon, and the other ministers genuflect when they approach the altar and when they depart from it, but not during the celebration of Mass itself.

Otherwise, all who pass before the Most Blessed Sacrament genuflect, unless they are moving in procession.

Ministers carrying the processional cross or candles bow their heads instead of genuflecting.

275. A bow signifies reverence and honor shown to the persons themselves or to the signs that represent them. There are two kinds of bow: a bow of the head and a bow of the body.

- a) A bow of the head is made when the three Divine Persons are named together and at the names of Jesus, of the Blessed Virgin Mary, and of the Saint in whose honor Mass is being celebrated.
- b) A bow of the body, that is to say, a profound bow, is made to the altar; during the prayers *Munda cor meum* (*Cleanse my heart*) and *In spiritu humilitatis* (*With humble spirit*); in the Creed at the words *et incarnatus est* (*and by the Holy Spirit . . . and became man*); in the Roman Canon at the *Supplices te rogamus* (*In humble prayer we ask you, almighty God*). The same kind of bow is made by the Deacon when he asks for a blessing before the proclamation of the Gospel. In addition, the Priest bows slightly as he pronounces the words of the Lord at the Consecration.

Incensation

276. Thurification or incensation is an expression of reverence and of prayer, as is signified in Sacred Scripture (cf. Ps 140 [141]:2; Rev 8:3).

Incense may be used optionally in any form of Mass:

a) during the Entrance Procession;
b) at the beginning of Mass, to incense the cross and the altar;
c) at the procession before the Gospel and the proclamation of the Gospel itself;
d) after the bread and the chalice have been placed on the altar, to incense the offerings, the cross, and the altar, as well as the Priest and the people;
e) at the elevation of the host and the chalice after the Consecration.

277. The Priest, having put incense into the thurible, blesses it with the Sign of the Cross, without saying anything.

Before and after an incensation, a profound bow is made to the person or object that is incensed, except for the altar and the offerings for the Sacrifice of the Mass.

Three swings of the thurible are used to incense: the Most Blessed Sacrament, a relic of the Holy Cross and images of the Lord exposed for public veneration, the offerings for the Sacrifice of the Mass, the altar cross, the *Book of the Gospels*, the paschal candle, the Priest, and the people.

Two swings of the thurible are used to incense relics and images of the Saints exposed for public veneration; this should be done, however, only at the beginning of the celebration, following the incensation of the altar.

The altar is incensed with single swings of the thurible in this way:

a) if the altar is freestanding with respect to the wall, the Priest incenses walking around it;
b) if the altar is not freestanding, the Priest incenses it while walking first to the right hand side, then to the left.

The cross, if situated on the altar or near it, is incensed by the Priest before he incenses the altar; otherwise, he incenses it when he passes in front of it.

The Priest incenses the offerings with three swings of the thurible or by making the Sign of the Cross over the offerings with the thurible before going on to incense the cross and the altar.

The Purification

278. Whenever a fragment of the host adheres to his fingers, especially after the fraction or after the Communion of the faithful, the Priest should wipe his fingers over the paten or, if necessary, wash them. Likewise, he should also gather any fragments that may have fallen outside the paten.

279. The sacred vessels are purified by the Priest, the Deacon, or an instituted acolyte after Communion or after Mass, in so far as possible at the credence table. The purification of the chalice is done with water alone or with wine and water, which is then consumed by whoever does the purification. The paten is wiped clean as usual with the purificator.

Care is to be taken that whatever may remain of the Blood of Christ after the distribution of Communion is consumed immediately and completely at the altar.

280. If a host or any particle should fall, it is to be picked up reverently; and if any of the Precious Blood is spilled, the area where the spill occurred should be washed with water, and this water should then be poured into the *sacrarium* in the sacristy.

Communion under Both Kinds

281. Holy Communion has a fuller form as a sign when it takes place under both kinds. For in this form the sign of the Eucharistic banquet is more clearly evident and clearer expression is given to the divine will by which the new and eternal Covenant is ratified in the Blood of the Lord, as also the connection between the Eucharistic banquet and the eschatological banquet in the Kingdom of the Father.[104]

282. Sacred pastors should take care to ensure that the faithful who participate in the rite or are present at it, are made aware by the most suitable means possible of the Catholic teaching on the form of Holy Communion as laid down by the Ecumenical Council of Trent. Above all, they should instruct the Christian faithful that the Catholic faith teaches that Christ, whole and entire, and the true Sacrament, is received even under only one species, and hence that as regards the resulting fruits, those who receive under only one species are not deprived of any grace that is necessary for salvation.[105]

Furthermore, they should teach that the Church, in her administration of the Sacraments, has the power to lay down or alter whatever provisions, apart from the substance of the Sacraments, that she judges to be more readily conducive to reverence for the Sacraments and the good of the recipients, in view of changing conditions, times, and places.[106] However, at the same time the faithful should be instructed to participate more readily in this sacred rite, by which the sign of the Eucharistic banquet is made more fully evident.

283. In addition to those cases given in the ritual books, Communion under both kinds is permitted for:

   a) Priests who are not able to celebrate or concelebrate Mass;
   b) the Deacon and others who perform some duty at the Mass;
   c) members of communities at the Conventual Mass or the "community" Mass, along with seminarians, and all those engaged in a retreat or taking part in a spiritual or pastoral gathering.

The Diocesan Bishop may establish norms for Communion under both kinds for his own diocese, which are also to be observed in churches of religious and at celebrations with small groups. The Diocesan Bishop is also given the faculty to permit Communion under both kinds whenever it may seem appropriate to the Priest to whom a community has been entrusted as its own shepherd, provided that the faithful have been well instructed and that there is no danger of profanation of the Sacrament or of the rite's becoming difficult because of the large number of participants or for some other cause.

In all that pertains to Communion under both kinds, the *Norms for the Distribution and Reception of Holy Communion under Both Kinds in the Dioceses of the United States of America* are to be followed (particularly nos. 27-54).

284. When Communion is distributed under both kinds:

   a) the chalice is usually administered by a Deacon or, in the absence of a Deacon, by a Priest, or even by a duly instituted acolyte or another extraordinary minister of Holy Communion, or by one of the faithful who, in a case of necessity, has been entrusted with this duty for a single occasion;
   b) whatever may remain of the Blood of Christ is consumed at the altar by the Priest or the Deacon or the duly instituted acolyte who ministered the chalice. The same then purifies, wipes, and arranges the sacred vessels in the usual way.

---

104   Cf. Sacred Congregation of Rites, Instruction, *Eucharisticum mysterium*, May 25, 1967, no. 32: *Acta Apostolicae Sedis* 59 (1967), p. 558.
105   Cf. Ecumenical Council of Trent, Session XXI, *Doctrina de communione sub utraque specie et parvulorum*, July 16, 1562, chapters 1-3: Denzinger-Schönmetzer, nos. 1725-1729.
106   Cf. *ibidem*, chapter 2: Denzinger-Schönmetzer, no. 1728.

Any of the faithful who wish to receive Holy Communion under the species of bread alone should be given Communion in this form.

285. For Communion under both kinds the following should be prepared:

   a) If Communion from the chalice is done by drinking directly from the chalice, a chalice of a sufficiently large size or several chalices are prepared. However, care should be taken lest beyond what is needed of the Blood of Christ remains to be consumed at the end of the celebration.
   b) If Communion from the chalice is done by intinction, the hosts should be neither too thin nor too small, but rather a little thicker than usual, so that after being intincted partly into the Blood of Christ they can still be easily distributed.

286. If Communion of the Blood of Christ is carried out by communicants' drinking from the chalice, each communicant, after receiving the Body of Christ, moves to the minister of the chalice and stands facing him. The minister says, *The Blood of Christ*, the communicant replies, *Amen*, and the minister hands over the chalice, which the communicant raises to his or her mouth. Each communicant drinks a little from the chalice, hands it back to the minister, and then withdraws; the minister wipes the rim of the chalice with the purificator.

287. If Communion from the chalice is carried out by intinction, each communicant, holding a Communion-plate under the mouth, approaches the Priest who holds a vessel with the sacred particles, with a minister standing at his side and holding the chalice. The Priest takes a host, intincts it partly in the chalice and, showing it, says, *The Body and Blood of Christ*. The communicant replies, *Amen*, receives the Sacrament in the mouth from the Priest, and then withdraws.

CHAPTER V
THE ARRANGEMENT AND ORNAMENTATION OF CHURCHES FOR THE CELEBRATION OF THE EUCHARIST

I. GENERAL PRINCIPLES

288. For the celebration of the Eucharist, the People of God are normally gathered together in a church or, if there is no church or if it is too small, then in another respectable place that is nonetheless worthy of so great a mystery. Therefore, churches or other places should be suitable for carrying out the sacred action and for ensuring the active participation of the faithful. Moreover, sacred buildings and requisites for divine worship should be truly worthy and beautiful and be signs and symbols of heavenly realities.[107]

289. Consequently, the Church constantly seeks the noble assistance of the arts and admits the artistic expressions of all peoples and regions.[108] In fact, just as she is intent on preserving the works of art and the artistic treasures handed down from past centuries[109] and, in so far as necessary, on adapting them to new needs, so also she strives to promote new works of art that are in harmony with the character of each successive age.[110]

On account of this, in appointing artists and choosing works of art to be admitted into a church, what should be looked for is that true excellence in art which nourishes faith and devotion and accords authentically with both the meaning and the purpose for which it is intended.[111]

290. All churches should be dedicated or at least blessed. Cathedrals and parish churches, however, are to be dedicated with a solemn rite.

291. For the proper construction, restoration, and arrangement of sacred buildings, all those involved should consult the diocesan commission for the Sacred Liturgy and sacred art. Moreover, the Diocesan Bishop should employ the counsel and help of this commission whenever it comes to laying down norms on this matter, approving plans for new buildings, and making decisions on the more important matters.[112]

292. The ornamentation of a church should contribute toward its noble simplicity rather than to ostentation. Moreover, in the choice of elements attention should be paid to authenticity and there should be the intention of fostering the instruction of the faithful and the dignity of the entire sacred place.

---

107 Cf. Second Ecumenical Council of the Vatican, Constitution on the Sacred Liturgy, *Sacrosanctum Concilium*, nos. 122-124; Decree on the Ministry and Life of Priests, *Presbyterorum ordinis*, no. 5; Sacred Congregation of Rites, Instruction, *Inter Oecumenici*, September 26, 1964, no. 90: *Acta Apostolicae Sedis* 56 (1964), p. 897; Instruction, *Eucharisticum mysterium*, May 25, 1967, no. 24: *Acta Apostolicae Sedis* 59 (1967), p. 554; *Code of Canon Law*, can. 932 §1.
108 Cf. Second Ecumenical Council of the Vatican, Constitution on the Sacred Liturgy, *Sacrosanctum Concilium*, no. 123.
109 Cf. Sacred Congregation of Rites, Instruction, *Eucharisticum mysterium*, May 25, 1967, no. 24: *Acta Apostolicae Sedis* 59 (1967), p. 554.
110 Cf. Second Ecumenical Council of the Vatican, Constitution on the Sacred Liturgy, *Sacrosanctum Concilium*, nos. 123, 129; Sacred Congregation of Rites, Instruction, *Inter Oecumenici*, September 26, 1964, no. 13c: *Acta Apostolicae Sedis* 56 (1964), p. 880.
111 Cf. Second Ecumenical Council of the Vatican, Constitution on the Sacred Liturgy, *Sacrosanctum Concilium*, no. 123.
112 Cf. *ibidem*, no. 126; Sacred Congregation of Rites, Instruction, *Inter Oecumenici*, September 26, 1964, no. 91: *Acta Apostolicae Sedis* 56 (1964), p. 898.

293. The suitable arrangement of a church, and of what goes with it, in such a way as to meet appropriately the needs of our own age requires not only that care be taken as regards whatever pertains more immediately to the celebration of sacred actions but also that the faithful be provided with whatever is conducive to their appropriate comfort and is normally provided in places where people habitually gather.

294. The People of God which is gathered for Mass is coherently and hierarchically ordered, and this finds its expression in the variety of ministries and the variety of actions according to the different parts of the celebration. Hence the general arrangement of the sacred building must be such that in some way it conveys the image of the assembled congregation and allows the appropriate ordering of all the participants, as well as facilitating each in the proper carrying out of his function.

The faithful and the *schola cantorum* (choir) shall have a place that facilitates their active participation.[113]

The Priest Celebrant, the Deacon, and the other ministers have places in the sanctuary. There, also, should be prepared seats for concelebrants, but if their number is great, seats should be arranged in another part of the church, though near the altar.

All these elements, even though they must express the hierarchical structure and the diversity of functions, should nevertheless bring about a close and coherent unity that is clearly expressive of the unity of the entire holy people. Indeed, the nature and beauty of the place and all its furnishings should foster devotion and express visually the holiness of the mysteries celebrated there.

II. ARRANGEMENT OF THE SANCTUARY FOR THE SACRED SYNAXIS

295. The sanctuary is the place where the altar stands, the Word of God is proclaimed, and the Priest, the Deacon, and the other ministers exercise their functions. It should be appropriately marked off from the body of the church either by its being somewhat elevated or by a particular structure and ornamentation. It should, moreover, be large enough to allow the Eucharist to be easily celebrated and seen.[114]

The Altar and Its Ornamentation

296. The altar, on which is effected the Sacrifice of the Cross made present under sacramental signs, is also the table of the Lord to which the People of God is convoked to participate in the Mass, and it is also the center of the thanksgiving that is accomplished through the Eucharist.

297. The celebration of the Eucharist in a sacred place is to take place on an altar; however, outside a sacred place, it may take place on a suitable table, always with the use of a cloth, a corporal, a cross, and candles.

298. It is desirable that in every church there be a fixed altar, since this more clearly and permanently signifies Christ Jesus, the Living Stone (1 Pt 2:4; cf. Eph 2:20). In other places set aside for sacred celebrations, the altar may be movable.

An altar is said to be fixed if it is so constructed as to be attached to the floor and not removable; it is said to be movable if it can be displaced.

299. The altar should be built separate from the wall, in such a way that it is possible to walk around it easily and that Mass can be celebrated at it facing the people, which is desirable wherever possible.

---

113   Cf. Sacred Congregation of Rites, Instruction, *Inter Oecumenici*, September 26, 1964, nos. 97-98: *Acta Apostolicae Sedis* 56 (1964), p. 899.
114   Cf. *ibidem*, no. 91: p. 898.

Moreover, the altar should occupy a place where it is truly the center toward which the attention of the whole congregation of the faithful naturally turns.[115] The altar should usually be fixed and dedicated.

300. An altar, whether fixed or movable, should be dedicated according to the rite prescribed in the Roman Pontifical; but it is permissible for a movable altar simply to be blessed.

301. In keeping with the Church's traditional practice and with what the altar signifies, the table of a fixed altar should be of stone and indeed of natural stone. In the Dioceses of the United States of America, wood which is dignified, solid, and well-crafted may be used, provided that the altar is structurally immobile. As to the supports or base for supporting the table, these may be made of any material, provided it is dignified and solid.

A movable altar may be constructed of any noble and solid material suited to liturgical use, according to the traditions and usages of the different regions.

302. The practice of the deposition of relics of Saints, even those not Martyrs, under the altar to be dedicated is fittingly retained. However, care should be taken to ensure the authenticity of such relics.

303. In building new churches, it is preferable for a single altar to be erected, one that in the gathering of the faithful will signify the one Christ and the one Eucharist of the Church.

In already existing churches, however, when the old altar is so positioned that it makes the people's participation difficult but cannot be moved without damage to artistic value, another fixed altar, skillfully made and properly dedicated, should be erected and the sacred rites celebrated on it alone. In order that the attention of the faithful not be distracted from the new altar, the old altar should not be decorated in any special way.

304. Out of reverence for the celebration of the memorial of the Lord and for the banquet in which the Body and Blood of the Lord are offered, there should be, on an altar where this is celebrated, at least one cloth, white in color, whose shape, size, and decoration are in keeping with the altar's structure. When, in the Dioceses of the United States of America, other cloths are used in addition to the altar cloth, then those cloths may be of other colors possessing Christian honorific or festive significance according to longstanding local usage, provided that the uppermost cloth covering the mensa (i.e., the altar cloth itself) is always white in color.

305. Moderation should be observed in the decoration of the altar.

During Advent the floral decoration of the altar should be marked by a moderation suited to the character of this time of year, without expressing in anticipation the full joy of the Nativity of the Lord. During Lent it is forbidden for the altar to be decorated with flowers. Exceptions, however, are *Laetare* Sunday (Fourth Sunday of Lent), Solemnities, and Feasts.

Floral decoration should always show moderation and be arranged around the altar rather than on the altar table.

306. For only what is required for the celebration of the Mass may be placed on the altar table: namely, from the beginning of the celebration until the proclamation of the Gospel, the *Book of the Gospels*; then from the Presentation of the Gifts until the purification of the vessels, the chalice with the paten, a ciborium, if necessary, and, finally, the corporal, the purificator, the pall, and the Missal.

In addition, arranged discreetly, there should be whatever may be needed to amplify the Priest's voice.

---

115 Cf. *ibidem*.

307. The candlesticks required for the different liturgical services for reasons of reverence or the festive character of the celebration (cf. no. 117) should be appropriately placed either on the altar or around it, according to the design of the altar and the sanctuary, so that the whole may be harmonious and the faithful may not be impeded from a clear view of what takes place at the altar or what is placed upon it.

308. Likewise, either on the altar or near it, there is to be a cross, with the figure of Christ crucified upon it, a cross clearly visible to the assembled people. It is desirable that such a cross should remain near the altar even outside of liturgical celebrations, so as to call to mind for the faithful the saving Passion of the Lord.

The Ambo

309. The dignity of the Word of God requires that in the church there be a suitable place from which it may be proclaimed and toward which the attention of the faithful naturally turns during the Liturgy of the Word.[116]

It is appropriate that generally this place be a stationary ambo and not simply a movable lectern. The ambo must be located in keeping with the design of each church in such a way that the ordained ministers and readers may be clearly seen and heard by the faithful.

From the ambo only the readings, the Responsorial Psalm, and the Easter Proclamation (*Exsultet*) are to be proclaimed; likewise it may be used for giving the Homily and for announcing the intentions of the Universal Prayer. The dignity of the ambo requires that only a minister of the word should stand at it.

It is appropriate that before being put into liturgical use a new ambo be blessed according to the rite described in the Roman Ritual.[117]

The Chair for the Priest Celebrant and Other Seats

310. The chair of the Priest Celebrant must signify his function of presiding over the gathering and of directing the prayer. Thus the more suitable place for the chair is facing the people at the head of the sanctuary, unless the design of the building or other features prevent this: as, for example, if on account of too great a distance, communication between the Priest and the congregation would be difficult, or if the tabernacle were to be positioned in the center behind the altar. In any case, any appearance of a throne is to be avoided.[118] It is appropriate that before being put into liturgical use, the chair be blessed according to the rite described in the Roman Ritual.[119]

Likewise, seats should be arranged in the sanctuary for concelebrating Priests as well as for Priests who are present at the celebration in choir dress but without concelebrating.

The seat for the Deacon should be placed near that of the celebrant. For the other ministers seats should be arranged so that they are clearly distinguishable from seats for the clergy and so that the ministers are easily able to carry out the function entrusted to them.[120]

---

116 Cf. Sacred Congregation of Rites, Instruction, *Inter Oecumenici*, September 26, 1964, no. 92: *Acta Apostolicae Sedis* 56 (1964), p. 899.
117 Cf. Rituale Romanum, *De Benedictionibus*, editio typica, 1984, Ordo benedictionis occasione data auspicandi novum ambonem, nos. 900-918.
118 Cf. Sacred Congregation of Rites, Instruction, *Inter Oecumenici*, September 26, 1964, no. 92: *Acta Apostolicae Sedis* 56 (1964), p. 898.
119 Cf. Rituale Romanum, *De Benedictionibus*, editio typica, 1984, Ordo benedictionis occasione data auspicandi novam cathedram seu sedem praesidentiae, nos. 880-899.
120 Cf. Sacred Congregation of Rites, Instruction, *Inter Oecumenici*, September 26, 1964, no. 92: *Acta Apostolicae Sedis* 56 (1964), p. 898.

III. THE ARRANGEMENT OF THE CHURCH

The Places for the Faithful

311. Places for the faithful should be arranged with appropriate care so that they are able to participate in the sacred celebrations, duly following them with their eyes and their attention. It is desirable that benches or seating usually should be provided for their use. However, the custom of reserving seats for private persons is to be reprobated.[121] Moreover, benches or seating should be so arranged, especially in newly built churches, that the faithful can easily take up the bodily postures required for the different parts of the celebration and can have easy access for the reception of Holy Communion.

Care should be taken to ensure that the faithful be able not only to see the Priest, the Deacon, and the readers but also, with the aid of modern technical means, to hear them without difficulty.

The Place for the Schola Cantorum *and the Musical Instruments*

312. The *schola cantorum* (choir) should be so positioned with respect to the arrangement of each church that its nature may be clearly evident, namely as part of the assembled community of the faithful undertaking a specific function. The positioning should also help the choir to exercise this function more easily and allow each choir member full sacramental participation in the Mass in a convenient manner.[122]

313. The organ and other lawfully approved musical instruments should be placed in a suitable place so that they can sustain the singing of both the choir and the people and be heard with ease by everybody if they are played alone. It is appropriate that before being put into liturgical use, the organ be blessed according to the rite described in the Roman Ritual.[123]

In Advent the use of the organ and other musical instruments should be marked by a moderation suited to the character of this time of year, without expressing in anticipation the full joy of the Nativity of the Lord.

In Lent the playing of the organ and musical instruments is allowed only in order to support the singing. Exceptions, however, are *Laetare* Sunday (Fourth Sunday of Lent), Solemnities, and Feasts.

The Place for the Reservation of the Most Holy Eucharist

314. In accordance with the structure of each church and legitimate local customs, the Most Blessed Sacrament should be reserved in a tabernacle in a part of the church that is truly noble, prominent, conspicuous, worthily decorated, and suitable for prayer.[124]

The tabernacle should usually be the only one, be irremovable, be made of solid and inviolable material that is not transparent, and be locked in such a way that the danger of profanation is prevented to the greatest extent possible.[125] Moreover, it is appropriate that before it is put into liturgical use, the tabernacle be blessed according to the rite described in the Roman Ritual.[126]

---

121 Cf. Second Ecumenical Council of the Vatican, Constitution on the Sacred Liturgy, *Sacrosanctum Concilium*, no. 32.
122 Cf. Sacred Congregation of Rites, Instruction, *Musicam sacram*, March 5, 1967, no. 23: *Acta Apostolicae Sedis* 59 (1967), p. 307.
123 Cf. Rituale Romanum, *De Benedictionibus*, editio typica, 1984, Ordo benedictionis organi, nos. 1052-1067.
124 Cf. Sacred Congregation of Rites, Instruction, *Eucharisticum mysterium*, May 25, 1967, no. 54: *Acta Apostolicae Sedis* 59 (1967), p. 568; cf. also Instruction, *Inter Oecumenici*, September 26, 1964, no. 95: *Acta Apostolicae Sedis* 56 (1964), p. 898.
125 Cf. Sacred Congregation of Rites, Instruction, *Eucharisticum mysterium*, May 25, 1967, no. 52: *Acta Apostolicae Sedis* 59 (1967), p. 568; Sacred Congregation of Rites, Instruction, *Inter Oecumenici*, September 26, 1964, no. 95: *Acta Apostolicae Sedis* 56 (1964), p. 898; Sacred Congregation for the Sacraments, Instruction, *Nullo umquam tempore*, May 28, 1938, no. 4: *Acta Apostolicae Sedis* 30 (1938), pp. 199-200; Rituale Romanum, *De sacra Communione et de cultu mysterii eucharistici extra Missam*, editio typica, 1973, nos. 10-11; *Code of Canon Law*, can. 938 §3.
126 Cf. Rituale Romanum, *De Benedictionibus*, editio typica,1984, Ordo benedictionis occasione data auspicandi novum tabernaculum eucharisticum, nos. 919-929.

315. It is more appropriate as a sign that on an altar on which Mass is celebrated there not be a tabernacle in which the Most Holy Eucharist is reserved.[127]

Consequently, it is preferable that the tabernacle be located, according to the judgment of the Diocesan Bishop:

a) either in the sanctuary, apart from the altar of celebration, in a appropriate form and place, not excluding its being positioned on an old altar no longer used for celebration (cf. no. 303);
b) or even in some chapel suitable for the private adoration and prayer of the faithful[128] and organically connected to the church and readily noticeable by the Christian faithful.

316. In accordance with traditional custom, near the tabernacle a special lamp, fueled by oil or wax, should shine permanently to indicate the presence of Christ and honor it.[129]

317. In no way should any of the other things be forgotten which are prescribed by law concerning the reservation of the Most Holy Eucharist.[130]

Sacred Images

318. In the earthly Liturgy, the Church participates, by a foretaste, in that heavenly Liturgy which is celebrated in the holy city of Jerusalem, toward which she journeys as a pilgrim, and where Christ is seated at the right hand of God; and by venerating the memory of the Saints, she hopes one day to have some share and fellowship with them.[131]

Thus, in sacred buildings images of the Lord, of the Blessed Virgin Mary, and of the Saints, in accordance with most ancient tradition of the Church, should be displayed for veneration by the faithful[132] and should be so arranged so as to lead the faithful toward the mysteries of faith celebrated there. Care should, therefore, be taken that their number not be increased indiscriminately, and moreover that they be arranged in proper order so as not to draw the attention of the faithful to themselves and away from the celebration itself.[133] There should usually be only one image of any given Saint. Generally speaking, in the ornamentation and arrangement of a church, as far as images are concerned, provision should be made for the devotion of the entire community as well as for the beauty and dignity of the images.

---

127 Cf. Sacred Congregation of Rites, Instruction, *Eucharisticum mysterium*, May 25, 1967, no. 55: *Acta Apostolicae Sedis* 59 (1967), p. 569.
128 Cf. Sacred Congregation of Rites, Instruction, *Eucharisticum mysterium*, May 25, 1967, no. 53: *Acta Apostolicae Sedis* 59 (1967), p. 568; Rituale Romanum, *De sacra Communione et de cultu mysterii eucharistici extra Missam*, editio typica, 1973, no. 9; *Code of Canon Law*, can. 938 §2; John Paul II, Apostolic Letter, *Dominicae Cenae*, February 24, 1980, no. 3: *Acta Apostolicae Sedis* (1980), pp. 117-119.
129 Cf. *Code of Canon Law*, can. 940; Sacred Congregation of Rites, Instruction, *Eucharisticum mysterium*, May 25, 1967, no. 57: *Acta Apostolicae Sedis* 59 (1967), p. 569; Rituale Romanum, *De sacra Communione et de cultu mysterii eucharistici extra Missam*, editio typica, 1973, no. 11.
130 Cf. particularly in Sacred Congregation for the Sacraments, Instruction, *Nullo umquam tempore*, May 28, 1938: *Acta Apostolicae Sedis* 30 (1938), pp. 198-207; *Code of Canon Law*, cc. 934-944.
131 Cf. Second Ecumenical Council of the Vatican, Constitution on the Sacred Liturgy, *Sacrosanctum Concilium*, no. 8.
132 Cf. Pontificale Romanum, *Ordo Dedicationis ecclesiae et altaris*, editio typica, 1977, chapter IV, no. 10; Rituale Romanum, *De Benedictionibus*, editio typica, 1984, Ordo ad benedicendas imagines quae fidelium venerationi publicae exhibentur, nos. 984-1031.
133 Cf. Second Ecumenical Council of the Vatican, Constitution on the Sacred Liturgy, *Sacrosanctum Concilium*, no. 125.

CHAPTER VI
THE REQUISITES FOR THE CELEBRATION OF MASS

I. THE BREAD AND WINE FOR CELEBRATING THE EUCHARIST

319. Following the example of Christ, the Church has always used bread and wine with water to celebrate the Lord's Supper.

320. The bread for celebrating the Eucharist must be made only from wheat, must be recently made, and, according to the ancient tradition of the Latin Church, must be unleavened.

321. By reason of the sign, it is required that the material for the Eucharistic Celebration truly have the appearance of food. Therefore, it is desirable that the Eucharistic Bread, even though unleavened and made in the traditional form, be fashioned in such a way that the Priest at Mass with the people is truly able to break it into parts and distribute these to at least some of the faithful. However, small hosts are not at all excluded when the large number of those receiving Holy Communion or other pastoral reasons call for them. Moreover, the gesture of the fraction or breaking of bread, which was quite simply the term by which the Eucharist was known in apostolic times, will bring out more clearly the force and importance of the sign of the unity of all in the one bread, and of the sign of charity by the fact that the one bread is distributed among the brothers and sisters.

322. The wine for the celebration of the Eucharist must be from the fruit of the vine (cf. Lk 22:18), natural, and unadulterated, that is, without admixture of extraneous substances.

323. Diligent care should be taken to ensure that the bread and wine intended for the Eucharist are kept in a perfect state of conservation: that is, that the wine does not turn to vinegar nor the bread spoil or become too hard to be broken easily.

324. If after the Consecration or as he receives Communion, the Priest notices that not wine but only water was poured into the chalice, he pours the water into some container, pours wine with water into the chalice and consecrates it, saying the part of narrative relating to the Consecration of the chalice, without being obliged to consecrate the bread again.

II. SACRED FURNISHINGS IN GENERAL

325. As in the case of the building of churches, so also regarding all sacred furnishings, the Church admits the manner of art of each individual region and accepts those adaptations that are in keeping with the culture and traditions of the individual nations, provided that all are suited to the purpose for which the sacred furnishings are intended.[134]

In this matter as well, that noble simplicity should be ensured which is the best accompaniment of genuine art.

326. In choosing materials for sacred furnishings, besides those which are traditional, others are admissible that, according to the mentality of our own age, are considered to be noble and are durable, and

---

[134] Cf. Second Ecumenical Council of the Vatican, Constitution on the Sacred Liturgy, *Sacrosanctum Concilium*, no. 128.

well suited for sacred use. In the Dioceses of the United States of America these materials may include wood, stone, or metal which are solid and appropriate to the purpose for which they are employed.

III. SACRED VESSELS

327. Among the requisites for the celebration of Mass, the sacred vessels are held in special honor, and among these especially the chalice and paten, in which the bread and wine are offered and consecrated and from which they are consumed.

328. Sacred vessels should be made from precious metal. If they are made from metal that rusts or from a metal less precious than gold, they should generally be gilded on the inside.

329. In the Dioceses of the United States of America, sacred vessels may also be made from other solid materials which in the common estimation in each region are considered precious or noble, for example, ebony or other harder woods, provided that such materials are suitable for sacred use. In this case, preference is always to be given to materials that do not easily break or deteriorate. This applies to all vessels that are intended to hold the hosts, such as the paten, the ciborium, the pyx, the monstrance, and others of this kind.

330. As regards chalices and other vessels that are intended to serve as receptacles for the Blood of the Lord, they are to have a bowl of material that does not absorb liquids. The base, on the other hand, may be made of other solid and worthy materials.

331. For the Consecration of hosts, a large paten may fittingly be used, on which is placed the bread both for the Priest and the Deacon and also for the other ministers and for the faithful.

332. As regards the form of the sacred vessels, it is for the artist to fashion them in a manner that is more particularly in keeping with the customs of each region, provided the individual vessels are suitable for their intended liturgical use and are clearly distinguishable from vessels intended for everyday use.

333. As for the blessing of sacred vessels, the rites prescribed in the liturgical books should be followed.[135]

334. The practice should be kept of building in the sacristy a *sacrarium* into which is poured the water from the washing of sacred vessels and linens (cf. no. 280).

IV. SACRED VESTMENTS

335. In the Church, which is the Body of Christ, not all members have the same function. This diversity of offices is shown outwardly in the celebration of the Eucharist by the diversity of sacred vestments, which must therefore be a sign of the function proper to each minister. Moreover, these same sacred vestments should also contribute to the decoration of the sacred action itself. The vestments worn by Priests and Deacons, as well as the attire worn by lay ministers, are blessed before being put into liturgical use according to the rite described in the Roman Ritual.[136]

---

[135] Cf. Pontificale Romanum, *Ordo Dedicationis ecclesiae et altaris*, editio typica, 1977, Ordo benedictionis calicis et patenae; Rituale Romanum, *De Benedictionibus*, editio typica, 1984, Ordo benedictionis rerum quæ in liturgicis celebrationibus usurpantur, nos. 1068-1084.

[136] Cf. Rituale Romanum, *De Benedictionibus*, editio typica, 1984, Ordo benedictionis rerum quae in liturgicis celebrationibus usurpantur, no. 1070.

336. The sacred garment common to all ordained and instituted ministers of any rank is the alb, to be tied at the waist with a cincture unless it is made so as to fit even without such. Before the alb is put on, should this not completely cover the ordinary clothing at the neck, an amice should be used. The alb may not be exchanged for a surplice, not even over a cassock, on occasions when a chasuble or dalmatic is to be worn or when, according to the norms, only a stole is worn without a chasuble or dalmatic.

337. The vestment proper to the Priest Celebrant at Mass and during other sacred actions directly connected with Mass is the chasuble worn, unless otherwise indicated, over the alb and stole.

338. The vestment proper to the Deacon is the dalmatic, worn over the alb and stole; however, the dalmatic may be omitted out of necessity or on account of a lesser degree of solemnity.

339. In the Dioceses of the United States of America, acolytes, altar servers, readers, and other lay ministers may wear the alb or other appropriate and dignified clothing.

340. The stole is worn by the Priest around his neck and hanging down in front of his chest, while it is worn by the Deacon over his left shoulder and drawn diagonally across the chest to the right side, where it is fastened.

341. The cope is worn by the Priest in processions and during other sacred actions, in accordance with the rubrics proper to the individual rites.

342. As regards the form of sacred vestments, Conferences of Bishops may determine and propose to the Apostolic See adaptations that correspond to the needs and the usages of the individual regions.[137]

343. For making sacred vestments, in addition to traditional materials, natural fabrics proper to each region may be used, and also artificial fabrics that are in keeping with the dignity of the sacred action and the sacred person. The Conference of Bishops will be the judge of this matter.[138]

344. It is fitting that the beauty and nobility of each vestment not be sought in an abundance of overlaid ornamentation, but rather in the material used and in the design. Ornamentation on vestments should, moreover, consist of figures, that is, of images or symbols, that denote sacred use, avoiding anything unbecoming to this.

345. Diversity of color in the sacred vestments has as its purpose to give more effective expression even outwardly whether to the specific character of the mysteries of faith to be celebrated or to a sense of Christian life's passage through the course of the liturgical year.

346. As regards the color of sacred vestments, traditional usage should be observed, namely:
   a) The color white is used in the Offices and Masses during Easter Time and Christmas Time; on the Solemnity of the Most Holy Trinity; and furthermore on celebrations of the Lord other than of his Passion, celebrations of the Blessed Virgin Mary, of the Holy Angels, and of Saints who were not Martyrs; on the Solemnities of All Saints (November 1) and of the Nativity of St. John the Baptist (June 24); and on the Feasts of St. John the Evangelist (December 27), of the Chair of St. Peter (February 22), and of the Conversion of St. Paul (January 25).
   b) The color red is used on Palm Sunday of the Lord's Passion and on Friday of Holy Week (Good Friday), on Pentecost Sunday, on celebrations of the Lord's Passion, on the "birthday" feast days of Apostles and Evangelists, and on celebrations of Martyr Saints.

---
137 Cf. Second Ecumenical Council of the Vatican, Constitution on the Sacred Liturgy, *Sacrosanctum Concilium*, no. 128.
138 Cf. *ibidem*.

c) The color green is used in the Offices and Masses of Ordinary Time.
d) The color violet or purple is used in Advent and Lent. It may also be worn in Offices and Masses for the Dead.
e) Besides the color violet, the colors white or black may be used at funeral services and at other Offices and Masses for the Dead in the Dioceses of the United States of America.
f) The color rose may be used, where it is the practice, on *Gaudete* Sunday (Third Sunday of Advent) and on *Laetare* Sunday (Fourth Sunday of Lent).
g) On more solemn days, festive, that is, more precious, sacred vestments may be used even if not of the color of the day.
h) The colors gold or silver may be worn on more solemn occasions in the Dioceses of the United States of America.

347. Ritual Masses are celebrated in their proper color, in white, or in a festive color; Masses for Various Needs, on the other hand, are celebrated in the color proper to the day or the time of year or in violet if they have a penitential character, for example, nos. 31, 33, or 38; Votive Masses are celebrated in the color suited to the Mass itself or even in the color proper to the day or the time of the year.

V. OTHER THINGS INTENDED FOR CHURCH USE

348. Besides the sacred vessels and the sacred vestments, for which some particular material is prescribed, other furnishings that either are intended for direct liturgical use[139] or are in any other way admitted into a church should be worthy and in keeping with their particular intended purpose.

349. Special care must be taken to ensure that the liturgical books, particularly the *Book of the Gospels* and the Lectionary, which are intended for the proclamation of the Word of God and hence receive special veneration, are to be in a liturgical action truly signs and symbols of higher realities and hence should be truly worthy, dignified, and beautiful.

350. Furthermore, every care is to be taken with respect to those things directly associated with the altar and the celebration of the Eucharist, for example, the altar cross and the cross carried in procession.

351. Every effort should be made, even in minor matters, to observe appropriately the requirements of art and to ensure that a noble simplicity is combined with elegance.

---

139 For blessing objects that are intended for liturgical use in churches, cf. Rituale Romanum, *De Benedictionibus*, editio typica, 1984, part III.

CHAPTER VII
THE CHOICE OF THE MASS AND ITS PARTS

352. The pastoral effectiveness of a celebration will be greatly increased if the texts of the readings, the prayers, and the liturgical chants correspond as aptly as possible to the needs, the preparation, and the culture of the participants. This will be achieved by appropriate use of the many possibilities of choice described below.

Hence in arranging the celebration of Mass, the Priest should be attentive rather to the common spiritual good of the People of God than to his own inclinations. He should also remember that choices of this kind are to be made in harmony with those who exercise some part in the celebration, including the faithful, as regards the parts that more directly pertain to them.

Since, indeed, many possibilities are provided for choosing the different parts of the Mass, it is necessary for the Deacon, the readers, the psalmist, the cantor, the commentator, and the choir to know properly before the celebration the texts that concern each and that are to be used, and it is necessary that nothing be in any sense improvised. For harmonious ordering and carrying out of the rites will greatly help in disposing the faithful for participation in the Eucharist.

I. THE CHOICE OF MASS

353. On Solemnities the Priest is obliged to follow the Calendar of the church where he is celebrating.

354. On Sundays, on the weekdays during Advent, Christmas Time, Lent, and Easter Time, on Feasts, and on Obligatory Memorials:

   a) If Mass is celebrated with the people, the Priest should follow the Calendar of the church where he is celebrating;
   b) If Mass is celebrated with the participation of one minister only, the Priest may choose either the Calendar of the church or his proper Calendar.

355. On Optional Memorials,

   a) On the weekdays of Advent from December 17 to December 24, on days within the Octave of the Nativity of the Lord, and on the weekdays of Lent, except Ash Wednesday and during Holy Week, the Mass texts for the current liturgical day are used; but the Collect may be taken from a Memorial which happens to be inscribed in the General Calendar for that day, except on Ash Wednesday and during Holy Week. On weekdays of Easter Time, Memorials of Saints may rightly be celebrated in full.
   b) On weekdays of Advent before December 17, on weekdays of Christmas Time from January 2, and on weekdays of Easter Time, one of the following may be chosen: either the Mass of the weekday, or the Mass of the Saint or of one of the Saints whose Memorial is observed, or the Mass of any Saint inscribed in the *Martyrology* for that day.
   c) On weekdays in Ordinary Time, there may be chosen either the Mass of the weekday, or the Mass of an Optional Memorial which happens to occur on that day, or the Mass of any Saint inscribed in the *Martyrology* for that day, or a Mass for Various Needs, or a Votive Mass.

If he celebrates with the people, the Priest will take care not to omit too frequently and without sufficient reason the readings assigned each day in the Lectionary to the weekdays, for the Church desires that a richer portion at the table of God's Word should be spread before the people.[140]

For the same reason he should choose Masses for the Dead in moderation, for every Mass is offered for both the living and the dead, and there is a commemoration of the dead in the Eucharistic Prayer.

---
140 Cf. Second Ecumenical Council of the Vatican, Constitution on the Sacred Liturgy, *Sacrosanctum Concilium*, no. 51.

Where, however, the Optional Memorials of the Blessed Virgin Mary or of the Saints are dear to the faithful, the legitimate devotion of the latter should be satisfied.

Moreover, as regards the option of choosing between a Memorial inscribed in the General Calendar and one inserted in a diocesan or religious Calendar, preference should be given, all else being equal and in keeping with tradition, to the Memorial in the particular Calendar.

II. THE CHOICE OF TEXTS FOR THE MASS

356. In choosing texts for the different parts of the Mass, whether for the time of the year or for Saints, the norms that follow should be observed.

The Readings

357. Sundays and Solemnities have assigned to them three readings, that is, from a Prophet, an Apostle, and a Gospel, by which the Christian people are instructed in the continuity of the work of salvation according to God's wonderful design. These readings should be followed strictly. In Easter Time, according to the tradition of the Church, instead of being from the Old Testament, the reading is taken from the Acts of the Apostles.

For Feasts, two readings are assigned. If, however, according to the norms a Feast is raised to the rank of a Solemnity, a third reading is added, and this is taken from the Common.

For Memorials of Saints, unless proper readings are given, the readings assigned for the weekday are normally used. In certain cases, particularized readings are provided, that is to say, readings which highlight some particular aspect of the spiritual life or activity of the Saint. The use of such readings is not to be insisted upon, unless a pastoral reason truly suggests it.

358. In the Lectionary for weekdays, readings are provided for each day of every week throughout the entire course of the year; hence, these readings will in general be used on the days to which they are assigned, unless there occurs a Solemnity, a Feast, or Memorial that has its own New Testament readings, that is to say, readings in which mention is made of the Saint being celebrated.

Should, however, the continuous reading during the week from time to time be interrupted, on account of some Solemnity or Feast, or some particular celebration, then the Priest shall be permitted, bearing in mind the scheme of readings for the entire week, either to combine parts omitted with other readings or to decide which readings are to be given preference over others.

In Masses for special groups, the Priest shall be allowed to choose texts more particularly suited to the particular celebration, provided they are taken from the texts of an approved Lectionary.

359. In addition, in the Lectionary a special selection of texts from Sacred Scripture is given for Ritual Masses into which certain Sacraments or Sacramentals are incorporated, or for Masses that are celebrated for certain needs.

Sets of readings of this kind have been so prescribed so that through a more apt hearing of the Word of God the faithful may be led to a fuller understanding of the mystery in which they are participating, and may be educated to a more ardent love of the Word of God.

Therefore, the texts proclaimed in the celebration are to be chosen keeping in mind both an appropriate pastoral reason and the options allowed in this matter.

360. At times, a longer and shorter form of the same text is given. In choosing between these two forms, a pastoral criterion should be kept in mind. On such an occasion, attention should be paid to the capacity of the faithful to listen with fruit to a reading of greater or lesser length, and to their capacity to hear a more complete text, which is then explained in the Homily.[141]

---

141 Missale Romanum, *Ordo lectionum Missae*, editio typica altera, 1981, Praenotanda, no. 80.

361. When a possibility is given of choosing between one or other text laid down, or suggested as optional, attention shall be paid to the good of participants, whether, that is to say, it is a matter of using an easier text or one more appropriate for a given gathering, or of repeating or setting aside a text that is assigned as proper to some particular celebration while being optional for another,[142] just as pastoral advantage may suggest.

Such a situation may arise either when the same text would have to be read again within a few days, as, for example, on a Sunday and on a subsequent weekday, or when it is feared that a certain text might give rise to some difficulties for a particular group of the Christian faithful. However, care should be taken that, when choosing scriptural passages, parts of Sacred Scripture are not permanently excluded.

362. The adaptations to the *Ordo Lectionum Missae* as contained in the Lectionary for Mass for use in the Dioceses of the United States of America should be carefully observed.

The Orations

363. In any Mass the orations proper to that Mass are used, unless otherwise noted.

On Memorials of Saints, the proper Collect is said or, if this is lacking, one from an appropriate Common. As to the Prayer over the Offerings and the Prayer after Communion, unless these are proper, they may be taken either from the Common or from the weekday of the current time of year.

On the weekdays in Ordinary Time, however, besides the orations from the previous Sunday, orations from another Sunday in Ordinary Time may be used, or one of the Prayers for Various Needs provided in the Missal. However, it shall always be permissible to use from these Masses the Collect alone.

In this way a richer collection of texts is provided, by which the prayer life of the faithful is more abundantly nourished.

However, during the more important times of the year, provision has already been made for this by means of the orations proper to these times of the year that exist for each weekday in the Missal.

The Eucharistic Prayer

364. The numerous Prefaces with which the *Roman Missal* is endowed have as their purpose to bring out more fully the motives for thanksgiving within the Eucharistic Prayer and to set out more clearly the different facets of the mystery of salvation.

365. The choice between the Eucharistic Prayers found in the Order of Mass is suitably guided by the following norms:

a) Eucharistic Prayer I, or the Roman Canon, which may always be used, is especially suited for use on days to which a proper text for the *Communicantes (In communion with those whose memory we venerate)* is assigned or in Masses endowed with a proper form of the *Hanc igitur (Therefore, Lord, we pray)* and also in the celebrations of the Apostles and of the Saints mentioned in the Prayer itself; likewise it is especially suited for use on Sundays, unless for pastoral reasons Eucharistic Prayer III is preferred.

b) Eucharistic Prayer II, on account of its particular features, is more appropriately used on weekdays or in special circumstances. Although it is provided with its own Preface, it may also be used with other Prefaces, especially those that sum up the mystery of salvation, for example, the Common Prefaces. When Mass is celebrated for a particular deceased person, the special formula given may be used at the proper point, namely, before the part *Remember also our brothers and sisters.*

---

142 *Ibidem*, no. 81.

c) Eucharistic Prayer III may be said with any Preface. Its use should be preferred on Sundays and festive days. If, however, this Eucharistic Prayer is used in Masses for the Dead, the special formula for a deceased person may be used, to be included at the proper place, namely after the words: *in your compassion, O merciful Father, gather to yourself all your children scattered throughout the world.*

d) Eucharistic Prayer IV has an invariable Preface and gives a fuller summary of salvation history. It may be used when a Mass has no Preface of its own and on Sundays in Ordinary Time. On account of its structure, no special formula for a deceased person may be inserted into this prayer.

The Chants

366. It is not permitted to substitute other chants for those found in the Order of Mass, for example, at the *Agnus Dei (Lamb of God).*

367. In choosing the chants between the readings, as well as the chants at the Entrance, at the Offertory, and at Communion, the norms laid down in their proper places are to be observed (cf. nos. 40-41, 47-48, 61-64, 74, 86-88).

CHAPTER VIII
MASSES AND PRAYERS FOR VARIOUS NEEDS AND OCCASIONS AND MASSES FOR THE DEAD

I. MASSES AND PRAYERS FOR VARIOUS NEEDS AND OCCASIONS

368. Since the liturgy of the Sacraments and Sacramentals has as its effect that for the faithful who are properly disposed almost every event in life is sanctified by the divine grace that flows from the Paschal Mystery,[143] and because the Eucharist is the Sacrament of Sacraments, the Missal provides examples of Mass formularies and orations that may be used in the various occasions of Christian life for the needs of the whole world or for the needs of the Church, whether universal or local.

369. In view of the rather broad possibilities of choice among the readings and orations, it is desirable that Masses for Various Needs and Occasions be used in moderation, that is, when truly required.

370. In all the Masses for Various Needs and Occasions, unless expressly indicated otherwise, it is permissible to use the weekday readings and also the chants between them, if they are suited to the celebration.

371. Among Masses of this kind are included Ritual Masses, Masses for Various Needs and Occasions, and Votive Masses.

372. Ritual Masses are connected to the celebration of certain Sacraments or Sacramentals. They are prohibited on Sundays of Advent, Lent, and Easter, on Solemnities, on the days within the Octave of Easter, on the Commemoration of All the Faithful Departed (All Souls' Day), on Ash Wednesday, and during Holy Week, and furthermore due regard is to be had for the norms set out in the ritual books or in the Masses themselves.

373. Masses for Various Needs and Occasions are used in certain situations either as occasion arises or at fixed times.
   Days or periods of prayer for the fruits of the earth, prayer for human rights and equality, prayer for world justice and peace, and penitential observances outside Lent are to be observed in the Dioceses of the United States of America at times to be designated by the Diocesan Bishop.
   In all the Dioceses of the United States of America, January 22 (or January 23, when January 22 falls on a Sunday) shall be observed as a particular day of prayer for the full restoration of the legal guarantee of the right to life and of penance for violations to the dignity of the human person committed through acts of abortion. The liturgical celebrations for this day may be the Mass "For Giving Thanks to God for the Gift of Human Life" (no. 48/1 of the Masses and Prayers for Various Needs and Occasions), celebrated with white vestments, or the Mass "For the Preservation of Peace and Justice" (no. 30 of the Masses and Prayers for Various Needs and Occasions), celebrated with violet vestments.

374. If any case of a graver need or of pastoral advantage should arise, at the direction of the Diocesan Bishop or with his permission, an appropriate Mass may be celebrated on any day except Solemnities,

---

143   Cf. Second Ecumenical Council of the Vatican, Constitution on the Sacred Liturgy, *Sacrosanctum Concilium*, no. 61.

the Sundays of Advent, Lent, and Easter, days within the Octave of Easter, the Commemoration of All the Faithful Departed (All Souls' Day), Ash Wednesday, and the days of Holy Week.

375. Votive Masses of the mysteries of the Lord or in honor of the Blessed Virgin Mary or of the Angels or of any given Saint or of all the Saints may be said in response to the devotion of the faithful on weekdays in Ordinary Time, even if an Optional Memorial occurs. However, it is not permitted to celebrate as Votive Masses those that refer to mysteries related to events in the life of the Lord or of the Blessed Virgin Mary, with the exception of the Mass of the Immaculate Conception, since their celebration is an integral part of the course of the liturgical year.

376. On days when there occurs an Obligatory Memorial or on a weekday of Advent up to and including December 16, of Christmas Time from January 2, and of Easter Time after the Octave of Easter, Masses for Various Needs and Occasions and Votive Masses are in principle forbidden. If, however, some real necessity or pastoral advantage calls for it, in the estimation of the rector of the church or the Priest Celebrant himself, a Mass appropriate to the same may be used in a celebration with the people.

377. On weekdays in Ordinary Time when an Optional Memorial occurs or when the Office is of the weekday, it is permissible to celebrate any Mass for Various Needs and Occasions, or use any prayer for the same, but to the exclusion of Ritual Masses.

378. Particularly recommended is the Saturday commemoration of the Blessed Virgin Mary, because it is to the Mother of the Redeemer that in the Liturgy of the Church firstly and before all the Saints veneration is given.[144]

II. MASSES FOR THE DEAD

379. The Church offers the Eucharistic Sacrifice of Christ's Pasch for the dead so that, since all the members of Christ's Body are in communion with one another, what implores spiritual help for some, may bring comforting hope to others.

380. Among the Masses for the Dead, the Funeral Mass holds first place. It may be celebrated on any day except for Solemnities that are Holydays of Obligation, Thursday of Holy Week (Holy Thursday), the Paschal Triduum, and the Sundays of Advent, Lent, and Easter, with due regard also for all the other requirements of the norm of the law.[145]

381. A Mass for the Dead, on receiving the news of a death, for the final burial, or the first anniversary, may be celebrated even on days within the Octave of the Nativity of the Lord, on days when an Obligatory Memorial occurs, and on weekdays other than Ash Wednesday or the weekdays of Holy Week.

Other Masses for the Dead or "daily" Masses, may be celebrated on weekdays in Ordinary Time on which Optional Memorials occur or when the Office is of the weekday, provided such Masses are actually applied for the dead.

382. At Funeral Masses there should usually be a short Homily, but to the exclusion of a funeral eulogy of any kind.

---

144 Cf. Second Ecumenical Council of the Vatican, Dogmatic Constitution on the Church, *Lumen gentium*, no. 54; Paul VI, Apostolic Exhortation, *Marialis cultus*, February 2, 1974, no. 9: *Acta Apostolicae Sedis* 66 (1974), pp. 122-123.
145 Cf. particularly *Code of Canon Law*, cc. 1176-1185; Rituale Romanum, *Ordo Exsequiarum*, editio typica, 1969.

383. The faithful, and especially those of the deceased's family, should be urged to participate in the Eucharistic Sacrifice offered for the deceased person, also by receiving Holy Communion.

384. If the Funeral Mass is directly joined to the rite of burial, once the Prayer after Communion has been said and omitting the Concluding Rites, there takes place the Rite of Final Commendation or Farewell. This rite is celebrated only if the body is present.

385. In the arranging and choosing of the variable parts of the Mass for the Dead, especially the Funeral Mass (for example, orations, readings, and the Universal Prayer), pastoral considerations bearing upon the deceased, the family, and those attending should be kept in mind.

Moreover, pastors should take into special account those who are present at a liturgical celebration or who hear the Gospel on the occasion of the funeral and who may be non-Catholics or Catholics who never or hardly ever participate in the Eucharist or who seem even to have lost the faith. For Priests are ministers of Christ's Gospel for all.

CHAPTER IX
ADAPTATIONS WITHIN THE COMPETENCE OF BISHOPS AND BISHOPS' CONFERENCES

386. The renewal of the *Roman Missal* carried out in our time in accordance with the decrees of the Second Vatican Ecumenical Council has taken great care that all the faithful may display in the celebration of the Eucharist that full, conscious, and active participation that is required by the very nature of the Liturgy and to which the faithful, in virtue of their status as such, have a right and duty.[146]

However, in order that such a celebration may correspond all the more fully to the norms and the spirit of the Sacred Liturgy, certain further adaptations are set out in this Instruction and in the Order of Mass and entrusted to the judgment either of the Diocesan Bishop or of the Conferences of Bishops.

387. The Diocesan Bishop, who is to be regarded as the High Priest of his flock, from whom the life in Christ of his faithful in some sense derives and upon whom it depends,[147] must promote, regulate, and be vigilant over the liturgical life in his diocese. It is to him that in this Instruction is entrusted the regulating of the discipline of concelebration (cf. nos. 202, 374) and the establishing of norms regarding the function of serving the Priest at the altar (cf. no. 107), the distribution of Holy Communion under both kinds (cf. no. 283), and the construction and ordering of churches (cf. no. 291). It is above all for him, moreover, to nourish the spirit of the Sacred Liturgy in the Priests, Deacons, and faithful.

388. Those adaptations spoken of below that necessitate a wider degree of coordination are to be decided, in accord with the norm of law, in the Conference of Bishops.

389. It is the competence, in the first place, of the Conferences of Bishops to prepare and approve an edition of this *Roman Missal* in the authorized vernacular languages, so that, once their decisions have been accorded the *recognitio* of the Apostolic See, the edition may be used in the regions to which it pertains.[148]

The *Roman Missal*, whether in Latin or in legitimately approved vernacular translations, is to be published in its entirety.

390. It is for the Conferences of Bishops to formulate the adaptations indicated in this *General Instruction* and in the Order of Mass and, once their decisions have been accorded the *recognitio* of the Apostolic See, to introduce them into the Missal itself. They are such as these:

- the gestures and bodily posture of the faithful (cf. no. 43);
- the gestures of veneration toward the altar and the *Book of the Gospels* (cf. no. 273);
- the texts of the chants at the Entrance, at the Presentation of the Gifts, and at Communion (cf. nos. 48, 74, 87);
- the readings from Sacred Scripture to be used in special circumstances (cf. no. 362);
- the form of the gesture of peace (cf. no. 82);
- the manner of receiving Holy Communion (cf. nos. 160, 283);
- the materials for the altar and sacred furnishings, especially the sacred vessels, and also the materials, form, and color of the liturgical vestments (cf. nos. 301, 326, 329, 339, 342-346).

It shall be permissible for Directories or pastoral Instructions that the Conferences of Bishops judge useful to be included, with the prior *recognitio* of the Apostolic See, in the *Roman Missal* at an appropriate place.

---

146   Cf. Second Ecumenical Council of the Vatican, Constitution on the Sacred Liturgy, *Sacrosanctum Concilium*, no. 14.
147   Cf. *ibidem*, no. 41.
148   Cf. *Code of Canon Law*, can. 838 §3.

391. It is for the same Conferences of Bishops to attend to the translations of the biblical texts that are used in the celebration of Mass, exercising special care in this. For it is out of the Sacred Scripture that the readings are read and are explained in the Homily and that Psalms are sung, and it is by the influence of Sacred Scripture and at its prompting that prayers, orations, and liturgical chants are fashioned in such a way that it is from Sacred Scripture that actions and signs derive their meaning.[149]

Language should be used that corresponds to the capacity for understanding of the faithful and is suitable for public proclamation, while maintaining those characteristics that are proper to the different ways of speaking used in the biblical books.

392. It shall also be for Conferences of Bishops to prepare with care a translation of the other texts, so that, even though the character of each language is respected, the meaning of the original Latin text is fully and faithfully rendered. In accomplishing this task, it is desirable that the different literary genres used at Mass be taken into account, such as the presidential prayers, the antiphons, the acclamations, the responses, the litanies of supplication, and so on.

It should be borne in mind that the primary purpose of the translation of the texts is not for meditation, but rather for their proclamation or singing during an actual celebration.

Language should be used that is accommodated to the faithful of the region, but is noble and marked by literary quality, even though there will always be a necessity for some catechesis on the biblical and Christian meaning of certain words and expressions.

Moreover, it is preferable that in regions that share the same language, the same translation be used in so far as possible for liturgical texts, especially for biblical texts and for the Order of Mass.[150]

393. Bearing in mind the important place that singing has in a celebration as a necessary or integral part of the Liturgy,[151] all musical settings for the texts of the Ordinary of Mass, for the people's responses and acclamations, and for the special rites that occur in the course of the liturgical year must be submitted to the Secretariat of Divine Worship of the United States Conference of Catholic Bishops for review and approval prior to publication.

While the organ is to be accorded pride of place, other wind, stringed, or percussion instruments may be admitted into divine worship in the Dioceses of the United States of America, according to longstanding local usage, in so far as these are truly suitable for sacred use, or can be made suitable.

394. Each diocese should have its own Calendar and Proper of Masses. For its part, the Conference of Bishops should draw up a proper Calendar for the nation or, together with other Conferences, a Calendar for a wider territory, to be approved by the Apostolic See.[152]

In carrying out this task, to the greatest extent possible the Lord's Day is to be preserved and safeguarded, as the primordial feast day, and hence other celebrations, unless they are truly of the greatest importance, should not have precedence over it.[153] Care should likewise be taken that the liturgical year as revised by decree of the Second Vatican Council not be obscured by secondary elements.

In the drawing up of the Calendar of a nation, the Rogation Days and Ember Days should be indicated (cf. no. 373), as well as the forms and texts for their celebration,[154] and other special measures should also be kept in mind.

It is appropriate that in publishing the Missal, celebrations proper to an entire nation or territory be inserted at the proper place among the celebrations of the General Calendar, while those proper to a region or diocese should have a place in a special appendix.

---

149 Cf. Second Ecumenical Council of the Vatican, Constitution on the Sacred Liturgy, *Sacrosanctum Concilium*, no. 24.
150 Cf. *ibidem*, no. 36 §3.
151 Cf. *ibidem*, no. 112.
152 Cf. *Universal Norms on the Liturgical Year and the Calendar*, nos. 48-51, infra, p. 99; Sacred Congregation for Divine Worship, Instruction, *Calendaria particularia*, June 24, 1970, nos. 4, 8: *Acta Apostolicae Sedis* 62 (1970), pp. 652-653.
153 Cf. Second Ecumenical Council of the Vatican, Constitution on the Sacred Liturgy, *Sacrosanctum Concilium*, no. 106.
154 Cf. *Universal Norms on the Liturgical Year and the Calendar*, nos. 48-51, infra, p. 99; Sacred Congregation for Divine Worship, Instruction, *Calendaria particularia*, June 24, 1970, no. 38: *Acta Apostolicae Sedis* 62 (1970), p. 660.

395. Finally, if the participation of the faithful and their spiritual welfare require variations and profounder adaptations in order for the sacred celebration to correspond with the culture and traditions of the different nations, then Conferences of Bishops may propose these to the Apostolic See in accordance with article 40 of the Constitution on the Sacred Liturgy for introduction with the Apostolic See's consent, especially in the case of nations to whom the Gospel has been more recently proclaimed.[155] The special norms handed down by means of the *Instruction on the Roman Liturgy and Inculturation*[156] should be attentively observed.

As regards the procedures in this matter, these should be observed:

Firstly, a detailed preliminary proposal should be set before the Apostolic See, so that, after the necessary faculty has been granted, the detailed working out of the individual points of adaptation may proceed.

Once these proposals have been duly approved by the Apostolic See, experiments should be carried out for specified periods and at specified places. When the period of experimentation is concluded, the Conference of Bishops shall decide, if the case requires, upon pursuing the adaptations and shall submit a mature formulation of the matter to the judgment of the Apostolic See.[157]

396. However, before proceeding to new adaptations, especially profounder ones, great care shall be taken to promote due instruction of the clergy and the faithful in a wise and orderly manner, so as to take advantage of the faculties already foreseen and to apply fully the pastoral norms in keeping with the spirit of the celebration.

397. The principle shall moreover be respected, according to which each particular Church must be in accord with the universal Church not only regarding the doctrine of the faith and sacramental signs, but also as to the usages universally received from apostolic and unbroken tradition. These are to be kept not only so that errors may be avoided, but also so that the faith may be handed on in its integrity, since the Church's rule of prayer (*lex orandi*) corresponds to her rule of faith (*lex credendi*).[158]

The Roman Rite constitutes a notable and precious part of the liturgical treasure and patrimony of the Catholic Church; its riches are conducive to the good of the universal Church, so that their loss would gravely harm her.

This Rite has in the course of the centuries not only preserved the liturgical usages that arose in the city of Rome, but has also in a deep, organic, and harmonious way integrated into itself certain other usages derived from the customs and culture of different peoples and of various particular Churches whether of the West or the East, so acquiring a certain supra-regional character. As to our own times, the identity and unitary expression of this Rite is found in the typical editions of the liturgical books promulgated by authority of the Supreme Pontiff, and in the liturgical books corresponding to them approved for their territories by the Conferences of Bishops and endowed with the *recognitio* of the Apostolic See.[159]

398. The norm established by the Second Vatican Council, namely that in the liturgical renewal innovations should not be made unless required by true and certain usefulness to the Church, nor without exercising caution to ensure that new forms grow in some sense organically from forms already existing,[160] must also be applied to implementation of the inculturation of the Roman Rite as such.[161]

---

155 Cf. Second Ecumenical Council of the Vatican, Constitution on the Sacred Liturgy, *Sacrosanctum Concilium*, nos. 37-40.
156 Cf. Congregation for Divine Worship and the Discipline of the Sacraments, Instruction, *Varietates legitimae*, January 25, 1994, nos. 54, 62-69: *Acta Apostolicae Sedis* 87 (1995), pp. 308-309, 311-313.
157 Cf. *ibidem*, nos. 66-68: *Acta Apostolicae Sedis* 87 (1995), p. 313.
158 Cf. *ibidem*, nos. 26-27: *Acta Apostolicae Sedis* 87 (1995), pp. 298-299.
159 Cf. John Paul II, Apostolic Letter, *Vicesimus quintus annus*, December 4, 1988, no. 16: *Acta Apostolicae Sedis* 81 (1989), p. 912; Congregation for Divine Worship and the Discipline of the Sacraments, Instruction, *Varietates legitimae*, January 25, 1994, nos. 2, 36: *Acta Apostolicae Sedis* 87 (1995), pp. 288, 302.
160 Cf. Second Ecumenical Council of the Vatican, Constitution on the Sacred Liturgy, *Sacrosanctum Concilium*, no. 23.
161 Cf. Congregation for Divine Worship and the Discipline of the Sacraments, Instruction, *Varietates legitimae*, January 25, 1994, no. 46: *Acta Apostolicae Sedis* 87 (1995), p. 306.

Inculturation, moreover, requires a necessary length of time, lest the authentic liturgical tradition suffer hasty and incautious contamination.

Finally, the pursuit of inculturation does not have as its purpose in any way the creation of new families of rites, but aims rather at meeting the needs of a particular culture, though in such a way that adaptations introduced either into the Missal or coordinated with other liturgical books are not at variance with the proper character of the Roman Rite.[162]

399. And so, the *Roman Missal*, though in a diversity of languages and with some variety of customs,[163] must in the future be safeguarded as an instrument and an outstanding sign of the integrity and unity of the Roman Rite.[164]

---

162 Cf. *ibidem,* no. 36: *Acta Apostolicae Sedis* 87 (1995), p. 302.
163 Cf. *ibidem,* no. 54: *Acta Apostolicae Sedis* 87 (1995), pp. 308-309.
164 Cf. Second Ecumenical Council of the Vatican, Constitution on the Sacred Liturgy, *Sacrosanctum Concilium,* no. 38; Paul VI, Apostolic Constitution, *Missale Romanum,* above, p. 13.

NORMS FOR THE DISTRIBUTION AND RECEPTION OF HOLY COMMUNION UNDER BOTH KINDS IN THE DIOCESES OF THE UNITED STATES OF AMERICA

CONGREGATION FOR DIVINE WORSHIP AND DISCIPLINE OF THE SACRAMENTS

Prot. N. 1383/01/L

THE UNITED STATES OF AMERICA

In response to the request of His Excellency, the Most Reverend Joseph Fiorenza, Bishop of Galveston-Houston, President of the Conference of Bishops of the United States of America, made in a letter dated June 21, 2001, and by virtue of the faculties granted to this Congregation by the Supreme Pontiff JOHN PAUL II, we grant recognition of the text entitled, "Norms for the Distribution and Reception of Holy Communion under Both Kinds in the Dioceses of the United States of America," as found in the attached copy, and which shall be inserted into future editions of the Roman Missal published in English for use in the dioceses of the this same Conference.

Mention of the recognition granted by this Congregation must be included in the published text of these norms.

All things to the contrary notwithstanding.

From the Congregation for Divine Worship and Discipline of the Sacraments, March 22, 2002.

JORGE A. Card. MEDINA ESTÉVEZ
Prefect

✠ FRANCESCO PIO TAMBURRINO
Archbishop Secretary

UNITED STATES CONFERENCE OF CATHOLIC BISHOPS

DECREE

On June 15, 2001, the Latin members of the United States Conference of Catholic Bishops approved the attached "Norms for the Distribution and Reception of Holy Communion under Both Kinds in the Dioceses of the United States of America."

In accord with the approval of these norms and following the confirmation of this action by the Congregation for Divine Worship and the Discipline of the Sacraments on March 22, 2002 (Prot. 1383/01/L), they are hereby published as particular law for all Latin celebrations of the Sacred Liturgy in the dioceses of the United States of America.

The effective date of this decree will be April 7, 2002, the Second Sunday of Easter.

Given at the General Secretariat of the United States Conference of Catholic Bishops, Washington, D.C. on March 28, 2002, Holy Thursday.

✠ Most Rev. WILTON D. GREGORY
Bishop of Belleville
President, United States Conference of Catholic Bishops

Reverend Monsignor WILLIAM P. FAY
General Secretary

PART I
HOLY COMMUNION:
THE BODY AND BLOOD OF THE LORD JESUS

The Mystery of the Holy Eucharist

1. On the night before he died, Christ gathered his Apostles in the upper room to celebrate the Last Supper and to give us the inestimable gift of his Body and Blood. "He did this in order to perpetuate the sacrifice of the Cross throughout the centuries until He should come again, and so to entrust to His beloved spouse, the Church, a memorial of His death and resurrection. . . ."[1] Thus, in the eucharistic Liturgy we are joined with Christ on the altar of the cross and at the table of the upper room in "the sacrificial memorial in which the sacrifice of the cross is perpetuated and [in] the sacred banquet of communion with the Lord's body and blood."[2]

2. Like all acts of the sacred Liturgy, the Eucharist uses signs to convey sacred realities. *Sacrosanctum Concilium: Constitution on the Sacred Liturgy* reminds us that "the sanctification of man is manifested by signs perceptible to the senses, and is effected in a way which is proper to each of these signs."[3] In a preeminent way the eucharistic Liturgy uses the signs of bread and wine in obedience to the Lord's command and after their transformation gives them to us as the Body and Blood of Christ in the act of communion. It is by taking and sharing the eucharistic bread and chalice—"signs perceptible to the senses" —that we obey the Lord's command and grow in the likeness of the Lord whose Body and Blood they both signify and contain.

3. The Eucharist constitutes "the Church's entire spiritual wealth, that is, Christ Himself, our Passover and living bread."[4] It is the "Sacrament of Sacraments."[5] Through it "the work of our redemption is accomplished."[6] He who is the "living bread that came down from heaven" (Jn 6:51) assures us, "Whoever eats my flesh and drinks my blood has eternal life, and I will raise him on the last day. For my flesh is true food, and my blood is true drink" (Jn 6:54-55).

4. The eyes of faith enable the believer to recognize the ineffable depths of the mystery that is the Holy Eucharist. The *Catechism of the Catholic Church* offers us a number of images from our tradition to refer to this most sacred reality: Eucharistic assembly (*synaxis*), action of thanksgiving, breaking of the bread, memorial, holy sacrifice, Lord's Supper, holy and divine Liturgy, Holy Communion, and Holy Mass.[7] The eucharistic species of bread and wine derive from the work of human hands. In the action of the Eucharist this bread and this wine are transformed and become our spiritual food and drink. It is Christ, the true vine, who gives life to the branches (cf. Jn 15:1-6). As bread from heaven (cf. Jn 6:41), bread of angels, the chalice of salvation, and the medicine of immortality,[8] the Eucharist is the promise of eternal life to all who eat and drink it (cf. Jn 6:50-51). The Eucharist is a sacred meal, "a sacrament of love, a sign of unity, a bond of charity"[9] in which Christ calls us as his friends to share in the banquet of

---

1 Second Ecumenical Council of the Vatican, Constitution on the Sacred Liturgy, *Sacrosanctum Concilium*, no. 47. (All Vatican II citations here refer to the following edition: Walter M. Abbott, ed., *The Documents of Vatican II* [New York: Guild Press, 1966].)
2 United States Catholic Conference–Libreria Editrice Vaticana, *Catechism of the Catholic Church* [CCC] (2000), no. 1382.
3 Second Ecumenical Council of the Vatican, Constitution on the Sacred Liturgy, *Sacrosanctum Concilium*, no. 7.
4 Second Vatican Council, *Presbyterorum Ordinis: Decree on the Ministry and Life of Priests* [PO] (December 7, 1965), no. 5.
5 Congregation for Divine Worship and the Discipline of the Sacraments, *General Instruction of the Roman Missal* [GIRM] (2000), no. 368.
6 *The Roman Missal*, Prayer over the Offerings, Holy Thursday Mass of the Lord's Supper, p. 303.
7 CCC, nos. 1328-1332.
8 Cf. St. Ignatius of Antioch, *Ad. Eph.*, 20, 2.
9 Second Ecumenical Council of the Vatican, Constitution on the Sacred Liturgy, *Sacrosanctum Concilium*, no. 47.

the kingdom of heaven (cf. Jn 15:15). This bread and chalice were given to his disciples at the Last Supper. This spiritual food has been the daily bread and sustenance for his disciples throughout the ages. The bread and wine of the Lord's Supper—his Body and Blood—as broken and poured out constitute the irreplaceable food for the journey of the "pilgrim church on earth."[10] The Eucharist perpetuates the sacrifice of Christ, offered once and for all for us and for our salvation, making present the victory and triumph of Christ's death and resurrection.[11] It is strength for those who journey in hope through this life and who desire to dwell with God in the life to come. Our final sharing in the Eucharist is *viaticum*, the food for the final journey of the believer to heaven itself. Through these many images, the Church helps us to see the Eucharist as union with Christ from whom she came, through whom she lives, and towards whom she directs her life.[12]

Holy Communion

5. While the heart of the celebration of the Eucharist is the Eucharistic Prayer, the consummation of the Mass is found in Holy Communion, whereby the people purchased for the Father by his beloved Son eat and drink the Body and Blood of Christ. They are thereby joined together as members of Christ's mystical Body, sharing the one life of the Spirit. In the great sacrament of the altar, they are joined to Christ Jesus and to one another.

It was also Christ's will that this sacrament be received as the soul's spiritual food to sustain and build up those who live with his life, as he said, "He who eats me, he also shall live because of me" (Jn 6:57). This sacrament is also to be a remedy to free us from our daily defects and to keep us from mortal sin. It was Christ's will, moreover, that this sacrament be a pledge of our future glory and our everlasting happiness and, likewise, a symbol of that one body of which he is the head (cf. Lk 22:19 and 1 Cor 11:3). He willed that we, as members of this body should be united to it by firm bonds of faith, hope, and love, so that we might all say the same thing, and that there might be no dissensions among us (cf. 1 Cor 1:10).[13]

As Catholics, we fully participate in the celebration of the Eucharist when we receive Holy Communion. We are encouraged to receive Communion devoutly and frequently. In order to be properly disposed to receive Communion, participants should not be conscious of grave sin and normally should have fasted for one hour. A person who is conscious of grave sin is not to receive the Body and Blood of the Lord without prior sacramental confession except for a grave reason where there is no opportunity for confession. In this case, the person is to be mindful of the obligation to make an act of perfect contrition, including the intention of confessing as soon as possible (canon 916). A frequent reception of the Sacrament of Penance is encouraged for all.[14]

Union with Christ

6. The Lord himself gave us the Eucharist at the Last Supper. The eucharistic sacrifice "is wholly directed toward the intimate union of the faithful with Christ through communion."[15] It is Christ himself who is received in Holy Communion, who said to his disciples, "Take and eat, this is my body." Giving thanks, he then took the chalice and said: "Take and drink, this is the cup of my blood. Do this in remembrance of me" (Mt 26:26-27; 1 Cor 11:25).

---

10   *The Roman Missal*, Eucharistic Prayer III, p. 654.
11   Second Ecumenical Council of the Vatican, Constitution on the Sacred Liturgy, *Sacrosanctum Concilium*, no. 6.
12   Cf. Second Vatican Council, *Lumen Gentium: Dogmatic Constitution on the Church* (November 21, 1964), no. 3.
13   Council of Trent, Session xiii (October 11, 1551), *De ratione institutionis ss. huius sacramenti*. (Latin text in Henricus Denzinger and Adolfus Schönmetzer, eds., *Enchiridion Symbolorum: Definitionum et Declarationum de Rebus Fidei et Morum* [DS] [Barcinone: Herder, 1976], 1638. English text in John F. Clarkson et al., *The Church Teaches* [TCT] [St. Louis, Mo.: B. Herder, 1955], 720.)
14   National Conference of Catholic Bishops, *Guidelines for the Reception of Communion* (Washington, D.C., 1996).
15   CCC, no. 1382.

7. Bread and wine are presented by the faithful and placed upon the altar by the Priest. These are simple gifts, but they were foreshadowed in the Old Testament and chosen by Christ himself for the Eucharistic sacrifice. When these gifts of bread and wine are offered by the Priest in the name of the Church to the Father in the great Eucharistic Prayer of thanksgiving, they are transformed by the Holy Spirit into the Body and Blood of the only-begotten Son of the Father. Finally, when the one bread is broken, the unity of the faithful is expressed and through Communion they "receive from the one bread the Lord's Body and from the one chalice the Lord's Blood in the same way that the Apostles received them from the hands of Christ himself."[16] Hence the import of the words of the hymn adapted from the *Didache*:

> As grain once scattered on the hillsides
> was in this broken bread made one
> so from all lands your church be gathered
> into your kingdom by your Son.[17]

Christ Himself Is Present in the Eucharistic Species

8. Christ is "truly, really, and substantially contained"[18] in Holy Communion. His presence is not momentary nor simply signified, but wholly and permanently real under each of the consecrated species of bread and wine.[19]

9. The Council of Trent teaches that "the true body and blood of our Lord, together with his soul and divinity, exist under the species of bread and wine. His body exists under the species of bread and his blood under the species of wine, according to the import of his words."[20]

10. The Church also teaches and believes that "immediately after the consecration the true body of our Lord and his true blood exist along with his soul and divinity under the form of bread and wine. The body is present under the form of bread and the blood under the form of wine, by virtue of the words [of Christ]. The same body, however, is under the form of wine and the blood under the form of bread, and the soul under either form, by virtue of the natural link and concomitance by which the parts of Christ the Lord, who has now risen from the dead and will die no more, are mutually united."[21]

11. Since, however, by reason of the sign value, sharing in both eucharistic species reflects more fully the sacred realities that the Liturgy signifies, the Church in her wisdom has made provisions in recent years so that more frequent eucharistic participation from both the sacred host and the chalice of salvation might be made possible for the laity in the Latin Church.

---

16 GIRM, no. 72(c).
17 F. Bland Tucker, trans., "Father, We Thank Thee, Who Hast Planted," a hymn adapted from the *Didache*, c. 110 (The Church Pension Fund, 1940).
18 Council of Trent, Session xiii (October 11, 1551), *Canones de ss. Eucharistiae sacramento*, can. 1 (DS 1651; TCT 728).
19 Cf. Council of Trent, Session xiii (October 11, 1551), *Decretum de ss. Eucharistiae sacramento*, cap. IV, *De transubstantione* (DS 1642; TCT 722): "Because Christ our Redeemer said that it was truly his body that he was offering under the species of bread (see Matthew 26:26ff.; Mark 14:22ff.; Luke 22:19ff.; 1 Corinthians 11:24ff.), it has always been the conviction of the Church, and this holy council now again declares it that, by the consecration of the bread and wine a change takes place in which the whole substance of bread is changed into the substance of the Body of Christ our Lord and the whole substance of the wine into the substance of his blood. This change the holy Catholic Church fittingly and properly names transubstantiation."
20 Council of Trent, Session xiii (October 11, 1551), *Decretum de ss. Eucharistiae sacramento*, cap. III, *De excellentia ss. Eucharistiae super reliqua sacramenta* (DS 1640; TCT 721).
21 *Ibid.* (DS 1640; Norman P. Tanner, ed., *Decrees of the Ecumenical Councils*, Vol. 2: *Trent to Vatican II* [London: Sheed & Ward, 1990], 695.)

Holy Communion as an Act of Faith

12. Christ's presence in the Eucharist challenges human understanding, logic, and ultimately reason. His presence cannot be known by the senses, but only through faith[22]—a faith that is continually deepened through that communion which takes place between the Lord and his faithful in the very act of the celebration of the Eucharist. Thus the Fathers frequently warned the faithful that by relying solely on their senses they would see only bread and wine. Rather, they exhorted the members of the Church to recall the word of Christ by whose power the bread and wine have been transformed into his own Body and Blood.[23]

13. The teaching of St. Cyril of Jerusalem assists the Church even today in understanding this great mystery:
> We have been instructed in these matters and filled with an unshakable faith that what seems to be bread is not bread, though it tastes like it, but the Body of Christ, and that what seems to be wine is not wine, though it tastes like it, but the Blood of Christ.[24]

14. The act of Communion, therefore, is also an act of faith. For when the minister says, "The Body of Christ" or "The Blood of Christ," the communicant's "Amen" is a profession in the presence of the saving Christ, body and blood, soul and divinity, who now gives life to the believer.

15. The communicant makes this act of faith in the total presence of the Lord Jesus Christ whether in Communion under one form or in Communion under both kinds. It should never be construed, therefore, that Communion under the form of bread alone or Communion under the form of wine alone is somehow an incomplete act or that Christ is not fully present to the communicant. The Church's unchanging teaching from the time of the Fathers through the ages—notably in the ecumenical councils of Lateran IV, Constance, Florence, Trent, and Vatican II—has witnessed to a constant unity of faith in the presence of Christ in both elements.[25] Clearly there are some pastoral circumstances that require eucharistic sharing in one species only, such as when Communion is brought to the sick or when one is unable to receive either the Body of the Lord or the Precious Blood due to an illness. Even in the earliest days of the Church's life, when Communion under both species was the norm, there were always instances when the Eucharist was received under only the form of bread or wine. Those who received Holy Communion at home or who were sick would usually receive under only one species, as would the whole Church during the Good Friday Liturgy.[26] Thus, the Church has always taught the doctrine of concomitance, by which we know that under each species alone, the whole Christ is sacramentally present and we "receive all the fruit of Eucharistic grace."[27]

16. At the same time an appreciation for reception of "the whole Christ" through one species should not diminish in any way the fuller sign value of reception of Holy Communion under both kinds. For just as Christ offered his whole self, body and blood, as a sacrifice for our sins, so too is our reception of his Body and Blood under both kinds an especially fitting participation in his memorial of eternal life.

---

22   Cf. CCC, no. 1381.
23   Cf. Paul VI, *Mysterium Fidei: On the Doctrine and Worship of the Eucharist* (September 3, 1965), no. 47 (in International Committee on English in the Liturgy, *Documents on the Liturgy, 1963-1979: Conciliar, Papal, and Curial Texts* [DOL] [1982] 176, no. 1192).
24   *Ibid.*, no. 48 (DOL 176, no. 1193).
25   Cf. GIRM, no. 281.
26   Cf. St. Cyprian, *De Lapsis*, 25, on Communion of infants and children; on Communion of the sick and dying, cf. *Statuta ecclesiae antiqua*, can. 76.
27   CCC, no. 1390.

Holy Communion Under Both Kinds

17. From the first days of the Church's celebration of the Eucharist, Holy Communion consisted of the reception of both species in fulfillment of the Lord's command to "take and eat... take and drink." The distribution of Holy Communion to the faithful under both kinds was thus the norm for more than a millennium of Catholic liturgical practice.

18. The practice of Holy Communion under both kinds at Mass continued until the late eleventh century, when the custom of distributing the Eucharist to the faithful under the form of bread alone began to grow. By the twelfth century theologians such as Peter Cantor speak of Communion under one kind as a "custom" of the Church.[28] This practice spread until the Council of Constance in 1415 decreed that Holy Communion under the form of bread alone would be distributed to the faithful.

19. In 1963, the Fathers of the Second Vatican Council authorized the extension of the faculty for Holy Communion under both kinds in *Sacrosanctum Concilium*:

> The dogmatic principles which were laid down by the Council of Trent remaining intact, Communion under both kinds may be granted when the bishops think fit, not only to clerics and religious, but also to the laity, in cases to be determined by the Apostolic See....[29]

20. The Council's decision to restore Holy Communion under both kinds at the bishop's discretion took expression in the first edition of the *Missale Romanum* and enjoys an even more generous application in the third typical edition of the *Missale Romanum*:

> Holy Communion has a fuller form as a sign when it takes place under both kinds. For in this form the sign of the Eucharistic banquet is more clearly evident and clearer expression is given to the divine will by which the new and eternal Covenant is ratified in the Blood of the Lord, as also the connection between the Eucharistic banquet and the eschatological banquet in the Kingdom of the Father.[30]

The *General Instruction* further states that "at the same time the faithful should be instructed to participate more readily in this sacred rite, by which the sign of the Eucharistic banquet is made more fully evident."[31]

21. The extension of the faculty for the distribution of Holy Communion under both kinds does not represent a change in the Church's immemorial beliefs concerning the Holy Eucharist. Rather, today the Church finds it salutary to restore a practice, when appropriate, that for various reasons was not opportune when the Council of Trent was convened in 1545.[32] But with the passing of time, and under the guidance of the Holy Spirit, the reform of the Second Vatican Council has resulted in the restoration of a practice by which the faithful are again able to experience "a fuller sign of the Eucharistic banquet."[33]

---

28   Cf. Petrus Cantor, *Summa de Sacramentis et Animae Consiliis*, ed. J.-A. Dugauquier, *Analecta Medievalis Namurcensia*, vol. 4 (Louvain/Lille, 1954), I, 144.
29   Second Ecumenical Council of the Vatican, Constitution on the Sacred Liturgy, *Sacrosanctum Concilium*, no. 55.
30   GIRM, no. 281. The GIRM goes on to say, "The faithful who participate in the rite or are present at it, are made aware by the most suitable means possible of the Catholic teaching on the form of Holy Communion as laid down by the Ecumenical Council of Trent. Above all, they should instruct the Christian faithful that the Catholic faith teaches that Christ, whole and entire, and the true Sacrament, is received even under only one species, and hence that as regards the resulting fruits, those who receive under only one species are not deprived of any grace that is necessary for salvation.
   "Furthermore, they should teach that the Church, in her administration of the Sacraments, has the power to lay down or alter whatever provisions, apart from the substance of the Sacraments, that she judges to be more readily conducive to reverence for the Sacraments and the good of the recipients, in view of changing conditions, times, and places" (no. 282).
31   *Ibid.*, no. 282.
32   Cf. Council of Trent, Session xxi (July 16, 1562), *De doctrina de communione sub utraque specie et parvulorum* (DS 1725-1734; TCT 739-745).
33   *Ibid.*

PART II
NORMS FOR THE DISTRIBUTION OF HOLY COMMUNION UNDER BOTH KINDS

The Purpose of These Norms

22. In response to a provision of the *General Instruction of the Roman Missal*, the United States Conference of Catholic Bishops herein describes the methods of distributing Holy Communion to the faithful under both kinds and approves the following norms, with the proper *recognitio* of the Apostolic See.[34] The purpose of these norms is to ensure the reverent and careful distribution of Holy Communion under both kinds.

When Communion Under Both Kinds May Be Given

23. The revised *Missale Romanum*, third typical edition, significantly expands those opportunities when Holy Communion may be offered under both kinds. In addition to those instances specified by individual ritual books, the *General Instruction* states that Communion under both kinds may be permitted as follows:

   a. for Priests who are not able to celebrate or concelebrate
   b. for the Deacon and others who perform some duty at Mass
   c. members of communities at the Conventual Mass or the "community" Mass, along with seminarians, and all those engaged in a retreat or taking part in a spiritual or pastoral gathering[35]

24. The *General Instruction* then indicates that the Diocesan Bishop may lay down norms for the distribution of Communion under both kinds for his own diocese, which must be observed. . . . The Diocesan Bishop also has the faculty to allow Communion under both kinds, whenever it seems appropriate to the Priest to whom charge of a given community has been entrusted as [its] own pastor, provided that the faithful have been well instructed and there is no danger of the profanation of the Sacrament or that the rite would be difficult to carry out on account of the number of participants or for some other reason.[36]

   In practice, the need to avoid obscuring the role of the Priest and the Deacon as the ordinary ministers of Holy Communion by an excessive use of extraordinary minister might in some circumstances constitute a reason either for limiting the distribution of Holy Communion under both species or for using intinction instead of distributing the Precious Blood from the chalice.

   Norms established by the Diocesan Bishop must be observed wherever the Eucharist is celebrated in the diocese, "which are also to be observed in churches of religious and at celebrations with small groups."[37]

---

34 Cf. GIRM, no. 283. The text before approval of Adaptations for the Dioceses of the United States of America read, "As to the manner of distributing Holy Communion under both kinds to the faithful and the extent of the faculty for doing so, the Conferences of Bishops may publish norms, once their decisions have received the *recognitio* of the Apostolic See."
35 *Ibid.*
36 *Ibid.*
37 *Ibid.*

Catechesis for Receiving the Body and Blood of the Lord

25. When Communion under both kinds is first introduced by the Diocesan Bishop and also whenever the opportunity for instruction is present, the faithful should be properly catechized on the following matters in the light of the teaching and directives of the *General Instruction*:

  a. the ecclesial nature of the Eucharist as the common possession of the whole Church;
  b. the Eucharist as the memorial of Christ's sacrifice, his death and resurrection, and as the sacred banquet;
  c. the real presence of Christ in the eucharistic elements, whole and entire—in each element of consecrated bread and wine (the doctrine of concomitance);
  d. the kinds of reverence due at all times to the sacrament, whether within the eucharistic Liturgy or outside the celebration;[38] and
  e. the role that ordinary and, if necessary, extraordinary ministers of the Eucharist are assigned in the eucharistic assembly.

The Minister of Holy Communion

26. By virtue of his sacred ordination, the bishop or Priest offers the sacrifice in the person of Christ, the Head of the Church. He receives gifts of bread and wine from the faithful, offers the sacrifice to God, and returns to them the very Body and Blood of Christ, as from the hands of Christ himself.[39] Thus bishops and Priests are considered the ordinary ministers of Holy Communion. In addition the Deacon who assists the bishop or Priest in distributing Communion is an ordinary minister of Holy Communion. When the Eucharist is distributed under both forms, "the Deacon himself administers the chalice."[40]

27. In every celebration of the Eucharist there should be a sufficient number of ministers for Holy Communion so that it can be distributed in an orderly and reverent manner. Bishops, Priests, and Deacons distribute Holy Communion by virtue of their office as ordinary ministers of the Body and Blood of the Lord.[41]

Extraordinary Ministers of Holy Communion

28. When the size of the congregation or the incapacity of the bishop, Priest, or Deacon requires it, the celebrant may be assisted by other bishops, Priests, or Deacons.[42] If such ordinary ministers of Holy Communion are not present, "the Priest may call upon extraordinary ministers to assist him, that is, duly instituted acolytes or even other faithful who have been duly deputed for this purpose. In case of necessity, the Priest may depute suitable faithful for this single occasion."[43] Extraordinary ministers of Holy Communion should receive sufficient spiritual, theological, and practical preparation to fulfill their role with knowledge and reverence. When recourse is had to Extraordinary Minister of Holy Communion, especially in the distribution of Holy Communion under both kinds, their number should not be increased beyond what is required for the orderly and reverent distribution of the Body and Blood of the Lord. In all matters such Extraordinary Ministers of Holy Communion should follow the guidance of the Diocesan Bishop.

---

38 Cf. Congregation of Rites, *Eucharisticum Mysterium: On Worship of the Eucharist* [EM] (May 25, 1967), part I, "General Principles to Be Given Prominence in Catechizing the People on the Eucharistic Mystery" (DOL 179, nos. 1234-1244).
39 Cf. GIRM, no. 93.
40 GIRM, no. 182.
41 Cf. GIRM, no. 108.
42 Cf. GIRM, no. 162.
43 GIRM, no. 162. Cf. also Sacred Congregation for the Discipline of the Sacraments, *Immensae Caritatis: Instruction on Facilitating Reception of Communion in Certain Circumstances*, section 1.I.c (DOL 264, no. 2075).

Reverence

29. All ministers of Holy Communion should show the greatest reverence for the Most Holy Eucharist by their demeanor, their attire, and the manner in which they handle the consecrated bread or wine. Should there be any mishap—as when, for example, the consecrated wine is spilled from the chalice—then the affected "area . . . should be washed with water, and this water should be then poured into the sacrarium."[44]

Planning

30. When Holy Communion is to be distributed under both species, careful planning should be undertaken so that:

- enough bread and wine are made ready for the communication of the faithful at each Mass.[45] As a general rule, Holy Communion is given from hosts consecrated at the same Mass and not from those reserved in the tabernacle. Precious Blood may not be reserved at one Mass for use at another;[46] and
- a suitable number of ministers of Holy Communion are provided at each Mass. For Communion from the chalice, it is desirable that there be generally two ministers of the Precious Blood for each minister of the Body of Christ, lest the liturgical celebration be unduly prolonged.

31. Even when Communion will be ministered in the form of bread alone to the congregation, care should be taken that sufficient amounts of the elements are consecrated so that the Precious Blood may be distributed to all concelebrating Priests.

Preparations

32. Before Mass begins, wine and hosts should be provided in vessels of appropriate size and number. The presence on the altar of a single chalice and one large paten can signify the one bread and one chalice by which we are gathered "into one Body by the Holy Spirit . . . [and] may truly become a living sacrifice in Christ."[47] When this is not possible, care should be taken that the number of vessels should not exceed the need.

33. The unity of all in the one bread will be better expressed when the bread to be broken is of sufficient size that at least some of the faithful are able to receive a piece broken from it. When the number of the faithful is great, however, a single large bread may be used for the breaking of the bread with small breads provided for the rest of the faithful.[48]

34. Sacred vessels, which "hold a place of honor," should be of noble materials, appropriate to their use, and in conformity to the requirements of liturgical law, as specified in the *General Instruction of the Roman Missal*, nos. 327-332.

---

44 GIRM, no. 280.
45 Cf. EM, no. 31 (DOL 179, no. 1260): "The faithful share more fully in the celebration of the eucharist through sacramental communion. It is strongly recommended that they should receive it as a rule in the Mass itself and at that point in the celebration which is prescribed by the rite, that is, right after the communion of the Priest celebrant.
   "In order that the communion may stand out more clearly even through signs as a participation in the sacrifice actually being celebrated, steps should be taken that enable the faithful to receive hosts consecrated at that Mass."
46 Cf. GIRM, no. 284b: "Whatever may remain of the Blood of Christ [after the distribution of Holy Communion] is consumed at the altar by the Priest or the Deacon or the duly instituted acolyte who ministered the chalice."
47 *The Roman Missal*, Eucharistic Prayer IV, p. 660.
48 Cf. GIRM, no. 321.

35. Before being used, vessels for the celebration must be blessed by the bishop or Priest according to the *Rite of Blessing a Chalice and Paten*.[49]

At the Preparation of the Gifts

36. The altar is prepared with corporal, purificator, Missal, and chalice (unless the chalice is prepared at a side table) by the Deacon and the servers. The gifts of bread and wine are brought forward by the faithful and received by the Priest or Deacon or at a convenient place.[50] If one chalice is not sufficient for Holy Communion to be distributed under both kinds to the Priest concelebrants or Christ's faithful, several chalices are placed on a corporal on the altar in an appropriate place, filled with wine. It is praiseworthy that the main chalice be larger than the other chalices prepared for distribution.[51]

At the Breaking of the Bread

37. As the *Agnus Dei* or *Lamb of God* is begun, the Bishop or Priest alone, or with the assistance of the Deacon, and if necessary of concelebrating Priests, breaks the eucharistic bread. Other empty ciboria or patens are then brought to the altar if this is necessary. The Deacon or Priest places the consecrated bread in several ciboria or patens, if necessary, as required for the distribution of Holy Communion. If it is not possible to accomplish this distribution in a reasonable time, the celebrant may call upon the assistance of other Deacons or concelebrating Priests.

38. If extraordinary ministers of Holy Communion are required by pastoral need, they should not approach the altar before the Priest has received Communion. After the Priest has concluded his own Communion, he distributes Communion to the extraordinary ministers, assisted by the Deacon, and then hands the sacred vessels to them for distribution of Holy Communion to the people.

39. All receive Holy Communion in the manner described by the *General Instruction to the Roman Missal*, whether Priest concelebrants (cf. GIRM, nos. 159, 242, 243, 246), Deacons (cf. GIRM, nos. 182, 244, 246), or extraordinary ministers of Holy Communion (cf. GIRM, no. 284). Neither Deacons nor lay ministers may ever receive Holy Communion in the manner of a concelebrating Priest. The practice of extraordinary ministers of Holy Communion waiting to receive Holy Communion until after the distribution of Holy Communion is not in accord with liturgical law.

40. After all eucharistic ministers have received Communion, the bishop or Priest celebrant reverently hands vessels containing the Body or the Blood of the Lord to the Deacons or extraordinary ministers who will assist with the distribution of Holy Communion. The Deacon may assist the Priest in handing the vessels containing the Body and Blood of the Lord to the extraordinary ministers of Holy Communion.

Distribution of the Body and Blood of the Lord

41. Holy Communion under the form of bread is offered to the communicant with the words "The Body of Christ." The communicant may choose whether to receive the Body of Christ in the hand or on the tongue. When receiving in the hand, the communicant should be guided by the words of St. Cyril of Jerusalem: "When you approach, take care not to do so with your hand stretched out and your fingers open or apart, but rather place your left hand as a throne beneath your right, as befits one who is about to receive the King. Then receive him, taking care that nothing is lost."[52]

---

49   Cf. GIRM, no. 333.
50   Cf. *ibid.*, no. 73.
51   Cf. Congregation for Divine Worship and the Discipline of the Sacraments, Instruction, *Redemptionis Sacramentum* (2004), nos. 105-106. These sentences were added to correspond to this Instruction.
52   Cat. Myst. V, 21-22.

42. Among the ways of ministering the Precious Blood as prescribed by the *General Instruction of the Roman Missal*, Communion from the chalice is generally the preferred form in the Latin Church, provided that it can be carried out properly according to the norms and without any risk of even apparent irreverence toward the Blood of Christ.[53]

43. The chalice is offered to the communicant with the words "The Blood of Christ," to which the communicant responds, "Amen."

44. The chalice may never be left on the altar or another place to be picked up by the communicant for self-communication (except in the case of concelebrating bishops or Priests), nor may the chalice be passed from one communicant to another. There shall always be a minister of the chalice.

45. After each communicant has received the Blood of Christ, the minister carefully wipes both sides of the rim of the chalice with a purificator. This action is a matter of both reverence and hygiene. For the same reason, the minister turns the chalice slightly after each communicant has received the Precious Blood.

46. It is the choice of the communicant, not the minister, to receive from the chalice.

47. Children are encouraged to receive Communion under both kinds provided that they are properly instructed and that they are old enough to receive from the chalice.

Other Forms of Distribution of the Precious Blood

48. Distribution of the Precious Blood by a spoon or through a straw is not customary in the Latin dioceses of the United States of America.

49. Holy Communion may be distributed by intinction in the following manner: "Each communicant, while holding a Communion-plate under the mouth, approaches the Priest who holds a vessel with the sacred particles, with a minister standing at his side and holding the chalice. The Priest takes a host, intincts it partly in the chalice and, showing it, says: 'The Body and Blood of Christ.' The communicant replies, 'Amen,' receives the Sacrament in the mouth from the Priest, and then withdraws."[54]

50. The communicant, including the extraordinary minister, is never allowed to self-communicate, even by means of intinction. Communion under either form, bread or wine, must always be given by an ordinary or extraordinary minister of Holy Communion.

Purification of Sacred Vessels

51. After Communion the consecrated bread that remains is to be reserved in the tabernacle. Care should be taken with any fragments remaining on the corporal or in the sacred vessels. The Deacon returns to the altar with the Priest and collects and consumes any remaining fragments.

52. When more of the Precious Blood remains than was necessary for Communion, and if not consumed by the bishop or Priest celebrant, the Deacon, standing at the altar, "immediately and reverently consumes all of the Blood of Christ that remains, assisted, if the case requires, by other Deacons

---

53 Cf. Sacred Congregation for Divine Worship, *Sacramentali Communione: Instruction Extending the Practice of Communion Under Both Kinds* (June 29, 1970), no. 6 (DOL 270, no. 2115).
54 GIRM, no. 287.

and Priests."[55] When there are extraordinary ministers of Holy Communion, they may consume what remains of the Precious Blood from their chalice of distribution with permission of the Diocesan Bishop.

53. The sacred vessels are to be purified by the Priest, the Deacon or an instituted acolyte.[56] The chalice and other vessels may be taken to a side table, where they are cleansed and arranged in the usual way. Other sacred vessels that held the Precious Blood are purified in the same way as chalices. Provided the remaining consecrated bread has been consumed or reserved and the remaining Precious Blood has been consumed, "it is also permitted to leave vessels needing to be purified on a corporal, suitably covered, on the credence table, and to purify them immediately after Mass, following the Dismissal of the people."[57]

54. The Precious Blood may not be reserved, except for giving Communion to someone who is sick. Only sick people who are unable to receive Communion under the form of bread may receive it under the form of wine alone at the discretion of the Priest. If not consecrated at a Mass in the presence of the sick person, the Blood of the Lord is kept in a properly covered vessel and is placed in the tabernacle after Communion. The Precious Blood should be carried to the sick in a vessel that is closed in such a way as to eliminate all danger of spilling. If some of the Precious Blood remains after the sick person has received Communion, it should be consumed by the minister, who should also see to it that the vessel is properly purified.

55. The reverence due to the Precious Blood of the Lord demands that it be fully consumed after Communion is completed and never be poured into the ground or the sacrarium.

Conclusion

56. The norms and directives established by the Church for the celebration of any liturgical rite always have as their immediate goal the proper and careful celebration of those rites. However, such directives also have as their purpose the fostering of celebrations that glorify God and deepen the faith, hope, and charity of the participants in liturgical worship. The ordered preparation and celebration of the Mass, and of Holy Communion in particular, should always profoundly affect the faith of communicants in all its aspects and dimensions. In the case of the distribution of Holy Communion under both kinds, Christian faith in the real presence of Christ in the Holy Eucharist can only be renewed and deepened in the life of the faithful by this esteemed practice.

57. In all other matters pertaining to the Rite of Communion under both kinds, the directives of the *General Instruction*, nos. 281-287, are to be consulted.

---

55   GIRM, no. 182.
56   Cf. GIRM, no. 279.
57   GIRM, no. 183.

UNIVERSAL NORMS ON THE LITURGICAL YEAR AND THE GENERAL ROMAN CALENDAR

APOSTOLIC LETTER
MOTU PROPRIO

APPROVAL OF THE UNIVERSAL NORMS ON THE LITURGICAL YEAR AND THE NEW GENERAL ROMAN CALENDAR

POPE PAUL VI

The Paschal Mystery's celebration is of supreme importance in Christian worship, as we are clearly taught by the sacred Second Vatican Council, and its meaning is unfolded over the course of days, of weeks, and of the whole year. From this it follows that it is necessary that this same Paschal Mystery of Christ be placed in clearer light in the reform of the liturgical year, for which norms were given by the Sacred Synod itself, with regard at once to the arrangement of what is known as the Proper of Time and of the Proper of Saints and to the revision of the Roman Calendar.[1]

I

For in fact, with the passage of centuries, it has happened that, partly from the increase in the number of vigils, religious festivals and their extension over an octave, and partly from the gradual introduction of new elements into the liturgical year, the Christian faithful had come not rarely to practice particular pious exercises in such a way that their minds seemed to have become somewhat distracted from the principal mysteries of divine redemption.

Yet everybody knows that several decisions were issued by Our Predecessors Saint Pius X and John XXIII, of blessed memory, with the intention on the one hand that Sunday, restored to its original dignity, should be truly considered by all as "the primordial feast day,"[2] and on the other that the liturgical celebration of Holy Lent should be restored. It is no less true that Our Predecessor Pius XII, of blessed memory, ordered by means of a decree[3] that in the Western Church during Easter Night the solemn vigil be restored, so that during it the People of God might renew their spiritual covenant with Christ the risen Lord in the course of celebrating the Sacraments of Christian Initiation.

That is to say, these Supreme Pontiffs, following the teaching of the holy Fathers and holding firmly to the doctrine handed down by the Catholic Church, rightly considered not only that in the course of the liturgical year those deeds are commemorated by means of which Christ Jesus in dying brought us salvation, and the memory of past actions is recalled, so that the Christian faithful, even

---

1 Cf. Second Vatican Council, Constitution on the Sacred Liturgy, *Sacrosanctum Concilium*, nos. 102-111.
2 *Ibidem*, no. 106.
3 Cf. Sacred Congregation of Rites, Decree, *Dominicae Resurrectionis*, February 9, 1951: *Acta Apostolicae Sedis* 43 (1951), pp. 128-129.

the more simple of them, may receive spiritual instruction and nourishment, but these Popes also taught that the celebration of the liturgical year "possesses a distinct sacramental power and efficacy to strengthen Christian life."[4] This is also Our own mind and teaching.

Rightly and properly, therefore, as we celebrate the "mystery of the Nativity of Christ"[5] and his appearance in the world, we pray that "we may be inwardly transformed through him whom we recognize as outwardly like ourselves,"[6] and that while we celebrate Christ's Pasch, we ask almighty God that those who have been reborn with Christ may "hold fast in their lives to the Sacrament they have received in faith."[7] For, in the words of the Second Vatican Council, "honoring thus the mysteries of redemption, the Church opens to the faithful the riches of her Lord's powers and merits, so that these are in some way made present in every age in order that the faithful may touch them and be filled with the grace of salvation."[8]

Hence the purpose of the revision of the liturgical year and of the norms accomplishing its reform, is nothing other than that through faith, hope, and charity the faithful may share more deeply in "the whole mystery of Christ, unfolded through the cycle of the year."[9]

II

We see no contradiction between what has already been said and the clear brightness that shines from the feasts of the Blessed Virgin Mary, "who is joined by an inseparable bond to the saving work of her Son,"[10] and the Memorials of the Saints, to which the birthdays of "our Lords the Martyrs and Victors"[11] are rightly joined, since "the feasts of the Saints proclaim the wonderful works of Christ in his servants and offer the faithful fitting examples for their imitation."[12] Furthermore, the Catholic Church has always held firmly and with assurance that in the feasts of the Saints the Paschal Mystery of Christ is proclaimed and renewed.[13]

Therefore, since it cannot be denied that with the passage of centuries more feasts of the Saints were introduced than was appropriate, the Sacred Synod duly cautioned: "Lest the feasts of the Saints take precedence over the feasts commemorating the very mysteries of salvation, many of them should be left to be celebrated by a particular Church or nation or religious family; and only those should be extended to the Universal Church that commemorate Saints having universal importance."[14]

Furthermore, to put these decrees of the Ecumenical Council into effect, the names of some Saints have been removed from the General Calendar, and likewise permission has been granted for the observation of the Memorials of some other Saints to be made optional, and that their cult be appropriately restored to their own regions. As a result, the removal from the Roman Calendar of the names of certain Saints not known throughout the world has allowed the addition of names of some Martyrs from regions to which the announcement of the Gospel spread in later times. Thus the single catalog displays in equal dignity, as representatives of all peoples, as it were, some who either shed their blood for Christ or were outstanding in their most signal virtues.

For these reasons we regard the new General Calendar drawn up for use in the Latin Rite as being more in keeping with the spiritual attitudes and sentiments of these times and to be a clearer

---

4 Sacred Congregation of Rites, General Decree *Maxima redemptionis nostrae mysteria*, November 16, 1955: *Acta Apostolicae Sedis* 47 (1955), p. 839.
5 St. Leo the Great, *Sermo XXVII in Nativitate Domini* 7, 1: PL 54, 216.
6 Cf. *Missale Romanum* [editio typica, 1962], Epiphany, oration [Collect 2 for the Baptism of the Lord, below, p. 202].
7 Cf. *Missale Romanum* [editio typica, 1962], Tuesday of Easter Week, oration [Collect of Monday within the Octave of Easter, below, p. 389].
8 Second Vatican Council, Constitution on the Sacred Liturgy, *Sacrosanctum Concilium*, no. 102.
9 Cf. *ibidem*, no. 102.
10 *Ibidem*, no. 103.
11 Cf. B. Mariani (ed.), *Breviarium Syriacum* (5th century), Rome 1956, p. 27.
12 Cf. Second Vatican Council, Constitution on the Sacred Liturgy, *Sacrosanctum Concilium*, no. 111.
13 Cf. *ibidem*, no. 104.
14 Cf. *ibidem*, no. 111.

reflection of that characteristic of the Church which is her universality, since it proposes henceforth names of outstanding men to put before the whole People of God clear examples of holiness, developed in many different ways. There is no need to speak of the immense spiritual value of this for the whole multitude of Christians.

Therefore, after most carefully pondering all these matters before the Lord, with Our Apostolic Authority We approve the new General Roman Calendar drawn up by the Consilium for the Implementation of the Constitution on the Sacred Liturgy and likewise the universal norms governing the ordering of the liturgical year, so that they may come into force on the first day of the month of January in the coming year, 1970, in accordance with the decrees that the Sacred Congregation of Rites has prepared in conjunction with the aforementioned Consilium, which are to remain in force until the publication of the duly renewed Roman Missal and Breviary.

Whatsoever we have laid down *motu proprio* in these Our Letters we order to be held firm and valid, notwithstanding, to the extent necessary, the Constitutions and Apostolic Ordinances issued by Our Predecessors, or other prescriptions worthy of mention and derogation.

Given in Rome, at Saint Peter's, on the fourteenth day of the month of February in the year 1969, the sixth of Our Pontificate.

PAUL VI, POPE

UNIVERSAL NORMS ON THE LITURGICAL YEAR AND THE CALENDAR

CHAPTER I

THE LITURGICAL YEAR

1. Holy Church celebrates the saving work of Christ on prescribed days in the course of the year with sacred remembrance. Each week, on the day called the Lord's Day, she commemorates the Resurrection of the Lord, which she also celebrates once a year in the great Paschal Solemnity, together with his blessed Passion. In fact, throughout the course of the year the Church unfolds the entire mystery of Christ and observes the birthdays of the Saints.

During the different periods of the liturgical year, in accord with traditional discipline, the Church completes the education of the faithful by means of both spiritual and bodily devotional practices, instruction, prayer, works of penance, and works of mercy.[1]

2. The principles that follow can and must be applied both to the Roman Rite and all other Rites; however, the practical norms are to be understood as applying solely to the Roman Rite, except in the case of those that by their very nature also affect the other Rites.[2]

TITLE I—THE LITURGICAL DAYS

I. The Liturgical Day in General

3. Each and every day is sanctified by the liturgical celebrations of the People of God, especially by the Eucharistic Sacrifice and the Divine Office.

The liturgical day runs from midnight to midnight. However, the celebration of Sunday and of Solemnities begins already on the evening of the previous day.

II. Sunday

4. On the first day of each week, which is known as the Day of the Lord or the Lord's Day, the Church, by an apostolic tradition that draws its origin from the very day of the Resurrection of Christ, celebrates the Paschal Mystery. Hence, Sunday must be considered the primordial feast day.[3]

5. Because of its special importance, the celebration of Sunday gives way only to Solemnities and Feasts of the Lord; indeed, the Sundays of Advent, Lent, and Easter have precedence over all Feasts of the Lord and over all Solemnities. In fact, Solemnities occurring on these Sundays are transferred to the following Monday unless they occur on Palm Sunday or on Sunday of the Lord's Resurrection.

6. Sunday excludes in principle the permanent assigning of any other celebration. However:

    a) the Sunday within the Octave of the Nativity is the Feast of the Holy Family;
    b) the Sunday following January 6 is the Feast of the Baptism of the Lord;
    c) the Sunday after Pentecost is the Solemnity of the Most Holy Trinity;

---

1   Cf. Second Vatican Council, Constitution on the Sacred Liturgy, *Sacrosanctum Concilium*, nos. 102-105.
2   Cf. *ibidem*, no. 3.
3   Cf. *ibidem*, no. 106.

d) the Last Sunday in Ordinary Time is the Solemnity of Our Lord Jesus Christ, King of the Universe.

7. Where the Solemnities of the Epiphany, the Ascension and the Most Holy Body and Blood of Christ are not observed as Holydays of Obligation, they should be assigned to a Sunday as their proper day in this manner:

 a) the Epiphany is assigned to the Sunday that falls between January 2 and January 8;
 b) the Ascension to the Seventh Sunday of Easter;
 c) the Solemnity of the Most Holy Body and Blood of Christ to the Sunday after Trinity Sunday.

III. Solemnities, Feasts, and Memorials

8. In the cycle of the year, as she celebrates the mystery of Christ, the Church also venerates with a particular love the Blessed Mother of God, Mary, and proposes to the devotion of the faithful the Memorials of the Martyrs and other Saints.[4]

9. The Saints who have universal importance are celebrated in an obligatory way throughout the whole Church; other Saints are either inscribed in the calendar, but for optional celebration, or are left to be honored by a particular Church, or nation, or religious family.[5]

10. Celebrations, according to the importance assigned to them, are hence distinguished one from another and termed: Solemnity, Feast, Memorial.

11. Solemnities are counted among the most important days, whose celebration begins with First Vespers (Evening Prayer I) on the preceding day. Some Solemnities are also endowed with their own Vigil Mass, which is to be used on the evening of the preceding day, if an evening Mass is celebrated.

12. The celebration of the two greatest Solemnities, Easter and the Nativity, is extended over eight days. Each Octave is governed by its own rules.

13. Feasts are celebrated within the limits of the natural day; accordingly they have no First Vespers (Evening Prayer I), except in the case of Feasts of the Lord that fall on a Sunday in Ordinary Time or in Christmas Time and which replace the Sunday Office.

14. Memorials are either obligatory or optional; their observance is integrated into the celebration of the occurring weekday in accordance with the norms set forth in the *General Instruction of the Roman Missal* and of the Liturgy of the Hours.
 Obligatory Memorials which fall on weekdays of Lent may only be celebrated as Optional Memorials.
 If several Optional Memorials are inscribed in the Calendar on the same day, only one may be celebrated, the others being omitted.

15. On Saturdays in Ordinary Time when no Obligatory Memorial occurs, an Optional Memorial of the Blessed Virgin Mary may be celebrated.

---

4 Cf. *ibidem*, nos. 103-104.
5 Cf. *ibidem*, no. 111.

IV. Weekdays

16. The days of the week that follow Sunday are called weekdays; however, they are celebrated differently according to the importance of each.

   a) Ash Wednesday and the weekdays of Holy Week, from Monday up to and including Thursday, take precedence over all other celebrations.
   b) The weekdays of Advent from December 17 up to and including December 24 and all the weekdays of Lent have precedence over Obligatory Memorials.
   c) Other weekdays give way to all Solemnities and Feasts and are combined with Memorials.

TITLE II—THE CYCLE OF THE YEAR

17. Over the course of the year the Church celebrates the whole mystery of Christ, from the Incarnation to Pentecost Day and the days of waiting for the Advent of the Lord.[6]

I. The Paschal Triduum

18. Since Christ accomplished his work of human redemption and of the perfect glorification of God principally through his Paschal Mystery, in which by dying he has destroyed our death, and by rising restored our life, the sacred Paschal Triduum of the Passion and Resurrection of the Lord shines forth as the high point of the entire liturgical year.[7] Therefore the preeminence that Sunday has in the week, the Solemnity of Easter has in the liturgical year.[8]

19. The Paschal Triduum of the Passion and Resurrection of the Lord begins with the evening Mass of the Lord's Supper, has its center in the Easter Vigil, and closes with Vespers (Evening Prayer) of the Sunday of the Resurrection.

20. On Friday of the Passion of the Lord[9] (Good Friday) and, if appropriate, also on Holy Saturday until the Easter Vigil,[10] the sacred Paschal Fast is everywhere observed.

21. The Easter Vigil, in the holy night when the Lord rose again, is considered the "mother of all holy Vigils,"[11] in which the Church, keeping watch, awaits the Resurrection of Christ and celebrates it in the Sacraments. Therefore, the entire celebration of this sacred Vigil must take place at night, so that it both begins after nightfall and ends before the dawn on the Sunday.

II. Easter Time

22. The fifty days from the Sunday of the Resurrection to Pentecost Sunday are celebrated in joy and exultation as one feast day, indeed as one "great Sunday."[12]

These are the days above all others in which the *Alleluia* is sung.

---

6   Cf. *ibidem*, no. 102.
7   Cf. *ibidem*, no. 5.
8   Cf. *ibidem*, no. 106.
9   Cf. Paul VI, Apostolic Constitution, *Paenitemini*, February 17, 1966, II §3: *Acta Apostolicae Sedis* 58 (1966), p. 184.
10 Cf. Second Vatican Council, Constitution on the Sacred Liturgy, *Sacrosanctum Concilium*, no. 110.
11 St. Augustine, *Sermo:* 219: PL 38, 1088.
12 St. Athanasius, *Epistula. festalis:* PG 26, 1366.

ON THE LITURGICAL YEAR

23. The Sundays of this time of year are considered to be Sundays of Easter and are called, after Easter Sunday itself, the Second, Third, Fourth, Fifth, Sixth, and Seventh Sundays of Easter. This sacred period of fifty days concludes with Pentecost Sunday.

24. The first eight days of Easter Time constitute the Octave of Easter and are celebrated as Solemnities of the Lord.

25. On the fortieth day after Easter the Ascension of the Lord is celebrated, except where, not being observed as a Holyday of Obligation, it has been assigned to the Seventh Sunday of Easter (cf. no. 7).

26. The weekdays from the Ascension up to and including the Saturday before Pentecost prepare for the coming of the Holy Spirit, the Paraclete.

III. Lent

27. Lent is ordered to preparing for the celebration of Easter, since the Lenten liturgy prepares for celebration of the Paschal Mystery both catechumens, by the various stages of Christian Initiation, and the faithful, who recall their own Baptism and do penance.[13]

28. The forty days of Lent run from Ash Wednesday up to but excluding the Mass of the Lord's Supper exclusive.

From the beginning of Lent until the Paschal Vigil, the *Alleluia* is not said.

29. On Ash Wednesday, the beginning of Lent, which is observed everywhere as a fast day,[14] ashes are distributed.

30. The Sundays of this time of year are called the First, Second, Third, Fourth, and Fifth Sundays of Lent. The Sixth Sunday, on which Holy Week begins, is called "Palm Sunday of the Passion of the Lord."

31. Holy Week is ordered to the commemoration of Christ's Passion, beginning with his Messianic entrance into Jerusalem.

On Thursday of Holy Week, in the morning, the Bishop concelebrates Mass with his presbyterate and blesses the holy oils and consecrates the chrism.

IV. Christmas Time

32. After the annual celebration of the Paschal Mystery, the Church has no more ancient custom than celebrating the memorial of the Nativity of the Lord and of his first manifestations, and this takes place in Christmas Time.

33. Christmas Time runs from First Vespers (Evening Prayer I) of the Nativity of the Lord up to and including the Sunday after Epiphany or after January 6.

34. The Vigil Mass of the Nativity is used on the evening of December 24, either before or after First Vespers (Evening Prayer I).

On the day of the Nativity of the Lord, following ancient Roman tradition, Mass may be celebrated three times, that is, in the night, at dawn, and during the day.

---

13 Cf. Second Vatican Council, Constitution on the Sacred Liturgy, *Sacrosanctum Concilium*, no. 109.
14 Cf. Paul VI, Apostolic Constitution, *Paenitemini*, February 17, 1966, II §3: *Acta Apostolicae Sedis* 58 (1966), p. 184.

35. The Nativity of the Lord has its own Octave, arranged thus:

   a) Sunday within the Octave or, if there is no Sunday, December 30, is the Feast of the Holy Family of Jesus, Mary, and Joseph;
   b) December 26 is the Feast of Saint Stephen, the First Martyr;
   c) December 27 is the Feast of Saint John, Apostle and Evangelist;
   d) December 28 is the Feast of the Holy Innocents;
   e) December 29, 30, and 31 are days within the Octave;
   f) January 1, the Octave Day of the Nativity of the Lord, is the Solemnity of Mary, the Holy Mother of God, and also the commemoration of the conferral of the Most Holy Name of Jesus.

36. The Sunday falling between January 2 and January 5 is the Second Sunday after the Nativity.

37. The Epiphany of the Lord is celebrated on January 6, unless, where it is not observed as a Holyday of Obligation, it has been assigned to the Sunday occurring between January 2 and 8 (cf. no. 7).

38. The Sunday falling after January 6 is the Feast of the Baptism of the Lord.

V. Advent

39. Advent has a twofold character, for it is a time of preparation for the Solemnities of Christmas, in which the First Coming of the Son of God to humanity is remembered, and likewise a time when, by remembrance of this, minds and hearts are led to look forward to Christ's Second Coming at the end of time. For these two reasons, Advent is a period of devout and expectant delight.

40. Advent begins with First Vespers (Evening Prayer I) of the Sunday that falls on or closest to November 30 and it ends before First Vespers (Evening Prayer I) of Christmas.

41. The Sundays of this time of year are named the First, Second, Third, and Fourth Sundays of Advent.

42. The weekdays from December 17 up to and including December 24 are ordered in a more direct way to preparing for the Nativity of the Lord.

VI. Ordinary Time

43. Besides the times of year that have their own distinctive character, there remain in the yearly cycle thirty-three or thirty-four weeks in which no particular aspect of the mystery of Christ is celebrated, but rather the mystery of Christ itself is honored in its fullness, especially on Sundays. This period is known as Ordinary Time.

44. Ordinary Time begins on the Monday which follows the Sunday occurring after January 6 and extends up to and including the Tuesday before the beginning of Lent; it begins again on the Monday after Pentecost Sunday and ends before First Vespers (Evening Prayer I) of the First Sunday of Advent.

During these times of the year there is used the series of formularies given for the Sundays and weekdays of this time both in the Missal and in the Liturgy of the Hours (Vol. III-IV).

VII. Rogation Days and Ember Days

45. On Rogation and Ember Days the Church is accustomed to entreat the Lord for the various needs of humanity, especially for the fruits of the earth and for human labor, and to give thanks to him publicly.

46. In order that the Rogation Days and Ember Days may be adapted to the different regions and different needs of the faithful, the Conferences of Bishops should arrange the time and manner in which they are held.

Consequently, concerning their duration, whether they are to last one or more days, or be repeated in the course of the year, norms are to be established by the competent authority, taking into consideration local needs.

47. The Mass for each day of these celebrations should be chosen from among the Masses for Various Needs, and should be one which is more particularly appropriate to the purpose of the supplications.

CHAPTER II
THE CALENDAR

TITLE I—THE CALENDAR AND CELEBRATIONS TO BE INSCRIBED IN IT

48. The ordering of the celebration of the liturgical year is governed by a calendar, which is either general or particular, depending on whether it has been laid down for the use of the entire Roman Rite, or for the use of a Particular Church or religious family.

49. In the General Calendar is inscribed both the entire cycle of celebrations of the mystery of salvation in the Proper of Time, and that of those Saints who have universal significance and therefore are obligatorily celebrated by everyone, and of other Saints who demonstrate the universality and continuity of sainthood within the People of God.

Particular calendars, on the other hand, contain celebrations of a more proper character, appropriately combined organically with the general cycle.[15] For individual Churches or religious families show special honor to those Saints who are proper to them for some particular reason.

Particular calendars, however, are to be drawn up by the competent authority and approved by the Apostolic See.

50. In drawing up a particular calendar, attention should be paid to the following:

a) The Proper of Time, that is, the cycle of Times, Solemnities, and Feasts by which the mystery of redemption is unfolded and honored during the liturgical year, must always be kept intact and enjoy its rightful preeminence over particular celebrations.

b) Proper celebrations must be combined organically with universal celebrations, with attention to the rank and precedence indicated for each in the Table of Liturgical Days. So that particular calendars may not be overburdened, individual Saints should have only one celebration in the course of the liturgical year, although, where pastoral reasons recommend it, there may be another celebration in the form of an Optional Memorial marking the *translatio* or *inventio* of the bodies of Patron Saints or Founders of Churches or of religious families.

c) Celebrations granted by indult should not duplicate other celebrations already occurring in the cycle of the mystery of salvation, nor should their number be increased out of proportion.

51. Although it is appropriate for each diocese to have its own Calendar and Proper for the Office and Mass, there is nevertheless nothing to prevent entire provinces, regions, nations, or even larger areas, having Calendars and Propers in common, prepared by cooperation among all concerned.

This principle may also be similarly observed in the case of religious calendars for several provinces under the same civil jurisdiction.

52. A particular calendar is prepared by the insertion in the General Calendar of proper Solemnities, Feasts and Memorials, that is:

a) in a diocesan calendar, besides celebrations of Patrons and of the dedication of the cathedral church, the Saints and Blessed who have special connections with the diocese, e.g., by their birth, residence over a long period, or their death;

---

15   Cf. Sacred Congregation for Divine Worship, Instruction, *Calendaria particularia*, June 24,1970: *Acta Apostolicae Sedis* 62 (1970), pp. 651-663.

b) in a religious calendar, besides celebrations of the Title, the Founder and the Patron, those Saints and Blessed who were members of that religious family or had a special relationship with it;
c) in calendars for individual churches, besides the proper celebrations of the diocese or religious family, celebrations proper to the church that are listed in the Table of Liturgical Days, and Saints whose body is kept in the church. Members of religious families, too, join the community of the local Church in celebrating the anniversary of the dedication of the cathedral church and the principal Patrons of the place and of the wider region where they live.

53. When a diocese or religious family has the distinction of having many Saints and Blessed, care must be taken so that the calendar of the entire diocese or entire institute does not become overburdened. Consequently:

a) A common celebration can, first of all, be held of all the Saints and Blessed of a diocese or religious family, or of some category among them.
b) Only the Saints and Blessed of particular significance for the entire diocese or the entire religious family should be inscribed in the calendar as an individual celebration.
c) The other Saints or Blessed should be celebrated only in those places with which they have closer ties or where their bodies are kept.

54. Proper celebrations should be inscribed in the Calendar as Obligatory or Optional Memorials, unless other provisions have been made for them in the Table of Liturgical Days, or there are special historical or pastoral reasons. There is no reason, however, why some celebrations may not be observed in certain places with greater solemnity than in the rest of the diocese or religious family.

55. Celebrations inscribed in a particular calendar must be observed by all who are bound to follow that calendar and may only be removed from the calendar or changed in rank with the approval of the Apostolic See.

TITLE II—THE PROPER DAY FOR CELEBRATIONS

56. The Church's practice has been to celebrate the Saints on their "birthday," a practice that it is appropriate to follow when proper celebrations are inscribed in particular calendars.

However, even though proper celebrations have special importance for individual particular Churches or individual religious families, it is greatly expedient that there be as much unity as possible in the celebration of Solemnities, Feasts and Obligatory Memorials inscribed in the General Calendar.

Consequently in inscribing proper celebrations in a particular calendar, the following should be observed:

a) Celebrations that are also listed in the General Calendar are to be inscribed on the same date in a particular calendar, with a change if necessary in the rank of celebration.
   The same must be observed with regard to a diocesan or religious calendar for the inscription of celebrations proper to a single church.
b) Celebrations of Saints not found in the General Calendar should be assigned to their "birthday." If this is not known, the celebrations should be assigned to a date proper to the Saint for some other reason, e.g., the date of ordination or of the *inventio* or *translatio* of the Saint's body; otherwise to a day that is free from other celebrations in the particular Calendar.
c) If, on the other hand, the "birthday" or other proper day is impeded by another obligatory celebration, even of lower rank, in the General Calendar or in a particular calendar, the celebration should be assigned to the closest date not so impeded.

d) However, if it is a question of celebrations that for pastoral reasons cannot be transferred to another date, the impeding celebration must itself be transferred.
e) Other celebrations, termed celebrations by indult, should be inscribed on a date more pastorally appropriate.
f) In order that the cycle of the liturgical year shine forth in all its clarity, but that the celebration of the Saints not be permanently impeded, dates that usually fall during Lent and the Octave of Easter, as well as the weekdays from December 17 to December 31, should remain free of any particular celebration, unless it is a question of Obligatory Memorials, of Feasts found in the Table of Liturgical Days under no. 8: a, b, c, d, or of Solemnities that cannot be transferred to another time of the year.

The Solemnity of Saint Joseph, where it is observed as a Holyday of Obligation, should it fall on Palm Sunday of the Lord's Passion, is anticipated on the preceding Saturday, March 18. Where, on the other hand, it is not observed as a Holyday of Obligation, it may be transferred by the Conference of Bishops to another day outside Lent.

57. If any Saints or Blessed are inscribed together in the Calendar, they are always celebrated together, whenever their celebrations are of equal rank, even though one or more of them may be more proper. If, however, the celebration of one or more of these Saints or Blessed is of a higher rank, the Office of this or those Saints or Blessed alone is celebrated and the celebration of the others is omitted, unless it is appropriate to assign them to another date in the form of an Obligatory Memorial.

58. For the pastoral good of the faithful, it is permitted to observe on Sundays in Ordinary Time those celebrations that fall during the week and that are agreeable to the devotion of the faithful, provided the celebrations rank above that Sunday in the Table of Liturgical Days. The Mass of such celebrations may be used at all the celebrations of Mass at which the people are present.

59. Precedence among liturgical days, as regards their celebration, is governed solely by the following Table.

TABLE OF LITURGICAL DAYS
ACCORDING TO THEIR ORDER OF PRECEDENCE

I

1. The Paschal Triduum of the Passion and Resurrection of the Lord.

2. The Nativity of the Lord, the Epiphany, the Ascension, and Pentecost.
Sundays of Advent, Lent, and Easter.
Ash Wednesday.
Weekdays of Holy Week from Monday up to and including Thursday.
Days within the Octave of Easter.

3. Solemnities inscribed in the General Calendar, whether of the Lord, of the Blessed Virgin Mary, or of Saints.
The Commemoration of All the Faithful Departed.

4. Proper Solemnities, namely:

   a) The Solemnity of the principal Patron of the place, city, or state.
   b) The Solemnity of the dedication and of the anniversary of the dedication of one's own church.
   c) The Solemnity of the Title of one's own church.
   d) The Solemnity either of the Title
                        or of the Founder
                        or of the principal Patron of an Order or Congregation.

II

5. Feasts of the Lord inscribed in the General Calendar.

6. Sundays of Christmas Time and the Sundays in Ordinary Time.

7. Feasts of the Blessed Virgin Mary and of the Saints in the General Calendar.

8. Proper Feasts, namely:

   a) The Feast of the principal Patron of the diocese.
   b) The Feast of the anniversary of the dedication of the cathedral church.
   c) The Feast of the principal Patron of a region or province, or a country, or of a wider territory.
   d) The Feast of the Title, Founder, or principal Patron of an Order or Congregation and of a religious province, without prejudice to the prescriptions given under no. 4.
   e) Other Feasts proper to an individual church.
   f) Other Feasts inscribed in the Calendar of each diocese or Order or Congregation.

9. Weekdays of Advent from December 17 up to and including December 24.
Days within the Octave of Christmas.
Weekdays of Lent.

III

10. Obligatory Memorials in the General Calendar.

11. Proper Obligatory Memorials, namely:

a) The Memorial of a secondary Patron of the place, diocese, region, or religious province.
b) Other Obligatory Memorials inscribed in the Calendar of each diocese, or Order or Congregation.

12. Optional Memorials, which, however, may be celebrated, in the special manner described in the *General Instruction* of the Roman Missal and of the Liturgy of the Hours, even on the days listed in no. 9.
In the same manner Obligatory Memorials may be celebrated as Optional Memorials if they happen to fall on Lenten weekdays.

13. Weekdays of Advent up to and including December 16.
Weekdays of Christmas Time from January 2 until the Saturday after the Epiphany.
Weekdays of the Easter Time from Monday after the Octave of Easter up to and including the Saturday before Pentecost.
Weekdays in Ordinary Time.

60. If several celebrations fall on the same day, the one that holds the highest rank according to the Table of Liturgical Days is observed. However, a Solemnity impeded by a liturgical day that takes precedence over it should be transferred to the closest day not listed under nos. 1-8 in the Table of Precedence, provided that what is laid down in no. 5 is observed. As to the Solemnity of the Annunciation of the Lord, whenever it falls on any day of Holy Week, it shall always be transferred to the Monday after the Second Sunday of Easter.
Other celebrations are omitted in that year.

61. Should on the other hand, Vespers (Evening Prayer) of the current day's Office and First Vespers (Evening Prayer I) of the following day be assigned for celebration on the same day, then Vespers (Evening Prayer) of the celebration with the higher rank in the Table of Liturgical Days takes precedence; in cases of equal rank, Vespers (Evening Prayer) of the current day takes precedence.

GENERAL ROMAN CALENDAR

[including the Proper Calendar for the Dioceses of the United States of America]

JANUARY

Cal.	1	The Octave Day of the Nativity of the Lord: SOLEMNITY OF MARY, THE HOLY MOTHER OF GOD	Solemnity
IV	2	Sts Basil the Great and Gregory Nazianzen, Bishops and Doctors of the Church	Memorial
III	3	*The Most Holy Name of Jesus**	
Eve	4	[USA] St Elizabeth Ann Seton, Religious	Memorial
Nones	5	[USA] St John Neumann, Bishop	Memorial
VIII	6	[USA] *St André Bessette, Religious*	
VII	7	*St Raymond of Penyafort, Priest*	
VI	8		
V	9		
IV	10		
III	11		
Eve	12		
Ides	13	*St Hilary, Bishop and Doctor of the Church*	
XIX	14		
XVIII	15		
XVII	16		
XVI	17	St Anthony, Abbot	Memorial
XV	18		
XIV	19		
XIII	20	*St Fabian, Pope and Martyr*	
		St Sebastian, Martyr	
XII	21	St Agnes, Virgin and Martyr	Memorial
XI	22	[USA] Day of Prayer for the Legal Protection of Unborn Children**	
X	23	[USA] *St Vincent, Deacon and Martyr*	
IX	24	St Francis de Sales, Bishop and Doctor of the Church	Memorial
VIII	25	THE CONVERSION OF ST PAUL THE APOSTLE	Feast
VII	26	Sts Timothy and Titus, Bishops	Memorial
VI	27	*St Angela Merici, Virgin*	
V	28	St Thomas Aquinas, Priest and Doctor of the Church	Memorial
IV	29		
III	30		
Eve	31	St John Bosco, Priest	Memorial

[USA] Sunday between January 2 and January 8:
        THE EPIPHANY OF THE LORD   Solemnity

Sunday after January 6: THE BAPTISM OF THE LORD   Feast

    When the Solemnity of the Epiphany is transferred to the Sunday that occurs on January 7 or 8, the Feast of the Baptism of the Lord is celebrated on the following Monday.

* When the rank of the celebration is not indicated, it is an Optional Memorial.
** January 23, when January 22 falls on a Sunday

FEBRUARY

Cal.	1		
IV	2	THE PRESENTATION OF THE LORD	Feast
III	3	*St Blaise, Bishop and Martyr*	
		St Ansgar, Bishop	
Eve	4		
Nones	5	St Agatha, Virgin and Martyr	Memorial
VIII	6	St Paul Miki and Companions, Martyrs	Memorial
VII	7		
VI	8	*St Jerome Emiliani*	
		St Josephine Bakhita, Virgin	
V	9		
IV	10	St Scholastica, Virgin	Memorial
III	11	*Our Lady of Lourdes*	
Eve	12		
Ides	13		
XVI	14	Sts Cyril, Monk, and Methodius, Bishop	Memorial
XV	15		
XIV	16		
XIII	17	*The Seven Holy Founders of the Servite Order*	
XII	18		
XI	19		
X	20		
IX	21	*St Peter Damian, Bishop and Doctor of the Church*	
VIII	22	THE CHAIR OF ST PETER THE APOSTLE	Feast
VII	23	St Polycarp, Bishop and Martyr	Memorial
VI	24		
V	25		
IV	26		
III	27		
Eve	28		

MARCH

Cal.	1		
VI	2		
V	3	[USA] *St Katharine Drexel, Virgin*	
IV	4	*St Casimir*	
III	5		
Eve	6		
Nones	7	Sts Perpetua and Felicity, Martyrs	Memorial
VIII	8	*St John of God, Religious*	
VII	9	*St Frances of Rome, Religious*	
VI	10		
V	11		
IV	12		
III	13		
Eve	14		
Ides	15		
XVII	16		
XVI	17	*St Patrick, Bishop*	
XV	18	*St Cyril of Jerusalem, Bishop and Doctor of the Church*	
XIV	19	ST JOSEPH, SPOUSE OF THE BLESSED VIRGIN MARY	Solemnity
XIII	20		
XII	21		
XI	22		
X	23	*St Turibius of Mogrovejo, Bishop*	
IX	24		
VIII	25	THE ANNUNCIATION OF THE LORD	Solemnity
VII	26		
VI	27		
V	28		
IV	29		
III	30		
Eve	31		

APRIL

Cal.	1		
IV	2	St Francis of Paola, Hermit	
III	3		
Eve	4	St Isidore, Bishop and Doctor of the Church	
Nones	5	St Vincent Ferrer, Priest	
VIII	6		
VII	7	St John Baptist de la Salle, Priest	Memorial
VI	8		
V	9		
IV	10		
III	11	St Stanislaus, Bishop and Martyr	Memorial
Eve	12		
Ides	13	St Martin I, Pope and Martyr	
XVIII	14		
XVII	15		
XVI	16		
XV	17		
XIV	18		
XIII	19		
XII	20		
XI	21	St Anselm, Bishop and Doctor of the Church	
X	22		
IX	23	St George, Martyr	
		St Adalbert, Bishop and Martyr	
VIII	24	St Fidelis of Sigmaringen, Priest and Martyr	
VII	25	ST MARK, EVANGELIST	Feast
VI	26		
V	27		
IV	28	St Peter Chanel, Priest and Martyr	
		St Louis Grignion de Montfort, Priest	
III	29	St Catherine of Siena, Virgin and Doctor of the Church	Memorial
Eve	30	St Pius V, Pope	

MAY

Cal.	1	*St Joseph the Worker*	
VI	2	St Athanasius, Bishop and Doctor of the Church	Memorial
V	3	STS PHILIP AND JAMES, APOSTLES	Feast
IV	4		
III	5		
Eve	6		
Nones	7		
VIII	8		
VII	9		
VI	10	[USA] *St Damien de Veuster, Priest*	
V	11		
IV	12	*Sts Nereus and Achilleus, Martyrs*	
		St Pancras, Martyr	
III	13	*Our Lady of Fatima*	
Eve	14	ST MATTHIAS, APOSTLE	Feast
Ides	15	[USA] *St Isidore*	
XVII	16		
XVI	17		
XV	18	*St John I, Pope and Martyr*	
XIV	19		
XIII	20	*St Bernardine of Siena, Priest*	
XII	21	*St Christopher Magallanes, Priest, and Companions, Martyrs*	
XI	22	*St Rita of Cascia, Religious*	
X	23		
IX	24		
VIII	25	*St Bede the Venerable, Priest and Doctor of the Church*	
		St Gregory VII, Pope	
		St Mary Magdalene de' Pazzi, Virgin	
VII	26	St Philip Neri, Priest	Memorial
VI	27	*St Augustine of Canterbury, Bishop*	
V	28		
IV	29		
III	30		
Eve	31	THE VISITATION OF THE BLESSED VIRGIN MARY	Feast

First Sunday after Pentecost
　　　　　THE MOST HOLY TRINITY　　　　　　　　　　Solemnity

[USA] Sunday after the Most Holy Trinity
　　　　　THE MOST HOLY BODY AND BLOOD OF CHRIST　Solemnity

JUNE

Cal.	1	St Justin, Martyr	Memorial
IV	2	*Sts Marcellinus and Peter, Martyrs*	
III	3	St Charles Lwanga and Companions, Martyrs	Memorial
Eve	4		
Nones	5	St Boniface, Bishop and Martyr	Memorial
VIII	6	*St Norbert, Bishop*	
VII	7		
VI	8		
V	9	*St Ephrem, Deacon and Doctor of the Church*	
IV	10		
III	11	St Barnabas, Apostle	Memorial
Eve	12		
Ides	13	St Anthony of Padua, Priest and Doctor of the Church	Memorial
XVIII	14		
XVII	15		
XVI	16		
XV	17		
XIV	18		
XIII	19	*St Romuald, Abbot*	
XII	20		
XI	21	St Aloysius Gonzaga, Religious	Memorial
X	22	*St Paulinus of Nola, Bishop*	
		Sts John Fisher, Bishop, and Thomas More, Martyrs	
IX	23		
VIII	24	THE NATIVITY OF ST JOHN THE BAPTIST	Solemnity
VII	25		
VI	26		
V	27	*St Cyril of Alexandria, Bishop and Doctor of the Church*	
IV	28	St Irenaeus, Bishop and Martyr	Memorial
III	29	STS PETER AND PAUL, APOSTLES	Solemnity
Eve	30	*The First Martyrs of the Holy Roman Church*	

Friday after the Second Sunday after Pentecost
    THE MOST SACRED HEART OF JESUS   Solemnity

Saturday after the Second Sunday after Pentecost
    The Immaculate Heart of the Blessed Virgin Mary   Memorial

JULY

Cal.	1	[USA] Bl Junípero Serra, Priest	
VI	2		
V	3	ST THOMAS, APOSTLE	Feast
IV	4	[USA] Independence Day	
III	5	St Anthony Zaccaria, Priest	
		[USA] St Elizabeth of Portugal	
Eve	6	St Maria Goretti, Virgin and Martyr	
Nones	7		
VIII	8		
VII	9	St Augustine Zhao Rong, Priest, and Companions, Martyrs	
VI	10		
V	11	St Benedict, Abbot	Memorial
IV	12		
III	13	St Henry	
Eve	14	[USA] Bl Kateri Tekakwitha, Virgin	Memorial
Ides	15	St Bonaventure, Bishop and Doctor of the Church	Memorial
XVII	16	Our Lady of Mount Carmel	
XVI	17		
XV	18	[USA] St Camillus de Lellis, Priest	
XIV	19		
XIII	20	St Apollinaris, Bishop and Martyr	
XII	21	St Lawrence of Brindisi, Priest and Doctor of the Church	
XI	22	St Mary Magdalene	Memorial
X	23	St Bridget, Religious	
IX	24	St Sharbel Makhlūf, Priest	
VIII	25	ST JAMES, APOSTLE	Feast
VII	26	Sts Joachim and Anne, Parents of the Blessed Virgin Mary	Memorial
VI	27		
V	28		
IV	29	St Martha	Memorial
III	30	St Peter Chrysologus, Bishop and Doctor of the Church	
Eve	31	St Ignatius of Loyola, Priest	Memorial

AUGUST

Cal.	1	St Alphonsus Mary Liguori, Bishop and Doctor of the Church	Memorial
IV	2	*St Eusebius of Vercelli, Bishop*	
		St Peter Julian Eymard, Priest	
III	3		
Eve	4	St John Mary Vianney, Priest	Memorial
Nones	5	*The Dedication of the Basilica of St Mary Major*	
VIII	6	THE TRANSFIGURATION OF THE LORD	Feast
VII	7	*St Sixtus II, Pope, and Companions, Martyrs*	
		St Cajetan, Priest	
VI	8	St Dominic, Priest	Memorial
V	9	*St Teresa Benedicta of the Cross, Virgin and Martyr*	
IV	10	ST LAWRENCE, DEACON AND MARTYR	Feast
III	11	St Clare, Virgin	Memorial
Eve	12	*St Jane Frances de Chantal, Religious*	
Ides	13	*Sts Pontian, Pope, and Hippolytus, Priest, Martyrs*	
XIX	14	St Maximilian Mary Kolbe, Priest and Martyr	Memorial
XVIII	15	THE ASSUMPTION OF THE BLESSED VIRGIN MARY	Solemnity
XVII	16	*St Stephen of Hungary*	
XVI	17		
XV	18		
XIV	19	*St John Eudes, Priest*	
XIII	20	St Bernard, Abbot and Doctor of the Church	Memorial
XII	21	St Pius X, Pope	Memorial
XI	22	The Queenship of the Blessed Virgin Mary	Memorial
X	23	*St Rose of Lima, Virgin*	
IX	24	ST BARTHOLOMEW, APOSTLE	Feast
VIII	25	*St Louis*	
		St Joseph Calasanz, Priest	
VII	26		
VI	27	St Monica	Memorial
V	28	St Augustine, Bishop and Doctor of the Church	Memorial
IV	29	The Passion of St John the Baptist	Memorial
III	30		
Eve	31		

SEPTEMBER

Cal.	1		
IV	2		
III	3	St Gregory the Great, Pope and Doctor of the Church	Memorial
Eve	4		
Nones	5		
VIII	6		
VII	7		
VI	8	THE NATIVITY OF THE BLESSED VIRGIN MARY	Feast
V	9	[USA] St Peter Claver, Priest	Memorial
IV	10		
III	11		
Eve	12	*The Most Holy Name of Mary*	
Ides	13	St John Chrysostom, Bishop and Doctor of the Church	Memorial
XVIII	14	THE EXALTATION OF THE HOLY CROSS	Feast
XVII	15	Our Lady of Sorrows	Memorial
XVI	16	Sts Cornelius, Pope, and Cyprian, Bishop, Martyrs	Memorial
XV	17	*St Robert Bellarmine, Bishop and Doctor of the Church*	
XIV	18		
XIII	19	*St Januarius, Bishop and Martyr*	
XII	20	Sts Andrew Kim Tae-gŏn, Priest, Paul Chŏng Ha-sang, and Companions, Martyrs	Memorial
XI	21	ST MATTHEW, APOSTLE AND EVANGELIST	Feast
X	22		
IX	23	St Pius of Pietrelcina, Priest	Memorial
VIII	24		
VII	25		
VI	26	*Sts Cosmas and Damian, Martyrs*	
V	27	St Vincent de Paul, Priest	Memorial
IV	28	*St Wenceslaus, Martyr*	
		St Lawrence Ruiz and Companions, Martyrs	
III	29	STS MICHAEL, GABRIEL AND RAPHAEL, ARCHANGELS	Feast
Eve	30	St Jerome, Priest and Doctor of the Church	Memorial

OCTOBER

Cal.	1	St Thérèse of the Child Jesus, Virgin and Doctor of the Church	Memorial
VI	2	The Holy Guardian Angels	Memorial
V	3		
IV	4	St Francis of Assisi	Memorial
III	5		
Eve	6	*St Bruno, Priest*	
		[USA] *Bl Marie Rose Durocher, Virgin*	
Nones	7	Our Lady of the Rosary	Memorial
VIII	8		
VII	9	*St Denis, Bishop, and Companions, Martyrs*	
		St John Leonardi, Priest	
VI	10		
V	11		
IV	12		
III	13		
Eve	14	*St Callistus I, Pope and Martyr*	
Ides	15	St Teresa of Jesus, Virgin and Doctor of the Church	Memorial
XVII	16	*St Hedwig, Religious*	
		St Margaret Mary Alacoque, Virgin	
XVI	17	St Ignatius of Antioch, Bishop and Martyr	Memorial
XV	18	St Luke, Evangelist	Feast
XIV	19	[USA] Sts John de Brébeuf and Isaac Jogues, Priests, and Companions, Martyrs	Memorial
XIII	20	[USA] *St Paul of the Cross, Priest*	
XII	21		
XI	22		
X	23	*St John of Capestrano, Priest*	
IX	24	*St Anthony Mary Claret, Bishop*	
VIII	25		
VII	26		
VI	27		
V	28	Sts Simon and Jude, Apostles	Feast
IV	29		
III	30		
Eve	31		

NOVEMBER

Cal.	1	ALL SAINTS	Solemnity
IV	2	THE COMMEMORATION OF ALL THE FAITHFUL DEPARTED (ALL SOULS' DAY)	
III	3	*St Martin de Porres, Religious*	
Eve	4	St Charles Borromeo, Bishop	Memorial
Nones	5		
VIII	6		
VII	7		
VI	8		
V	9	THE DEDICATION OF THE LATERAN BASILICA	Feast
IV	10	St Leo the Great, Pope and Doctor of the Church	Memorial
III	11	St Martin of Tours, Bishop	Memorial
Eve	12	St Josaphat, Bishop and Martyr	Memorial
Ides	13	[USA] St Frances Xavier Cabrini, Virgin	Memorial
XVIII	14		
XVII	15	*St Albert the Great, Bishop and Doctor of the Church*	
XVI	16	*St Margaret of Scotland*	
		St Gertrude, Virgin	
XV	17	St Elizabeth of Hungary, Religious	Memorial
XIV	18	*The Dedication of the Basilicas of Sts Peter and Paul, Apostles*	
		[USA] *St Rose Philippine Duchesne, Virgin*	
XIII	19		
XII	20		
XI	21	The Presentation of the Blessed Virgin Mary	Memorial
X	22	St Cecilia, Virgin and Martyr	Memorial
IX	23	*St Clement I, Pope and Martyr*	
		St Columban, Abbot	
		[USA] *Bl Miguel Agustín Pro, Priest and Martyr*	
VIII	24	St Andrew Dũng-Lạc, Priest, and Companions, Martyrs	Memorial
VII	25	*St Catherine of Alexandria, Virgin and Martyr*	
VI	26		
V	27		
IV	28		
III	29		
Eve	30	ST ANDREW, APOSTLE	Feast

Last Sunday in Ordinary Time:
OUR LORD JESUS CHRIST,
KING OF THE UNIVERSE — Solemnity

[USA] Fourth Thursday: *Thanksgiving Day*

DECEMBER

Cal.	1		
IV	2		
III	3	St Francis Xavier, Priest	Memorial
Eve	4	*St John Damascene, Priest and Doctor of the Church*	
Nones	5		
VIII	6	*St Nicholas, Bishop*	
VII	7	St Ambrose, Bishop and Doctor of the Church	Memorial
VI	8	[USA] THE IMMACULATE CONCEPTION OF THE BLESSED VIRGIN MARY (Patronal Feastday of the United States of America)	Solemnity
V	9	*St Juan Diego Cuauhtlatoatzin*	
IV	10		
III	11	*St Damasus I, Pope*	
Eve	12	[USA] Our Lady of Guadalupe	Feast
Ides	13	St Lucy, Virgin and Martyr	Memorial
XIX	14	St John of the Cross, Priest and Doctor of the Church	Memorial
XVIII	15		
XVII	16		
XVI	17		
XV	18		
XIV	19		
XIII	20		
XII	21	*St Peter Canisius, Priest and Doctor of the Church*	
XI	22		
X	23	*St John of Kanty, Priest*	
IX	24		
VIII	25	THE NATIVITY OF THE LORD (CHRISTMAS)	Solemnity
VII	26	St Stephen, The First Martyr	Feast
VI	27	St John, Apostle and Evangelist	Feast
V	28	The Holy Innocents, Martyrs	Feast
IV	29	*St Thomas Becket, Bishop and Martyr*	
III	30		
Eve	31	*St Sylvester I, Pope*	

Sunday within the Octave of the Nativity, or, if there is no Sunday, December 30:
The Holy Family of Jesus, Mary, and Joseph   Feast

SPECIAL DAYS OF PRAYER FOR THE DIOCESES OF THE UNITED STATES OF AMERICA

I n all the Dioceses of the United States of America, January 22 (or January 23, when January 22 falls on a Sunday) shall be observed as a particular day of prayer for the full restoration of the legal guarantee of the right to life and of penance for violations to the dignity of the human person committed through acts of abortion. The liturgical celebrations for this day may be the Mass "For Giving Thanks to God for the Gift of Human Life" (no. 48/1 of the Masses and Prayers for Various Needs and Occasions), celebrated with white vestments, or the Mass "For the Preservation of Peace and Justice" (no. 30 of the Masses and Prayers for Various Needs and Occasions), celebrated with violet vestments.

TABLE OF PRINCIPAL CELEBRATIONS OF THE LITURGICAL YEAR

A.D.	Lectionary Cycles		Ash Wednesday	Easter	Ascension	Pentecost
	Dominical Cycle	Sunday Cycle				
2010	c	C-A	17 February	4 April	13 May	23 May
2011	b	A-B	9 March	24 April	2 June	12 June
2012*	A g	B-C	22 February	8 April	17 May	27 May
2013	f	C-A	13 February	31 March	9 May	19 May
2014	e	A-B	5 March	20 April	29 May	8 June
2015	d	B-C	18 February	5 April	14 May	24 May
2016*	c b	C-A	10 February	27 March	5 May	15 May
2017	A	A-B	1 March	16 April	25 May	4 June
2018	g	B-C	14 February	1 April	10 May	20 May
2019	f	C-A	6 March	21 April	30 May	9 June
2020*	e d	A-B	26 February	12 April	21 May	31 May
2021	c	B-C	17 February	4 April	13 May	23 May
2022	b	C-A	2 March	17 April	26 May	5 June
2023	A	A-B	22 February	9 April	18 May	28 May
2024*	g f	B-C	14 February	31 March	9 May	19 May
2025	e	C-A	5 March	20 April	29 May	8 June
2026	d	A-B	18 February	5 April	14 May	24 May
2027	c	B-C	10 February	28 March	6 May	16 May
2028*	b A	C-A	1 March	16 April	25 May	4 June
2029	g	A-B	14 February	1 April	10 May	20 May
2030	f	B-C	6 March	21 April	30 May	9 June
2031	e	C-A	26 February	13 April	22 May	1 June
2032*	d c	A-B	11 February	28 March	6 May	16 May
2033	b	B-C	2 March	17 April	26 May	5 June
2034	A	C-A	22 February	9 April	18 May	28 May
2035	g	A-B	7 February	25 March	3 May	13 May
2036*	f e	B-C	27 February	13 April	22 May	1 June
2037	d	C-A	18 February	5 April	14 May	24 May
2038	c	A-B	10 March	25 April	3 June	13 June
2039	b	B-C	23 February	10 April	19 May	29 May

* Leap Years

(continued) TABLE OF PRINCIPAL CELEBRATIONS OF THE LITURGICAL YEAR

A.D.	Ordinary Time					First Sunday of Advent
	Before Lent		After Easter Time			
	Up Until	Weeks	From		From Week	
2010	16 February	6	24 May		8	28 November
2011	8 March	9	13 June		11	27 November
2012*	21 February	7	28 May		8	2 December
2013	12 February	5	20 May		7	1 December
2014	4 March	8	9 June		10	30 November
2015	17 February	6	25 May		8	29 November
2016*	9 February	5	16 May		7	27 November
2017	28 February	8	5 June		9	3 December
2018	13 February	6	21 May		7	2 December
2019	5 March	8	10 June		10	1 December
2020*	25 February	7	1 June		9	29 November
2021	16 February	6	24 May		8	28 November
2022	1 March	8	6 June		10	27 November
2023	21 February	7	29 May		8	3 December
2024*	13 February	6	20 May		7	1 December
2025	4 March	8	9 June		10	30 November
2026	17 February	6	25 May		8	29 November
2027	9 February	5	17 May		7	28 November
2028*	29 February	8	5 June		9	3 December
2029	13 February	6	21 May		7	2 December
2030	5 March	8	10 June		10	1 December
2031	25 February	7	2 June		9	30 November
2032*	10 February	5	17 May		7	28 November
2033	1 March	8	6 June		10	27 November
2034	21 February	7	29 May		8	3 December
2035	6 February	5	14 May		6	2 December
2036*	26 February	7	2 June		9	30 November
2037	17 February	6	25 May		8	29 November
2038	9 March	9	14 June		11	28 November
2039	22 February	7	30 May		9	27 November

* Leap Years

PROPER OF TIME

ADVENT
FIRST SUNDAY OF ADVENT

Entrance Antiphon
Cf. Ps 25 (24): 1-3

To you, I lift up my soul, O my God.
In you, I have trusted; let me not be put to shame.
Nor let my enemies exult over me; and let none who hope in you be put to shame.

The Gloria in excelsis (Glory to God in the highest) is not said.

Collect

Grant your faithful, we pray, almighty God,
the resolve to run forth to meet your Christ
with righteous deeds at his coming,
so that, gathered at his right hand,
they may be worthy to possess the heavenly Kingdom.
Through our Lord Jesus Christ, your Son,
who lives and reigns with you in the unity of the Holy Spirit,
one God, for ever and ever.

The Creed is said.

Prayer over the Offerings

Accept, we pray, O Lord, these offerings we make,
gathered from among your gifts to us,
and may what you grant us to celebrate devoutly here below
gain for us the prize of eternal redemption.
Through Christ our Lord.

Preface I of Advent, p. 534.

Communion Antiphon
Ps 85 (84): 13

The Lord will bestow his bounty, and our earth shall yield its increase.

Prayer after Communion

May these mysteries, O Lord,
in which we have participated,
profit us, we pray,
for even now, as we walk amid passing things,
you teach us by them to love the things of heaven
and hold fast to what endures.
Through Christ our Lord.

A formula of Solemn Blessing, p. 674, may be used.

Monday

Entrance Antiphon
Cf. Jer 31: 10; Is 35: 4

Hear the word of the Lord, O nations;
declare it to the distant lands:
Behold, our Savior will come; you need no longer fear.

Collect

Keep us alert, we pray, O Lord our God,
as we await the advent of Christ your Son,
so that, when he comes and knocks,
he may find us watchful in prayer
and exultant in his praise.
Who lives and reigns with you in the unity of the Holy Spirit,
one God, for ever and ever.

Prayer over the Offerings

Accept, we pray, O Lord, these offerings we make,
gathered from among your gifts to us,
and may what you grant us to celebrate devoutly here below
gain for us the prize of eternal redemption.
Through Christ our Lord.

Preface I of Advent, p. 534.

Communion Antiphon
Cf. Ps 106 (105): 4-5; Is 38: 3

Come, O Lord, visit us in peace,
that we may rejoice before you with a blameless heart.

Prayer after Communion

May these mysteries, O Lord,
in which we have participated,
profit us, we pray,
for even now, as we walk amid passing things,
you teach us by them
to love the things of heaven
and hold fast to what endures.
Through Christ our Lord.

Tuesday

Entrance Antiphon
Cf. Zec 14: 5, 7

Behold, the Lord will come, and all his holy ones with him;
and on that day there will be a great light.

Collect

Look with favor, Lord God, on our petitions,
and in our trials grant us your compassionate help,
that, consoled by the presence of your Son,
whose coming we now await,
we may be tainted no longer
by the corruption of former ways.
Through our Lord Jesus Christ, your Son,
who lives and reigns with you in the unity of the Holy Spirit,
one God, for ever and ever.

Prayer over the Offerings

Be pleased, O Lord, with our humble prayers and offerings,
and, since we have no merits to plead our cause,
come, we pray, to our rescue
with the protection of your mercy.
Through Christ our Lord.

Preface I of Advent, p. 534.

Communion Antiphon
Cf. 2 Tm 4: 8

The Just Judge will bestow a crown of righteousness
on those who eagerly await his coming.

Prayer after Communion

Replenished by the food of spiritual nourishment,
we humbly beseech you, O Lord,
that, through our partaking in this mystery,
you may teach us to judge wisely the things of earth
and hold firm to the things of heaven.
Through Christ our Lord.

Wednesday

Entrance Antiphon
Cf. Hb 2: 3; 1 Cor 4: 5

The Lord will come and he will not delay.
He will illumine what is hidden in darkness
and reveal himself to all the nations.

Collect
**Prepare our hearts, we pray, O Lord our God,
by your divine power,
so that at the coming of Christ your Son
we may be found worthy of the banquet of eternal life
and merit to receive heavenly nourishment from his hands.
Who lives and reigns with you in the unity of the Holy Spirit,
one God, for ever and ever.**

Prayer over the Offerings
**May the sacrifice of our worship, Lord, we pray,
be offered to you unceasingly,
to complete what was begun in sacred mystery
and powerfully accomplish for us your saving work.
Through Christ our Lord.**

Preface I of Advent, p. 534.

Communion Antiphon
Cf. Is 40: 10; 35: 5

Behold, our Lord will come with power
and will enlighten the eyes of his servants.

Prayer after Communion
**We implore your mercy, Lord,
that this divine sustenance
may cleanse us of our faults
and prepare us for the coming feasts.
Through Christ our Lord.**

Thursday

Entrance Antiphon   Cf. Ps 119 (118): 151-152

You, O Lord, are close, and all your ways are truth.
From of old I have known of your decrees, for you are eternal.

Collect

Stir up your power, O Lord,
and come to our help with mighty strength,
that what our sins impede
the grace of your mercy may hasten.
Through our Lord Jesus Christ, your Son,
who lives and reigns with you in the unity of the Holy Spirit,
one God, for ever and ever.

Prayer over the Offerings

Accept, we pray, O Lord, these offerings we make,
gathered from among your gifts to us,
and may what you grant us to celebrate devoutly here below
gain for us the prize of eternal redemption.
Through Christ our Lord.

Preface I of Advent, p. 534.

Communion Antiphon   Ti 2: 12-13

Let us live justly and devoutly in this age,
as we await the blessed hope
and the coming of the glory of our great God.

Prayer after Communion

May these mysteries, O Lord,
in which we have participated,
profit us, we pray,
for even now, as we walk amid passing things,
you teach us by them
to love the things of heaven
and hold fast to what endures.
Through Christ our Lord.

Friday

Entrance Antiphon

Behold, the Lord will come
descending with splendor to visit his people with peace,
and he will bestow on them eternal life.

Collect

**Stir up your power, we pray, O Lord, and come,
that with you to protect us,
we may find rescue
from the pressing dangers of our sins,
and with you to set us free,
we may be found worthy of salvation.
Who live and reign with God the Father
in the unity of the Holy Spirit,
one God, for ever and ever.**

Prayer over the Offerings

**Be pleased, O Lord, with our humble prayers and offerings,
and, since we have no merits to plead our cause,
come, we pray, to our rescue
with the protection of your mercy.
Through Christ our Lord.**

Preface I of Advent, p. 534.

Communion Antiphon *Cf. Phil 3: 20-21*

We await a savior, the Lord Jesus Christ,
who will change our mortal bodies,
to conform with his glorified body.

Prayer after Communion

**Replenished by the food of spiritual nourishment,
we humbly beseech you, O Lord,
that, through our partaking in this mystery,
you may teach us to judge wisely the things of earth
and hold firm to the things of heaven.
Through Christ our Lord.**

Saturday

Entrance Antiphon
Cf. Ps 80 (79): 4, 2

Come and show us your face, O Lord,
who are seated upon the Cherubim, and we will be saved.

Collect

O God, who sent your Only Begotten Son into this world
to free the human race from its ancient enslavement,
bestow on those who devoutly await him
the grace of your compassion from on high,
that we may attain the prize of true freedom.
Through our Lord Jesus Christ, your Son,
who lives and reigns with you in the unity of the Holy Spirit,
one God, for ever and ever.

Prayer over the Offerings

May the sacrifice of our worship, Lord, we pray,
be offered to you unceasingly,
to complete what was begun in sacred mystery
and powerfully accomplish for us your saving work.
Through Christ our Lord.

Preface I of Advent, p. 534.

Communion Antiphon
Cf. Rev 22: 12

Behold, I am coming soon
and my recompense is with me, says the Lord,
to bestow a reward according to the deeds of each.

Prayer after Communion

We implore your mercy, Lord,
that this divine sustenance
may cleanse us of our faults
and prepare us for the coming feasts.
Through Christ our Lord.

SECOND SUNDAY OF ADVENT

Entrance Antiphon Cf. Is 30: 19, 30
O people of Sion, behold,
the Lord will come to save the nations,
and the Lord will make the glory of his voice heard
in the joy of your heart.

The Gloria in excelsis (Glory to God in the highest) is not said.

Collect

**Almighty and merciful God,
may no earthly undertaking hinder those
who set out in haste to meet your Son,
but may our learning of heavenly wisdom
gain us admittance to his company.
Who lives and reigns with you in the unity of the Holy Spirit,
one God, for ever and ever.**

The Creed is said.

Prayer over the Offerings

**Be pleased, O Lord, with our humble prayers and offerings,
and, since we have no merits to plead our cause,
come, we pray, to our rescue
with the protection of your mercy.
Through Christ our Lord.**

Preface I of Advent, p. 534.

Communion Antiphon Bar 5: 5; 4: 36
Jerusalem, arise and stand upon the heights,
and behold the joy which comes to you from God.

Prayer after Communion

**Replenished by the food of spiritual nourishment,
we humbly beseech you, O Lord,
that, through our partaking in this mystery,
you may teach us to judge wisely the things of earth
and hold firm to the things of heaven.
Through Christ our Lord.**

A formula of Solemn Blessing, p. 674, may be used.

Monday

Entrance Antiphon   Cf. Jer 31: 10; Is 35: 4

Hear the word of the Lord, O nations;
declare it to the distant lands:
Behold, our Savior will come; you need no longer fear.

Collect

May our prayer of petition
rise before you, we pray, O Lord,
that, with purity unblemished,
we, your servants, may come, as we desire,
to celebrate the great mystery
of the Incarnation of your Only Begotten Son.
Who lives and reigns with you in the unity of the Holy Spirit,
one God, for ever and ever.

Prayer over the Offerings

Accept, we pray, O Lord, these offerings we make,
gathered from among your gifts to us,
and may what you grant us to celebrate devoutly here below
gain for us the prize of eternal redemption.
Through Christ our Lord.

Preface I of Advent, p. 534.

Communion Antiphon   Cf. Ps 106 (105): 4-5; Is 38: 3

Come, O Lord, visit us in peace,
that we may rejoice before you with a blameless heart.

Prayer after Communion

May these mysteries, O Lord,
in which we have participated,
profit us, we pray,
for even now, as we walk amid passing things,
you teach us by them
to love the things of heaven
and hold fast to what endures.
Through Christ our Lord.

Tuesday

Entrance Antiphon   Cf. Zec 14: 5, 7

Behold, the Lord will come, and all his holy ones with him;
and on that day there will be a great light.

Collect

O God, who have shown forth your salvation
to all the ends of the earth,
grant, we pray,
that we may look forward in joy
to the glorious Nativity of Christ.
Who lives and reigns with you in the unity of the Holy Spirit,
one God, for ever and ever.

Prayer over the Offerings

Be pleased, O Lord, with our humble prayers and offerings,
and, since we have no merits to plead our cause,
come, we pray, to our rescue
with the protection of your mercy.
Through Christ our Lord.

Preface I of Advent, p. 534.

Communion Antiphon   Cf. 2 Tm 4: 8

The Just Judge will bestow a crown of righteousness
on those who eagerly await his coming.

Prayer after Communion

Replenished by the food of spiritual nourishment,
we humbly beseech you, O Lord,
that, through our partaking in this mystery,
you may teach us to judge wisely the things of earth
and hold firm to the things of heaven.
Through Christ our Lord.

Wednesday

Entrance Antiphon
Cf. Hb 2: 3; 1 Cor 4: 5

The Lord will come and he will not delay.
He will illumine what is hidden in darkness
and reveal himself to all the nations.

Collect

**Almighty God, who command us
to prepare the way for Christ the Lord,
grant in your kindness, we pray,
that no infirmity may weary us
as we long for the comforting presence
of our heavenly physician.
Who lives and reigns with you in the unity of the Holy Spirit,
one God, for ever and ever.**

Prayer over the Offerings

**May the sacrifice of our worship, Lord, we pray,
be offered to you unceasingly,
to complete what was begun in sacred mystery
and powerfully accomplish for us your saving work.
Through Christ our Lord.**

Preface I of Advent, p. 534.

Communion Antiphon
Cf. Is 40: 10; 35: 5

Behold, our Lord will come with power
and will enlighten the eyes of his servants.

Prayer after Communion

**We implore your mercy, Lord,
that this divine sustenance
may cleanse us of our faults
and prepare us for the coming feasts.
Through Christ our Lord.**

Thursday

Entrance Antiphon   Cf. Ps 119 (118): 151-152

You, O Lord, are close, and all your ways are truth.
From of old I have known of your decrees, for you are eternal.

Collect

Stir up our hearts, O Lord,
to make ready the paths
of your Only Begotten Son,
that through his coming,
we may be found worthy to serve you
with minds made pure.
Through our Lord Jesus Christ, your Son,
who lives and reigns with you in the unity of the Holy Spirit,
one God, for ever and ever.

Prayer over the Offerings

Accept, we pray, O Lord, these offerings we make,
gathered from among your gifts to us,
and may what you grant us to celebrate devoutly here below
gain for us the prize of eternal redemption.
Through Christ our Lord.

Preface I of Advent, p. 534.

Communion Antiphon   Ti 2: 12-13

Let us live justly and devoutly in this age,
as we await the blessed hope
and the coming of the glory of our great God.

Prayer after Communion

May these mysteries, O Lord,
in which we have participated,
profit us, we pray,
for even now, as we walk amid passing things,
you teach us by them
to love the things of heaven
and hold fast to what endures.
Through Christ our Lord.

Friday

Entrance Antiphon
Behold, the Lord will come
descending with splendor to visit his people with peace,
and he will bestow on them eternal life.

Collect
Grant that your people, we pray, almighty God,
may be ever watchful
for the coming of your Only Begotten Son,
that, as the author of our salvation himself has taught us,
we may hasten, alert and with lighted lamps,
to meet him when he comes.
Who lives and reigns with you in the unity of the Holy Spirit,
one God, for ever and ever.

Prayer over the Offerings
Be pleased, O Lord, with our humble prayers and offerings,
and, since we have no merits to plead our cause,
come, we pray, to our rescue
with the protection of your mercy.
Through Christ our Lord.

Preface I of Advent, p. 534.

Communion Antiphon   Cf. Phil 3: 20-21
We await a savior, the Lord Jesus Christ,
who will change our mortal bodies,
to conform with his glorified body.

Prayer after Communion
Replenished by the food of spiritual nourishment,
we humbly beseech you, O Lord,
that, through our partaking in this mystery,
you may teach us to judge wisely the things of earth
and hold firm to the things of heaven.
Through Christ our Lord.

Saturday

Entrance Antiphon
Cf. Ps 80 (79): 4, 2

Come and show us your face, O Lord,
who are seated upon the Cherubim, and we will be saved.

Collect

**May the splendor of your glory dawn in our hearts,
we pray, almighty God,
that all shadows of the night may be scattered
and we may be shown to be children of light
by the advent of your Only Begotten Son.
Who lives and reigns with you in the unity of the Holy Spirit,
one God, for ever and ever.**

Prayer over the Offerings

**May the sacrifice of our worship, Lord, we pray,
be offered to you unceasingly,
to complete what was begun in sacred mystery
and powerfully accomplish for us your saving work.
Through Christ our Lord.**

Preface I of Advent, p. 534.

Communion Antiphon
Cf. Rev 22: 12

Behold, I am coming soon
and my recompense is with me, says the Lord,
to bestow a reward according to the deeds of each.

Prayer after Communion

**We implore your mercy, Lord,
that this divine sustenance
may cleanse us of our faults
and prepare us for the coming feasts.
Through Christ our Lord.**

THIRD SUNDAY OF ADVENT

In this Mass the color violet or rose is used.

Entrance Antiphon   *Phil 4: 4-5*
    Rejoice in the Lord always; again I say, rejoice.
    Indeed, the Lord is near.

The Gloria in excelsis (Glory to God in the highest) is not said.

Collect
    O God, who see how your people
    faithfully await the feast of the Lord's Nativity,
    enable us, we pray,
    to attain the joys of so great a salvation
    and to celebrate them always
    with solemn worship and glad rejoicing.
    Through our Lord Jesus Christ, your Son,
    who lives and reigns with you in the unity of the Holy Spirit,
    one God, for ever and ever.

The Creed is said.

Prayer over the Offerings
    May the sacrifice of our worship, Lord, we pray,
    be offered to you unceasingly,
    to complete what was begun in sacred mystery
    and powerfully accomplish for us your saving work.
    Through Christ our Lord.

Preface I or II of Advent, pp. 534-537.

Communion Antiphon   *Cf. Is 35: 4*
    Say to the faint of heart: Be strong and do not fear.
    Behold, our God will come, and he will save us.

Prayer after Communion
    We implore your mercy, Lord,
    that this divine sustenance may cleanse us of our faults
    and prepare us for the coming feasts.
    Through Christ our Lord.

A formula of Solemn Blessing, p. 674, may be used.

When during the week a Mass of the weekday is to be said, the texts given below are used, unless the day is one of the Advent weekdays that occur from December 17 to 24.

Monday

Entrance Antiphon
Cf. Jer 31: 10; Is 35: 4

Hear the word of the Lord, O nations;
declare it to the distant lands:
Behold, our Savior will come; you need no longer fear.

Collect

Incline a merciful ear to our cry, we pray, O Lord,
and, casting light on the darkness of our hearts,
visit us with the grace of your Son.
Who lives and reigns with you in the unity of the Holy Spirit,
one God, for ever and ever.

Prayer over the Offerings

Accept, we pray, O Lord, these offerings we make,
gathered from among your gifts to us,
and may what you grant us to celebrate devoutly here below
gain for us the prize of eternal redemption.
Through Christ our Lord.

Preface I of Advent, p. 534.

Communion Antiphon
Cf. Ps 106 (105): 4-5; Is 38: 3

Come, O Lord, visit us in peace,
that we may rejoice before you with a blameless heart.

Prayer after Communion

May these mysteries, O Lord,
in which we have participated,
profit us, we pray,
for even now, as we walk amid passing things,
you teach us by them
to love the things of heaven
and hold fast to what endures.
Through Christ our Lord.

Tuesday

Entrance Antiphon
Cf. Zec 14: 5, 7
Behold, the Lord will come, and all his holy ones with him;
and on that day there will be a great light.

Collect
O God, who through your Only Begotten Son
have made us a new creation,
look kindly, we pray,
on the handiwork of your mercy,
and at your Son's coming
cleanse us from every stain of the old way of life.
Through our Lord Jesus Christ, your Son,
who lives and reigns with you in the unity of the Holy Spirit,
one God, for ever and ever.

Prayer over the Offerings
Be pleased, O Lord, with our humble prayers and offerings,
and since we have no merits to plead our cause,
come, we pray, to our rescue
with the protection of your mercy.
Through Christ our Lord.

Preface I of Advent, p. 534.

Communion Antiphon
Cf. 2 Tm 4: 8
The Just Judge will bestow a crown of righteousness
on those who eagerly await his coming.

Prayer after Communion
Replenished by the food of spiritual nourishment,
we humbly beseech you, O Lord,
that, through our partaking in this mystery,
you may teach us to judge wisely the things of earth
and hold firm to the things of heaven.
Through Christ our Lord.

Wednesday

Entrance Antiphon
Cf. Hb 2: 3; 1 Cor 4: 5

The Lord will come and he will not delay.
He will illumine what is hidden in darkness
and reveal himself to all the nations.

Collect

Grant, we pray, almighty God,
that the coming solemnity of your Son
may bestow healing upon us in this present life
and bring us the rewards of life eternal.
Through our Lord Jesus Christ, your Son,
who lives and reigns with you in the unity of the Holy Spirit,
one God, for ever and ever.

Prayer over the Offerings

May the sacrifice of our worship, Lord, we pray,
be offered to you unceasingly,
to complete what was begun in sacred mystery
and powerfully accomplish for us your saving work.
Through Christ our Lord.

Preface I of Advent, p. 534.

Communion Antiphon
Cf. Is 40: 10; 35: 5

Behold, our Lord will come with power
and will enlighten the eyes of his servants.

Prayer after Communion

We implore your mercy, Lord,
that this divine sustenance
may cleanse us of our faults
and prepare us for the coming feasts.
Through Christ our Lord.

Thursday

Entrance Antiphon
Cf. Ps 119 (118): 151-152

You, O Lord, are close, and all your ways are truth.
From of old I have known of your decrees, for you are eternal.

Collect

Unworthy servants that we are, O Lord,
grieved by the guilt of our deeds,
we pray that you may gladden us
by the saving advent of your Only Begotten Son.
Who lives and reigns with you in the unity of the Holy Spirit,
one God, for ever and ever.

Prayer over the Offerings

Accept, we pray, O Lord, these offerings we make,
gathered from among your gifts to us,
and may what you grant us to celebrate devoutly here below
gain for us the prize of eternal redemption.
Through Christ our Lord.

Preface I of Advent, p. 534.

Communion Antiphon
Ti 2: 12-13

Let us live justly and devoutly in this age,
as we await the blessed hope
and the coming of the glory of our great God.

Prayer after Communion

May these mysteries, O Lord,
in which we have participated,
profit us, we pray,
for even now, as we walk amid passing things,
you teach us by them
to love the things of heaven
and hold fast to what endures.
Through Christ our Lord.

Friday

Entrance Antiphon
Behold, the Lord will come
descending with splendor to visit his people with peace,
and he will bestow on them eternal life.

Collect
May your grace, almighty God,
always go before us and follow after,
so that we, who await with heartfelt desire
the coming of your Only Begotten Son,
may receive your help both now and in the life to come.
Through our Lord Jesus Christ, your Son,
who lives and reigns with you in the unity of the Holy Spirit,
one God, for ever and ever.

Prayer over the Offerings
Be pleased, O Lord, with our humble prayers and offerings,
and, since we have no merits to plead our cause,
come, we pray, to our rescue
with the protection of your mercy.
Through Christ our Lord.

Preface I of Advent, p. 534.

Communion Antiphon   Cf. Phil 3: 20-21
We await a savior, the Lord Jesus Christ,
who will change our mortal bodies,
to conform with his glorified body.

Prayer after Communion
Replenished by the food of spiritual nourishment,
we humbly beseech you, O Lord,
that, through our partaking in this mystery,
you may teach us to judge wisely the things of earth
and hold firm to the things of heaven.
Through Christ our Lord.

FOURTH SUNDAY OF ADVENT

Entrance Antiphon
Cf. Is 45: 8

Drop down dew from above, you heavens,
and let the clouds rain down the Just One;
let the earth be opened and bring forth a Savior.

The Gloria in excelsis (Glory to God in the highest) is not said.

Collect

Pour forth, we beseech you, O Lord,
your grace into our hearts,
that we, to whom the Incarnation of Christ your Son
was made known by the message of an Angel,
may by his Passion and Cross
be brought to the glory of his Resurrection.
Who lives and reigns with you in the unity of the Holy Spirit,
one God, for ever and ever.

The Creed is said.

Prayer over the Offerings

May the Holy Spirit, O Lord,
sanctify these gifts laid upon your altar,
just as he filled with his power
    the womb of the Blessed Virgin Mary.
Through Christ our Lord.

Preface II of Advent, p. 536.

Communion Antiphon
Is 7: 14

Behold, a Virgin shall conceive and bear a son;
and his name will be called Emmanuel.

Prayer after Communion

Having received this pledge of eternal redemption,
we pray, almighty God,
that, as the feast day of our salvation draws ever nearer,
so we may press forward all the more eagerly
to the worthy celebration of the mystery of your Son's Nativity.
Who lives and reigns for ever and ever.

A formula of Solemn Blessing, p. 674, may be used.

THE WEEKDAYS OF ADVENT
from December 17 to 24

The following Masses are used on the days to which they are assigned, with the exception of Sunday, which retains its own Mass.

December 17

Entrance Antiphon
Cf. Is 49: 13

Rejoice, O heavens, and exult, O earth,
for our Lord will come to show mercy to his poor.

Collect

O God, Creator and Redeemer of human nature,
who willed that your Word should take flesh
in an ever-virgin womb,
look with favor on our prayers,
that your Only Begotten Son,
having taken to himself our humanity,
may be pleased to grant us a share in his divinity.
Who lives and reigns with you in the unity of the Holy Spirit,
one God, for ever and ever.

Prayer over the Offerings

Sanctify these gifts of your Church, O Lord,
and grant that through these venerable mysteries
we may be nourished with the bread of heaven.
Through Christ our Lord.

Preface II of Advent, p. 536.

Communion Antiphon
Cf. Hg 2: 7

Behold, the Desired of all the nations will come,
and the house of the Lord will be filled with glory.

Prayer after Communion

Nourished by these divine gifts, almighty God,
we ask you to grant our desire:
that, aflame with your Spirit,
we may shine like bright torches
before your Christ when he comes.
Who lives and reigns for ever and ever.

December 18

Entrance Antiphon
Christ our King is coming,
he is the Lamb foretold by John.

Collect
**Grant, we pray, almighty God,
that we, who are weighed down from of old
by slavery beneath the yoke of sin,
may be set free by the newness
of the long-awaited Nativity
of your Only Begotten Son.
Who lives and reigns with you in the unity of the Holy Spirit,
one God, for ever and ever.**

Prayer over the Offerings
**May the sacrifice to be offered to you, O Lord,
make us acceptable to your name,
that we may merit for all eternity
to be the companions of Christ,
by whose Death our own mortality was healed.
Who lives and reigns for ever and ever.**

Preface II of Advent, p. 536.

Communion Antiphon   Mt 1: 23
His name will be called Emmanuel,
which means God-with-us.

Prayer after Communion
**May we receive your mercy
in the midst of your temple, O Lord,
and show fitting honor
to the coming solemnities of our redemption.
Through Christ our Lord.**

December 19

Entrance Antiphon
Cf. Heb 10: 37

He who is to come will come and will not delay,
and now there will be no fear within our land,
for he is our Savior.

Collect

O God, who through the child-bearing of the holy Virgin
graciously revealed the radiance of your glory to the world,
grant, we pray,
that we may venerate with integrity of faith
the mystery of so wondrous an Incarnation
and always celebrate it with due reverence.
Through our Lord Jesus Christ, your Son,
who lives and reigns with you in the unity of the Holy Spirit,
one God, for ever and ever.

Prayer over the Offerings

Look with favor, we pray, O Lord,
on the offerings we lay upon your altars,
that what we bring despite our weakness
may be sanctified by your power.
Through Christ our Lord.

Preface II of Advent, p. 536.

Communion Antiphon
Lk 1: 78-79

The Dawn from on high will visit us,
guiding our feet in the way of peace.

Prayer after Communion

As we give thanks, almighty God,
for these gifts you have bestowed,
graciously arouse in us, we pray,
the desire for those yet to come,
that we may welcome the Nativity of our Savior
and honor it with minds made pure.
Through Christ our Lord.

December 20

Entrance Antiphon
Cf. Is 11: 1; 40: 5; Lk 3: 6

A branch shall sprout from the root of Jesse,
and the glory of the Lord will fill the whole earth,
and all flesh will see the salvation of God.

Collect
O God, eternal majesty, whose ineffable Word
the immaculate Virgin received through the message of an Angel
and so became the dwelling-place of divinity,
filled with the light of the Holy Spirit,
grant, we pray, that by her example
we may in humility hold fast to your will.
Through our Lord Jesus Christ, your Son,
who lives and reigns with you in the unity of the Holy Spirit,
one God, for ever and ever.

Prayer over the Offerings
Look, O Lord, we pray,
upon the one sacrifice of your Son,
that, by participating in this mystery,
we may possess at last the gifts we have awaited
and for which our faith bids us hope.
Through Christ our Lord.

Preface II of Advent, p. 536.

Communion Antiphon
Lk 1: 31

The Angel said to Mary:
Behold, you will conceive and bear a son,
and you shall name him Jesus.

Prayer after Communion
Grant divine protection, O Lord,
to those you renew with this heavenly gift,
that to those who delight in your mysteries
you may give the joy of true peace.
Through Christ our Lord.

December 21

Entrance Antiphon
Cf. Is 7: 14; 8: 10

The Lord and Ruler will be coming soon,
and his name will be called Emmanuel,
because he will be God-with-us.

Collect

**Hear in kindness, O Lord,
the prayers of your people,
that those who rejoice
at the coming of your Only Begotten Son in our flesh
may, when at last he comes in glory,
gain the reward of eternal life.
Through our Lord Jesus Christ, your Son,
who lives and reigns with you in the unity of the Holy Spirit,
one God, for ever and ever.**

Prayer over the Offerings

**Be pleased, O Lord, to accept the offerings of your Church,
for in your mercy you have given them to be offered
and by your power you transform them
into the mystery of our salvation.
Through Christ our Lord.**

Preface II of Advent, p. 536.

Communion Antiphon
Lk 1: 45

Blessed are you who have believed,
that what was spoken to you by the Lord would be fulfilled.

Prayer after Communion

**Lord, may participation in this divine mystery
provide enduring protection for your people,
so that, being subject to your glorious majesty in dedicated service,
they may know abundant health in mind and body.
Through Christ our Lord.**

December 22

Entrance Antiphon
Ps 24 (23): 7

O gates, lift high your heads; grow higher, ancient doors.
Let him enter, the king of glory!

Collect

O God, who, seeing the human race fallen into death,
willed to redeem it by the coming of your Only Begotten Son,
grant, we pray,
that those who confess his Incarnation with humble fervor
may merit his company as their Redeemer.
Who lives and reigns with you in the unity of the Holy Spirit,
one God, for ever and ever.

Prayer over the Offerings

Trusting in your compassion, O Lord,
we come eagerly with our offerings to your sacred altar,
that, through the purifying action of your grace,
we may be cleansed by the very mysteries we serve.
Through Christ our Lord.

Preface II of Advent, p. 536.

Communion Antiphon
Lk 1: 46, 49

My soul proclaims the greatness of the Lord,
for the Almighty has done great things for me.

Prayer after Communion

May reception of your Sacrament strengthen us, O Lord,
so that we may go out to meet our Savior
with worthy deeds when he comes
and merit the rewards of the blessed.
Through Christ our Lord.

December 23

Entrance Antiphon
Cf. Is 9: 5; Ps 72 (71): 17

A child shall be born for us,
and he will be called God, the Almighty;
every tribe of the earth shall be blest in him.

Collect

Almighty ever-living God,
as we see how the Nativity of your Son
according to the flesh draws near,
we pray that to us, your unworthy servants,
mercy may flow from your Word,
who chose to become flesh of the Virgin Mary
and establish among us his dwelling,
Jesus Christ our Lord.
Who lives and reigns with you in the unity of the Holy Spirit,
one God, for ever and ever.

Prayer over the Offerings

May this oblation,
by which divine worship in its fullness
has been inaugurated for us,
be our perfect reconciliation with you, O Lord,
that we may celebrate with minds made pure
the Nativity of our Redeemer.
Who lives and reigns for ever and ever.

Preface II of Advent, p. 536.

Communion Antiphon
Rev 3: 20

Behold, I stand at the door and knock:
if anyone hears my voice and opens the door to me,
I will enter his house and dine with him, and he with me.

Prayer after Communion

Grant your peace, O Lord,
to those you have nourished with these heavenly gifts,
that we may be ready, with lighted lamps,
to meet your dearly beloved Son at his coming.
Who lives and reigns for ever and ever.

December 24
The Morning Mass

Entrance Antiphon
Cf. Gal 4: 4

Behold, when the fullness of time had come,
God sent his Son into the world.

Collect
Come quickly, we pray, Lord Jesus,
and do not delay,
that those who trust in your compassion
may find solace and relief in your coming.
Who live and reign with God the Father
in the unity of the Holy Spirit,
one God, for ever and ever.

Prayer over the Offerings
Graciously make your own, O Lord,
the offerings which we bring,
that, partaking of them, we be cleansed of our sins
and merit to stand ready with pure hearts
for the coming in glory of your Son.
Who lives and reigns for ever and ever.

Preface II of Advent, p. 536.

Communion Antiphon
Lk 1: 68

Blessed be the Lord, the God of Israel!
He has visited his people and redeemed them.

Prayer after Communion
Grant to us who find new vigor, O Lord,
in these your wondrous gifts,
that, as we prepare to celebrate in adoration
the festivities of your Son's Nativity,
so we may possess in gladness
his everlasting rewards.
Who lives and reigns for ever and ever.

CHRISTMAS TIME
December 25

THE NATIVITY OF THE LORD [CHRISTMAS]
Solemnity

At the Vigil Mass

This Mass is used on the evening of December 24, either before or after First Vespers (Evening Prayer I) of the Nativity.

Entrance Antiphon   Cf. Ex 16: 6-7

    Today you will know that the Lord will come, and he will save us,
    and in the morning you will see his glory.

The Gloria in excelsis (Glory to God in the highest) is said.

Collect

O God, who gladden us year by year
as we wait in hope for our redemption,
grant that, just as we joyfully welcome
your Only Begotten Son as our Redeemer,
we may also merit to face him confidently
when he comes again as our Judge.
Who lives and reigns with you in the unity of the Holy Spirit,
one God, for ever and ever.

The Creed is said. All kneel at the words and by the Holy Spirit was incarnate.

Prayer over the Offerings

As we look forward, O Lord,
to the coming festivities,
may we serve you all the more eagerly
for knowing that in them
you make manifest the beginnings of our redemption.
Through Christ our Lord.

Preface I, II or III of the Nativity of the Lord, pp. 538-543.

When the Roman Canon is used, the proper form of the Communicantes (In communion with those) is said.

Communion Antiphon   Cf. Is 40: 5

    The glory of the Lord will be revealed,
    and all flesh will see the salvation of our God.

Prayer after Communion

Grant, O Lord, we pray,
that we may draw new vigor
from celebrating the Nativity of your Only Begotten Son,
by whose heavenly mystery we receive both food and drink.
Who lives and reigns for ever and ever.

A formula of Solemn Blessing, p. 674, may be used.

At the Mass during the Night

On the Nativity of the Lord all Priests may celebrate or concelebrate three Masses, provided the Masses are celebrated at their proper times.

Entrance Antiphon
Ps 2: 7

The Lord said to me: You are my Son.
It is I who have begotten you this day.

Or:

Let us all rejoice in the Lord, for our Savior has been born in the world.
Today true peace has come down to us from heaven.

The Gloria in excelsis (Glory to God in the highest) is said.

Collect

O God, who have made this most sacred night
radiant with the splendor of the true light,
grant, we pray, that we, who have known the mysteries of his
　　light on earth,
may also delight in his gladness in heaven.
Who lives and reigns with you in the unity of the Holy Spirit,
one God, for ever and ever.

The Creed is said. All kneel at the words and by the Holy Spirit was incarnate.

Prayer over the Offerings

May the oblation of this day's feast
be pleasing to you, O Lord, we pray,
that through this most holy exchange
we may be found in the likeness of Christ,
in whom our nature is united to you.
Who lives and reigns for ever and ever.

Preface I, II or III of the Nativity of the Lord, pp. 538-543.

When the Roman Canon is used, the proper form of the Communicantes (In communion with those) is said.

Communion Antiphon Jn 1: 14
The Word became flesh, and we have seen his glory.

Prayer after Communion
**Grant us, we pray, O Lord our God,
that we, who are gladdened by participation
in the feast of our Redeemer's Nativity,
may through an honorable way of life become worthy of union
   with him.
Who lives and reigns for ever and ever.**

A formula of Solemn Blessing, p. 674, may be used.

At the Mass at Dawn

Entrance Antiphon   Cf. Is 9: 1, 5; Lk 1: 33

Today a light will shine upon us, for the Lord is born for us;
and he will be called Wondrous God,
Prince of peace, Father of future ages:
and his reign will be without end.

The Gloria in excelsis (Glory to God in the highest) is said.

Collect

Grant, we pray, almighty God,
that, as we are bathed in the new radiance of your incarnate Word,
the light of faith, which illumines our minds,
may also shine through in our deeds.
Through our Lord Jesus Christ, your Son,
who lives and reigns with you in the unity of the Holy Spirit,
one God, for ever and ever.

The Creed is said. All kneel at the words and by the Holy Spirit was incarnate.

Prayer over the Offerings

May our offerings be worthy, we pray, O Lord,
of the mysteries of the Nativity this day,
that, just as Christ was born a man and also shone forth as God,
so these earthly gifts may confer on us what is divine.
Through Christ our Lord.

Preface I, II or III of the Nativity of the Lord, pp. 538-543.

When the Roman Canon is used, the proper form of the Communicantes (In communion with those) is said.

Communion Antiphon   Cf. Zec 9: 9

Rejoice, O Daughter Sion; lift up praise, Daughter Jerusalem:
Behold, your King will come, the Holy One and Savior of the world.

Prayer after Communion

Grant us, Lord, as we honor with joyful devotion
the Nativity of your Son,
that we may come to know with fullness of faith
the hidden depths of this mystery
and to love them ever more and more.
Through Christ our Lord.

A formula of Solemn Blessing, p. 674, may be used.

At the Mass during the Day

Entrance Antiphon
Cf. Is 9: 5

A child is born for us, and a son is given to us;
his scepter of power rests upon his shoulder,
and his name will be called Messenger of great counsel.

The Gloria in excelsis (Glory to God in the highest) is said.

Collect

**O God, who wonderfully created the dignity of human nature
and still more wonderfully restored it,
grant, we pray,
that we may share in the divinity of Christ,
who humbled himself to share in our humanity.
Who lives and reigns with you in the unity of the Holy Spirit,
one God, for ever and ever.**

The Creed is said. All kneel at the words *and by the Holy Spirit was incarnate*.

Prayer over the Offerings

**Make acceptable, O Lord, our oblation on this solemn day,
when you manifested the reconciliation
that makes us wholly pleasing in your sight
and inaugurated for us the fullness of divine worship.
Through Christ our Lord.**

Preface I, II or III of the Nativity of the Lord, pp. 538-543.

When the Roman Canon is used, the proper form of the Communicantes (In communion with those) is said.

Communion Antiphon
Cf. Ps 98 (97): 3

All the ends of the earth have seen the salvation of our God.

Prayer after Communion

**Grant, O merciful God,
that, just as the Savior of the world, born this day,
is the author of divine generation for us,
so he may be the giver even of immortality.
Who lives and reigns for ever and ever.**

A formula of Solemn Blessing, p. 674, may be used.

The Sunday within the Octave of the Nativity of the Lord [Christmas], or, if there is no Sunday, December 30.

THE HOLY FAMILY OF JESUS, MARY AND JOSEPH

Feast

Entrance Antiphon

Lk 2: 16

The shepherds went in haste,
and found Mary and Joseph and the Infant lying in a manger.

The Gloria in excelsis (Glory to God in the highest) is said.

Collect

O God, who were pleased to give us
the shining example of the Holy Family,
graciously grant that we may imitate them
in practicing the virtues of family life and in the bonds of charity,
and so, in the joy of your house,
delight one day in eternal rewards.
Through our Lord Jesus Christ, your Son,
who lives and reigns with you in the unity of the Holy Spirit,
one God, for ever and ever.

When this Feast is celebrated on Sunday, the Creed is said.

Prayer over the Offerings

We offer you, Lord, the sacrifice of conciliation,
humbly asking that,
through the intercession of the Virgin Mother of God and
    Saint Joseph,
you may establish our families firmly in your grace and your
    peace.
Through Christ our Lord.

Preface I, II or III of the Nativity of the Lord, pp. 538-543.

When the Roman Canon is used, the proper form of the Communicantes (In communion with those) is said.

Communion Antiphon   Bar 3: 38
Our God has appeared on the earth, and lived among us.

Prayer after Communion

Bring those you refresh with this heavenly Sacrament,
most merciful Father,
to imitate constantly the example of the Holy Family,
so that, after the trials of this world,
we may share their company for ever.
Through Christ our Lord.

December 29

Fifth Day within the Octave of the Nativity of the Lord [Christmas]

Entrance Antiphon
Jn 3: 16

God so loved the world that he gave his Only Begotten Son,
so that all who believe in him may not perish,
but may have eternal life.

The Gloria in excelsis (Glory to God in the highest) is said.

Collect
Almighty and invisible God,
who dispersed the darkness of this world
by the coming of your light,
look, we pray, with serene countenance upon us,
that we may acclaim with fitting praise
the greatness of the Nativity of your Only Begotten Son.
Who lives and reigns with you in the unity of the Holy Spirit,
one God, for ever and ever.

Prayer over the Offerings
Receive our oblation, O Lord,
by which is brought about a glorious exchange,
that, by offering what you have given,
we may merit to receive your very self.
Through Christ our Lord.

Preface I, II or III of the Nativity of the Lord, pp. 538-543.

When the Roman Canon is used, the proper form of the Communicantes (In communion with those) is said.

Communion Antiphon
Lk 1: 78

Through the tender mercy of our God,
the Dawn from on high will visit us.

Prayer after Communion
Grant, we pray, almighty God,
that, by the power of these holy mysteries,
our life may be constantly sustained.
Through Christ our Lord.

December 30

Sixth Day within the Octave of the Nativity of the Lord [Christmas]

When there is no Sunday within the Octave of the Nativity [Christmas], the Feast of the Holy Family of Jesus, Mary and Joseph is celebrated on this day (cf. pp. 176-177).

Entrance Antiphon — Wis 18: 14-15

When a profound silence covered all things
and night was in the middle of its course,
your all-powerful Word, O Lord,
bounded from heaven's royal throne.

The Gloria in excelsis (Glory to God in the highest) is said.

Collect

Grant, we pray, almighty God,
that the newness of the Nativity in the flesh
of your Only Begotten Son may set us free,
for ancient servitude holds us bound
beneath the yoke of sin.
Through our Lord Jesus Christ, your Son,
who lives and reigns with you in the unity of the Holy Spirit,
one God, for ever and ever.

Prayer over the Offerings

Receive with favor, O Lord, we pray,
the offerings of your people,
that what they profess with devotion and faith
may be theirs through these heavenly mysteries.
Through Christ our Lord.

Preface I, II or III of the Nativity of the Lord, pp. 538-543.

When the Roman Canon is used, the proper form of the Communicantes (In communion with those) is said.

Communion Antiphon — Jn 1: 16

From his fullness we have all received,
grace upon grace.

Prayer after Communion

O God, who touch us through our partaking of your Sacrament,
work, we pray, the effects of its power in our hearts,
that we may be made fit to receive your gift
through this very gift itself.
Through Christ our Lord.

December 31

Seventh Day within the Octave of the Nativity of the Lord [Christmas]

Entrance Antiphon
Is 9: 5

A child is born for us, and a son is given to us;
his scepter of power rests upon his shoulder,
and his name will be called Messenger of great counsel.

The Gloria in excelsis (Glory to God in the highest) is said.

Collect

**Almighty ever-living God,
who in the Nativity of your Son
established the beginning and fulfillment of all religion,
grant, we pray, that we may be numbered
among those who belong to him,
in whom is the fullness of human salvation.
Who lives and reigns with you in the unity of the Holy Spirit,
one God, for ever and ever.**

Prayer over the Offerings

O God, who give us the gift of true prayer and of peace,
graciously grant that, through this offering,
we may do fitting homage to your divine majesty
and, by partaking of the sacred mystery,
we may be faithfully united in mind and heart.
Through Christ our Lord.

Preface I, II or III of the Nativity of the Lord, pp. 538-543.

When the Roman Canon is used, the proper form of the Communicantes (In communion with those) is said.

Communion Antiphon   1 Jn 4: 9
God sent his Only Begotten Son into the world,
so that we might have life through him.

Prayer after Communion

May your people, O Lord,
whom you guide and sustain in many ways,
experience, both now and in the future,
the remedies which you bestow,
that, with the needed solace of things that pass away,
they may strive with ever deepened trust for things eternal.
Through Christ our Lord.

January 1
The Octave Day of the Nativity of the Lord [Christmas]

SOLEMNITY OF MARY, THE HOLY MOTHER OF GOD

Entrance Antiphon

Hail, Holy Mother, who gave birth to the King
who rules heaven and earth for ever.

Or: Cf. Is 9: 1, 5; Lk 1: 33

Today a light will shine upon us, for the Lord is born for us;
and he will be called Wondrous God,
Prince of peace, Father of future ages:
and his reign will be without end.

The Gloria in excelsis (Glory to God in the highest) is said.

Collect

O God, who through the fruitful virginity of Blessed Mary
bestowed on the human race
the grace of eternal salvation,
grant, we pray,
that we may experience the intercession of her,
through whom we were found worthy
to receive the author of life,
our Lord Jesus Christ, your Son.
Who lives and reigns with you in the unity of the Holy Spirit,
one God, for ever and ever.

The Creed is said.

Prayer over the Offerings

O God, who in your kindness begin all good things
and bring them to fulfillment,
grant to us, who find joy in the Solemnity of the
    holy Mother of God,
that, just as we glory in the beginnings of your grace,
so one day we may rejoice in its completion.
Through Christ our Lord.

Preface I of the Blessed Virgin Mary (on the Solemnity of the Motherhood), pp. 590-591.

When the Roman Canon is used, the proper form of the Communicantes (In communion with those) is said.

Communion Antiphon
Heb 13: 8

Jesus Christ is the same yesterday, today, and for ever.

Prayer after Communion

We have received this heavenly Sacrament with joy, O Lord:
grant, we pray,
that it may lead us to eternal life,
for we rejoice to proclaim the blessed ever-Virgin Mary
Mother of your Son and Mother of the Church.
Through Christ our Lord.

A formula of Solemn Blessing, p. 675, may be used.

On the days following, when the Mass of the weekday is to be said, the texts given below are used, p. 190.

SECOND SUNDAY AFTER THE NATIVITY [CHRISTMAS]

Entrance Antiphon
Wis 18: 14-15

When a profound silence covered all things
and night was in the middle of its course,
your all-powerful Word, O Lord, bounded from heaven's royal throne.

The Gloria in excelsis (Glory to God in the highest) is said.

Collect

Almighty ever-living God,
splendor of faithful souls,
graciously be pleased to fill the world with your glory,
and show yourself to all peoples by the radiance of your light.
Through our Lord Jesus Christ, your Son,
who lives and reigns with you in the unity of the Holy Spirit,
one God, for ever and ever.

The Creed is said.

Prayer over the Offerings

Sanctify, O Lord, the offerings we make
on the Nativity of your Only Begotten Son,
for by it you show us the way of truth
and promise the life of the heavenly Kingdom.
Through Christ our Lord.

Preface I, II or III of the Nativity of the Lord, pp. 538-543.

Communion Antiphon
Cf. Jn 1: 12

To all who would accept him,
he gave the power to become children of God.

Prayer after Communion

Lord our God, we humbly ask you,
that, through the working of this mystery,
our offenses may be cleansed
and our just desires fulfilled.
Through Christ our Lord.

A formula of Solemn Blessing, p. 674, may be used.

[In the Dioceses of the United States]
Sunday between January 2 and January 8

THE EPIPHANY OF THE LORD
Solemnity

At the Vigil Mass

This Mass is used on the evening of the day before the Solemnity, either before or after First Vespers (Evening Prayer I) of the Epiphany.

Entrance Antiphon
Cf. Bar 5: 5

Arise, Jerusalem, and look to the East
and see your children gathered from the rising to the setting of the sun.

The Gloria in excelsis (Glory to God in the highest) is said.

Collect

May the splendor of your majesty, O Lord, we pray,
shed its light upon our hearts,
that we may pass through the shadows of this world
and reach the brightness of our eternal home.
Through our Lord Jesus Christ, your Son,
who lives and reigns with you in the unity of the Holy Spirit,
one God, for ever and ever.

The Creed is said.

Prayer over the Offerings

Accept we pray, O Lord, our offerings,
in honor of the appearing of your Only Begotten Son
and the first fruits of the nations,
that to you praise may be rendered
and eternal salvation be ours.
Through Christ our Lord.

Preface of the Epiphany of the Lord, pp. 544-545.

Communion Antiphon
Cf. Rev 21: 23

The brightness of God illumined the holy city Jerusalem,
and the nations will walk by its light.

Prayer after Communion

Renewed by sacred nourishment,
we implore your mercy, O Lord,
that the star of your justice
may shine always bright in our minds
and that our true treasure may ever consist in our confession of you.
Through Christ our Lord.

A formula of Solemn Blessing, p. 676, may be used.

At the Mass during the Day

Entrance Antiphon
Cf. Mal 3: 1; 1 Chr 29: 12

Behold, the Lord, the Mighty One, has come;
and kingship is in his grasp, and power and dominion.

The Gloria in excelsis (Glory to God in the highest) is said.

Collect

O God, who on this day
revealed your Only Begotten Son to the nations
by the guidance of a star,
grant in your mercy
that we, who know you already by faith,
may be brought to behold the beauty of your sublime glory.
Through our Lord Jesus Christ, your Son,
who lives and reigns with you in the unity of the Holy Spirit,
one God, for ever and ever.

Where it is the practice, if appropriate, the moveable Feasts of the current year may be proclaimed after the Gospel, according to the formula given below, pp. 1448-1449.

The Creed is said.

Prayer over the Offerings

Look with favor, Lord, we pray,
on these gifts of your Church,
in which are offered now not gold or frankincense or myrrh,
but he who by them is proclaimed,
sacrificed and received, Jesus Christ.
Who lives and reigns for ever and ever.

Preface of the Epiphany of the Lord, pp. 544-545.

When the Roman Canon is used, the proper form of the Communicantes (In communion with those) is said.

Communion Antiphon Cf. Mt 2: 2

We have seen his star in the East,
and have come with gifts to adore the Lord.

Prayer after Communion

Go before us with heavenly light, O Lord,
always and everywhere,
that we may perceive with clear sight
and revere with true affection
the mystery in which you have willed us to participate.
Through Christ our Lord.

A formula of Solemn Blessing, p. 676, may be used.

WEEKDAYS OF CHRISTMAS TIME
from January 2
to the Saturday before the Feast of
the Baptism of the Lord

These Masses are used on the weekdays to which they are assigned, with the Collect selected as indicated.

Monday

Entrance Antiphon
A holy day has dawned upon us:
Come, you nations, and adore the Lord,
for a great light has come down upon the earth.

Collect
Before the Solemnity of the Epiphany

Grant your people, O Lord, we pray,
unshakable strength of faith,
so that all who profess that your Only Begotten Son
is with you for ever in your glory
and was born of the Virgin Mary
in a body truly like our own
may be freed from present trials
and given a place in abiding gladness.
Through our Lord Jesus Christ, your Son,
who lives and reigns with you in the unity of the Holy Spirit,
one God, for ever and ever.

After the Solemnity of the Epiphany

O God, whose eternal Word adorns the face of the heavens
yet accepted from the Virgin Mary the frailty of our flesh,
grant, we pray,
that he who appeared among us as the splendor of truth
may go forth in the fullness of power
for the redemption of the world.
Who lives and reigns with you in the unity of the Holy Spirit,
one God, for ever and ever.

Prayer over the Offerings

Receive our oblation, O Lord,
by which is brought about a glorious exchange,
that, by offering what you have given,
we may merit to receive your very self.
Through Christ our Lord.

Preface of the Nativity (pp. 538-543) before the Solemnity of the Epiphany; Preface of the Epiphany (pp. 544-545) or of the Nativity (pp. 538-543) after the Solemnity.

Communion Antiphon Jn 1: 14

We have seen his glory, the glory of an only Son coming from the Father,
filled with grace and truth.

Prayer after Communion

Grant, we pray, almighty God,
that, by the power of these holy mysteries,
our life may be constantly sustained.
Through Christ our Lord.

Tuesday

Entrance Antiphon
Ps 118 (117): 26-27

Blessed is he who comes in the name of the Lord:
The Lord is God and has given us light.

Collect

Before the Solemnity of the Epiphany

O God, who in the blessed childbearing of the holy Virgin Mary
kept the flesh of your Son
free from the sentence incurred by the human race,
grant, we pray,
that we, who have been taken up into this new creation,
may be freed from the ancient taint of sin.
Through our Lord Jesus Christ, your Son,
who lives and reigns with you in the unity of the Holy Spirit,
one God, for ever and ever.

After the Solemnity of the Epiphany

O God, whose Only Begotten Son
has appeared in our very flesh,
grant, we pray, that we may be inwardly transformed
through him whom we recognize as outwardly like ourselves.
Who lives and reigns with you in the unity of the Holy Spirit,
one God, for ever and ever.

Prayer over the Offerings

Receive with favor, O Lord, we pray, the offerings of your people,
that what they profess with devotion and faith
may be theirs through these heavenly mysteries.
Through Christ our Lord.

Preface of the Nativity (pp. 538-543) before the Solemnity of the Epiphany; Preface of the Epiphany (pp. 544-545) or of the Nativity (pp. 538-543) after the Solemnity.

Communion Antiphon   Eph 2: 4; Rom 8: 3

Because of that great love of his with which God loved us,
he sent his Son in the likeness of sinful flesh.

Prayer after Communion

O God, who touch us through our partaking of your Sacrament,
work, we pray, the effects of its power in our hearts,
that we may be made fit to receive your gift
through this very gift itself.
Through Christ our Lord.

Wednesday

Entrance Antiphon
Is 9: 1

A people who walked in darkness has seen a great light;
for those dwelling in a land of deep gloom, a light has shone.

Collect

Before the Solemnity of the Epiphany

**Grant us, almighty God, that the bringer of your salvation,
who for the world's redemption came forth with newness of heavenly light,
may dawn afresh in our hearts and bring us constant renewal.
Who lives and reigns with you in the unity of the Holy Spirit,
one God, for ever and ever.**

After the Solemnity of the Epiphany

**O God, who bestow light on all the nations,
grant your peoples the gladness of lasting peace
and pour into our hearts that brilliant light
by which you purified the minds of our fathers in faith.
Through our Lord Jesus Christ, your Son,
who lives and reigns with you in the unity of the Holy Spirit,
one God, for ever and ever.**

Prayer over the Offerings

O God, who give us the gift of true prayer and of peace,
graciously grant that, through this offering,
we may do fitting homage to your divine majesty
and, by partaking of the sacred mystery,
we may be faithfully united in mind and heart.
Through Christ our Lord.

Preface of the Nativity (pp. 538-543) before the Solemnity of the Epiphany; Preface of the Epiphany (pp. 544-545) or of the Nativity (pp. 538-543) after the Solemnity.

Communion Antiphon   1 Jn 1: 2
That life which was with the Father became visible, and has appeared to us.

Prayer after Communion

May your people, O Lord,
whom you guide and sustain in many ways,
experience, both now and in the future,
the remedies which you bestow,
that, with the needed solace of things that pass away,
they may strive with ever deepened trust for things eternal.
Through Christ our Lord.

Thursday

Entrance Antiphon
Cf. Jn 1: 1

In the beginning and before all ages, the Word was God
and he humbled himself to be born the Savior of the world.

Collect

Before the Solemnity of the Epiphany

O God, who by the Nativity of your Only Begotten Son
wondrously began for your people the work of redemption,
grant, we pray, to your servants such firmness of faith,
that by his guidance they may attain the glorious prize you
  have promised.
Through our Lord Jesus Christ, your Son,
who lives and reigns with you in the unity of the Holy Spirit,
one God, for ever and ever.

After the Solemnity of the Epiphany

O God, who through your Son raised up your eternal light for
  all nations,
grant that your people may come to acknowledge
the full splendor of their Redeemer,
that, bathed ever more in his radiance,
they may reach everlasting glory.
Through our Lord Jesus Christ, your Son,
who lives and reigns with you in the unity of the Holy Spirit,
one God, for ever and ever.

Prayer over the Offerings

**Receive our oblation, O Lord,
by which is brought about a glorious exchange,
that, by offering what you have given,
we may merit to receive your very self.
Through Christ our Lord.**

Preface of the Nativity (pp. 538-543) before the Solemnity of the Epiphany; Preface of the Epiphany (pp. 544-545) or of the Nativity (pp. 538-543) after the Solemnity.

Communion Antiphon

Jn 3: 16

God so loved the world that he gave his Only Begotten Son,
so that all who believe in him may not perish, but may have eternal life.

Prayer after Communion

**Grant, we pray, almighty God,
that, by the power of these holy mysteries,
our life may be constantly sustained.
Through Christ our Lord.**

Friday

Entrance Antiphon   Ps 112 (111): 4

A light has risen in the darkness for the upright of heart;
the Lord is generous, merciful and just.

Collect

Before the Solemnity of the Epiphany

Cast your kindly light upon your faithful, Lord, we pray,
and with the splendor of your glory
set their hearts ever aflame,
that they may never cease to acknowledge their Savior
and may truly hold fast to him.
Who lives and reigns with you in the unity of the Holy Spirit,
one God, for ever and ever.

After the Solemnity of the Epiphany

Grant, we ask, almighty God,
that the Nativity of the Savior of the world,
made known by the guidance of a star,
may be revealed ever more fully to our minds.
Through our Lord Jesus Christ, your Son,
who lives and reigns with you in the unity of the Holy Spirit,
one God, for ever and ever.

Prayer over the Offerings

Receive with favor, O Lord, we pray, the offerings of your people,
that what they profess with devotion and faith
may be theirs through these heavenly mysteries.
Through Christ our Lord.

Preface of the Nativity (pp. 538-543) before the Solemnity of the Epiphany; Preface of the Epiphany (pp. 544-545) or of the Nativity (pp. 538-543) after the Solemnity.

Communion Antiphon   1 Jn 4: 9

By this the love of God was revealed to us:
God sent his Only Begotten Son into the world,
so that we might have life through him.

Prayer after Communion

O God, who touch us through our partaking of your Sacrament,
work, we pray, the effects of its power in our hearts,
that we may be made fit to receive your gift
through this very gift itself.
Through Christ our Lord.

Saturday

Entrance Antiphon
Gal 4: 4-5

God sent his Son, born of a woman,
so that we might receive adoption as children.

Collect

Before the Solemnity of the Epiphany

**Almighty ever-living God,
who were pleased to shine forth with new light
through the coming of your Only Begotten Son,
grant, we pray,
that, just as he was pleased to share our bodily form
through the childbearing of the Virgin Mary,
so we, too, may one day merit
to become companions in his kingdom of grace.
Who lives and reigns with you in the unity of the Holy Spirit,
one God, for ever and ever.**

After the Solemnity of the Epiphany

**Almighty ever-living God,
who through your Only Begotten Son
have made us a new creation for yourself,
grant, we pray,
that by your grace we may be found in the likeness of him,
in whom our nature is united to you.
Who lives and reigns with you in the unity of the Holy Spirit,
one God, for ever and ever.**

Prayer over the Offerings

O God, who give us the gift of true prayer and of peace,
graciously grant that, through this offering,
we may do fitting homage to your divine majesty
and, by partaking of the sacred mystery,
we may be faithfully united in mind and heart.
Through Christ our Lord.

Preface of the Nativity (pp. 538-543) before the Solemnity of the Epiphany; Preface of the Epiphany (p. 544-545) or of the Nativity (pp. 538-543) after the Solemnity.

Communion Antiphon   Jn 1: 16
From his fullness we have all received,
grace upon grace.

Prayer after Communion

May your people, O Lord,
whom you guide and sustain in many ways,
experience, both now and in the future,
the remedies which you bestow,
that, with the needed solace of things that pass away,
they may strive with ever deepened trust for things eternal.
Through Christ our Lord.

Sunday after the Epiphany of the Lord
THE BAPTISM OF THE LORD
Feast

Where the Solemnity of the Epiphany is transferred to Sunday, if this Sunday occurs on January 7 or 8, the Feast of the Baptism of the Lord is celebrated on the following Monday.

Entrance Antiphon   Cf. Mt 3: 16-17
After the Lord was baptized, the heavens were opened,
and the Spirit descended upon him like a dove,
and the voice of the Father thundered:
This is my beloved Son, with whom I am well pleased.

The Gloria in excelsis (Glory to God in the highest) is said.

Collect
**Almighty ever-living God,
who, when Christ had been baptized in the River Jordan
and as the Holy Spirit descended upon him,
solemnly declared him your beloved Son,
grant that your children by adoption,
reborn of water and the Holy Spirit,
may always be well pleasing to you.
Through our Lord Jesus Christ, your Son,
who lives and reigns with you in the unity of the Holy Spirit,
one God, for ever and ever.**

Or:

**O God, whose Only Begotten Son
has appeared in our very flesh,
grant, we pray, that we may be inwardly transformed
through him whom we recognize as outwardly like ourselves.
Who lives and reigns with you in the unity of the Holy Spirit,
one God, for ever and ever.**

The Creed is said.

Prayer over the Offerings

Accept, O Lord, the offerings
we have brought to honor the revealing of your beloved Son,
so that the oblation of your faithful
may be transformed into the sacrifice of him
who willed in his compassion
to wash away the sins of the world.
Who lives and reigns for ever and ever.

Preface: The Baptism of the Lord.

V. The Lord be with you.   R. And with your spir-it.

V. Lift up your hearts.   R. We lift them up to the Lord.

V. Let us give thanks to the Lord our God.   R. It is right and just.

It is truly right and just, our duty and our sal-va-tion, al-ways and everywhere to give you thanks, Lord, holy Father, almighty and e--ter-nal God. For in the waters of the Jordan you revealed with signs and wonders a new Bap-tism, so that through the voice that came down from heav-en we might come to be-lieve in your Word dwell-ing a-mong us, and by the Spirit's descending in the likeness of a dove we might know that Christ your Servant has been anointed with the oil of glad-ness and sent to bring the good news to the poor. And so, with the Pow-ers of heav-en,

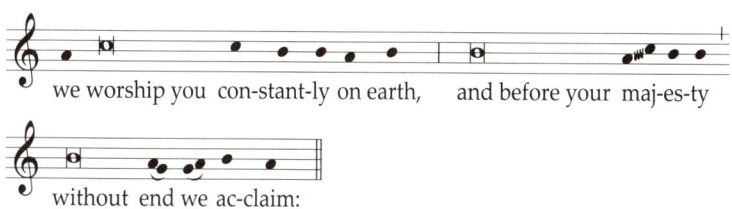

we worship you con-stant-ly on earth, and before your maj-es-ty without end we ac-claim:

Holy, Holy, Holy Lord God of hosts . . .

Text without music:
V. **The Lord be with you.**
R. And with your spirit.

V. **Lift up your hearts.**
R. We lift them up to the Lord.

V. **Let us give thanks to the Lord our God.**
R. It is right and just.

It is truly right and just, our duty and our salvation,
always and everywhere to give you thanks,
Lord, holy Father, almighty and eternal God.

For in the waters of the Jordan
you revealed with signs and wonders a new Baptism,
so that through the voice that came down from heaven
we might come to believe in your Word dwelling among us,
and by the Spirit's descending in the likeness of a dove
we might know that Christ your Servant
has been anointed with the oil of gladness
and sent to bring the good news to the poor.

And so, with the Powers of heaven,
we worship you constantly on earth,
and before your majesty
without end we acclaim:

Holy, Holy, Holy Lord God of hosts . . .

Communion Antiphon
Jn 1: 32, 34

Behold the One of whom John said:
I have seen and testified that this is the Son of God.

Prayer after Communion

**Nourished with these sacred gifts,
we humbly entreat your mercy, O Lord,
that, faithfully listening to your Only Begotten Son,
we may be your children in name and in truth.
Through Christ our Lord.**

Ordinary Time lasts from the Monday after this Sunday to the Tuesday before Lent. For Masses both on Sundays and on weekdays, the texts given below, pp. 459 ff., are used.

LENT

1. It is strongly recommended that the tradition of gathering the local Church after the fashion of the Roman "stations" be kept and promoted, especially during Lent and at least in larger towns and cities, in a way best suited to individual places.

    Such gatherings of the faithful can take place, especially with the chief Pastor of the diocese presiding, on Sundays or on other more convenient days during the week, either at the tombs of the Saints, or in the principal churches or shrines of a city, or even in the more frequently visited places of pilgrimage in the diocese.

    If a procession precedes a Mass celebrated for such a gathering, according to circumstances and local conditions, the faithful gather at a smaller church or some other suitable place other than in the church to which the procession will head.

    After greeting the people, the Priest says a Collect of The Mystery of the Holy Cross (cf. below, p. 1331), For the Forgiveness of Sins (cf. below, pp. 1306-1307), or For the Church, especially For the Particular Church (cf. below, p. 1242), or one of the Prayers over the People. Then the procession makes its way to the church in which Mass will be celebrated and meanwhile the Litany of the Saints is sung. Invocations to the Patron Saint or the Founder Saint and to the Saints of the local Church may be inserted at the appropriate point in the Litany.

    When the procession reaches the church, the Priest venerates the altar and, if appropriate, incenses it. Afterwards, omitting the Introductory Rites and, if appropriate, the **Kyrie**, he says the Collect of the Mass, and then continues the Mass in the usual way.

2. At these gatherings, instead of Mass, some celebration of the Word of God may also take place, especially in the form of the penitential celebrations given in the Roman Ritual for Lent.

3. On weekdays of Lent, at the end of Mass and before the final blessing, the Prayer over the People indicated for each day may appropriately be used.

4. During Lent, it is not permitted to decorate the altar with flowers, and the use of musical instruments is allowed only so as to support the singing. Nevertheless, **Laetare** Sunday (the Fourth Sunday of Lent), Solemnities, and Feasts are exceptions to this rule.

ASH WEDNESDAY

In the course of today's Mass, ashes are blessed and distributed. These are made from the olive branches or branches of other trees that were blessed the previous year.

Introductory Rites and Liturgy of the Word

Entrance Antiphon Wis 11: 24, 25, 27

You are merciful to all, O Lord,
and despise nothing that you have made.
You overlook people's sins, to bring them to repentance,
and you spare them, for you are the Lord our God.

The Penitential Act is omitted, and the Distribution of Ashes takes its place.

Collect

**Grant, O Lord, that we may begin with holy fasting
this campaign of Christian service,
so that, as we take up battle against spiritual evils,
we may be armed with weapons of self-restraint.
Through our Lord Jesus Christ, your Son,
who lives and reigns with you in the unity of the Holy Spirit,
one God, for ever and ever.**

Blessing and Distribution of Ashes

After the Homily, the Priest, standing with hands joined, says:

Dear brethren (brothers and sisters), let us humbly ask God our Father
that he be pleased to bless with the abundance of his grace
these ashes, which we will put on our heads in penitence.

After a brief prayer in silence, and, with hands extended, he continues:

O God, who are moved by acts of humility
and respond with forgiveness to works of penance,
lend your merciful ear to our prayers
and in your kindness pour out the grace of your ✠ blessing
on your servants who are marked with these ashes,
that, as they follow the Lenten observances,
they may be worthy to come with minds made pure
to celebrate the Paschal Mystery of your Son.
Through Christ our Lord.
R. **Amen.**

Or:

O God, who desire not the death of sinners,
but their conversion,
mercifully hear our prayers
and in your kindness be pleased to bless ✠ these ashes,
which we intend to receive upon our heads,
that we, who acknowledge we are but ashes
and shall return to dust,
may, through a steadfast observance of Lent,
gain pardon for sins and newness of life
after the likeness of your Risen Son.
Who lives and reigns for ever and ever.
R. **Amen.**

He sprinkles the ashes with holy water, without saying anything.

Then the Priest places ashes on the head of all those present who come to him, and says to each one:

Repent, and believe in the Gospel.

Or:

Remember that you are dust, and to dust you shall return.

Meanwhile, the following are sung:

Antiphon 1

Let us change our garments to sackcloth and ashes,
let us fast and weep before the Lord,
that our God, rich in mercy, might forgive us our sins.

Antiphon 2
Cf. Jl 2: 17; Est 4: 17

Let the priests, the ministers of the Lord,
stand between the porch and the altar and weep and cry out:
Spare, O Lord, spare your people;
do not close the mouths of those who sing your praise, O Lord.

Antiphon 3
Ps 51 (50): 3

Blot out my transgressions, O Lord.

This may be repeated after each verse of Psalm 51 (50) (Have mercy on me, O God).

Responsory
Cf. Bar 3: 2; Ps 79 (78): 9

R. Let us correct our faults which we have committed in ignorance, let us not be taken unawares by the day of our death, looking in vain for leisure to repent. * Hear us, O Lord, and show us your mercy, for we have sinned against you.

V. **Help us, O God our Savior; for the sake of your name, O Lord, set us free. * Hear us, O Lord . . .**

Another appropriate chant may also be sung.

After the distribution of ashes, the Priest washes his hands and proceeds to the Universal Prayer, and continues the Mass in the usual way.

The Creed is not said.

The Liturgy of the Eucharist

Prayer over the Offerings
As we solemnly offer
the annual sacrifice for the beginning of Lent,
we entreat you, O Lord,
that, through works of penance and charity,
we may turn away from harmful pleasures
and, cleansed from our sins, may become worthy
to celebrate devoutly the Passion of your Son.
Who lives and reigns for ever and ever.

Preface III or IV of Lent, pp. 550-553.

Communion Antiphon   Cf. Ps 1: 2-3
He who ponders the law of the Lord day and night
will yield fruit in due season.

Prayer after Communion
May the Sacrament we have received sustain us, O Lord,
that our Lenten fast may be pleasing to you
and be for us a healing remedy.
Through Christ our Lord.

Prayer over the People

For the dismissal, the Priest stands facing the people and, extending his hands over them, says this prayer:

Pour out a spirit of compunction, O God,
on those who bow before your majesty,
and by your mercy may they merit the rewards you promise
to those who do penance.
Through Christ our Lord.

The blessing and distribution of ashes may also take place outside Mass. In this case, the rite is preceded by a Liturgy of the Word, with the Entrance Antiphon, the Collect, and the readings with their chants as at Mass. Then there follow the Homily and the blessing and distribution of ashes. The rite is concluded with the Universal Prayer, the Blessing, and the Dismissal of the Faithful.

Thursday after Ash Wednesday

Entrance Antiphon
Cf. Ps 55 (54): 17-20, 23

When I cried to the Lord, he heard my voice;
he rescued me from those who attack me.
Entrust your cares to the Lord, and he will support you.

Collect

**Prompt our actions with your inspiration, we pray, O Lord,
and further them with your constant help,
that all we do may always begin from you
and by you be brought to completion.
Through our Lord Jesus Christ, your Son,
who lives and reigns with you in the unity of the Holy Spirit,
one God, for ever and ever.**

Prayer over the Offerings

**Regard with favor, O Lord, we pray,
the offerings we set upon this sacred altar,
that, bestowing on us your pardon,
our oblations may give honor to your name.
Through Christ our Lord.**

Preface of Lent, pp. 546-553.

Communion Antiphon
Cf. Ps 51 (50): 12

Create a pure heart for me, O God;
renew a steadfast spirit within me.

Prayer after Communion

**Having received the blessing of your heavenly gifts,
we humbly beseech you, almighty God,
that they may always be for us
a source both of pardon and of salvation.
Through Christ our Lord.**

Prayer over the People
for optional use

**Almighty God,
who have made known to your people
the ways of eternal life,
lead them by that path, we pray,
to you, the unfading light.
Through Christ our Lord.**

Friday after Ash Wednesday

Entrance Antiphon
Ps 30 (29): 11

    The Lord heard and had mercy on me;
    the Lord became my helper.

Collect

**Show gracious favor, O Lord, we pray,
to the works of penance we have begun,
that we may have strength to accomplish with sincerity
the bodily observances we undertake.
Through our Lord Jesus Christ, your Son,
who lives and reigns with you in the unity of the Holy Spirit,
one God, for ever and ever.**

Prayer over the Offerings

**We offer, O Lord, the sacrifice of our Lenten observance,
praying that it may make our intentions acceptable to you
and add to our powers of self-restraint.
Through Christ our Lord.**

Preface of Lent, pp. 546-553.

Communion Antiphon
Ps 25 (24): 4

    O Lord, make me know your ways,
    teach me your paths.

Prayer after Communion

**We pray, almighty God,
that, through partaking of this mystery,
we may be cleansed of all our misdeeds,
and so be suited for the remedies of your compassion.
Through Christ our Lord.**

Prayer over the People
for optional use

**For your mighty deeds, O God of mercy,
may your people offer endless thanks,
and, by observing the age-old disciplines
along their pilgrim journey,
may they merit to come and behold you for ever.
Through Christ our Lord.**

Saturday after Ash Wednesday

Entrance Antiphon   Cf. Ps 69 (68): 17

> Answer us, Lord, for your mercy is kind;
> in the abundance of your mercies, look upon us.

Collect

> Almighty ever-living God,
> look with compassion on our weakness
> and ensure us your protection
> by stretching forth the right hand of your majesty.
> Through our Lord Jesus Christ, your Son,
> who lives and reigns with you in the unity of the Holy Spirit,
> one God, for ever and ever.

Prayer over the Offerings

> Accept, we pray, O Lord,
> the sacrifice of conciliation and praise,
> and grant that, cleansed by its working,
> we may offer minds well pleasing to you.
> Through Christ our Lord.

Preface of Lent, pp. 546-553.

Communion Antiphon   Mt 9: 13

> I desire mercy, not sacrifice, says the Lord,
> for I did not come to call the just but sinners.

Prayer after Communion

> Nourished with the gift of heavenly life,
> we pray, O Lord,
> that what remains for us a mystery in this present life
> may be for us a help to reach eternity.
> Through Christ our Lord.

Prayer over the People   *for optional use*

> Abide graciously, O Lord, with your people,
> who have touched the sacred mysteries,
> that no dangers may bring affliction
> to those who trust in you, their protector.
> Through Christ our Lord.

FIRST SUNDAY OF LENT

On this Sunday is celebrated the rite of "election" or "enrollment of names" for the catechumens who are to be admitted to the Sacraments of Christian Initiation at the Easter Vigil, using the proper prayers and intercessions as given below, pp. 1119-1120.

Entrance Antiphon
Cf. Ps 91 (90): 15-16

When he calls on me, I will answer him;
I will deliver him and give him glory,
I will grant him length of days.

The Gloria in excelsis (Glory to God in the highest) is not said.

Collect

**Grant, almighty God,
through the yearly observances of holy Lent,
that we may grow in understanding
of the riches hidden in Christ
and by worthy conduct pursue their effects.
Through our Lord Jesus Christ, your Son,
who lives and reigns with you in the unity of the Holy Spirit,
one God, for ever and ever.**

The Creed is said.

Prayer over the Offerings

**Give us the right dispositions, O Lord, we pray,
to make these offerings,
for with them we celebrate the beginning
of this venerable and sacred time.
Through Christ our Lord.**

Preface: The Temptation of the Lord.

V. The Lord be with you.   R. And with your spirit.

V. Lift up your hearts.   R. We lift them up to the Lord.

V. Let us give thanks to the Lord our God.   R. It is right and just.

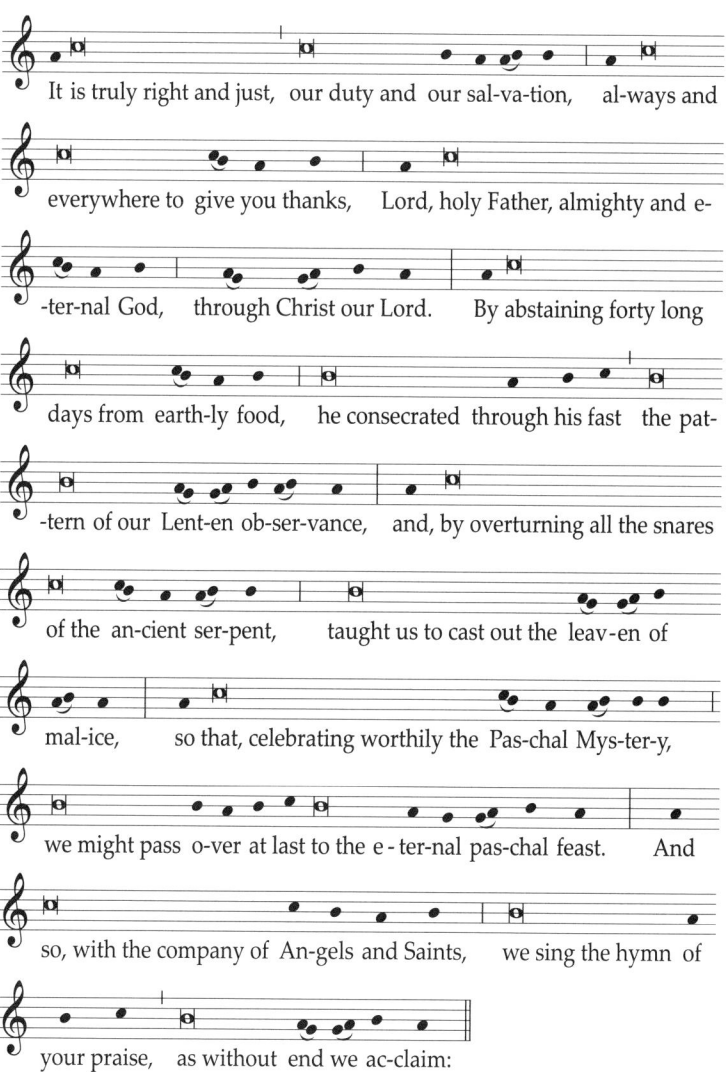

Holy, Holy, Holy Lord God of hosts . . .

Text without music:
℣. **The Lord be with you.**
℟. And with your spirit.

℣. **Lift up your hearts.**
℟. We lift them up to the Lord.

℣. **Let us give thanks to the Lord our God.**
℟. It is right and just.

**It is truly right and just, our duty and our salvation,
always and everywhere to give you thanks,
Lord, holy Father, almighty and eternal God,
through Christ our Lord.**

**By abstaining forty long days from earthly food,
he consecrated through his fast
the pattern of our Lenten observance
and, by overturning all the snares of the ancient serpent,
taught us to cast out the leaven of malice,
so that, celebrating worthily the Paschal Mystery,
we might pass over at last to the eternal paschal feast.**

**And so, with the company of Angels and Saints,
we sing the hymn of your praise,
as without end we acclaim:**

Holy, Holy, Holy Lord God of hosts . . .

Communion Antiphon
Mt 4: 4
One does not live by bread alone,
but by every word that comes forth from the mouth of God.

Or:
Cf. Ps 91 (90): 4

The Lord will conceal you with his pinions,
and under his wings you will trust.

Prayer after Communion
**Renewed now with heavenly bread,
by which faith is nourished, hope increased,
and charity strengthened,
we pray, O Lord,
that we may learn to hunger for Christ,
the true and living Bread,
and strive to live by every word
which proceeds from your mouth.
Through Christ our Lord.**

Prayer over the People
**May bountiful blessing, O Lord, we pray,
come down upon your people,
that hope may grow in tribulation,
virtue be strengthened in temptation,
and eternal redemption be assured.
Through Christ our Lord.**

Monday

Entrance Antiphon — Cf. Ps 123 (122): 2-3

Like the eyes of slaves on the hand of their lords,
so our eyes are on the Lord our God, till he show us his mercy.
Have mercy on us, Lord, have mercy.

Collect

Convert us, O God our Savior,
and instruct our minds by heavenly teaching,
that we may benefit from the works of Lent.
Through our Lord Jesus Christ, your Son,
who lives and reigns with you in the unity of the Holy Spirit,
one God, for ever and ever.

Prayer over the Offerings

May this devout oblation be acceptable to you, O Lord,
that by your power it may sanctify our manner of life
and gain for us your conciliation and pardon.
Through Christ our Lord.

Preface of Lent, pp. 546-553.

Communion Antiphon — Mt 25: 40, 34

Amen, I say to you:
Whatever you did for one of the least of my brethren,
you did it for me, says the Lord.
Come, you blessed of my Father,
receive the kingdom prepared for you from the foundation of the world.

Prayer after Communion

We pray, O Lord, that, in receiving your Sacrament,
we may experience help in mind and body
so that, kept safe in both,
we may glory in the fullness of heavenly healing.
Through Christ our Lord.

Prayer over the People — for optional use

Enlighten the minds of your people, Lord, we pray,
with the light of your glory,
that they may see what must be done
and have the strength to do what is right.
Through Christ our Lord.

Tuesday

Entrance Antiphon
Cf. Ps 90 (89): 1-2

O Lord, you have been our refuge, from generation to generation;
from age to age, you are.

Collect

Look upon your family, Lord,
that, through the chastening effects of bodily discipline,
our minds may be radiant in your presence
with the strength of our yearning for you.
Through our Lord Jesus Christ, your Son,
who lives and reigns with you in the unity of the Holy Spirit,
one God, for ever and ever.

Prayer over the Offerings

Receive, O Creator, almighty God,
what we bring from your bountiful goodness,
and be pleased to transform
this temporal sustenance you have given us,
that it may bring us eternal life.
Through Christ our Lord.

Preface of Lent, pp. 546-553.

Communion Antiphon
Cf. Ps 4: 2

When I called, the God of justice gave me answer;
from anguish you released me;
have mercy, O Lord, and hear my prayer!

Prayer after Communion

Grant us through these mysteries, Lord,
that by moderating earthly desires
we may learn to love the things of heaven.
Through Christ our Lord.

Prayer over the People
for optional use

May your faithful be strengthened, O God, by your blessing:
in grief, may you be their consolation,
in tribulation, their power to endure,
and in peril, their protection.
Through Christ our Lord.

Wednesday

Entrance Antiphon   Cf. Ps 25 (24): 6, 2, 22

Remember your compassion, O Lord,
and your merciful love, for they are from of old.
Let not our enemies exult over us.
Redeem us, O God of Israel, from all our distress.

Collect

Look kindly, Lord, we pray,
on the devotion of your people,
that those who by self-denial are restrained in body
may by the fruit of good works be renewed in mind.
Through our Lord Jesus Christ, your Son,
who lives and reigns with you in the unity of the Holy Spirit,
one God, for ever and ever.

Prayer over the Offerings

We offer to you, O Lord,
what you have given to be dedicated to your name,
that, just as for our benefit you make these gifts a Sacrament,
so you may let them become for us an eternal remedy.
Through Christ our Lord.

Preface of Lent, pp. 546-553.

Communion Antiphon   Cf. Ps 5: 12

All who take refuge in you shall be glad, O Lord,
and ever cry out their joy, and you shall dwell among them.

Prayer after Communion

O God, who never cease to nourish us by your Sacrament,
grant that the refreshment you give us through it
may bring us unending life.
Through Christ our Lord.

Prayer over the People   *for optional use*

Watch over your people, Lord,
and in your kindness cleanse them from all sins,
for if evil has no dominion over them,
no trial can do them harm.
Through Christ our Lord.

Thursday

Entrance Antiphon   *Cf. Ps 5: 2-3*
To my words give ear, O Lord; give heed to my sighs.
Attend to the sound of my cry, my King and my God.

Collect

**Bestow on us, we pray, O Lord,
a spirit of always pondering on what is right
and of hastening to carry it out,
and, since without you we cannot exist,
may we be enabled to live according to your will.
Through our Lord Jesus Christ, your Son,
who lives and reigns with you in the unity of the Holy Spirit,
one God, for ever and ever.**

Prayer over the Offerings

**Be merciful, O Lord, to those who approach you in supplication,
and, accepting the oblations and prayers of your people,
turn the hearts of us all towards you.
Through Christ our Lord.**

Preface of Lent, pp. 546-553.

Communion Antiphon   *Mt 7: 8*
Everyone who asks, receives; and the one who seeks, finds;
and to the one who knocks, the door will be opened.

Prayer after Communion

**We pray, O Lord our God,
that, as you have given these most sacred mysteries
to be the safeguard of our salvation,
so you may make them a healing remedy for us,
both now and in time to come.
Through Christ our Lord.**

Prayer over the People   *for optional use*

**May the mercy they have hoped for, O Lord,
come to those who make supplication to you,
and may the riches of heaven be given them,
that they may know what it is right to ask
and receive what they have sought.
Through Christ our Lord.**

Friday

Entrance Antiphon   Cf. Ps 25 (24): 17-18
Set me free from my distress, O Lord.
See my lowliness and suffering,
and take away all my sins.

Collect
Grant that your faithful, O Lord, we pray,
may be so conformed to the paschal observances,
that the bodily discipline now solemnly begun
may bear fruit in the souls of all.
Through our Lord Jesus Christ, your Son,
who lives and reigns with you in the unity of the Holy Spirit,
one God, for ever and ever.

Prayer over the Offerings
Accept the sacrificial offerings, O Lord,
by which, in your power and kindness,
you willed us to be reconciled to yourself
and our salvation to be restored.
Through Christ our Lord.

Preface of Lent, pp. 546-553.

Communion Antiphon   Ez 33: 11
As I live, says the Lord, I do not desire the death of the sinner,
but rather that he turn back and live.

Prayer after Communion
May the holy refreshment of your Sacrament
restore us anew, O Lord,
and, cleansing us of old ways,
take us up into the mystery of salvation.
Through Christ our Lord.

Prayer over the People   *for optional use*
Look with favor on your people, O Lord,
that what their observance outwardly declares
it may inwardly bring about.
Through Christ our Lord.

Saturday

Entrance Antiphon
Cf. Ps 19 (18): 8

The law of the Lord is perfect; it revives the soul.
The decrees of the Lord are steadfast; they give wisdom to the simple.

Collect
Turn our hearts to you, eternal Father,
and grant that, seeking always the one thing necessary
and carrying out works of charity,
we may be dedicated to your worship.
Through our Lord Jesus Christ, your Son,
who lives and reigns with you in the unity of the Holy Spirit,
one God, for ever and ever.

Prayer over the Offerings
May these blessed mysteries
by which we are restored, O Lord, we pray,
make us worthy of the gift they bestow.
Through Christ our Lord.

Preface of Lent, pp. 546-553.

Communion Antiphon
Mt 5: 48

Be perfect, as your heavenly Father is perfect, says the Lord.

Prayer after Communion
Show unceasing favor, O Lord,
to those you refresh with this divine mystery,
and accompany with salutary consolations
those you have imbued with heavenly teaching.
Through Christ our Lord.

Prayer over the People
for optional use

May the blessing for which they have longed
strengthen your faithful, O God,
so that, never straying from your will,
they may always rejoice in your benefits.
Through Christ our Lord.

SECOND SUNDAY OF LENT

Entrance Antiphon   Cf. Ps 27 (26): 8-9

Of you my heart has spoken: Seek his face.
It is your face, O Lord, that I seek;
hide not your face from me.

Or: Cf. Ps 25 (24): 6, 2, 22

Remember your compassion, O Lord,
and your merciful love, for they are from of old.
Let not our enemies exult over us.
Redeem us, O God of Israel, from all our distress.

The Gloria in excelsis (Glory to God in the highest) is not said.

Collect

**O God, who have commanded us
to listen to your beloved Son,
be pleased, we pray,
to nourish us inwardly by your word,
that, with spiritual sight made pure,
we may rejoice to behold your glory.
Through our Lord Jesus Christ, your Son,
who lives and reigns with you in the unity of the Holy Spirit,
one God, for ever and ever.**

The Creed is said.

Prayer over the Offerings

**May this sacrifice, O Lord, we pray,
cleanse us of our faults
and sanctify your faithful in body and mind
for the celebration of the paschal festivities.
Through Christ our Lord.**

Preface: The Transfiguration of the Lord.

V. The Lord be with you.   R. And with your spir-it.

V. Lift up your hearts.   R. We lift them up to the Lord.

SECOND SUNDAY OF LENT

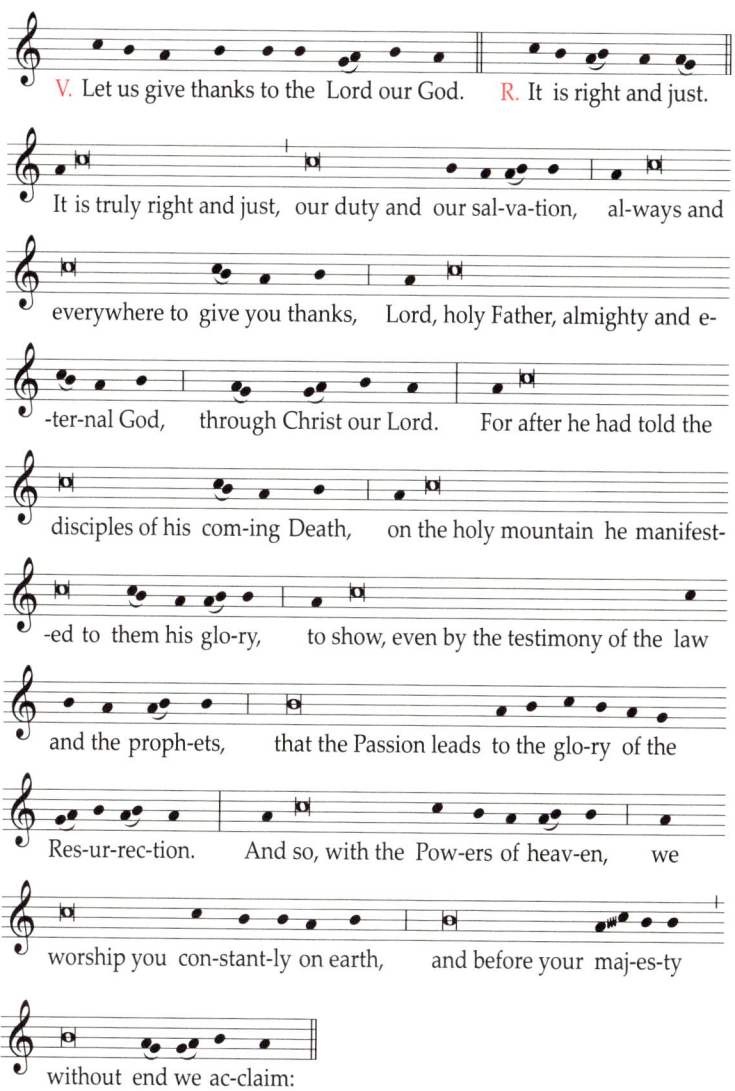

V. Let us give thanks to the Lord our God.   R. It is right and just.

It is truly right and just, our duty and our sal-va-tion, al-ways and everywhere to give you thanks, Lord, holy Father, almighty and e-ter-nal God, through Christ our Lord. For after he had told the disciples of his com-ing Death, on the holy mountain he manifest-ed to them his glo-ry, to show, even by the testimony of the law and the proph-ets, that the Passion leads to the glo-ry of the Res-ur-rec-tion. And so, with the Pow-ers of heav-en, we worship you con-stant-ly on earth, and before your maj-es-ty without end we ac-claim:

Holy, Holy, Holy Lord God of hosts . . .

Text without music:
℣. **The Lord be with you.**
℟. And with your spirit.

℣. **Lift up your hearts.**
℟. We lift them up to the Lord.

℣. **Let us give thanks to the Lord our God.**
℟. It is right and just.

It is truly right and just, our duty and our salvation,
always and everywhere to give you thanks,
Lord, holy Father, almighty and eternal God,
through Christ our Lord.

For after he had told the disciples of his coming Death,
on the holy mountain he manifested to them his glory,
to show, even by the testimony of the law and the prophets,
that the Passion leads to the glory of the Resurrection.

And so, with the Powers of heaven,
we worship you constantly on earth,
and before your majesty
without end we acclaim:

Holy, Holy, Holy Lord God of hosts . . .

Communion Antiphon
Mt 17: 5

This is my beloved Son, with whom I am well pleased;
listen to him.

Prayer after Communion

**As we receive these glorious mysteries,
we make thanksgiving to you, O Lord,
for allowing us while still on earth
to be partakers even now of the things of heaven.
Through Christ our Lord.**

Prayer over the People

**Bless your faithful, we pray, O Lord,
with a blessing that endures for ever,
and keep them faithful
to the Gospel of your Only Begotten Son,
so that they may always desire and at last attain
that glory whose beauty he showed in his own Body,
to the amazement of his Apostles.
Through Christ our Lord.**

Monday

Entrance Antiphon   *Cf. Ps 26 (25): 11-12*
    Redeem me, O Lord, and have mercy on me.
    My foot stands on level ground;
    I will bless the Lord in the assembly.

Collect
    O God, who have taught us
    to chasten our bodies
    for the healing of our souls,
    enable us, we pray,
    to abstain from all sins,
    and strengthen our hearts
    to carry out your loving commands.
    Through our Lord Jesus Christ, your Son,
    who lives and reigns with you in the unity of the Holy Spirit,
    one God, for ever and ever.

Prayer over the Offerings
    Accept in your goodness these our prayers, O Lord,
    and set free from worldly attractions
    those you allow to serve the heavenly mysteries.
    Through Christ our Lord.

    Preface of Lent, pp. 546-553.

Communion Antiphon   *Lk 6: 36*
    Be merciful, as your Father is merciful, says the Lord.

Prayer after Communion
    May this Communion, O Lord,
    cleanse us of wrongdoing
    and make us heirs to the joy of heaven.
    Through Christ our Lord.

Prayer over the People   *for optional use*
    Confirm the hearts of your faithful, O Lord, we pray,
    and strengthen them by the power of your grace,
    that they may be constant in making supplication to you
    and sincere in love for one another.
    Through Christ our Lord.

Tuesday

Entrance Antiphon   Cf. Ps 13 (12): 4-5

Give light to my eyes lest I fall asleep in death,
lest my enemy say: I have overcome him.

Collect

Guard your Church, we pray, O Lord, in your unceasing mercy,
and, since without you mortal humanity is sure to fall,
may we be kept by your constant helps from all harm
and directed to all that brings salvation.
Through our Lord Jesus Christ, your Son,
who lives and reigns with you in the unity of the Holy Spirit,
one God, for ever and ever.

Prayer over the Offerings

Be pleased to work your sanctification within us
by means of these mysteries, O Lord,
and by it may we be cleansed of earthly faults
and led to the gifts of heaven.
Through Christ our Lord.

Preface of Lent, pp. 546-553.

Communion Antiphon   Ps 9: 2-3

I will recount all your wonders.
I will rejoice in you and be glad,
and sing psalms to your name, O Most High.

Prayer after Communion

May the refreshment of this sacred table,
O Lord, we pray,
bring us an increase in devoutness of life
and the constant help of your work of conciliation.
Through Christ our Lord.

Prayer over the People   for optional use

Graciously hear the cries of your faithful, O Lord,
and relieve the weariness of their souls,
that, having received your forgiveness,
they may ever rejoice in your blessing.
Through Christ our Lord.

Wednesday

Entrance Antiphon
Cf. Ps 38 (37): 22-23

Forsake me not, O Lord! My God, be not far from me!
Make haste and come to my help, O Lord, my strong salvation!

Collect

Keep your family, O Lord,
schooled always in good works,
and so comfort them with your protection here
as to lead them graciously to gifts on high.
Through our Lord Jesus Christ, your Son,
who lives and reigns with you in the unity of the Holy Spirit,
one God, for ever and ever.

Prayer over the Offerings

Look with favor, Lord,
on the sacrificial gifts we offer you,
and by this holy exchange
undo the bonds of our sins.
Through Christ our Lord.

Preface of Lent, pp. 546-553.

Communion Antiphon
Mt 20: 28

The Son of Man did not come to be served but to serve,
and to give his life as a ransom for many.

Prayer after Communion

Grant, we pray, O Lord our God,
that what you have given us as the pledge of immortality
may work for our eternal salvation.
Through Christ our Lord.

Prayer over the People
for optional use

Bestow upon your servants, Lord,
abundance of grace and protection;
grant health of mind and body;
grant fullness of fraternal charity,
and make them always devoted to you.
Through Christ our Lord.

Thursday

Entrance Antiphon   Cf. Ps 139 (138): 23-24

Test me, O God, and know my thoughts.
See that my path is not wicked,
and lead me in the way everlasting.

Collect

O God, who delight in innocence and restore it,
direct the hearts of your servants to yourself,
that, caught up in the fire of your Spirit,
we may be found steadfast in faith
and effective in works.
Through our Lord Jesus Christ, your Son,
who lives and reigns with you in the unity of the Holy Spirit,
one God, for ever and ever.

Prayer over the Offerings

By this present sacrifice, we pray, O Lord,
sanctify our observance,
that what Lenten discipline outwardly declares
it may inwardly bring about.
Through Christ our Lord.

Preface of Lent, pp. 546-553.

Communion Antiphon   Ps 119 (118): 1

Blessed are those whose way is blameless,
who walk in the law of the Lord.

Prayer after Communion

May this sacrifice, O God,
remain active in its effects
and work ever more strongly within us.
Through Christ our Lord.

Prayer over the People   for optional use

Abide with your servants, O Lord,
who implore the help of your grace,
that they may receive from you
the support and guidance of your protection.
Through Christ our Lord.

Friday

Entrance Antiphon   *Cf. Ps 31 (30): 2, 5*

In you, O Lord, I put my trust, let me never be put to shame;
release me from the snare they have hidden for me,
for you indeed are my refuge.

Collect

Grant, we pray, almighty God,
that, purifying us by the sacred practice of penance,
you may lead us in sincerity of heart
to attain the holy things to come.
Through our Lord Jesus Christ, your Son,
who lives and reigns with you in the unity of the Holy Spirit,
one God, for ever and ever.

Prayer over the Offerings

May your merciful grace prepare your servants, O God,
for the worthy celebration of these mysteries,
and lead them to it by a devout way of life.
Through Christ our Lord.

Preface of Lent, pp. 546-553.

Communion Antiphon   *1 Jn 4: 10*

God loved us, and sent his Son
as expiation for our sins.

Prayer after Communion

Having received this pledge of eternal salvation,
we pray, O Lord,
that we may set our course so well
as to attain the redemption you promise.
Through Christ our Lord.

Prayer over the People   *for optional use*

Grant your people, O Lord, we pray,
health of mind and body,
that by constancy in good deeds
they may always merit the defense of your protection.
Through Christ our Lord.

Saturday

Entrance Antiphon
Ps 145 (144): 8-9

The Lord is kind and full of compassion, slow to anger, abounding in mercy.
How good is the Lord to all, compassionate to all his creatures.

Collect

O God, who grant us by glorious healing remedies while still on earth
to be partakers of the things of heaven,
guide us, we pray, through this present life
and bring us to that light in which you dwell.
Through our Lord Jesus Christ, your Son,
who lives and reigns with you in the unity of the Holy Spirit,
one God, for ever and ever.

Prayer over the Offerings

Through these sacred gifts, we pray, O Lord,
may our redemption yield its fruits,
restraining us from unruly desires
and leading us onward to the gifts of salvation.
Through Christ our Lord.

Preface of Lent, pp. 546-553.

Communion Antiphon
Lk 15: 32

You must rejoice, my son,
for your brother was dead and has come to life;
he was lost and is found.

Prayer after Communion

May your divine Sacrament, O Lord, which we have received,
fill the inner depths of our heart
and, by its working mightily within us,
make us partakers of its grace.
Through Christ our Lord.

Prayer over the People
for optional use

May the ears of your mercy be open, O Lord,
to the prayers of those who call upon you;
and that you may grant what they desire,
have them ask what is pleasing to you.
Through Christ our Lord.

THIRD SUNDAY OF LENT

On this Sunday is celebrated the first scrutiny in preparation for the Baptism of the catechumens who are to be admitted to the Sacraments of Christian Initiation at the Easter Vigil, using the proper prayers and intercessions as given below, pp. 1121-1123.

Entrance Antiphon
Cf. Ps 25 (24): 15-16

My eyes are always on the Lord,
for he rescues my feet from the snare.
Turn to me and have mercy on me,
for I am alone and poor.

Or:
Cf. Ez 36: 23-26

When I prove my holiness among you,
I will gather you from all the foreign lands;
and I will pour clean water upon you
and cleanse you from all your impurities,
and I will give you a new spirit, says the Lord.

The Gloria in excelsis (Glory to God in the highest) is not said.

Collect

O God, author of every mercy and of all goodness,
who in fasting, prayer and almsgiving
have shown us a remedy for sin,
look graciously on this confession of our lowliness,
that we, who are bowed down by our conscience,
may always be lifted up by your mercy.
Through our Lord Jesus Christ, your Son,
who lives and reigns with you in the unity of the Holy Spirit,
one God, for ever and ever.

The Creed is said.

Prayer over the Offerings

Be pleased, O Lord, with these sacrificial offerings,
and grant that we who beseech pardon for our own sins,
may take care to forgive our neighbor.
Through Christ our Lord.

When the Gospel of the Samaritan Woman is not read, Preface I or II of Lent, pp. 546-549, is used.

Preface: The Samaritan Woman.

V. The Lord be with you.   R. And with your spir-it.

V. Lift up your hearts.   R. We lift them up to the Lord.

V. Let us give thanks to the Lord our God.   R. It is right and just.

It is truly right and just, our duty and our sal-va-tion, al-ways and everywhere to give you thanks, Lord, holy Father, almighty and e--ter-nal God, through Christ our Lord. For when he asked the Samaritan woman for wa-ter to drink, he had already created the gift of faith with-in her and so ardently did he thirst for her faith, that he kin-dled in her the fire of di-vine love. And so we, too, give you thanks and with the An-gels praise your mighty deeds, as we ac-claim:

Holy, Holy, Holy Lord God of hosts . . .

Text without music:
V. **The Lord be with you.**
R. And with your spirit.

V. **Lift up your hearts.**
R. We lift them up to the Lord.

V. **Let us give thanks to the Lord our God.**
R. It is right and just.

It is truly right and just, our duty and our salvation,
always and everywhere to give you thanks,
Lord, holy Father, almighty and eternal God,
through Christ our Lord.

For when he asked the Samaritan woman for water to drink,
he had already created the gift of faith within her
and so ardently did he thirst for her faith,
that he kindled in her the fire of divine love.

And so we, too, give you thanks
and with the Angels
praise your mighty deeds, as we acclaim:

Holy, Holy, Holy Lord God of hosts . . .

Communion Antiphon

When the Gospel of the Samaritan Woman is read: Jn 4: 13-14
> For anyone who drinks it, says the Lord,
> the water I shall give will become in him
> a spring welling up to eternal life.

When another Gospel is read: Cf. Ps 84 (83): 4-5
> The sparrow finds a home,
> and the swallow a nest for her young:
> by your altars, O Lord of hosts, my King and my God.
> Blessed are they who dwell in your house,
> for ever singing your praise.

Prayer after Communion

**As we receive the pledge
of things yet hidden in heaven
and are nourished while still on earth
with the Bread that comes from on high,
we humbly entreat you, O Lord,
that what is being brought about in us in mystery
may come to true completion.
Through Christ our Lord.**

Prayer over the People

**Direct, O Lord, we pray, the hearts of your faithful,
and in your kindness grant your servants this grace:
that, abiding in the love of you and their neighbor,
they may fulfill the whole of your commands.
Through Christ our Lord.**

Monday

Entrance Antiphon   Ps 84 (83): 3

My soul is longing and yearning for the courts of the Lord.
My heart and my flesh cry out to the living God.

Collect

May your unfailing compassion, O Lord,
cleanse and protect your Church,
and, since without you she cannot stand secure,
may she be always governed by your grace.
Through our Lord Jesus Christ, your Son,
who lives and reigns with you in the unity of the Holy Spirit,
one God, for ever and ever.

Prayer over the Offerings

May what we offer you, O Lord,
in token of our service,
be transformed by you into the sacrament of salvation.
Through Christ our Lord.

Preface of Lent, pp. 546-553.

Communion Antiphon   Ps 117 (116): 1, 2

O praise the Lord, all you nations,
for his merciful love towards us is great.

Prayer after Communion

May communion in this your Sacrament,
we pray, O Lord,
bring with it purification and the unity that is your gift.
Through Christ our Lord.

Prayer over the People   for optional use

May your right hand, we ask, O Lord,
protect this people that makes entreaty to you:
graciously purify them and give them instruction,
that, finding solace in this life,
they may reach the good things to come.
Through Christ our Lord.

Tuesday

Entrance Antiphon   Cf. Ps 17 (16): 6, 8

To you I call, for you will surely heed me, O God;
turn your ear to me; hear my words.
Guard me as the apple of your eye;
in the shadow of your wings protect me.

Collect

May your grace not forsake us, O Lord, we pray,
but make us dedicated to your holy service
and at all times obtain for us your help.
Through our Lord Jesus Christ, your Son,
who lives and reigns with you in the unity of the Holy Spirit,
one God, for ever and ever.

Prayer over the Offerings

Grant us, O Lord, we pray,
that this saving sacrifice may cleanse us of our faults
and become an oblation
pleasing to your almighty power.
Through Christ our Lord.

Preface of Lent, pp. 546-553.

Communion Antiphon   Cf. Ps 15 (14): 1-2

Lord, who may abide in your tent,
and dwell on your holy mountain?
Whoever walks without fault and does what is just.

Prayer after Communion

May the holy partaking of this mystery
give us life, O Lord, we pray,
and grant us both pardon and protection.
Through Christ our Lord.

Prayer over the People   for optional use

O God, founder and ruler of your people,
drive away the sins that assail them,
that they may always be pleasing to you
and ever safe under your protection.
Through Christ our Lord.

Wednesday

Entrance Antiphon   Cf. Ps 119 (118): 133

Let my steps be guided by your promise; may evil never rule me.

Collect

Grant, we pray, O Lord,
that, schooled through Lenten observance
and nourished by your word,
through holy restraint
we may be devoted to you with all our heart
and be ever united in prayer.
Through our Lord Jesus Christ, your Son,
who lives and reigns with you in the unity of the Holy Spirit,
one God, for ever and ever.

Prayer over the Offerings

Accept, O Lord, we pray, the prayers of your people
along with these sacrificial offerings,
and defend those who celebrate your mysteries
from every kind of danger.
Through Christ our Lord.

Preface of Lent, pp. 546-553.

Communion Antiphon   Cf. Ps 16 (15): 11

You will show me the path of life,
the fullness of joy in your presence, O Lord.

Prayer after Communion

May the heavenly banquet, at which we have been fed,
sanctify us, O Lord,
and, cleansing us of all errors,
make us worthy of your promises from on high.
Through Christ our Lord.

Prayer over the People   for optional use

Give to your people, our God,
a resolve that is pleasing to you,
for, by conforming them to your teachings,
you bestow on them every favor.
Through Christ our Lord.

THIRD WEEK OF LENT

Thursday

Entrance Antiphon
I am the salvation of the people, says the Lord.
Should they cry to me in any distress,
I will hear them, and I will be their Lord for ever.

Collect
We implore your majesty most humbly, O Lord,
that, as the feast of our salvation draws ever closer,
so we may press forward all the more eagerly
towards the worthy celebration of the Paschal Mystery.
Through our Lord Jesus Christ, your Son,
who lives and reigns with you in the unity of the Holy Spirit,
one God, for ever and ever.

Prayer over the Offerings
Cleanse your people, Lord, we pray,
from every taint of wickedness,
that their gifts may be pleasing to you;
and do not let them cling to false joys,
for you promise them the rewards of your truth.
Through Christ our Lord.

Preface of Lent, pp. 546-553.

Communion Antiphon
Ps 119 (118): 4-5

You have laid down your precepts to be carefully kept;
may my ways be firm in keeping your statutes.

Prayer after Communion
Graciously raise up, O Lord,
those you renew with this Sacrament,
that we may come to possess your salvation
both in mystery and in the manner of our life.
Through Christ our Lord.

Prayer over the People
for optional use

We call on your loving kindness
and trust in your mercy, O Lord,
that, since we have from you all that we are,
through your grace we may seek what is right
and have strength to do the good we desire.
Through Christ our Lord.

Friday

Entrance Antiphon
Ps 86 (85): 8, 10

Among the gods there is none like you, O Lord,
for you are great and do marvelous deeds; you alone are God.

Collect

Pour your grace into our hearts, we pray, O Lord,
that we may be constantly drawn away from unruly desires
and obey by your own gift the heavenly teaching you give us.
Through our Lord Jesus Christ, your Son,
who lives and reigns with you in the unity of the Holy Spirit,
one God, for ever and ever.

Prayer over the Offerings

Look with favor, we pray, Lord,
on the offerings we dedicate,
that they may be pleasing in your sight
and always be salutary for us.
Through Christ our Lord.

Preface of Lent, pp. 546-553.

Communion Antiphon
Cf. Mk 12: 33

To love God with all your heart, and your neighbor as yourself,
is worth more than any sacrifice.

Prayer after Communion

May your strength be at work in us, O Lord,
pervading our minds and bodies,
that what we have received
by participating in this Sacrament
may bring us the fullness of redemption.
Through Christ our Lord.

Prayer over the People
for optional use

Look graciously, O Lord,
upon the faithful who implore your mercy,
that, trusting in your kindness,
they may spread far and wide
the gifts your charity has bestowed.
Through Christ our Lord.

Saturday

Entrance Antiphon
Ps 103 (102): 2-3

Bless the Lord, O my soul, and never forget all his benefits;
it is he who forgives all your sins.

Collect

Rejoicing in this annual celebration
of our Lenten observance,
we pray, O Lord,
that, with our hearts set on the paschal mysteries,
we may be gladdened by their full effects.
Through our Lord Jesus Christ, your Son,
who lives and reigns with you in the unity of the Holy Spirit,
one God, for ever and ever.

Prayer over the Offerings

O God, by whose grace it comes to pass
that we may approach your mysteries
with minds made pure,
grant, we pray,
that, in reverently handing them on,
we may offer you fitting homage.
Through Christ our Lord.

Preface of Lent, pp. 546-553.

Communion Antiphon
Lk 18: 13

The tax collector stood at a distance, beating his breast and saying:
O God, be merciful to me, a sinner.

Prayer after Communion

May we truly revere, O merciful God,
these holy gifts, by which you ceaselessly nourish us,
and may we always partake of them
with abundant faith in our heart.
Through Christ our Lord.

Prayer over the People
for optional use

Hold out to your faithful people, Lord,
the right hand of heavenly assistance,
that they may seek you with all their heart
and merit the granting of what they ask.
Through Christ our Lord.

FOURTH SUNDAY OF LENT

In this Mass, the color violet or rose is used. Instrumental music is permitted, and the altar may be decorated with flowers.

On this Sunday is celebrated the second scrutiny in preparation for the Baptism of the catechumens who are to be admitted to the Sacraments of Christian Initiation at the Easter Vigil, using the proper prayers and intercessions as given below, p. 1124.

Entrance Antiphon
Cf. Is 66: 10-11

Rejoice, Jerusalem, and all who love her.
Be joyful, all who were in mourning;
exult and be satisfied at her consoling breast.

The Gloria in excelsis (Glory to God in the highest) is not said.

Collect

**O God, who through your Word
reconcile the human race to yourself in a wonderful way,
grant, we pray,
that with prompt devotion and eager faith
the Christian people may hasten
toward the solemn celebrations to come.
Through our Lord Jesus Christ, your Son,
who lives and reigns with you in the unity of the Holy Spirit,
one God, for ever and ever.**

The Creed is said.

Prayer over the Offerings

**We place before you with joy these offerings,
which bring eternal remedy, O Lord,
praying that we may both faithfully revere them
and present them to you, as is fitting,
for the salvation of all the world.
Through Christ our Lord.**

When the Gospel of the Man Born Blind is not read, Preface I or II of Lent, pp. 546-549, is used.

Preface: The Man Born Blind.

V. The Lord be with you.   R. And with your spir-it.

V. Lift up your hearts.   R. We lift them up to the Lord.

V. Let us give thanks to the Lord our God.   R. It is right and just.

It is truly right and just, our duty and our sal-va-tion, al-ways and everywhere to give you thanks, Lord, holy Father, almighty and e- -ter-nal God, through Christ our Lord. By the mystery of the Incarnation, he has led the human race that walked in dark-ness into the ra-di-ance of the faith and has brought those born in slavery to an-cient sin through the waters of re-gen-er-a-tion to make them your a-dopt-ed chil-dren. There-fore, all creatures of heaven and earth sing a new song in ad-o-ra-tion, and we, with all the host of An-gels, cry out, and with-out end ac-claim:

Holy, Holy, Holy Lord God of hosts . . .

Text without music:
℣. **The Lord be with you.**
℟. And with your spirit.

℣. **Lift up your hearts.**
℟. We lift them up to the Lord.

℣. **Let us give thanks to the Lord our God.**
℟. It is right and just.

**It is truly right and just, our duty and our salvation,
always and everywhere to give you thanks,
Lord, holy Father, almighty and eternal God,
through Christ our Lord.**

**By the mystery of the Incarnation,
he has led the human race that walked in darkness
into the radiance of the faith
and has brought those born in slavery to ancient sin
through the waters of regeneration
to make them your adopted children.**

**Therefore, all creatures of heaven and earth
sing a new song in adoration,
and we, with all the host of Angels,
cry out, and without end acclaim:**

Holy, Holy, Holy Lord God of hosts . . .

Communion Antiphon

When the Gospel of the Man Born Blind is read: Cf. Jn 9: 11, 38
>The Lord anointed my eyes: I went, I washed,
>I saw and I believed in God.

When the Gospel of the Prodigal Son is read: Lk 15: 32
>You must rejoice, my son,
>for your brother was dead and has come to life;
>he was lost and is found.

When another Gospel is read: Cf. Ps 122 (121): 3-4
>Jerusalem is built as a city bonded as one together.
>It is there that the tribes go up, the tribes of the Lord,
>to praise the name of the Lord.

Prayer after Communion

**O God, who enlighten everyone who comes into this world,
illuminate our hearts, we pray,
with the splendor of your grace,
that we may always ponder
what is worthy and pleasing to your majesty
and love you in all sincerity.
Through Christ our Lord.**

Prayer over the People

**Look upon those who call to you, O Lord,
and sustain the weak;
give life by your unfailing light
to those who walk in the shadow of death,
and bring those rescued by your mercy from every evil
to reach the highest good.
Through Christ our Lord.**

Monday

Entrance Antiphon   *Cf. Ps 31 (30): 7-8*
As for me, I trust in the Lord.
Let me be glad and rejoice in your mercy,
for you have seen my affliction.

Collect
O God, who renew the world
through mysteries beyond all telling,
grant, we pray,
that your Church may be guided by your eternal design
and not be deprived of your help in this present age.
Through our Lord Jesus Christ, your Son,
who lives and reigns with you in the unity of the Holy Spirit,
one God, for ever and ever.

Prayer over the Offerings
May we receive, O Lord, we pray,
the effects of this offering dedicated to you,
so that we may be cleansed from old earthly ways
and be renewed by growth in heavenly life.
Through Christ our Lord.

Preface of Lent, pp. 546-553.

Communion Antiphon   *Ez 36: 27*
I will place my spirit within you
and make you walk according to my laws;
and my judgments you shall keep and observe, says the Lord.

Prayer after Communion
May your holy gifts, O Lord, we pray,
give us life by making us new,
and, by sanctifying us, lead us to things eternal.
Through Christ our Lord.

Prayer over the People   *for optional use*
Renew your people within and without, O Lord,
and, since it is your will
that they be unhindered by bodily delights,
give them, we pray,
perseverance in their spiritual intent.
Through Christ our Lord.

Tuesday

Entrance Antiphon
Cf. Is 55: 1

All who are thirsty, come to the waters, says the Lord.
Though you have no money, come and drink with joy.

Collect

May the venerable exercises of holy devotion
shape the hearts of your faithful, O Lord,
to welcome worthily the Paschal Mystery
and proclaim the praises of your salvation.
Through our Lord Jesus Christ, your Son,
who lives and reigns with you in the unity of the Holy Spirit,
one God, for ever and ever.

Prayer over the Offerings

We offer to you, O Lord,
these gifts which you yourself have bestowed;
may they attest to your care as Creator
for this our mortal life,
and effect in us the healing
that brings us immortality.
Through Christ our Lord.

Preface of Lent, pp. 546-553.

Communion Antiphon
Cf. Ps 23 (22): 1-2

The Lord is my shepherd; there is nothing I shall want.
Fresh and green are the pastures where he gives me repose,
near restful waters he leads me.

Prayer after Communion

Purify our minds, O Lord, we pray,
and renew them with this heavenly Sacrament,
that we may find help for our bodies
now and likewise in times to come.
Through Christ our Lord.

Prayer over the People
for optional use

Grant, O merciful God,
that your people may remain always devoted to you
and may constantly receive from your kindness
whatever is for their good.
Through Christ our Lord.

Wednesday

Entrance Antiphon Ps 69 (68): 14

I pray to you, O Lord, for a time of your favor.
In your great mercy, answer me, O God,
with your salvation that never fails.

Collect

O God, who reward the merits of the just
and offer pardon to sinners who do penance,
have mercy, we pray, on those who call upon you,
that the admission of our guilt
may serve to obtain your pardon for our sins.
Through our Lord Jesus Christ, your Son,
who lives and reigns with you in the unity of the Holy Spirit,
one God, for ever and ever.

Prayer over the Offerings

May the power of this sacrifice, O Lord, we pray,
mercifully wipe away what is old in us,
and increase in us grace of salvation and newness of life.
Through Christ our Lord.

Preface of Lent, pp. 546-553.

Communion Antiphon Jn 3: 17

God did not send his Son into the world
to judge the world,
but that the world might be saved through him.

Prayer after Communion

May your heavenly gifts, O Lord, we pray,
which you bestow as a heavenly remedy on your people,
not bring judgment to those who receive them.
Through Christ our Lord.

Prayer over the People for optional use

May your servants be shielded, O Lord,
by the protection of your loving-kindness,
that, doing what is good in this world,
they may reach you, their highest good.
Through Christ our Lord.

Thursday

Entrance Antiphon   Cf. Ps 105 (104): 3-4

    Let the hearts that seek the Lord rejoice;
    turn to the Lord and his strength;
    constantly seek his face.

Collect

    We invoke your mercy in humble prayer, O Lord,
    that you may cause us, your servants,
    corrected by penance and schooled by good works,
    to persevere sincerely in your commands
    and come safely to the paschal festivities.
    Through our Lord Jesus Christ, your Son,
    who lives and reigns with you in the unity of the Holy Spirit,
    one God, for ever and ever.

Prayer over the Offerings

    Grant, we pray, almighty God,
    that what we offer in sacrifice
    may cleanse us in our frailty from every evil
    and always grant us your protection.
    Through Christ our Lord.

Preface of Lent, pp. 546-553.

Communion Antiphon   Jer 31: 33

    I will place my law within them, and I will write it upon their hearts;
    and I will be their God, and they shall be my people, says the Lord.

Prayer after Communion

    May this Sacrament we have received purify us, we pray, O Lord,
    and grant your servants freedom from all blame,
    that those bound by a guilty conscience
    may glory in the fullness of heavenly remedy.
    Through Christ our Lord.

Prayer over the People   for optional use

    O God, protector of all who hope in you,
    bless your people, keep them safe,
    defend them, prepare them,
    that, free from sin and safe from the enemy,
    they may persevere always in your love.
    Through Christ our Lord.

Friday

Entrance Antiphon   Cf. Ps 54 (53): 3-4

O God, save me by your name;
by your power, defend my cause.
O God, hear my prayer;
give ear to the words of my mouth.

Collect

O God, who have prepared
fitting helps for us in our weakness,
grant, we pray, that we may receive
their healing effects with joy
and reflect them in a holy way of life.
Through our Lord Jesus Christ, your Son,
who lives and reigns with you in the unity of the Holy Spirit,
one God, for ever and ever.

Prayer over the Offerings

May this sacrifice, almighty God,
cleanse us by its mighty power
and lead us to approach its source
with ever greater purity.
Through Christ our Lord.

Preface of Lent, pp. 546-553.

Communion Antiphon   Eph 1: 7

In Christ, we have redemption by his Blood,
and forgiveness of our sins,
in accord with the riches of his grace.

Prayer after Communion

Grant, we pray, O Lord,
that, as we pass from old to new,
so, with former ways left behind,
we may be renewed in holiness of mind.
Through Christ our Lord.

Prayer over the People   *for optional use*

Look upon your servants, O Lord,
and in your goodness protect with heavenly assistance
those who trust in your mercy.
Through Christ our Lord.

Saturday

Entrance Antiphon   Cf. Ps 18 (17): 5, 7

The waves of death rose about me;
the pains of the netherworld surrounded me.
In my anguish I called to the Lord,
and from his holy temple he heard my voice.

Collect

May the working of your mercy, O Lord, we pray,
direct our hearts aright,
for without your grace
we cannot find favor in your sight.
Through our Lord Jesus Christ, your Son,
who lives and reigns with you in the unity of the Holy Spirit,
one God, for ever and ever.

Prayer over the Offerings

Be pleased, O Lord, we pray,
with these oblations you receive from our hands,
and, even when our wills are defiant,
constrain them mercifully to turn to you.
Through Christ our Lord.

Preface of Lent, pp. 546-553.

Communion Antiphon   Cf. 1 Pt 1: 18-19

By the precious Blood of Christ,
the Blood of a spotless and unblemished Lamb,
we have been redeemed.

Prayer after Communion

May your holy gifts purify us, O Lord, we pray,
and by their working render us fully pleasing to you.
Through Christ our Lord.

Prayer over the People   for optional use

Look upon your people, O Lord,
and, as they draw near to the coming festivities,
bestow upon them abundance of heavenly grace,
that, helped by the consolations of this world,
they may be impelled more readily
towards higher goods that cannot be seen.
Through Christ our Lord.

FIFTH SUNDAY OF LENT

In the Dioceses of the United States, the practice of covering crosses and images throughout the church from this Sunday may be observed. Crosses remain covered until the end of the Celebration of the Lord's Passion on Good Friday, but images remain covered until the beginning of the Easter Vigil.

On this Sunday is celebrated the third scrutiny in preparation for the Baptism of the catechumens who are to be admitted to the Sacraments of Christian Initiation at the Easter Vigil, using the proper prayers and intercessions as given below, p. 1125.

Entrance Antiphon
Cf. Ps 43 (42): 1-2

Give me justice, O God,
and plead my cause against a nation that is faithless.
From the deceitful and cunning rescue me,
for you, O God, are my strength.

The Gloria in excelsis (Glory to God in the highest) is not said.

Collect

**By your help, we beseech you, Lord our God,
may we walk eagerly in that same charity
with which, out of love for the world,
your Son handed himself over to death.
Through our Lord Jesus Christ, your Son,
who lives and reigns with you in the unity of the Holy Spirit,
one God, for ever and ever.**

The Creed is said.

Prayer over the Offerings

**Hear us, almighty God,
and, having instilled in your servants
the teachings of the Christian faith,
graciously purify them
by the working of this sacrifice.
Through Christ our Lord.**

When the Gospel of Lazarus is not read, Preface I or II of Lent, pp. 546-549, is used.

Preface: Lazarus.

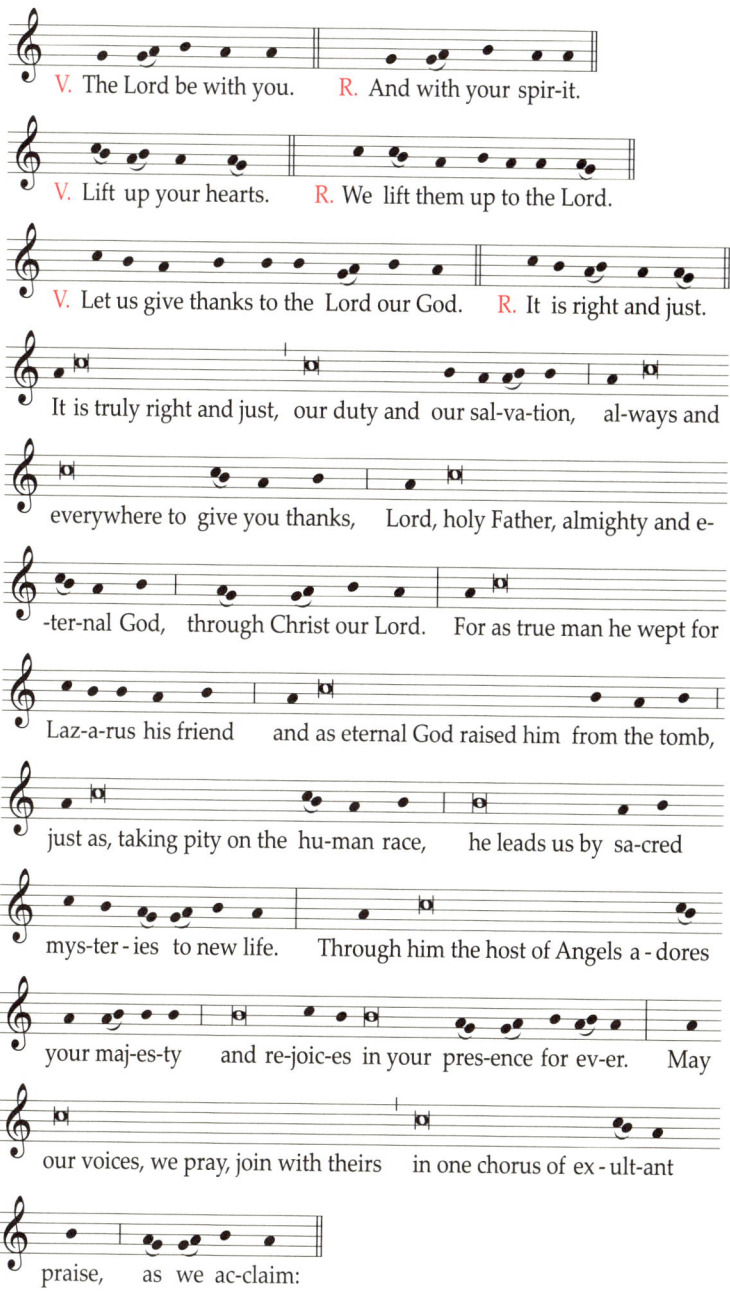

V. The Lord be with you. R. And with your spir-it.

V. Lift up your hearts. R. We lift them up to the Lord.

V. Let us give thanks to the Lord our God. R. It is right and just.

It is truly right and just, our duty and our sal-va-tion, al-ways and everywhere to give you thanks, Lord, holy Father, almighty and e--ter-nal God, through Christ our Lord. For as true man he wept for Laz-a-rus his friend and as eternal God raised him from the tomb, just as, taking pity on the hu-man race, he leads us by sa-cred mys-ter-ies to new life. Through him the host of Angels a-dores your maj-es-ty and re-joic-es in your pres-ence for ev-er. May our voices, we pray, join with theirs in one chorus of ex-ult-ant praise, as we ac-claim:

Holy, Holy, Holy Lord God of hosts . . .

Text without music:
V. **The Lord be with you.**
R. And with your spirit.

V. **Lift up your hearts.**
R. We lift them up to the Lord.

V. **Let us give thanks to the Lord our God.**
R. It is right and just.

It is truly right and just, our duty and our salvation,
always and everywhere to give you thanks,
Lord, holy Father, almighty and eternal God,
through Christ our Lord.

For as true man he wept for Lazarus his friend
and as eternal God raised him from the tomb,
just as, taking pity on the human race,
he leads us by sacred mysteries to new life.

Through him the host of Angels adores your majesty
and rejoices in your presence for ever.
May our voices, we pray, join with theirs
in one chorus of exultant praise, as we acclaim:

Holy, Holy, Holy Lord God of hosts . . .

Communion Antiphon

When the Gospel of Lazarus is read: Cf. Jn 11: 26
    Everyone who lives and believes in me
    will not die for ever, says the Lord.

When the Gospel of the Adulterous Woman is read: Jn 8: 10-11
    Has no one condemned you, woman? No one, Lord.
    Neither shall I condemn you. From now on, sin no more.

When another Gospel is read: Jn 12: 24
    Amen, Amen I say to you: Unless a grain of wheat
    falls to the ground and dies, it remains a single grain.
    But if it dies, it bears much fruit.

Prayer after Communion

We pray, almighty God,
that we may always be counted among the members of Christ,
in whose Body and Blood we have communion.
Who lives and reigns for ever and ever.

Prayer over the People

Bless, O Lord, your people,
who long for the gift of your mercy,
and grant that what, at your prompting, they desire
they may receive by your generous gift.
Through Christ our Lord.

Monday

Entrance Antiphon
Cf. Ps 56 (55): 2

Have mercy on me, O God, for people assail me;
they fight me all day long and oppress me.

Collect

O God, by whose wondrous grace
we are enriched with every blessing,
grant us so to pass from former ways to newness of life,
that we may be made ready for the glory of the heavenly Kingdom.
Through our Lord Jesus Christ, your Son,
who lives and reigns with you in the unity of the Holy Spirit,
one God, for ever and ever.

Prayer over the Offerings

Grant, we pray, O Lord,
that, preparing to celebrate the holy mysteries,
we may bring before you as the fruit of bodily penance
a joyful purity of heart.
Through Christ our Lord.

Preface I of the Passion of the Lord, p. 554.

Communion Antiphon

When the Gospel of the Adulterous Woman is read: Jn 8: 10-11
> Has no one condemned you, woman? No one, Lord.
> Neither shall I condemn you. From now on, sin no more.

When another Gospel is read: Jn 8: 12
> I am the light of the world, says the Lord;
> whoever follows me will not walk in the darkness,
> but will have the light of life.

Prayer after Communion

Strengthened by the blessing of your Sacraments, we pray, O Lord,
that through them we may constantly be cleansed of our faults
and, by following Christ,
hasten our steps upward toward you.
Through Christ our Lord.

Prayer over the People   *for optional use*

Set free from their sins, O Lord, we pray,
the people who call upon you,
that, living a holy way of life,
they may be kept safe from every trial.
Through Christ our Lord.

Tuesday

Entrance Antiphon
Ps 27 (26): 14

> Wait for the Lord; be strong;
> be stouthearted, and wait for the Lord!

Collect

> Grant us, we pray, O Lord,
> perseverance in obeying your will,
> that in our days the people dedicated to your service
> may grow in both merit and number.
> Through our Lord Jesus Christ, your Son,
> who lives and reigns with you in the unity of the Holy Spirit,
> one God, for ever and ever.

Prayer over the Offerings

> We offer you, O Lord, the sacrifice of conciliation,
> that, being moved to compassion,
> you may both pardon our offenses
> and direct our wavering hearts.
> Through Christ our Lord.

Preface I of the Passion of the Lord, p. 554.

Communion Antiphon
Jn 12: 32

> When I am lifted up from the earth,
> I will draw all to myself, says the Lord.

Prayer after Communion

> Grant, we pray, almighty God,
> that, ever seeking what is divine,
> we may always be worthy
> to approach these heavenly gifts.
> Through Christ our Lord.

Prayer over the People
for optional use

> O God, who choose to show mercy not anger
> to those who hope in you,
> grant that your faithful may weep, as they should,
> for the evil they have done,
> and so merit the grace of your consolation.
> Through Christ our Lord.

Wednesday

Entrance Antiphon
Cf. Ps 18 (17): 48-49

My deliverer from angry nations, you set me above my assailants;
you saved me from the violent man, O Lord.

Collect

Enlighten, O God of compassion,
the hearts of your children, sanctified by penance,
and in your kindness
grant those you stir to a sense of devotion
a gracious hearing when they cry out to you.
Through our Lord Jesus Christ, your Son,
who lives and reigns with you in the unity of the Holy Spirit,
one God, for ever and ever.

Prayer over the Offerings

Receive back, O Lord, these sacrificial offerings,
which you have given to be offered
to the honor of your name,
and grant that they may become remedies for our healing.
Through Christ our Lord.

Preface I of the Passion of the Lord, p. 554.

Communion Antiphon
Col 1: 13-14

God has brought us to the kingdom of his beloved Son,
in whom we have redemption through his Blood,
the forgiveness of sins.

Prayer after Communion

May the mysteries we have received, O Lord,
bring us heavenly medicine,
that they may purge all evil from our heart
and strengthen us with eternal protection.
Through Christ our Lord.

Prayer over the People
for optional use

Attend, almighty God,
to the prayers of your people,
and, as you endow them
with confident hope in your compassion,
let them feel as ever the effects of your mercy.
Through Christ our Lord.

Thursday

Entrance Antiphon
Heb 9: 15

Christ is mediator of a New Covenant,
so that by means of his death, those who are called
may receive the promise of an eternal inheritance.

Collect

Be near, O Lord, to those who plead before you,
and look kindly on those who place their hope in your mercy,
that, cleansed from the stain of their sins,
they may persevere in holy living
and be made full heirs of your promise.
Through our Lord Jesus Christ, your Son,
who lives and reigns with you in the unity of the Holy Spirit,
one God, for ever and ever.

Prayer over the Offerings

Look with favor, Lord, we pray,
on these sacrificial offerings,
that they may profit our conversion
and the salvation of all the world.
Through Christ our Lord.

Preface I of the Passion of the Lord, p. 554.

Communion Antiphon
Rom 8: 32

God did not spare his own Son, but handed him over for us all;
with him, he has given us all things.

Prayer after Communion

**Nourished by your saving gifts,
we beseech your mercy, Lord,
that by this same Sacrament,
with which you feed us in the present age,
you may make us partakers of life eternal.
Through Christ our Lord.**

Prayer over the People
for optional use

**Be gracious to your people, Lord, we pray,
that, as from day to day they reject what does not please you,
they may be filled instead with delight at your commands.
Through Christ our Lord.**

Friday

Entrance Antiphon   Ps 31 (30): 10, 16, 18

Have mercy on me, O Lord, for I am in distress.
Deliver me from the hands of my enemies and those who pursue me.
O Lord, let me never be put to shame, for I call on you.

Collect

**Pardon the offenses of your peoples, we pray, O Lord,
and in your goodness set us free
from the bonds of the sins
we have committed in our weakness.
Through our Lord Jesus Christ, your Son,
who lives and reigns with you in the unity of the Holy Spirit,
one God, for ever and ever.**

Or:

**O God, who in this season
give your Church the grace
to imitate devoutly the Blessed Virgin Mary
in contemplating the Passion of Christ,
grant, we pray, through her intercession,
that we may cling more firmly each day
to your Only Begotten Son
and come at last to the fullness of his grace.
Who lives and reigns with you in the unity of the Holy Spirit,
one God, for ever and ever.**

Prayer over the Offerings

Grant, O merciful God, that we may be worthy
to serve ever fittingly at your altars,
and there to be saved by constant participation.
Through Christ our Lord.

Preface I of the Passion of the Lord, p. 554.

Communion Antiphon   1 Pt 2: 24

Jesus bore our sins in his own body on the cross,
so that dead to sin, we might live for righteousness.
By his wounds we have been healed.

Prayer after Communion

May the unfailing protection
of the sacrifice we have received
never leave us, O Lord,
and may it always drive far from us
all that would do us harm.
Through Christ our Lord.

Prayer over the People   for optional use

Grant, we pray, almighty God,
that your servants, who seek the grace of your protection,
may be free from every evil
and serve you in peace of mind.
Through Christ our Lord.

Saturday

Entrance Antiphon
Cf. Ps 22 (21): 20, 7

O Lord, do not stay afar off;
my strength, make haste to help me!
For I am a worm and no man,
scorned by everyone, despised by the people.

Collect
O God, who have made all those reborn in Christ
a chosen race and a royal priesthood,
grant us, we pray, the grace to will and to do what you command,
that the people called to eternal life
may be one in the faith of their hearts
and the homage of their deeds.
Through our Lord Jesus Christ, your Son,
who lives and reigns with you in the unity of the Holy Spirit,
one God, for ever and ever.

Prayer over the Offerings
May the gifts we offer from our fasting
be acceptable to you, O Lord, we pray,
and, as an expiation for our sins,
may they make us worthy of your grace
and lead us to what you promise for eternity.
Through Christ our Lord.

Preface I of the Passion of the Lord, p. 554.

Communion Antiphon
Cf. Jn 11: 52
Christ was handed over,
to gather into one the scattered children of God.

Prayer after Communion
We entreat your majesty most humbly, O Lord,
that, as you feed us with the nourishment
which comes from the most holy Body and Blood of your Son,
so you may make us sharers of his divine nature.
Who lives and reigns for ever and ever.

Prayer over the People
for optional use
Have mercy, Lord, on your Church,
as she brings you her supplications,
and be attentive to those who incline their hearts before you:
do not allow, we pray, those you have redeemed
by the Death of your Only Begotten Son,
to be harmed by their sins or weighed down by their trials.
Through Christ our Lord.

HOLY WEEK

PALM SUNDAY OF THE PASSION OF THE LORD

1. On this day the Church recalls the entrance of Christ the Lord into Jerusalem to accomplish his Paschal Mystery. Accordingly, the memorial of this entrance of the Lord takes place at all Masses, by means of the Procession or the Solemn Entrance before the principal Mass or the Simple Entrance before other Masses. The Solemn Entrance, but not the Procession, may be repeated before other Masses that are usually celebrated with a large gathering of people.

   It is desirable that, where neither the Procession nor the Solemn Entrance can take place, there be a sacred celebration of the Word of God on the messianic entrance and on the Passion of the Lord, either on Saturday evening or on Sunday at a convenient time.

The Commemoration of the Lord's Entrance into Jerusalem

First Form: The Procession

2. At an appropriate hour, a gathering takes place at a smaller church or other suitable place other than inside the church to which the procession will go. The faithful hold branches in their hands.

3. Wearing the red sacred vestments as for Mass, the Priest and the Deacon, accompanied by other ministers, approach the place where the people are gathered. Instead of the chasuble, the Priest may wear a cope, which he leaves aside when the procession is over, and puts on a chasuble.

4. Meanwhile, the following antiphon or another appropriate chant is sung.

Ant. Mt 21: 9

Ho-san-na to the Son of Da-vid; bless-ed is he who comes in the name of the Lord, the King of Is-ra-el. Ho-san-na in the high-est.

Or:

Ho-san-na fi-li-o Da-vid: be-ne-dí-ctus qui ve-nit in nó-mi-ne Dó-mi-ni. Rex Is-ra-el: Ho-san-na in ex-cél-sis.

5. After this, the Priest and people sign themselves, while the Priest says: In the name of the Father, and of the Son, and of the Holy Spirit. Then he greets the people in the usual way. A brief address is given, in which the faithful are invited to participate actively and consciously in the celebration of this day, in these or similar words:

**Dear brethren (brothers and sisters),
since the beginning of Lent until now
we have prepared our hearts by penance and charitable works.
Today we gather together to herald with the whole Church
the beginning of the celebration
of our Lord's Paschal Mystery,
that is to say, of his Passion and Resurrection.
For it was to accomplish this mystery
that he entered his own city of Jerusalem.
Therefore, with all faith and devotion,
let us commemorate
the Lord's entry into the city for our salvation,
following in his footsteps,
so that, being made by his grace partakers of the Cross,
we may have a share also in his Resurrection and in his life.**

6. After the address, the Priest says one of the following prayers with hands extended.

Let us pray.
Almighty ever-living God,
sanctify ✠ these branches with your blessing,
that we, who follow Christ the King in exultation,
may reach the eternal Jerusalem through him.
Who lives and reigns for ever and ever.
R. Amen.

Or:

Increase the faith of those who place their hope in you, O God,
and graciously hear the prayers of those who call on you,
that we, who today hold high these branches
to hail Christ in his triumph,
may bear fruit for you by good works accomplished in him.
Who lives and reigns for ever and ever.
R. Amen.

He sprinkles the branches with holy water without saying anything.

7. Then a Deacon or, if there is no Deacon, a Priest, proclaims in the usual way the Gospel concerning the Lord's entrance according to one of the four Gospels. If appropriate, incense may be used.

"Blessed is he who comes in the name of the Lord"

Year A:
✠ A reading from the holy Gospel according to Matthew. 21: 1-11

¹ When Jesus and the disciples drew near Jerusalem and
came to Bethphage on the Mount of Olives, Jesus sent
two disciples, ² saying to them,
"Go into the village opposite you,
and immediately you will find an ass tethered,
and a colt with her.
Untie them and bring them here to me.
³ And if anyone should say anything to you, reply,
'The master has need of them.' Then he will send them
at once."
⁴ This happened so that what had been spoken through the
prophet
might be fulfilled:
⁵ Say to daughter Zion,
"Behold, your king comes to you, meek and riding
on an ass,
and on a colt, the foal of a beast of burden."
⁶ The disciples went and did as Jesus had ordered them.
⁷ They brought the ass and the colt and laid their cloaks
over them, and he sat upon them.
⁸ The very large crowd spread their cloaks on the road,
while others cut branches from the trees and strewed
them on the road.
⁹ The crowds preceding him and those following
kept crying out and saying:
"Hosanna to the Son of David;
blessed is he who comes in the name of the Lord;
hosanna in the highest."
¹⁰ And when he entered Jerusalem
the whole city was shaken and asked, "Who is this?"
¹¹ And the crowds replied,
"This is Jesus the prophet, from Nazareth in Galilee."

The Gospel of the Lord.

Year B:
✠ A reading from the holy Gospel according to Mark. 11: 1-10

¹ When Jesus and his disciples drew near to Jerusalem, to
  Bethphage and Bethany at the Mount of Olives,
he sent two of his disciples ² and said to them,
  "Go into the village opposite you, and immediately on
    entering it,
  you will find a colt tethered on which no one has ever sat.
  Untie it and bring it here.
³ If anyone should say to you,
  'Why are you doing this?' reply,
  'The Master has need of it
  and will send it back here at once.'"
⁴ So they went off
  and found a colt tethered at a gate outside on the street,
    and they untied it.
⁵ Some of the bystanders said to them,
  "What are you doing, untying the colt?"
⁶ They answered them just as Jesus had told them to, and
    they permitted them to do it.
⁷ So they brought the colt to Jesus and put their cloaks over it.
  And he sat on it.
⁸ Many people spread their cloaks on the road, and others
    spread leafy branches
  that they had cut from the fields.
⁹ Those preceding him as well as those following kept
    crying out: "Hosanna!
  Blessed is he who comes in the name of the Lord!
¹⁰ Blessed is the kingdom of our father David that is
    to come!
  Hosanna in the highest!"
The Gospel of the Lord.

Or:

✠ A reading from the holy Gospel according to John. 12: 12-16

¹² When the great crowd that had come to the feast heard
that Jesus was coming to Jerusalem,
¹³ they took palm branches and went out to meet him, and
cried out:
"Hosanna!
Blessed is he who comes in the name of the Lord, the king
of Israel."
¹⁴ Jesus found an ass and sat upon it, as is written:
¹⁵ Fear no more, O daughter Zion;
see, your king comes, seated upon an ass's colt.
¹⁶ His disciples did not understand this at first, but when
Jesus had been glorified
they remembered that these things were written about
him and that they had done this for him.

The Gospel of the Lord.

Year C

✠ A reading from the holy Gospel according to Luke. 19: 28-40

²⁸ Jesus proceeded on his journey up to Jerusalem.
²⁹ As he drew near to Bethphage and Bethany at the place
called the Mount of Olives,
he sent two of his disciples.
³⁰ He said, "Go into the village opposite you,
and as you enter it you will find a colt tethered on which
no one has ever sat.
Untie it and bring it here.
³¹ And if anyone should ask you,
'Why are you untying it?' you will answer,
'The Master has need of it.' "
³² So those who had been sent went off
and found everything just as he had told them.
³³ And as they were untying the colt, its owners said to
them, "Why are you untying this colt?"
³⁴ They answered,
"The Master has need of it."

35 So they brought it to Jesus,
threw their cloaks over the colt,
and helped Jesus to mount.
36 As he rode along,
the people were spreading their cloaks on the road;
37 and now as he was approaching the slope of the Mount of
Olives, the whole multitude of his disciples
began to praise God aloud with joy
for all the mighty deeds they had seen.
38 They proclaimed:
"Blessed is the king who comes in the name of the Lord.
39 Peace in heaven and glory in the highest."
Some of the Pharisees in the crowd said to him, "Teacher,
rebuke your disciples."
40 He said in reply,
"I tell you, if they keep silent, the stones will cry out!"
The Gospel of the Lord.

8. After the Gospel, a brief homily may be given. Then, to begin the Procession, an invitation may be given by a Priest or a Deacon or a lay minister, in these or similar words:

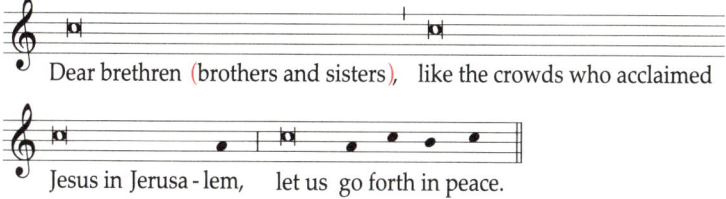

Dear brethren (brothers and sisters), like the crowds who acclaimed Jesus in Jerusalem, let us go forth in peace.

**Dear brethren (brothers and sisters),
like the crowds who acclaimed Jesus in Jerusalem,
let us go forth in peace.**

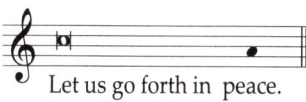

Let us go forth in peace.

Or:

Let us go forth in peace.

In this latter case, all respond:

In the name of Christ. A-men.

9. The Procession to the church where Mass will be celebrated then sets off in the usual way. If incense is used, the thurifer goes first, carrying a thurible with burning incense, then an acolyte or another minister, carrying a cross decorated with palm branches according to local custom, between two ministers with lighted candles. Then follow the Deacon carrying the Book of the Gospels, the Priest with the ministers, and, after them, all the faithful carrying branches.

As the Procession moves forward, the following or other suitable chants in honor of Christ the King are sung by the choir and people.

Antiphon 1

The children of the Hebrews, carrying olive branches,
went to meet the Lord, crying out and saying:
Hosanna in the highest.

If appropriate, this antiphon is repeated between the strophes of the following Psalm.

Psalm 24 (23)

The Lord's is the earth and its fullness, *
the world, and those who dwell in it.
It is he who set it on the seas;*
on the rivers he made it firm.

(The antiphon is repeated)

Who shall climb the mountain of the LORD?*
The clean of hands and pure of heart,
whose soul is not set on vain things, †
who has not sworn deceitful words.*

(The antiphon is repeated)

Blessings from the LORD shall he receive,*
and right reward from the God who saves him.
Such are the people who seek him,*
who seek the face of the God of Jacob.

(The antiphon is repeated)

O gates, lift high your heads; †
grow higher, ancient doors.*
Let him enter, the king of glory!
Who is this king of glory?*
The LORD, the mighty, the valiant;
the LORD, the valiant in war.

(The antiphon is repeated)

O gates, lift high your heads; †
grow higher, ancient doors.*
Let him enter, the king of glory!
Who is this king of glory?*
He, the LORD of hosts,
he is the king of glory.

(The antiphon is repeated)

Antiphon 2

The children of the Hebrews spread their garments on the road,
crying out and saying: Hosanna to the Son of David;
blesssed is he who comes in the name of the Lord.

If appropriate, this antiphon is repeated between the strophes of the following Psalm.

Psalm 47 (46)

All peoples, clap your hands.*
Cry to God with shouts of joy!
For the LORD, the Most high, is awesome,*
the great king over all the earth.

(The antiphon is repeated)

He humbles peoples under us*
and nations under our feet.
Our heritage he chose for us,*
the pride of Jacob whom he loves.
God goes up with shouts of joy.*
The LORD goes up with trumpet blast.

(The antiphon is repeated)

Sing praise for God; sing praise!*
Sing praise to our king; sing praise!
God is king of all earth.*
Sing praise with all your skill.

(The antiphon is repeated)

God reigns over the nations.*
God sits upon his holy throne.
The princes of the peoples are assembled
with the people of the God of Abraham. †
The rulers of the earth belong to God,*
who is greatly exalted.

(The antiphon is repeated)

Hymn to Christ the King

> Chorus:
> Glory and honor and praise be to you, Christ, King and Redeemer,
> to whom young children cried out loving Hosannas with joy.
> All repeat: Glory and honor . . .
>
> Chorus:
> Israel's King are you, King David's magnificent offspring;
> you are the ruler who come blest in the name of the Lord.
> All repeat: Glory and honor . . .
>
> Chorus:
> Heavenly hosts on high unite in singing your praises;
> men and women on earth and all creation join in.
> All repeat: Glory and honor . . .
>
> Chorus:
> Bearing branches of palm, Hebrews came crowding to greet you;
> see how with prayers and hymns we come to pay you our vows.
> All repeat: Glory and honor . . .
>
> Chorus:
> They offered gifts of praise to you, so near to your Passion;
> see how we sing this song now to you reigning on high.
> All repeat: Glory and honor . . .
>
> Chorus:
> Those you were pleased to accept; now accept our gifts of devotion,
> good and merciful King, lover of all that is good.
> All repeat: Glory and honor . . .

10. As the procession enters the church, there is sung the following responsory or another chant, which should speak of the Lord's entrance.

    R. As the Lord entered the holy city, the children of the Hebrews proclaimed the resurrection of life. *Waving their branches of palm, they cried: Hosanna in the Highest.

    V. When the people heard that Jesus was coming to Jerusalem, they went out to meet him. *Waving their branches.

11. When the Priest arrives at the altar, he venerates it and, if appropriate, incenses it. Then he goes to the chair, where he puts aside the cope, if he has worn one, and puts on the chasuble. Omitting the other Introductory Rites of the Mass and, if appropriate, the **Kyrie** (Lord, have mercy), he says the Collect of the Mass, and then continues the Mass in the usual way.

Second Form: The Solemn Entrance

12. When a procession outside the church cannot take place, the entrance of the Lord is celebrated inside the church by means of a Solemn Entrance before the principal Mass.

13. Holding branches in their hands, the faithful gather either outside, in front of the church door, or inside the church itself. The Priest and ministers and a representative group of the faithful go to a suitable place in the church outside the sanctuary, where at least the greater part of the faithful can see the rite.

14. While the Priest approaches the appointed place, the antiphon **Hosanna** or another appropriate chant is sung. Then the blessing of branches and the proclamation of the Gospel of the Lord's entrance into Jerusalem take place as above (nos. **5-7**). After the Gospel, the Priest processes solemnly with the ministers and the representative group of the faithful through the church to the sanctuary, while the responsory **As the Lord entered** (no. 10) or another appropriate chant is sung.

15. Arriving at the altar, the Priest venerates it. He then goes to the chair and, omitting the Introductory Rites of the Mass and, if appropriate, the **Kyrie** (Lord, have mercy), he says the Collect of the Mass, and then continues the Mass in the usual way.

Third Form: The Simple Entrance

16. At all other Masses of this Sunday at which the Solemn Entrance is not held, the memorial of the Lord's entrance into Jerusalem takes place by means of a Simple Entrance.

17. While the Priest proceeds to the altar, the Entrance Antiphon with its Psalm (no. 18) or another chant on the same theme is sung. Arriving at the altar, the Priest venerates it and goes to the chair. After the Sign of the Cross, he greets the people and continues the Mass in the usual way.

    At other Masses, in which singing at the entrance cannot take place, the Priest, as soon as he has arrived at the altar and venerated it, greets the people, reads the Entrance Antiphon, and continues the Mass in the usual way.

18. **Entrance Antiphon**   Cf. Jn 12: 1, 12-13; Ps 24 (23): 9-10
    Six days before the Passover,
    when the Lord came into the city of Jerusalem,
    the children ran to meet him;
    in their hands they carried palm branches
    and with a loud voice cried out:
    *Hosanna in the highest!

    Blessed are you, who have come in your abundant mercy!
    O gates, lift high your heads;
    grow higher, ancient doors.
    Let him enter, the king of glory!
    Who is this king of glory?
    He, the Lord of hosts, he is the king of glory.
    *Hosanna in the highest!

    Blessed are you, who have come in your abundant mercy!

At the Mass

19. After the Procession or Solemn Entrance the Priest begins the Mass with the Collect.

20. **Collect**
 Almighty ever-living God,
 who as an example of humility for the human race to follow
 caused our Savior to take flesh and submit to the Cross,
 graciously grant that we may heed his lesson of patient suffering
 and so merit a share in his Resurrection.
 Who lives and reigns with you in the unity of the Holy Spirit,
 one God, for ever and ever.

21. The narrative of the Lord's Passion is read without candles and without incense, with no greeting or signing of the book. It is read by a Deacon or, if there is no Deacon, by a Priest. It may also be read by readers, with the part of Christ, if possible, reserved to a Priest.
 Deacons, but not others, ask for the blessing of the Priest before singing the Passion, as at other times before the Gospel.

22. After the narrative of the Passion, a brief homily should take place, if appropriate. A period of silence may also be observed.

 The Creed is said, and the Universal Prayer takes place.

23. **Prayer over the Offerings**
 Through the Passion of your Only Begotten Son, O Lord,
 may our reconciliation with you be near at hand,
 so that, though we do not merit it by our own deeds,
 yet by this sacrifice made once for all,
 we may feel already the effects of your mercy.
 Through Christ our Lord.

24. **Preface: The Passion of the Lord.**

V. The Lord be with you. R. And with your spir-it.

V. Lift up your hearts. R. We lift them up to the Lord.

V. Let us give thanks to the Lord our God. R. It is right and just.

It is truly right and just, our duty and our sal-va-tion, al-ways and everywhere to give you thanks, Lord, holy Father, almighty and e- -ter-nal God, through Christ our Lord. For, though innocent, he suffered will-ing-ly for sin-ners and accepted unjust con-dem- -na-tion to save the guil-ty. His Death has washed a-way our sins, and his Res-ur-rec-tion has purchased our jus-ti-fi-ca-tion. And so, with all the An-gels, we praise you, as in joyful cele-bra-tion we ac-claim:

Holy, Holy, Holy Lord God of hosts . . .

Text without music:
V. **The Lord be with you.**
R. And with your spirit.

V. **Lift up your hearts.**
R. We lift them up to the Lord.

V. **Let us give thanks to the Lord our God.**
R. It is right and just.

It is truly right and just, our duty and our salvation,
always and everywhere to give you thanks,
Lord, holy Father, almighty and eternal God,
through Christ our Lord.

For, though innocent, he suffered willingly for sinners
and accepted unjust condemnation to save the guilty.
His Death has washed away our sins,
and his Resurrection has purchased our justification.

And so, with all the Angels,
we praise you, as in joyful celebration we acclaim:

Holy, Holy, Holy Lord God of hosts . . .

25. **Communion Antiphon** — Mt 26: 42
Father, if this chalice cannot pass without my drinking it,
your will be done.

26. **Prayer after Communion**
Nourished with these sacred gifts,
we humbly beseech you, O Lord,
that, just as through the death of your Son
you have brought us to hope for what we believe,
so by his Resurrection
you may lead us to where you call.
Through Christ our Lord.

27. **Prayer over the People**
Look, we pray, O Lord, on this your family,
for whom our Lord Jesus Christ
did not hesitate to be delivered into the hands of the wicked
and submit to the agony of the Cross.
Who lives and reigns for ever and ever.

MONDAY OF HOLY WEEK

Entrance Antiphon   Cf. Ps 35 (34): 1-2; 140 (139): 8

Contend, O Lord, with my contenders; fight those who fight me.
Take up your buckler and shield; arise in my defense, Lord, my mighty help.

Collect

Grant, we pray, almighty God,
that, though in our weakness we fail,
we may be revived through the Passion of your Only Begotten Son.
Who lives and reigns with you in the unity of the Holy Spirit,
one God, for ever and ever.

Prayer over the Offerings

Look graciously, O Lord,
upon the sacred mysteries we celebrate here,
and may what you have mercifully provided
to cancel the judgment we incurred
bear for us fruit in eternal life.
Through Christ our Lord.

Preface II of the Passion of the Lord, p. 556.

Communion Antiphon   Cf. Ps 102 (101): 3

Do not hide your face from me in the day of my distress.
Turn your ear towards me; on the day when I call, speedily answer me.

Prayer after Communion

Visit your people, O Lord, we pray,
and with ever-watchful love
look upon the hearts dedicated to you by means of these
    sacred mysteries,
so that under your protection
we may keep safe this remedy of eternal salvation,
which by your mercy we have received.
Through Christ our Lord.

Prayer over the People   for optional use

May your protection, O Lord, we pray,
defend the humble
and keep ever safe those who trust in your mercy,
that they may celebrate the paschal festivities
not only with bodily observance
but above all with purity of mind.
Through Christ our Lord.

TUESDAY OF HOLY WEEK

Entrance Antiphon Cf. Ps 27 (26): 12

Do not leave me to the will of my foes, O Lord,
for false witnesses rise up against me
and they breathe out violence.

Collect

Almighty ever-living God,
grant us so to celebrate
the mysteries of the Lord's Passion
that we may merit to receive your pardon.
Through our Lord Jesus Christ, your Son,
who lives and reigns with you in the unity of the Holy Spirit,
one God, for ever and ever.

Prayer over the Offerings

Look favorably, O Lord, we pray,
on these offerings of your family,
and to those you make partakers of these sacred gifts
grant a share in their fullness.
Through Christ our Lord.

Preface II of the Passion of the Lord, p. 556.

Communion Antiphon Rom 8: 32

God did not spare his own Son,
but handed him over for us all.

Prayer after Communion

Nourished by your saving gifts,
we beseech your mercy, Lord,
that by this same Sacrament,
with which you have fed us in the present age
you may make us partakers of life eternal.
Through Christ our Lord.

Prayer over the People for optional use

May your mercy, O God,
cleanse the people that are subject to you
from all seduction of former ways
and make them capable of new holiness.
Through Christ our Lord.

WEDNESDAY OF HOLY WEEK

Entrance Antiphon
Cf. Phil 2: 10, 8, 11

At the name of Jesus, every knee should bend,
of those in heaven and on the earth and under the earth,
for the Lord became obedient to death, death on a cross:
therefore Jesus Christ is Lord, to the glory of God the Father.

Collect

O God, who willed your Son to submit for our sake
to the yoke of the Cross,
so that you might drive from us the power of the enemy,
grant us, your servants, to attain the grace of the resurrection.
Through our Lord Jesus Christ, your Son,
who lives and reigns with you in the unity of the Holy Spirit,
one God, for ever and ever.

Prayer over the Offerings

Receive, O Lord, we pray, the offerings made here,
and graciously grant
that, celebrating your Son's Passion in mystery,
we may experience the grace of its effects.
Through Christ our Lord.

Preface II of the Passion of the Lord, p. 556.

Communion Antiphon
Mt 20: 28

The Son of Man did not come to be served but to serve
and to give his life as a ransom for many.

Prayer after Communion

Endow us, almighty God, with the firm conviction
that through your Son's Death in time,
to which the revered mysteries bear witness,
we may be assured of perpetual life.
Through Christ our Lord.

Prayer over the People
for optional use

Grant your faithful, O Lord, we pray,
to partake unceasingly of the paschal mysteries
and to await with longing the gifts to come,
that, persevering in the Sacraments of their rebirth,
they may be led by Lenten works to newness of life.
Through Christ our Lord.

THURSDAY OF HOLY WEEK [HOLY THURSDAY]

1. In accordance with a most ancient tradition of the Church, on this day all Masses without the people are forbidden.

The Chrism Mass

2. The blessing of the Oil of the Sick and of the Oil of Catechumens and the consecration of the Chrism are carried out by the Bishop, according to the Rite described in the Roman Pontifical, usually on this day, at a proper Mass to be celebrated during the morning.

3. If, however, it is very difficult for the clergy and the people to gather with the Bishop on this day, the Chrism Mass may be anticipated on another day, but near to Easter.

4. This Mass, which the Bishop concelebrates with his presbyterate, should be, as it were, a manifestation of the Priests' communion with their Bishop. Accordingly it is desirable that all the Priests participate in it, insofar as is possible, and during it receive Communion even under both kinds. To signify the unity of the presbyterate of the diocese, the Priests who concelebrate with the Bishop should be from different regions of the diocese.

5. In accord with traditional practice, the blessing of the Oil of the Sick takes place before the end of the Eucharistic Prayer, but the blessing of the Oil of Catechumens and the consecration of the Chrism take place after Communion. Nevertheless, for pastoral reasons, it is permitted for the entire rite of blessing to take place after the Liturgy of the Word.

6. **Entrance Antiphon**   Rev 1: 6

   Jesus Christ has made us into a kingdom, priests for his God and Father.
   To him be glory and power for ever and ever. Amen.

   The Gloria in excelsis (Glory to God in the highest) is said.

7. **Collect**

   O God, who anointed your Only Begotten Son with the Holy Spirit and made him Christ and Lord,
   graciously grant
   that, being made sharers in his consecration,
   we may bear witness to your Redemption in the world.
   Through our Lord Jesus Christ, your Son,
   who lives and reigns with you in the unity of the Holy Spirit,
   one God, for ever and ever.

8. After the reading of the Gospel, the Bishop preaches the Homily in which, taking his starting point from the text of the readings proclaimed in the Liturgy of the Word, he speaks to the people and to his Priests about priestly anointing, urging the Priests to be faithful in their office and calling on them to renew publicly their priestly promises.

THE CHRISM MASS

Renewal of Priestly Promises

9. After the Homily, the Bishop speaks with the Priests in these or similar words.

**Beloved sons,
on the anniversary of that day
when Christ our Lord conferred his priesthood
on his Apostles and on us,
are you resolved to renew,
in the presence of your Bishop and God's holy people,
the promises you once made?**

The Priests, all together, respond: **I am.**

**Are you resolved to be more united with the Lord Jesus
and more closely conformed to him,
denying yourselves and confirming those promises
about sacred duties towards Christ's Church
which, prompted by love of him,
you willingly and joyfully pledged
on the day of your priestly ordination?**

Priests: **I am.**

**Are you resolved to be faithful stewards of the mysteries of God
in the Holy Eucharist and the other liturgical rites
and to discharge faithfully the sacred office of teaching,
following Christ the Head and Shepherd,
not seeking any gain,
but moved only by zeal for souls?**

Priests: **I am.**

Then, turned towards the people, the Bishop continues:

**As for you, dearest sons and daughters,
pray for your Priests,
that the Lord may pour out his gifts abundantly upon them,
and keep them faithful as ministers of Christ, the High Priest,
so that they may lead you to him,
who is the source of salvation.**

People: Christ, hear us. Christ, graciously hear us.

And pray also for me,
that I may be faithful to the apostolic office
entrusted to me in my lowliness
and that in your midst I may be made day by day
a living and more perfect image of Christ,
the Priest, the Good Shepherd,
the Teacher and the Servant of all.

People: Christ, hear us. Christ, graciously hear us.

May the Lord keep us all in his charity
and lead all of us,
shepherds and flock,
to eternal life.

All: Amen.

10. The Creed is not said.

11. **Prayer over the Offerings**

May the power of this sacrifice, O Lord, we pray,
mercifully wipe away what is old in us
and increase in us grace of salvation and newness of life.
Through Christ our Lord.

THE CHRISM MASS 293

12. **Preface: The Priesthood of Christ and the Ministry of Priests.**

V. The Lord be with you.   R. And with your spir-it.

V. Lift up your hearts.   R. We lift them up to the Lord.

V. Let us give thanks to the Lord our God.   R. It is right and just.

It is truly right and just, our duty and our sal-va-tion, al-ways and everywhere to give you thanks, Lord, holy Father, almighty and e-ter-nal God. For by the anointing of the Ho-ly Spir-it you made your Only Begotten Son High Priest of the new and e-ter-nal cov-e-nant, and by your wondrous design were pleased to de-cree that his one Priest-hood should con-tin-ue in the Church. For Christ not only adorns with a royal priesthood the people he has made his own, but with a brother's kindness he also chooses men

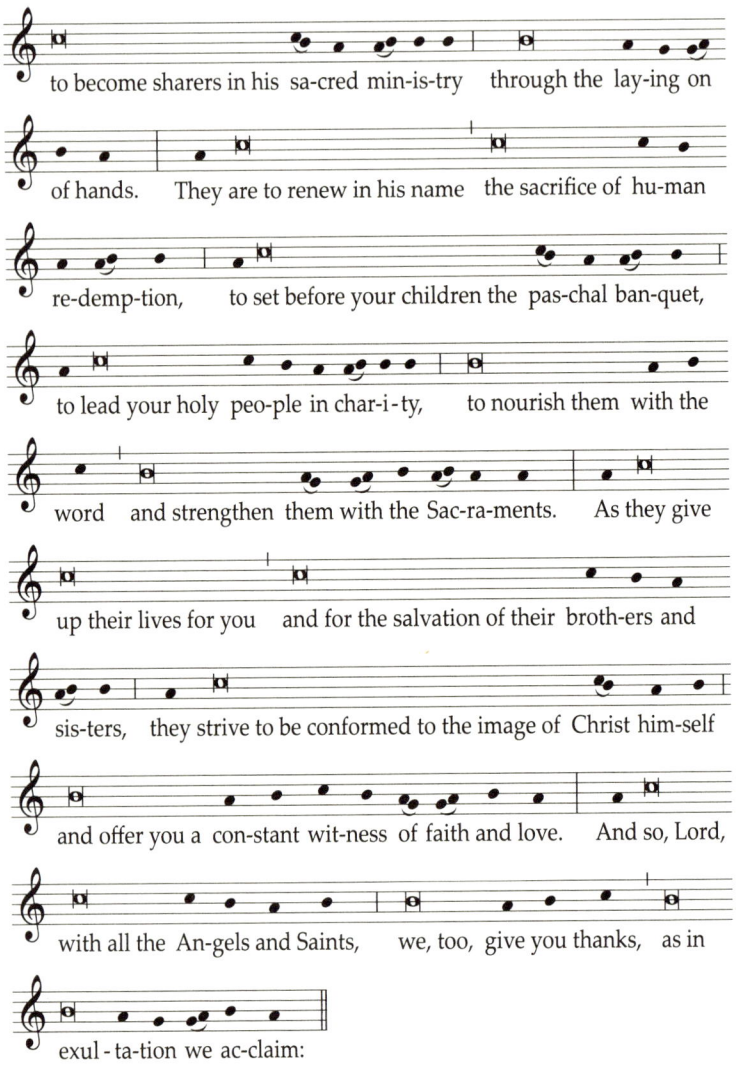

to become sharers in his sacred ministry through the laying on of hands. They are to renew in his name the sacrifice of human redemption, to set before your children the paschal banquet, to lead your holy people in charity, to nourish them with the word and strengthen them with the Sacraments. As they give up their lives for you and for the salvation of their brothers and sisters, they strive to be conformed to the image of Christ himself and offer you a constant witness of faith and love. And so, Lord, with all the Angels and Saints, we, too, give you thanks, as in exultation we acclaim:

Holy, Holy, Holy Lord God of hosts . . .

Text without music:

V. **The Lord be with you.**
R. And with your spirit.

V. **Lift up your hearts.**
R. We lift them up to the Lord.

V. **Let us give thanks to the Lord our God.**
R. It is right and just.

It is truly right and just, our duty and our salvation,
always and everywhere to give you thanks,
Lord, holy Father, almighty and eternal God.

For by the anointing of the Holy Spirit
you made your Only Begotten Son
High Priest of the new and eternal covenant,
and by your wondrous design were pleased to decree
that his one Priesthood should continue in the Church.

For Christ not only adorns with a royal priesthood
the people he has made his own,
but with a brother's kindness he also chooses men
to become sharers in his sacred ministry
through the laying on of hands.

They are to renew in his name
the sacrifice of human redemption,
to set before your children the paschal banquet,
to lead your holy people in charity,
to nourish them with the word
and strengthen them with the Sacraments.

As they give up their lives for you
and for the salvation of their brothers and sisters,
they strive to be conformed to the image of Christ himself
and offer you a constant witness of faith and love.

And so, Lord, with all the Angels and Saints,
we, too, give you thanks, as in exultation we acclaim:

Holy, Holy, Holy Lord God of hosts . . .

13. **Communion Antiphon** Ps 89 (88): 2
I will sing for ever of your mercies, O Lord;
through all ages my mouth will proclaim your fidelity.

14. **Prayer after Communion**
We beseech you, almighty God,
that those you renew by your Sacraments
may merit to become the pleasing fragrance of Christ.
Who lives and reigns for ever and ever.

15. The reception of the Holy Oils may take place in individual parishes either before the celebration of the Evening Mass of the Lord's Supper or at another time that seems more appropriate.

THE SACRED
PASCHAL TRIDUUM

1. In the Sacred Triduum, the Church solemnly celebrates the greatest mysteries of our redemption, keeping by means of special celebrations the memorial of her Lord, crucified, buried, and risen.

    The Paschal Fast should also be kept sacred. It is to be celebrated everywhere on the Friday of the Lord's Passion and, where appropriate, prolonged also through Holy Saturday as a way of coming, with spirit uplifted, to the joys of the Lord's Resurrection.

2. For a fitting celebration of the Sacred Triduum, a sufficient number of lay ministers is required, who must be carefully instructed as to what they are to do.

    The singing of the people, the ministers, and the Priest Celebrant has a special importance in the celebrations of these days, for when texts are sung, they have their proper impact.

    Pastors should, therefore, not fail to explain to the Christian faithful, as best they can, the meaning and order of the celebrations and to prepare them for active and fruitful participation.

3. The celebrations of the Sacred Triduum are to be carried out in cathedral and parochial churches and only in those churches in which they can be performed with dignity, that is, with a good attendance of the faithful, an appropriate number of ministers, and the means to sing at least some of the parts.

    Consequently, it is desirable that small communities, associations, and special groups of various kinds join together in these churches to carry out the sacred celebrations in a more noble manner.

THURSDAY OF THE LORD'S SUPPER
At the Evening Mass

1. The Mass of the Lord's Supper is celebrated in the evening, at a convenient time, with the full participation of the whole local community and with all the Priests and ministers exercising their office.

2. All Priests may concelebrate even if they have already concelebrated the Chrism Mass on this day, or if they have to celebrate another Mass for the good of the Christian faithful.

3. Where a pastoral reason requires it, the local Ordinary may permit another Mass to be celebrated in churches and oratories in the evening and, in case of genuine necessity, even in the morning, but only for the faithful who are in no way able to participate in the evening Mass. Care should, nevertheless, be taken that celebrations of this sort do not take place for the advantage of private persons or special small groups, and do not prejudice the evening Mass.

4. Holy Communion may only be distributed to the faithful during Mass; but it may be brought to the sick at any hour of the day.

5. The altar may be decorated with flowers with a moderation that accords with the character of this day. The tabernacle should be entirely empty; but a sufficient amount of bread should be consecrated in this Mass for the Communion of the clergy and the people on this and the following day.

6. **Entrance Antiphon** *Cf. Gal 6: 14*
We should glory in the Cross of our Lord Jesus Christ,
in whom is our salvation, life and resurrection,
through whom we are saved and delivered.

7. The Gloria in excelsis (Glory to God in the highest) is said. While the hymn is being sung, bells are rung, and when it is finished, they remain silent until the Gloria in excelsis of the Easter Vigil, unless, if appropriate, the Diocesan Bishop has decided otherwise. Likewise, during this same period, the organ and other musical instruments may be used only so as to support the singing.

8. **Collect**
**O God, who have called us to participate
in this most sacred Supper,
in which your Only Begotten Son,
when about to hand himself over to death,
entrusted to the Church a sacrifice new for all eternity,
the banquet of his love,
grant, we pray,
that we may draw from so great a mystery,
the fullness of charity and of life.
Through our Lord Jesus Christ, your Son,
who lives and reigns with you in the unity of the Holy Spirit,
one God, for ever and ever.**

9. After the proclamation of the Gospel, the Priest gives a homily in which light is shed on the principal mysteries that are commemorated in this Mass, namely, the institution of the Holy Eucharist and of the priestly Order, and the commandment of the Lord concerning fraternal charity.

The Washing of Feet

10. After the Homily, where a pastoral reason suggests it, the Washing of Feet follows.

11. The men who have been chosen are led by the ministers to seats prepared in a suitable place. Then the Priest (removing his chasuble if necessary) goes to each one, and, with the help of the ministers, pours water over each one's feet and then dries them.

12. Meanwhile some of the following antiphons or other appropriate chants are sung.

Antiphon 1
Cf. Jn 13: 4, 5, 15

After the Lord had risen from supper,
he poured water into a basin
and began to wash the feet of his disciples:
he left them this example.

Antiphon 2
Cf. Jn 13: 12, 13, 15

The Lord Jesus, after eating supper with his disciples,
washed their feet and said to them:
Do you know what I, your Lord and Master, have done for you?
I have given you an example, that you should do likewise.

Antiphon 3
Jn 13: 6, 7, 8

Lord, are you to wash my feet? Jesus said to him in answer:
If I do not wash your feet, you will have no share with me.

V. So he came to Simon Peter and Peter said to him:
—Lord.

V. What I am doing, you do not know for now,
but later you will come to know.
—Lord.

Antiphon 4   Cf. Jn 13: 14
If I, your Lord and Master, have washed your feet,
how much more should you wash each other's feet?

Antiphon 5   Jn 13: 35
This is how all will know that you are my disciples:
if you have love for one another.

℣. Jesus said to his disciples:
—This is how.

Antiphon 6   Jn 13: 34
I give you a new commandment,
that you love one another
as I have loved you, says the Lord.

Antiphon 7   1 Cor 13: 13
Let faith, hope and charity, these three, remain among you,
but the greatest of these is charity.

℣. Now faith, hope and charity, these three, remain;
but the greatest of these is charity.
—Let.

13. After the Washing of Feet, the Priest washes and dries his hands, puts the chasuble back on, and returns to the chair, and from there he directs the Universal Prayer.

The Creed is not said.

The Liturgy of the Eucharist

14. At the beginning of the Liturgy of the Eucharist, there may be a procession of the faithful in which gifts for the poor may be presented with the bread and wine.

    Meanwhile the following, or another appropriate chant, is sung.

    Ant. Where true charity is dwelling, God is present there.

    V. By the love of Christ we have been brought together:
    V. let us find in him our gladness and our pleasure;
    V. may we love him and revere him, God the living,
    V. and in love respect each other with sincere hearts.

    Ant. Where true charity is dwelling, God is present there.

    V. So when we as one are gathered all together,
    V. let us strive to keep our minds free of division;
    V. may there be an end to malice, strife and quarrels,
    V. and let Christ our God be dwelling here among us.

    Ant. Where true charity is dwelling, God is present there.

    V. May your face thus be our vision, bright in glory,
    V. Christ our God, with all the blessed Saints in heaven:
    V. such delight is pure and faultless, joy unbounded,
    V. which endures through countless ages world without end. Amen.

15. **Prayer over the Offerings**

    **Grant us, O Lord, we pray,
    that we may participate worthily in these mysteries,
    for whenever the memorial of this sacrifice is celebrated
    the work of our redemption is accomplished.
    Through Christ our Lord.**

16. **Preface: The Sacrifice and the Sacrament of Christ.**

V. The Lord be with you.   R. And with your spir-it.

V. Lift up your hearts.   R. We lift them up to the Lord.

V. Let us give thanks to the Lord our God.   R. It is right and just.

It is truly right and just, our duty and our sal-va-tion, al-ways and everywhere to give you thanks, Lord, holy Father, almighty and e- -ter-nal God, through Christ our Lord. For he is the true and eter- -nal Priest, who instituted the pattern of an ever-last-ing sac-ri-fice and was the first to offer himself as the sav-ing Vic-tim, command- -ing us to make this of-fer-ing as his me-mo-ri-al. As we eat his flesh that was sacrificed for us, we are made strong, and, as we drink his Blood that was poured out for us, we are washed clean.

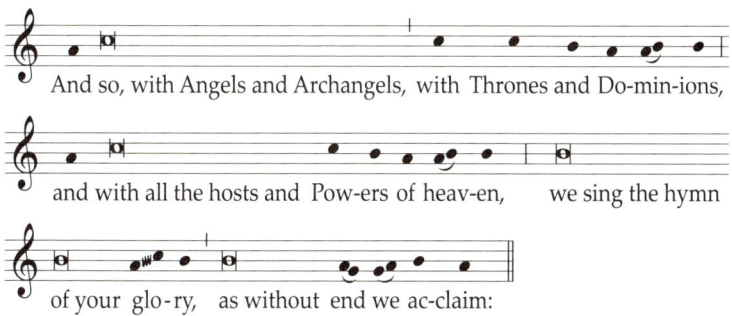

And so, with Angels and Archangels, with Thrones and Dominions, and with all the hosts and Powers of heaven, we sing the hymn of your glory, as without end we acclaim:

Holy, Holy, Holy Lord God of hosts . . .

Text without music: Preface I of the Most Holy Eucharist, p. 588.

17. When the Roman Canon is used, this special form of it is said, with proper formulas for the Communicantes (In communion with those), Hanc igitur (Therefore, Lord, we pray), and Qui pridie (On the day before he was to suffer).

18. The Priest, with hands extended, says:

To you, therefore, most merciful Father,   Celebrant alone
we make humble prayer and petition
through Jesus Christ, your Son, our Lord:

He joins his hands and says:
that you accept

He makes the Sign of the Cross once over the bread and chalice together, saying:
and bless ✶ these gifts, these offerings,
these holy and unblemished sacrifices,

With hands extended, he continues:
which we offer you firstly
for your holy catholic Church.
Be pleased to grant her peace,
to guard, unite and govern her
throughout the whole world,
together with your servant N. our Pope
and N. our Bishop,*
and all those who, holding to the truth,
hand on the catholic and apostolic faith.

---

* Mention may be made here of the Coadjutor Bishop, or Auxiliary Bishops, as noted in the *General Instruction of the Roman Missal*, no. 149.

19. Commemoration of the Living.

> **Remember, Lord, your servants N. and N.**

Celebrant or one concelebrant

The Priest joins his hands and prays briefly for those for whom he intends to pray.

Then, with hands extended, he continues:

> **and all gathered here,**
> **whose faith and devotion are known to you.**
> **For them we offer you this sacrifice of praise**
> **or they offer it for themselves**
> **and all who are dear to them:**
> **for the redemption of their souls,**
> **in hope of health and well-being,**
> **and paying their homage to you,**
> **the eternal God, living and true.**

20. Within the Action.

> **Celebrating the most sacred day**
> **on which our Lord Jesus Christ**
> **was handed over for our sake,**
> **and in communion with those whose memory we venerate,**
> **especially the glorious ever-Virgin Mary,**
> **Mother of our God and Lord, Jesus Christ,**
> **and † blessed Joseph, her Spouse**
> **your blessed Apostles and Martyrs,**
> **Peter and Paul, Andrew,**
> > **(James, John,**
> > **Thomas, James, Philip,**
> > **Bartholomew, Matthew, Simon and Jude;**
> > **Linus, Cletus, Clement, Sixtus,**
> > **Cornelius, Cyprian,**
> > **Lawrence, Chrysogonus,**
> > **John and Paul,**
> > **Cosmas and Damian)**
> > **and all your Saints;**
> **we ask that through their merits and prayers,**
> **in all things we may be defended**
> **by your protecting help.**
> **(Through Christ our Lord. Amen.)**

Celebrant or one concelebrant

MASS OF THE LORD'S SUPPER

21. With hands extended, the Priest continues:

Therefore, Lord, we pray: *Celebrant alone*
graciously accept this oblation of our service,
that of your whole family,
which we make to you
as we observe the day
on which our Lord Jesus Christ
handed on the mysteries of his Body and Blood
for his disciples to celebrate;
order our days in your peace,
and command that we be delivered from eternal damnation
and counted among the flock of those you have chosen.

He joins his hands.

(Through Christ our Lord. Amen.)

22. Holding his hands extended over the offerings, he says:

Be pleased, O God, we pray,   *Celebrant with*
to bless, acknowledge,   *concelebrants*
and approve this offering in every respect;
make it spiritual and acceptable,
so that it may become for us
the Body and Blood of your most beloved Son,
our Lord Jesus Christ.

He joins his hands.

23. *In the formulas that follow, the words of the Lord should be pronounced clearly and distinctly, as the nature of these words requires.*

> **On the day before he was to suffer**
> **for our salvation and the salvation of all,**
> **that is today,**

He takes the bread and, holding it slightly raised above the altar, continues:

> **he took bread in his holy and venerable hands,**

He raises his eyes.

> **and with eyes raised to heaven**
> **to you, O God, his almighty Father,**
> **giving you thanks, he said the blessing,**
> **broke the bread**
> **and gave it to his disciples, saying:**

He bows slightly.

> **TAKE THIS, ALL OF YOU, AND EAT OF IT,**
> **FOR THIS IS MY BODY,**
> **WHICH WILL BE GIVEN UP FOR YOU.**

He shows the consecrated host to the people, places it again on the paten, and genuflects in adoration.

24. *After this, the Priest continues:*

> **In a similar way, when supper was ended,**

He takes the chalice and, holding it slightly raised above the altar, continues:

> **he took this precious chalice**
> **in his holy and venerable hands,**
> **and once more giving you thanks, he said the blessing**
> **and gave the chalice to his disciples, saying:**

He bows slightly.

> **TAKE THIS, ALL OF YOU, AND DRINK FROM IT,**
> **FOR THIS IS THE CHALICE OF MY BLOOD,**
> **THE BLOOD OF THE NEW AND ETERNAL COVENANT,**
> **WHICH WILL BE POURED OUT FOR YOU AND FOR MANY**
> **FOR THE FORGIVENESS OF SINS.**
>
> **DO THIS IN MEMORY OF ME.**

He shows the chalice to the people, places it on the corporal, and genuflects in adoration.

25. Then he says:
> **The mystery of faith.**   *Celebrant alone*

And the people continue, acclaiming:
> **We proclaim your Death, O Lord,**
> **and profess your Resurrection**
> **until you come again.**

Or:

> **When we eat this Bread and drink this Cup,**
> **we proclaim your Death, O Lord,**
> **until you come again.**

Or:

> **Save us, Savior of the world,**
> **for by your Cross and Resurrection**
> **you have set us free.**

26. Then the Priest, with hands extended, says: *Celebrant with concelebrants*
> **Therefore, O Lord,**
> **as we celebrate the memorial of the blessed Passion,**
> **the Resurrection from the dead,**
> **and the glorious Ascension into heaven**
> **of Christ, your Son, our Lord,**
> **we, your servants and your holy people,**
> **offer to your glorious majesty**
> **from the gifts that you have given us,**
> **this pure victim,**
> **this holy victim,**
> **this spotless victim,**
> **the holy Bread of eternal life**
> **and the Chalice of everlasting salvation.**

27. **Be pleased to look upon these offerings**
with a serene and kindly countenance,
and to accept them,
as once you were pleased to accept
the gifts of your servant Abel the just,
the sacrifice of Abraham, our father in faith,
and the offering of your high priest Melchizedek,
a holy sacrifice, a spotless victim.

28. *Bowing, with hands joined, he continues:*

**In humble prayer we ask you, almighty God:
command that these gifts be borne
by the hands of your holy Angel
to your altar on high
in the sight of your divine majesty,
so that all of us, who through this participation at the altar
receive the most holy Body and Blood of your Son,**

He stands upright and signs himself with the Sign of the Cross, saying:

may be filled with every grace and heavenly blessing.

He joins his hands.

(Through Christ our Lord. Amen.)

29. *Commemoration of the Dead.*

With hands extended, the Priest says:

**Remember also, Lord, your servants N. and N.,
who have gone before us with the sign of faith
and rest in the sleep of peace.**

Celebrant or one concelebrant

He joins his hands and prays briefly for those who have died and for whom he intends to pray.

Then, with hands extended he continues:

**Grant them, O Lord, we pray,
and all who sleep in Christ,
a place of refreshment, light and peace.**

He joins his hands.

(Through Christ our Lord. Amen.)

MASS OF THE LORD'S SUPPER

30. *He strikes his breast with his right hand, saying:*
    To us, also, your servants, who, though sinners, *Celebrant or one concelebrant*
    And, with hands extended he continues:
    hope in your abundant mercies,
    graciously grant some share
    and fellowship with your holy Apostles and Martyrs:
    with John the Baptist, Stephen,
       Matthias, Barnabas,
       (Ignatius, Alexander,
       Marcellinus, Peter,
       Felicity, Perpetua,
       Agatha, Lucy,
       Agnes, Cecilia, Anastasia)
    and all your Saints;
    admit us, we beseech you,
    into their company,
    not weighing our merits,
    but granting us your pardon,

    He joins his hands.
    through Christ our Lord. *Celebrant alone*

31. *And he continues:*
    Through whom
    you continue to make all these good things, O Lord;
    you sanctify them, fill them with life,
    bless them, and bestow them upon us.

32. *He takes the chalice and the paten with the host and, elevating both, he says:*
    Through him, and with him, and in him, *Celebrant alone or with concelebrants*
    O God, almighty Father,
    in the unity of the Holy Spirit,
    all honor and glory is yours,
    for ever and ever.

    The people acclaim:
    Amen.

    Then follows the Communion Rite, p. 663.

33. At an appropriate moment during Communion, the Priest entrusts the Eucharist from the table of the altar to Deacons or acolytes or other extraordinary ministers, so that afterwards it may be brought to the sick who are to receive Holy Communion at home.

34. **Communion Antiphon**   1 Cor 11: 24-25
   This is the Body that will be given up for you;
   this is the Chalice of the new covenant in my Blood, says the Lord;
   do this, whenever you receive it, in memory of me.

35. After the distribution of Communion, a ciborium with hosts for Communion on the following day is left on the altar. The Priest, standing at the chair, says the Prayer after Communion.

36. **Prayer after Communion**
   Grant, almighty God,
   that, just as we are renewed
   by the Supper of your Son in this present age,
   so we may enjoy his banquet for all eternity.
   Who lives and reigns for ever and ever.

The Transfer of the Most Blessed Sacrament

37. After the Prayer after Communion, the Priest puts incense in the thurible while standing, blesses it and then, kneeling, incenses the Blessed Sacrament three times. Then, having put on a white humeral veil, he rises, takes the ciborium, and covers it with the ends of the veil.

38. A procession is formed in which the Blessed Sacrament, accompanied by torches and incense, is carried through the church to a place of repose prepared in a part of the church or in a chapel suitably decorated. A lay minister with a cross, standing between two other ministers with lighted candles leads off. Others carrying lighted candles follow. Before the Priest carrying the Blessed Sacrament comes the thurifer with a smoking thurible. Meanwhile, the hymn **Pange, lingua** (exclusive of the last two stanzas) or another eucharistic chant is sung.

39. When the procession reaches the place of repose, the Priest, with the help of the Deacon if necessary, places the ciborium in the tabernacle, the door of which remains open. Then he puts incense in the thurible and, kneeling, incenses the Blessed Sacrament, while **Tantum ergo Sacramentum** or another eucharistic chant is sung. Then the Deacon or the Priest himself places the Sacrament in the tabernacle and closes the door.

40. After a period of adoration in silence, the Priest and ministers genuflect and return to the sacristy.

41. At an appropriate time, the altar is stripped and, if possible, the crosses are removed from the church. It is expedient that any crosses which remain in the church be veiled.

42. Vespers (Evening Prayer) is not celebrated by those who have attended the Mass of the Lord's Supper.

43. The faithful are invited to continue adoration before the Blessed Sacrament for a suitable length of time during the night, according to local circumstances, but after midnight the adoration should take place without solemnity.

44. If the celebration of the Passion of the Lord on the following Friday does not take place in the same church, the Mass is concluded in the usual way and the Blessed Sacrament is placed in the tabernacle.

FRIDAY OF THE PASSION OF THE LORD
[GOOD FRIDAY]

1. On this and the following day, by a most ancient tradition, the Church does not celebrate the Sacraments at all, except for Penance and the Anointing of the Sick.

2. On this day, Holy Communion is distributed to the faithful only within the celebration of the Lord's Passion; but it may be brought at any hour of the day to the sick who cannot participate in this celebration.

3. The altar should be completely bare: without a cross, without candles and without cloths.

The Celebration of the Passion of the Lord

4. On the afternoon of this day, about three o'clock (unless a later hour is chosen for a pastoral reason), there takes place the celebration of the Lord's Passion consisting of three parts, namely, the Liturgy of the Word, the Adoration of the Cross, and Holy Communion.

    In the United States, if the size or nature of a parish or other community indicates the pastoral need for an additional liturgical service, the Diocesan Bishop may permit the service to be repeated later. This liturgy by its very nature may not, however, be celebrated in the absence of a Priest.

5. The Priest and the Deacon, if a Deacon is present, wearing red vestments as for Mass, go to the altar in silence and, after making a reverence to the altar, prostrate themselves or, if appropriate, kneel and pray in silence for a while. All others kneel.

6. Then the Priest, with the ministers, goes to the chair where, facing the people, who are standing, he says, with hands extended, one of the following prayers, omitting the invitation **Let us pray.**

Prayer

Remember your mercies, O Lord,
and with your eternal protection sanctify your servants,
for whom Christ your Son,
by the shedding of his Blood,
established the Paschal Mystery.
Who lives and reigns for ever and ever.
R. Amen.

Or:

O God, who by the Passion of Christ your Son, our Lord,
abolished the death inherited from ancient sin
by every succeeding generation,
grant that just as, being conformed to him,
we have borne by the law of nature
the image of the man of earth,
so by the sanctification of grace
we may bear the image of the Man of heaven.
Through Christ our Lord.
R. Amen.

FIRST PART:
THE LITURGY OF THE WORD

7. Then all sit and the First Reading, from the Book of the Prophet Isaiah (52: 13-53: 12), is read with its Psalm.

8. The Second Reading, from the Letter to the Hebrews (4: 14-16; 5: 7-9), follows, and then the chant before the Gospel.

9. Then the narrative of the Lord's Passion according to John (18: 1–19: 42) is read in the same way as on the preceding Sunday.

10. After the reading of the Lord's Passion, the Priest gives a brief homily and, at its end, the faithful may be invited to spend a short time in prayer.

The Solemn Intercessions

11. The Liturgy of the Word concludes with the Solemn Intercessions, which take place in this way: the Deacon, if a Deacon is present, or if he is not, a lay minister, stands at the ambo, and sings or says the invitation in which the intention is expressed. Then all pray in silence for a while, and afterwards the Priest, standing at the chair or, if appropriate, at the altar, with hands extended, sings or says the prayer.

    The faithful may remain either kneeling or standing throughout the entire period of the prayers.

12. Before the Priest's prayer, in accord with tradition, it is permissible to use the Deacon's invitations Let us kneel — Let us stand, with all kneeling for silent prayer.

    Text with music:

    Let us kneel.   Let us stand.

    The Conferences of Bishops may provide other invitations to introduce the prayer of the Priest.

13. In a situation of grave public need, the Diocesan Bishop may permit or order the addition of a special intention.

    I. **For Holy Church**

    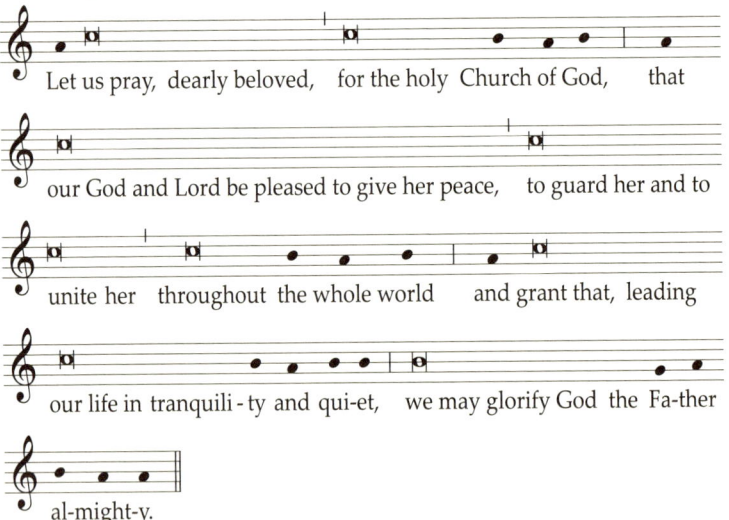

    The prayer is sung in the simple tone or, if the invitations Let us kneel — Let us stand are used, in the solemn tone.

Let us pray, dearly beloved, for the holy Church of God,
that our God and Lord be pleased to give her peace,
to guard her and to unite her throughout the whole world
and grant that, leading our life in tranquility and quiet,
we may glorify God the Father almighty.

Prayer in silence. Then the Priest says:

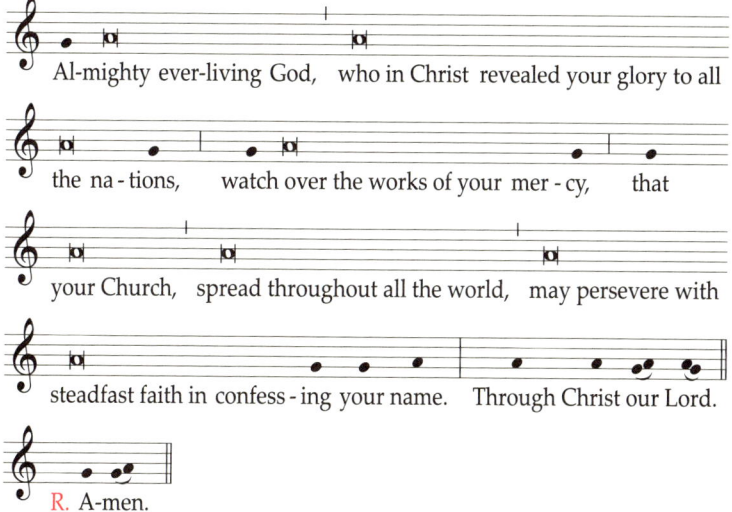

Almighty ever-living God,
who in Christ revealed your glory to all the nations,
watch over the works of your mercy,
that your Church, spread throughout all the world,
may persevere with steadfast faith in confessing your name.
Through Christ our Lord.
R. Amen.

II. For the Pope

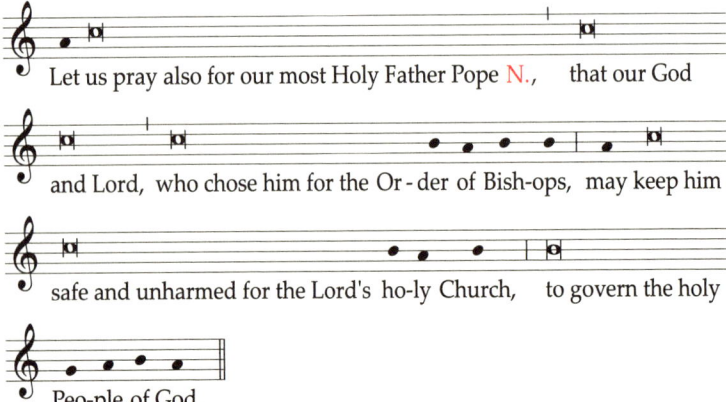

Let us pray also for our most Holy Father Pope N., that our God and Lord, who chose him for the Order of Bishops, may keep him safe and unharmed for the Lord's holy Church, to govern the holy People of God.

**Let us pray also for our most Holy Father Pope N.,
that our God and Lord,
who chose him for the Order of Bishops,
may keep him safe and unharmed for the Lord's holy Church,
to govern the holy People of God.**

Prayer in silence. Then the Priest says:

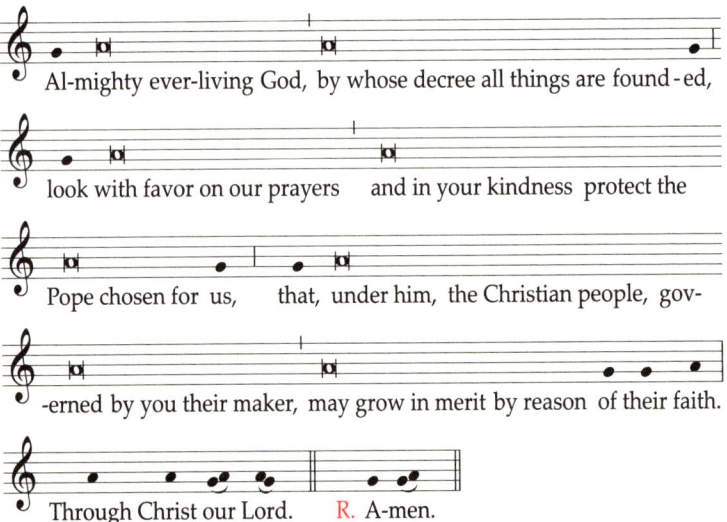

Almighty ever-living God, by whose decree all things are founded, look with favor on our prayers and in your kindness protect the Pope chosen for us, that, under him, the Christian people, governed by you their maker, may grow in merit by reason of their faith. Through Christ our Lord. R. Amen.

Almighty ever-living God,
by whose decree all things are founded,
look with favor on our prayers
and in your kindness protect the Pope chosen for us,
that, under him, the Christian people,
governed by you their maker,
may grow in merit by reason of their faith.
Through Christ our Lord.
R. Amen.

III. **For all orders and degrees of the faithful**

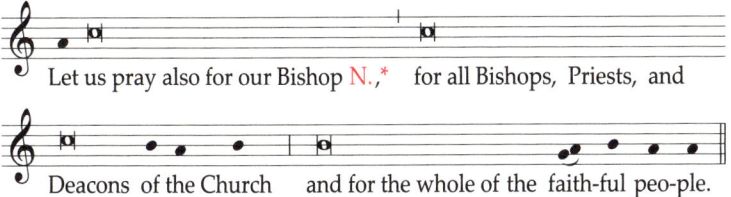

Let us pray also for our Bishop N.,* for all Bishops, Priests, and Deacons of the Church and for the whole of the faithful people.

Let us pray also for our Bishop N.,*
for all Bishops, Priests, and Deacons of the Church
and for the whole of the faithful people.

---

* Mention may be made here of the Coadjutor Bishop, or Auxiliary Bishops, as noted in the *General Instruction of the Roman Missal*, no. 149.

Prayer in silence. Then the Priest says:

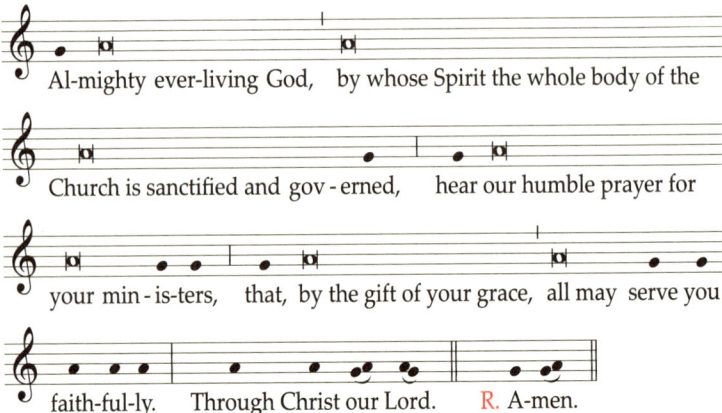

Al-mighty ever-living God, by whose Spirit the whole body of the Church is sanctified and gov-erned, hear our humble prayer for your min-is-ters, that, by the gift of your grace, all may serve you faith-ful-ly. Through Christ our Lord. R. A-men.

**Almighty ever-living God,
by whose Spirit the whole body of the Church
is sanctified and governed,
hear our humble prayer for your ministers,
that, by the gift of your grace,
all may serve you faithfully.
Through Christ our Lord.**
R. Amen.

IV. **For catechumens**

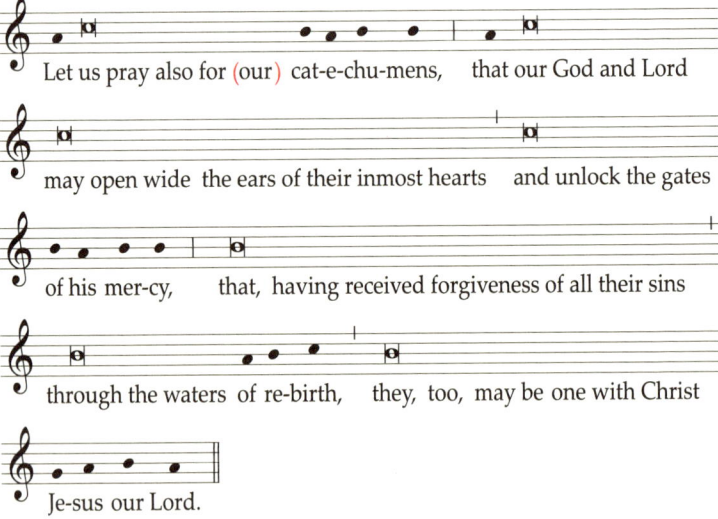

Let us pray also for (our) cat-e-chu-mens, that our God and Lord may open wide the ears of their inmost hearts and unlock the gates of his mer-cy, that, having received forgiveness of all their sins through the waters of re-birth, they, too, may be one with Christ Je-sus our Lord.

Let us pray also for (our) catechumens,
that our God and Lord
may open wide the ears of their inmost hearts
and unlock the gates of his mercy,
that, having received forgiveness of all their sins
through the waters of rebirth,
they, too, may be one with Christ Jesus our Lord.

Prayer in silence. Then the Priest says:

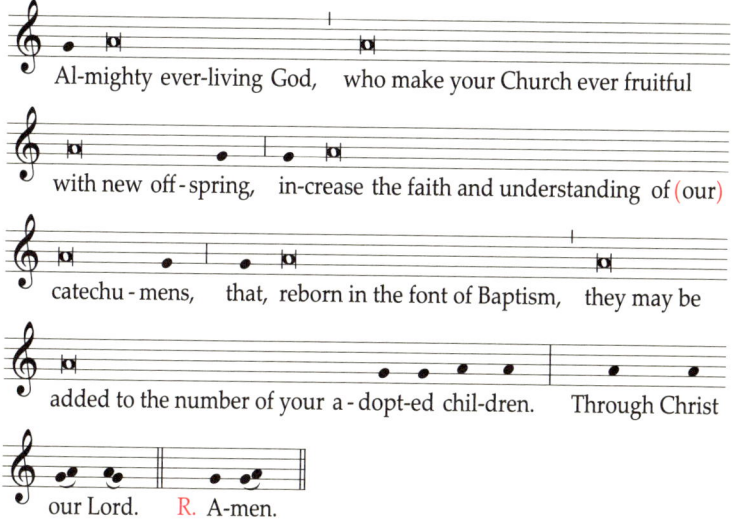

Al-mighty ever-living God, who make your Church ever fruitful with new off-spring, in-crease the faith and understanding of (our) catechu-mens, that, reborn in the font of Baptism, they may be added to the number of your a-dopt-ed chil-dren. Through Christ our Lord. R. A-men.

Almighty ever-living God,
who make your Church ever fruitful with new offspring,
increase the faith and understanding of (our) catechumens,
that, reborn in the font of Baptism,
they may be added to the number of your adopted children.
Through Christ our Lord.
R. Amen.

V. **For the unity of Christians**

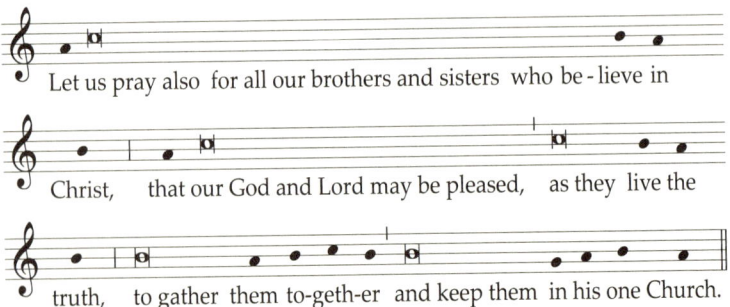

Let us pray also for all our brothers and sisters who believe in Christ, that our God and Lord may be pleased, as they live the truth, to gather them together and keep them in his one Church.

Prayer in silence. Then the Priest says:

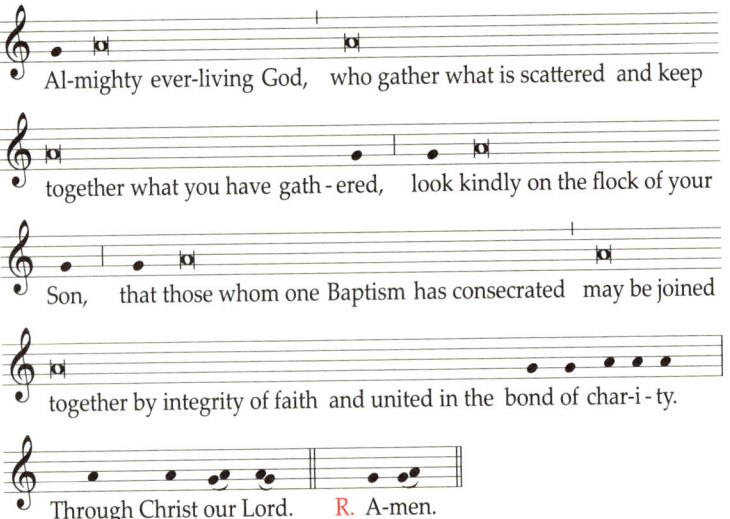

Almighty ever-living God,
who gather what is scattered
and keep together what you have gathered,
look kindly on the flock of your Son,
that those whom one Baptism has consecrated
may be joined together by integrity of faith
and united in the bond of charity.
Through Christ our Lord.
R. Amen.

VI. For the Jewish people

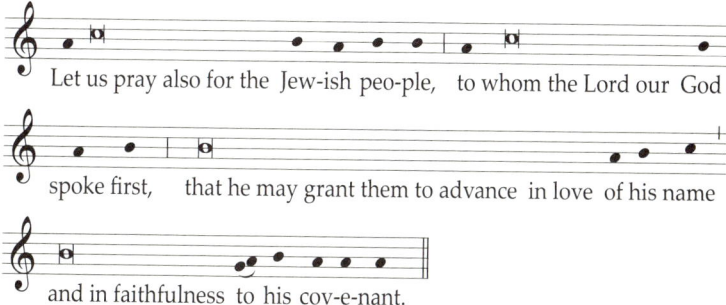

Let us pray also for the Jewish people, to whom the Lord our God spoke first, that he may grant them to advance in love of his name and in faithfulness to his cov-e-nant.

**Let us pray also for the Jewish people,
to whom the Lord our God spoke first,
that he may grant them to advance in love of his name
and in faithfulness to his covenant.**

Prayer in silence. Then the Priest says:

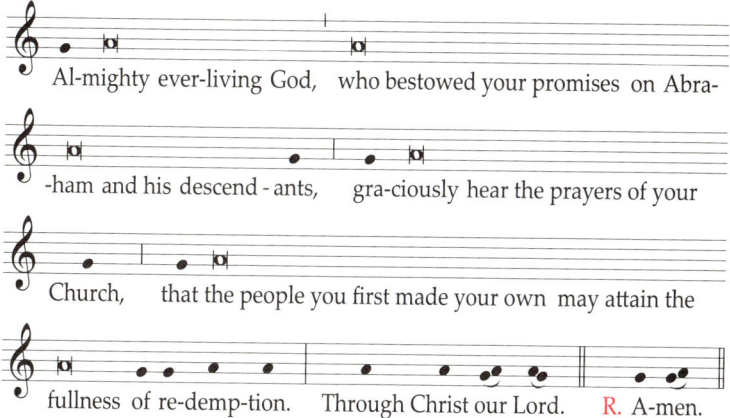

Al-mighty ever-living God, who bestowed your promises on Abra-ham and his descend-ants, gra-ciously hear the prayers of your Church, that the people you first made your own may attain the fullness of re-demp-tion. Through Christ our Lord. R. A-men.

**Almighty ever-living God,
who bestowed your promises on Abraham and his descendants,
graciously hear the prayers of your Church,
that the people you first made your own
may attain the fullness of redemption.
Through Christ our Lord.
R. Amen.**

VII. **For those who do not believe in Christ**

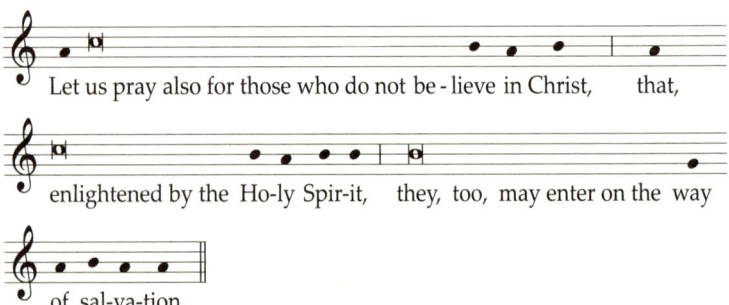

Let us pray also for those who do not believe in Christ, that, enlightened by the Holy Spirit, they, too, may enter on the way of salvation.

**Let us pray also for those who do not believe in Christ,
that, enlightened by the Holy Spirit,
they, too, may enter on the way of salvation.**

Prayer in silence. Then the Priest says:

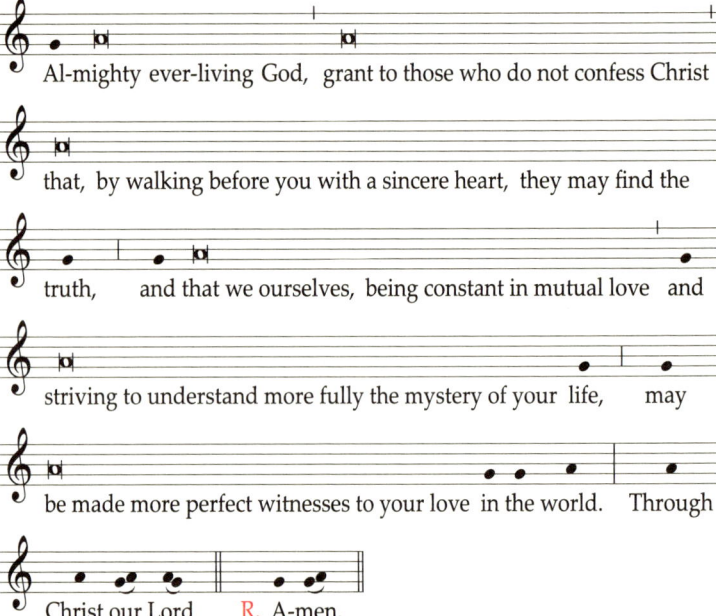

Almighty ever-living God, grant to those who do not confess Christ that, by walking before you with a sincere heart, they may find the truth, and that we ourselves, being constant in mutual love and striving to understand more fully the mystery of your life, may be made more perfect witnesses to your love in the world. Through Christ our Lord. R. Amen.

**Almighty ever-living God,
grant to those who do not confess Christ
that, by walking before you with a sincere heart,
they may find the truth
and that we ourselves, being constant in mutual love
and striving to understand more fully the mystery of your life,
may be made more perfect witnesses to your love in the world.
Through Christ our Lord.**
R. Amen.

VIII. For those who do not believe in God

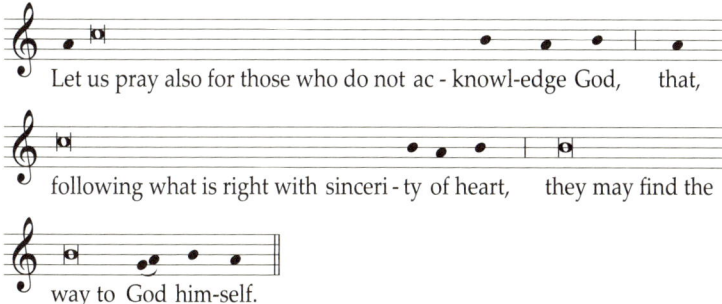

Let us pray also for those who do not ac-knowl-edge God, that, following what is right with sinceri-ty of heart, they may find the way to God him-self.

Let us pray also for those who do not acknowledge God, that, following what is right in sincerity of heart, they may find the way to God himself.

Prayer in silence. Then the Priest says:

Al-mighty ever-living God, who created all people to seek you al-ways by desiring you and, by finding you, come to rest, grant, we pray, that, despite every harmful obstacle, all may recognize the signs of your fatherly love and the witness of the good works done by those who believe in you, and so in gladness confess you, the one true God and Father of our hu-man race. Through Christ our Lord.

R. A-men.

Almighty ever-living God,
who created all people
to seek you always by desiring you
and, by finding you, come to rest,
grant, we pray,
that, despite every harmful obstacle,
all may recognize the signs of your fatherly love
and the witness of the good works
done by those who believe in you,
and so in gladness confess you,
the one true God and Father of our human race.
Through Christ our Lord.
℟. Amen.

IX. **For those in public office**

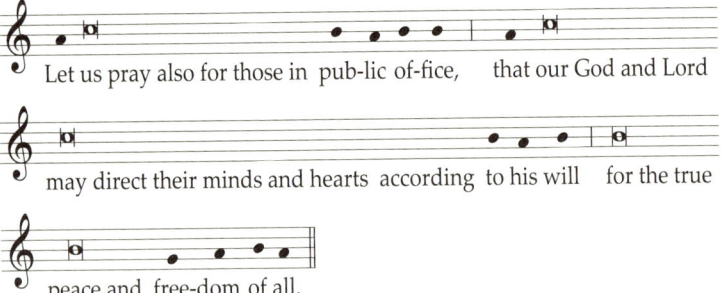

Let us pray also for those in pub-lic of-fice, that our God and Lord may direct their minds and hearts according to his will for the true peace and free-dom of all.

Let us pray also for those in public office,
that our God and Lord
may direct their minds and hearts according to his will
for the true peace and freedom of all.

THE PASSION OF THE LORD

Prayer in silence. Then the Priest says:

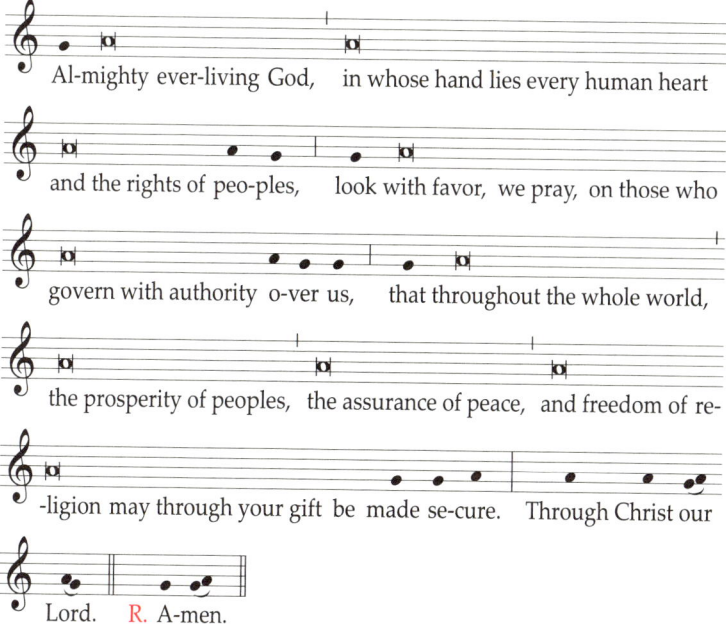

Almighty ever-living God,
in whose hand lies every human heart
and the rights of peoples,
look with favor, we pray,
on those who govern with authority over us,
that throughout the whole world,
the prosperity of peoples,
the assurance of peace,
and freedom of religion
may through your gift be made secure.
Through Christ our Lord.
R. Amen.

X. **For those in tribulation**

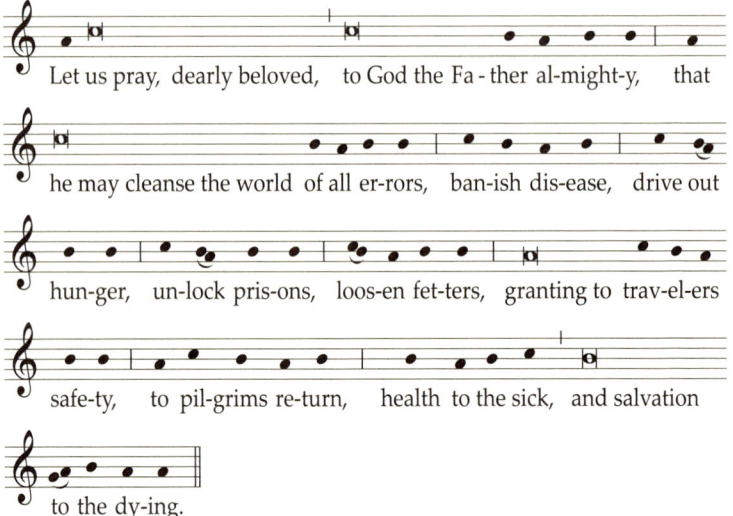

Let us pray, dearly beloved, to God the Father almighty, that he may cleanse the world of all errors, banish disease, drive out hunger, unlock prisons, loosen fetters, granting to travelers safety, to pilgrims return, health to the sick, and salvation to the dying.

**Let us pray, dearly beloved,
to God the Father almighty,
that he may cleanse the world of all errors,
banish disease, drive out hunger,
unlock prisons, loosen fetters,
granting to travelers safety, to pilgrims return,
health to the sick, and salvation to the dying.**

Prayer in silence. Then the Priest says:

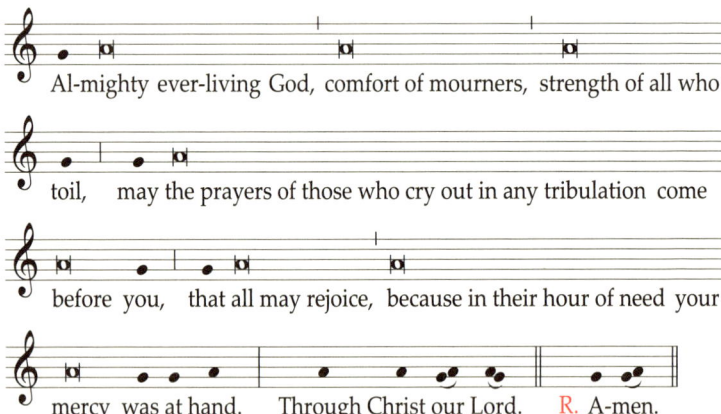

Almighty ever-living God, comfort of mourners, strength of all who toil, may the prayers of those who cry out in any tribulation come before you, that all may rejoice, because in their hour of need your mercy was at hand. Through Christ our Lord. R. Amen.

Almighty ever-living God,
comfort of mourners, strength of all who toil,
may the prayers of those who cry out in any tribulation
come before you,
that all may rejoice,
because in their hour of need
your mercy was at hand.
Through Christ our Lord.
R. Amen.

Second Part:
The Adoration of the Holy Cross

14. After the Solemn Intercessions, the solemn Adoration of the Holy Cross takes place. Of the two forms of the showing of the Cross presented here, the more appropriate one, according to pastoral needs, should be chosen.

The Showing of the Holy Cross

First Form

15. The Deacon accompanied by ministers, or another suitable minister, goes to the sacristy, from which, in procession, accompanied by two ministers with lighted candles, he carries the Cross, covered with a violet veil, through the church to the middle of the sanctuary.

The Priest, standing before the altar and facing the people, receives the Cross, uncovers a little of its upper part and elevates it while beginning the Ecce lignum Crucis (Behold the wood of the Cross). He is assisted in singing by the Deacon or, if need be, by the choir. All respond, Come, let us adore. At the end of the singing, all kneel and for a brief moment adore in silence, while the Priest stands and holds the Cross raised.

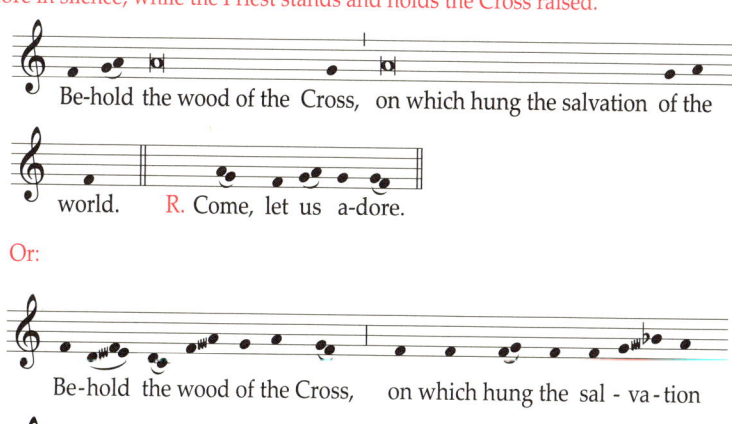

Be-hold the wood of the Cross, on which hung the salvation of the world. R. Come, let us a-dore.

Or:

Be-hold the wood of the Cross, on which hung the sal-va-tion of the world. R. Come, let us a-dore.

Or:

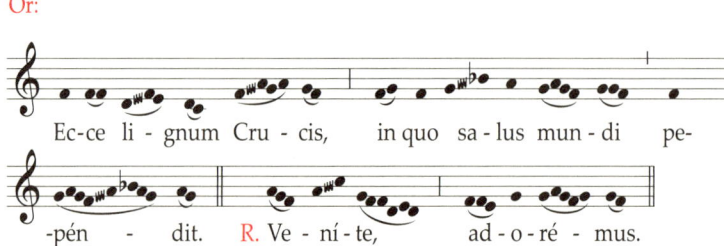

Ec-ce li-gnum Cru-cis, in quo sa-lus mun-di pe--pén - dit. R. Ve-ní-te, ad-o-ré-mus.

**Behold the wood of the Cross,
on which hung the salvation of the world.**
R. Come, let us adore.

Then the Priest uncovers the right arm of the Cross and again, raising up the Cross, begins, Behold the wood of the Cross and everything takes place as above.

Finally, he uncovers the Cross entirely and, raising it up, he begins the invitation Behold the wood of the Cross a third time and everything takes place like the first time.

Second Form

16. The Priest or the Deacon accompanied by ministers, or another suitable minister, goes to the door of the church, where he receives the unveiled Cross, and the ministers take lighted candles; then the procession sets off through the church to the sanctuary. Near the door, in the middle of the church and before the entrance of the sanctuary, the one who carries the Cross elevates it, singing, Behold the wood of the Cross, to which all respond, Come, let us adore. After each response all kneel and for a brief moment adore in silence, as above.

The Adoration of the Holy Cross

17. Then, accompanied by two ministers with lighted candles, the Priest or the Deacon carries the Cross to the entrance of the sanctuary or to another suitable place and there puts it down or hands it over to the ministers to hold. Candles are placed on the right and left sides of the Cross.

18. For the Adoration of the Cross, first the Priest Celebrant alone approaches, with the chasuble and his shoes removed, if appropriate. Then the clergy, the lay ministers, and the faithful approach, moving as if in procession, and showing reverence to the Cross by a simple genuflection or by some other sign appropriate to the usage of the region, for example, by kissing the Cross.

19. Only one Cross should be offered for adoration. If, because of the large number of people, it is not possible for all to approach individually, the Priest, after some of the clergy and faithful have adored, takes the Cross and, standing in the middle before the altar, invites the people in a few words to adore the Holy Cross and afterwards holds the Cross elevated higher for a brief time, for the faithful to adore it in silence.

20. While the adoration of the Holy Cross is taking place, the antiphon Crucem tuam adoramus (We adore your Cross, O Lord), the Reproaches, the hymn Crux fidelis (Faithful Cross) or other suitable chants are sung, during which all who have already adored the Cross remain seated.

Chants to Be Sung during the Adoration of the Holy Cross

Ant. We adore your Cross, O Lord,
we praise and glorify your holy Resurrection,
for behold, because of the wood of a tree
joy has come to the whole world.

May God have mercy on us and bless us; Cf. Ps 67 (66): 2
may he let his face shed its light upon us
and have mercy on us.

And the antiphon is repeated: We adore . . .

The Reproaches

Parts assigned to one of the two choirs separately are indicated by the numbers 1 (first choir) and 2 (second choir); parts sung by both choirs together are marked: 1 and 2. Some of the verses may also be sung by two cantors.

I

1 and 2 My people, what have I done to you?
Or how have I grieved you? Answer me!
1   Because I led you out of the land of Egypt,
    you have prepared a Cross for your Savior.
1   Hagios o Theos,
2   Holy is God,
1   Hagios Ischyros,
2   Holy and Mighty,
1   Hagios Athanatos, eleison himas.
2   Holy and Immortal One, have mercy on us.

1 and 2 Because I led you out through the desert forty years
and fed you with manna and brought you into a land of plenty,
you have prepared a Cross for your Savior.
1   Hagios o Theos,
2   Holy is God,
1   Hagios Ischyros,
2   Holy and Mighty,
1   Hagios Athanatos, eleison himas.
2   Holy and Immortal One, have mercy on us.

1 and 2 What more should I have done for you and have not done?
Indeed, I planted you as my most beautiful chosen vine
and you have turned very bitter for me,
for in my thirst you gave me vinegar to drink
and with a lance you pierced your Savior's side.
1   Hagios o Theos,
2   Holy is God,

1 Hagios Ischyros,
2 Holy and Mighty,
1 Hagios Athanatos, eleison himas.
2 Holy and Immortal One, have mercy on us.

II

Cantors:
> I scourged Egypt for your sake with its firstborn sons,
> and you scourged me and handed me over.

1 and 2 repeat:
> My people, what have I done to you?
> Or how have I grieved you? Answer me!

Cantors:
> I led you out from Egypt as Pharoah lay sunk in the Red Sea,
> and you handed me over to the chief priests.

1 and 2 repeat:
> My people . . .

Cantors:
> I opened up the sea before you,
> and you opened my side with a lance.

1 and 2 repeat:
> My people . . .

Cantors:
> I went before you in a pillar of cloud,
> and you led me into Pilate's palace.

1 and 2 repeat:
> My people . . .

Cantors:
> I fed you with manna in the desert,
> and on me you rained blows and lashes.

1 and 2 repeat:
> My people . . .

Cantors:
> I gave you saving water from the rock to drink,
> and for drink you gave me gall and vinegar.

1 and 2 repeat:
> My people . . .

Cantors:
> I struck down for you the kings of the Canaanites,
> and you struck my head with a reed.

THE PASSION OF THE LORD   333

1 and 2 repeat:
>My people . . .

Cantors:
>I put in your hand a royal scepter,
>and you put on my head a crown of thorns.

1 and 2 repeat:
>My people . . .

Cantors:
>I exalted you with great power,
>and you hung me on the scaffold of the Cross.

1 and 2 repeat:
>My people . . .

Hymn

All:
>Faithful Cross the Saints rely on,
>Noble tree beyond compare!
>Never was there such a scion,
>Never leaf or flower so rare.
>Sweet the timber, sweet the iron,
>Sweet the burden that they bear!

Cantors:
>Sing, my tongue, in exultation
>Of our banner and device!
>Make a solemn proclamation
>Of a triumph and its price:
>How the Savior of creation
>Conquered by his sacrifice!

All:
>Faithful Cross the Saints rely on,
>Noble tree beyond compare!
>Never was there such a scion,
>Never leaf or flower so rare.

Cantors:
>For, when Adam first offended,
>Eating that forbidden fruit,
>Not all hopes of glory ended
>With the serpent at the root:
>Broken nature would be mended
>By a second tree and shoot.

All:
> Sweet the timber, sweet the iron,
> Sweet the burden that they bear!

Cantors:
> Thus the tempter was outwitted
> By a wisdom deeper still:
> Remedy and ailment fitted,
> Means to cure and means to kill;
> That the world might be acquitted,
> Christ would do his Father's will.

All:
> Faithful Cross the Saints rely on,
> Noble tree beyond compare!
> Never was there such a scion,
> Never leaf or flower so rare.

Cantors:
> So the Father, out of pity
> For our self-inflicted doom,
> Sent him from the heavenly city
> When the holy time had come:
> He, the Son and the Almighty,
> Took our flesh in Mary's womb.

All:
> Sweet the timber, sweet the iron,
> Sweet the burden that they bear!

Cantors:
> Hear a tiny baby crying,
> Founder of the seas and strands;
> See his virgin Mother tying
> Cloth around his feet and hands;
> Find him in a manger lying
> Tightly wrapped in swaddling-bands!

All:
> Faithful Cross the Saints rely on,
> Noble tree beyond compare!
> Never was there such a scion,
> Never leaf or flower so rare.

Cantors:
> So he came, the long-expected,
> Not in glory, not to reign;
> Only born to be rejected,
> Choosing hunger, toil and pain,

Till the scaffold was erected
And the Paschal Lamb was slain.

All:

Sweet the timber, sweet the iron,
Sweet the burden that they bear!

Cantors:

No disgrace was too abhorrent:
Nailed and mocked and parched he died;
Blood and water, double warrant,
Issue from his wounded side,
Washing in a mighty torrent
Earth and stars and oceantide.

All:

Faithful Cross the Saints rely on,
Noble tree beyond compare!
Never was there such a scion,
Never leaf or flower so rare.

Cantors:

Lofty timber, smooth your roughness,
Flex your boughs for blossoming;
Let your fibers lose their toughness,
Gently let your tendrils cling;
Lay aside your native gruffness,
Clasp the body of your King!

All:

Sweet the timber, sweet the iron,
Sweet the burden that they bear!

Cantors:

Noblest tree of all created,
Richly jeweled and embossed:
Post by Lamb's blood consecrated;
Spar that saves the tempest-tossed;
Scaffold-beam which, elevated,
Carries what the world has cost!

All:

Faithful Cross the Saints rely on,
Noble tree beyond compare!
Never was there such a scion,
Never leaf or flower so rare.

The following conclusion is never to be omitted:

All:
Wisdom, power, and adoration
To the blessed Trinity
For redemption and salvation
Through the Paschal Mystery,
Now, in every generation,
And for all eternity. Amen.

In accordance with local circumstances or popular traditions and if it is pastorally appropriate, the Stabat Mater may be sung, as found in the Graduale Romanum, or another suitable chant in memory of the compassion of the Blessed Virgin Mary.

21. When the adoration has been concluded, the Cross is carried by the Deacon or a minister to its place at the altar. Lighted candles are placed around or on the altar or near the Cross.

Third Part:
Holy Communion

22. A cloth is spread on the altar, and a corporal and the Missal put in place. Meanwhile the Deacon or, if there is no Deacon, the Priest himself, putting on a humeral veil, brings the Blessed Sacrament back from the place of repose to the altar by a shorter route, while all stand in silence. Two ministers with lighted candles accompany the Blessed Sacrament and place their candlesticks around or upon the altar.

When the Deacon, if a Deacon is present, has placed the Blessed Sacrament upon the altar and uncovered the ciborium, the Priest goes to the altar and genuflects.

23. Then the Priest, with hands joined, says aloud:

**At the Savior's command
and formed by divine teaching,
we dare to say:**

The Priest, with hands extended says, and all present continue:

**Our Father, who art in heaven,
hallowed be thy name;
thy kingdom come,
thy will be done
on earth as it is in heaven.
Give us this day our daily bread,
and forgive us our trespasses,
as we forgive those who trespass against us;
and lead us not into temptation,
but deliver us from evil.**

Text with music, p. 663.

24. With hands extended, the Priest continues alone:

> Deliver us, Lord, we pray, from every evil,
> graciously grant peace in our days,
> that, by the help of your mercy,
> we may be always free from sin
> and safe from all distress,
> as we await the blessed hope
> and the coming of our Savior, Jesus Christ.

He joins his hands.

The people conclude the prayer, acclaiming:

> For the kingdom, the power and the glory are yours now and for ever.

Text with music, p. 664.

25. Then the Priest, with hands joined, says quietly:

> May the receiving of your Body and Blood,
> Lord Jesus Christ,
> not bring me to judgment and condemnation,
> but through your loving mercy
> be for me protection in mind and body
> and a healing remedy.

26. The Priest then genuflects, takes a particle, and, holding it slightly raised over the ciborium, while facing the people, says aloud:

> Behold the Lamb of God,
> behold him who takes away the sins of the world.
> Blessed are those called to the supper of the Lamb.

And together with the people he adds once:

> Lord, I am not worthy
> that you should enter under my roof,
> but only say the word
> and my soul shall be healed.

27. And facing the altar, he reverently consumes the Body of Christ, saying quietly: May the Body of Christ keep me safe for eternal life.

28. He then proceeds to distribute Communion to the faithful. During Communion, Psalm 22 (21) or another appropriate chant may be sung.

29. When the distribution of Communion has been completed, the ciborium is taken by the Deacon or another suitable minister to a place prepared outside the church or, if circumstances so require, it is placed in the tabernacle.

30. Then the Priest says: Let us pray, and, after a period of sacred silence, if circumstances so suggest, has been observed, he says the Prayer after Communion.

Almighty ever-living God,
who have restored us to life
by the blessed Death and Resurrection of your Christ,
preserve in us the work of your mercy,
that, by partaking of this mystery,
we may have a life unceasingly devoted to you.
Through Christ our Lord.
R. Amen.

31. For the Dismissal the Deacon or, if there is no Deacon, the Priest himself, may say the invitation Bow down for the blessing.

    Then the Priest, standing facing the people and extending his hands over them, says this Prayer over the People:

    May abundant blessing, O Lord, we pray,
    descend upon your people,
    who have honored the Death of your Son
    in the hope of their resurrection:
    may pardon come,
    comfort be given,
    holy faith increase,
    and everlasting redemption be made secure.
    Through Christ our Lord.
    R. Amen.

32. And all, after genuflecting to the Cross, depart in silence.

33. After the celebration, the altar is stripped, but the Cross remains on the altar with two or four candlesticks.

34. Vespers (Evening Prayer) is not celebrated by those who have been present at the solemn afternoon liturgical celebration.

HOLY SATURDAY

1. On Holy Saturday the Church waits at the Lord's tomb in prayer and fasting, meditating on his Passion and Death and on his Descent into Hell, and awaiting his Resurrection.

2. The Church abstains from the Sacrifice of the Mass, with the sacred table left bare, until after the solemn Vigil, that is, the anticipation by night of the Resurrection, when the time comes for paschal joys, the abundance of which overflows to occupy fifty days.

3. Holy Communion may only be given on this day as Viaticum.

EASTER TIME

EASTER SUNDAY OF THE RESURRECTION OF THE LORD

THE EASTER VIGIL IN THE HOLY NIGHT

1. By most ancient tradition, this is the night of keeping vigil for the Lord (Ex 12: 42), in which, following the Gospel admonition (Lk 12: 35-37), the faithful, carrying lighted lamps in their hands, should be like those looking for the Lord when he returns, so that at his coming he may find them awake and have them sit at his table.

2. Of this night's Vigil, which is the greatest and most noble of all solemnities, there is to be only one celebration in each church. It is arranged, moreover, in such a way that after the Lucernarium and Easter Proclamation (which constitutes the first part of this Vigil), Holy Church meditates on the wonders the Lord God has done for his people from the beginning, trusting in his word and promise (the second part, that is, the Liturgy of the Word) until, as day approaches, with new members reborn in Baptism (the third part), the Church is called to the table the Lord has prepared for his people, the memorial of his Death and Resurrection until he comes again (the fourth part).

3. The entire celebration of the Easter Vigil must take place during the night, so that it begins after nightfall and ends before daybreak on the Sunday.

4. The Mass of the Vigil, even if it is celebrated before midnight, is a paschal Mass of the Sunday of the Resurrection.

5. Anyone who participates in the Mass of the night may receive Communion again at Mass during the day. A Priest who celebrates or concelebrates the Mass of the night may again celebrate or concelebrate Mass during the day.

    The Easter Vigil takes the place of the Office of Readings.

6. The Priest is usually assisted by a Deacon. If, however, there is no Deacon, the duties of his Order, except those indicated below, are assumed by the Priest Celebrant or by a concelebrant.

    The Priest and Deacon vest as at Mass, in white vestments.

7. Candles should be prepared for all who participate in the Vigil. The lights of the church are extinguished.

First Part:
The Solemn Beginning of the Vigil or Lucernarium

The Blessing of the Fire and Preparation of the Candle

8. A blazing fire is prepared in a suitable place outside the church. When the people are gathered there, the Priest approaches with the ministers, one of whom carries the paschal candle. The processional cross and candles are not carried.

   Where, however, a fire cannot be lit outside the church, the rite is carried out as in no. 13, below.

9. The Priest and faithful sign themselves while the Priest says: In the name of the Father, and of the Son, and of the Holy Spirit, and then he greets the assembled people in the usual way and briefly instructs them about the night vigil in these or similar words:

   **Dear brethren (brothers and sisters),
   on this most sacred night,
   in which our Lord Jesus Christ
   passed over from death to life,
   the Church calls upon her sons and daughters,
   scattered throughout the world,
   to come together to watch and pray.
   If we keep the memorial
   of the Lord's paschal solemnity in this way,
   listening to his word and celebrating his mysteries,
   then we shall have the sure hope
   of sharing his triumph over death
   and living with him in God.**

10. Then the Priest blesses the fire, saying with hands extended:

    Let us pray.

    **O God, who through your Son
    bestowed upon the faithful the fire of your glory,
    sanctify ✠ this new fire, we pray,
    and grant that,
    by these paschal celebrations,
    we may be so inflamed with heavenly desires,
    that with minds made pure
    we may attain festivities of unending splendor.
    Through Christ our Lord.**
    R. **Amen.**

11. After the blessing of the new fire, one of the ministers brings the paschal candle to the Priest, who cuts a cross into the candle with a stylus. Then he makes the Greek letter Alpha above the cross, the letter Omega below, and the four numerals of the current year between the arms of the cross, saying meanwhile:

1. **Christ yesterday and today**
   (he cuts a vertical line);
2. **the Beginning and the End**
   (he cuts a horizontal line);
3. **the Alpha**
   (he cuts the letter Alpha above the vertical line);
4. **and the Omega**
   (he cuts the letter Omega below the vertical line).
5. **All time belongs to him**
   (he cuts the first numeral of the current year in the upper left corner of the cross);
6. **and all the ages**
   (he cuts the second numeral of the current year in the upper right corner of the cross).
7. **To him be glory and power**
   (he cuts the third numeral of the current year in the lower left corner of the cross);
8. **through every age and for ever. Amen.**
   (he cuts the fourth numeral of the current year in the lower right corner of the cross).

12. When the cutting of the cross and of the other signs has been completed, the Priest may insert five grains of incense into the candle in the form of a cross, meanwhile saying:

1. **By his holy**
2. **and glorious wounds,**
3. **may Christ the Lord**
4. **guard us**
5. **and protect us. Amen.**

1

4 2 5

3

13. Where, because of difficulties that may occur, a fire is not lit, the blessing of fire is adapted to the circumstances. When the people are gathered in the church as on other occasions, the Priest comes to the door of the church, along with the ministers carrying the paschal candle. The people, insofar as is possible, turn to face the Priest.

    The greeting and address take place as in no. 9 above; then the fire is blessed and the candle is prepared, as above in nos. 10-12.

14. The Priest lights the paschal candle from the new fire, saying:

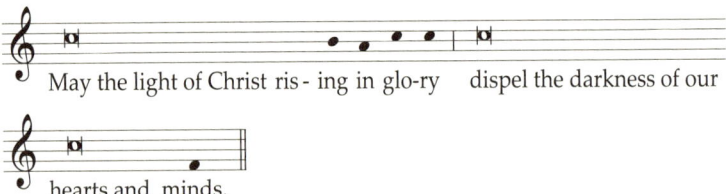
May the light of Christ rising in glory dispel the darkness of our hearts and minds.

**May the light of Christ rising in glory
dispel the darkness of our hearts and minds.**

As regards the preceding elements, Conferences of Bishops may also establish other forms more adapted to the culture of the different peoples.

Procession

15. When the candle has been lit, one of the ministers takes burning coals from the fire and places them in the thurible, and the Priest puts incense into it in the usual way. The Deacon or, if there is no Deacon, another suitable minister, takes the paschal candle and a procession forms. The thurifer with the smoking thurible precedes the Deacon or other minister who carries the paschal candle. After them follows the Priest with the ministers and the people, all holding in their hands unlit candles.

At the door of the church the Deacon, standing and raising up the candle, sings:

The Light of Christ.

Or:

Lu-men Chris-ti.

The Light of Christ.

And all reply:

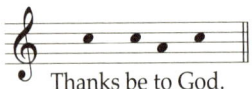
Thanks be to God.

Or:

De-o grá-ti-as.

Thanks be to God.

The Priest lights his candle from the flame of the paschal candle.

16. Then the Deacon moves forward to the middle of the church and, standing and raising up the candle, sings a second time:

The Light of Christ.

And all reply:

Thanks be to God.

All light their candles from the flame of the paschal candle and continue in procession.

17. When the Deacon arrives before the altar, he stands facing the people, raises up the candle and sings a third time:

The Light of Christ.

And all reply:

Thanks be to God.

Then the Deacon places the paschal candle on a large candlestand prepared next to the ambo or in the middle of the sanctuary.

And lights are lit throughout the church, except for the altar candles.

The Easter Proclamation
(Exsultet)

18. Arriving at the altar, the Priest goes to his chair, gives his candle to a minister, puts incense into the thurible and blesses the incense as at the Gospel at Mass. The Deacon goes to the Priest and saying, Your blessing, Father, asks for and receives a blessing from the Priest, who says in a low voice:

May the Lord be in your heart and on your lips,
that you may proclaim his paschal praise worthily and well,
in the name of the Father and of the Son, ✠ and of the Holy Spirit.

The Deacon replies: **Amen.**

This blessing is omitted if the Proclamation is made by someone who is not a Deacon.

19. The Deacon, after incensing the book and the candle, proclaims the Easter Proclamation (Exsultet) at the ambo or at a lectern, with all standing and holding lighted candles in their hands.

The Easter Proclamation may be made, in the absence of a Deacon, by the Priest himself or by another concelebrating Priest. If, however, because of necessity, a lay cantor sings the Proclamation, the words Therefore, dearest friends up to the end of the invitation are omitted, along with the greeting The Lord be with you.

The Proclamation may also be sung in the shorter form (pp. 357-361).

Longer Form of the Easter Proclamation

Text without music:

Longer Form of the Easter Proclamation

Exult, let them exult, the hosts of heaven,
exult, let Angel ministers of God exult,
let the trumpet of salvation
sound aloud our mighty King's triumph!
Be glad, let earth be glad, as glory floods her,
ablaze with light from her eternal King,
let all corners of the earth be glad,
knowing an end to gloom and darkness.
Rejoice, let Mother Church also rejoice,
arrayed with the lightning of his glory,
let this holy building shake with joy,
filled with the mighty voices of the peoples.

(Therefore, dearest friends,
standing in the awesome glory of this holy light,
invoke with me, I ask you,
the mercy of God almighty,
that he, who has been pleased to number me,
though unworthy, among the Levites,
may pour into me his light unshadowed,
that I may sing this candle's perfect praises).

(V. The Lord be with you.
R. And with your spirit.)

V. Lift up your hearts.
R. We lift them up to the Lord.

V. Let us give thanks to the Lord our God.
R. It is right and just.

It is truly right and just,
with ardent love of mind and heart
and with devoted service of our voice,
to acclaim our God invisible, the almighty Father,
and Jesus Christ, our Lord, his Son, his Only Begotten.

Who for our sake paid Adam's debt to the eternal Father,
and, pouring out his own dear Blood,
wiped clean the record of our ancient sinfulness.

These, then, are the feasts of Passover,
in which is slain the Lamb, the one true Lamb,
whose Blood anoints the doorposts of believers.

This is the night,
when once you led our forebears, Israel's children,
from slavery in Egypt
and made them pass dry-shod through the Red Sea.

This is the night
that with a pillar of fire
banished the darkness of sin.

This is the night
that even now, throughout the world,
sets Christian believers apart from worldly vices
and from the gloom of sin,
leading them to grace
and joining them to his holy ones.

This is the night,
when Christ broke the prison-bars of death
and rose victorious from the underworld.

Our birth would have been no gain,
had we not been redeemed.
O wonder of your humble care for us!
O love, O charity beyond all telling,
to ransom a slave you gave away your Son!

O truly necessary sin of Adam,
destroyed completely by the Death of Christ!

O happy fault
that earned so great, so glorious a Redeemer!

O truly blessed night,
worthy alone to know the time and hour
when Christ rose from the underworld!

This is the night
of which it is written:
The night shall be as bright as day,
dazzling is the night for me,
and full of gladness.

The sanctifying power of this night
dispels wickedness, washes faults away,
restores innocence to the fallen, and joy to mourners,
drives out hatred, fosters concord, and brings down the mighty.

On this, your night of grace, O holy Father,
accept this candle, a solemn offering,
the work of bees and of your servants' hands,
an evening sacrifice of praise,
this gift from your most holy Church.

But now we know the praises of this pillar,
which glowing fire ignites for God's honor,
a fire into many flames divided,
yet never dimmed by sharing of its light,
for it is fed by melting wax,
drawn out by mother bees
to build a torch so precious.

O truly blessed night,
when things of heaven are wed to those of earth,
and divine to the human.

Therefore, O Lord,
we pray you that this candle,
hallowed to the honor of your name,
may persevere undimmed,
to overcome the darkness of this night.
Receive it as a pleasing fragrance,
and let it mingle with the lights of heaven.
May this flame be found still burning
by the Morning Star:
the one Morning Star who never sets,
Christ your Son,
who, coming back from death's domain,
has shed his peaceful light on humanity,
and lives and reigns for ever and ever.
R. Amen.

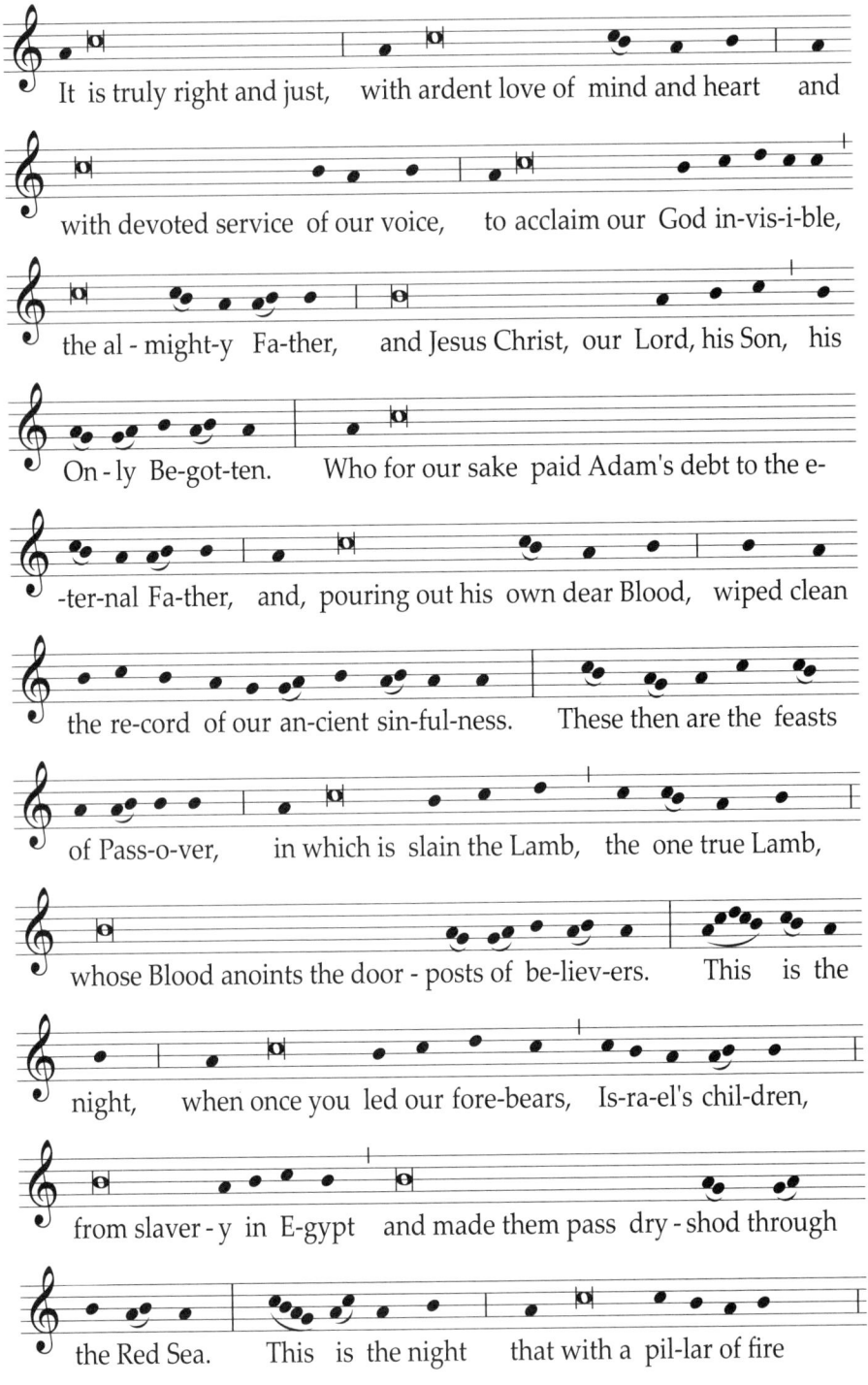

THE EASTER VIGIL

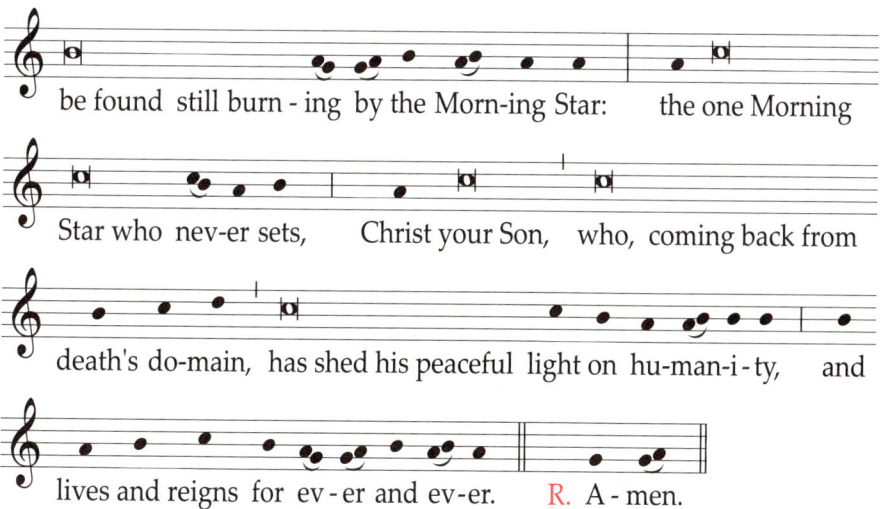

Shorter Form of the Easter Proclamation

E xult, let them exult, the hosts of heaven,
exult, let Angel ministers of God exult,
let the trumpet of salvation
sound aloud our mighty King's triumph!
Be glad, let earth be glad, as glory floods her,
ablaze with light from her eternal King,
let all corners of the earth be glad,
knowing an end to gloom and darkness.
Rejoice, let Mother Church also rejoice,
arrayed with the lightning of his glory,
let this holy building shake with joy,
filled with the mighty voices of the peoples.

(V. The Lord be with you.
R. And with your spirit.)

V. Lift up your hearts.
R. We lift them up to the Lord.

V. Let us give thanks to the Lord our God.
R. It is right and just.

It is truly right and just,
with ardent love of mind and heart
and with devoted service of our voice,
to acclaim our God invisible, the almighty Father,
and Jesus Christ, our Lord, his Son, his Only Begotten.

Who for our sake paid Adam's debt to the eternal Father,
and, pouring out his own dear Blood,
wiped clean the record of our ancient sinfulness.

These then are the feasts of Passover,
in which is slain the Lamb, the one true Lamb,
whose Blood anoints the doorposts of believers.

This is the night,
when once you led our forebears, Israel's children,
from slavery in Egypt
and made them pass dry-shod through the Red Sea.

This is the night
that with a pillar of fire
banished the darkness of sin.

This is the night
that which even now, throughout the world,
sets Christian believers apart from worldly vices
and from the gloom of sin,
leading them to grace
and joining them to his holy ones.

This is the night,
when Christ broke the prison-bars of death
and rose victorious from the underworld.

O wonder of your humble care for us!
O love, O charity beyond all telling,
to ransom a slave you gave away your Son!

O truly necessary sin of Adam,
destroyed completely by the Death of Christ!

O happy fault
that earned so great, so glorious a Redeemer!
The sanctifying power of this night
dispels wickedness, washes faults away,
restores innocence to the fallen, and joy to mourners.

O truly blessed night,
when things of heaven are wed to those of earth
and divine to the human.

On this, your night of grace, O holy Father,
accept this candle, a solemn offering,
the work of bees and of your servants' hands,
an evening sacrifice of praise,
this gift from your most holy Church.

Therefore, O Lord,
we pray you that this candle,
hallowed to the honor of your name,
may persevere undimmed,
to overcome the darkness of this night.
Receive it as a pleasing fragrance,
and let it mingle with the lights of heaven.
May this flame be found still burning
by the Morning Star:
the one Morning Star who never sets,
Christ your Son,
who, coming back from death's domain,
has shed his peaceful light on humanity,
and lives and reigns for ever and ever.
R. Amen.

Second Part:
The Liturgy of the Word

20. In this Vigil, the mother of all Vigils, nine readings are provided, namely seven from the Old Testament and two from the New (the Epistle and Gospel), all of which should be read whenever this can be done, so that the character of the Vigil, which demands an extended period of time, may be preserved.

21. Nevertheless, where more serious pastoral circumstances demand it, the number of readings from the Old Testament may be reduced, always bearing in mind that the reading of the Word of God is a fundamental part of this Easter Vigil. At least three readings should be read from the Old Testament, both from the Law and from the Prophets, and their respective Responsorial Psalms should be sung. Never, moreover, should the reading of chapter 14 of Exodus with its canticle be omitted.

22. After setting aside their candles, all sit. Before the readings begin, the Priest instructs the people in these or similar words:

**Dear brethren (brothers and sisters),
now that we have begun our solemn Vigil,
let us listen with quiet hearts to the Word of God.
Let us meditate on how God in times past saved his people
and in these, the last days, has sent us his Son as our Redeemer.
Let us pray that our God may complete this paschal work
   of salvation
by the fullness of redemption.**

23. Then the readings follow. A reader goes to the ambo and proclaims the reading. Afterwards a psalmist or a cantor sings or says the Psalm with the people making the response. Then all rise, the Priest says, Let us pray and, after all have prayed for a while in silence, he says the prayer corresponding to the reading. In place of the Responsorial Psalm a period of sacred silence may be observed, in which case the pause after Let us pray is omitted.

Prayers after the Readings

24. After the first reading (On creation: Gn 1: 1–2: 2 or 1: 1, 26-31a) and the Psalm (104 [103] or 33 [32]).

Let us pray.

**Almighty ever-living God,
who are wonderful in the ordering of all your works,
may those you have redeemed understand
that there exists nothing more marvelous
than the world's creation in the beginning
except that, at the end of the ages,
Christ our Passover has been sacrificed.
Who lives and reigns for ever and ever.
R. Amen.**

Or, On the creation of man:

**O God, who wonderfully created human nature
and still more wonderfully redeemed it,
grant us, we pray,
to set our minds against the enticements of sin,
that we may merit to attain eternal joys.
Through Christ our Lord.
R. Amen.**

25. After the second reading (On Abraham's sacrifice: Gn 22: 1-18 or 1-2, 9a, 10-13, 15-18) and the Psalm (16 [15]).

Let us pray.

**O God, supreme Father of the faithful,
who increase the children of your promise
by pouring out the grace of adoption
throughout the whole world
and who through the Paschal Mystery
make your servant Abraham father of nations,
as once you swore,
grant, we pray,
that your peoples may enter worthily
into the grace to which you call them.
Through Christ our Lord.
R. Amen.**

26. After the third reading (On the passage through the Red Sea: Ex 14: 15-15: 1) and its canticle (Ex 15).

Let us pray.

O God, whose ancient wonders
remain undimmed in splendor even in our day,
for what you once bestowed on a single people,
freeing them from Pharaoh's persecution
by the power of your right hand,
now you bring about as the salvation of the nations
through the waters of rebirth,
grant, we pray, that the whole world
may become children of Abraham
and inherit the dignity of Israel's birthright.
Through Christ our Lord.
R. Amen.

Or:

O God, who by the light of the New Testament
have unlocked the meaning
of wonders worked in former times,
so that the Red Sea prefigures the sacred font
and the nation delivered from slavery
foreshadows the Christian people,
grant, we pray, that all nations,
obtaining the privilege of Israel by merit of faith,
may be reborn by partaking of your Spirit.
Through Christ our Lord.
R. Amen.

27. After the fourth reading (On the new Jerusalem: Is 54: 5-14) and the Psalm (30 [29]).

Let us pray.

Almighty ever-living God,
surpass, for the honor of your name,
what you pledged to the Patriarchs by reason of their faith,
and through sacred adoption increase the children of
    your promise,
so that what the Saints of old never doubted would come to pass
your Church may now see in great part fulfilled.
Through Christ our Lord.
R. Amen.

THE EASTER VIGIL

Alternatively, other prayers may be used from among those which follow the readings that have been omitted.

28. After the fifth reading (On salvation freely offered to all: Is 55: 1-11) and the canticle (Is 12).

    Let us pray.

    **Almighty ever-living God,
    sole hope of the world,
    who by the preaching of your Prophets
    unveiled the mysteries of this present age,
    graciously increase the longing of your people,
    for only at the prompting of your grace
    do the faithful progress in any kind of virtue.
    Through Christ our Lord.**
    R. Amen.

29. After the sixth reading (On the fountain of wisdom: Bar 3: 9-15, 31–4: 4) and the Psalm (19 [18]).

    Let us pray.

    **O God, who constantly increase your Church
    by your call to the nations,
    graciously grant
    to those you wash clean in the waters of Baptism
    the assurance of your unfailing protection.
    Through Christ our Lord.**
    R. Amen.

30. After the seventh reading (On a new heart and new spirit: Ez 36: 16-28) and the Psalm (42-43 [41-42]).

    Let us pray.

    **O God of unchanging power and eternal light,
    look with favor on the wondrous mystery of the whole Church
    and serenely accomplish the work of human salvation,
    which you planned from all eternity;
    may the whole world know and see
    that what was cast down is raised up,
    what had become old is made new,
    and all things are restored to integrity through Christ,
    just as by him they came into being.
    Who lives and reigns for ever and ever.**
    R. Amen.

    Or:

**O God, who by the pages of both Testaments
instruct and prepare us to celebrate the Paschal Mystery,
grant that we may comprehend your mercy,
so that the gifts we receive from you this night
may confirm our hope of the gifts to come.
Through Christ our Lord.
R. Amen.**

31. After the last reading from the Old Testament with its Responsorial Psalm and its prayer, the altar candles are lit, and the Priest intones the hymn Gloria in excelsis Deo (Glory to God in the highest), which is taken up by all, while bells are rung, according to local custom.

Gló-ri - a   in   ex - cél - sis   De - o.

32. When the hymn is concluded, the Priest says the Collect in the usual way.

Let us pray.

**O God, who make this most sacred night radiant
with the glory of the Lord's Resurrection,
stir up in your Church a spirit of adoption,
so that, renewed in body and mind,
we may render you undivided service.
Through our Lord Jesus Christ, your Son,
who lives and reigns with you in the unity of the Holy Spirit,
one God, for ever and ever.**

33. Then the reader proclaims the reading from the Apostle.

34. After the Epistle has been read, all rise, then the Priest solemnly intones the Alleluia three times, raising his voice by a step each time, with all repeating it. If necessary, the psalmist intones the Alleluia.

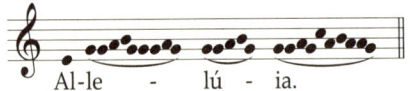
Al-le - lú - ia.

Then the psalmist or cantor proclaims Psalm 118 (117) with the people responding Alleluia.

35. The Priest, in the usual way, puts incense in the thurible and blesses the Deacon. At the Gospel lights are not carried, but only incense.

36. After the Gospel, the Homily, even if brief, is not to be omitted.

Third Part:
Baptismal Liturgy

37. After the Homily the Baptismal Liturgy begins. The Priest goes with the ministers to the baptismal font, if this can be seen by the faithful. Otherwise a vessel with water is placed in the sanctuary.

38. Catechumens, if there are any, are called forward and presented by their godparents in front of the assembled Church or, if they are small children, are carried by their parents and godparents.

39. Then, if there is to be a procession to the baptistery or to the font, it forms immediately. A minister with the paschal candle leads off, and those to be baptized follow him with their godparents, then the ministers, the Deacon, and the Priest. During the procession, the Litany (no. 43) is sung. When the Litany is completed, the Priest gives the address (no. 40).

40. If, however, the Baptismal Liturgy takes place in the sanctuary, the Priest immediately makes an introductory statement in these or similar words.

If there are candidates to be baptized:

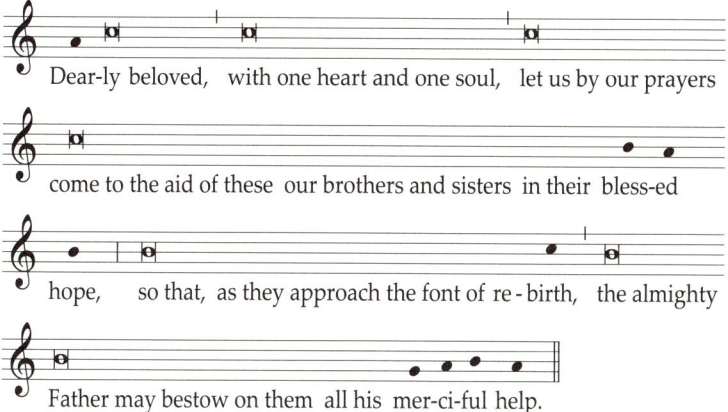

Dear-ly beloved, with one heart and one soul, let us by our prayers come to the aid of these our brothers and sisters in their bless-ed hope, so that, as they approach the font of re-birth, the almighty Father may bestow on them all his mer-ci-ful help.

**Dearly beloved,
with one heart and one soul, let us by our prayers
come to the aid of these our brothers and sisters in their
blessed hope,
so that, as they approach the font of rebirth,
the almighty Father may bestow on them
all his merciful help.**

If the font is to be blessed, but no one is to be baptized:

Dear-ly beloved, let us humbly invoke upon this font the grace of God the al-might-y Fa-ther, that those who from it are born a-new may be numbered among the children of a-dop-tion in Christ.

**Dearly beloved,
let us humbly invoke upon this font
the grace of God the almighty Father,
that those who from it are born anew
may be numbered among the children of adoption in Christ.**

41. The Litany is sung by two cantors, with all standing (because it is Easter Time) and responding.
    If, however, there is to be a procession of some length to the baptistery, the Litany is sung during the procession; in this case, those to be baptized are called forward before the procession begins, and the procession takes place led by the paschal candle, followed by the catechumens with their godparents, then the ministers, the Deacon, and the Priest. The address should occur before the Blessing of Water.

42. If no one is to be baptized and the font is not to be blessed, the Litany is omitted, and the Blessing of Water (no. 54) takes place at once.

43. In the Litany the names of some Saints may be added, especially the Titular Saint of the church and the Patron Saints of the place and of those to be baptized.

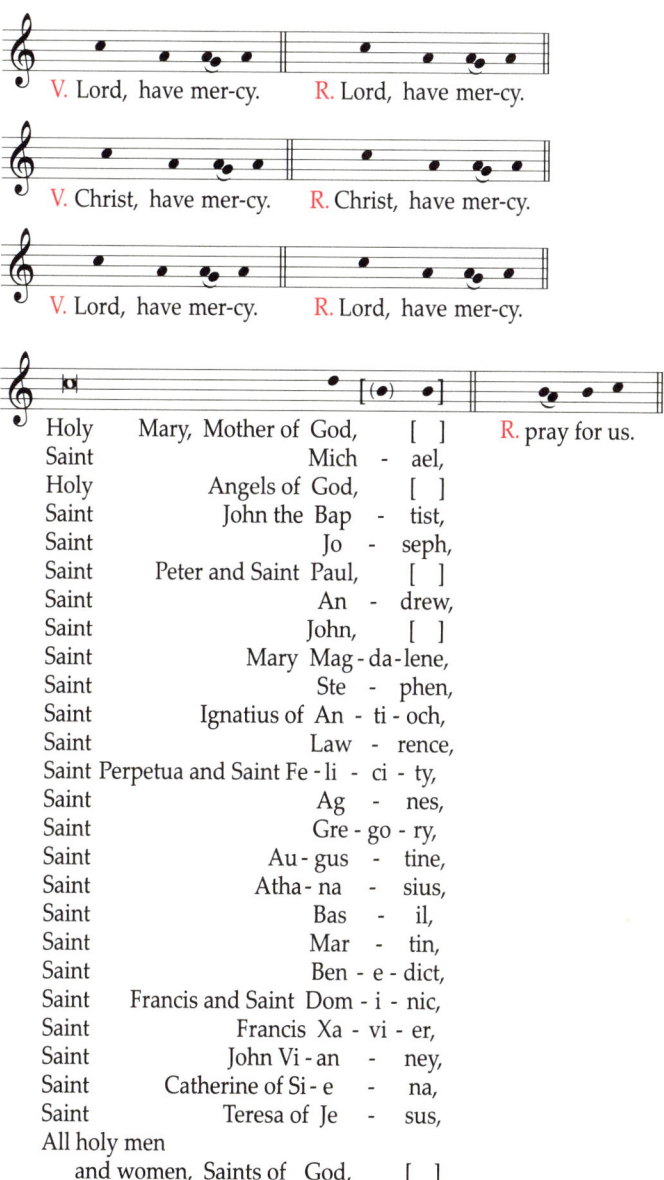

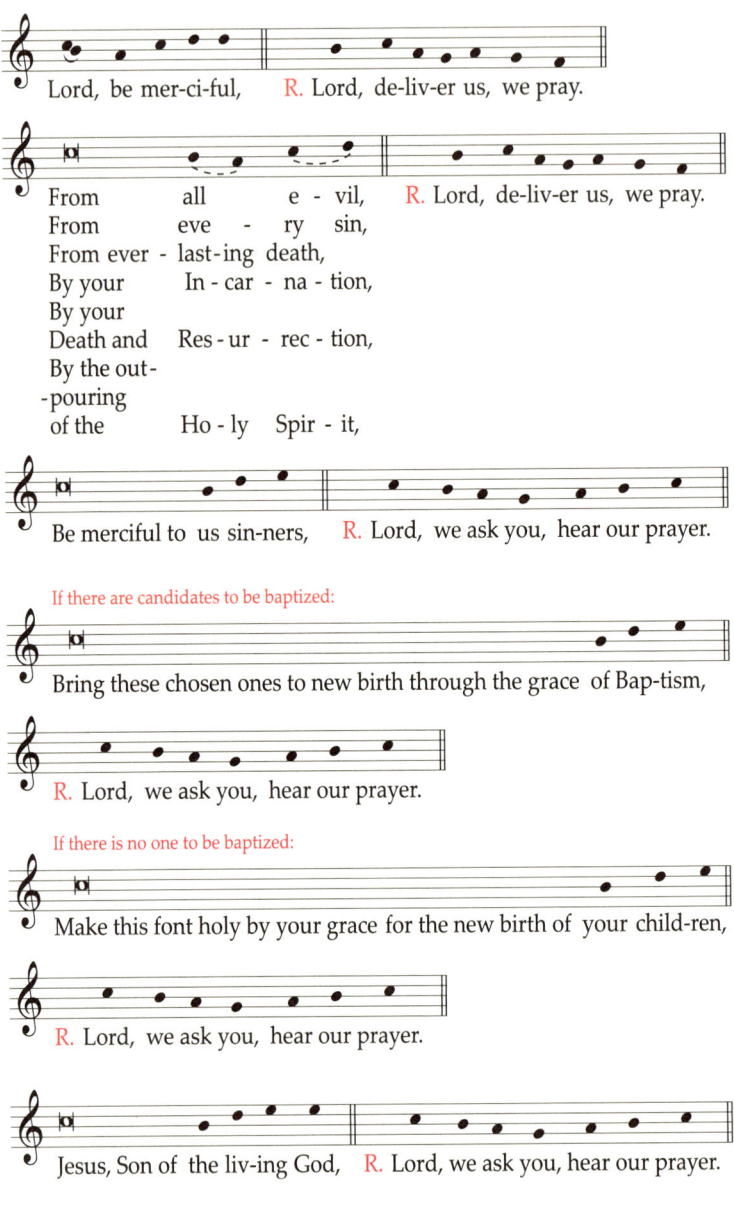

If there are candidates to be baptized, the Priest, with hands extended, says the following prayer:

**Almighty ever-living God,
be present by the mysteries of your great love
and send forth the spirit of adoption
to create the new peoples
brought to birth for you in the font of Baptism,
so that what is to be carried out by our humble service
may be brought to fulfillment by your mighty power.
Through Christ our Lord.**
R. Amen.

Blessing of Baptismal Water

44. The Priest then blesses the baptismal water, saying the following prayer with hands extended:

O God, who by invisible power accomplish a wondrous effect through sacra-men-tal signs and who in many ways have pre-pared water, your cre-a-tion, to show forth the grace of Bap-tism;

O God, whose Spirit in the first moments of the world's creation hovered o-ver the wa-ters, so that the very substance of wa-ter would even then take to itself the pow-er to sanc-ti-fy;

O God, who by the outpouring of the flood foreshadowed re-gen-er-a-tion, so that from the mystery of one and the same ele-ment of wa-ter would come an end to vice and a be-gin-ning of vir-tue;

O God, who caused the children of Abraham to pass dry-shod through the Red Sea, so that the chosen people, set free from slav-

THE EASTER VIGIL

And, if appropriate, lowering the paschal candle into the water either once or three times, he continues:

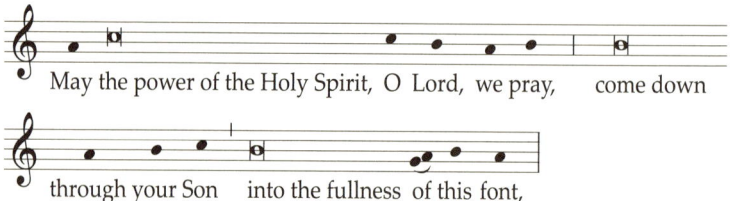

May the power of the Holy Spirit, O Lord, we pray, come down through your Son into the fullness of this font,

and, holding the candle in the water, he continues:

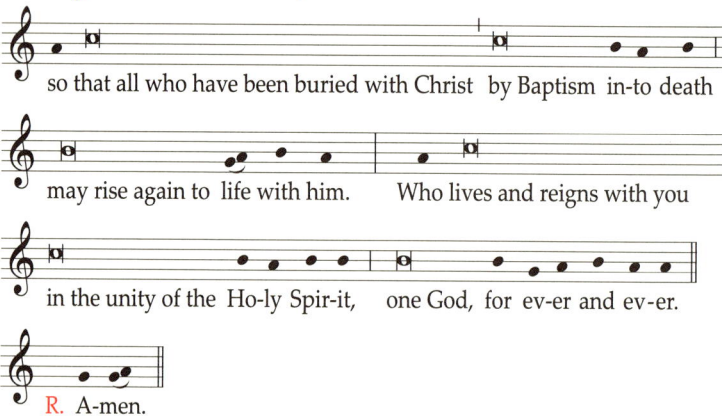

so that all who have been buried with Christ by Baptism in-to death may rise again to life with him. Who lives and reigns with you in the unity of the Ho-ly Spir-it, one God, for ev-er and ev-er.

R. A-men.

45. Then the candle is lifted out of the water, as the people acclaim:

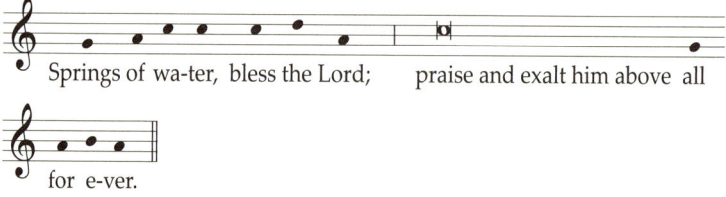

Springs of wa-ter, bless the Lord; praise and exalt him above all for e-ver.

Text without music:
46. The Priest then blesses the baptismal water, saying the following prayer with hands extended:

O God, who by invisible power
accomplish a wondrous effect
through sacramental signs
and who in many ways have prepared water, your creation,
to show forth the grace of Baptism;

O God, whose Spirit
in the first moments of the world's creation
hovered over the waters,
so that the very substance of water
would even then take to itself the power to sanctify;

O God, who by the outpouring of the flood
foreshadowed regeneration,
so that from the mystery of one and the same element of water
would come an end to vice and a beginning of virtue;

O God, who caused the children of Abraham
to pass dry-shod through the Red Sea,
so that the chosen people,
set free from slavery to Pharaoh,
would prefigure the people of the baptized;

O God, whose Son,
baptized by John in the waters of the Jordan,
was anointed with the Holy Spirit,
and, as he hung upon the Cross,
gave forth water from his side along with blood,
and after his Resurrection, commanded his disciples:
"Go forth, teach all nations, baptizing them
in the name of the Father and of the Son and of the Holy Spirit,"
look now, we pray, upon the face of your Church
and graciously unseal for her the fountain of Baptism.

May this water receive by the Holy Spirit
the grace of your Only Begotten Son,
so that human nature, created in your image
and washed clean through the Sacrament of Baptism
from all the squalor of the life of old,
may be found worthy to rise to the life of newborn children
through water and the Holy Spirit.

And, if appropriate, lowering the paschal candle into the water either once or three times, he continues:

**May the power of the Holy Spirit,
O Lord, we pray,
come down through your Son
into the fullness of this font,**

and, holding the candle in the water, he continues:

**so that all who have been buried with Christ
by Baptism into death
may rise again to life with him.
Who lives and reigns with you in the unity of the Holy Spirit,
one God, for ever and ever.**

℟. **Amen.**

47. *Then the candle is lifted out of the water, as the people acclaim:*

    **Springs of water, bless the Lord;
    praise and exalt him above all for ever.**

48. *After the blessing of baptismal water and the acclamation of the people, the Priest, standing, puts the prescribed questions to the adults and the parents or godparents of the children, as is set out in the respective Rites of the Roman Ritual, in order for them to make the required renunciation.*

    If the anointing of the adults with the Oil of Catechumens has not taken place beforehand, as part of the immediately preparatory rites, it occurs at this moment.

49. *Then the Priest questions the adults individually about the faith and, if there are children to be baptized, he requests the triple profession of faith from all the parents and godparents together, as is indicated in the respective Rites.*

    Where many are to be baptized on this night, it is possible to arrange the rite so that, immediately after the response of those to be baptized and of the godparents and the parents, the Celebrant asks for and receives the renewal of baptismal promises of all present.

50. *When the interrogation is concluded, the Priest baptizes the adult elect and the children.*

51. *After the Baptism, the Priest anoints the infants with chrism. A white garment is given to each, whether adults or children. Then the Priest or Deacon receives the paschal candle from the hand of the minister, and the candles of the newly baptized are lighted. For infants the rite of Ephphetha is omitted.*

52. *Afterwards, unless the baptismal washing and the other explanatory rites have occurred in the sanctuary, a procession returns to the sanctuary, formed as before, with the newly baptized or the godparents or parents carrying lighted candles. During this procession, the baptismal canticle* Vidi aquam *(I saw water) or another appropriate chant is sung (no. 56).*

53. *If adults have been baptized, the Bishop or, in his absence, the Priest who has conferred Baptism, should at once administer the Sacrament of Confirmation to them in the sanctuary, as is indicated in the Roman Pontifical or Roman Ritual.*

The Blessing of Water

54. If no one present is to be baptized and the font is not to be blessed, the Priest introduces the faithful to the blessing of water, saying:

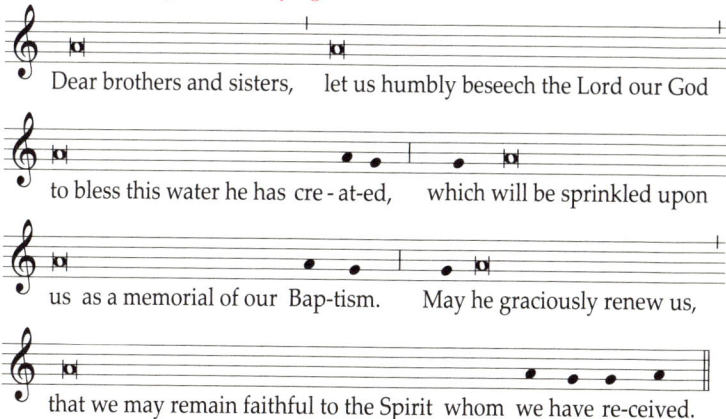

Dear brothers and sisters, let us humbly beseech the Lord our God to bless this water he has cre-at-ed, which will be sprinkled upon us as a memorial of our Bap-tism. May he graciously renew us, that we may remain faithful to the Spirit whom we have re-ceived.

And after a brief pause in silence, he proclaims the following prayer with hands extended:

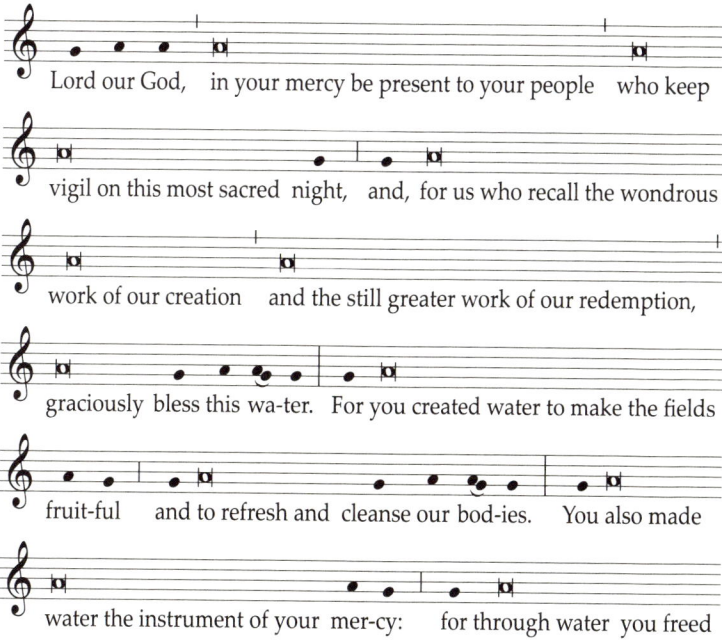

Lord our God, in your mercy be present to your people who keep vigil on this most sacred night, and, for us who recall the wondrous work of our creation and the still greater work of our redemption, graciously bless this wa-ter. For you created water to make the fields fruit-ful and to refresh and cleanse our bod-ies. You also made water the instrument of your mer-cy: for through water you freed

Text without music:
Dear brothers and sisters,
let us humbly beseech the Lord our God
to bless this water he has created,
which will be sprinkled upon us
as a memorial of our Baptism.
May he graciously renew us,
that we may remain faithful to the Spirit
whom we have received.

And after a brief pause in silence, he proclaims the following prayer, with hands extended:
Lord our God,
in your mercy be present to your people
who keep vigil on this most sacred night,
and, for us who recall the wondrous work of our creation
and the still greater work of our redemption,
graciously bless this water.
For you created water to make the fields fruitful
and to refresh and cleanse our bodies.
You also made water the instrument of your mercy:
for through water you freed your people from slavery
and quenched their thirst in the desert;
through water the Prophets proclaimed the new covenant
you were to enter upon with the human race;
and last of all,
through water, which Christ made holy in the Jordan,
you have renewed our corrupted nature
in the bath of regeneration.
Therefore, may this water be for us
a memorial of the Baptism we have received,
and grant that we may share
in the gladness of our brothers and sisters,
who at Easter have received their Baptism.
Through Christ our Lord.
R. Amen.

The Renewal of Baptismal Promises

55. When the Rite of Baptism (and Confirmation) has been completed or, if this has not taken place, after the blessing of water, all stand, holding lighted candles in their hands, and renew the promise of baptismal faith, unless this has already been done together with those to be baptized (cf. no. 49).

The Priest addresses the faithful in these or similar words:

Dear brethren (brothers and sisters), through the Paschal Mystery
we have been buried with Christ in Baptism,
so that we may walk with him in newness of life.
And so, now that our Lenten observance is concluded,
let us renew the promises of Holy Baptism,
by which we once renounced Satan and his works
and promised to serve God in the holy Catholic Church.
And so I ask you:

Priest: **Do you renounce Satan?**
All: I do.

Priest: **And all his works?**
All: I do.

Priest: **And all his empty show?**
All: I do.

Or:

Priest: **Do you renounce sin,**
so as to live in the freedom of the children of God?
All: I do.

Priest: **Do you renounce the lure of evil,**
so that sin may have no mastery over you?
All: I do.

Priest: **Do you renounce Satan,**
the author and prince of sin?
All: I do.

THE EASTER VIGIL

If the situation warrants, this second formula may be adapted by Conferences of Bishops according to local needs.

Then the Priest continues:

Priest: **Do you believe in God,**
the Father almighty,
Creator of heaven and earth?

All: **I do.**

Priest: **Do you believe in Jesus Christ, his only Son, our Lord,**
who was born of the Virgin Mary,
suffered death and was buried,
rose again from the dead
and is seated at the right hand of the Father?

All: **I do.**

Priest: **Do you believe in the Holy Spirit,**
the holy Catholic Church,
the communion of saints,
the forgiveness of sins,
the resurrection of the body,
and life everlasting?

All: **I do.**

And the Priest concludes:

And may almighty God, the Father of our Lord Jesus Christ,
who has given us new birth by water and the Holy Spirit
and bestowed on us forgiveness of our sins,
keep us by his grace,
in Christ Jesus our Lord,
for eternal life.

All: **Amen.**

56. *The Priest sprinkles the people with the blessed water, while all sing:*

Antiphon

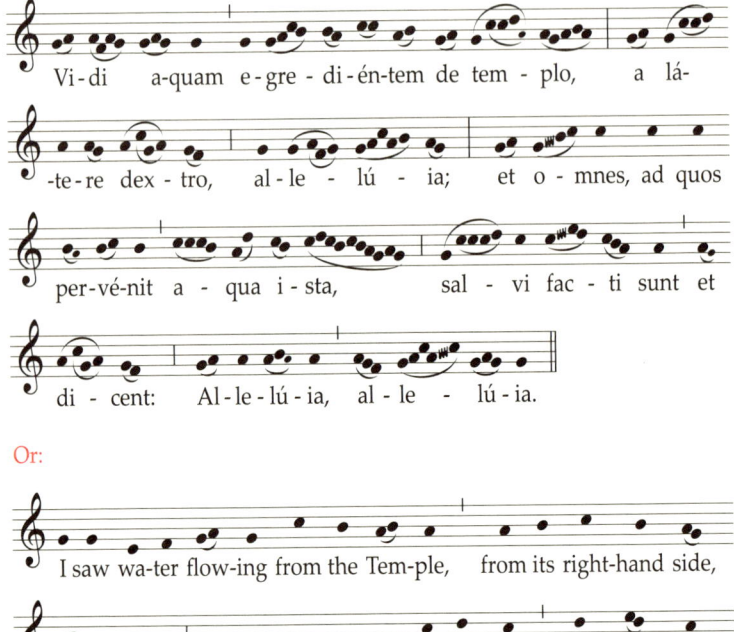

Vi-di a-quam e-gre-di-én-tem de tem-plo, a lá-te-re dex-tro, al-le-lú-ia; et o-mnes, ad quos per-vé-nit a-qua i-sta, sal-vi fac-ti sunt et di-cent: Al-le-lú-ia, al-le-lú-ia.

Or:

I saw wa-ter flow-ing from the Tem-ple, from its right-hand side, al-le-lu-ia; and all to whom this wa-ter came were saved and shall say: Al-le-lu-ia, al-le-lu-ia.

Ant. I saw water flowing from the Temple,
from its right-hand side, alleluia;
and all to whom this water came were saved
and shall say: Alleluia, alleluia.

Another chant that is baptismal in character may also be sung.

57. Meanwhile the newly baptized are led to their place among the faithful.
    If the blessing of baptismal water has not taken place in the baptistery, the Deacon and the ministers reverently carry the vessel of water to the font.
    If the blessing of the font has not occurred, the blessed water is put aside in an appropriate place.

58. After the sprinkling, the Priest returns to the chair where, omitting the Creed, he directs the Universal Prayer, in which the newly baptized participate for the first time.

Fourth Part:
The Liturgy of the Eucharist

59. The Priest goes to the altar and begins the Liturgy of the Eucharist in the usual way.

60. It is desirable that the bread and wine be brought forward by the newly baptized or, if they are children, by their parents or godparents.

61. **Prayer over the Offerings**

    Accept, we ask, O Lord,
    the prayers of your people
    with the sacrificial offerings,
    that what has begun in the paschal mysteries
    may, by the working of your power,
    bring us to the healing of eternity.
    Through Christ our Lord.

62. Preface I of Easter: The Paschal Mystery (. . . on this night above all . . .), p. 558.

63. In the Eucharistic Prayer, a commemoration is made of the baptized and their godparents in accord with the formulas which are found in the Roman Missal and Roman Ritual for each of the Eucharistic Prayers.

64. Before the Ecce Agnus Dei (Behold the Lamb of God), the Priest may briefly address the newly baptized about receiving their first Communion and about the excellence of this great mystery, which is the climax of Initiation and the center of the whole of Christian life.

65. It is desirable that the newly baptized receive Holy Communion under both kinds, together with their godfathers, godmothers, and Catholic parents and spouses, as well as their lay catechists. It is even appropriate that, with the consent of the Diocesan Bishop, where the occasion suggests this, all the faithful be admitted to Holy Communion under both kinds.

66. **Communion Antiphon**   1 Cor 5: 7-8

    Christ our Passover has been sacrificed;
    therefore let us keep the feast
    with the unleavened bread of purity and truth, alleluia.

    Psalm 118 (117) may appropriately be sung.

67. **Prayer after Communion**

    Pour out on us, O Lord, the Spirit of your love,
    and in your kindness make those you have nourished
    by this paschal Sacrament
    one in mind and heart.
    Through Christ our Lord.

68. **Solemn Blessing**

May almighty God bless you
through today's Easter Solemnity
and, in his compassion,
defend you from every assault of sin.
R. Amen.

And may he, who restores you to eternal life
in the Resurrection of his Only Begotten,
endow you with the prize of immortality.
R. Amen.

Now that the days of the Lord's Passion have drawn to a close,
may you who celebrate the gladness of the Paschal Feast
come with Christ's help, and exulting in spirit,
to those feasts that are celebrated in eternal joy.
R. Amen.

And may the blessing of almighty God,
the Father, and the Son, ✠ and the Holy Spirit,
come down on you and remain with you for ever.
R. Amen.

The final blessing formula from the Rite of Baptism of Adults or of Children may also be used, according to circumstances.

69. To dismiss the people the Deacon or, if there is no Deacon, the Priest himself sings or says:

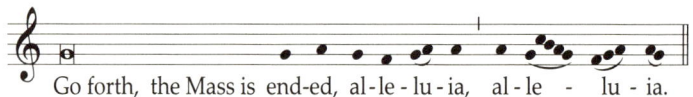
Go forth, the Mass is end-ed, al-le-lu-ia, al-le - lu - ia.

Or:

Go in peace, al-le-lu-ia, al-le - lu - ia.

All reply:

Thanks be to God, al-le-lu-ia, al-le - lu - ia.

This practice is observed throughout the Octave of Easter.

70. The paschal candle is lit in all the more solemn liturgical celebrations of this period.

At the Mass during the Day

71. **Entrance Antiphon**   Cf. Ps 139 (138): 18, 5-6

   I have risen, and I am with you still, alleluia.
   You have laid your hand upon me, alleluia.
   Too wonderful for me, this knowledge, alleluia, alleluia.

   Or: Lk 24: 34; cf. Rev 1: 6

   The Lord is truly risen, alleluia.
   To him be glory and power
   for all the ages of eternity, alleluia, alleluia.

   The Gloria in excelsis (Glory to God in the highest) is said.

72. **Collect**

   **O God, who on this day,
   through your Only Begotten Son,
   have conquered death
   and unlocked for us the path to eternity,
   grant, we pray, that we who keep
   the solemnity of the Lord's Resurrection
   may, through the renewal brought by your Spirit,
   rise up in the light of life.
   Through our Lord Jesus Christ, your Son,
   who lives and reigns with you in the unity of the Holy Spirit,
   one God, for ever and ever.**

   The Creed is said.

   However, in Easter Sunday Masses which are celebrated with a congregation, the rite of the renewal of baptismal promises may take place after the Homily, according to the text used at the Easter Vigil (p. 382). In that case the Creed is omitted.

73. **Prayer over the Offerings**

   **Exultant with paschal gladness, O Lord,
   we offer the sacrifice
   by which your Church
   is wondrously reborn and nourished.
   Through Christ our Lord.**

74. Preface I of Easter, The Paschal Mystery, pp. 558-559.

   When the Roman Canon is used, the proper forms of the Communicantes (In communion with those) and Hanc igitur (Therefore, Lord, we pray) are said.

75. **Communion Antiphon** 1 Cor 5: 7-8
   Christ our Passover has been sacrificed, alleluia;
   therefore let us keep the feast with the unleavened bread
   of purity and truth, alleluia, alleluia.

76. **Prayer after Communion**
   **Look upon your Church, O God,
   with unfailing love and favor,
   so that, renewed by the paschal mysteries,
   she may come to the glory of the resurrection.
   Through Christ our Lord.**

77. To impart the blessing at the end of Mass, the Priest may appropriately use the formula of Solemn Blessing for the Mass of the Easter Vigil, p. 386.

78. For the dismissal of the people, there is sung (as above no. 69) or said:
   Go forth, the Mass is ended, alleluia, alleluia.
   Or:
   Go in peace, alleluia, alleluia.
   R. Thanks be to God, alleluia, alleluia.

MONDAY WITHIN THE OCTAVE OF EASTER

Entrance Antiphon   Ex 13: 5, 9

The Lord has led you into a land flowing with milk and honey,
that the law of the Lord may always be on your lips, alleluia.

Or:

The Lord has risen from the dead, as he said;
let us all exult and rejoice,
for he reigns for all eternity, alleluia.

The Gloria in excelsis (Glory to God in the highest) is said.

Collect

O God, who give constant increase
to your Church by new offspring,
grant that your servants may hold fast in their lives
to the Sacrament they have received in faith.
Through our Lord Jesus Christ, your Son,
who lives and reigns with you in the unity of the Holy Spirit,
one God, for ever and ever.

Prayer over the Offerings

Accept graciously, O Lord, we pray,
the offerings of your peoples,
that, renewed by confession of your name and by Baptism,
they may attain unending happiness.
Through Christ our Lord.

Preface I of Easter, p. 558.

When the Roman Canon is used, the proper forms of the Communicantes (In communion with those) and Hanc igitur (Therefore, Lord, we pray) are said.

Communion Antiphon   Rom 6: 9

Christ, having risen from the dead, dies now no more;
death will no longer have dominion over him, alleluia.

Prayer after Communion

May the grace of this paschal Sacrament
abound in our minds, we pray, O Lord,
and make those you have set on the way of eternal salvation
worthy of your gifts.
Through Christ our Lord.

TUESDAY WITHIN THE OCTAVE OF EASTER

Entrance Antiphon
Cf. Sir 15: 3-4

He gave them the water of wisdom to drink;
it will be made strong in them and will not be moved;
it will raise them up for ever, alleluia.

The Gloria in excelsis (Glory to God in the highest) is said.

Collect

O God, who have bestowed on us paschal remedies,
endow your people with heavenly gifts,
so that, possessed of perfect freedom,
they may rejoice in heaven
over what gladdens them now on earth.
Through our Lord Jesus Christ, your Son,
who lives and reigns with you in the unity of the Holy Spirit,
one God, for ever and ever.

Prayer over the Offerings

Accept in compassion, Lord, we pray,
the offerings of your family,
that under your protective care
they may never lose what they have received,
but attain the gifts that are eternal.
Through Christ our Lord.

Preface I of Easter, p. 558.

When the Roman Canon is used, the proper forms of the Communicantes (In communion with those) and Hanc igitur (Therefore, Lord, we pray) are said.

Communion Antiphon
Col 3: 1-2

If you have risen with Christ, seek the things that are above,
where Christ is seated at the right hand of God;
mind the things that are above, alleluia.

Prayer after Communion

Hear us, almighty God,
and, as you have bestowed on your family
the perfect grace of Baptism,
so prepare their hearts
for the reward of eternal happiness.
Through Christ our Lord.

WEDNESDAY WITHIN THE OCTAVE OF EASTER

Entrance Antiphon
Cf. Mt 25: 34

Come, you blessed of my Father;
receive the kingdom prepared for you
from the foundation of the world, alleluia.

The Gloria in excelsis (Glory to God in the highest) is said.

Collect
O God, who gladden us year by year
with the solemnity of the Lord's Resurrection,
graciously grant
that, by celebrating these present festivities,
we may merit through them to reach eternal joys.
Through our Lord Jesus Christ, your Son,
who lives and reigns with you in the unity of the Holy Spirit,
one God, for ever and ever.

Prayer over the Offerings
Receive, we pray, O Lord,
the sacrifice which has redeemed the human race,
and be pleased to accomplish in us
salvation of mind and body.
Through Christ our Lord.

Preface I of Easter, p. 558.

When the Roman Canon is used, the proper forms of the Communicantes (In communion with those) and Hanc igitur (Therefore, Lord, we pray) are said.

Communion Antiphon
Cf. Lk 24: 35

The disciples recognized the Lord Jesus
in the breaking of the bread, alleluia.

Prayer after Communion
We pray, O Lord,
that the reverent reception of the Sacrament of your Son
may cleanse us from our old ways
and transform us into a new creation.
Through Christ our Lord.

THURSDAY WITHIN THE OCTAVE OF EASTER

Entrance Antiphon
Wis 10: 20-21

They praised in unison your conquering hand, O Lord,
for wisdom opened mouths that were mute
and gave eloquence to the tongues of infants, alleluia.

The Gloria in excelsis (Glory to God in the highest) is said.

Collect

O God, who have united the many nations
in confessing your name,
grant that those reborn in the font of Baptism
may be one in the faith of their hearts
and the homage of their deeds.
Through our Lord Jesus Christ, your Son,
who lives and reigns with you in the unity of the Holy Spirit,
one God, for ever and ever.

Prayer over the Offerings

Graciously be pleased, O Lord,
to accept the sacrificial gifts we offer joyfully
both for those who have been reborn
and in hope of your increased help from heaven.
Through Christ our Lord.

Preface I of Easter, p. 558.

When the Roman Canon is used, the proper forms of the Communicantes (In communion with those) and Hanc igitur (Therefore, Lord, we pray) are said.

Communion Antiphon
Cf. 1 Pt 2: 9

O chosen people, proclaim the mighty works of him
who called you out of darkness into his wonderful light, alleluia.

Prayer after Communion

Hear, O Lord, our prayers,
that this most holy exchange,
by which you have redeemed us,
may bring your help in this present life
and ensure for us eternal gladness.
Through Christ our Lord.

FRIDAY WITHIN THE OCTAVE OF EASTER

Entrance Antiphon *Cf. Ps 78 (77): 53*
The Lord led his people in hope,
while the sea engulfed their foes, alleluia.

The Gloria in excelsis (Glory to God is the highest) is said.

Collect
Almighty ever-living God,
who gave us the Paschal Mystery
in the covenant you established
for reconciling the human race,
so dispose our minds, we pray,
that what we celebrate by professing the faith
we may express in deeds.
Through our Lord Jesus Christ, your Son,
who lives and reigns with you in the unity of the Holy Spirit,
one God, for ever and ever.

Prayer over the Offerings
Perfect within us, O Lord, we pray,
the solemn exchange brought about by these paschal offerings,
that we may be drawn from earthly desires
to a longing for the things of heaven.
Through Christ our Lord.

Preface I of Easter, p. 558.

When the Roman Canon is used, the proper forms of the Communicantes (In communion with those) and Hanc igitur (Therefore, Lord, we pray) are said.

Communion Antiphon *Cf. Jn 21: 12-13*
Jesus said to his disciples: Come and eat.
And he took bread and gave it to them, alleluia.

Prayer after Communion
Keep safe, O Lord, we pray,
those whom you have saved by your kindness
that, redeemed by the Passion of your Son,
they may rejoice in his Resurrection.
Who lives and reigns for ever and ever.

SATURDAY WITHIN THE OCTAVE OF EASTER

Entrance Antiphon
Ps 105 (104): 43

The Lord brought out his people with joy,
his chosen ones with shouts of rejoicing, alleluia.

The Gloria in excelsis (Glory to God in the highest) is said.

Collect

O God, who by the abundance of your grace
give increase to the peoples who believe in you,
look with favor on those you have chosen
and clothe with blessed immortality
those reborn through the Sacrament of Baptism.
Through our Lord Jesus Christ, your Son,
who lives and reigns with you in the unity of the Holy Spirit,
one God, for ever and ever.

Prayer over the Offerings

Grant, we pray, O Lord,
that we may always find delight in these paschal mysteries,
so that the renewal constantly at work within us
may be the cause of our unending joy.
Through Christ our Lord.

Preface I of Easter, p. 558.

When the Roman Canon is used, the proper forms of the Communicantes (In communion with those) and Hanc igitur (Therefore, Lord, we pray) are said.

Communion Antiphon
Gal 3: 27

All of you who have been baptized in Christ
have put on Christ, alleluia.

Prayer after Communion

Look with kindness upon your people, O Lord,
and grant, we pray,
that those you were pleased to renew by eternal mysteries
may attain in their flesh
the incorruptible glory of the resurrection.
Through Christ our Lord.

SECOND SUNDAY OF EASTER
(or of Divine Mercy)

Entrance Antiphon
1 Pt 2: 2

Like newborn infants, you must long for the pure, spiritual milk,
that in him you may grow to salvation, alleluia.

Or:

4 Esdr 2: 36-37

Receive the joy of your glory, giving thanks to God,
who has called you into the heavenly kingdom, alleluia.

The Gloria in excelsis (Glory to God in the highest) is said.

Collect

**God of everlasting mercy,
who in the very recurrence of the paschal feast
kindle the faith of the people you have made your own,
increase, we pray, the grace you have bestowed,
that all may grasp and rightly understand
in what font they have been washed,
by whose Spirit they have been reborn,
by whose Blood they have been redeemed.
Through our Lord Jesus Christ, your Son,
who lives and reigns with you in the unity of the Holy Spirit,
one God, for ever and ever.**

The Creed is said.

Prayer over the Offerings

Accept, O Lord, we pray,
the oblations of your people
(and of those you have brought to new birth),
that, renewed by confession of your name and by Baptism,
they may attain unending happiness.
Through Christ our Lord.

Preface I of Easter (. . . on this day above all . . .), p. 558.

When the Roman Canon is used, the proper forms of the Communicantes (In communion with those) and Hanc igitur (Therefore, Lord, we pray) are said.

Communion Antiphon   Cf. Jn 20: 27

Bring your hand and feel the place of the nails,
and do not be unbelieving but believing, alleluia.

Prayer after Communion

Grant, we pray, almighty God,
that our reception of this paschal Sacrament
may have a continuing effect
in our minds and hearts.
Through Christ our Lord.

A formula of Solemn Blessing, p. 677, may be used.

For the dismissal of the people, there is sung (as above, p. 386) or said: Go forth, the Mass is ended, alleluia, alleluia. Or: Go in peace, alleluia, alleluia. The people respond: Thanks be to God, alleluia, alleluia.

Monday

Entrance Antiphon
Rom 6: 9

Christ, having risen from the dead, dies now no more;
death will no longer have dominion over him, alleluia.

Collect

Grant, we pray, almighty God,
that we, who have been renewed by paschal remedies,
transcending the likeness of our earthly parentage,
may be transformed in the image of our heavenly maker.
Through our Lord Jesus Christ, your Son,
who lives and reigns with you in the unity of the Holy Spirit,
one God, for ever and ever.

Prayer over the Offerings

Receive, O Lord, we pray,
these offerings of your exultant Church,
and, as you have given her cause for such great gladness,
grant also that the gifts we bring
may bear fruit in perpetual happiness.
Through Christ our Lord.

Preface of Easter, pp. 558-567.

Communion Antiphon
Jn 20: 19

Jesus stood in the midst of his disciples and said to them:
Peace be with you, alleluia.

Prayer after Communion

Look with kindness upon your people, O Lord,
and grant, we pray,
that those you were pleased to renew by eternal mysteries
may attain in their flesh
the incorruptible glory of the resurrection.
Through Christ our Lord.

Tuesday

Entrance Antiphon
Rev 19: 7, 6

Let us rejoice and be glad and give glory to God,
for the Lord our God the Almighty reigns, alleluia.

Collect

Enable us, we pray, almighty God,
to proclaim the power of the risen Lord,
that we, who have received the pledge of his gift,
may come to possess all he gives
when it is fully revealed.
Through our Lord Jesus Christ, your Son,
who lives and reigns with you in the unity of the Holy Spirit,
one God, for ever and ever.

Prayer over the Offerings

Grant, we pray, O Lord,
that we may always find delight in these paschal mysteries,
so that the renewal constantly at work within us
may be the cause of our unending joy.
Through Christ our Lord.

Preface of Easter, pp. 558-567.

Communion Antiphon
Cf. Lk 24: 46, 26

The Christ had to suffer and rise from the dead,
and so enter into his glory, alleluia.

Prayer after Communion

Hear, O Lord, our prayers,
that this most holy exchange,
by which you have redeemed us,
may bring your help in this present life
and ensure for us eternal gladness.
Through Christ our Lord.

Wednesday

Entrance Antiphon
Cf. Ps 18 (17): 50; 22 (21): 23

I will praise you, Lord, among the nations;
I will tell of your name to my kin, alleluia.

Collect
As we recall year by year the mysteries
by which, through the restoration of its original dignity,
human nature has received the hope of rising again,
we earnestly beseech your mercy, Lord,
that what we celebrate in faith
we may possess in unending love.
Through our Lord Jesus Christ, your Son,
who lives and reigns with you in the unity of the Holy Spirit,
one God, for ever and ever.

Prayer over the Offerings
O God, who by the wonderful exchange effected in this sacrifice
have made us partakers of the one supreme Godhead,
grant, we pray,
that, as we have come to know your truth,
we may make it ours by a worthy way of life.
Through Christ our Lord.

Preface of Easter, pp. 558-567.

Communion Antiphon
Cf. Jn 15: 16, 19

I have chosen you from the world, says the Lord,
and have appointed you to go and bear fruit,
fruit that will last, alleluia.

Prayer after Communion
Graciously be present to your people, we pray, O Lord,
and lead those you have imbued with heavenly mysteries
to pass from former ways to newness of life.
Through Christ our Lord.

Thursday

Entrance Antiphon
Cf. Ps 68 (67): 8-9, 20

O God, when you went forth before your people,
marching with them and living among them,
the earth trembled, heavens poured down rain, alleluia.

Collect

O God, who for the salvation of the world
brought about the paschal sacrifice,
be favorable to the supplications of your people,
so that Christ our High Priest, interceding on our behalf,
may by his likeness to ourselves
bring us reconciliation,
and by his equality with you
free us from our sins.
Through our Lord Jesus Christ, your Son,
who lives and reigns with you in the unity of the Holy Spirit,
one God, for ever and ever.

Prayer over the Offerings

May our prayers rise up to you, O Lord,
together with the sacrificial offerings,
so that, purified by your graciousness,
we may be conformed to the mysteries of your mighty love.
Through Christ our Lord.

Preface of Easter, pp. 558-567.

Communion Antiphon
Mt 28: 20

Behold, I am with you always,
even to the end of the age, alleluia.

Prayer after Communion

Almighty ever-living God,
who restore us to eternal life
in the Resurrection of Christ,
increase in us, we pray, the fruits of this paschal Sacrament
and pour into our hearts the strength of this saving food.
Through Christ our Lord.

Friday

Entrance Antiphon
Rev 5: 9-10

You have redeemed us, Lord, by your Blood,
from every tribe and tongue and people and nation,
and have made us into a kingdom, priests for our God, alleluia.

Collect

O God, hope and light of the sincere,
we humbly entreat you to dispose our hearts
to offer you worthy prayer
and ever to extol you
by dutiful proclamation of your praise.
Through our Lord Jesus Christ, your Son,
who lives and reigns with you in the unity of the Holy Spirit,
one God, for ever and ever.

Prayer over the Offerings

Accept in compassion, Lord, we pray,
the offerings of your family,
that under your protective care
they may never lose what they have received,
but attain the gifts that are eternal.
Through Christ our Lord.

Preface of Easter, pp. 558-567.

Communion Antiphon
Rom 4: 25

Christ our Lord was handed over for our transgressions
and was raised again for our justification, alleluia.

Prayer after Communion

Keep safe, O Lord, we pray,
those whom you have saved by your kindness,
that, redeemed by the Passion of your Son,
they may rejoice in his Resurrection.
Who lives and reigns for ever and ever.

Saturday

Entrance Antiphon   Cf. 1 Pt 2: 9

    O chosen people, proclaim the mighty works of him
    who called you out of darkness into his wonderful light, alleluia.

Collect

    Set aside, O Lord,
    the bond of sentence written for us by the law of sin,
    which in the Paschal Mystery you canceled
    through the Resurrection of Christ your Son.
    Who lives and reigns with you in the unity of the Holy Spirit,
    one God, for ever and ever.

    Or:

    O God, who willed that through the paschal mysteries
    the gates of mercy should stand open for your faithful,
    look upon us and have mercy,
    that as we follow, by your gift, the way you desire for us,
    so may we never stray from the paths of life.
    Through our Lord Jesus Christ, your Son,
    who lives and reigns with you in the unity of the Holy Spirit,
    one God, for ever and ever.

Prayer over the Offerings

    Sanctify graciously these gifts, O Lord, we pray,
    and, accepting the oblation of this spiritual sacrifice,
    make of us an eternal offering to you.
    Through Christ our Lord.

    Preface of Easter, pp. 558-567.

Communion Antiphon   Jn 17: 24

    Father, I wish that, where I am,
    those you gave me may also be with me,
    that they may see the glory that you gave me, alleluia.

Prayer after Communion

    We have partaken of the gifts of this sacred mystery,
    humbly imploring, O Lord,
    that what your Son commanded us to do
    in memory of him
    may bring us growth in charity.
    Through Christ our Lord.

THIRD SUNDAY OF EASTER

Entrance Antiphon   Cf. Ps 66 (65): 1-2

Cry out with joy to God, all the earth;
O sing to the glory of his name.
O render him glorious praise, alleluia.

The Gloria in excelsis (Glory to God in the highest) is said.

Collect

May your people exult for ever, O God,
in renewed youthfulness of spirit,
so that, rejoicing now in the restored glory of our adoption,
we may look forward in confident hope
to the rejoicing of the day of resurrection.
Through our Lord Jesus Christ, your Son,
who lives and reigns with you in the unity of the Holy Spirit,
one God, for ever and ever.

The Creed is said.

Prayer over the Offerings

Receive, O Lord, we pray,
these offerings of your exultant Church,
and, as you have given her cause for such great gladness,
grant also that the gifts we bring
may bear fruit in perpetual happiness.
Through Christ our Lord.

Preface of Easter, pp. 558-567.

Communion Antiphon
Lk 24: 35

> The disciples recognized the Lord Jesus
> in the breaking of the bread, alleluia.

Optional for Year B:
Lk 24: 46-47

> The Christ had to suffer and on the third day rise from the dead;
> in his name repentance and remission of sins
> must be preached to all the nations, alleluia.

Optional for Year C:
Cf. Jn 21: 12-13

> Jesus said to his disciples: Come and eat.
> And he took bread and gave it to them, alleluia.

Prayer after Communion

**Look with kindness upon your people, O Lord,
and grant, we pray,
that those you were pleased to renew by eternal mysteries
may attain in their flesh
the incorruptible glory of the resurrection.
Through Christ our Lord.**

A formula of Solemn Blessing, p. 677, may be used.

Monday

Entrance Antiphon
> The Good Shepherd has risen,
> who laid down his life for his sheep
> and willingly died for his flock, alleluia.

Collect
> Grant, we pray, almighty God,
> that, putting off our old self with all its ways,
> we may live as Christ did,
> for through the healing paschal remedies
> you have conformed us to his nature.
> Who lives and reigns with you in the unity of the Holy Spirit,
> one God, for ever and ever.

Prayer over the Offerings
> May our prayers rise up to you, O Lord,
> together with the sacrificial offerings,
> so that, purified by your graciousness,
> we may be conformed to the mysteries of your mighty love.
> Through Christ our Lord.

Preface of Easter, pp. 558-567.

Communion Antiphon — Jn 14: 27
> Peace I leave with you; my peace I give to you.
> Not as the world gives do I give it to you, says the Lord, alleluia.

Prayer after Communion
> Almighty ever-living God,
> who restore us to eternal life
> in the Resurrection of Christ,
> increase in us, we pray, the fruits of this paschal Sacrament
> and pour into our hearts the strength of this saving food.
> Through Christ our Lord.

Tuesday

Entrance Antiphon   Rev 19: 5; 12: 10

Sing praise to our God,
all you who fear God, both small and great,
for now salvation and strength have come,
and the power of his Christ, alleluia.

Collect

O God, who open wide the gates of the heavenly Kingdom
to those reborn of water and the Holy Spirit,
pour out on your servants
an increase of the grace you have bestowed,
that, having been purged of all sins,
they may lack nothing
that in your kindness you have promised.
Through our Lord Jesus Christ, your Son,
who lives and reigns with you in the unity of the Holy Spirit,
one God, for ever and ever.

Prayer over the Offerings

Receive, O Lord, we pray,
these offerings of your exultant Church,
and, as you have given her cause for such great gladness,
grant also that the gifts we bring
may bear fruit in perpetual happiness.
Through Christ our Lord.

Preface of Easter, pp. 558-567.

Communion Antiphon   Rom 6: 8

If we have died with Christ,
we believe that we shall also live with Christ, alleluia.

Prayer after Communion

Look with kindness upon your people, O Lord,
and grant, we pray,
that those you were pleased to renew by eternal mysteries
may attain in their flesh
the incorruptible glory of the resurrection.
Through Christ our Lord.

Wednesday

Entrance Antiphon
Cf. Ps 71 (70): 8, 23

Let my mouth be filled with your praise, that I may sing aloud;
my lips shall shout for joy, when I sing to you, alleluia.

Collect

**Be present to your family, O Lord, we pray,
and graciously ensure
those you have endowed with the grace of faith
an eternal share in the Resurrection of your Only Begotten Son.
Who lives and reigns with you in the unity of the Holy Spirit,
one God, for ever and ever.**

Prayer over the Offerings

**Grant, we pray, O Lord,
that we may always find delight in these paschal mysteries,
so that the renewal constantly at work within us
may be the cause of our unending joy.
Through Christ our Lord.**

Preface of Easter, pp. 558-567.

Communion Antiphon

The Lord has risen and shone his light upon us,
whom he has redeemed by his Blood, alleluia.

Prayer after Communion

**Hear, O Lord, our prayers,
that this most holy exchange,
by which you have redeemed us,
may bring your help in this present life
and ensure for us eternal gladness.
Through Christ our Lord.**

Thursday

Entrance Antiphon   *Cf. Ex 15: 1-2*
    Let us sing to the Lord, for he has gloriously triumphed.
    The Lord is my strength and my might;
    he has become my salvation, alleluia.

Collect
    Almighty ever-living God,
    let us feel your compassion more readily
    during these days when, by your gift,
    we have known it more fully,
    so that those you have freed from the darkness of error
    may cling more firmly to the teachings of your truth.
    Through our Lord Jesus Christ, your Son,
    who lives and reigns with you in the unity of the Holy Spirit,
    one God, for ever and ever.

Prayer over the Offerings
    O God, who by the wonderful exchange effected in this sacrifice
    have made us partakers of the one supreme Godhead,
    grant, we pray,
    that, as we have come to know your truth,
    we may make it ours by a worthy way of life.
    Through Christ our Lord.

Preface of Easter, pp. 558-567.

Communion Antiphon   *2 Cor 5: 15*
    Christ died for all, that those who live
    may live no longer for themselves,
    but for him, who died for them and is risen, alleluia.

Prayer after Communion
    Graciously be present to your people, we pray, O Lord,
    and lead those you have imbued with heavenly mysteries
    to pass from former ways to newness of life.
    Through Christ our Lord.

Friday

Entrance Antiphon   Rev 5: 12
Worthy is the Lamb who was slain,
to receive power and divinity,
and wisdom and strength and honor, alleluia.

Collect
Grant, we pray, almighty God,
that we, who have come to know
the grace of the Lord's Resurrection,
may, through the love of the Spirit,
ourselves rise to newness of life.
Through our Lord Jesus Christ, your Son,
who lives and reigns with you in the unity of the Holy Spirit,
one God, for ever and ever.

Prayer over the Offerings
Graciously sanctify these gifts, O Lord, we pray,
and, accepting the oblation of this spiritual sacrifice,
make of us an eternal offering to you.
Through Christ our Lord.

Preface of Easter, pp. 558-567.

Communion Antiphon
The Crucified is risen from the dead
and has redeemed us, alleluia.

Prayer after Communion
We have partaken of the gifts of this sacred mystery,
humbly imploring, O Lord,
that what your Son commanded us to do
in memory of him
may bring us growth in charity.
Through Christ our Lord.

Saturday

Entrance Antiphon
Col 2: 12

You have been buried with Christ in Baptism,
through which you also rose again
by faith in the working of God,
who raised him from the dead, alleluia.

Collect

**O God, who in the font of Baptism
have made new those who believe in you,
keep safe those reborn in Christ,
that, defeating every onslaught of error,
they may faithfully preserve the grace of your blessing.
Through our Lord Jesus Christ, your Son,
who lives and reigns with you in the unity of the Holy Spirit,
one God, for ever and ever.**

Prayer over the Offerings

**Accept in compassion, Lord, we pray,
the offerings of your family,
that under your protective care
they may never lose what they have received,
but attain the gifts that are eternal.
Through Christ our Lord.**

Preface of Easter, pp. 558-567.

Communion Antiphon
Jn 17: 20-21

Father, I pray for them, that they may be one in us,
so that the world may believe it was you who sent me,
says the Lord, alleluia.

Prayer after Communion

**Keep safe, O Lord, we pray,
those whom you have saved by your kindness,
that, redeemed by the Passion of your Son,
they may rejoice in his Resurrection.
Who lives and reigns for ever and ever.**

FOURTH SUNDAY OF EASTER

Entrance Antiphon
Cf. Ps 33 (32): 5-6

The merciful love of the Lord fills the earth;
by the word of the Lord the heavens were made, alleluia.

The Gloria in excelsis (Glory to God in the highest) is said.

Collect

**Almighty ever-living God,
lead us to a share in the joys of heaven,
so that the humble flock may reach
where the brave Shepherd has gone before.
Who lives and reigns with you in the unity of the Holy Spirit,
one God, for ever and ever.**

The Creed is said.

Prayer over the Offerings

**Grant, we pray, O Lord,
that we may always find delight in these paschal mysteries,
so that the renewal constantly at work within us
may be the cause of our unending joy.
Through Christ our Lord.**

Preface of Easter, pp. 558-567.

Communion Antiphon

The Good Shepherd has risen,
who laid down his life for his sheep
and willingly died for his flock, alleluia.

Prayer after Communion

**Look upon your flock, kind Shepherd,
and be pleased to settle in eternal pastures
the sheep you have redeemed
by the Precious Blood of your Son.
Who lives and reigns for ever and ever.**

A formula of Solemn Blessing, p. 677, may be used.

Monday

Entrance Antiphon
Rom 6: 9

Christ, having risen from the dead, dies now no more;
death will no longer have dominion over him, alleluia.

Collect

O God, perfect light of the blessed,
by whose gift we celebrate the paschal mysteries on earth,
bring us, we pray,
to rejoice in the full measure of your grace
for ages unending.
Through our Lord Jesus Christ, your Son,
who lives and reigns with you in the unity of the Holy Spirit,
one God, for ever and ever.

Prayer over the Offerings

Receive, O Lord, we pray,
these offerings of your exultant Church,
and, as you have given her cause for such great gladness,
grant also that the gifts we bring
may bear fruit in perpetual happiness.
Through Christ our Lord.

Preface of Easter, pp. 558-567.

Communion Antiphon
Jn 20: 19

Jesus stood in the midst of his disciples
and said to them: Peace be with you, alleluia.

Prayer after Communion

Look with kindness upon your people, O Lord,
and grant, we pray,
that those you were pleased to renew by eternal mysteries
may attain in their flesh
the incorruptible glory of the resurrection.
Through Christ our Lord.

Tuesday

Entrance Antiphon
Rev 19: 7, 6

> Let us rejoice and be glad and give glory to God,
> for the Lord our God the Almighty reigns, alleluia.

Collect

> Grant, we pray, almighty God,
> that, celebrating the mysteries of the Lord's Resurrection,
> we may merit to receive the joy of our redemption.
> Through our Lord Jesus Christ, your Son,
> who lives and reigns with you in the unity of the Holy Spirit,
> one God, for ever and ever.

Prayer over the Offerings

> Grant, we pray, O Lord,
> that we may always find delight in these paschal mysteries,
> so that the renewal constantly at work within us
> may be the cause of our unending joy.
> Through Christ our Lord.

Preface of Easter, pp. 558-567.

Communion Antiphon
Cf. Lk 24: 46, 26

> The Christ had to suffer and rise from the dead,
> and so enter into his glory, alleluia.

Prayer after Communion

> Hear, O Lord, our prayers,
> that this most holy exchange,
> by which you have redeemed us,
> may bring your help in this present life
> and ensure for us eternal gladness.
> Through Christ our Lord.

Wednesday

Entrance Antiphon   Cf. Ps 18 (17): 50; 22 (21): 23

I will praise you, Lord, among the nations;
I will tell of your name to my kin, alleluia.

Collect

O God, life of the faithful,
glory of the humble, blessedness of the just,
listen kindly to the prayers
of those who call on you,
that they who thirst for what you generously promise
may always have their fill of your plenty.
Through our Lord Jesus Christ, your Son,
who lives and reigns with you in the unity of the Holy Spirit,
one God, for ever and ever.

Prayer over the Offerings

O God, who by the wonderful exchange effected in this sacrifice
have made us partakers of the one supreme Godhead,
grant, we pray,
that, as we have come to know your truth,
we may make it ours by a worthy way of life.
Through Christ our Lord.

Preface of Easter, pp. 558-567.

Communion Antiphon   Cf. Jn 15: 16, 19

I have chosen you from the world, says the Lord,
and have appointed you to go out and bear fruit,
fruit that will last, alleluia.

Prayer after Communion

Graciously be present to your people, we pray, O Lord,
and lead those you have imbued with heavenly mysteries
to pass from former ways to newness of life.
Through Christ our Lord.

Thursday

Entrance Antiphon
Cf. Ps 68 (67): 8-9, 20

O God, when you went forth before your people,
marching with them and living among them,
the earth trembled, heavens poured down rain, alleluia.

Collect

O God, who restore human nature
to yet greater dignity than at its beginnings,
look upon the amazing mystery of your loving kindness,
and in those you have chosen to make new
through the wonder of rebirth
may you preserve the gifts
of your enduring grace and blessing.
Through our Lord Jesus Christ, your Son,
who lives and reigns with you in the unity of the Holy Spirit,
one God, for ever and ever.

Prayer over the Offerings

May our prayers rise up to you, O Lord,
together with the sacrificial offerings,
so that, purified by your graciousness,
we may be conformed to the mysteries of your mighty love.
Through Christ our Lord.

Preface of Easter, pp. 558-567.

Communion Antiphon
Mt 28: 20

Behold, I am with you always,
even to the end of the age, alleluia.

Prayer after Communion

Almighty ever-living God,
who restore us to eternal life
in the Resurrection of Christ,
increase in us, we pray, the fruits of this paschal Sacrament
and pour into our hearts the strength of this saving food.
Through Christ our Lord.

Friday

Entrance Antiphon   Rev 5: 9-10

You have redeemed us, Lord, by your Blood,
from every tribe and tongue and people and nation,
and have made us into a kingdom, priests for our God, alleluia.

Collect

O God, author of our freedom and of our salvation,
listen to the voice of our pleading
and grant that those you have redeemed
by the shedding of your Son's Blood
may have life through you
and, under your protection,
rejoice for ever unharmed.
Through our Lord Jesus Christ, your Son,
who lives and reigns with you in the unity of the Holy Spirit,
one God, for ever and ever.

Prayer over the Offerings

Accept in compassion, Lord, we pray,
the offerings of your family,
that under your protective care
they may never lose what they have received,
but attain the gifts that are eternal.
Through Christ our Lord.

Preface of Easter, pp. 558-567.

Communion Antiphon   Rom 4: 25

Christ our Lord was handed over for our transgressions
and was raised again for our justification, alleluia.

Prayer after Communion

Keep safe, O Lord, we pray,
those whom you have saved by your kindness,
that, redeemed by the Passion of your Son,
they may rejoice in his Resurrection.
Who lives and reigns for ever and ever.

Saturday

Entrance Antiphon
Cf. 1 Pt 2: 9

O chosen people, proclaim the mighty works of him
who called you out of darkness into his wonderful light, alleluia.

Collect

**O God, who in the celebration of Easter
graciously give to the world
the healing of heavenly remedies,
show benevolence to your Church,
that our present observance
may benefit us for eternal life.
Through our Lord Jesus Christ, your Son,
who lives and reigns with you in the unity of the Holy Spirit,
one God, for ever and ever.**

Prayer over the Offerings

**Graciously sanctify these gifts, O Lord, we pray,
and, accepting the oblation of this spiritual sacrifice,
make of us an eternal offering to you.
Through Christ our Lord.**

Preface of Easter, pp. 558-567.

Communion Antiphon
Jn 17: 24

Father, I wish that, where I am,
those you gave me may also be with me,
that they may see the glory that you gave me, alleluia.

Prayer after Communion

**We have partaken of the gifts of this sacred mystery,
humbly imploring, O Lord,
that what your Son commanded us to do
in memory of him
may bring us growth in charity.
Through Christ our Lord.**

FIFTH SUNDAY OF EASTER

Entrance Antiphon   Cf. Ps 98 (97): 1-2
O sing a new song to the Lord,
for he has worked wonders;
in the sight of the nations
he has shown his deliverance, alleluia.

The Gloria in excelsis (Glory to God in the highest) is said.

Collect

**Almighty ever-living God,
constantly accomplish the Paschal Mystery within us,
that those you were pleased to make new in Holy Baptism
may, under your protective care, bear much fruit
and come to the joys of life eternal.
Through our Lord Jesus Christ, your Son,
who lives and reigns with you in the unity of the Holy Spirit,
one God, for ever and ever.**

The Creed is said.

Prayer over the Offerings

**O God, who by the wonderful exchange effected in this sacrifice
have made us partakers of the one supreme Godhead,
grant, we pray,
that, as we have come to know your truth,
we may make it ours by a worthy way of life.
Through Christ our Lord.**

Preface of Easter, pp. 558-567.

Communion Antiphon   Cf. Jn 15: 1, 5
I am the true vine and you are the branches, says the Lord.
Whoever remains in me, and I in him, bears fruit in plenty, alleluia.

Prayer after Communion

**Graciously be present to your people, we pray, O Lord,
and lead those you have imbued with heavenly mysteries
to pass from former ways to newness of life.
Through Christ our Lord.**

A formula of Solemn Blessing, p. 677, may be used.

Monday

Entrance Antiphon
The Good Shepherd has risen,
who laid down his life for his sheep
and willingly died for his flock, alleluia.

Collect
May your right hand, O Lord, we pray,
encompass your family with perpetual help,
so that, defended from all wickedness
by the Resurrection of your Only Begotten Son,
we may make our way by means of your heavenly gifts.
Through our Lord Jesus Christ, your Son,
who lives and reigns with you in the unity of the Holy Spirit,
one God, for ever and ever.

Prayer over the Offerings
May our prayers rise up to you, O Lord,
together with the sacrificial offerings,
so that, purified by your graciousness,
we may be conformed to the mysteries of your mighty love.
Through Christ our Lord.

Preface of Easter, pp. 558-567.

Communion Antiphon Jn 14: 27
Peace I leave with you; my peace I give to you.
Not as the world gives do I give it to you,
says the Lord, alleluia.

Prayer after Communion
Almighty ever-living God,
who restore us to eternal life
in the Resurrection of Christ,
increase in us, we pray, the fruits of this paschal Sacrament
and pour into our hearts the strength of this saving food.
Through Christ our Lord.

Tuesday

Entrance Antiphon
Rev 19: 5; 12: 10

Sing praise to our God,
all you who fear God, both small and great,
for now salvation and strength have come,
and the power of his Christ, alleluia.

Collect

O God, who restore us to eternal life
in the Resurrection of Christ,
grant your people constancy in faith and hope,
that we may never doubt the promises
of which we have learned from you.
Through our Lord Jesus Christ, your Son,
who lives and reigns with you in the unity of the Holy Spirit,
one God, for ever and ever.

Prayer over the Offerings

Receive, O Lord, we pray,
these offerings of your exultant Church,
and, as you have given her cause for such great gladness,
grant also that the gifts we bring
may bear fruit in perpetual happiness.
Through Christ our Lord.

Preface of Easter, pp. 558-567.

Communion Antiphon
Rom 6: 8

If we have died with Christ,
we believe that we shall also live with Christ, alleluia.

Prayer after Communion

Look with kindness upon your people, O Lord,
and grant, we pray,
that those you were pleased to renew by eternal mysteries
may attain in their flesh
the incorruptible glory of the resurrection.
Through Christ our Lord.

Wednesday

Entrance Antiphon
Cf. Ps 71 (70): 8, 23

Let my mouth be filled with your praise, that I may sing aloud;
my lips shall shout for joy, when I sing to you, alleluia.

Collect
O God, restorer and lover of innocence,
direct the hearts of your servants towards yourself,
that those you have set free from the darkness of unbelief
may never stray from the light of your truth.
Through our Lord Jesus Christ, your Son,
who lives and reigns with you in the unity of the Holy Spirit,
one God, for ever and ever.

Prayer over the Offerings
Grant, we pray, O Lord,
that we may always find delight in these paschal mysteries,
so that the renewal constantly at work within us
may be the cause of our unending joy.
Through Christ our Lord.

Preface of Easter, pp. 558-567.

Communion Antiphon
The Lord has risen and shone his light upon us,
whom he has redeemed by his Blood, alleluia.

Prayer after Communion
Hear, O Lord, our prayers,
that this most holy exchange,
by which you have redeemed us,
may bring your help in this present life
and ensure for us eternal gladness.
Through Christ our Lord.

Thursday

Entrance Antiphon
Cf. Ex 15: 1-2

Let us sing to the Lord, for he has gloriously triumphed.
The Lord is my strength and my might;
he has become my salvation, alleluia.

Collect

O God, by whose grace,
though sinners, we are made just
and, though pitiable, made blessed,
stand, we pray, by your works,
stand by your gifts,
that those justified by faith
may not lack the courage of perseverance.
Through our Lord Jesus Christ, your Son,
who lives and reigns with you in the unity of the Holy Spirit,
one God, for ever and ever.

Prayer over the Offerings

O God, who by the wonderful exchange effected in this sacrifice
have made us partakers of the one supreme Godhead,
grant, we pray,
that, as we have come to know your truth,
we may make it ours by a worthy way of life.
Through Christ our Lord.

Preface of Easter, pp. 558-567.

Communion Antiphon
2 Cor 5: 15

Christ died for all, that those who live
may live no longer for themselves,
but for him who died for them and is risen, alleluia.

Prayer after Communion

Graciously be present to your people, we pray, O Lord,
and lead those you have imbued with heavenly mysteries
to pass from former ways to newness of life.
Through Christ our Lord.

Friday

Entrance Antiphon
Rev 5: 12

Worthy is the Lamb who was slain,
to receive power and divinity,
and wisdom and strength and honor, alleluia.

Collect
Grant us, Lord, we pray,
that, being rightly conformed to the paschal mysteries,
what we celebrate in joy
may protect and save us with perpetual power.
Through our Lord Jesus Christ, your Son,
who lives and reigns with you in the unity of the Holy Spirit,
one God, for ever and ever.

Prayer over the Offerings
Graciously sanctify these gifts, O Lord, we pray,
and, accepting the oblation of this spiritual sacrifice,
make of us an eternal offering to you.
Through Christ our Lord.

Preface of Easter, pp. 558-567.

Communion Antiphon
The Crucified is risen from the dead
and has redeemed us, alleluia.

Prayer after Communion
We have partaken of the gifts of this sacred mystery,
humbly imploring, O Lord,
that what your Son commanded us to do
in memory of him
may bring us growth in charity.
Through Christ our Lord.

Saturday

Entrance Antiphon   Col 2: 12
You have been buried with Christ in Baptism,
through which you also rose again
by faith in the working of God,
who raised him from the dead, alleluia.

Collect

Almighty and eternal God,
who through the regenerating power of Baptism
have been pleased to confer on us heavenly life,
grant, we pray,
that those you render capable of immortality
by justifying them
may by your guidance
attain the fullness of glory.
Through our Lord Jesus Christ, your Son,
who lives and reigns with you in the unity of the Holy Spirit,
one God, for ever and ever.

Prayer over the Offerings

Accept in compassion, Lord, we pray,
the offerings of your family,
that under your protective care
they may never lose what they have received,
but attain the gifts that are eternal.
Through Christ our Lord.

Preface of Easter, pp. 558-567.

Communion Antiphon   Jn 17: 20-21
Father, I pray for them, that they may be one in us,
so that the world may believe it was you who sent me,
says the Lord, alleluia.

Prayer after Communion

Keep safe, O Lord, we pray,
those whom you have saved by your kindness,
that, redeemed by the Passion of your Son,
they may rejoice in his Resurrection.
Who lives and reigns for ever and ever.

SIXTH SUNDAY OF EASTER

Entrance Antiphon   Cf. Is 48: 20

    Proclaim a joyful sound and let it be heard;
    proclaim to the ends of the earth:
    The Lord has freed his people, alleluia.

The Gloria in excelsis (Glory to God in the highest) is said.

Collect

    Grant, almighty God,
    that we may celebrate with heartfelt devotion these days of joy,
    which we keep in honor of the risen Lord,
    and that what we relive in remembrance
    we may always hold to in what we do.
    Through our Lord Jesus Christ, your Son,
    who lives and reigns with you in the unity of the Holy Spirit,
    one God, for ever and ever.

The Creed is said.

Prayer over the Offerings

    May our prayers rise up to you, O Lord,
    together with the sacrificial offerings,
    so that, purified by your graciousness,
    we may be conformed to the mysteries of your mighty love.
    Through Christ our Lord.

Preface of Easter, pp. 558-567.

Communion Antiphon   Jn 14: 15-16

    If you love me, keep my commandments, says the Lord,
    and I will ask the Father and he will send you another Paraclete,
    to abide with you for ever, alleluia.

Prayer after Communion

    Almighty ever-living God,
    who restore us to eternal life in the Resurrection of Christ,
    increase in us, we pray, the fruits of this paschal Sacrament
    and pour into our hearts the strength of this saving food.
    Through Christ our Lord.

A formula of Solemn Blessing, p. 677, may be used.

Monday

Entrance Antiphon   Rom 6: 9

    Christ, having risen from the dead, dies now no more;
    death will no longer have dominion over him, alleluia.

Collect

    Grant, O merciful God,
    that we may experience at all times
    the fruit produced by the paschal observances.
    Through our Lord Jesus Christ, your Son,
    who lives and reigns with you in the unity of the Holy Spirit,
    one God, for ever and ever.

Prayer over the Offerings

    Receive, O Lord, we pray,
    these offerings of your exultant Church,
    and, as you have given her cause for such great gladness,
    grant also that the gifts we bring
    may bear fruit in perpetual happiness.
    Through Christ our Lord.

Preface of Easter, pp. 558-567.

Communion Antiphon   Jn 20: 19

    Jesus stood in the midst of his disciples
    and said to them: Peace be with you, alleluia.

Prayer after Communion

    Look with kindness upon your people, O Lord,
    and grant, we pray,
    that those you were pleased to renew by eternal mysteries
    may attain in their flesh
    the incorruptible glory of the resurrection.
    Through Christ our Lord.

Tuesday

Entrance Antiphon *Rev 19: 7, 6*
Let us rejoice and be glad and give glory to God,
for the Lord our God the Almighty reigns, alleluia.

Collect
**Grant, almighty and merciful God,
that we may in truth receive a share
in the Resurrection of Christ your Son.
Who lives and reigns with you in the unity of the Holy Spirit,
one God, for ever and ever.**

Prayer over the Offerings
**Grant, we pray, O Lord,
that we may always find delight in these paschal mysteries,
so that the renewal constantly at work within us
may be the cause of our unending joy.
Through Christ our Lord.**

Preface of Easter, pp. 558-567.

Communion Antiphon *Cf. Lk 24: 46, 26*
The Christ had to suffer and rise from the dead,
and so enter into his glory, alleluia.

Prayer after Communion
**Hear, O Lord, our prayers,
that this most holy exchange,
by which you have redeemed us,
may bring your help in this present life
and ensure for us eternal gladness.
Through Christ our Lord.**

Wednesday
At the Morning Mass

In regions where the Solemnity of the Ascension occurs on the following Sunday, this Mass is also used in the evening.

Entrance Antiphon
Cf. Ps 18 (17): 50; 22 (21): 23

>I will praise you, Lord, among the nations;
>I will tell of your name to my kin, alleluia.

Collect

>Grant, we pray, O Lord,
>that, as we celebrate in mystery
>the solemnities of your Son's Resurrection,
>so, too, we may be worthy
>to rejoice at his coming with all the Saints.
>Through our Lord Jesus Christ, your Son,
>who lives and reigns with you in the unity of the Holy Spirit,
>one God, for ever and ever.

Prayer over the Offerings

>O God, who by the wonderful exchange effected in this sacrifice
>have made us partakers of the one supreme Godhead,
>grant, we pray,
>that, as we have come to know your truth,
>we may make it ours by a worthy way of life.
>Through Christ our Lord.

Preface of Easter, pp. 558-567.

Communion Antiphon
Cf. Jn 15: 16, 19

>I have chosen you from the world, says the Lord,
>and have appointed you to go out and bear fruit,
>fruit that will last, alleluia.

Prayer after Communion

>Graciously be present to your people, we pray, O Lord,
>and lead those you have imbued with heavenly mysteries
>to pass from former ways to newness of life.
>Through Christ our Lord.

THE ASCENSION OF THE LORD

Solemnity

Where the Solemnity of the Ascension is not to be observed as a Holyday of Obligation, it is assigned to the Seventh Sunday of Easter as its proper day.

At the Vigil Mass

This Mass is used on the evening of the day before the Solemnity, either before or after First Vespers (Evening Prayer I) of the Ascension.

Entrance Antiphon
Ps 68 (67): 33, 35

You kingdoms of the earth, sing to God;
praise the Lord, who ascends above the highest heavens;
his majesty and might are in the skies, alleluia.

The Gloria in excelsis (Glory to God in the highest) is said.

Collect

O God, whose Son today ascended to the heavens
as the Apostles looked on,
grant, we pray, that, in accordance with his promise,
we may be worthy for him to live with us always on earth,
and we with him in heaven.
Who lives and reigns with you in the unity of the Holy Spirit,
one God, for ever and ever.

The Creed is said.

Prayer over the Offerings

O God, whose Only Begotten Son, our High Priest,
is seated ever-living at your right hand to intercede for us,
grant that we may approach with confidence the throne of grace
and there obtain your mercy.
Through Christ our Lord.

Preface I or II of the Ascension, pp. 568-571.

When the Roman Canon is used, the proper form of the Communicantes (In communion with those) is said.

Communion Antiphon
Cf. Heb 10: 12

Christ, offering a single sacrifice for sins,
is seated for ever at God's right hand, alleluia.

Prayer after Communion

May the gifts we have received from your altar, Lord,
kindle in our hearts a longing for the heavenly homeland
and cause us to press forward, following in the Savior's footsteps,
to the place where for our sake he entered before us.
Who lives and reigns for ever and ever.

A formula of Solemn Blessing, p. 678, may be used.

At the Mass during the Day

Entrance Antiphon   Acts 1: 11

Men of Galilee, why gaze in wonder at the heavens?
This Jesus whom you saw ascending into heaven
will return as you saw him go, alleluia.

The Gloria in excelsis (Glory to God in the highest) is said.

Collect

Gladden us with holy joys, almighty God,
and make us rejoice with devout thanksgiving,
for the Ascension of Christ your Son
is our exaltation,
and, where the Head has gone before in glory,
the Body is called to follow in hope.
Through our Lord Jesus Christ, your Son,
who lives and reigns with you in the unity of the Holy Spirit,
one God, for ever and ever.

Or:

Grant, we pray, almighty God,
that we, who believe that your Only Begotten Son, our Redeemer,
ascended this day to the heavens,
may in spirit dwell already in heavenly realms.
Who lives and reigns with you in the unity of the Holy Spirit,
one God, for ever and ever.

The Creed is said.

Prayer over the Offerings

We offer sacrifice now in supplication, O Lord,
to honor the wondrous Ascension of your Son:
grant, we pray,
that through this most holy exchange
we, too, may rise up to the heavenly realms.
Through Christ our Lord.

Preface I or II of the Ascension of the Lord, pp. 568-571.

When the Roman Canon is used, the proper form of the Communicantes (In communion with those) is said.

Communion Antiphon

Mt 28: 20

Behold, I am with you always,
even to the end of the age, alleluia.

Prayer after Communion

Almighty ever-living God,
who allow those on earth to celebrate divine mysteries,
grant, we pray,
that Christian hope may draw us onward
to where our nature is united with you.
Through Christ our Lord.

A formula of Solemn Blessing, p. 678, may be used.

Thursday

In regions where the Solemnity of the Ascension occurs on the following Sunday.

Entrance Antiphon
Cf. Ps 68 (67): 8-9, 20

O God, when you went forth before your people,
marching with them and living among them,
the earth trembled, heavens poured down rain, alleluia.

Collect

O God, who made your people
partakers in your redemption,
grant, we pray,
that we may perpetually render thanks
for the Resurrection of the Lord.
Who lives and reigns with you in the unity of the Holy Spirit,
one God, for ever and ever.

Prayer over the Offerings

May our prayers rise up to you, O Lord,
together with the sacrificial offerings,
so that, purified by your graciousness,
we may be conformed to the mysteries of your mighty love.
Through Christ our Lord.

Preface of Easter, pp. 558-567.

Communion Antiphon
Mt 28: 20

Behold, I am with you always,
even to the end of the age, alleluia.

Prayer after Communion

Almighty ever-living God,
who restore us to eternal life
in the Resurrection of Christ,
increase in us, we pray, the fruits of this paschal Sacrament
and pour into our hearts the strength of this saving food.
Through Christ our Lord.

Friday

Entrance Antiphon
Rev 5: 9-10

You have redeemed us, Lord, by your Blood
from every tribe and tongue and people and nation,
and have made us into a kingdom, priests for our God, alleluia.

Collect

O God, who restore us to eternal life
in the Resurrection of Christ,
raise us up, we pray, to the author of our salvation,
who is seated at your right hand,
so that, when our Savior comes again in majesty,
those you have given new birth in Baptism
may be clothed with blessed immortality.
Through our Lord Jesus Christ, your Son,
who lives and reigns with you in the unity of the Holy Spirit,
one God, for ever and ever.

In regions where the Solemnity of the Ascension is celebrated on the following Sunday:

Hear our prayers, O Lord,
so that what was promised
by the sanctifying power of your Word
may everywhere be accomplished
through the working of the Gospel
and that all your adopted children may attain
what the testimony of truth has foretold.
Through our Lord Jesus Christ, your Son,
who lives and reigns with you in the unity of the Holy Spirit,
one God, for ever and ever.

Prayer over the Offerings

Accept in compassion, Lord, we pray,
the offerings of your family,
that under your protective care
they may never lose what they have received,
but attain the gifts that are eternal.
Through Christ our Lord.

Preface of Easter, or of the Ascension, pp. 558-571.

Communion Antiphon   Rom 4: 25

Christ our Lord was handed over for our transgressions
and was raised again for our justification, alleluia.

Prayer after Communion

Keep safe, O Lord, we pray,
those whom you have saved by your kindness,
that, redeemed by the Passion of your Son,
they may rejoice in his Resurrection.
Who lives and reigns for ever and ever.

Saturday

Entrance Antiphon Cf. 1 Pt 2: 9
O chosen people, proclaim the mighty works of him
who called you out of darkness into his wonderful light, alleluia.

Collect
O God, whose Son, at his Ascension to the heavens,
was pleased to promise the Holy Spirit to the Apostles,
grant, we pray,
that, just as they received manifold gifts of heavenly teaching,
so on us, too, you may bestow spiritual gifts.
Through our Lord Jesus Christ, your Son,
who lives and reigns with you in the unity of the Holy Spirit,
one God, for ever and ever.

In regions where the Solemnity of the Ascension is celebrated on the following Sunday:
Constantly shape our minds, we pray, O Lord,
by the practice of good works,
that, trying always for what is better,
we may strive to hold ever fast to the Paschal Mystery.
Through our Lord Jesus Christ, your Son,
who lives and reigns with you in the unity of the Holy Spirit,
one God, for ever and ever.

Prayer over the Offerings
Graciously sanctify these gifts, O Lord, we pray,
and, accepting the oblation of this spiritual sacrifice,
make of us an eternal offering to you.
Through Christ our Lord.

Preface of Easter, or of the Ascension, pp. 558-571.

Communion Antiphon Jn 17: 24
Father, I wish that, where I am,
those you gave me may also be with me,
that they may see the glory that you gave me, alleluia.

Prayer after Communion
We have partaken of the gifts of this sacred mystery,
humbly imploring, O Lord,
that what your Son commanded us to do in memory of him
may bring us growth in charity.
Through Christ our Lord.

SEVENTH SUNDAY OF EASTER

Entrance Antiphon
Cf. Ps 27 (26): 7-9

O Lord, hear my voice, for I have called to you;
of you my heart has spoken: Seek his face;
hide not your face from me, alleluia.

The Gloria in excelsis (Glory to God in the highest) is said.

Collect
Graciously hear our supplications, O Lord,
so that we, who believe that the Savior of the human race
is with you in your glory,
may experience, as he promised,
until the end of the world,
his abiding presence among us.
Who lives and reigns with you in the unity of the Holy Spirit,
one God, for ever and ever.

The Creed is said.

Prayer over the Offerings
Accept, O Lord, the prayers of your faithful
with the sacrificial offerings,
that through these acts of devotedness
we may pass over to the glory of heaven.
Through Christ our Lord.

Preface of Easter, or of the Ascension, pp. 558-571.

Communion Antiphon
Jn 17: 22

Father, I pray that they may be one
as we also are one, alleluia.

Prayer after Communion
Hear us, O God our Savior,
and grant us confidence,
that through these sacred mysteries
there will be accomplished in the body of the whole Church
what has already come to pass in Christ her Head.
Who lives and reigns for ever and ever.

A formula of Solemn Blessing, p. 677, may be used.

Monday

Entrance Antiphon
Acts 1: 8

You will receive the power of the Holy Spirit coming upon you,
and you will be my witnesses,
even to the ends of the earth, alleluia.

Collect

**May the power of the Holy Spirit
come to us, we pray, O Lord,
that we may keep your will faithfully in mind
and express it in a devout way of life.
Through our Lord Jesus Christ, your Son,
who lives and reigns with you in the unity of the Holy Spirit,
one God, for ever and ever.**

Prayer over the Offerings

**May this unblemished sacrifice purify us, O Lord,
and impart to our minds
the force of grace from on high.
Through Christ our Lord.**

Preface of Easter, or of the Ascension, pp. 558-571.

Communion Antiphon
Jn 14: 18; 16: 22

I will not leave you orphans, says the Lord;
I will come to you again, and your heart will rejoice, alleluia.

Prayer after Communion

**Graciously be present to your people, we pray, O Lord,
and lead those you have imbued with heavenly mysteries
to pass from former ways to newness of life.
Through Christ our Lord.**

Tuesday

Entrance Antiphon
Rev 1: 17-18

> I am the first and the last,
> I was dead and am now alive.
> Behold, I am alive for ever and ever, alleluia.

Collect

> Grant, we pray, almighty and merciful God,
> that the Holy Spirit, coming near
> and dwelling graciously within us,
> may make of us a perfect temple of his glory.
> Through our Lord Jesus Christ, your Son,
> who lives and reigns with you in the unity of the Holy Spirit,
> one God, for ever and ever.

Prayer over the Offerings

> Accept, O Lord, the prayers of your faithful
> with the sacrificial offerings,
> that through these acts of devotedness
> we may pass over to the glory of heaven.
> Through Christ our Lord.

Preface of Easter, or of the Ascension, pp. 558-571.

Communion Antiphon
Jn 14: 26

> The Holy Spirit, whom the Father will send in my name,
> will teach you all things and remind you of all I have told you,
> says the Lord, alleluia.

Prayer after Communion

> We have partaken of the gifts of this sacred mystery,
> humbly imploring, O Lord,
> that what your Son commanded us to do
> in memory of him
> may bring us growth in charity.
> Through Christ our Lord.

Wednesday

Entrance Antiphon
Ps 47 (46): 2

All peoples, clap your hands.
Cry to God with shouts of joy, alleluia.

Collect
Graciously grant to your Church, O merciful God,
that, gathered by the Holy Spirit,
she may be devoted to you with all her heart
and united in purity of intent.
Through our Lord Jesus Christ, your Son,
who lives and reigns with you in the unity of the Holy Spirit,
one God, for ever and ever.

Prayer over the Offerings
Accept, O Lord, we pray,
the sacrifices instituted by your commands,
and through the sacred mysteries,
which we celebrate as our dutiful service,
graciously complete the sanctifying work
by which you are pleased to redeem us.
Through Christ our Lord.

Preface of Easter, or of the Ascension, pp. 558-571.

Communion Antiphon
Jn 15: 26-27

When the Paraclete comes, whom I will send you,
the Spirit of Truth who proceeds from the Father,
he will bear witness to me,
and you also will bear witness, says the Lord, alleluia.

Prayer after Communion
May our partaking of this divine Sacrament, O Lord,
constantly increase your grace within us,
and, by cleansing us with its power,
make us always ready to receive so great a gift.
Through Christ our Lord.

Thursday

Entrance Antiphon
Heb 4: 16

With boldness let us approach the throne of grace,
that we may receive mercy
and find grace as a timely help, alleluia.

Collect

May your Spirit, O Lord, we pray,
imbue us powerfully with spiritual gifts,
that he may give us a mind pleasing to you
and graciously conform us to your will.
Through our Lord Jesus Christ, your Son,
who lives and reigns with you in the unity of the Holy Spirit,
one God, for ever and ever.

Prayer over the Offerings

Graciously sanctify these gifts, O Lord, we pray,
and, accepting the oblation of this spiritual sacrifice,
make of us an eternal offering to you.
Through Christ our Lord.

Preface of Easter, or of the Ascension, pp. 558-571.

Communion Antiphon
Jn 16: 7

I tell you the truth, it is for your good that I go;
for if I do not go away, the Paraclete will not come to you,
says the Lord, alleluia.

Prayer after Communion

May the mysteries we have received, O Lord, we pray,
enlighten us by the instruction they bring
and restore us through our participation in them,
that we may merit the gifts of the Spirit.
Through Christ our Lord.

Friday

Entrance Antiphon
Rev 1: 5-6

Christ loved us and washed us clean of our sins by his Blood,
and made us into a kingdom,
priests for his God and Father, alleluia.

Collect

O God, who by the glorification of your Christ
and the light of the Holy Spirit
have unlocked for us the gates of eternity,
grant, we pray,
that, partaking of so great a gift,
our devotion may grow deeper
and our faith be strengthened.
Through our Lord Jesus Christ, your Son,
who lives and reigns with you in the unity of the Holy Spirit,
one God, for ever and ever.

Prayer over the Offerings

Look mercifully, O Lord, we pray,
upon the sacrificial gifts of your people,
and, that they may become acceptable to you,
let the coming of the Holy Spirit
cleanse our consciences.
Through Christ our Lord.

Preface of Easter, or of the Ascension, pp. 558-571.

Communion Antiphon
Jn 16: 13

When the Spirit of truth comes,
he will teach you all truth, says the Lord, alleluia.

Prayer after Communion

O God, by whose mysteries
we are cleansed and nourished,
grant, we pray,
that this banquet which you give us
may bring everlasting life.
Through Christ our Lord.

Saturday
At the Morning Mass

Entrance Antiphon   Acts 1: 14

The disciples devoted themselves with one accord to prayer
with the women, and Mary the Mother of Jesus,
and his brethren, alleluia.

Collect

Grant, we pray, almighty God,
that we, who have celebrated the paschal festivities,
may by your gift hold fast to them
in the way that we live our lives.
Through our Lord Jesus Christ, your Son,
who lives and reigns with you in the unity of the Holy Spirit,
one God, for ever and ever.

Prayer over the Offerings

May the Holy Spirit coming near, we pray, O Lord,
prepare our minds for the divine Sacrament,
since the Spirit himself is the remission of all sins.
Through Christ our Lord.

Preface of Easter, or of the Ascension, pp. 558-571.

Communion Antiphon   Jn 16: 14

The Holy Spirit will glorify me,
for he will take from what is mine and declare it to you,
says the Lord, alleluia.

Prayer after Communion

Hear in your compassion our prayers, O Lord,
that, as we have been brought
from things of the past to new mysteries,
so, with former ways left behind,
we may be made new in holiness of mind.
Through Christ our Lord.

PENTECOST SUNDAY

Solemnity

At the Vigil Mass
Extended form

This Vigil Mass may be celebrated on the Saturday evening, either before or after First Vespers (Evening Prayer I) of Pentecost Sunday.

1. In churches where the Vigil Mass is celebrated in an extended form, this may be done as follows.

2. a) If First Vespers (Evening Prayer I) celebrated in choir or in common immediately precede Mass, the celebration may begin either from the introductory verse and the hymn (Veni, creator Spiritus) or else from the singing of the Entrance Antiphon with the procession and greeting of the Priest; in either case the Penitential Act is omitted (cf. *General Instruction of the Liturgy of the Hours*, nos. 94 and 96).

    Then the Psalmody prescribed for Vespers follows, up to but not including the Short Reading.

    After the Psalmody, omitting the Penitential Act, and if appropriate, the Kyrie (Lord, have mercy), the Priest says the prayer Grant, we pray, almighty God, that the splendor, as at the Vigil Mass.

3. b) If Mass is begun in the usual way, after the Kyrie (Lord, have mercy), the Priest says the prayer Grant, we pray, almighty God, that the splendor, as at the Vigil Mass.

    Then the Priest may address the people in these or similar words:

    **Dear brethren (brothers and sisters),
    we have now begun our Pentecost Vigil,
    after the example of the Apostles and disciples,
    who with Mary, the Mother of Jesus, persevered in prayer,
    awaiting the Spirit promised by the Lord;
    like them, let us, too, listen with quiet hearts to the Word of God.
    Let us meditate on how many great deeds
    God in times past did for his people
    and let us pray that the Holy Spirit,
    whom the Father sent as the first fruits for those who believe,
    may bring to perfection his work in the world.**

4. Then follow the readings proposed as options in the Lectionary. A reader goes to the ambo and proclaims the reading. Afterwards a psalmist or a cantor sings or says the Psalm with the people making the response. Then all rise, the Priest says, Let us pray and, after all have prayed for a while in silence, he says the prayer corresponding to the reading. In place of the Responsorial Psalm a period of sacred silence may be observed, in which case the pause after Let us pray is omitted.

Prayers after the Readings

5. After the first reading (On Babel: Gn 11: 1-9) and the Psalm (33 [32]: 10-11, 12-13, 14-15; R. v. 12b).

Let us pray.

**Grant, we pray, almighty God,
that your Church may always remain that holy people,
formed as one by the unity of Father, Son and Holy Spirit,
which manifests to the world
the Sacrament of your holiness and unity
and leads it to the perfection of your charity.
Through Christ our Lord.**
R. **Amen.**

6. After the second reading (On God's Descent on Mount Sinai: Ex 19: 3-8, 16-20b) and the canticle (Dn 3: 52, 53, 54, 55, 56; R. v. 52b) or the Psalm (19 [18]: 8, 9, 10, 11; R. Jn 6: 68c).

Let us pray.

**O God, who in fire and lightning
gave the ancient Law to Moses on Mount Sinai
and on this day manifested the new covenant
in the fire of the Spirit,
grant, we pray,
that we may always be aflame with that same Spirit
whom you wondrously poured out on your Apostles,
and that the new Israel,
gathered from every people,
may receive with rejoicing
the eternal commandment of your love.
Through Christ our Lord.**
R. **Amen.**

PENTECOST SUNDAY

7. After the third reading (On the dry bones and God's spirit: Ez 37: 1-14) and the Psalm (107 [106]: 2-3, 4-5, 6-7, 8-9; R. v. 1 or Alleluia).

Let us pray.

Lord, God of power,
who restore what has fallen
and preserve what you have restored,
increase, we pray, the peoples
to be renewed by the sanctification of your name,
that all who are washed clean by holy Baptism
may always be directed by your prompting.
Through Christ our Lord.
R. Amen.

Or:

O God, who have brought us to rebirth by the word of life,
pour out upon us your Holy Spirit,
that, walking in oneness of faith,
we may attain in our flesh
the incorruptible glory of the resurrection.
Through Christ our Lord.
R. Amen.

Or:

May your people exult for ever, O God,
in renewed youthfulness of spirit,
so that, rejoicing now in the restored glory of our adoption,
we may look forward in confident hope
to the rejoicing of the day of resurrection.
Through Christ our Lord.
R. Amen.

8. After the fourth reading (On the outpouring of the Spirit: Joel 3: 1-5) and the Psalm (104 [103]: 1-2a, 24, 35c, 27-28, 29bc-30; R. v. 30 or Alleluia).

Let us pray.

Fulfill for us your gracious promise,
O Lord, we pray, so that by his coming
the Holy Spirit may make us witnesses before the world
to the Gospel of our Lord Jesus Christ.
Who lives and reigns for ever and ever.
R. Amen.

9. Then the Priest intones the hymn Gloria in excelsis Deo (Glory to God in the highest).

Gló-ri-a in ex-cél-sis De-o.

10. When the hymn is concluded, the Priest says the Collect in the usual way: Almighty ever-living God, who willed, as here below.

11. Then the reader proclaims the reading from the Apostle (Rom 8: 22-27), and Mass continues in the usual way.

12. If Vespers (Evening Prayer) are joined to Mass, after Communion with the Communion Antiphon (On the last day), the Magnificat is sung, with its Vespers antiphon (Veni, Sancte Spiritus); then the Prayer after Communion is said and the rest follows as usual.

13. It is appropriate that the formula of Solemn Blessing be used, p. 678.

    To dismiss the people the Deacon or, if there is no Deacon, the Priest himself sings or says:

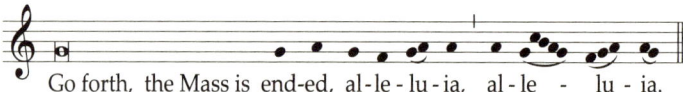
Go forth, the Mass is end-ed, al-le-lu-ia, al-le - lu - ia.

Or:

Go in peace, al-le-lu-ia, al-le - lu - ia.

And the people reply:

Thanks be to God, al-le-lu-ia, al-le - lu - ia.

At the Vigil Mass
Simple form

This Mass is used on the Saturday evening, either before or after First Vespers (Evening Prayer I) of Pentecost Sunday.

Entrance Antiphon
Rom 5: 5; cf. 8: 11

The love of God has been poured into our hearts
through the Spirit of God dwelling within us, alleluia.

The Gloria in excelsis (Glory to God in the highest) is said.

Collect

Almighty ever-living God,
who willed the Paschal Mystery
to be encompassed as a sign in fifty days,
grant that from out of the scattered nations
the confusion of many tongues
may be gathered by heavenly grace
into one great confession of your name.
Through our Lord Jesus Christ, your Son,
who lives and reigns with you in the unity of the Holy Spirit,
one God, for ever and ever.

Or:

Grant, we pray, almighty God,
that the splendor of your glory
may shine forth upon us
and that, by the bright rays of the Holy Spirit,
the light of your light may confirm the hearts
of those born again by your grace.
Through our Lord Jesus Christ, your Son,
who lives and reigns with you in the unity of the Holy Spirit,
one God, for ever and ever.

The Creed is said.

Prayer over the Offerings

Pour out upon these gifts the blessing of your Spirit,
we pray, O Lord,
so that through them your Church may be imbued with such love
that the truth of your saving mystery
may shine forth for the whole world.
Through Christ our Lord.

Preface of Pentecost as in the following Mass, pp. 454-456.

When the Roman Canon is used, the proper form of the Communicantes (In communion with those) is said.

Communion Antiphon
Jn 7: 37

On the last day of the festival, Jesus stood and cried out:
If anyone is thirsty, let him come to me and drink, alleluia.

Prayer after Communion

May these gifts we have consumed
benefit us, O Lord,
that we may always be aflame with the same Spirit,
whom you wondrously poured out on your Apostles.
Through Christ our Lord.

A formula of Solemn Blessing, p. 678, may be used.

To dismiss the people the Deacon or, if there is no Deacon, the Priest himself sings (as above p. 386) or says:

Go forth, the Mass is ended, alleluia, alleluia.

Or:

Go in peace, alleluia, alleluia.

And the people reply:

Thanks be to God, alleluia, alleluia.

PENTECOST SUNDAY

At the Mass during the Day

Entrance Antiphon
Wis 1: 7

The Spirit of the Lord has filled the whole world
and that which contains all things
understands what is said, alleluia.

Or:
Rom 5: 5; cf. 8: 11

The love of God has been poured into our hearts
through the Spirit of God dwelling within us, alleluia.

The Gloria in excelsis (Glory to God in the highest) is said.

Collect

O God, who by the mystery of today's great feast
sanctify your whole Church in every people and nation,
pour out, we pray, the gifts of the Holy Spirit
across the face of the earth
and, with the divine grace that was at work
when the Gospel was first proclaimed,
fill now once more the hearts of believers.
Through our Lord Jesus Christ, your Son,
who lives and reigns with you in the unity of the Holy Spirit,
one God, for ever and ever.

The Creed is said.

Prayer over the Offerings

Grant, we pray, O Lord,
that, as promised by your Son,
the Holy Spirit may reveal to us more abundantly
the hidden mystery of this sacrifice
and graciously lead us into all truth.
Through Christ our Lord.

Preface: The mystery of Pentecost.

V. The Lord be with you.   R. And with your spirit.

V. Lift up your hearts.   R. We lift them up to the Lord.

V. Let us give thanks to the Lord our God.   R. It is right and just.

It is truly right and just, our duty and our salvation, always and everywhere to give you thanks, Lord, holy Father, almighty and eternal God. For, bringing your Paschal Mystery to completion, you bestowed the Holy Spirit today on those you made your adopted children by uniting them to your Only Begotten Son. This same Spirit, as the Church came to birth, opened to all peoples the knowledge of God and brought together the many languages of the earth in profession of the one faith. Therefore,

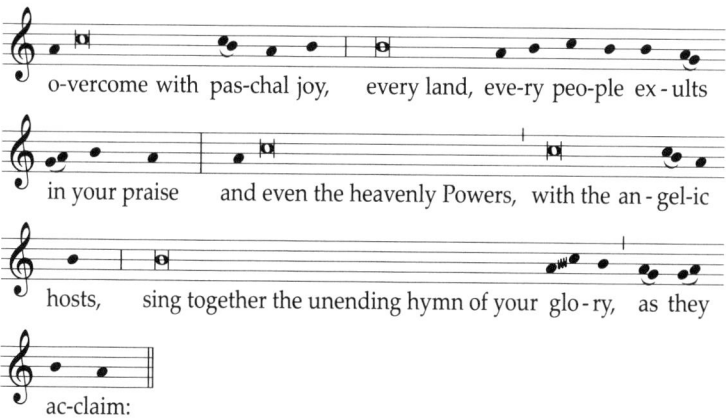

o-vercome with pas-chal joy, every land, eve-ry peo-ple ex-ults in your praise and even the heavenly Powers, with the an-gel-ic hosts, sing together the unending hymn of your glo-ry, as they ac-claim:

Holy, Holy, Holy Lord God of hosts . . .

Text without music:

V. **The Lord be with you.**
R. And with your spirit.

V. **Lift up your hearts.**
R. We lift them up to the Lord.

V. **Let us give thanks to the Lord our God.**
R. It is right and just.

**It is truly right and just, our duty and our salvation,
always and everywhere to give you thanks,
Lord, holy Father, almighty and eternal God.**

**For, bringing your Paschal Mystery to completion,
you bestowed the Holy Spirit today
on those you made your adopted children
by uniting them to your Only Begotten Son.
This same Spirit, as the Church came to birth,
opened to all peoples the knowledge of God
and brought together the many languages of the earth
in profession of the one faith.**

**Therefore, overcome with paschal joy,
every land, every people exults in your praise
and even the heavenly Powers, with the angelic hosts,
sing together the unending hymn of your glory,
as they acclaim:**

Holy, Holy, Holy Lord God of hosts . . .

When the Roman Canon is used, the proper form of the Communicantes (In communion with those) *is said.*

Communion Antiphon   Acts 2: 4, 11

They were all filled with the Holy Spirit
and spoke of the marvels of God, alleluia.

Prayer after Communion

O God, who bestow heavenly gifts upon your Church,
safeguard, we pray, the grace you have given,
that the gift of the Holy Spirit poured out upon her
may retain all its force
and that this spiritual food
may gain her abundance of eternal redemption.
Through Christ our Lord.

A formula of Solemn Blessing, p. 678, may be used.

To dismiss the people the Deacon or, if there is no Deacon, the Priest himself sings or says:

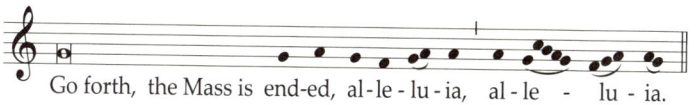
Go forth, the Mass is end-ed, al-le-lu-ia, al-le - lu - ia.

Or:

Go in peace, al-le-lu-ia, al-le - lu - ia.

And the people reply:

Thanks be to God, al-le-lu-ia, al-le - lu - ia.

With Easter Time now concluded, the paschal candle is extinguished. It is desirable to keep the paschal candle in the baptistery with due honor so that it is lit at the celebration of Baptism and the candles of those baptized are lit from it.

Where the Monday or Tuesday after Pentecost are days on which the faithful are obliged or accustomed to attend Mass, the Mass of Pentecost Sunday may be repeated, or a Mass of the Holy Spirit, pp. 1338-1345, may be said.

ORDINARY TIME

1. Ordinary Time contains thirty-three or thirty-four weeks. It begins on the Monday following the Sunday after January 6 and continues until the beginning of Lent; it begins again on the Monday after Pentecost Sunday and ends on the Saturday before the First Sunday of Advent.

2. The numbering of Sundays and weeks in Ordinary Time is calculated as follows:
   a) The Sunday on which the Feast of the Baptism of the Lord occurs takes the place of the first Sunday in Ordinary Time; the week that follows is counted as the first week in Ordinary Time. The remaining Sundays and weeks are numbered in order until the beginning of Lent.
   b) If there are thirty-four weeks in Ordinary Time, after Pentecost the series is resumed with the week that follows immediately the last week celebrated before Lent; it should be noted, however, that the Masses of Pentecost Sunday and of the Solemnity of the Most Holy Trinity take the place of the Sunday Masses. If, however, there are thirty-three weeks in Ordinary Time, the first week that would otherwise follow Pentecost is omitted.

3. Thus, in the Missal, thirty-four Masses for the Sundays and weekdays in Ordinary Time are found. They are used in this way:
   a) On Sundays the Mass corresponding to the number of the Sunday in Ordinary Time is ordinarily used, unless there occurs a Solemnity or a Feast of the Lord which takes the place of the Sunday.
   b) On weekdays, however, any of the thirty-four Masses may be used, provided the pastoral needs of the faithful are taken into consideration.

4. The Gloria in excelsis (Glory to God in the highest) and the Creed are said on Sundays; on weekdays, however, both are omitted.

5. Unless a Eucharistic Prayer is used that has a proper Preface, on Sundays one of the Prefaces for Sundays in Ordinary Time is said, pp. 572-587; but on weekdays, a Common Preface is said, pp. 610-621.

6. Two antiphons are provided for Communion, the first from the Psalms, and the second for the most part from the Gospel. One or the other may be selected, as circumstances suggest, but preference should be given to an antiphon that is in harmony with the Gospel of the Mass.

SUNDAY AND DAILY MASSES
FIRST WEEK IN ORDINARY TIME

On the first Sunday in Ordinary Time there occurs the Feast of the Baptism of the Lord, pp. 202-206.

Entrance Antiphon
Upon a lofty throne, I saw a man seated,
whom a host of angels adore, singing in unison:
Behold him, the name of whose empire is eternal.

Collect
**Attend to the pleas of your people with heavenly care,
O Lord, we pray,
that they may see what must be done
and gain strength to do what they have seen.
Through our Lord Jesus Christ, your Son,
who lives and reigns with you in the unity of the Holy Spirit,
one God, for ever and ever.**

Prayer over the Offerings
**May your people's oblation, O Lord, find favor with you, we pray,
that it may restore them to holiness
and obtain what they devoutly entreat.
Through Christ our Lord.**

Communion Antiphon
Ps 36 (35): 10

With you, O Lord, is the fountain of life,
and in your light we see light.

Or:

Jn 10: 10

I have come that they may have life,
and have it more abundantly, says the Lord.

Prayer after Communion
**Humbly we ask you, almighty God,
be graciously pleased to grant
that those you renew with your Sacraments
may also serve with lives pleasing to you.
Through Christ our Lord.**

SECOND SUNDAY IN ORDINARY TIME

Entrance Antiphon   Ps 66 (65): 4
All the earth shall bow down before you, O God,
and shall sing to you,
shall sing to your name, O Most High!

Collect
Almighty ever-living God,
who govern all things,
both in heaven and on earth,
mercifully hear the pleading of your people
and bestow your peace on our times.
Through our Lord Jesus Christ, your Son,
who lives and reigns with you in the unity of the Holy Spirit,
one God, for ever and ever.

Prayer over the Offerings
Grant us, O Lord, we pray,
that we may participate worthily in these mysteries,
for whenever the memorial of this sacrifice is celebrated
the work of our redemption is accomplished.
Through Christ our Lord.

Communion Antiphon   Cf. Ps 23 (22): 5
You have prepared a table before me,
and how precious is the chalice that quenches my thirst.

Or: 1 Jn 4: 16

We have come to know and to believe
in the love that God has for us.

Prayer after Communion
Pour on us, O Lord, the Spirit of your love,
and in your kindness
make those you have nourished
by this one heavenly Bread
one in mind and heart.
Through Christ our Lord.

THIRD SUNDAY IN ORDINARY TIME

Entrance Antiphon
Cf. Ps 96 (95): 1, 6

O sing a new song to the Lord;
sing to the Lord, all the earth.
In his presence are majesty and splendor,
strength and honor in his holy place.

Collect

Almighty ever-living God,
direct our actions according to your good pleasure,
that in the name of your beloved Son
we may abound in good works.
Through our Lord Jesus Christ, your Son,
who lives and reigns with you in the unity of the Holy Spirit,
one God, for ever and ever.

Prayer over the Offerings

Accept our offerings, O Lord, we pray,
and in sanctifying them
grant that they may profit us for salvation.
Through Christ our Lord.

Communion Antiphon
Cf. Ps 34 (33): 6

Look toward the Lord and be radiant;
let your faces not be abashed.

Or:
Jn 8: 12

I am the light of the world, says the Lord;
whoever follows me will not walk in darkness,
but will have the light of life.

Prayer after Communion

Grant, we pray, almighty God,
that, receiving the grace
by which you bring us to new life,
we may always glory in your gift.
Through Christ our Lord.

FOURTH SUNDAY IN ORDINARY TIME

Entrance Antiphon   Ps 106 (105): 47

Save us, O Lord our God!
And gather us from the nations,
to give thanks to your holy name,
and make it our glory to praise you.

Collect

Grant us, Lord our God,
that we may honor you with all our mind,
and love everyone in truth of heart.
Through our Lord Jesus Christ, your Son,
who lives and reigns with you in the unity of the Holy Spirit,
one God, for ever and ever.

Prayer over the Offerings

O Lord, we bring to your altar
these offerings of our service:
be pleased to receive them, we pray,
and transform them
into the Sacrament of our redemption.
Through Christ our Lord.

Communion Antiphon   Cf. Ps 31 (30): 17-18

Let your face shine on your servant.
Save me in your merciful love.
O Lord, let me never be put to shame, for I call on you.

Or: Mt 5: 3-4

Blessed are the poor in spirit,
for theirs is the Kingdom of Heaven.
Blessed are the meek, for they shall possess the land.

Prayer after Communion

Nourished by these redeeming gifts,
we pray, O Lord,
that through this help to eternal salvation
true faith may ever increase.
Through Christ our Lord.

FIFTH SUNDAY IN ORDINARY TIME

Entrance Antiphon
Ps 95 (94): 6-7

O come, let us worship God
and bow low before the God who made us,
for he is the Lord our God.

Collect

Keep your family safe, O Lord, with unfailing care,
that, relying solely on the hope of heavenly grace,
they may be defended always by your protection.
Through our Lord Jesus Christ, your Son,
who lives and reigns with you in the unity of the Holy Spirit,
one God, for ever and ever.

Prayer over the Offerings

O Lord our God,
who once established these created things
to sustain us in our frailty,
grant, we pray,
that they may become for us now
the Sacrament of eternal life.
Through Christ our Lord.

Communion Antiphon
Cf. Ps 107 (106): 8-9

Let them thank the Lord for his mercy,
his wonders for the children of men,
for he satisfies the thirsty soul,
and the hungry he fills with good things.

Or:
Mt 5: 5-6

Blessed are those who mourn, for they shall be consoled.
Blessed are those who hunger and thirst for righteousness,
for they shall have their fill.

Prayer after Communion

O God, who have willed that we be partakers
in the one Bread and the one Chalice,
grant us, we pray, so to live
that, made one in Christ,
we may joyfully bear fruit
for the salvation of the world.
Through Christ our Lord.

SIXTH SUNDAY IN ORDINARY TIME

Entrance Antiphon   Cf. Ps 31 (30): 3-4

Be my protector, O God,
a mighty stronghold to save me.
For you are my rock, my stronghold!
Lead me, guide me, for the sake of your name.

Collect

O God, who teach us that you abide
in hearts that are just and true,
grant that we may be so fashioned by your grace
as to become a dwelling pleasing to you.
Through our Lord Jesus Christ, your Son,
who lives and reigns with you in the unity of the Holy Spirit,
one God, for ever and ever.

Prayer over the Offerings

May this oblation, O Lord, we pray,
cleanse and renew us
and may it become for those who do your will
the source of eternal reward.
Through Christ our Lord.

Communion Antiphon   Cf. Ps 78 (77): 29-30

They ate and had their fill,
and what they craved the Lord gave them;
they were not disappointed in what they craved.

Or: Jn 3: 16

God so loved the world
that he gave his Only Begotten Son,
so that all who believe in him may not perish,
but may have eternal life.

Prayer after Communion

Having fed upon these heavenly delights,
we pray, O Lord,
that we may always long
for that food by which we truly live.
Through Christ our Lord.

SEVENTH SUNDAY IN ORDINARY TIME

Entrance Antiphon
Ps 13 (12): 6

O Lord, I trust in your merciful love.
My heart will rejoice in your salvation.
I will sing to the Lord who has been bountiful with me.

Collect

Grant, we pray, almighty God,
that, always pondering spiritual things,
we may carry out in both word and deed
that which is pleasing to you.
Through our Lord Jesus Christ, your Son,
who lives and reigns with you in the unity of the Holy Spirit,
one God, for ever and ever.

Prayer over the Offerings

As we celebrate your mysteries, O Lord,
with the observance that is your due,
we humbly ask you,
that what we offer to the honor of your majesty
may profit us for salvation.
Through Christ our Lord.

Communion Antiphon
Ps 9: 2-3

I will recount all your wonders,
I will rejoice in you and be glad,
and sing psalms to your name, O Most High.

Or:
Jn 11: 27

Lord, I have come to believe that you are the Christ,
the Son of the living God, who is coming into this world.

Prayer after Communion

Grant, we pray, almighty God,
that we may experience the effects of the salvation
which is pledged to us by these mysteries.
Through Christ our Lord.

EIGHTH SUNDAY IN ORDINARY TIME

Entrance Antiphon   Cf. Ps 18 (17): 19-20

The Lord became my protector.
He brought me out to a place of freedom;
he saved me because he delighted in me.

Collect

Grant us, O Lord, we pray,
that the course of our world
may be directed by your peaceful rule
and that your Church may rejoice,
untroubled in her devotion.
Through our Lord Jesus Christ, your Son,
who lives and reigns with you in the unity of the Holy Spirit,
one God, for ever and ever.

Prayer over the Offerings

O God, who provide gifts to be offered to your name
and count our oblations as signs
of our desire to serve you with devotion,
we ask of your mercy
that what you grant as the source of merit
may also help us to attain merit's reward.
Through Christ our Lord.

Communion Antiphon   Cf. Ps 13 (12): 6

I will sing to the Lord who has been bountiful with me,
sing psalms to the name of the Lord Most High.

Or: Mt 28: 20

Behold, I am with you always,
even to the end of the age, says the Lord.

Prayer after Communion

Nourished by your saving gifts,
we beseech your mercy, Lord,
that by this same Sacrament
with which you feed us in the present age,
you may make us partakers of life eternal.
Through Christ our Lord.

NINTH SUNDAY IN ORDINARY TIME

Entrance Antiphon
Cf. Ps 25 (24): 16, 18

Turn to me and have mercy on me, O Lord,
for I am alone and poor.
See my lowliness and suffering
and take away all my sins, my God.

Collect

O God, whose providence never fails in its design,
keep from us, we humbly beseech you,
all that might harm us
and grant all that works for our good.
Through our Lord Jesus Christ, your Son,
who lives and reigns with you in the unity of the Holy Spirit,
one God, for ever and ever.

Prayer over the Offerings

Trusting in your compassion, O Lord,
we come eagerly with our offerings to your sacred altar,
that, through the purifying action of your grace,
we may be cleansed by the very mysteries we serve.
Through Christ our Lord.

Communion Antiphon
Cf. Ps 17 (16): 6

To you I call, for you will surely heed me, O God;
turn your ear to me; hear my words.

Or:
Mk 11: 23, 24

Amen, I say to you: Whatever you ask for in prayer,
believe you will receive it,
and it will be yours, says the Lord.

Prayer after Communion

Govern by your Spirit, we pray, O Lord,
those you feed with the Body and Blood of your Son,
that, professing you not just in word or in speech,
but also in works and in truth,
we may merit to enter the Kingdom of Heaven.
Through Christ our Lord.

TENTH SUNDAY IN ORDINARY TIME

Entrance Antiphon
Cf. Ps 27 (26): 1-2

The Lord is my light and my salvation; whom shall I fear?
The Lord is the stronghold of my life; whom should I dread?
When those who do evil draw near, they stumble and fall.

Collect

**O God, from whom all good things come,
grant that we, who call on you in our need,
may at your prompting discern what is right,
and by your guidance do it.
Through our Lord Jesus Christ, your Son,
who lives and reigns with you in the unity of the Holy Spirit,
one God, for ever and ever.**

Prayer over the Offerings

**Look kindly upon our service, O Lord, we pray,
that what we offer
may be an acceptable oblation to you
and lead us to grow in charity.
Through Christ our Lord.**

Communion Antiphon
Ps 18 (17): 3

The Lord is my rock, my fortress, and my deliverer;
my God is my saving strength.

Or:
1 Jn 4: 16

God is love, and whoever abides in love
abides in God, and God in him.

Prayer after Communion

**May your healing work, O Lord,
free us, we pray, from doing evil
and lead us to what is right.
Through Christ our Lord.**

ELEVENTH SUNDAY IN ORDINARY TIME

Entrance Antiphon
Cf. Ps 27 (26): 7, 9

O Lord, hear my voice, for I have called to you; be my help.
Do not abandon or forsake me, O God, my Savior!

Collect

O God, strength of those who hope in you,
graciously hear our pleas,
and, since without you mortal frailty can do nothing,
grant us always the help of your grace,
that in following your commands
we may please you by our resolve and our deeds.
Through our Lord Jesus Christ, your Son,
who lives and reigns with you in the unity of the Holy Spirit,
one God, for ever and ever.

Prayer over the Offerings

O God, who in the offerings presented here
provide for the twofold needs of human nature,
nourishing us with food
and renewing us with your Sacrament,
grant, we pray,
that the sustenance they provide
may not fail us in body or in spirit.
Through Christ our Lord.

Communion Antiphon
Ps 27 (26): 4

There is one thing I ask of the Lord, only this do I seek:
to live in the house of the Lord all the days of my life.

Or: *Jn 17: 11*

Holy Father, keep in your name those you have given me,
that they may be one as we are one, says the Lord.

Prayer after Communion

As this reception of your Holy Communion, O Lord,
foreshadows the union of the faithful in you,
so may it bring about unity in your Church.
Through Christ our Lord.

TWELFTH SUNDAY IN ORDINARY TIME

Entrance Antiphon   Cf. Ps 28 (27): 8-9

The Lord is the strength of his people,
a saving refuge for the one he has anointed.
Save your people, Lord, and bless your heritage,
and govern them for ever.

Collect

Grant, O Lord,
that we may always revere and love your holy name,
for you never deprive of your guidance
those you set firm on the foundation of your love.
Through our Lord Jesus Christ, your Son,
who lives and reigns with you in the unity of the Holy Spirit,
one God, for ever and ever.

Prayer over the Offerings

Receive, O Lord, the sacrifice of conciliation and praise
and grant that, cleansed by its action,
we may make offering of a heart pleasing to you.
Through Christ our Lord.

Communion Antiphon   Ps 145 (144): 15

The eyes of all look to you, Lord,
and you give them their food in due season.

Or: Jn 10: 11, 15

I am the Good Shepherd,
and I lay down my life for my sheep, says the Lord.

Prayer after Communion

Renewed and nourished
by the Sacred Body and Precious Blood of your Son,
we ask of your mercy, O Lord,
that what we celebrate with constant devotion
may be our sure pledge of redemption.
Through Christ our Lord.

THIRTEENTH SUNDAY IN ORDINARY TIME

Entrance Antiphon
Ps 47 (46): 2

All peoples, clap your hands.
Cry to God with shouts of joy!

Collect

O God, who through the grace of adoption
chose us to be children of light,
grant, we pray,
that we may not be wrapped in the darkness of error
but always be seen to stand in the bright light of truth.
Through our Lord Jesus Christ, your Son,
who lives and reigns with you in the unity of the Holy Spirit,
one God, for ever and ever.

Prayer over the Offerings

O God, who graciously accomplish
the effects of your mysteries,
grant, we pray,
that the deeds by which we serve you
may be worthy of these sacred gifts.
Through Christ our Lord.

Communion Antiphon
Cf. Ps 103 (102): 1

Bless the Lord, O my soul,
and all within me, his holy name.

Or:
Jn 17: 20-21

O Father, I pray for them, that they may be one in us,
that the world may believe that you have sent me, says the Lord.

Prayer after Communion

May this divine sacrifice we have offered and received
fill us with life, O Lord, we pray,
so that, bound to you in lasting charity,
we may bear fruit that lasts for ever.
Through Christ our Lord.

FOURTEENTH SUNDAY IN ORDINARY TIME

Entrance Antiphon   Cf. Ps 48 (47): 10-11

Your merciful love, O God,
we have received in the midst of your temple.
Your praise, O God, like your name,
reaches the ends of the earth;
your right hand is filled with saving justice.

Collect

O God, who in the abasement of your Son
have raised up a fallen world,
fill your faithful with holy joy,
for on those you have rescued from slavery to sin
you bestow eternal gladness.
Through our Lord Jesus Christ, your Son,
who lives and reigns with you in the unity of the Holy Spirit,
one God, for ever and ever.

Prayer over the Offerings

May this oblation dedicated to your name
purify us, O Lord,
and day by day bring our conduct
closer to the life of heaven.
Through Christ our Lord.

Communion Antiphon   Ps 34 (33): 9

Taste and see that the Lord is good;
blessed the man who seeks refuge in him.

Or: Mt 11: 28

Come to me, all who labor and are burdened,
and I will refresh you, says the Lord.

Prayer after Communion

Grant, we pray, O Lord,
that, having been replenished by such great gifts,
we may gain the prize of salvation
and never cease to praise you.
Through Christ our Lord.

FIFTEENTH SUNDAY IN ORDINARY TIME

Entrance Antiphon   Cf. Ps 17 (16):15

As for me, in justice I shall behold your face;
I shall be filled with the vision of your glory.

Collect

O God, who show the light of your truth
to those who go astray,
so that they may return to the right path,
give all who for the faith they profess
are accounted Christians
the grace to reject whatever is contrary to the name of Christ
and to strive after all that does it honor.
Through our Lord Jesus Christ, your Son,
who lives and reigns with you in the unity of the Holy Spirit,
one God, for ever and ever.

Prayer over the Offerings

Look upon the offerings of the Church, O Lord,
as she makes her prayer to you,
and grant that, when consumed by those who believe,
they may bring ever greater holiness.
Through Christ our Lord.

Communion Antiphon   Cf. Ps 84 (83): 4-5

The sparrow finds a home,
and the swallow a nest for her young:
by your altars, O Lord of hosts, my King and my God.
Blessed are they who dwell in your house,
for ever singing your praise.

Or: Jn 6: 57

Whoever eats my flesh and drinks my blood
remains in me and I in him, says the Lord.

Prayer after Communion

Having consumed these gifts, we pray, O Lord,
that, by our participation in this mystery,
its saving effects upon us may grow.
Through Christ our Lord.

SIXTEENTH SUNDAY IN ORDINARY TIME

Entrance Antiphon   Ps 54 (53): 6, 8

See, I have God for my help.
The Lord sustains my soul.
I will sacrifice to you with willing heart,
and praise your name, O Lord, for it is good.

Collect

Show favor, O Lord, to your servants
and mercifully increase the gifts of your grace,
that, made fervent in hope, faith and charity,
they may be ever watchful in keeping your commands.
Through our Lord Jesus Christ, your Son,
who lives and reigns with you in the unity of the Holy Spirit,
one God, for ever and ever.

Prayer over the Offerings

O God, who in the one perfect sacrifice
brought to completion varied offerings of the law,
accept, we pray, this sacrifice from your faithful servants
and make it holy, as you blessed the gifts of Abel,
so that what each has offered to the honor of your majesty
may benefit the salvation of all.
Through Christ our Lord.

Communion Antiphon   Ps 111 (110): 4-5

The Lord, the gracious, the merciful,
has made a memorial of his wonders;
he gives food to those who fear him.

Or: Rev 3: 20

Behold, I stand at the door and knock, says the Lord.
If anyone hears my voice and opens the door to me,
I will enter his house and dine with him, and he with me.

Prayer after Communion

Graciously be present to your people, we pray, O Lord,
and lead those you have imbued with heavenly mysteries
to pass from former ways to newness of life.
Through Christ our Lord.

SEVENTEENTH SUNDAY IN ORDINARY TIME

Entrance Antiphon
Cf. Ps 68 (67): 6-7, 36

God is in his holy place,
God who unites those who dwell in his house;
he himself gives might and strength to his people.

Collect

O God, protector of those who hope in you,
without whom nothing has firm foundation, nothing is holy,
bestow in abundance your mercy upon us
and grant that, with you as our ruler and guide,
we may use the good things that pass
in such a way as to hold fast even now
to those that ever endure.
Through our Lord Jesus Christ, your Son,
who lives and reigns with you in the unity of the Holy Spirit,
one God, for ever and ever.

Prayer over the Offerings

Accept, O Lord, we pray, the offerings
which we bring from the abundance of your gifts,
that through the powerful working of your grace
these most sacred mysteries may sanctify our present way of life
and lead us to eternal gladness.
Through Christ our Lord.

Communion Antiphon
Ps 103 (102): 2

Bless the Lord, O my soul,
and never forget all his benefits.

Or:
Mt 5: 7-8

Blessed are the merciful, for they shall receive mercy.
Blessed are the clean of heart, for they shall see God.

Prayer after Communion

We have consumed, O Lord, this divine Sacrament,
the perpetual memorial of the Passion of your Son;
grant, we pray, that this gift,
which he himself gave us with love beyond all telling,
may profit us for salvation.
Through Christ our Lord.

EIGHTEENTH SUNDAY IN ORDINARY TIME

Entrance Antiphon
Ps 70 (69): 2, 6

O God, come to my assistance;
O Lord, make haste to help me!
You are my rescuer, my help;
O Lord, do not delay.

Collect

Draw near to your servants, O Lord,
and answer their prayers with unceasing kindness,
that, for those who glory in you as their Creator and guide,
you may restore what you have created
and keep safe what you have restored.
Through our Lord Jesus Christ, your Son,
who lives and reigns with you in the unity of the Holy Spirit,
one God, for ever and ever.

Prayer over the Offerings

Graciously sanctify these gifts, O Lord, we pray,
and, accepting the oblation of this spiritual sacrifice,
make of us an eternal offering to you.
Through Christ our Lord.

Communion Antiphon
Wis 16: 20

You have given us, O Lord, bread from heaven,
endowed with all delights and sweetness in every taste.

Or:
Jn 6: 35

I am the bread of life, says the Lord;
whoever comes to me will not hunger
and whoever believes in me will not thirst.

Prayer after Communion

Accompany with constant protection, O Lord,
those you renew with these heavenly gifts
and, in your never-failing care for them,
make them worthy of eternal redemption.
Through Christ our Lord.

NINETEENTH SUNDAY IN ORDINARY TIME

Entrance Antiphon Cf. Ps 74 (73): 20, 19, 22, 23
Look to your covenant, O Lord,
and forget not the life of your poor ones for ever.
Arise, O God, and defend your cause,
and forget not the cries of those who seek you.

Collect
Almighty ever-living God,
whom, taught by the Holy Spirit,
we dare to call our Father,
bring, we pray, to perfection in our hearts
the spirit of adoption as your sons and daughters,
that we may merit to enter into the inheritance
which you have promised.
Through our Lord Jesus Christ, your Son,
who lives and reigns with you in the unity of the Holy Spirit,
one God, for ever and ever.

Prayer over the Offerings
Be pleased, O Lord, to accept the offerings of your Church,
for in your mercy you have given them to be offered
and by your power you transform them
into the mystery of our salvation.
Through Christ our Lord.

Communion Antiphon Ps 147: 12, 14
O Jerusalem, glorify the Lord,
who gives you your fill of finest wheat.

Or: Cf. Jn 6: 51

The bread that I will give, says the Lord,
is my flesh for the life of the world.

Prayer after Communion
May the communion in your Sacrament
that we have consumed, save us, O Lord,
and confirm us in the light of your truth.
Through Christ our Lord.

TWENTIETH SUNDAY IN ORDINARY TIME

Entrance Antiphon   Ps 84 (83): 10-11

Turn your eyes, O God, our shield;
and look on the face of your anointed one;
one day within your courts
is better than a thousand elsewhere.

Collect

O God, who have prepared for those who love you
good things which no eye can see,
fill our hearts, we pray, with the warmth of your love,
so that, loving you in all things and above all things,
we may attain your promises,
which surpass every human desire.
Through our Lord Jesus Christ, your Son,
who lives and reigns with you in the unity of the Holy Spirit,
one God, for ever and ever.

Prayer over the Offerings

Receive our oblation, O Lord,
by which is brought about a glorious exchange,
that, by offering what you have given,
we may merit to receive your very self.
Through Christ our Lord.

Communion Antiphon   Ps 130 (129): 7

With the Lord there is mercy;
in him is plentiful redemption.

Or: Jn 6: 51-52

I am the living bread that came down from heaven, says the Lord.
Whoever eats of this bread will live for ever.

Prayer after Communion

Made partakers of Christ through these Sacraments,
we humbly implore your mercy, Lord,
that, conformed to his image on earth,
we may merit also to be his coheirs in heaven.
Who lives and reigns for ever and ever.

TWENTY-FIRST SUNDAY IN ORDINARY TIME

Entrance Antiphon — Cf. Ps 86 (85): 1-3

Turn your ear, O Lord, and answer me;
save the servant who trusts in you, my God.
Have mercy on me, O Lord, for I cry to you all the day long.

Collect

O God, who cause the minds of the faithful
to unite in a single purpose,
grant your people to love what you command
and to desire what you promise,
that, amid the uncertainties of this world,
our hearts may be fixed on that place
where true gladness is found.
Through our Lord Jesus Christ, your Son,
who lives and reigns with you in the unity of the Holy Spirit,
one God, for ever and ever.

Prayer over the Offerings

O Lord, who gained for yourself a people by adoption
through the one sacrifice offered once for all,
bestow graciously on us, we pray,
the gifts of unity and peace in your Church.
Through Christ our Lord.

Communion Antiphon — Cf. Ps 104 (103): 13-15

The earth is replete with the fruits of your work, O Lord;
you bring forth bread from the earth
and wine to cheer the heart.

Or: — Cf. Jn 6: 54

Whoever eats my flesh and drinks my blood
has eternal life, says the Lord,
and I will raise him up on the last day.

Prayer after Communion

Complete within us, O Lord, we pray,
the healing work of your mercy
and graciously perfect and sustain us,
so that in all things we may please you.
Through Christ our Lord.

TWENTY-SECOND SUNDAY IN ORDINARY TIME

Entrance Antiphon
Cf. Ps 86 (85): 3, 5

Have mercy on me, O Lord, for I cry to you all the day long.
O Lord, you are good and forgiving,
full of mercy to all who call to you.

Collect

God of might, giver of every good gift,
put into our hearts the love of your name,
so that, by deepening our sense of reverence,
you may nurture in us what is good
and, by your watchful care,
keep safe what you have nurtured.
Through our Lord Jesus Christ, your Son,
who lives and reigns with you in the unity of the Holy Spirit,
one God, for ever and ever.

Prayer over the Offerings

May this sacred offering, O Lord,
confer on us always the blessing of salvation,
that what it celebrates in mystery
it may accomplish in power.
Through Christ our Lord.

Communion Antiphon
Ps 31 (30): 20

How great is the goodness, Lord,
that you keep for those who fear you.

Or:
Mt 5: 9-10

Blessed are the peacemakers,
for they shall be called children of God.
Blessed are they who are persecuted for the sake of righteousness,
for theirs is the Kingdom of Heaven.

Prayer after Communion

Renewed by this bread from the heavenly table,
we beseech you, Lord,
that, being the food of charity,
it may confirm our hearts
and stir us to serve you in our neighbor.
Through Christ our Lord.

TWENTY-THIRD SUNDAY IN ORDINARY TIME

Entrance Antiphon   Ps 119 (118): 137, 124

You are just, O Lord, and your judgment is right;
treat your servant in accord with your merciful love.

Collect

O God, by whom we are redeemed and receive adoption,
look graciously upon your beloved sons and daughters,
that those who believe in Christ
may receive true freedom
and an everlasting inheritance.
Through our Lord Jesus Christ, your Son,
who lives and reigns with you in the unity of the Holy Spirit,
one God, for ever and ever.

Prayer over the Offerings

O God, who give us the gift of true prayer and of peace,
graciously grant that, through this offering,
we may do fitting homage to your divine majesty
and, by partaking of the sacred mystery,
we may be faithfully united in mind and heart.
Through Christ our Lord.

Communion Antiphon   Cf. Ps 42 (41): 2-3

Like the deer that yearns for running streams,
so my soul is yearning for you, my God;
my soul is thirsting for God, the living God.

Or: Jn 8: 12

I am the light of the world, says the Lord;
whoever follows me will not walk in darkness,
but will have the light of life.

Prayer after Communion

Grant that your faithful, O Lord,
whom you nourish and endow with life
through the food of your Word and heavenly Sacrament,
may so benefit from your beloved Son's great gifts
that we may merit an eternal share in his life.
Who lives and reigns for ever and ever.

TWENTY-FOURTH SUNDAY IN ORDINARY TIME

Entrance Antiphon
Cf. Sir 36: 18

Give peace, O Lord, to those who wait for you,
that your prophets be found true.
Hear the prayers of your servant,
and of your people Israel.

Collect

Look upon us, O God,
Creator and ruler of all things,
and, that we may feel the working of your mercy,
grant that we may serve you with all our heart.
Through our Lord Jesus Christ, your Son,
who lives and reigns with you in the unity of the Holy Spirit,
one God, for ever and ever.

Prayer over the Offerings

Look with favor on our supplications, O Lord,
and in your kindness accept these, your servants' offerings,
that what each has offered to the honor of your name
may serve the salvation of all.
Through Christ our Lord.

Communion Antiphon
Cf. Ps 36 (35): 8

How precious is your mercy, O God!
The children of men seek shelter in the shadow of your wings.

Or:
Cf. 1 Cor 10: 16

The chalice of blessing that we bless
is a communion in the Blood of Christ;
and the bread that we break
is a sharing in the Body of the Lord.

Prayer after Communion

May the working of this heavenly gift, O Lord, we pray,
take possession of our minds and bodies,
so that its effects, and not our own desires,
may always prevail in us.
Through Christ our Lord.

TWENTY-FIFTH SUNDAY IN ORDINARY TIME

Entrance Antiphon

I am the salvation of the people, says the Lord.
Should they cry to me in any distress,
I will hear them, and I will be their Lord for ever.

Collect

O God, who founded all the commands of your sacred Law
upon love of you and of our neighbor,
grant that, by keeping your precepts,
we may merit to attain eternal life.
Through our Lord Jesus Christ, your Son,
who lives and reigns with you in the unity of the Holy Spirit,
one God, for ever and ever.

Prayer over the Offerings

Receive with favor, O Lord, we pray,
the offerings of your people,
that what they profess with devotion and faith
may be theirs through these heavenly mysteries.
Through Christ our Lord.

Communion Antiphon   Ps 119 (118): 4-5

You have laid down your precepts to be carefully kept;
may my ways be firm in keeping your statutes.

Or: Jn 10: 14

I am the Good Shepherd, says the Lord;
I know my sheep, and mine know me.

Prayer after Communion

Graciously raise up, O Lord,
those you renew with this Sacrament,
that we may come to possess your redemption
both in mystery and in the manner of our life.
Through Christ our Lord.

TWENTY-SIXTH SUNDAY IN ORDINARY TIME

Entrance Antiphon
Dn 3: 31, 29, 30, 43, 42

All that you have done to us, O Lord,
you have done with true judgment,
for we have sinned against you
and not obeyed your commandments.
But give glory to your name
and deal with us according to the bounty of your mercy.

Collect

**O God, who manifest your almighty power
above all by pardoning and showing mercy,
bestow, we pray, your grace abundantly upon us
and make those hastening to attain your promises
heirs to the treasures of heaven.
Through our Lord Jesus Christ, your Son,
who lives and reigns with you in the unity of the Holy Spirit,
one God, for ever and ever.**

Prayer over the Offerings

**Grant us, O merciful God,
that this our offering may find acceptance with you
and that through it the wellspring of all blessing
may be laid open before us.
Through Christ our Lord.**

Communion Antiphon
Cf. Ps 119 (118): 49-50

Remember your word to your servant, O Lord,
by which you have given me hope.
This is my comfort when I am brought low.

Or:
1 Jn 3: 16

By this we came to know the love of God:
that Christ laid down his life for us;
so we ought to lay down our lives for one another.

Prayer after Communion

**May this heavenly mystery, O Lord,
restore us in mind and body,
that we may be coheirs in glory with Christ,
to whose suffering we are united
whenever we proclaim his Death.
Who lives and reigns for ever and ever.**

TWENTY-SEVENTH SUNDAY IN ORDINARY TIME

Entrance Antiphon
Cf. Est 4: 17

Within your will, O Lord, all things are established,
and there is none that can resist your will.
For you have made all things, the heaven and the earth,
and all that is held within the circle of heaven;
you are the Lord of all.

Collect

**Almighty ever-living God,
who in the abundance of your kindness
surpass the merits and the desires of those who entreat you,
pour out your mercy upon us
to pardon what conscience dreads
and to give what prayer does not dare to ask.
Through our Lord Jesus Christ, your Son,
who lives and reigns with you in the unity of the Holy Spirit,
one God, for ever and ever.**

Prayer over the Offerings

**Accept, O Lord, we pray,
the sacrifices instituted by your commands
and, through the sacred mysteries,
which we celebrate with dutiful service,
graciously complete the sanctifying work
by which you are pleased to redeem us.
Through Christ our Lord.**

Communion Antiphon
Lam 3: 25

The Lord is good to those who hope in him,
to the soul that seeks him.

Or:

Cf. 1 Cor 10: 17

Though many, we are one bread, one body,
for we all partake of the one Bread and one Chalice.

Prayer after Communion

**Grant us, almighty God,
that we may be refreshed and nourished
by the Sacrament which we have received,
so as to be transformed into what we consume.
Through Christ our Lord.**

TWENTY-EIGHTH SUNDAY IN ORDINARY TIME

Entrance Antiphon   Ps 130 (129): 3-4

If you, O Lord, should mark iniquities,
Lord, who could stand?
But with you is found forgiveness,
O God of Israel.

Collect

May your grace, O Lord, we pray,
at all times go before us and follow after
and make us always determined
to carry out good works.
Through our Lord Jesus Christ, your Son,
who lives and reigns with you in the unity of the Holy Spirit,
one God, for ever and ever.

Prayer over the Offerings

Accept, O Lord, the prayers of your faithful
with the sacrificial offerings,
that, through these acts of devotedness,
we may pass over to the glory of heaven.
Through Christ our Lord.

Communion Antiphon   Cf. Ps 34 (33): 11

The rich suffer want and go hungry,
but those who seek the Lord lack no blessing.

Or: 1 Jn 3: 2

When the Lord appears, we shall be like him,
for we shall see him as he is.

Prayer after Communion

We entreat your majesty most humbly, O Lord,
that, as you feed us with the nourishment
which comes from the most holy Body and Blood of your Son,
so you may make us sharers of his divine nature.
Who lives and reigns for ever and ever.

TWENTY-NINTH SUNDAY IN ORDINARY TIME

Entrance Antiphon
Cf. Ps 17 (16): 6, 8

> To you I call; for you will surely heed me, O God;
> turn your ear to me; hear my words.
> Guard me as the apple of your eye;
> in the shadow of your wings protect me.

Collect

> **Almighty ever-living God,**
> **grant that we may always conform our will to yours**
> **and serve your majesty in sincerity of heart.**
> **Through our Lord Jesus Christ, your Son,**
> **who lives and reigns with you in the unity of the Holy Spirit,**
> **one God, for ever and ever.**

Prayer over the Offerings

> **Grant us, Lord, we pray,**
> **a sincere respect for your gifts,**
> **that, through the purifying action of your grace,**
> **we may be cleansed by the very mysteries we serve.**
> **Through Christ our Lord.**

Communion Antiphon
Cf. Ps 33 (32): 18-19

> Behold, the eyes of the Lord
> are on those who fear him,
> who hope in his merciful love,
> to rescue their souls from death,
> to keep them alive in famine.

Or:
Mk 10: 45

> The Son of Man has come
> to give his life as a ransom for many.

Prayer after Communion

> **Grant, O Lord, we pray,**
> **that, benefiting from participation in heavenly things,**
> **we may be helped by what you give in this present age**
> **and prepared for the gifts that are eternal.**
> **Through Christ our Lord.**

THIRTIETH SUNDAY IN ORDINARY TIME

Entrance Antiphon   Cf. Ps 105 (104): 3-4

Let the hearts that seek the Lord rejoice;
turn to the Lord and his strength;
constantly seek his face.

Collect

Almighty ever-living God,
increase our faith, hope and charity,
and make us love what you command,
so that we may merit what you promise.
Through our Lord Jesus Christ, your Son,
who lives and reigns with you in the unity of the Holy Spirit,
one God, for ever and ever.

Prayer over the Offerings

Look, we pray, O Lord,
on the offerings we make to your majesty,
that whatever is done by us in your service
may be directed above all to your glory.
Through Christ our Lord.

Communion Antiphon   Cf. Ps 20 (19): 6

We will ring out our joy at your saving help
and exult in the name of our God.

Or: Eph 5: 2

Christ loved us and gave himself up for us,
as a fragrant offering to God.

Prayer after Communion

May your Sacraments, O Lord, we pray,
perfect in us what lies within them,
that what we now celebrate in signs
we may one day possess in truth.
Through Christ our Lord.

THIRTY-FIRST SUNDAY IN ORDINARY TIME

Entrance Antiphon
Cf. Ps 38 (37): 22-23

Forsake me not, O Lord, my God;
be not far from me!
Make haste and come to my help,
O Lord, my strong salvation!

Collect
**Almighty and merciful God,
by whose gift your faithful offer you
right and praiseworthy service,
grant, we pray,
that we may hasten without stumbling
to receive the things you have promised.
Through our Lord Jesus Christ, your Son,
who lives and reigns with you in the unity of the Holy Spirit,
one God, for ever and ever.**

Prayer over the Offerings
May these sacrificial offerings, O Lord,
become for you a pure oblation,
and for us a holy outpouring of your mercy.
Through Christ our Lord.

Communion Antiphon
Cf. Ps 16 (15): 11

You will show me the path of life,
the fullness of joy in your presence, O Lord.

Or:

Jn 6: 58

Just as the living Father sent me
and I have life because of the Father,
so whoever feeds on me
shall have life because of me, says the Lord.

Prayer after Communion
May the working of your power, O Lord,
increase in us, we pray,
so that, renewed by these heavenly Sacraments,
we may be prepared by your gift
for receiving what they promise.
Through Christ our Lord.

THIRTY-SECOND SUNDAY IN ORDINARY TIME

Entrance Antiphon Cf. Ps 88 (87): 3
Let my prayer come into your presence.
Incline your ear to my cry for help, O Lord.

Collect
Almighty and merciful God,
graciously keep from us all adversity,
so that, unhindered in mind and body alike,
we may pursue in freedom of heart
the things that are yours.
Through our Lord Jesus Christ, your Son,
who lives and reigns with you in the unity of the Holy Spirit,
one God, for ever and ever.

Prayer over the Offerings
Look with favor, we pray, O Lord,
upon the sacrificial gifts offered here,
that, celebrating in mystery the Passion of your Son,
we may honor it with loving devotion.
Through Christ our Lord.

Communion Antiphon Cf. Ps 23 (22): 1-2
The Lord is my shepherd; there is nothing I shall want.
Fresh and green are the pastures where he gives me repose,
near restful waters he leads me.

Or: Cf. Lk 24: 35

The disciples recognized the Lord Jesus in the breaking of bread.

Prayer after Communion
Nourished by this sacred gift, O Lord,
we give you thanks and beseech your mercy,
that, by the pouring forth of your Spirit,
the grace of integrity may endure
in those your heavenly power has entered.
Through Christ our Lord.

THIRTY-THIRD SUNDAY IN ORDINARY TIME

Entrance Antiphon
Jer 29: 11, 12, 14

The Lord said: I think thoughts of peace and not of affliction.
You will call upon me, and I will answer you,
and I will lead back your captives from every place.

Collect

Grant us, we pray, O Lord our God,
the constant gladness of being devoted to you,
for it is full and lasting happiness
to serve with constancy
the author of all that is good.
Through our Lord Jesus Christ, your Son,
who lives and reigns with you in the unity of the Holy Spirit,
one God, for ever and ever.

Prayer over the Offerings

Grant, O Lord, we pray,
that what we offer in the sight of your majesty
may obtain for us the grace of being devoted to you
and gain us the prize of everlasting happiness.
Through Christ our Lord.

Communion Antiphon
Ps 73 (72): 28

To be near God is my happiness,
to place my hope in God the Lord.

Or:

Mk 11: 23-24

Amen, I say to you: Whatever you ask in prayer,
believe that you will receive,
and it shall be given to you, says the Lord.

Prayer after Communion

We have partaken of the gifts of this sacred mystery,
humbly imploring, O Lord,
that what your Son commanded us to do
in memory of him
may bring us growth in charity.
Through Christ our Lord.

THIRTY-FOURTH WEEK IN ORDINARY TIME

On the last Sunday in Ordinary Time there occurs the Solemnity of our Lord Jesus Christ, King of the Universe, pp. 505-509.

Entrance Antiphon *Cf. Ps 85 (84): 9*
The Lord speaks of peace to his people and his holy ones
and to those who turn to him.

Collect
Stir up the will of your faithful, we pray, O Lord,
that, striving more eagerly
to bring your divine work to fruitful completion,
they may receive in greater measure
the healing remedies your kindness bestows.
Through our Lord Jesus Christ, your Son,
who lives and reigns with you in the unity of the Holy Spirit,
one God, for ever and ever.

Prayer over the Offerings
Accept, O Lord, the sacred offerings
which at your bidding we dedicate to your name
and, in order that through these gifts
we may become worthy of your love,
grant us unfailing obedience to your commands.
Through Christ our Lord.

Communion Antiphon *Ps 117 (116): 1, 2*
O praise the Lord, all you nations,
for his merciful love towards us is great.

Or: *Mt 28: 20*

Behold, I am with you always,
even to the end of the age, says the Lord.

Prayer after Communion
We pray, almighty God,
that those to whom you give the joy
of participating in divine mysteries
may never be parted from you.
Through Christ our Lord.

THE SOLEMNITIES OF THE LORD DURING ORDINARY TIME

First Sunday after Pentecost
THE MOST HOLY TRINITY
Solemnity

Entrance Antiphon

Blest be God the Father,
and the Only Begotten Son of God,
and also the Holy Spirit,
for he has shown us his merciful love.

The Gloria in excelsis (Glory to God in the highest) is said.

Collect

God our Father, who by sending into the world
the Word of truth and the Spirit of sanctification
made known to the human race your wondrous mystery,
grant us, we pray, that in professing the true faith,
we may acknowledge the Trinity of eternal glory
and adore your Unity, powerful in majesty.
Through our Lord Jesus Christ, your Son,
who lives and reigns with you in the unity of the Holy Spirit,
one God, for ever and ever.

The Creed is said.

Prayer over the Offerings

Sanctify by the invocation of your name,
we pray, O Lord our God,
this oblation of our service,
and by it make of us an eternal offering to you.
Through Christ our Lord.

Preface: The mystery of the Most Holy Trinity.

V. The Lord be with you.   R. And with your spir-it.

V. Lift up your hearts.   R. We lift them up to the Lord.

V. Let us give thanks to the Lord our God.   R. It is right and just.

It is truly right and just, our duty and our sal-va-tion, al-ways and everywhere to give you thanks, Lord, holy Father, almighty and e--ter-nal God. For with your Only Begotten Son and the Holy Spirit you are one God, one Lord: not in the unity of a sin-gle per-son, but in a Trini-ty of one sub-stance. For what you have revealed to us of your glo-ry we believe equally of your Son and of the Ho-ly Spir-it, so that, in the confessing of the true and e-ter-nal God-head, you might be adored in what is proper to each Per-son,

THE MOST HOLY TRINITY

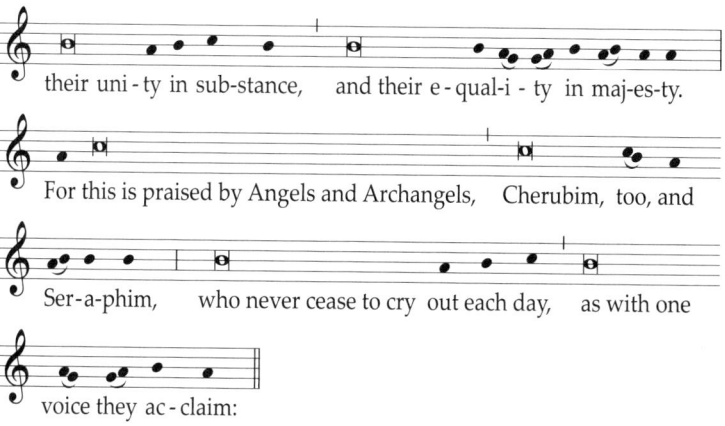

Holy, Holy, Holy Lord God of hosts . . .

Text without music:
V. **The Lord be with you.**
R. And with your spirit.

V. **Lift up your hearts.**
R. We lift them up to the Lord.

V. **Let us give thanks to the Lord our God.**
R. It is right and just.

It is truly right and just, our duty and our salvation,
always and everywhere to give you thanks,
Lord, holy Father, almighty and eternal God.

For with your Only Begotten Son and the Holy Spirit
you are one God, one Lord:
not in the unity of a single person,
but in a Trinity of one substance.

For what you have revealed to us of your glory
we believe equally of your Son
and of the Holy Spirit,
so that, in the confessing of the true and eternal Godhead,
you might be adored in what is proper to each Person,
their unity in substance,
and their equality in majesty.

For this is praised by Angels and Archangels,
Cherubim, too, and Seraphim,
who never cease to cry out each day,
as with one voice they acclaim:

Holy, Holy, Holy Lord God of hosts . . .

Communion Antiphon
Gal 4: 6

Since you are children of God,
God has sent into your hearts the Spirit of his Son,
the Spirit who cries out: Abba, Father.

Prayer after Communion

May receiving this Sacrament, O Lord our God,
bring us health of body and soul,
as we confess your eternal holy Trinity and undivided Unity.
Through Christ our Lord.

[In the Dioceses of the United States]
Sunday after the Most Holy Trinity
THE MOST HOLY BODY AND BLOOD OF CHRIST (CORPUS CHRISTI)

Solemnity

Entrance Antiphon
Cf. Ps 81 (80): 17

He fed them with the finest wheat
and satisfied them with honey from the rock.

The Gloria in excelsis (Glory to God in the highest) is said.

Collect

O God, who in this wonderful Sacrament
have left us a memorial of your Passion,
grant us, we pray,
so to revere the sacred mysteries of your Body and Blood
that we may always experience in ourselves
the fruits of your redemption.
Who live and reign with God the Father
in the unity of the Holy Spirit,
one God, for ever and ever.

The Creed is said.

Prayer over the Offerings

Grant your Church, O Lord, we pray,
the gifts of unity and peace,
whose signs are to be seen in mystery
in the offerings we here present.
Through Christ our Lord.

THE SOLEMNITIES OF THE LORD

Preface: The fruits of the Most Holy Eucharist.

V. The Lord be with you.   R. And with your spir-it.

V. Lift up your hearts.   R. We lift them up to the Lord.

V. Let us give thanks to the Lord our God.   R. It is right and just.

It is truly right and just, our duty and our sal-va-tion, al-ways and everywhere to give you thanks, Lord, holy Father, almighty and e--ter-nal God, through Christ our Lord. For at the Last Supper with his A-pos-tles, es-tablishing for the ages to come the saving memo--rial of the Cross, he offered himself to you as the un-blem-ished Lamb, the acceptable gift of per-fect praise. Nour-ishing your faithful by this sa-cred mys-ter-y, you make them holy, so that the human race, bounded by one world, may be enlightened by one

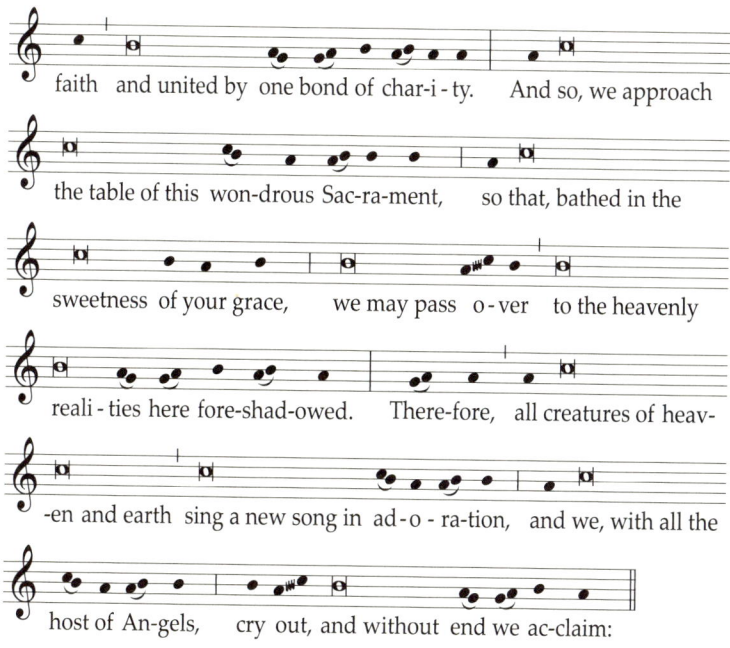

faith and united by one bond of charity. And so, we approach the table of this wondrous Sacrament, so that, bathed in the sweetness of your grace, we may pass over to the heavenly realities here foreshadowed. Therefore, all creatures of heaven and earth sing a new song in adoration, and we, with all the host of Angels, cry out, and without end we acclaim:

Holy, Holy, Holy Lord God of hosts . . .

Text without music: Preface II or I of the Most Holy Eucharist, pp. 588-589.

Communion Antiphon
Jn 6: 57

Whoever eats my flesh and drinks my blood
remains in me and I in him, says the Lord.

Prayer after Communion

Grant, O Lord, we pray,
that we may delight for all eternity
in that share in your divine life,
which is foreshadowed in the present age
by our reception of your precious Body and Blood.
Who live and reign for ever and ever.

It is desirable that a procession take place after the Mass in which the Host to be carried in the procession is consecrated. However, nothing prohibits a procession from taking place even after a public and lengthy period of adoration following the Mass. If a procession takes place after Mass, when the Communion of the faithful is over, the monstrance in which the consecrated host has been placed is set on the altar. When the Prayer after Communion has been said, the Concluding Rites are omitted and the procession forms.

Friday after the Second Sunday after Pentecost
THE MOST SACRED HEART OF JESUS
Solemnity

Entrance Antiphon
Ps 33 (32): 11, 19

The designs of his Heart are from age to age,
to rescue their souls from death,
and to keep them alive in famine.

The Gloria in excelsis (Glory to God in the highest) is said.

Collect

Grant, we pray, almighty God,
that we, who glory in the Heart of your beloved Son
and recall the wonders of his love for us,
may be made worthy to receive
an overflowing measure of grace
from that fount of heavenly gifts.
Through our Lord Jesus Christ, your Son,
who lives and reigns with you in the unity of the Holy Spirit,
one God, for ever and ever.

Or:

O God, who in the Heart of your Son,
wounded by our sins,
bestow on us in mercy
the boundless treasures of your love,
grant, we pray,
that, in paying him the homage of our devotion,
we may also offer worthy reparation.
Through our Lord Jesus Christ, your Son,
who lives and reigns with you in the unity of the Holy Spirit,
one God, for ever and ever.

The Creed is said.

Prayer over the Offerings

Look, O Lord, we pray, on the surpassing charity
in the Heart of your beloved Son,
that what we offer may be a gift acceptable to you
and an expiation of our offenses.
Through Christ our Lord.

THE MOST SACRED HEART OF JESUS

Preface: The boundless charity of Christ.

V. The Lord be with you. R. And with your spir-it.

V. Lift up your hearts. R. We lift them up to the Lord.

V. Let us give thanks to the Lord our God. R. It is right and just.

It is truly right and just, our duty and our sal-va-tion, al-ways and everywhere to give you thanks, Lord, holy Father, almighty and e-ter-nal God, through Christ our Lord. For raised up high on the Cross, he gave himself up for us with a won-der-ful love and poured out blood and water from his pierced side, the well-spring of the Church's Sac-ra-ments, so that, won over to the open heart of the Sav-ior, all might draw wa-ter joy-ful-ly from the springs of sal-va-tion. And so, with all the An-gels and Saints, we praise you, as without end we ac-claim:

Holy, Holy, Holy Lord God of hosts . . .

Text without music:
V. The Lord be with you.
R. And with your spirit.

V. Lift up your hearts.
R. We lift them up to the Lord.

V. Let us give thanks to the Lord our God.
R. It is right and just.

It is truly right and just, our duty and our salvation,
always and everywhere to give you thanks,
Lord, holy Father, almighty and eternal God,
through Christ our Lord.

For raised up high on the Cross,
he gave himself up for us with a wonderful love
and poured out blood and water from his pierced side,
the wellspring of the Church's Sacraments,
so that, won over to the open heart of the Savior,
all might draw water joyfully from the springs of salvation.

And so, with all the Angels and Saints,
we praise you, as without end we acclaim:

Holy, Holy, Holy Lord God of hosts . . .

Communion Antiphon
Cf. Jn 7: 37-38

Thus says the Lord:
Let whoever is thirsty come to me and drink.
Streams of living water will flow
from within the one who believes in me.

Or:
Jn 19: 34

One of the soldiers opened his side with a lance,
and at once there came forth blood and water.

Prayer after Communion

May this sacrament of charity, O Lord,
make us fervent with the fire of holy love,
so that, drawn always to your Son,
we may learn to see him in our neighbor.
Through Christ our Lord.

Last Sunday in Ordinary Time
OUR LORD JESUS CHRIST, KING OF THE UNIVERSE

Solemnity

Entrance Antiphon   Rev 5: 12; 1: 6

    How worthy is the Lamb who was slain,
    to receive power and divinity,
    and wisdom and strength and honor.
    To him belong glory and power for ever and ever.

The Gloria in excelsis (Glory to God in the highest) is said.

Collect

    Almighty ever-living God,
    whose will is to restore all things
    in your beloved Son, the King of the universe,
    grant, we pray,
    that the whole creation, set free from slavery,
    may render your majesty service
    and ceaselessly proclaim your praise.
    Through our Lord Jesus Christ, your Son,
    who lives and reigns with you in the unity of the Holy Spirit,
    one God, for ever and ever.

The Creed is said.

Prayer over the Offerings

    As we offer you, O Lord, the sacrifice
    by which the human race is reconciled to you,
    we humbly pray
    that your Son himself may bestow on all nations
    the gifts of unity and peace.
    Through Christ our Lord.

Preface: Christ, King of the Universe.

V. The Lord be with you. R. And with your spir-it.

V. Lift up your hearts. R. We lift them up to the Lord.

V. Let us give thanks to the Lord our God. R. It is right and just.

It is truly right and just, our duty and our sal-va-tion, al-ways and everywhere to give you thanks, Lord, holy Father, almighty and e-ter-nal God. For you anointed your Only Begotten Son, our Lord Jesus Christ, with the oil of glad-ness as e-ter-nal Priest and King of all cre-a-tion, so that, by offering himself on the altar of the Cross as a spotless sacrifice to bring us peace, he might accom-plish the mys-ter-ies of hu-man re-demp-tion and, making all created things subject to his rule, he might present to the immen-

OUR LORD JESUS CHRIST, KING OF THE UNIVERSE

-sity of your maj-es-ty   an eternal and u-ni-ver-sal king-dom,   a king-dom of truth and life,   a kingdom of ho-li-ness and grace, a kingdom of jus-tice, love and peace.   And so, with Angels and Archangels,   with Thrones and Do-min-ions,   and with all the hosts and Pow-ers of heav-en,   we sing the hymn of your glo-ry, as without end we ac-claim:

Holy, Holy, Holy Lord God of hosts . . .

Text without music:
℣. **The Lord be with you.**
℟. And with your spirit.

℣. **Lift up your hearts.**
℟. We lift them up to the Lord.

℣. **Let us give thanks to the Lord our God.**
℟. It is right and just.

It is truly right and just, our duty and our salvation,
always and everywhere to give you thanks,
Lord, holy Father, almighty and eternal God.

For you anointed your Only Begotten Son,
our Lord Jesus Christ, with the oil of gladness
as eternal Priest and King of all creation,
so that, by offering himself on the altar of the Cross
as a spotless sacrifice to bring us peace,
he might accomplish the mysteries of human redemption
and, making all created things subject to his rule,
he might present to the immensity of your majesty
an eternal and universal kingdom,
a kingdom of truth and life,
a kingdom of holiness and grace,
a kingdom of justice, love and peace.

And so, with Angels and Archangels,
with Thrones and Dominions,
and with all the hosts and Powers of heaven,
we sing the hymn of your glory,
as without end we acclaim:

Holy, Holy, Holy Lord God of hosts . . .

Communion Antiphon
Ps 29 (28): 10-11

The Lord sits as King for ever.
The Lord will bless his people with peace.

Prayer after Communion

Having received the food of immortality,
we ask, O Lord,
that, glorying in obedience
to the commands of Christ, the King of the universe,
we may live with him eternally in his heavenly Kingdom.
Who lives and reigns for ever and ever.

THE ORDER OF MASS

THE INTRODUCTORY RITES

1. When the people are gathered, the Priest approaches the altar with the ministers while the Entrance Chant is sung.

    When he has arrived at the altar, after making a profound bow with the ministers, the Priest venerates the altar with a kiss and, if appropriate, incenses the cross and the altar. Then, with the ministers, he goes to the chair.

    When the Entrance Chant is concluded, the Priest and the faithful, standing, sign themselves with the Sign of the Cross, while the Priest, facing the people, says:

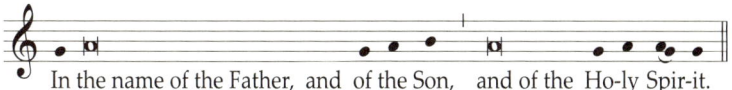
In the name of the Father, and of the Son, and of the Ho-ly Spir-it.

In the name of the Father, and of the Son, and of the Holy Spirit.

The people reply:

A-men.

Amen.

2. Then the Priest, extending his hands, greets the people, saying:

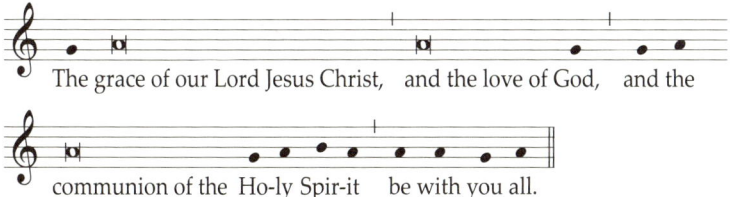
The grace of our Lord Jesus Christ, and the love of God, and the communion of the Ho-ly Spir-it be with you all.

**The grace of our Lord Jesus Christ,
and the love of God,
and the communion of the Holy Spirit
be with you all.**

Or:

Grace to you and peace from God our Father and the Lord Jesus Christ.

Grace to you and peace from God our Father and the Lord Jesus Christ.

Or:

The Lord be with you.

The Lord be with you.

The people reply:

And with your spirit.

And with your spirit.

In this first greeting a Bishop, instead of The Lord be with you, says:

Peace be with you.

Peace be with you.

3. The Priest, or a Deacon or another minister, may very briefly introduce the faithful to the Mass of the day.

Penitential Act*

4. Then follows the Penitential Act, to which the Priest invites the faithful, saying:

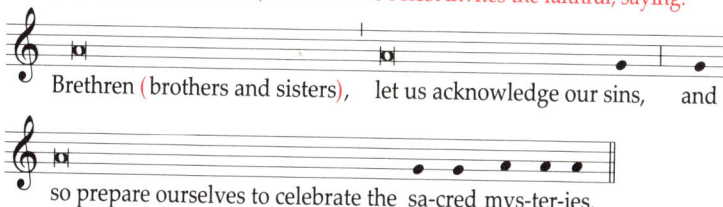

Brethren (brothers and sisters), let us acknowledge our sins, and so prepare ourselves to celebrate the sacred mysteries.

A brief pause for silence follows. Then all recite together the formula of general confession:

**I confess to almighty God
and to you, my brothers and sisters,
that I have greatly sinned,
in my thoughts and in my words,
in what I have done and in what I have failed to do,**

And, striking their breast, they say:

**through my fault, through my fault,
through my most grievous fault;**

Then they continue:

**therefore I ask blessed Mary ever-Virgin,
all the Angels and Saints,
and you, my brothers and sisters,
to pray for me to the Lord our God.**

The absolution by the Priest follows:

**May almighty God have mercy on us,
forgive us our sins,
and bring us to everlasting life.**

---

* From time to time on Sundays, especially in Easter Time, instead of the customary Penitential Act, the blessing and sprinkling of water may take place (as in Appendix II, pp. 1453-1456) as a reminder of Baptism.

The people reply:

Amen.

Or:

5. The Priest invites the faithful to make the Penitential Act:

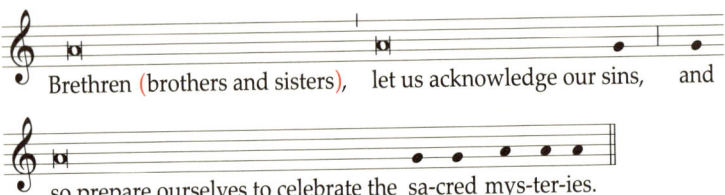

Brethren (brothers and sisters), let us acknowledge our sins, and so prepare ourselves to celebrate the sacred mysteries.

A brief pause for silence follows.

The Priest then says:

Have mercy on us, O Lord.

The people reply:

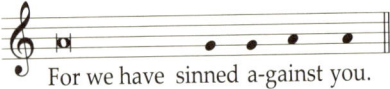

For we have sinned against you.

The Priest:

Show us, O Lord, your mercy.

The people:

And grant us your salvation.

The absolution by the Priest follows:

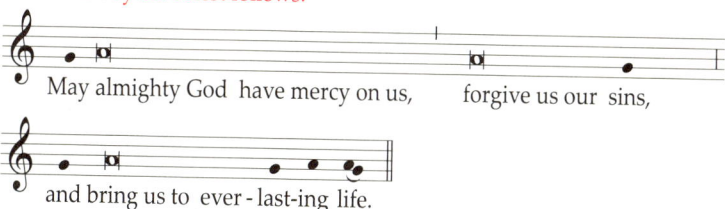

May almighty God have mercy on us,
forgive us our sins,
and bring us to everlasting life.

The people reply:

Amen.

Or:

6. The Priest invites the faithful to make the Penitential Act:

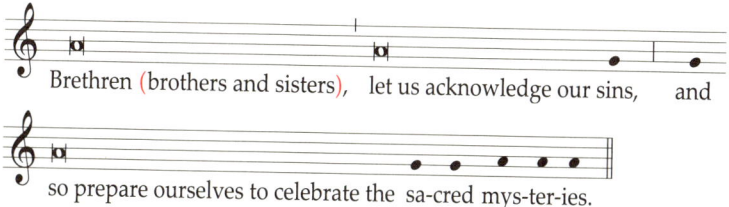

Brethren (brothers and sisters), let us acknowledge our sins, and so prepare ourselves to celebrate the sacred mysteries.

A brief pause for silence follows.

518 THE ORDER OF MASS

The Priest, or a Deacon or another minister, then says the following or other invocations*
with Kyrie, eleison (Lord, have mercy):

---

* Sample invocations are found in Appendix VI, pp. 1474-1480.

THE ORDER OF MASS

The absolution by the Priest follows:

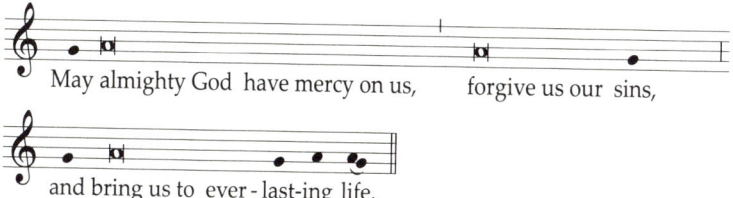

May almighty God have mercy on us, forgive us our sins, and bring us to ever-last-ing life.

The people reply:

A-men.

The Priest, or a Deacon or another minister, then says the following or other invocations* with Kyrie, eleison (Lord, have mercy):

**You were sent to heal the contrite of heart:
Lord, have mercy.**   Or: **Kyrie, eleison.**

The people reply:

   Lord, have mercy.   Or: Kyrie, eleison.

The Priest:

**You came to call sinners:
Christ, have mercy.**   Or: **Christe, eleison.**

The people:

   Christ, have mercy.   Or: Christe, eleison.

The Priest:

**You are seated at the right hand of the Father to intercede for us:
Lord, have mercy.**   Or: **Kyrie, eleison.**

The people:

   Lord, have mercy.   Or: Kyrie, eleison.

The absolution by the Priest follows:

**May almighty God have mercy on us,
forgive us our sins,
and bring us to everlasting life.**

The people reply:

   Amen.

---

* Sample invocations are found in Appendix VI, pp. 1474-1480.

7. The Kyrie, eleison (Lord, have mercy) invocations follow, unless they have just occurred in a formula of the Penitential Act.

V. **Lord, have mercy.** R. Lord, have mercy.
V. **Christ, have mercy.** R. Christ, have mercy.
V. **Lord, have mercy.** R. Lord, have mercy.

Or:

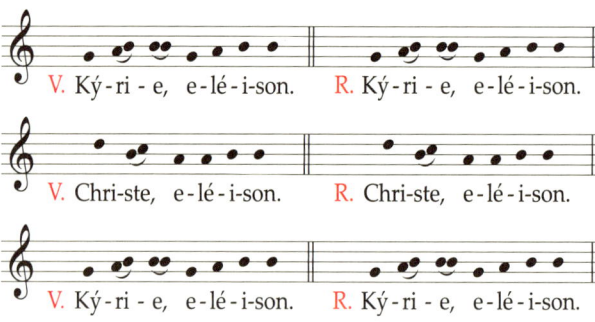

Or:

V. **Kyrie, eleison.** R. Kyrie, eleison.
V. **Christe, eleison.** R. Christe, eleison.
V. **Kyrie, eleison.** R. Kyrie, eleison.

THE ORDER OF MASS

521

8. Then, when it is prescribed, this hymn is either sung or said:

Glo-ry to God in the high-est,

and on earth peace to peo-ple of good will.

We praise you, we bless you, we a-dore you, we glo-ri-fy you,

we give you thanks for your great glo-ry,

Lord God, heav-en-ly King, O God, al-might-y Fa-ther.

Lord Je-sus Christ, On-ly Be-got-ten Son,

Lord God, Lamb of God, Son of the Fa-ther,

you take a-way the sins of the world, have mer-cy on us;

you take a-way the sins of the world, re-ceive our prayer;

you are seat-ed at the right hand of the Fa-ther, have mer-cy on us.

For you a-lone are the Ho-ly One, you a-lone are the Lord,

you a-lone are the Most High, Je-sus Christ, with the Ho-ly Spir-it,

in the glo-ry of God the Fa - ther. A - men.

Glory to God in the highest,
and on earth peace to people of good will.

We praise you,
we bless you,
we adore you,
we glorify you,
we give you thanks for your great glory,
Lord God, heavenly King,
O God, almighty Father.

Lord Jesus Christ, Only Begotten Son,
Lord God, Lamb of God, Son of the Father,
you take away the sins of the world,
   have mercy on us;
you take away the sins of the world,
   receive our prayer;
you are seated at the right hand of the Father,
   have mercy on us.

For you alone are the Holy One,
you alone are the Lord,
you alone are the Most High,
Jesus Christ,
with the Holy Spirit,
in the glory of God the Father.
Amen.

9. When this hymn is concluded, the Priest, with hands joined, says:

Let us pray.

And all pray in silence with the Priest for a while.

Then the Priest, with hands extended, says the Collect prayer, at the end of which the people acclaim:

Amen.

THE LITURGY OF THE WORD

10. Then the reader goes to the ambo and reads the First Reading, while all sit and listen.

    To indicate the end of the reading, the reader acclaims:

    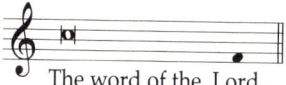

    The word of the Lord.

    All reply:

    Thanks be to God.

11. The psalmist or cantor sings or says the Psalm, with the people making the response.

12. After this, if there is to be a Second Reading, a reader reads it from the ambo, as above.

    To indicate the end of the reading, the reader acclaims:

    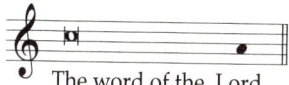

    The word of the Lord.

    All reply:

    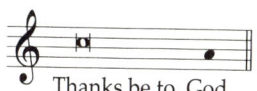

    Thanks be to God.

13. There follows the Alleluia or another chant laid down by the rubrics, as the liturgical time requires.

14. Meanwhile, if incense is used, the Priest puts some into the thurible. After this, the Deacon who is to proclaim the Gospel, bowing profoundly before the Priest, asks for the blessing, saying in a low voice:

    Your blessing, Father.

    The Priest says in a low voice:

    May the Lord be in your heart and on your lips,
    that you may proclaim his Gospel worthily and well,
    in the name of the Father, and of the Son, ✠ and of the Holy Spirit.

    The Deacon signs himself with the Sign of the Cross and replies:

    Amen.

If, however, a Deacon is not present, the Priest, bowing before the altar, says quietly:

**Cleanse my heart and my lips, almighty God,
that I may worthily proclaim your holy Gospel.**

15. The Deacon, or the Priest, then proceeds to the ambo, accompanied, if appropriate, by ministers with incense and candles. There he says:

The Lord be with you.

The people reply:

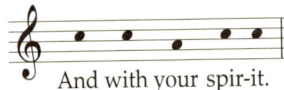

And with your spirit.

The Deacon, or the Priest:

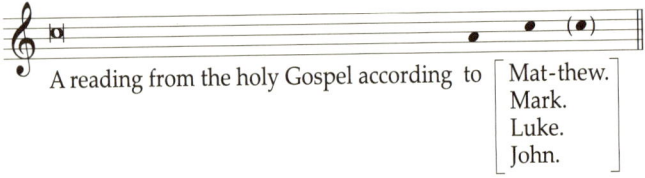

A reading from the holy Gospel according to N.

and, at the same time, he makes the Sign of the Cross on the book and on his forehead, lips, and breast.

The people acclaim:

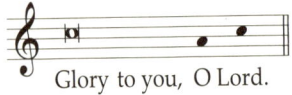

Glory to you, O Lord.

Then the Deacon, or the Priest, incenses the book, if incense is used, and proclaims the Gospel.

16. At the end of the Gospel, the Deacon, or the Priest, acclaims:

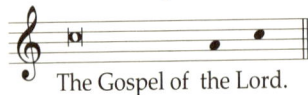

The Gospel of the Lord.

All reply:

Praise to you, Lord Jesus Christ.

Praise to you, Lord Jesus Christ.

Then he kisses the book, saying quietly:

**Through the words of the Gospel
may our sins be wiped away.**

17. Then follows the Homily, which is to be preached by a Priest or Deacon on all Sundays and Holydays of Obligation; on other days, it is recommended.

18. At the end of the Homily, the Symbol or Profession of Faith or Creed, when prescribed, is either sung or said:

I be-lieve in one God, the Fa-ther al-might-y, mak-er of heav-en and earth, of all things vis-i-ble and in-vis-i-ble.

I be-lieve in one Lord Je-sus Christ, the Only Be-got-ten Son of God, born of the Father be-fore all a-ges. God from God, Light from Light, true God from true God, be-got-ten, not made, con-sub-stan-tial with the Fa-ther; through him all things were made. For us men and for our sal-va-tion he came down from

At the words that follow, up to and including and became man, *all bow.*

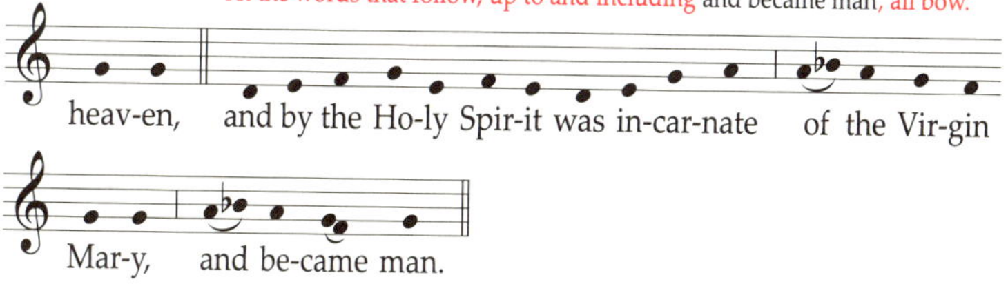

heav-en, and by the Ho-ly Spir-it was in-car-nate of the Vir-gin Mar-y, and be-came man.

THE ORDER OF MASS

An alternate musical setting of the Creed may be found in Appendix I, pp. 1439-1441.

I believe in one God,
the Father almighty,
maker of heaven and earth,
of all things visible and invisible.

I believe in one Lord Jesus Christ,
the Only Begotten Son of God,
born of the Father before all ages.
God from God, Light from Light,
true God from true God,
begotten, not made, consubstantial with the Father;
through him all things were made.
For us men and for our salvation
he came down from heaven,

At the words that follow, up to and including and became man, all bow.

and by the Holy Spirit was incarnate of the Virgin Mary,
and became man.

For our sake he was crucified under Pontius Pilate,
he suffered death and was buried,
and rose again on the third day
in accordance with the Scriptures.
He ascended into heaven
and is seated at the right hand of the Father.
He will come again in glory
to judge the living and the dead
and his kingdom will have no end.

I believe in the Holy Spirit, the Lord, the giver of life,
who proceeds from the Father and the Son,
who with the Father and the Son is adored and glorified,
who has spoken through the prophets.

I believe in one, holy, catholic and apostolic Church.
I confess one Baptism for the forgiveness of sins
and I look forward to the resurrection of the dead
and the life of the world to come. Amen.

19. Instead of the Niceno-Constantinopolitan Creed, especially during Lent and Easter Time, the baptismal Symbol of the Roman Church, known as the Apostles' Creed, may be used.

> **I believe in God,
> the Father almighty,
> Creator of heaven and earth,
> and in Jesus Christ, his only Son, our Lord,**
>
> At the words that follow, up to and including the Virgin Mary, all bow.
>
> **who was conceived by the Holy Spirit,
> born of the Virgin Mary,
> suffered under Pontius Pilate,
> was crucified, died and was buried;
> he descended into hell;
> on the third day he rose again from the dead;
> he ascended into heaven,
> and is seated at the right hand of God the Father almighty;
> from there he will come to judge the living and the dead.**
>
> **I believe in the Holy Spirit,
> the holy catholic Church,
> the communion of saints,
> the forgiveness of sins,
> the resurrection of the body,
> and life everlasting. Amen.**

20. Then follows the Universal Prayer, that is, the Prayer of the Faithful or Bidding Prayers.

The Liturgy of the Eucharist

21. When all this has been done, the Offertory Chant begins. Meanwhile, the ministers place the corporal, the purificator, the chalice, the pall, and the Missal on the altar.

22. It is desirable that the faithful express their participation by making an offering, bringing forward bread and wine for the celebration of the Eucharist and perhaps other gifts to relieve the needs of the Church and of the poor.

23. The Priest, standing at the altar, takes the paten with the bread and holds it slightly raised above the altar with both hands, saying in a low voice:

    **Blessed are you, Lord God of all creation,
    for through your goodness we have received
    the bread we offer you:
    fruit of the earth and work of human hands,
    it will become for us the bread of life.**

    Then he places the paten with the bread on the corporal.

    If, however, the Offertory Chant is not sung, the Priest may speak these words aloud; at the end, the people may acclaim:

    Blessed be God for ever.

24. The Deacon, or the Priest, pours wine and a little water into the chalice, saying quietly:

    **By the mystery of this water and wine
    may we come to share in the divinity of Christ
    who humbled himself to share in our humanity.**

25. The Priest then takes the chalice and holds it slightly raised above the altar with both hands, saying in a low voice:

    **Blessed are you, Lord God of all creation,
    for through your goodness we have received
    the wine we offer you:
    fruit of the vine and work of human hands,
    it will become our spiritual drink.**

    Then he places the chalice on the corporal.

    If, however, the Offertory Chant is not sung, the Priest may speak these words aloud; at the end, the people may acclaim:

    Blessed be God for ever.

26. After this, the Priest, bowing profoundly, says quietly:

    **With humble spirit and contrite heart
    may we be accepted by you, O Lord,
    and may our sacrifice in your sight this day
    be pleasing to you, Lord God.**

27. If appropriate, he also incenses the offerings, the cross, and the altar. A Deacon or other minister then incenses the Priest and the people.

28. Then the Priest, standing at the side of the altar, washes his hands, saying quietly:

**Wash me, O Lord, from my iniquity
and cleanse me from my sin.**

29. Standing at the middle of the altar, facing the people, extending and then joining his hands, he says:

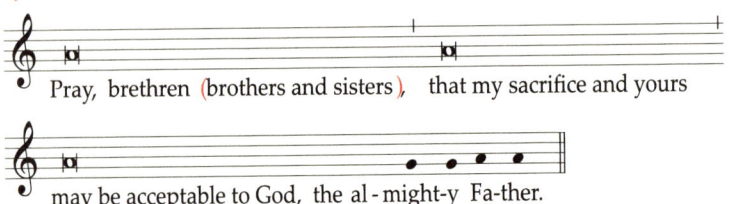

**Pray, brethren (brothers and sisters),
that my sacrifice and yours
may be acceptable to God,
the almighty Father.**

The people rise and reply:

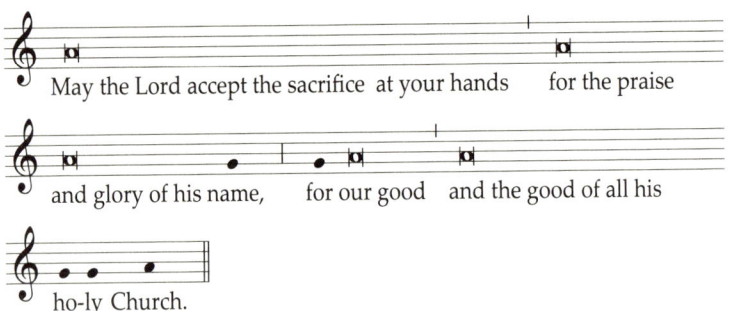

May the Lord accept the sacrifice at your hands
for the praise and glory of his name,
for our good
and the good of all his holy Church.

30. Then the Priest, with hands extended, says the Prayer over the Offerings, at the end of which the people acclaim:

Amen.

THE EUCHARISTIC PRAYER

31. Then the Priest begins the Eucharistic Prayer.

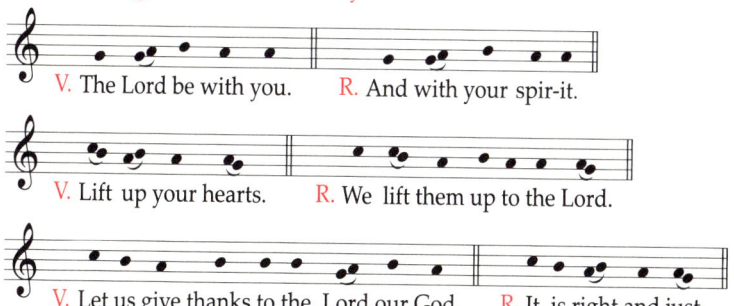

Extending his hands, he says:
The Lord be with you.

The people reply:
And with your spirit.

The Priest, raising his hands, continues:
Lift up your hearts.

The people:
We lift them up to the Lord.

The Priest, with hands extended, adds:
Let us give thanks to the Lord our God.

The people:
It is right and just.

The Priest, with hands extended, continues the Preface.

At the end of the Preface he joins his hands and concludes the Preface with the people, singing or saying aloud:

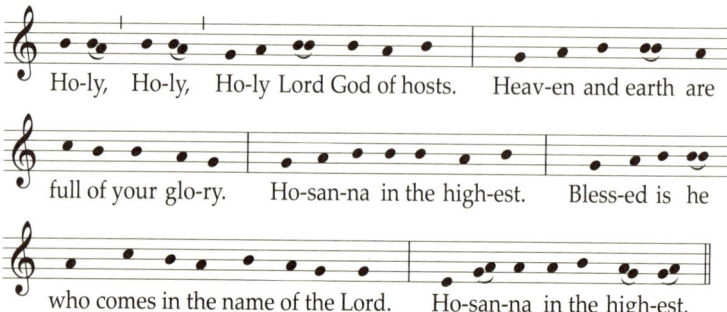

Ho-ly, Ho-ly, Ho-ly Lord God of hosts. Heav-en and earth are full of your glo-ry. Ho-san-na in the high-est. Bless-ed is he who comes in the name of the Lord. Ho-san-na in the high-est.

Holy, Holy, Holy Lord God of hosts.
Heaven and earth are full of your glory.
Hosanna in the highest.
Blessed is he who comes in the name of the Lord.
Hosanna in the highest.

Or:

San-ctus, San-ctus, San-ctus Dó-mi-nus De-us Sá-ba-oth. Ple-ni sunt cæ-li et ter-ra gló-ri-a tu-a. Ho-sán-na in ex-cél-sis. Be-ne-dí-ctus qui ve-nit in nó-mi-ne Dó-mi-ni. Ho-sán-na in ex-cél-sis.

32. In all Masses, the Priest celebrant is permitted to sing parts of the Eucharistic Prayer provided with musical notation below, pp. 693ff., especially the principal parts.

In Eucharistic Prayer I, the Roman Canon, the words included in brackets may be omitted.

PREFACE I OF ADVENT

The two comings of Christ

33. The following Preface is said in Masses of Advent from the First Sunday of Advent to December 16 and in other Masses that are celebrated in Advent and have no proper Preface.

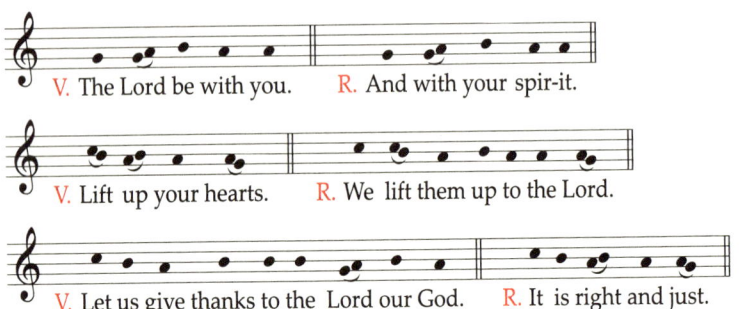

V. The Lord be with you. R. And with your spir-it.

V. Lift up your hearts. R. We lift them up to the Lord.

V. Let us give thanks to the Lord our God. R. It is right and just.

It is truly right and just, our duty and our salvation,
always and everywhere to give you thanks,
Lord, holy Father, almighty and eternal God,
through Christ our Lord.

For he assumed at his first coming
the lowliness of human flesh,
and so fulfilled the design you formed long ago,
and opened for us the way to eternal salvation,
that, when he comes again in glory and majesty
and all is at last made manifest,
we who watch for that day
may inherit the great promise
in which now we dare to hope.

And so, with Angels and Archangels,
with Thrones and Dominions,
and with all the hosts and Powers of heaven,
we sing the hymn of your glory,
as without end we acclaim:

Holy, Holy, Holy Lord God of hosts . . .

THE EUCHARISTIC PRAYER

Holy, Holy, Holy Lord God of hosts . . .

PREFACE II OF ADVENT

The twofold expectation of Christ

34. The following Preface is said in Masses of Advent from December 17 to December 24 and in other Masses that are celebrated in Advent and have no proper Preface.

V. The Lord be with you.   R. And with your spirit.

V. Lift up your hearts.   R. We lift them up to the Lord.

V. Let us give thanks to the Lord our God.   R. It is right and just.

It is truly right and just, our duty and our salvation,
always and everywhere to give you thanks,
Lord, holy Father, almighty and eternal God,
through Christ our Lord.

For all the oracles of the prophets foretold him,
the Virgin Mother longed for him
with love beyond all telling,
John the Baptist sang of his coming
and proclaimed his presence when he came.

It is by his gift that already we rejoice
at the mystery of his Nativity,
so that he may find us watchful in prayer
and exultant in his praise.

And so, with Angels and Archangels,
with Thrones and Dominions,
and with all the hosts and Powers of heaven,
we sing the hymn of your glory,
as without end we acclaim:

Holy, Holy, Holy Lord God of hosts . . .

Holy, Holy, Holy Lord God of hosts . . .

PREFACE I OF THE NATIVITY OF THE LORD

Christ the Light

35. The following Preface is said in Masses of the Nativity of the Lord and of its Octave Day, and within the Octave, even in Masses that otherwise might have a proper Preface, with the exception of Masses that have a proper Preface concerning the divine mysteries or divine Persons. It is also used on weekdays of Christmas Time.

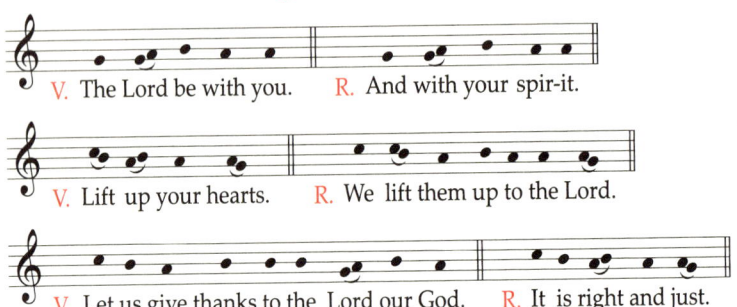

V. The Lord be with you. R. And with your spir-it.

V. Lift up your hearts. R. We lift them up to the Lord.

V. Let us give thanks to the Lord our God. R. It is right and just.

It is truly right and just, our duty and our salvation,
always and everywhere to give you thanks,
Lord, holy Father, almighty and eternal God.

For in the mystery of the Word made flesh
a new light of your glory has shone upon the eyes of our mind,
so that, as we recognize in him God made visible,
we may be caught up through him in love of things invisible.

And so, with Angels and Archangels,
with Thrones and Dominions,
and with all the hosts and Powers of heaven,
we sing the hymn of your glory,
as without end we acclaim:

Holy, Holy, Holy Lord God of hosts . . .

When the Roman Canon is used, there is a proper Communicantes, p. 637. At the Vigil Mass and the Mass during the Night of the Nativity of the Lord: Celebrating the most sacred night, etc., is said, while Celebrating the most sacred day, etc., is then said throughout the Octave of the Nativity of the Lord.

THE EUCHARISTIC PRAYER

It is truly right and just, our duty and our sal-va-tion, al-ways and everywhere to give you thanks, Lord, holy Father, almighty and e--ter-nal God. For in the mystery of the Word made flesh a new light of your glory has shone upon the eyes of our mind, so that, as we recognize in him God made vis-i-ble, we may be caught up through him in love of things in-vis-i-ble. And so, with Angels and Archangels, with Thrones and Do-min-ions, and with all the hosts and Pow-ers of heav-en, we sing the hymn of your glo-ry, as without end we ac-claim:

Holy, Holy, Holy Lord God of hosts . . .

PREFACE II OF THE NATIVITY OF THE LORD

The restoration of all things in the Incarnation

36. The following Preface is said in Masses of the Nativity of the Lord and of its Octave Day, and within the Octave, even in Masses that otherwise might have a proper Preface, with the exception of Masses that have a proper Preface concerning the divine mysteries or divine Persons. It is also used on weekdays of Christmas Time.

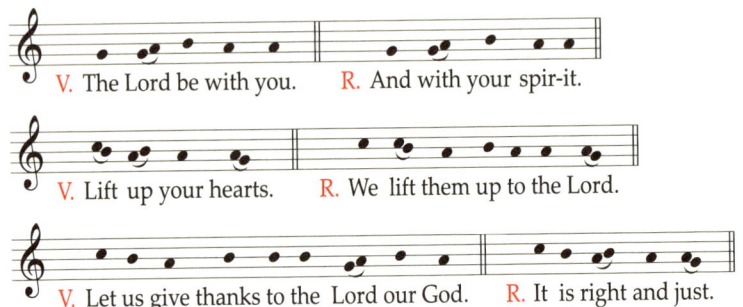

V. The Lord be with you.   R. And with your spir-it.

V. Lift up your hearts.   R. We lift them up to the Lord.

V. Let us give thanks to the Lord our God.   R. It is right and just.

It is truly right and just, our duty and our salvation,
always and everywhere to give you thanks,
Lord, holy Father, almighty and eternal God,
through Christ our Lord.

For on the feast of this awe-filled mystery,
though invisible in his own divine nature,
he has appeared visibly in ours;
and begotten before all ages,
he has begun to exist in time;
so that, raising up in himself all that was cast down,
he might restore unity to all creation
and call straying humanity back to the heavenly Kingdom.

And so, with all the Angels, we praise you,
as in joyful celebration we acclaim:

Holy, Holy, Holy Lord God of hosts . . .

When the Roman Canon is used, there is a proper Communicantes, p. 637. At the Vigil Mass and the Mass during the Night of the Nativity of the Lord: Celebrating the most sacred night, etc., is said, while Celebrating the most sacred day, etc., is then said throughout the Octave of the Nativity of the Lord.

THE EUCHARISTIC PRAYER

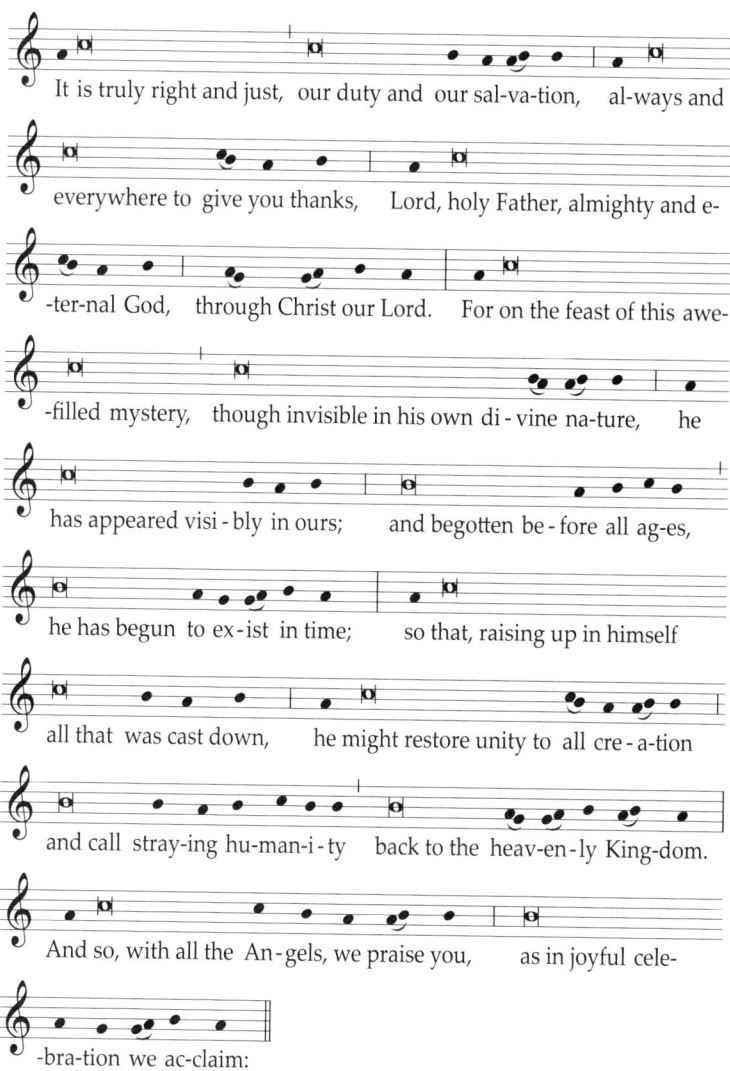

It is truly right and just, our duty and our salvation, always and everywhere to give you thanks, Lord, holy Father, almighty and eternal God, through Christ our Lord. For on the feast of this awe-filled mystery, though invisible in his own divine nature, he has appeared visibly in ours; and begotten before all ages, he has begun to exist in time; so that, raising up in himself all that was cast down, he might restore unity to all creation and call straying humanity back to the heavenly Kingdom. And so, with all the Angels, we praise you, as in joyful celebration we acclaim:

Holy, Holy, Holy Lord God of hosts . . .

PREFACE III OF THE NATIVITY OF THE LORD

The exchange in the Incarnation of the Word

37. The following Preface is said in Masses of the Nativity of the Lord and of its Octave Day, and within the Octave, even in Masses that otherwise might have a proper Preface, with the exception of Masses that have a proper Preface concerning the divine mysteries or divine Persons. It is also used on weekdays of Christmas Time.

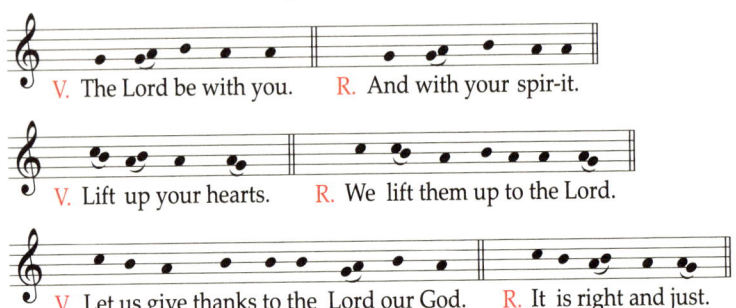

V. The Lord be with you.   R. And with your spirit.

V. Lift up your hearts.   R. We lift them up to the Lord.

V. Let us give thanks to the Lord our God.   R. It is right and just.

It is truly right and just, our duty and our salvation,
always and everywhere to give you thanks,
Lord, holy Father, almighty and eternal God,
through Christ our Lord.

For through him the holy exchange that restores our life
has shone forth today in splendor:
when our frailty is assumed by your Word
not only does human mortality receive unending honor
but by this wondrous union we, too, are made eternal.

And so, in company with the choirs of Angels,
we praise you, and with joy we proclaim:

Holy, Holy, Holy Lord God of hosts . . .

When the Roman Canon is used, there is a proper Communicantes, p. 637. At the Vigil Mass and the Mass during the Night of the Nativity of the Lord: Celebrating the most sacred night, etc., is said, while Celebrating the most sacred day, etc., is then said throughout the Octave of the Nativity of the Lord.

THE EUCHARISTIC PRAYER

Holy, Holy, Holy Lord God of hosts . . .

PREFACE OF THE EPIPHANY OF THE LORD

Christ the light of the nations

38. The following Preface is said in Masses of the Solemnity of the Epiphany. This Preface, or one of the Prefaces of the Nativity, may be said even on days after the Epiphany up to the Saturday that precedes the Feast of the Baptism of the Lord.

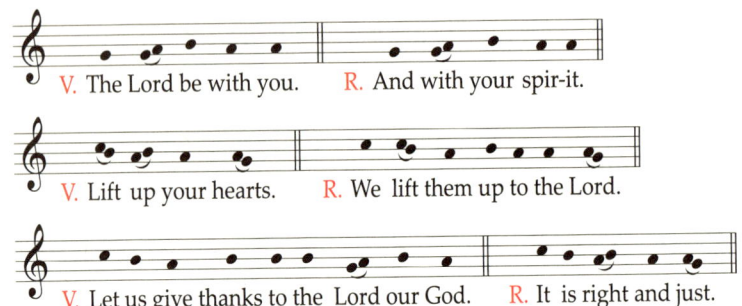

V. The Lord be with you. R. And with your spir-it.

V. Lift up your hearts. R. We lift them up to the Lord.

V. Let us give thanks to the Lord our God. R. It is right and just.

It is truly right and just, our duty and our salvation,
always and everywhere to give you thanks,
Lord, holy Father, almighty and eternal God.

For today you have revealed the mystery
of our salvation in Christ
as a light for the nations,
and, when he appeared in our mortal nature,
you made us new by the glory of his immortal nature.

And so, with Angels and Archangels,
with Thrones and Dominions,
and with all the hosts and Powers of heaven,
we sing the hymn of your glory,
as without end we acclaim:

Holy, Holy, Holy Lord God of hosts . . .

When the Roman Canon is used on the Solemnity of the Epiphany, there is a proper Communicantes, p. 637.

THE EUCHARISTIC PRAYER

It is truly right and just, our duty and our sal-va-tion, al-ways and everywhere to give you thanks, Lord, holy Father, almighty and e- -ter-nal God. For today you have revealed the mystery of our salva- -tion in Christ as a light for the na-tions, and, when he appeared in our mor-tal na-ture, you made us new by the glory of his im-mor-tal na-ture. And so, with Angels and Archangels, with Thrones and Do-min-ions, and with all the hosts and Pow-ers of heav-en, we sing the hymn of your glo-ry, as without end we ac-claim:

Holy, Holy, Holy Lord God of hosts . . .

PREFACE I OF LENT

The spiritual meaning of Lent

39. The following Preface is said in Masses of Lent, especially on Sundays when a more specific Preface is not prescribed.

V. The Lord be with you. R. And with your spirit.

V. Lift up your hearts. R. We lift them up to the Lord.

V. Let us give thanks to the Lord our God. R. It is right and just.

It is truly right and just, our duty and our salvation,
always and everywhere to give you thanks,
Lord, holy Father, almighty and eternal God,
through Christ our Lord.

For by your gracious gift each year
your faithful await the sacred paschal feasts
with the joy of minds made pure,
so that, more eagerly intent on prayer
and on the works of charity,
and participating in the mysteries
by which they have been reborn,
they may be led to the fullness of grace
that you bestow on your sons and daughters.

And so, with Angels and Archangels,
with Thrones and Dominions,
and with all the hosts and Powers of heaven,
we sing the hymn of your glory,
as without end we acclaim:

Holy, Holy, Holy Lord God of hosts . . .

THE EUCHARISTIC PRAYER

It is truly right and just, our duty and our sal-va-tion, al-ways and everywhere to give you thanks, Lord, holy Father, almighty and e--ter-nal God, through Christ our Lord. For by your gracious gift each year your faithful await the sacred pas-chal feasts with the joy of minds made pure, so that, more eagerly in-tent on prayer and on the works of char-i-ty, and participating in the mysteries by which they have been re-born, they may be led to the full-ness of grace that you bestow on your sons and daugh-ters. And so, with Angels and Archangels, with Thrones and Do-min-ions, and with all the hosts and Pow-ers of heav-en, we sing the hymn of your glo-ry, as without end we ac-claim:

Holy, Holy, Holy Lord God of hosts . . .

PREFACE II OF LENT

Spiritual penance

40. The following Preface is said in Masses of Lent, especially on Sundays when a more specific Preface is not prescribed.

V. The Lord be with you.   R. And with your spirit.

V. Lift up your hearts.   R. We lift them up to the Lord.

V. Let us give thanks to the Lord our God.   R. It is right and just.

It is truly right and just, our duty and our salvation,
always and everywhere to give you thanks,
Lord, holy Father, almighty and eternal God.

For you have given your children a sacred time
for the renewing and purifying of their hearts,
that, freed from disordered affections,
they may so deal with the things of this passing world
as to hold rather to the things that eternally endure.

And so, with all the Angels and Saints,
we praise you, as without end we acclaim:

Holy, Holy, Holy Lord God of hosts . . .

THE EUCHARISTIC PRAYER

It is truly right and just, our duty and our sal-va-tion, al-ways and everywhere to give you thanks, Lord, holy Father, almighty and e- -ter-nal God. For you have given your children a sa-cred time for the renewing and puri-fy-ing of their hearts, that, freed from dis- -or-dered af-fec-tions, they may so deal with the things of this pass-ing world as to hold rather to the things that e-ter-nal-ly en-dure. And so, with all the An-gels and Saints, we praise you, as without end we ac-claim:

Holy, Holy, Holy Lord God of hosts . . .

PREFACE III OF LENT

The fruits of abstinence

41. The following Preface is said in Masses of the weekdays of Lent and on days of fasting.

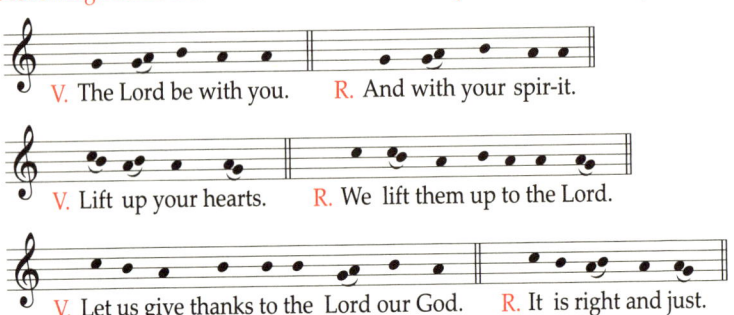

V. The Lord be with you.   R. And with your spir-it.

V. Lift up your hearts.   R. We lift them up to the Lord.

V. Let us give thanks to the Lord our God.   R. It is right and just.

It is truly right and just, our duty and our salvation,
always and everywhere to give you thanks,
Lord, holy Father, almighty and eternal God.

For you will that our self-denial should give you thanks,
humble our sinful pride,
contribute to the feeding of the poor,
and so help us imitate you in your kindness.

And so we glorify you with countless Angels,
as with one voice of praise we acclaim:

Holy, Holy, Holy Lord God of hosts . . .

It is truly right and just, our duty and our sal-va-tion, al-ways and everywhere to give you thanks, Lord, holy Father, almighty and e--ter-nal God. For you will that our self-denial should give you thanks, hum-ble our sin-ful pride, contribute to the feeding of the poor, and so help us imitate you in your kind-ness. And so we glorify you with count-less An-gels, as with one voice of praise we ac-claim:

Holy, Holy, Holy Lord God of hosts . . .

PREFACE IV OF LENT

The fruits of fasting

42. The following Preface is said in Masses of the weekdays of Lent and on days of fasting.

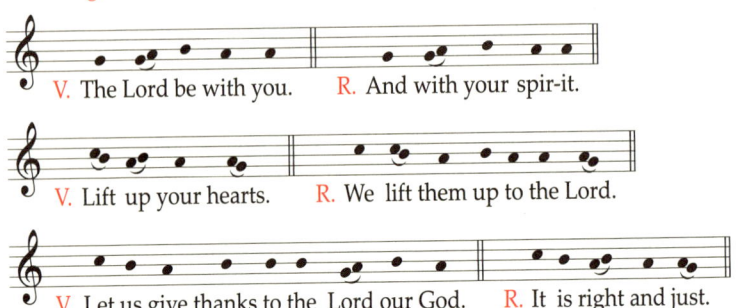

V. The Lord be with you.   R. And with your spir-it.

V. Lift up your hearts.   R. We lift them up to the Lord.

V. Let us give thanks to the Lord our God.   R. It is right and just.

It is truly right and just, our duty and our salvation,
always and everywhere to give you thanks,
Lord, holy Father, almighty and eternal God.

For through bodily fasting you restrain our faults,
raise up our minds,
and bestow both virtue and its rewards,
through Christ our Lord.

Through him the Angels praise your majesty,
Dominions adore and Powers tremble before you.
Heaven and the Virtues of heaven and the blessed Seraphim
worship together with exultation.
May our voices, we pray, join with theirs
in humble praise, as we acclaim:

Holy, Holy, Holy Lord God of hosts . . .

THE EUCHARISTIC PRAYER

It is truly right and just, our duty and our sal-va-tion, al-ways and everywhere to give you thanks, Lord, holy Father, almighty and e- -ter-nal God. For through bodily fasting you re-strain our faults, raise up our minds, and bestow both virtue and its rewards, through Christ our Lord. Through him the Angels praise your maj-es-ty, Do-min-ions a-dore and Powers trem-ble be-fore you. Heav-en and the Virtues of heaven and the bless-ed Ser-a-phim worship to-geth-er with ex-ul-ta-tion. May our voices, we pray, join with theirs in hum-ble praise, as we ac-claim:

Holy, Holy, Holy Lord God of hosts . . .

PREFACE I OF THE PASSION OF THE LORD

The power of the Cross

43. The following Preface is said during the Fifth Week of Lent and in Masses of the mysteries of the Cross and Passion of the Lord.

V. The Lord be with you.   R. And with your spirit.

V. Lift up your hearts.   R. We lift them up to the Lord.

V. Let us give thanks to the Lord our God.   R. It is right and just.

It is truly right and just, our duty and our salvation,
always and everywhere to give you thanks,
Lord, holy Father, almighty and eternal God.

For through the saving Passion of your Son
the whole world has received a heart
to confess the infinite power of your majesty,
since by the wondrous power of the Cross
your judgment on the world is now revealed
and the authority of Christ crucified.

And so, Lord, with all the Angels and Saints,
we, too, give you thanks, as in exultation we acclaim:

Holy, Holy, Holy Lord God of hosts . . .

Holy, Holy, Holy Lord God of hosts . . .

PREFACE II OF THE PASSION OF THE LORD

The victory of the Passion

44. The following Preface is said on Monday, Tuesday, and Wednesday of Holy Week.

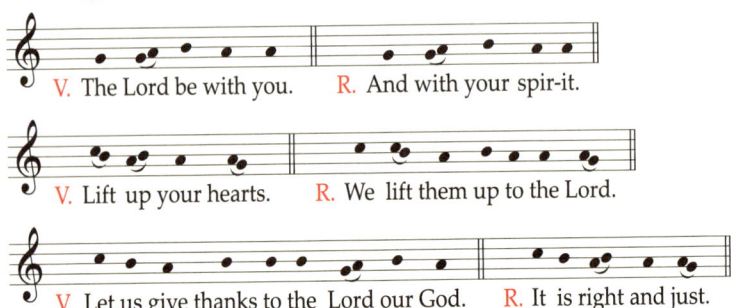

V. The Lord be with you. R. And with your spir-it.

V. Lift up your hearts. R. We lift them up to the Lord.

V. Let us give thanks to the Lord our God. R. It is right and just.

It is truly right and just, our duty and our salvation,
always and everywhere to give you thanks,
Lord, holy Father, almighty and eternal God,
through Christ our Lord.
For the days of his saving Passion
and glorious Resurrection are approaching,
by which the pride of the ancient foe is vanquished
and the mystery of our redemption in Christ is celebrated.

Through him the host of Angels adores your majesty
and rejoices in your presence for ever.
May our voices, we pray, join with theirs
in one chorus of exultant praise, as we acclaim:

Holy, Holy, Holy Lord God of hosts . . .

THE EUCHARISTIC PRAYER

It is truly right and just, our duty and our salvation, always and everywhere to give you thanks, Lord, holy Father, almighty and eternal God, through Christ our Lord. For the days of his saving Passion and glorious Resurrection are approaching, by which the pride of the ancient foe is vanquished and the mystery of our redemption in Christ is celebrated. Through him the host of Angels adores your majesty and rejoices in your presence for ever. May our voices, we pray, join with theirs in one chorus of exultant praise, as we acclaim:

Holy, Holy, Holy Lord God of hosts . . .

PREFACE I OF EASTER

The Paschal Mystery

45. The following Preface is said during Easter Time.

At the Easter Vigil, is said on this night; on Easter Sunday and throughout the Octave of Easter, is said on this day; on other days of Easter Time, is said in this time.

V. The Lord be with you. R. And with your spir-it.

V. Lift up your hearts. R. We lift them up to the Lord.

V. Let us give thanks to the Lord our God. R. It is right and just.

It is truly right and just, our duty and our salvation,
at all times to acclaim you, O Lord,
but (on this night / on this day / in this time) above all
to laud you yet more gloriously,
when Christ our Passover has been sacrificed.

For he is the true Lamb
who has taken away the sins of the world;
by dying he has destroyed our death,
and by rising, restored our life.

Therefore, overcome with paschal joy,
every land, every people exults in your praise
and even the heavenly Powers, with the angelic hosts,
sing together the unending hymn of your glory,
as they acclaim:

Holy, Holy, Holy Lord God of hosts . . .

When the Roman Canon is used, there is a proper Communicantes and a proper Hanc igitur, as below, p. 637. In the Communicantes at the Easter Vigil, Celebrating the most sacred night, etc. is said.

THE EUCHARISTIC PRAYER

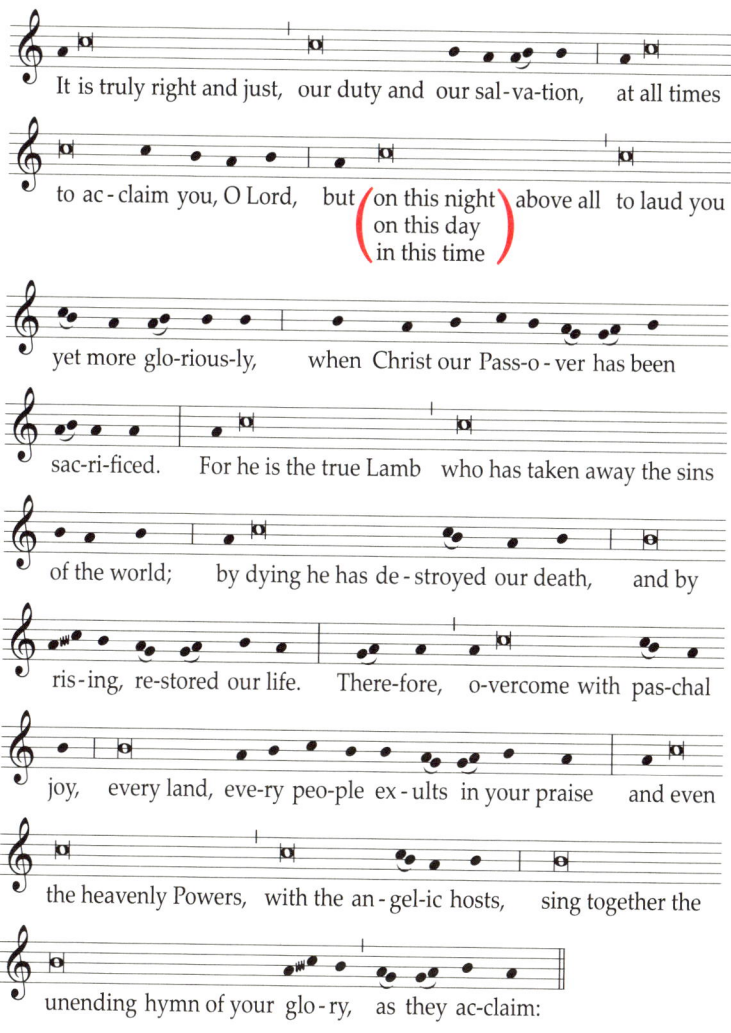

It is truly right and just, our duty and our sal-va-tion, at all times to ac-claim you, O Lord, but (on this night / on this day / in this time) above all to laud you yet more glo-rious-ly, when Christ our Pass-o-ver has been sac-ri-ficed. For he is the true Lamb who has taken away the sins of the world; by dying he has de-stroyed our death, and by ris-ing, re-stored our life. There-fore, o-vercome with pas-chal joy, every land, eve-ry peo-ple ex-ults in your praise and even the heavenly Powers, with the an-gel-ic hosts, sing together the unending hymn of your glo-ry, as they ac-claim:

Holy, Holy, Holy Lord God of hosts . . .

PREFACE II OF EASTER

New life in Christ

46. The following Preface is said during Easter Time.

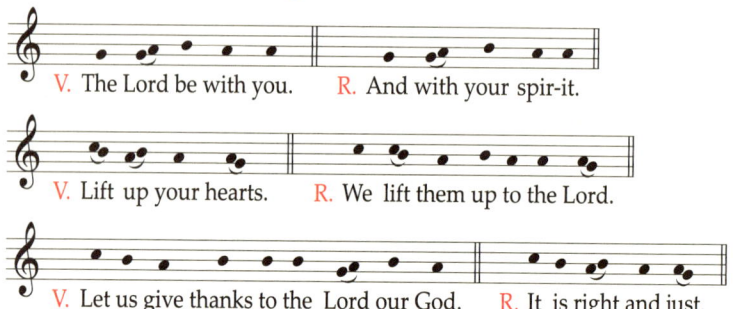

V. The Lord be with you.   R. And with your spir-it.

V. Lift up your hearts.   R. We lift them up to the Lord.

V. Let us give thanks to the Lord our God.   R. It is right and just.

It is truly right and just, our duty and our salvation,
at all times to acclaim you, O Lord,
but in this time above all to laud you yet more gloriously,
when Christ our Passover has been sacrificed.

Through him the children of light rise to eternal life
and the halls of the heavenly Kingdom
are thrown open to the faithful;
for his Death is our ransom from death,
and in his rising the life of all has risen.

Therefore, overcome with paschal joy,
every land, every people exults in your praise
and even the heavenly Powers, with the angelic hosts,
sing together the unending hymn of your glory,
as they acclaim:

Holy, Holy, Holy Lord God of hosts . . .

THE EUCHARISTIC PRAYER

Holy, Holy, Holy Lord God of hosts ...

PREFACE III OF EASTER

Christ living and always interceding for us

47. The following Preface is said during Easter Time.

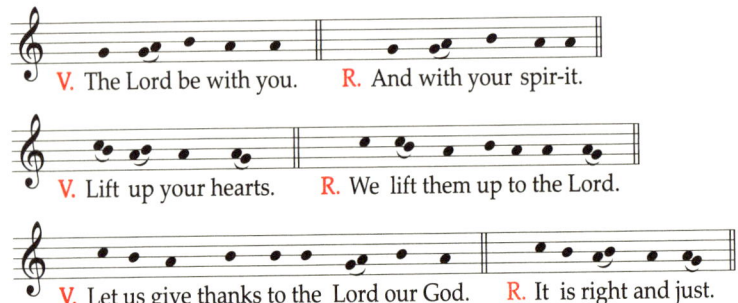

V. The Lord be with you. R. And with your spir-it.

V. Lift up your hearts. R. We lift them up to the Lord.

V. Let us give thanks to the Lord our God. R. It is right and just.

It is truly right and just, our duty and our salvation,
at all times to acclaim you, O Lord,
but in this time above all to laud you yet more gloriously,
when Christ our Passover has been sacrificed.

He never ceases to offer himself for us
but defends us and ever pleads our cause before you:
he is the sacrificial Victim who dies no more,
the Lamb, once slain, who lives for ever.

Therefore, overcome with paschal joy,
every land, every people exults in your praise
and even the heavenly Powers, with the angelic hosts,
sing together the unending hymn of your glory,
as they acclaim:

Holy, Holy, Holy Lord God of hosts . . .

THE EUCHARISTIC PRAYER

It is truly right and just, our duty and our sal-va-tion, at all times to ac-claim you, O Lord, but in this time above all to laud you yet more glo-rious-ly, when Christ our Pass-o-ver has been sac-ri-ficed. He never ceases to offer him-self for us but defends us and ever pleads our cause be-fore you: he is the sacrificial Vic--tim who dies no more, the Lamb, once slain, who lives for ev-er. There-fore, o-vercome with pas-chal joy, every land, eve-ry peo-ple ex-ults in your praise and even the heavenly Powers, with the an-gel-ic hosts, sing together the unending hymn of your glo-ry, as they ac-claim:

Holy, Holy, Holy Lord God of hosts . . .

PREFACE IV OF EASTER

The restoration of the universe through the Paschal Mystery

48. The following Preface is said during Easter Time.

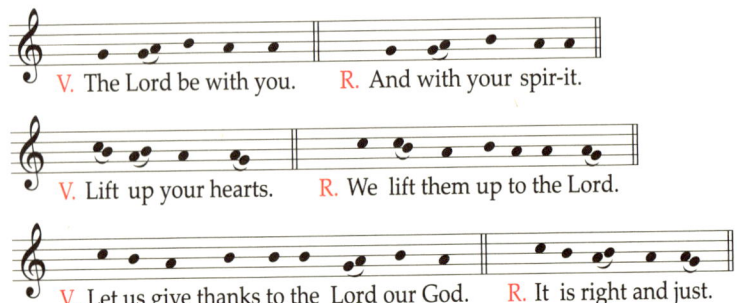

V. The Lord be with you.   R. And with your spir-it.

V. Lift up your hearts.   R. We lift them up to the Lord.

V. Let us give thanks to the Lord our God.   R. It is right and just.

It is truly right and just, our duty and our salvation,
at all times to acclaim you, O Lord,
but in this time above all to laud you yet more gloriously,
when Christ our Passover has been sacrificed.

For, with the old order destroyed,
a universe cast down is renewed,
and integrity of life is restored to us in Christ.

Therefore, overcome with paschal joy,
every land, every people exults in your praise
and even the heavenly Powers, with the angelic hosts,
sing together the unending hymn of your glory,
as they acclaim:

Holy, Holy, Holy Lord God of hosts . . .

Holy, Holy, Holy Lord God of hosts . . .

PREFACE V OF EASTER

Christ, Priest and Victim

49. The following Preface is said during Easter Time.

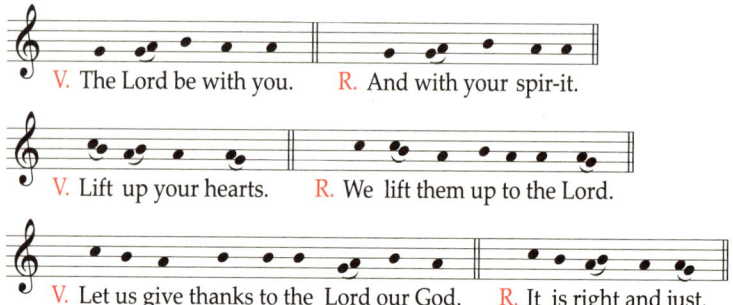

V. The Lord be with you. R. And with your spir-it.

V. Lift up your hearts. R. We lift them up to the Lord.

V. Let us give thanks to the Lord our God. R. It is right and just.

It is truly right and just, our duty and our salvation,
at all times to acclaim you, O Lord,
but in this time above all to laud you yet more gloriously,
when Christ our Passover has been sacrificed.

By the oblation of his Body,
he brought the sacrifices of old to fulfillment
in the reality of the Cross
and, by commending himself to you for our salvation,
showed himself the Priest, the Altar, and the Lamb of sacrifice.

Therefore, overcome with paschal joy,
every land, every people exults in your praise
and even the heavenly Powers, with the angelic hosts,
sing together the unending hymn of your glory,
as they acclaim:

Holy, Holy, Holy Lord God of hosts . . .

THE EUCHARISTIC PRAYER

Holy, Holy, Holy Lord God of hosts . . .

PREFACE I OF THE ASCENSION OF THE LORD

The mystery of the Ascension

50. The following Preface is said on the day of the Ascension of the Lord. It may be said on the days between the Ascension and Pentecost in all Masses that have no proper Preface.

V. The Lord be with you.　R. And with your spir-it.

V. Lift up your hearts.　R. We lift them up to the Lord.

V. Let us give thanks to the Lord our God.　R. It is right and just.

It is truly right and just, our duty and our salvation,
always and everywhere to give you thanks,
Lord, holy Father, almighty and eternal God.
For the Lord Jesus, the King of glory,
conqueror of sin and death,
ascended (today) to the highest heavens,
as the Angels gazed in wonder.

Mediator between God and man,
judge of the world and Lord of hosts,
he ascended, not to distance himself from our lowly state
but that we, his members, might be confident of following
where he, our Head and Founder, has gone before.

Therefore, overcome with paschal joy,
every land, every people exults in your praise
and even the heavenly Powers, with the angelic hosts,
sing together the unending hymn of your glory,
as they acclaim:

Holy, Holy, Holy Lord God of hosts . . .

When the Roman Canon is used on the Ascension, there is a proper Communicantes, p. 637.

THE EUCHARISTIC PRAYER

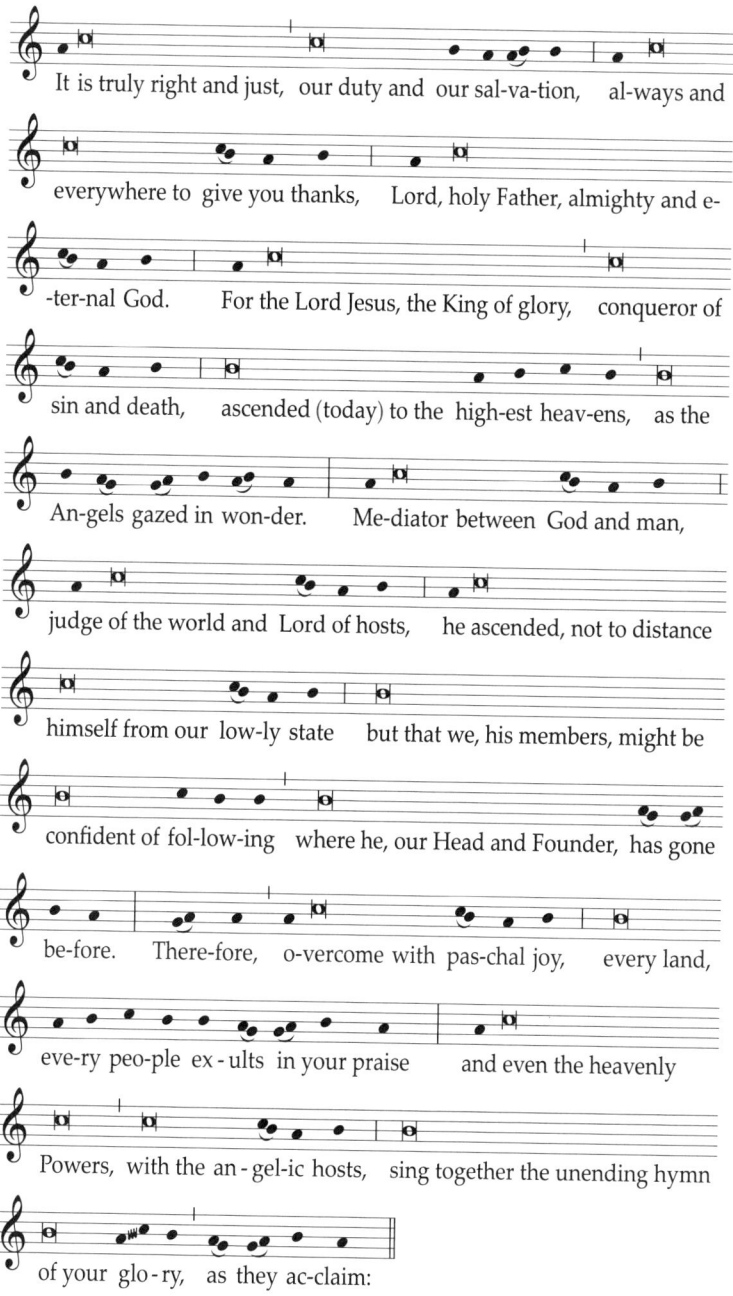

It is truly right and just, our duty and our sal-va-tion, al-ways and everywhere to give you thanks, Lord, holy Father, almighty and e-ter-nal God. For the Lord Jesus, the King of glory, conqueror of sin and death, ascended (today) to the high-est heav-ens, as the An-gels gazed in won-der. Me-diator between God and man, judge of the world and Lord of hosts, he ascended, not to distance himself from our low-ly state but that we, his members, might be confident of fol-low-ing where he, our Head and Founder, has gone be-fore. There-fore, o-vercome with pas-chal joy, every land, eve-ry peo-ple ex-ults in your praise and even the heavenly Powers, with the an-gel-ic hosts, sing together the unending hymn of your glo-ry, as they ac-claim:

Holy, Holy, Holy Lord God of hosts . . .

PREFACE II OF THE ASCENSION OF THE LORD

The mystery of the Ascension

51. The following Preface is said on the day of the Ascension of the Lord. It may be said on the days between the Ascension and Pentecost in all Masses that have no proper Preface.

V. The Lord be with you.   R. And with your spir-it.

V. Lift up your hearts.   R. We lift them up to the Lord.

V. Let us give thanks to the Lord our God.   R. It is right and just.

It is truly right and just, our duty and our salvation,
always and everywhere to give you thanks,
Lord, holy Father, almighty and eternal God,
through Christ our Lord.

For after his Resurrection
he plainly appeared to all his disciples
and was taken up to heaven in their sight,
that he might make us sharers in his divinity.

Therefore, overcome with paschal joy,
every land, every people exults in your praise
and even the heavenly Powers, with the angelic hosts,
sing together the unending hymn of your glory,
as they acclaim:

Holy, Holy, Holy Lord God of hosts . . .

When the Roman Canon is used on the Ascension, there is a proper *Communicantes*, p. 637.

Holy, Holy, Holy Lord God of hosts . . .

PREFACE I OF THE SUNDAYS IN ORDINARY TIME

The Paschal Mystery and the People of God

52. The following Preface is said on Sundays in Ordinary Time.

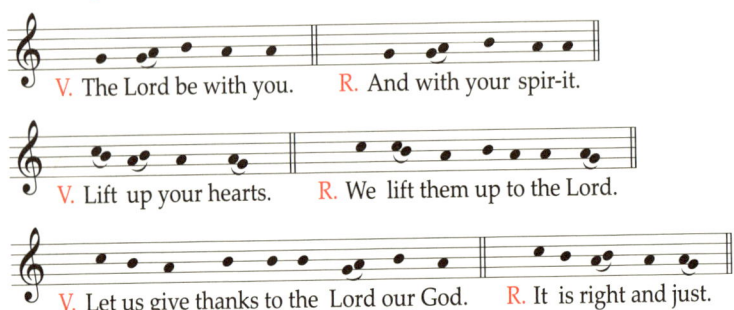

V. The Lord be with you. R. And with your spirit.

V. Lift up your hearts. R. We lift them up to the Lord.

V. Let us give thanks to the Lord our God. R. It is right and just.

It is truly right and just, our duty and our salvation,
always and everywhere to give you thanks,
Lord, holy Father, almighty and eternal God,
through Christ our Lord.

For through his Paschal Mystery,
he accomplished the marvelous deed,
by which he has freed us from the yoke of sin and death,
summoning us to the glory of being now called
a chosen race, a royal priesthood,
a holy nation, a people for your own possession,
to proclaim everywhere your mighty works,
for you have called us out of darkness
into your own wonderful light.

And so, with Angels and Archangels,
with Thrones and Dominions,
and with all the hosts and Powers of heaven,
we sing the hymn of your glory,
as without end we acclaim:

Holy, Holy, Holy Lord God of hosts . . .

THE EUCHARISTIC PRAYER

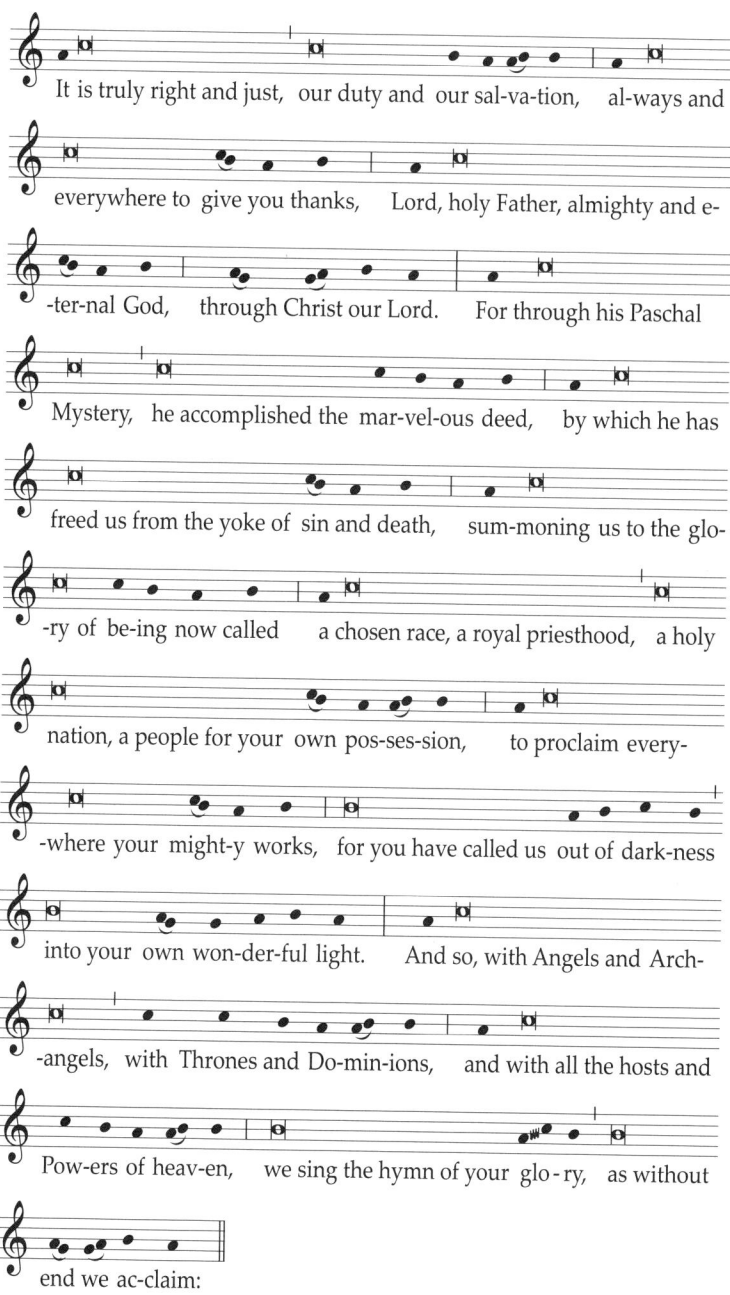

It is truly right and just, our duty and our salvation, always and everywhere to give you thanks, Lord, holy Father, almighty and eternal God, through Christ our Lord. For through his Paschal Mystery, he accomplished the marvelous deed, by which he has freed us from the yoke of sin and death, summoning us to the glory of being now called a chosen race, a royal priesthood, a holy nation, a people for your own possession, to proclaim everywhere your mighty works, for you have called us out of darkness into your own wonderful light. And so, with Angels and Archangels, with Thrones and Dominions, and with all the hosts and Powers of heaven, we sing the hymn of your glory, as without end we acclaim:

Holy, Holy, Holy Lord God of hosts . . .

PREFACE II OF THE SUNDAYS IN ORDINARY TIME

The mystery of salvation

53. The following Preface is said on Sundays in Ordinary Time.

V. The Lord be with you. R. And with your spir-it.

V. Lift up your hearts. R. We lift them up to the Lord.

V. Let us give thanks to the Lord our God. R. It is right and just.

It is truly right and just, our duty and our salvation,
always and everywhere to give you thanks,
Lord, holy Father, almighty and eternal God,
through Christ our Lord.

For out of compassion for the waywardness that is ours,
he humbled himself and was born of the Virgin;
by the passion of the Cross he freed us from unending death,
and by rising from the dead he gave us life eternal.

And so, with Angels and Archangels,
with Thrones and Dominions,
and with all the hosts and Powers of heaven,
we sing the hymn of your glory,
as without end we acclaim:

Holy, Holy, Holy Lord God of hosts . . .

THE EUCHARISTIC PRAYER

It is truly right and just, our duty and our salvation, always and everywhere to give you thanks, Lord, holy Father, almighty and eternal God, through Christ our Lord. For out of compassion for the waywardness that is ours, he humbled himself and was born of the Virgin; by the passion of the Cross he freed us from unending death, and by rising from the dead he gave us life eternal. And so, with Angels and Archangels, with Thrones and Dominions, and with all the hosts and Powers of heaven, we sing the hymn of your glory, as without end we acclaim:

Holy, Holy, Holy Lord God of hosts . . .

PREFACE III OF THE SUNDAYS IN ORDINARY TIME

The salvation of man by a man

54. The following Preface is said on Sundays in Ordinary Time.

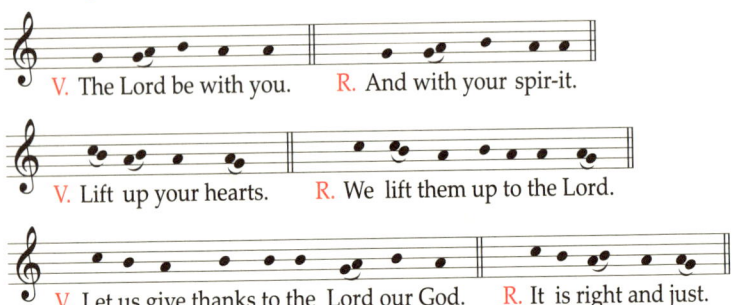

V. The Lord be with you.   R. And with your spirit.

V. Lift up your hearts.   R. We lift them up to the Lord.

V. Let us give thanks to the Lord our God.   R. It is right and just.

It is truly right and just, our duty and our salvation,
always and everywhere to give you thanks,
Lord, holy Father, almighty and eternal God.

For we know it belongs to your boundless glory,
that you came to the aid of mortal beings with your divinity
and even fashioned for us a remedy out of mortality itself,
that the cause of our downfall
might become the means of our salvation,
through Christ our Lord.

Through him the host of Angels adores your majesty
and rejoices in your presence for ever.
May our voices, we pray, join with theirs
in one chorus of exultant praise, as we acclaim:

Holy, Holy, Holy Lord God of hosts . . .

THE EUCHARISTIC PRAYER

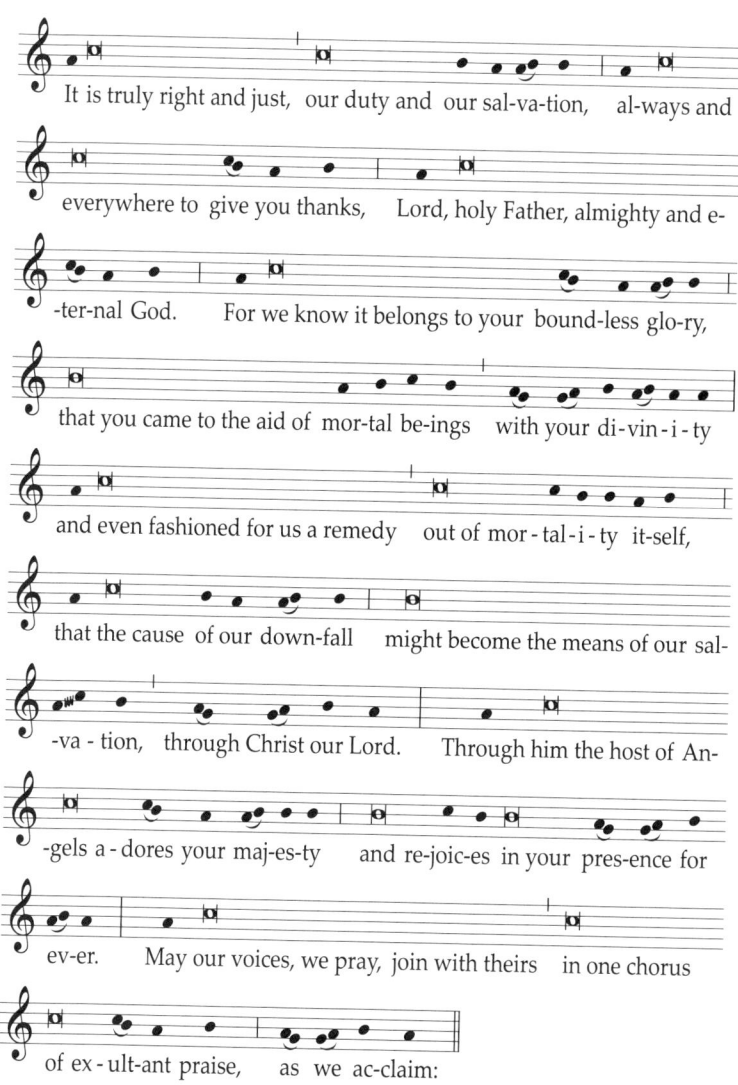

Holy, Holy, Holy Lord God of hosts ...

PREFACE IV OF THE SUNDAYS IN ORDINARY TIME

The history of salvation

55. The following Preface is said on Sundays in Ordinary Time.

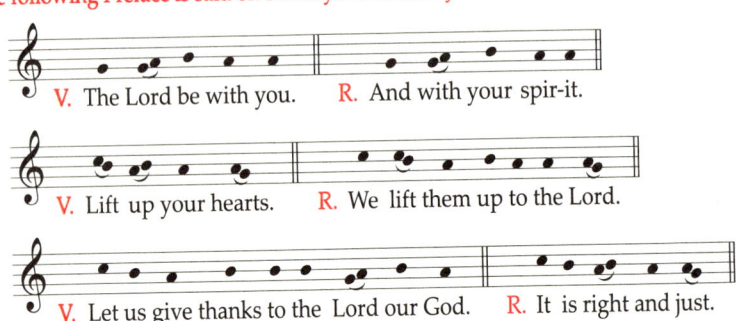

V. The Lord be with you. R. And with your spirit.

V. Lift up your hearts. R. We lift them up to the Lord.

V. Let us give thanks to the Lord our God. R. It is right and just.

It is truly right and just, our duty and our salvation,
always and everywhere to give you thanks,
Lord, holy Father, almighty and eternal God,
through Christ our Lord.

For by his birth he brought renewal
to humanity's fallen state,
and by his suffering, canceled out our sins;
by his rising from the dead
he has opened the way to eternal life,
and by ascending to you, O Father,
he has unlocked the gates of heaven.

And so, with the company of Angels and Saints,
we sing the hymn of your praise,
as without end we acclaim:

Holy, Holy, Holy Lord God of hosts . . .

THE EUCHARISTIC PRAYER

It is truly right and just, our duty and our sal-va-tion, al-ways and everywhere to give you thanks, Lord, holy Father, almighty and e--ter-nal God, through Christ our Lord. For by his birth he brought renewal to humanity's fall-en state, and by his suf-fer-ing, can--celled out our sins; by his rising from the dead he has opened the way to e-ter-nal life, and by ascending to you, O Fa-ther, he has unlocked the gates of heav-en. And so, with the company of An-gels and Saints, we sing the hymn of your praise, as without end we ac-claim:

Holy, Holy, Holy Lord God of hosts . . .

PREFACE V OF THE SUNDAYS IN ORDINARY TIME

Creation

56. The following Preface is said on Sundays in Ordinary Time.

V. The Lord be with you. R. And with your spir-it.

V. Lift up your hearts. R. We lift them up to the Lord.

V. Let us give thanks to the Lord our God. R. It is right and just.

It is truly right and just, our duty and our salvation,
always and everywhere to give you thanks,
Lord, holy Father, almighty and eternal God.

For you laid the foundations of the world
and have arranged the changing of times and seasons;
you formed man in your own image
and set humanity over the whole world in all its wonder,
to rule in your name over all you have made
and for ever praise you in your mighty works,
through Christ our Lord.

And so, with all the Angels, we praise you,
as in joyful celebration we acclaim:

Holy, Holy, Holy Lord God of hosts . . .

THE EUCHARISTIC PRAYER

It is truly right and just, our duty and our sal-va-tion, al-ways and everywhere to give you thanks, Lord, holy Father, almighty and e- -ter-nal God. For you laid the foundations of the world and have arranged the chang-ing of times and sea-sons; you formed man in your own im-age and set humanity over the whole world in all its won-der, to rule in your name over all you have made and for ever praise you in your might-y works, through Christ our Lord. And so, as with all the An-gels, we praise you, as in joyful cele- -bra-tion we ac-claim:

Holy, Holy, Holy Lord God of hosts . . .

PREFACE VI OF THE SUNDAYS IN ORDINARY TIME

The pledge of the eternal Passover

57. The following Preface is said on Sundays in Ordinary Time.

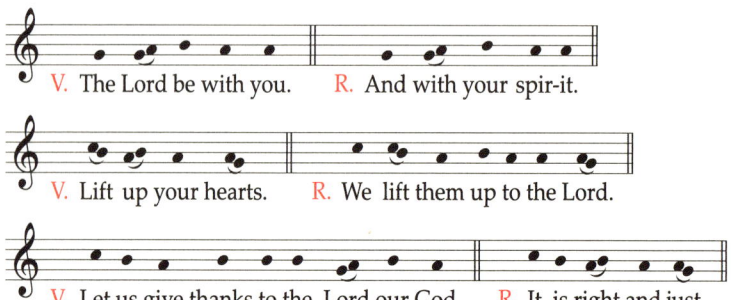

V. The Lord be with you. R. And with your spir-it.

V. Lift up your hearts. R. We lift them up to the Lord.

V. Let us give thanks to the Lord our God. R. It is right and just.

It is truly right and just, our duty and our salvation,
always and everywhere to give you thanks,
Lord, holy Father, almighty and eternal God.

For in you we live and move and have our being,
and while in this body
we not only experience the daily effects of your care,
but even now possess the pledge of life eternal.

For, having received the first fruits of the Spirit,
through whom you raised up Jesus from the dead,
we hope for an everlasting share in the Paschal Mystery.

And so, with all the Angels, we praise you,
as in joyful celebration we acclaim:

Holy, Holy, Holy Lord God of hosts . . .

THE EUCHARISTIC PRAYER

Holy, Holy, Holy Lord God of hosts . . .

PREFACE VII OF THE SUNDAYS IN ORDINARY TIME

Salvation through the obedience of Christ

58. The following Preface is said on Sundays in Ordinary Time.

V. The Lord be with you.   R. And with your spir-it.

V. Lift up your hearts.   R. We lift them up to the Lord.

V. Let us give thanks to the Lord our God.   R. It is right and just.

It is truly right and just, our duty and our salvation,
always and everywhere to give you thanks,
Lord, holy Father, almighty and eternal God.

For you so loved the world
that in your mercy you sent us the Redeemer,
to live like us in all things but sin,
so that you might love in us what you loved in your Son,
by whose obedience we have been restored to those gifts of yours
that, by sinning, we had lost in disobedience.

And so, Lord, with all the Angels and Saints,
we, too, give you thanks, as in exultation we acclaim:

Holy, Holy, Holy Lord God of hosts . . .

Holy, Holy, Holy Lord God of hosts . . .

PREFACE VIII OF THE SUNDAYS IN ORDINARY TIME

The Church united by the unity of the Trinity

59. The following Preface is said on Sundays in Ordinary Time.

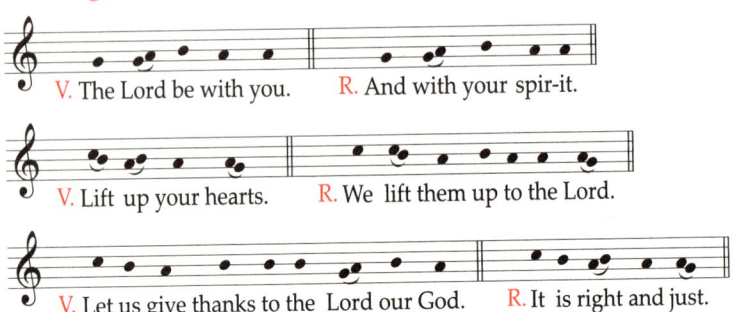

V. The Lord be with you.   R. And with your spirit.

V. Lift up your hearts.   R. We lift them up to the Lord.

V. Let us give thanks to the Lord our God.   R. It is right and just.

It is truly right and just, our duty and our salvation,
always and everywhere to give you thanks,
Lord, holy Father, almighty and eternal God.

For, when your children were scattered afar by sin,
through the Blood of your Son and the power of the Spirit,
you gathered them again to yourself,
that a people, formed as one by the unity of the Trinity,
made the body of Christ and the temple of the Holy Spirit,
might, to the praise of your manifold wisdom,
be manifest as the Church.

And so, in company with the choirs of Angels,
we praise you, and with joy we proclaim:

Holy, Holy, Holy Lord God of hosts . . .

THE EUCHARISTIC PRAYER

Holy, Holy, Holy Lord God of hosts . . .

PREFACE I OF THE MOST HOLY EUCHARIST

The Sacrifice and the Sacrament of Christ

60. The following Preface is said in the Mass of the Lord's Supper (text with music, p. 304). It may also be said on the Solemnity of the Most Holy Body and Blood of Christ (Corpus Christi) and in Votive Masses of the Most Holy Eucharist.

V. **The Lord be with you.**
R. And with your spirit.

V. **Lift up your hearts.**
R. We lift them up to the Lord.

V. **Let us give thanks to the Lord our God.**
R. It is right and just.

It is truly right and just, our duty and our salvation,
always and everywhere to give you thanks,
Lord, holy Father, almighty and eternal God,
through Christ our Lord.

For he is the true and eternal Priest,
who instituted the pattern of an everlasting sacrifice
and was the first to offer himself as the saving Victim,
commanding us to make this offering as his memorial.
As we eat his flesh that was sacrificed for us,
we are made strong,
and, as we drink his Blood that was poured out for us,
we are washed clean.

And so, with Angels and Archangels,
with Thrones and Dominions,
and with all the hosts and Powers of heaven,
we sing the hymn of your glory,
as without end we acclaim:

Holy, Holy, Holy Lord God of hosts . . .

When the Roman Canon is used in the Mass of the Lord's Supper, there is a proper *Communicantes, Hanc igitur* and *Qui pridie.* For ease of use, the entire Canon has been printed with these incorporated, pp. 635-643.

PREFACE II OF THE MOST HOLY EUCHARIST

The fruits of the Most Holy Eucharist

61. The following Preface is said on the Solemnity of the Most Holy Body and Blood of Christ (Corpus Christi) and in Votive Masses of the Most Holy Eucharist (text with music, p. 500).

V. **The Lord be with you.**
R. And with your spirit.

V. **Lift up your hearts.**
R. We lift them up to the Lord.

V. **Let us give thanks to the Lord our God.**
R. It is right and just.

**It is truly right and just, our duty and our salvation,
always and everywhere to give you thanks,
Lord, holy Father, almighty and eternal God,
through Christ our Lord.**

**For at the Last Supper with his Apostles,
establishing for the ages to come the saving memorial of the Cross,
he offered himself to you as the unblemished Lamb,
the acceptable gift of perfect praise.**

**Nourishing your faithful by this sacred mystery,
you make them holy, so that the human race,
bounded by one world,
may be enlightened by one faith
and united by one bond of charity.**

**And so, we approach the table of this wondrous Sacrament,
so that, bathed in the sweetness of your grace,
we may pass over to the heavenly realities here foreshadowed.**

**Therefore, all creatures of heaven and earth
sing a new song in adoration,
and we, with all the host of Angels,
cry out, and without end we acclaim:**

Holy, Holy, Holy Lord God of hosts . . .

PREFACE I OF THE BLESSED VIRGIN MARY

The Motherhood of the Blessed Virgin Mary

62. The following Preface is said in Masses of the Blessed Virgin Mary, with the mention at the appropriate place of the particular celebration, as indicated in the individual Masses.

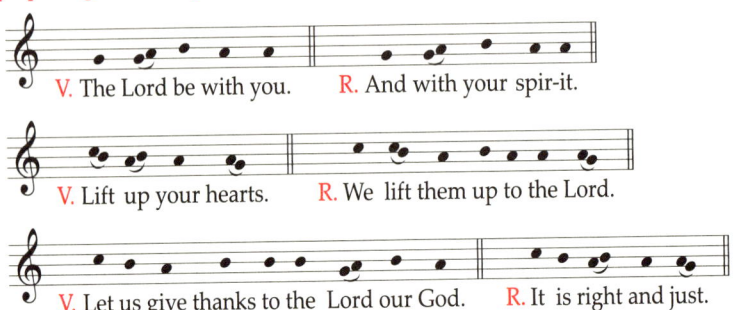

V. The Lord be with you. R. And with your spir-it.

V. Lift up your hearts. R. We lift them up to the Lord.

V. Let us give thanks to the Lord our God. R. It is right and just.

It is truly right and just, our duty and our salvation,
always and everywhere to give you thanks,
Lord, holy Father, almighty and eternal God,
and to praise, bless, and glorify your name
(on the Solemnity of the Motherhood /
on the feast day / on the Nativity / in veneration)
of the Blessed ever-Virgin Mary.

For by the overshadowing of the Holy Spirit
she conceived your Only Begotten Son,
and without losing the glory of virginity,
brought forth into the world the eternal Light,
Jesus Christ our Lord.

Through him the Angels praise your majesty,
Dominions adore and Powers tremble before you.
Heaven and the Virtues of heaven and the blessed Seraphim
worship together with exultation.
May our voices, we pray, join with theirs
in humble praise, as we acclaim:

Holy, Holy, Holy Lord God of hosts . . .

THE EUCHARISTIC PRAYER

It is truly right and just, our duty and our sal-va-tion, al-ways and everywhere to give you thanks, Lord, holy Father, almighty and e-ter-nal God, and to praise, bless, and glori-fy your name

(on the Solemnity of the Motherhood
on the feast day
on the Nativity
in veneration)

of the Blessed ev-er-Vir-gin Mar-y. For by the overshadowing of the Holy Spirit she conceived your Only Be-got-ten Son, and without losing the glory of virginity, brought forth into the world the e-ter-nal Light, Je-sus Christ our Lord. Through him the Angels praise your maj-es-ty, Domin--ions a-dore and Powers trem-ble be-fore you. Heav-en and the Virtues of heaven and the bless-ed Ser-a-phim worship to-geth-er with ex-ul-ta-tion. May our voices, we pray, join with theirs in hum-ble praise, as we ac-claim:

Holy, Holy, Holy Lord God of hosts . . .

PREFACE II OF THE BLESSED VIRGIN MARY

The Church praises God with the words of Mary

63. The following Preface is said in Masses of the Blessed Virgin Mary.

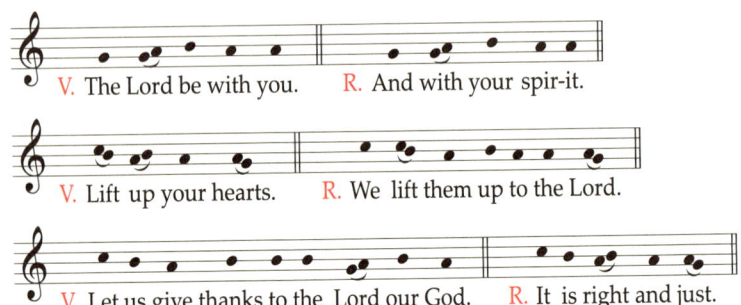

V. The Lord be with you. R. And with your spir-it.

V. Lift up your hearts. R. We lift them up to the Lord.

V. Let us give thanks to the Lord our God. R. It is right and just.

It is truly right and just, our duty and our salvation,
to praise your mighty deeds in the exaltation of all the Saints,
and especially, as we celebrate the memory of the Blessed Virgin Mary,
to proclaim your kindness as we echo her thankful hymn of praise.

For truly even to earth's ends you have done great things
and extended your abundant mercy from age to age:
when you looked on the lowliness of your handmaid,
you gave us through her the author of our salvation,
your Son, Jesus Christ, our Lord.

Through him the host of Angels adores your majesty
and rejoices in your presence for ever.
May our voices, we pray, join with theirs
in one chorus of exultant praise, as we acclaim:

Holy, Holy, Holy Lord God of hosts . . .

THE EUCHARISTIC PRAYER

It is truly right and just, our duty and our sal-va-tion, to praise your mighty deeds in the exaltation of all the Saints, and especial-ly, as we celebrate the memory of the Blessed Vir-gin Mar-y, to pro-claim your kind-ness as we echo her thank-ful hymn of praise. For truly even to earth's ends you have done great things and ex-tended your a-bun-dant mer-cy from age to age: when you looked on the lowliness of your hand-maid, you gave us through her the author of our sal-va-tion, your Son, Je-sus Christ, our Lord. Through him the host of Angels a-dores your maj-es-ty and re-joic-es in your pres-ence for ev-er. May our voices, we pray, join with theirs in one chorus of ex-ult-ant praise, as we ac-claim:

Holy, Holy, Holy Lord God of hosts . . .

PREFACE I OF APOSTLES

The Apostles, shepherds of God's people

64. The following Preface is said in Masses of the Apostles, especially of Saints Peter and Paul.

V. The Lord be with you.   R. And with your spir-it.

V. Lift up your hearts.   R. We lift them up to the Lord.

V. Let us give thanks to the Lord our God.   R. It is right and just.

It is truly right and just, our duty and our salvation,
always and everywhere to give you thanks,
Lord, holy Father, almighty and eternal God.

For you, eternal Shepherd, do not desert your flock,
but through the blessed Apostles
watch over it and protect it always,
so that it may be governed
by those you have appointed shepherds
to lead it in the name of your Son.

And so, with Angels and Archangels,
with Thrones and Dominions,
and with all the hosts and Powers of heaven,
we sing the hymn of your glory,
as without end we acclaim:

Holy, Holy, Holy Lord God of hosts . . .

Holy, Holy, Holy Lord God of hosts . . .

PREFACE II OF APOSTLES

The apostolic foundation and witness

65. The following Preface is said in Masses of the Apostles and Evangelists.

V. The Lord be with you.   R. And with your spir-it.

V. Lift up your hearts.   R. We lift them up to the Lord.

V. Let us give thanks to the Lord our God.   R. It is right and just.

It is truly right and just, our duty and our salvation,
always and everywhere to give you thanks,
Lord, holy Father, almighty and eternal God,
through Christ our Lord.

For you have built your Church
to stand firm on apostolic foundations,
to be a lasting sign of your holiness on earth
and offer all humanity your heavenly teaching.

Therefore, now and for ages unending,
with all the host of Angels,
we sing to you with all our hearts,
crying out as we acclaim:

Holy, Holy, Holy Lord God of hosts . . .

Holy, Holy, Holy Lord God of hosts . . .

PREFACE I OF SAINTS

The glory of the Saints

66. The following Preface is said in Masses of All Saints, of Patron Saints and of Saints who are Titulars of a church, and on Solemnities and Feasts of Saints, unless a proper Preface is to be said. This Preface may be said also on Memorials of Saints.

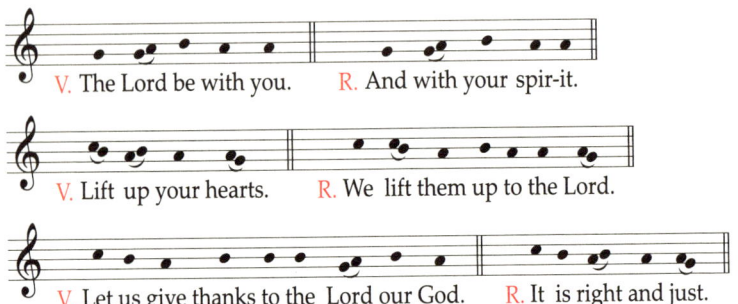

V. The Lord be with you. R. And with your spirit.

V. Lift up your hearts. R. We lift them up to the Lord.

V. Let us give thanks to the Lord our God. R. It is right and just.

It is truly right and just, our duty and our salvation,
always and everywhere to give you thanks,
Lord, holy Father, almighty and eternal God.

For you are praised in the company of your Saints
and, in crowning their merits, you crown your own gifts.
By their way of life you offer us an example,
by communion with them you give us companionship,
by their intercession, sure support,
so that, encouraged by so great a cloud of witnesses,
we may run as victors in the race before us
and win with them the imperishable crown of glory,
through Christ our Lord.

And so, with the Angels and Archangels,
and with the great multitude of the Saints,
we sing the hymn of your praise,
as without end we acclaim:

Holy, Holy, Holy Lord God of hosts . . .

THE EUCHARISTIC PRAYER

It is truly right and just, our duty and our sal-va-tion, al-ways and everywhere to give you thanks, Lord, holy Father, almighty and e--ter-nal God. For you are praised in the company of your Saints and, in crown-ing their mer-its, you crown your own gifts. By their way of life you offer us an ex-am-ple, by communion with them you gave us com-pan-ion-ship, by their inter-ces-sion, sure sup-port, so that, encouraged by so great a cloud of wit-ness-es, we may run as victors in the race be-fore us and win with them the imperishable crown of glo-ry, through Christ our Lord. And so, with the Angels and Arch-an-gels, and with the great mul--titude of the Saints, we sing the hymn of your praise, as without end we ac-claim:

Holy, Holy, Holy Lord God of hosts . . .

PREFACE II OF SAINTS

The action of the Saints

67. The following Preface is said in Masses of All Saints, of Patron Saints and of Saints who are Titulars of a church, and on Solemnities and Feasts of Saints, unless a proper Preface is to be said. This Preface may be said also on Memorials of Saints.

V. The Lord be with you. R. And with your spir-it.

V. Lift up your hearts. R. We lift them up to the Lord.

V. Let us give thanks to the Lord our God. R. It is right and just.

It is truly right and just, our duty and our salvation,
always and everywhere to give you thanks,
Lord, holy Father, almighty and eternal God,
through Christ our Lord.

For in the marvelous confession of your Saints,
you make your Church fruitful with strength ever new
and offer us sure signs of your love.
And that your saving mysteries may be fulfilled,
their great example lends us courage,
their fervent prayers sustain us in all we do.

And so, Lord, with all the Angels and Saints,
we, too, give you thanks, as in exultation we acclaim:

Holy, Holy, Holy Lord God of hosts . . .

THE EUCHARISTIC PRAYER

Holy, Holy, Holy Lord God of hosts . . .

PREFACE I OF HOLY MARTYRS

The sign and example of martyrdom

68. The following Preface is said on the Solemnities and Feasts of Holy Martyrs. It may also be said on their Memorials.

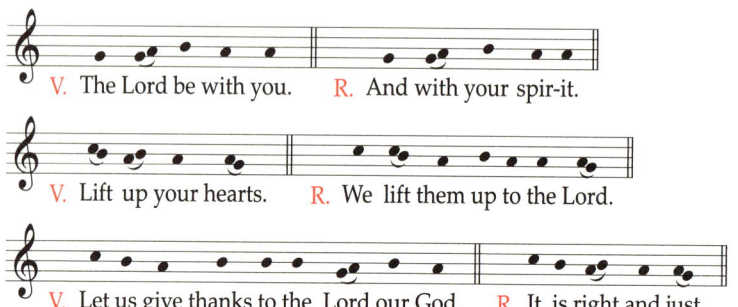

V. The Lord be with you.   R. And with your spir-it.

V. Lift up your hearts.   R. We lift them up to the Lord.

V. Let us give thanks to the Lord our God.   R. It is right and just.

It is truly right and just, our duty and our salvation,
always and everywhere to give you thanks,
Lord, holy Father, almighty and eternal God.

For the blood of your blessed Martyr N.,
poured out like Christ's to glorify your name,
shows forth your marvelous works,
by which in our weakness you perfect your power
and on the feeble bestow strength to bear you witness,
through Christ our Lord.

And so, with the Powers of heaven,
we worship you constantly on earth,
and before your majesty
without end we acclaim:

Holy, Holy, Holy Lord God of hosts . . .

THE EUCHARISTIC PRAYER

It is truly right and just, our duty and our salvation, always and everywhere to give you thanks, Lord, holy Father, almighty and eternal God. For the blood of your blessed Martyr N., poured out like Christ's to glorify your name, shows forth your marvelous works, by which in our weakness you perfect your power and on the feeble bestow strength to bear you witness, through Christ our Lord. And so, with the Powers of heaven, we worship you constantly on earth, and before your majesty without end we acclaim:

Holy, Holy, Holy Lord God of hosts . . .

PREFACE II OF HOLY MARTYRS

The wonders of God in the victory of the Martyrs

69. The following Preface is said on the Solemnities and Feasts of Holy Martyrs. It may also be said on their Memorials.

V. The Lord be with you. R. And with your spirit.

V. Lift up your hearts. R. We lift them up to the Lord.

V. Let us give thanks to the Lord our God. R. It is right and just.

It is truly right and just, our duty and our salvation,
always and everywhere to give you thanks,
Lord, holy Father, almighty and eternal God.

For you are glorified when your Saints are praised;
their very sufferings are but wonders of your might:
in your mercy you give ardor to their faith,
to their endurance you grant firm resolve,
and in their struggle the victory is yours,
through Christ our Lord.

Therefore, all creatures of heaven and earth
sing a new song in adoration,
and we, with all the host of Angels,
cry out, and without end we acclaim:

Holy, Holy, Holy Lord God of hosts . . .

THE EUCHARISTIC PRAYER

It is truly right and just, our duty and our sal-va-tion, al-ways and everywhere to give you thanks, Lord, holy Father, almighty and e-ter-nal God. For you are glorified when your Saints are praised; their ver-y suf-fer-ings are but won-ders of your might: in your mercy you give ardor to their faith, to their endurance you grant firm re-solve, and in their strug-gle the victory is yours, through Christ our Lord. There-fore, all creatures of heaven and earth sing a new song in ad-o-ra-tion, and we, with all the host of An-gels, cry out, and without end we ac-claim:

Holy, Holy, Holy Lord God of hosts . . .

PREFACE OF HOLY PASTORS

The presence of holy Pastors in the Church

70. The following Preface is said on the Solemnities and Feasts of Holy Pastors. It may also be said on their Memorials.

V. The Lord be with you. R. And with your spirit.

V. Lift up your hearts. R. We lift them up to the Lord.

V. Let us give thanks to the Lord our God. R. It is right and just.

It is truly right and just, our duty and our salvation,
always and everywhere to give you thanks,
Lord, holy Father, almighty and eternal God,
through Christ our Lord.

For, as on the festival of Saint N. you bid your Church rejoice,
so, too, you strengthen her by the example of his holy life,
teach her by his words of preaching,
and keep her safe in answer to his prayers.

And so, with the company of Angels and Saints,
we sing the hymn of your praise,
as without end we acclaim:

Holy, Holy, Holy Lord God of hosts . . .

THE EUCHARISTIC PRAYER

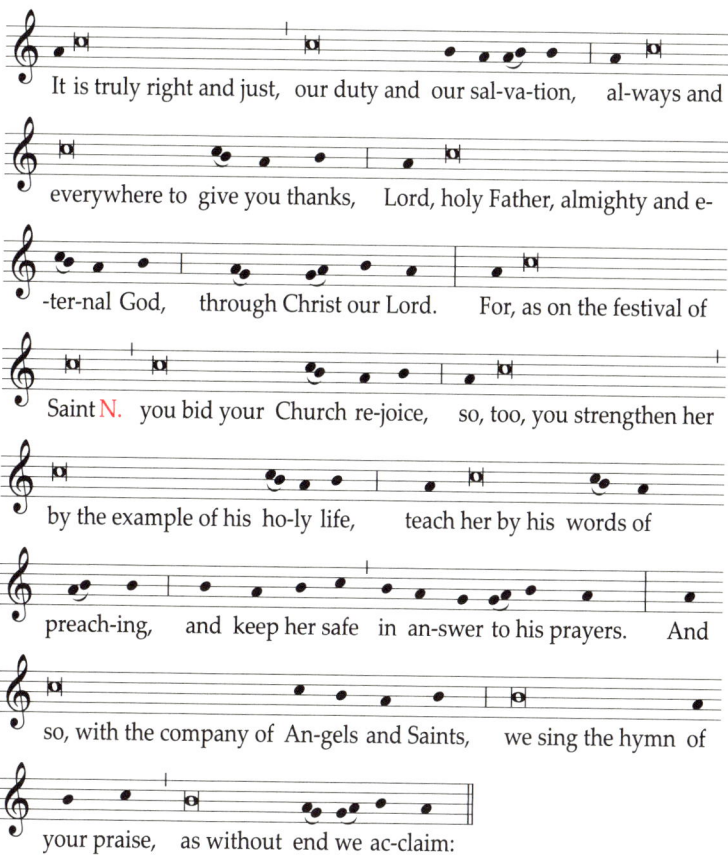

It is truly right and just, our duty and our salvation, always and everywhere to give you thanks, Lord, holy Father, almighty and eternal God, through Christ our Lord. For, as on the festival of Saint N. you bid your Church rejoice, so, too, you strengthen her by the example of his holy life, teach her by his words of preaching, and keep her safe in answer to his prayers. And so, with the company of Angels and Saints, we sing the hymn of your praise, as without end we acclaim:

Holy, Holy, Holy Lord God of hosts . . .

PREFACE OF HOLY VIRGINS AND RELIGIOUS

The sign of a life consecrated to God

71. The following Preface is said on the Solemnities and Feasts of Holy Virgins and Religious. It may also be said on their Memorials.

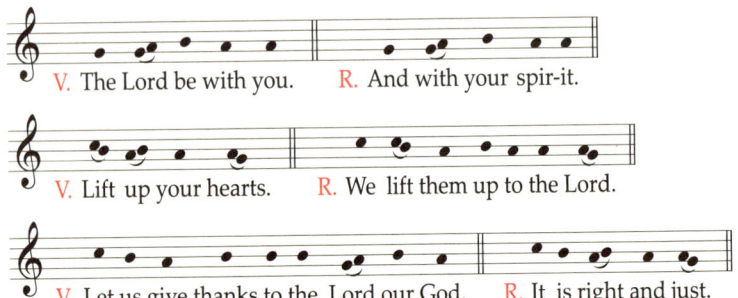

V. The Lord be with you.   R. And with your spirit.

V. Lift up your hearts.   R. We lift them up to the Lord.

V. Let us give thanks to the Lord our God.   R. It is right and just.

It is truly right and just, our duty and our salvation,
always and everywhere to give you thanks,
Lord, holy Father, almighty and eternal God.

For in the Saints who consecrated themselves to Christ
for the sake of the Kingdom of Heaven,
it is right to celebrate the wonders of your providence,
by which you call human nature back to its original holiness
and bring it to experience on this earth
the gifts you promise in the new world to come.

And so, with all the Angels and Saints,
we praise you, as without end we acclaim:

Holy, Holy, Holy Lord God of hosts . . .

Holy, Holy, Holy Lord God of hosts . . .

COMMON PREFACE I

The renewal of all things in Christ

72. The following Preface is said in Masses that have no proper Preface, and for which a Preface related to a specific liturgical time is not indicated.

V. The Lord be with you.   R. And with your spirit.

V. Lift up your hearts.   R. We lift them up to the Lord.

V. Let us give thanks to the Lord our God.   R. It is right and just.

It is truly right and just, our duty and our salvation,
always and everywhere to give you thanks,
Lord, holy Father, almighty and eternal God,
through Christ our Lord.

In him you have been pleased to renew all things,
giving us all a share in his fullness.
For though he was in the form of God, he emptied himself
and by the blood of his Cross brought peace to all creation.
Therefore he has been exalted above all things,
and to all who obey him,
has become the source of eternal salvation.

And so, with Angels and Archangels,
with Thrones and Dominions,
and with all the hosts and Powers of heaven,
we sing the hymn of your glory,
as without end we acclaim:

Holy, Holy, Holy Lord God of hosts . . .

THE EUCHARISTIC PRAYER

It is truly right and just, our duty and our salvation, always and everywhere to give you thanks, Lord, holy Father, almighty and eternal God, through Christ our Lord. In him you have been pleased to renew all things, giving us all a share in his fullness. For though he was in the form of God, he emptied himself and by the blood of his Cross brought peace to all creation. Therefore he has been exalted above all things, and to all who obey him, has become the source of eternal salvation. And so, with Angels and Archangels, with Thrones and Dominions, and with all the hosts and Powers of heaven, we sing the hymn of your glory, as without end we acclaim:

Holy, Holy, Holy Lord God of hosts ...

COMMON PREFACE II

Salvation through Christ

73. The following Preface is said in Masses that have no proper Preface, and for which a Preface related to a specific liturgical time is not indicated.

V. The Lord be with you.   R. And with your spirit.

V. Lift up your hearts.   R. We lift them up to the Lord.

V. Let us give thanks to the Lord our God.   R. It is right and just.

It is truly right and just, our duty and our salvation,
always and everywhere to give you thanks,
Lord, holy Father, almighty and eternal God.

For in goodness you created man
and, when he was justly condemned,
in mercy you redeemed him,
through Christ our Lord.

Through him the Angels praise your majesty,
Dominions adore and Powers tremble before you.
Heaven and the Virtues of heaven and the blessed Seraphim
worship together with exultation.
May our voices, we pray, join with theirs
in humble praise, as we acclaim:

Holy, Holy, Holy Lord God of hosts . . .

THE EUCHARISTIC PRAYER

Holy, Holy, Holy Lord God of hosts . . .

COMMON PREFACE III

Praise to God for the creation and restoration of the human race

74. The following Preface is said in Masses that have no proper Preface, and for which a Preface related to a specific liturgical time is not indicated.

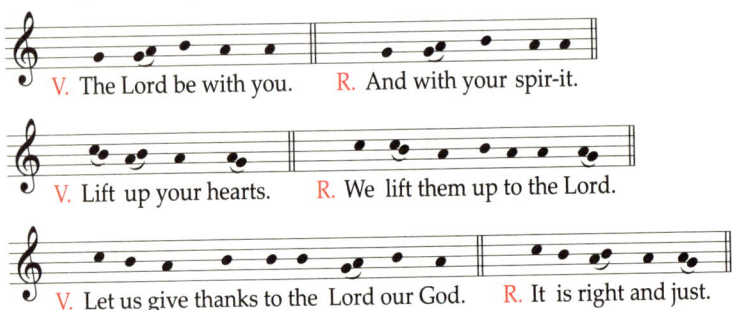

V. The Lord be with you.   R. And with your spir-it.

V. Lift up your hearts.   R. We lift them up to the Lord.

V. Let us give thanks to the Lord our God.   R. It is right and just.

It is truly right and just, our duty and our salvation,
always and everywhere to give you thanks,
Lord, holy Father, almighty and eternal God.

For just as through your beloved Son
you created the human race,
so also through him
with great goodness you formed it anew.

And so, it is right that all your creatures serve you,
all the redeemed praise you,
and all your Saints with one heart bless you.
Therefore, we, too, extol you with all the Angels,
as in joyful celebration we acclaim:

Holy, Holy, Holy Lord God of hosts . . .

THE EUCHARISTIC PRAYER

It is truly right and just, our duty and our salvation, always and everywhere to give you thanks, Lord, holy Father, almighty and eternal God. For just as through your beloved Son you created the human race, so also through him with great goodness you formed it anew. And so, it is right that all your creatures serve you, all the redeemed praise you, and all your Saints with one heart bless you. Therefore, we, too, extol you with all the Angels, as in joyful celebration we acclaim:

Holy, Holy, Holy Lord God of hosts . . .

COMMON PREFACE IV

Praise, the gift of God

75. The following Preface is said in Masses that have no proper Preface, and for which a Preface related to a specific liturgical time is not indicated.

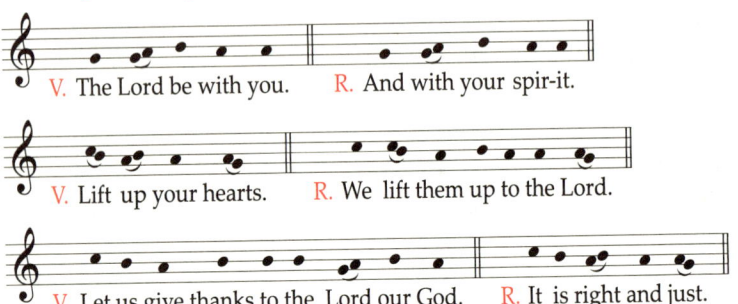

V. The Lord be with you.   R. And with your spirit.

V. Lift up your hearts.   R. We lift them up to the Lord.

V. Let us give thanks to the Lord our God.   R. It is right and just.

It is truly right and just, our duty and our salvation,
always and everywhere to give you thanks,
Lord, holy Father, almighty and eternal God.

For, although you have no need of our praise,
yet our thanksgiving is itself your gift,
since our praises add nothing to your greatness
but profit us for salvation,
through Christ our Lord.

And so, in company with the choirs of Angels,
we praise you, and with joy we proclaim:

Holy, Holy, Holy Lord God of hosts . . .

Holy, Holy, Holy Lord God of hosts . . .

COMMON PREFACE V

The proclamation of the mystery of Christ

76. The following Preface is said in Masses that have no proper Preface, and for which a Preface related to a specific liturgical time is not indicated.

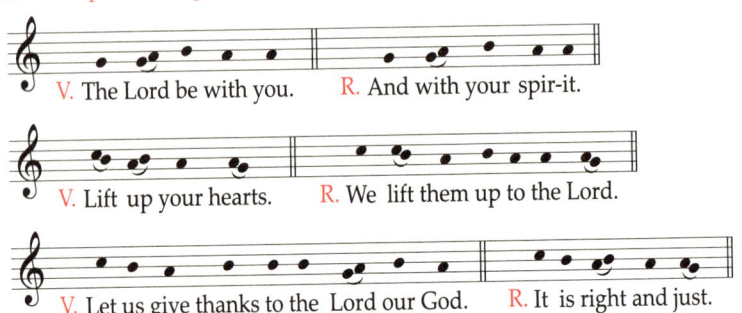

V. The Lord be with you. R. And with your spir-it.

V. Lift up your hearts. R. We lift them up to the Lord.

V. Let us give thanks to the Lord our God. R. It is right and just.

It is truly right and just, our duty and our salvation,
always and everywhere to give you thanks,
Lord, holy Father, almighty and eternal God,
through Christ our Lord.

His Death we celebrate in love,
his Resurrection we confess with living faith,
and his Coming in glory we await with unwavering hope.

And so, with all the Angels and Saints,
we praise you, as without end we acclaim:

Holy, Holy, Holy Lord God of hosts …

THE EUCHARISTIC PRAYER

It is truly right and just, our duty and our salvation, always and everywhere to give you thanks, Lord, holy Father, almighty and eternal God, through Christ our Lord. His Death we celebrate in love, his Resurrection we confess with living faith, and his Coming in glory we await with unwavering hope. And so, with all the Angels and Saints, we praise you, as without end we acclaim:

Holy, Holy, Holy Lord God of hosts . . .

COMMON PREFACE VI

The mystery of salvation in Christ

77. The following Preface is said in Masses that have no proper Preface, and for which a Preface related to a specific liturgical time is not indicated.

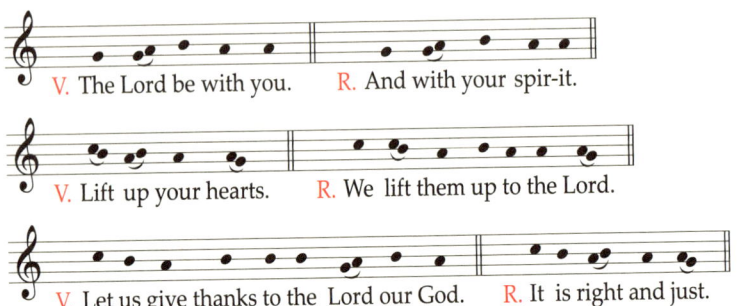

V. The Lord be with you. R. And with your spir-it.

V. Lift up your hearts. R. We lift them up to the Lord.

V. Let us give thanks to the Lord our God. R. It is right and just.

It is truly right and just, our duty and our salvation,
always and everywhere to give you thanks, Father most holy,
through your beloved Son, Jesus Christ,
your Word through whom you made all things,
whom you sent as our Savior and Redeemer,
incarnate by the Holy Spirit and born of the Virgin.

Fulfilling your will and gaining for you a holy people,
he stretched out his hands as he endured his Passion,
so as to break the bonds of death and manifest the resurrection.

And so, with the Angels and all the Saints,
we declare your glory,
as with one voice we acclaim:

Holy, Holy, Holy Lord God of hosts . . .

THE EUCHARISTIC PRAYER

Holy, Holy, Holy Lord God of hosts . . .

PREFACE I FOR THE DEAD

The hope of resurrection in Christ

78. *The following Preface is said in Masses for the Dead.*

V. The Lord be with you.   R. And with your spirit.

V. Lift up your hearts.   R. We lift them up to the Lord.

V. Let us give thanks to the Lord our God.   R. It is right and just.

It is truly right and just, our duty and our salvation,
always and everywhere to give you thanks,
Lord, holy Father, almighty and eternal God,
through Christ our Lord.

In him the hope of blessed resurrection has dawned,
that those saddened by the certainty of dying
might be consoled by the promise of immortality to come.
Indeed for your faithful, Lord,
life is changed not ended,
and, when this earthly dwelling turns to dust,
an eternal dwelling is made ready for them in heaven.

And so, with Angels and Archangels,
with Thrones and Dominions,
and with all the hosts and Powers of heaven,
we sing the hymn of your glory,
as without end we acclaim:

Holy, Holy, Holy Lord God of hosts . . .

THE EUCHARISTIC PRAYER

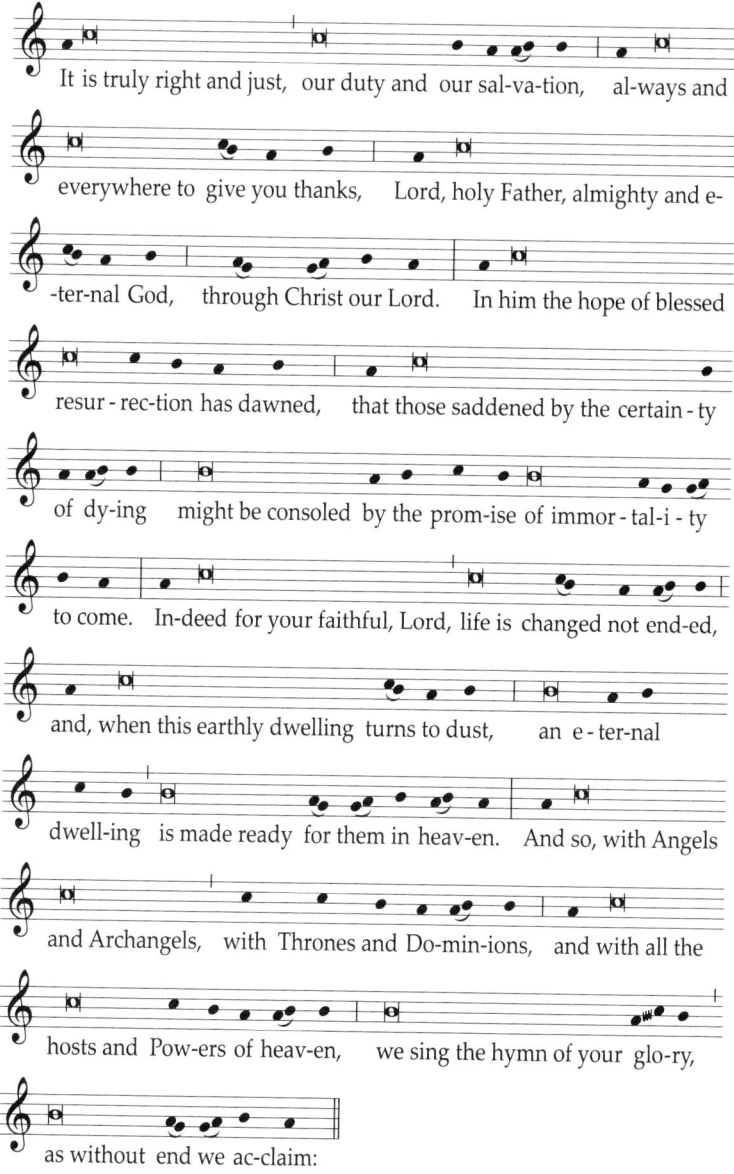

It is truly right and just, our duty and our sal-va-tion, al-ways and everywhere to give you thanks, Lord, holy Father, almighty and e- -ter-nal God, through Christ our Lord. In him the hope of blessed resur-rec-tion has dawned, that those saddened by the certain-ty of dy-ing might be consoled by the prom-ise of immor-tal-i-ty to come. In-deed for your faithful, Lord, life is changed not end-ed, and, when this earthly dwelling turns to dust, an e-ter-nal dwell-ing is made ready for them in heav-en. And so, with Angels and Archangels, with Thrones and Do-min-ions, and with all the hosts and Pow-ers of heav-en, we sing the hymn of your glo-ry, as without end we ac-claim:

Holy, Holy, Holy Lord God of hosts . . .

PREFACE II FOR THE DEAD

Christ died so that we might live

79. The following Preface is said in Masses for the Dead.

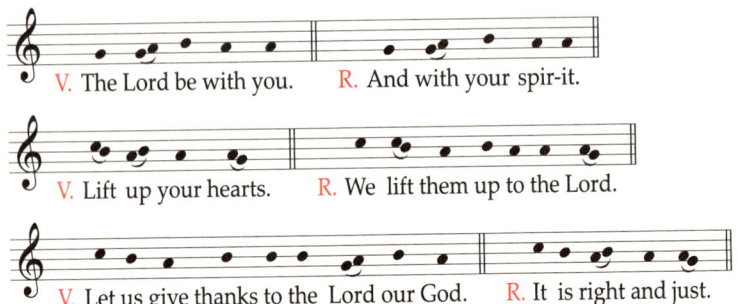

V. The Lord be with you.   R. And with your spir-it.

V. Lift up your hearts.   R. We lift them up to the Lord.

V. Let us give thanks to the Lord our God.   R. It is right and just.

It is truly right and just, our duty and our salvation,
always and everywhere to give you thanks,
Lord, holy Father, almighty and eternal God,
through Christ our Lord.

For as one alone he accepted death,
so that we might all escape from dying;
as one man he chose to die,
so that in your sight we all might live for ever.

And so, in company with the choirs of Angels,
we praise you, and with joy we proclaim:

Holy, Holy, Holy Lord God of hosts . . .

Holy, Holy, Holy Lord God of hosts . . .

PREFACE III FOR THE DEAD

Christ, the salvation and the life

80. The following Preface is said in Masses for the Dead.

V. The Lord be with you. R. And with your spir-it.

V. Lift up your hearts. R. We lift them up to the Lord.

V. Let us give thanks to the Lord our God. R. It is right and just.

It is truly right and just, our duty and our salvation,
always and everywhere to give you thanks,
Lord, holy Father, almighty and eternal God,
through Christ our Lord.

For he is the salvation of the world,
the life of the human race,
the resurrection of the dead.

Through him the host of Angels adores your majesty
and rejoices in your presence for ever.
May our voices, we pray, join with theirs
in one chorus of exultant praise, as we acclaim:

Holy, Holy, Holy Lord God of hosts . . .

THE EUCHARISTIC PRAYER 627

It is truly right and just, our duty and our salvation, always and everywhere to give you thanks, Lord, holy Father, almighty and eternal God, through Christ our Lord. For he is the salvation of the world, the life of the human race, the resurrection of the dead. Through him the host of Angels adores your majesty and rejoices in your presence for ever. May our voices, we pray, join with theirs in one chorus of exultant praise, as we acclaim:

Holy, Holy, Holy Lord God of hosts ...

PREFACE IV FOR THE DEAD

From earthly life to heavenly glory

81. The following Preface is said in Masses for the Dead.

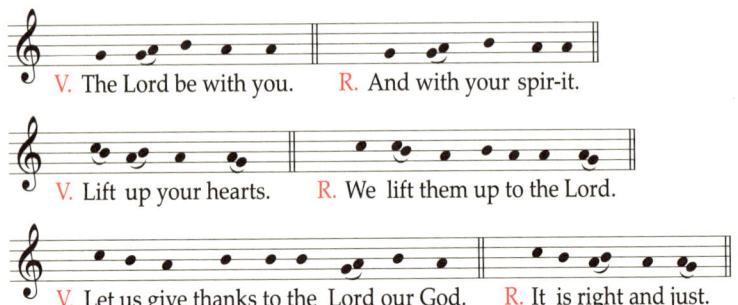

V. The Lord be with you.   R. And with your spirit.

V. Lift up your hearts.   R. We lift them up to the Lord.

V. Let us give thanks to the Lord our God.   R. It is right and just.

It is truly right and just, our duty and our salvation,
always and everywhere to give you thanks,
Lord, holy Father, almighty and eternal God.

For it is at your summons that we come to birth,
by your will that we are governed,
and at your command that we return,
on account of sin,
to that earth from which we came.

And when you give the sign,
we who have been redeemed by the Death of your Son,
shall be raised up to the glory of his Resurrection.

And so, with the company of Angels and Saints,
we sing the hymn of your praise,
as without end we acclaim:

Holy, Holy, Holy Lord God of hosts . . .

Holy, Holy, Holy Lord God of hosts . . .

PREFACE V FOR THE DEAD

Our resurrection through the victory of Christ

82. The following Preface is said in Masses for the Dead.

V. The Lord be with you.   R. And with your spir-it.

V. Lift up your hearts.   R. We lift them up to the Lord.

V. Let us give thanks to the Lord our God.   R. It is right and just.

It is truly right and just, our duty and our salvation,
always and everywhere to give you thanks,
Lord, holy Father, almighty and eternal God.

For even though by our own fault we perish,
yet by your compassion and your grace,
when seized by death according to our sins,
we are redeemed through Christ's great victory,
and with him called back into life.

And so, with the Powers of heaven,
we worship you constantly on earth,
and before your majesty
without end we acclaim:

Holy, Holy, Holy Lord God of hosts . . .

THE EUCHARISTIC PRAYER

It is truly right and just, our duty and our sal-va-tion, al-ways and everywhere to give you thanks, Lord, holy Father, almighty and e--ter-nal God. For even though by our own fault we per-ish, yet by your compassion and your grace, when seized by death according to our sins, we are redeemed through Christ's great vic-to-ry, and with him called back in-to life. And so, with the Pow-ers of heav-en, we worship you con-stant-ly on earth, and before your maj-es-ty without end we ac-claim:

Holy, Holy, Holy Lord God of hosts . . .

THE EUCHARISTIC PRAYERS

EUCHARISTIC PRAYER I
(THE ROMAN CANON)

83. V. **The Lord be with you.**
R. And with your spirit.

V. **Lift up your hearts.**
R. We lift them up to the Lord.

V. **Let us give thanks to the Lord our God.**
R. It is right and just.

Then follows the Preface to be used in accord with the rubrics, which concludes:

Holy, Holy, Holy Lord God of hosts.
Heaven and earth are full of your glory.
Hosanna in the highest.
Blessed is he who comes in the name of the Lord.
Hosanna in the highest.

84. The Priest, with hands extended, says:

To you, therefore, most merciful Father,   Celebrant alone
we make humble prayer and petition
through Jesus Christ, your Son, our Lord:

He joins his hands and says:

that you accept

He makes the Sign of the Cross once over the bread and chalice together, saying:

and bless ✠ these gifts, these offerings,
these holy and unblemished sacrifices,

With hands extended, he continues:

which we offer you firstly
for your holy catholic Church.
Be pleased to grant her peace,
to guard, unite and govern her
throughout the whole world,
together with your servant N. our Pope
and N. our Bishop,*
and all those who, holding to the truth,
hand on the catholic and apostolic faith.

---

* Mention may be made here of the Coadjutor Bishop, or Auxiliary Bishops, as noted in the *General Instruction of the Roman Missal*, no. 149.

85. Commemoration of the Living.

Remember, Lord, your servants N. and N. *Celebrant or one concelebrant*

The Priest joins his hands and prays briefly for those for whom he intends to pray.

Then, with hands extended, he continues:

and all gathered here,
whose faith and devotion are known to you.
For them, we offer you this sacrifice of praise
or they offer it for themselves
and all who are dear to them:
for the redemption of their souls,
in hope of health and well-being,
and paying their homage to you,
the eternal God, living and true.

86. Within the Action.

In communion with those whose memory we venerate, *Celebrant or one concelebrant*
especially the glorious ever-Virgin Mary,
Mother of our God and Lord, Jesus Christ,
† and blessed Joseph, her Spouse,
your blessed Apostles and Martyrs,
Peter and Paul, Andrew,
   (James, John,
   Thomas, James, Philip,
   Bartholomew, Matthew,
   Simon and Jude;
   Linus, Cletus, Clement, Sixtus,
   Cornelius, Cyprian,
   Lawrence, Chrysogonus,
   John and Paul,
   Cosmas and Damian)
and all your Saints;
we ask that through their merits and prayers,
in all things we may be defended
by your protecting help.
(Through Christ our Lord. Amen.)

PROPER FORMS OF THE *COMMUNICANTES*

On the Nativity of the Lord and throughout the Octave

Celebrating the most sacred night (day)
on which blessed Mary the immaculate Virgin
brought forth the Savior for this world,
and in communion with those whose memory we venerate,
especially the glorious ever-Virgin Mary,
Mother of our God and Lord, Jesus Christ, †

On the Epiphany of the Lord

Celebrating the most sacred day
on which your Only Begotten Son,
eternal with you in your glory,
appeared in a human body, truly sharing our flesh,
and in communion with those whose memory we venerate,
especially the glorious ever-Virgin Mary,
Mother of our God and Lord, Jesus Christ, †

From the Mass of the Easter Vigil until the Second Sunday of Easter

Celebrating the most sacred night (day)
of the Resurrection of our Lord Jesus Christ in the flesh,
and in communion with those whose memory we venerate,
especially the glorious ever-Virgin Mary,
Mother of our God and Lord, Jesus Christ, †

On the Ascension of the Lord

Celebrating the most sacred day
on which your Only Begotten Son, our Lord,
placed at the right hand of your glory
our weak human nature,
which he had united to himself,
and in communion with those whose memory we venerate,
especially the glorious ever-Virgin Mary,
Mother of our God and Lord, Jesus Christ, †

On Pentecost Sunday

Celebrating the most sacred day of Pentecost,
on which the Holy Spirit
appeared to the Apostles in tongues of fire,
and in communion with those whose memory we venerate,
especially the glorious ever-Virgin Mary,
Mother of our God and Lord, Jesus Christ, †

87. *With hands extended, the Priest continues:*

Therefore, Lord, we pray: *Celebrant alone*
graciously accept this oblation of our service,
that of your whole family;
order our days in your peace,
and command that we be delivered from eternal damnation
and counted among the flock of those you have chosen.

He joins his hands.

(Through Christ our Lord. Amen.)

From the Mass of the Easter Vigil until the Second Sunday of Easter

Therefore, Lord, we pray:
graciously accept this oblation of our service,
that of your whole family,
which we make to you
also for those to whom you have been pleased to give
the new birth of water and the Holy Spirit,
granting them forgiveness of all their sins;
order our days in your peace,
and command that we be delivered from eternal damnation
and counted among the flock of those you have chosen.

He joins his hands.

(Through Christ our Lord. Amen.)

---

88. *Holding his hands extended over the offerings, he says:*

Be pleased, O God, we pray,   *Celebrant*
to bless, acknowledge,   *with concelebrants*
and approve this offering in every respect;
make it spiritual and acceptable,
so that it may become for us
the Body and Blood of your most beloved Son,
our Lord Jesus Christ.

He joins his hands.

89. In the formulas that follow, the words of the Lord should be pronounced clearly and distinctly, as the nature of these words requires.

> **On the day before he was to suffer,**

He takes the bread and, holding it slightly raised above the altar, continues:

> **he took bread in his holy and venerable hands,**

He raises his eyes.

> **and with eyes raised to heaven**
> **to you, O God, his almighty Father,**
> **giving you thanks, he said the blessing,**
> **broke the bread**
> **and gave it to his disciples, saying:**

He bows slightly.

> **TAKE THIS, ALL OF YOU, AND EAT OF IT,**
> **FOR THIS IS MY BODY,**
> **WHICH WILL BE GIVEN UP FOR YOU.**

He shows the consecrated host to the people, places it again on the paten, and genuflects in adoration.

90. *After this, the Priest continues:*

> **In a similar way, when supper was ended,**

He takes the chalice and, holding it slightly raised above the altar, continues:

> **he took this precious chalice**
> **in his holy and venerable hands,**
> **and once more giving you thanks, he said the blessing**
> **and gave the chalice to his disciples, saying:**

He bows slightly.

> **TAKE THIS, ALL OF YOU, AND DRINK FROM IT,**
> **FOR THIS IS THE CHALICE OF MY BLOOD,**
> **THE BLOOD OF THE NEW AND ETERNAL COVENANT,**
> **WHICH WILL BE POURED OUT FOR YOU AND FOR MANY**
> **FOR THE FORGIVENESS OF SINS.**
>
> **DO THIS IN MEMORY OF ME.**

He shows the chalice to the people, places it on the corporal, and genuflects in adoration.

91. Then he says:

The mystery of faith.

And the people continue, acclaiming:

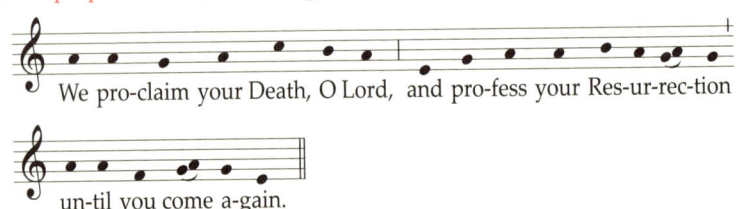

We proclaim your Death, O Lord,
and profess your Resurrection
until you come again.

Or:

When we eat this Bread and drink this Cup,
we proclaim your Death, O Lord,
until you come again.

Or:

Save us, Savior of the world,
for by your Cross and Resurrection
you have set us free.

EUCHARISTIC PRAYER I

92. *Then the Priest, with hands extended, says:*   *Celebrant*
    with concelebrants
    Therefore, O Lord,
    as we celebrate the memorial of the blessed Passion,
    the Resurrection from the dead,
    and the glorious Ascension into heaven
    of Christ, your Son, our Lord,
    we, your servants and your holy people,
    offer to your glorious majesty
    from the gifts that you have given us,
    this pure victim,
    this holy victim,
    this spotless victim,
    the holy Bread of eternal life
    and the Chalice of everlasting salvation.

93. Be pleased to look upon these offerings
    with a serene and kindly countenance,
    and to accept them,
    as once you were pleased to accept
    the gifts of your servant Abel the just,
    the sacrifice of Abraham, our father in faith,
    and the offering of your high priest Melchizedek,
    a holy sacrifice, a spotless victim.

94. *Bowing, with hands joined, he continues:*
    In humble prayer we ask you, almighty God:
    command that these gifts be borne
    by the hands of your holy Angel
    to your altar on high
    in the sight of your divine majesty,
    so that all of us, who through this participation at the altar
    receive the most holy Body and Blood of your Son,

    He stands upright again and signs himself with the Sign of the Cross, saying:
    may be filled with every grace and heavenly blessing.

    He joins his hands.
    (Through Christ our Lord. Amen.)

95. Commemoration of the Dead.

With hands extended, the Priest says: *Celebrant or one concelebrant*

**Remember also, Lord, your servants N. and N.,
who have gone before us with the sign of faith
and rest in the sleep of peace.**

He joins his hands and prays briefly for those who have died and for whom he intends to pray.

Then, with hands extended, he continues:

**Grant them, O Lord, we pray,
and all who sleep in Christ,
a place of refreshment, light and peace.**

He joins his hands.

(Through Christ our Lord. Amen.)

96. *He strikes his breast with his right hand, saying:* *Celebrant or one concelebrant*

To us, also, your servants, who, though sinners,

And, with hands extended, he continues:

**hope in your abundant mercies,
graciously grant some share
and fellowship with your holy Apostles and Martyrs:
with John the Baptist, Stephen,
Matthias, Barnabas,
   (Ignatius, Alexander,
   Marcellinus, Peter,
   Felicity, Perpetua,
   Agatha, Lucy,
   Agnes, Cecilia, Anastasia)
and all your Saints;
admit us, we beseech you,
into their company,
not weighing our merits,
but granting us your pardon,**

He joins his hands.

through Christ our Lord.

EUCHARISTIC PRAYER I

97. And he continues:

Through whom   Celebrant alone
you continue to make all these good things, O Lord;
you sanctify them, fill them with life,
bless them, and bestow them upon us.

98. He takes the chalice and the paten with the host and, raising both, he says:

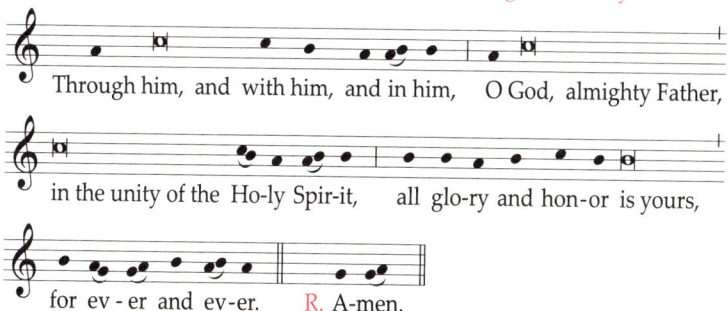

Through him, and with him, and in him,   Celebrant alone
O God, almighty Father,   or with concelebrants
in the unity of the Holy Spirit,
all glory and honor is yours,
for ever and ever.

The people acclaim:
Amen.

Then follows the Communion Rite, p. 663.

EUCHARISTIC PRAYER II

99. Although it is provided with its own Preface (text with music, p. 721), this Eucharistic Prayer may also be used with other Prefaces, especially those that present an overall view of the mystery of salvation, such as the Common Prefaces.

V. **The Lord be with you.**
R. And with your spirit.

V. **Lift up your hearts.**
R. We lift them up to the Lord.

V. **Let us give thanks to the Lord our God.**
R. It is right and just.

It is truly right and just, our duty and our salvation,
always and everywhere to give you thanks, Father most holy,
through your beloved Son, Jesus Christ,
your Word through whom you made all things,
whom you sent as our Savior and Redeemer,
incarnate by the Holy Spirit and born of the Virgin.

Fulfilling your will and gaining for you a holy people,
he stretched out his hands as he endured his Passion,
so as to break the bonds of death and manifest the resurrection.

And so, with the Angels and all the Saints
we declare your glory,
as with one voice we acclaim:

Holy, Holy, Holy Lord God of hosts.
Heaven and earth are full of your glory.
Hosanna in the highest.
Blessed is he who comes in the name of the Lord.
Hosanna in the highest.

100. *The Priest, with hands extended, says:*

> You are indeed Holy, O Lord,   *Celebrant alone*
> the fount of all holiness.

101. *He joins his hands and, holding them extended over the offerings, says:*

> Make holy, therefore, these gifts, we pray,   *Celebrant*
> by sending down your Spirit upon them like the dewfall,   *with concelebrants*

*He joins his hands
and makes the Sign of the Cross once over the bread and the chalice together, saying:*

> so that they may become for us
> the Body and ✠ Blood of our Lord Jesus Christ.

He joins his hands.

102. *In the formulas that follow, the words of the Lord should be pronounced clearly and distinctly, as the nature of these words requires.*

> At the time he was betrayed
> and entered willingly into his Passion,

He takes the bread and, holding it slightly raised above the altar, continues:

> he took bread and, giving thanks, broke it,
> and gave it to his disciples, saying:

He bows slightly.

> Take this, all of you, and eat of it,
> for this is my Body,
> which will be given up for you.

He shows the consecrated host to the people, places it again on the paten, and genuflects in adoration.

EUCHARISTIC PRAYER II

103. After this, he continues:

In a similar way, when supper was ended,

He takes the chalice and, holding it slightly raised above the altar, continues:

**he took the chalice
and, once more giving thanks,
he gave it to his disciples, saying:**

He bows slightly.

**Take this, all of you, and drink from it,
for this is the chalice of my Blood,
the Blood of the new and eternal covenant,
which will be poured out for you and for many
for the forgiveness of sins.**

Do this in memory of me.

He shows the chalice to the people, places it on the corporal, and genuflects in adoration.

104. Then he says:

The mystery of faith.   Celebrant alone

And the people continue, acclaiming:

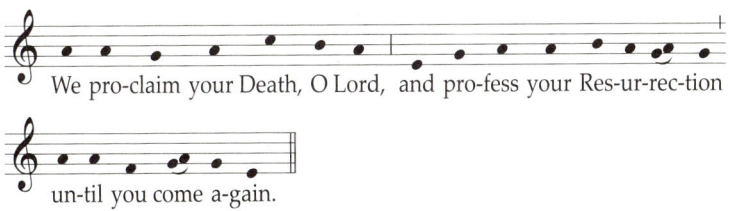

We proclaim your Death, O Lord,
and profess your Resurrection
until you come again.

Or:

When we eat this Bread and drink this Cup,
we proclaim your Death, O Lord,
until you come again.

Or:

Save us, Savior of the world,
for by your Cross and Resurrection
you have set us free.

105. Then the Priest, with hands extended, says:

> **Therefore, as we celebrate**   Celebrant
> **the memorial of his Death and Resurrection,**   with concelebrants
> **we offer you, Lord,**
> **the Bread of life and the Chalice of salvation,**
> **giving thanks that you have held us worthy**
> **to be in your presence and minister to you.**
>
> **Humbly we pray**
> **that, partaking of the Body and Blood of Christ,**
> **we may be gathered into one by the Holy Spirit.**
>
> **Remember, Lord, your Church,**   Celebrant or
> **spread throughout the world,**   one concelebrant
> **and bring her to the fullness of charity,**
> **together with N. our Pope and N. our Bishop***
> **and all the clergy.**

---

*   Mention may be made here of the Coadjutor Bishop, or Auxiliary Bishops, as noted in the *General Instruction of the Roman Missal*, no. 149.

In Masses for the Dead, the following may be added:
**Remember your servant N.,
whom you have called (today)
from this world to yourself.
Grant that he (she) who was united with your Son in a death like his,
may also be one with him in his Resurrection.**

**Remember also our brothers and sisters
who have fallen asleep in the hope of the resurrection,
and all who have died in your mercy:
welcome them into the light of your face.
Have mercy on us all, we pray,
that with the Blessed Virgin Mary, Mother of God,
with the blessed Apostles,
and all the Saints who have pleased you throughout the ages,
we may merit to be coheirs to eternal life,
and may praise and glorify you**

He joins his hands.
through your Son, Jesus Christ.

106. He takes the chalice and the paten with the host and, raising both, he says:

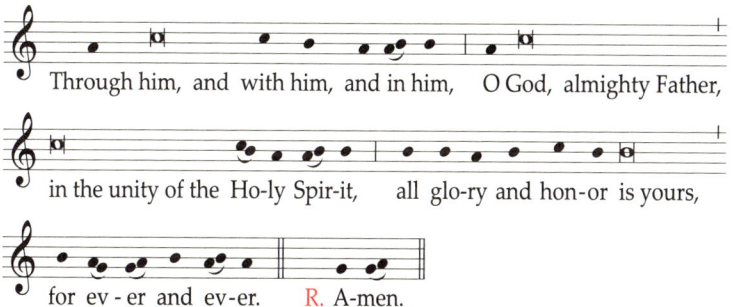

Through him, and with him, and in him, O God, almighty Father, in the unity of the Ho-ly Spir-it, all glo-ry and hon-or is yours, for ev-er and ev-er. R. A-men.

Through him, and with him, and in him,   Celebrant
O God, almighty Father,   with concelebrants
in the unity of the Holy Spirit,
all glory and honor is yours,
for ever and ever.

The people acclaim:
Amen.

Then follows the Communion Rite, p. 663.

EUCHARISTIC PRAYER III

107. V. **The Lord be with you.**
R. And with your spirit.

V. **Lift up your hearts.**
R. We lift them up to the Lord.

V. **Let us give thanks to the Lord our God.**
R. It is right and just.

Then follows the Preface to be used in accord with the rubrics, which concludes:

Holy, Holy, Holy Lord God of hosts.
Heaven and earth are full of your glory.
Hosanna in the highest.
Blessed is he who comes in the name of the Lord.
Hosanna in the highest.

108. *The Priest, with hands extended, says:*

You are indeed Holy, O Lord, *Celebrant alone*
and all you have created
rightly gives you praise,
for through your Son our Lord Jesus Christ,
by the power and working of the Holy Spirit,
you give life to all things and make them holy,
and you never cease to gather a people to yourself,
so that from the rising of the sun to its setting
a pure sacrifice may be offered to your name.

109. *He joins his hands and, holding them extended over the offerings, says:*

Therefore, O Lord, we humbly implore you: *Celebrant*
by the same Spirit graciously make holy *with concelebrants*
these gifts we have brought to you for consecration,

He joins his hands
and makes the Sign of the Cross once over the bread and chalice together, saying:

that they may become the Body and ✚ Blood
of your Son our Lord Jesus Christ,

He joins his hands.

at whose command we celebrate these mysteries.

110. In the formulas that follow, the words of the Lord should be pronounced clearly and distinctly, as the nature of these words requires.

For on the night he was betrayed

He takes the bread and, holding it slightly raised above the altar, continues:

**he himself took bread,
and, giving you thanks, he said the blessing,
broke the bread and gave it to his disciples, saying:**

He bows slightly.

**Take this, all of you, and eat of it,
for this is my Body,
which will be given up for you.**

He shows the consecrated host to the people, places it again on the paten, and genuflects in adoration.

111. After this, he continues:

In a similar way, when supper was ended,

He takes the chalice and, holding it slightly raised above the altar, continues:

**he took the chalice,
and, giving you thanks, he said the blessing,
and gave the chalice to his disciples, saying:**

He bows slightly.

**Take this, all of you, and drink from it,
for this is the chalice of my Blood,
the Blood of the new and eternal covenant,
which will be poured out for you and for many
for the forgiveness of sins.**

Do this in memory of me.

He shows the chalice to the people, places it on the corporal, and genuflects in adoration.

112. Then he says:

The mys-ter-y of faith.

The mystery of faith. Celebrant alone

And the people continue, acclaiming:

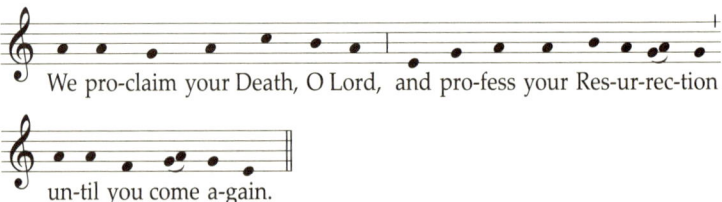

We proclaim your Death, O Lord,
and profess your Resurrection
until you come again.

Or:

When we eat this Bread and drink this Cup,
we proclaim your Death, O Lord,
until you come again.

Or:

Save us, Savior of the world,
for by your Cross and Resurrection
you have set us free.

113. Then the Priest, with hands extended, says:

Therefore, O Lord, as we celebrate the memorial   Celebrant
of the saving Passion of your Son,   with concelebrants
his wondrous Resurrection
and Ascension into heaven,
and as we look forward to his second coming,
we offer you in thanksgiving
this holy and living sacrifice.

Look, we pray, upon the oblation of your Church
and, recognizing the sacrificial Victim by whose death
you willed to reconcile us to yourself,
grant that we, who are nourished
by the Body and Blood of your Son
and filled with his Holy Spirit,
may become one body, one spirit in Christ.

May he make of us   Celebrant or
an eternal offering to you,   one concelebrant
so that we may obtain an inheritance with your elect,
especially with the most Blessed Virgin Mary, Mother of God,
with your blessed Apostles and glorious Martyrs
(with Saint N.: the Saint of the day or Patron Saint)
and with all the Saints,
on whose constant intercession in your presence
we rely for unfailing help.

May this Sacrifice of our reconciliation, *Celebrant or one concelebrant*
we pray, O Lord,
advance the peace and salvation of all the world.
Be pleased to confirm in faith and charity
your pilgrim Church on earth,
with your servant N. our Pope and N. our Bishop,*
the Order of Bishops, all the clergy,
and the entire people you have gained for your own.

Listen graciously to the prayers of this family,
whom you have summoned before you:
in your compassion, O merciful Father,
gather to yourself all your children
scattered throughout the world.

† To our departed brothers and sisters *Celebrant or one concelebrant*
and to all who were pleasing to you
at their passing from this life,
give kind admittance to your kingdom.
There we hope to enjoy for ever the fullness of your glory

He joins his hands.
through Christ our Lord,
through whom you bestow on the world all that is good. †

114. He takes the chalice and the paten with the host and, raising both, he says:

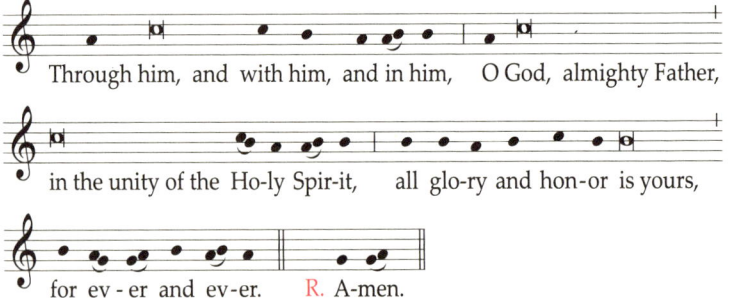

Through him, and with him, and in him, O God, almighty Father,
in the unity of the Ho-ly Spir-it, all glo-ry and hon-or is yours,
for ev-er and ev-er. ℟. A-men.

---

* Mention may be made here of the Coadjutor Bishop, or Auxiliary Bishops, as noted in the *General Instruction of the Roman Missal*, no. 149.

Through him, and with him, and in him, *Celebrant alone*
O God, almighty Father, *or with concelebrants*
in the unity of the Holy Spirit,
all glory and honor is yours,
for ever and ever.

The people acclaim:
Amen.

Then follows the Communion Rite, p. 663.

---

115. When this Eucharistic Prayer is used in Masses for the Dead, the following may be said:
    † **Remember your servant N.**
    whom you have called (today)
    from this world to yourself.
    Grant that he (she) who was united with your Son in a death like his,
    may also be one with him in his Resurrection,
    when from the earth
    he will raise up in the flesh those who have died,
    and transform our lowly body
    after the pattern of his own glorious body.
    To our departed brothers and sisters, too,
    and to all who were pleasing to you
    at their passing from this life,
    give kind admittance to your kingdom.
    There we hope to enjoy for ever the fullness of your glory,
    when you will wipe away every tear from our eyes.
    For seeing you, our God, as you are,
    we shall be like you for all the ages
    and praise you without end,

    He joins his hands.
    through Christ our Lord,
    through whom you bestow on the world all that is good. †

EUCHARISTIC PRAYER IV

116. It is not permitted to change the Preface of this Eucharistic Prayer because of the structure of the Prayer itself, which presents a summary of the history of salvation (text with music, p. 736).

V. The Lord be with you.
R. And with your spirit.

V. Lift up your hearts.
R. We lift them up to the Lord.

V. Let us give thanks to the Lord our God.
R. It is right and just.

It is truly right to give you thanks,
truly just to give you glory, Father most holy,
for you are the one God living and true,
existing before all ages and abiding for all eternity,
dwelling in unapproachable light;
yet you, who alone are good, the source of life,
have made all that is,
so that you might fill your creatures with blessings
and bring joy to many of them by the glory of your light.

And so, in your presence are countless hosts of Angels,
who serve you day and night
and, gazing upon the glory of your face,
glorify you without ceasing.

With them we, too, confess your name in exultation,
giving voice to every creature under heaven,
as we acclaim:

Holy, Holy, Holy Lord God of hosts.
Heaven and earth are full of your glory.
Hosanna in the highest.
Blessed is he who comes in the name of the Lord.
Hosanna in the highest.

117. *The Priest, with hands extended, says:*   *Celebrant alone*

>We give you praise, Father most holy,
>   for you are great
>and you have fashioned all your works
>in wisdom and in love.
>You formed man in your own image
>and entrusted the whole world to his care,
>so that in serving you alone, the Creator,
>he might have dominion over all creatures.
>And when through disobedience he had lost your friendship,
>you did not abandon him to the domain of death.
>For you came in mercy to the aid of all,
>so that those who seek might find you.
>Time and again you offered them covenants
>and through the prophets
>taught them to look forward to salvation.
>
>And you so loved the world, Father most holy,
>that in the fullness of time
>you sent your Only Begotten Son to be our Savior.
>Made incarnate by the Holy Spirit
>and born of the Virgin Mary,
>he shared our human nature
>in all things but sin.
>To the poor he proclaimed the good news of salvation,
>to prisoners, freedom,
>and to the sorrowful of heart, joy.
>To accomplish your plan,
>he gave himself up to death,
>and, rising from the dead,
>he destroyed death and restored life.
>
>And that we might live no longer for ourselves
>but for him who died and rose again for us,
>he sent the Holy Spirit from you, Father,
>as the first fruits for those who believe,
>so that, bringing to perfection his work in the world,
>he might sanctify creation to the full.

118. He joins his hands and, holding them extended over the offerings, says:

Celebrant with concelebrants

**Therefore, O Lord, we pray:
may this same Holy Spirit
graciously sanctify these offerings,**

He joins his hands and makes the Sign of the Cross once over the bread and chalice together, saying:

**that they may become
the Body and ✠ Blood of our Lord Jesus Christ**

He joins his hands.

**for the celebration of this great mystery,
which he himself left us
as an eternal covenant.**

119. In the formulas that follow, the words of the Lord should be pronounced clearly and distinctly, as the nature of these words requires.

**For when the hour had come
for him to be glorified by you, Father most holy,
having loved his own who were in the world,
he loved them to the end:
and while they were at supper,**

He takes the bread and, holding it slightly raised above the altar, continues:

**he took bread, blessed and broke it,
and gave it to his disciples, saying:**

He bows slightly.

**TAKE THIS, ALL OF YOU, AND EAT OF IT,
FOR THIS IS MY BODY,
WHICH WILL BE GIVEN UP FOR YOU.**

He shows the consecrated host to the people, places it again on the paten, and genuflects in adoration.

EUCHARISTIC PRAYER IV

120. After this, he continues:

In a similar way,

He takes the chalice and, holding it slightly raised above the altar, continues:

**taking the chalice filled with the fruit of the vine,
he gave thanks,
and gave the chalice to his disciples, saying:**

He bows slightly.

**TAKE THIS, ALL OF YOU, AND DRINK FROM IT,
FOR THIS IS THE CHALICE OF MY BLOOD,
THE BLOOD OF THE NEW AND ETERNAL COVENANT,
WHICH WILL BE POURED OUT FOR YOU AND FOR MANY
FOR THE FORGIVENESS OF SINS.**

DO THIS IN MEMORY OF ME.

He shows the chalice to the people, places it on the corporal, and genuflects in adoration.

121. Then he says:

The mys-ter-y of faith.

The mystery of faith. Celebrant alone

And the people continue, acclaiming:

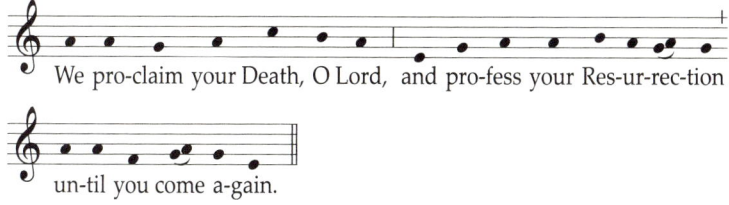
We pro-claim your Death, O Lord, and pro-fess your Res-ur-rec-tion un-til you come a-gain.

**We proclaim your Death, O Lord,
and profess your Resurrection
until you come again.**

Or:

When we eat this Bread and drink this Cup,
we proclaim your Death, O Lord,
until you come again.

Or:

Save us, Savior of the world,
for by your Cross and Resurrection
you have set us free.

122. Then, with hands extended, the Priest says:

Celebrant with concelebrants

**Therefore, O Lord,
as we now celebrate the memorial of our redemption,
we remember Christ's Death
and his descent to the realm of the dead,
we proclaim his Resurrection
and his Ascension to your right hand,
and, as we await his coming in glory,
we offer you his Body and Blood,
the sacrifice acceptable to you
which brings salvation to the whole world.**

**Look, O Lord, upon the Sacrifice
which you yourself have provided for your Church,
and grant in your loving kindness
to all who partake of this one Bread and one Chalice
that, gathered into one body by the Holy Spirit,
they may truly become a living sacrifice in Christ
to the praise of your glory.**

> Therefore, Lord, remember now
> all for whom we offer this sacrifice:
> especially your servant N. our Pope,
> N. our Bishop,* and the whole Order of Bishops,
> all the clergy,
> those who take part in this offering,
> those gathered here before you,
> your entire people,
> and all who seek you with a sincere heart.
>
> Remember also
> those who have died in the peace of your Christ
> and all the dead,
> whose faith you alone have known.

Celebrant or one concelebrant

> To all of us, your children,
> grant, O merciful Father,
> that we may enter into a heavenly inheritance
> with the Blessed Virgin Mary, Mother of God,
> and with your Apostles and Saints in your kingdom.
> There, with the whole of creation,
> freed from the corruption of sin and death,
> may we glorify you through Christ our Lord,

Celebrant or one concelebrant

He joins his hands.

> through whom you bestow on the world all that is good.

---

* Mention may be made here of the Coadjutor Bishop, or Auxiliary Bishops, as noted in the *General Instruction of the Roman Missal*, no. 149.

123. He takes the chalice and the paten with the host and, raising both, he says:

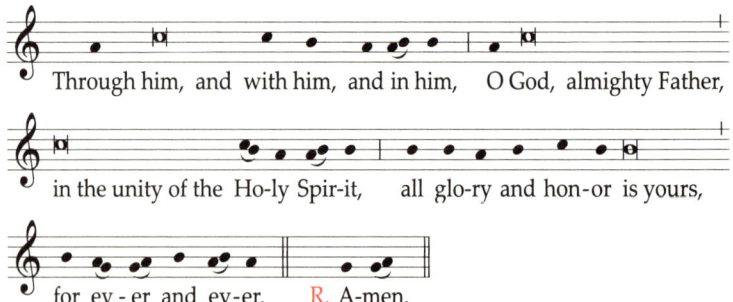

Through him, and with him, and in him, O God, almighty Father,
in the unity of the Ho-ly Spir-it, all glo-ry and hon-or is yours,
for ev-er and ev-er. R. A-men.

Through him, and with him, and in him,   Celebrant alone
O God, almighty Father,   or with concelebrants
in the unity of the Holy Spirit,
all glory and honor is yours,
for ever and ever.

The people acclaim:
Amen.

Then follows the Communion Rite, p. 663.

THE COMMUNION RITE

124. After the chalice and paten have been set down, the Priest, with hands joined, says:

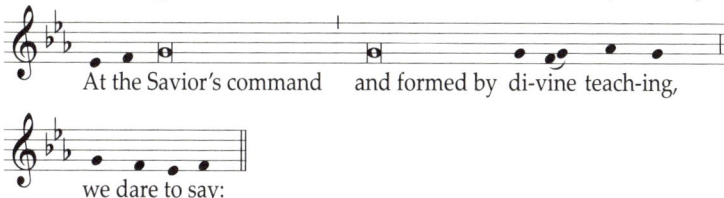

**At the Savior's command
and formed by divine teaching,
we dare to say:**

He extends his hands and, together with the people, continues:

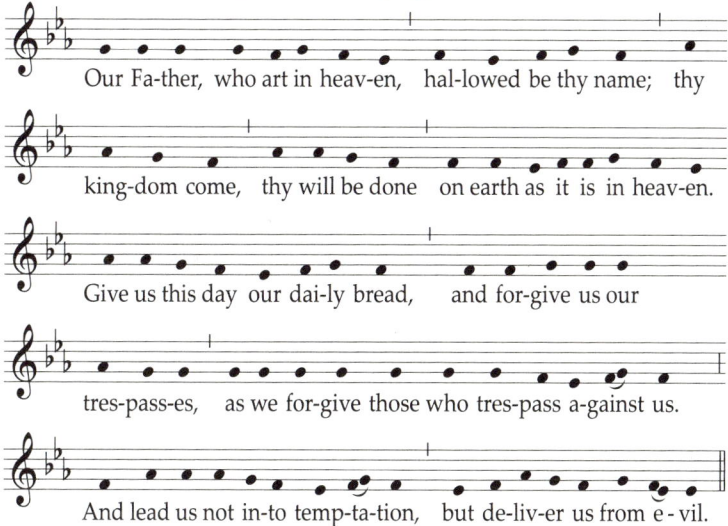

**Our Father, who art in heaven,
hallowed be thy name;
thy kingdom come,
thy will be done
on earth as it is in heaven.
Give us this day our daily bread,
and forgive us our trespasses,
as we forgive those who trespass against us;
and lead us not into temptation,
but deliver us from evil.**

Or:

Pa-ter nos-ter, qui es in cae-lis: san-cti-fi-cé-tur no-men tu-um; ad-vé-ni-at reg-num tu-um; fi-at vo-lún-tas tu-a, si-cut in cae-lo, et in ter-ra. Pa-nem nos-trum co-ti-di-á-num da no-bis hó-di-e; et di-mít-te no-bis dé-bi-ta nos-tra, si-cut et nos di-mít-ti-mus de-bi-tó-ri-bus nos-tris; et ne nos in-dú-cas in ten-ta-ti-ó-nem; sed lí-be-ra nos a ma-lo.

Alternate musical settings of the Lord's Prayer may be found in Appendix I, pp. **1443-1444**.

125. With hands extended, the Priest alone continues, saying:

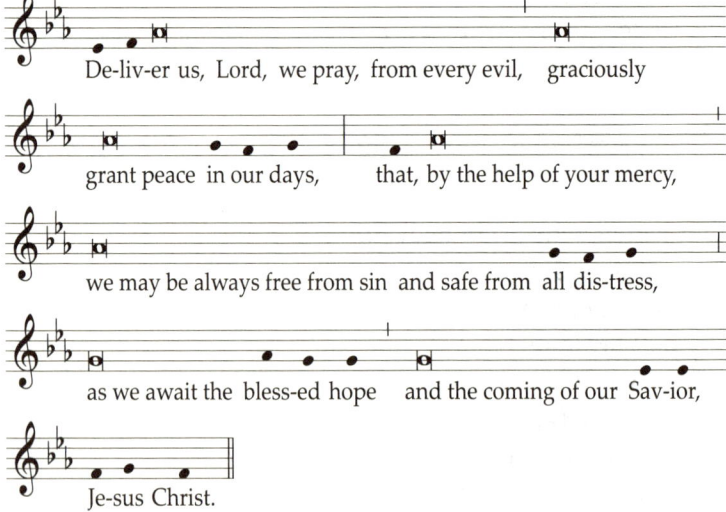

De-liv-er us, Lord, we pray, from every evil, graciously grant peace in our days, that, by the help of your mercy, we may be always free from sin and safe from all dis-tress, as we await the bless-ed hope and the coming of our Sav-ior, Je-sus Christ.

Deliver us, Lord, we pray, from every evil,
graciously grant peace in our days,
that, by the help of your mercy,
we may be always free from sin
and safe from all distress,
as we await the blessed hope
and the coming of our Savior, Jesus Christ.

He joins his hands.

The people conclude the prayer, acclaiming:

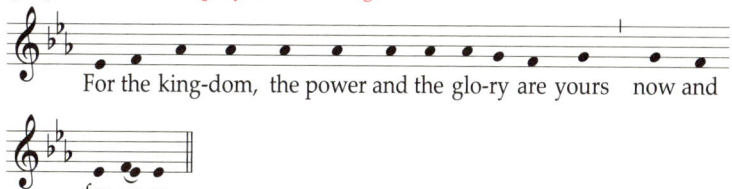

For the kingdom,
the power and the glory are yours
now and for ever.

126. Then the Priest, with hands extended, says aloud:

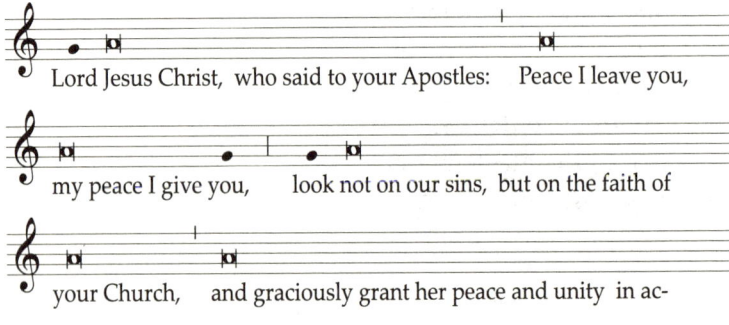

Lord Jesus Christ, who said to your Apostles: Peace I leave you, my peace I give you, look not on our sins, but on the faith of your Church, and graciously grant her peace and unity in accordance with your will.

He joins his hands.

Who live and reign for ever and ever.

The people reply:

Amen.

127. The Priest, turned towards the people, extending and then joining his hands, adds:

The peace of the Lord be with you always.

The people reply:

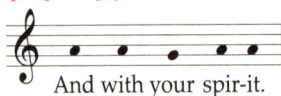

And with your spirit.

128. Then, if appropriate, the Deacon, or the Priest, adds:

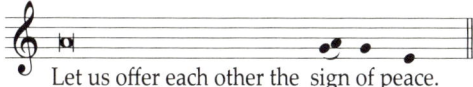
Let us offer each other the sign of peace.

Let us offer each other the sign of peace.

And all offer one another a sign, in keeping with local customs, that expresses peace, communion, and charity. The Priest gives the sign of peace to a Deacon or minister.

129. Then he takes the host, breaks it over the paten, and places a small piece in the chalice, saying quietly:

**May this mingling of the Body and Blood
of our Lord Jesus Christ
bring eternal life to us who receive it.**

130. Meanwhile the following is sung or said:

Lamb of God, you take away the sins of the world,
have mercy on us.
Lamb of God, you take away the sins of the world,
have mercy on us.
Lamb of God, you take away the sins of the world,
grant us peace.

Or:

A-gnus De-i, * qui tol-lis pec-cá-ta mun-di: mi-se-ré-re no-bis.

A-gnus De-i, * qui tol-lis pec-cá-ta mun-di: mi-se-ré-re no-bis.

A-gnus De-i, * qui tol-lis pec-cá-ta mun-di: do-na no-bis pa-cem.

The invocation may even be repeated several times if the fraction is prolonged. Only the final time, however, is grant us peace said.

131. Then the Priest, with hands joined, says quietly:

**Lord Jesus Christ, Son of the living God,
who, by the will of the Father
and the work of the Holy Spirit,
through your Death gave life to the world,
free me by this, your most holy Body and Blood,
from all my sins and from every evil;
keep me always faithful to your commandments,
and never let me be parted from you.**

Or:

**May the receiving of your Body and Blood,
Lord Jesus Christ,
not bring me to judgment and condemnation,
but through your loving mercy
be for me protection in mind and body
and a healing remedy.**

THE ORDER OF MASS

132. The Priest genuflects, takes the host and, holding it slightly raised above the paten or above the chalice, while facing the people, says aloud:

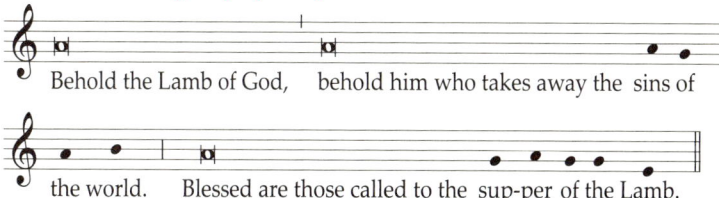

Behold the Lamb of God, behold him who takes away the sins of the world. Blessed are those called to the sup-per of the Lamb.

**Behold the Lamb of God,
behold him who takes away the sins of the world.
Blessed are those called to the supper of the Lamb.**

And together with the people he adds once:

Lord, I am not worthy that you should enter un-der my roof, but only say the word and my soul shall be healed.

**Lord, I am not worthy
that you should enter under my roof,
but only say the word
and my soul shall be healed.**

133. The Priest, facing the altar, says quietly:

   **May the Body of Christ
   keep me safe for eternal life.**

   And he reverently consumes the Body of Christ.

   Then he takes the chalice and says quietly:

   **May the Blood of Christ
   keep me safe for eternal life.**

   And he reverently consumes the Blood of Christ.

134. After this, he takes the paten or ciborium and approaches the communicants. The Priest raises a host slightly and shows it to each of the communicants, saying:

   The Body of Christ.

   The communicant replies:

   Amen.

   And receives Holy Communion.

   If a Deacon also distributes Holy Communion, he does so in the same manner.

135. If any are present who are to receive Holy Communion under both kinds, the rite described in the proper place is to be followed.

136. While the Priest is receiving the Body of Christ, the Communion Chant begins.

137. When the distribution of Communion is over, the Priest or a Deacon or an acolyte purifies the paten over the chalice and also the chalice itself.

    While he carries out the purification, the Priest says quietly:

    What has passed our lips as food, O Lord,
    may we possess in purity of heart,
    that what has been given to us in time
    may be our healing for eternity.

138. Then the Priest may return to the chair. If appropriate, a sacred silence may be observed for a while, or a psalm or other canticle of praise or a hymn may be sung.

139. Then, standing at the altar or at the chair and facing the people, with hands joined, the Priest says:

    Let us pray.

    All pray in silence with the Priest for a while, unless silence has just been observed. Then the Priest, with hands extended, says the Prayer after Communion, at the end of which the people acclaim:

    Amen.

THE CONCLUDING RITES

140. If they are necessary, any brief announcements to the people follow here.

141. Then the dismissal takes place. The Priest, facing the people and extending his hands, says:

The Lord be with you.

The Lord be with you.

The people reply:

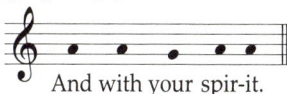
And with your spir-it.

And with your spirit.

The Priest blesses the people, saying:

May almighty God bless you,   the Father, and the Son, ✠ and the Ho-ly Spir-it.

**May almighty God bless you,
the Father, and the Son, ✠ and the Holy Spirit.**

The people reply:

A-men.

Amen.

---

142. On certain days or occasions, this formula of blessing is preceded, in accordance with the rubrics, by another more solemn formula of blessing or by a prayer over the people (cf. pp. **674ff.**).

143. In a Pontifical Mass, the celebrant receives the miter and, extending his hands, says:

The Lord be with you.

The Lord be with you.

All reply:

And with your spir-it.

And with your spirit.

The celebrant says:

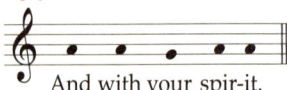
Blessed be the name of the Lord.

Blessed be the name of the Lord.

All reply:

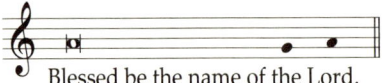
Now and for ev-er.

Now and for ever.

The celebrant says:

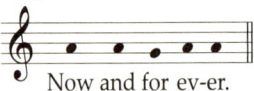
Our help is in the name of the Lord.

Our help is in the name of the Lord.

All reply:

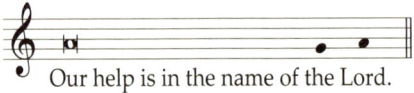
Who made heav-en and earth.

Who made heaven and earth.

Then the celebrant receives the pastoral staff, if he uses it, and says:

May almighty God bless you,

May almighty God bless you,

making the Sign of the Cross over the people three times, he adds:

the Father, ✠ and the Son, ✠ and the Holy ✠ Spirit.

All:

Amen.

---

144. Then the Deacon, or the Priest himself, with hands joined and facing the people, says:

Go forth, the Mass is ended.

Or:

Go and announce the Gospel of the Lord.

Or:

Go in peace, glorifying the Lord by your life.

Or:

Go in peace.

The people reply:

Thanks be to God.

145. Then the Priest venerates the altar as usual with a kiss, as at the beginning. After making a profound bow with the ministers, he withdraws.

146. If any liturgical action follows immediately, the rites of dismissal are omitted.

BLESSINGS AT THE END OF MASS AND PRAYERS OVER THE PEOPLE

SOLEMN BLESSINGS

The following blessings may be used, at the discretion of the Priest, at the end of the celebration of Mass, or of a Liturgy of the Word, or of the Office, or of the Sacraments.

The Deacon or, in his absence, the Priest himself, says the invitation: Bow down for the blessing. Then the Priest, with hands extended over the people, says the blessing, with all responding: Amen.

I. For Celebrations in the Different Liturgical Times

1. Advent

   May the almighty and merciful God,
   by whose grace you have placed your faith
   in the First Coming of his Only Begotten Son
   and yearn for his coming again,
   sanctify you by the radiance of Christ's Advent
   and enrich you with his blessing.
   R. Amen.

   As you run the race of this present life,
   may he make you firm in faith,
   joyful in hope and active in charity.
   R. Amen.

   So that, rejoicing now with devotion
   at the Redeemer's coming in the flesh,
   you may be endowed with the rich reward of eternal life
   when he comes again in majesty.
   R. Amen.

   And may the blessing of almighty God,
   the Father, and the Son, ✠ and the Holy Spirit,
   come down on you and remain with you for ever.
   R. Amen.

2. The Nativity of the Lord

   May the God of infinite goodness,
   who by the Incarnation of his Son has driven darkness from the world
   and by that glorious Birth has illumined this most holy night (day),
   drive far from you the darkness of vice
   and illumine your hearts with the light of virtue.
   R. Amen.

May God, who willed that the great joy
of his Son's saving Birth
be announced to shepherds by the Angel,
fill your minds with the gladness he gives
and make you heralds of his Gospel.
R. Amen.

And may God, who by the Incarnation
brought together the earthly and heavenly realm,
fill you with the gift of his peace and favor
and make you sharers with the Church in heaven.
R. Amen.

And may the blessing of almighty God,
the Father, and the Son, ✠ and the Holy Spirit,
come down on you and remain with you for ever.
R. Amen.

3. The Beginning of the Year

May God, the source and origin of all blessing,
grant you grace,
pour out his blessing in abundance,
and keep you safe from harm throughout the year.
R. Amen.

May he give you integrity in the faith,
endurance in hope,
and perseverance in charity
with holy patience to the end.
R. Amen.

May he order your days and your deeds in his peace,
grant your prayers in this and in every place,
and lead you happily to eternal life.
R. Amen.

And may the blessing of almighty God,
the Father, and the Son, ✠ and the Holy Spirit,
come down on you and remain with you for ever.
R. Amen.

4. The Epiphany of the Lord

May God, who has called you
out of darkness into his wonderful light,
pour out in kindness his blessing upon you
and make your hearts firm
in faith, hope and charity.
R. Amen.

And since in all confidence you follow Christ,
who today appeared in the world
as a light shining in darkness,
may God make you, too,
a light for your brothers and sisters.
R. Amen.

And so when your pilgrimage is ended,
may you come to him
whom the Magi sought as they followed the star
and whom they found with great joy, the Light from Light,
who is Christ the Lord.
R. Amen.

And may the blessing of almighty God,
the Father, and the Son, ✠ and the Holy Spirit,
come down on you and remain with you for ever.
R. Amen.

5. The Passion of the Lord

May God, the Father of mercies,
who has given you an example of love
in the Passion of his Only Begotten Son,
grant that, by serving God and your neighbor,
you may lay hold of the wondrous gift of his blessing.
R. Amen.

So that you may receive the reward of everlasting life from him,
through whose earthly Death
you believe that you escape eternal death.
R. Amen.

And by following the example of his self-abasement,
may you possess a share in his Resurrection.
R. Amen.

And may the blessing of almighty God,
the Father, and the Son, ✠ and the Holy Spirit,
come down on you and remain with you for ever.
R. Amen.

6. Easter Time

May God, who by the Resurrection of his Only Begotten Son
was pleased to confer on you
the gift of redemption and of adoption,
give you gladness by his blessing.
R. Amen.

May he, by whose redeeming work
you have received the gift of everlasting freedom,
make you heirs to an eternal inheritance.
R. Amen.

And may you, who have already risen with Christ
in Baptism through faith,
by living in a right manner on this earth,
be united with him in the homeland of heaven.
R. Amen.

And may the blessing of almighty God,
the Father, and the Son, ✠ and the Holy Spirit,
come down on you and remain with you for ever.
R. Amen.

7. The Ascension of the Lord

**May almighty God bless you,
for on this very day his Only Begotten Son
pierced the heights of heaven
and unlocked for you the way
to ascend to where he is.**
R. Amen.

**May he grant that,
as Christ after his Resurrection
was seen plainly by his disciples,
so when he comes as Judge
he may show himself merciful to you for all eternity.**
R. Amen.

**And may you, who believe he is seated
with the Father in his majesty,
know with joy the fulfillment of his promise
to stay with you until the end of time.**
R. Amen.

**And may the blessing of almighty God,
the Father, and the Son, ✠ and the Holy Spirit,
come down on you and remain with you for ever.**
R. Amen.

8. The Holy Spirit

**May God, the Father of lights,
who was pleased to enlighten the disciples' minds
by the outpouring of the Spirit, the Paraclete,
grant you gladness by his blessing
and make you always abound with the gifts of the same Spirit.**
R. Amen.

**May the wondrous flame that appeared above the disciples,
powerfully cleanse your hearts from every evil
and pervade them with its purifying light.**
R. Amen.

**And may God, who has been pleased to unite many tongues
in the profession of one faith,
give you perseverance in that same faith
and, by believing, may you journey from hope to clear vision.**
R. Amen.

And may the blessing of almighty God,
the Father, and the Son, ✠ and the Holy Spirit,
come down on you and remain with you for ever.
R. Amen.

9. Ordinary Time I

May the Lord bless you and keep you.
R. Amen.

May he let his face shine upon you
and show you his mercy.
R. Amen.

May he turn his countenance towards you
and give you his peace.
R. Amen.

And may the blessing of almighty God,
the Father, and the Son, ✠ and the Holy Spirit,
come down on you and remain with you for ever.
R. Amen.

10. Ordinary Time II

May the peace of God,
which surpasses all understanding,
keep your hearts and minds
in the knowledge and love of God,
and of his Son, our Lord Jesus Christ.
R. Amen.

And may the blessing of almighty God,
the Father, and the Son, ✠ and the Holy Spirit,
come down on you and remain with you for ever.
R. Amen.

11. Ordinary Time III

> May almighty God bless you in his kindness
> and pour out saving wisdom upon you.
> R. Amen.
>
> May he nourish you always with the teachings of the faith
> and make you persevere in holy deeds.
> R. Amen.
>
> May he turn your steps towards himself
> and show you the path of charity and peace.
> R. Amen.
>
> And may the blessing of almighty God,
> the Father, and the Son, ✠ and the Holy Spirit,
> come down on you and remain with you for ever.
> R. Amen.

12. Ordinary Time IV

> May the God of all consolation order your days in his peace
> and grant you the gifts of his blessing.
> R. Amen.
>
> May he free you always from every distress
> and confirm your hearts in his love.
> R. Amen.
>
> So that on this life's journey
> you may be effective in good works,
> rich in the gifts of hope, faith and charity,
> and may come happily to eternal life.
> R. Amen.
>
> And may the blessing of almighty God,
> the Father, and the Son, ✠ and the Holy Spirit,
> come down on you and remain with you for ever.
> R. Amen.

13. Ordinary Time V

May almighty God always keep every adversity far from you
and in his kindness pour out upon you the gifts of his blessing.
R. Amen.

May God keep your hearts attentive to his words,
that they may be filled with everlasting gladness.
R. Amen.

And so, may you always understand what is good and right,
and be found ever hastening along
in the path of God's commands,
made coheirs with the citizens of heaven.
R. Amen.

And may the blessing of almighty God,
the Father, and the Son, ✠ and the Holy Spirit,
come down on you and remain with you for ever.
R. Amen.

14. Ordinary Time VI

May God bless you with every heavenly blessing,
make you always holy and pure in his sight,
pour out in abundance upon you the riches of his glory,
and teach you with the words of truth;
may he instruct you in the Gospel of salvation,
and ever endow you with fraternal charity.
Through Christ our Lord.
R. Amen.

And may the blessing of almighty God,
the Father, and the Son, ✠ and the Holy Spirit,
come down on you and remain with you for ever.
R. Amen.

II. For Celebrations of the Saints

15. The Blessed Virgin Mary

May God, who through the childbearing of the Blessed Virgin Mary
willed in his great kindness to redeem the human race,
be pleased to enrich you with his blessing.
R. Amen.

May you know always and everywhere the protection of her,
through whom you have been found worthy to receive the author of life.
R. Amen.

May you, who have devoutly gathered on this day,
carry away with you the gifts of spiritual joys and heavenly rewards.
R. Amen.

And may the blessing of almighty God,
the Father, and the Son, ✠ and the Holy Spirit,
come down on you and remain with you for ever.
R. Amen.

16. Saints Peter and Paul, Apostles

May almighty God bless you,
for he has made you steadfast in Saint Peter's saving confession
and through it has set you on the solid rock of the Church's faith.
R. Amen.

And having instructed you
by the tireless preaching of Saint Paul,
may God teach you constantly by his example
to win brothers and sisters for Christ.
R. Amen.

So that by the keys of St Peter and the words of St Paul,
and by the support of their intercession,
God may bring us happily to that homeland
that Peter attained on a cross
and Paul by the blade of a sword.
R. Amen.

And may the blessing of almighty God,
the Father, and the Son, ✠ and the Holy Spirit,
come down on you and remain with you for ever.
R. Amen.

17. The Apostles

May God, who has granted you
to stand firm on apostolic foundations,
graciously bless you through the glorious merits
of the holy Apostles N. and N. (the holy Apostle N.).
R. Amen.

And may he, who endowed you
with the teaching and example of the Apostles,
make you, under their protection,
witnesses to the truth before all.
R. Amen.

So that through the intercession of the Apostles,
you may inherit the eternal homeland,
for by their teaching you possess firmness of faith.
R. Amen.

And may the blessing of almighty God,
the Father, and the Son, ✠ and the Holy Spirit,
come down on you and remain with you for ever.
R. Amen.

18. All Saints

May God, the glory and joy of the Saints,
who has caused you to be strengthened
by means of their outstanding prayers,
bless you with unending blessings.
R. Amen.

Freed through their intercession from present ills
and formed by the example of their holy way of life,
may you be ever devoted
to serving God and your neighbor.
R. Amen.

So that, together with all,
you may possess the joys of the homeland,
where Holy Church rejoices
that her children are admitted in perpetual peace
to the company of the citizens of heaven.
R. Amen.

And may the blessing of almighty God,
the Father, and the Son, ✠ and the Holy Spirit,
come down on you and remain with you for ever.
R. Amen.

III. Other Blessings

19. For the Dedication of a Church

May God, the Lord of heaven and earth,
who has gathered you today for the dedication of this church,
make you abound in heavenly blessings.
R. Amen.

And may he, who has willed that all his scattered children
should be gathered together in his Son,
grant that you may become his temple
and the dwelling place of the Holy Spirit.
R. Amen.

And so, when you are thoroughly cleansed,
may God dwell within you
and grant you to possess with all the Saints
the inheritance of eternal happiness.
R. Amen.

And may the blessing of almighty God,
the Father, ✠ and the Son, ✠ and the Holy ✠ Spirit,
come down on you and remain with you for ever.
R. Amen.

20. In Celebrations for the Dead

May the God of all consolation bless you,
for in his unfathomable goodness he created the human race,
and in the Resurrection of his Only Begotten Son
he has given believers the hope of rising again.
R. Amen.

To us who are alive, may God grant pardon for our sins,
and to all the dead, a place of light and peace.
R. Amen.

So may we all live happily for ever with Christ,
whom we believe truly rose from the dead.
R. Amen.

And may the blessing of almighty God,
the Father, and the Son, ✠ and the Holy Spirit,
come down on you and remain with you for ever.
R. Amen.

PRAYERS OVER THE PEOPLE

The following prayers may be used, at the discretion of the Priest, at the end of the celebration of Mass, or of a Liturgy of the Word, or of the Office, or of the Sacraments.

The Deacon or, in his absence, the Priest himself, says the invitation: Bow down for the blessing. Then the Priest, with hands outstretched over the people, says the prayer, with all responding: Amen.

After the prayer, the Priest always adds: And may the blessing of almighty God, the Father, and the Son, ✠ and the Holy Spirit, come down on you and remain with you for ever. R. Amen.

1. Be gracious to your people, O Lord,
   and do not withhold consolation on earth
   from those you call to strive for heaven.
   Through Christ our Lord.

2. Grant, O Lord, we pray,
   that the Christian people
   may understand the truths they profess
   and love the heavenly liturgy
   in which they participate.
   Through Christ our Lord.

3. May your people receive your holy blessing,
   O Lord, we pray,
   and, by that gift,
   spurn all that would harm them
   and obtain what they desire.
   Through Christ our Lord.

4. Turn your people to you with all their heart,
   O Lord, we pray,
   for you protect even those who go astray,
   but when they serve you with undivided heart,
   you sustain them with still greater care.
   Through Christ our Lord.

5. Graciously enlighten your family, O Lord, we pray,
   that by holding fast to what is pleasing to you,
   they may be worthy to accomplish all that is good.
   Through Christ our Lord.

6. Bestow pardon and peace, O Lord, we pray,
   upon your faithful,
   that they may be cleansed from every offense
   and serve you with untroubled hearts.
   Through Christ our Lord.

7. May your heavenly favor, O Lord, we pray,
   increase in number the people subject to you
   and make them always obedient to your commands.
   Through Christ our Lord.

8. Be propitious to your people, O God,
   that, freed from every evil,
   they may serve you with all their heart
   and ever stand firm under your protection.
   Through Christ our Lord.

9. May your family always rejoice together, O God,
   over the mysteries of redemption they have celebrated,
   and grant its members the perseverance
   to attain the effects that flow from them.
   Through Christ our Lord.

10. Lord God, from the abundance of your mercies
    provide for your servants and ensure their safety,
    so that, strengthened by your blessings,
    they may at all times abound in thanksgiving
    and bless you with unending exultation.
    Through Christ our Lord.

11. Keep your family, we pray, O Lord,
    in your constant care,
    so that, under your protection,
    they may be free from all troubles
    and by good works show dedication to your name.
    Through Christ our Lord.

12. Purify your faithful, both in body and in mind,
    O Lord, we pray,
    so that, feeling the compunction you inspire,
    they may be able to avoid harmful pleasures
    and ever feed upon your delights.
    Through Christ our Lord.

13. May the effects of your sacred blessing, O Lord,
    make themselves felt among your faithful,
    to prepare with spiritual sustenance the minds of all,
    that they may be strengthened by the power of your love
    to carry out works of charity.
    Through Christ our Lord.

14. The hearts of your faithful submitted to your name,
    entreat your help, O Lord,
    and since without you they can do nothing that is just,
    grant by your abundant mercy
    that they may both know what is right
    and receive all that they need for their good.
    Through Christ our Lord.

15. Hasten to the aid of your faithful people
    who call upon you, O Lord, we pray,
    and graciously give strength in their human weakness,
    so that, being dedicated to you in complete sincerity,
    they may find gladness in your remedies
    both now and in the life to come.
    Through Christ our Lord.

16. Look with favor on your family, O Lord,
    and bestow your endless mercy on those who seek it:
    and just as without your mercy,
    they can do nothing truly worthy of you,
    so through it,
    may they merit to obey your saving commands.
    Through Christ our Lord.

17. Bestow increase of heavenly grace
    on your faithful, O Lord;
    may they praise you with their lips,
    with their souls, with their lives;
    and since it is by your gift that we exist,
    may our whole lives be yours.
    Through Christ our Lord.

18. Direct your people, O Lord, we pray,
    with heavenly instruction,
    that by avoiding every evil
    and pursuing all that is good,
    they may earn not your anger
    but your unending mercy.
    Through Christ our Lord.

19. Be near to those who call on you, O Lord,
    and graciously grant your protection
    to all who place their hope in your mercy,
    that they may remain faithful in holiness of life
    and, having enough for their needs in this world,
    they may be made full heirs of your promise for eternity.
    Through Christ our Lord.

20. Bestow the grace of your kindness
    upon your supplicant people, O Lord,
    that, formed by you, their creator,
    and restored by you, their sustainer,
    through your constant action they may be saved.
    Through Christ our Lord.

21. May your faithful people, O Lord, we pray,
    always respond to the promptings of your love
    and, moved by wholesome compunction,
    may they do gladly what you command,
    so as to receive the things you promise.
    Through Christ our Lord.

22. May the weakness of your devoted people
    stir your compassion, O Lord, we pray,
    and let their faithful pleading win your mercy,
    that what they do not presume upon by their merits
    they may receive by your generous pardon.
    Through Christ our Lord.

23. In defense of your children, O Lord, we pray,
    stretch forth the right hand of your majesty,
    so that, obeying your fatherly will,
    they may have the unfailing protection
    of your fatherly care.
    Through Christ our Lord.

24. Look, O Lord, on the prayers of your family,
    and grant them the assistance they humbly implore,
    so that, strengthened by the help they need,
    they may persevere in confessing your name.
    Through Christ our Lord.

25. Keep your family safe, O Lord, we pray,
    and grant them the abundance of your mercies,
    that they may find growth
    through the teachings and the gifts of heaven.
    Through Christ our Lord.

26. May your faithful people rejoice, we pray, O Lord,
    to be upheld by your right hand,
    and, progressing in the Christian life,
    may they delight in good things
    both now and in the time to come.
    Through Christ our Lord.

On Feasts of Saints

27. May the Christian people exult, O Lord,
    at the glorification of the illustrious members of your Son's Body,
    and may they gain a share in the eternal lot
    of the Saints on whose feast day
    they reaffirm their devotion to you,
    rejoicing with them for ever in your glory.
    Through Christ our Lord.

28. Turn the hearts of your people
    always to you, O Lord, we pray,
    and, as you give them the help of such great patrons as these,
    grant also the unfailing help of your protection.
    Through Christ our Lord.

CHANTS FOR THE EUCHARISTIC PRAYER

EUCHARISTIC PRAYER I
or THE ROMAN CANON

The Priest, with hands extended, sings:

To you, therefore, most merciful Father, we make humble prayer and petition through Jesus Christ, your Son, our Lord:

He joins his hands and makes the Sign of the Cross once over the bread and chalice together, singing:

that you accept and bless ✠ these gifts, these of-fer-ings, these holy

With hands extended, the Priest continues:

and unblemished sacrifices, which we offer you firstly for your holy cath-o-lic Church. Be pleased to grant her peace, to guard, unite and govern her throughout the whole world, to-geth-er with your servant N. our Pope and N. our Bishop,* and all those who, holding to the truth, hand on the catholic and apos-tol-ic faith.

---

* Mention may be made here of the Coadjutor Bishop, or Auxiliary Bishops, as noted in the *General Instruction of the Roman Missal*. no. 149.

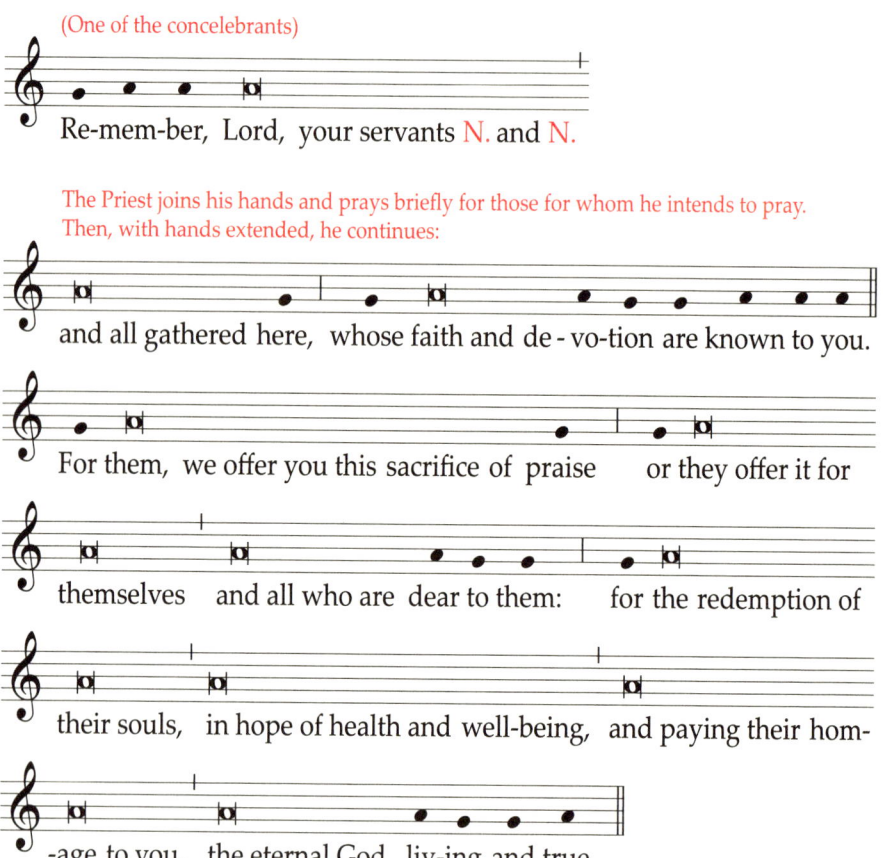

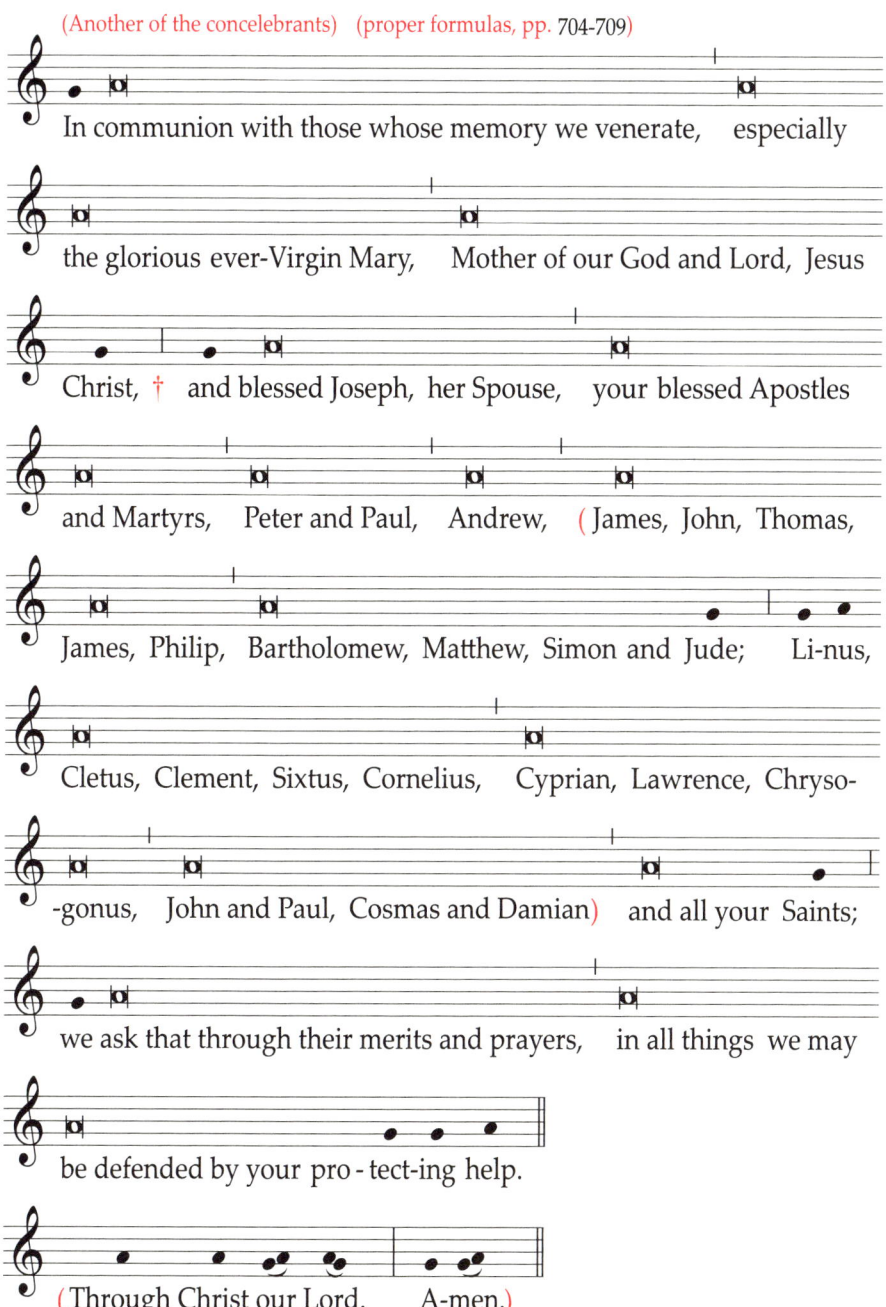

With hands extended, the principal celebrant continues (proper formulas, pp. 704-709):

There-fore, Lord, we pray: graciously accept this oblation of our service, that of your whole fa-mi-ly; or-der our days in your peace, and command that we be delivered from eternal damnation and counted among the flock of those you have cho-sen.

(He joins his hands.)

(Through Christ our Lord. A-men.)

Holding his hands extended over the offerings, he sings (together with the concelebrants):

Be pleased, O God, we pray, to bless, acknowledge, and approve this offering in every re - spect; make it spiritual and acceptable, so that it may become for us the Body and Blood of your most be--loved Son, our Lord Je-sus Christ.

He joins his hands.

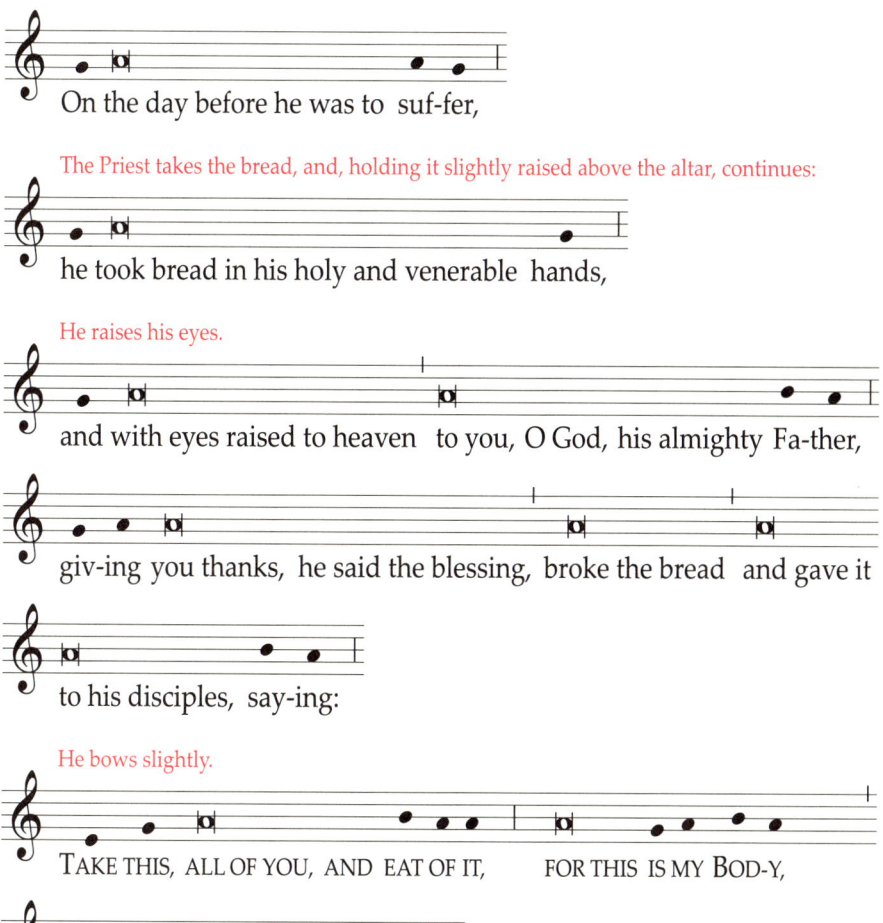

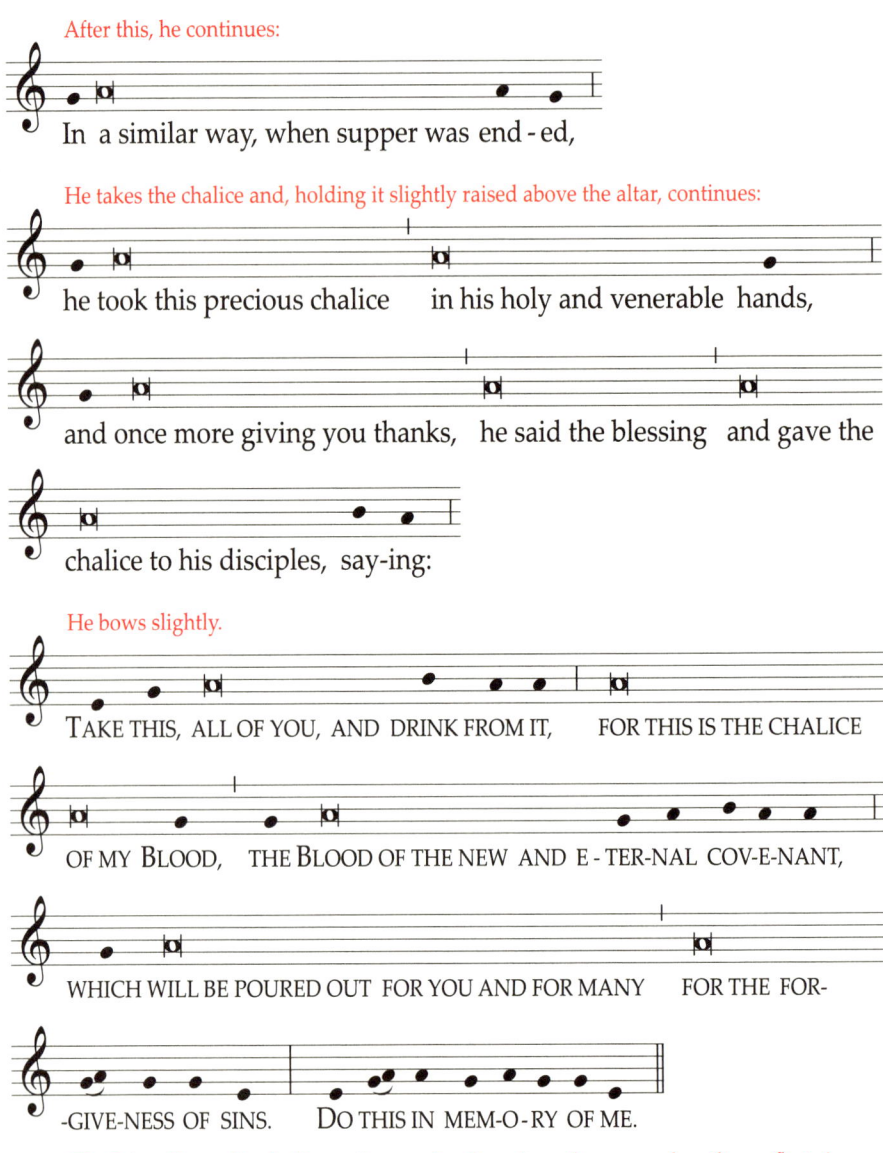

EUCHARISTIC PRAYER I 699

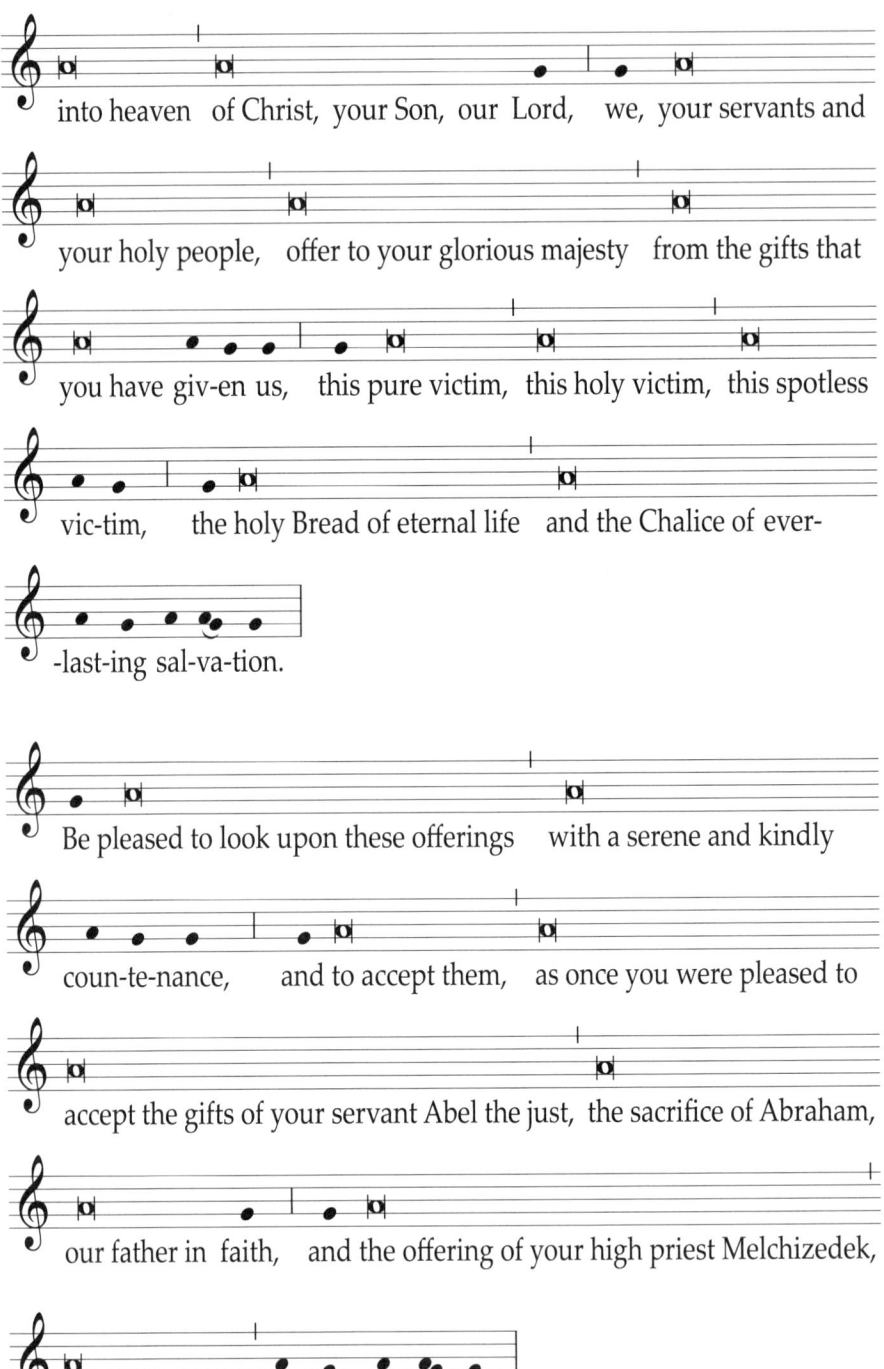

EUCHARISTIC PRAYER I 701

Bowing, with hands joined, he continues:

In humble prayer we ask you, almighty God, com-mand that these gifts be borne by the hands of your holy Angel to your altar on high in the sight of your divine maj-es-ty, so that all of us who through this participation at the altar receive the most holy Body and Blood

He stands upright again and signs himself with the Sign of the Cross, singing:

of your Son, may be filled with every grace and heav-en-ly bless-ing.

(He joins his hands.)

(Through Christ our Lord. A-men.)

With hands extended, the Priest sings (one of the concelebrants):

Re-mem-ber also, Lord, your servants N. and N., who have gone before us with the sign of faith and rest in the sleep of peace.

EUCHARISTIC PRAYER I 703

He joins his hands.

through Christ our Lord.

And the principal celebrant continues, with hands joined:

Through whom you continue to make all these good things, O Lord;

you sanctify them, fill them with life, bless them, and be-stow

them up-on us.

He takes the chalice and the paten with the host and raising both, he sings (together with the concelebrants):

Through him, and with him, and in him, O God, almighty Father,

in the unity of the Ho-ly Spir-it, all glo-ry and hon-or is yours,

for ev-er and ev-er. R. A-men.

Then follows the Communion Rite, p. 663.

PROPER FORMS OF THE *COMMUNICANTES* AND *HANC IGITUR*

On the Nativity of the Lord and throughout the Octave

Cel-ebrating the most sacred night/day on which blessed Mary the im-maculate Virgin brought forth the Savior for this world, and in com-munion with those whose memory we ven-er-ate, es-pecially the glorious ever-Virgin Mary, Mother of our God and Lord, Jesus Christ, †

On the Epiphany of the Lord

Cel-ebrating the most sacred day on which your Only Begotten Son, eternal with you in your glory, appeared in a human body, truly sharing our flesh, and in communion with those whose memory we ven-er-ate, es-pecially the glorious ever-Virgin Mary, Mother of our God and Lord, Jesus Christ, †

EUCHARISTIC PRAYER I

Thursday of the Lord's Supper

Cel-ebrating the most sacred day on which our Lord Jesus Christ was handed over for our sake, and in communion with those whose memory we ven-er-ate, es-pecially the glorious ever-Virgin Mary, Mother of our God and Lord, Jesus Christ, †

With hands extended, the Priest continues:

There-fore, Lord, we pray: graciously accept this oblation of our service, that of your whole fa-mi-ly, which we make to you as we observe the day on which our Lord Jesus Christ handed on the mys--teries of his Body and Blood for his disciples to cel-e-brate; or-der our days in your peace, and command that we be delivered from eternal damnation and counted among the flock of those you have

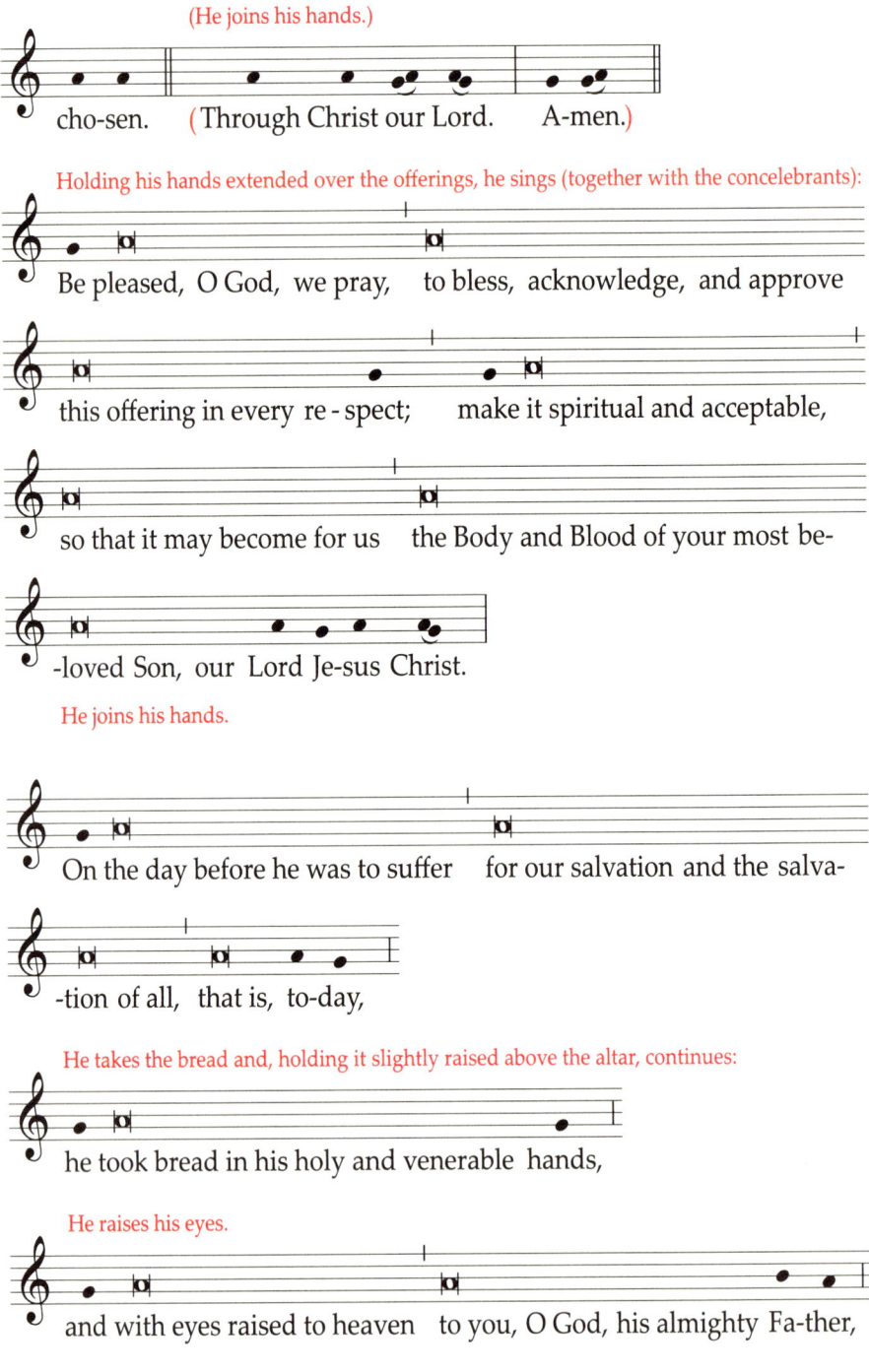

giv-ing you thanks, he said the blessing, broke the bread and gave it to his disciples, say-ing:

He bows slightly.

TAKE THIS, ALL OF YOU, AND EAT OF IT, FOR THIS IS MY BOD-Y, WHICH WILL BE GIV-EN UP FOR YOU.

He shows the consecrated host to the people, places it again on the paten, and genuflects in adoration.

From the Mass of the Easter Vigil until the Second Sunday of Easter

Cel-ebrating the most sacred $\frac{\text{night}}{\text{day}}$ of the Resurrection of our Lord Jesus Christ in the flesh, and in communion with those whose mem--ory we ven-er-ate, es-pecially the glorious ever-Virgin Mary, Mother of our God and Lord, Jesus Christ, †

There-fore, Lord, we pray: graciously accept this oblation of our service, that of your whole fa-mi-ly, which we make to you also for those to whom you have been pleased to give the new birth of water and the Holy Spirit, granting them forgiveness of all their sins; or-der our days in your peace, and command that we be delivered from eternal damnation and counted among the flock of those you

(He joins his hands.)

have cho-sen. (Through Christ our Lord. A-men.)

On the Ascension of the Lord

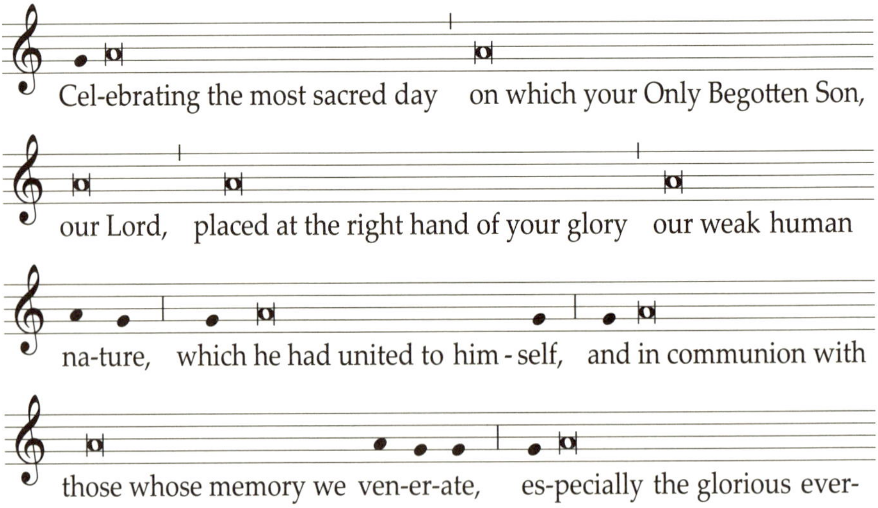

Cel-ebrating the most sacred day on which your Only Begotten Son, our Lord, placed at the right hand of your glory our weak human na-ture, which he had united to him-self, and in communion with those whose memory we ven-er-ate, es-pecially the glorious ever-

-Virgin Mary, Mother of our God and Lord, Jesus Christ, †

On Pentecost Sunday

Cel-ebrating the most sacred day of Pentecost, on which the Holy Spirit appeared to the Apostles in tongues of fire, and in commun- -ion with those whose memory we ven-er-ate, es-pecially the glori- -ous ever-Virgin Mary, Mother of our God and Lord, Jesus Christ, †

EUCHARISTIC PRAYER I
or THE ROMAN CANON
(Solemn Tone)

The Priest, with hands extended, sings:

To you, therefore, most merciful Father, we make humble prayer and petition through Jesus Christ, your Son, our Lord:

He joins his hands and makes the Sign of the Cross once over the bread and chalice together, singing:

that you accept and bless ✠ these gifts, these of-fer-ings, these holy

With hands extended, he continues:

and unblemished sacrifices, which we offer you firstly for your holy cath-o-lic Church. Be pleased to grant her peace, to guard, unite and govern her throughout the whole world, to-geth-er with your servant N. our Pope and N. our Bishop,* and all those who, holding to the truth, hand on the catholic and apos-tol-ic faith.

---

* Mention may be made here of the Coadjutor Bishop, or Auxiliary Bishops, as noted in the *General Instruction of the Roman Missal*, no. 149.

EUCHARISTIC PRAYER I (SOLEMN TONE)   711

(One of the concelebrants)

Re-mem-ber, Lord, your servants N. and N.

The Priest joins his hands and prays briefly for those for whom he intends to pray. Then, with hands extended, he continues:

and all gathered here, whose faith and de-vo-tion are known to you.

For them, we offer you this sacrifice of praise   or they offer it for themselves   and all who are dear to them: for the redemption of their souls,   in hope of health and well-being,   and paying their hom--age to you,   the eternal God, liv-ing and true.

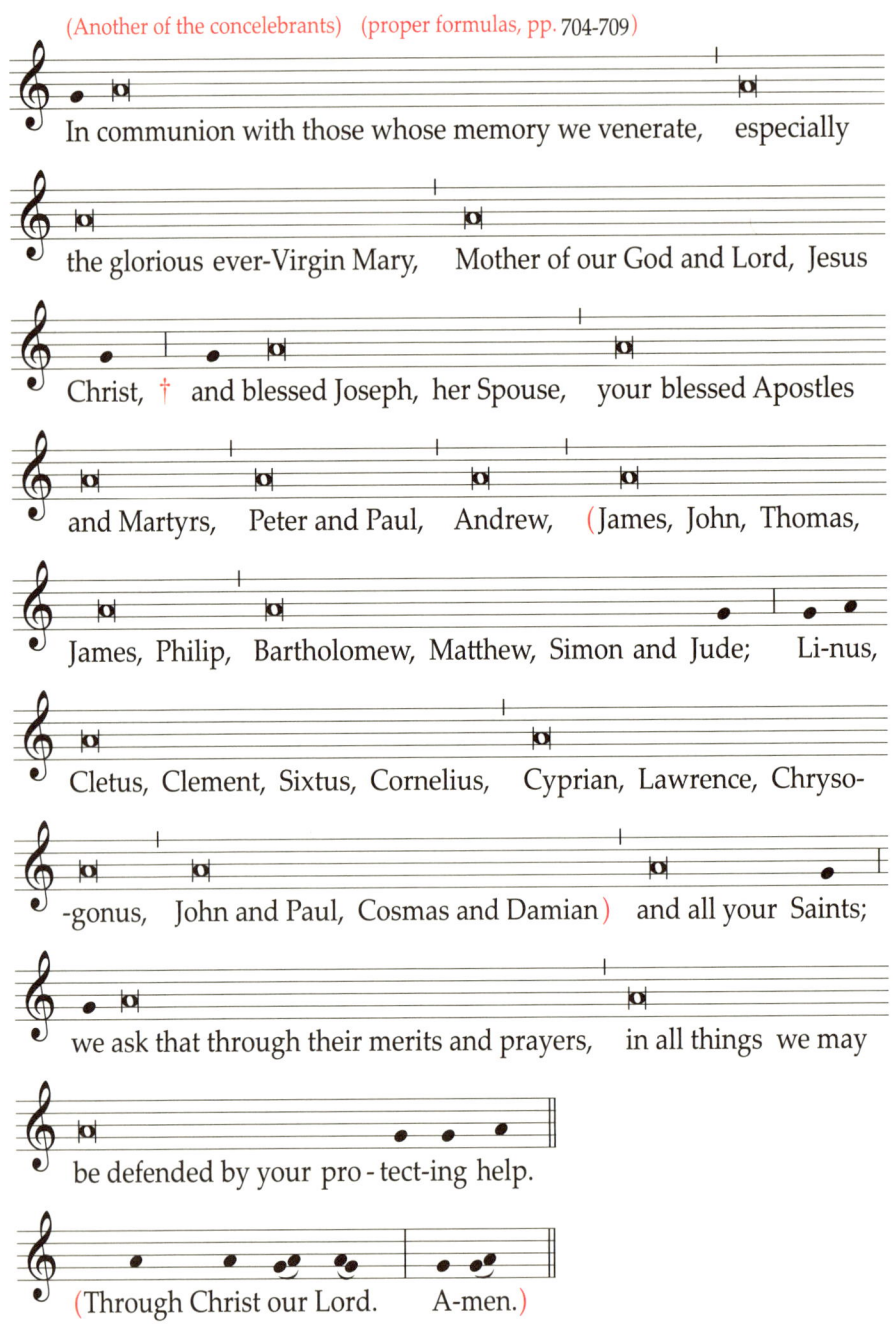

EUCHARISTIC PRAYER I (SOLEMN TONE)

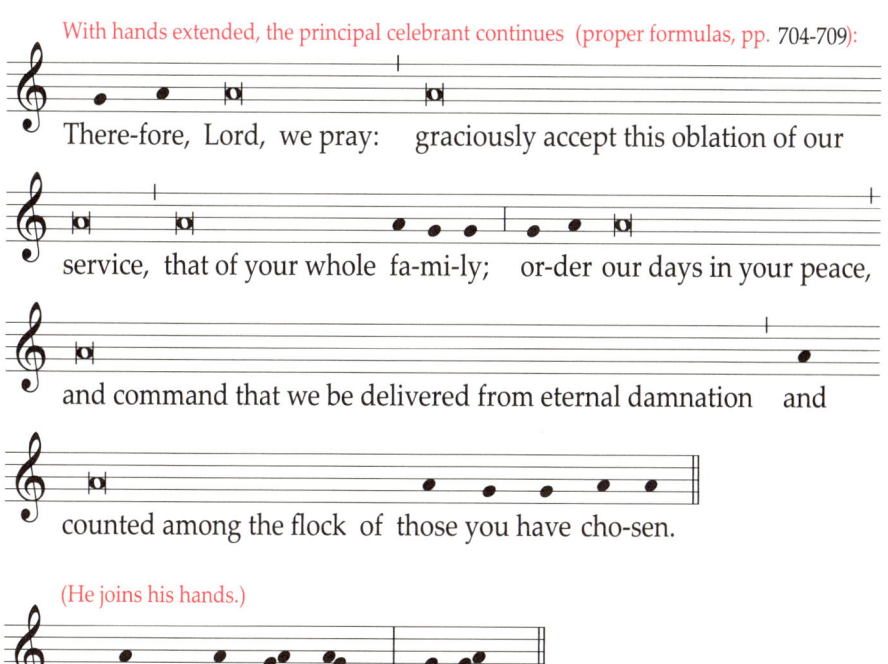

With hands extended, the principal celebrant continues (proper formulas, pp. 704-709):

There-fore, Lord, we pray: graciously accept this oblation of our service, that of your whole fa-mi-ly; or-der our days in your peace, and command that we be delivered from eternal damnation and counted among the flock of those you have cho-sen.

(He joins his hands.)

(Through Christ our Lord. A-men.)

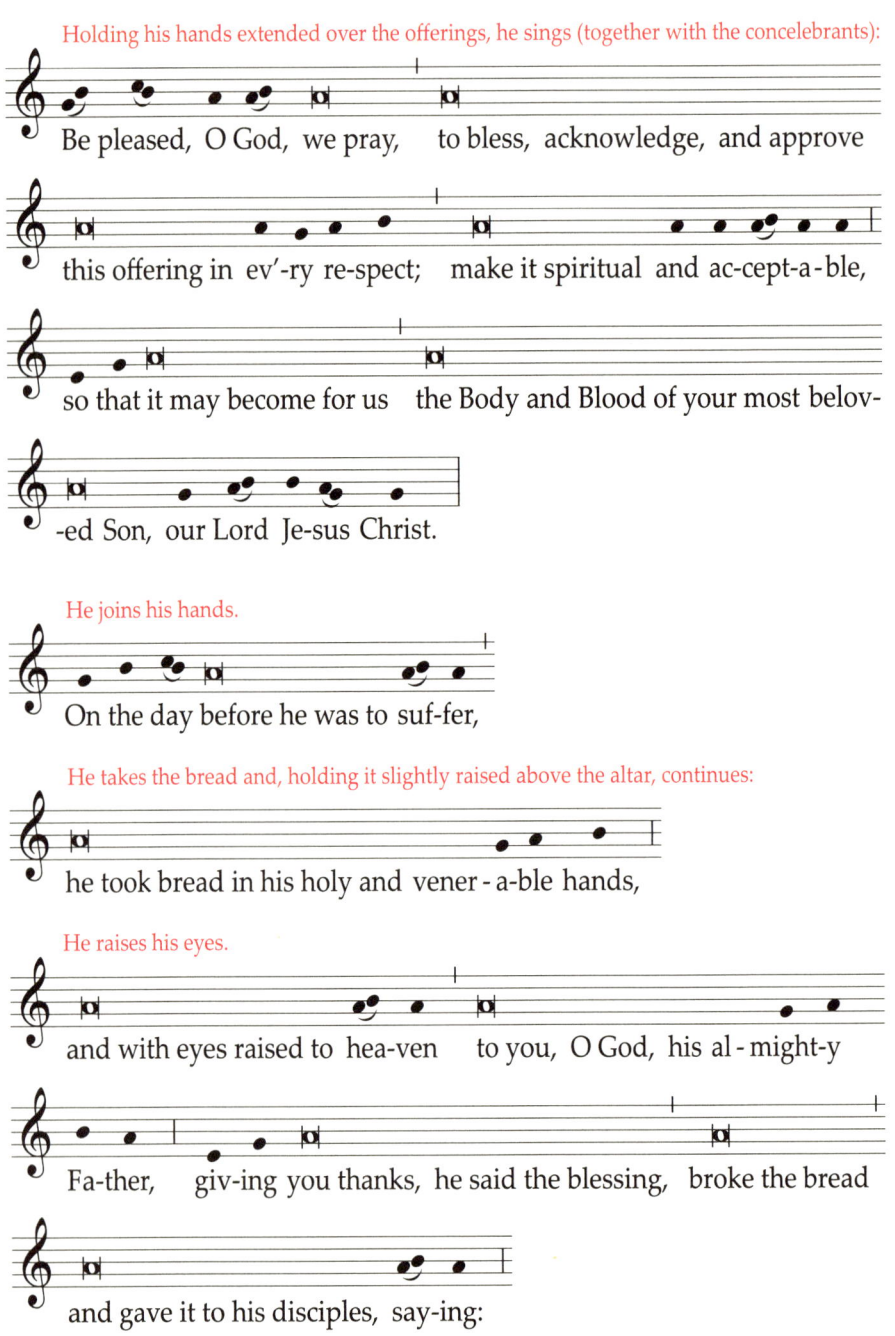

EUCHARISTIC PRAYER I (SOLEMN TONE) 715

He bows slightly.

Take this, all of you, and eat of it,   for this is my Bod-y,

which will be giv-en up for you.

He shows the consecrated host to the people, places it again on the paten, and genuflects in adoration.

After this, he continues:

In a sim-i-lar way, when supper was end-ed,

He takes the chalice and, holding it slightly raised above the altar, continues:

he took this precious chalice   in his holy and vener - a-ble hands,

and once more giving you thanks, he said the blessing   and gave the

chalice to his disciples, say-ing:

He bows slightly.

Take this, all of you, and drink from it,   for this is the chalice

of my Blood,   the Blood of the new and e - ter-nal cov-e-nant,

which will be poured out for you and for man-y   for the

FOR-GIVE-NESS OF SINS. DO THIS IN MEM-O-RY OF ME.

The Priest shows the chalice to the people, places it on the corporal, and genuflects in adoration.

Then he sings: Or:

The mys-ter-y of faith.   The mys-ter-y of faith.

And the people continue, acclaiming:

We pro-claim your Death, O Lord, and pro-fess your Res-ur-rec-tion un-til you come a-gain.

Or:

When we eat this Bread and drink this Cup, we pro-claim your Death, O Lord, un-til you come a-gain.

Or:

Save us, Sav-ior of the world, for by your Cross and Res-ur-rec-tion you have set us free.

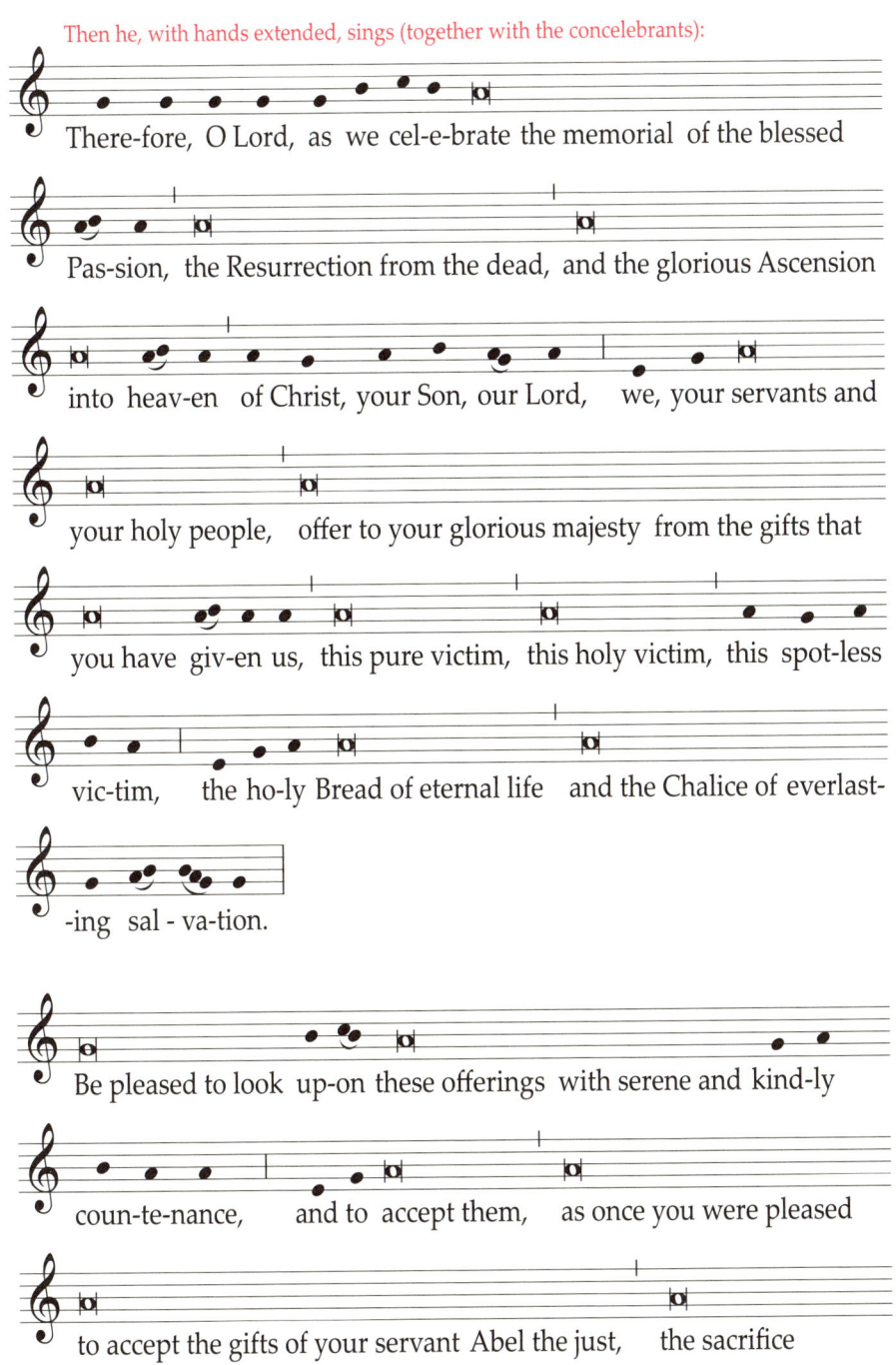

EUCHARISTIC PRAYER I (SOLEMN TONE) 719

With hands extended, the Priest sings (one of the concelebrants):

Re-mem-ber also, Lord, your servants N. and N., who have gone before us with the sign of faith and rest in the sleep of peace.

He joins his hands and prays briefly for those who have died and for whom he intends to pray.
Then, with hands extended, he continues:

Grant them, O Lord, we pray, and all who sleep in Christ, a place of

(He joins his hands.)

refreshment, light and peace. (Through Christ our Lord. A-men.)

(Another of the concelebrants)
He strikes his breast with his right hand, singing: *And, with hands extended, he continues:*

To us, also, your servants, who, though sinners, hope in your abun--dant mercies, graciously grant some share and fellowship with your holy Apostles and Mar-tyrs: with John the Baptist, Stephen, Mat--thias, Barnabas, (Ignatius, Alexander, Marcellinus, Peter, Felicity, Perpetua, Agatha, Lucy, Agnes, Cecilia, Anastasia) and all your

Saints; ad-mit us, we beseech you, into their company, not weigh--ing our merits, but granting us your par-don,

He joins his hands.

through Christ our Lord.

And the principal celebrant continues, with hands joined:

Through whom you continue to make all these good things, O Lord;

you sanctify them, fill them with life, bless them, and be-stow them up-on us.

He takes the chalice and the paten with the host and raising both, he sings (together with the concelebrants):

Through him, and with him, and in him, O God, almighty Father, in the unity of the Ho-ly Spir-it, all glo-ry and hon-or is yours, for ev-er and ev-er. R. A-men.

Then follows the Communion Rite, p. 663.

EUCHARISTIC PRAYER II

Although it is provided with its own Preface, this Eucharistic Prayer may also be used with other Prefaces, especially those that present an overall view of the mystery of salvation, such as the Common Prefaces.

V. The Lord be with you.   R. And with your spir-it.

V. Lift up your hearts.   R. We lift them up to the Lord.

V. Let us give thanks to the Lord our God.   R. It is right and just.

It is truly right and just, our duty and our sal-va-tion, al-ways and everywhere to give you thanks, Fa-ther most ho-ly, through your beloved Son, Je-sus Christ, your Word through whom you made all things, whom you sent as our Savior and Re-deem-er, incarnate by the Ho-ly Spir-it and born of the Vir-gin. Ful-filling your will and gaining for you a ho-ly peo-ple, he stretched out his hands as he en-dured his Pas-sion, so as to break the bonds of death

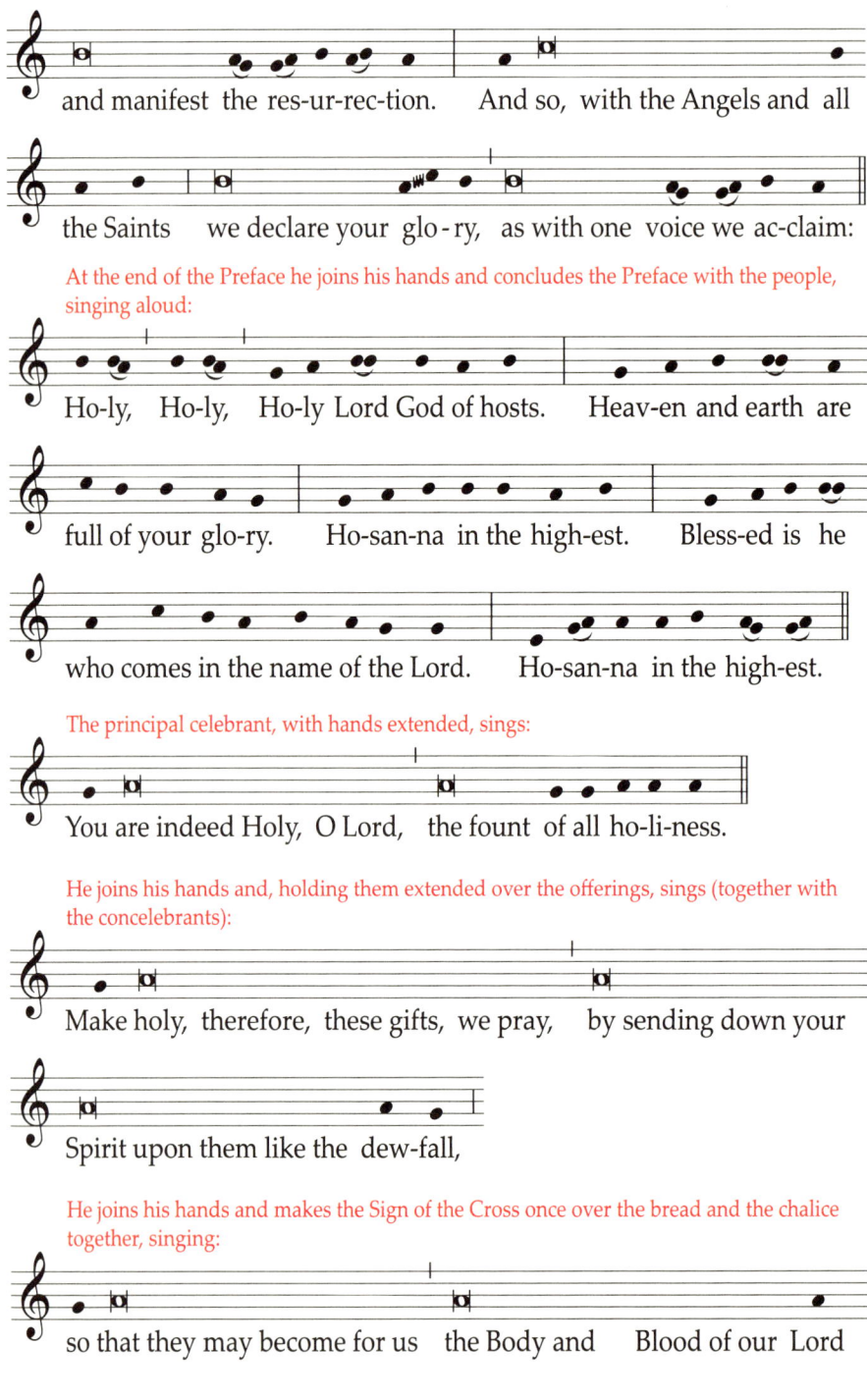

and manifest the res-ur-rec-tion. And so, with the Angels and all the Saints we declare your glo-ry, as with one voice we ac-claim:

At the end of the Preface he joins his hands and concludes the Preface with the people, singing aloud:

Ho-ly, Ho-ly, Ho-ly Lord God of hosts. Heav-en and earth are full of your glo-ry. Ho-san-na in the high-est. Bless-ed is he who comes in the name of the Lord. Ho-san-na in the high-est.

The principal celebrant, with hands extended, sings:

You are indeed Holy, O Lord, the fount of all ho-li-ness.

He joins his hands and, holding them extended over the offerings, sings (together with the concelebrants):

Make holy, therefore, these gifts, we pray, by sending down your Spirit upon them like the dew-fall,

He joins his hands and makes the Sign of the Cross once over the bread and the chalice together, singing:

so that they may become for us the Body and Blood of our Lord

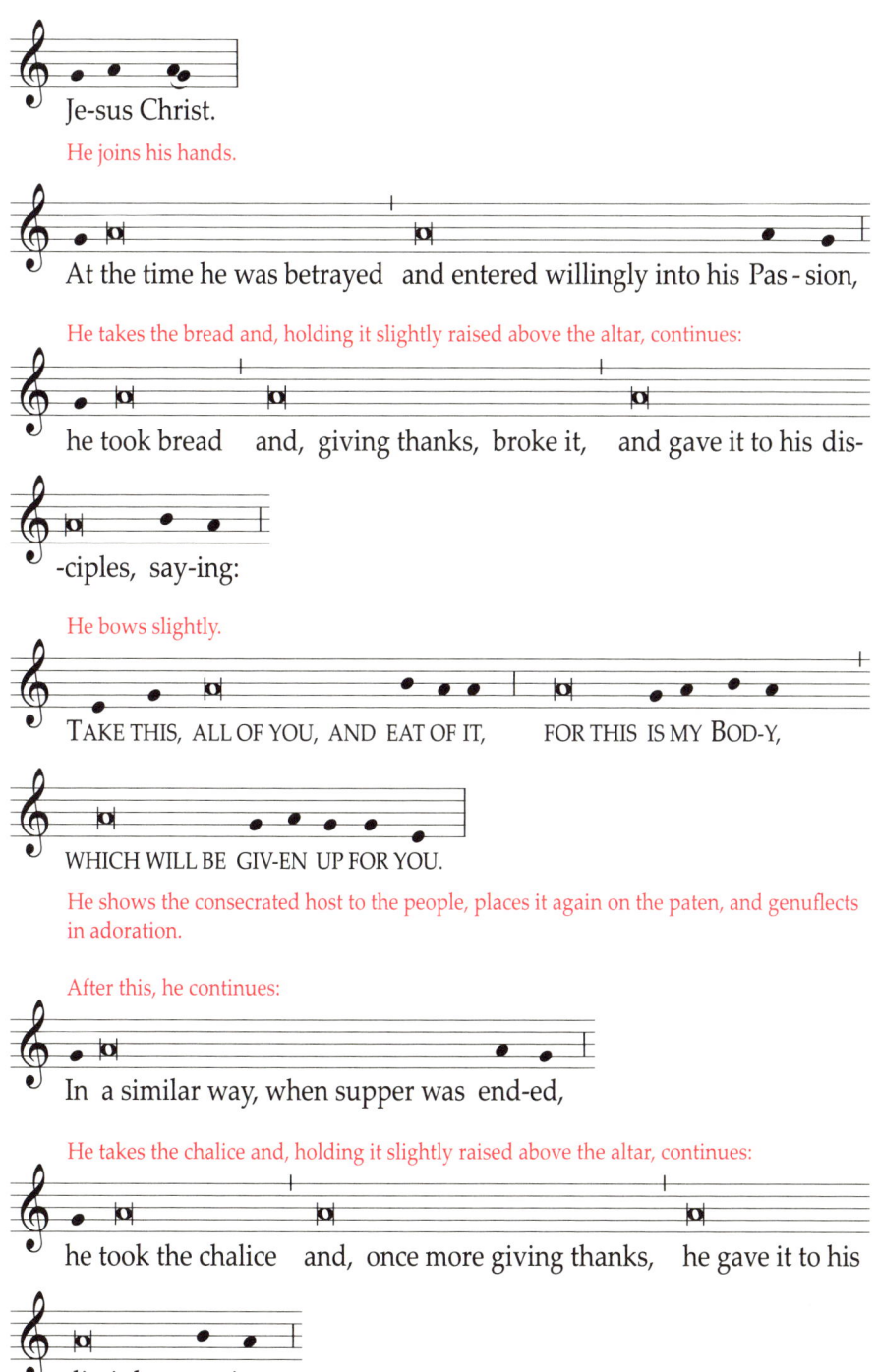

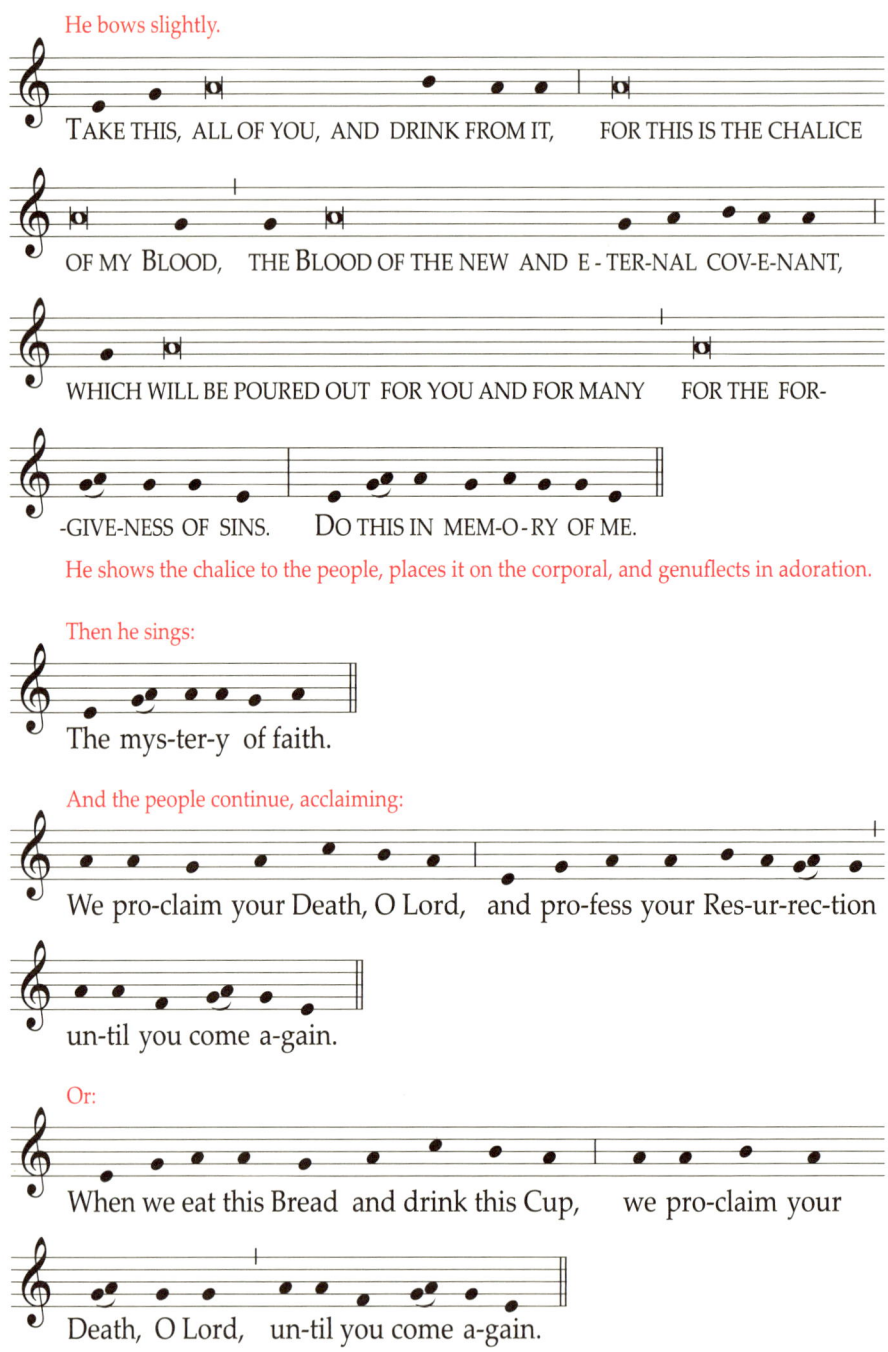

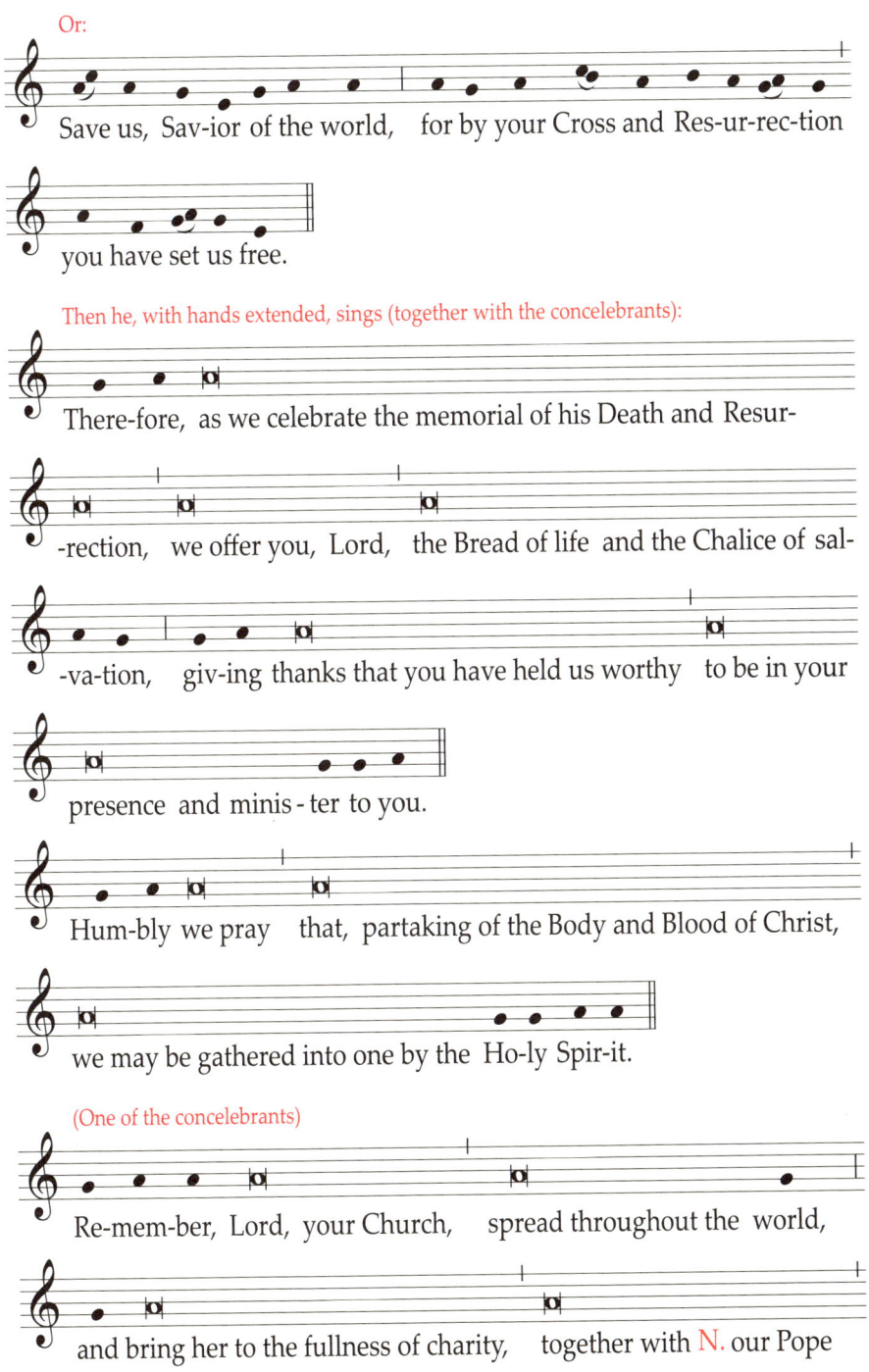

Or:

Save us, Sav-ior of the world, for by your Cross and Res-ur-rec-tion you have set us free.

Then he, with hands extended, sings (together with the concelebrants):

There-fore, as we celebrate the memorial of his Death and Resur-rection, we offer you, Lord, the Bread of life and the Chalice of sal-va-tion, giv-ing thanks that you have held us worthy to be in your presence and minis-ter to you.

Hum-bly we pray that, partaking of the Body and Blood of Christ, we may be gathered into one by the Ho-ly Spir-it.

(One of the concelebrants)

Re-mem-ber, Lord, your Church, spread throughout the world, and bring her to the fullness of charity, together with N. our Pope

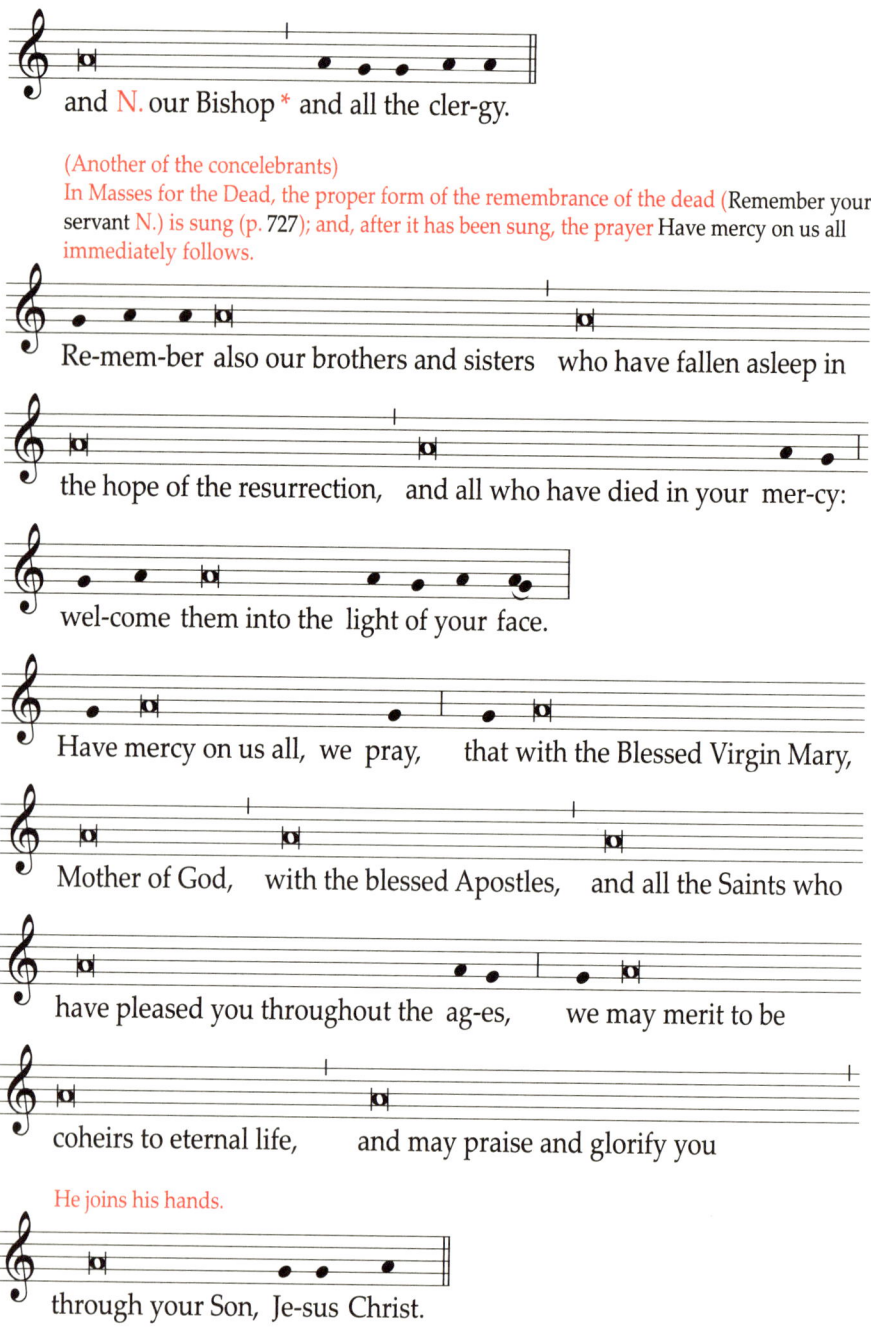

EUCHARISTIC PRAYER III 727

He takes the chalice and paten with the host and raising both, he sings (together with the concelebrants):

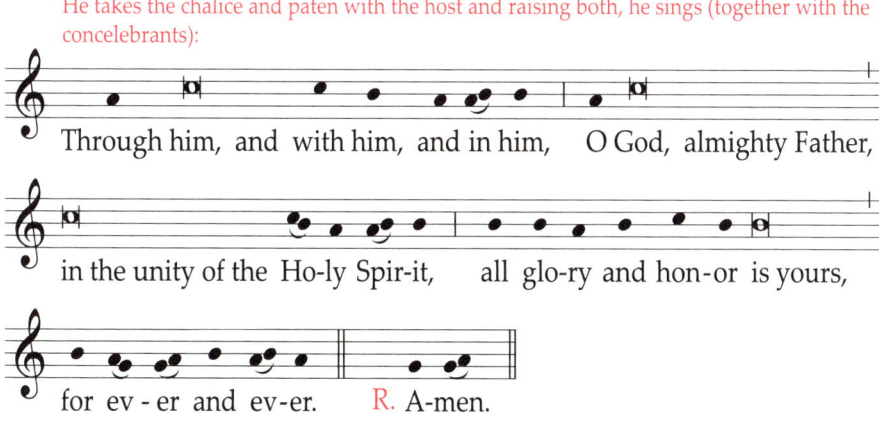

Through him, and with him, and in him, O God, almighty Father, in the unity of the Ho-ly Spir-it, all glo-ry and hon-or is yours, for ev-er and ev-er. ℟. A-men.

Then follows the Communion Rite, p. 663.

In Masses for the Dead, the following may be sung:

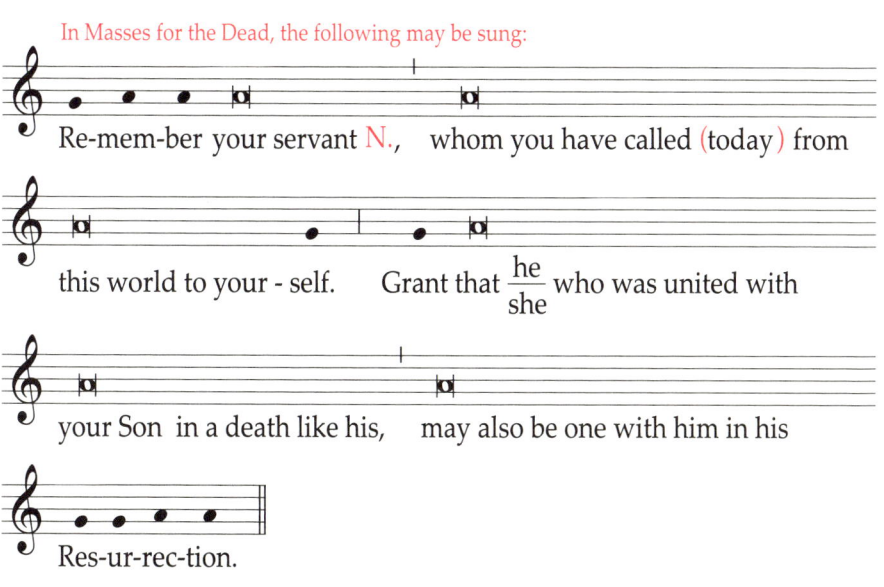

Re-mem-ber your servant N., whom you have called (today) from this world to your-self. Grant that he/she who was united with your Son in a death like his, may also be one with him in his Res-ur-rec-tion.

EUCHARISTIC PRAYER III

The principal celebrant, with hands extended, sings:

You are indeed Holy, O Lord,   and all you have created rightly gives you praise,   for through your Son our Lord Jesus Christ, by the power and working of the Holy Spirit,   you give life to all things and make them ho-ly,   and you never cease to gather a people to yourself,   so that from the rising of the sun to its setting a pure sacrifice may be offered to your name.

He joins his hands and, holding them extended over the offerings, sings (together with the concelebrants):

There-fore, O Lord, we humbly implore you: by the same Spirit graciously make holy   these gifts we have brought to you for conse-

He joins his hands and makes the Sign of the Cross once over the bread and chalice together, singing:

-cra-tion,   that they may become the Body and   Blood of your Son

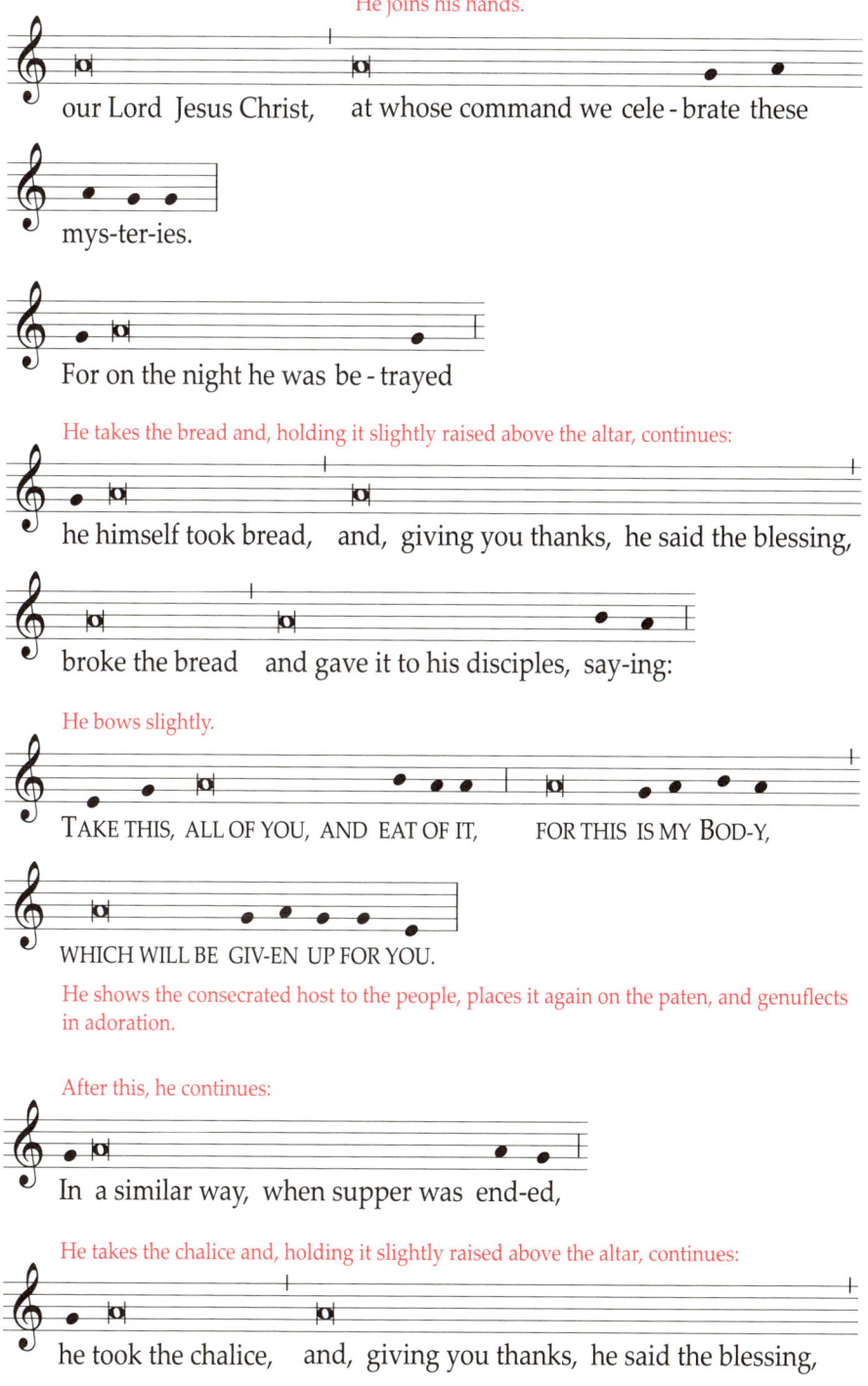

and gave the chalice to his disciples, say-ing:

He bows slightly.

Take this, all of you, and drink from it,   for this is the chalice

of my Blood,   the Blood of the new and e-ter-nal cov-e-nant,

which will be poured out for you and for many   for the for-

-give-ness of sins.   Do this in mem-o-ry of me.

He shows the chalice to the people, places it on the corporal, and genuflects in adoration.

Then he sings:

The mys-ter-y of faith.

And the people continue, acclaiming:

We pro-claim your Death, O Lord,   and pro-fess your Res-ur-rec-tion

un-til you come a-gain.

Or:

When we eat this Bread and drink this Cup,   we pro-claim your

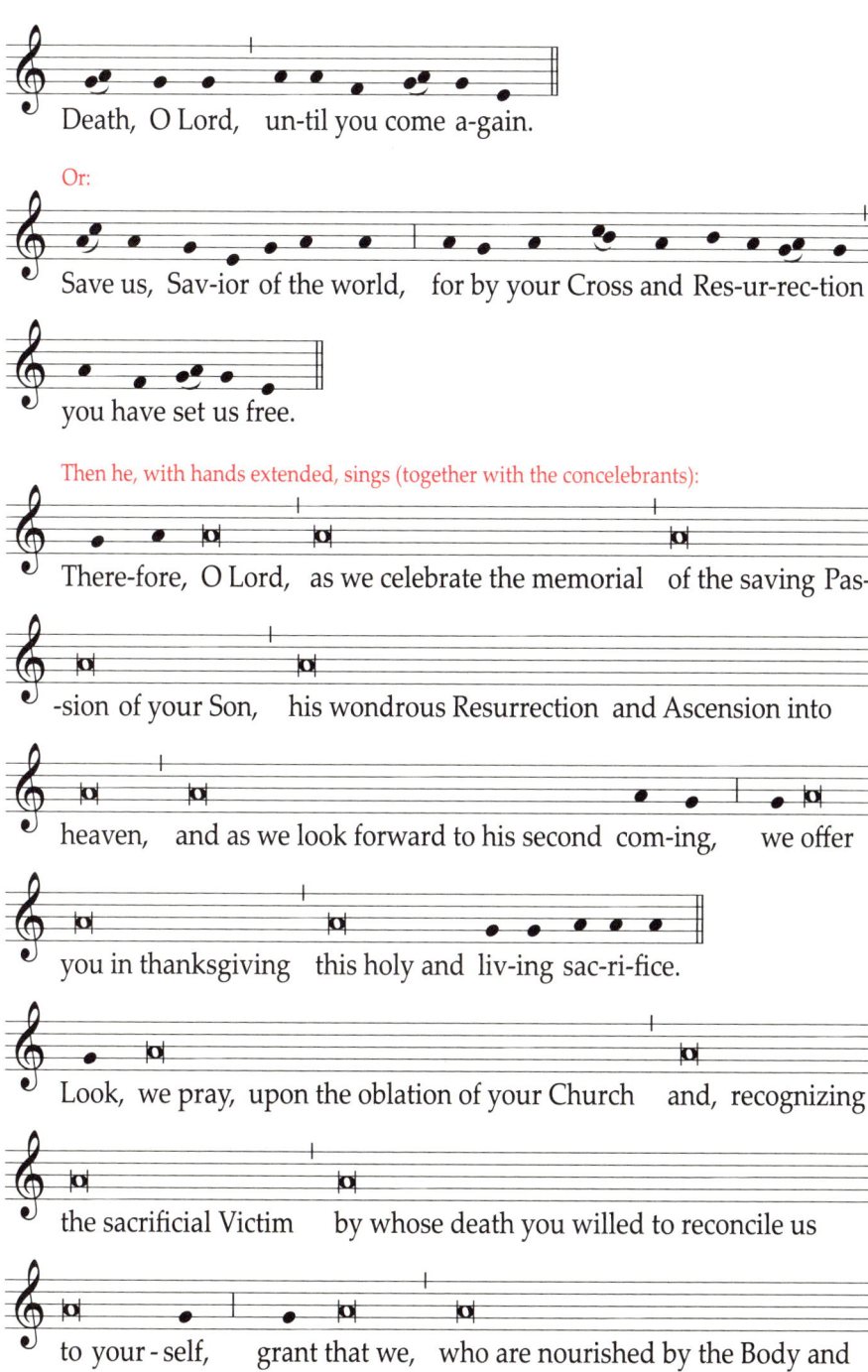

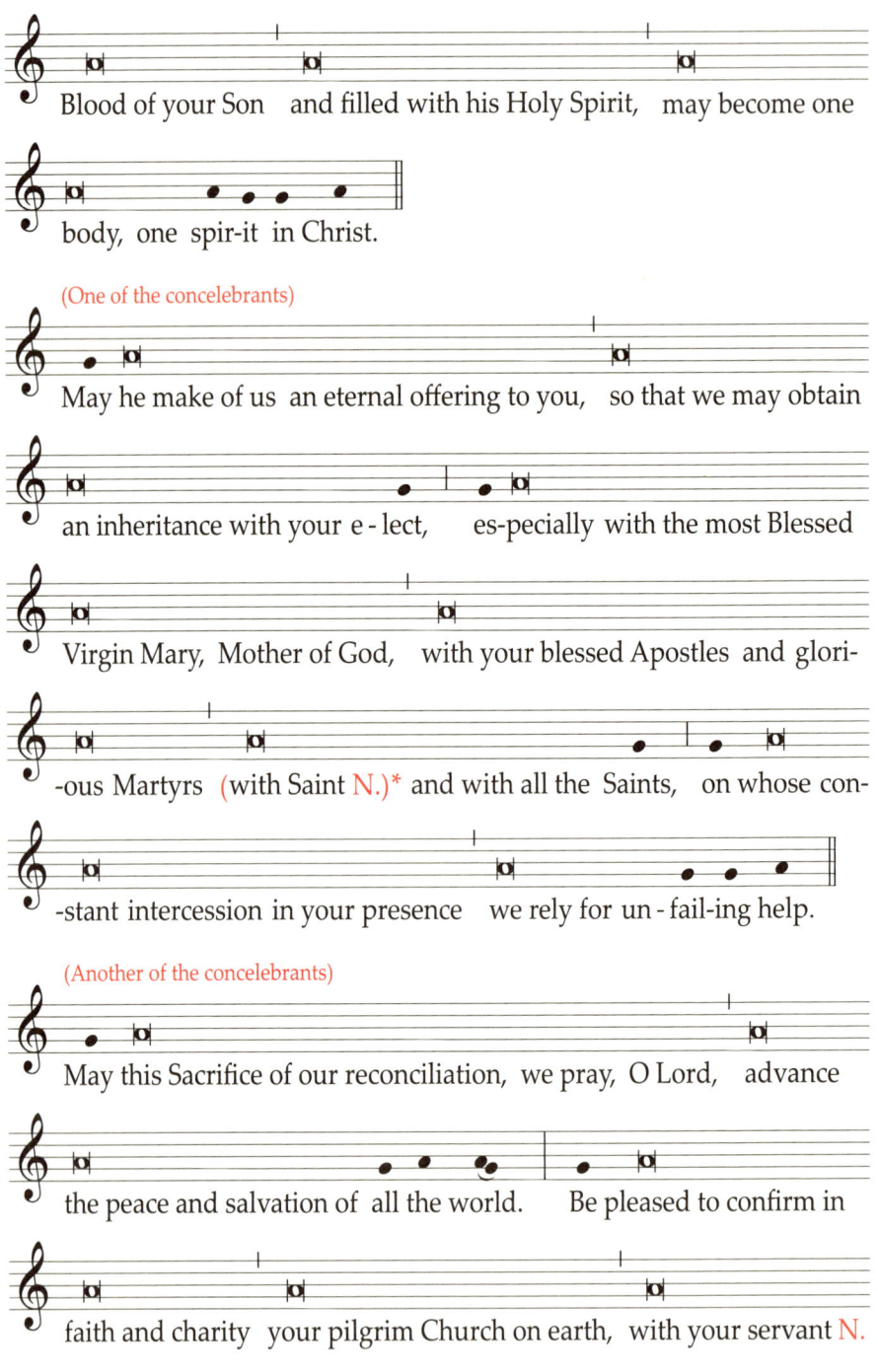

EUCHARISTIC PRAYER III

our Pope   and N. our Bishop,*   the Order of Bishops,   all the clergy,

and the entire people you have gained for your own.

Lis-ten graciously to the prayers of this family,   whom you have sum-

-moned be-fore you: in your compassion, O merciful Father, gather

to yourself all your children   scattered through-out the world.

In Masses for the Dead, the proper form of the remembrance of the dead (Remember your servant N.) *is said* (pp. 734-735); *and, after it has been said, the doxology* (Through him) *immediately follows.*

† To our departed brothers and sisters   and to all who were pleasing

to you at their passing from this life,   give kind admittance to your

king-dom.   There we hope to enjoy for ever the fullness of your

He joins his hands.

glory   through Christ our Lord,   through whom you bestow on the

---

* Mention may be made here of the Coadjutor Bishop, or Auxiliary Bishops, as noted in the *General Instruction of the Roman Missal*, no. 149.

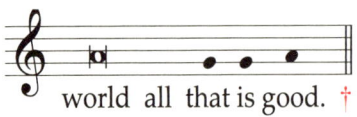
world all that is good. †

He takes the chalice and the paten with the host and raising both, he sings (together with the concelebrants):

Through him, and with him, and in him, O God, almighty Father, in the unity of the Ho-ly Spir-it, all glo-ry and hon-or is yours,

for ev-er and ev-er. ℟. A-men.

Then follows the Communion Rite, p. 663.

In Masses for the Dead, the following may be sung:

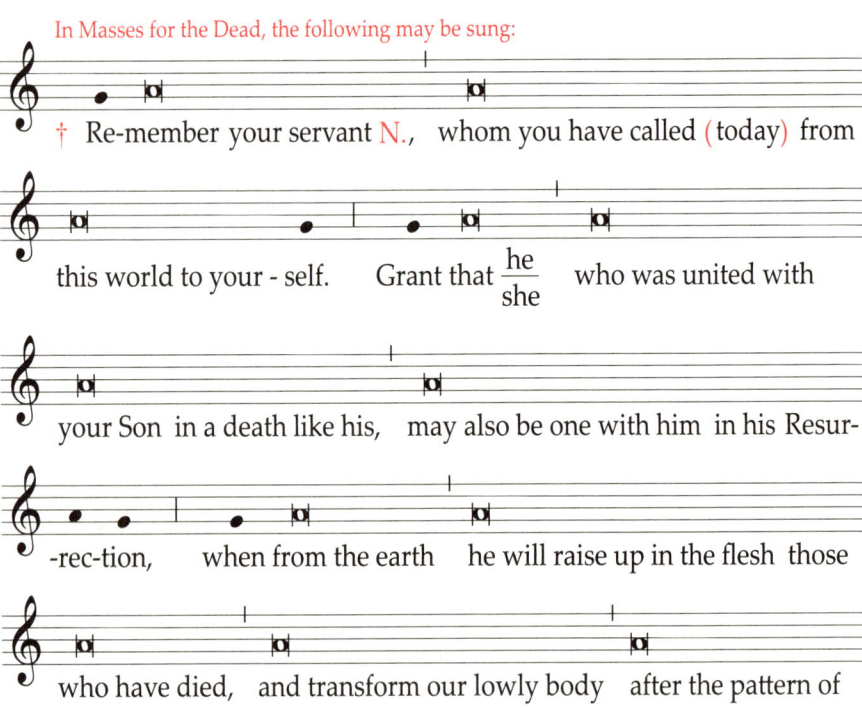
† Re-member your servant N., whom you have called (today) from this world to your-self. Grant that $\frac{he}{she}$ who was united with your Son in a death like his, may also be one with him in his Resur--rec-tion, when from the earth he will raise up in the flesh those who have died, and transform our lowly body after the pattern of

EUCHARISTIC PRAYER IV

his own glorious body. To our departed brothers and sisters, too,

and to all who were pleasing to you at their passing from this life,

give kind admittance to your kingdom. There we hope to enjoy for

ever the fullness of your glory, when you will wipe away every tear

from our eyes. For seeing you, our God, as you are, we shall be

He joins his hands.

like you for all the ages and praise you without end, through Christ

our Lord, through whom you bestow on the world all that is good. †

EUCHARISTIC PRAYER IV

It is not permitted to change the Preface of this Eucharistic Prayer because of the structure of the Prayer itself, which presents a summary of the history of salvation.

V. The Lord be with you.   R. And with your spir-it.

V. Lift up your hearts.   R. We lift them up to the Lord.

V. Let us give thanks to the Lord our God.   R. It is right and just.

It is truly right to give you thanks, tru-ly just to give you glory, Fa-ther most ho-ly, for you are the one God liv-ing and true, ex--isting before all ages and abiding for all e-ter-ni-ty, dwelling in un-ap-proach-a-ble light; yet you, who alone are good, the source of life, have made all that is, so that you might fill your crea-tures with bless-ings and bring joy to many of them by the glo-ry of your light. And so, in your presence are countless hosts of An-gels,

EUCHARISTIC PRAYER IV   739

-ful of heart, joy.   To accomplish your plan,   he gave himself up to

death,   and, rising from the dead,   he destroyed death and re-

-stored life.   And that we might live no longer for ourselves   but for

him who died and rose a - gain for us,   he sent the Holy Spirit from

you, Father, as the first fruits for those who be - lieve,   so that, bring-

-ing to perfection his work in the world,   he might sanctify creation

to the full.

He joins his hands and, holding them extended over the offerings, sings (together with the concelebrants):

There-fore, O Lord, we pray: may this same Holy Spirit graciously

He joins his hands and makes the Sign of the Cross once over the bread and chalice together, singing:

sanctify these of-fer-ings,   that they may become the Body and

He joins his hands.

Blood of our Lord Jesus Christ   for the celebration of this great mys-

-tery, which he himself left us as an e-ter-nal cov-e-nant.

For when the hour had come for him to be glorified by you, Father

most holy, having loved his own who were in the world, he loved

them to the end: and while they were at supper,

He takes the bread and, holding it slightly raised above the altar, continues:

he took bread, blessed and broke it, and gave it to his disciples,

say-ing:

He bows slightly.

TAKE THIS, ALL OF YOU, AND EAT OF IT, FOR THIS IS MY BOD-Y,

WHICH WILL BE GIV-EN UP FOR YOU.

He shows the consecrated host to the people, places it again on the paten, and genuflects in adoration.

After this, he continues: He takes the chalice and, holding it slightly raised above the altar, continues:

In a similar way, taking the chalice filled with the fruit of the vine,

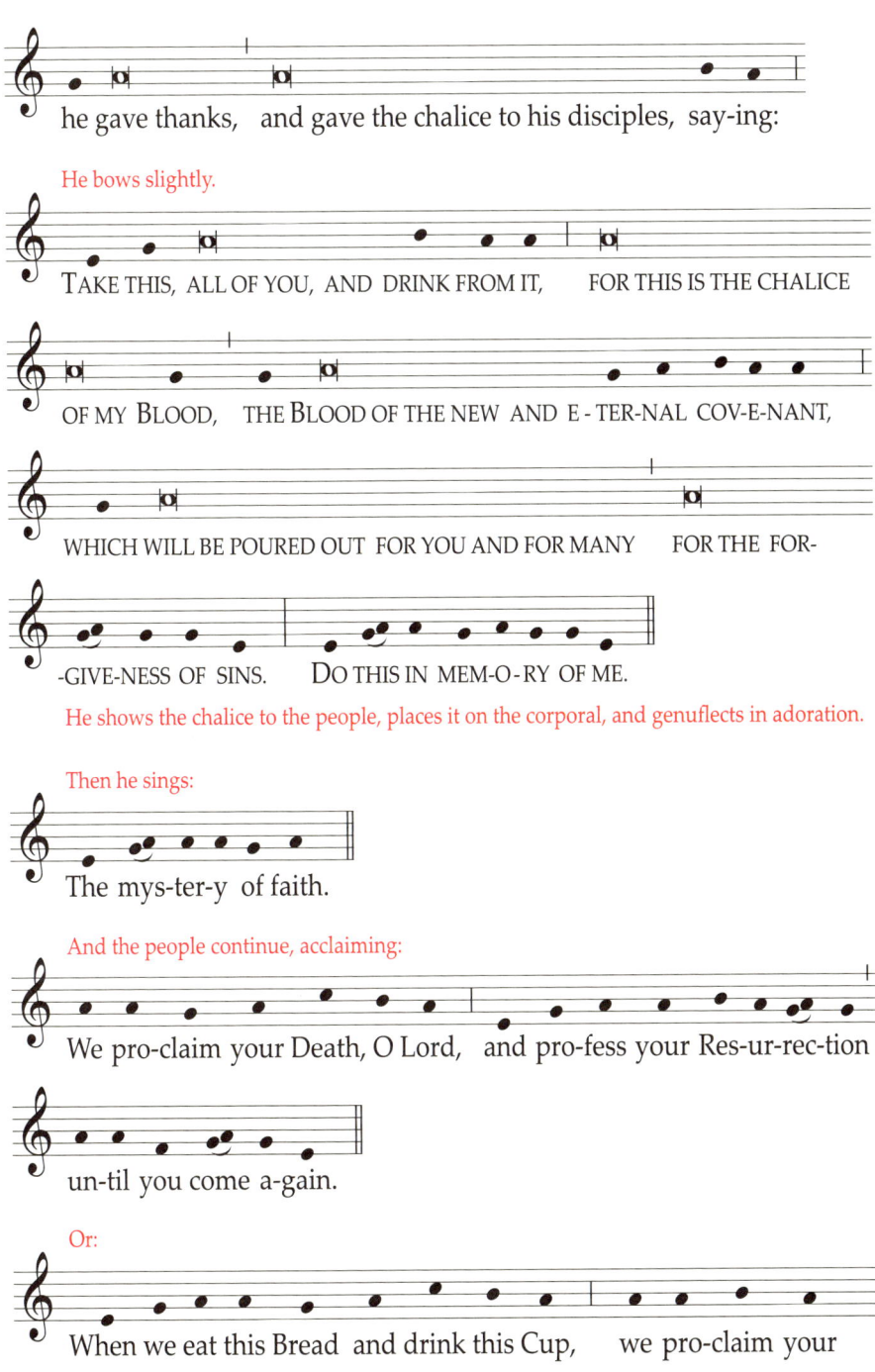

EUCHARISTIC PRAYER IV

741

he gave thanks, and gave the chalice to his disciples, say-ing:

He bows slightly.

TAKE THIS, ALL OF YOU, AND DRINK FROM IT, FOR THIS IS THE CHALICE OF MY BLOOD, THE BLOOD OF THE NEW AND E - TER-NAL COV-E-NANT, WHICH WILL BE POURED OUT FOR YOU AND FOR MANY FOR THE FOR- -GIVE-NESS OF SINS. DO THIS IN MEM-O-RY OF ME.

He shows the chalice to the people, places it on the corporal, and genuflects in adoration.

Then he sings:

The mys-ter-y of faith.

And the people continue, acclaiming:

We pro-claim your Death, O Lord, and pro-fess your Res-ur-rec-tion un-til you come a-gain.

Or:

When we eat this Bread and drink this Cup, we pro-claim your

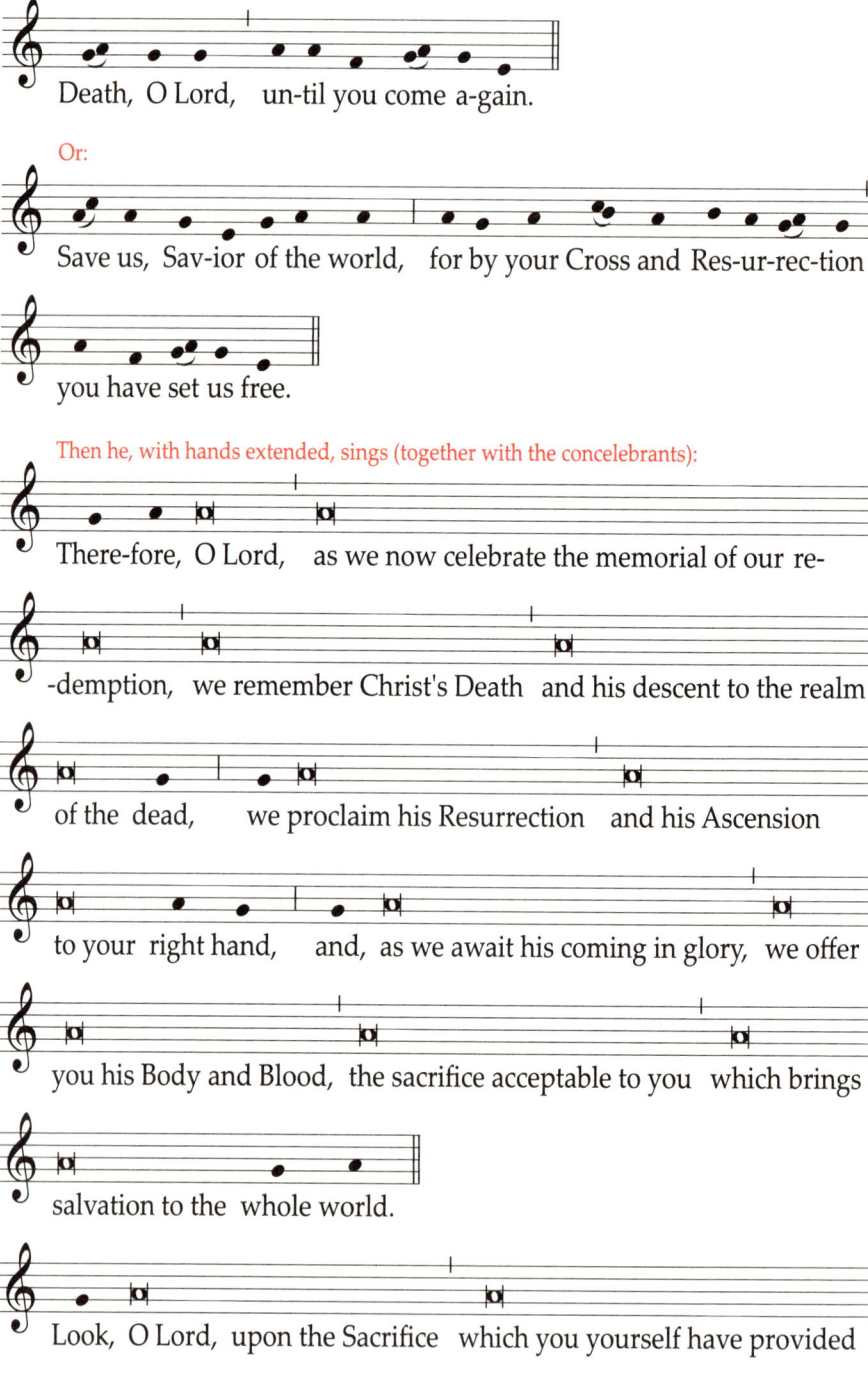

EUCHARISTIC PRAYER IV

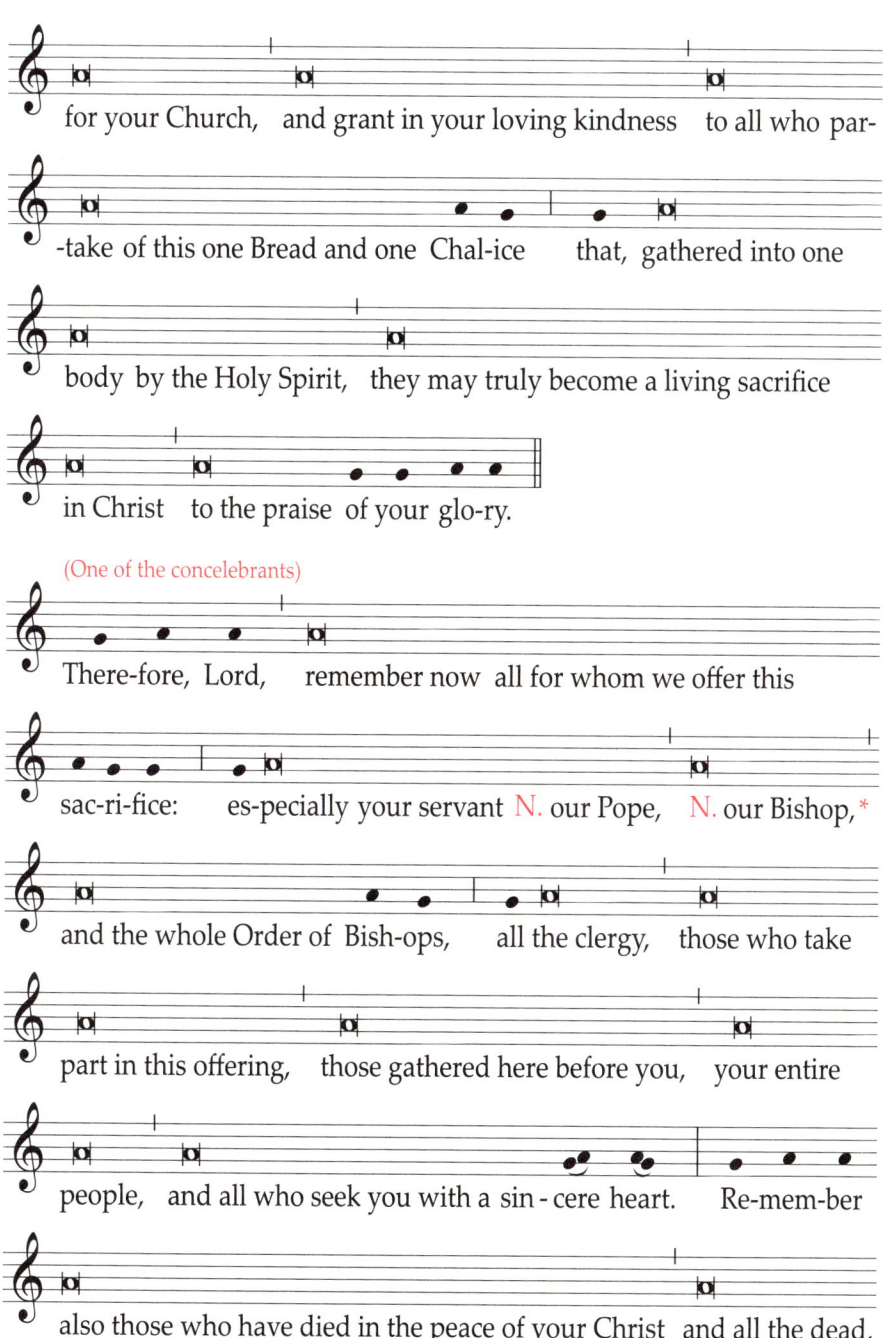

for your Church, and grant in your loving kindness to all who par- -take of this one Bread and one Chal-ice that, gathered into one body by the Holy Spirit, they may truly become a living sacrifice in Christ to the praise of your glo-ry.

(One of the concelebrants)

There-fore, Lord, remember now all for whom we offer this sac-ri-fice: es-pecially your servant N. our Pope, N. our Bishop,* and the whole Order of Bish-ops, all the clergy, those who take part in this offering, those gathered here before you, your entire people, and all who seek you with a sin-cere heart. Re-mem-ber also those who have died in the peace of your Christ and all the dead,

* Mention may be made here of the Coadjutor Bishop, or Auxiliary Bishops, as noted in the *General Instruction of the Roman Missal,* no. 149.

THE ORDER OF MASS WITH THE PARTICIPATION OF A SINGLE MINISTER

THE INTRODUCTORY RITES

1. The Priest approaches the altar with the minister and after making a profound bow with the minister, venerates the altar with a kiss and goes to the chair.
    Then the minister or the Priest himself recites the Entrance Antiphon and the Priest and the minister, standing, sign themselves with the Sign of the Cross, while the Priest, facing the minister, says:

    In the name of the Father, and of the Son, and of the Holy Spirit.

    The minister replies:

    Amen.

2. Then the Priest, facing the minister and extending his hands, greets him, saying:

    The Lord be with you.

    The minister replies:

    And with your spirit.

    Other formulas of greeting may also be used, as found in the Order of Mass (pp. 513-514).

3. Then the Priest and the minister recite together the formula of general confession:

    I confess to almighty God
    and to you, my brother,
    that I have greatly sinned,
    in my thoughts and in my words,
    in what I have done and in what I have failed to do,

    And, striking their breast, they say:

    through my fault, through my fault,
    through my most grievous fault;

    Then they continue:

    therefore I ask blessed Mary ever-Virgin,
    all the Angels and Saints,
    and you, my brother,
    to pray for me to the Lord our God.

    The absolution by the Priest follows:

    May almighty God have mercy on us,
    forgive us our sins,
    and bring us to everlasting life.

    The minister replies:

    Amen.

    Other formulas for the Penitential Act may also be used, as found in the Order of Mass (pp. 515-519).

4. The Kyrie, eleison (Lord, have mercy) invocations follow, the Priest reciting them in alternation with the minister:

> Priest: **Lord, have mercy.**   Minister: Lord, have mercy.
> Priest: **Christ, have mercy.**   Minister: Christ, have mercy.
> Priest: **Lord, have mercy.**   Minister: Lord, have mercy.

Or:

> Priest: **Kyrie, eleison.**   Minister: Kyrie, eleison.
> Priest: **Christe, eleison.**   Minister: Christe, eleison.
> Priest: **Kyrie, eleison.**   Minister: Kyrie, eleison.

5. Then, when it is prescribed, the Priest and the minister recite together the hymn Gloria in excelsis (Glory to God in the highest).

6. When this hymn is concluded, the Priest, with hands joined, says:

> **Let us pray.**

After a moment of prayer in silence, he extends his hands and says the Collect prayer, at the end of which the minister acclaims:

> Amen.

THE LITURGY OF THE WORD

7. Then the minister or the Priest himself reads the First Reading, the Psalm and the Second Reading, if there is to be one, along with the other chant.

8. Then the Priest, bowing profoundly before the altar, says quietly:

> **Cleanse my heart and my lips, almighty God,**
> **that I may worthily proclaim your holy Gospel.**

9. After this, with hands joined, he says:

> **The Lord be with you.**

The minister replies:

> And with your spirit.

The Priest:

> **A reading from the holy Gospel according to N.**

and, at the same time, he makes the Sign of the Cross on the book and on his forehead, lips, and breast.

The minister acclaims:

> Glory to you, O Lord.

Then the Priest proclaims the Gospel, at the end of which he acclaims:

> **The Gospel of the Lord.**

The minister replies:
Praise to you, Lord Jesus Christ.

Then the Priest kisses the book, saying quietly:
**Through the words of the Gospel
may our sins be wiped away.**

10. When it is prescribed, the Priest and the minister recite together the Symbol or Profession of Faith or Creed.

11. After this there may follow the Universal Prayer, that is, the Prayer of the Faithful or Bidding Prayers. In it the Priest says the introduction and conclusion and the minister the intentions.

THE LITURGY OF THE EUCHARIST

12. The minister places the corporal, the purificator and the chalice on the altar, unless this was already done at the beginning of Mass. The Priest goes to the middle of the altar.

13. Then the minister brings the paten with the bread, which the Priest takes and holds slightly raised above the altar with both hands, saying:

**Blessed are you, Lord God of all creation,
for through your goodness we have received
the bread we offer you:
fruit of the earth and work of human hands,
it will become for us the bread of life.**

Then he places the paten with the bread on the corporal.

At the end, the minister may acclaim:
Blessed be God for ever.

14. After this the Priest pours wine and a little water into the chalice, saying quietly:

**By the mystery of this water and wine
may we come to share in the divinity of Christ
who humbled himself to share in our humanity.**

15. Then he takes the chalice and holds it slightly raised above the altar with both hands, saying:

**Blessed are you, Lord God of all creation,
for through your goodness we have received
the wine we offer you:
fruit of the vine and work of human hands,
it will become our spiritual drink.**

Then he places the chalice on the corporal.

At the end, the minister may acclaim:
Blessed be God for ever.

16. After this, the Priest, bowing profoundly, says quietly:

**With humble spirit and contrite heart
may we be accepted by you, O Lord,
and may our sacrifice in your sight this day
be pleasing to you, Lord God.**

17. Then standing at the side of the altar, he washes his hands, saying quietly:

**Wash me, O Lord, from my iniquity
and cleanse me from my sin.**

18. Standing at the middle of the altar, facing the minister, extending and then joining his hands, he says:

**Pray, brethren (brothers and sisters),
that my sacrifice and yours
may be acceptable to God,
the almighty Father.**

The minister replies:

**May the Lord accept the sacrifice at your hands
for the praise and glory of his name,
for our good
and the good of all his holy Church.**

Then the Priest, with hands extended, says the Prayer over the Offerings, at the end of which the minister acclaims: **Amen.**

19. Then the Priest says the Eucharistic Prayer, according to the norms indicated in each Eucharistic Prayer (pp. 635-662 and 757-798).

THE COMMUNION RITE

20. After the doxology at the end of the Eucharistic Prayer, and after the chalice and paten have been set down, the Priest, with hands joined, says:

**At the Savior's command
and formed by divine teaching,
we dare to say:**

WITH THE PARTICIPATION OF A SINGLE MINISTER

He extends his hands and, together with the minister, continues:

**Our Father, who art in heaven,
hallowed be thy name;
thy kingdom come,
thy will be done
on earth as it is in heaven.
Give us this day our daily bread,
and forgive us our trespasses,
as we forgive those who trespass against us;
and lead us not into temptation,
but deliver us from evil.**

21. *With hands extended, the Priest alone continues, saying:*

    **Deliver us, Lord, we pray, from every evil,
    graciously grant peace in our days,
    that, by the help of your mercy,
    we may be always free from sin
    and safe from all distress,
    as we await the blessed hope
    and the coming of our Savior, Jesus Christ.**

    He joins his hands.

    The minister concludes the prayer, acclaiming:

    For the kingdom, the power and the glory are yours now and for ever.

22. *Then the Priest, with hands extended, says aloud:*

    **Lord Jesus Christ,
    who said to your Apostles:
    Peace I leave you, my peace I give you,
    look not on our sins,
    but on the faith of your Church,
    and graciously grant her peace and unity
    in accordance with your will.**

    He joins his hands.

    Who live and reign for ever and ever.

    The minister replies:

    Amen.

23. *The Priest, facing the minister, extending and then joining his hands, adds:*
    The peace of the Lord be with you always.

    The minister replies:
    And with your spirit.

    Then, if appropriate, the Priest gives the sign of peace to the minister.

24. *Then he takes the host and breaks it over the paten, while the minister says:*
    Lamb of God, you take away the sins of the world, have mercy on us.
    Lamb of God, you take away the sins of the world, have mercy on us.
    Lamb of God, you take away the sins of the world, grant us peace.

    The Priest places a small piece in the chalice, saying quietly:
    May this mingling of the Body and Blood
    of our Lord Jesus Christ
    bring eternal life to us who receive it.

25. *Then the Priest, with hands joined, says quietly:*
    Lord Jesus Christ, Son of the living God,
    who, by the will of the Father
    and the work of the Holy Spirit,
    through your Death gave life to the world,
    free me by this, your most holy Body and Blood,
    from all my sins and from every evil;
    keep me always faithful to your commandments,
    and never let me be parted from you.

    Or:

    May the receiving of your Body and Blood,
    Lord Jesus Christ,
    not bring me to judgment and condemnation,
    but through your loving mercy
    be for me protection in mind and body
    and a healing remedy.

26. The Priest genuflects, takes the host and, holding it slightly raised above the paten or above the chalice, while facing the minister, says aloud:

> Behold the Lamb of God,
> behold him who takes away the sins of the world.
> Blessed are those called to the supper of the Lamb.

And together with the minister he adds once:

> **Lord, I am not worthy**
> **that you should enter under my roof,**
> **but only say the word**
> **and my soul shall be healed.**

If the minister is not to receive Communion, the Priest, having taken up the host, immediately says, Lord, I am not worthy, etc.

27. The Priest then says quietly:

> **May the Body of Christ**
> **keep me safe for eternal life.**

And he reverently consumes the Body of Christ.

Then he takes the chalice and says quietly:

> **May the Blood of Christ**
> **keep me safe for eternal life.**

And he reverently consumes the Blood of Christ.

28. Meanwhile the minister recites the Communion Antiphon.

29. After this, the Priest takes the paten and approaches the minister, if he is to receive Communion, and raises a host slightly, showing it to the minister and saying:

> **The Body of Christ.**

The minister replies:

> Amen.

And receives Holy Communion.

30. Then the Priest purifies the paten over the chalice and also the chalice itself. The chalice, paten, corporal and purificator are taken by the minister to the credence table or left on the altar.

While he carries out the purification, the Priest says quietly:

> **What has passed our lips as food, O Lord,**
> **may we possess in purity of heart,**
> **that what has been given to us in time**
> **may be our healing for eternity.**

31. A sacred silence may be observed for a while.

32. Then, with hands joined, the Priest says:

Let us pray.

After a brief pause for silence, unless silence has just been observed, he extends his hands and says the Prayer after Communion, at the end of which the minister acclaims:

Amen.

THE CONCLUDING RITES

33. Then the Priest, facing the minister and extending his hands, says:

The Lord be with you.

The minister replies:

And with your spirit.

The Priest blesses the minister, saying:

May almighty God bless you,
the Father, and the Son, ✠ **and the Holy Spirit.**

The minister replies:

Amen.

34. Then the Priest venerates the altar with a kiss, and after making a profound bow with the minister, he withdraws.

APPENDIX TO THE ORDER OF MASS

Eucharistic Prayer for Reconciliation I
in a concelebration

The Preface and You are indeed Holy, O Lord to just as you yourself are holy inclusive are said by the principal celebrant alone, with hands extended.

From Look, we pray to we, too, are your sons and daughters inclusive is said together by all the concelebrants, with hands extended toward the offerings.

From But before to who heals every division inclusive, all the concelebrants together speak in this manner:

a) The part But before, with hands joined.
b) While speaking the words of the Lord, each extends his right hand toward the bread and toward the chalice, if this seems appropriate; as the host and the chalice are elevated at the Consecration, however, the concelebrants look toward them and then bow profoundly.
c) The parts Therefore, as we celebrate the memorial and Look kindly, most compassionate Father, with hands extended.

It is appropriate that the intercession Be pleased to keep us always in communion of mind and heart be assigned to one or other of the concelebrants, who pronounces this prayer alone, with hands extended.

The following parts especially may be sung: But before; As he ate with them; In a similar way; Therefore, as we celebrate the memorial; Look kindly, most compassionate Father, as well as the concluding doxology.

The concluding doxology of the Eucharistic Prayer is pronounced by the principal celebrant alone, or by all the concelebrants together with the principal celebrant.

EUCHARISTIC PRAYERS FOR RECONCILIATION

The Eucharistic Prayers for Reconciliation may be used in Masses in which the mystery of reconciliation is conveyed to the faithful in a special way, as, for example, in the Masses for Promoting Harmony, For Reconciliation, For the Preservation of Peace and Justice, In Time of War or Civil Disturbance, For the Forgiveness of Sins, For Charity, of the Mystery of the Holy Cross, of the Most Holy Eucharist, of the Most Precious Blood of our Lord Jesus Christ, as well as in Masses during Lent. Although these Eucharistic Prayers have been provided with a proper Preface, they may also be used with other Prefaces that refer to penance and conversion, as, for example, the Prefaces of Lent.

I

V. The Lord be with you.   R. And with your spir-it.

V. Lift up your hearts.   R. We lift them up to the Lord.

V. Let us give thanks to the Lord our God.   R. It is right and just.

It is truly right and just that we should always give you thanks, Lord, holy Father, almighty and e-ter-nal God. For you do not cease to spur us on to possess a more a-bun-dant life and, being rich in mercy, you constantly of-fer par-don and call on sin-ners to trust in your for-give-ness a-lone. Nev-er did you turn away from us, and, though time and again we have bro-ken your cov-e-nant, you

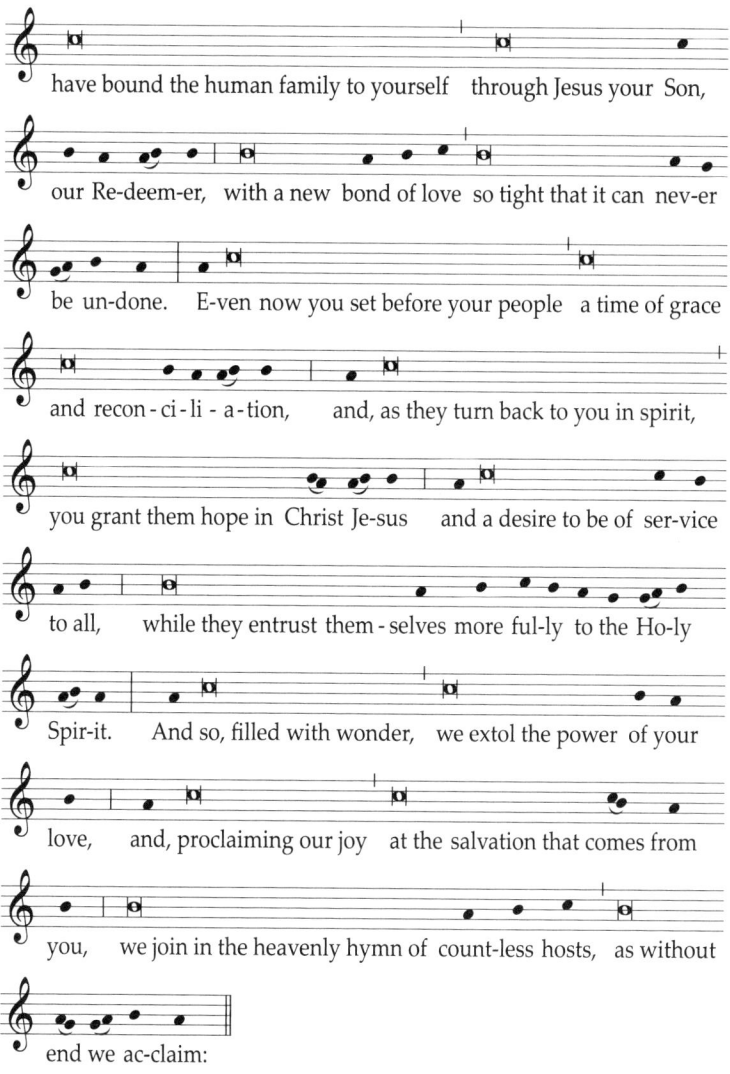

Holy, Holy, Holy Lord God of hosts . . .

Text without music:

1. ℣. **The Lord be with you.**
    ℞. And with your spirit.

    ℣. **Lift up your hearts.**
    ℞. We lift them up to the Lord.

    ℣. **Let us give thanks to the Lord our God.**
    ℞. It is right and just.

    It is truly right and just
    that we should always give you thanks,
    Lord, holy Father, almighty and eternal God.

    For you do not cease to spur us on
    to possess a more abundant life
    and, being rich in mercy,
    you constantly offer pardon
    and call on sinners
    to trust in your forgiveness alone.

    Never did you turn away from us,
    and, though time and again we have broken your covenant,
    you have bound the human family to yourself
    through Jesus your Son, our Redeemer,
    with a new bond of love so tight
    that it can never be undone.

    Even now you set before your people
    a time of grace and reconciliation,
    and, as they turn back to you in spirit,
    you grant them hope in Christ Jesus
    and a desire to be of service to all,
    while they entrust themselves
    more fully to the Holy Spirit.

    And so, filled with wonder,
    we extol the power of your love,
    and, proclaiming our joy
    at the salvation that comes from you,
    we join in the heavenly hymn of countless hosts,
    as without end we acclaim:

EUCHARISTIC PRAYER FOR RECONCILIATION I

Holy, Holy, Holy Lord God of hosts.
Heaven and earth are full of your glory.
Hosanna in the highest.
Blessed is he who comes in the name of the Lord.
Hosanna in the highest.

2. *The Priest, with hands extended, says:*

You are indeed Holy, O Lord,   *Celebrant alone*
and from the world's beginning
are ceaselessly at work,
so that the human race may become holy,
just as you yourself are holy.

3. *He joins his hands and, holding them extended over the offerings, says:*

Look, we pray, upon your people's offerings   *Celebrant*
and pour out on them the power of your Spirit,   *with concelebrants*

He joins his hands and makes the Sign of the Cross once over the bread and chalice together, saying:

that they may become the Body and ✠ Blood

He joins his hands.

of your beloved Son, Jesus Christ,
in whom we, too, are your sons and daughters.

Indeed, though we once were lost
and could not approach you,
you loved us with the greatest love:
for your Son, who alone is just,
handed himself over to death,
and did not disdain to be nailed for our sake
to the wood of the Cross.

But before his arms were outstretched between heaven and earth,
to become the lasting sign of your covenant,
he desired to celebrate the Passover with his disciples.

4. In the formulas that follow, the words of the Lord should be pronounced clearly and distinctly, as the nature of these words requires.

As he ate with them,

He takes the bread and, holding it slightly raised above the altar, continues:

**he took bread
and, giving you thanks, he said the blessing,
broke the bread and gave it to them, saying:**

He bows slightly.

**TAKE THIS, ALL OF YOU, AND EAT OF IT,
FOR THIS IS MY BODY,
WHICH WILL BE GIVEN UP FOR YOU.**

He shows the consecrated host to the people, places it again on the paten, and genuflects in adoration.

5. *After this, he continues:*

**In a similar way, when supper was ended,
knowing that he was about to reconcile all things in himself
through his Blood to be shed on the Cross,**

He takes the chalice and, holding it slightly raised above the altar, continues:

**he took the chalice, filled with the fruit of the vine,
and once more giving you thanks,
handed the chalice to his disciples, saying:**

He bows slightly.

**TAKE THIS, ALL OF YOU, AND DRINK FROM IT,
FOR THIS IS THE CHALICE OF MY BLOOD,
THE BLOOD OF THE NEW AND ETERNAL COVENANT,
WHICH WILL BE POURED OUT FOR YOU AND FOR MANY
FOR THE FORGIVENESS OF SINS.**

DO THIS IN MEMORY OF ME.

He shows the chalice to the people, places it on the corporal, and genuflects in adoration.

EUCHARISTIC PRAYER FOR RECONCILIATION I

6. Then he says:

The mystery of faith. *Celebrant alone*

And the people continue, acclaiming:

We proclaim your Death, O Lord,
and profess your Resurrection
until you come again.

Or:

When we eat this Bread and drink this Cup,
we proclaim your Death, O Lord,
until you come again.

Or:

Save us, Savior of the world,
for by your Cross and Resurrection
you have set us free.

7. Then the Priest, with hands extended, says:

Therefore, as we celebrate *Celebrant*
the memorial of your Son Jesus Christ, *with concelebrants*
who is our Passover and our surest peace,
we celebrate his Death and Resurrection from the dead,
and looking forward to his blessed Coming,
we offer you, who are our faithful and merciful God,
this sacrificial Victim
who reconciles to you the human race.

Look kindly, most compassionate Father,
on those you unite to yourself
by the Sacrifice of your Son,
and grant that, by the power of the Holy Spirit,
as they partake of this one Bread and one Chalice,
they may be gathered into one Body in Christ,
who heals every division.

Be pleased to keep us always   Celebrant or
in communion of mind and heart,   one concelebrant
together with N. our Pope and N. our Bishop.[*]
Help us to work together
for the coming of your Kingdom,
until the hour when we stand before you,
Saints among the Saints in the halls of heaven,
with the Blessed Virgin Mary, Mother of God,
the blessed Apostles and all the Saints,
and with our deceased brothers and sisters,
whom we humbly commend to your mercy.

Then, freed at last from the wound of corruption
and made fully into a new creation,
we shall sing to you with gladness

He joins his hands.
   the thanksgiving of Christ,
   who lives for all eternity.

8.   *He takes the chalice and the paten with the host and, raising both, he says:*
   Through him, and with him, and in him,   Celebrant alone
   O God, almighty Father,   or with
   in the unity of the Holy Spirit,   concelebrants
   all glory and honor is yours,
   for ever and ever.

The people acclaim:
   Amen.

Then follows the Communion Rite, p. 663.

---

[*]   Mention may be made here of the Coadjutor Bishop, or Auxiliary Bishops, as noted in the *General Instruction of the Roman Missal*, no. 149.

Eucharistic Prayer for Reconciliation II
in a concelebration

The Preface and You, therefore, almighty Father to handed over to death inclusive are said by the principal celebrant alone, with hands extended.

From And now, celebrating the reconciliation to when we celebrate these mysteries inclusive is spoken together by all the concelebrants, with hands extended toward the offerings.

From For when about to give his life to the Sacrifice of perfect reconciliation inclusive, all the concelebrants together speak in this manner:

a) The part For when about to give his life, with hands joined.
b) While speaking the words of the Lord, each extends his right hand toward the bread and toward the chalice, if this seems appropriate; as the host and the chalice are elevated at the Consecration, however, the concelebrants look toward them and then bow profoundly.
c) The part Celebrating therefore the memorial, with hands extended.

It is appropriate that the intercessions May he make your Church and Just as you have gathered us now be assigned to one or other of the concelebrants, who pronounces this prayer alone, with hands extended.

The following parts especially may be sung: And now, celebrating the reconciliation; For when about to give his life; In a similar way on that same evening; Celebrating therefore the memorial, as well as the concluding doxology.

The concluding doxology of the Eucharistic Prayer is pronounced by the principal celebrant alone, or by all the concelebrants together with the principal celebrant.

EUCHARISTIC PRAYER FOR RECONCILIATION

II

V. The Lord be with you.   R. And with your spirit.

V. Lift up your hearts.   R. We lift them up to the Lord.

V. Let us give thanks to the Lord our God.   R. It is right and just.

It is truly right and just that we should give you thanks and praise, O God, almighty Father, for all you do in this world, through our Lord Jesus Christ. For though the human race is divided by dissension and discord, yet we know that by testing us you change our hearts to prepare them for reconciliation. Even more, by your Spirit you move human hearts that enemies may speak to each other again, adversaries join hands, and peoples seek to meet together. By the working of your power

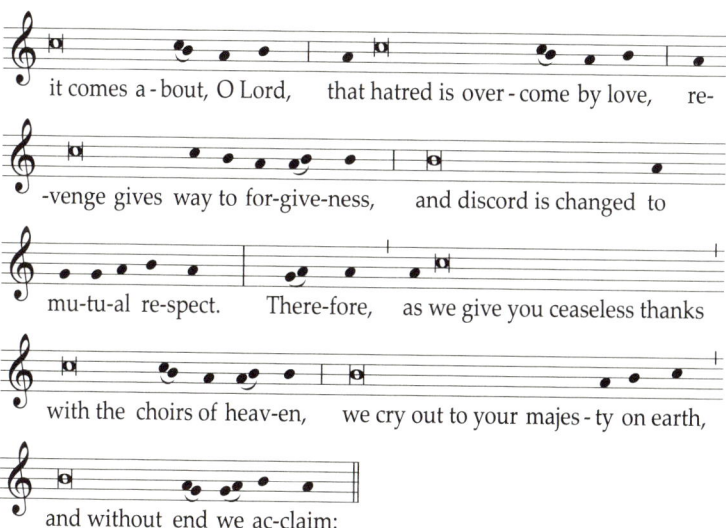

it comes a-bout, O Lord, that hatred is over-come by love, re-venge gives way to for-give-ness, and discord is changed to mu-tu-al re-spect. There-fore, as we give you ceaseless thanks with the choirs of heav-en, we cry out to your majes-ty on earth, and without end we ac-claim:

Holy, Holy, Holy Lord God of hosts ...

Text without music:

1. V. **The Lord be with you.**
R. And with your spirit.

V. **Lift up your hearts.**
R. We lift them up to the Lord.

V. **Let us give thanks to the Lord our God.**
R. It is right and just.

It is truly right and just
that we should give you thanks and praise,
O God, almighty Father,
for all you do in this world,
through our Lord Jesus Christ.

For though the human race
is divided by dissension and discord,
yet we know that by testing us
you change our hearts
to prepare them for reconciliation.

Even more, by your Spirit you move human hearts
that enemies may speak to each other again,
adversaries join hands,
and peoples seek to meet together.

By the working of your power
it comes about, O Lord,
that hatred is overcome by love,
revenge gives way to forgiveness,
and discord is changed to mutual respect.

Therefore, as we give you ceaseless thanks
with the choirs of heaven,
we cry out to your majesty on earth,
and without end we acclaim:

Holy, Holy, Holy Lord God of hosts.
Heaven and earth are full of your glory.
Hosanna in the highest.
Blessed is he who comes in the name of the Lord.
Hosanna in the highest.

2. *The Priest, with hands extended, says:*

You, therefore, almighty Father,   *Celebrant alone*
we bless through Jesus Christ your Son,
who comes in your name.
He himself is the Word that brings salvation,
the hand you extend to sinners,
the way by which your peace is offered to us.
When we ourselves had turned away from you
on account of our sins,
you brought us back to be reconciled, O Lord,
so that, converted at last to you,
we might love one another
through your Son,
whom for our sake you handed over to death.

3. *He joins his hands and, holding them extended over the offerings, says:*

And now, celebrating the reconciliation   *Celebrant*
Christ has brought us,   *with concelebrants*
we entreat you:
sanctify these gifts by the outpouring of your Spirit,

He joins his hands and makes the Sign of the Cross once over the bread and chalice together, saying:

**that they may become the Body and ✠ Blood of your Son,
whose command we fulfill when we celebrate these mysteries.**

He joins his hands.

4. *In the formulas that follow, the words of the Lord should be pronounced clearly and distinctly, as the nature of these words requires.*

   **For when about to give his life to set us free,
   as he reclined at supper,**

   He takes the bread and, holding it slightly raised above the altar, continues:

   **he himself took bread into his hands,
   and, giving you thanks, he said the blessing,
   broke the bread and gave it to his disciples, saying:**

   He bows slightly.

   **Take this, all of you, and eat of it,
   for this is my Body,
   which will be given up for you.**

   He shows the consecrated host to the people, places it again on the paten, and genuflects in adoration.

5. *After this, he continues:*

   In a similar way, on that same evening,

   He takes the chalice and, holding it slightly raised above the altar, continues:

   **he took the chalice of blessing in his hands,
   confessing your mercy,
   and gave the chalice to his disciples, saying:**

   He bows slightly.

   **Take this, all of you, and drink from it,
   for this is the chalice of my Blood,
   the Blood of the new and eternal covenant,
   which will be poured out for you and for many
   for the forgiveness of sins.

   Do this in memory of me.**

   He shows the chalice to the people, places it on the corporal, and genuflects in adoration.

6. Then he says:
> **The mystery of faith.**   *Celebrant alone*

And the people continue, acclaiming:
> **We proclaim your Death, O Lord,**
> **and profess your Resurrection**
> **until you come again.**

Or:

> **When we eat this Bread and drink this Cup,**
> **we proclaim your Death, O Lord,**
> **until you come again.**

Or:

> **Save us, Savior of the world,**
> **for by your Cross and Resurrection**
> **you have set us free.**

7. Then the Priest, with hands extended, says:
> **Celebrating, therefore, the memorial**   *Celebrant*
> **of the Death and Resurrection of your Son,**   *with concelebrants*
> **who left us this pledge of his love,**
> **we offer you what you have bestowed on us,**
> **the Sacrifice of perfect reconciliation.**

> **Holy Father, we humbly beseech you**
> **to accept us also, together with your Son,**
> **and in this saving banquet**
> **graciously to endow us with his very Spirit,**
> **who takes away everything**
> **that estranges us from one another.**

> **May he make your Church a sign of unity**   *Celebrant or*
> **and an instrument of your peace among all people**   *one concelebrant*
> **and may he keep us in communion**
> **with N. our Pope and N. our Bishop***
> **and all the Bishops**
> **and your entire people.**

---

*   Mention may be made here of the Coadjutor Bishop, or Auxiliary Bishops, as noted in the *General Instruction of the Roman Missal*, no. 149.

> Just as you have gathered us now *(Celebrant or one concelebrant)*
>> at the table of your Son,
> so also bring us together,
> with the glorious Virgin Mary, Mother of God,
> with your blessed Apostles and all the Saints,
> with our brothers and sisters
> and those of every race and tongue
> who have died in your friendship.
> Bring us to share with them the unending banquet of unity
> in a new heaven and a new earth,
> where the fullness of your peace will shine forth
>
> *He joins his hands.*
> **in Christ Jesus our Lord.**

8. *He takes the chalice and the paten with the host and, raising both, he says:*

> **Through him, and with him, and in him,** *(Celebrant alone or with concelebrants)*
> **O God, almighty Father,**
> **in the unity of the Holy Spirit,**
> **all glory and honor is yours,**
> **for ever and ever.**

The people acclaim:
Amen.

Then follows the Communion Rite, p. 663.

Eucharistic Prayer for Various Needs
in a concelebration

The Preface and You are indeed Holy to and breaks the bread inclusive are said by the principal celebrant alone, with hands extended.

From Therefore, Father most merciful to of our Lord Jesus Christ inclusive is spoken together by all the concelebrants, with hands extended toward the offerings.

From On the day before he was to suffer to in whose Body and Blood we have communion inclusive, all the concelebrants together speak in this manner:

a) The part On the day before he was to suffer, with hands joined.
b) While speaking the words of the Lord, each extends his right hand toward the bread and toward the chalice, if this seems appropriate; as the host and the chalice are elevated at the Consecration, however, the concelebrants look toward them and then bow profoundly.
c) The parts Therefore, holy Father and Look with favor on the oblation of your Church, with hands extended.

It is appropriate that the intercessions Lord, renew your Church; or And so, having called us to your table; or By our partaking; or Bring your Church, O Lord; as well as Remember our brothers and sisters; be assigned to one or other of the concelebrants, who pronounces these prayers alone, with hands extended.

The following parts especially may be sung: On the day before he was to suffer; In a similar way; Therefore, holy Father; Look with favor on the oblation of your Church, as well as the concluding doxology.

The concluding doxology of the Eucharistic Prayer is pronounced by the principal celebrant alone, or by all the concelebrants along with the principal celebrant.

EUCHARISTIC PRAYER FOR USE IN MASSES FOR VARIOUS NEEDS

I

The Church on the Path of Unity

1. The following form of this Eucharistic Prayer is appropriately used with Mass formularies such as, For the Church, For the Pope, For the Bishop, For the Election of a Pope or a Bishop, For a Council or Synod, For Priests, For the Priest Himself, For Ministers of the Church, and For a Spiritual or Pastoral Gathering.

V. The Lord be with you.   R. And with your spirit.

V. Lift up your hearts.   R. We lift them up to the Lord.

V. Let us give thanks to the Lord our God.   R. It is right and just.

It is truly right and just to give you thanks and raise to you a hymn of glory and praise, O Lord, Father of infinite goodness.

For by the word of your Son's Gospel you have brought together one Church from every people, tongue, and nation, and, having filled her with life by the power of your Spirit, you never cease through her to gather the whole human race into one. Manifesting the covenant of your love, she dispenses without ceasing

the blessed hope of your Kingdom and shines bright as the sign of your faithfulness, which in Christ Jesus our Lord you promised would last for eternity. And so, with all the Powers of heaven, we worship you constantly on earth, while, with all the Church, as one voice we acclaim:

Holy, Holy, Holy Lord God of hosts . . .

Text without music:

V. **The Lord be with you.**
R. And with your spirit.

V. **Lift up your hearts.**
R. We lift them up to the Lord.

V. **Let us give thanks to the Lord our God.**
R. It is right and just.

It is truly right and just to give you thanks
and raise to you a hymn of glory and praise,
O Lord, Father of infinite goodness.

For by the word of your Son's Gospel
you have brought together one Church
from every people, tongue, and nation,
and, having filled her with life by the power of your Spirit,
you never cease through her
to gather the whole human race into one.

Manifesting the covenant of your love,
she dispenses without ceasing
the blessed hope of your Kingdom
and shines bright as the sign of your faithfulness,
which in Christ Jesus our Lord
you promised would last for eternity.

And so, with all the Powers of heaven,
we worship you constantly on earth,
while, with all the Church,
as one voice we acclaim:

Holy, Holy, Holy Lord God of hosts.
Heaven and earth are full of your glory.
Hosanna in the highest.
Blessed is he who comes in the name of the Lord.
Hosanna in the highest.

2. *The Priest, with hands extended, says:*

You are indeed Holy and to be glorified, O God,   *Celebrant alone*
who love the human race
and who always walk with us on the journey of life.
Blessed indeed is your Son,
present in our midst
when we are gathered by his love,
and when, as once for the disciples, so now for us,
he opens the Scriptures and breaks the bread.

3. *He joins his hands and, holding them extended over the offerings, says:*

   Therefore, Father most merciful,   *Celebrant*
   we ask that you send forth your Holy Spirit   *with concelebrants*
   to sanctify these gifts of bread and wine,

   He joins his hands and makes the Sign of the Cross once over the bread and chalice together, saying:

   that they may become for us
   the Body and ✠ Blood

   He joins his hands.

   of our Lord Jesus Christ.

4. *In the formulas that follow, the words of the Lord should be pronounced clearly and distinctly, as the nature of these words requires.*

   On the day before he was to suffer,
   on the night of the Last Supper,

   He takes the bread and, holding it slightly raised above the altar, continues:

   he took bread and said the blessing,
   broke the bread and gave it to his disciples, saying:

   He bows slightly.

   TAKE THIS, ALL OF YOU, AND EAT OF IT,
   FOR THIS IS MY BODY,
   WHICH WILL BE GIVEN UP FOR YOU.

   He shows the consecrated host to the people, places it again on the paten, and genuflects in adoration.

5. *After this, he continues:*

   In a similar way, when supper was ended,

   He takes the chalice and, holding it slightly raised above the altar, continues:

   he took the chalice, gave you thanks
   and gave the chalice to his disciples, saying:

   He bows slightly.

   TAKE THIS, ALL OF YOU, AND DRINK FROM IT,
   FOR THIS IS THE CHALICE OF MY BLOOD,
   THE BLOOD OF THE NEW AND ETERNAL COVENANT,
   WHICH WILL BE POURED OUT FOR YOU AND FOR MANY
   FOR THE FORGIVENESS OF SINS.

   DO THIS IN MEMORY OF ME.

   He shows the chalice to the people, places it on the corporal, and genuflects in adoration.

6. Then he says:
The mystery of faith. Celebrant alone

And the people continue, acclaiming:
We proclaim your Death, O Lord,
and profess your Resurrection
until you come again.

Or:

When we eat this Bread and drink this Cup,
we proclaim your Death, O Lord,
until you come again.

Or:

Save us, Savior of the world,
for by your Cross and Resurrection
you have set us free.

7. Then the Priest, with hands extended, says: *Celebrant with concelebrants*
Therefore, holy Father,
as we celebrate the memorial of Christ your Son, our Savior,
whom you led through his Passion and Death on the Cross
to the glory of the Resurrection,
and whom you have seated at your right hand,
we proclaim the work of your love until he comes again
and we offer you the Bread of life
and the Chalice of blessing.

Look with favor on the oblation of your Church,
in which we show forth
the paschal Sacrifice of Christ that has been handed on to us,
and grant that, by the power of the Spirit of your love,
we may be counted now and until the day of eternity
among the members of your Son,
in whose Body and Blood we have communion.

Lord, renew your Church (which is in N.)   *Celebrant or one concelebrant*
by the light of the Gospel.
Strengthen the bond of unity
between the faithful and the pastors of your people,
together with N. our Pope, N. our Bishop,[*]
and the whole Order of Bishops,
that in a world torn by strife
your people may shine forth
as a prophetic sign of unity and concord.

Remember our brothers and sisters (N. and N.),   *Celebrant alone or with concelebrants*
who have fallen asleep in the peace of your Christ,
and all the dead, whose faith you alone have known.
Admit them to rejoice in the light of your face,
and in the resurrection give them the fullness of life.

Grant also to us,
when our earthly pilgrimage is done,
that we may come to an eternal dwelling place
and live with you for ever;
there, in communion with the Blessed Virgin Mary, Mother of God,
with the Apostles and Martyrs,
(with Saint N.: the Saint of the day or Patron)
and with all the Saints,
we shall praise and exalt you

He joins his hands.

through Jesus Christ, your Son.

8. *He takes the chalice and the paten with the host and, raising both, he says:*

   Through him, and with him, and in him,   *Celebrant alone or with concelebrants*
   O God, almighty Father,
   in the unity of the Holy Spirit,
   all glory and honor is yours,
   for ever and ever.

The people acclaim:

Amen.

Then follows the Communion Rite, p. 663.

---

[*] Mention may be made here of the Coadjutor Bishop, or Auxiliary Bishops, as noted in the *General Instruction of the Roman Missal*, no. 149.

II

God Guides His Church along the Way of Salvation

1. The following form of this Eucharistic Prayer is appropriately used with Mass formularies such as, For the Church, For Vocations to Holy Orders, For the Laity, For the Family, For Religious, For Vocations to Religious Life, For Charity, For Relatives and Friends, and For Giving Thanks to God.

V. The Lord be with you.   R. And with your spir-it.

V. Lift up your hearts.   R. We lift them up to the Lord.

V. Let us give thanks to the Lord our God.   R. It is right and just.

It is truly right and just, our duty and our sal-va-tion, al-ways and everywhere to give you thanks, Lord, holy Father, creator of the world and source of all life. For you never forsake the works of your wis-dom, but by your prov-i-dence are even now at work in our midst. With mighty hand and out-stretched arm you led your peo-ple Is-ra-el through the de-sert. Now, as your Church makes her pilgrim journey in the world, you always accompany her by the power of the Ho-ly Spir-it and lead her along the paths of time

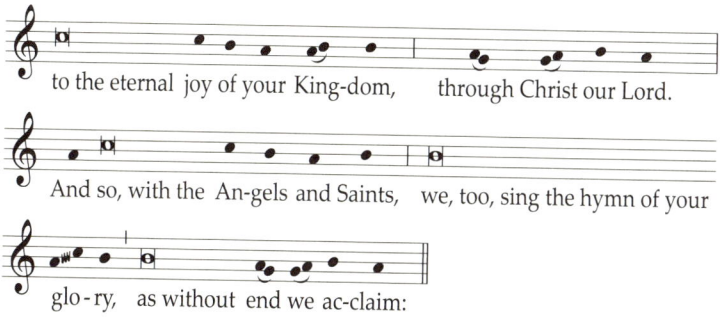

Holy, Holy, Holy Lord God of hosts . . .

Text without music:

V. **The Lord be with you.**
R. And with your spirit.

V. **Lift up your hearts.**
R. We lift them up to the Lord.

V. **Let us give thanks to the Lord our God.**
R. It is right and just.

It is truly right and just, our duty and our salvation,
always and everywhere to give you thanks,
Lord, holy Father,
creator of the world and source of all life.

For you never forsake the works of your wisdom,
but by your providence are even now at work in our midst.
With mighty hand and outstretched arm
you led your people Israel through the desert.
Now, as your Church makes her pilgrim journey in the world,
you always accompany her
by the power of the Holy Spirit
and lead her along the paths of time
to the eternal joy of your Kingdom,
through Christ our Lord.

And so, with the Angels and Saints,
we, too, sing the hymn of your glory,
as without end we acclaim:

Holy, Holy, Holy Lord God of hosts.
Heaven and earth are full of your glory.
Hosanna in the highest.
Blessed is he who comes in the name of the Lord.
Hosanna in the highest.

2. The Priest, with hands extended, says:

Celebrant alone

You are indeed Holy and to be glorified, O God,
who love the human race
and who always walk with us on the journey of life.
Blessed indeed is your Son,
present in our midst
when we are gathered by his love
and when, as once for the disciples, so now for us,
he opens the Scriptures and breaks the bread.

3. He joins his hands and, holding them extended over the offerings, says:

Celebrant with concelebrants

Therefore, Father most merciful,
we ask that you send forth your Holy Spirit
to sanctify these gifts of bread and wine,

He joins his hands and makes the Sign of the Cross once over the bread and chalice together, saying:

that they may become for us
the Body and ✠ Blood

He joins his hands.

of our Lord Jesus Christ.

4. In the formulas that follow, the words of the Lord should be pronounced clearly and distinctly, as the nature of these words requires.

On the day before he was to suffer,
on the night of the Last Supper,

He takes the bread and, holding it slightly raised above the altar, continues:

he took bread and said the blessing,
broke the bread and gave it to his disciples, saying:

He bows slightly.

TAKE THIS, ALL OF YOU, AND EAT OF IT,
FOR THIS IS MY BODY,
WHICH WILL BE GIVEN UP FOR YOU.

He shows the consecrated host to the people, places it again on the paten, and genuflects in adoration.

EUCHARISTIC PRAYER FOR USE IN MASSES FOR VARIOUS NEEDS II

5. *After this, he continues:*

   In a similar way, when supper was ended,

   He takes the chalice and, holding it slightly raised above the altar, continues:

   he took the chalice, gave you thanks
   and gave the chalice to his disciples, saying:

   He bows slightly.

   Take this, all of you, and drink from it,
   for this is the chalice of my Blood,
   the Blood of the new and eternal covenant,
   which will be poured out for you and for many
   for the forgiveness of sins.

   Do this in memory of me.

   He shows the chalice to the people, places it on the corporal, and genuflects in adoration.

6. *Then he says:*

   The mystery of faith. *Celebrant alone*

   And the people continue, acclaiming:

   We proclaim your Death, O Lord,
   and profess your Resurrection
   until you come again.

   Or:

   When we eat this Bread and drink this Cup,
   we proclaim your Death, O Lord,
   until you come again.

   Or:

   Save us, Savior of the world,
   for by your Cross and Resurrection
   you have set us free.

7. *Then the Priest, with hands extended, says:*

Celebrant with concelebrants

Therefore, holy Father,
as we celebrate the memorial
    of Christ your Son, our Savior,
whom you led through his Passion and Death on the Cross
to the glory of the Resurrection,
and whom you have seated at your right hand,
we proclaim the work of your love until he comes again
and we offer you the Bread of life
and the Chalice of blessing.

Look with favor on the oblation of your Church,
in which we show forth
the paschal Sacrifice of Christ that has been handed on to us,
and grant that, by the power of the Spirit of your love,
we may be counted now and until the day of eternity
among the members of your Son,
in whose Body and Blood we have communion.

Celebrant or one concelebrant

And so, having called us to your table, Lord,
confirm us in unity,
so that, together with N. our Pope and N. our Bishop,*
with all Bishops, Priests and Deacons,
and your entire people,
as we walk your ways with faith and hope,
we may strive to bring joy and trust into the world.

Celebrant or one concelebrant

Remember our brothers and sisters (N. and N.),
who have fallen asleep in the peace of your Christ,
and all the dead, whose faith you alone have known.
Admit them to rejoice in the light of your face,
and in the resurrection give them the fullness of life.

---

* Mention may be made here of the Coadjutor Bishop, or Auxiliary Bishops, as noted in the *General Instruction of the Roman Missal*, no. 149.

Grant also to us,
when our earthly pilgrimage is done,
that we may come to an eternal dwelling place
and live with you for ever;
there, in communion with the Blessed Virgin Mary, Mother of God,
with the Apostles and Martyrs,
(with Saint N.: the Saint of the day or Patron)
and with all the Saints,
we shall praise and exalt you

He joins his hands.

through Jesus Christ, your Son.

8. *He takes the chalice and the paten with the host and, raising both, he says:*

Through him, and with him, and in him,
O God, almighty Father,
in the unity of the Holy Spirit,
all glory and honor is yours,
for ever and ever.

Celebrant alone or with concelebrants

The people acclaim:

Amen.

Then follows the Communion Rite, p. 663.

III

Jesus, the Way to the Father

1. The following form of this Eucharistic Prayer is appropriately used with Mass formularies such as, For the Evangelization of Peoples, For Persecuted Christians, For the Nation or State, For Those in Public Office, For a Governing Assembly, At the Beginning of the Civil Year, and For the Progress of Peoples.

V. The Lord be with you.   R. And with your spir-it.

V. Lift up your hearts.   R. We lift them up to the Lord.

V. Let us give thanks to the Lord our God.   R. It is right and just.

It is truly right and just, our duty and our sal-va-tion, al-ways and everywhere to give you thanks, ho-ly Father, Lord of heav-en and earth, through Christ our Lord. For by your Word you cre-at-ed the world and you govern all things in har-mo-ny. You gave us the same Word made flesh as Mediator, and he has spoken your words to us and called us to fol-low him. He is the way that leads us to you, the truth that sets us free, the life that fills us with glad-ness. Through your Son you gather men and women,

EUCHARISTIC PRAYER FOR USE IN MASSES FOR VARIOUS NEEDS III

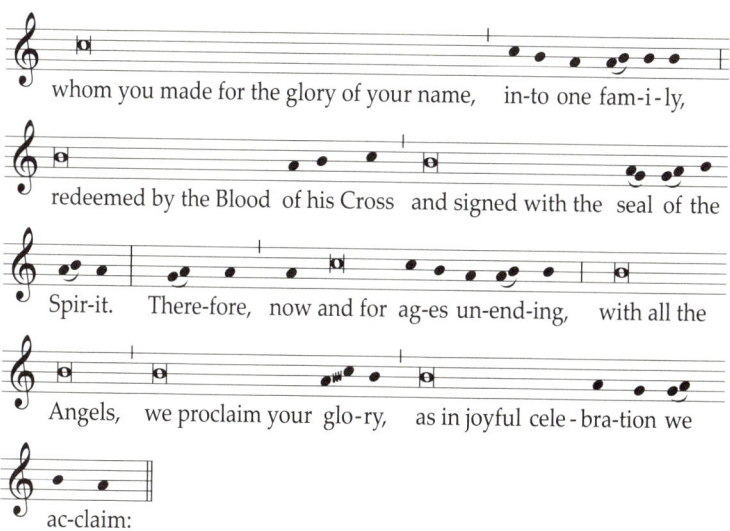

whom you made for the glory of your name, in-to one fam-i-ly, redeemed by the Blood of his Cross and signed with the seal of the Spir-it. There-fore, now and for ag-es un-end-ing, with all the Angels, we proclaim your glo-ry, as in joyful cele-bra-tion we ac-claim:

Holy, Holy, Holy Lord God of hosts . . .

Text without music:

V. **The Lord be with you.**
R. And with your spirit.

V. **Lift up your hearts.**
R. We lift them up to the Lord.

V. **Let us give thanks to the Lord our God.**
R. It is right and just.

It is truly right and just, our duty and our salvation,
always and everywhere to give you thanks,
holy Father, Lord of heaven and earth,
through Christ our Lord.

For by your Word you created the world
and you govern all things in harmony.
You gave us the same Word made flesh as Mediator,
and he has spoken your words to us
and called us to follow him.
He is the way that leads us to you,
the truth that sets us free,
the life that fills us with gladness.

Through your Son
you gather men and women,
whom you made for the glory of your name,
into one family,
redeemed by the Blood of his Cross
and signed with the seal of the Spirit.

Therefore, now and for ages unending,
with all the Angels,
we proclaim your glory,
as in joyful celebration we acclaim:

Holy, Holy, Holy Lord God of hosts.
Heaven and earth are full of your glory.
Hosanna in the highest.
Blessed is he who comes in the name of the Lord.
Hosanna in the highest.

2. *The Priest, with hands extended, says:*

You are indeed Holy and to be glorified, O God,   *Celebrant alone*
who love the human race
and who always walk with us on the journey of life.
Blessed indeed is your Son,
present in our midst
when we are gathered by his love
and when, as once for the disciples, so now for us,
he opens the Scriptures and breaks the bread.

3. *He joins his hands and, holding them extended over the offerings, says:*

Therefore, Father most merciful,   *Celebrant*
we ask that you send forth your Holy Spirit   *with concelebrants*
to sanctify these gifts of bread and wine,

He joins his hands and makes the Sign of the Cross once over the bread and chalice together, saying:

that they may become for us
the Body and ✠ Blood

He joins his hands.

of our Lord Jesus Christ.

4. In the formulas that follow, the words of the Lord should be pronounced clearly and distinctly, as the nature of these words requires.

> **On the day before he was to suffer,**
> **on the night of the Last Supper,**

He takes the bread and, holding it slightly raised above the altar, continues:

> **he took bread and said the blessing,**
> **broke the bread and gave it to his disciples, saying:**

He bows slightly.

> **TAKE THIS, ALL OF YOU, AND EAT OF IT,**
> **FOR THIS IS MY BODY,**
> **WHICH WILL BE GIVEN UP FOR YOU.**

He shows the consecrated host to the people, places it again on the paten, and genuflects in adoration.

5. *After this, he continues:*

> **In a similar way, when supper was ended,**

He takes the chalice and, holding it slightly raised above the altar, continues:

> **he took the chalice, gave you thanks**
> **and gave the chalice to his disciples, saying:**

He bows slightly.

> **TAKE THIS, ALL OF YOU, AND DRINK FROM IT,**
> **FOR THIS IS THE CHALICE OF MY BLOOD,**
> **THE BLOOD OF THE NEW AND ETERNAL COVENANT,**
> **WHICH WILL BE POURED OUT FOR YOU AND FOR MANY**
> **FOR THE FORGIVENESS OF SINS.**
>
> **DO THIS IN MEMORY OF ME.**

He shows the chalice to the people, places it on the corporal, and genuflects in adoration.

6. *Then he says:*

> **The mystery of faith.**   *Celebrant alone*

And the people continue, acclaiming:

> We proclaim your Death, O Lord,
> and profess your Resurrection
> until you come again.
>
> *Or:*
>
> When we eat this Bread and drink this Cup,
> we proclaim your Death, O Lord,
> until you come again.

Or:

Save us, Savior of the world,
for by your Cross and Resurrection
you have set us free.

7. Then the Priest, with hands extended, says:

Therefore, holy Father, Celebrant with concelebrants
as we celebrate the memorial of Christ your Son, our Savior,
whom you led through his Passion and Death on the Cross
to the glory of the Resurrection,
and whom you have seated at your right hand,
we proclaim the work of your love until he comes again
and we offer you the Bread of life
and the Chalice of blessing.

Look with favor on the oblation of your Church,
in which we show forth
the paschal Sacrifice of Christ that has been handed on to us,
and grant that, by the power of the Spirit of your love,
we may be counted now and until the day of eternity
among the members of your Son,
in whose Body and Blood we have communion.

By our partaking of this mystery, almighty Father, Celebrant or one concelebrant
give us life through your Spirit,
grant that we may be conformed to the image of your Son,
and confirm us in the bond of communion,
together with N. our Pope and N. our Bishop,*
with all other Bishops,
with Priests and Deacons,
and with your entire people.

Grant that all the faithful of the Church,
looking into the signs of the times by the light of faith,
may constantly devote themselves
to the service of the Gospel.

---

* Mention may be made here of the Coadjutor Bishop, or Auxiliary Bishops, as noted in the *General Instruction of the Roman Missal*, no. 149.

Keep us attentive to the needs of all
that, sharing their grief and pain,
their joy and hope,
we may faithfully bring them the good news of salvation
and go forward with them
along the way of your Kingdom.

Remember our brothers and sisters **(N. and N.)**, *Celebrant or one concelebrant*
who have fallen asleep in the peace of your Christ,
and all the dead, whose faith you alone have known.
Admit them to rejoice in the light of your face,
and in the resurrection give them the fullness of life.

Grant also to us,
when our earthly pilgrimage is done,
that we may come to an eternal dwelling place
and live with you for ever;
there, in communion with the Blessed Virgin Mary, Mother of God,
with the Apostles and Martyrs,
(with Saint N.: the Saint of the day or Patron)
and with all the Saints,
we shall praise and exalt you

He joins his hands.

through Jesus Christ, your Son.

8. *He takes the chalice and the paten with the host and, raising both, he says:*

   Through him, and with him, and in him, *Celebrant alone or with concelebrants*
   O God, almighty Father,
   in the unity of the Holy Spirit,
   all glory and honor is yours,
   for ever and ever.

The people acclaim:

Amen.

Then follows the Communion Rite, p. 663.

IV

Jesus, Who Went About Doing Good

1. The following form of this Eucharistic Prayer is appropriately used with Mass formularies such as, For Refugees and Exiles, In Time of Famine or For Those Suffering Hunger, For Our Oppressors, For Those Held in Captivity, For Those in Prison, For the Sick, For the Dying, For the Grace of a Happy Death, and In Any Need.

V. The Lord be with you.   R. And with your spir-it.

V. Lift up your hearts.   R. We lift them up to the Lord.

V. Let us give thanks to the Lord our God.   R. It is right and just.

It is truly right and just, our duty and our sal-va-tion, al-ways and everywhere to give you thanks, Fa-ther of mercies and faith-ful God. For you have given us Jesus Christ, your Son, as our Lord and Re-deem-er. He always showed compassion for children and for the poor, for the sick and for sin-ners, and he be-came a neigh-bor to the oppressed and the af-flict-ed. By word and deed he an-nounced to the world that you are our Fa-ther and that you care for all your sons and daugh-ters. And so, with all the An-gels

and Saints, we exalt and bless your name and sing the hymn of your glo-ry, as without end we ac-claim:

Holy, Holy, Holy Lord God of hosts . . .

Text without music:

V. **The Lord be with you.**
R. And with your spirit.

V. **Lift up your hearts.**
R. We lift them up to the Lord.

V. **Let us give thanks to the Lord our God.**
R. It is right and just.

It is truly right and just, our duty and our salvation,
always and everywhere to give you thanks,
Father of mercies and faithful God.

For you have given us Jesus Christ, your Son,
as our Lord and Redeemer.

He always showed compassion
for children and for the poor,
for the sick and for sinners,
and he became a neighbor
to the oppressed and the afflicted.

By word and deed he announced to the world
that you are our Father
and that you care for all your sons and daughters.

And so, with all the Angels and Saints,
we exalt and bless your name
and sing the hymn of your glory,
as without end we acclaim:

Holy, Holy, Holy Lord God of hosts.
Heaven and earth are full of your glory.
Hosanna in the highest.
Blessed is he who comes in the name of the Lord.
Hosanna in the highest.

2. *The Priest, with hands extended, says:*   *Celebrant alone*

   You are indeed Holy and to be glorified, O God,
   who love the human race
   and who always walk with us on the journey of life.
   Blessed indeed is your Son,
   present in our midst
   when we are gathered by his love
   and when, as once for the disciples, so now for us,
   he opens the Scriptures and breaks the bread.

3. *He joins his hands and, holding them extended over the offerings, says:*   *Celebrant with concelebrants*

   Therefore, Father most merciful,
   we ask that you send forth your Holy Spirit
   to sanctify these gifts of bread and wine,

   He joins his hands and makes the Sign of the Cross once over the bread and chalice together, saying:

   that they may become for us
   the Body and ✠ Blood

   He joins his hands.

   of our Lord Jesus Christ.

4. *In the formulas that follow, the words of the Lord should be pronounced clearly and distinctly, as the nature of these words requires.*

   On the day before he was to suffer,
   on the night of the Last Supper,

   He takes the bread and, holding it slightly raised above the altar, continues:

   he took bread and said the blessing,
   broke the bread and gave it to his disciples, saying:

   He bows slightly.

   TAKE THIS, ALL OF YOU, AND EAT OF IT,
   FOR THIS IS MY BODY,
   WHICH WILL BE GIVEN UP FOR YOU.

   He shows the consecrated host to the people, places it again on the paten, and genuflects in adoration.

5. *After this, he continues:*

In a similar way, when supper was ended,

He takes the chalice and, holding it slightly raised above the altar, continues:

**he took the chalice, gave you thanks
and gave the chalice to his disciples, saying:**

He bows slightly.

**Take this, all of you, and drink from it,
for this is the chalice of my Blood,
the Blood of the new and eternal covenant,
which will be poured out for you and for many
for the forgiveness of sins.**

Do this in memory of me.

He shows the chalice to the people, places it on the corporal, and genuflects in adoration.

6. *Then he says:*

The mystery of faith. *Celebrant alone*

And the people continue, acclaiming:

We proclaim your Death, O Lord,
and profess your Resurrection
until you come again.

Or:

When we eat this Bread and drink this Cup,
we proclaim your Death, O Lord,
until you come again.

Or:

Save us, Savior of the world,
for by your Cross and Resurrection
you have set us free.

7. Then the Priest, with hands extended, says: Celebrant
                                with concelebrants

> **Therefore, holy Father,**
> **as we celebrate the memorial of Christ your Son, our Savior,**
> **whom you led through his Passion and Death on the Cross**
> **to the glory of the Resurrection,**
> **and whom you have seated at your right hand,**
> **we proclaim the work of your love until he comes again**
> **and we offer you the Bread of life**
> **and the Chalice of blessing.**
>
> **Look with favor on the oblation of your Church,**
> **in which we show forth**
> **the paschal Sacrifice of Christ that has been handed on to us,**
> **and grant that, by the power of the Spirit of your love,**
> **we may be counted now and until the day of eternity**
> **among the members of your Son,**
> **in whose Body and Blood we have communion.**

                              Celebrant or
                            one concelebrant

> **Bring your Church, O Lord,**
> **to perfect faith and charity,**
> **together with N. our Pope and N. our Bishop,**[*]
> **with all Bishops, Priests and Deacons,**
> **and the entire people you have made your own.**
>
> **Open our eyes**
> **to the needs of our brothers and sisters;**
> **inspire in us words and actions**
> **to comfort those who labor and are burdened.**
> **Make us serve them truly,**
> **after the example of Christ and at his command.**
> **And may your Church stand as a living witness**
> **to truth and freedom,**
> **to peace and justice,**
> **that all people may be raised up to a new hope.**

---

[*] Mention may be made here of the Coadjutor Bishop, or Auxiliary Bishops, as noted in the *General Instruction of the Roman Missal*, no. 149.

EUCHARISTIC PRAYER FOR USE IN MASSES FOR VARIOUS NEEDS IV

Remember our brothers and sisters **(N. and N.)**, *(Celebrant or one concelebrant)*
who have fallen asleep in the peace of your Christ,
and all the dead, whose faith you alone have known.
Admit them to rejoice in the light of your face,
and in the resurrection give them the fullness of life.
Grant also to us,
when our earthly pilgrimage is done,
that we may come to an eternal dwelling place
and live with you for ever;
there, in communion with the Blessed Virgin Mary, Mother of God,
with the Apostles and Martyrs,
(with Saint N.: the Saint of the day or Patron)
and with all the Saints,
we shall praise and exalt you

He joins his hands.

through Jesus Christ, your Son.

8. *He takes the chalice and the paten with the host and, raising both, he says:*

Through him, and with him, and in him, *(Celebrant alone or with concelebrants)*
O God, almighty Father,
in the unity of the Holy Spirit,
all glory and honor is yours,
for ever and ever.

The people acclaim:

Amen.

Then follows the Communion Rite, p. 663.

PROPER OF SAINTS

1. The rank of the celebration, namely Solemnity, Feast, or Memorial, is indicated for each day. If no other indication is given, the celebration is an Optional Memorial.

2. For each Solemnity and Feast a complete proper Mass is provided. This is therefore said as printed.

3. As regards Memorials, the following are to be observed:
    a) The proper texts proposed for certain days are always to be used.
    b) Whenever there is a reference to a particular Common, the more appropriate texts should be chosen according to the principles explained at the beginning of the Commons. The page reference given in each case only indicates a text that is particularly suitable.
    c) If, however, a reference is given to several Commons, one or other of them may be used, with due regard for pastoral concerns; it is always allowed to exchange texts among several Masses of the same Common.
        For example, if a Saint is both a Martyr and a Bishop, either the Common of Martyrs or the Common of Pastors (for Bishops) may be used.
    d) Moreover, as well as the Commons that refer to a particular category of Saint (e.g., of Martyrs, Virgins, Pastors, etc.), it is always permitted to use the texts from the Common of Holy Men and Women, which refers to Sainthood in general.
    e) The Prayers over the Offerings and after Communion, unless they are proper, are taken either from the Common or from the current time of the liturgical year.

4. The Masses contained in this Proper of Saints are also used as Votive Masses, with the exception of Masses of the mysteries of the life of the Lord and of the Blessed Virgin Mary (cf. *General Instruction of the Roman Missal,* no. 375) and also of Masses of certain Saints for whom a special Votive Mass is provided. When Masses of the Proper of Saints are used as Votive Masses, words in the prayers indicating the heavenly birthday or the Solemnity or Feast are not used but are replaced by the word **memorial** or **commemoration.**

JANUARY

January 2
Saints Basil the Great and Gregory Nazianzen, Bishops and Doctors of the Church
Memorial

Entrance Antiphon — Cf. Sir 44: 15, 14

Let the peoples recount the wisdom of the Saints,
and let the Church proclaim their praise.
Their names will live on and on.

Collect

O God, who were pleased to give light to your Church
by the example and teaching
of the Bishops Saints Basil and Gregory,
grant, we pray,
that in humility we may learn your truth
and practice it faithfully in charity.
Through our Lord Jesus Christ, your Son,
who lives and reigns with you in the unity of the Holy Spirit,
one God, for ever and ever.

Prayer over the Offerings

Accept this sacrifice from your people, we pray, O Lord,
and make what is offered for your glory,
in honor of Saints Basil and Gregory,
a means to our eternal salvation.
Through Christ our Lord.

Communion Antiphon — Cf. 1 Cor 1: 23-24

We proclaim Christ crucified;
Christ, the power of God and the wisdom of God.

Prayer after Communion

May partaking at the heavenly table, almighty God,
confirm and increase strength from on high
in all who celebrate the feast day of Saints Basil and Gregory,
that we may preserve in integrity the gift of faith
and walk in the path of salvation you trace for us.
Through Christ our Lord.

January 3
The Most Holy Name of Jesus

Entrance Antiphon   Phil 2: 10-11

At the name of Jesus, every knee should bend,
of those in heaven and on earth and under the earth,
and every tongue confess
that Jesus Christ is Lord, to the glory of God the Father.

Collect

O God, who founded the salvation of the human race
on the Incarnation of your Word,
give your peoples the mercy they implore,
so that all may know there is no other name to be invoked
but the Name of your Only Begotten Son.
Who lives and reigns with you in the unity of the Holy Spirit,
one God, for ever and ever.

Prayer over the Offerings

Bringing you these offerings
from what your bounty bestows on us,
we pray, O Lord,
that, just as you have given to Christ,
obedient even until death, the Name that saves,
so you may grant us protection by its power.
Through Christ our Lord.

Communion Antiphon   Ps 8: 2

O Lord, our Lord, how majestic is your name
through all the earth!

Prayer after Communion

May the sacrificial gifts offered to your majesty, O Lord,
to honor Christ's Name
and which we have now received,
fill us, we pray, with your abundant grace,
so that we may come to rejoice
that our names, too, are written in heaven.
Through Christ our Lord.

[In the Dioceses of the United States]

January 4
Saint Elizabeth Ann Seton, Religious
Memorial

Entrance Antiphon
Cf. Prv 14: 1-2

Behold a wise woman who has built her house.
She feared the Lord and walked in the right path.

Or:
Cf. Ps 24 (23): 6

This is the generation
which seeks the face of the God of Jacob.

Collect

O God, who crowned with the gift of true faith
Saint Elizabeth Ann Seton's burning zeal to find you,
grant by her intercession and example
that we may always seek you with diligent love
and find you in daily service with sincere faith.
Through our Lord Jesus Christ, your Son,
who lives and reigns with you in the unity of the Holy Spirit,
one God, for ever and ever.

Prayer over the Offerings

O Lord, we ask that you look graciously
upon our gifts placed on your altar
in celebration of Saint Elizabeth Ann Seton,
and grant by the power at work in this sacrifice,
that we may be more deeply inserted into the mystery of your Son.
Who lives and reigns for ever and ever.

Communion Antiphon
Jn 6: 51

I am the living bread from heaven, says the Lord.
Whoever eats this bread will live for ever;
the bread I shall give is my flesh for the life of the world.

Prayer after Communion

As we partake of the sacrament of our salvation,
while recalling the memory of Saint Elizabeth Ann Seton,
we humbly ask you, O Lord,
that we may be inflamed with a burning desire for the heavenly table,
and by its power consecrate our life faithfully to you.
Through Christ our Lord.

[In the Dioceses of the United States]

January 5
Saint John Neumann, Bishop
Memorial

Entrance Antiphon
Ps 16 (15): 5-6

O Lord, my allotted portion and my cup,
you it is who hold fast my lot.
For me the measuring lines have fallen on pleasant sites;
fair to me indeed is my inheritance.

Collect

O God, who called the Bishop Saint John Neumann,
renowned for his charity and pastoral service,
to shepherd your people in America,
grant by his intercession
that, as we foster the Christian education of youth
and are strengthened by the witness of brotherly love,
we may constantly increase the family of your Church.
Through our Lord Jesus Christ, your Son,
who lives and reigns with you in the unity of the Holy Spirit,
one God, for ever and ever.

Prayer over the Offerings

Merciful Father,
look upon the gifts we have placed on your altar
and grant that we may reflect
the image of Christ your Son,
just as you granted to Saint John Neumann
to imitate what he celebrated.
Through Christ our Lord.

Communion Antiphon
Mt 19: 29

Everyone who has given up home,
brothers, or sisters, father or mother,
wife or children or property for my sake
will receive many times as much and inherit everlasting life.

Prayer after Communion

Refreshed by our participation in the memorial
of the Death and Resurrection of your Son,
we ask, O Lord,
that by the example of Saint John Neumann,
we may experience the power of this Sacrament
and remain constantly in the Church
by the bond of unity and truth.
Through Christ our Lord.

[In the Dioceses of the United States]

January 6
Saint André Bessette, Religious

From the Common of Holy Men and Women: For Religious (p. 1107).

Collect

Lord our God, friend of the lowly,
who gave your servant, Saint André Bessette,
a great devotion to Saint Joseph
and a special commitment to the poor and afflicted,
help us through his intercession
to follow his example of prayer and love
and so come to share with him in your glory.
Through our Lord Jesus Christ, your Son,
who lives and reigns with you in the unity of the Holy Spirit,
one God, for ever and ever.

January 7
Saint Raymond of Penyafort, Priest

From the Common of Pastors: For One Pastor (p. 1078).

Collect

O God, who adorned the Priest Saint Raymond
with the virtue of outstanding mercy and compassion
for sinners and for captives,
grant us, through his intercession,
that, released from slavery to sin,
we may carry out in freedom of spirit
what is pleasing to you.
Through our Lord Jesus Christ, your Son,
who lives and reigns with you in the unity of the Holy Spirit,
one God, for ever and ever.

January 13
Saint Hilary, Bishop and Doctor of the Church

From the Common of Pastors: For a Bishop (p. 1074), or from the Common of Doctors of the Church (p. 1088).

Collect

Grant, we pray, almighty God,
that we may rightly understand and truthfully profess
the divinity of your Son,
which the Bishop Saint Hilary taught with such constancy.
Through our Lord Jesus Christ, your Son,
who lives and reigns with you in the unity of the Holy Spirit,
one God, for ever and ever.

January 17
Saint Anthony, Abbot
Memorial

Entrance Antiphon
Cf. Ps 92 (91): 13-14

The just will flourish like the palm tree,
and grow like a Lebanon cedar,
planted in the house of the Lord,
in the courts of the house of our God.

Collect

O God, who brought the Abbot Saint Anthony
to serve you by a wondrous way of life in the desert,
grant, through his intercession,
that, denying ourselves,
we may always love you above all things.
Through our Lord Jesus Christ, your Son,
who lives and reigns with you in the unity of the Holy Spirit,
one God, for ever and ever.

Prayer over the Offerings

May these offerings of our service,
placed on your altar in commemoration of Saint Anthony,
be acceptable to you, O Lord, we pray,
and grant that, released from earthly attachments,
we may have our riches in you alone.
Through Christ our Lord.

Communion Antiphon
Cf. Mt 19: 21

If you would be perfect,
go, sell what you have, give to the poor,
and follow me, says the Lord.

Prayer after Communion

Nourished for our healing by your Sacraments, O Lord,
may we escape every snare of the enemy unharmed,
just as by your grace Saint Anthony won glorious victories
over the powers of darkness.
Through Christ our Lord.

January 20
Saint Fabian, Pope and Martyr

From the Common of Martyrs: For One Martyr (p. 1059), or from the Common of Pastors: For a Pope (p. 1071).

Collect

O God, glory of your Priests,
grant, we pray,
that, helped by the intercession of your Martyr Saint Fabian,
we may make progress by communion in the faith
and by worthy service.
Through our Lord Jesus Christ, your Son,
who lives and reigns with you in the unity of the Holy Spirit,
one God, for ever and ever.

Saint Sebastian, Martyr

From the Common of Martyrs: For One Martyr (p. 1059).

Collect

Grant us, we pray, O Lord, a spirit of fortitude,
so that, taught by the glorious example
of your Martyr Saint Sebastian,
we may learn to obey you rather than men.
Through our Lord Jesus Christ, your Son,
who lives and reigns with you in the unity of the Holy Spirit,
one God, for ever and ever.

January 21
Saint Agnes, Virgin and Martyr
Memorial

From the Common of Martyrs: For a Virgin Martyr (p. 1068), or from the Common of Virgins: For One Virgin (p. 1092).

Collect

Almighty ever-living God,
who choose what is weak in the world to confound the strong,
mercifully grant,
that we, who celebrate the heavenly birthday of your
 Martyr Saint Agnes,
may follow her constancy in the faith.
Through our Lord Jesus Christ, your Son,
who lives and reigns with you in the unity of the Holy Spirit,
one God, for ever and ever.

[In the Dioceses of the United States]
January 22*
(*January 23, when January 22 falls on a Sunday)
Day of Prayer for the Legal Protection of Unborn Children

From the Masses and Prayers for Various Needs and Occasions: For Giving Thanks to God for the Gift of Human Life (no. 48/1), with white vestments (p. 1321); or For the Preservation of Peace and Justice (no. 30), with violet vestments (p. 1297).

[In the Dioceses of the United States]
January 23
Saint Vincent, Deacon and Martyr

From the Common of Martyrs: For One Martyr (p. 1059).

Collect

Almighty ever-living God,
mercifully pour out your Spirit upon us,
so that our hearts may possess that strong love
by which the Martyr Saint Vincent
triumphed over all bodily torments.
Through our Lord Jesus Christ, your Son,
who lives and reigns with you in the unity of the Holy Spirit,
one God, for ever and ever.

January 24
Saint Francis de Sales, Bishop and Doctor of the Church
Memorial

From the Common of Pastors: For a Bishop (p. 1074), or from the Common of Doctors of the Church (p. 1088).

Collect

O God, who for the salvation of souls
willed that the Bishop Saint Francis de Sales
become all things to all,
graciously grant that, following his example,
we may always display the gentleness of your charity
in the service of our neighbor.
Through our Lord Jesus Christ, your Son,
who lives and reigns with you in the unity of the Holy Spirit,
one God, for ever and ever.

Prayer over the Offerings

Through this saving sacrifice which we offer you, O Lord,
kindle in our hearts that divine fire of the Holy Spirit
with which you wonderfully inflamed
the most gentle soul of Saint Francis de Sales.
Through Christ our Lord.

Prayer after Communion

Grant, we pray, almighty God,
that through the Sacrament we have received,
we may imitate on earth
the charity and meekness of Saint Francis de Sales
and so attain like him the glory of heaven.
Through Christ our Lord.

January 25
THE CONVERSION OF SAINT PAUL THE APOSTLE
Feast

Entrance Antiphon
2 Tm 1: 12; 4: 8

> I know the one in whom I have believed
> and I am sure that he, the just judge, the mighty,
> will keep safe what is my due until that day.

The Gloria in excelsis (Glory to God in the highest) is said.

Collect

> O God, who taught the whole world
> through the preaching of the blessed Apostle Paul,
> draw us, we pray, nearer to you
> through the example of him whose conversion we celebrate today,
> and so make us witnesses to your truth in the world.
> Through our Lord Jesus Christ, your Son,
> who lives and reigns with you in the unity of the Holy Spirit,
> one God, for ever and ever.

Prayer over the Offerings

> As we celebrate the divine mysteries, O Lord, we pray,
> may the Spirit fill us with that light of faith
> with which he constantly enlightened the blessed Apostle Paul
> for the spreading of your glory.
> Through Christ our Lord.

Preface I of the Apostles, p. 594.

Communion Antiphon
Cf. Gal 2: 20

> I live by faith in the Son of God,
> who has loved me
> and given himself up for me.

Prayer after Communion

> May the Sacrament we have received, O Lord our God,
> stir up in us that fire of charity
> with which the blessed Apostle Paul burned ardently
> as he bore his concern for all the Churches.
> Through Christ our Lord.

The Solemn Blessing formula on p. 683 may be used.

January 26
Saints Timothy and Titus, Bishops
Memorial

Entrance Antiphon
Ps 96 (95): 3-4

Tell among the nations his glory,
and his wonders among all the peoples,
for the Lord is great and highly to be praised.

Collect

O God, who adorned Saints Timothy and Titus
with apostolic virtues,
grant, through the intercession of them both,
that, living justly and devoutly in this present age,
we may merit to reach our heavenly homeland.
Through our Lord Jesus Christ, your Son,
who lives and reigns with you in the unity of the Holy Spirit,
one God, for ever and ever.

Prayer over the Offerings

Receive, O Lord, we pray, the offerings of your people,
which we bring in celebration of Saints Timothy and Titus,
and, in your kindness, render us fully acceptable
by giving us sincerity of heart.
Through Christ our Lord.

Communion Antiphon
Mk 16: 15; Mt 28: 20

Go into all the world, and proclaim the Gospel.
I am with you always, says the Lord.

Prayer after Communion

May the Sacrament we have received, O Lord our God,
nourish in us that faith
taught by the preaching of the Apostles
and kept safe by the labors of Saints Timothy and Titus.
Through Christ our Lord.

January 27
Saint Angela Merici, Virgin

From the Common of Virgins: For One Virgin (p. 1092), or from the Common of Holy Men and Women: For Educators (p. 1111).

Collect

May the Virgin Saint Angela never fail to commend us
to your compassion, O Lord, we pray,
that, following the lessons of her charity and prudence,
we may hold fast to your teaching
and express it in what we do.
Through our Lord Jesus Christ, your Son,
who lives and reigns with you in the unity of the Holy Spirit,
one God, for ever and ever.

January 28
Saint Thomas Aquinas, Priest and Doctor of the Church
Memorial

From the Common of Doctors of the Church (p. 1088), or from the Common of Pastors: For One Pastor (p. 1078).

Collect

O God, who made Saint Thomas Aquinas
outstanding in his zeal for holiness
and his study of sacred doctrine,
grant us, we pray,
that we may understand what he taught
and imitate what he accomplished.
Through our Lord Jesus Christ, your Son,
who lives and reigns with you in the unity of the Holy Spirit,
one God, for ever and ever.

January 31
Saint John Bosco, Priest
Memorial

From the Common of Pastors: For One Pastor (p. 1078), or from the Common of Holy Men and Women: For Educators (p. 1111).

Collect

O God, who raised up the Priest Saint John Bosco
as a father and teacher of the young,
grant, we pray,
that, aflame with the same fire of love,
we may seek out souls and serve you alone.
Through our Lord Jesus Christ, your Son,
who lives and reigns with you in the unity of the Holy Spirit,
one God, for ever and ever.

FEBRUARY

February 2
THE PRESENTATION OF THE LORD
Feast

The Blessing of Candles and the Procession

First Form: The Procession

1. At an appropriate hour, a gathering takes place at a smaller church or other suitable place other than inside the church to which the procession will go. The faithful hold in their hands unlighted candles.

2. The Priest, wearing white vestments as for Mass, approaches with the ministers. Instead of the chasuble, the Priest may wear a cope, which he leaves aside after the procession is over.

3. While the candles are being lit, the following antiphon or another appropriate chant is sung.

Be-hold, our Lord will come with power, to en-light-en the eyes of his ser-vants, al-le-lu-ia.

Or:

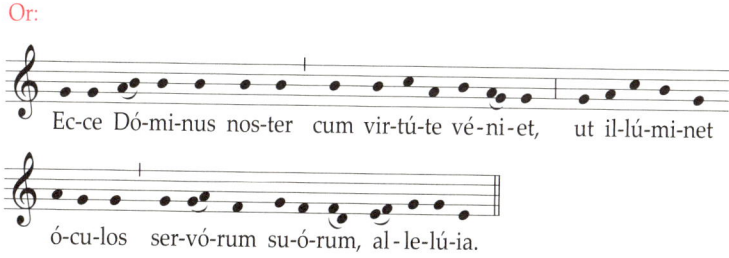

Ec-ce Dó-mi-nus nos-ter cum vir-tú-te vé-ni-et, ut il-lú-mi-net ó-cu-los ser-vó-rum su-ó-rum, al-le-lú-ia.

4. When the chant is concluded, the Priest, facing the people, says: In the name of the Father, and of the Son, and of the Holy Spirit. Then the Priest greets the people in the usual way, and next he gives an introductory address, encouraging the faithful to celebrate the rite of this feast day actively and consciously. He may use these or similar words:

Dear brethren (brothers and sisters),
forty days have passed since we celebrated the joyful feast
of the Nativity of the Lord.
Today is the blessed day
when Jesus was presented in the Temple by Mary and Joseph.
Outwardly he was fulfilling the Law,
but in reality he was coming to meet his believing people.
Prompted by the Holy Spirit,
Simeon and Anna came to the Temple.
Enlightened by the same Spirit,
they recognized the Lord
and confessed him with exultation.
So let us also, gathered together by the Holy Spirit,
proceed to the house of God to encounter Christ.
There we shall find him
and recognize him in the breaking of the bread,
until he comes again, revealed in glory.

5. After the address the Priest blesses the candles, saying, with hands extended:

Let us pray.

O God, source and origin of all light,
who on this day showed to the just man Simeon
the Light for revelation to the Gentiles,
we humbly ask that,
in answer to your people's prayers,
you may be pleased to sanctify with your blessing ✠ these candles,
which we are eager to carry in praise of your name,
so that, treading the path of virtue,
we may reach that light which never fails.
Through Christ our Lord.
R. Amen.

Or:

O God, true light, who create light eternal,
spreading it far and wide,
pour, we pray, into the hearts of the faithful
the brilliance of perpetual light,
so that all who are brightened in your holy temple
by the splendor of these candles
may happily reach the light of your glory.
Through Christ our Lord.
R. Amen.

He sprinkles the candles with holy water without saying anything, and puts incense into the thurible for the procession.

6. Then the Priest receives from the Deacon or a minister the lighted candle prepared for him and the procession begins, with the Deacon announcing (or, if there is no Deacon, the Priest himself):

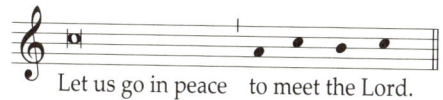
Let us go in peace to meet the Lord.

Or:

Let us go forth in peace.

In this case, all respond:

In the name of Christ. A-men.

7. All carry lighted candles. As the procession moves forward, one or other of the antiphons that follow is sung, namely the antiphon *A light for revelation* with the canticle (Lk 2: 29-32), or the antiphon *Sion, adorn your bridal chamber* or another appropriate chant.

I

Ant.

Lk 2: 29-32

A light for re-ve-la-tion to the Gen-tiles and the glo-ry of your peo-ple Is-ra-el.

Or:

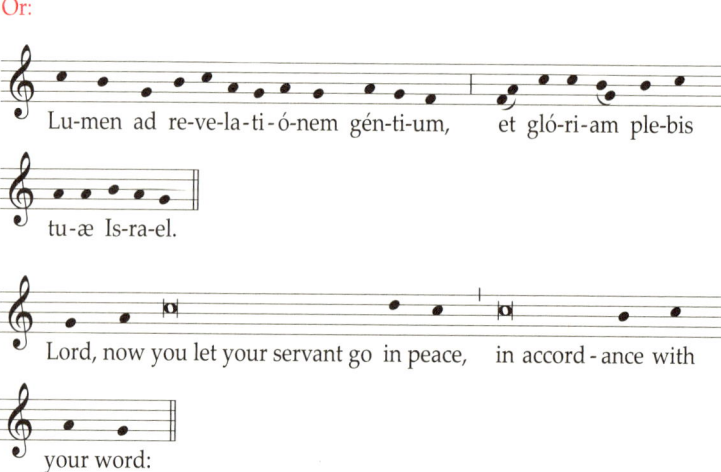

Lu-men ad re-ve-la-ti-ó-nem gén-ti-um, et gló-ri-am ple-bis tu-æ Is-ra-el.

Lord, now you let your servant go in peace, in accord-ance with your word:

Ant.

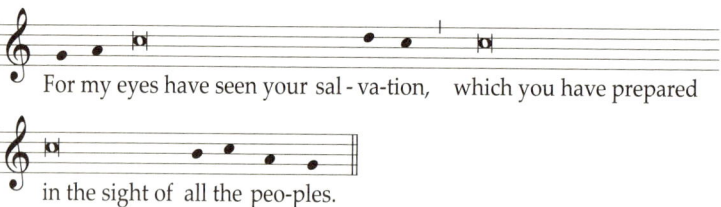

For my eyes have seen your sal-va-tion, which you have prepared in the sight of all the peo-ples.

Ant.

Text without music:

> Ant. A light for revelation to the Gentiles
> and the glory of your people Israel.
>
> Lord, now you let your servant go in peace,
> in accordance with your word.
>
> Ant. A light for revelation to the Gentiles . . .
> For my eyes have seen your salvation.
>
> Ant. A light for revelation to the Gentiles . . .
> Which you have prepared in the sight of all peoples.
>
> Ant. A light for revelation to the Gentiles . . .

II

> Ant. Sion, adorn your bridal chamber and welcome Christ the King; take Mary in your arms, who is the gate of heaven, for she herself is carrying the King of glory and new light. A Virgin she remains, though bringing in her hands the Son before the morning star begotten, whom Simeon, taking in his arms announced to the peoples as Lord of life and death and Savior of the world.

8. As the procession enters the church, the Entrance Antiphon of the Mass is sung. When the Priest has arrived at the altar, he venerates it and, if appropriate, incenses it. Then he goes to the chair, where he takes off the cope, if he used it in the procession, and puts on a chasuble. After the singing of the hymn Gloria in excelsis (Glory to God in the highest), he says the Collect as usual. The Mass continues in the usual manner.

Second Form: The Solemn Entrance

9. Whenever a procession cannot take place, the faithful gather in church, holding candles in their hands. The Priest, wearing white sacred vestments as for Mass, together with the ministers and a representative group of the faithful, goes to a suitable place, either in front of the church door or inside the church itself, where at least a large part of the faithful can conveniently participate in the rite.

10. When the Priest reaches the place appointed for the blessing of the candles, candles are lit while the antiphon Behold, our Lord (no. 3) or another appropriate chant is sung.

11. Then, after the greeting and address, the Priest blesses the candles, as above nos. 4-5; and then the procession to the altar takes place, with singing (nos. 6-7). For Mass, what is indicated in no. 8 above is observed.

At the Mass

Entrance Antiphon   Cf. Ps 48 (47): 10-11

Your merciful love, O God,
we have received in the midst of your temple.
Your praise, O God, like your name,
reaches the ends of the earth;
your right hand is filled with saving justice.

The Gloria in excelsis (Glory to God in the highest) is said.

Collect

**Almighty ever-living God,
we humbly implore your majesty
that, just as your Only Begotten Son
was presented on this day in the Temple
in the substance of our flesh,
so, by your grace,
we may be presented to you with minds made pure.
Through our Lord Jesus Christ, your Son,
who lives and reigns with you in the unity of the Holy Spirit,
one God, for ever and ever.**

When this Feast falls on a Sunday, the Creed is said.

Prayer over the Offerings

May the offering made with exultation by your Church
be pleasing to you, O Lord, we pray,
for you willed that your Only Begotten Son
be offered to you for the life of the world
as the Lamb without blemish.
Who lives and reigns for ever and ever.

Preface: The mystery of the Presentation of the Lord.

V. The Lord be with you. R. And with your spir-it.

V. Lift up your hearts. R. We lift them up to the Lord.

V. Let us give thanks to the Lord our God. R. It is right and just.

It is truly right and just, our duty and our sal-va-tion, al-ways and everywhere to give you thanks, Lord, holy Father, almighty and e-ter-nal God. For your co-eternal Son was presented on this day in the Tem-ple and revealed by the Spirit as the glo-ry of Is-ra-el and Light of the na-tions. And so, we, too, go forth, rejoicing to encounter your Sal-va-tion, and with the Angels and Saints praise you, as without end we ac-claim:

Holy, Holy, Holy Lord God of hosts . . .

Text without music:

V. **The Lord be with you.**
R. And with your spirit.

V. **Lift up your hearts.**
R. We lift them up to the Lord.

V. **Let us give thanks to the Lord our God.**
R. It is right and just.

It is truly right and just, our duty and our salvation,
always and everywhere to give you thanks,
Lord, holy Father, almighty and eternal God.

For your co-eternal Son was presented on this day in the Temple
and revealed by the Spirit
as the glory of Israel and Light of the nations.

And so, we, too, go forth, rejoicing to encounter your Salvation,
and with the Angels and Saints
praise you, as without end we acclaim:

Holy, Holy, Holy Lord God of hosts . . .

Communion Antiphon
Lk 2: 30-31

My eyes have seen your salvation,
which you prepared in the sight of all the peoples.

Prayer after Communion

By these holy gifts which we have received, O Lord,
bring your grace to perfection within us,
and, as you fulfilled Simeon's expectation
that he would not see death
until he had been privileged to welcome the Christ,
so may we, going forth to meet the Lord,
obtain the gift of eternal life.
Through Christ our Lord.

February 3
Saint Blaise, Bishop and Martyr

From the Common of Martyrs: For One Martyr (p. 1059), or from the Common of Pastors: For a Bishop (p. 1074).

Collect

> Hear, O Lord, the supplications your people make
> under the patronage of the Martyr Saint Blaise,
> and grant that they may rejoice in peace in this present life,
> and find help for life eternal.
> Through our Lord Jesus Christ, your Son,
> who lives and reigns with you in the unity of the Holy Spirit,
> one God, for ever and ever.

Saint Ansgar, Bishop

From the Common of Pastors: For Missionaries (p. 1084), or For a Bishop (p. 1074).

Collect

> O God, who willed to send the Bishop Saint Ansgar
> to enlighten many peoples,
> grant us, through his intercession,
> that we may always walk in the light of your truth.
> Through our Lord Jesus Christ, your Son,
> who lives and reigns with you in the unity of the Holy Spirit,
> one God, for ever and ever.

February 5
Saint Agatha, Virgin and Martyr
Memorial

From the Common of Martyrs: For a Virgin Martyr (p. 1068), or from the Common of Virgins: For One Virgin (p. 1092).

Collect

May the Virgin Martyr Saint Agatha
implore your compassion for us, O Lord, we pray,
for she found favor with you
by the courage of her martyrdom
and the merit of her chastity.
Through our Lord Jesus Christ, your Son,
who lives and reigns with you in the unity of the Holy Spirit,
one God, for ever and ever.

February 6
Saint Paul Miki and Companions, Martyrs
Memorial

From the Common of Martyrs: For Several Martyrs (p. 1052).

Collect

O God, strength of all the Saints,
who through the Cross were pleased to call
the Martyrs Saint Paul Miki and companions to life,
grant, we pray, that by their intercession
we may hold with courage even until death
to the faith that we profess.
Through our Lord Jesus Christ, your Son,
who lives and reigns with you in the unity of the Holy Spirit,
one God, for ever and ever.

February 8
Saint Jerome Emiliani

From the Common of Holy Men and Women: For Educators (p. 1111).

Collect

O God, Father of mercies,
who sent Saint Jerome Emiliani as a helper and father to orphans,
grant, through his intercession,
that we may preserve faithfully the spirit of adoption,
by which we are called, and truly are, your children.
Through our Lord Jesus Christ, your Son,
who lives and reigns with you in the unity of the Holy Spirit,
one God, for ever and ever.

Saint Josephine Bakhita, Virgin

From the Common of Virgins: For One Virgin (p. 1092).

Collect

O God, who led Saint Josephine Bakhita from abject slavery
to the dignity of being your daughter and a bride of Christ,
grant, we pray, that by her example
we may show constant love for the Lord Jesus crucified,
remaining steadfast in charity
and prompt to show compassion.
Through our Lord Jesus Christ, your Son,
who lives and reigns with you in the unity of the Holy Spirit,
one God, for ever and ever.

February 10
Saint Scholastica, Virgin
Memorial

From the Common of Virgins: For One Virgin (p. 1092), or from the Common of Holy Men and Women: For a Nun (p. 1106).

Collect

As we celebrate anew the Memorial of the Virgin Saint Scholastica,
we pray, O Lord,
that, following her example,
we may serve you with pure love
and happily receive what comes from loving you.
Through our Lord Jesus Christ, your Son,
who lives and reigns with you in the unity of the Holy Spirit,
one God, for ever and ever.

February 11
Our Lady of Lourdes

From the Common of the Blessed Virgin Mary (p. 1039).

Collect

Grant us, O merciful God, protection in our weakness,
that we, who keep the Memorial of the Immaculate Mother of God,
may, with the help of her intercession,
rise up from our iniquities.
Through our Lord Jesus Christ, your Son,
who lives and reigns with you in the unity of the Holy Spirit,
one God, for ever and ever.

February 14
Saints Cyril, Monk, and Methodius, Bishop
Memorial

Entrance Antiphon

These are holy men who became friends of God,
glorious heralds of divine truth.

Collect

O God, who enlightened the Slavic peoples
through the brothers Saints Cyril and Methodius,
grant that our hearts may grasp the words of your teaching,
and perfect us as a people of one accord
in true faith and right confession.
Through our Lord Jesus Christ, your Son,
who lives and reigns with you in the unity of the Holy Spirit,
one God, for ever and ever.

Prayer over the Offerings

Look, O Lord, upon the offerings
which we bring before your majesty
in commemoration of Saints Cyril and Methodius,
and grant that these gifts may become the sign of a new humanity,
reconciled to you in loving charity.
Through Christ our Lord.

Communion Antiphon   Cf. Mk 16: 20

The disciples went forth and preached the Gospel,
while the Lord worked with them,
confirming the word through accompanying signs.

Prayer after Communion

O God, Father of all nations,
who make us sharers in the one Bread and the one Spirit
and heirs of the eternal banquet,
grant in your kindness
on this feast day of Saints Cyril and Methodius,
that the multitude of your children,
persevering in the same faith,
may be united in building up
the Kingdom of justice and peace.
Through Christ our Lord.

February 17
The Seven Holy Founders of the Servite Order

From the Common of Holy Men and Women: For Religious (p. 1107).

Collect

Impart to us, O Lord, in kindness
the filial devotion with which the holy brothers
venerated so devoutly the Mother of God
and led your people to yourself.
Through our Lord Jesus Christ, your Son,
who lives and reigns with you in the unity of the Holy Spirit,
one God, for ever and ever.

February 21
Saint Peter Damian, Bishop and Doctor of the Church

From the Common of Doctors of the Church (p. 1088), or from the Common of Pastors: For a Bishop (p. 1074).

Collect

Grant, we pray, almighty God,
that we may so follow the teaching and example
of the Bishop Saint Peter Damian,
that, putting nothing before Christ
and always ardent in the service of your Church,
we may be led to the joys of eternal light.
Through our Lord Jesus Christ, your Son,
who lives and reigns with you in the unity of the Holy Spirit,
one God, for ever and ever.

February 22
THE CHAIR OF SAINT PETER THE APOSTLE
Feast

Entrance Antiphon   Lk 22: 32

The Lord says to Simon Peter:
I have prayed for you that your faith may not fail,
and, once you have turned back, strengthen your brothers.

The Gloria in excelsis (Glory to God in the highest) is said.

Collect

Grant, we pray, almighty God,
that no tempests may disturb us,
for you have set us fast
on the rock of the Apostle Peter's confession of faith.
Through our Lord Jesus Christ, your Son,
who lives and reigns with you in the unity of the Holy Spirit,
one God, for ever and ever.

Prayer over the Offerings

Accept with favor, O Lord, we pray,
the prayers and offerings of your Church,
that, with Saint Peter as her shepherd,
she may come to an eternal inheritance,
for it is through his teaching
that she holds the faith in its integrity.
Through Christ our Lord.

Preface I of the Apostles, p. 594.

Communion Antiphon   Cf. Mt 16: 16, 18

Peter said to Jesus: You are the Christ, the Son of the living God.
And Jesus replied: You are Peter,
and upon this rock I will build my Church.

Prayer after Communion

O God, who at our celebration
of the feast day of the blessed Apostle Peter
have nourished us by communion in the Body and Blood of Christ,
grant, we pray, that this redeeming exchange
may be for us a Sacrament of unity and peace.
Through Christ our Lord.

The Solemn Blessing formula on p. 683 may be used.

February 23
Saint Polycarp, Bishop and Martyr
Memorial

From the Common of Martyrs: For One Martyr (p. 1059), or from the Common of Pastors: For a Bishop (p. 1074).

Collect

God of all creation,
who were pleased to give the Bishop Saint Polycarp
a place in the company of the Martyrs,
grant, through his intercession,
that, sharing with him in the chalice of Christ,
we may rise through the Holy Spirit to eternal life.
Through our Lord Jesus Christ, your Son,
who lives and reigns with you in the unity of the Holy Spirit,
one God, for ever and ever.

MARCH

[In the Dioceses of the United States]

March 3
Saint Katharine Drexel, Virgin

From the Common of Virgins: For One Virgin (p. 1092).

Collect

God of love,
you called Saint Katharine Drexel
to teach the message of the Gospel
and to bring the life of the Eucharist
to the Native American and African American peoples;
by her prayers and example,
enable us to work for justice
among the poor and the oppressed,
and keep us undivided in love
in the eucharistic community of your Church.
Through our Lord Jesus Christ, your Son,
who lives and reigns with you in the unity of the Holy Spirit,
one God, for ever and ever.

March 4
Saint Casimir

From the Common of Holy Men and Women: For One Saint (p. 1101).

Collect

Almighty God, to serve you is to reign;
grant that, with the help of Saint Casimir's intercession,
we may constantly serve you in holiness and justice.
Through our Lord Jesus Christ, your Son,
who lives and reigns with you in the unity of the Holy Spirit,
one God, for ever and ever.

March 7
Saints Perpetua and Felicity, Martyrs
Memorial

Entrance Antiphon
The souls of the Saints are rejoicing in heaven,
the Saints who followed the footsteps of Christ,
and since for love of him they shed their blood,
they now exult with Christ for ever.

Collect
O God, at the urging of whose love
the Martyrs Saints Perpetua and Felicity
defied their persecutors and overcame the torment of death,
grant, we ask, by their prayers, that we may ever grow in
    your love.
Through our Lord Jesus Christ, your Son,
who lives and reigns with you in the unity of the Holy Spirit,
one God, for ever and ever.

Prayer over the Offerings
As we joyfully offer, O Lord, this day's sacrifice,
recalling the heaven-sent victory of Saints Perpetua and Felicity,
we proclaim by it your mighty deeds
and rejoice at having gained their glorious intercession.
Through Christ our Lord.

Communion Antiphon   2 Cor 4: 11
For the sake of Jesus we are given up to death,
that the life of Jesus may be manifested in our mortal flesh.

Prayer after Communion
As we draw everlasting joys, O Lord,
from our participation in this Sacrament
and from the Memorial of Saints Perpetua and Felicity,
we humbly implore,
that by your gift we may truly understand
what you grant us to enact in diligent service.
Through Christ our Lord.

March 8
Saint John of God, Religious

From the Common of Holy Men and Women: For Religious (p. 1107), or For Those Who Practiced Works of Mercy (p. 1110).

Collect

O God, who filled Saint John of God
with a spirit of compassion,
grant, we pray,
that, giving ourselves to works of charity,
we may merit to be found among the elect in your Kingdom.
Through our Lord Jesus Christ, your Son,
who lives and reigns with you in the unity of the Holy Spirit,
one God, for ever and ever.

March 9
Saint Frances of Rome, Religious

From the Common of Holy Men and Women: For Holy Women (p. 1113), or For Religious (p. 1107).

Collect

O God, who have given us in Saint Frances of Rome
a singular model of both married and monastic life,
grant us perseverance in your service,
that in every circumstance of life we may see and follow you.
Through our Lord Jesus Christ, your Son,
who lives and reigns with you in the unity of the Holy Spirit,
one God, for ever and ever.

March 17
Saint Patrick, Bishop

From the Common of Pastors: For Missionaries (p. 1084), or For a Bishop (p. 1074).

Collect

O God, who chose the Bishop Saint Patrick
to preach your glory to the peoples of Ireland,
grant, through his merits and intercession,
that those who glory in the name of Christian
may never cease to proclaim your wondrous deeds to all.
Through our Lord Jesus Christ, your Son,
who lives and reigns with you in the unity of the Holy Spirit,
one God, for ever and ever.

March 18
Saint Cyril of Jerusalem, Bishop and Doctor of the Church

From the Common of Pastors: For a Bishop (p. 1074), or from the Common of Doctors of the Church (p. 1088).

Collect

O God, who through the Bishop Saint Cyril of Jerusalem
led your Church in a wonderful way
to a deeper sense of the mysteries of salvation,
grant us, through his intercession,
that we may so acknowledge your Son
as to have life ever more abundantly.
Through our Lord Jesus Christ, your Son,
who lives and reigns with you in the unity of the Holy Spirit,
one God, for ever and ever.

March 19
SAINT JOSEPH,
SPOUSE OF THE BLESSED VIRGIN MARY
Solemnity

Entrance Antiphon
Cf. Lk 12: 42

> Behold, a faithful and prudent steward,
> whom the Lord set over his household.

The Gloria in excelsis (Glory to God in the highest) is said.

Collect

> Grant, we pray, almighty God,
> that by Saint Joseph's intercession
> your Church may constantly watch over
> the unfolding of the mysteries of human salvation,
> whose beginnings you entrusted to his faithful care.
> Through our Lord Jesus Christ, your Son,
> who lives and reigns with you in the unity of the Holy Spirit,
> one God, for ever and ever.

The Creed is said.

Prayer over the Offerings

> We pray, O Lord,
> that, just as Saint Joseph served with loving care
> your Only Begotten Son, born of the Virgin Mary,
> so we may be worthy to minister
> with a pure heart at your altar.
> Through Christ our Lord.

Preface: The mission of Saint Joseph.

V. The Lord be with you. R. And with your spirit.

V. Lift up your hearts. R. We lift them up to the Lord.

V. Let us give thanks to the Lord our God. R. It is right and just.

It is truly right and just, our duty and our salvation, always and everywhere to give you thanks, Lord, holy Father, almighty and eternal God, and on the Solemnity of Saint Joseph to give you fitting praise, to glorify you and bless you. For this just man was given by you as spouse to the Virgin Mother of God and set as a wise and faithful servant in charge of your household to watch like a father over your Only Begotten Son, who was conceived by the overshadowing of the Holy Spirit, our Lord

Je-sus Christ. Through him the Angels praise your maj-es-ty, Domin-ions a-dore and Powers trem-ble be-fore you. Heav-en and the Virtues of heaven and the bless-ed Ser-a-phim worship to-geth-er with ex-ul-ta-tion. May our voices, we pray, join with theirs in hum-ble praise, as we ac-claim:

Holy, Holy, Holy Lord God of hosts . . .

Text without music:

V. **The Lord be with you.**
R. And with your spirit.

V. **Lift up your hearts.**
R. We lift them up to the Lord.

V. **Let us give thanks to the Lord our God.**
R. It is right and just.

It is truly right and just, our duty and our salvation,
always and everywhere to give you thanks,
Lord, holy Father, almighty and eternal God,
and on the Solemnity of Saint Joseph
to give you fitting praise,
to glorify you and bless you.

For this just man was given by you
as spouse to the Virgin Mother of God
and set as a wise and faithful servant
in charge of your household
to watch like a father over your Only Begotten Son,
who was conceived by the overshadowing of the Holy Spirit,
our Lord Jesus Christ.

Through him the Angels praise your majesty,
Dominions adore and Powers tremble before you.
Heaven and the Virtues of heaven and the blessed Seraphim
worship together with exultation.
May our voices, we pray, join with theirs
in humble praise, as we acclaim:

Holy, Holy, Holy Lord God of hosts . . .

Communion Antiphon   Mt 25: 21

Well done, good and faithful servant.
Come, share your master's joy.

Prayer after Communion

Defend with unfailing protection,
O Lord, we pray,
the family you have nourished
with food from this altar,
as they rejoice at the Solemnity of Saint Joseph,
and graciously keep safe your gifts among them.
Through Christ our Lord.

March 23
Saint Turibius of Mogrovejo, Bishop

From the Common of Pastors: For a Bishop (p. 1074).

Collect

O God, who gave increase to your Church
through the apostolic labors and zeal for truth
of the Bishop Saint Turibius,
grant that the people consecrated to you
may always receive new growth in faith and holiness.
Through our Lord Jesus Christ, your Son,
who lives and reigns with you in the unity of the Holy Spirit,
one God, for ever and ever.

March 25
THE ANNUNCIATION OF THE LORD
Solemnity

Whenever this Solemnity occurs during Holy Week, it is transferred to the Monday after the Second Sunday of Easter.

Entrance Antiphon
Heb 10: 5, 7

The Lord said, as he entered the world:
Behold, I come to do your will, O God.

The Gloria in excelsis *(Glory to God in the highest) is said.*

Collect

O God, who willed that your Word
should take on the reality of human flesh
in the womb of the Virgin Mary,
grant, we pray,
that we, who confess our Redeemer to be God and man,
may merit to become partakers even in his divine nature.
Who lives and reigns with you in the unity of the Holy Spirit,
one God, for ever and ever.

The Creed is said. At the words and was incarnate *all genuflect.*

Prayer over the Offerings

Be pleased, almighty God,
to accept your Church's offering,
so that she, who is aware that her beginnings
lie in the Incarnation of your Only Begotten Son,
may rejoice to celebrate his mysteries on this Solemnity.
Who lives and reigns for ever and ever.

Preface: The mystery of the Incarnation.

V. The Lord be with you.   R. And with your spir-it.

V. Lift up your hearts.   R. We lift them up to the Lord.

V. Let us give thanks to the Lord our God.   R. It is right and just.

It is truly right and just, our duty and our sal-va-tion, al-ways and everywhere to give you thanks, Lord, holy Father, almighty and e-ter-nal God, through Christ our Lord. For the Virgin Mary heard with faith that the Christ was to be born among men and for men's sake by the over-shad-ow-ing pow-er of the Ho-ly Spir-it. Lov-ingly she bore him in her im-mac-u-late womb, that the prom-ises to the children of Israel might come a-bout and the hope of na-tions be accomplished be-yond all tell-ing. Through him the

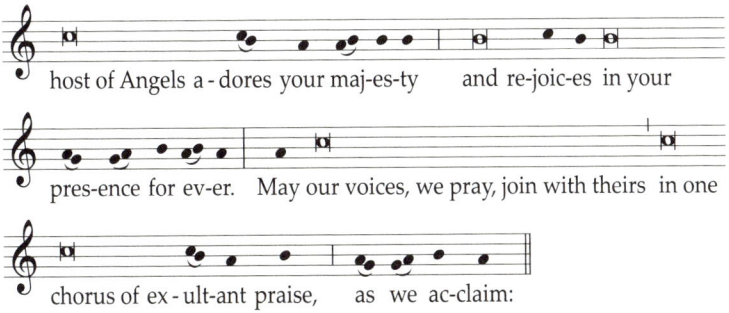
host of Angels a-dores your maj-es-ty and re-joic-es in your pres-ence for ev-er. May our voices, we pray, join with theirs in one chorus of ex-ult-ant praise, as we ac-claim:

Holy, Holy, Holy Lord God of hosts . . .

Text without music:

V. **The Lord be with you.**
R. And with your spirit.

V. **Lift up your hearts.**
R. We lift them up to the Lord.

V. **Let us give thanks to the Lord our God.**
R. It is right and just.

It is truly right and just, our duty and our salvation,
always and everywhere to give you thanks,
Lord, holy Father, almighty and eternal God,
through Christ our Lord.

For the Virgin Mary heard with faith
that the Christ was to be born among men and for men's sake
by the overshadowing power of the Holy Spirit.
Lovingly she bore him in her immaculate womb,
that the promises to the children of Israel might come about
and the hope of nations be accomplished beyond all telling.

Through him the host of Angels adores your majesty
and rejoices in your presence for ever.
May our voices, we pray, join with theirs
in one chorus of exultant praise, as we acclaim:

Holy, Holy, Holy Lord God of hosts . . .

Communion Antiphon
Is 7: 14

Behold, a Virgin shall conceive and bear a son;
and his name will be called Emmanuel.

Prayer after Communion

**Confirm in our minds the mysteries of the true faith,
we pray, O Lord,
so that, confessing that he who was conceived of the Virgin Mary
is true God and true man,
we may, through the saving power of his Resurrection,
merit to attain eternal joy.
Through Christ our Lord.**

APRIL

April 2
Saint Francis of Paola, Hermit

From the Common of Holy Men and Women: For Religious (p. 1107).

Collect

O God, exaltation of the lowly,
who raised Saint Francis of Paola to the glory of your Saints,
grant, we pray, that by his merits and example
we may happily attain the rewards promised to the humble.
Through our Lord Jesus Christ, your Son,
who lives and reigns with you in the unity of the Holy Spirit,
one God, for ever and ever.

April 4
Saint Isidore, Bishop and Doctor of the Church

From the Common of Pastors: For a Bishop (p. 1074), or from the Common of Doctors of the Church (p. 1088).

Collect

Graciously hear the prayers, O Lord,
which we make in commemoration of Saint Isidore,
that your Church may be aided by his intercession,
just as she has been instructed by his heavenly teaching.
Through our Lord Jesus Christ, your Son,
who lives and reigns with you in the unity of the Holy Spirit,
one God, for ever and ever.

April 5
Saint Vincent Ferrer, Priest

From the Common of Pastors: For Missionaries (p. 1084).

Collect

O God, who raised up the Priest Saint Vincent Ferrer
to minister by the preaching of the Gospel,
grant, we pray,
that, when the Judge comes,
whom Saint Vincent proclaimed on earth,
we may be among those blessed
to behold him reigning in heaven.
Who lives and reigns with you in the unity of the Holy Spirit,
one God, for ever and ever.

April 7
Saint John Baptist de la Salle, Priest
Memorial

From the Common of Pastors: For One Pastor (p. 1078), or from the Common of Holy Men and Women: For Educators (p. 1111).

Collect

O God, who chose Saint John Baptist de la Salle
to educate young Christians,
raise up, we pray, teachers in your Church
ready to devote themselves wholeheartedly
to the human and Christian formation of the young.
Through our Lord Jesus Christ, your Son,
who lives and reigns with you in the unity of the Holy Spirit,
one God, for ever and ever.

April 11
Saint Stanislaus, Bishop and Martyr
Memorial

From the Common of Martyrs: For One Martyr (p. 1059, or, during Easter Time, p. 1065), or from the Common of Pastors: For a Bishop (p. 1074).

Collect

O God, for whose honor the Bishop Saint Stanislaus
fell beneath the swords of his persecutors,
grant, we pray,
that we may persevere strong in faith even until death.
Through our Lord Jesus Christ, your Son,
who lives and reigns with you in the unity of the Holy Spirit,
one God, for ever and ever.

April 13
Saint Martin I, Pope and Martyr

From the Common of Martyrs: For One Martyr (p. 1059, or, during Easter Time, p. 1065), or from the Common of Pastors: For a Pope (p. 1071).

Collect

Grant, almighty God,
that we may withstand the trials of this world
with invincible firmness of purpose,
just as you did not allow your Martyr Pope Saint Martin the First
to be daunted by threats or broken by suffering.
Through our Lord Jesus Christ, your Son,
who lives and reigns with you in the unity of the Holy Spirit,
one God, for ever and ever.

April 21
Saint Anselm, Bishop and Doctor of the Church

From the Common of Pastors: For a Bishop (p. 1074), or from the Common of Doctors of the Church (p. 1088).

Collect

O God, who led the Bishop Saint Anselm
to seek out and teach the depths of your wisdom,
grant, we pray,
that our faith in you may so aid our understanding,
that what we believe by your command
may give delight to our hearts.
Through our Lord Jesus Christ, your Son,
who lives and reigns with you in the unity of the Holy Spirit,
one God, for ever and ever.

April 23
Saint George, Martyr

From the Common of Martyrs: For One Martyr during Easter Time (p. 1065).

Collect

Extolling your might, O Lord,
we humbly implore you,
that, as Saint George imitated the Passion of the Lord,
so he may lend us ready help in our weakness.
Through our Lord Jesus Christ, your Son,
who lives and reigns with you in the unity of the Holy Spirit,
one God, for ever and ever.

Saint Adalbert, Bishop and Martyr

From the Common of Martyrs: For One Martyr during Easter Time (p. 1065), or from the Common of Pastors: For a Bishop (p. 1074).

Collect

O God, who bestowed the crown of martyrdom
on the Bishop Saint Adalbert,
as he burned with zeal for souls,
grant, we pray, by his prayers,
that the obedience of the flock may never fail the shepherds,
nor the care of the shepherds be ever lacking to the flock.
Through our Lord Jesus Christ, your Son,
who lives and reigns with you in the unity of the Holy Spirit,
one God, for ever and ever.

April 24
Saint Fidelis of Sigmaringen, Priest and Martyr

From the Common of Martyrs: For One Martyr during Easter Time (p. 1065), or from the Common of Pastors: For One Pastor (p. 1078).

Collect

O God, who were pleased to award
the palm of martyrdom to Saint Fidelis
as, burning with love for you, he propagated the faith,
grant, we pray, through his intercession,
that, grounded in charity,
we may merit to know with him
the power of the Resurrection of Christ.
Who lives and reigns with you in the unity of the Holy Spirit,
one God, for ever and ever.

April 25
SAINT MARK, EVANGELIST
Feast

Entrance Antiphon   Mk 16: 15

Go into all the world,
and proclaim the Gospel to every creature, alleluia.

The Gloria in excelsis (Glory to God in the highest) is said.

Collect

O God, who raised up Saint Mark, your Evangelist,
and endowed him with the grace to preach the Gospel,
grant, we pray,
that we may so profit from his teaching
as to follow faithfully in the footsteps of Christ.
Who lives and reigns with you in the unity of the Holy Spirit,
one God, for ever and ever.

Prayer over the Offerings

As we venerate the glory of Saint Mark,
we offer you, Lord, the sacrifice of praise
and humbly beseech you,
that your Church may always persevere
in the preaching of the Gospel.
Through Christ our Lord.

Preface II of the Apostles, p. 596.

Communion Antiphon   Mt 28: 20

Behold, I am with you always,
even to the end of the age, says the Lord, alleluia.

Prayer after Communion

Grant, we pray, almighty God,
that what we have received from your holy altar
may sanctify us and make us strong
in the faith of the Gospel which Saint Mark proclaimed.
Through Christ our Lord.

April 28
Saint Peter Chanel, Priest and Martyr

From the Common of Martyrs: For One Martyr during Easter Time (p. 1065), or from the Common of Pastors: For Missionaries (p. 1084).

Collect

O God, who for the spreading of your Church
crowned Saint Peter Chanel with martyrdom,
grant that, in these days of paschal joy,
we may so celebrate the mysteries of Christ's Death and
　　Resurrection
as to bear worthy witness to newness of life.
Through our Lord Jesus Christ, your Son,
who lives and reigns with you in the unity of the Holy Spirit,
one God, for ever and ever.

Saint Louis Grignion de Montfort, Priest

From the Common of Pastors: For One Pastor (p. 1078).

Collect

O God, who willed to direct the steps of the Priest Saint Louis
along the way of salvation and of the love of Christ,
in the company of the Blessed Virgin,
grant us, by his example,
that, meditating on the mysteries of your love,
we may strive tirelessly for the building up of your Church.
Through our Lord Jesus Christ, your Son,
who lives and reigns with you in the unity of the Holy Spirit,
one God, for ever and ever.

Or:

Almighty and eternal God, who made the Priest Saint Louis
an outstanding witness and teacher
of total devotion to Christ your Son
through the hands of his Blessed Mother,
grant us that, following the same spiritual path,
we may constantly spread your Kingdom.
Through our Lord Jesus Christ, your Son,
who lives and reigns with you in the unity of the Holy Spirit,
one God, for ever and ever.

April 29
Saint Catherine of Siena, Virgin and Doctor of the Church
Memorial

Entrance Antiphon
Here is a wise virgin, from among the number of the prudent,
who went forth with lighted lamp to meet Christ, alleluia.

Collect
O God, who set Saint Catherine of Siena on fire with divine love
in her contemplation of the Lord's Passion
and her service of your Church,
grant, through her intercession,
that your people,
participating in the mystery of Christ,
may ever exult in the revelation of his glory.
Who lives and reigns with you in the unity of the Holy Spirit,
one God, for ever and ever.

Prayer over the Offerings
Accept, O Lord, the saving sacrifice we offer
in commemoration of Saint Catherine,
so that, instructed by her teaching,
we may give ever more fervent thanks
to you, the one true God.
Through Christ our Lord.

Communion Antiphon
Cf. 1 Jn 1: 7

If we walk in the light, as God is in the light,
then we have fellowship with one another,
and the blood of his Son Jesus Christ
cleanses us from all sin, alleluia.

Prayer after Communion
May the heavenly table
at which we have been fed, O Lord,
confer eternal life upon us,
as even in this world
it nourished the life of Saint Catherine.
Through Christ our Lord.

April 30
Saint Pius V, Pope

From the Common of Pastors: For a Pope (p. 1071).

Collect

O God, who in your providence
raised up Pope Saint Pius the Fifth in your Church
that the faith might be safeguarded
and more fitting worship be offered to you,
grant, through his intercession,
that we may participate in your mysteries
with lively faith and fruitful charity.
Through our Lord Jesus Christ, your Son,
who lives and reigns with you in the unity of the Holy Spirit,
one God, for ever and ever.

MAY

May 1
Saint Joseph the Worker

Entrance Antiphon   Ps 128 (127): 1-2

Blessed are all who fear the Lord and walk in his ways!
By the labor of your hands you shall eat;
blessed are you, and blessed will you be, alleluia.

Collect

O God, Creator of all things,
who laid down for the human race the law of work,
graciously grant
that by the example of Saint Joseph and under his patronage
we may complete the works you set us to do
and attain the rewards you promise.
Through our Lord Jesus Christ, your Son,
who lives and reigns with you in the unity of the Holy Spirit,
one God, for ever and ever.

Prayer over the Offerings

O God, fount of all mercy,
look upon our offerings,
which we bring before your majesty
in commemoration of Saint Joseph,
and mercifully grant that the gifts we offer
may become the means of protection for those who call upon you.
Through Christ our Lord.

Preface: The mission of Saint Joseph.

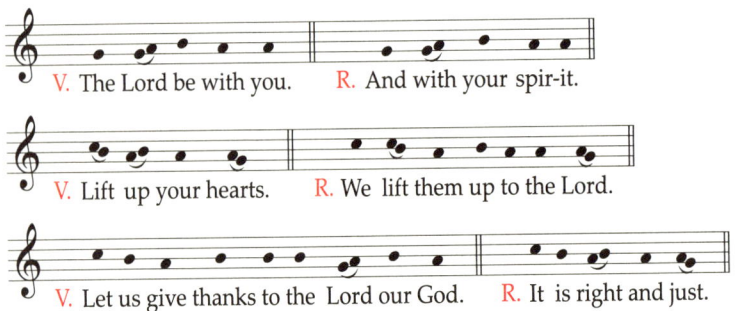

V. The Lord be with you.   R. And with your spir-it.

V. Lift up your hearts.   R. We lift them up to the Lord.

V. Let us give thanks to the Lord our God.   R. It is right and just.

It is truly right and just, our duty and our salvation, always and everywhere to give you thanks, Lord, holy Father, almighty and eternal God, and on the commemoration of Saint Joseph to give you fitting praise, to glorify you and bless you. For this just man was given by you as spouse to the Virgin Mother of God and set as a wise and faithful servant in charge of your household to watch like a father over your Only Begotten Son, who was conceived by the overshadowing of the Holy Spirit, our Lord Jesus Christ. Through him the Angels praise your majesty, Dominions adore and Powers tremble before you. Heaven and the Virtues of heaven and the blessed Seraphim worship together with exultation. May our voices, we pray, join with theirs in humble praise, as we acclaim:

Holy, Holy, Holy Lord God of hosts . . .

Text without music:
V. The Lord be with you.
R. And with your spirit.

V. Lift up your hearts.
R. We lift them up to the Lord.

V. Let us give thanks to the Lord our God.
R. It is right and just.

It is truly right and just, our duty and our salvation,
always and everywhere to give you thanks,
Lord, holy Father, almighty and eternal God,
and on the commemoration of Saint Joseph
to give you fitting praise,
to glorify you and bless you.

For this just man was given by you
as spouse to the Virgin Mother of God
and set as a wise and faithful servant
in charge of your household
to watch like a father over your Only Begotten Son,
who was conceived by the overshadowing of the Holy Spirit,
our Lord Jesus Christ.

Through him the Angels praise your majesty,
Dominions adore and Powers tremble before you.
Heaven and the Virtues of heaven and the blessed Seraphim
worship together with exultation.
May our voices, we pray, join with theirs
in humble praise, as we acclaim:

Holy, Holy, Holy Lord God of hosts . . .

Communion Antiphon   Cf. Col 3: 17
Whatever you do in word or deed,
do everything in the name of the Lord, giving thanks to God through him, alleluia.

Prayer after Communion
Having fed upon heavenly delights, we humbly ask you, O Lord,
that, by Saint Joseph's example,
cherishing in our hearts the signs of your love,
we may ever enjoy the fruit of perpetual peace.
Through Christ our Lord.

May 2
Saint Athanasius, Bishop and Doctor of the Church
Memorial

Entrance Antiphon
Cf. Sir 15: 5

In the midst of the Church he opened his mouth,
and the Lord filled him with the spirit of wisdom and understanding
and clothed him in a robe of glory, alleluia.

Collect

Almighty ever-living God,
who raised up the Bishop Saint Athanasius
as an outstanding champion of your Son's divinity,
mercifully grant,
that, rejoicing in his teaching and his protection,
we may never cease to grow in knowledge and love of you.
Through our Lord Jesus Christ, your Son,
who lives and reigns with you in the unity of the Holy Spirit,
one God, for ever and ever.

Prayer over the Offerings

Look, O Lord, upon the offerings we present to you
in commemoration of Saint Athanasius,
and may witnessing to your truth
bring salvation to those
who profess, as he did, an unblemished faith.
Through Christ our Lord.

Communion Antiphon
1 Cor 3: 11

No one can lay a foundation other than the one that is there,
namely, Jesus Christ, alleluia.

Prayer after Communion

Grant us, we pray, almighty God,
that the true divinity of your Only Begotten Son,
which we firmly profess with Saint Athanasius,
may, through this Sacrament, ever give us life and protection.
Through Christ our Lord.

May 3
SAINTS PHILIP AND JAMES, APOSTLES
Feast

Entrance Antiphon

These are the holy men
whom the Lord chose in his own perfect love;
to them he gave eternal glory, alleluia.

The Gloria in excelsis (Glory to God in the highest) is said.

Collect

O God, who gladden us each year
with the feast day of the Apostles Philip and James,
grant us, through their prayers,
a share in the Passion and Resurrection
of your Only Begotten Son,
so that we may merit to behold you for eternity.
Through our Lord Jesus Christ, your Son,
who lives and reigns with you in the unity of the Holy Spirit,
one God, for ever and ever.

Prayer over the Offerings

Receive, O Lord, the offerings we bring
for the feast day of the Apostles Philip and James
and bestow on us religion pure and undefiled.
Through Christ our Lord.

Preface of the Apostles, pp. 594-597.

Communion Antiphon
Cf. Jn 14: 8-9

Lord, show us the Father, and that will be enough for us.
Whoever has seen me, Philip, has seen the Father also, alleluia.

Prayer after Communion

Purify our minds, we pray, O Lord,
by these holy gifts we have received,
so that, contemplating you in your Son
together with the Apostles Philip and James,
we may be worthy to possess eternal life.
Through Christ our Lord.

The Solemn Blessing formula on p. 683 may be used.

[In the Dioceses of the United States]

May 10
Saint Damien de Veuster, Priest

From the Common of Pastors: For Missionaries (p. 1084).

Collect

Father of mercy,
who gave us in Saint Damien
a shining witness of love for the poorest and most abandoned,
grant that, by his intercession,
as faithful witnesses of the heart of your Son Jesus,
we too may be servants of the most needy and rejected.
Through our Lord Jesus Christ, your Son,
who lives and reigns with you in the unity of the Holy Spirit,
one God, for ever and ever.

May 12
Saints Nereus and Achilleus, Martyrs

From the Common of Martyrs: For Several Martyrs (p. 1052 or, during Easter Time, p. 1062).

Collect

Grant, we pray, almighty God,
that we, who know the great courage
of the glorious Martyrs Nereus and Achilleus
in confessing you,
may experience their loving intercession for us in your presence.
Through our Lord Jesus Christ, your Son,
who lives and reigns with you in the unity of the Holy Spirit,
one God, for ever and ever.

Saint Pancras, Martyr

From the Common of Martyrs: For One Martyr (p. 1059 or, during Easter Time, p. 1065).

Collect

May your Church rejoice, O God,
confident in the intercession of the Martyr Saint Pancras,
and by his glorious prayers
may she persevere in devotion to you
and stand ever firm.
Through our Lord Jesus Christ, your Son,
who lives and reigns with you in the unity of the Holy Spirit,
one God, for ever and ever.

May 13
Our Lady of Fatima

From the Common of the Blessed Virgin Mary (p. 1039).

Collect

O God, who chose the Mother of your Son to be our Mother also,
grant us that, persevering in penance and prayer
for the salvation of the world,
we may further more effectively each day the reign of Christ.
Who lives and reigns with you in the unity of the Holy Spirit,
one God, for ever and ever.

May 14
SAINT MATTHIAS, APOSTLE
Feast

Entrance Antiphon   Jn 15: 16

It was not you who chose me, says the Lord,
but I who chose you and appointed you to go and bear fruit,
fruit that will last (E.T. alleluia).

The Gloria in excelsis (Glory to God in the highest) is said.

Collect

O God, who assigned Saint Matthias
a place in the college of Apostles,
grant us, through his intercession,
that, rejoicing at how your love has been allotted to us,
we may merit to be numbered among the elect.
Through our Lord Jesus Christ, your Son,
who lives and reigns with you in the unity of the Holy Spirit,
one God, for ever and ever.

Prayer over the Offerings

Receive, O Lord, the offerings of your Church,
reverently presented for the Feast of Saint Matthias,
and through them strengthen us by the power of your grace.
Through Christ our Lord.

Preface of the Apostles, pp. 594-597.

Communion Antiphon   Jn 15: 12

This is my commandment: Love one another
as I love you, says the Lord (E.T. alleluia).

Prayer after Communion

Never cease, O Lord, we pray,
to fill your family with divine gifts,
and, through blessed Matthias' intercession for us,
graciously admit us to a share in the lot of the Saints in light.
Through Christ our Lord.

The Solemn Blessing formula on p. 683 may be used.

[In the Dioceses of the United States]

May 15
Saint Isidore

From the Common of Holy Men and Women: For One Saint (p. 1101).

Collect

Lord God, to whom belongs all creation,
and who call us to serve you
by caring for the gifts that surround us,
inspire us by the example of Saint Isidore
to share our food with the hungry
and to work for the salvation of all people.
Through our Lord Jesus Christ, your Son,
who lives and reigns with you in the unity of the Holy Spirit,
one God, for ever and ever.

May 18
Saint John I, Pope and Martyr

From the Common of Martyrs: For One Martyr (p. 1059 or, during Easter Time, p. 1065), or from the Common of Pastors: For a Pope (p. 1071).

Collect

O God, who reward faithful souls
and who have consecrated this day
by the martyrdom of Pope Saint John the First,
graciously hear the prayers of your people
and grant that we, who venerate his merits,
may imitate his constancy in the faith.
Through our Lord Jesus Christ, your Son,
who lives and reigns with you in the unity of the Holy Spirit,
one God, for ever and ever.

May 20
Saint Bernardine of Siena, Priest

From the Common of Pastors: For Missionaries (p. 1084), or from the Common of Holy Men and Women: For Religious (p. 1107).

Collect

O God, who gave the Priest Saint Bernardine of Siena
a great love for the holy Name of Jesus,
grant, through his merits and prayers,
that we may ever be set aflame
with the spirit of your love.
Through our Lord Jesus Christ, your Son,
who lives and reigns with you in the unity of the Holy Spirit,
one God, for ever and ever.

May 21
Saint Christopher Magallanes, Priest, and Companions, Martyrs

From the Common of Martyrs: For Several Martyrs (p. 1052 or, during Easter Time, p. 1062).

Collect

Almighty and eternal God,
who made the Priest Saint Christopher Magallanes and his companions
faithful to Christ the King even to the point of martyrdom,
grant us, through their intercession,
that, persevering in confession of the true faith,
we may always hold fast to the commandments of your love.
Through our Lord Jesus Christ, your Son,
who lives and reigns with you in the unity of the Holy Spirit,
one God, for ever and ever.

May 22
Saint Rita of Cascia, Religious

From the Common of Holy Men and Women: For Religious (p. 1107).

Collect

Bestow on us, we pray, O Lord,
the wisdom and strength of the Cross,
with which you were pleased to endow Saint Rita,
so that, suffering in every tribulation with Christ,
we may participate ever more deeply in his Paschal Mystery.
Who lives and reigns with you in the unity of the Holy Spirit,
one God, for ever and ever.

May 25
Saint Bede the Venerable, Priest and Doctor of the Church

From the Common of Doctors of the Church (p. 1088), or from the Common of Holy Men and Women: For a Monk (p. 1105).

Collect

O God, who bring light to your Church
through the learning of the Priest Saint Bede,
mercifully grant that your servants
may always be enlightened by his wisdom and helped by
   his merits.
Through our Lord Jesus Christ, your Son,
who lives and reigns with you in the unity of the Holy Spirit,
one God, for ever and ever.

Saint Gregory VII, Pope

From the Common of Pastors: For a Pope (p. 1071).

Collect

Give to your Church, we pray, O Lord,
that spirit of fortitude and zeal for justice
which you made to shine forth in Pope Saint Gregory the Seventh,
so that, rejecting evil, she may be free
to carry out in charity whatever is right.
Through our Lord Jesus Christ, your Son,
who lives and reigns with you in the unity of the Holy Spirit,
one God, for ever and ever.

Saint Mary Magdalene de' Pazzi, Virgin

From the Common of Virgins: For One Virgin (p. 1092), or from the Common of Holy Men and Women: For Religious (p. 1107).

Collect

O God, lover of virginity,
who adorned with heavenly gifts
the Virgin Saint Mary Magdalene de' Pazzi,
setting her on fire with your love,
grant, we pray, that we, who honor her today,
may imitate her example of purity and love.
Through our Lord Jesus Christ, your Son,
who lives and reigns with you in the unity of the Holy Spirit,
one God, for ever and ever.

May 26
Saint Philip Neri, Priest
Memorial

Entrance Antiphon   Rom 5: 5; cf. 8: 11

The love of God has been poured into our hearts
through the Spirit of God dwelling within us (E.T. alleluia).

Collect

O God, who never cease to bestow the glory of holiness
on the faithful servants you raise up for yourself,
graciously grant
that the Holy Spirit may kindle in us that fire
with which he wonderfully filled
the heart of Saint Philip Neri.
Through our Lord Jesus Christ, your Son,
who lives and reigns with you in the unity of the Holy Spirit,
one God, for ever and ever.

Prayer over the Offerings

As we offer you the sacrifice of praise, O Lord,
we ask that by the example of Saint Philip
we may always give ourselves cheerfully
for the glory of your name
and the service of our neighbor.
Through Christ our Lord.

Communion Antiphon

Jn 15: 9

As the Father loves me, so I also love you;
remain in my love, says the Lord (E.T. alleluia).

Prayer after Communion

Having fed upon these heavenly delights,
we pray, O Lord,
that in imitation of Saint Philip
we may always long for that food by which we truly live.
Through Christ our Lord.

May 27
Saint Augustine of Canterbury, Bishop

From the Common of Pastors: For Missionaries (p. 1084), or For a Bishop (p. 1074).

Collect

O God, who by the preaching
of the Bishop Saint Augustine of Canterbury
led the English peoples to the Gospel,
grant, we pray, that the fruits of his labors
may remain ever abundant in your Church.
Through our Lord Jesus Christ, your Son,
who lives and reigns with you in the unity of the Holy Spirit,
one God, for ever and ever.

May 31
THE VISITATION OF THE BLESSED VIRGIN MARY
Feast

Entrance Antiphon
Cf. Ps 66 (65): 16

Come and hear, all who fear God;
I will tell what the Lord did for my soul (E.T. alleluia).

The Gloria in excelsis (Glory to God in the highest) is said.

Collect

Almighty ever-living God,
who, while the Blessed Virgin Mary was carrying your Son in
  her womb,
inspired her to visit Elizabeth,
grant us, we pray,
that, faithful to the promptings of the Spirit,
we may magnify your greatness
with the Virgin Mary at all times.
Through our Lord Jesus Christ, your Son,
who lives and reigns with you in the unity of the Holy Spirit,
one God, for ever and ever.

Prayer over the Offerings

May our offering of this saving sacrifice
be acceptable to your majesty, O Lord,
as you were pleased to accept the charity
of the most Blessed Mother of your Only Begotten Son.
Who lives and reigns for ever and ever.

Preface II of the Blessed Virgin Mary, p. 592.

Communion Antiphon   Lk 1: 48-49

All generations will call me blessed,
for he who is mighty has done great things for me,
and holy is his name (E.T. alleluia).

Prayer after Communion

May your Church proclaim your greatness, O God,
for you have done great things for your faithful,
and, as Saint John the Baptist leapt with joy
when he first sensed the hidden presence of Christ,
so may your Church rejoice
to receive in this Sacrament the same ever-living Lord.
Who lives and reigns for ever and ever.

The Solemn Blessing formula on p. 682 may be used.

Saturday after the Second Sunday after Pentecost
The Immaculate Heart of the Blessed Virgin Mary
Memorial

Entrance Antiphon
Ps 13 (12): 6

My heart will rejoice in your salvation.
I will sing to the Lord, who has been bountiful with me.

Collect

O God, who prepared a fit dwelling place for the Holy Spirit
in the Heart of the Blessed Virgin Mary,
graciously grant that through her intercession
we may be a worthy temple of your glory.
Through our Lord Jesus Christ, your Son,
who lives and reigns with you in the unity of the Holy Spirit,
one God, for ever and ever.

Prayer over the Offerings

Look, O Lord, upon the prayers and offerings of your faithful,
presented in commemoration of Blessed Mary, the Mother of God,
that they may be pleasing to you
and may confer on us your help and forgiveness.
Through Christ our Lord.

Preface I of the Blessed Virgin Mary (on the feast day), p. 590, or II, p. 592.

Communion Antiphon
Lk 2: 19

Mary treasured all these words,
reflecting on them in her heart.

Prayer after Communion

Having been made partakers of eternal redemption,
we pray, O Lord,
that we, who commemorate the Mother of your Son,
may glory in the fullness of your grace
and experience its continued increase for our salvation.
Through Christ our Lord.

JUNE

June 1
Saint Justin, Martyr
Memorial

Entrance Antiphon   Cf. Ps 119 (118): 85, 46

The wicked have told me lies, but not so is your law:
I spoke of your decrees before kings,
and was not confounded (E.T. alleluia).

Collect

O God, who through the folly of the Cross
wondrously taught Saint Justin the Martyr
the surpassing knowledge of Jesus Christ,
grant us, through his intercession,
that, having rejected deception and error,
we may become steadfast in the faith.
Through our Lord Jesus Christ, your Son,
who lives and reigns with you in the unity of the Holy Spirit,
one God, for ever and ever.

Prayer over the Offerings

Grant us, we pray, O Lord,
that we may celebrate worthily these mysteries,
which Saint Justin strenuously defended.
Through Christ our Lord.

Communion Antiphon   Cf. 1 Cor 2: 2

I resolved to know nothing while I was with you
except Jesus Christ, and him crucified (E.T. alleluia).

Prayer after Communion

Refreshed by heavenly food,
we humbly implore you, O Lord,
that, attentive to the teaching of Saint Justin the Martyr,
we may abide at all times in thanksgiving
for the gifts we have received.
Through Christ our Lord.

June 2
Saints Marcellinus and Peter, Martyrs

From the Common of Martyrs: For Several Martyrs (p. 1052 or, during Easter Time, p. 1062).

Collect

O God, who surround us with protection
through the glorious confession
of the Martyrs Saints Marcellinus and Peter,
grant that we may profit by imitating them
and be upheld by their prayer.
Through our Lord Jesus Christ, your Son,
who lives and reigns with you in the unity of the Holy Spirit,
one God, for ever and ever.

June 3
Saint Charles Lwanga and Companions, Martyrs
Memorial

Entrance Antiphon
Cf. Wis 3: 6-7, 9

As gold in the furnace, the Lord put his chosen to the test;
as sacrificial offerings, he took them to himself;
and in due time they will be honored,
and grace and peace will be with the elect of God (E.T. alleluia).

Collect

O God, who have made the blood of Martyrs
the seed of Christians,
mercifully grant that the field which is your Church,
watered by the blood
shed by Saints Charles Lwanga and his companions,
may be fertile and always yield you an abundant harvest.
Through our Lord Jesus Christ, your Son,
who lives and reigns with you in the unity of the Holy Spirit,
one God, for ever and ever.

Prayer over the Offerings

We offer you sacrifice, O Lord, humbly praying
that, as you granted the blessed Martyrs
grace to die rather than sin,
so you may bring us to minister at your altar
in dedication to you alone.
Through Christ our Lord.

Communion Antiphon   Ps 116 (115): 15

How precious in the eyes of the Lord
is the death of his holy ones (E.T. alleluia).

Prayer after Communion

We have received this divine Sacrament, O Lord,
as we celebrate the victory of your holy Martyrs;
may what helped them to endure torment, we pray,
make us, in the face of trials,
steadfast in faith and in charity.
Through Christ our Lord.

June 5
Saint Boniface, Bishop and Martyr
Memorial

From the Common of Martyrs: For One Martyr (p. 1059 or, during Easter Time, p. 1065) or from the Common of Pastors: For Missionaries (p. 1084).

Collect

May the Martyr Saint Boniface be our advocate, O Lord,
that we may firmly hold the faith
he taught with his lips and sealed in his blood
and confidently profess it by our deeds.
Through our Lord Jesus Christ, your Son,
who lives and reigns with you in the unity of the Holy Spirit,
one God, for ever and ever.

June 6
Saint Norbert, Bishop

From the Common of Pastors: For a Bishop (p. 1074), or from the Common of Holy Men and Women: For Religious (p. 1107).

Collect

O God, who made the Bishop Saint Norbert
a servant of your Church
outstanding in his prayer and pastoral zeal,
grant, we ask, that by the help of his intercession,
the flock of the faithful
may always find shepherds after your own heart
and be fed in the pastures of salvation.
Through our Lord Jesus Christ, your Son,
who lives and reigns with you in the unity of the Holy Spirit,
one God, for ever and ever.

June 9
Saint Ephrem, Deacon and Doctor of the Church

From the Common of Doctors of the Church (p. 1088).

Collect

Pour into our hearts O Lord, we pray, the Holy Spirit,
at whose prompting the Deacon Saint Ephrem
exulted in singing of your mysteries
and from whom he received the strength
to serve you alone.
Through our Lord Jesus Christ, your Son,
who lives and reigns with you in the unity of the Holy Spirit,
one God, for ever and ever.

June 11
Saint Barnabas, Apostle
Memorial

Entrance Antiphon
Cf. Acts 11: 24

>Blessed is this holy man,
>who was worthy to be numbered among the Apostles,
>for he was a good man,
>filled with the Holy Spirit and with faith (E.T. alleluia).

Collect

>O God, who decreed that Saint Barnabas,
>a man filled with faith and the Holy Spirit,
>should be set apart to convert the nations,
>grant that the Gospel of Christ,
>which he strenuously preached,
>may be faithfully proclaimed by word and by deed.
>Through our Lord Jesus Christ, your Son,
>who lives and reigns with you in the unity of the Holy Spirit,
>one God, for ever and ever.

Prayer over the Offerings

>Sanctify with your blessing, we pray, O Lord,
>the offerings presented here,
>so that by your grace they may set us on fire
>with the flame of your love,
>by which Saint Barnabas
>brought the light of the Gospel to the nations.
>Through Christ our Lord.

Preface of the Apostles, pp. 594-597.

Communion Antiphon
Cf. Jn 15: 15

>I no longer call you slaves,
>because a slave does not know what his master is doing.
>But I have called you friends,
>because I have told you
>everything I have heard from my Father (E.T. alleluia).

Prayer after Communion

> As we receive the pledge of eternal life,
> we humbly implore you, Lord,
> that what we celebrate in sacramental signs
> on the Memorial of the blessed Apostle Barnabas
> we may one day behold unveiled.
> Through Christ our Lord.

June 13
Saint Anthony of Padua, Priest and Doctor of the Church
Memorial

From the Common of Pastors: For One Pastor (p. 1078), or from the Common of Doctors of the Church (p. 1088), or from the Common of Holy Men and Women: For Religious (p. 1107).

Collect

> Almighty ever-living God,
> who gave Saint Anthony of Padua to your people
> as an outstanding preacher
> and an intercessor in their need,
> grant that, with his assistance,
> as we follow the teachings of the Christian life,
> we may know your help in every trial.
> Through our Lord Jesus Christ, your Son,
> who lives and reigns with you in the unity of the Holy Spirit,
> one God, for ever and ever.

June 19
Saint Romuald, Abbot

From the Common of Holy Men and Women: For an Abbot (p. 1103).

Collect

> O God, who through Saint Romuald renewed
> the manner of life of hermits in your Church,
> grant that, denying ourselves and following Christ,
> we may merit to reach the heavenly realms on high.
> Through our Lord Jesus Christ, your Son,
> who lives and reigns with you in the unity of the Holy Spirit,
> one God, for ever and ever.

June 21
Saint Aloysius Gonzaga, Religious
Memorial

Entrance Antiphon   Cf. Ps 24 (23): 4, 3

The clean of hands and pure of heart
shall climb the mountain of the Lord
and stand in his holy place.

Collect

O God, giver of heavenly gifts,
who in Saint Aloysius Gonzaga
joined penitence to a wonderful innocence of life,
grant, through his merits and intercession,
that, though we have failed to follow him in innocence,
we may imitate him in penitence.
Through our Lord Jesus Christ, your Son,
who lives and reigns with you in the unity of the Holy Spirit,
one God, for ever and ever.

Prayer over the Offerings

Grant us, O Lord,
that by the example of Saint Aloysius,
we may take our place at the heavenly banquet,
clothed always in our wedding garment,
so that, by participation in this mystery,
we may possess the riches of your grace.
Through Christ our Lord.

Communion Antiphon   Ps 78 (77): 24-25

God gave them bread from heaven;
man ate the bread of Angels.

Prayer after Communion

Bring us, who have been fed
with the food of Angels, O Lord,
to serve you in purity of life,
and, following the example of Saint Aloysius,
whom we honor today,
may we persevere in constant thanksgiving.
Through Christ our Lord.

June 22
Saint Paulinus of Nola, Bishop

From the Common of Pastors: For a Bishop (p. 1074).

Collect

O God, who made the Bishop Saint Paulinus of Nola
outstanding for love of poverty and for pastoral care,
graciously grant that, as we celebrate his merits,
we may imitate the example of his charity.
Through our Lord Jesus Christ, your Son,
who lives and reigns with you in the unity of the Holy Spirit,
one God, for ever and ever.

Saints John Fisher, Bishop, and Thomas More, Martyrs

From the Common of Martyrs: For Several Martyrs (p. 1052).

Collect

O God, who in martyrdom
have brought true faith to its highest expression,
graciously grant
that, strengthened through the intercession
of Saints John Fisher and Thomas More,
we may confirm by the witness of our life
the faith we profess with our lips.
Through our Lord Jesus Christ, your Son,
who lives and reigns with you in the unity of the Holy Spirit,
one God, for ever and ever.

June 24
THE NATIVITY OF SAINT JOHN THE BAPTIST
Solemnity

At the Vigil Mass

This Mass is used on the evening of June 23, either before or after First Vespers (Evening Prayer I) of the Solemnity.

Entrance Antiphon
Lk 1: 15, 14

He will be great in the sight of the Lord
and will be filled with the Holy Spirit,
even from his mother's womb;
and many will rejoice at his birth.

The Gloria in excelsis *(Glory to God in the highest) is said.*

Collect

**Grant, we pray, almighty God,
that your family may walk in the way of salvation
and, attentive to what Saint John the Precursor urged,
may come safely to the One he foretold,
our Lord Jesus Christ.
Who lives and reigns with you in the unity of the Holy Spirit,
one God, for ever and ever.**

The Creed is said.

Prayer over the Offerings

**Look with favor, O Lord,
upon the offerings made by your people
on the Solemnity of Saint John the Baptist,
and grant that what we celebrate in mystery
we may follow with deeds of devoted service.
Through Christ our Lord.**

Proper Preface, as in the following Mass, pp. 880-881.

Communion Antiphon
Lk 1: 68

Blessed be the Lord, the God of Israel!
He has visited his people and redeemed them.

Prayer after Communion

May the marvelous prayer of Saint John the Baptist
accompany us who have eaten our fill
at this sacrificial feast, O Lord,
and, since Saint John proclaimed your Son
to be the Lamb who would take away our sins,
may he implore now for us your favor.
Through Christ our Lord.

At the Mass during the Day

Entrance Antiphon
Jn 1: 6-7; Lk 1: 17

A man was sent from God, whose name was John.
He came to testify to the light,
to prepare a people fit for the Lord.

The Gloria in excelsis (Glory to God in the highest) is said.

Collect

O God, who raised up Saint John the Baptist
to make ready a nation fit for Christ the Lord,
give your people, we pray,
the grace of spiritual joys
and direct the hearts of all the faithful
into the way of salvation and peace.
Through our Lord Jesus Christ, your Son,
who lives and reigns with you in the unity of the Holy Spirit,
one God, for ever and ever.

The Creed is said.

Prayer over the Offerings

We place these offerings on your altar, O Lord,
to celebrate with fitting honor the nativity of him
who both foretold the coming of the world's Savior
and pointed him out when he came.
Who lives and reigns for ever and ever.

And so, with the Pow-ers of heav-en, we worship you con-stant-ly on earth, and before your maj-es-ty without end we ac-claim:

Holy, Holy, Holy Lord God of hosts . . .

Text without music:

V. **The Lord be with you.**
R. And with your spirit.

V. **Lift up your hearts.**
R. We lift them up to the Lord.

V. **Let us give thanks to the Lord our God.**
R. It is right and just.

It is truly right and just, our duty and our salvation,
always and everywhere to give you thanks,
Lord, holy Father, almighty and eternal God,
through Christ our Lord.

In his Precursor, Saint John the Baptist,
we praise your great glory,
for you consecrated him for a singular honor
among those born of women.

His birth brought great rejoicing;
even in the womb he leapt for joy
at the coming of human salvation.
He alone of all the prophets
pointed out the Lamb of redemption.

And to make holy the flowing waters,
he baptized the very author of Baptism
and was privileged to bear him supreme witness
by the shedding of his blood.

And so, with the Powers of heaven,
we worship you constantly on earth,
and before your majesty
without end we acclaim:

Holy, Holy, Holy Lord God of hosts . . .

Communion Antiphon   Cf. Lk 1: 78
Through the tender mercy of our God,
the Dawn from on high will visit us.

Prayer after Communion
Having feasted at the banquet of the heavenly Lamb,
we pray, O Lord,
that, finding joy in the nativity of Saint John the Baptist,
your Church may know as the author of her rebirth
the Christ whose coming John foretold.
Who lives and reigns for ever and ever.

June 27
Saint Cyril of Alexandria,
Bishop and Doctor of the Church

From the Common of Pastors: For a Bishop (p. 1074), or from the Common of Doctors of the Church (p. 1088).

Collect
O God, who made the Bishop Saint Cyril of Alexandria
an invincible champion of the divine motherhood
of the most Blessed Virgin Mary,
grant, we pray,
that we, who believe she is truly the Mother of God,
may be saved through the Incarnation of Christ your Son.
Who lives and reigns with you in the unity of the Holy Spirit,
one God, for ever and ever.

June 28
Saint Irenaeus, Bishop and Martyr
Memorial

Entrance Antiphon
Mal 2: 6

> The law of truth was in his mouth;
> no dishonesty was found on his lips.
> He walked with me in integrity and peace,
> and turned many away from evil.

Collect

> O God, who called the Bishop Saint Irenaeus
> to confirm true doctrine and the peace of the Church,
> grant, we pray, through his intercession,
> that, being renewed in faith and charity,
> we may always be intent on fostering unity and concord.
> Through our Lord Jesus Christ, your Son,
> who lives and reigns with you in the unity of the Holy Spirit,
> one God, for ever and ever.

Prayer over the Offerings

> May the sacrifice we offer you with joy
> on the heavenly birthday of Saint Irenaeus
> bring you glory, O Lord,
> and instill in us a love of the truth,
> so that we may keep the Church's faith inviolate
> and her unity secure.
> Through Christ our Lord.

Communion Antiphon
Jn 15: 4-5

> Remain in me, as I remain in you, says the Lord.
> Whoever remains in me, and I in him, bears fruit in plenty.

Prayer after Communion

> Through these sacred mysteries, we pray, O Lord,
> give us in your compassion an increase of that faith
> which brought glory to the Bishop Saint Irenaeus
> as he maintained it even until death,
> and may the same faith bring to us, who truly follow it,
> justification in your sight.
> Through Christ our Lord.

June 29
SAINTS PETER AND PAUL, APOSTLES
Solemnity

At the Vigil Mass

This Mass is used on the evening of June 28, either before or after First Vespers (Evening Prayer I) of the Solemnity.

Entrance Antiphon

Peter the Apostle, and Paul the teacher of the Gentiles,
these have taught us your law, O Lord.

The Gloria in excelsis (Glory to God in the highest) is said.

Collect

Grant, we pray, O Lord our God,
that we may be sustained
by the intercession of the blessed Apostles Peter and Paul,
that, as through them you gave your Church
the foundations of her heavenly office,
so through them you may help her to eternal salvation.
Through our Lord Jesus Christ, your Son,
who lives and reigns with you in the unity of the Holy Spirit,
one God, for ever and ever.

The Creed is said.

Prayer over the Offerings

We bring offerings to your altar, O Lord,
as we glory in the solemn feast
of the blessed Apostles Peter and Paul,
so that the more we doubt our own merits,
the more we may rejoice that we are to be saved
by your loving kindness.
Through Christ our Lord.

Proper Preface, as in the following Mass, pp. 887-888.

Communion Antiphon

Cf. Jn 21: 15, 17

Simon, Son of John, do you love me more than these?
Lord, you know everything; you know that I love you.

Prayer after Communion

By this heavenly Sacrament, O Lord, we pray,
strengthen your faithful,
whom you have enlightened with the teaching of the Apostles.
Through Christ our Lord.

The Solemn Blessing formula on p. 682 may be used.

At the Mass during the Day

Entrance Antiphon

These are the ones who, living in the flesh,
planted the Church with their blood;
they drank the chalice of the Lord
and became the friends of God.

The Gloria in excelsis (Glory to God in the highest) is said.

Collect

O God, who on the Solemnity of the Apostles Peter and Paul
give us the noble and holy joy of this day,
grant, we pray, that your Church
may in all things follow the teaching
of those through whom she received
the beginnings of right religion.
Through our Lord Jesus Christ, your Son,
who lives and reigns with you in the unity of the Holy Spirit,
one God, for ever and ever.

The Creed is said.

Prayer over the Offerings

May the prayer of the Apostles, O Lord,
accompany the sacrificial gift
that we present to your name for consecration,
and may their intercession make us devoted to you
in celebration of the sacrifice.
Through Christ our Lord.

Preface: The twofold mission of Peter and Paul in the Church.

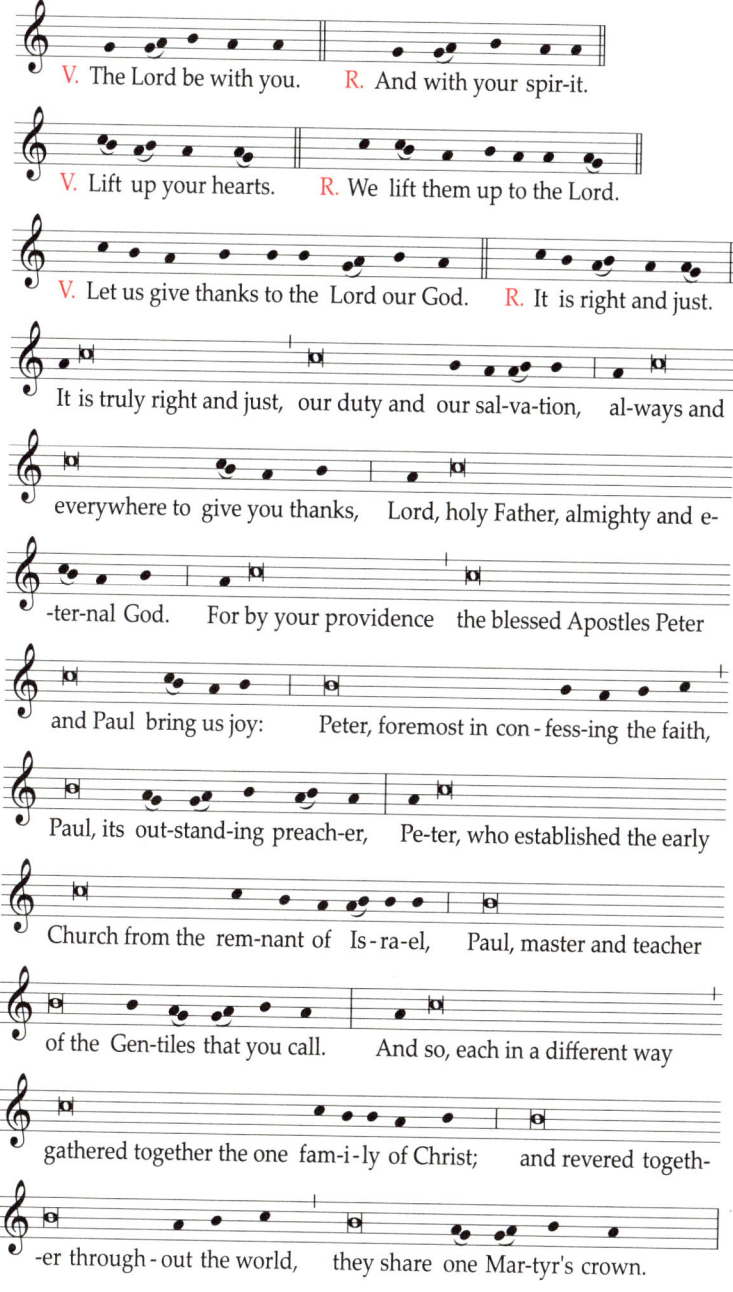

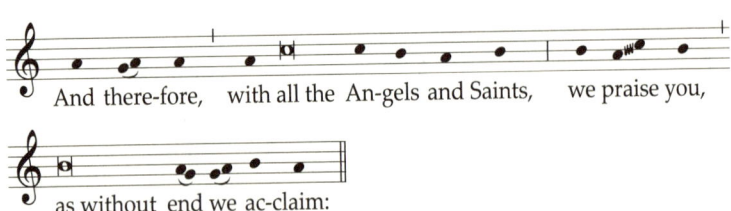

Holy, Holy, Holy Lord God of hosts ...

Text without music:

V. The Lord be with you.
R. And with your spirit.

V. Lift up your hearts.
R. We lift them up to the Lord.

V. Let us give thanks to the Lord our God.
R. It is right and just.

It is truly right and just, our duty and our salvation,
always and everywhere to give you thanks,
Lord, holy Father, almighty and eternal God.

For by your providence
the blessed Apostles Peter and Paul bring us joy:
Peter, foremost in confessing the faith,
Paul, its outstanding preacher,
Peter, who established the early Church from the remnant
   of Israel,
Paul, master and teacher of the Gentiles that you call.

And so, each in a different way
gathered together the one family of Christ;
and revered together throughout the world,
they share one Martyr's crown.

And therefore, with all the Angels and Saints,
we praise you, as without end we acclaim:

Holy, Holy, Holy Lord God of hosts ...

Communion Antiphon
Cf. Mt 16: 16, 18

Peter said to Jesus: You are the Christ, the Son of the living God.
And Jesus replied: You are Peter,
and upon this rock I will build my Church.

Prayer after Communion

Grant us, O Lord,
who have been renewed by this Sacrament,
so to live in the Church,
that, persevering in the breaking of the Bread
and in the teaching of the Apostles,
we may be one heart and one soul,
made steadfast in your love.
Through Christ our Lord.

The Solemn Blessing formula on p. 682 may be used.

For a Votive Mass of Saint Peter or of Saint Paul, cf. below, p. 1362, or p. 1363.

June 30
The First Martyrs of Holy Roman Church

From the Common of Martyrs: For Several Martyrs (p. 1052).

Collect

O God, who consecrated
the abundant first fruits of the Roman Church
by the blood of the Martyrs,
grant, we pray, that with firm courage
we may together draw strength from so great a struggle
and ever rejoice at the triumph of faithful love.
Through our Lord Jesus Christ, your Son,
who lives and reigns with you in the unity of the Holy Spirit,
one God, for ever and ever.

JULY

[In the Dioceses of the United States]

July 1
Blessed Junípero Serra, Priest

From the Common of Pastors: For Missionaries (p. 1084), or For One Pastor (p. 1078).

Collect

O God, who by your ineffable mercy
have been pleased through the labors
of your Priest Blessed Junípero Serra
to count many American peoples within your Church,
grant by his intercession
that we may so join our hearts to you in love,
as to carry always and everywhere before all people
the image of your Only Begotten Son.
Who lives and reigns with you in the unity of the Holy Spirit,
one God, for ever and ever.

July 3
SAINT THOMAS, APOSTLE
Feast

Entrance Antiphon
Cf. Ps 118 (117): 28, 21

You are my God, and I confess you;
you are my God, and I exalt you;
I will thank you, for you became my savior.

The Gloria in excelsis (Glory to God in the highest) is said.

Collect

Grant, almighty God,
that we may glory in the Feast of the blessed Apostle Thomas,
so that we may always be sustained by his intercession
and, believing, may have life
in the name of Jesus Christ your Son,
whom Thomas acknowledged as the Lord.
Who lives and reigns with you in the unity of the Holy Spirit,
one God, for ever and ever.

Prayer over the Offerings

We render you, O Lord, the service that is your due,
humbly imploring you to keep safe your gifts in us,
as we honor the confession of the Apostle Saint Thomas
and offer you a sacrifice of praise.
Through Christ our Lord.

Preface of the Apostles, pp. 594-597.

Communion Antiphon   Cf. Jn 20: 27

Bring your hand and feel the place of the nails,
and do not be unbelieving but believing.

Prayer after Communion

O God, as we truly receive in this Sacrament
the Body of your Only Begotten Son,
grant, we pray, that we may recognize him
with the Apostle Thomas by faith
as our Lord and our God
and proclaim him by our deeds and by our life.
Who lives and reigns for ever and ever.

The Solemn Blessing formula, p. 683, may be used.

[In the Dioceses of the United States]
July 4
Independence Day

Entrance Antiphon   Cf. Sir 36: 18, 19

Give peace, O Lord, to those who wait for you;
hear the prayers of your servants
and guide us in the way of justice.

The Gloria in excelsis (Glory to God in the highest) is said.

Collect

God of justice, Father of truth,
who guide creation in wisdom and goodness
to fulfillment in Christ your Son,
open our hearts to the truth of his Gospel,
that your peace may rule in our hearts
and your justice guide our lives.
Through our Lord Jesus Christ, your Son,
who lives and reigns with you in the unity of the Holy Spirit,
one God, for ever and ever.

Or:

Father of all nations and ages,
we recall the day when our country
claimed its place among the family of nations;
for what has been achieved we give you thanks,
for the work that still remains we ask your help,
and as you have called us from many peoples to be one nation,
grant that, under your providence,
our country may share your blessings
with all the peoples of the earth.
Through our Lord Jesus Christ, your Son,
who lives and reigns with you in the unity of the Holy Spirit,
one God, for ever and ever.

Prayer over the Offerings

Accept, Lord God, these gifts we bring to this altar
and, having taught us through the wisdom of the Gospel,
lead us to true justice and lasting peace.
Through Christ our Lord.

Or:

Father, who have molded into one
our nation, drawn from the peoples of many lands,
grant, that as the grains of wheat become one bread
and the many grapes one cup of wine,
so we may before all others be instruments of your peace.
Through Christ our Lord.

Preface: Independence Day I.

V. The Lord be with you.   R. And with your spirit.

V. Lift up your hearts.   R. We lift them up to the Lord.

V. Let us give thanks to the Lord our God.   R. It is right and just.

It is truly right and just, our duty and our salvation, always and everywhere to give you thanks, Lord, holy Father, almighty and eternal God, through Christ our Lord. He spoke to us a message of peace and taught us to live as brothers and sisters. His message took form in the vision of our founding fathers as they fashioned a nation where we might live as one. His message lives on in our midst as our task for today and a promise for tomorrow. And so, with hearts full of love, we join the angels today and every day of our lives, to sing your glory as we acclaim:

Holy, Holy, Holy Lord God of hosts . . .

Text without music:
V. **The Lord be with you.**
R. And with your spirit.

V. **Lift up your hearts.**
R. We lift them up to the Lord.

V. **Let us give thanks to the Lord our God.**
R. It is right and just.

It is truly right and just, our duty and our salvation,
always and everywhere to give you thanks,
Lord, holy Father, almighty and eternal God,
through Christ our Lord.

He spoke to us a message of peace
and taught us to live as brothers and sisters.
His message took form in the vision of our founding fathers
as they fashioned a nation
where we might live as one.
His message lives on in our midst
as our task for today
and a promise for tomorrow.

And so, with hearts full of love,
we join the angels today and every day of our lives,
to sing your glory as we acclaim:

Holy, Holy, Holy Lord God of hosts . . .

Or:

Preface: Independence Day II.

℣. The Lord be with you.　　℟. And with your spirit.

℣. Lift up your hearts.　　℟. We lift them up to the Lord.

℣. Let us give thanks to the Lord our God.　　℟. It is right and just.

It is truly right and just, our duty and our salvation, always and everywhere to give you thanks, Lord, holy Father, almighty and eternal God, through Christ our Lord. For we praise you as the God of creation, as the Father of Jesus, the Savior of the world, in whose image we seek to live. He loved the children of the lands he walked and enriched them with his witness of justice and truth. He lived and died that we might be reborn in the Spirit and filled with love for all people. And so, with hearts full of love, we join the angels today and every day of our lives, to sing your glory as we acclaim:

Holy, Holy, Holy Lord God of hosts . . .

Text without music:
V. The Lord be with you.
R. And with your spirit.

V. Lift up your hearts.
R. We lift them up to the Lord.

V. Let us give thanks to the Lord our God.
R. It is right and just.

It is truly right and just, our duty and our salvation,
always and everywhere to give you thanks,
Lord, holy Father, almighty and eternal God,
through Christ our Lord.

For we praise you as the God of creation,
as the Father of Jesus, the Savior of the world,
in whose image we seek to live.
He loved the children of the lands he walked
and enriched them with his witness of justice and truth.
He lived and died that we might be reborn in the Spirit
and filled with love for all people.

And so, with hearts full of love,
we join the angels today and every day of our lives,
to sing your glory as we acclaim:

Holy, Holy, Holy Lord God of hosts . . .

Communion Antiphon

Ps 36 (35):10

With you, O Lord, is the fountain of life, and in your light, we see light.

Prayer after Communion

By showing us in this Eucharist, O Lord,
a glimpse of the unity and joy
of your people in heaven,
deepen our unity and intensify our joy,
that all who believe in you
may work together to build the city of lasting peace.
Through Christ our Lord.

Or:

May the love we share in this Eucharist, heavenly Father,
flow in rich blessing throughout our land
and by your grace may we as a nation
place our trust in you
and seek to do your will.
Through Christ our Lord.

Solemn Blessing

May God the Father who has called us
to be one human family
fill your hearts with deep longing
for peace and harmony.
R. Amen.

May the Son of God who came to share our life
and make us children of the one Father
enable you to grow in wisdom and grace
before God and the human family.
R. Amen.

And may the Holy Spirit who is the bond of love
between the Father and the Son
unite in love all here present;
may he be the bond of love among you,
our nation, and all peoples.
R. Amen.

And may the blessing of almighty God,
the Father, and the Son, ✠ and the Holy Spirit,
come down on you and remain with you for ever.
R. Amen.

July 5
Saint Anthony Zaccaria, Priest

From the Common of Pastors: For One Pastor (p. 1078), or from the Common of Holy Men and Women: For Educators (p. 1111), or For Religious (p. 1107).

Collect

Grant, O Lord, that in the spirit of the Apostle Paul
we may pursue the surpassing knowledge of Jesus Christ,
for, having learned it,
Saint Anthony Zaccaria
constantly preached your saving word in the Church.
Through our Lord Jesus Christ, your Son,
who lives and reigns with you in the unity of the Holy Spirit,
one God, for ever and ever.

[In the Dioceses of the United States]
Saint Elizabeth of Portugal

From the Common of Holy Men and Women: For Those Who Practiced Works of Mercy (p. 1110).

Collect

O God, author of peace and lover of charity,
who adorned Saint Elizabeth of Portugal
with a marvelous grace for reconciling those in conflict,
grant, through her intercession,
that we may become peacemakers,
and so be called children of God.
Through our Lord Jesus Christ, your Son,
who lives and reigns with you in the unity of the Holy Spirit,
one God, for ever and ever.

July 6
Saint Maria Goretti, Virgin and Martyr

From the Common of Martyrs: For a Virgin Martyr (p. 1068), or from the Common of Virgins: For One Virgin (p. 1092).

Collect

O God, author of innocence and lover of chastity,
who bestowed the grace of martyrdom
on your handmaid, the Virgin Saint Maria Goretti, in her youth,
grant, we pray, through her intercession,
that, as you gave her a crown for her steadfastness,
so we, too, may be firm
in obeying your commandments.
Through our Lord Jesus Christ, your Son,
who lives and reigns with you in the unity of the Holy Spirit,
one God, for ever and ever.

July 9
Saint Augustine Zhao Rong, Priest, and Companions, Martyrs

From the Common of Martyrs: For Several Martyrs (p. 1052).

Collect

O God, who in your wonderful providence
have strengthened your Church
through the confession of the Martyrs
Saint Augustine Zhao and companions,
grant that your people,
faithful to the mission entrusted to it,
may enjoy ever greater freedom
and witness to the truth before the world.
Through our Lord Jesus Christ, your Son,
who lives and reigns with you in the unity of the Holy Spirit,
one God, for ever and ever.

July 11
Saint Benedict, Abbot
Memorial

Entrance Antiphon

There was a man of venerable life,
Benedict, blessed by grace and by name,
who, leaving home and patrimony
and desiring to please God alone,
sought out the habit of holy living.

Collect

O God, who made the Abbot Saint Benedict
an outstanding master in the school of divine service,
grant, we pray,
that, putting nothing before love of you,
we may hasten with a loving heart
in the way of your commands.
Through our Lord Jesus Christ, your Son,
who lives and reigns with you in the unity of the Holy Spirit,
one God, for ever and ever.

Prayer over the Offerings

Look kindly, Lord, upon these holy offerings,
which we make in honor of Saint Benedict,
and grant that,
by following his example in seeking you,
we may merit the gifts of unity in your service and of peace.
Through Christ our Lord.

Communion Antiphon   Lk 12: 42

This is the steward, faithful and prudent,
whom the Lord set over his household
to give them their allowance of food at the proper time.

Prayer after Communion

Having received this pledge of eternal life,
we humbly beseech you, O Lord,
that, attentive to the teaching of Saint Benedict,
we may faithfully serve your designs
and love one another with fervent charity.
Through Christ our Lord.

July 13
Saint Henry

From the Common of Holy Men and Women: For One Saint (p. 1101).

Collect

O God, whose abundant grace prepared Saint Henry
to be raised by you in a wonderful way
from the cares of earthly rule to heavenly realms,
grant, we pray, through his intercession,
that amid the uncertainties of this world
we may hasten towards you with minds made pure.
Through our Lord Jesus Christ, your Son,
who lives and reigns with you in the unity of the Holy Spirit,
one God, for ever and ever.

[In the Dioceses of the United States]
July 14
Blessed Kateri Tekakwitha, Virgin
Memorial

From the Common of Virgins: For One Virgin (p. 1092).

Collect

O God, who desired the Virgin Blessed Kateri Tekakwitha
to flower among Native Americans
in a life of innocence,
grant, through her intercession,
that when all are gathered into your Church
from every nation, tribe and tongue,
they may magnify you
in a single canticle of praise.
Through our Lord Jesus Christ, your Son,
who lives and reigns with you in the unity of the Holy Spirit,
one God, for ever and ever.

July 15
Saint Bonaventure, Bishop and Doctor of the Church
Memorial

From the Common of Pastors: For a Bishop (p. 1074) or from the Common of Doctors of the Church (p. 1088).

Collect

Grant, we pray, almighty God,
that, just as we celebrate the heavenly birthday
of the Bishop Saint Bonaventure,
we may benefit from his great learning
and constantly imitate the ardor of his charity.
Through our Lord Jesus Christ, your Son,
who lives and reigns with you in the unity of the Holy Spirit,
one God, for ever and ever.

July 16
Our Lady of Mount Carmel

From the Common of the Blessed Virgin Mary (p. 1039).

Collect

May the venerable intercession of the glorious Virgin Mary
come to our aid, we pray, O Lord,
so that, fortified by her protection,
we may reach the mountain which is Christ.
Who lives and reigns with you in the unity of the Holy Spirit,
one God, for ever and ever.

[In the Dioceses of the United States]

July 18
Saint Camillus de Lellis, Priest

From the Common of Holy Men and Women: For Those Who Practiced Works of Mercy (p. 1110).

Collect

O God, who adorned the Priest Saint Camillus
with a singular grace of charity towards the sick,
pour out upon us, by his merits,
a spirit of love for you,
so that, serving you in our neighbor,
we may, at the hour of our death,
pass safely over to you.
Through our Lord Jesus Christ, your Son,
who lives and reigns with you in the unity of the Holy Spirit,
one God, for ever and ever.

July 20
Saint Apollinaris, Bishop and Martyr

From the Common of Martyrs: For One Martyr (p. 1059), or from the Common of Pastors: For a Bishop (p. 1074).

Collect

Direct your faithful, Lord, in the way of eternal salvation,
which the Bishop Saint Apollinaris showed by his teaching
   and martyrdom,
and grant, through his intercession,
that we may so persevere in keeping your commandments
as to merit being crowned with him.
Through our Lord Jesus Christ, your Son,
who lives and reigns with you in the unity of the Holy Spirit,
one God, for ever and ever.

July 21
Saint Lawrence of Brindisi, Priest and Doctor of the Church

From the Common of Pastors: For One Pastor (p. 1078), or from the Common of Doctors of the Church (p. 1088), or from the Common of Holy Men and Women: For Religious (p. 1107).

Collect

O God, who for the glory of your name
and the salvation of souls
bestowed on the Priest Saint Lawrence of Brindisi
a spirit of counsel and fortitude,
grant, we pray, that in the same spirit,
we may know what must be done
and, through his intercession,
bring it to completion.
Through our Lord Jesus Christ, your Son,
who lives and reigns with you in the unity of the Holy Spirit,
one God, for ever and ever.

July 22
Saint Mary Magdalene
Memorial

Entrance Antiphon

Jn 20: 17

The Lord said to Mary Magdalene:
Go to my brothers and tell them:
I am going to my Father and your Father,
to my God and your God.

Collect

O God, whose Only Begotten Son
entrusted Mary Magdalene before all others
with announcing the great joy of the Resurrection,
grant, we pray,
that through her intercession and example
we may proclaim the living Christ
and come to see him reigning in your glory.
Who lives and reigns with you in the unity of the Holy Spirit,
one God, for ever and ever.

Prayer over the Offerings

Accept, O Lord, the offerings
presented in commemoration of Saint Mary Magdalene,
whose homage of charity
was graciously accepted by your Only Begotten Son.
Who lives and reigns for ever and ever.

Communion Antiphon 2 Cor 5: 14, 15

The love of Christ impels us,
so that those who live may live no longer for themselves,
but for him who died for them and was raised.

Prayer after Communion

May the holy reception of your mysteries, Lord,
instill in us that persevering love
with which Saint Mary Magdalene
clung resolutely to Christ her Master.
Who lives and reigns for ever and ever.

July 23
Saint Bridget, Religious

From the Common of Holy Men and Women: For Holy Women (p. 1113) or For Religious (p. 1107).

Collect

O God, who guided Saint Bridget of Sweden
along different paths of life
and wondrously taught her the wisdom of the Cross
as she contemplated the Passion of your Son,
grant us, we pray,
that, walking worthily in our vocation,
we may seek you in all things.
Through our Lord Jesus Christ, your Son,
who lives and reigns with you in the unity of the Holy Spirit,
one God, for ever and ever.

July 24
Saint Sharbel Makhlūf, Priest

From the Common of Pastors: For One Pastor (p. 1078), or from the Common of Holy Men and Women: For a Monk (p. 1105).

Collect

O God, who called the Priest Saint Sharbel Makhlūf
to the solitary combat of the desert
and imbued him with all manner of devotion,
grant us, we pray,
that, being made imitators of the Lord's Passion,
we may merit to be co-heirs of his Kingdom.
Who lives and reigns with you in the unity of the Holy Spirit,
one God, for ever and ever.

July 25
SAINT JAMES, APOSTLE
Feast

Entrance Antiphon
Cf. Mt 4: 18, 21

As he walked by the Sea of Galilee,
Jesus saw James the son of Zebedee and John his brother
mending their nets and he called them.

The Gloria in excelsis (Glory to God in the highest) is said.

Collect

Almighty ever-living God,
who consecrated the first fruits of your Apostles
by the blood of Saint James,
grant, we pray,
that your Church may be strengthened by his confession of faith
and constantly sustained by his protection.
Through our Lord Jesus Christ, your Son,
who lives and reigns with you in the unity of the Holy Spirit,
one God, for ever and ever.

Prayer over the Offerings

Cleanse us, Lord, by the saving baptism of your Son's Passion,
so that on the Feast of Saint James,
whom you willed to be the first among the Apostles
to drink of Christ's chalice of suffering,
we may offer a sacrifice pleasing to you.
Through Christ our Lord.

Preface of the Apostles, pp. 594-597.

Communion Antiphon

They drank the chalice of the Lord,
and became the friends of God.

Prayer after Communion

Help us, O Lord, we pray,
through the intercession of the blessed Apostle James,
on whose feast day we have received with joy your holy gifts.
Through Christ our Lord.

The Solemn Blessing formula, p. 683, may be used.

July 26
Saints Joachim and Anne,
Parents of the Blessed Virgin Mary
Memorial

Entrance Antiphon
Cf. Sir 44: 1, 25

Let us praise Joachim and Anne, to whom, in their generation,
the Lord gave him who was a blessing for all the nations.

Collect

O Lord, God of our Fathers,
who bestowed on Saints Joachim and Anne this grace,
that of them should be born the Mother of your incarnate Son,
grant, through the prayers of both,
that we may attain the salvation
you have promised to your people.
Through our Lord Jesus Christ, your Son,
who lives and reigns with you in the unity of the Holy Spirit,
one God, for ever and ever.

Prayer over the Offerings

Receive, we pray, O Lord,
these offerings of our homage,
and grant that we may merit a share in the same blessing
which you promised to Abraham and his descendants.
Through Christ our Lord.

Communion Antiphon
Cf. Ps 24 (23): 5

They received blessings from the Lord
and mercy from God their Savior.

Prayer after Communion

O God, who willed that your Only Begotten Son
should be born from among humanity
so that by a wonderful mystery
humanity might be born again from you,
we pray that, in your kindness,
you may sanctify by the spirit of adoption
those you have fed with the Bread you give your children.
Through Christ our Lord.

July 29
Saint Martha
Memorial

Entrance Antiphon
Cf. Lk 10: 38

Jesus entered a village,
where a woman named Martha welcomed him into her home.

Collect

Almighty ever-living God,
whose Son was pleased to be welcomed
in Saint Martha's house as a guest,
grant, we pray,
that through her intercession,
serving Christ faithfully in our brothers and sisters,
we may merit to be received by you
in the halls of heaven.
Through our Lord Jesus Christ, your Son,
who lives and reigns with you in the unity of the Holy Spirit,
one God, for ever and ever.

Prayer over the Offerings

As we proclaim your wonders in Saint Martha, O Lord,
we humbly implore your majesty,
that, as her homage of love was pleasing to you,
so, too, our dutiful service may find favor in your sight.
Through Christ our Lord.

Communion Antiphon Jn 11: 27

Martha said to Jesus:
You are the Christ, the Son of God,
who is coming into this world.

Prayer after Communion

May the holy reception of the Body and Blood
of your Only Begotten Son, O Lord,
turn us away from the cares of this fallen world,
so that, following the example of Saint Martha,
we may grow in sincere love for you on earth
and rejoice to behold you for eternity in heaven.
Through Christ our Lord.

July 30
Saint Peter Chrysologus, Bishop and Doctor of the Church

From the Common of Pastors: For a Bishop (p. 1074), or from the Common of Doctors of the Church (p. 1088).

Collect

O God, who made the Bishop Saint Peter Chrysologus
an outstanding preacher of your incarnate Word,
grant, through his intercession,
that we may constantly ponder in our hearts
the mysteries of your salvation
and faithfully express them in what we do.
Through our Lord Jesus Christ, your Son,
who lives and reigns with you in the unity of the Holy Spirit,
one God, for ever and ever.

July 31
Saint Ignatius of Loyola, Priest
Memorial

Entrance Antiphon
Cf. Phil 2: 10-11

At the name of Jesus, every knee should bend,
of those in heaven and on earth and under the earth,
and every tongue confess that Jesus Christ is Lord,
to the glory of God the Father.

Collect

O God, who raised up Saint Ignatius of Loyola in your Church
to further the greater glory of your name,
grant that by his help we may imitate him
in fighting the good fight on earth
and merit to receive with him a crown in heaven.
Through our Lord Jesus Christ, your Son,
who lives and reigns with you in the unity of the Holy Spirit,
one God, for ever and ever.

Prayer over the Offerings

May these offerings we make to you
as we celebrate Saint Ignatius
be pleasing, Lord God,
and grant that the sacred mysteries,
which you have made the fount of all holiness,
may sanctify us, too, in the truth.
Through Christ our Lord.

Communion Antiphon
Cf. Lk 12: 49

Thus says the Lord: I have come to cast fire on the earth,
and how I wish that it were kindled!

Prayer after Communion

May the sacrifice of praise
that we have offered with thanksgiving
in honor of Saint Ignatius, O Lord,
bring us to exalt your majesty without end.
Through Christ our Lord.

AUGUST

August 1
Saint Alphonsus Liguori, Bishop and Doctor of the Church
Memorial

From the Common of Pastors: For a Bishop (p. 1074), or from the Common of Doctors of the Church (p. 1088).

Collect

O God, who constantly raise up in your Church new examples
 of virtue,
grant that we may follow so closely in the footsteps
of the Bishop Saint Alphonsus in his zeal for souls
as to attain the same rewards that are his in heaven.
Through our Lord Jesus Christ, your Son,
who lives and reigns with you in the unity of the Holy Spirit,
one God, for ever and ever.

Prayer over the Offerings

Be pleased, O Lord, to enkindle our hearts
with the celestial fire of your Spirit,
just as you granted that Saint Alphonsus should celebrate
 these mysteries
and by them offer himself to you as a holy sacrifice.
Through Christ our Lord.

Prayer after Communion

O God, who gave us Saint Alphonsus
to be a faithful steward and preacher of this great mystery,
grant that your faithful
may receive it often and, receiving it,
praise you without end.
Through Christ our Lord.

August 2
Saint Eusebius of Vercelli, Bishop

From the Common of Pastors: For a Bishop (p. 1074).

Collect

Lead us, Lord God, to imitate the constancy of Saint Eusebius
in affirming the divinity of your Son,
so that, by preserving the faith he taught as your Bishop,
we may merit a share in the very life of your Son.
Who lives and reigns with you in the unity of the Holy Spirit,
one God, for ever and ever.

Saint Peter Julian Eymard, Priest

From the Common of Holy Men and Women: For Religious (p. 1107), or from the Common of Pastors: For One Pastor (p. 1078).

Collect

O God, who adorned Saint Peter Julian Eymard
with a wonderful love for the sacred mysteries
of the Body and Blood of your Son,
graciously grant
that we, too, may be worthy to receive
the delights he drew from this divine banquet.
Through our Lord Jesus Christ, your Son,
who lives and reigns with you in the unity of the Holy Spirit,
one God, for ever and ever.

August 4
Saint John Vianney, Priest
Memorial

From the Common of Pastors: For One Pastor (p. 1078).

Collect

Almighty and merciful God,
who made the Priest Saint John Vianney
wonderful in his pastoral zeal,
grant, we pray,
that through his intercession and example
we may in charity win brothers and sisters for Christ
and attain with them eternal glory.
Through our Lord Jesus Christ, your Son,
who lives and reigns with you in the unity of the Holy Spirit,
one God, for ever and ever.

August 5
The Dedication of the Basilica of Saint Mary Major

From the Common of the Blessed Virgin Mary (p. 1039).

Collect

Pardon the faults of your servants, we pray, O Lord,
that we, who cannot please you by our own deeds,
may be saved through the intercession
of the Mother of your Son and our Lord.
Who lives and reigns with you in the unity of the Holy Spirit,
one God, for ever and ever.

August 6
THE TRANSFIGURATION OF THE LORD
Feast

Entrance Antiphon
Cf. Mt 17: 5

In a resplendent cloud the Holy Spirit appeared.
The Father's voice was heard: This is my beloved Son,
with whom I am well pleased. Listen to him.

The Gloria in excelsis (Glory to God in the highest) is said.

Collect

O God, who in the glorious Transfiguration
of your Only Begotten Son
confirmed the mysteries of faith by the witness of the Fathers
and wonderfully prefigured our full adoption to sonship,
grant, we pray, to your servants,
that, listening to the voice of your beloved Son,
we may merit to become co-heirs with him.
Who lives and reigns with you in the unity of the Holy Spirit,
one God, for ever and ever.

When this Feast falls on a Sunday, the Creed is said.

Prayer over the Offerings

Sanctify, O Lord, we pray,
these offerings here made to celebrate
the glorious Transfiguration of your Only Begotten Son,
and by his radiant splendor
cleanse us from the stains of sin.
Through Christ our Lord.

Preface: The mystery of the Transfiguration.

℣. The Lord be with you.   ℟. And with your spir-it.

℣. Lift up your hearts.   ℟. We lift them up to the Lord.

℣. Let us give thanks to the Lord our God.   ℟. It is right and just.

It is truly right and just, our duty and our sal-va-tion, al-ways and everywhere to give you thanks, Lord, holy Father, almighty and e--ter-nal God, through Christ our Lord. For he revealed his glory in the presence of cho-sen wit-ness-es and filled with the greatest splendor that bod-i-ly form which he shares with all hu-man-i-ty, that the scandal of the Cross might be removed from the hearts of his dis-ci-ples and that he might show how in the Body of the whole Church is to be ful-filled what so wonderfully shone forth

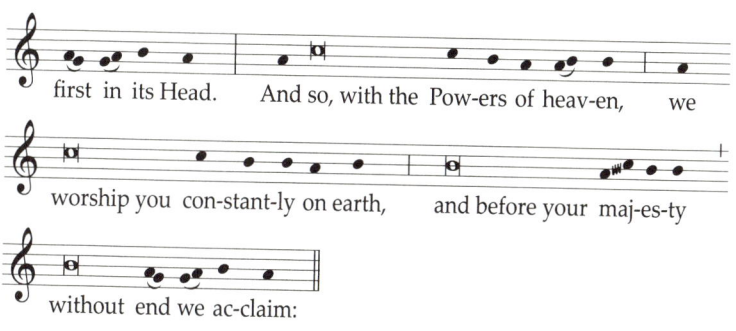

Holy, Holy, Holy Lord God of hosts . . .

Text without music:
V. **The Lord be with you.**
R. And with your spirit.

V. **Lift up your hearts.**
R. We lift them up to the Lord.

V. **Let us give thanks to the Lord our God.**
R. It is right and just.

It is truly right and just, our duty and our salvation,
always and everywhere to give you thanks,
Lord, holy Father, almighty and eternal God,
through Christ our Lord.

For he revealed his glory in the presence of chosen witnesses
and filled with the greatest splendor that bodily form
which he shares with all humanity,
that the scandal of the Cross
might be removed from the hearts of his disciples
and that he might show
how in the Body of the whole Church is to be fulfilled
what so wonderfully shone forth first in its Head.

And so, with the Powers of heaven,
we worship you constantly on earth,
and before your majesty
without end we acclaim:

Holy, Holy, Holy Lord God of hosts . . .

Communion Antiphon   Cf. 1 Jn 3: 2

When Christ appears, we shall be like him,
for we shall see him as he is.

Prayer after Communion

May the heavenly nourishment we have received,
O Lord, we pray,
transform us into the likeness of your Son,
whose radiant splendor you willed to make manifest
in his glorious Transfiguration.
Who lives and reigns for ever and ever.

August 7
Saint Sixtus II, Pope, and Companions, Martyrs

From the Common of Martyrs: For Several Martyrs (p. 1052).

Collect

By the power of the Holy Spirit,
we pray, almighty God,
make us docile in believing the faith
and courageous in confessing it,
just as you granted Saint Sixtus and his companions
that they might lay down their lives
for the sake of your word and in witness to Jesus.
Who lives and reigns with you in the unity of the Holy Spirit,
one God, for ever and ever.

Saint Cajetan, Priest

From the Common of Pastors: For One Pastor (p. 1078), or from the Common of Holy Men and Women: For Religious (p. 1107).

Collect

O God, who endowed the Priest Saint Cajetan
with the grace of imitating
the apostolic way of life,
grant us, through his example and intercession,
to trust in you at all times
and to seek unceasingly your Kingdom.
Through our Lord Jesus Christ, your Son,
who lives and reigns with you in the unity of the Holy Spirit,
one God, for ever and ever.

August 8
Saint Dominic, Priest
Memorial

Entrance Antiphon
Cf. Sir 15: 5

In the midst of the Church he opened his mouth,
and the Lord filled him with the spirit of wisdom and understanding
and clothed him in a robe of glory.

Collect

May Saint Dominic come to the help of your Church
by his merits and teaching, O Lord,
and may he, who was an outstanding preacher of your truth,
be a devoted intercessor on our behalf.
Through our Lord Jesus Christ, your Son,
who lives and reigns with you in the unity of the Holy Spirit,
one God, for ever and ever.

Prayer over the Offerings

Attend mercifully to the prayers we offer you, O Lord,
by the intercession of Saint Dominic,
and through the great power of this sacrifice
strengthen by the protection of your grace
those who champion the faith.
Through Christ our Lord.

Communion Antiphon
Lk 12: 42

This is the steward, faithful and prudent,
whom the Lord set over his household
to give them their allowance of food at the proper time.

Prayer after Communion

May your Church, O Lord,
receive with wholehearted reverence
the power of this heavenly Sacrament,
by which we have been nourished
on the commemoration of Saint Dominic,
and may your Church,
having flourished by means of his preaching,
be helped through his intercession.
Through Christ our Lord.

August 9
Saint Teresa Benedicta of the Cross, Virgin and Martyr

From the Common of Martyrs: For a Virgin Martyr (p. 1068), or from the Common of Virgins: For One Virgin (p. 1092).

Collect

God of our Fathers,
who brought the Martyr Saint Teresa Benedicta of the Cross
to know your crucified Son
and to imitate him even until death,
grant, through her intercession,
that the whole human race may acknowledge Christ as its Savior
and through him come to behold you for eternity.
Who lives and reigns with you in the unity of the Holy Spirit,
one God, for ever and ever.

August 10
SAINT LAWRENCE, DEACON AND MARTYR
Feast

Entrance Antiphon

This is the blessed Lawrence,
who gave himself up for the treasure of the Church:
for this he earned the suffering of martyrdom
to ascend with joy to the Lord Jesus Christ.

The Gloria in excelsis (Glory to God in the highest) is said.

Collect

O God, giver of that ardor of love for you
by which Saint Lawrence was outstandingly faithful in service
and glorious in martyrdom,
grant that we may love what he loved
and put into practice what he taught.
Through our Lord Jesus Christ, your Son,
who lives and reigns with you in the unity of the Holy Spirit,
one God, for ever and ever.

Prayer over the Offerings

Receive with favor, O Lord,
the offerings we joyfully make on the feast day of Saint Lawrence
and grant that they become a help to our salvation.
Through Christ our Lord.

Preface of Holy Martyrs, pp. 602-605.

Communion Antiphon
Cf. Jn 12: 26

Whoever serves me must follow me
and where I am there also will my servant be, says the Lord.

Prayer after Communion

Nourished by these sacred gifts,
we humbly implore you, Lord,
that the homage of dutiful service,
which we render on the feast of Saint Lawrence,
may bring us an increase of your saving grace.
Through Christ our Lord.

August 11
Saint Clare, Virgin
Memorial

From the Common of Virgins: For One Virgin (p. 1092), or from the Common of Holy Men and Women: For a Nun (p. 1106).

Collect

O God, who in your mercy led Saint Clare to a love of poverty,
grant, through her intercession,
that, following Christ in poverty of spirit,
we may merit to contemplate you
one day in the heavenly Kingdom.
Through our Lord Jesus Christ, your Son,
who lives and reigns with you in the unity of the Holy Spirit,
one God, for ever and ever.

August 12
Saint Jane Frances de Chantal, Religious

From the Common of Holy Men and Women: For Religious (p. 1107).

Collect

O God, who made Saint Jane Frances de Chantal
radiant with outstanding merits in different walks of life,
grant us, through her intercession,
that, walking faithfully in our vocation,
we may constantly be examples of shining light.
Through our Lord Jesus Christ, your Son,
who lives and reigns with you in the unity of the Holy Spirit,
one God, for ever and ever.

August 13
Saints Pontian, Pope, and Hippolytus, Priest, Martyrs

From the Common of Martyrs: For Several Martyrs (p. 1052), or from the Common of Pastors: For Several Pastors (p. 1077).

Collect

May the precious long-suffering of the just,
O Lord, we pray,
bring us a great increase of love for you
and always prompt in our hearts
constancy in the holy faith.
Through our Lord Jesus Christ, your Son,
who lives and reigns with you in the unity of the Holy Spirit,
one God, for ever and ever.

August 14
Saint Maximilian Kolbe, Priest and Martyr
Memorial

Entrance Antiphon
Mt 25: 34, 40

Come, you blessed of my Father, says the Lord.
Amen, I say to you:
Whatever you did for one of the least of my brethren,
you did it for me.

Collect

O God, who filled the Priest and Martyr Saint Maximilian Kolbe
with a burning love for the Immaculate Virgin Mary
and with zeal for souls and love of neighbor,
graciously grant, through his intercession,
that, striving for your glory by eagerly serving others,
we may be conformed, even until death, to your Son.
Who lives and reigns with you in the unity of the Holy Spirit,
one God, for ever and ever.

Prayer over the Offerings

We present our oblations to you, O Lord,
humbly praying that we may learn
from the example of Saint Maximilian
to offer our very lives to you.
Through Christ our Lord.

Communion Antiphon
Cf. Jn 15: 13

Greater love has no one
than to lay down his life for his friends, says the Lord.

Prayer after Communion

We pray, O Lord,
that, renewed by the Body and Blood of your Son,
we may be inflamed with the same fire of charity
that Saint Maximilian received from this holy banquet.
Through Christ our Lord.

August 15
THE ASSUMPTION
OF THE BLESSED VIRGIN MARY
Solemnity

At the Vigil Mass

This Mass is used on the evening of August 14, either before or after First Vespers (Evening Prayer I) of the Solemnity.

Entrance Antiphon

Glorious things are spoken of you, O Mary,
who today were exalted above the choirs of Angels
into eternal triumph with Christ.

The Gloria in excelsis (Glory to God in the highest) is said.

Collect

O God, who, looking on the lowliness of the Blessed Virgin Mary,
raised her to this grace,
that your Only Begotten Son was born of her according to the flesh
and that she was crowned this day with surpassing glory,
grant through her prayers,
that, saved by the mystery of your redemption,
we may merit to be exalted by you on high.
Through our Lord Jesus Christ, your Son,
who lives and reigns with you in the unity of the Holy Spirit,
one God, for ever and ever.

The Creed is said.

Prayer over the Offerings

Receive, we pray, O Lord,
the sacrifice of conciliation and praise,
which we celebrate on the Assumption of the holy Mother of God,
that it may lead us to your pardon
and confirm us in perpetual thanksgiving.
Through Christ our Lord.

Proper Preface, as in the following Mass, pp. 929-930.

Communion Antiphon　　　　　　　　　　　　　　　　　　　Cf. Lk 11: 27

Blessed is the womb of the Virgin Mary,
which bore the Son of the eternal Father.

Prayer after Communion

Having partaken of this heavenly table,
we beseech your mercy, Lord our God,
that we, who honor the Assumption of the Mother of God,
may be freed from every threat of harm.
Through Christ our Lord.

The Solemn Blessing formula, p. 682, may be used.

At the Mass during the Day

Entrance Antiphon
Cf. Rev 12: 1

A great sign appeared in heaven:
a woman clothed with the sun, and the moon beneath her feet,
and on her head a crown of twelve stars.

Or:

Let us all rejoice in the Lord,
as we celebrate the feast day in honor of the Virgin Mary,
at whose Assumption the Angels rejoice
and praise the Son of God.

The Gloria in excelsis (Glory to God in the highest) is said.

Collect

Almighty ever-living God,
who assumed the Immaculate Virgin Mary, the Mother of your Son,
body and soul into heavenly glory,
grant, we pray,
that, always attentive to the things that are above,
we may merit to be sharers of her glory.
Through our Lord Jesus Christ, your Son,
who lives and reigns with you in the unity of the Holy Spirit,
one God, for ever and ever.

The Creed is said.

Prayer over the Offerings

May this oblation, our tribute of homage,
rise up to you, O Lord,
and, through the intercession of the most Blessed Virgin Mary,
whom you assumed into heaven,
may our hearts, aflame with the fire of love,
constantly long for you.
Through Christ our Lord.

Preface: The Glory of Mary assumed into heaven.

V. The Lord be with you.   R. And with your spirit.

V. Lift up your hearts.   R. We lift them up to the Lord.

V. Let us give thanks to the Lord our God.   R. It is right and just.

It is truly right and just, our duty and our salvation, always and everywhere to give you thanks, Lord, holy Father, almighty and eternal God, through Christ our Lord. For today the Virgin Mother of God was assumed into heaven as the beginning and image of your Church's coming to perfection and a sign of sure hope and comfort to your pilgrim people; rightly you would not allow her to see the corruption of the tomb, since from her own body she marvelously brought forth your incarnate Son, the Author of all life. And so, in company with the choirs of Angels, we praise you, and with joy we proclaim:

Holy, Holy, Holy Lord God of hosts . . .

Text without music:
V. The Lord be with you.
R. And with your spirit.

V. Lift up your hearts.
R. We lift them up to the Lord.

V. Let us give thanks to the Lord our God.
R. It is right and just.

It is truly right and just, our duty and our salvation,
always and everywhere to give you thanks,
Lord, holy Father, almighty and eternal God,
through Christ our Lord.

For today the Virgin Mother of God
was assumed into heaven
as the beginning and image
of your Church's coming to perfection
and a sign of sure hope and comfort to your pilgrim people;
rightly you would not allow her
to see the corruption of the tomb
since from her own body she marvelously brought forth
your incarnate Son, the Author of all life.

And so, in company with the choirs of Angels,
we praise you, and with joy we proclaim:

Holy, Holy, Holy Lord God of hosts . . .

Communion Antiphon Lk 1: 48-49
All generations will call me blessed,
for he who is mighty has done great things for me.

Prayer after Communion
Having received the Sacrament of salvation,
we ask you to grant, O Lord,
that, through the intercession of the Blessed Virgin Mary,
whom you assumed into heaven,
we may be brought to the glory of the resurrection.
Through Christ our Lord.

The Solemn Blessing formula, p. 682, may be used.

August 16
Saint Stephen of Hungary

From the Common of Holy Men and Women: For One Saint (p. 1101).

Collect

Grant your Church, we pray, almighty God,
that she may have Saint Stephen of Hungary,
who fostered her growth while a king on earth,
as her glorious defender in heaven.
Through our Lord Jesus Christ, your Son,
who lives and reigns with you in the unity of the Holy Spirit,
one God, for ever and ever.

August 19
Saint John Eudes, Priest

From the Common of Pastors: For One Pastor (p. 1078), or from the Common of Holy Men and Women: For Religious (p. 1107).

Collect

O God, who wonderfully chose the Priest Saint John Eudes
to proclaim the unfathomable riches of Christ,
grant us, by his example and teachings,
that, growing in knowledge of you,
we may live faithfully by the light of the Gospel.
Through our Lord Jesus Christ, your Son,
who lives and reigns with you in the unity of the Holy Spirit,
one God, for ever and ever.

August 20
Saint Bernard, Abbot and Doctor of the Church
Memorial

Entrance Antiphon

Filled by the Lord with a spirit of understanding,
blessed Bernard ministered streams of clear teaching
to the people of God.

Collect

O God, who made of the Abbot Saint Bernard
a man consumed with zeal for your house
and a light shining and burning in your Church,
grant, through his intercession,
that we may be on fire with the same spirit
and walk always as children of light.
Through our Lord Jesus Christ, your Son,
who lives and reigns with you in the unity of the Holy Spirit,
one God, for ever and ever.

Prayer over the Offerings

We offer to your majesty, O Lord,
the Sacrament of unity and peace,
as we celebrate the Memorial of the Abbot Saint Bernard,
a man outstanding in word and deed,
who strove to bring order and concord to your Church.
Through Christ our Lord.

Communion Antiphon   Jn 15: 9

As the Father loves me, so I also love you;
remain in my love, says the Lord.

Prayer after Communion

May the food we have received, O Lord,
as we honor Saint Bernard,
work its effect in us,
so that, strengthened by his example
and instructed by his teaching,
we may be caught up in love of your incarnate Word.
Who lives and reigns for ever and ever.

August 21
Saint Pius X, Pope
Memorial

From the Common of Pastors: For a Pope (p. 1071).

Collect

O God, who to safeguard the Catholic faith
and to restore all things in Christ,
filled Pope Saint Pius the Tenth
with heavenly wisdom and apostolic fortitude,
graciously grant
that, following his teaching and example,
we may gain an eternal prize.
Through our Lord Jesus Christ, your Son,
who lives and reigns with you in the unity of the Holy Spirit,
one God, for ever and ever.

Prayer over the Offerings

Receive with kindness our oblations
and grant, O Lord, we pray,
that, following the teachings of Pope Saint Pius,
we may celebrate these divine mysteries with sincere reverence
and receive them in a spirit of faith.
Through Christ our Lord.

Prayer after Communion

Celebrating the Memorial of Pope Saint Pius,
we pray, O Lord our God,
that by the power of this heavenly table
we may be made constant in the faith
and be of one accord in your love.
Through Christ our Lord.

August 22
The Queenship of the Blessed Virgin Mary
Memorial

Entrance Antiphon
Cf. Ps 45 (44): 10

At your right stands the queen in robes of gold,
finely arrayed.

Collect
O God, who made the Mother of your Son
to be our Mother and our Queen,
graciously grant that, sustained by her intercession,
we may attain in the heavenly Kingdom
the glory promised to your children.
Through our Lord Jesus Christ, your Son,
who lives and reigns with you in the unity of the Holy Spirit,
one God, for ever and ever.

Prayer over the Offerings
As we observe this Memorial of the Blessed Virgin Mary,
we bring you our offerings, O Lord,
praying to be given strength by the humanity of Christ,
who offered himself to you on the Cross
as the unblemished oblation.
Who lives and reigns for ever and ever.

Preface I of the Blessed Virgin Mary (on the feast day), p. 590, or II, p. 592.

Communion Antiphon
Cf. Lk 1: 45

Blessed are you who have believed
that what was spoken to you by the Lord will be fulfilled.

Prayer after Communion
Having received this heavenly Sacrament,
we humbly pray, O Lord,
that we, who reverently celebrate the Memorial of the Blessed
    Virgin Mary,
may merit to be partakers at your eternal banquet.
Through Christ our Lord.

August 23
Saint Rose of Lima, Virgin

From the Common of Virgins: For One Virgin (p. 1092).

Collect

O God, you set Saint Rose of Lima on fire with your love,
so that, secluded from the world
in the austerity of a life of penance,
she might give herself to you alone;
grant, we pray, that through her intercession,
we may tread the paths of life on earth
and drink at the stream of your delights in heaven.
Through our Lord Jesus Christ, your Son,
who lives and reigns with you in the unity of the Holy Spirit,
one God, for ever and ever.

August 24
SAINT BARTHOLOMEW, APOSTLE
Feast

Entrance Antiphon   Cf. Ps 96 (95): 2-3

Proclaim the salvation of God day by day;
tell among the nations his glory.

The Gloria in excelsis (Glory to God in the highest) is said.

Collect

Strengthen in us, O Lord, the faith,
by which the blessed Apostle Bartholomew
clung wholeheartedly to your Son,
and grant that through the help of his prayers
your Church may become for all the nations
the sacrament of salvation.
Through our Lord Jesus Christ, your Son,
who lives and reigns with you in the unity of the Holy Spirit,
one God, for ever and ever.

Prayer over the Offerings

As we celebrate anew
the feast day of Saint Bartholomew, O Lord,
we pray that we may obtain your help
through the intercession of the Apostle,
in whose honor we bring you this sacrifice of praise.
Through Christ our Lord.

Preface of the Apostles, pp. 594-597.

Communion Antiphon

Lk 22: 29-30

I confer a kingdom on you,
just as my Father has conferred one on me,
that you may eat and drink at my table in my kingdom, says the Lord.

Prayer after Communion

As we celebrate the feast day
of the blessed Apostle Bartholomew,
we have received the pledge of eternal salvation, O Lord,
and we pray that it may be of help to us,
both now and for the life to come.
Through Christ our Lord.

The Solemn Blessing formula, p. 683, may be used.

August 25
Saint Louis

From the Common of Holy Men and Women: For One Saint (p. 1101).

Collect

O God, who brought Saint Louis
from the cares of earthly rule
to the glory of a heavenly realm,
grant, we pray, through his intercession,
that, by fulfilling our duties on earth,
we may seek out your eternal Kingdom.
Through our Lord Jesus Christ, your Son,
who lives and reigns with you in the unity of the Holy Spirit,
one God, for ever and ever.

Saint Joseph Calasanz, Priest

From the Common of Holy Men and Women: For Educators (p. 1111), or from the Common of Pastors: For One Pastor (p. 1078).

Collect

O God, who adorned the Priest Saint Joseph Calasanz
with such charity and patience
that he labored tirelessly
to educate children and endow them with every virtue,
grant, we pray, that we, who venerate him as a teacher of wisdom,
may constantly imitate him,
for he was a co-worker of your truth.
Through our Lord Jesus Christ, your Son,
who lives and reigns with you in the unity of the Holy Spirit,
one God, for ever and ever.

August 27
Saint Monica
Memorial

From the Common of Holy Men and Women: For Holy Women (p. 1113).

Collect

O God, who console the sorrowful
and who mercifully accepted
the motherly tears of Saint Monica
for the conversion of her son Augustine,
grant us, through the intercession of them both,
that we may bitterly regret our sins
and find the grace of your pardon.
Through our Lord Jesus Christ, your Son,
who lives and reigns with you in the unity of the Holy Spirit,
one God, for ever and ever.

August 28
Saint Augustine, Bishop and Doctor of the Church
Memorial

Entrance Antiphon
Cf. Sir 15: 5

In the midst of the Church he opened his mouth,
and the Lord filled him
with the spirit of wisdom and understanding
and clothed him in a robe of glory.

Collect

Renew in your Church, we pray, O Lord,
the spirit with which you endowed
your Bishop Saint Augustine
that, filled with the same spirit,
we may thirst for you,
the sole fount of true wisdom,
and seek you, the author of heavenly love.
Through our Lord Jesus Christ, your Son,
who lives and reigns with you in the unity of the Holy Spirit,
one God, for ever and ever.

Prayer over the Offerings

Celebrating the memorial of our salvation,
we humbly beseech your mercy, O Lord,
that this Sacrament of your loving kindness
may be for us the sign of unity
and the bond of charity.
Through Christ our Lord.

Communion Antiphon
Mt 23: 10, 8

Thus says the Lord: You have but one teacher, the Christ,
and you are all brothers.

Prayer after Communion

May partaking of Christ's table
sanctify us, we pray, O Lord,
that, being made members of his Body,
we may become what we have received.
Through Christ our Lord.

August 29
The Passion of Saint John the Baptist
Memorial

Entrance Antiphon
Cf. Ps 119 (118): 46-47

I spoke, O Lord, of your decrees before kings,
and was not confounded;
I pondered your commands and loved them greatly.

Collect

O God, who willed that Saint John the Baptist
should go ahead of your Son
both in his birth and in his death,
grant that, as he died a Martyr for truth and justice,
we, too, may fight hard
for the confession of what you teach.
Through our Lord Jesus Christ, your Son,
who lives and reigns with you in the unity of the Holy Spirit,
one God, for ever and ever.

Prayer over the Offerings

Through these offerings which we bring you, O Lord,
grant that we may make straight your paths,
as taught by that voice crying in the desert,
Saint John the Baptist,
who powerfully sealed his teaching
by the shedding of his blood.
Through Christ our Lord.

Preface: The mission of the Precursor.

V. The Lord be with you.
R. And with your spirit.

V. Lift up your hearts.
R. We lift them up to the Lord.

V. Let us give thanks to the Lord our God.
R. It is right and just.

It is truly right and just, our duty and our salvation,
always and everywhere to give you thanks,
Lord, holy Father, almighty and eternal God,
through Christ our Lord.

In his Precursor, Saint John the Baptist,
we praise your great glory,
for you consecrated him for a singular honor
among those born of women.

His birth brought great rejoicing;
even in the womb he leapt for joy
at the coming of human salvation.
He alone of all the prophets
pointed out the Lamb of redemption.

And to make holy the flowing waters,
he baptized the very author of Baptism
and was privileged to bear him supreme witness
by the shedding of his blood.

And so, with the Powers of heaven,
we worship you constantly on earth,
and before your majesty
without end we acclaim:

Holy, Holy, Holy Lord God of hosts . . .

Text with music, pp. 880-881.

Communion Antiphon
Jn 3: 27, 30

John answered and said:
He must increase; but I must decrease.

Prayer after Communion

Grant, O Lord,
as we celebrate the heavenly birth of Saint John the Baptist,
that we may revere, for what it signifies,
the saving Sacrament we have received
and, even more, may rejoice
at its clear effects in us.
Through Christ our Lord.

SEPTEMBER

September 3
Saint Gregory the Great, Pope and Doctor of the Church
Memorial

Entrance Antiphon

Blessed Gregory, raised upon the throne of Peter,
sought always the beauty of the Lord
and lived in celebration of that love.

Collect

O God, who care for your people with gentleness
and rule them in love,
through the intercession of Pope Saint Gregory,
endow, we pray, with a spirit of wisdom
those to whom you have given authority to govern,
that the flourishing of a holy flock
may become the eternal joy of the shepherds.
Through our Lord Jesus Christ, your Son,
who lives and reigns with you in the unity of the Holy Spirit,
one God, for ever and ever.

Prayer over the Offerings

Grant our supplication, we pray, O Lord,
that this sacrifice we present in celebration of Saint Gregory
may be for our good,
since through its offering
you have loosed the offenses of all the world.
Through Christ our Lord.

Communion Antiphon   Lk 12: 42

This is the steward, faithful and prudent,
whom the Lord set over his household
to give them their allowance of food at the proper time.

Prayer after Communion

> Through Christ the teacher, O Lord,
> instruct those you feed with Christ, the living Bread,
> that on the feast day of Saint Gregory
> they may learn your truth
> and express it in works of charity.
> Through Christ our Lord.

September 8
THE NATIVITY OF THE BLESSED VIRGIN MARY
Feast

Entrance Antiphon

> Let us celebrate with joy the Nativity of the Blessed Virgin Mary,
> for from her arose the sun of justice, Christ our God.

The Gloria in excelsis (Glory to God in the highest) is said.

Collect

> Impart to your servants, we pray, O Lord,
> the gift of heavenly grace,
> that the feast of the Nativity of the Blessed Virgin
> may bring deeper peace
> to those for whom the birth of her Son
> was the dawning of salvation.
> Through our Lord Jesus Christ, your Son,
> who lives and reigns with you in the unity of the Holy Spirit,
> one God, for ever and ever.

Prayer over the Offerings

> May the humanity of your Only Begotten Son
> come, O Lord, to our aid,
> and may he, who at his birth from the Blessed Virgin
> did not diminish but consecrated her integrity,
> by taking from us now our wicked deeds,
> make our oblation acceptable to you.
> Through Christ our Lord.
>
> Or:

As we celebrate with joy
the Nativity of the Blessed Virgin Mary,
we bring you our offerings, O Lord,
and we humbly pray to be given strength
by the humanity of your Son,
who from her was pleased to take flesh.
Who lives and reigns for ever and ever.

Preface I of the Blessed Virgin Mary (and on the Nativity), p. 590, or II, p. 592.

Communion Antiphon
Is 7: 14; Mt 1: 21
Behold, the Virgin will bear a son,
who will save his people from their sins.

Prayer after Communion
May your Church exult, O Lord,
for you have renewed her with these sacred mysteries,
as she rejoices in the Nativity of the Blessed Virgin Mary,
which was the hope and the daybreak of salvation
for all the world.
Through Christ our Lord.

The Solemn Blessing formula, p. 682, may be used.

[In the Dioceses of the United States]

September 9
Saint Peter Claver, Priest
Memorial

From the Common of Pastors: For One Pastor (p. 1078), or from the Common of Holy Men and Women: For Those Who Practiced Works of Mercy (p. 1110).

Collect
O God, who made Saint Peter Claver a slave of slaves
and strengthened him with wonderful charity and patience
as he came to their help,
grant, through his intercession,
that, seeking the things of Jesus Christ,
we may love our neighbor in deeds and in truth.
Through our Lord Jesus Christ, your Son,
who lives and reigns with you in the unity of the Holy Spirit,
one God, for ever and ever.

September 12
The Most Holy Name of Mary

Entrance Antiphon *Cf. Jdt 13: 18-19*

Blessed are you, O Virgin Mary, by the Lord God Most High,
above all women on the earth;
for he has so exalted your name
that your praise shall be undying on our lips.

Collect

Grant, we pray, almighty God,
that, for all who celebrate the glorious Name
of the Blessed Virgin Mary,
she may obtain your merciful favor.
Through our Lord Jesus Christ, your Son,
who lives and reigns with you in the unity of the Holy Spirit,
one God, for ever and ever.

Prayer over the Offerings

May the intercession of Blessed Mary ever-Virgin
commend our offerings,
we pray, O Lord,
and may it make us acceptable to your majesty
as we revere and venerate her Name.
Through Christ our Lord.

Communion Antiphon *Cf. Lk 1: 48*

All generations will call me blessed,
for God has looked on his lowly handmaid.

Prayer after Communion

May we obtain the grace of your blessing, O Lord,
through the intercession of Mary, the Mother of God,
that from her, whose holy Name we venerate,
we may obtain help in our every need.
Through Christ our Lord.

September 13
Saint John Chrysostom, Bishop and Doctor of the Church
Memorial

Entrance Antiphon
Cf. Dn 12: 3

Those who are wise will shine brightly
like the splendor of the firmament
and those who lead the many to justice shall be like the stars for ever.

Collect

O God, strength of those who hope in you,
who willed that the Bishop Saint John Chrysostom
should be illustrious by his wonderful eloquence
and his experience of suffering,
grant us, we pray,
that, instructed by his teachings,
we may be strengthened through the example
of his invincible patience.
Through our Lord Jesus Christ, your Son,
who lives and reigns with you in the unity of the Holy Spirit,
one God, for ever and ever.

Prayer over the Offerings

May the sacrifice which we gladly present
in commemoration of Saint John Chrysostom
be pleasing to you, O God,
for, taught by him,
we, too, give ourselves entirely to you in praise.
Through Christ our Lord.

Communion Antiphon
Cf. 1 Cor 1: 23-24

We proclaim Christ crucified;
Christ, the power of God and the wisdom of God.

Prayer after Communion

Grant, O merciful God,
that these mysteries we have received
as we commemorate Saint John Chrysostom,
may confirm us in your love
and enable us to be faithful in confessing your truth.
Through Christ our Lord.

September 14
THE EXALTATION OF THE HOLY CROSS
Feast

Entrance Antiphon
Cf. Gal 6: 14

We should glory in the Cross of our Lord Jesus Christ,
in whom is our salvation, life and resurrection,
through whom we are saved and delivered.

The Gloria in excelsis (Glory to God in the highest) is said.

Collect

O God, who willed that your Only Begotten Son
should undergo the Cross to save the human race,
grant, we pray,
that we, who have known his mystery on earth,
may merit the grace of his redemption in heaven.
Through our Lord Jesus Christ, your Son,
who lives and reigns with you in the unity of the Holy Spirit,
one God, for ever and ever.

When this Feast falls on a Sunday, the Creed is said.

Prayer over the Offerings

May this oblation, O Lord,
which on the altar of the Cross
canceled the offense of the whole world,
cleanse us, we pray, of all our sins.
Through Christ our Lord.

Preface: The victory of the glorious Cross.

V. The Lord be with you.   R. And with your spir-it.

V. Lift up your hearts.   R. We lift them up to the Lord.

V. Let us give thanks to the Lord our God.   R. It is right and just.

Holy, Holy, Holy Lord God of hosts . . .

Text without music:
V. The Lord be with you.
R. And with your spirit.

V. Lift up your hearts.
R. We lift them up to the Lord.

V. Let us give thanks to the Lord our God.
R. It is right and just.

It is truly right and just, our duty and our salvation,
always and everywhere to give you thanks,
Lord, holy Father, almighty and eternal God.

For you placed the salvation of the human race
on the wood of the Cross,
so that, where death arose,
life might again spring forth
and the evil one, who conquered on a tree,
might likewise on a tree be conquered,
through Christ our Lord.

Through him the Angels praise your majesty,
Dominions adore and Powers tremble before you.
Heaven and the Virtues of heaven and the blessed Seraphim
worship together with exultation.
May our voices, we pray, join with theirs
in humble praise, as we acclaim:

Holy, Holy, Holy Lord God of hosts . . .

Preface I of the Passion of the Lord, p. 554, may also be used.

Communion Antiphon   Jn 12: 32
When I am lifted up from the earth,
I will draw everyone to myself, says the Lord.

Prayer after Communion
Having been nourished by your holy banquet,
we beseech you, Lord Jesus Christ,
to bring those you have redeemed
by the wood of your life-giving Cross
to the glory of the resurrection.
Who live and reign for ever and ever.

September 15
Our Lady of Sorrows
Memorial

Entrance Antiphon Cf. Lk 2: 34-35

Simeon said to Mary: Behold, this child is destined
for the ruin and rising of many in Israel,
and to be a sign of contradiction;
and your own soul a sword will pierce.

Collect

O God, who willed
that, when your Son was lifted high on the Cross,
his Mother should stand close by and share his suffering,
grant that your Church,
participating with the Virgin Mary in the Passion of Christ,
may merit a share in his Resurrection.
Who lives and reigns with you in the unity of the Holy Spirit,
one God, for ever and ever.

Prayer over the Offerings

Receive, O merciful God, to the praise of your name
the prayers and sacrificial offerings
which we bring to you
as we venerate the Blessed Virgin Mary,
whom you graciously gave to us
as a most devoted Mother
when she stood by the Cross of Jesus.
Who lives and reigns for ever and ever.

Preface I of the Blessed Virgin Mary (on the feast day), p. 590, or II, p. 592.

Communion Antiphon Cf. 1 Pt 4: 13

Rejoice when you share in the sufferings of Christ,
that you may also rejoice exultantly when his glory is revealed.

Prayer after Communion

Having received the Sacrament of eternal redemption,
we humbly ask, O Lord,
that, honoring how the Blessed Virgin Mary
suffered with her Son,
we may complete in ourselves for the Church's sake
what is lacking in the sufferings of Christ.
Who lives and reigns for ever and ever.

September 16
Saints Cornelius, Pope, and Cyprian, Bishop, Martyrs
Memorial

From the Common of Martyrs: For Several Martyrs (p. 1052), or from the Common of Pastors: For a Bishop (p. 1074).

Collect

O God, who gave Saints Cornelius and Cyprian to your people
as diligent shepherds and valiant Martyrs,
grant that through their intercession
we may be strengthened in faith and constancy
and spend ourselves without reserve
for the unity of the Church.
Through our Lord Jesus Christ, your Son,
who lives and reigns with you in the unity of the Holy Spirit,
one God, for ever and ever.

Prayer over the Offerings

Receive, we pray, O Lord, the offerings of your people
in honor of the passion of your holy Martyrs
Saints Cornelius and Cyprian,
and may the gifts that gave them courage under persecution
make us, too, steadfast in all trials.
Through Christ our Lord.

Prayer after Communion

Through these mysteries which we have received,
we humbly beseech you, O Lord,
that by the example of the Martyrs
Saints Cornelius and Cyprian
we may be strengthened with the fortitude of your Spirit
to bear witness to the truth of the Gospel.
Through Christ our Lord.

September 17
Saint Robert Bellarmine, Bishop and Doctor of the Church

From the Common of Pastors: For a Bishop (p. 1074), or from the Common of Doctors of the Church (p. 1088).

Collect

O God, who adorned the Bishop Saint Robert Bellarmine
with wonderful learning and virtue
to vindicate the faith of your Church,
grant, through his intercession,
that in the integrity of that same faith
your people may always find joy.
Through our Lord Jesus Christ, your Son,
who lives and reigns with you in the unity of the Holy Spirit,
one God, for ever and ever.

September 19
Saint Januarius, Bishop and Martyr

From the Common of Martyrs: For One Martyr (p. 1059), or from the Common of Pastors: For a Bishop (p. 1074).

Collect

O God, who grant us to venerate
the memory of the Martyr Saint Januarius,
give us, we pray, the joy of his company
in blessed happiness for all eternity.
Through our Lord Jesus Christ, your Son,
who lives and reigns with you in the unity of the Holy Spirit,
one God, for ever and ever.

September 20
Saints Andrew Kim Tae-gŏn, Priest, and Paul Chŏng Ha-sang, and Companions, Martyrs
Memorial

Entrance Antiphon

The blood of the holy Martyrs
was poured out for Christ upon the earth;
therefore they have gained everlasting rewards.

Collect

O God, who have been pleased to increase
your adopted children in all the world,
and who made the blood of the Martyrs
Saint Andrew Kim Tae-gŏn and his companions
a most fruitful seed of Christians,
grant that we may be defended by their help
and profit always from their example.
Through our Lord Jesus Christ, your Son,
who lives and reigns with you in the unity of the Holy Spirit,
one God, for ever and ever.

Prayer over the Offerings

Look with favor, almighty God,
on the offerings of your people
and, through the intercession of the blessed Martyrs,
grant that we ourselves may become
a sacrifice acceptable to you
for the salvation of all the world.
Through Christ our Lord.

Communion Antiphon   Mt 10: 32

Everyone who acknowledges me before others
I will acknowledge before my heavenly Father, says the Lord.

Prayer after Communion

Nourished with the food of the valiant
as we celebrate the blessed Martyrs,
we humbly ask you, O Lord,
that, clinging faithfully to Christ,
we may labor in the Church for the salvation of all.
Through Christ our Lord.

September 21
SAINT MATTHEW, APOSTLE AND EVANGELIST
Feast

Entrance Antiphon
Cf. Mt 28: 19-20

Go and make disciples of all nations, baptizing them
and teaching them to observe all that I have commanded you,
says the Lord.

The Gloria in excelsis (Glory to God in the highest) is said.

Collect

O God, who with untold mercy
were pleased to choose as an Apostle
Saint Matthew, the tax collector,
grant that, sustained by his example and intercession,
we may merit to hold firm in following you.
Through our Lord Jesus Christ, your Son,
who lives and reigns with you in the unity of the Holy Spirit,
one God, for ever and ever.

Prayer over the Offerings

As we celebrate anew the memory of Saint Matthew,
we bring you sacrifices and prayers, O Lord,
humbly imploring you to look kindly on your Church,
whose faith you have nourished by the preaching of the Apostles.
Through Christ our Lord.

Preface of the Apostles, pp. 594-597.

Communion Antiphon
Mt 9: 13

I did not come to call the just, but sinners, says the Lord.

Prayer after Communion

Sharing in that saving joy, O Lord,
with which Saint Matthew welcomed
the Savior as a guest in his home, we pray:
grant that we may always be renewed
by the food we receive from Christ,
who came to call not the just, but sinners to salvation.
Who lives and reigns for ever and ever.

The Solemn Blessing formula, p. 683, may be used.

September 23
Saint Pius of Pietrelcina, Priest
Memorial

From the Common of Pastors: For One Pastor (p. 1078), or from the Common of Holy Men and Women: For Religious (p. 1107).

Collect

Almighty ever-living God, who, by a singular grace,
gave the Priest Saint Pius a share in the Cross of your Son
and, by means of his ministry,
renewed the wonders of your mercy,
grant that through his intercession
we may be united constantly to the sufferings of Christ,
and so brought happily to the glory of the resurrection.
Through our Lord Jesus Christ, your Son,
who lives and reigns with you in the unity of the Holy Spirit,
one God, for ever and ever.

September 26
Saints Cosmas and Damian, Martyrs

From the Common of Martyrs: For Several Martyrs (p. 1052).

Collect

May you be magnified, O Lord,
by the revered memory of your Saints Cosmas and Damian,
for with providence beyond words
you have conferred on them everlasting glory,
and on us, your unfailing help.
Through our Lord Jesus Christ, your Son,
who lives and reigns with you in the unity of the Holy Spirit,
one God, for ever and ever.

Prayer over the Offerings

In honor of the precious death of your just ones, O Lord,
we come to offer that sacrifice
from which all martyrdom draws its origin.
Through Christ our Lord.

Prayer after Communion

Preserve in us your gift, O Lord,
and may what we have received at your hands
as we commemorate the Martyrs Saints Cosmas and Damian,
bring us healing, salvation and peace.
Through Christ our Lord.

September 27
Saint Vincent de Paul, Priest
Memorial

Entrance Antiphon   Cf. Lk 4: 18

The Spirit of the Lord is upon me, for he has anointed me
and sent me to preach the good news to the poor,
to heal the broken-hearted.

Collect

O God, who for the relief of the poor
and the formation of the clergy
endowed the Priest Saint Vincent de Paul
with apostolic virtues,
grant, we pray, that, afire with that same spirit,
we may love what he loved
and put into practice what he taught.
Through our Lord Jesus Christ, your Son,
who lives and reigns with you in the unity of the Holy Spirit,
one God, for ever and ever.

Prayer over the Offerings

O God, who enabled Saint Vincent
to imitate what he celebrated in the divine mysteries,
grant that by the power of this sacrifice
we, too, may be transformed into an oblation acceptable to you.
Through Christ our Lord.

Communion Antiphon   Cf. Ps 107 (106): 8-9

Let them thank the Lord for his mercy,
his wonders for the children of men,
for he satisfies the thirsty soul,
and the hungry he fills with good things.

Prayer after Communion

Renewed by this heavenly Sacrament, O Lord,
we implore
that, just as we are prompted by Saint Vincent's example
to imitate your Son in his preaching of the Gospel to the poor,
so, too, we may be sustained by his prayers.
Through Christ our Lord.

September 28
Saint Wenceslaus, Martyr

From the Common of Martyrs: For One Martyr (p. 1059).

Collect

O God, who taught the Martyr Saint Wenceslaus
to place the heavenly Kingdom before an earthly one,
grant through his prayers that, denying ourselves,
we may hold fast to you with all our heart.
Through our Lord Jesus Christ, your Son,
who lives and reigns with you in the unity of the Holy Spirit,
one God, for ever and ever.

Saint Lawrence Ruiz and Companions, Martyrs

From the Common of Martyrs: For Several Martyrs (p. 1052).

Collect

Grant us, we pray, Lord God,
the same perseverance shown by your Martyrs
Saint Lawrence Ruiz and his companions
in serving you and their neighbor,
since those persecuted for the sake of righteousness
are blessed in your Kingdom.
Through our Lord Jesus Christ, your Son,
who lives and reigns with you in the unity of the Holy Spirit,
one God, for ever and ever.

September 29
SAINTS MICHAEL, GABRIEL AND RAPHAEL, ARCHANGELS
Feast

Entrance Antiphon
Cf. Ps 103 (102): 20

Bless the Lord, all you his angels, mighty in power,
fulfilling his word, and heeding his voice.

The Gloria in excelsis (Glory to God in the highest) is said.

Collect
O God, who dispose in marvelous order
ministries both angelic and human,
graciously grant
that our life on earth may be defended
by those who watch over us
as they minister perpetually to you in heaven.
Through our Lord Jesus Christ, your Son,
who lives and reigns with you in the unity of the Holy Spirit,
one God, for ever and ever.

Prayer over the Offerings
We offer you a sacrifice of praise, O Lord,
humbly entreating,
that, as these gifts are borne by the ministry of Angels
into the presence of your majesty,
so you may receive them favorably
and make them profitable for our salvation.
Through Christ our Lord.

Preface: God glorified through the Angels.

V. The Lord be with you. R. And with your spir-it.

V. Lift up your hearts. R. We lift them up to the Lord.

V. Let us give thanks to the Lord our God. R. It is right and just.

It is truly right and just, our duty and our sal-va-tion, al-ways and everywhere to give you thanks, Lord, holy Father, almighty and e--ter-nal God, and to praise you with-out end in your Arch-an-gels and An-gels. For the honor we pay the angelic creatures in whom you de-light redounds to your own sur-pas-sing glo-ry, and by their great dig-ni-ty and splen-dor you show how infinitely great you are, to be exalted a-bove all things, through Christ our Lord. Through him the multitude of Angels ex-tols your maj-es-ty, and we are united with them in exultant ad-o-ra-tion, as with one voice of praise we ac-claim:

Holy, Holy, Holy Lord God of hosts . . .

Text without music:
℣. **The Lord be with you.**
℞. And with your spirit.

℣. **Lift up your hearts.**
℞. We lift them up to the Lord.

℣. **Let us give thanks to the Lord our God.**
℞. It is right and just.

It is truly right and just, our duty and our salvation,
always and everywhere to give you thanks,
Lord, holy Father, almighty and eternal God,
and to praise you without end
in your Archangels and Angels.

For the honor we pay the angelic creatures
in whom you delight
redounds to your own surpassing glory,
and by their great dignity and splendor
you show how infinitely great you are,
to be exalted above all things,
through Christ our Lord.

Through him the multitude of Angels extols your majesty,
and we are united with them in exultant adoration,
as with one voice of praise we acclaim:

Holy, Holy, Holy Lord God of hosts . . .

Communion Antiphon   Ps 138 (137): 1
I will thank you, Lord, with all my heart;
in the presence of the Angels I will praise you.

Prayer after Communion
Having been nourished with heavenly Bread,
we beseech you humbly, O Lord,
that, drawing from it new strength,
under the faithful protection of your Angels,
we may advance boldly along the way of salvation.
Through Christ our Lord.

September 30
Saint Jerome, Priest and Doctor of the Church
Memorial

Entrance Antiphon   Cf. Ps 1: 2-3

Blessed indeed is he
who ponders the law of the Lord day and night:
he will yield his fruit in due season.

Collect

O God, who gave the Priest Saint Jerome
a living and tender love for Sacred Scripture,
grant that your people
may be ever more fruitfully nourished by your Word
and find in it the fount of life.
Through our Lord Jesus Christ, your Son,
who lives and reigns with you in the unity of the Holy Spirit,
one God, for ever and ever.

Prayer over the Offerings

Grant us, O Lord,
that, having meditated on your Word,
following the example of Saint Jerome,
we may more eagerly draw near
to offer your majesty the sacrifice of salvation.
Through Christ our Lord.

Communion Antiphon   Cf. Jer 15: 16

Lord God, your words were found and I consumed them;
your word became the joy and the happiness of my heart.

Prayer after Communion

May these holy gifts we have received, O Lord,
as we rejoice in celebrating Saint Jerome,
stir up the hearts of your faithful
so that, attentive to sacred teachings,
they may understand the path they are to follow
and, by following it, obtain life everlasting.
Through Christ our Lord.

OCTOBER

October 1
Saint Thérèse of the Child Jesus, Virgin and Doctor of the Church
Memorial

Entrance Antiphon   Cf. Dt 32: 10-12

The Lord led her and taught her,
and kept her as the apple of his eye.
Like an eagle spreading its wings
he took her up and bore her on his shoulders.
The Lord alone was her guide.

Collect

O God, who open your Kingdom
to those who are humble and to little ones,
lead us to follow trustingly in the little way of Saint Thérèse,
so that through her intercession
we may see your eternal glory revealed.
Through our Lord Jesus Christ, your Son,
who lives and reigns with you in the unity of the Holy Spirit,
one God, for ever and ever.

Prayer over the Offerings

As we proclaim your wonders in Saint Thérèse, O Lord,
we humbly implore your majesty,
that, as her merits were pleasing to you,
so, too, our dutiful service may find favor in your sight.
Through Christ our Lord.

Communion Antiphon   Mt 18: 3

Thus says the Lord:
Unless you turn and become like children,
you will not enter the Kingdom of Heaven.

Prayer after Communion

May the Sacrament we have received, O Lord,
kindle in us the force of that love
with which Saint Thérèse dedicated herself to you
and longed to obtain your mercy for all.
Through Christ our Lord.

October 2
The Holy Guardian Angels
Memorial

Entrance Antiphon
Cf. Dn 3: 58

Angels of the Lord, bless the Lord,
praise and exalt him above all for ever.

Collect

O God, who in your unfathomable providence
are pleased to send your holy Angels to guard us,
hear our supplication as we cry to you,
that we may always be defended by their protection
and rejoice eternally in their company.
Through our Lord Jesus Christ, your Son,
who lives and reigns with you in the unity of the Holy Spirit,
one God, for ever and ever.

Prayer over the Offerings

Receive, O Lord, the offerings we bring before you
as we venerate your holy Angels,
and graciously grant
that under their constant protection
we may be delivered from present dangers
and brought happily to life eternal.
Through Christ our Lord.

Preface: God glorified through the Angels.

V. **The Lord be with you.**
R. And with your spirit.

V. **Lift up your hearts.**
R. We lift them up to the Lord.

V. **Let us give thanks to the Lord our God.**
R. It is right and just.

It is truly right and just, our duty and our salvation,
always and everywhere to give you thanks,
Lord, holy Father, almighty and eternal God,
and to praise you without end
in your Archangels and Angels.

For the honor we pay the angelic creatures
in whom you delight
redounds to your own surpassing glory,
and by their great dignity and splendor
you show how infinitely great you are,
to be exalted above all things,
through Christ our Lord.

Through him the multitude of Angels extols your majesty,
and we are united with them in exultant adoration,
as with one voice of praise we acclaim:

Holy, Holy, Holy Lord God of hosts . . .

Text with music, p. 960.

Communion Antiphon
Cf. Ps 138 (137): 1

In the presence of the Angels I will praise you, my God.

Prayer after Communion

As you are pleased to nourish us for eternal life
with so great a Sacrament, O Lord,
direct us by the ministry of Angels
into the way of salvation and peace.
Through Christ our Lord.

October 4
Saint Francis of Assisi
Memorial

Entrance Antiphon

Francis, the man of God, left his home behind,
abandoned his inheritance and became poor and penniless,
but the Lord raised him up.

Collect

O God, by whose gift Saint Francis
was conformed to Christ in poverty and humility,
grant that, by walking in Francis' footsteps,
we may follow your Son,
and, through joyful charity,
come to be united with you.
Through our Lord Jesus Christ, your Son,
who lives and reigns with you in the unity of the Holy Spirit,
one God, for ever and ever.

Prayer over the Offerings

As we bring you these offerings, O Lord,
we pray that we may be rightly disposed
for the celebration of the mystery of the Cross,
which Saint Francis so ardently embraced.
Through Christ our Lord.

Communion Antiphon   Mt 5: 3

Blessed are the poor in spirit,
for theirs is the Kingdom of Heaven.

Prayer after Communion

Grant us, we pray, O Lord,
through these holy gifts which we have received,
that, imitating the charity and apostolic zeal of Saint Francis,
we may experience the effects of your love
and spread them everywhere for the salvation of all.
Through Christ our Lord.

October 6
Saint Bruno, Priest

From the Common of Holy Men and Women: For a Monk (p. 1105), or from the Common of Pastors: For One Pastor (p. 1078).

Collect

O God, who called Saint Bruno to serve you in solitude,
grant, through his intercession,
that amid the changes of this world
we may constantly look to you alone.
Through our Lord Jesus Christ, your Son,
who lives and reigns with you in the unity of the Holy Spirit,
one God, for ever and ever.

[In the Dioceses of the United States]
Blessed Marie Rose Durocher, Virgin

From the Common of Virgins: For One Virgin (p. 1092).

Collect

Lord, who enkindled in the heart of Blessed Marie Rose Durocher
the flame of ardent charity
and a great desire to cooperate
in the mission of the Church as a teacher,
grant us that same active love,
so that, in responding to the needs of the world today,
we may lead our brothers and sisters
to the blessedness of eternal life.
Through our Lord Jesus Christ, your Son,
who lives and reigns with you in the unity of the Holy Spirit,
one God, for ever and ever.

October 7
Our Lady of the Rosary
Memorial

Entrance Antiphon   Cf. Lk 1: 28, 42

Hail Mary, full of grace, the Lord is with you.
Blessed are you among women
and blessed is the fruit of your womb.

Collect

Pour forth, we beseech you, O Lord,
your grace into our hearts,
that we, to whom the Incarnation of Christ your Son
was made known by the message of an Angel,
may, through the intercession of the Blessed Virgin Mary,
by his Passion and Cross
be brought to the glory of his Resurrection.
Who lives and reigns with you in the unity of the Holy Spirit,
one God, for ever and ever.

Prayer over the Offerings

Grant, we pray, O Lord,
that we may be rightly conformed to these offerings we bring
and so honor the mysteries of your Only Begotten Son,
as to be made worthy of his promises.
Who lives and reigns for ever and ever.

Preface I of the Blessed Virgin Mary (on the feast day) p. 590, or II p. 592.

Communion Antiphon   Lk 1: 31

Behold, you will conceive in your womb and bear a son,
and you shall name him Jesus.

Prayer after Communion

We pray, O Lord our God,
that, just as we proclaim in this Sacrament
the Death and Resurrection of your Son,
so, being made partakers in his suffering,
we may also merit a share
in his consolation and his glory.
Who lives and reigns for ever and ever.

October 9
Saint Denis, Bishop, and Companions, Martyrs

From the Common of Martyrs: For Several Martyrs (p. 1052).

Collect

O God, who sent Saint Denis and his companions
to preach your glory to the nations
and strengthened them for their mission
with the virtue of constancy in suffering,
grant, we pray, that we may imitate them
in disdaining prosperity in this world
and in being undaunted by any trial.
Through our Lord Jesus Christ, your Son,
who lives and reigns with you in the unity of the Holy Spirit,
one God, for ever and ever.

Saint John Leonardi, Priest

From the Common of Pastors: For Missionaries (p. 1084), or from the Common of Holy Men and Women: For Those Who Practiced Works of Mercy (p. 1110).

Collect

O God, giver of all good things,
who through the Priest Saint John Leonardi
caused the Gospel to be announced to the nations,
grant, through his intercession,
that the true faith may always and everywhere prosper.
Through our Lord Jesus Christ, your Son,
who lives and reigns with you in the unity of the Holy Spirit,
one God, for ever and ever.

October 14
Saint Callistus I, Pope and Martyr

From the Common of Martyrs: For One Martyr (p. 1059), or from the Common of Pastors: For a Pope (p. 1071).

Collect

O God, who raised up Pope Saint Callistus the First
to serve the Church
and attend devoutly to Christ's faithful departed,
strengthen us, we pray, by his witness to the faith,
so that, rescued from the slavery of corruption,
we may merit an incorruptible inheritance.
Through our Lord Jesus Christ, your Son,
who lives and reigns with you in the unity of the Holy Spirit,
one God, for ever and ever.

October 15
Saint Teresa of Jesus, Virgin and Doctor of the Church
Memorial

Entrance Antiphon
Cf. Ps 42 (41): 2-3

Like the deer that yearns for running streams,
so my soul is yearning for you, my God;
my soul is thirsting for God, the living God.

Collect

O God, who through your Spirit
raised up Saint Teresa of Jesus
to show the Church the way to seek perfection,
grant that we may always be nourished
by the food of her heavenly teaching
and fired with longing for true holiness.
Through our Lord Jesus Christ, your Son,
who lives and reigns with you in the unity of the Holy Spirit,
one God, for ever and ever.

Prayer over the Offerings

May our offerings, O Lord, be acceptable to your majesty,
to whom the devoted service of Saint Teresa
was pleasing in such great measure.
Through Christ our Lord.

Communion Antiphon

Ps 89 (88): 2

I will sing for ever of your mercies, O Lord;
through all ages my mouth will proclaim your fidelity.

Prayer after Communion

Grant, O Lord our God,
that your obedient family,
whom you have fed with the Bread of heaven,
may follow the example of Saint Teresa
and rejoice to sing of your mercies for all eternity.
Through Christ our Lord.

October 16
Saint Hedwig, Religious

From the Common of Holy Men and Women: For Religious (p. 1107), or For Holy Women (p. 1113).

Collect

Grant, we pray, almighty God,
that the revered intercession of Saint Hedwig
may bring us heavenly aid,
just as her wonderful life
is an example of humility for all.
Through our Lord Jesus Christ, your Son,
who lives and reigns with you in the unity of the Holy Spirit,
one God, for ever and ever.

Saint Margaret Mary Alacoque, Virgin

From the Common of Virgins: For One Virgin (p. 1092).

Collect

Pour out on us, we pray, O Lord,
the spirit with which you so remarkably endowed
Saint Margaret Mary,
so that we may come to know
that love of Christ which surpasses all understanding
and be utterly filled with your fullness.
Through our Lord Jesus Christ, your Son,
who lives and reigns with you in the unity of the Holy Spirit,
one God, for ever and ever.

October 17
Saint Ignatius of Antioch, Bishop and Martyr
Memorial

Entrance Antiphon   *Cf. Gal 2: 19-20*

I am crucified with Christ, yet I live;
no longer I, but Christ lives in me.
I live by faith in the Son of God,
who has loved me and given himself up for me.

Collect

Almighty ever-living God,
who adorn the sacred body of your Church
with the confessions of holy Martyrs,
grant, we pray,
that, just as the glorious passion of Saint Ignatius of Antioch,
which we celebrate today,
brought him eternal splendor,
so it may be for us unending protection.
Through our Lord Jesus Christ, your Son,
who lives and reigns with you in the unity of the Holy Spirit,
one God, for ever and ever.

Prayer over the Offerings

> May this oblation and our homage be pleasing to you, O Lord,
> just as you accepted Saint Ignatius, the wheat of Christ,
> made pure bread through his martyrdom and passion.
> Through Christ our Lord.

Communion Antiphon

> I am the wheat of Christ to be ground by the teeth of beasts,
> that I may be found to be pure bread.

Prayer after Communion

> May the heavenly Bread we have received, O Lord,
> on the feast day of Saint Ignatius
> renew us, we pray,
> and make us Christians in name and in deed.
> Through Christ our Lord.

October 18
SAINT LUKE, EVANGELIST
Feast

Entrance Antiphon — Is 52: 7

> How beautiful upon the mountains are the feet of him
> who brings glad tidings of peace,
> bearing good news, announcing salvation!

The Gloria in excelsis (Glory to God in the highest) is said.

Collect

> Lord God, who chose Saint Luke
> to reveal by his preaching and writings
> the mystery of your love for the poor,
> grant that those who already glory in your name
> may persevere as one heart and one soul
> and that all nations may merit to see your salvation.
> Through our Lord Jesus Christ, your Son,
> who lives and reigns with you in the unity of the Holy Spirit,
> one God, for ever and ever.

Prayer over the Offerings

Grant through your heavenly gifts
that we may serve you in freedom of heart, we pray, O Lord,
so that the offerings we make on the feast day of Saint Luke
may bring us healing and give us glory.
Through Christ our Lord.

Preface II of the Apostles, p. 596.

Communion Antiphon

Cf. Lk 10: 1, 9

The Lord sent out disciples to proclaim throughout the towns:
The kingdom of God is at hand for you.

Prayer after Communion

Grant, we pray, almighty God,
that what we have received from your holy altar
may sanctify us and make us strong
in the faith of the Gospel which Saint Luke proclaimed.
Through Christ our Lord.

[In the Dioceses of the United States]

October 19
Saints John de Brébeuf and Isaac Jogues, Priests, and Companions, Martyrs
Memorial

From the Common of Martyrs: For Missionary Martyrs (p. 1066).

Collect

O God, who chose to manifest
the blessed hope of your eternal Kingdom
by the toil of Saints John de Brébeuf,
Isaac Jogues and their companions
and by the shedding of their blood,
graciously grant that through their intercession
the faith of Christians may be strengthened day by day.
Through our Lord Jesus Christ, your Son,
who lives and reigns with you in the unity of the Holy Spirit,
one God, for ever and ever.

[In the Dioceses of the United States]
October 20
Saint Paul of the Cross, Priest

Entrance Antiphon
Cf. 1 Cor 2: 2

I resolved to know nothing while I was with you
except for Jesus Christ, and him crucified.

Collect
May the Priest Saint Paul,
whose only love was the Cross,
obtain for us your grace, O Lord,
so that, urged on more strongly by his example,
we may each embrace our own cross with courage.
Through our Lord Jesus Christ, your Son,
who lives and reigns with you in the unity of the Holy Spirit,
one God, for ever and ever.

Prayer over the Offerings
Look upon the sacrificial gifts we offer, almighty God,
in commemoration of Saint Paul of the Cross
and grant that we who celebrate the mysteries of the Lord's Passion
may imitate what we now enact.
Through Christ our Lord.

Communion Antiphon
1 Cor 1: 23, 24

We proclaim Christ crucified;
Christ, the power of God and the wisdom of God.

Prayer after Communion
O God, who in Saint Paul
have wonderfully made known the mystery of the Cross,
graciously grant
that, drawing strength from this sacrifice,
we may cling faithfully to Christ
and labor in the Church for the salvation of all.
Through Christ our Lord.

October 23
Saint John of Capistrano, Priest

From the Common of Pastors: For Missionaries (p. 1084), or from the Common of Holy Men and Women: For Religious (p. 1107).

Collect

O God, who raised up Saint John of Capistrano
to comfort your faithful people in tribulation,
place us, we pray, under your safe protection
and keep your Church in everlasting peace.
Through our Lord Jesus Christ, your Son,
who lives and reigns with you in the unity of the Holy Spirit,
one God, for ever and ever.

October 24
Saint Anthony Mary Claret, Bishop

From the Common of Pastors: For Missionaries (p. 1084), or For a Bishop (p. 1074).

Collect

O God, who for the evangelization of peoples
strengthened the Bishop Saint Anthony Mary Claret
with admirable charity and long-suffering,
grant, through his intercession,
that, seeking the things that are yours,
we may earnestly devote ourselves
to winning our brothers and sisters for Christ.
Who lives and reigns with you in the unity of the Holy Spirit,
one God, for ever and ever.

October 28
SAINTS SIMON AND JUDE, APOSTLES
Feast

Entrance Antiphon

These are the holy men
whom the Lord chose in his own perfect love;
to them he gave eternal glory.

The Gloria in excelsis (Glory to God in the highest) is said.

Collect

O God, who by the blessed Apostles
have brought us to acknowledge your name,
graciously grant,
through the intercession of Saints Simon and Jude,
that the Church may constantly grow
by increase of the peoples who believe in you.
Through our Lord Jesus Christ, your Son,
who lives and reigns with you in the unity of the Holy Spirit,
one God, for ever and ever.

Prayer over the Offerings

As we venerate the perpetual glory
of the holy Apostles Simon and Jude, O Lord,
we ask that you receive our prayers
and lead us to worthy celebration of the sacred mysteries.
Through Christ our Lord.

Preface of the Apostles, pp. 594-597.

Communion Antiphon   Jn 14: 23

Whoever loves me will keep my word, says the Lord;
and my Father will love him, and we will come to him,
and make our home with him.

Prayer after Communion

Having received this Sacrament, O Lord,
we humbly implore you in the Holy Spirit,
that what we do to honor the glorious passion
of the Apostles Simon and Jude
may keep us ever in your love.
Through Christ our Lord.

The Solemn Blessing formula, p. 683, may be used.

NOVEMBER

November 1
ALL SAINTS
Solemnity

Entrance Antiphon

Let us all rejoice in the Lord,
as we celebrate the feast day in honor of all the Saints,
at whose festival the Angels rejoice
and praise the Son of God.

The Gloria in excelsis *(Glory to God in the highest) is said.*

Collect

Almighty ever-living God,
by whose gift we venerate in one celebration
the merits of all the Saints,
bestow on us, we pray,
through the prayers of so many intercessors,
an abundance of the reconciliation with you
for which we earnestly long.
Through our Lord Jesus Christ, your Son,
who lives and reigns with you in the unity of the Holy Spirit,
one God, for ever and ever.

The Creed is said.

Prayer over the Offerings

May these offerings we bring in honor of all the Saints
be pleasing to you, O Lord,
and grant that, just as we believe the Saints
to be already assured of immortality,
so we may experience their concern for our salvation.
Through Christ our Lord.

Preface: The glory of Jerusalem, our mother.

V. The Lord be with you.   R. And with your spirit.

V. Lift up your hearts.   R. We lift them up to the Lord.

V. Let us give thanks to the Lord our God.   R. It is right and just.

It is truly right and just, our duty and our salvation, always and everywhere to give you thanks, Lord, holy Father, almighty and eternal God. For today by your gift we celebrate the festival of your city, the heavenly Jerusalem, our mother, where the great array of our brothers and sisters already gives you eternal praise. Towards her, we eagerly hasten as pilgrims advancing by faith, rejoicing in the glory bestowed upon those exalted members of the Church through whom you give us, in our frailty, both strength and

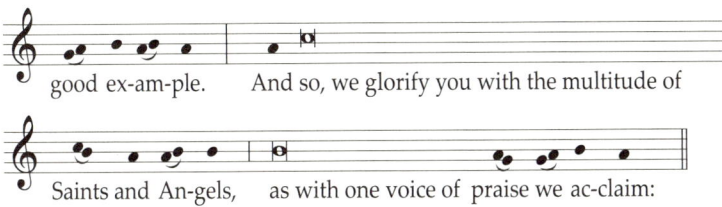

good ex-am-ple. And so, we glorify you with the multitude of Saints and An-gels, as with one voice of praise we ac-claim:

Holy, Holy, Holy Lord God of hosts . . .

Text without music:
V. **The Lord be with you.**
R. And with your spirit.

V. **Lift up your hearts.**
R. We lift them up to the Lord.

V. **Let us give thanks to the Lord our God.**
R. It is right and just.

**It is truly right and just, our duty and our salvation,
always and everywhere to give you thanks,
Lord, holy Father, almighty and eternal God.**

**For today by your gift we celebrate the festival of your city,
the heavenly Jerusalem, our mother,
where the great array of our brothers and sisters
already gives you eternal praise.**

**Towards her, we eagerly hasten as pilgrims advancing by faith,
rejoicing in the glory bestowed upon those exalted members of the Church
through whom you give us, in our frailty, both strength and good example.**

**And so, we glorify you with the multitude of Saints and Angels,
as with one voice of praise we acclaim:**

Holy, Holy, Holy Lord God of hosts . . .

Communion Antiphon   Mt 5: 8-10
   Blessed are the clean of heart, for they shall see God.
   Blessed are the peacemakers,
   for they shall be called children of God.
   Blessed are they who are persecuted for the sake of righteousness,
   for theirs is the Kingdom of Heaven.

Prayer after Communion
   As we adore you, O God, who alone are holy
   and wonderful in all your Saints,
   we implore your grace,
   so that, coming to perfect holiness in the fullness of your love,
   we may pass from this pilgrim table
   to the banquet of our heavenly homeland.
   Through Christ our Lord.

The Solemn Blessing formula, p. 683, may be used.

For the Votive Mass of All Saints, cf. below, p. 1366.

November 2
THE COMMEMORATION
OF ALL THE FAITHFUL DEPARTED
(All Souls' Day)

The Masses that follow may be used at the discretion of the celebrant.*

Even when November 2 falls on a Sunday, the Mass celebrated is that of the Commemoration of All the Faithful Departed.

1

Entrance Antiphon   Cf. 1 Thes 4: 14; 1 Cor 15: 22
   Just as Jesus died and has risen again,
   so through Jesus God will bring with him
   those who have fallen asleep;
   and as in Adam all die,
   so also in Christ will all be brought to life.

---

* On this day, any Priest may celebrate three Masses, observing, nevertheless, what was established by Benedict XV in the Apostolic Constitution, *Incruentum altaris sacrificium*, August 10, 1915: *Acta Apostolicae Sedis* 7 (1915) pp. 401–404.

Collect

Listen kindly to our prayers, O Lord,
and, as our faith in your Son,
raised from the dead, is deepened,
so may our hope of resurrection for your departed servants
also find new strength.
Through our Lord Jesus Christ, your Son,
who lives and reigns with you in the unity of the Holy Spirit,
one God, for ever and ever.

Prayer over the Offerings

Look favorably on our offerings, O Lord,
so that your departed servants
may be taken up into glory with your Son,
in whose great mystery of love we are all united.
Who lives and reigns for ever and ever.

Preface for the Dead, pp. 622-631.

Communion Antiphon

Cf. Jn 11: 25-26

I am the Resurrection and the Life, says the Lord.
Whoever believes in me, even though he dies, will live,
and everyone who lives and believes in me will not die for ever.

Prayer after Communion

Grant we pray, O Lord, that your departed servants,
for whom we have celebrated this paschal Sacrament,
may pass over to a dwelling place of light and peace.
Through Christ our Lord.

The Solemn Blessing formula, p. 684, may be used.

2

Entrance Antiphon   Cf. 4 Esdr 2: 34-35

Eternal rest grant unto them, O Lord,
and let perpetual light shine upon them.

Collect

O God, glory of the faithful and life of the just,
by the Death and Resurrection of whose Son
we have been redeemed,
look mercifully on your departed servants,
that, just as they professed the mystery of our resurrection,
so they may merit to receive the joys of eternal happiness.
Through our Lord Jesus Christ, your Son,
who lives and reigns with you in the unity of the Holy Spirit,
one God, for ever and ever.

Prayer over the Offerings

Almighty and merciful God,
by means of these sacrificial offerings
wash away, we pray, in the Blood of Christ,
the sins of your departed servants,
for you purify unceasingly by your merciful forgiveness
those you once cleansed in the waters of Baptism.
Through Christ our Lord.

Preface for the Dead, pp. 622-631.

Communion Antiphon   Cf. 4 Esdr 2: 35, 34

Let perpetual light shine upon them, O Lord,
with your Saints for ever, for you are merciful.

Prayer after Communion

Having received the Sacrament of your Only Begotten Son,
who was sacrificed for us and rose in glory,
we humbly implore you, O Lord,
for your departed servants,
that, cleansed by the paschal mysteries,
they may glory in the gift of the resurrection to come.
Through Christ our Lord.

The Solemn Blessing formula, p. 684, may be used.

NOVEMBER

3

Entrance Antiphon — Cf. Rom 8: 11

God, who raised Jesus from the dead,
will give life also to your mortal bodies, through his Spirit that dwells in you.

Collect

O God, who willed that your Only Begotten Son,
having conquered death,
should pass over into the realm of heaven,
grant, we pray, to your departed servants
that, with the mortality of this life overcome,
they may gaze eternally on you,
their Creator and Redeemer.
Through our Lord Jesus Christ, your Son,
who lives and reigns with you in the unity of the Holy Spirit,
one God, for ever and ever.

Prayer over the Offerings

Receive, Lord, in your kindness,
the sacrificial offering we make
for all your servants who sleep in Christ,
that, set free from the bonds of death
by this singular sacrifice,
they may merit eternal life.
Through Christ our Lord.

Preface for the Dead, pp. 622-631.

Communion Antiphon — Cf. Phil 3: 20-21

We await a savior, the Lord Jesus Christ,
who will change our mortal bodies, to conform with his glorified body.

Prayer after Communion

Through these sacrificial gifts
which we have received, O Lord,
bestow on your departed servants your great mercy
and, to those you have endowed with the grace of Baptism,
grant also the fullness of eternal joy.
Through Christ our Lord.

The Solemn Blessing formula, p. 684, may be used.

November 3
Saint Martin de Porres, Religious

From the Common of Holy Men and Women: For Religious (p. 1107).

Collect

O God, who led Saint Martin de Porres
by the path of humility to heavenly glory,
grant that we may so follow his radiant example in this life
as to merit to be exalted with him in heaven.
Through our Lord Jesus Christ, your Son,
who lives and reigns with you in the unity of the Holy Spirit,
one God, for ever and ever.

November 4
Saint Charles Borromeo, Bishop
Memorial

From the Common of Pastors: For a Bishop (p. 1074).

Collect

Preserve in the midst of your people,
we ask, O Lord, the spirit with which you filled
the Bishop Saint Charles Borromeo,
that your Church may be constantly renewed
and, by conforming herself to the likeness of Christ,
may show his face to the world.
Who lives and reigns with you in the unity of the Holy Spirit,
one God, for ever and ever.

Prayer over the Offerings

Look, O Lord, upon the offering placed on your altar
in commemoration of Saint Charles,
and grant by the power of this sacrifice
that, as you made him an attentive pastor,
outstanding in the merit of his virtues,
so you may make us abound in good fruit by our works.
Through Christ our Lord.

Prayer after Communion

May the sacred mysteries of which we have partaken,
O Lord, we pray, give us that determination
which made Saint Charles faithful in ministry
and fervent in charity.
Through Christ our Lord.

November 9
THE DEDICATION OF THE LATERAN BASILICA
Feast

In the basilica itself, the Mass of the Common of the Dedication of a Church is used (p. 1032).

Entrance Antiphon
Cf. Rev 21: 2

I saw the holy city, a new Jerusalem,
coming down out of heaven from God,
prepared like a bride adorned for her husband.

Or:

Cf. Rev 21: 3

Behold God's dwelling with the human race.
He will dwell with them and they will be his people,
and God himself with them will be their God.

The Gloria in excelsis (Glory to God in the highest) is said.

Collect

O God, who from living and chosen stones
prepare an eternal dwelling for your majesty,
increase in your Church the spirit of grace you have bestowed,
so that by new growth your faithful people
may build up the heavenly Jerusalem.
Through our Lord Jesus Christ, your Son,
who lives and reigns with you in the unity of the Holy Spirit,
one God, for ever and ever.

Or:

O God, who were pleased to call your Church the Bride,
grant that the people that serves your name
may revere you, love you and follow you,
and may be led by you
to attain your promises in heaven.
Through our Lord Jesus Christ, your Son,
who lives and reigns with you in the unity of the Holy Spirit,
one God, for ever and ever.

When this Feast falls on a Sunday, the Creed is said.

Prayer over the Offerings

Accept, we pray, O Lord, the offering made here
and grant that by it those who seek your favor
may receive in this place
the power of the Sacraments
and the answer to their prayers.
Through Christ our Lord.

Preface: The mystery of the Church, the Bride of Christ and the Temple of the Spirit.

V. The Lord be with you.   R. And with your spir-it.

V. Lift up your hearts.   R. We lift them up to the Lord.

V. Let us give thanks to the Lord our God.   R. It is right and just.

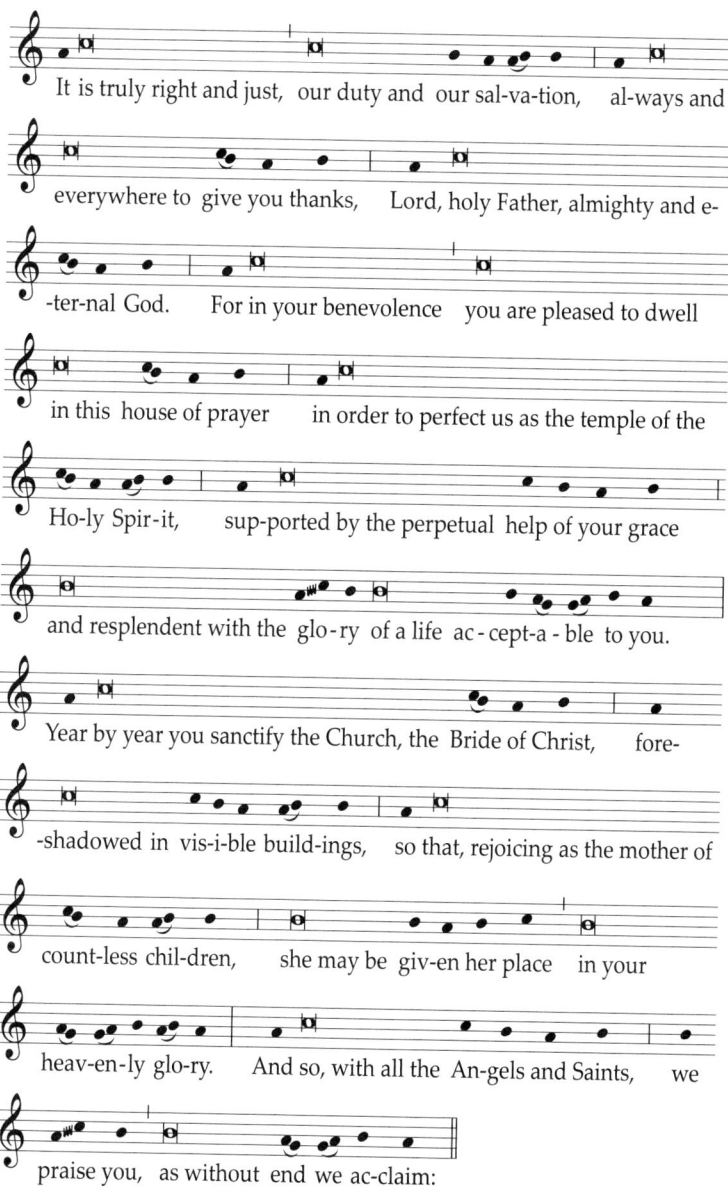

Holy, Holy, Holy Lord God of hosts ...

Text without music:

V. **The Lord be with you.**
R. And with your spirit.

V. **Lift up your hearts.**
R. We lift them up to the Lord.

V. **Let us give thanks to the Lord our God.**
R. It is right and just.

It is truly right and just, our duty and our salvation,
always and everywhere to give you thanks,
Lord, holy Father, almighty and eternal God.

For in your benevolence you are pleased
to dwell in this house of prayer
in order to perfect us as the temple of the Holy Spirit,
supported by the perpetual help of your grace
and resplendent with the glory of a life acceptable to you.

Year by year you sanctify the Church, the Bride of Christ,
foreshadowed in visible buildings,
so that, rejoicing as the mother of countless children,
she may be given her place in your heavenly glory.

And so, with all the Angels and Saints,
we praise you, as without end we acclaim:

Holy, Holy, Holy Lord God of hosts . . .

Communion Antiphon   Cf. 1 Pt 2: 5

Be built up like living stones,
into a spiritual house, a holy priesthood.

Prayer after Communion

O God, who chose to foreshadow for us
the heavenly Jerusalem
through the sign of your Church on earth,
grant, we pray,
that, by our partaking of this Sacrament,
we may be made the temple of your grace
and may enter the dwelling place of your glory.
Through Christ our Lord.

The Solemn Blessing formula, p. 684, may be used.

November 10
Saint Leo the Great, Pope and Doctor of the Church
Memorial

Entrance Antiphon
Cf. Sir 45: 30

The Lord established for him a covenant of peace,
and made him the prince,
that he might have the dignity of the priesthood for ever.

Collect

O God, who never allow the gates of hell
to prevail against your Church,
firmly founded on the apostolic rock,
grant her, we pray,
that through the intercession of Pope Saint Leo,
she may stand firm in your truth
and know the protection of lasting peace.
Through our Lord Jesus Christ, your Son,
who lives and reigns with you in the unity of the Holy Spirit,
one God, for ever and ever.

Prayer over the Offerings

Through the offerings made here, we pray, O Lord,
graciously shed light on your Church,
so that your flock may everywhere prosper
and that under your governance
the shepherds may become pleasing to your name.
Through Christ our Lord.

Communion Antiphon
Mt 16: 16, 18

Peter said to Jesus:
You are the Christ, the Son of the living God.
And Jesus replied: You are Peter,
and upon this rock I will build my Church.

Prayer after Communion

Be pleased, O Lord, we pray,
to govern the Church you have nourished by this holy meal,
so that, firmly directed,
she may enjoy ever greater freedom
and persevere in integrity of religion.
Through Christ our Lord.

November 11
Saint Martin of Tours, Bishop
Memorial

Entrance Antiphon
Cf. 1 Sm 2: 35

I shall raise up for myself a faithful priest
who will act in accord with my heart and my mind, says the Lord.

Collect

O God, who are glorified in the Bishop Saint Martin
both by his life and death,
make new, we pray,
the wonders of your grace in our hearts,
that neither death nor life
may separate us from your love.
Through our Lord Jesus Christ, your Son,
who lives and reigns with you in the unity of the Holy Spirit,
one God, for ever and ever.

Prayer over the Offerings

Sanctify these offerings, we pray, Lord God,
which we joyfully present in honor of Saint Martin,
so that through them our life may always be directed
whether in tribulation or in prosperity.
Through Christ our Lord.

Communion Antiphon
Cf. Mt 25: 40

Amen, I say to you:
Whatever you did for one of the least of my brethren,
you did it for me, says the Lord.

Prayer after Communion

Grant to us who have been restored
by this Sacrament of unity, O Lord,
perfect harmony with your will in all things,
that, just as Saint Martin submitted himself entirely to you,
so we, too, may glory in being truly yours.
Through Christ our Lord.

November 12
Saint Josaphat, Bishop and Martyr
Memorial

Entrance Antiphon

Because of the Lord's covenant and the ancestral laws,
the Saints of God persevered in loving brotherhood,
for there was always one spirit in them, and one faith.

Collect

Stir up in your Church, we pray, O Lord,
the Spirit that filled Saint Josaphat
as he laid down his life for the sheep,
so that through his intercession
we, too, may be strengthened by the same Spirit
and not be afraid to lay down our life for others.
Through our Lord Jesus Christ, your Son,
who lives and reigns with you in the unity of the Holy Spirit,
one God, for ever and ever.

Prayer over the Offerings

Most merciful God,
pour out your blessing upon these offerings
and confirm us in the faith
that Saint Josaphat professed by the shedding of his blood.
Through Christ our Lord.

Communion Antiphon

Mt. 10: 39

Whoever loses his life for my sake,
will find it in eternity, says the Lord.

Prayer after Communion

May this heavenly table, O Lord,
bestow on us a spirit of fortitude and peace,
so that, following Saint Josaphat's example,
we may willingly spend our lives
working for the honor and unity of the Church.
Through Christ our Lord.

[In the Dioceses of the United States]

November 13
Saint Frances Xavier Cabrini, Virgin
Memorial

From the Common of Virgins: For One Virgin (p. 1092), or from the Common of Holy Men and Women: For Those Who Practiced Works of Mercy (p. 1110).

Collect

God our Father,
who called Saint Frances Xavier Cabrini from Italy
to serve the immigrants of America,
by her example,
teach us to have concern for the stranger,
the sick, and all those in need,
and by her prayers help us to see Christ
in all the men and women we meet.
Through our Lord Jesus Christ, your Son,
who lives and reigns with you in the unity of the Holy Spirit,
one God, for ever and ever.

November 15
Saint Albert the Great, Bishop and Doctor of the Church

From the Common of Pastors: For a Bishop (p. 1074), or from the Common of Doctors of the Church (p. 1088).

Collect

O God, who made the Bishop Saint Albert great
by his joining of human wisdom to divine faith,
grant, we pray, that we may so adhere to the truths he taught,
that through progress in learning
we may come to a deeper knowledge and love of you.
Through our Lord Jesus Christ, your Son,
who lives and reigns with you in the unity of the Holy Spirit,
one God, for ever and ever.

November 16
Saint Margaret of Scotland

From the Common of Holy Men and Women: For Those Who Practiced Works of Mercy (p. 1110).

Collect

O God, who made Saint Margaret of Scotland wonderful
in her outstanding charity towards the poor,
grant that through her intercession and example
we may reflect among all humanity
the image of your divine goodness.
Through our Lord Jesus Christ, your Son,
who lives and reigns with you in the unity of the Holy Spirit,
one God, for ever and ever.

Saint Gertrude, Virgin

From the Common of Virgins: For One Virgin (p. 1092), or from the Common of Holy Men and Women: For a Nun (p. 1106).

Collect

O God, who prepared a delightful dwelling for yourself
in the heart of the Virgin Saint Gertrude,
graciously bring light, through her intercession,
to the darkness of our hearts,
that we may joyfully experience you present and at work
    within us.
Through our Lord Jesus Christ, your Son,
who lives and reigns with you in the unity of the Holy Spirit,
one God, for ever and ever.

November 17
Saint Elizabeth of Hungary, Religious
Memorial

From the Common of Holy Men and Women: For Those Who Practiced Works of Mercy (p. 1110).

Collect

O God, by whose gift Saint Elizabeth of Hungary
recognized and revered Christ in the poor,
grant, through her intercession,
that we may serve with unfailing charity
the needy and those afflicted.
Through our Lord Jesus Christ, your Son,
who lives and reigns with you in the unity of the Holy Spirit,
one God, for ever and ever.

November 18
The Dedication of the Basilicas
of Saints Peter and Paul, Apostles

Entrance Antiphon
Cf. Ps 45 (44): 17-18

You will make them princes over all the earth;
they will remember your name through all generations.
Thus the peoples will praise you for ever, from age to age.

Collect

Defend your Church, O Lord,
by the protection of the holy Apostles,
that, as she received from them
the beginnings of her knowledge of things divine,
so through them she may receive,
even to the end of the world,
an increase in heavenly grace.
Through our Lord Jesus Christ, your Son,
who lives and reigns with you in the unity of the Holy Spirit,
one God, for ever and ever.

Prayer over the Offerings

As we bring you this offering of our service,
we beseech your mercy, Lord,
that the truth handed down to us
by the ministry of the Apostles Peter and Paul
may endure undefiled in our hearts.
Through Christ our Lord.

Preface of the Apostles, pp. 594-597.

Communion Antiphon
Cf. Jn 6: 69, 70

O Lord, you have the words of eternal life,
and we have come to believe
that you are the Christ, the Son of God.

Prayer after Communion

May your people, we pray, O Lord,
nourished by the Bread of heaven,
rejoice in commemorating the Apostles Peter and Paul,
for it is through your gift
that we are governed under their patronage.
Through Christ our Lord.

[In the Dioceses of the United States]
Saint Rose Philippine Duchesne, Virgin

From the Common of Virgins: For One Virgin (p. 1092).

Collect

Almighty God, who filled the heart of Saint Rose Philippine Duchesne
with charity and missionary zeal,
and gave her the desire
to make you known among all peoples,
grant us to follow her way
and fill us with that same love and zeal
to extend your Kingdom to the ends of the earth.
Through our Lord Jesus Christ, your Son,
who lives and reigns with you in the unity of the Holy Spirit,
one God, for ever and ever.

November 21
The Presentation of the Blessed Virgin Mary
Memorial

From the Common of the Blessed Virgin Mary (p. 1039).

Collect

As we venerate the glorious memory
of the most holy Virgin Mary,
grant, we pray, O Lord, through her intercession,
that we, too, may merit to receive
from the fullness of your grace.
Through our Lord Jesus Christ, your Son,
who lives and reigns with you in the unity of the Holy Spirit,
one God, for ever and ever.

November 22
Saint Cecilia, Virgin and Martyr
Memorial

From the Common of Martyrs: For a Virgin Martyr (p. 1068), or from the Common of Virgins: For One Virgin (p. 1092).

Collect

O God, who gladden us each year
with the feast day of your handmaid Saint Cecilia,
grant, we pray,
that what has been devoutly handed down concerning her
may offer us examples to imitate
and proclaim the wonders worked in his servants
by Christ your Son.
Who lives and reigns with you in the unity of the Holy Spirit,
one God, for ever and ever.

November 23
Saint Clement I, Pope and Martyr

From the Common of Martyrs: For One Martyr (p. 1059), or from the Common of Pastors: For a Pope (p. 1071).

Collect

Almighty ever-living God,
who are wonderful in the virtue of all your Saints,
grant us joy in the yearly commemoration of Saint Clement,
who, as a Martyr and High Priest of your Son,
bore out by his witness what he celebrated in mystery
and confirmed by example what he preached with his lips.
Through our Lord Jesus Christ, your Son,
who lives and reigns with you in the unity of the Holy Spirit,
one God, for ever and ever.

Saint Columban, Abbot

From the Common of Pastors: For Missionaries (p. 1084), or from the Common of Holy Men and Women: For an Abbot (p. 1103).

Collect

O God, who in Saint Columban
wonderfully joined the work of evangelization
to zeal for the monastic life,
grant, we pray,
that through his intercession and example
we may strive to seek you above all things
and to bring increase to your faithful people.
Through our Lord Jesus Christ, your Son,
who lives and reigns with you in the unity of the Holy Spirit,
one God, for ever and ever.

[In the Dioceses of the United States]
Blessed Miguel Agustín Pro, Priest and Martyr

From the Common of Martyrs: For One Martyr (p. 1059), or from the Common of Pastors: For One Pastor (p. 1078).

Collect

Our God and Father,
who conferred upon your servant Blessed Miguel Agustín Pro
the grace of ardently seeking your greater glory
   and the salvation of others,
grant, through his intercession and example,
that by faithfully and joyfully performing our daily duties
and effectively assisting those around us,
we may serve you with zeal
and ever seek your glory.
Through our Lord Jesus Christ, your Son,
who lives and reigns with you in the unity of the Holy Spirit,
one God, for ever and ever.

November 24
Saint Andrew Dũng-Lạc, Priest, and Companions, Martyrs
Memorial

Entrance Antiphon
Cf. Gal 6: 14; cf. 1 Cor 1: 18

May we never boast, except in the Cross of our Lord Jesus Christ.
For the word of the Cross is the power of God
to us who have been saved.

Collect

O God, source and origin of all fatherhood,
who kept the Martyrs Saint Andrew Dũng-Lạc and his companions
faithful to the Cross of your Son,
even to the shedding of their blood,
grant, through their intercession,
that, spreading your love among our brothers and sisters,
we may be your children both in name and in truth.
Through our Lord Jesus Christ, your Son,
who lives and reigns with you in the unity of the Holy Spirit,
one God, for ever and ever.

Prayer over the Offerings

Receive, O holy Father, the offerings we bring
as we venerate the passion of the holy Martyrs,
so that amid the trials of this life
we may always be found faithful
and may offer ourselves to you
as an acceptable sacrifice.
Through Christ our Lord.

Communion Antiphon
Mt 5: 10

Blessed are they who are persecuted for the sake of righteousness,
for theirs is the Kingdom of Heaven.

Prayer after Communion

Renewed by the one Bread
as we commemorate the holy Martyrs,
we humbly beseech you, O Lord,
that, abiding as one in your love,
we may merit by endurance an eternal prize.
Through Christ our Lord.

November 25
Saint Catherine of Alexandria, Virgin and Martyr

From the Common of Martyrs: For a Virgin Martyr (p. 1068), or from the Common of Virgins: For One Virgin (p. 1092).

Collect

Almighty ever-living God,
who gave Saint Catherine of Alexandria to your people
as a Virgin and an invincible Martyr,
grant that through her intercession
we may be strengthened in faith and constancy
and spend ourselves without reserve
for the unity of the Church.
Through our Lord Jesus Christ, your Son,
who lives and reigns with you in the unity of the Holy Spirit,
one God, for ever and ever.

November 30
SAINT ANDREW, APOSTLE
Feast

Entrance Antiphon
Cf. Mt 4: 18-19

    Beside the Sea of Galilee,
    the Lord saw two brothers, Peter and Andrew,
    and he said to them:
    Come after me and I will make you fishers of men.

The Gloria in excelsis (Glory to God in the highest) is said.

Collect
**We humbly implore your majesty, O Lord,
that, just as the blessed Apostle Andrew
was for your Church a preacher and pastor,
so he may be for us a constant intercessor before you.
Through our Lord Jesus Christ, your Son,
who lives and reigns with you in the unity of the Holy Spirit,
one God, for ever and ever.**

Prayer over the Offerings
**Grant us, almighty God, that through these offerings,
which we bring on the feast day of Saint Andrew,
we may please you by what we have brought
and be given life by what you have accepted.
Through Christ our Lord.**

Preface of the Apostles, pp. 594-597.

Communion Antiphon
Cf. Jn 1: 41-42

    Andrew told his brother Simon:
    We have found the Messiah, the Christ,
    and he brought him to Jesus.

Prayer after Communion
**May communion in your Sacrament strengthen us, O Lord,
so that by the example of the blessed Apostle Andrew
we, who carry in our body the Death of Christ,
may merit to live with him in glory.
Who lives and reigns for ever and ever.**

The Solemn Blessing formula, p. 683, may be used.

[In the Dioceses of the United States]
Fourth Thursday in November
Thanksgiving Day

Entrance Antiphon   Eph 5: 19-20

Sing and make music to the Lord in your hearts,
always thanking God the Father for all things
in the name of our Lord Jesus Christ.

Collect

Father all-powerful,
your gifts of love are countless
and your goodness infinite;
as we come before you on Thanksgiving Day
with gratitude for your kindness,
open our hearts to have concern
for every man, woman, and child,
so that we may share your gifts in loving service.
Through our Lord Jesus Christ, your Son,
who lives and reigns with you in the unity of the Holy Spirit,
one God, for ever and ever.

Prayer over the Offerings

God our Father,
from whose hand we have received generous gifts
so that we might learn to share your blessings in gratitude,
accept these gifts of bread and wine,
and let the perfect sacrifice of Jesus
draw us closer to all our brothers and sisters in the human family.
Through Christ our Lord.

Preface: Thanksgiving Day.

V. The Lord be with you. R. And with your spirit.

V. Lift up your hearts. R. We lift them up to the Lord.

V. Let us give thanks to the Lord our God. R. It is right and just.

It is truly right and just, our duty and our salvation, always and everywhere to give you thanks, Lord, holy Father, almighty and eternal God, through Christ our Lord. You have entrusted to us the great gift of freedom, a gift that calls forth responsibility and commitment to the truth that all have a fundamental dignity before you. In Jesus, through his death and resurrection, we find our ultimate redemption, freedom from sin, and every blessing. And so, with hearts full of love, we join the angels today and every day of our lives, to sing your glory as we acclaim:

Holy, Holy, Holy Lord God of hosts . . .

Text without music:
℣. The Lord be with you.
℟. And with your spirit.

℣. Lift up your hearts.
℟. We lift them up to the Lord.

℣. Let us give thanks to the Lord our God.
℟. It is right and just.

It is truly right and just, our duty and our salvation,
always and everywhere to give you thanks,
Lord, holy Father, almighty and eternal God,
through Christ our Lord.

You have entrusted to us
the great gift of freedom,
a gift that calls forth
responsibility and commitment
to the truth that all have a fundamental dignity before you.
In Jesus, through his Death and Resurrection,
we find our ultimate redemption,
freedom from sin,
and every blessing.

As so, with hearts full of love,
we join the angels, today and every day of our lives,
to sing your glory as we acclaim:

Holy, Holy, Holy Lord God of hosts . . .

Communion Antiphon Ps 138 (137): 1
I will thank you, Lord, with all my heart,
for you have heard the words of my mouth.
Or: Ps 116 (115): 12-13
How can I repay the Lord for all his goodness to me?
The chalice of salvation I will raise, and I will call on the name of the Lord.

Prayer after Communion
In this celebration, O Lord our God,
you have shown us the depths of your love for all your children;
help us, we pray, to reach out in love to all your people,
so that we may share with them
the good things of time and eternity.
Through Christ our Lord.

DECEMBER

December 3
Saint Francis Xavier, Priest
Memorial

Entrance Antiphon
Ps 18 (17): 50; 22 (21): 23

I will praise you, Lord, among the nations;
I will tell of your name to my kin.

Collect

O God, who through the preaching of Saint Francis Xavier
won many peoples to yourself,
grant that the hearts of the faithful
may burn with the same zeal for the faith
and that Holy Church may everywhere rejoice
in an abundance of offspring.
Through our Lord Jesus Christ, your Son,
who lives and reigns with you in the unity of the Holy Spirit,
one God, for ever and ever.

Prayer over the Offerings

Receive, O Lord, these offerings we bring you
in commemoration of Saint Francis Xavier,
and grant that, as he journeyed to distant lands
out of longing for the salvation of souls,
so we, too, bearing effective witness to the Gospel,
may, with our brothers and sisters,
eagerly hasten towards you.
Through Christ our Lord.

Communion Antiphon
Mt 10: 27

What I say to you in the darkness
speak in the light, says the Lord,
what you hear whispered,
proclaim on the housetops.

Prayer after Communion

May your mysteries, O God,
kindle in us that fire of charity
with which Saint Francis Xavier burned for the salvation of souls,
so that, walking ever more worthily in our vocation,
we may obtain with him the reward you promise
to those who labor well in your harvest.
Through Christ our Lord.

December 4
Saint John Damascene, Priest and Doctor of the Church

From the Common of Pastors: For One Pastor (p. 1078), or from the Common of Doctors of the Church (p. 1088).

Collect

Grant, we pray, O Lord,
that we may be helped by the prayers
of the Priest Saint John Damascene,
so that the true faith,
which he excelled in teaching,
may always be our light and our strength.
Through our Lord Jesus Christ, your Son,
who lives and reigns with you in the unity of the Holy Spirit,
one God, for ever and ever.

December 6
Saint Nicholas, Bishop

From the Common of Pastors: For a Bishop (p. 1074).

Collect

We humbly implore your mercy, Lord:
protect us in all dangers
through the prayers of the Bishop Saint Nicholas,
that the way of salvation may lie open before us.
Through our Lord Jesus Christ, your Son,
who lives and reigns with you in the unity of the Holy Spirit,
one God, for ever and ever.

December 7
Saint Ambrose, Bishop and Doctor of the Church
Memorial

Entrance Antiphon
Cf. Sir 15: 5

In the midst of the Church he opened his mouth,
and the Lord filled him with the spirit of wisdom and understanding
and clothed him in a robe of glory.

Collect

O God, who made the Bishop Saint Ambrose
a teacher of the Catholic faith
and a model of apostolic courage,
raise up in your Church men after your own heart
to govern her with courage and wisdom.
Through our Lord Jesus Christ, your Son,
who lives and reigns with you in the unity of the Holy Spirit,
one God, for ever and ever.

Prayer over the Offerings

As we celebrate the divine mysteries, O Lord, we pray,
may the Holy Spirit fill us with that light of faith
by which he constantly enlightened Saint Ambrose
for the spreading of your glory.
Through Christ our Lord.

Communion Antiphon
Cf. Ps 1: 2, 3

He who ponders the law of the Lord day and night
will yield fruit in due season.

Prayer after Communion

Lead us, who have been strengthened
by the power of this Sacrament, O Lord,
so to profit from the teaching of Saint Ambrose
that, hastening fearlessly along your paths,
we may be prepared for the delights of the eternal banquet.
Through Christ our Lord.

December 8

**THE IMMACULATE CONCEPTION
OF THE BLESSED VIRGIN MARY**

**PATRONAL FEASTDAY OF THE
UNITED STATES OF AMERICA**

Solemnity

Entrance Antiphon

Is 61: 10

> I rejoice heartily in the Lord,
> in my God is the joy of my soul;
> for he has clothed me with a robe of salvation,
> and wrapped me in a mantle of justice,
> like a bride adorned with her jewels.

The Gloria in excelsis (Glory to God in the highest) is said.

Collect

> O God, who by the Immaculate Conception of the Blessed Virgin
> prepared a worthy dwelling for your Son,
> grant, we pray,
> that, as you preserved her from every stain
> by virtue of the Death of your Son, which you foresaw,
> so, through her intercession,
> we, too, may be cleansed and admitted to your presence.
> Through our Lord Jesus Christ, your Son,
> who lives and reigns with you in the unity of the Holy Spirit,
> one God, for ever and ever.

The Creed is said.

Prayer over the Offerings

> Graciously accept the saving sacrifice
> which we offer you, O Lord,
> on the Solemnity of the Immaculate Conception
> of the Blessed Virgin Mary,
> and grant that, as we profess her,
> on account of your prevenient grace,
> to be untouched by any stain of sin,
> so, through her intercession,
> we may be delivered from all our faults.
> Through Christ our Lord.

Preface: The mystery of Mary and the Church.

V. The Lord be with you.   R. And with your spir-it.

V. Lift up your hearts.   R. We lift them up to the Lord.

V. Let us give thanks to the Lord our God.   R. It is right and just.

It is truly right and just, our duty and our sal-va-tion, al-ways and everywhere to give you thanks, Lord, holy Father, almighty and e- -ter-nal God.   For you preserved the most Blessed Virgin Mary from all stain of o-rig-i-nal sin, so that in her, endowed with the rich fullness of your grace, you might prepare a worthy Mother for your Son and signify the beginning of the Church, his beautiful Bride with-out spot or wrin-kle.   She, the most pure Virgin, was to bring forth a Son, the in-no-cent Lamb who would wipe a-way

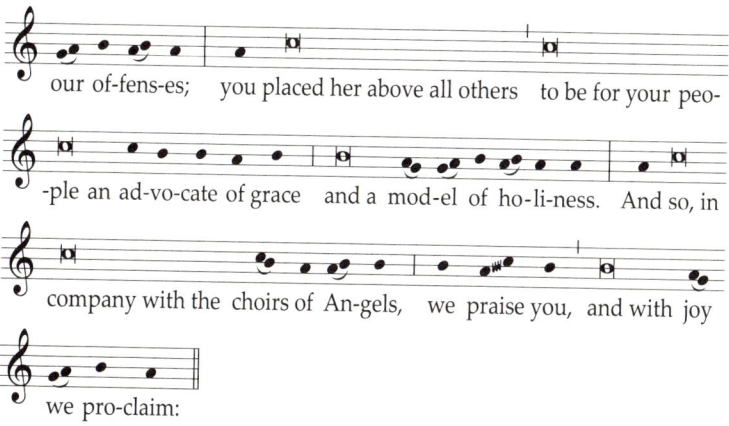

our of-fens-es; you placed her above all others to be for your peo-ple an ad-vo-cate of grace and a mod-el of ho-li-ness. And so, in company with the choirs of An-gels, we praise you, and with joy we pro-claim:

Holy, Holy, Holy Lord God of hosts . . .

Text without music:

V. **The Lord be with you.**
R. And with your spirit.

V. **Lift up your hearts.**
R. We lift them up to the Lord.

V. **Let us give thanks to the Lord our God.**
R. It is right and just.

It is truly right and just, our duty and our salvation,
always and everywhere to give you thanks,
Lord, holy Father, almighty and eternal God.

For you preserved the most Blessed Virgin Mary
from all stain of original sin,
so that in her, endowed with the rich fullness of your grace,
you might prepare a worthy Mother for your Son
and signify the beginning of the Church,
his beautiful Bride without spot or wrinkle.

She, the most pure Virgin, was to bring forth a Son,
the innocent Lamb who would wipe away our offenses;
you placed her above all others
to be for your people an advocate of grace
and a model of holiness.

And so, in company with the choirs of Angels,
we praise you, and with joy we proclaim:

Holy, Holy, Holy Lord God of hosts . . .

Communion Antiphon

Glorious things are spoken of you, O Mary,
for from you arose the sun of justice,
Christ our God.

Prayer after Communion

May the Sacrament we have received,
O Lord our God,
heal in us the wounds of that fault
from which in a singular way
you preserved Blessed Mary in her Immaculate Conception.
Through Christ our Lord.

The Solemn Blessing formula, p. 682, may be used.

December 9
Saint Juan Diego Cuauhtlatoatzin

From the Common of Holy Men and Women: For One Saint (p. 1101).

Collect

O God, who by means of Saint Juan Diego showed
the love of the most holy Virgin Mary for your people,
grant, through his intercession,
that, by following the counsels our Mother gave at Guadalupe,
we may be ever constant in fulfilling your will.
Through our Lord Jesus Christ, your Son,
who lives and reigns with you in the unity of the Holy Spirit,
one God, for ever and ever.

December 11
Saint Damasus I, Pope

From the Common of Pastors: For a Pope (p. 1071).

Collect

Grant, we pray, O Lord,
that we may constantly exalt the merits of your Martyrs,
whom Pope Saint Damasus so venerated and loved.
Through our Lord Jesus Christ, your Son,
who lives and reigns with you in the unity of the Holy Spirit,
one God, for ever and ever.

[In the Dioceses of the United States]
December 12
OUR LADY OF GUADALUPE
Feast

Entrance Antiphon
Rev 12: 1

A great sign appeared in the sky, a woman clothed with the sun,
with the moon under her feet, and on her head a crown of twelve stars.

The Gloria in excelsis (Glory to God in the highest) is said.

Collect

O God, Father of mercies,
who placed your people under the singular protection
of your Son's most holy Mother,
grant that all who invoke the Blessed Virgin of Guadalupe,
may seek with ever more lively faith
the progress of peoples in the ways of justice and of peace.
Through our Lord Jesus Christ, your Son,
who lives and reigns with you in the unity of the Holy Spirit,
one God, for ever and ever.

Prayer over the Offerings

Accept, O Lord, the gifts we present to you
on this feast of Our Lady of Guadalupe,
and grant that this sacrifice
may strengthen us to fulfill your commandments
as true children of the Virgin Mary.
Through Christ our Lord.

Preface I or II of the Blessed Virgin Mary, pp. 590-593.

Communion Antiphon
Lk 1: 52

The Lord has cast down the mighty from their thrones,
and has lifted up the lowly.

Or:
Cf. Ps 147 (146): 20

God has not acted thus for any other nation;
to no other people had he shown his love so clearly.

Prayer after Communion

Lord God, may the Body and Blood of your Son,
which we receive in this sacrament,
reconcile us always in your love;
and may we who rejoice in Our Lady of Guadalupe
live united and at peace in this world
until the day of the Lord dawns in glory.
Through Christ our Lord.

December 13
Saint Lucy, Virgin and Martyr
Memorial

From the Common of Martyrs: For a Virgin Martyr (p. 1068), or from the Common of Virgins: For One Virgin (p. 1092).

Collect

May the glorious intercession
of the Virgin and Martyr Saint Lucy
give us new heart, we pray, O Lord,
so that we may celebrate her heavenly birthday
in this present age
and so behold things eternal.
Through our Lord Jesus Christ, your Son,
who lives and reigns with you in the unity of the Holy Spirit,
one God, for ever and ever.

December 14
Saint John of the Cross, Priest and Doctor of the Church
Memorial

Entrance Antiphon
Gal 6: 14

May I never boast,
except in the Cross of our Lord Jesus Christ,
through which the world has been crucified to me,
and I to the world.

Collect

O God, who gave the Priest Saint John
an outstanding dedication to perfect self-denial
and love of the Cross,
grant that, by imitating him closely at all times,
we may come to contemplate eternally your glory.
Through our Lord Jesus Christ, your Son,
who lives and reigns with you in the unity of the Holy Spirit,
one God, for ever and ever.

Prayer over the Offerings

Look upon the sacrificial gifts we offer, almighty God,
in commemoration of Saint John of the Cross
and grant that we, who celebrate
the mysteries of the Lord's Passion,
may imitate what we now enact.
Through Christ our Lord.

Communion Antiphon
Cf. Mt 16: 24

Whoever wishes to come after me must deny himself,
take up his cross, and follow me, says the Lord.

Prayer after Communion

O God, who in Saint John
have wonderfully made known the mystery of the Cross,
graciously grant
that, drawing strength from this sacrifice,
we may cling faithfully to Christ
and labor in the Church for the salvation of all.
Through Christ our Lord.

December 21
Saint Peter Canisius, Priest and Doctor of the Church

From the Common of Pastors: For One Pastor (p. 1078), or from the Common of Doctors of the Church (p. 1088).

Collect

O God, who for the defense of the Catholic faith
made the Priest Saint Peter Canisius
strong in virtue and in learning,
grant, through his intercession,
that those who seek the truth
may joyfully find you, their God,
and that your faithful people
may persevere in confessing you.
Through our Lord Jesus Christ, your Son,
who lives and reigns with you in the unity of the Holy Spirit,
one God, for ever and ever.

December 23
Saint John of Kanty, Priest

From the Common of Pastors: For One Pastor (p. 1078), or from the Common of Holy Men and Women: For Those Who Practiced Works of Mercy (p. 1110).

Collect

Grant, we pray, almighty God,
that by the example of the Priest Saint John of Kanty
we may advance in the knowledge of holy things
and, by showing compassion to all,
may gain forgiveness in your sight.
Through our Lord Jesus Christ, your Son,
who lives and reigns with you in the unity of the Holy Spirit,
one God, for ever and ever.

December 26
SAINT STEPHEN, THE FIRST MARTYR
Feast

Entrance Antiphon

The gates of heaven were opened for blessed Stephen,
who was found to be first among the number of the Martyrs
and therefore is crowned triumphant in heaven.

The Gloria in excelsis (Glory to God in the highest) is said.

Collect

Grant, Lord, we pray,
that we may imitate what we worship,
and so learn to love even our enemies,
for we celebrate the heavenly birthday
of a man who knew how to pray even for his persecutors.
Through our Lord Jesus Christ, your Son,
who lives and reigns with you in the unity of the Holy Spirit,
one God, for ever and ever.

Prayer over the Offerings

May these offerings of our devotion today,
be acceptable to you, we pray, O Lord,
for they are prompted
by the glorious commemoration of Saint Stephen the Martyr.
Through Christ our Lord.

Preface of the Nativity of the Lord, pp. 538-543.

Communion Antiphon
Acts 7: 58

As they were stoning Stephen, he called out:
Lord Jesus, receive my spirit.

Prayer after Communion

For the many mercies which surround us
we give thanks to you, O Lord,
who save us through the Nativity of your Son
and gladden us with the celebration of the blessed
   Martyr Stephen.
Through Christ our Lord.

December 27
SAINT JOHN, APOSTLE AND EVANGELIST
Feast

Entrance Antiphon

This is John, who reclined on the Lord's breast at supper,
the blessed Apostle, to whom celestial secrets were revealed
and who spread the words of life through all the world.

Or: Cf. Sir 15: 5

In the midst of the Church he opened his mouth,
and the Lord filled him
with the spirit of wisdom and understanding
and clothed him in a robe of glory.

The Gloria in excelsis (Glory to God in the highest) is said.

Collect

O God, who through the blessed Apostle John
have unlocked for us the secrets of your Word,
grant, we pray,
that we may grasp with proper understanding
what he has so marvelously brought to our ears.
Through our Lord Jesus Christ, your Son,
who lives and reigns with you in the unity of the Holy Spirit,
one God, for ever and ever.

Prayer over the Offerings

Sanctify the offerings we have made, O Lord, we pray,
and grant that from the banquet of this supper
we may draw the hidden wisdom of the eternal Word,
just as, from this same source,
you revealed it to your Apostle John.
Through Christ our Lord.

Preface of the Nativity of the Lord, pp. 538-543.

Communion Antiphon   Jn 1: 14, 16

The Word became flesh and made his dwelling among us,
and from his fullness we have all received.

Prayer after Communion

Grant, we pray, almighty God,
that the Word made flesh,
proclaimed by the blessed Apostle John,
may, through this mystery which we have celebrated,
ever dwell among us.
Through Christ our Lord.

December 28
THE HOLY INNOCENTS, MARTYRS
Feast

Entrance Antiphon

The innocents were slaughtered as infants for Christ;
spotless, they follow the Lamb
and sing for ever: Glory to you, O Lord.

The Gloria in excelsis (Glory to God in the highest) is said.

Collect

O God, whom the Holy Innocents confessed
and proclaimed on this day,
not by speaking but by dying,
grant, we pray,
that the faith in you which we confess with our lips
may also speak through our manner of life.
Through our Lord Jesus Christ, your Son,
who lives and reigns with you in the unity of the Holy Spirit,
one God, for ever and ever.

Prayer over the Offerings

Receive, O Lord, we pray,
the offerings of your devoted servants
and purify us as we faithfully serve these, your mysteries,
by which you grant justification
even to those who lack understanding.
Through Christ our Lord.

Preface of the Nativity of the Lord, pp. 538-543.

Communion Antiphon   Cf. Rev 14: 4
Behold those redeemed as the first fruits
of the human race for God and the Lamb,
and who follow the Lamb wherever he goes.

Prayer after Communion
Grant, O Lord, abundant salvation to your faithful
as they receive your holy gifts
on the feast day of these, your Saints,
who, though still unable to profess your Son in speech,
were crowned with heavenly grace
on account of his birth.
Who lives and reigns for ever and ever.

December 29
Saint Thomas Becket, Bishop and Martyr

From the Common of Martyrs: For One Martyr (p. 1059), or from the Common of Pastors: For a Bishop (p. 1074).

Collect
O God, who gave the Martyr Saint Thomas Becket
the courage to give up his life for the sake of justice,
grant, through his intercession,
that, renouncing our life
for the sake of Christ in this world,
we may find it in heaven.
Through our Lord Jesus Christ, your Son,
who lives and reigns with you in the unity of the Holy Spirit,
one God, for ever and ever.

December 31
Saint Sylvester I, Pope

From the Common of Pastors: For a Pope (p. 1071).

Collect

Come, O Lord, to the help of your people,
sustained by the intercession of Pope Saint Sylvester,
so that, running the course of this present life under
    your guidance,
we may happily attain life without end.
Through our Lord Jesus Christ, your Son,
who lives and reigns with you in the unity of the Holy Spirit,
one God, for ever and ever.

COMMONS

1. For convenience, the individual Commons each offer several Masses with all the elements, namely antiphons and prayers, included.

    It is permitted for the Priest, as appropriate, to exchange antiphons and prayers of the same Common, choosing those texts which seem more suitable for pastoral reasons.

    In addition, for Masses of Memorials, the Prayers over the Offerings and the Prayers after Communion may also be taken from the weekdays of the current liturgical time as well as from these Commons.

2. In the Common of Martyrs and in the Common of Holy Men and Women, all the prayers that are given for men may also be used for women, with the necessary change of gender.

3. In the individual Commons, texts in the singular may always be used for several Saints, with the necessary change to the plural. Similarly, texts in the plural may be used for an individual, with the necessary change to the singular.

4. Masses that are designated for specific times or circumstances should only be used for these.

COMMON OF THE DEDICATION OF A CHURCH

The formularies of the Mass for the Dedication of a Church and of the Mass for the Dedication of an Altar are to be found among the Ritual Masses (pp. 1221-1233).

ON THE ANNIVERSARY OF THE DEDICATION

I. In the Church that was Dedicated

Entrance Antiphon   Ps 68 (67): 36
Wonderful are you, O God in your holy place.
The God of Israel himself gives his people strength and courage.
Blessed be God (E.T. alleluia)!

The Gloria in excelsis (Glory to God in the highest) is said.

Collect
O God, who year by year renew for us the day
when this your holy temple was consecrated,
hear the prayers of your people
and grant that in this place
for you there may always be pure worship
and for us, fullness of redemption.
Through our Lord Jesus Christ, your Son,
who lives and reigns with you in the unity of the Holy Spirit,
one God, for ever and ever.

The Creed is said.

Prayer over the Offerings
Recalling the day when you were pleased
to fill your house with glory and holiness, O Lord,
we pray that you may make of us
a sacrificial offering always acceptable to you.
Through Christ our Lord.

COMMON OF THE DEDICATION OF A CHURCH

Preface: The mystery of the Temple of God, which is the Church.

V. The Lord be with you.　　R. And with your spir-it.

V. Lift up your hearts.　　R. We lift them up to the Lord.

V. Let us give thanks to the Lord our God.　　R. It is right and just.

It is truly right and just, our duty and our sal-va-tion, al-ways and everywhere to give you thanks, Lord, holy Father, almighty and e-ter-nal God, through Christ our Lord. For in this visible house that you have let us build and where you never cease to show favor to the family on pilgrimage to you in this place, you wonderfully manifest and accomplish the mys-ter-y of your com-mun-ion with us. Here you build up for yourself the temple that we are and cause your Church, spread throughout the world, to grow ever more and more as the Lord's own Bod-y, till she reaches her fullness in the vi-sion of peace, the heavenly cit-y of Je-ru-sa-lem. And

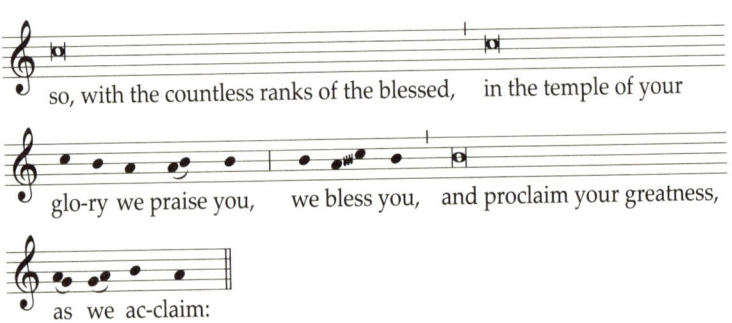

Holy, Holy, Holy Lord God of hosts . . .

Text without music:

V. **The Lord be with you.**
R. And with your spirit.

V. **Lift up your hearts.**
R. We lift them up to the Lord.

V. **Let us give thanks to the Lord our God.**
R. It is right and just.

It is truly right and just, our duty and our salvation,
always and everywhere to give you thanks,
Lord, holy Father, almighty and eternal God,
through Christ our Lord.

For in this visible house that you have let us build
and where you never cease to show favor
to the family on pilgrimage to you in this place,
you wonderfully manifest and accomplish
the mystery of your communion with us.

Here you build up for yourself the temple that we are
and cause your Church, spread throughout the world,
to grow ever more and more as the Lord's own Body,
till she reaches her fullness in the vision of peace,
the heavenly city of Jerusalem.

And so, with the countless ranks of the blessed,
in the temple of your glory we praise you,
we bless you and proclaim your greatness, as we acclaim:

Holy, Holy, Holy Lord God of hosts . . .

Communion Antiphon
Cf. 1 Cor 3: 16-17

You are the temple of God, and the Spirit of God dwells in you.
The temple of God, which you are, is holy (E.T. alleluia).

Prayer after Communion

May the people consecrated to you, O Lord, we pray,
receive the fruits and joy of your blessing,
that the festive homage
they have offered you today in the body
may redound upon them as a spiritual gift.
Through Christ our Lord.

Blessing at the End of Mass

May God, the Lord of heaven and earth,
who has gathered you today
in memory of the dedication of this church,
make you abound in heavenly blessings.
R. Amen.

And may he, who has willed that all his scattered children
be gathered together in his Son,
grant that you may become his temple
and the dwelling place of the Holy Spirit.
R. Amen.

Thus, may you be made thoroughly clean,
so that God may dwell within you
and you may possess with all the Saints
the inheritance of eternal happiness.
R. Amen.

And may the blessing of almighty God,
the Father, and the Son, ✠ and the Holy Spirit,
come down on you and remain with you for ever.
R. Amen.

II. Outside the Church that was Dedicated

Entrance Antiphon
Cf. Rev 21: 2

I saw the holy city, a new Jerusalem,
coming down out of heaven from God
prepared like a bride adorned for her husband (E.T. alleluia).

Or:

Cf. Rev 21: 3

Behold God's dwelling with the human race.
He will dwell with them
and they will be his people,
and God himself with them will be their God (E.T. alleluia).

The Gloria in excelsis (Glory to God in the highest) is said.

Collect

O God, who from living and chosen stones
prepare an eternal dwelling for your majesty,
increase in your Church the grace you have bestowed,
so that by unceasing growth
your faithful people may build up the heavenly Jerusalem.
Through our Lord Jesus Christ, your Son,
who lives and reigns with you in the unity of the Holy Spirit,
one God, for ever and ever.

Or:

O God, who were pleased to call your Church the Bride,
grant that the people that serves your name
may revere you, love you and follow you,
and may be led by you
to attain your promises in heaven.
Through our Lord Jesus Christ, your Son,
who lives and reigns with you in the unity of the Holy Spirit,
one God, for ever and ever.

COMMON OF THE DEDICATION OF A CHURCH

Prayer over the Offerings

Accept, we pray, O Lord, the offering made here
and grant that by it those who seek your favor
may receive in this place
the grace of the Sacraments
and an answer to their prayers.
Through Christ our Lord.

Preface: The mystery of the Church, the Bride of Christ and Temple of the Spirit.

V. The Lord be with you.
R. And with your spirit.

V. Lift up your hearts.
R. We lift them up to the Lord.

V. Let us give thanks to the Lord our God.
R. It is right and just.

It is truly right and just, our duty and our salvation,
always and everywhere to give you thanks,
Lord, holy Father, almighty and eternal God.

For in your benevolence you are pleased
to dwell in this house of prayer
in order to perfect us as the temple of the Holy Spirit,
supported by the perpetual help of your grace
and resplendent with the glory of a life acceptable to you.

Year by year you sanctify the Church, the Bride of Christ,
foreshadowed in visible buildings,
so that, rejoicing as the mother of countless children,
she may be given her place in your heavenly glory.

And so, with all the Angels and Saints,
we praise you, as without end we acclaim:

Holy, Holy, Holy Lord God of hosts . . .

Text with music, pp. 988-989.

Communion Antiphon   Cf. 1 Pt 2: 5

Be built up like living stones,
into a spiritual house, a holy priesthood (E.T. alleluia).

Or: Cf. Mt 21: 13; Lk 11: 10

My house shall be a house of prayer, says the Lord:
in that house, everyone who asks receives, and the one who seeks finds,
and to the one who knocks, the door will be opened (E.T. alleluia).

Prayer after Communion

O God, who chose to foreshadow for us
the heavenly Jerusalem
through the sign of your Church on earth,
grant, we pray,
that, by our partaking of this Sacrament,
we may be made the temple of your grace
and may enter the dwelling place of your glory.
Through Christ our Lord.

COMMON OF THE BLESSED VIRGIN MARY

These Masses are also used for celebrating the Memorial of the Blessed Virgin Mary on Saturday, and in Votive Masses of the Blessed Virgin Mary. In all the prayers, where the word "commemoration" is found, "memorial" may also be used, as appropriate.

I. In Ordinary Time

These formularies may be used in accordance with the norms, even in Lent, should a celebration of the Blessed Virgin Mary occur that is duly inscribed in a proper calendar.

1

Entrance Antiphon

Hail, Holy Mother, who gave birth to the King
who rules heaven and earth for ever.

Collect

Grant, Lord God, that we, your servants,
may rejoice in unfailing health of mind and body,
and, through the glorious intercession of Blessed Mary ever-Virgin,
may we be set free from present sorrow
and come to enjoy eternal happiness.
Through our Lord Jesus Christ, your Son,
who lives and reigns with you in the unity of the Holy Spirit,
one God, for ever and ever.

Prayer over the Offerings

Receive, O Lord, we ask, the prayers of your people
with the sacrificial offerings,
that, through the intercession of Blessed Mary,
the Mother of your Son,
no petition may go unanswered,
no request be made in vain.
Through Christ our Lord.

Or:

May the humanity of your Only Begotten Son
come, O Lord, to our aid,
and may he, who at his birth from the Blessed Virgin
did not diminish but consecrated her integrity,
by taking from us now our wicked deeds,
make our oblation acceptable to you.
Through Christ our Lord.

Preface I of the Blessed Virgin Mary (for Votive Masses: and to praise, bless, and glorify your name in veneration of), p. 590, or II, p. 592.

Communion Antiphon
Cf. Lk 11: 27

Blessed is the womb of the Virgin Mary,
which bore the Son of the eternal Father.

Prayer after Communion

As we receive this heavenly Sacrament,
we beseech, O Lord, your mercy,
that we, who rejoice in commemorating the Blessed Virgin Mary,
may by imitating her
serve worthily the mystery of our redemption.
Through Christ our Lord.

2

Entrance Antiphon
Blessed are you, O Virgin Mary, who bore the Creator of all things.
You became the Mother of your Maker,
and you remain for ever Virgin.

Collect
Grant us, O merciful God,
protection in our weakness,
that we, who keep the Memorial of the holy Mother of God,
may, with the help of her intercession,
rise up from our iniquities.
Through our Lord Jesus Christ, your Son,
who lives and reigns with you in the unity of the Holy Spirit,
one God, for ever and ever.

Prayer over the Offerings

As we honor the memory of the Mother of your Son,
we pray, O Lord,
that the oblation of this sacrifice
may, by your grace, make of us an eternal offering to you.
Through Christ our Lord.

Preface I of the Blessed Virgin Mary (for Votive Masses: and to praise, bless, and glorify your name in veneration of), p. 590, or II, p. 592.

Communion Antiphon   Lk 1: 49

He who is mighty has done great things for me,
and holy is his name.

Prayer after Communion

Having been made partakers of eternal redemption,
we pray, O Lord,
that we, who commemorate the Mother of your Son,
may glory in the fullness of your grace
and experience its continued increase for our salvation.
Through Christ our Lord.

3

Entrance Antiphon   Cf. Jdt 13: 18-19

Blessed are you, O Virgin Mary, by the Lord God Most High,
above all women on the earth;
for he has so exalted your name
that your praise shall be undying on our lips.

Collect

As we venerate the glorious memory
of the most holy Virgin Mary,
grant, we pray, O Lord, through her intercession,
that we, too, may merit to receive
from the fullness of your grace.
Through our Lord Jesus Christ, your Son,
who lives and reigns with you in the unity of the Holy Spirit,
one God, for ever and ever.

Prayer over the Offerings

We offer you the sacrifice of praise, O Lord,
as we rejoice in commemorating the Mother of your Son;
grant, we pray,
that through this most holy exchange
we may advance towards eternal redemption.
Through Christ our Lord.

Preface I of the Blessed Virgin Mary (for Votive Masses: and to praise, bless, and glorify your name in veneration of), p. 590, or II, p. 592.

Communion Antiphon
Cf. Lk 1: 48

All generations will call me blessed,
for God has looked on his lowly handmaid.

Prayer after Communion

Renewed with this heavenly food,
we humbly implore you, Lord,
that, having received your Son, born of the tender Virgin,
under sacramental signs,
we may profess him in words
and hold fast to him in deeds.
Who lives and reigns for ever and ever.

4

Entrance Antiphon
Cf. Ps 45 (44): 13, 15, 16

All the richest of the people long to see your face:
behind her, her maiden companions are escorted to the King;
her attendants are escorted to you amid gladness and joy.

Collect

Pardon the faults of your servants, we pray, O Lord,
that we, who cannot please you by our own deeds,
may be saved through the intercession
of the Mother of your Son and our Lord.
Who lives and reigns with you in the unity of the Holy Spirit,
one God, for ever and ever.

COMMON OF THE BLESSED VIRGIN MARY

Prayer over the Offerings

Accept, O Lord, the offerings we bring you
and grant that, enlightened by the Holy Spirit
and encouraged by the example of the Blessed Virgin Mary,
our hearts may always seek out
    and treasure the things that are yours.
Through Christ our Lord.

Preface I of the Blessed Virgin Mary (for Votive Masses: and to praise, bless, and glorify your name in veneration of), p. 590, or II, p. 592.

Communion Antiphon

Praise the Lord our God,
for in Mary his handmaid
he has fulfilled his promise of mercy to the house of Israel.

Prayer after Communion

Having received the Sacrament of salvation and of faith,
we humbly beseech you, O Lord,
that we, who devoutly honor the Blessed Virgin Mary,
may be worthy to share with her in the charity of heaven.
Through Christ our Lord.

5

Entrance Antiphon
Cf. Lk 1: 28, 42

Hail, Mary, full of grace, the Lord is with you.
Blessed are you among women,
and blessed is the fruit of your womb.

Collect

O God, who chose the Blessed Virgin Mary,
foremost among the poor and humble,
to be the Mother of the Savior,
grant, we pray, that, following her example,
we may offer you the homage of sincere faith
and place in you all our hope of salvation.
Through our Lord Jesus Christ, your Son,
who lives and reigns with you in the unity of the Holy Spirit,
one God, for ever and ever.

Prayer over the Offerings

Receive, O Lord, the offerings of our devotion,
and grant that we, who celebrate
your Son's work of boundless charity,
may, through the example of the Blessed Virgin Mary,
be confirmed in love of you and of our neighbor.
Through Christ our Lord.

Preface I of the Blessed Virgin Mary (for Votive Masses: and to praise, bless, and glorify your name in veneration of), p. 590, or II, p. 592.

Communion Antiphon   Cf. Ps 87 (86): 3; Lk 1: 49

Glorious things are spoken of you, O Virgin Mary,
for he who is mighty has done great things for you.

Prayer after Communion

Grant to your Church, O Lord,
that, strengthened by the power of this Sacrament,
she may eagerly walk in the pathways of the Gospel,
until she reaches the blessed vision of peace,
which the Virgin Mary, your lowly handmaid,
already enjoys eternally in glory.
Through Christ our Lord.

6

Entrance Antiphon

The rod of Jesse has blossomed;
the Virgin has brought forth one who is both God and man.
God has restored peace,
reconciling in himself the depths and the heights.

Collect

May the venerable intercession of Blessed Mary ever-Virgin
come to our aid, we pray, O Lord,
and free us from every danger,
so that we may rejoice in your peace.
Through our Lord Jesus Christ, your Son,
who lives and reigns with you in the unity of the Holy Spirit,
one God, for ever and ever.

COMMON OF THE BLESSED VIRGIN MARY

Prayer over the Offerings

We offer you, O Lord,
these offerings of conciliation and praise,
humbly asking that,
following the example of the Blessed Virgin Mary,
we may present our very selves
as a holy sacrifice pleasing to you.
Through Christ our Lord.

Preface I of the Blessed Virgin Mary (for Votive Masses: and to praise, bless, and glorify your name in veneration of), p. 590, or II, p. 592.

Communion Antiphon
Ps 45 (44): 3

Graciousness is poured out upon your lips,
for God has blessed you for ever more.

Prayer after Communion

Having nourished us with heavenly food, O Lord,
grant that, according to the example of the Blessed Virgin Mary,
we may serve you in purity of life
and magnify you, with her, in wholehearted praise.
Through Christ our Lord.

7

Entrance Antiphon
Cf. Lk 1: 47-48

Mary said: My spirit rejoices in God my Savior,
because the Lord has looked on his lowly handmaid.

Collect

O God, who were pleased to choose Blessed Mary
as the virginal chamber where your Word would dwell,
grant, we pray, that under her protection,
we may participate joyfully in her commemoration.
Through our Lord Jesus Christ, your Son,
who lives and reigns with you in the unity of the Holy Spirit,
one God, for ever and ever.

Prayer over the Offerings

May the offerings your people make
in commemoration of Blessed Mary
be acceptable to you, O Lord,
for by her virginity she pleased you
and in humility conceived your Son, our Lord.
Who lives and reigns for ever and ever.

Preface I of the Blessed Virgin Mary (for Votive Masses: and to praise, bless, and glorify your name in veneration of), p. 590, or II, p. 592.

Communion Antiphon
Lk 2: 19

Mary treasured all these words,
reflecting on them in her heart.

Prayer after Communion

Having been made partakers of this spiritual food,
we pray, O Lord our God,
that, steadily imitating the Blessed Virgin Mary,
we may always be found intent on service of the Church
and may know the joys of doing your will.
Through Christ our Lord.

8

Entrance Antiphon

Happy are you, holy Virgin Mary, and most worthy of all praise,
for from you arose the sun of justice, Christ our God,
through whom we have been saved and redeemed.

Collect

Grant, we pray, almighty God, that your faithful,
who rejoice under the patronage of the most holy Virgin Mary,
may be freed by her motherly intercession
from all evils on earth
and merit the attainment of eternal joys in heaven.
Through our Lord Jesus Christ, your Son,
who lives and reigns with you in the unity of the Holy Spirit,
one God, for ever and ever.

Prayer over the Offerings

> Look, O Lord, upon the prayers and offerings of your faithful,
> presented in commemoration of Blessed Mary, the Mother of God,
> that they may be pleasing to you
> and may confer on us your help and forgiveness.
> Through Christ our Lord.

Preface I of the Blessed Virgin Mary (for Votive Masses: and to praise, bless, and glorify your name in veneration of), p. 590, or II, p. 592.

Communion Antiphon   Cf. Lk 1: 48

> The Lord has looked on his lowly handmaid;
> behold, henceforth all generations will call me blessed.

Prayer after Communion

> Renewed by the Sacrament of salvation,
> we humbly beseech you, Lord,
> that we, who have honored in veneration
> the memory of the Blessed Virgin Mary, Mother of God,
> may merit to experience in perpetuity the fruits of your redemption.
> Through Christ our Lord.

II. In Advent

Entrance Antiphon   Cf. Is 45: 8

Drop down dew from above, you heavens,
and let the clouds rain down the Just One;
let the earth be opened and bring forth a Savior.

Or: Cf. Lk 1: 30-32

The angel said to Mary: You have found favor with God.
Behold, you will conceive and bear a son,
and he will be called Son of the Most High.

Collect

O God, who willed that at the message of an Angel
your Word should take flesh
in the womb of the Blessed Virgin Mary,
grant that we, who pray to you
and believe her to be truly the Mother of God,
may be helped by her interceding before you.
Through our Lord Jesus Christ, your Son,
who lives and reigns with you in the unity of the Holy Spirit,
one God, for ever and ever.

Or:

O God, who, fulfilling the promise made to our Fathers,
chose the Blessed Virgin Mary
to become the Mother of the Savior,
grant that we may follow her example,
for her humility was pleasing to you
and her obedience profitable to us.
Through our Lord Jesus Christ, your Son,
who lives and reigns with you in the unity of the Holy Spirit,
one God, for ever and ever.

Prayer over the Offerings

Accept, O Lord, these offerings,
and by your power change them into the Sacrament of salvation,
in which, fulfilling the sacrifices of the Fathers,
is offered the true Lamb, Jesus Christ your Son,
born of the ever-Virgin Mary in a way beyond all telling.
Who lives and reigns for ever and ever.

Preface I of the Blessed Virgin Mary, p. 590, or II, p. 592. Preface II of Advent, p. 536, may also be used.

Communion Antiphon

Cf. Is 7: 14

Behold, a Virgin shall conceive and bear a son,
and his name will be called Emmanuel.

Prayer after Communion

May the mysteries we have received,
O Lord our God,
always show forth your mercy in us,
that we, who commemorate in faith the Mother of your Son,
may be saved by his Incarnation.
Who lives and reigns for ever and ever.

III. In Christmas Time

Entrance Antiphon

In childbirth she brought forth the King, whose name is eternal.
She keeps a mother's joy with a virgin's honor.
None like her was seen before, and none thereafter.

Or:

O Virgin Mother of God,
he whom the whole world cannot contain
cloistered himself within your womb, made man for us.

Collect

O God, who through the fruitful virginity of Blessed Mary
bestowed on the human race the grace of eternal salvation,
grant, we pray,
that we may experience the intercession of her,
through whom we were found worthy to receive the author of life,
our Lord Jesus Christ, your Son.
Who lives and reigns with you in the unity of the Holy Spirit,
one God, for ever and ever.

Or:

O God, who willed that your Word, begotten from all eternity,
should come forth from the womb of the Blessed Virgin Mary,
grant, we pray, through her intercession,
that he may light up our darkness
with the splendor of his presence,
and from his fullness give us joy and peace.
Who lives and reigns with you in the unity of the Holy Spirit,
one God, for ever and ever.

Prayer over the Offerings

As we celebrate the blessed days which you made sacred
by the Nativity of your Only Begotten Son,
born into time as the offspring of the Virgin Mary,
we pray, O Lord, that this oblation may sanctify us,
and may grant us new birth in him.
Who lives and reigns for ever and ever.

Preface I of the Blessed Virgin Mary, p. 590, or II, p. 592.

Communion Antiphon   Cf. Lk 11: 27

Blessed is the womb of the Virgin Mary,
which bore the Son of the eternal Father.

Prayer after Communion

Renewed by the Body and Blood of your incarnate Word,
we pray, O Lord, that these divine mysteries,
which we have joyfully received
as we commemorate the Blessed Virgin Mary,
may make us sharers for eternity in the divinity of your Son.
Who lives and reigns for ever and ever.

IV. In Easter Time

Entrance Antiphon
Cf. Ps 30 (29): 12

You have changed my mourning into dancing, O Lord,
and have girded me with joy, alleluia.

Collect
O God, who have been pleased to gladden the world
by the Resurrection of your Son our Lord Jesus Christ,
grant, we pray,
that through his Mother, the Virgin Mary,
we may receive the joys of everlasting life.
Through our Lord Jesus Christ, your Son,
who lives and reigns with you in the unity of the Holy Spirit,
one God, for ever and ever.

Prayer over the Offerings
Receive, holy Father, this offering of our humility,
which we bring you with joy
as we commemorate the Blessed Virgin Mary,
and grant, we pray, that it may be for us,
who are joined to the sacrifice of Christ,
our consolation on earth and our eternal salvation.
Who lives and reigns for ever and ever.

Preface I of the Blessed Virgin Mary, p. 590, or II, p. 592.

Communion Antiphon
Rejoice, O Virgin Mother,
for Christ has risen from the tomb, alleluia.

Prayer after Communion
Renewed by this paschal Sacrament,
we pray, O Lord,
that we, who honor the memory of the Mother of your Son,
may show forth in our mortal flesh the life of Jesus.
Who lives and reigns for ever and ever.

During Easter Time, the Mass of Our Lady, Queen of Apostles, may also be used, pp. 1351-1352.

COMMON OF MARTYRS

I. Outside Easter Time

A. For Several Martyrs

1

Entrance Antiphon
The souls of the Saints are rejoicing in heaven,
the Saints who followed the footsteps of Christ,
and since for love of him they shed their blood,
they now exult with Christ for ever.

Or:

Holy men shed their glorious blood for the Lord;
they loved Christ in their life,
they imitated him in their death,
and therefore were crowned in triumph.

Collect
Grant a joyful outcome to our prayers, O Lord,
so that we, who each year
devoutly honor the day of the passion of the holy Martyrs N. and N.,
may also imitate the constancy of their faith.
Through our Lord Jesus Christ, your Son,
who lives and reigns with you in the unity of the Holy Spirit,
one God, for ever and ever.

Prayer over the Offerings
Receive, holy Father, the offerings we bring
in commemoration of the holy Martyrs,
and grant that we, your servants,
may be found steadfast in confessing your name.
Through Christ our Lord.

COMMON OF MARTYRS

Communion Antiphon
Lk 22: 28-30

It is you who have stood by me in my trials;
and I confer a kingdom on you, says the Lord,
that you may eat and drink at my table in my kingdom.

Or:

See how rich is the Saints' reward from God;
they died for Christ and will live for ever.

Prayer after Communion

O God, who in your holy Martyrs
have wonderfully made known the mystery of the Cross,
graciously grant
that, drawing strength from this sacrifice,
we may cling faithfully to Christ
and labor in the Church for the salvation of all.
Through Christ our Lord.

2

Entrance Antiphon
Cf. Ps 34 (33): 20-21

Many are the trials of the just,
but from them all the Lord will rescue them.
The Lord will keep guard over all their bones;
not one of their bones shall be broken.

Or:
Cf. Rev 7: 14; Dn 3: 95

These are they who come out of the great ordeal
and have washed their robes in the blood of the Lamb.
For God's sake they handed their bodies over for punishment,
and they have earned unfading crowns.

Collect

Almighty ever-living God,
who gave Saints N. and N.
the grace of suffering for Christ,
come, in your divine mercy, we pray,
to the help of our own weakness,
that, as your Saints did not hesitate to die for your sake,
we, too, may live bravely in confessing you.
Through our Lord Jesus Christ, your Son,
who lives and reigns with you in the unity of the Holy Spirit,
one God, for ever and ever.

Prayer over the Offerings
May the sacrifice soon to be consecrated
be acceptable to you, O Lord, we pray,
in commemoration of this precious martyrdom,
so that it may cleanse our sins
and commend to you the prayers of your servants.
Through Christ our Lord.

Communion Antiphon *Cf. Jn 15: 13*
Greater love has no one
than to lay down his life for his friends, says the Lord.

Or: *Lk 12: 4*

I say to you, my friends:
Do not be afraid of those who kill the body.

Prayer after Communion
Grant us, O Lord, we pray,
that, being nourished by the Bread of heaven
and made one Body in Christ,
we may never be separated from his love
and, after the example of your holy Martyrs **N.** and **N.**,
may bravely overcome all things
for the sake of him who loved us.
Who lives and reigns for ever and ever.

3

Entrance Antiphon *Cf. Ps 37 (36): 39*
From the Lord comes the salvation of the just;
he is their stronghold in time of distress.

Or: *Cf. Wis 3: 6-7, 9*

As gold in the furnace, the Lord put his chosen to the test;
as sacrificial offerings he took them to himself;
and in due time they will be honored,
and grace and peace will be with the elect of God.

COMMON OF MARTYRS

Collect

May the sight of the great number
of your holy Martyrs gladden us, O Lord,
making our faith stronger
and bringing us consolation by the prayers of them all.
Through our Lord Jesus Christ, your Son,
who lives and reigns with you in the unity of the Holy Spirit,
one God, for ever and ever.

Or:

May the prayer of the blessed Martyrs N. and N.,
being pleasing to you, O Lord,
commend us, we pray,
and confirm us in the profession of your truth.
Through our Lord Jesus Christ, your Son,
who lives and reigns with you in the unity of the Holy Spirit,
one God, for ever and ever.

Prayer over the Offerings

Receive, we pray, O Lord, the offerings of your people
in honor of the passion of your holy Martyrs,
and may the gifts that gave blessed N. and N.
courage under persecution
make us, too, steadfast in all trials.
Through Christ our Lord.

Communion Antiphon   Cf. Mk 8: 35

Whoever loses his life for my sake
and for the sake of the Gospel will save it, says the Lord.

Or: Cf. Wis 3: 4

Even if before men, indeed, they be punished,
yet is their hope full of immortality.

Prayer after Communion

Preserve in us your gift, O Lord,
and may what we have received at your hands
for the feast day of the blessed Martyrs N. and N.
bring us salvation and peace.
Through Christ our Lord.

4

Entrance Antiphon   Cf. Ps 34 (33): 18

When the just cried out, the Lord heard them
and rescued them in all their distress.

Or:

Because of the Lord's covenant and the ancestral laws,
the Saints of God persevered in loving brotherhood,
for there was always one spirit in them, and one faith.

Collect

O God, who gladden us each year
with the feast day of blessed N. and N.,
grant in your mercy
that we, who honor their heavenly birthday,
may also imitate their courage in suffering.
Through our Lord Jesus Christ, your Son,
who lives and reigns with you in the unity of the Holy Spirit,
one God, for ever and ever.

Or:

O God, who bestowed on Saints N. and N.
the grace of coming to such surpassing glory,
grant to your servants, we pray,
through your Martyrs' merits,
pardon for their sins and freedom from every trial.
Through our Lord Jesus Christ, your Son,
who lives and reigns with you in the unity of the Holy Spirit,
one God, for ever and ever.

Prayer over the Offerings

We bring you sacrificial offerings, O Lord,
to commemorate blessed N. and N.,
humbly entreating
that, as you gave them the bright light of holy faith,
so you may grant us pardon and peace.
Through Christ our Lord.

COMMON OF MARTYRS

Communion Antiphon
2 Cor 4: 11

For the sake of Jesus we are given up to death,
that the life of Jesus may be manifested in our mortal flesh.

Or:
Mt 10: 28

Do not be afraid of those who kill the body
but cannot kill the soul, says the Lord.

Prayer after Communion

**Through this heavenly Sacrament, O Lord,
grant us manifold grace
on the celebration of the blessed Martyrs N. and N.,
that from so great a struggle
we may learn to be united in unwavering patience
and to exult in the victory they won for love of you.
Through Christ our Lord.**

5

Entrance Antiphon

The blood of the holy Martyrs
was poured out for Christ upon the earth;
therefore they have gained everlasting rewards.

Or:
Cf. Wis 3: 1-2, 3

The souls of the just are in the hand of God
and no torment shall touch them.
They seemed, in the view of the foolish, to be dead,
but they are in peace.

Collect

**Grant us in your compassion, O Lord, we pray,
an increase of that faith
which brought glory to your holy Martyrs N. and N.
as they maintained it even to the shedding of their blood,
and may the same faith bring to us, who truly follow it,
justification in your sight.
Through our Lord Jesus Christ, your Son,
who lives and reigns with you in the unity of the Holy Spirit,
one God, for ever and ever.**

Prayer over the Offerings

>Look with favor, we pray, O Lord,
>upon these sacrificial gifts offered here
>that, celebrating in mystery the Passion of your Son,
>we may, by following the example of blessed **N.** and **N.**,
>honor it with loving devotion.
>Through Christ our Lord.

>Or:

>May this sacrifice, O Lord,
>which we bring for the triumph of blessed **N.** and **N.**,
>constantly kindle in our hearts the fire of your love
>and prepare them for the rewards
>you have promised to those who persevere.
>Through Christ our Lord.

Communion Antiphon — Cf. Rom 8: 38-39

>Neither death nor life nor any created thing
>will be able to separate us from the love of Christ.

Or: — Mt 10: 30, 31

>The hairs on your head are counted.
>So do not be afraid; you are worth more than many sparrows.

Prayer after Communion

>Having been fed, O Lord,
>on the commemoration of your blessed Martyrs **N.** and **N.**,
>with the precious Body and Blood of your Only Begotten Son,
>we humbly pray:
>grant that by steadfast charity we may abide in you,
>draw life from you, and to you be drawn.
>Through Christ our Lord.

COMMON OF MARTYRS

B. For One Martyr

1

Entrance Antiphon

This holy man fought to the death for the law of his God
and did not fear the words of the godless,
for he was built on solid rock.

Or: Cf. Wis 10: 12

The Lord granted him a stern struggle,
that he might know that wisdom is mightier than all else.

Collect

Almighty and merciful God,
who brought your Martyr blessed N.
to overcome the torments of his (her) passion,
grant that we, who celebrate the day of his (her) triumph,
may remain invincible under your protection
against the snares of the enemy.
Through our Lord Jesus Christ, your Son,
who lives and reigns with you in the unity of the Holy Spirit,
one God, for ever and ever.

Prayer over the Offerings

Sanctify our offerings by your blessing,
O Lord, we pray,
and by your grace may we be set afire
with that flame of your love
through which Saint N. overcame every bodily torment.
Through Christ our Lord.

Or:

May the offerings we bring in commemoration of blessed N.
be acceptable to you, we pray, O Lord,
so that they may be pleasing to your majesty
just as the shedding of this Martyr's blood
was precious in your sight.
Through Christ our Lord.

Communion Antiphon   Cf. Mt 16: 24
   Whoever wishes to come after me, must deny himself,
   take up his cross, and follow me, says the Lord.

   Or: Mt 10: 39

   Whoever loses his life for my sake,
   will find it in eternity, says the Lord.

Prayer after Communion
   May the sacred mysteries of which we have partaken,
   O Lord, we pray,
   give us that determination which made your blessed Martyr N.
   faithful in your service
   and victorious in suffering.
   Through Christ our Lord.

2

Entrance Antiphon
   This truly is a Martyr,
   who shed his (her) blood for the name of Christ,
   who did not fear the threats of judges
   but attained the heavenly kingdom.

   Or: Cf. Phil 3: 8, 10

   He (She) counted all as loss in order to know Christ
   and to have a share in his sufferings,
   conforming himself (herself) to his death.

Collect
   Almighty ever-living God,
   by whose gift blessed N. fought
   for righteousness' sake even until death,
   grant, we pray, through his (her) intercession,
   that we may bear every adversity for the sake of your love
   and hasten with all our strength towards you who alone are life.
   Through our Lord Jesus Christ, your Son,
   who lives and reigns with you in the unity of the Holy Spirit,
   one God, for ever and ever.

Prayer over the Offerings

Most merciful God,
pour out your blessing upon these offerings
and confirm us in the faith
that blessed N. professed by the shedding of his (her) blood.
Through Christ our Lord.

Or:

We offer you sacrificial gifts, O Lord,
to commemorate your blessed Martyr N.,
whom no temptation could separate
from the unity of the Body of Christ.
Who lives and reigns for ever and ever.

Communion Antiphon Cf. Jn 15: 1, 5

I am the true vine and you are the branches, says the Lord.
Whoever remains in me, and I in him, bears fruit in plenty.

Or: Jn 8: 12

Whoever follows me will not walk in darkness,
but will have the light of life, says the Lord.

Prayer after Communion

Made new by these sacred mysteries, we pray, O Lord,
that, imitating the wondrous constancy of blessed N.,
we may merit an eternal reward for suffering endured.
Through Christ our Lord.

II. During Easter Time

A. For Several Martyrs

1

Entrance Antiphon   *Cf. Mt 25: 34*

Come, you blessed of my Father;
receive the kingdom prepared for you
from the foundation of the world, alleluia.

Or: *Cf. Rev 7:13-14*

These who are clothed in white robes
are they who survived the time of great distress
and have washed their robes in the blood of the Lamb, alleluia.

Collect

By the power of the Holy Spirit
we pray, almighty God:
make us docile in believing the faith
and courageous in confessing it,
just as you granted the blessed Martyrs N. and N.
that they might lay down their lives
for the sake of your word and in witness to Jesus.
Who lives and reigns with you in the unity of the Holy Spirit,
one God, for ever and ever.

Or:

O God, from whom faith draws perseverance and
    weakness strength,
grant, through the example and prayers of the Martyrs N. and N.,
that we may share in the Passion and Resurrection
of your Only Begotten Son,
so that with the Martyrs
we may attain perfect joy in your presence.
Through our Lord Jesus Christ, your Son,
who lives and reigns with you in the unity of the Holy Spirit,
one God, for ever and ever.

Prayer over the Offerings

In honor of the precious death of your just ones, O Lord,
we come to offer that sacrifice
from which all martyrdom draws its origin.
Through Christ our Lord.

Communion Antiphon
Cf. Rev 2: 7

To the victor I will give the right to eat from the tree of life,
which is in the paradise of my God, alleluia.

Or:
Cf. Ps 33 (32): 1

Ring out your joy to the Lord, O you just,
for praise is fitting for the upright, alleluia.

Prayer after Communion

As we celebrate by this divine banquet
the heavenly victory of the blessed Martyrs N. and N.,
we beseech you, Lord, to bestow victory
on those who eat here below of the Bread of life
and to allow them to eat as victors from the tree of life in paradise.
Through Christ our Lord.

2

Entrance Antiphon
Cf. Rev 12: 11

These are the Saints who were victorious
because of the blood of the Lamb,
and in the face of death refused to cling to life;
therefore they reign with Christ for ever, alleluia.

Or:
Cf. Mt 25: 34

Rejoice, you Saints, in the presence of the Lamb;
a kingdom has been prepared for you
from the foundation of the world, alleluia.

Collect

May the glorious feast day of your blessed Martyrs N. and N.
gladden us, we pray, O Lord,
for, as they boldly confessed the Passion and Resurrection
of your Only Begotten Son,
you led them to shed their costly blood in a glorious death.
Through our Lord Jesus Christ, your Son,
who lives and reigns with you in the unity of the Holy Spirit,
one God, for ever and ever.

Prayer over the Offerings

Look with such serenity and kindness,
we pray, O Lord,
upon these present offerings,
that they may be filled with the blessing of the Holy Spirit
and may stir up in our hearts that powerful love
through which the holy Martyrs N. and N.
overcame every bodily torment.
Through Christ our Lord.

Communion Antiphon
Cf. 2 Tm 2: 11-12

If we have died with Christ, we shall also live with him;
if we persevere, we shall also reign with him, alleluia.

Or:
Cf. Mt 5: 12

Rejoice and be glad,
for your reward will be great in heaven, alleluia.

Prayer after Communion

Renewed by the sustenance of the one Bread, O Lord,
on the commemoration of the blessed Martyrs N. and N.,
we humbly pray
that you may confirm us ever in your charity
and make us walk in newness of life.
Through Christ our Lord.

COMMON OF MARTYRS

B. For One Martyr

Entrance Antiphon
Cf. 4 Esdr 2: 35

Perpetual light will shine on your Saints, O Lord,
and life without end for ever, alleluia.

Or:

This is the one who was not deserted by God on the day of struggle
and now wears a crown of victory
for faithfulness to the Lord's commands, alleluia.

Collect

O God, who were pleased to give light to your Church
by adorning blessed N. with the victory of martyrdom,
graciously grant
that, as he (she) imitated the Lord's Passion,
so we may, by following in his (her) footsteps,
be worthy to attain eternal joys.
Through our Lord Jesus Christ, your Son,
who lives and reigns with you in the unity of the Holy Spirit,
one God, for ever and ever.

Prayer over the Offerings

Receive, we pray, O Lord,
the sacrifice of conciliation and praise
which we offer to your majesty
in commemoration of the blessed Martyr N.,
that it may lead us to obtain pardon
and confirm us in perpetual thanksgiving.
Through Christ our Lord.

Communion Antiphon
Jn 12: 24

Unless a grain of wheat falls into the ground and dies,
it remains just a grain of wheat;
but if it dies, it produces much fruit, alleluia.

Or:
Ps 116 (115): 15

How precious in the eyes of the Lord
is the death of his holy ones, alleluia.

Prayer after Communion

We have received your heavenly gifts,
rejoicing at this feast day, O Lord;
grant, we pray, that we, who in this divine banquet
proclaim the Death of your Son,
may merit to be partakers with the holy Martyrs
in his Resurrection and his glory.
Who lives and reigns for ever and ever.

III. For Missionary Martyrs

A. For Several Missionary Martyrs

Entrance Antiphon   Cf. Gal 6: 14; 1 Cor 1: 18

May we never boast,
except in the Cross of our Lord Jesus Christ.
For the word of the Cross is the power of God
to us who have been saved (E.T. alleluia).

Collect

We humbly beseech the mercy of your majesty,
almighty and merciful God,
that, as you have poured the knowledge
of your Only Begotten Son into the hearts of the peoples
by the preaching of the blessed Martyrs N. and N.,
so, through their intercession,
we may be made steadfast in the faith.
Through our Lord Jesus Christ, your Son,
who lives and reigns with you in the unity of the Holy Spirit,
one God, for ever and ever.

Prayer over the Offerings

As we venerate the passion of your Martyrs N. and N.,
grant that through this sacrifice, O Lord,
we may proclaim worthily the Death of your Only Begotten Son,
who, not content with encouraging the Martyrs by word,
strengthened them likewise by example.
Who lives and reigns for ever and ever.

Communion Antiphon

Mt 5: 10

Blessed are they who are persecuted for the sake of righteousness,
for theirs is the Kingdom of Heaven (E.T. alleluia).

Or:

Mt 10: 32

Everyone who acknowledges me before others
I will acknowledge before my heavenly Father,
says the Lord (E.T. alleluia).

Prayer after Communion

Having fed upon heavenly delights,
we humbly ask you, O Lord,
that by the example of blessed N. and N.
we may bear in our hearts
the marks of your Son's charity and suffering
and ever enjoy the fruit of perpetual peace.
Through Christ our Lord.

B. For One Missionary Martyr

Entrance Antiphon

Cf. Phil 2: 30

This Saint went as far as death,
handing over his life to destruction
for the work of Christ (E.T. alleluia).

Collect

Grant, we pray, almighty God,
that we may follow with due devotion the faith of blessed N.,
who, for spreading the faith,
merited the crown of martyrdom.
Through our Lord Jesus Christ, your Son,
who lives and reigns with you in the unity of the Holy Spirit,
one God, for ever and ever.

Prayer over the Offerings

As we commemorate the martyrdom of blessed N., O Lord,
we make our offerings at your altar,
praying that we, who celebrate the mysteries of our Lord's Passion,
may imitate what we now do.
Through Christ our Lord.

Communion Antiphon   Mk 8: 35

    Whoever loses his life for the sake of the Gospel
    will save it, says the Lord (E.T. alleluia).

Prayer after Communion

    As we celebrate the heavenly banquet,
    we beseech you, Lord,
    that, in following such a great example of faith,
    we may be encouraged by the remembrance of the blessed Martyr N.
    and led on by his (her) gracious intercession.
    Through Christ our Lord.

IV. For a Virgin Martyr

Entrance Antiphon

    Behold, now she follows the Lamb who was crucified for us,
    powerful in virginity, modesty her offering,
    a sacrifice on the altar of chastity (E.T. alleluia).

Or:

    Blessed is the virgin
    who by denying herself and taking up her cross
    imitated the Lord, the spouse of virgins
    and prince of martyrs (E.T. alleluia).

Collect

    O God, who gladden us today
    with the annual commemoration of blessed N.,
    graciously grant
    that we may be helped by her merits,
    just as our lives are lit up by the splendor
    of her example of chastity and fortitude.
    Through our Lord Jesus Christ, your Son,
    who lives and reigns with you in the unity of the Holy Spirit,
    one God, for ever and ever.

Prayer over the Offerings

May the offerings we bring in celebration of blessed N.
win your gracious acceptance, O Lord, we pray,
just as the struggle of her suffering and passion
was pleasing to you.
Through Christ our Lord.

Communion Antiphon   Rev 7: 17

The Lamb who is at the center of the throne
will lead them to the springs of the waters of life (E.T. alleluia).

Prayer after Communion

O God, who bestowed on blessed N. a crown among the Saints
for her twofold triumph of virginity and martyrdom,
grant, we pray, through the power of this Sacrament,
that, bravely overcoming every evil,
we may attain the glory of heaven.
Through Christ our Lord.

V. For a Holy Woman Martyr

Entrance Antiphon

For the Kingdom of Heaven belongs to these women,
who despised life in the world,
and have reached the rewards of the kingdom
and washed their robes in the blood of the Lamb (E.T. alleluia).

Collect

O God, by whose gift strength is made perfect in weakness,
grant to all who honor the glory of blessed N.
that she, who drew from you the strength to triumph,
may likewise always obtain from you
the grace of victory for us.
Through our Lord Jesus Christ, your Son,
who lives and reigns with you in the unity of the Holy Spirit,
one God, for ever and ever.

Prayer over the Offerings

As we joyfully offer, O Lord, this day's sacrifice,
recalling the heaven-sent victory of blessed N.,
we proclaim by it your mighty deeds
and rejoice at having gained her glorious intercession.
Through Christ our Lord.

Communion Antiphon   *Rev 12: 11-12*

They did not cling to their lives even in the face of death;
therefore rejoice, you heavens,
and you who dwell in them (E.T. alleluia).

Prayer after Communion

As we draw everlasting joys, O Lord,
from our participation in this Sacrament
and from the commemoration of blessed N.,
we humbly implore
that by your gift we may truly understand
what you grant us to enact in diligent service.
Through Christ our Lord.

COMMON OF PASTORS

I. For a Pope or for a Bishop

1

Entrance Antiphon

> The Lord chose him for himself as high priest,
> and, opening his treasure house,
> made him rich in all good things (E.T. alleluia).

> Or: Cf. Sir 50: 1; 44: 16, 22

> Behold a great priest, who in his days pleased God;
> therefore, in accordance with his promise,
> the Lord gave him growth for the good of his people (E.T. alleluia).

Collect

For a Pope:

> Almighty ever-living God,
> who chose blessed N. to preside over your whole people
> and benefit them by word and example,
> keep safe, we pray, by his intercession,
> the shepherds of your Church
> along with the flocks entrusted to their care,
> and direct them in the way of eternal salvation.
> Through our Lord Jesus Christ, your Son,
> who lives and reigns with you in the unity of the Holy Spirit,
> one God, for ever and ever.

For a Bishop:

> O God, who in blessed N.
> were pleased to provide for your Church
> the example of a good shepherd,
> mercifully grant that through his intercession
> we may merit an eternal place in your pastures.
> Through our Lord Jesus Christ, your Son,
> who lives and reigns with you in the unity of the Holy Spirit,
> one God, for ever and ever.

Prayer over the Offerings

Accept this sacrifice from your people, we pray, O Lord,
and make what is offered for your glory,
in honor of blessed N.,
a means to our eternal salvation.
Through Christ our Lord.

Communion Antiphon
Cf. Jn 10: 11

The Good Shepherd has laid down his life
for his sheep (E.T. alleluia).

Prayer after Communion

May the Sacrament we have received, O Lord our God,
stir up in us that fire of charity
with which blessed N. burned ardently
as he gave himself unceasingly for your Church.
Through Christ our Lord.

2

Entrance Antiphon
Cf. Sir 45: 30

The Lord established for him a covenant of peace,
and made him the prince,
that he might have the dignity of the priesthood for ever (E.T. alleluia).

Collect

For a Pope:

O God, who gave blessed N. to be shepherd of the whole Church
and made him resplendent with wondrous virtue and teaching,
grant that we, who venerate the merits of such a Bishop,
may shine with good deeds before others
and burn with love before you.
Through our Lord Jesus Christ, your Son,
who lives and reigns with you in the unity of the Holy Spirit,
one God, for ever and ever.

COMMON OF PASTORS

For a Pope:

O God, who made blessed N. the Vicar of Peter
and committed to him the care of the universal Church,
by his intercession keep your beloved flock ever safe,
so that with integrity of faith and perfect charity
your Church may journey to her heavenly homeland.
Through our Lord Jesus Christ, your Son,
who lives and reigns with you in the unity of the Holy Spirit,
one God, for ever and ever.

For a Bishop:

Grant, we pray, almighty God,
that we may venerate fittingly the memory of the Bishop blessed N.,
and, as you willed that his word and example
should benefit those over whom he presided,
so may we always experience
the support of his intercession before you.
Through our Lord Jesus Christ, your Son,
who lives and reigns with you in the unity of the Holy Spirit,
one God, for ever and ever.

Prayer over the Offerings

Grant our supplication, we pray, O Lord,
that this sacrifice we present on the feast day of blessed N.
may be for our good,
since through its offering
you have loosed the offenses of all the world.
Through Christ our Lord.

Communion Antiphon   Cf. Jn 21: 17

Lord, you know everything:
you know that I love you (E.T. alleluia).

Prayer after Communion

May the power of the gifts we have received, Lord God,
on this feast day of blessed N.
fill us with its effects,
both to sustain our mortal life
and to gain us the joy of unending happiness.
Through Christ our Lord.

II. For a Bishop

1

Entrance Antiphon   Cf. Ez 34: 11, 23-24

I will look after my sheep, says the Lord,
and I will appoint a shepherd to pasture them,
and I, the Lord, will be their God (E.T. alleluia).

Or: Cf. Lk 12: 42

This is the steward, faithful and prudent,
whom the Lord set over his household
to give them their allowance of food at the proper time (E.T. alleluia).

Collect

Almighty ever-living God,
who chose blessed N.
to preside as Bishop over your holy people,
we pray that, by his merits,
you may bestow on us the grace of your loving kindness.
Through our Lord Jesus Christ, your Son,
who lives and reigns with you in the unity of the Holy Spirit,
one God, for ever and ever.

Or:

Almighty and eternal God,
who gave your holy Church blessed N. as Bishop,
grant that what he taught when moved by the divine Spirit
may always stay firm in our hearts;
and as by your gift we embrace him as our patron,
may we also have him as our defender
to entreat your mercy.
Through our Lord Jesus Christ, your Son,
who lives and reigns with you in the unity of the Holy Spirit,
one God, for ever and ever.

Prayer over the Offerings

Look with favor, O Lord, we pray,
on the offerings we set upon this sacred altar
on the feast day of blessed N.,
that, bestowing on us your pardon,
our oblations may give honor to your name.
Through Christ our Lord.

Communion Antiphon

Cf. Jn 15: 16

It was not you who chose me, says the Lord,
but I who chose you and appointed you to go and bear fruit,
fruit that will last (E.T. alleluia).

Or:

Cf. Lk 12: 36-37

Blessed is that servant, whom his lord finds awake
when he comes and knocks at the gate (E.T. alleluia).

Prayer after Communion

Renewed by the sacred mysteries,
we humbly pray, O Lord,
that, following the example of blessed N.,
we may strive to profess what he believed
and to practice what he taught.
Through Christ our Lord.

2

Entrance Antiphon

Cf. 1 Sm 2: 35

I shall raise up for myself a faithful priest
who will act in accord with my heart and my mind,
says the Lord (E.T. alleluia).

Or:

Cf. Lk 12: 42

This is the steward, faithful and prudent,
whom the Lord set over his household,
to give them their allowance of food at the proper time (E.T. alleluia).

Collect

O God, who wonderfully numbered
among your holy shepherds blessed N.,
a man aflame with divine charity
and outstanding for that faith that overcomes the world,
grant, we pray, that through his intercession
we, too, persevering in faith and charity,
may merit to be sharers of his glory.
Through our Lord Jesus Christ, your Son,
who lives and reigns with you in the unity of the Holy Spirit,
one God, for ever and ever.

Or:

Lord God, who graciously imbued
blessed N. with heavenly doctrine,
grant, through his intercession,
that we may keep that same teaching faithfully
and express it in what we do.
Through our Lord Jesus Christ, your Son,
who lives and reigns with you in the unity of the Holy Spirit,
one God, for ever and ever.

Prayer over the Offerings

Receive, O Lord, these offerings of your people,
on the feast day of blessed N.,
so that through them, according to our confident hope,
we may experience the help of your loving kindness.
Through Christ our Lord.

Communion Antiphon — Jn 10: 10

I have come that they may have life,
and have it more abundantly, says the Lord (E.T. alleluia).

Or: — Mk 16: 17-18

These are the signs that will follow those who believe in me, says the Lord:
they will cast out demons.
They will lay hands on the sick, and they will recover (E.T. alleluia).

COMMON OF PASTORS

Prayer after Communion

Replenished by the sacred Body and the precious Blood of your Son,
we pray, O Lord our God,
that what we celebrate with loving devotion,
may be our sure pledge of redemption.
Through Christ our Lord.

III. For Pastors

A. For Several Pastors

Entrance Antiphon

Jer 3: 15

I will appoint over you shepherds after my own heart,
who will shepherd you wisely and prudently (E.T. alleluia).

Or:

Cf. Dn 3: 84, 87

Priests of God, bless the Lord;
praise the Lord, all who are holy and humble of heart (E.T. alleluia).

Collect

O God, who to pasture your people
filled (the Bishops) blessed N. and N. with a spirit of truth and of love,
grant that, as we celebrate their feast day with honor,
we may benefit by imitating them
and be given relief through their intercession.
Through our Lord Jesus Christ, your Son,
who lives and reigns with you in the unity of the Holy Spirit,
one God, for ever and ever.

Prayer over the Offerings

We offer you a sacrifice of praise
in commemoration of your Saints, O Lord,
by which we trust to be delivered
from evils both present and to come.
Through Christ our Lord.

Communion Antiphon
Mt 20: 28

The Son of Man did not come to be served but to serve,
and to give his life as a ransom for many (E.T. alleluia).

Prayer after Communion
We have received this heavenly Sacrament, O Lord,
as we commemorate your Saints N. and N.;
grant, we pray, that what we celebrate in time
we may attain with eternal joy.
Through Christ our Lord.

B. For One Pastor

1

Entrance Antiphon
Cf. Ps 132 (131): 9

Your priests, O Lord, shall be clothed with justice;
your holy ones shall ring out their joy (E.T. alleluia).

Collect
We humbly ask you, almighty God,
that at the intercession of (the Bishop) blessed N.
you may multiply your gifts among us
and order our days in peace.
Through our Lord Jesus Christ, your Son,
who lives and reigns with you in the unity of the Holy Spirit,
one God, for ever and ever.

Prayer over the Offerings
Receive, O Lord, we pray,
the offerings placed on your altar
in commemoration of blessed N.,
so that, as you brought him glory,
you may, through these sacred mysteries,
grant to us your pardon.
Through Christ our Lord.

COMMON OF PASTORS

Communion Antiphon
Cf. Mt 24: 46-47

Blessed is the servant whom the Lord finds watching
when he comes. Amen, I say to you:
He will put that servant in charge of all his property (E.T. alleluia).

Or:
Lk 12: 42

This is the steward, faithful and prudent,
whom the Lord set over his household,
to give them their allowance of food at the proper time (E.T. alleluia).

Prayer after Communion

May partaking at the heavenly table, almighty God,
confirm and increase strength from on high
in all who celebrate the feast day of blessed N.,
that we may preserve in integrity the gift of faith
and walk in the path of salvation you trace for us.
Through Christ our Lord.

2

Entrance Antiphon
Cf. Lk 4: 18

The Spirit of the Lord is upon me,
for he has anointed me
and sent me to preach the good news to the poor,
to heal the broken-hearted (E.T. alleluia).

Or:
Cf. Sir 45: 20

The Lord chose him as a priest for himself,
to offer him a sacrifice of praise (E.T. alleluia).

Collect

O God, light of the faithful and shepherd of souls,
who set (the Bishop) blessed N. in the Church
to feed your sheep by his words and form them by his example,
grant that through his intercession
we may keep the faith he taught by his words
and follow the way he showed by his example.
Through our Lord Jesus Christ, your Son,
who lives and reigns with you in the unity of the Holy Spirit,
one God, for ever and ever.

Prayer over the Offerings

We humbly implore your majesty, almighty God,
that, just as the offerings made in honor of blessed N.
bear witness to the glory of divine power,
so they may impart to us the effects of your salvation.
Through Christ our Lord.

Communion Antiphon   Mt 28: 20

Behold, I am with you always,
even to the end of the age, says the Lord (E.T. alleluia).

Prayer after Communion

May the mysteries we have received, O Lord,
prepare us, we pray, for the eternal joys
that, as a faithful steward, blessed N. came to deserve.
Through Christ our Lord.

Or:

Make us, who have been nourished
by this sacred meal, almighty God,
always follow the example of blessed N.
in serving you with constant devotion
and assisting all with untiring charity.
Through Christ our Lord.

IV. For Founders of Churches

A. For One Founder

Entrance Antiphon
Cf. Is 59: 21; 56: 7

> Thus says the Lord: My words, which I have put into your mouth,
> will remain for ever on your lips
> and your gifts will be accepted on my altar (E.T. alleluia).

Collect

> Almighty and merciful God,
> who were pleased to enlighten our forebears
> by the preaching of blessed N.,
> grant, we pray,
> that, glorying in the name of Christian,
> we may show continually in our deeds the faith that we profess.
> Through our Lord Jesus Christ, your Son,
> who lives and reigns with you in the unity of the Holy Spirit,
> one God, for ever and ever.

Or:

> Look, O Lord, upon your family,
> which (the Bishop) blessed N.
> engendered by the Word of truth
> and fed with the Sacrament of life,
> that your grace, which has made them faithful through his ministry,
> may through his prayers make them fervent in charity.
> Through our Lord Jesus Christ, your Son,
> who lives and reigns with you in the unity of the Holy Spirit,
> one God, for ever and ever.

Prayer over the Offerings

> Grant our supplication, we pray, almighty God,
> that these sacrificial offerings of your people,
> which we bring you in commemoration of blessed N.,
> you may graciously mingle with the gifts of heaven.
> Through Christ our Lord.

Communion Antiphon
Cf. Mk 10: 45

The Son of Man has come to give his life
as a ransom for many (E.T. alleluia).

Or:
1 Cor 3: 11

No one can lay a foundation
other than the one that is there,
namely, Jesus Christ (E.T. alleluia).

Prayer after Communion

**As we rejoice at the feast day of blessed N.,
we have received the pledge of eternal redemption, O Lord,
and we pray that it may be of help to us,
both now and for the life to come.
Through Christ our Lord.**

B. For Several Founders

Entrance Antiphon

These are the holy men
whom the Lord chose in his own perfect love;
to them he gave eternal glory;
their teaching is a light for the Church (E.T. alleluia).

Collect

**O Lord, who through the apostolic ministry of Saints N. and N.
gave your Church the beginnings of religion,
look on her with kindness
and grant her, we pray, through their intercession,
constant increase in Christian devotion.
Through our Lord Jesus Christ, your Son,
who lives and reigns with you in the unity of the Holy Spirit,
one God, for ever and ever.**

Or:

O God, who called our forebears
by the preaching of (the Bishops) blessed N. and N.
into the wonderful light of the Gospel,
grant that through their intercession
we may grow in grace and in the knowledge
of our Lord Jesus Christ, your Son.
Who lives and reigns with you in the unity of the Holy Spirit,
one God, for ever and ever.

Prayer over the Offerings

Receive, O Lord, we pray, the offerings of your people,
which we bring for the feast day of Saints N. and N.,
and in your kindness render us fully acceptable
by giving us sincerity of heart.
Through Christ our Lord.

Communion Antiphon

Cf. Jn 15: 15

I no longer call you slaves,
because a slave does not know what his master is doing.
But I have called you friends,
because I have told you
everything I have heard from my Father (E.T. alleluia).

Or:

1 Pt 2: 9

O chosen people, proclaim the mighty works of him
who called you out of darkness into his wonderful light (E.T. alleluia).

Prayer after Communion

May the Savior we have welcomed at this altar, O Lord,
gladden us on the feast day of Saints N. and N.,
on which, with longing for your favor,
we honor the precious beginnings of our faith
and proclaim your wonders in your Saints.
Through Christ our Lord.

V. For Missionaries

For Missionary Martyrs, pp. 1066-1068.

1

Entrance Antiphon
O chosen people, proclaim the mighty works of him
who called you out of darkness into his wonderful light (E.T. alleluia).

Or: *Ps 18 (17): 50; 22 (21): 23*

I will praise you, Lord, among the nations;
I will tell of your name to my kin (E.T. alleluia).

Collect
O God, who through (the Bishop) blessed N.
brought peoples without faith
from darkness to the light of truth,
grant us, through his intercession,
that we may stand firm in faith
and remain constant in the hope of the Gospel he preached.
Through our Lord Jesus Christ, your Son,
who lives and reigns with you in the unity of the Holy Spirit,
one God, for ever and ever.

Or:

Almighty ever-living God,
who have made sacred this day's rejoicing at the glorification of
    blessed N.,
graciously grant
that we may strive always to keep
and to put into practice the faith
which, with unquenchable zeal, he strove to proclaim.
Through our Lord Jesus Christ, your Son,
who lives and reigns with you in the unity of the Holy Spirit,
one God, for ever and ever.

Prayer over the Offerings

Look upon the sacrificial gifts we offer, almighty God,
on the feast day of blessed N.,
and grant that we, who celebrate the mysteries of the
   Lord's Passion,
may imitate what we now do.
Through Christ our Lord.

Communion Antiphon

Ez 34: 15

I will pasture my sheep;
I myself will give them rest, says the Lord (E.T. alleluia).

Or:

Mt 10: 27

What I say to you in the darkness
speak in the light, says the Lord;
what you hear whispered proclaim on the housetops (E.T. alleluia).

Prayer after Communion

By the power of this mystery, O Lord,
confirm your servants in the true faith,
that they may everywhere profess in word and deed
the faith for which blessed N. never ceased to labor
and for which he spent his whole life.
Through Christ our Lord.

2

Entrance Antiphon

Cf. Is 52: 7

How beautiful upon the mountains are the feet
of him who brings glad tidings of peace,
bearing good news, announcing salvation (E.T. alleluia).

Collect

O God, who gave increase to your Church
through the zeal for religion
and apostolic labors of blessed N.,
grant, through his intercession,
that she may always receive
new growth in faith and in holiness.
Through our Lord Jesus Christ, your Son,
who lives and reigns with you in the unity of the Holy Spirit,
one God, for ever and ever.

Prayer over the Offerings

Look with favor on our supplications, O Lord,
and free us from every fault,
so that through the purifying action of your grace
we may be cleansed by the very mysteries
through which we render you service.
Through Christ our Lord.

Communion Antiphon   Mk 16: 15; Mt 28: 20

Go into all the world, and proclaim the Gospel.
I am with you always, says the Lord (E.T. alleluia).

Or: Jn 15: 4-5

Remain in me, as I remain in you, says the Lord.
Whoever remains in me
and I in him bears fruit in plenty (E.T. alleluia).

Prayer after Communion

May the Sacrament we have received, O Lord our God,
nourish in us that faith
taught by the preaching of the Apostles
and kept safe by the labors of blessed N.
Through Christ our Lord.

3

Entrance Antiphon   Ps 96 (95): 3-4

Tell among the nations his glory,
and his wonders among all the peoples,
for the Lord is great and highly to be praised (E.T. alleluia).

Collect

O God, by whose untold mercy
blessed **N.** preached the good news
of the unfathomable riches of Christ,
grant that through his intercession
we may grow in knowledge of you
and, bearing fruit in every good work,
faithfully walk in your presence,
in accord with the truth of the Gospel.
Through our Lord Jesus Christ, your Son,
who lives and reigns with you in the unity of the Holy Spirit,
one God, for ever and ever.

Prayer over the Offerings

As we celebrate the memory of blessed **N.**,
we pray, O Lord, that you may pour out your blessing from heaven
on these offerings we have made to you,
so that in partaking of them
we may be without fault
and be replenished with heavenly food.
Through Christ our Lord.

Communion Antiphon
Cf. Lk 10: 1, 9

The Lord sent out disciples
to proclaim throughout the towns:
The kingdom of God is at hand for you (E.T. alleluia).

Or:
Cf. Mt 13: 8, 23

This is the seed that fell on rich soil:
those who with a good and perfect heart
patiently bring forth fruit (E.T. alleluia).

Prayer after Communion

May your holy gifts which we have received
fill us with life, O Lord,
so that we, who rejoice in commemorating blessed **N.**,
may also profit from his example of apostolic virtue.
Through Christ our Lord.

COMMON OF DOCTORS OF THE CHURCH

1

Entrance Antiphon *Cf. Sir 15: 5*

In the midst of the Church he opened his mouth,
and the Lord filled him with the spirit of wisdom and understanding
and clothed him in a robe of glory (E.T. alleluia).

Or: *Ps 37 (36): 30-31*

The mouth of the just man utters wisdom,
and his tongue tells forth what is just;
the law of his God is in his heart (E.T. alleluia).

Collect

Almighty and eternal God,
who gave your holy Church blessed N. as Doctor (and Bishop),
grant that what he taught when moved by the divine Spirit
may always stay firm in our hearts;
and, as by your gift we embrace him as our patron,
may we also have him as our defender to entreat your mercy.
Through our Lord Jesus Christ, your Son,
who lives and reigns with you in the unity of the Holy Spirit,
one God, for ever and ever.

Prayer over the Offerings

May the sacrifice which we gladly present on the feast day of blessed N.,
be pleasing to you, O God,
for, taught by him, we, too, give ourselves entirely to you in praise.
Through Christ our Lord.

COMMON OF DOCTORS OF THE CHURCH

Communion Antiphon
Cf. Lk 12: 42

Behold a faithful and prudent steward
to give them their allowance of food at the proper time (E.T. alleluia).

Or:
Cf. Ps 1: 2-3

He who ponders the law of the Lord day and night
will yield his fruit in due season (E.T. alleluia).

Prayer after Communion

**Through Christ the teacher, O Lord,
instruct those you feed with Christ, the living Bread,
that on the feast day of blessed N. they may learn your truth
and express it in works of charity.
Through Christ our Lord.**

2

Entrance Antiphon
Cf. Dn 12: 3

Those who are wise will shine brightly
like the splendor of the firmament
and those who lead the many to justice
shall be like the stars for ever (E.T. alleluia).

Or:
Cf. Sir 44: 15, 14

Let the peoples recount the wisdom of the Saints,
and let the Church proclaim their praise.
Their names will live on and on (E.T. alleluia).

Collect

**Lord God, who graciously imbued blessed N. with
   heavenly doctrine,
grant, through his intercession,
that we may keep that same teaching faithfully
and express it in what we do.
Through our Lord Jesus Christ, your Son,
who lives and reigns with you in the unity of the Holy Spirit,
one God, for ever and ever.**

Prayer over the Offerings

As we celebrate the divine mysteries,
O Lord, we pray,
may the Holy Spirit fill us with that light of faith
by which he constantly enlightened blessed N.
for the spreading of your glory.
Through Christ our Lord.

Communion Antiphon
Cf. 1 Cor 1: 23-24

We proclaim Christ crucified;
Christ, the power of God and the wisdom of God (E.T. alleluia).

Prayer after Communion

Refreshed by heavenly food,
we humbly implore you, O Lord,
that, attentive to the teaching of blessed N.,
we may abide at all times in thanksgiving
for the gifts we have received.
Through Christ our Lord.

COMMON OF VIRGINS

For a Virgin Martyr, pp. 1068-1069.

I. For Several Virgins

Entrance Antiphon
Cf. Ps 148: 12-14

Let the virgins praise the name of the Lord,
for his name alone is exalted;
his splendor is above heaven and earth (E.T. alleluia).

Or:

Cf. Ps 45 (44): 16

The virgins to the King are escorted amid gladness and joy;
they are led within the temple to the Lord and King (E.T. alleluia).

Collect

Bestow your mercy upon us, Lord, we pray,
that, as we rejoice with loving devotion
on the feast day of the Virgins blessed N. and N.,
so by your gift we may know the eternal delight of their company.
Through our Lord Jesus Christ, your Son,
who lives and reigns with you in the unity of the Holy Spirit,
one God, for ever and ever.

Prayer over the Offerings

As we proclaim your wonders, O Lord,
in the commemoration of the holy Virgins N. and N.,
we bring you these offerings and prayers;
grant, we ask,
that, as their merits are pleasing to you,
so, too, our dutiful service may find favor in your sight.
Through Christ our Lord.

Communion Antiphon
Cf. Mt 25: 10

The bridegroom has come, and the virgins who were ready
have gone with him into the wedding feast (E.T. alleluia).

Or:

Jn 14: 21, 23

Whoever loves me will be loved by my Father,
and I will come to him and reveal myself to him (E.T. alleluia).

Prayer after Communion

May the mysteries we have received, O Lord,
on this feast day of the Virgins blessed N. and N.
constantly bestir and enlighten us, we pray,
so that we may stand ready for the coming of your Son
and be admitted to his wedding feast on high.
Through Christ our Lord.

II. For One Virgin

1

Entrance Antiphon

Here is a wise virgin, from among the number of the prudent,
who went forth with lighted lamp to meet Christ (E.T. alleluia).

Or:

How beautiful you are, O virgin of Christ,
who were worthy to receive the Lord's crown,
the crown of perpetual virginity (E.T. alleluia).

Collect

Hear us, God our Savior,
that, as we rejoice in commemorating the Virgin blessed N.,
we may be instructed by her loving devotion.
Through our Lord Jesus Christ, your Son,
who lives and reigns with you in the unity of the Holy Spirit,
one God, for ever and ever.

Prayer over the Offerings

As we proclaim your wonders, O Lord,
in the Virgin blessed N.,
we humbly implore your majesty
that, as her merits are pleasing to you,
so, too, our dutiful service may find favor in your sight.
Through Christ our Lord.

COMMON OF VIRGINS

Communion Antiphon
Cf. Mt 25: 6

    Behold, the Bridegroom is coming;
    come out to meet Christ the Lord (E.T. alleluia).

    Or:
Cf. Ps 27 (26): 4

    There is one thing I ask of the Lord, only this do I seek:
    to live in the house of the Lord all the days of my life (E.T. alleluia).

Prayer after Communion

**Renewed by partaking of this divine gift,
we pray, O Lord our God,
that by the example of the blessed N.,
bearing in our body the Death of Jesus,
we may strive to hold fast to you alone.
Through Christ our Lord.**

2

Entrance Antiphon

    Let us rejoice and exult for joy:
    for the Lord of all has shown his love
    for a holy and glorious virgin (E.T. alleluia).

    Or:

    Here is a wise virgin whom the Lord found watching;
    when they took up their lamps
    she brought oil with her
    and when the Lord came
    she went in with him to the wedding feast (E.T. alleluia).

Collect

**Lord God, who gave the holy Virgin N. gift upon gift from heaven,
grant, we pray,
that, imitating her virtues on earth,
we may delight with her in the joys of eternity.
Through our Lord Jesus Christ, your Son,
who lives and reigns with you in the unity of the Holy Spirit,
one God, for ever and ever.**

Or, for a Virgin foundress:

Grant, O Lord our God,
that the Virgin blessed N., your faithful spouse,
may stir up in our hearts the flame of divine love,
which she inspired in other virgins
to the enduring glory of your Church.
Through our Lord Jesus Christ, your Son,
who lives and reigns with you in the unity of the Holy Spirit,
one God, for ever and ever.

Prayer over the Offerings

May we receive, O Lord, we pray,
the effects of this offering dedicated to you,
so that we may be cleansed from old earthly ways
and, through the example of blessed N.,
be renewed by growth in heavenly life.
Through Christ our Lord.

Communion Antiphon

Cf. Mt 25: 4, 6

The five wise virgins brought flasks of oil with their lamps.
Then at midnight, the cry went up:
Behold, the Bridegroom is coming;
come out to meet Christ the Lord (E.T. alleluia).

Prayer after Communion

May the holy reception of the Body and Blood
of your Only Begotten Son, O Lord,
turn us away from the cares of this fleeting world,
so that, following the example of blessed N.,
we may grow in sincere love for you on earth
and rejoice to behold you for eternity in heaven.
Through Christ our Lord.

COMMON OF VIRGINS

3

Entrance Antiphon

Come, bride of Christ, receive the crown,
which the Lord has prepared for you for eternity (E.T. alleluia).

Or:

For love of the Lord Jesus Christ,
she despised the kingdom of the world
and all worldly things (E.T. alleluia).

Collect

O God, who declare that you abide in hearts that are pure,
grant that through the intercession of the Virgin blessed N.
we may be so fashioned by your grace,
that we become a dwelling pleasing to you.
Through our Lord Jesus Christ, your Son,
who lives and reigns with you in the unity of the Holy Spirit,
one God, for ever and ever.

Or:

Hear our prayers, we ask, O Lord,
that we, who devoutly honor the virtue of the Virgin blessed N.,
may be worthy to abide in love of you
and to grow in it always until the end.
Through our Lord Jesus Christ, your Son,
who lives and reigns with you in the unity of the Holy Spirit,
one God, for ever and ever.

Prayer over the Offerings

Receive, O Lord, the homage of our humble service,
which we present to you
in commemoration of the Virgin blessed N.,
and grant through the one unblemished sacrifice
that we may constantly burn
with devoted and holy love in your sight.
Through Christ our Lord.

Communion Antiphon Cf. Lk 10: 42

The wise virgin has chosen the better part,
and it will not be taken from her (E.T. alleluia).

Or: Mt 25: 6

At midnight, the cry went up:
Behold, the Bridegroom is coming; come out to meet him (E.T. alleluia)!

Prayer after Communion

**Renewed by heavenly Bread,
we humbly beseech your mercy, O Lord,
that we, who rejoice in commemorating blessed N.,
may obtain pardon for our offenses,
health for our bodies,
and grace and eternal glory for our souls.
Through Christ our Lord.**

COMMON OF HOLY MEN AND WOMEN

The following Masses, if indicated for a particular category of Saints, are used for Saints of that category. Other Masses, however, may be used for all categories of Saints.

I. For All Categories of Saints

A. For Several Saints

1

Entrance Antiphon   Cf. Ps 145 (144): 10-11

May all your works thank you, O Lord,
and all your Holy ones bless you.
They shall speak of the glory of your reign,
and declare your mighty deeds (E.T. alleluia).

Collect

Almighty and eternal God,
who by glorifying the Saints,
bestow on us fresh proofs of your love,
graciously grant
that, commended by their intercession
   and spurred on by their example,
we may be faithful in imitating your Only Begotten Son.
Who lives and reigns with you in the unity of the Holy Spirit,
one God, for ever and ever.

Prayer over the Offerings

Give favorable hearing to our prayers, O Lord, we pray,
and safeguard us through the intercession of your Saints,
that we may give worthy service at your altar.
Through Christ our Lord.

Communion Antiphon   Cf. Ps 68 (67): 4

The just shall rejoice at the presence of God;
they shall exult with glad rejoicing (E.T. alleluia).

Or: Lk 12: 37

Blessed are those servants
whom the lord finds vigilant on his arrival.
Amen, I say to you:
He will gird himself, seat them at table,
and proceed to wait on them (E.T. alleluia).

Prayer after Communion

Almighty ever-living God,
Father of all consolation and peace,
grant your family,
gathered to praise your name in celebration of the Saints,
that through the mysteries of your Only Begotten Son,
which they have here received,
they may obtain the pledge of eternal redemption.
Through Christ our Lord.

2

Entrance Antiphon   Cf. Ps 64 (63): 11

The just will rejoice in the Lord and hope in him,
and all upright hearts will be praised (E.T. alleluia).

Collect

O God, who see that in our weakness we fail,
mercifully restore us to your love by the example of your Saints.
Through our Lord Jesus Christ, your Son,
who lives and reigns with you in the unity of the Holy Spirit,
one God, for ever and ever.

Prayer over the Offerings

Grant us, we pray, almighty God,
that the humble offering we make
may be pleasing to you in honor of your Saints
and may purify us both in body and in mind.
Through Christ our Lord.

Communion Antiphon
Cf. Jn 12: 26

> Whoever serves me must follow me,
> and where I am, there also will my servant be (E.T. alleluia).

Prayer after Communion

On the heavenly birthday of your Saints, we pray, O Lord,
that we, who are nourished by the gift of this Sacrament,
may delight for all eternity
in the good things with which even now
by your grace you nurture us.
Through Christ our Lord.

3

Entrance Antiphon
Cf. Ps 92 (91): 13-14

> The just will flourish like the palm tree,
> and grow like a Lebanon cedar,
> planted in the house of the Lord,
> in the courts of the house of our God (E.T. alleluia).

Collect

May the prayer and integrity of the Saints,
O Lord, we pray,
obtain help for your faithful,
that they may gain a share in the eternal inheritance
of those whom they celebrate with devotion.
Through our Lord Jesus Christ, your Son,
who lives and reigns with you in the unity of the Holy Spirit,
one God, for ever and ever.

Prayer over the Offerings

Give to those who make
sacrificial offerings at your altar, O Lord,
that spirit of devotion
which you instilled in your Saints,
so that we may approach these sacred rites
with a pure mind and a fervent heart
and celebrate a sacrifice that is pleasing to you
and ensures your favor for us.
Through Christ our Lord.

Communion Antiphon   Mt 11: 28

Come to me, all who labor and are burdened,
and I will refresh you, says the Lord (E.T. alleluia).

Prayer after Communion

May the communion in your Sacrament that we have consumed,
save us, O Lord,
and confirm us in the light of your truth.
Through Christ our Lord.

4

Entrance Antiphon   Jer 17: 7-8

Blessed is the man who trusts in the Lord,
whose hope is the Lord.
He is like a tree planted beside the waters
that stretches out its roots to the stream:
it fears not the heat when it comes (E.T. alleluia).

Collect

Grant, we pray, almighty God,
that the example of your Saints may spur us on to a better life,
so that we, who celebrate the memory of blessed N. and N.,
may also imitate without ceasing their deeds.
Through our Lord Jesus Christ, your Son,
who lives and reigns with you in the unity of the Holy Spirit,
one God, for ever and ever.

Prayer over the Offerings

As we make our offerings at this sacred altar, O Lord,
on the feast day of your Saints,
we ask your mercy,
that this oblation may render you supreme glory
and win for us an abundance of your grace.
Through Christ our Lord.

Communion Antiphon

Jn 15: 9

As the Father loves me, so I also love you;
remain in my love, says the Lord (E.T. alleluia).

Prayer after Communion

We pray, O Lord our God,
that the divine mysteries,
which we celebrate in commemoration of your Saints,
may bring about in us salvation and eternal peace.
Through Christ our Lord.

B. For One Saint

1

Entrance Antiphon

Cf. Ps 21 (20): 2-3

In your strength, O Lord, the just one rejoices;
how greatly your salvation makes him glad!
You have granted him his soul's desire (E.T. alleluia).

Collect

O God, who in your Saints have given an example
and brought us protection in our weakness
to help us tread the path of salvation,
mercifully grant
that we, who honor the heavenly birthday of blessed N.,
may, through his (her) example, make our way to you.
Through our Lord Jesus Christ, your Son,
who lives and reigns with you in the unity of the Holy Spirit,
one God, for ever and ever.

Prayer over the Offerings

Through the present oblation, O Lord,
which we offer in commemoration of blessed N.,
bestow on your faithful, we pray,
the gifts of unity and peace.
Through Christ our Lord.

Communion Antiphon   Cf. Mt 16: 24

Whoever wishes to come after me,
must deny himself, take up his cross,
and follow me, says the Lord (E.T. alleluia).

Or, for those who served in public office: Mt 6: 33

Seek first the kingdom of God, and his righteousness,
and all these things will be given you besides, says the Lord (E.T. alleluia).

Prayer after Communion

May the Sacrament we have received, O Lord,
in commemoration of blessed N.,
sanctify our minds and hearts,
that we may merit to be made sharers in the divine nature.
Through Christ our Lord.

2

Entrance Antiphon   Mal 2: 6

The law of truth was in his mouth;
no dishonesty was found on his lips.
He walked with me in integrity and peace,
and turned many away from evil (E.T. alleluia).

Collect

O God, who alone are holy
and without whom no one is good,
command, we pray, through the intercession of blessed N.,
that we be numbered among those
who do not deserve to be deprived of your glory.
Through our Lord Jesus Christ, your Son,
who lives and reigns with you in the unity of the Holy Spirit,
one God, for ever and ever.

Prayer over the Offerings
May the sacrifices we offer to your majesty, O Lord,
on this feast day of blessed N.
be effective for our salvation
and pleasing to you in your loving kindness.
Through Christ our Lord.

Communion Antiphon   Mt 5: 8-9
Blessed are the clean of heart, for they shall see God.
Blessed are the peacemakers,
for they shall be called children of God (E.T. alleluia).

Prayer after Communion
Nourished by these sacred gifts,
we humbly implore you, Lord,
that the homage of dutiful service,
which we render on the feast day of blessed N.,
may bring us an increase of your saving grace.
Through Christ our Lord.

II. For Monks and Religious

A. For an Abbot

Entrance Antiphon   Cf. Ps 92 (91): 13-14
The just will flourish like the palm tree,
and grow like a Lebanon cedar,
planted in the house of the Lord,
in the courts of the house of our God (E.T. alleluia).

Or: Ps 37 (36): 30-31

The mouth of the just man utters wisdom,
and his tongue tells forth what is right.
The law of his God is in his heart (E.T. alleluia).

Collect

Grant us, O Lord,
that amid the uncertainties of this world
we may cling with all our heart to the things of heaven,
for through the Abbot blessed N.
you have given us a model of evangelical perfection.
Through our Lord Jesus Christ, your Son,
who lives and reigns with you in the unity of the Holy Spirit,
one God, for ever and ever.

Prayer over the Offerings

Grant those who approach your altar, O Lord,
that spirit of devotion
with which the blessed Abbot N. was on fire,
so that, pure of heart and fervent in charity,
we may offer you a worthy sacrifice.
Through Christ our Lord.

Communion Antiphon

Cf. Lk 12: 42

This is the steward, faithful and prudent,
whom the Lord set over his household,
to give them their allowance of food at the proper time (E.T. alleluia).

Or:

Mt 23: 11

The greatest among you must be your servant,
says the Lord (E.T. alleluia).

Prayer after Communion

By the power of this Sacrament which we have received,
renew our hearts, O Lord,
so that by the example of the Abbot blessed N.,
being wise in the things above
and not in the things of earth here below,
we may merit to appear in glory with Christ.
Who lives and reigns for ever and ever.

B. For a Monk

Entrance Antiphon

Where brothers unite to glorify God,
there the Lord will give blessing (E.T. alleluia).

Or: Cf. Ps 71 (70): 8, 23

Let my mouth be filled with your praise, that I may sing aloud;
my lips shall shout for joy, when I sing to you (E.T. alleluia).

Collect

**O God, who in your kindness
called your servant blessed N. to the following of Christ,
grant, we pray, through his intercession,
that, denying ourselves,
we may hold fast to you with all our heart.
Through our Lord Jesus Christ, your Son,
who lives and reigns with you in the unity of the Holy Spirit,
one God, for ever and ever.**

Prayer over the Offerings

Receive, O Lord, we pray,
the offerings made for the salvation of your people,
so that through the intercession of blessed N.
we may flee the enticements of sin
and draw near to the company of heaven.
Through Christ our Lord.

Communion Antiphon

Cf. Lk 8: 15

Those who keep God's word with a good and perfect heart
patiently bring forth fruit (E.T. alleluia).

Or: Cf. Ps 84 (83): 5

Blessed are they who dwell in your house,
for ever singing your praise (E.T. alleluia).

Prayer after Communion

Grant our request, we pray, O Lord our God,
that, defended by the protection of blessed N.,
we may live by this Sacrament of your wisdom
in serenity and moderation.
Through Christ our Lord.

C. For a Nun

Entrance Antiphon   Cf. Ps 52 (51): 10

I am like a growing olive tree in the house of God.
I trust in the mercy of God, for ever and ever (E.T. alleluia).

Or:

I despised the kingdom of the world and all worldly finery
for love of my Lord, Jesus Christ,
whom I have seen, whom I have loved,
in whom I have believed, in whom has been my delight (E.T. alleluia).

Collect

O God, who called your handmaid blessed N.
to seek you before all else,
grant that, serving you, through her example and intercession,
with a pure and humble heart,
we may come at last to your eternal glory.
Through our Lord Jesus Christ, your Son,
who lives and reigns with you in the unity of the Holy Spirit,
one God, for ever and ever.

Prayer over the Offerings

We bring the offerings of our devotion
to be consecrated by you, O Lord,
in commemoration of blessed N.,
for by the consolation you give us in this life
you show that we should not lose hope
of what is promised for eternity.
Through Christ our Lord.

Communion Antiphon
Ps 45 (44): 2

My heart overflows with noble words.
To the king I address the song I have made (E.T. alleluia).

Or:
Lk 10: 42

One thing is necessary:
she has chosen the better part,
which shall not be taken away from her (E.T. alleluia).

Prayer after Communion

Renewed, O Lord, at the wellsprings of salvation,
we humbly entreat you
that through the intercession of blessed N.,
holding more closely day by day to Christ,
we may merit to be coheirs in his Kingdom of grace.
Who lives and reigns for ever and ever.

D. For Religious

1

Entrance Antiphon
Cf. Ps 16 (15): 5

O Lord, it is you who are my portion and cup;
you yourself who secure my portion (E.T. alleluia).

Or, for a Woman Religious:
Cf. Hos 2: 21-22

The Lord has taken her as his bride for ever
in faithfulness and mercy (E.T. alleluia).

Collect

O God, by whose gift blessed N.
persevered in imitating Christ, poor and lowly,
grant us through his (her) intercession
that, faithfully walking in our own vocation,
we may reach the perfection
you have set before us in your Son.
Who lives and reigns with you in the unity of the Holy Spirit,
one God, for ever and ever.

Prayer over the Offerings

Most merciful God,
who were pleased to create in blessed N.
the New Man in your image, the old having passed away,
graciously grant, we pray,
that, renewed like him (her),
we may offer you the acceptable sacrifice of conciliation.
Through Christ our Lord.

Communion Antiphon
Cf. Mt 19: 27-29

Amen, I say to you: That you who have left all and followed me
will receive a hundredfold and possess eternal life (E.T. alleluia).

Or, for a woman Religious:
Cf. Lam 3: 24-25

The Lord is my portion:
he is good to the soul that seeks him (E.T. alleluia).

Prayer after Communion

By the power of this Sacrament, Lord, we pray,
lead us always in your love,
through the example of blessed N.,
and bring to fulfillment the good work you have begun in us
until the day of Christ Jesus.
Who lives and reigns for ever and ever.

2

Entrance Antiphon
Cf. Ps 24 (23): 5-6

These are the holy ones, who have received blessings from the Lord,
and mercy from the God who saves them,
such is the people who seek the Lord (E.T. alleluia).

Or:
Cf. Ps 105 (104): 3-4

Let the hearts that seek the Lord rejoice;
turn to the Lord and his strength;
constantly seek his face (E.T. alleluia).

COMMON OF HOLY MEN AND WOMEN

Collect

O God, who called blessed N.
to seek your Kingdom in this world
through the pursuit of perfect charity,
grant, we pray, through his (her) intercession
that we may advance with joyful spirit along the way of love.
Through our Lord Jesus Christ, your Son,
who lives and reigns with you in the unity of the Holy Spirit,
one God, for ever and ever.

Prayer over the Offerings

May these offerings of our service,
placed on your altar in commemoration of blessed N.,
be acceptable to you, O Lord, we pray,
and grant that, released from earthly attachments,
we may have our riches in you alone.
Through Christ our Lord.

Communion Antiphon

Ps 34 (33): 9

Taste and see that the Lord is good;
blessed the man who seeks refuge in him (E.T. alleluia).

Or:

Mt 5: 3

Blessed are the poor in spirit,
for theirs is the Kingdom of Heaven (E.T. alleluia).

Prayer after Communion

We pray, almighty God,
that we, who are fortified by the power of this Sacrament,
may learn through the example of blessed N.
to seek you always above all things
and to bear in this world the likeness of the New Man.
Through Christ our Lord.

III. For Those Who Practiced Works of Mercy

Entrance Antiphon   *Cf. Mt 25: 34, 36, 40*

Come, you blessed of my Father, says the Lord:
I was sick, and you visited me.
Amen, I say to you: Whatever you did
for one of the least of my brethren you did it for me (E.T. alleluia).

Or: *Ps 112 (111): 9*

Open-handed, he gives to the poor;
his justice stands firm for ever.
His might shall be exalted in glory (E.T. alleluia).

Collect

O God, who have taught your Church
to keep all the heavenly commandments
by love of you as God and love of neighbor;
grant that, practicing the works of charity
after the example of blessed N.,
we may be worthy to be numbered among the blessed in your Kingdom.
Through our Lord Jesus Christ, your Son,
who lives and reigns with you in the unity of the Holy Spirit,
one God, for ever and ever.

Prayer over the Offerings

Receive, O Lord, the offerings of your people,
and grant that we, who celebrate
your Son's work of boundless charity,
may, by the example of blessed N.,
be confirmed in love of you and of our neighbor.
Through Christ our Lord.

Communion Antiphon

Cf. Jn 15: 13

Greater love has no one
than to lay down his life for his friends (E.T. alleluia).

Or:

Cf. Jn 13: 35

This is how all will know that you are my disciples:
if you have love for one another, says the Lord (E.T. alleluia).

Prayer after Communion

Grant, we pray, O Lord,
that we, who are renewed by these sacred mysteries,
may follow the example of blessed **N.**,
who honored you with tireless devotion
and, by surpassing charity, was of service to your people.
Through Christ our Lord.

Or:

Having fed upon the delights of the Sacrament of salvation, O Lord,
we humbly implore your faithful love,
that, imitating, by your grace, the charity of blessed **N.**,
we may also be made partakers with him **(her)** in glory.
Through Christ our Lord.

IV. For Educators

Entrance Antiphon

Cf. Mk 10: 14

Let the children come to me; do not prevent them,
for the kingdom of God belongs to such as these (E.T. alleluia).

Or:

Cf. Mt 5: 19

Whoever obeys and teaches the commandments of the Lord
will be called great in the Kingdom of Heaven,
says the Lord (E.T. alleluia).

Collect

O God, who raised up blessed N. in your Church
to show others the way of salvation,
grant us, by his (her) example,
so to follow Christ the master,
that we may come with our neighbor into your presence.
Through our Lord Jesus Christ, your Son,
who lives and reigns with you in the unity of the Holy Spirit,
one God, for ever and ever.

Prayer over the Offerings

May the oblation made by your consecrated people
in commemoration of blessed N.
be acceptable to you, we pray, O Lord,
and grant that by participation in this mystery
we may reflect the pattern of your love.
Through Christ our Lord.

Communion Antiphon Mt 18: 3

Unless you turn and become like children,
you will not enter the Kingdom of Heaven, says the Lord (E.T. alleluia).

Or: Jn 8: 12

Whoever follows me will not walk in darkness,
but will have the light of life, says the Lord (E.T. alleluia).

Prayer after Communion

May this holy meal give us strength, almighty God,
so that, by the example of blessed N.,
we may show in our hearts and by our deeds
both fraternal charity and the light of truth.
Through Christ our Lord.

V. For Holy Women

For a Holy Woman Martyr, pp. 1069-1070.

1

Entrance Antiphon
Cf. Prv 31: 30, 28

The woman who fears the Lord will herself be praised.
Her children have called her most blessed,
her husband has sung her praises (E.T. alleluia).

Or:

Cf. Prv 31: 20, 27

She reaches out her hands to the needy
and extends her arms to the poor.
She did not eat her food in idleness (E.T. alleluia).

Collect

O God, who gladden us each year with the feast day of blessed N.,
grant, we pray, that we, who are called to honor her,
may also follow her example of holy living.
Through our Lord Jesus Christ, your Son,
who lives and reigns with you in the unity of the Holy Spirit,
one God, for ever and ever.

Or, for several:

Grant, we pray, almighty God,
that the revered intercession of blessed N. and N.
may bring us heavenly aid,
just as their wonderful lives
point the way to salvation for us all.
Through our Lord Jesus Christ, your Son,
who lives and reigns with you in the unity of the Holy Spirit,
one God, for ever and ever.

Prayer over the Offerings

We bring you these sacrificial gifts, O Lord,
to commemorate blessed N.,
humbly entreating
that they may bestow on us both pardon and salvation.
Through Christ our Lord.

Communion Antiphon
Cf. Mt 13: 45-46

The Kingdom of Heaven is like a merchant
who travels in search of fine pearls
and who, on finding one of great price,
sold everything and bought it (E.T. alleluia).

Prayer after Communion

May the working of this divine Sacrament
enlighten and inflame us, almighty God,
on this feast day of blessed N.,
that we may be ever fervent with holy desires
and abound in good works.
Through Christ our Lord.

2

Entrance Antiphon
Cf. Prv 14: 1-2

Behold a wise woman who has built her house.
She feared the Lord and walked in the right path (E.T. alleluia).

Collect

O God, the exaltation of the lowly,
who willed that blessed N. should excel
in the beauty of her charity and patience,
grant, through her merits and intercession,
that, carrying our cross each day,
we may always persevere in love for you.
Through our Lord Jesus Christ, your Son,
who lives and reigns with you in the unity of the Holy Spirit,
one God, for ever and ever.

COMMON OF HOLY MEN AND WOMEN

Or:

Pour out upon us, Lord,
the spirit of knowledge and love of you,
with which you filled your handmaid blessed N.,
so that, serving you sincerely in imitation of her,
we may be pleasing to you
by our faith and our works.
Through our Lord Jesus Christ, your Son,
who lives and reigns with you in the unity of the Holy Spirit,
one God, for ever and ever.

Prayer over the Offerings

Look with favor, O Lord,
on the sacrificial offering of your people,
and what they devoutly celebrate in honor of blessed N.
may they experience in its power to save.
Through Christ our Lord.

Communion Antiphon

Mt 12: 50

Whoever does the will of my heavenly Father
is my brother, and sister, and mother, says the Lord (E.T. alleluia).

Prayer after Communion

We are replenished, O Lord, with the gifts
we have received on the feast day of blessed N.;
grant, we pray,
that we may be purified by their effects
and strengthened by the help they bring.
Through Christ our Lord.

RITUAL MASSES

Ritual Masses are prohibited on the Sundays of Advent, Lent, and Easter, on Solemnities, on days within the Octave of Easter, on the Commemoration of All the Faithful Departed (All Souls' Day), on Ash Wednesday and on the weekdays of Holy Week. The norms given in the ritual books and in connection with the Masses themselves are to be observed.

I. FOR THE CONFERRAL OF THE SACRAMENTS OF CHRISTIAN INITIATION

All the prayers given for a man may be adapted for a woman, with the necessary change of gender, or adapted for several individuals, with the necessary change to the plural.

1. FOR THE ELECTION OR ENROLLMENT OF NAMES

The rite of "election" or "enrollment of names" for catechumens who are to be admitted to the Sacraments of Christian Initiation at the Easter Vigil should be celebrated during the Mass of the First Sunday of Lent (pp. 216-219). If, for pastoral reasons, it is celebrated apart from this Sunday, the Mass that follows may be used with the color violet on any day except those listed in nos. 1-4 of the Table of Liturgical Days. The Mass of the Friday of the Fourth Week of Lent may also be used (p. 254).

Entrance Antiphon Cf. Ps 105 (104): 3-4

Let the hearts that seek the Lord rejoice;
turn to the Lord and his strength;
constantly seek his face.

Collect

O God, who though you are ever the cause
of the salvation of the human race
now gladden your people with grace in still greater measure,
look mercifully, we pray, upon your chosen ones,
that your compassionate and protecting help
may defend both those yet to be born anew
and those already reborn.
Through our Lord Jesus Christ, your Son,
who lives and reigns with you in the unity of the Holy Spirit,
one God, for ever and ever.

Prayer over the Offerings
>Almighty ever-living God,
>who restore us by the Sacrament of Baptism
>to eternal life as we confess your name,
>receive, we beseech you,
>the offerings and prayers of your servants
>and command that those who hope in you
>may have their desires fulfilled
>and their sins canceled out.
>Through Christ our Lord.

The Preface of the current liturgical time is said.

Communion Antiphon   *Eph 1: 7*
>In Christ, we have redemption by his Blood
>and forgiveness of our sins, in accord with the riches of his grace.

Prayer after Communion
>May this Sacrament we have received
>purify us, we pray, O Lord,
>and grant your servants freedom from all blame,
>that those bound by a guilty conscience
>may glory in the fullness of heavenly remedy.
>Through Christ our Lord.

2. FOR THE CELEBRATION OF THE SCRUTINIES

These Masses may be used with the color violet when the Scrutinies for the catechumens who are to be admitted to the Sacraments of Christian Initiation at the Easter Vigil are celebrated at the time proper for them, namely, on the Third, Fourth, and Fifth Sundays of Lent. If, however, for pastoral reasons, the Scrutinies cannot take place on these Sundays, other appropriate weekdays may be chosen in Lent, or, whenever Baptism is to be conferred outside the Easter Vigil, also at other times of the year. Nevertheless, in the first Mass of the Scrutinies, the Gospel of the Samaritan Woman is always read, in the second, that of the Man born blind, in the third, that of Lazarus, as given respectively for the Third, Fourth, and Fifth Sundays of Lent.

A
For the First Scrutiny

Entrance Antiphon   Ez 36: 23-26

When I prove my holiness among you,
I will gather you from all the foreign lands
and I will pour clean water upon you
and cleanse you from all your impurities,
and I will give you a new spirit, says the Lord.

Or: Cf. Is 55: 1

Come to the waters, you who are thirsty, says the Lord;
you who have no money, come and drink joyfully.

Collect

Grant, we pray, O Lord,
that these chosen ones may come worthily and wisely
to the confession of your praise,
so that in accordance with that first dignity
which they lost by original sin
they may be fashioned anew through your glory.
Through our Lord Jesus Christ, your Son,
who lives and reigns with you in the unity of the Holy Spirit,
one God, for ever and ever.

Prayer over the Offerings

May your merciful grace prepare your servants, O Lord,
for the worthy celebration of these mysteries
and lead them to it by a devout way of life.
Through Christ our Lord.

The Preface of the Third Sunday of Lent is said (p. 237).

When the Roman Canon is used, in the section Memento Domine (Remember, Lord, your servants) there is a commemoration of the godparents, and the proper form of the Hanc igitur (Therefore, Lord, we pray), is said.

Proper form of Memento Domine (Remember, Lord, your servants):

Remember, Lord, your servants
who are to present your chosen ones
for the holy grace of your Baptism,

Here the names of the godparents are read out.

and all gathered here,
whose faith and devotion are known to you ...

Proper form of the Hanc igitur (Therefore, Lord, we pray):

Therefore, Lord, we pray:
graciously accept this oblation
which we make to you for your servants,
whom you have been pleased
to enroll, choose and call for eternal life
and for the blessed gift of your grace.
(Through Christ our Lord. Amen.)

When Eucharistic Prayer II is used, after the words and all the clergy, the following is added:

Remember also, Lord, your servants
who are to present these chosen ones
at the font of rebirth.

When Eucharistic Prayer III is used, after the words the entire people you have gained for your own, the following is added:

Assist your servants with your grace,
O Lord, we pray,
that they may lead these chosen ones by word and example
to new life in Christ, our Lord.

Communion Antiphon
Cf. Jn 4: 14

For anyone who drinks it, says the Lord,
the water I shall give will become in him a spring
welling up to eternal life.

Prayer after Communion

Give help, O Lord, we pray,
by the grace of your redemption
and be pleased to protect and prepare
those you are to initiate
through the Sacraments of eternal life.
Through Christ our Lord.

B

For the Second Scrutiny

Entrance Antiphon   Cf. Ps 25 (24): 15-16

My eyes are always on the Lord, for he rescues my feet from the snare.
Turn to me and have mercy on me, for I am alone and poor.

Collect

Almighty ever-living God,
give to your Church an increase in spiritual joy,
so that those once born of earth
may be reborn as citizens of heaven.
Through our Lord Jesus Christ, your Son,
who lives and reigns with you in the unity of the Holy Spirit,
one God, for ever and ever.

Prayer over the Offerings

We place before you with joy these offerings,
which bring eternal remedy, O Lord,
praying that we may both faithfully revere them
and present them to you, as is fitting,
for those who seek salvation.
Through Christ our Lord.

The Preface of the Fourth Sunday of Lent is said (p. 247).

The commemoration of the godparents in the Eucharistic Prayers takes place as above (p. 1122) and, if the Roman Canon is used, the proper form of the Hanc igitur (Therefore, Lord, we pray) *is said, as in the First Scrutiny (p. 1122).*

Communion Antiphon   Cf. Jn 9: 11, 38

The Lord anointed my eyes; I went, I washed,
I saw and I believed in God.

Prayer after Communion

Sustain your family always in your kindness,
O Lord, we pray,
correct them, set them in order,
graciously protect them under your rule,
and in your unfailing goodness
direct them along the way of salvation.
Through Christ our Lord.

C

For the Third Scrutiny

Entrance Antiphon
Cf. Ps 18 (17): 5-7

> The waves of death rose about me;
> the pains of the netherworld surrounded me.
> In my anguish I called to the Lord;
> and from his holy temple he heard my voice.

Collect

> **Grant, O Lord, to these chosen ones**
> **that, instructed in the holy mysteries,**
> **they may receive new life at the font of Baptism**
> **and be numbered among the members of your Church.**
> **Through our Lord Jesus Christ, your Son,**
> **who lives and reigns with you in the unity of the Holy Spirit,**
> **one God, for ever and ever.**

Prayer over the Offerings

> **Hear us, almighty God,**
> **and, having instilled in your servants**
> **the first fruits of the Christian faith,**
> **graciously purify them by the working of this sacrifice.**
> **Through Christ our Lord.**

The Preface of the Fifth Sunday of Lent is said (p. 257).

The commemoration of the godparents in the Eucharistic Prayers takes place as above (p. 1122) and, if the Roman Canon is used, the proper form of the Hanc igitur (Therefore, Lord, we pray) is said, as in the First Scrutiny (p. 1122).

Communion Antiphon
Cf. Jn 11: 26

> Everyone who lives and believes in me
> will not die for ever, says the Lord.

Prayer after Communion

> **May your people be at one, O Lord, we pray,**
> **and in wholehearted submission to you**
> **may they obtain this grace:**
> **that, safe from all distress,**
> **they may readily live out their joy at being saved**
> **and remember in loving prayer those to be reborn.**
> **Through Christ our Lord.**

3. FOR THE CONFERRAL OF BAPTISM

The Sacraments of Christian Initiation are usually conferred on adults during the Vigil of the Holy Night of Easter. If, however, they are celebrated apart from the Paschal Solemnity because of necessity, this Mass may be used with the color white or a festive color on days when Ritual Masses are permitted.

This Mass may also be said for the conferral of the Baptism of infants, under the same conditions.

In this Mass, the Penitential Act, the Kyrie and the Creed are omitted. The Gloria in excelsis (Glory to God in the highest), however, is said.

A

Entrance Antiphon Cf. Eph 4: 24

Put on the new man,
created in the image of God
in righteousness and holiness of truth (E.T. alleluia).

Collect

O God, who bring us to participate in the mystery
of the Passion and Resurrection of your Son,
grant, we pray,
that, strengthened by the spirit of adoption as your children,
we may always walk in newness of life.
Through our Lord Jesus Christ, your Son,
who lives and reigns with you in the unity of the Holy Spirit,
one God, for ever and ever.

Prayer over the Offerings

O Lord, who have graciously gathered into your priestly people
those you have conformed to the likeness of your Son
(and perfected with the seal of chrism),
be pleased, we ask you,
to look upon them as acceptable sacrifices
and to receive them favorably
together with the offerings of your Church.
Through Christ our Lord.

During Easter Time, Preface II of Easter (p. 560) may be used, and during other periods of the year, Preface I of the Sundays in Ordinary Time (p. 572).

When the Roman Canon is used, in the section Memento Domine (Remember, Lord, your servants), there is a commemoration of the godparents:

**Remember, Lord, your servants
who have presented your chosen ones
for the holy grace of your Baptism,**

Here the names of the godparents are read out.

**and all gathered here,
whose faith and devotion are known to you . . .**

In the Eucharistic Prayers, a commemoration of the newly baptized is included according to these formulas:

a) In Eucharistic Prayer I, the proper form of the Hanc igitur (Therefore, Lord, we pray) is said:

**Therefore, Lord, we pray:
graciously accept this oblation of our service,
that of your whole family,
which we offer you
also for those to whom you have been pleased to give
the new birth of water and the Holy Spirit,
granting them forgiveness of all their sins
so as to find them in Christ Jesus our Lord;
and command that their names be written
in the book of the living.
(Through Christ our Lord. Amen.)**

b) In the intercessions of Eucharistic Prayer II, after the words and all the clergy, the following is added:

**Remember also, Lord, the newly baptized
who, through Baptism (and Confirmation),
have today been joined to your family,
that they may follow Christ, your Son,
with a generous heart and a willing spirit.
Remember also our brothers and sisters . . .**

c) In the intercessions of Eucharistic Prayer III, after the words whom you have summoned before you, the following is added:

> Strengthen, we pray, in their holy purpose
> your servants who by the cleansing waters of rebirth
> (and the bestowing of the Holy Spirit)
> have today been joined to your people
> and grant that they may always walk in newness of life.
> In your compassion, O merciful Father,
> gather to yourself all your children
> scattered throughout the world.
> To our departed brothers and sisters . . .

d) In the intercessions of Eucharistic Prayer IV, the commemoration of the newly baptized is inserted in this way:

> Therefore, Lord, remember now
> all for whom we offer this sacrifice:
> especially your servant N. our Pope,
> N. our Bishop, and the whole Order of Bishops,
> and all the clergy.
> Be mindful, too, of those who take part in this offering,
> those gathered here before you,
> especially the newly baptized,
> whom today you have brought to new birth
> by water and the Holy Spirit,
> your entire people,
> and all who seek you with a sincere heart.

Communion Antiphon   Cf. 1 Jn 3: 1

> See what love the Father has bestowed on us,
> that we may be called and may truly be the children of God (E.T. alleluia).

Prayer after Communion

> Grant, O Lord, we pray,
> that, nourished with the Sacrament of your Son's Body and Blood,
> we may grow in the communion of his Spirit
> and in love for one another,
> and so, through ardent charity,
> reach the full stature of the Body of Christ.
> Who lives and reigns for ever and ever.

B

Entrance Antiphon
Ti 3: 5, 7

God has saved us through the bath
that gives rebirth and renewal in the Holy Spirit,
that, justified by his grace, we may become heirs
with the hope of eternal life (E.T. alleluia).

Collect

O God, who bring us to rebirth by the word of life,
grant that, accepting it with a sincere heart,
we may be eager to live by the truth
and may bear abundant fruits of fraternal charity.
Through our Lord Jesus Christ, your Son,
who lives and reigns with you in the unity of the Holy Spirit,
one God, for ever and ever.

Prayer over the Offerings

Open the door to your supper, O Lord,
for those who approach the bread that is prepared
and the wine that has been mixed,
so that, celebrating the heavenly banquet with gladness,
we may be numbered as fellow citizens of the Saints
and members of your household.
Through Christ our Lord.

During Easter Time, Preface II of Easter (p. 560) may be used, and during other periods of the year, Preface I of the Sundays in Ordinary Time (p. 572).

In the Eucharistic Prayers there are proper intercessions (pp. 1127-1128).

Communion Antiphon
Cf. 1 Jn 3: 2

Now we are God's children,
and what we shall be has not yet been revealed (E.T. alleluia).

Prayer after Communion

Grant, O Lord,
that by the power of this Sacrament
we, who have proclaimed in celebration
the glorious mystery of your Son's Death and Resurrection,
may also profess it by our manner of life.
Through Christ our Lord.

4. FOR THE CONFERRAL OF CONFIRMATION

This Mass is used, with the color red or white, or a festive color, at the conferral of Confirmation on days when Ritual Masses are permitted. The Gloria in excelsis (Glory to God in the highest) is said. The Creed, however, is omitted.

A

Entrance Antiphon   *Ez 36: 25-26*

Thus says the Lord:
I will pour clean water upon you
and I will give you a new heart;
a new spirit I will put within you (E.T. alleluia).

Collect

Grant, we pray, almighty and merciful God,
that the Holy Spirit, coming near
and dwelling graciously within us,
may make of us a perfect temple of his glory.
Through our Lord Jesus Christ, your Son,
who lives and reigns with you in the unity of the Holy Spirit,
one God, for ever and ever.

Or:

Fulfill for us your gracious promise, O Lord, we pray,
so that by his coming
the Holy Spirit may make us witnesses before the world
to the Gospel of our Lord Jesus Christ.
Who lives and reigns with you in the unity of the Holy Spirit,
one God, for ever and ever.

Other prayers to be used at choice (p. 1134).

Prayer over the Offerings

Receive in your mercy, O Lord,
the prayers of your servants
and grant that, being conformed more perfectly to your Son,
they may grow steadily in bearing witness to him,
as they share in the memorial of his redemption,
by which he gained for us your Holy Spirit.
Through Christ our Lord.

Preface I of the Holy Spirit (p. 1339) or Preface II (p. 1342) may be used.

When the Roman Canon is used, the proper form of the Hanc igitur (Therefore, Lord, we pray) *is said:*

**Therefore, Lord, we pray:
graciously accept this oblation of our service,
that of your whole family,
which we offer you
also for those reborn in Baptism,
whom you have been pleased to confirm
by bestowing the Holy Spirit,
and in your mercy, keep safe in them your grace.
(Through Christ our Lord. Amen.)**

When Eucharistic Prayer II is used, after the words and all the clergy, *the following is added:*

**Remember also, Lord, your servants
whom you have been pleased to confirm today
by bestowing the Holy Spirit,
and keep them in your grace.**

When Eucharistic Prayer III is used, after the words the entire people you have gained for your own, *the following is added:*

**Remember also, Lord,
your servants reborn in Baptism
whom you have been pleased to confirm
by bestowing the Holy Spirit,
and in your mercy, keep safe in them your grace.**

Communion Antiphon   Cf. Heb 6: 4

Rejoice in the Lord, all you who have been enlightened,
who have tasted the gift from heaven
and have been made sharers in the Holy Spirit (E.T. alleluia).

Prayer after Communion

**Accompany with your blessing
from this day forward, O Lord,
those who have been anointed with the Holy Spirit
and nourished by the Sacrament of your Son,
so that, with all trials overcome,
they may gladden your Church by their holiness
and, through their works and their charity,
foster her growth in the world.
Through Christ our Lord.**

Solemn Blessing at the End of Mass

The Bishop, with hands extended over the newly confirmed, says:

May God the Father almighty bless you,
whom he has made his adopted sons and daughters
reborn from water and the Holy Spirit,
and may he keep you worthy of his fatherly love.
R. Amen.

May his Only Begotten Son,
who promised that the Spirit of truth would abide in his Church,
bless you and confirm you by his power
in the confession of the true faith.
R. Amen.

May the Holy Spirit,
who kindles the fire of charity in the hearts of disciples,
bless you and lead you blameless and gathered as one
into the joy of the Kingdom of God.
R. Amen.

And he blesses all the people, adding:

And may almighty God bless all of you, who are gathered here,
the Father, ✠ and the Son, ✠ and the Holy ✠ Spirit.
R. Amen.

Or:

Prayer over the People

The Bishop, with hands extended over the newly confirmed and the people, says:

Confirm, O God,
what you have brought about in us,
and preserve in the hearts of your faithful
the gifts of the Holy Spirit:
may they never be ashamed
to confess Christ crucified before the world
and by devoted charity
may they ever fulfill his commands.
Who lives and reigns for ever and ever.
R. Amen.

And may the blessing of almighty God,
the Father, ✠ and the Son, ✠ and the Holy ✠ Spirit,
come down on you and remain with you for ever.
R. Amen.

B

Entrance Antiphon   Rom 5: 5; cf. 8: 11

> The love of God has been poured into our hearts
> through the Spirit of God dwelling within us (E.T. alleluia).

Collect

> **Graciously pour out your Holy Spirit upon us,**
> **we pray, O Lord,**
> **so that, walking in oneness of faith**
> **and strengthened by the power of his love,**
> **we may come to the measure of the full stature of Christ.**
> **Who lives and reigns with you in the unity of the Holy Spirit,**
> **one God, for ever and ever.**

Other prayers to be used at choice (p. 1134).

Prayer over the Offerings

> **Accept graciously these your servants, O Lord,**
> **together with your Only Begotten Son,**
> **so that, signed with his Cross and with a spiritual anointing,**
> **they may constantly offer themselves to you**
> **in union with him**
> **and merit each day a greater outpouring of your Spirit.**
> **Through Christ our Lord.**

Preface I of the Holy Spirit (p. 1339) or Preface II (p. 1342) may be used.

In the Eucharistic Prayers there are proper intercessions (pp. 1127-1128).

Communion Antiphon   Cf. Ps 34 (33): 6, 9

> Look towards him and be radiant;
> let your faces not be abashed.
> Taste and see that the Lord is good.
> Blessed the man who seeks refuge in him (E.T. alleluia).

Prayer after Communion

>   Instruct, O Lord, in the fullness of the Law
>   those you have endowed with the gifts of your Spirit
>   and nourished by the Body of your Only Begotten Son,
>   that they may constantly show to the world
>   the freedom of your adopted children
>   and, by the holiness of their lives,
>   exercise the prophetic mission of your people.
>   Through Christ our Lord.

Solemn Blessing or Prayer over the People (p. 1132).

C

Other Prayers to be used if appropriate.

Collect

>   May the Paraclete who proceeds from you,
>   we pray, O Lord,
>   enlighten our minds and lead us into all truth,
>   just as your Son has promised.
>   Who lives and reigns with you in the unity of the Holy Spirit,
>   one God, for ever and ever.

Prayer over the Offerings

>   Accept the oblation of your family,
>   we pray, O Lord,
>   that those who have received the gift of the Holy Spirit
>   may keep safe what they have received
>   and come to eternal rewards.
>   Through Christ our Lord.

Prayer after Communion

>   Pour on us, O Lord, the Spirit of your love
>   and, in your kindness,
>   make those you have nourished by this one heavenly Bread
>   one in mind and heart.
>   Through Christ our Lord.

II. FOR THE CONFERRAL OF THE ANOINTING OF THE SICK

Whenever Holy Anointing is conferred during Mass, on days when Ritual Masses are permitted, the Mass for the Sick (pp. 1313-1315) may be used with the color white.

All the prayers given for a man may be adapted for a woman, with the necessary change of gender; in addition, those expressed in the plural may be used for individuals, with the necessary change to the singular.

At the end of Mass, a formula of blessing chosen from those that follow may be used.

May God the Father bless you.
R. Amen.

May the Son of God heal you.
R. Amen.

May the Holy Spirit shed light upon you.
R. Amen.

May God guard your body and save your soul.
R. Amen.

May he enlighten your heart and lead you to life on high.
R. Amen.

And may almighty God bless all of you, who are gathered here, the Father, and the Son, ✠ and the Holy Spirit.
R. Amen.

Or:

May the Lord Jesus Christ be with you to defend you.
R. Amen.

May he go before you to lead you and behind you to guard you.
R. Amen.

May he look upon you, keep you safe and bless you.
R. Amen.

And may almighty God bless all of you, who are gathered here, the Father, and the Son, ✠ and the Holy Spirit.
R. Amen.

III. FOR THE ADMINISTERING OF VIATICUM

This Mass may be used with the color white on days when Ritual Masses are permitted.
All the prayers given for a man may be adapted for a woman, with the necessary change of gender; in addition, those expressed in the plural form may be used for individuals, with the necessary change to the singular.

Entrance Antiphon *Cf. Ps 81 (80): 17*

> He fed them with the finest wheat,
> and satisfied them with honey from the rock (E.T. alleluia).

Or: *Cf. Is 53: 4*

> Truly the Lord has borne our infirmities,
> and he has carried our sorrows (E.T. alleluia).

Collect

> O God, whose Son is for us the way, the truth and the life,
> look lovingly upon your servant N.
> and grant that, trusting in your promises
> and strengthened by the Body of your Son,
> he (she) may journey in peace to your Kingdom.
> Through our Lord Jesus Christ, your Son,
> who lives and reigns with you in the unity of the Holy Spirit,
> one God, for ever and ever.

Prayer over the Offerings

> Look graciously on our sacrifice, holy Father,
> that it may present to you the Paschal Lamb,
> whose Passion has unlocked the gates of paradise,
> and by your grace lead your servant N. to the gift of eternal life.
> Through Christ our Lord.

Communion Antiphon
Jn 6: 54

Whoever eats my flesh and drinks my blood has eternal life, says the Lord, and I will raise him on the last day (E.T. alleluia).

Or:

Col 1: 24

In my flesh I am completing what is lacking in the afflictions of Christ on behalf of his body, which is the Church (E.T. alleluia).

Prayer after Communion

O Lord, eternal health and salvation
of those who believe in you,
grant, we pray, that your servant N.,
renewed by heavenly food and drink,
may safely reach your Kingdom of light and life.
Through Christ our Lord.

IV. FOR THE CONFERRAL OF HOLY ORDERS

1. FOR THE ORDINATION OF A BISHOP

This Ritual Mass may be used with the color white or a festive color, except on Solemnities, on the Sundays of Advent, Lent, and Easter, on days within the Octave of Easter, and on Feasts of the Apostles. When these days occur, the Mass of the day is said.

A
For the Ordination of one Bishop

Entrance Antiphon   Cf. Lk 4: 18
The Spirit of the Lord is upon me, for he has anointed me
and sent me to preach the good news to the poor,
to heal the broken-hearted (E.T. alleluia).

The Gloria in excelsis (Glory to God in the highest) is said.

Collect
O God, who out of the abundance of your untold grace alone
choose to set your servant and Priest N.
over your Church of N. this day,
grant that he may carry out worthily the office of Bishop
and, under your governance in all things,
he may direct by word and example
the people entrusted to his care.
Through our Lord Jesus Christ, your Son,
who lives and reigns with you in the unity of the Holy Spirit,
one God, for ever and ever.

Or, especially when a non-residential Bishop is ordained:

O God, eternal Shepherd,
who, governing your flock with watchful care,
choose to join N., your servant and Priest,
to the College of Bishops this day,
grant, we pray, that by his holiness of life
he may everywhere prove to be a true witness to Christ.
Who lives and reigns with you in the unity of the Holy Spirit,
one God, for ever and ever.

The Creed is said in accordance with the rubrics; the Universal Prayer is omitted.

Prayer over the Offerings

If the newly ordained Bishop presides at the Liturgy of the Eucharist, he says:

**We offer you the sacrifice of praise, O Lord,
for the deepening of our service of you,
so that what you have conferred on us,
unworthy as we are,
you may graciously bring to fulfillment.
Through Christ our Lord.**

If, however, the principal ordaining Bishop presides at the Liturgy of the Eucharist, he says:

**May this oblation, O Lord,
which we have presented for your Church
and for N., your servant and Bishop,
become an offering acceptable to you;
and for the good of the flock,
may he whom you have raised up among your people to be High Priest
be endowed, by your gift, with apostolic virtues.
Through Christ our Lord.**

This Preface may be said:

Preface: The Priesthood of Christ and the ministry of Priests.

℣. **The Lord be with you.**
℟. And with your spirit.

℣. **Lift up your hearts.**
℟. We lift them up to the Lord.

℣. **Let us give thanks to the Lord our God.**
℟. It is right and just.

It is truly right and just, our duty and our salvation,
always and everywhere to give you thanks,
Lord, holy Father, almighty and eternal God.

For by the anointing of the Holy Spirit
you made your Only Begotten Son
High Priest of the new and eternal covenant,
and by your wondrous design were pleased to decree
that his one Priesthood should continue in the Church.

For Christ not only adorns with a royal priesthood
the people he has made his own,
but with a brother's kindness he also chooses men
to become sharers in his sacred ministry
through the laying on of hands.

They are to renew in his name
the sacrifice of human redemption,
to set before your children the paschal banquet,
to lead your holy people in charity,
to nourish them with the word
and strengthen them with the Sacraments.

As they give up their lives for you
and for the salvation of their brothers and sisters,
they strive to be conformed to the image of Christ himself
and offer you a constant witness of faith and love.

And so, Lord, with all the Angels and Saints,
we, too, give you thanks, as in exultation we acclaim:

Holy, Holy, Holy Lord God of hosts . . .

Text with music, pp. 293-294.

Mention of the newly ordained Bishop is made according to the following formulas:

a) In Eucharistic Prayer I, the newly ordained Bishop says the proper form of the Hanc igitur (Therefore, Lord, we pray):

Therefore, Lord, we pray:
graciously accept this oblation of our service,
that of your whole family,
which we make to you
also for me, your unworthy servant,
whom you have been pleased to raise to the Order of Bishops;
and in your mercy, keep safe your gifts in me,
so that what I have received by divine commission
I may fulfill by divine assistance.
(Through Christ our Lord. Amen.)

Another Bishop, however, says:

Therefore, Lord, we pray:
graciously accept this oblation of our service,
that of your whole family,
which we make to you
also for your servant N.,
whom you have been pleased to raise to the Order of Bishops;
and in your mercy, keep safe your gifts in him,
so that what he has received by divine commission
he may fulfill by divine assistance.
(Through Christ our Lord. Amen.)

b) In Eucharistic Prayer II, after the words *we may be gathered into one by the Holy Spirit*, the newly ordained Bishop says:

Remember, Lord, your Church,
spread throughout the world,
and bring her to the fullness of charity,
together with N. our Pope
(and N. our Bishop),
and me, your unworthy servant,
whom you have willed to provide today as shepherd for the
**   Church (of N.),**
and all the clergy.
Remember also our brothers and sisters . . .

Another Bishop, however, says:

Remember, Lord, your Church,
spread throughout the world,
and bring her to the fullness of charity,
together with **N.** our Pope
and **N.** our Bishop,
(and your servant **N.**),
whom you have willed to provide today as shepherd for the
   Church **(of N.)**,
and all the clergy.
Remember also our brothers and sisters . . .

c) In Eucharistic Prayer III, after the words advance the peace and salvation of all the world, the newly ordained Bishop says:

Be pleased to confirm in faith and charity
your pilgrim Church on earth,
with your servant **N.** our Pope
(and N. our Bishop**)**,
and me, your unworthy servant,
who have been ordained today as shepherd for the Church **(of N.)**,
with the Order of Bishops, all the clergy,
and the entire people you have gained for your own.
Listen graciously to the prayers of this family . . .

Another Bishop, however, says:

Be pleased to confirm in faith and charity
your pilgrim Church on earth,
with your servant **N.** our Pope
and **N.** our Bishop,
(and your servant **N.**),
who has been ordained today as shepherd for the Church **(of N.)**,
with the Order of Bishops, all the clergy,
and the entire people you have gained for your own.
Listen graciously to the prayers of this family . . .

d) If the proper Preface is not used, Eucharistic Prayer IV may be said; in the intercessions of this prayer, after the words to the praise of your glory, *the newly ordained Bishop says:*

Therefore, Lord, remember now
all for whom we offer this sacrifice:
especially your servant N. our Pope,
(N. our Bishop),
and me, your unworthy servant,
whom today you have been pleased to choose
for the service of your people,
with the whole Order of Bishops,
and all the clergy.
Be mindful also of those who take part in this offering,
those gathered here before you,
your entire people,
and all who seek you with a sincere heart.
Remember also
those who have died in the peace of your Christ . . .

Another Bishop, however, says:

Therefore, Lord, remember now
all for whom we offer this sacrifice:
especially your servant N. our Pope,
N. our Bishop,
(and this your servant N.),
whom today you have been pleased to choose
for the service of your people,
with the whole Order of Bishops,
and all the clergy.
Be mindful also of those who take part in this offering,
those gathered here before you,
your entire people,
and all who seek you with a sincere heart.
Remember also
those who have died in the peace of your Christ . . .

Communion Antiphon   Jn 17: 17-18

Holy Father, consecrate them in the truth.
As you sent me into the world,
so I sent them into the world, says the Lord (E.T. alleluia).

Prayer after Communion

If the newly ordained Bishop presides at the Liturgy of the Eucharist, he says:

Complete within us, O Lord, we pray,
the healing work of your mercy,
and graciously perfect and sustain us,
so that in all things we may please you.
Through Christ our Lord.

If, however, the principal ordaining Bishop presides at the Liturgy of the Eucharist, he says:

By the power of this Sacrament, O Lord,
increase the gifts of your grace
in N., your servant and Bishop,
that he may serve you worthily in the pastoral ministry
and receive the eternal rewards of a faithful steward.
Through Christ our Lord.

Solemn Blessing at the End of Mass

If the newly ordained Bishop presides at the Liturgy of the Eucharist, he imparts the following blessing, with hands extended over the people:

O God, who care for your people with gentleness
and rule them in love,
endow with the Spirit of wisdom
those to whom you have handed on authority to govern,
that from the flourishing of a holy flock
may come eternal joy for its shepherds.
R. Amen.

As in your majestic power
you allot the number of our days
and the measure of our years,
look favorably upon our humble service
and confer on our time the abundance of your peace.
R. Amen.

Give a happy outcome to the tasks
that through your grace you have laid upon me,
whom you have raised to the rank of Bishop;
make me pleasing to you in the fulfillment of my duties,
and so guide the hearts of people and pastor,
that the obedience of the flock may never fail the shepherd
nor the care of the shepherd be lacking for the flock.
R. Amen.

And he blesses all the people, adding:

And may almighty God bless all of you, who are gathered here, the Father, ✠ and the Son, ✠ and the Holy ✠ Spirit.
R. Amen.

If, however, the principal ordaining Bishop presides at the Liturgy of the Eucharist, he imparts the following blessing, with hands extended over the newly ordained Bishop:

May the Lord bless you and keep you;
and as he has willed to set you as High Priest over his people,
so may he make you happy in this present life
and grant you a share in the happiness that is eternal.
R. Amen.

May he grant that the clergy and people
he has chosen to unite by his gracious help
be happily governed by his providence and your stewardship
for many years to come.
R. Amen.

May they obey God's commandments,
freed from adversity,
and may they abound in all that is good,
submitting in faith to your ministry,
so that they may enjoy peace and tranquility in the present age
and with you be found worthy
to share the company of the citizens of eternity.
R. Amen.

And he blesses all the people, adding:

And may almighty God bless all of you, who are gathered here, the Father, ✠ and the Son, ✠ and the Holy ✠ Spirit.
R. Amen.

B
For the Ordination of Several Bishops

Entrance Antiphon   Cf. Lk 4: 18

The Spirit of the Lord is upon me, for he has anointed me
and sent me to preach the good news to the poor,
to heal the broken-hearted (E.T. alleluia).

The Gloria in excelsis (Glory to God in the highest) is said.

Collect

O God, who out of the abundance of your untold grace alone
choose to raise these Priests, your servants,
to the ministry of the high priesthood this day,
grant that they may carry out worthily the office of Bishop
and, under your governance in all things,
they may direct by word and example
the people entrusted to their care.
Through our Lord Jesus Christ, your Son,
who lives and reigns with you in the unity of the Holy Spirit,
one God, for ever and ever.

Or, especially if non-resident Bishops are ordained:

O God, eternal Shepherd,
who, governing your flock with watchful care,
choose to join these your servants and Priests
to the College of Bishops this day,
grant, we pray, that by their holiness of life
they may everywhere prove to be true witnesses to Christ.
Who lives and reigns with you in the unity of the Holy Spirit,
one God, for ever and ever.

The Creed is said in accordance with the rubrics; the Universal Prayer is omitted.

Prayer over the Offerings

If a newly ordained Bishop presides at the Liturgy of the Eucharist, he says:

We offer you the sacrifice of praise, O Lord,
for the deepening of our service of you,
so that what you have conferred on us,
unworthy as we are,
you may graciously bring to fulfillment.
Through Christ our Lord.

If, however, the principal ordaining Bishop presides at the Liturgy of the Eucharist, he says:

May this oblation, O Lord,
which we have presented for your Church
and for these your servants, newly ordained as Bishops,
become an offering acceptable to you;
and for the good of the flock,
may those you have raised up
among your people to be High Priests
be endowed, by your gift, with apostolic virtues.
Through Christ our Lord.

Preface: The Priesthood of Christ and the ministry of Priests (pp. 293-294).

Mention of the newly ordained Bishops is made according to the following formulas:

a) In Eucharistic Prayer I, a newly ordained Bishop says the proper form of the Hanc igitur *(Therefore, Lord, we pray):*

Therefore, Lord, we pray:
graciously accept this oblation of our service,
that of your whole family,
which we make to you
also for me, your unworthy servant,
and for these your servants, **N. N.**,
whom you have been pleased to raise to the Order of Bishops;
and in your mercy, keep safe your gifts in us,
so that what we have received by divine commission
we may fulfill by divine assistance.
(Through Christ our Lord. Amen.**)**

Another Bishop, however, says:

Therefore, Lord, we pray:
graciously accept this oblation of our service,
that of your whole family,
which we make to you
also for these your servants, **N. N.**,
whom you have been pleased to raise to the Order of Bishops;
and in your mercy, keep safe your gifts in them,
so that what they have received by divine commission
they may fulfill by divine assistance.
(Through Christ our Lord. Amen.**)**

b) In Eucharistic Prayer II, after the words we may be gathered into one by the Holy Spirit, a newly ordained Bishop says:

**Remember, Lord, your Church,
spread throughout the world,
and bring her to the fullness of charity,
together with N. our Pope
(and N. our Bishop),
me, your unworthy servant,
and these your servants, N. N.,
whom you have willed to provide today
as shepherds for the Church,
and all the clergy.
Remember also our brothers and sisters . . .**

c) In Eucharistic Prayer III, after the words advance the peace and salvation of all the world, a newly ordained Bishop says:

**Be pleased to confirm in faith and charity
your pilgrim Church on earth,
with your servant N. our Pope
(and N. our Bishop),
and me, your unworthy servant,
and these your servants, N. N.,
who have been ordained today as shepherds for the Church,
with the Order of Bishops, all the clergy,
and the entire people you have gained for your own.
Listen graciously to the prayers of this family . . .**

d) *If the proper Preface is not used, Eucharistic Prayer IV may be said; in the intercessions of this prayer, after the words* to the praise of your glory, *a newly ordained Bishop says:*

> Therefore, Lord, remember now
> all for whom we offer this sacrifice:
> especially your servant N. our Pope,
> (N. our Bishop),
> me, your unworthy servant,
> and these your servants, N. N.,
> whom today you have been pleased to choose
> for the service of your people,
> with the whole Order of Bishops,
> and all the clergy.
> Be mindful also of those who take part in this offering,
> those gathered here before you,
> your entire people,
> and all who seek you with a sincere heart.
> Remember also
> those who have died in the peace of your Christ . . .

Communion Antiphon   Jn 17: 17-18

> Holy Father, consecrate them in the truth.
> As you sent me into the world,
> so I sent them into the world, says the Lord (E.T. alleluia).

Prayer after Communion

If a newly ordained Bishop presides at the Liturgy of the Eucharist, he says:

> Complete within us, O Lord, we pray,
> the healing work of your mercy,
> and graciously perfect and sustain us,
> so that in all things we may please you.
> Through Christ our Lord.

If, however, the principal ordaining Bishop presides at the Liturgy of the Eucharist, he says:

> By the power of this Sacrament, O Lord,
> increase the gifts of your grace
> in these your servants and Bishops,
> that they may serve you worthily in the pastoral ministry
> and receive the eternal rewards of faithful stewards.
> Through Christ our Lord.

Solemn Blessing at the End of Mass

If a newly ordained Bishop presides at the Liturgy of the Eucharist, he imparts the following blessing, with hands extended over the people:

O God, who care for your people with gentleness
and rule them with love,
endow with the Spirit of wisdom
those to whom you have handed on authority to govern,
that from the flourishing of a holy flock
may come eternal joy for its shepherds.
R. Amen.

As in your majestic power you allot
the number of our days and the measure of our years,
look favorably upon our humble service
and confer on our time the abundance of your peace.
R. Amen.

Give a happy outcome to the tasks
that through your grace you have laid upon me,
whom you have raised to the rank of Bishop;
make us pleasing to you in the fulfillment of our duties,
and so guide the hearts of people and pastors,
that the obedience of the flock may never fail the shepherds
nor the care of the shepherds be lacking to the flock.
R. Amen.

And he blesses all the people, adding:

And may almighty God bless all of you, who are gathered here,
the Father, ✠ and the Son, ✠ and the Holy ✠ Spirit.
R. Amen.

If, however, the principal ordaining Bishop presides at the Liturgy of the Eucharist, he imparts the following blessing, with hands extended over the newly ordained Bishops:

May the Lord bless you and keep you;
and as he has willed to set you as High Priests over his people,
so may he make you happy in this present life
and grant you a share in the happiness that is eternal.
R. Amen.

May God grant that the clergy and people
he has chosen to unite by his gracious help
be happily governed by his providence and your stewardship
for many years to come.
R. Amen.

May they obey God's commandments,
freed from adversity,
and may they abound in all that is good,
submitting in faith to your ministry,
so that they will enjoy peace and tranquility in the present age
and with you be found worthy
to share the company of the citizens of eternity.
R. Amen.

And he blesses all the people, adding:

And may almighty God bless all of you, who are gathered here,
the Father, ✠ and the Son, ✠ and the Holy ✠ Spirit.
R. Amen.

2. FOR THE ORDINATION OF PRIESTS

This Ritual Mass may be used, with the color white or a festive color, except on Solemnities, on the Sundays of Advent, Lent, and Easter, and on days within the Octave of Easter. When these days occur, the Mass of the day is said.

A
For the Ordination of Several Priests

Entrance Antiphon — Jer 3: 15

I will appoint over you shepherds after my own heart,
who will shepherd you wisely and prudently (E.T. alleluia).

The Gloria in excelsis (Glory to God in the highest) is said.

Collect

Lord our God, who in governing your people
make use of the ministry of Priests,
grant a persevering obedience to your will
to these Deacons of your Church,
whom you graciously choose today
for the office of the priesthood,
so that by their ministry and life
they may gain glory for you in Christ.
Who lives and reigns with you in the unity of the Holy Spirit,
one God, for ever and ever.

The Creed is said in accordance with the rubrics; the Universal Prayer is omitted.

Prayer over the Offerings

O God, who have willed that your Priests
should minister at the holy altar and serve your people,
grant by the power of this sacrifice, we pray,
that the labors of your servants may constantly please you
and in your Church bear that fruit which lasts for ever.
Through Christ our Lord.

Preface: The Priesthood of Christ and the ministry of Priests.

V. The Lord be with you.
R. And with your spirit.

V. Lift up your hearts.
R. We lift them up to the Lord.

V. Let us give thanks to the Lord our God.
R. It is right and just.

It is truly right and just, our duty and our salvation,
always and everywhere to give you thanks,
Lord, holy Father, almighty and eternal God.

For by the anointing of the Holy Spirit
you made your Only Begotten Son
High Priest of the new and eternal covenant,
and by your wondrous design were pleased to decree
that his one Priesthood should continue in the Church.

For Christ not only adorns with a royal priesthood
the people he has made his own,
but with a brother's kindness he also chooses men
to become sharers in his sacred ministry
through the laying on of hands.

They are to renew in his name
the sacrifice of human redemption,
to set before your children the paschal banquet,
to lead your holy people in charity,
to nourish them with your word
and strengthen them with the Sacraments.

As they give up their lives for you
and for the salvation of their brothers and sisters,
they strive to be conformed to the image of Christ himself
and offer you a constant witness of faith and love.

And so, Lord, with all the Angels and Saints,
we, too, give you thanks, as in exultation we acclaim:

Holy, Holy, Holy Lord God of hosts . . .

Text with music, pp. 293-294.

Mention of the newly ordained Priests in the Eucharistic Prayers is made according to the following formulas:

a) In Eucharistic Prayer I, the proper form of the Hanc igitur (Therefore, Lord, we pray) is said:

Therefore, Lord, we pray:
graciously accept this oblation of our service,
that of your whole family,
which we make to you
also for these your servants,
whom you have been pleased to raise to the Order of Priesthood;
and in your mercy, keep safe your gifts in them,
so that what they have received by divine commission
they may fulfill by divine assistance.
(Through Christ our Lord. Amen.)

b) In Eucharistic Prayer II, after the words we may be gathered into one by the Holy Spirit, the following is said:

Remember, Lord, your Church,
spread throughout the world,
and bring her to the fullness of charity,
together with N. our Pope
and N. our Bishop.
Be mindful also of these your servants,
whom you have willed to provide today as Priests for the Church,
and all the clergy.
Remember also our brothers and sisters . . .

c) In Eucharistic Prayer III, after the words advance the peace and salvation of all the world, the following is said:

Be pleased to confirm in faith and charity
your pilgrim Church on earth,
with your servant N. our Pope
and N. our Bishop,
with the Order of Bishops,
these your servants,
who have been ordained today as Priests for the Church,
all the clergy,
and the entire people you have gained for your own.
Listen graciously to the prayers of this family . . .

d) If the proper Preface is not used, Eucharistic Prayer IV may be said; in the intercessions of this prayer, after the words to the praise of your glory, the following is said:

Therefore, Lord, remember now
all for whom we offer this sacrifice:
especially your servant N. our Pope,
and N. our Bishop,
with the whole Order of Bishops,
these your servants,
whom today you have been pleased to choose
for the priestly service of your people,
and all the clergy.
Be mindful also of those who take part in this offering,
those gathered here before you,
your entire people,
and all who seek you with a sincere heart.
Remember also
those who have died in the peace of your Christ . . .

Communion Antiphon
Mk 16: 15; Mt 28: 20

Go into all the world, and proclaim the Gospel.
I am with you always, says the Lord (E.T. alleluia).

Prayer after Communion

May the divine sacrifice
we have offered and received, O Lord,
give new life to your Priests and to all your servants,
that, united to you in unfailing love,
they may receive the grace
of giving worthy service to your majesty.
Through Christ our Lord.

Solemn Blessing at the End of Mass

The Bishop, with hands extended over the newly ordained Priests and the people, says:

May God, who founded the Church and guides her still,
protect you constantly with his grace,
that you may faithfully discharge the duties of the Priesthood.
R. Amen.

May he make you servants and witnesses in the world
to divine charity and truth
and faithful ministers of reconciliation.
R. Amen.

And may he make you true shepherds
to provide the living Bread and word of life to the faithful,
that they may continue to grow in the unity of the Body of Christ.
R. Amen.

And he blesses all the people, adding:

And may almighty God bless all of you, who are gathered here,
the Father, ✠ and the Son, ✠ and the Holy ✠ Spirit.
R. Amen.

B

For the Ordination of One Priest

Entrance Antiphon
Jer 3: 15

I will appoint over you shepherds after my own heart,
who will shepherd you wisely and prudently (E.T. alleluia).

The Gloria in excelsis (Glory to God in the highest) is said.

Collect

Lord our God, who in governing your people
make use of the ministry of Priests,
grant a persevering obedience to your will
to this Deacon of your Church,
whom you graciously choose today
for the office of the priesthood,
so that by his ministry and life
he may gain glory for you in Christ.
Who lives and reigns with you in the unity of the Holy Spirit,
one God, for ever and ever.

The Creed is said in accordance with the rubrics; the Universal Prayer is omitted.

Prayer over the Offerings

O God, who have willed that your Priests
should minister at the holy altar and serve your people,
grant by the power of this sacrifice, we pray,
that the labors of your servants may constantly please you
and in your Church bear that fruit which lasts for ever.
Through Christ our Lord.

Preface: The Priesthood of Christ and the ministry of Priests.

V. The Lord be with you.
R. And with your spirit.

V. Lift up your hearts.
R. We lift them up to the Lord.

V. Let us give thanks to the Lord our God.
R. It is right and just.

It is truly right and just, our duty and our salvation,
always and everywhere to give you thanks,
Lord, holy Father, almighty and eternal God.

For by the anointing of the Holy Spirit
you made your Only Begotten Son
High Priest of the new and eternal covenant,
and by your wondrous design were pleased to decree
that his one Priesthood should continue in the Church.

For Christ not only adorns with a royal priesthood
the people he has made his own,
but with a brother's kindness he also chooses men
to become sharers in his sacred ministry
through the laying on of hands.

They are to renew in his name
the sacrifice of human redemption,
to set before your children the paschal banquet,
to lead your holy people in charity,
to nourish them with the word
and strengthen them with the Sacraments.

As they give up their lives for you
and for the salvation of their brothers and sisters,
they strive to be conformed to the image of Christ himself
and offer you a constant witness of faith and love.

And so, Lord, with all the Angels and Saints,
we, too, give you thanks, as in exultation we acclaim:

Holy, Holy, Holy Lord God of hosts . . .

Text with music, pp. 293-294.

Mention of the newly ordained Priest in the Eucharistic Prayers is made according to the following formulas:

a) In Eucharistic Prayer I, the proper form of the Hanc igitur (Therefore, Lord, we pray) is said:

Therefore, Lord, we pray:
graciously accept this oblation of our service,
that of your whole family,
which we make to you
also for this your servant,
whom you have been pleased to raise to the Order of Priesthood;
and in your mercy, keep safe your gifts in him,
so that what he has received by divine commission
he may fulfill by divine assistance.
(Through Christ our Lord. Amen.)

b) In Eucharistic Prayer II, after the words we may be gathered into one by the Holy Spirit, the following is said:

Remember, Lord, your Church,
spread throughout the world,
and bring her to the fullness of charity,
together with N. our Pope
and N. our Bishop.
Be mindful also of this your servant,
whom you have willed to provide today as a Priest for the Church,
and all the clergy.
Remember also our brothers and sisters . . .

c) In Eucharistic Prayer III, after the words advance the peace and salvation of all the world, the following is said:

Be pleased to confirm in faith and charity
your pilgrim Church on earth,
with your servant N. our Pope
and N. our Bishop,
with the Order of Bishops,
this your servant,
who has been ordained today as a Priest for the Church,
all the clergy,
and the entire people you have gained for your own.
Listen graciously to the prayers of this family . . .

d) If the proper Preface is not used, Eucharistic Prayer IV may be said; in the intercessions of this prayer, after the words for the praise of your glory, the following is said:

Therefore, Lord, remember now
all for whom we offer this sacrifice:
especially your servant N. our Pope,
and N. our Bishop,
with the whole Order of Bishops,
this your servant,
whom today you have been pleased to choose
for the priestly service of your people,
and all the clergy.
Be mindful also of those who take part in this offering,
those gathered here before you,
your entire people,
and all who seek you with a sincere heart.
Remember also
those who have died in the peace of your Christ . . .

Communion Antiphon
Mk 16: 15; Mt 28: 20

Go into all the world, and proclaim the Gospel.
I am with you always, says the Lord (E.T. alleluia).

Prayer after Communion

May the divine sacrifice
we have offered and received, O Lord,
give new life to your Priests and to all your servants,
that, united to you in unfailing love,
they may receive the grace
of giving worthy service to your majesty.
Through Christ our Lord.

Solemn Blessing at the End of Mass

The Bishop, with hands extended over the newly ordained Priest and the people, says:

May God, who founded the Church and guides her still,
protect you constantly with his grace,
that you may faithfully discharge the duties of the Priesthood.
R. Amen.

May he make you a servant and a witness in the world
to divine charity and truth
and a faithful minister of reconciliation.
R. Amen.

And may he make you a true shepherd
to provide the living Bread and word of life to the faithful,
that they may continue to grow in the unity of the Body of Christ.
R. Amen.

And he blesses all the people, adding:

And may almighty God bless all of you, who are gathered here,
the Father, ✠ and the Son, ✠ and the Holy ✠ Spirit.
R. Amen.

3. FOR THE ORDINATION OF DEACONS

This Ritual Mass may be used, with the color white or a festive color, except on Solemnities, on the Sundays of Advent, Lent, and Easter, and on days within the Octave of Easter. When these days occur, the Mass of the day is said.

A

For the Ordination of Several Deacons

Entrance Antiphon   Jn 12: 26

Whoever serves me must follow me,
and where I am, there also will my servant be (E.T. alleluia).

The Gloria in excelsis *(Glory to God in the highest) is said.*

Collect

O God, who have taught the ministers of your Church
to seek not to be served
but to serve their brothers and sisters,
grant, we pray, that these your servants,
whom you graciously choose today for the office of Deacon,
may be effective in action, gentle in ministry,
and constant in prayer.
Through our Lord Jesus Christ, your Son,
who lives and reigns with you in the unity of the Holy Spirit,
one God, for ever and ever.

The Creed is said in accordance with the rubrics; the Universal Prayer is omitted.

Prayer over the Offerings

Holy Father, whose Son chose to wash the disciples' feet
and so set us an example,
accept, we pray, the oblations of our service,
and grant that, offering ourselves as a spiritual sacrifice,
we may be filled with a spirit of humility and zeal.
Through Christ our Lord.

Preface: Christ, source of all ministry in the Church.

V. The Lord be with you.   R. And with your spir-it.

V. Lift up your hearts.   R. We lift them up to the Lord.

V. Let us give thanks to the Lord our God.   R. It is right and just.

It is truly right and just, our duty and our sal-va-tion, al-ways and everywhere to give you thanks, Lord, holy Father, almighty and e-ter-nal God. For by the anointing of the Ho-ly Spir-it you

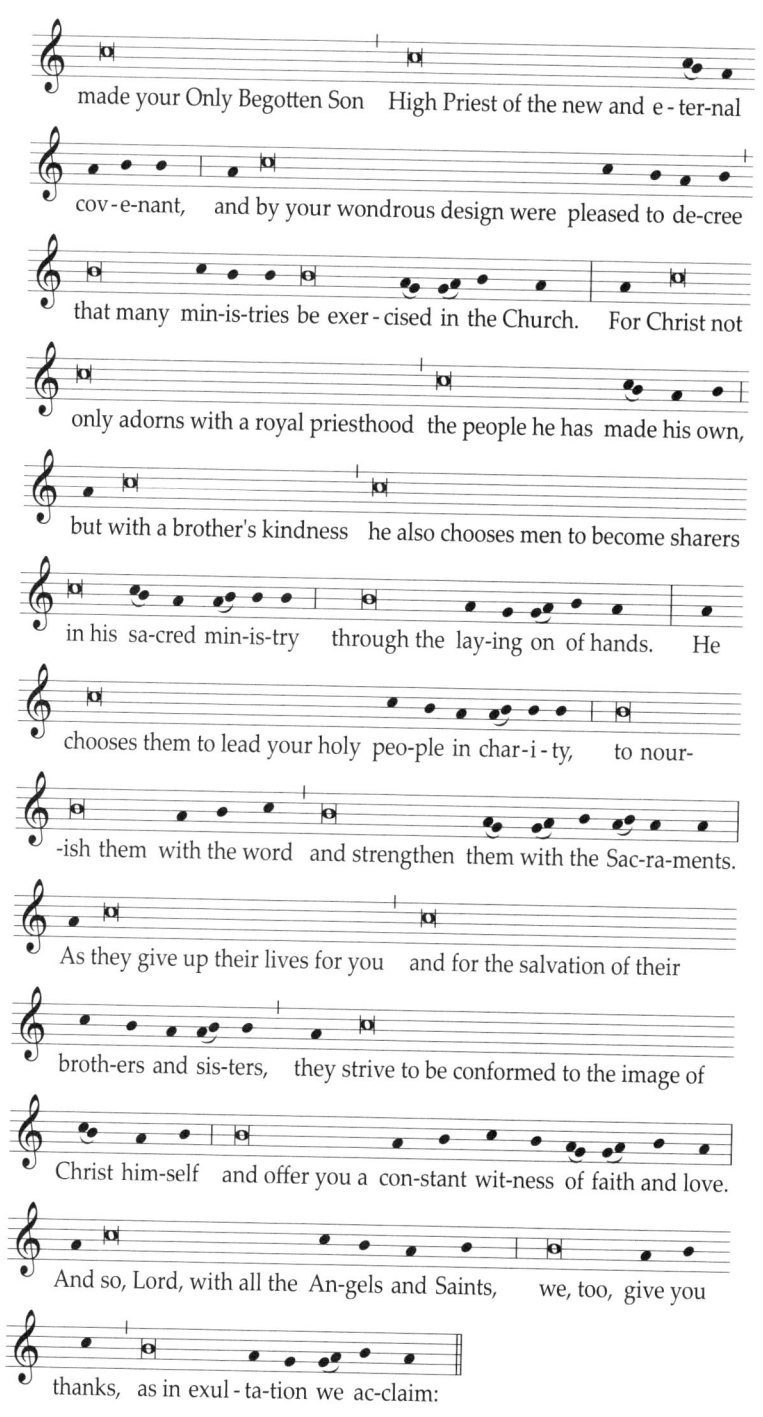

Holy, Holy, Holy Lord God of hosts . . .

Text without music:

V. **The Lord be with you.**
R. And with your spirit.

V. **Lift up your hearts.**
R. We lift them up to the Lord.

V. **Let us give thanks to the Lord our God.**
R. It is right and just.

It is truly right and just, our duty and our salvation,
always and everywhere to give you thanks,
Lord, holy Father, almighty and eternal God.

For by the anointing of the Holy Spirit
you made your Only Begotten Son
High Priest of the new and eternal covenant,
and by your wondrous design were pleased to decree
that many ministries be exercised in the Church.

For Christ not only adorns with a royal priesthood
the people he has made his own,
but with a brother's kindness he also chooses men
to become sharers in his sacred ministry
through the laying on of hands.

He chooses them to lead your holy people in charity,
to nourish them with the word
and strengthen them with the Sacraments.

As they give up their lives for you
and for the salvation of their brothers and sisters,
they strive to be conformed to the image of Christ himself
and offer you a constant witness of faith and love.

And so, Lord, with all the Angels and Saints,
we, too, give you thanks, as in exultation we acclaim:

Holy, Holy, Holy Lord God of hosts . . .

Mention of the newly ordained Deacons in the Eucharistic Prayers is made according to the following formulas:

a) In Eucharistic Prayer I, the proper form of the Hanc igitur (Therefore, Lord, we pray) is said:

Therefore, Lord, we pray:
graciously accept this oblation of our service,
that of your whole family,
which we make to you
also for your servants
whom you have been pleased to raise to the Order of the Diaconate;
and in your mercy, keep safe your gifts in them,
so that what they have received by divine commission
they may fulfill by divine assistance.
(Through Christ our Lord. Amen.)

b) In Eucharistic Prayer II, after the words we may be gathered into one by the Holy Spirit, the following is said:

Remember, Lord, your Church,
spread throughout the world,
and bring her to the fullness of charity,
together with N. our Pope
and N. our Bishop.
Be mindful also of these your servants,
whom you have willed to provide today as ministers for the Church,
and all the clergy.
Remember also our brothers and sisters . . .

c) In Eucharistic Prayer III, after the words advance the peace and salvation of all the world, the following is said:

Be pleased to confirm in faith and charity
your pilgrim Church on earth,
with your servant N. our Pope
and N. our Bishop,
with the Order of Bishops,
these your servants,
who have been ordained today as ministers for the Church,
all the clergy,
and the entire people you have gained for your own.
Listen graciously to the prayers of this family . . .

d) If the proper Preface is not used, Eucharistic Prayer IV may be said; in its intercession, after the words to the praise of your glory, the following is said:

Therefore, Lord, remember now
all for whom we offer this sacrifice:
especially your servant N. our Pope,
and N. our Bishop,
with the whole Order of Bishops,
these your servants,
whom today you have been pleased to choose
for the diaconal service of your people,
and all the clergy.
Be mindful also of those who take part in this offering,
those gathered here before you,
your entire people,
and all who seek you with a sincere heart.
Remember also
those who have died in the peace of your Christ . . .

Communion Antiphon   Mt 20: 28

The Son of Man did not come to be served but to serve
and to give his life as a ransom for many (E.T. alleluia).

Prayer after Communion

Grant, O Lord, to your servants,
whom you have replenished with heavenly food and drink,
that, for the sake of your glory and the salvation of believers,
they may be found faithful
as ministers of the Gospel, of the Sacraments and of charity.
Through Christ our Lord.

Solemn Blessing at the End of Mass

The Bishop, with hands extended over the newly ordained Deacons and the people, says:

May God, who has called you to the service of others in his Church,
give you great zeal for all,
especially the afflicted and the poor.
R. Amen.

May he, who has entrusted you with preaching the Gospel of Christ,
help you, as you live according to his word,
to be its sincere and fervent witnesses.
R. Amen.

May he, who has appointed you stewards of his mysteries,
make you imitators of his Son, Jesus Christ,
and ministers of unity and peace in the world.
R. Amen.

And he blesses all the people, adding:

And may almighty God bless all of you, who are gathered here,
the Father, ✠ and the Son, ✠ and the Holy ✠ Spirit.
R. Amen.

B
For the Ordination of One Deacon

Entrance Antiphon
Jn 12: 26

Whoever serves me must follow me,
and where I am, there also will my servant be (E.T. alleluia).

The Gloria in excelsis (Glory to God in the highest) is said.

Collect
O God, who have taught the ministers of your Church
to seek not to be served
but to serve their brothers and sisters,
grant, we pray, that this your servant,
whom you graciously choose today for the office of Deacon,
may be effective in action, gentle in ministry,
and constant in prayer.
Through our Lord Jesus Christ, your Son,
who lives and reigns with you in the unity of the Holy Spirit,
one God, for ever and ever.

The Creed is said in accordance with the rubrics; the Universal Prayer is omitted.

Prayer over the Offerings
Holy Father, whose Son chose to wash the disciples' feet
and so set us an example,
accept, we pray, the oblations of our service,
and grant that, offering ourselves as a spiritual sacrifice,
we may be filled with a spirit of humility and zeal.
Through Christ our Lord.

Preface: Christ, source of all ministry in the Church.

℣. **The Lord be with you.**
℟. And with your spirit.

℣. **Lift up your hearts.**
℟. We lift them up to the Lord.

℣. **Let us give thanks to the Lord our God.**
℟. It is right and just.

It is truly right and just, our duty and our salvation,
always and everywhere to give you thanks,
Lord, holy Father, almighty and eternal God.

For by the anointing of the Holy Spirit
you made your Only Begotten Son
High Priest of the new and eternal covenant,
and by your wondrous design were pleased to decree
that many ministries be exercised in the Church.

For Christ not only adorns with a royal priesthood
the people he has made his own,
but with a brother's kindness he also chooses men
to become sharers in his sacred ministry
through the laying on of hands.

He chooses them to lead your holy people in charity,
to nourish them with the word
and strengthen them with the Sacraments.

As they give up their lives for you
and for the salvation of their brothers and sisters,
they strive to be conformed to the image of Christ himself
and offer you a constant witness of faith and love.

And so, Lord, with all the Angels and Saints,
we, too, give you thanks, as in exultation we acclaim:

Holy, Holy, Holy Lord God of hosts . . .

Text with music, pp. 1162-1163.

Mention of the newly ordained Deacon in the Eucharistic Prayers is made according to the following formulas:

a) In Eucharistic Prayer I, the proper form of the Hanc igitur (Therefore, Lord, we pray) *is said:*

Therefore, Lord, we pray:
graciously accept this oblation of our service,
that of your whole family,
which we make to you
also for your servant
whom you have been pleased to raise
to the Order of the Diaconate;
and in your mercy, keep safe your gifts in him,
so that what he has received by divine commission
he may fulfill by divine assistance.
(Through Christ our Lord. Amen.)

b) In Eucharistic Prayer II, after the words we may be gathered into one by the Holy Spirit, *the following is said:*

Remember, Lord, your Church,
spread throughout the world,
and bring her to the fullness of charity,
together with N. our Pope
and N. our Bishop.
Be mindful also of this your servant,
whom you have willed to provide today
as a minister for the Church,
and all the clergy.
Remember also our brothers and sisters . . .

c) In Eucharistic Prayer III, after the words advance the peace and salvation of all the world, *the following is said:*

Be pleased to confirm in faith and charity
your pilgrim Church on earth,
with your servant N. our Pope
and N. our Bishop,
with the Order of Bishops,
this your servant,
who has been ordained today as a minister for the Church,
all the clergy,
and the entire people you have gained for your own.
Listen graciously to the prayers of this family . . .

d) If the proper Preface is not used, Eucharistic Prayer IV may be said; in its intercession, after the words to the praise of your glory, the following is said:

**Therefore, Lord, remember now
all for whom we offer this sacrifice:
especially your servant N. our Pope,
and N. our Bishop,
with the whole Order of Bishops,
this your servant,
whom today you have been pleased to choose
for the diaconal service of your people,
and all the clergy.
Be mindful also of those who take part in this offering,
those gathered here before you,
your entire people,
and all who seek you with a sincere heart.
Remember also
those who have died in the peace of your Christ . . .**

Communion Antiphon   Mt 20: 28

The Son of Man did not come to be served but to serve
and to give his life as a ransom for many (E.T. alleluia).

Prayer after Communion

**Grant, O Lord, to your servant,
whom you have replenished with heavenly food and drink,
that, for the sake of your glory and the salvation of believers,
he may be found faithful
as a minister of the Gospel, of the Sacraments and of charity.
Through Christ our Lord.**

Solemn Blessing at the End of Mass

The Bishop, with hands extended over the newly ordained Deacon and the people, says:

**May God, who has called you to the service of others in his Church,
give you great zeal for all,
especially the afflicted and the poor.**

R. Amen.

**May he, who has entrusted you with preaching the Gospel of Christ,
help you, as you live according to his word,
to be its sincere and fervent witness.**

R. Amen.

**May he, who has appointed you a steward of his mysteries,
make you an imitator of his Son, Jesus Christ,
and a minister of unity and peace in the world.**

R. Amen.

And he blesses all the people, adding:

**And may almighty God bless all of you, who are gathered here,
the Father, ✠ and the Son, ✠ and the Holy ✠ Spirit.**

R. Amen.

4. FOR THE ORDINATION OF DEACONS AND PRIESTS IN THE SAME CELEBRATION

In the Ordination of Deacons and Priests to be conferred in the same liturgical celebration, this Ritual Mass may be used, with the color white or a festive color, except on Solemnities, on the Sundays of Advent, Lent, and Easter, and on days within the Octave of Easter. When these days occur, the Mass of the day is said.

Entrance Antiphon
Jn 12: 26

Whoever serves me must follow me,
and where I am, there also will my servant be (E.T. alleluia).

The Gloria in excelsis (Glory to God in the highest) is said.

Collect

O God, who have willed to provide
shepherds for your people,
pour out a spirit of reverence
and fortitude in your Church,
to make these your servants worthy ministers at your altar
and ardent yet gentle heralds of your Gospel.
Through our Lord Jesus Christ, your Son,
who lives and reigns with you in the unity of the Holy Spirit,
one God, for ever and ever.

<small>The Creed is said in accordance with the rubrics; the Universal Prayer is omitted.</small>

Prayer over the Offerings

Holy Father, whose Son chose to wash the disciples' feet
and so set us an example,
accept, we pray, the oblations of our service,
and grant that, offering ourselves as a spiritual sacrifice,
we may be filled with a spirit of humility and zeal.
Through Christ our Lord.

<small>The Preface *Christ, source of all ministry in the Church* (p. 1169) is said.</small>

<small>Mention of the newly ordained in the Eucharistic Prayers is made according to the following formulas:</small>

<small>a) In Eucharistic Prayer I, the proper form of the *Hanc igitur* (Therefore, Lord, we pray) is said:</small>

Therefore, Lord, we pray:
graciously accept this oblation of our service,
that of your whole family,
which we make to you
also for these your servants,
whom you have been pleased to raise
to the Orders of the Diaconate and of the Priesthood;
and in your mercy, keep safe your gifts in them,
so that what they have received by divine commission
they may fulfill by divine assistance.
(Through Christ our Lord. Amen.)

b) In Eucharistic Prayer II, after the words we may be gathered into one by the Holy Spirit, the following is said:

Remember, Lord, your Church,
spread throughout the world,
and bring her to the fullness of charity,
together with N. our Pope
and N. our Bishop.
Be mindful also of these your servants,
whom you have willed to provide today
as Deacons and Priests for the Church,
and all the clergy.
Remember also our brothers and sisters . . .

c) In Eucharistic Prayer III, after the words advance the peace and salvation of all the world, the following is said:

Be pleased to confirm in faith and charity
your pilgrim Church on earth,
with your servant N. our Pope
and N. our Bishop,
with the Order of Bishops,
these your servants,
who have been ordained today
as Deacons and Priests for the Church,
all the clergy,
and the entire people you have gained for your own.
Listen graciously to the prayers of this family . . .

d) If the proper Preface is not used, Eucharistic Prayer IV may be said; in its intercession, after the words *to the praise of your glory*, the following is said:

> Therefore, Lord, remember now
> all for whom we offer this sacrifice:
> especially your servant N. our Pope,
> and N. our Bishop,
> with the whole Order of Bishops,
> these your servants,
> whom today you have been pleased to choose
> for the diaconal and priestly service of your people,
> and all the clergy.
> Be mindful also of those who take part in this offering,
> those gathered here before you,
> your entire people,
> and all who seek you with a sincere heart.
> Remember also
> those who have died in the peace of your Christ . . .

Communion Antiphon
Jn 17: 17-18

> Holy Father, consecrate them in the truth.
> As you sent me into the world,
> so I sent them into the world, says the Lord (E.T. alleluia).

Prayer after Communion

> Grant, O Lord, to your servants,
> whom you have replenished with heavenly food and drink,
> that, for the sake of your glory and the salvation of believers,
> they may be found faithful
> as ministers of the Gospel, of the Sacraments and of charity.
> Through Christ our Lord.

Solemn Blessing at the End of Mass

The Bishop, with hands extended over the newly ordained Priests and Deacons, says:

May God, who founded the Church and guides her still,
protect you constantly with his grace,
that you may faithfully discharge your duties.

℟. Amen.

May he, who has entrusted Deacons
with preaching the Gospel
and of serving both altar and people,
make you fervent witnesses to the Gospel
and ministers of charity in the world.

℟. Amen.

May he make you who are Priests true shepherds
to provide the living Bread and word of life to the faithful,
that they may continue to grow in the unity of the Body of Christ.

℟. Amen.

And he blesses all the people, adding:

And may almighty God bless all of you, who are gathered here,
the Father, ✠ and the Son, ✠ and the Holy ✠ Spirit.

℟. Amen.

V. FOR THE CELEBRATION OF MARRIAGE

Whenever Marriage is celebrated during Mass, this Ritual Mass is used, with the color white or a festive color.

However, on those days listed in nos. 1-4 of the Table of Liturgical Days, the Mass of the day is used, retaining the Nuptial Blessing in the Mass and, if appropriate, the proper formula for the final blessing.

If, however, during Christmas Time and Ordinary Time, the parish community participates in a Sunday Mass during which Marriage is celebrated, the Mass of the Sunday is used.

Although complete Mass formularies are given here for the sake of convenience, all texts, especially the prayers and the Nuptial Blessing, may be exchanged, if appropriate, with others.

A

Entrance Antiphon
Cf. Ps 20 (19): 3, 5

> May the Lord send you help from the holy place
> and give you support from Sion.
> May he grant you your hearts' desire
> and fulfill every one of your designs (E.T. alleluia).

The Penitential Act is omitted. The Gloria in excelsis (Glory to God in the highest) is said.

Collect

> Be attentive to our prayers, O Lord,
> and in your kindness uphold
> what you have established for the increase of the human race,
> so that the union you have created
> may be kept safe by your assistance.
> Through our Lord Jesus Christ, your Son,
> who lives and reigns with you in the unity of the Holy Spirit,
> one God, for ever and ever.

Or:

> O God, who in creating the human race
> willed that man and wife should be one,
> join, we pray, in a bond of inseparable love
> these your servants who are to be united in the covenant of Marriage,
> so that, as you make their love fruitful,
> they may become, by your grace, witnesses to charity itself.
> Through our Lord Jesus Christ, your Son,
> who lives and reigns with you in the unity of the Holy Spirit,
> one God, for ever and ever.

Prayer over the Offerings

Receive, we pray, O Lord,
the offering made on the occasion
of this sealing of the sacred bond of Marriage,
and, just as your goodness is its origin,
may your providence guide its course.
Through Christ our Lord.

Preface: The dignity of the marriage covenant.

V. The Lord be with you.   R. And with your spir-it.

V. Lift up your hearts.   R. We lift them up to the Lord.

V. Let us give thanks to the Lord our God.   R. It is right and just.

It is truly right and just, our duty and our sal-va-tion, al-ways and everywhere to give you thanks, Lord, holy Father, almighty and e- -ter-nal God. For you have forged the covenant of marriage as a sweet yoke of har-mo-ny and an unbreakable bond of peace, so that the chaste and fruitful love of ho-ly Mat-rimony may serve to increase the children you a-dopt as your own. By your providence and grace, O Lord, you accomplish the wonder of this two-fold de-sign: that, while the birth of children brings beauty to the world,

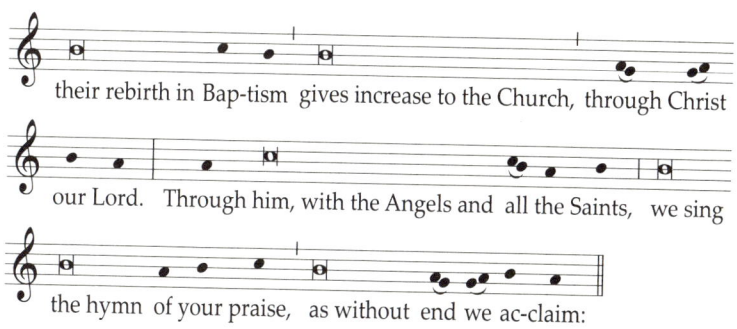

Holy, Holy, Holy Lord God of hosts . . .

Text without music:

℣. **The Lord be with you.**
℟. And with your spirit.

℣. **Lift up your hearts.**
℟. We lift them up to the Lord.

℣. **Let us give thanks to the Lord our God.**
℟. It is right and just.

It is truly right and just, our duty and our salvation,
always and everywhere to give you thanks,
Lord, holy Father, almighty and eternal God.

For you have forged the covenant of marriage
as a sweet yoke of harmony
and an unbreakable bond of peace,
so that the chaste and fruitful love of holy Matrimony
may serve to increase the children you adopt as your own.

By your providence and grace, O Lord,
you accomplish the wonder of this twofold design:
that, while the birth of children brings beauty to the world,
their rebirth in Baptism gives increase to the Church,
through Christ our Lord.

Through him, with the Angels and all the Saints,
we sing the hymn of your praise,
as without end we acclaim:

Holy, Holy, Holy Lord God of hosts . . .

A commemoration of the husband and wife in the Eucharistic Prayers is made according to the following formulas:

a) In Eucharistic Prayer I, the proper form of the Hanc igitur (Therefore, Lord, we pray) is said. The words in parentheses may be omitted, if the occasion so suggests:

Therefore, Lord, we pray:
graciously accept this oblation of our service,
the offering of your servants N. and N.
and of your whole family,
who entreat your majesty on their behalf;
and as you have brought them to their wedding day,
so (gladden them with your gift of the children they desire and)
bring them in your kindness
to the length of days for which they hope.
(Through Christ our Lord. Amen.)

b) In Eucharistic Prayer II, after the words and all the clergy, the following is added:

Be mindful also, Lord, of N. and N.,
whom you have brought to their wedding day,
so that by your grace
they may abide in mutual love and in peace.

c) In Eucharistic Prayer III, after the words whom you have summoned before you, the following is added:

Strengthen, we pray, in the grace of Marriage N. and N.,
whom you have brought happily to their wedding day,
that under your protection
they may always be faithful in their lives
to the covenant they have sealed in your presence.
In your compassion, O merciful Father,
gather to yourself all your children
scattered throughout the world.
To our departed brothers and sisters . . .

Nuptial Blessing

After the Our Father, the prayer Deliver us is omitted. The Priest, standing and facing the bride and bridegroom, invokes upon them God's blessing, and this is never omitted.

In the invitation, if one or both of the spouses will not be receiving Communion, the words in parentheses are omitted. In the prayer, the words in parentheses may be omitted if it seems that circumstances suggest it, for example, if the bride and bridegroom are advanced in years.

The bride and bridegroom approach the altar or, if appropriate, they remain at their place and kneel.

The Priest, with hands joined, calls upon those present to pray, saying:

Dear brothers and sisters,
let us humbly pray to the Lord
that on these his servants, now married in Christ,
he may mercifully pour out
the blessing of his grace
and make of one heart in love
(by the Sacrament of Christ's Body and Blood)
those he has joined by a holy covenant.

And all pray in silence for a while.

Then the Priest, with hands extended over the bride and bridegroom, continues:

O God, who by your mighty power
created all things out of nothing,
and, when you had set in place
the beginnings of the universe,
formed man and woman in your own image,
making the woman an inseparable helpmate to the man,
that they might no longer be two, but one flesh,
and taught that what you were pleased to make one
must never be divided;

O God, who consecrated the bond of Marriage
by so great a mystery
that in the wedding covenant you foreshadowed
the Sacrament of Christ and his Church;

O God, by whom woman is joined to man
and the companionship they had in the beginning
is endowed with the one blessing
not forfeited by original sin
nor washed away by the flood.

Look now with favor on these your servants,
joined together in Marriage,
who ask to be strengthened by your blessing.
Send down on them the grace of the Holy Spirit
and pour your love into their hearts,
that they may remain faithful in the Marriage covenant.

May the grace of love and peace
abide in your daughter N.,
and let her always follow the example of those holy women
whose praises are sung in the Scriptures.
May her husband entrust his heart to her,
so that, acknowledging her as his equal
and his joint heir to the life of grace,
he may show her due honor
and cherish her always
with the love that Christ has for his Church.

And now, Lord, we implore you:
may these your servants
hold fast to the faith and keep your commandments;
made one in the flesh,
may they be blameless in all they do;
and with the strength that comes from the Gospel,
may they bear true witness to Christ before all;
(may they be blessed with children,
and prove themselves virtuous parents,
who live to see their children's children).

And grant that,
reaching at last together the fullness of years
for which they hope,
they may come to the life of the blessed
in the Kingdom of Heaven.
Through Christ our Lord.
R. Amen.

The prayer Lord Jesus Christ is omitted, and The peace of the Lord is said immediately.

Then the bride and bridegroom and all present offer one another a sign, in keeping with local customs, that expresses peace, communion and charity.

Communion Antiphon

Cf. Eph 5: 25, 27

Christ loved the Church and handed himself over for her,
to present her as a holy and spotless bride for himself (E.T. alleluia).

Prayer after Communion

By the power of this sacrifice, O Lord,
accompany with your loving favor
what in your providence you have instituted,
so as to make of one heart in love
those you have already joined in this holy union
(and replenished with the one Bread and the one Chalice).
Through Christ our Lord.

Solemn Blessing at the End of Mass

The Priest, with hands extended over the bride and bridegroom, says:

May God the eternal Father
keep you of one heart in love for one another,
that the peace of Christ may dwell in you
and abide always in your home.
R. Amen.

May you be blessed in your children,
have solace in your friends
and enjoy true peace with everyone.
R. Amen.

May you be witnesses in the world to God's charity,
so that the afflicted and needy who have known your kindness
may one day receive you thankfully
into the eternal dwelling of God.
R. Amen.

And he blesses all the people, adding:

And may almighty God bless all of you, who are gathered here,
the Father, and the Son, ✠ and the Holy Spirit.
R. Amen.

B

Entrance Antiphon
Cf. Ps 90 (89): 14, 17

At dawn, O Lord, fill us with your merciful love,
and we shall exult and rejoice all our days.
Let the favor of the Lord our God be upon us
and upon the work of our hands (E.T. alleluia).

The Penitential Act is omitted. The Gloria in excelsis (Glory to God in the highest) is said.

Collect

Be attentive to our prayers, O Lord,
and in your kindness
pour out your grace on these your servants (N. and N.),
that, coming together before your altar,
they may be confirmed in love for one another.
Through our Lord Jesus Christ, your Son,
who lives and reigns with you in the unity of the Holy Spirit,
one God, for ever and ever.

Or:

O God, who consecrated the bond of Marriage
by so great a mystery
that in the wedding covenant you foreshadow
the Sacrament of Christ and his Church,
grant, we pray, to these your servants,
that what they receive in faith
they may live out in deeds.
Through our Lord Jesus Christ, your Son,
who lives and reigns with you in the unity of the Holy Spirit,
one God, for ever and ever.

Prayer over the Offerings

Receive in your kindness, Lord,
the offerings we bring in gladness before you,
and in your fatherly love
watch over those you have joined in a sacramental covenant.
Through Christ our Lord.

Preface: The great Sacrament of Matrimony.

V. The Lord be with you. R. And with your spir-it.

V. Lift up your hearts. R. We lift them up to the Lord.

V. Let us give thanks to the Lord our God. R. It is right and just.

FOR THE CELEBRATION OF MARRIAGE

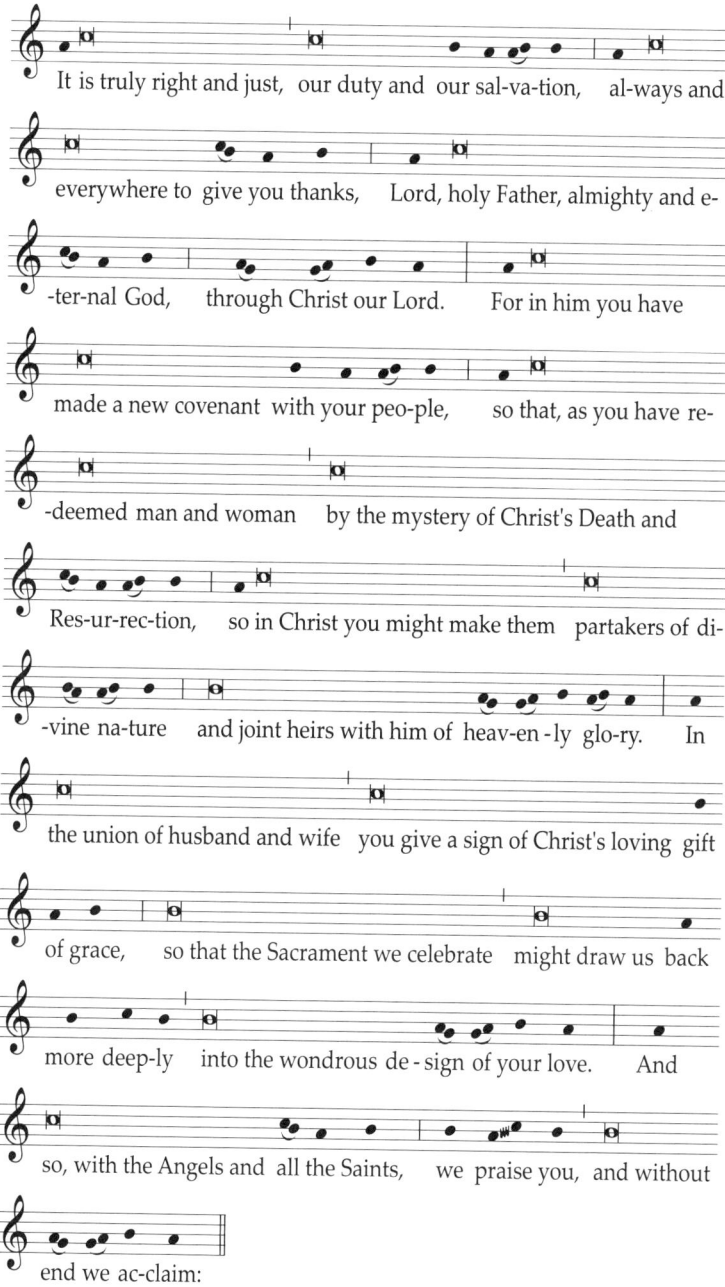

It is truly right and just, our duty and our salvation, always and everywhere to give you thanks, Lord, holy Father, almighty and eternal God, through Christ our Lord. For in him you have made a new covenant with your people, so that, as you have redeemed man and woman by the mystery of Christ's Death and Resurrection, so in Christ you might make them partakers of divine nature and joint heirs with him of heavenly glory. In the union of husband and wife you give a sign of Christ's loving gift of grace, so that the Sacrament we celebrate might draw us back more deeply into the wondrous design of your love. And so, with the Angels and all the Saints, we praise you, and without end we acclaim:

Holy, Holy, Holy Lord God of hosts . . .

Text without music:
V. The Lord be with you.
R. And with your spirit.

V. Lift up your hearts.
R. We lift them up to the Lord.

V. Let us give thanks to the Lord our God.
R. It is right and just.

It is truly right and just, our duty and our salvation,
always and everywhere to give you thanks,
Lord, holy Father, almighty and eternal God,
through Christ our Lord.

For in him you have made a new covenant with your people,
so that, as you have redeemed man and woman
by the mystery of Christ's Death and Resurrection,
so in Christ you might make them partakers of divine nature
and joint heirs with him of heavenly glory.

In the union of husband and wife
you give a sign of Christ's loving gift of grace,
so that the Sacrament we celebrate
might draw us back more deeply
into the wondrous design of your love.

And so, with the Angels and all the Saints,
we praise you, and without end we acclaim:

Holy, Holy, Holy Lord God of hosts . . .

In the Eucharistic Prayers there are proper intercessions (pp. 1127-1128).

Nuptial Blessing

After the Our Father, the prayer Deliver us is omitted. The Priest, standing and facing the bride and bridegroom, invokes upon them God's blessing, and this is never omitted.

In the invitation, if one or both of the spouses will not be receiving Communion, the words in parentheses are omitted. In the prayer, the words in parentheses may be omitted if it seems that circumstances suggest it, for example, if the bride and bridegroom are advanced in years.

The bride and bridegroom approach the altar or, if appropriate, they remain at their place and kneel.

The Priest, with hands joined, calls upon those present to pray, saying:

Let us pray to the Lord for this bride and groom,
who come to the altar as they begin their married life,
that (partaking of the Body and Blood of Christ)
they may always be bound together by love for one another.

And all pray in silence for a while.

Then the Priest, with hands extended over the bride and bridegroom, continues:

Holy Father,
who formed man in your own image,
male and female you created them,
so that as husband and wife, united in body and heart,
they might fulfill their calling in the world;

O God, who, to reveal the great design you formed in your love,
willed that the love of spouses for each other
should foreshadow the covenant you graciously made with
    your people,
so that, by fulfillment of the sacramental sign,
the mystical marriage of Christ with his Church
might become manifest
in the union of husband and wife among your faithful;

Graciously stretch out your right hand
over these your servants (N. and N.), we pray,
and pour into their hearts the power of the Holy Spirit.

Grant, O Lord,
that, as they enter upon this sacramental union,
they may share with one another the gifts of your love
and, by being for each other a sign of your presence,
become one heart and one mind.

May they also sustain, O Lord, by their deeds
the home they are forming
(and prepare their children
to become members of your heavenly household
by raising them in the way of the Gospel).

Graciously crown with your blessings your daughter N.,
so that, by being a good wife (and mother),
she may bring warmth to her home with a love that is pure
and adorn it with welcoming graciousness.

Bestow a heavenly blessing also, O Lord,
on N., your servant,
that he may be a worthy, good and
faithful husband (and a provident father).

Grant, holy Father, that, desiring to approach your table
as a couple joined in Marriage in your presence,
they may one day have the joy
of taking part in your great banquet in heaven.
Through Christ our Lord.
R. Amen.

The prayer Lord Jesus Christ *is omitted, and* The peace of the Lord *is said immediately. Then the bride and bridegroom and all present offer a sign, in keeping with local customs, that expresses peace, communion and charity.*

Communion Antiphon

Jn 13: 34

I give you a new commandment, that you love one another
as I have loved you, says the Lord (E.T. alleluia).

Prayer after Communion

Having been made partakers at your table,
we pray, O Lord,
that those who are united by the Sacrament of Marriage
may always hold fast to you
and proclaim your name to the world.
Through Christ our Lord.

Solemn Blessing at the End of Mass

The Priest, with hands extended over the bride and bridegroom, says:

May God the all-powerful Father grant you his joy
and bless you in your children.
R. Amen.

May the Only Begotten Son of God
stand by you with compassion in good times and in bad.
R. Amen.

May the Holy Spirit of God
always pour forth his love into your hearts.
R. Amen.

And he blesses all the people, adding:

And may almighty God bless all of you, who are gathered here,
the Father, and the Son, ✠ and the Holy Spirit.
R. Amen.

C

Entrance Antiphon Cf. Ps 145 (144): 2, 9

I will bless you day after day, O Lord,
and praise your name for ever and ever,
for you are kind to all
and compassionate to all your creatures (E.T. alleluia).

The Penitential Act is omitted. The Gloria in excelsis *(Glory to God in the highest) is said.*

Collect

Grant, we pray, almighty God,
that these your servants,
now to be joined by the Sacrament of Matrimony,
may grow in the faith they profess
and enrich your Church with faithful offspring.
Through our Lord Jesus Christ, your Son,
who lives and reigns with you in the unity of the Holy Spirit,
one God, for ever and ever.

Or:

O God, who since the beginning of the world
have blessed the increase of offspring,
show favor to our supplications
and pour forth the help of your blessing
on these your servants (**N.** and **N.**),
so that in the union of Marriage
they may be bound together
in mutual affection,
in likeness of mind,
and in shared holiness.
Through our Lord Jesus Christ, your Son,
who lives and reigns with you in the unity of the Holy Spirit,
one God, for ever and ever.

Prayer over the Offerings

Show favor to our supplications, O Lord,
and receive with a kindly countenance
the oblations we offer for these your servants,
joined now in a holy covenant,
that through these mysteries
they may be strengthened in love for one another and for you.
Through Christ our Lord.

Preface: Matrimony as a sign of divine love.

V. The Lord be with you.   R. And with your spirit.

V. Lift up your hearts.   R. We lift them up to the Lord.

V. Let us give thanks to the Lord our God.   R. It is right and just.

It is truly right and just, our duty and our salvation, always and everywhere to give you thanks, Lord, holy Father, almighty and eternal God. For you willed that the human race, created by the gift of your goodness, should be raised to such high dignity that in the union of husband and wife you might bestow a true image of your love. For those you created out of charity you call to the law of charity without ceasing and grant them a share in your eternal charity. And so, the Sacrament of holy Matrimony, as the abiding sign of your own love, consecrates the love of man

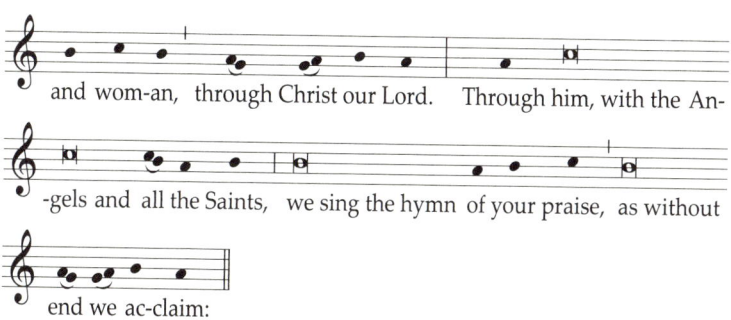

and wom-an, through Christ our Lord. Through him, with the An-gels and all the Saints, we sing the hymn of your praise, as without end we ac-claim:

Holy, Holy, Holy Lord God of hosts . . .

Text without music:

V. **The Lord be with you.**
R. And with your spirit.

V. **Lift up your hearts.**
R. We lift them up to the Lord.

V. **Let us give thanks to the Lord our God.**
R. It is right and just.

It is truly right and just, our duty and our salvation,
always and everywhere to give you thanks,
Lord, holy Father, almighty and eternal God.

For you willed that the human race,
created by the gift of your goodness,
should be raised to such high dignity
that in the union of husband and wife
you might bestow a true image of your love.

For those you created out of charity
you call to the law of charity without ceasing
and grant them a share in your eternal charity.

And so, the Sacrament of holy Matrimony,
as the abiding sign of your own love,
consecrates the love of man and woman,
through Christ our Lord.

Through him, with the Angels and all the Saints,
we sing the hymn of your praise,
as without end we acclaim:

Holy, Holy, Holy Lord God of hosts . . .

In the Eucharistic Prayers there are proper intercessions (pp. 1127-1128).

Nuptial Blessing

After the Our Father, the prayer Deliver us is omitted. The Priest, standing and facing the bride and bridegroom, invokes upon them God's blessing, and this is never omitted.

In the invitation, if one or both of the spouses will not be receiving Communion, the words in parentheses are omitted. In the prayer, the words in parentheses may be omitted if it seems that circumstances suggest it, for example, if the bride and bridegroom are advanced in years.

The bride and bridegroom approach the altar or, if appropriate, they remain at their place and kneel.

The Priest, with hands joined, calls upon those present to pray, saying:

Let us humbly invoke by our prayers, dear brothers and sisters, God's blessing upon this bride and groom, that in his kindness he may favor with his help those on whom he has bestowed the Sacrament of Matrimony.

All pray in silence for a while.

Then the Priest, with hands extended over the bride and bridegroom, continues:

Holy Father, maker of the whole world, who created man and woman in your own image and willed that their union be crowned with your blessing, we humbly beseech you for these your servants, who are joined today in the Sacrament of Matrimony.

May your abundant blessing, Lord, come down upon this bride, N., and upon N., her companion for life, and may the power of your Holy Spirit set their hearts aflame from on high, so that, living out together the gift of Matrimony, they may (adorn their family with children and) enrich the Church.

In happiness may they praise you, O Lord,
in sorrow may they seek you out;
may they have the joy of your presence
to assist them in their toil,
and know that you are near
to comfort them in their need;
let them pray to you in the holy assembly
and bear witness to you in the world,
and after a happy old age,
together with the circle of friends that surrounds them,
may they come to the Kingdom of Heaven.
Through Christ our Lord.
R. Amen.

The prayer Lord Jesus Christ is omitted and The peace of the Lord is said immediately.

Then the bride and bridegroom and all present offer one another a sign, in keeping with local customs, that expresses peace, communion and charity.

Communion Antiphon   Ps 34 (33): 2, 9

I will bless the Lord at all times,
praise of him is always in my mouth.
Taste and see that the Lord is good;
blessed the man who seeks refuge in him (E.T. alleluia).

Prayer after Communion

Grant, we pray, almighty God,
that the power of the Sacrament we have received
may find growth in these your servants
and that the effects of the sacrifice we have offered
may be felt by us all.
Through Christ our Lord.

Solemn Blessing at the End of Mass

The Priest, with hands extended over the bride and bridegroom, says:

**May the Lord Jesus,
who graced the marriage at Cana by his presence,
bless you and your loved ones.**
R. Amen.

**May he, who loved the Church to the end,
unceasingly pour his love into your hearts.**
R. Amen.

**May the Lord grant
that, bearing witness to faith in his Resurrection,
you may await with joy the blessed hope to come.**
R. Amen.

And he blesses all the people, adding:

**And may almighty God bless all of you, who are gathered here,
the Father, and the Son, ✠ and the Holy Spirit.**
R. Amen.

Masses for the Anniversaries of Marriage are found among the Masses for Various Needs (pp. 1259-1261).

VI. FOR THE BLESSING OF AN ABBOT OR AN ABBESS

This Mass may be used, with the color white or a festive color, on days when Ritual Masses are permitted.

1

For the Blessing of an Abbot

Entrance Antiphon Cf. Jn 15: 16

It was not you who chose me, says the Lord,
but I who chose you and appointed you to go and bear fruit,
fruit that will last (E.T. alleluia).

Or: Cf. Col 3: 14-15

And over all things put on love,
which is the bond of perfection,
and let the peace of Christ rule in your hearts (E.T. alleluia).

The Gloria in excelsis (Glory to God in the highest) is said.

Collect

Grant, we pray, O Lord, to your servant N.,
whom you have chosen as Abbot of this community of N.,
that by his deeds and his teaching
he may guide the hearts of his brothers
toward those things that are right,
and so receive joyfully with them
the recompense of an eternal reward
from you, the most loving Shepherd.
Through our Lord Jesus Christ, your Son,
who lives and reigns with you in the unity of the Holy Spirit,
one God, for ever and ever.

The Creed is said in accordance with the rubrics; the Universal Prayer is omitted.

Prayer over the Offerings

Receive, we pray, O Lord, the oblation of your servants
and grant that, offering themselves as a spiritual sacrifice,
they may constantly be filled
with true humility, with obedience and with peace.
Through Christ our Lord.

The Preface of Religious Life (pp. 1210-1212) may be said.

Mention of the newly blessed Abbot in the Eucharistic Prayers is made according to the following formulas:

a) In Eucharistic Prayer I, the proper form of the Hanc igitur (Therefore, Lord, we pray) is said.

Therefore, Lord, we pray:
graciously accept this oblation of our service,
that of your whole family,
which we make to you
also for your servant N.,
whom you have been pleased to choose
for the governance of this community;
and in your mercy, keep safe your gifts in him,
so that what he has received by your grace
may strengthen the hearts of his brothers.
(Through Christ our Lord. Amen.)

b) In Eucharistic Prayer II, after the words we may be gathered into one by the Holy Spirit, the following is said:

Remember, Lord, your Church,
spread throughout the world,
and bring her to the fullness of charity,
together with N. our Pope and N. our Bishop.
Be mindful also of this your servant,
whom you have willed to provide today
as Abbot for this community,
and all the clergy.
Remember also our brothers and sisters . . .

c) In Eucharistic Prayer III, after the words advance the peace and salvation of all the world, the following is said:

**Be pleased to confirm in faith and charity
your pilgrim Church on earth,
with your servant N. our Pope and N. our Bishop,
the Order of Bishops,
this your servant N.,
who today has been chosen as Abbot of this community,
all the clergy,
and the entire people you have gained for your own.
Listen graciously to the prayers of this family . . .**

d) If the proper Preface is not used, Eucharistic Prayer IV may be said; in its intercession, after the words to the praise of your glory, the following is said:

**Therefore, Lord, remember now
all for whom we offer this sacrifice:
especially your servant N. our Pope,
and N. our Bishop,
with the whole Order of Bishops,
and this your servant N.,
whom today you have been pleased to choose
for the service of this community,
and all the clergy.
Be mindful also of those who take part in this offering,
those gathered here before you,
your entire people,
and all who seek you with a sincere heart.
Remember also
those who have died in the peace of your Christ . . .**

Communion Antiphon   Mt 20: 28

The Son of Man did not come to be served but to serve
and to give his life as a ransom for many (E.T. alleluia).

Or:

Where true charity is dwelling, God is present there.
By the love of Christ we have been brought together (E.T. alleluia).

Prayer after Communion

> Look with favor on your family, Lord,
> and grant that we, who have celebrated the mystery of faith,
> may hasten tirelessly along the path of the Gospel,
> glorifying you in all things.
> Through Christ our Lord.

Solemn Blessing at the End of Mass

The Prelate, with hands extended over the newly blessed Abbot, says:

> May God, from whom all fatherhood takes its name,
> grant that you be strengthened with power in your inner self
> according to the riches of his glory.
> R. Amen.

> May God grant you to hasten in the way of his commands
> in company with your brothers,
> openheartedly and in the joy of Christ.
> R. Amen.

> By the grace of God,
> may this monastic family, gathered in the name of the Lord,
> come, with you as guide, to a heavenly way of life.
> R. Amen.

And the Prelate blesses all the people, adding:

> And may almighty God bless all of you, who are gathered here,
> the Father, ✠ and the Son, ✠ and the Holy ✠ Spirit.
> R. Amen.

If, however, the newly blessed Abbot presides at the Liturgy of the Eucharist, he imparts the blessing using the pontifical rite, or he may say the formula that follows, with his hands extended over the congregation:

> May God, the Father of mercy, keep you in his good favor,
> and, as he has chosen to set me as Abbot over you,
> so may he make us all companions in eternal happiness.
> R. Amen.

> May the Lord Jesus Christ grant you
> to hasten in the way of his commands,
> openheartedly and in brotherly joy.
> R. Amen.

May the Holy Spirit grant us all
to carry out with one accord the works of holiness and life,
that we may be imitators of our fathers,
one in mind and heart.
R. Amen.

And the Abbot blesses all the people, adding:

And may almighty God bless all of you, who are gathered here,
the Father, ✠ and the Son, ✠ and the Holy ✠ Spirit.
R. Amen.

2

For the Blessing of an Abbess

Entrance Antiphon
Cf. Jn 15: 16

It was not you who chose me, says the Lord,
but I who chose you and appointed you to go and bear fruit,
fruit that will last (E.T. alleluia).

Or:

Cf. Col 3: 14-15

And over all things put on love,
which is the bond of perfection,
and let the peace of Christ rule in your hearts (E.T. alleluia).

The Gloria in excelsis (Glory to God in the highest) is said.

Collect

Grant, we pray, O Lord, to your servant N.,
whom you have chosen as Abbess of this community of N.,
that by her deeds and her teaching
she may guide the hearts of her sisters
toward those things that are right,
and so receive joyfully with them
the recompense of an eternal reward
from you, the most loving Shepherd.
Through our Lord Jesus Christ, your Son,
who lives and reigns with you in the unity of the Holy Spirit,
one God, for ever and ever.

The Creed is said in accordance with the rubrics; the Universal Prayer is omitted.

Prayer over the Offerings
Receive, we pray, O Lord,
the oblation of your servants
and grant that, offering themselves as a spiritual sacrifice,
they may constantly be filled
with true humility, with obedience and with peace.
Through Christ our Lord.

The Preface of Religious Life (pp. 1210-1212) may be said.

The commemoration of the newly blessed Abbess in the Eucharistic Prayers takes place according to the following formulas:

a) In Eucharistic Prayer I, the proper form of the Hanc igitur (Therefore, Lord, we pray) is said:

Therefore, Lord, we pray:
graciously accept this oblation of our service,
that of your whole family,
which we make to you,
also for your servant N.,
whom you have been pleased to choose
for the governance of this community;
and in your mercy, keep safe your gifts in her,
so that what she has received by your grace
may strengthen the hearts of her sisters.
(Through Christ our Lord. Amen.)

b) In Eucharistic Prayer II, after the words and all the clergy, the following is said:

Be mindful also of this your servant,
whom you have willed to provide today
as Abbess of this community.
Remember also our brothers and sisters . . .

c) In Eucharistic Prayer III, after the words the entire people you have gained for your own, the following is said:

Strengthen also, Lord,
in the service of her sisters
this your servant,
who has been chosen today
as Abbess of this community.
Listen graciously to the prayers of this family . . .

FOR THE BLESSING OF AN ABBESS

d) *If the proper Preface is not used, Eucharistic Prayer IV may be said: in its intercession, after the words* to the praise of your glory, *the following is said:*

> Therefore, Lord, remember now
> all for whom we offer this sacrifice:
> especially your servant N. our Pope,
> and N. our Bishop,
> with the whole Order of Bishops,
> all the clergy,
> and this your servant N.,
> whom today you have been pleased to choose
> for the service of this community.
> Be mindful also of those who take part in this offering,
> those gathered here before you,
> your entire people,
> and all who seek you with a sincere heart.
> Remember also
> those who have died in the peace of your Christ …

Communion Antiphon
Mt 20: 28

The Son of Man did not come to be served but to serve
and to give his life as a ransom for many (E.T. alleluia).

Or:

Where true charity is dwelling, God is present there.
By the love of Christ we have been brought together (E.T. alleluia).

Prayer after Communion

> Look with favor on your family, Lord,
> and grant that we, who have celebrated the mystery of faith,
> may hasten tirelessly along the path of the Gospel,
> glorifying you in all things.
> Through Christ our Lord.

Solemn Blessing at the End of Mass

The Prelate, with hands extended over the newly blessed Abbess, says:

May God, who for the good of the Church
has united these servants in the love of his Son,
give you a spirit of devoted care
to direct the family entrusted to you
in the quest of perfection.
R. Amen.

May God grant you to hasten in the way of his commands
in company with your sisters,
openheartedly and in the joy of Christ.
R. Amen.

By the grace of God,
may this monastic family, gathered in the name of the Lord,
come, with you as guide, to a heavenly way of life.
R. Amen.

And he blesses all the people, adding:

And may almighty God bless all of you, who are gathered here,
the Father, ✠ and the Son, ✠ and the Holy ✠ Spirit.
R. Amen.

VII. FOR THE CONSECRATION OF VIRGINS

This Ritual Mass may be used, with the color white or a festive color, on days when Ritual Masses are permitted.
   The prayers should be adapted, with the necessary change to the singular, if only one virgin is to be consecrated.

Entrance Antiphon

Cf. Ps 105 (104): 4-5

Turn to the Lord and his strength;
constantly seek his face.
Remember the wonders he has done (E.T. alleluia).

The Gloria in excelsis (Glory to God in the highest) is said.

Collect

Grant, we pray, O Lord, to these your servants,
in whom you have instilled a resolve to live in virginity,
that the work you have begun in them
may be brought to fulfillment
and that they may be found worthy
to complete what they now begin,
so as to bring you a full and perfect offering.
Through our Lord Jesus Christ, your Son,
who lives and reigns with you in the unity of the Holy Spirit,
one God, for ever and ever.

The Creed is said in accordance with the rubrics; the Universal Prayer is omitted.

Prayer over the Offerings

As we offer sacrificial gifts, we pray, O Lord,
grant generously to these your servants
perseverance in the resolve they have made their own,
so that, when the doors are opened
at the coming of the most high King,
they may merit to enter with joy into the heavenly Kingdom.
Through Christ our Lord.

The Preface of Religious Life (pp. 1210-1212) may be said.

The commemoration of the consecrated virgins in the Eucharistic Prayers takes place according to the following formulas:

a) In Eucharistic Prayer I, the proper form of the Hanc igitur (Therefore, Lord, we pray) is said:

**Therefore, Lord, we pray:
graciously accept this oblation of our service,
and of these your servants,
which we make to you on their day of consecration;
sanctify this offering in your mercy,
so that they who by your gift
have today united themselves more closely to your Son
may hasten gladly to meet him
when he comes in glory at the end of time.
(Through Christ our Lord. Amen.)**

b) In the intercessions of Eucharistic Prayer II, after the words *and all the clergy*, the following is added:

**Be mindful also, Lord, of these sisters,
whom you have consecrated today by a spiritual anointing
so that, with lighted lamps of charity and faith,
they may constantly serve you and your people
as they await the advent of Christ the Bridegroom.
Remember also our brothers and sisters . . .**

c) In the intercessions of Eucharistic Prayer III, after the words *the entire people you have gained for your own*, the following is added:

**Strengthen in their holy resolve, O Lord,
these your servants,
who seek to follow your Christ in faithful devotion,
giving a witness of evangelical life
and of sisterly love.
Listen graciously to the prayers of this family . . .**

d) If the proper Preface is not used, Eucharistic Prayer IV may be said; in its intercession, after the words *to the praise of your glory*, mention of the consecrated may be inserted in this way:

**Therefore, Lord, remember now
all for whom we offer this sacrifice:
especially your servant N. our Pope
and N. our Bishop,
with the whole Order of Bishops,
and all the clergy.**

Be mindful also of these sisters,
whom you have dedicated today in perpetuity
to divine worship and the service of humanity,
those who take part in this offering,
those gathered here before you,
your entire people,
and all who seek you with a sincere heart.
Remember also
those who have died in the peace of your Christ . . .

Communion Antiphon

Ps 42 (41): 2

Like the deer that yearns for running streams,
so my soul is yearning for you, my God (E.T. alleluia).

Prayer after Communion

Replenished by these sacred gifts, O Lord,
we humbly pray
that the way of life chosen by your servants N. and N.
may constantly benefit the advancement of human society
and unceasingly profit the growth of the Church.
Through Christ our Lord.

Solemn Blessing at the End of Mass

The Bishop, with hands extended over the virgins newly consecrated to God, says:

May the almighty Father, by his protection,
keep intact the resolve he has poured into your hearts
to live in blessed virginity.

R. Amen.

May the Lord Jesus, who unites to himself
the hearts of sacred virgins in a nuptial covenant,
make your hearts fruitful by the word that is God's seed.

R. Amen.

May the Holy Spirit,
who came down upon the Blessed Virgin
and, descending today, has consecrated your hearts,
fire you with zeal for the service of God and the Church.

R. Amen.

And he blesses all the people, adding:

And may almighty God bless all of you,
who are gathered for these sacred rites,
the Father, ✠ and the Son, ✠ and the Holy ✠ Spirit.

R. Amen.

Or:

May God, who inspires and brings to completion every holy design,
guard you always with his grace,
that you may faithfully discharge the duties of your calling.

R. Amen.

May God make you partakers of divine charity
and its witness and sign before all nations.

R. Amen.

May God graciously make lasting in heaven
the bonds by which he has united you to Christ on earth.

R. Amen.

And he blesses all the people, adding:

And may almighty God bless all of you,
who are gathered for these sacred rites,
the Father, ✠ and the Son, ✠ and the Holy ✠ Spirit.

R. Amen.

VIII. FOR RELIGIOUS PROFESSION

The Masses on the day of first profession, on the day of perpetual profession, and on the day of the renewal of vows may be used, with the color white or a festive color, on days when Ritual Masses are permitted.

All the prayers given for a man may be adapted for a woman, with the necessary change of gender; in addition those expressed in the plural form, may be used for individuals, with a necessary change to the singular.

1. FOR FIRST RELIGIOUS PROFESSION

Entrance Antiphon *Cf. Ps 40 (39): 8-9*

Behold, I come, O Lord, that I may do your will.
O my God, I have vowed it,
and your law lies deep within me (E.T. alleluia).

The Gloria in excelsis (Glory to God in the highest) is said.

Collect

O Lord, who have inspired these our brothers (sisters)
with the resolve to follow Christ more closely,
grant them, we pray,
a blessed end to the journey they now begin,
so that they may be found worthy to offer you
a perfect gift of loving service.
Through our Lord Jesus Christ, your Son,
who lives and reigns with you in the unity of the Holy Spirit,
one God, for ever and ever.

Prayer over the Offerings

Receive, O Lord, we pray,
the oblations and prayers we offer you
as we celebrate the beginnings of religious profession,
and grant that the first fruits of your servants
may be transformed by your grace into a plentiful harvest.
Through Christ our Lord.

Proper Preface (pp. 1210-1212).

Communion Antiphon
Mk 3: 35

Whoever does the will of God
is my brother and sister and mother, says the Lord (E.T. alleluia).

Prayer after Communion

**May the mysteries we have received
fill us with joy, O Lord,
and grant that by their power
these your servants may faithfully fulfill
the duties of the religious life they have begun
and may offer you willing service.
Through Christ our Lord.**

2. FOR PERPETUAL PROFESSION

A

Entrance Antiphon
Cf. Ps 122 (121): 1-2

> I rejoiced when they said to me:
> Let us go to the house of the Lord.
> Now our feet are standing
> within your gates, O Jerusalem (E.T. alleluia).

The Gloria in excelsis (Glory to God in the highest) *is said.*

Collect

> O God, who willed that the grace of Baptism
> should flourish in these your servants,
> so that they might strive to follow more closely
> in the footsteps of your Son,
> grant, we pray,
> that, constantly seeking evangelical perfection,
> they may add to the holiness of your Church
> and increase her apostolic zeal.
> Through our Lord Jesus Christ, your Son,
> who lives and reigns with you in the unity of the Holy Spirit,
> one God, for ever and ever.

The Creed is said in accordance with the rubrics; the Universal Prayer is omitted.

Prayer over the Offerings

> Receive the gifts and intentions of your servants, O Lord,
> and confirm in your love
> those who profess the evangelical counsels.
> Through Christ our Lord.

Preface: Religious life as service of God through the imitation of Christ.

V. The Lord be with you.   R. And with your spir-it.

V. Lift up your hearts.   R. We lift them up to the Lord.

V. Let us give thanks to the Lord our God.   R. It is right and just.

It is truly right and just, our duty and our sal-va-tion, al-ways and everywhere to give you thanks, Lord, holy Father, almighty and e-ter-nal God, through Christ our Lord. He is the unblemished flower, who sprang from the root of the Vir-gin and declared the pure of heart bless-ed, teaching by his way of life the sur-pas-sing worth of chas-ti-ty. He chose always to hold fast to what is pleas-ing to you and, becoming obedient for our sake even un-til death, he willingly offered him-self to you as a perfect and a

FOR RELIGIOUS PROFESSION

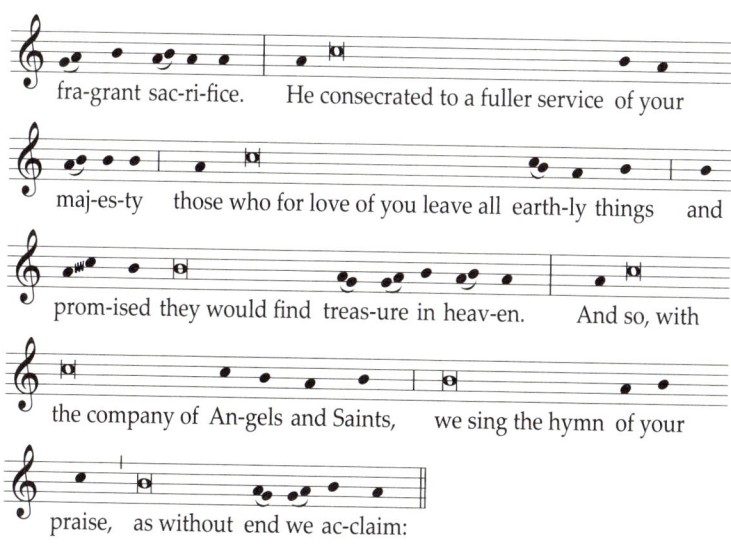

fra-grant sac-ri-fice. He consecrated to a fuller service of your maj-es-ty those who for love of you leave all earth-ly things and prom-ised they would find treas-ure in heav-en. And so, with the company of An-gels and Saints, we sing the hymn of your praise, as without end we ac-claim:

Holy, Holy, Holy Lord God of hosts . . .

Text without music:

V. **The Lord be with you.**
R. And with your spirit.

V. **Lift up your hearts.**
R. We lift them up to the Lord.

V. **Let us give thanks to the Lord our God.**
R. It is right and just.

It is truly right and just, our duty and our salvation,
always and everywhere to give you thanks,
Lord, holy Father, almighty and eternal God,
through Christ our Lord.

He is the unblemished flower,
who sprang from the root of the Virgin
and declared the pure of heart blessed,
teaching by his way of life the surpassing worth of chastity.

He chose always to hold fast to what is pleasing to you
and, becoming obedient for our sake even until death,
he willingly offered himself to you
as a perfect and a fragrant sacrifice.

He consecrated to a fuller service of your majesty
those who for love of you leave all earthly things
and promised they would find treasure in heaven.

And so, with the company of Angels and Saints,
we sing the hymn of your praise,
as without end we acclaim:

Holy, Holy, Holy Lord God of hosts . . .

In the Eucharistic Prayers, the oblation of the professed is appropriately commemorated according to the following formulas:

For Men:

a) In Eucharistic Prayer I, the proper form of the Hanc igitur (Therefore, Lord, we pray) is said.

Therefore, Lord, we pray:
graciously accept this oblation of our service,
and of these your servants,
which we make to you on their profession day;
sanctify this offering in your mercy,
so that those who by your gift
have dedicated their lives to you today
may, at the glorious coming of your Son,
be admitted to the joy of the eternal Pasch.
(Through Christ our Lord. Amen.)

b) In the intercessions of Eucharistic Prayer II, after the words *and all the clergy*, the following is added:

Be mindful also, Lord, of these brothers,
who have dedicated themselves today
to your perpetual service,
and grant that they may always raise
their hearts and minds to you
and glorify your name.
Remember also our brothers and sisters . . .

c) In the intercessions of Eucharistic Prayer III, after the words *the entire people you have gained for your own*, the following is added:

Strengthen in their holy resolve, O Lord,
these your servants,
who today have bound themselves to you perpetually
in the sacred bonds of religious profession,
and grant that they may show forth in your Church
the new and eternal life
purchased for us by Christ's redemption.
Listen graciously to the prayers of this family . . .

d) If the proper Preface is not used, Eucharistic Prayer IV may be said; in its intercession, after the words *to the praise of your glory*, a commemoration of the professed may be inserted in this way:

Therefore, Lord, remember now
all for whom we offer this sacrifice:
especially your servant N. our Pope
and N. our Bishop,
the whole Order of Bishops,
and all the clergy.
Be mindful also of these brothers,
who consecrate themselves to you more closely today
by perpetual profession,
those who take part in this offering,
those gathered here before you,
your entire people,
and all who seek you with a sincere heart.
Remember also
those who have died in the peace of your Christ . . .

For Women:

a) In Eucharistic Prayer I, the proper form of the Hanc igitur (Therefore, Lord, we pray) is said.

Therefore, Lord, we pray:
graciously accept this oblation of our service,
and of these your servants,
which we make to you on their profession day;
sanctify this offering in your mercy,
so that they who by your gift
have today united themselves more closely to your Son
may hasten gladly to meet him
when he comes in glory at the end of time.
(Through Christ our Lord. Amen.)

b) In the intercessions of Eucharistic Prayer II, after the words *and all the clergy*, the following is added:

Be mindful also, Lord, of these sisters,
who have left all things for your sake
in order to find you in all things
and, forgetful of themselves, to look to the needs of all.
Remember also our brothers and sisters . . .

c) In the intercessions of Eucharistic Prayer III, after the words *the entire people you have gained for your own*, the following is added:

Strengthen in their holy resolve, O Lord,
these your servants,
who seek to follow your Christ in faithful devotion,
giving a witness of evangelical life and of fraternal love.
Listen graciously to the prayers of this family . . .

d) If the proper Preface is not used, Eucharistic Prayer IV may be said; in its intercession, after the words *to the praise of your glory*, a commemoration of the professed may be inserted in this way:

Therefore, Lord, remember now
all for whom we offer this sacrifice:
especially your servant N. our Pope
and N. our Bishop,
with the whole Order of Bishops,
and all the clergy.
Be mindful also of these sisters,
who today have consecrated themselves to you perpetually
by a sacred pledge,
those who take part in this offering,
those gathered here before you,
your entire people,
and all who seek you with a sincere heart.
Remember also
those who have died in the peace of your Christ . . .

Communion Antiphon
Gal 2: 19-20

I am crucified with Christ
yet I live, no longer I,
but Christ lives in me (E.T. alleluia).

Prayer after Communion

Having received with reverence the divine mysteries,
we humbly beseech you, O Lord,
to inflame with the fire of the Holy Spirit these your servants,
bound to you now by an act of sacred offering,
and to admit them for ever to the company of your Son.
Who lives and reigns for ever and ever.

Solemn Blessing at the End of Mass

The Priest, with hands extended over the professed, says:

May God, the inspirer of every good resolve,
foster your purposes and strengthen your hearts,
that what you have promised
you may keep with persevering faith.
R. Amen.

May he grant you to hasten in the joy of Christ
along the narrow way you have chosen,
rejoicing to bear the burdens of your brothers (sisters).
R. Amen.

May the charity of God make of you a family
brought together in the Lord's name,
to show forth the image of the love of Christ.
R. Amen.

And he blesses all the people, adding:

And may almighty God bless all of you,
who are gathered for these sacred rites,
the Father, and the Son, ✠ and the Holy Spirit.
R. Amen.

B

Entrance Antiphon
Cf. Ps 66 (65): 13-14

My offering I bring to your house, O Lord;
to you I will pay my vows,
the vows which my lips have promised (E.T. alleluia).

The Gloria in excelsis (Glory to God in the highest) is said.

Collect

O Lord, holy Father, graciously confirm
the resolve of your servants N. and N.
and grant that the grace of Baptism,
which they desire to be strengthened by new bonds,
may produce in them its full effect,
so that they may render due worship to your majesty
and spread with apostolic zeal the Kingdom of Christ.
Who lives and reigns with you in the unity of the Holy Spirit,
one God, for ever and ever.

The Creed is said in accordance with the rubrics; the Universal Prayer is omitted.

Prayer over the Offerings

Receive in your kindness, O Lord,
the offerings of your servants
and transform them into the Sacrament of redemption,
filling with the gifts of the Holy Spirit
those whom with a father's care
you have called to imitate more closely your Son.
Who lives and reigns for ever and ever.

Preface and proper intercessions (pp. 1210-1215).

Communion Antiphon

Ps 34 (33): 9

Taste and see that the Lord is good;
blessed the man who seeks refuge in him (E.T. alleluia).

Prayer after Communion

May we be filled with joy, O Lord,
by today's celebration of a solemn pledge
and the reverent reception of this divine Sacrament;
grant, we pray, in your mercy,
that this twofold act of devotion
may stir with burning charity the hearts of your servants
to serve the Church and the human family.
Through Christ our Lord.

Solemn Blessing at the End of Mass

The Priest, with hands extended over the professed, says:

May God, who inspires and brings to completion every holy design,
guard you always with his grace,
that you may faithfully discharge the duties of your calling.
℟. Amen.

May God make you partakers of divine charity
and its witness and sign before all nations.
℟. Amen.

May God graciously make lasting in heaven
the bonds by which he has united you to Christ on earth.
℟. Amen.

And he blesses all the people, adding:

And may almighty God bless all of you,
who are gathered for these sacred rites,
the Father, and the Son, ✠ and the Holy Spirit.
℟. Amen.

Masses for the Anniversaries of Religious Profession are found among the Masses for Various Needs (pp. 1264-1265).

3. FOR THE RENEWAL OF VOWS

The Entrance and Communion Antiphons may be taken, if appropriate, from one of the preceding Masses (pp. 1207-1217).

Collect

O God, who direct the course of all things
and rule over the whole human race,
look upon these your sons (daughters),
who wish to confirm their offering of themselves to you,
and grant, we pray, that day by day,
they may be bound more closely
to the mystery of the Church
and devote themselves ever more
to the good of the human family.
Through our Lord Jesus Christ, your Son,
who lives and reigns with you in the unity of the Holy Spirit,
one God, for ever and ever.

Prayer over the Offerings

Look with gracious favor, O Lord,
on the offerings of your people,
to which these, our brothers (sisters),
add their renewed oblation
of chastity, poverty and obedience;
transform, we pray, these earthly gifts
into the Sacrament of eternal life,
and conform those who make this offering
in mind and heart
to the likeness of your Son.
Who lives and reigns for ever and ever.

Proper Preface (pp. 1210-1212).

Prayer after Communion

Having received, O Lord, this heavenly Sacrament
we humbly ask that these your servants,
who, with such trust in your grace from on high,
have renewed their resolve of determined service,
may be strengthened by the power of Christ
and fortified by the protection of the Holy Spirit.
Through Christ our Lord.

IX. FOR THE INSTITUTION OF LECTORS AND ACOLYTES

If the Rite of Institution is celebrated during Mass, the Mass for the Ministers of the Church (p. 1255) may be used, with the color white or a festive color.

When, however, the days listed in nos. 1-9 of the Table of Liturgical Days occur, the Mass of the day is said.

X. FOR THE DEDICATION OF A CHURCH AND AN ALTAR

1. FOR THE DEDICATION OF A CHURCH

When a church is dedicated, the proper Ritual Mass is always used, with the color white or a festive color. The dedication of a church, however, is not to take place during the Paschal Triduum, on the Nativity of the Lord, on the Epiphany, on the Ascension, on Pentecost Sunday, on Ash Wednesday, on the weekdays of Holy Week, or on the Commemoration of All the Faithful Departed (All Souls' Day).

Entrance Antiphon
Cf. Ps 68 (67): 6, 7, 36

God is in his holy place,
God who unites those who dwell in his house;
he himself gives might and strength to his people (E.T. alleluia).

Or, with Psalm 121:

Cf. Ps 122 (121): 1

Let us go rejoicing to the house of the Lord (E.T. alleluia).

The Gloria in excelsis (Glory to God in the highest) is said.

Collect

Almighty ever-living God,
pour out your grace upon this place
and extend the gift of your help
to all who call upon you,
that the power of your word and of the Sacraments
may strengthen here the hearts of all the faithful.
Through our Lord Jesus Christ, your Son,
who lives and reigns with you in the unity of the Holy Spirit,
one God, for ever and ever.

The Creed is said; the Universal Prayer is omitted.

Prayer over the Offerings

May the gifts of your joyful Church
be acceptable to you, O Lord,
so that your people, gathering in this holy house,
may come through these mysteries to everlasting salvation.
Through Christ our Lord.

Eucharistic Prayer I or III is said with this Preface, which is an integral part of the Rite of the Dedication of a Church.

Preface: The mystery of God's Temple.

V. The Lord be with you.　　R. And with your spir-it.

V. Lift up your hearts.　　R. We lift them up to the Lord.

V. Let us give thanks to the Lord our God.　　R. It is right and just.

It is truly right and just, our duty and our sal-va-tion, al-ways and everywhere to give you thanks, Fa-ther most ho-ly. For you have made the whole world a temple of your glo-ry, that your name might everywhere be ex-tolled, yet you allow us to consecrate to you apt places for the di-vine mys-ter-ies. And so, we dedicate joyfully to your maj-es-ty this house of prayer, built by hu-man la-bor. Here is foreshadowed the mystery of the true Tem-ple, here is pre-fig-ured the heav-en-ly Je-ru-sa-lem. For you made

FOR THE DEDICATION OF A CHURCH AND AN ALTAR

the Body of your Son, born of the tender Virgin, the Temple conse-crated to you, in which the full-ness of the God-head might dwell. You also established the Church as a ho-ly cit-y, built upon the foundation of the A-pos-tles, with Christ Jesus him-self the chief cor-ner-stone: a city to be built of cho-sen stones, giv-en life by the Spirit and bond-ed by char-i-ty, where for endless ages you will be all in all and the light of Christ will shine un-dimmed for ev-er. Through him, O Lord, with all the An-gels and Saints, we give you thanks, as in exul-ta-tion we ac-claim:

Holy, Holy, Holy Lord God of hosts . . .

Text without music:

V. The Lord be with you.
R. And with your spirit.

V. Lift up your hearts.
R. We lift them up to the Lord.

V. Let us give thanks to the Lord our God.
R. It is right and just.

It is truly right and just, our duty and our salvation,
always and everywhere to give you thanks,
Father most holy.

For you have made the whole world a temple of your glory,
that your name might everywhere be extolled,
yet you allow us to consecrate to you
apt places for the divine mysteries.

And so, we dedicate joyfully to your majesty
this house of prayer, built by human labor.

Here is foreshadowed the mystery of the true Temple,
here is prefigured the heavenly Jerusalem.

For you made the Body of your Son, born of the tender Virgin,
the Temple consecrated to you,
in which the fullness of the Godhead might dwell.

You also established the Church as a holy city,
built upon the foundation of the Apostles,
with Christ Jesus himself the chief cornerstone:
a city to be built of chosen stones,
given life by the Spirit and bonded by charity,
where for endless ages you will be all in all
and the light of Christ will shine undimmed for ever.

Through him, O Lord, with all the Angels and Saints,
we give you thanks, as in exultation we acclaim:

Holy, Holy, Holy Lord God of hosts . . .

FOR THE DEDICATION OF A CHURCH AND AN ALTAR

When Mass is already celebrated regularly in the church, Eucharistic Prayer I or III is said with this Preface.

Preface: From the mystery of the Temple of God, which is the Church.

V. The Lord be with you.
R. And with your spirit.

V. Lift up your hearts.
R. We lift them up to the Lord.

V. Let us give thanks to the Lord our God.
R. It is right and just.

It is truly right and just, our duty and our salvation,
always and everywhere to give you thanks,
Lord, holy Father, almighty and eternal God,
through Christ our Lord.

For in this visible house that you have let us build
and where you never cease to show favor
to the family on pilgrimage to you in this place,
you wonderfully manifest and accomplish
the mystery of your communion with us.
Here you build up for yourself the temple that we are
and cause your Church, spread throughout the world,
to grow ever more and more as the Lord's own Body,
till she reaches her fullness in the vision of peace,
the heavenly city of Jerusalem.

And so, with the countless ranks of the blessed,
in the temple of your glory we praise you,
we bless you and proclaim your greatness, as we acclaim:

Holy, Holy, Holy Lord God of hosts . . .

Text with music, pp. 1033-1034.

In the Eucharistic prayers, the dedication of the church is commemorated according to the following formulas:

a) In Eucharistic Prayer I, the proper form of the Hanc igitur (Therefore, Lord, we pray) is said:

**Therefore, Lord, we pray:
graciously accept this oblation of our service,
and of these your servants,
who in a spirit of faith
have offered to you this church (in honor of N.)
and built it with tireless labor.
(Through Christ our Lord. Amen.)**

b) In the intercessions of Eucharistic Prayer III, after the words the entire people you have gained for your own, the following is said:

**Listen graciously to the prayers of this family,
who dedicate this church to you:
may it be for your family a house of salvation
and a place for the celebration of your heavenly Sacraments.
Here may the Gospel of peace resound
and the sacred mysteries be celebrated,
so that your faithful,
formed by the word of life and by divine grace
on their pilgrim way through the earthly city,
may merit to reach the eternal Jerusalem.
There, in your compassion, O merciful Father,
gather to yourself all your children
scattered throughout the world.
To our departed brothers and sisters
and to all . . .**

Communion Antiphon

Cf. Mt 21: 13; Lk 11: 10

My house shall be a house of prayer, says the Lord:
in that house, everyone who asks receives,
and the one who seeks finds,
and to the one who knocks, the door will be opened (E.T. alleluia).

Or:

Cf. Ps 128 (127): 3

Like shoots of the olive,
may the children of the Church be gathered
around the table of the Lord (E.T. alleluia).

Prayer after Communion

Through these holy gifts we have received,
O Lord, we pray,
instill in our minds an increase of your truth,
so that we may constantly adore you in your holy temple
and glory in your sight with all the Saints.
Through Christ our Lord.

Solemn Blessing at the End of Mass

The Bishop, with hands extended over the people, says:

May God, the Lord of heaven and earth,
who has gathered you today for the dedication of this church,
make you abound in heavenly blessings.
R. Amen.

May God, who has willed that all his scattered children
be gathered in his Son,
grant that you become his temple
and the dwelling place of the Holy Spirit.
R. Amen.

May you be made thoroughly clean,
so that God may dwell within you
and you may possess with all the Saints
the inheritance of eternal happiness.
R. Amen.

And may the blessing of almighty God,
the Father, ✠ and the Son, ✠ and the Holy ✠ Spirit,
come down on you and remain with you for ever.
R. Amen.

Masses for the Anniversary of Dedication are found among the Commons (pp. 1032-1038).

2. FOR THE DEDICATION OF AN ALTAR

When an altar is dedicated, the proper Ritual Mass is normally used, with the color white or a festive color. The dedication of an altar, however, is not to take place during the Paschal Triduum, on Ash Wednesday, on the weekdays of Holy Week, or on the Commemoration of All the Faithful Departed (All Souls' Day). On the Nativity of the Lord, on the Epiphany, on the Ascension, on Pentecost Sunday, as well as on the Sundays of Advent, Lent, and Easter, the Mass of the day is used, except for the Prayer over the Offerings and the Preface, which are intimately connected to the rite itself.

Entrance Antiphon

Ps 84 (83): 10-11

Turn your eyes, our God, our shield,
and look on the face of your anointed one;
one day within your courts
is better than a thousand elsewhere (E.T. alleluia).

Or:

Ps 43 (42): 4

I will come to the altar of God,
to God who restores the joy of my youth (E.T. alleluia).

The Gloria in excelsis (Glory to God in the highest) is said.

Collect

O God, who willed to draw all things
to your Son, lifted high on the altar of the Cross,
fill your Church, we pray, with heavenly grace
as she dedicates to you this altar,
the table at which you will plentifully nourish
the faithful you gather as one
and will shape day by day,
through the outpouring of the Spirit,
a people consecrated to yourself.
Through our Lord Jesus Christ, your Son,
who lives and reigns with you in the unity of the Holy Spirit,
one God, for ever and ever.

The Creed is said; the Universal Prayer is omitted.

Prayer over the Offerings

May your Holy Spirit come down upon this altar,
we pray, O Lord our God,
to sanctify the gifts of your people
and graciously to cleanse the hearts of all who receive them.
Through Christ our Lord.

Eucharistic Prayer I or III is said with this Preface, which is an integral part of the Rite of the Dedication of an Altar.

Preface: Christ himself is the altar.

V. The Lord be with you.   R. And with your spir-it.

V. Lift up your hearts.   R. We lift them up to the Lord.

V. Let us give thanks to the Lord our God.   R. It is right and just.

It is truly right and just, our duty and our sal-va-tion, al-ways and everywhere to give you thanks, Lord, holy Father, almighty and e--ter-nal God, through Christ our Lord. Hav-ing become both the true Priest and the true ob-la-tion, he has taught us to celebrate for ever the memorial of the Sac-ri-fice that he himself of-fered to you on the al-tar of the Cross. There-fore, Lord, your people have raised this al-tar, which we dedicate to you with joy-ful praise. Tru-ly this is an ex-alt-ed place, where the Sacrifice of Christ is ever

FOR THE DEDICATION OF A CHURCH AND AN ALTAR

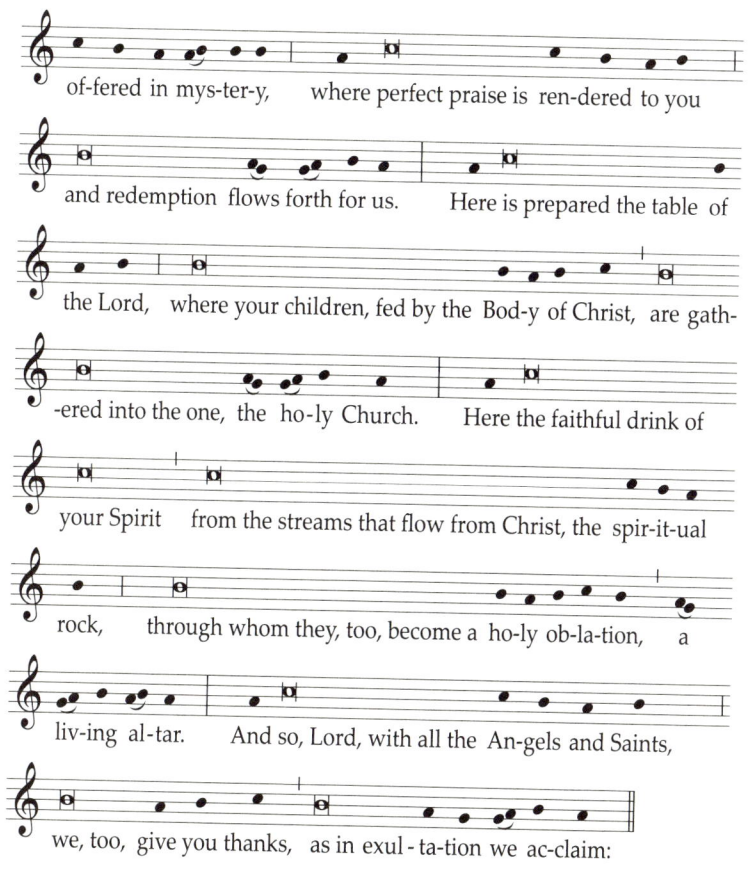

of-fered in mys-ter-y, where perfect praise is ren-dered to you and redemption flows forth for us. Here is prepared the table of the Lord, where your children, fed by the Bod-y of Christ, are gath-ered into the one, the ho-ly Church. Here the faithful drink of your Spirit from the streams that flow from Christ, the spir-it-ual rock, through whom they, too, become a ho-ly ob-la-tion, a liv-ing al-tar. And so, Lord, with all the An-gels and Saints, we, too, give you thanks, as in exul-ta-tion we ac-claim:

Holy, Holy, Holy Lord God of hosts . . .

Text without music:

V. **The Lord be with you.**
R. And with your spirit.

V. **Lift up your hearts.**
R. We lift them up to the Lord.

V. **Let us give thanks to the Lord our God.**
R. It is right and just.

It is truly right and just, our duty and our salvation,
always and everywhere to give you thanks,
Lord, holy Father, almighty and eternal God,
through Christ our Lord.

Having become both the true Priest and the true oblation,
he has taught us to celebrate for ever
the memorial of the Sacrifice
that he himself offered to you on the altar of the Cross.

Therefore, Lord, your people have raised this altar,
which we dedicate to you with joyful praise.

Truly this is an exalted place,
where the Sacrifice of Christ is ever offered in mystery,
where perfect praise is rendered to you
and redemption flows forth for us.

Here is prepared the table of the Lord,
where your children, fed by the Body of Christ,
are gathered into the one, the holy Church.

Here the faithful drink of your Spirit
from the streams that flow from Christ, the spiritual rock,
through whom they, too, become a holy oblation, a living altar.

And so, Lord, with all the Angels and Saints,
we, too, give you thanks, as in exultation we acclaim:

Holy, Holy, Holy Lord God of hosts . . .

Communion Antiphon Cf. Ps 84 (83): 4-5

The sparrow finds a home,
and the swallow a nest for her young:
by your altars, O Lord of hosts, my King and my God.
Blessed are they who dwell in your house,
for ever singing your praise (E.T. alleluia).

Or: Cf. Ps 128 (127): 3

Like shoots of the olive,
may the children of the Church be gathered
around the table of the Lord (E.T. alleluia).

Prayer after Communion

Keep us, O Lord, ever close to your altar
where the Sacrament of sacrifice is celebrated,
so that, united in faith and charity,
we, who by Christ are nourished,
into Christ may be transformed.
Who lives and reigns for ever and ever.

Solemn Blessing at the End of Mass

The Bishop, with hands extended over the people, says:

May God, who adorns you with a royal priesthood,
grant that, as you exercise it in holiness,
you may share worthily in the sacrifice of Christ.
R. Amen.

And may he, who gathers you at one table
and renews you with one Bread,
make of you one heart and one soul.
R. Amen.

By the example of your love
may you draw to Christ
those to whom you proclaim him.
R. Amen.

And may the blessing of almighty God,
the Father, ✠ and the Son, ✠ and the Holy ✠ Spirit,
come down on you and remain with you for ever.
R. Amen.

MASSES AND PRAYERS FOR VARIOUS NEEDS AND OCCASIONS

1. This section groups together Masses and prayers for various intentions, which may be used in many situations, and for various needs and occasions.

   The texts found in the first two parts may be used either in a Mass with the people or in a Mass without the people. The texts collected in the third part may, in general, be used in Masses celebrated without the people, unless at times a pastoral reason suggests otherwise.

2. In case of some grave need, a corresponding Mass may be said on the instructions of the local Ordinary or with his permission, on any day except on Solemnities, the Sundays of Advent, Lent, and Easter, days within the Octave of Easter, the Commemoration of All the Faithful Departed (All Souls' Day), Ash Wednesday, and on the weekdays of Holy Week.

   If, however, some real necessity or pastoral advantage requires it, in the judgment of the rector of the church or the Priest celebrant himself, an appropriate Mass or a Collect may be used in a celebration with the people even if on that day there occurs an Obligatory Memorial or a weekday of Advent up to and including December 16, or a weekday of Christmas Time from January 2 or a weekday of Easter Time after the Octave of Easter.

   During Easter Time, **Alleluia** is added to the Entrance Antiphon and Communion Antiphon, unless this would be not in accord with the sense.

3. In a Mass for a weekday in Ordinary Time, the Priest may always use all the prayers of this series, or even only the Collect, observing what is indicated in no. 1.

4. As for the Eucharistic Prayer which may be used with formularies of the Masses for Various Needs, see Appendix to the Order of Mass, p. 755.

5. In certain Masses, the liturgical texts given for a man may be adapted for a woman, with the necessary change of gender; in addition, those expressed in the plural may be used for individuals, with the necessary change to the singular.

6. These Masses may be said with the color proper to the day or the liturgical time or with the color violet if they have a penitential character, see e.g., nos. 31, 33, 38 (cf. the *General Instruction*, no. 347).

I. FOR HOLY CHURCH

1. FOR THE CHURCH

A

Entrance Antiphon *Cf. Eph 1: 9-10*

God has made known to us the mystery of his will,
to bring together all things in Christ,
all things in heaven and on earth in him.

Collect

O God, who in your wonderful providence
decreed that Christ's kingdom
should be extended throughout the earth
and that all should become partakers of his saving redemption,
grant, we pray, that your Church
may be the universal sacrament of salvation
and that Christ may be revealed to all
as the hope of the nations and their Savior.
Who lives and reigns with you in the unity of the Holy Spirit,
one God, for ever and ever.

Prayer over the Offerings

Look upon the offerings of the people consecrated to you,
O merciful God,
and, through the power of this Sacrament,
grant that the multitude of those who believe in you
may constantly be made a chosen race,
a royal priesthood, a holy nation, a people of your own.
Through Christ our Lord.

Preface VIII of the Sundays in Ordinary Time, p. 586.

Communion Antiphon *Rev 22: 17, 20*

The Spirit and the bride say: Come.
Amen. Come, Lord Jesus.

Prayer after Communion

O God, who constantly feed and strengthen the Church
with your Sacraments,
grant to us,
who have been nourished at the heavenly table,
that, by obeying your teachings of love,
we may become for the human family
a life-giving leaven and a means to salvation.
Through Christ our Lord.

B

Entrance Antiphon   Rev 7: 9

I had a vision of a great multitude, which no one could count,
from every nation, race, people, and tongue.

Collect

O God, in the covenant of your Christ
you never cease to gather to yourself from all nations
a people growing together in unity through the Spirit;
grant, we pray, that your Church,
faithful to the mission entrusted to her,
may continually go forward with the human family
and always be the leaven and the soul of human society,
to renew it in Christ and transform it into the family of God.
Through our Lord Jesus Christ, your Son,
who lives and reigns with you in the unity of the Holy Spirit,
one God, for ever and ever.

Prayer over the Offerings

Receive with kindness the offerings we bring you, O Lord,
and grant that your Church,
which came forth from the side of Christ as he slept on the Cross,
may ever draw her holiness from participation in this mystery,
living by it always and responding worthily to her founder,
Jesus Christ our Lord.
Who lives and reigns for ever and ever.

Preface VIII of the Sundays in Ordinary Time, p. 586.

Communion Antiphon

Jn 19: 34

> One of the soldiers opened his side with a lance,
> and at once there came forth blood and water.

> Or:

Rev 7: 12

> Blessing and glory and wisdom and thanksgiving,
> honor and power and might
> be to our God for ever and ever. Amen.

Prayer after Communion

**Nourished by the Sacrament of your Son,
we implore you, Lord,
to make fruitful the work of your Church,
for by it you constantly reveal
the fullness of the mystery of salvation to the poor,
whom you have called to an honored place in your eternal Kingdom.
Through Christ our Lord.**

C

Entrance Antiphon

Mt 18: 20

> Where two or three are gathered together in my name,
> there am I in the midst of them.

> Or:

Rom 12: 5

> Though many, we are one body in Christ
> and individually parts of one another.

Collect

**Grant, we pray, almighty God,
that your Church may always remain that holy people,
formed as one by the unity of Father, Son and Holy Spirit,
which manifests to the world
the Sacrament of your holiness and unity
and leads it to the perfection of your charity.
Through our Lord Jesus Christ, your Son,
who lives and reigns with you in the unity of the Holy Spirit,
one God, for ever and ever.**

Prayer over the Offerings

Celebrating the memorial of your Son's boundless love,
we humbly beseech you, O Lord,
that through the ministry of your Church
the fruits of his saving work
may advance the salvation of all the world.
Through Christ our Lord.

Preface for the Unity of Christians, p. 1274.

Communion Antiphon

Cf. 1 Cor 10: 17

Though many, we are one bread, one body,
for we all partake of the one Bread and one Chalice.

Prayer after Communion

O God, who by this wonderful Sacrament
give courage and comfort to the Church,
grant that through these holy gifts
your people may hold fast to Christ,
so that, by the tasks they carry out in this present age,
they may in freedom build up your eternal Kingdom.
Through Christ our Lord.

D

Entrance Antiphon

Cf. Jn 17: 20-21

Father, I pray for those who will believe in me,
that they may be one in us,
so that the world may believe it was you who sent me.

Collect

Almighty ever-living God,
who in Christ revealed your glory to all the nations,
watch over the works of your mercy,
that Holy Church, spread throughout the whole world,
may persevere with steadfast faith in confessing your name.
Through our Lord Jesus Christ, your Son,
who lives and reigns with you in the unity of the Holy Spirit,
one God, for ever and ever.

Prayer over the Offerings

O God, who constantly sanctify your Church
through the same sacrifice by which you have made her clean,
grant that, united to Christ her Head,
she may offer herself to you with him
and be united with you in purity of will.
Through Christ our Lord.

Preface VIII of the Sundays in Ordinary Time, p. 586.

Communion Antiphon
Jn 15: 5

Whoever remains in me and I in him bears fruit in plenty,
because without me you can do nothing, says the Lord.

Prayer after Communion

Be pleased, O Lord, we pray,
to govern the Church you have nourished by this holy meal,
so that, firmly directed,
she may enjoy ever greater freedom
and persevere in integrity of religion.
Through Christ our Lord.

E
For the Particular Church

Entrance Antiphon
Rev 1: 5-6

To Jesus Christ who loves us
and has washed us clean of our sins by his Blood,
who has made us into a kingdom, priests for his God and Father.
To him be glory and power for ever and ever. Amen.

Collect

O God, who in each pilgrim Church throughout the world
make visible the one, holy, catholic and apostolic Church,
graciously grant
that your faithful may be so united to their shepherd
and gathered together in the Holy Spirit
through the Gospel and the Eucharist,
as to worthily embody the universality of your people
and become a sign and instrument in the world of the presence
of Christ.
Who lives and reigns with you in the unity of the Holy Spirit,
one God, for ever and ever.

Prayer over the Offerings

Celebrating the memorial of your Son's boundless love,
we humbly beseech you, O Lord,
that through the ministry of your Church
the fruits of his saving work
may advance the salvation of all the world.
Through Christ our Lord.

Preface VIII of the Sundays in Ordinary Time, p. 586.

Communion Antiphon

Rev 3: 20

Behold, I stand at the door and knock, says the Lord.
If anyone hears my voice and opens the door to me,
I will enter his house and dine with him, and he with me.

Prayer after Communion

In this your Church, O Lord,
may integrity of faith, holiness of life,
fraternal charity and pure religion
flourish and abide until the end,
and, as you do not fail to feed her
with the Body of your Son and with your word,
so also never cease, we pray,
to guide her under your protection.
Through Christ our Lord.

2. FOR THE POPE

Especially on the Anniversary of Election

This Mass is said, with the color white, on the anniversary of the election of the Pope in places wherever special celebrations are held, provided they do not occur on a Sunday of Advent, Lent or Easter, on a Solemnity, on Ash Wednesday, or on a weekday of Holy Week.

Entrance Antiphon   Mt 16: 18-19

> You are Peter, and upon this rock I will build my Church,
> and the gates of the netherworld shall not prevail against it.
> To you I will give the keys to the Kingdom of Heaven.

Collect

> O God, who in your providential design
> willed that your Church be built
> upon blessed Peter, whom you set over the other Apostles,
> look with favor, we pray, on N. our Pope
> and grant that he, whom you have made Peter's successor,
> may be for your people a visible source and foundation
> of unity in faith and of communion.
> Through our Lord Jesus Christ, your Son,
> who lives and reigns with you in the unity of the Holy Spirit,
> one God, for ever and ever.

Or:

> O God, shepherd and ruler of all the faithful,
> look favorably on your servant N.,
> whom you have set at the head of your Church as her shepherd;
> grant, we pray, that by word and example
> he may be of service to those over whom he presides
> so that, together with the flock entrusted to his care,
> he may come to everlasting life.
> Through our Lord Jesus Christ, your Son,
> who lives and reigns with you in the unity of the Holy Spirit,
> one God, for ever and ever.

Or:

O God, who chose your servant **N.**
in succession to the Apostle Peter
as shepherd of the whole flock,
look favorably on the supplications of your people
and grant that, as Vicar of Christ on earth,
he may confirm his brethren
and that the whole Church may be in communion with him
in the bond of unity, love and peace,
so that in you, the shepherd of souls,
all may know the truth and attain life eternal.
Through our Lord Jesus Christ, your Son,
who lives and reigns with you in the unity of the Holy Spirit,
one God, for ever and ever.

Prayer over the Offerings

Be pleased, we pray, O Lord,
with the offerings presented here
and govern with unfailing protection your holy Church,
together with **N.** our Pope,
whom you have chosen to be her shepherd.
Through Christ our Lord.

Communion Antiphon
Jn 21: 15, 17

Simon, son of John, do you love me more than these?
Lord, you know everything; you know that I love you.

Prayer after Communion

Having been made sharers at the heavenly table,
we humbly entreat you, Lord:
by the power of this mystery,
strengthen your Church in unity and charity
and, as you have entrusted your servant **N.** with the office of shepherd,
grant him always salvation and protection,
together with the flock entrusted to his care.
Through Christ our Lord.

3. FOR THE BISHOP
Especially on the Anniversary of Ordination

This Mass is said on the anniversary of the Ordination of the Bishop wherever special celebrations are held, provided they do not occur on a Sunday of Advent, Lent or Easter, on a Solemnity, on Ash Wednesday, or on a weekday of Holy Week.

Entrance Antiphon *Ez 34: 11, 23, 24*

I will look after my sheep, says the Lord,
and I will appoint a shepherd to pasture them,
and I, the Lord, will be their God.

Collect

O God, eternal shepherd of the faithful,
who tend your Church in countless ways
and rule over her in love,
grant, we pray, that N., your servant,
whom you have set over your people,
may preside in the place of Christ
over the flock whose shepherd he is,
and be faithful as a teacher of doctrine,
a Priest of sacred worship
and as one who serves them by governing.
Through our Lord Jesus Christ, your Son,
who lives and reigns with you in the unity of the Holy Spirit,
one God, for ever and ever.

Or:

O God, shepherd and ruler of all the faithful,
look favorably on your servant,
whom you have set at the head
of your Church of N. as her shepherd;
grant, we pray, that by word and example
he may be of service to those over whom he presides,
so that, together with the flock entrusted to his care,
he may come to everlasting life.
Through our Lord Jesus Christ, your Son,
who lives and reigns with you in the unity of the Holy Spirit,
one God, for ever and ever.

Or:

O Lord, who for the feeding of your flock
have set your servant N. over it
as a successor to the Apostles,
grant him, we pray,
a spirit of counsel and fortitude,
a spirit of knowledge and piety,
so that, by faithfully governing the people entrusted to him,
he may build up in the world the sacrament of the Church.
Through our Lord Jesus Christ, your Son,
who lives and reigns with you in the unity of the Holy Spirit,
one God, for ever and ever.

Prayer over the Offerings

May this oblation, O Lord,
which we have presented for your servant N.,
become an offering acceptable to you,
and, for the good of the flock,
may he, whom you have raised up
among your people to be High Priest,
be endowed, by your gift, with apostolic virtues.
Through Christ our Lord.

Communion Antiphon *Mt 20: 28*

The Son of Man did not come to be served but to serve,
and to give his life as a ransom for many.

Prayer after Communion

By the power of this Sacrament, O Lord,
increase the gifts of your grace
in N., your servant and our Bishop,
that he may serve you worthily in the pastoral ministry
and receive the eternal rewards of a faithful steward.
Through Christ our Lord.

4. FOR THE ELECTION OF A POPE OR A BISHOP

Entrance Antiphon
                        1 Sm 2: 35

> I will raise up for myself a faithful priest,
> who shall do according to my heart and mind;
> I will establish a lasting house for him
> and he shall walk before me all his days.

Collect

> O God, eternal shepherd,
> who govern your flock with unfailing care,
> grant in your boundless fatherly love
> a pastor for your Church
> who will please you by his holiness
> and to us show watchful care.
> Through our Lord Jesus Christ, your Son,
> who lives and reigns with you in the unity of the Holy Spirit,
> one God, for ever and ever.

Prayer over the Offerings

> May your abundant kindness favor us, O Lord,
> that, through the sacred offerings we reverently bring to you,
> we may come to rejoice that a pastor pleasing to your majesty
> presides over your holy Church.
> Through Christ our Lord.

Communion Antiphon
                           Jn 15: 16

> I chose you and appointed you to go and bear fruit, says the Lord,
> fruit that will last.

Prayer after Communion

> As we have been renewed, O Lord,
> with the supreme Sacrament of salvation,
> the Body and Blood of your Only Begotten Son,
> may the wondrous grace of your majesty
> gladden us with the gift of a shepherd
> who will instruct your people by his virtues
> and imbue the minds of the faithful with the truth of the Gospel.
> Through Christ our Lord.

5. FOR A COUNCIL OR A SYNOD

Entrance Antiphon   Cf. Col 3: 14-15

And over all things put on love,
which is the bond of perfection,
and let the peace of Christ rule in your hearts.

Collect

O Lord, ruler and guardian of your Church,
pour out, we pray, upon your servants
a spirit of truth, understanding and peace,
that they may strive with all their heart
to know what is pleasing to you
and then pursue it with all their strength.
Through our Lord Jesus Christ, your Son,
who lives and reigns with you in the unity of the Holy Spirit,
one God, for ever and ever.

Or:

O God, who care for your peoples with gentleness
and rule them in love,
endow with a spirit of wisdom
those to whom you have handed on authority to govern,
that your people may be led to know the truth more fully
and to grow in holiness according to your will.
Through our Lord Jesus Christ, your Son,
who lives and reigns with you in the unity of the Holy Spirit,
one God, for ever and ever.

Prayer over the Offerings

Look upon the offerings of your servants,
O God of all compassion,
and bestow on them the grace of your light,
that they may have a true understanding
of what is right in your eyes
and boldly carry it out.
Through Christ our Lord.

Preface II of the Holy Spirit, p. 1342.

Communion Antiphon

Where true charity is dwelling, God is present there.
By the love of Christ we have been brought together.

Prayer after Communion

Grant, we pray, O merciful God,
that the holy gifts we have received
may confirm your servants in the truth
and prompt them to seek the honor of your name.
Through Christ our Lord.

6. FOR PRIESTS

Entrance Antiphon
Cf. Lk 4: 18

The Spirit of the Lord is upon me, for he has anointed me
and sent me to preach good news to the poor,
to heal the broken-hearted
and to let the oppressed go free.

Collect

O God, who made your Only Begotten Son eternal High Priest,
grant that those he has chosen
as ministers and stewards of your mysteries
may be found faithful in carrying out
the ministry they have received.
Through our Lord Jesus Christ, your Son,
who lives and reigns with you in the unity of the Holy Spirit,
one God, for ever and ever.

Or:

Lord our God, who in governing your people
make use of the ministry of Priests,
grant to these men
a persevering obedience to your will,
so that by their ministry and life
they may gain glory for you in Christ.
Who lives and reigns with you in the unity of the Holy Spirit,
one God, for ever and ever.

Prayer over the Offerings

O God, who have willed that your Priests
should minister at the holy altar and serve your people,
grant by the power of this sacrifice, we pray,
that their labors may constantly please you
and in your Church bear that fruit which lasts for ever.
Through Christ our Lord.

Communion Antiphon
Jn 17: 17-18

Holy Father, consecrate them in the truth;
your word is truth.
As you sent me into the world,
so I sent them into the world, says the Lord.

Prayer after Communion

May the divine sacrifice
we have offered and received, O Lord,
give new life to your Priests and to all your servants,
that, united to you in unfailing love,
they may receive the grace
of giving worthy service to your majesty.
Through Christ our Lord.

7. FOR THE PRIEST HIMSELF

A
Especially for a Priest with the Care of Souls

Entrance Antiphon Cf. Col 1: 25, 28

I have become a servant of the Church
according to God's commission given to me for you.
We proclaim Christ, that we may present everyone perfect in Christ Jesus.

Collect

O God, who have willed that I preside over your family
not by any merit of mine
but out of the abundance of your untold grace alone,
grant that I may carry out worthily the ministry of the priestly office
and, under your governance in all things,
may direct the people entrusted to my care.
Through our Lord Jesus Christ, your Son,
who lives and reigns with you in the unity of the Holy Spirit,
one God, for ever and ever.

Prayer over the Offerings

O God, powerful and kindly ruler of days and seasons,
look in mercy on the ministry given me by your grace
and, through the power of this oblation,
direct the hearts of Priest and people to be so disposed
that the obedience of the flock may never fail the shepherd,
nor the care of the shepherd be lacking for the flock.
Through Christ our Lord.

Communion Antiphon Jn 15: 9

As the Father loves me, so I also love you;
remain in my love, says the Lord.

Prayer after Communion

Almighty ever-living God,
source and perfection of every virtue,
grant, we pray, that by participation in this mystery
I may do what is right and preach what is true,
so that by my deeds and by my words
I may offer to the faithful instruction in your grace.
Through Christ our Lord.

FOR THE PRIEST HIMSELF

B

Entrance Antiphon
Ps 16 (15): 2, 5

I say to the Lord: You are my Lord.
My goodness lies in you alone.
O Lord it is you who are my portion and cup;
you yourself who secure my lot.

Collect

Incline your merciful ear to my prayers,
O God of all compassion,
and enlighten my heart by the grace of the Holy Spirit,
that I may worthily celebrate your mysteries,
faithfully serve your Church
and love you with eternal charity.
Through our Lord Jesus Christ, your Son,
who lives and reigns with you in the unity of the Holy Spirit,
one God, for ever and ever.

Prayer over the Offerings

Receive, almighty God,
these offerings we bring you in veneration
and, as you look upon your Christ,
who is both Priest and Victim,
grant that I, who share in his priesthood,
may always offer myself
as a spiritual sacrifice pleasing to you.
Through Christ our Lord.

Communion Antiphon
Cf. Lk 22: 28-30

Jesus said to those who stood by him in his trials:
I confer a kingdom on you, that you may eat and drink at my table.

Prayer after Communion

As you strengthen me with the Bread of heaven
and gladden me with the chalice of the new covenant,
bring me, holy Father, to serve you faithfully
and to spend my life boldly and zealously
for the salvation of all humanity.
Through Christ our Lord.

C
On the Anniversary of His Ordination

Entrance Antiphon
Cf. Jn 15: 16

It was not you who chose me, says the Lord,
but I who chose you and appointed you to go out and bear fruit,
fruit that will last.

Collect

Holy Father, who, by no merit of my own, chose me
for communion with the eternal priesthood of your Christ
and for the ministry of your Church,
grant that I may be an ardent yet gentle preacher of the Gospel
and a faithful steward of your mysteries.
Through our Lord Jesus Christ, your Son,
who lives and reigns with you in the unity of the Holy Spirit,
one God, for ever and ever.

Prayer over the Offerings

We offer you the sacrifice of praise, O Lord,
for the deepening of our service of you,
so that what you have conferred on us,
unworthy as we are,
you may graciously bring to fulfillment.
Through Christ our Lord.

Communion Antiphon
Cf. 1 Cor 10: 16

The chalice of blessing that we bless
is a communion in the Blood of Christ;
and the bread that we break
is a sharing in the Body of the Lord.

Prayer after Communion

For the glory of your name, O Lord,
I have joyfully celebrated the mystery of faith
to mark the anniversary of my priestly ordination,
so that I may be in truth
what I have handled mystically in this sacrifice.
Through Christ our Lord.

8. FOR MINISTERS OF THE CHURCH

Entrance Antiphon
Cf. 1 Cor 12: 4-6

> There are different graces but the same Spirit,
> different ministries but the same Lord,
> different works but the same God,
> who accomplishes everything in everyone.

Collect

> O God, who have taught the ministers of your Church
> to seek not to be served, but to serve their brothers and sisters,
> grant, we pray,
> that they may be effective in action, gentle in ministry,
> and constant in prayer.
> Through our Lord Jesus Christ, your Son,
> who lives and reigns with you in the unity of the Holy Spirit,
> one God, for ever and ever.

Prayer over the Offerings

> Holy Father, whose Son chose to wash the disciples' feet
> and so set us an example,
> accept, we pray, the oblations of our service,
> and grant that, offering ourselves as a spiritual sacrifice,
> we may be filled with a spirit of humility and zeal.
> Through Christ our Lord.

Communion Antiphon
Lk 12: 37

> Blessed are those servants whom the lord finds vigilant on his arrival.
> Amen, I say to you:
> He will gird himself, seat them at table,
> and proceed to wait on them.

Prayer after Communion

> Grant, O Lord, to your servants,
> whom you have replenished with heavenly food and drink,
> that, for the sake of your glory and the salvation of believers,
> they may be found faithful as ministers of the Gospel,
> of the Sacraments and of charity.
> Through Christ our Lord.

9. FOR VOCATIONS TO HOLY ORDERS

Entrance Antiphon
Mt 9: 38

Ask the Lord of the harvest
to send out laborers for his harvest,
says Jesus to his disciples.

Collect

O God, who willed to provide shepherds for your people,
pour out in your Church a spirit of piety and fortitude,
to raise up worthy ministers for your altars
and make them ardent yet gentle heralds of your Gospel.
Through our Lord Jesus Christ, your Son,
who lives and reigns with you in the unity of the Holy Spirit,
one God, for ever and ever.

Prayer over the Offerings

Look kindly, we pray, O Lord,
on the prayers and offerings of your people,
that the stewards of your mysteries may grow in number
and persevere always in your love.
Through Christ our Lord.

Communion Antiphon
1 Jn 3: 16

By this we came to know the love of God:
that Christ laid down his life for us;
so we ought to lay down our lives for our brothers.

Prayer after Communion

Renewed with the Bread of the heavenly table,
we entreat you, O Lord,
that through this Sacrament of charity
the seeds you sow with great abundance in the field of your Church
may come to maturity,
so that many may make it their choice in life
to serve you in their brothers and sisters.
Through Christ our Lord.

10. FOR THE LAITY

Entrance Antiphon
Mt 13: 33

The Kingdom of Heaven is like yeast that a woman took
and mixed with three measures of wheat flour,
until the whole batch was leavened.

Collect

O God, who have sent the power of the Gospel
like leaven into the world,
grant that your faithful,
whom you have called to live amid the world and its affairs,
may be fervent with the Christian spirit
and, through the tasks they carry out in this present age,
may constantly build up your Kingdom.
Through our Lord Jesus Christ, your Son,
who lives and reigns with you in the unity of the Holy Spirit,
one God, for ever and ever.

Prayer over the Offerings

O God, who willed to save the whole world
by the sacrifice of your Son,
grant through the power of this oblation
that your servants living in the lay state,
whom you do not cease to call to the apostolate,
may imbue the world with the spirit of Christ
and be the leaven of its sanctification.
Through Christ our Lord.

Communion Antiphon   Ps 100 (99): 2
Cry out with joy to the Lord, all the earth.
Serve the Lord with gladness.
Come before him, singing for joy, alleluia.

Or: Jn 15: 8

By this is my Father glorified,
that you bear much fruit and become my disciples, says the Lord.

Prayer after Communion

As we draw upon the fullness of your grace,
we pray, O Lord,
that your faithful,
who by your will are engaged in the things of this world,
may be strengthened by the power of the Eucharistic Banquet,
to be tireless witnesses to the truth of the Gospel
and may ever make your Church present and active
amid the affairs of this age.
Through Christ our Lord.

11. ON THE ANNIVERSARIES OF MARRIAGE

On the main anniversaries of marriage, as for example, on the twenty-fifth, fiftieth, or sixtieth anniversary, whenever Masses for Various Needs are permitted, the Mass for Giving Thanks to God (pp. 1323-1324) may be used with the prayers given below.

The same prayers may also be used, if appropriate, at Mass on a weekday in Ordinary Time. In these celebrations, a special remembrance of the Sacrament of Marriage may appropriately be made, using the forms which are indicated in the Roman Ritual (*Order of Celebrating Marriage*, nos. 272-286).

A

On Any Anniversary

Collect

O God, Creator of all things,
who in the beginning made man and woman
that they might form the marriage bond,
bless and strengthen the union of your servants N. and N.,
that they may show forth an ever more perfect image
of the union of Christ with his Church.
Through our Lord Jesus Christ, your Son,
who lives and reigns with you in the unity of the Holy Spirit,
one God, for ever and ever.

Prayer over the Offerings

O God, who made blood and water
flow from the side of Christ
as a sign of the mysteries of human rebirth,
be pleased, we pray, to receive
the offerings we make in thanksgiving
on behalf of your servants N. and N.
and endow their marriage with your many gifts.
Through Christ our Lord.

Prayer after Communion

Open wide in joy and love, O Lord,
the hearts of these your servants,
who have been refreshed with food and drink from on high,
that their home may be a place of decency and peace
and welcome everyone with love.
Through Christ our Lord.

B

On the Twenty-Fifth Anniversary

Collect

O Lord, who have joined these your servants N. and N.
in the unbreakable bond of marriage
and have been pleased to sustain them
in communion of spirit amid toil and joy,
increase, we pray, and purify their love,
so that (together with their children) they may rejoice
in the sanctification they bring to each other.
Through our Lord Jesus Christ, your Son,
who lives and reigns with you in the unity of the Holy Spirit,
one God, for ever and ever.

Prayer over the Offerings

Be pleased, O God, to receive these offerings
in thanksgiving for your servants N. and N.,
so that from them they may draw peace and joy in abundance.
Through Christ our Lord.

Prayer after Communion

O God, who have graciously welcomed this married couple N. and N.
(together with their children and friends)
to the table of your family,
grant that they may continue to grow
in strong and eager communion with each other,
so that by your gift they may be united,
until they reach the heavenly banquet.
Through Christ our Lord.

C
On the Fiftieth Anniversary

Collect

O God, almighty Father,
for the sake of the good works they have done
through their long life together,
look kindly on this husband and wife N. and N.
(with the children they have brought to life and faith)
and, as you sealed the beginnings of their love
by a wonderful Sacrament,
so bless their fruitful old age.
Through our Lord Jesus Christ, your Son,
who lives and reigns with you in the unity of the Holy Spirit,
one God, for ever and ever.

Prayer over the Offerings

Be pleased, O God, to receive these offerings,
presented in thanksgiving for your servants N. and N.,
who have lived as one in true fidelity these many years
and who ask of your bounty all the blessings of unity and peace.
Through Christ our Lord.

Prayer after Communion

Having tasted the delights of your table,
we entreat you, O Lord,
to keep this married couple N. and N.
safe and holy in the years ahead,
until you welcome them both,
in the fullness of their days,
to your heavenly banquet.
Through Christ our Lord.

12. FOR THE FAMILY

Entrance Antiphon   Eph 6: 2-3

Honor your father and mother.
This is the first commandment with a promise,
that it may go well with you
and that you may have a long life on earth.

Collect

O God, in whose eternal design
family life has its firm foundation,
look with compassion on the prayers of your servants
and grant that, following the example
of the Holy Family of your Only Begotten Son
in practicing the virtues of family life and in the bonds of charity,
we may, in the joy of your house,
delight one day in eternal rewards.
Through our Lord Jesus Christ, your Son,
who lives and reigns with you in the unity of the Holy Spirit,
one God, for ever and ever.

Prayer over the Offerings

We offer you, Lord, the sacrifice of conciliation,
humbly asking that you may establish our families
firmly in your grace and your peace.
Through Christ our Lord.

Communion Antiphon   Is 49: 15

Can a mother forget her infant?
Even should she forget, I will never forget you, says the Lord.

Prayer after Communion

Bring those you refresh with this heavenly Sacrament,
most merciful Father,
to imitate constantly the example
of the Holy Family of your Only Begotten Son,
so that, after the trials of this world,
they may share their company for ever.
Through Christ our Lord.

13. FOR RELIGIOUS

A

Entrance Antiphon   Ps 37 (36): 3-4

Trust in the Lord and do good,
and you will dwell in the land and be secure.
Find your delight in the Lord,
and he will grant your heart's desire.

Collect

O God, who inspire and bring to fulfillment every good intention,
direct your servants into the way of eternal salvation,
and, as they have left all things to devote themselves entirely to you,
grant that, following Christ and renouncing the things of this world,
they may faithfully serve you and their neighbor
in a spirit of poverty and in humility of heart.
Through our Lord Jesus Christ, your Son,
who lives and reigns with you in the unity of the Holy Spirit,
one God, for ever and ever.

Prayer over the Offerings

Sanctify, we pray, O Lord,
through these holy things we offer you,
the servants you have gathered in your name,
so that, faithfully fulfilling their vows to you,
they may serve your majesty in sincerity of heart.
Through Christ our Lord.

Communion Antiphon   1 Kgs 19: 7

The angel of the Lord said to Elijah:
Get up and eat, else the journey will be too much for you!

Or: Rev 22: 17, 20

The Spirit and the bride say: Come.
Amen. Come, Lord Jesus.

Prayer after Communion

Grant, O Lord, that your servants,
gathered in your love and partaking of the one Bread,
may be of one heart in prompting each other
in the pursuit of charity and good works,
so that through a holy way of life
they may always and everywhere be true witnesses to Christ.
Who lives and reigns for ever and ever.

B

On the Twenty-Fifth or Fiftieth Anniversary of Religious Profession

Entrance Antiphon

Cf. Ps 40 (39): 8-9

Behold, I come, O Lord, that I may do your will.
I have vowed it, and your law lies deep within me.

Collect

O Lord, faithful God,
grant, we pray, that we may give you thanks
for your kindness towards our brother (sister) N.,
who today is eager to renew the gift received from you;
strengthen in him (her) a spirit of perfect charity,
so that each day he (she) may more fervently serve your glory
and the work of your salvation.
Through our Lord Jesus Christ, your Son,
who lives and reigns with you in the unity of the Holy Spirit,
one God, for ever and ever.

Prayer over the Offerings

Receive with our oblation, O Lord,
the offering of himself (herself),
which our brother (sister) N. desires to reaffirm today,
and by the power of the Holy Spirit
graciously conform him (her) more fully
to the image of your beloved Son.
Who lives and reigns for ever and ever.

Communion Antiphon

Ps 42 (41): 2

Like the deer that yearns for running streams,
so my soul is yearning for you, my God.

Prayer after Communion

We have partaken, O Lord,
of the Body and Blood of your Son,
which you have given us on this joyful anniversary;
grant, we pray, that our brother (sister) N.,
refreshed with heavenly food and drink,
may proceed happily on the journey towards you
already long begun.
Through Christ our Lord.

14. FOR VOCATIONS TO RELIGIOUS LIFE

Entrance Antiphon
Mt 19: 21

If you would be perfect,
go, sell what you have, give to the poor,
and follow me, says the Lord.

Collect
Holy Father, who, though urging all the faithful to perfect charity,
never cease to prompt many to follow more closely
in the footsteps of your Son,
grant, we pray, that those you have chosen for this special calling
may, by their way of life,
show to the Church and the world a clear sign of your Kingdom.
Through our Lord Jesus Christ, your Son,
who lives and reigns with you in the unity of the Holy Spirit,
one God, for ever and ever.

Or, to be said by a religious Priest:

Look with favor on your family, O Lord,
and increase it always with new offspring,
so that it may lead its sons (daughters)
towards their goal of perfect charity
and work effectively for the salvation of all.
Through our Lord Jesus Christ, your Son,
who lives and reigns with you in the unity of the Holy Spirit,
one God, for ever and ever.

Prayer over the Offerings
Receive in compassion, holy Father,
the offerings we bring you,
and grant fraternal communion and spiritual freedom
to all who set out joyfully to imitate your Son
by following the narrow way.
Through Christ our Lord.

Communion Antiphon
Cf. Mt 19: 27-29

Amen, I say to you: That you who have left all and followed me will receive a hundredfold and possess eternal life, says the Lord.

Prayer after Communion

Strengthen your servants, O Lord,
with this spiritual food and drink,
so that, always faithful to the call of the Gospel,
they may make present everywhere
the living image of your Son.
Who lives and reigns for ever and ever.

Or, to be said by a religious Priest:

By the power of this Sacrament
give us, Lord, we pray,
perseverance in obeying your will,
that we may bear witness to your love before the world
and seek with courage those good things
which alone will last for ever.
Through Christ our Lord.

15. FOR PROMOTING HARMONY

Entrance Antiphon
Acts 4: 32-33

The community of believers was of one heart and mind.
The Apostles bore witness to the Resurrection of the Lord Jesus,
and great favor was accorded them all, alleluia.

Collect

O God, who are perfect unity and true charity,
grant your faithful one heart and one mind,
that the body of your Church,
which rests on the confession of the truth,
may flourish in harmony
and be made strong in enduring unity.
Through our Lord Jesus Christ, your Son,
who lives and reigns with you in the unity of the Holy Spirit,
one God, for ever and ever.

Or:

O God, who have taught your Church
to keep all the heavenly commandments
by loving you and loving our neighbor,
grant us a spirit of peace and grace,
so that your entire family
may be devoted to you wholeheartedly
and united in purity of intent.
Through our Lord Jesus Christ, your Son,
who lives and reigns with you in the unity of the Holy Spirit,
one God, for ever and ever.

Prayer over the Offerings

O God, who renew us in your image
through your Sacraments and your commandments,
mercifully guide our footsteps in your paths,
that through these sacrificial offerings which we bring
we may possess the gift of charity,
for which you have taught us to hope.
Through Christ our Lord.

Preface of the Unity of Christians, p. 1274.

Communion Antiphon   Jn 17: 20-21

Father, I pray for those who will believe in me,
that they may be one in us,
so that the world may believe it was you who sent me, says the Lord.

Prayer after Communion

We have received, O Lord, the Sacrament of unity;
grant us, we pray,
that, living in your house in holy accord,
we may possess the peace we hand on
and preserve the peace we have received.
Through Christ our Lord.

16. FOR RECONCILIATION

The words in this Mass printed within parentheses are said on the occasion of a special penitential time.

Entrance Antiphon

I am the salvation of the people, says the Lord.
Should they cry to me in any distress,
I will hear them, and I will be their Lord for ever.

Collect

God of mercy and reconciliation,
who offer your people special days of salvation
so that they may recognize you as Creator and Father of all,
mercifully come to our help, we pray,
(throughout this acceptable time),
so that, receiving gladly from you the message of peace,
we may serve your will to restore all things in Christ.
Who lives and reigns with you in the unity of the Holy Spirit,
one God, for ever and ever.

Or, especially during Easter Time:

O God, author of true freedom,
whose will it is to shape all men and women
into a single people released from slavery,
(and who offer us a time of grace and blessing,)
grant to your Church, we pray,
that, as she receives new growth in freedom,
she may appear more clearly to the world
as the universal sacrament of salvation,
manifesting and making present
the mystery of your love for all.
Through our Lord Jesus Christ, your Son,
who lives and reigns with you in the unity of the Holy Spirit,
one God, for ever and ever.

Prayer over the Offerings

Remember, Lord, that your Son,
who is our peace and our reconciliation,
has canceled the sin of the world with his Blood,
and, as you look mercifully on your Church's offerings,
grant that we (who joyfully celebrate this time of grace)
may extend to all the freedom of Christ.
Who lives and reigns for ever and ever.

One or other of the Eucharistic Prayers for Reconciliation may be used, p. 757 and p. 765.

Communion Antiphon   Mt 11: 28

Come to me, all who labor and are burdened,
and I will refresh you, says the Lord.

Or: Jn 16: 24

Ask, and you will receive,
so that your joy may be complete, says the Lord.

Prayer after Communion

May the Sacrament of your Son, which we have received,
increase our strength, we pray, O Lord,
that from this mystery of unity
we may drink deeply of love's power
and everywhere promote your peace.
Through Christ our Lord.

17. FOR THE UNITY OF CHRISTIANS

This Mass may be used whenever there are special celebrations for the unity of Christians, provided it does not occur on a Sunday of Advent, Lent or Easter, or on any Solemnity.

A

Entrance Antiphon — Jn 10: 14-15

I am the Good Shepherd,
and I know my sheep and mine know me, says the Lord,
just as the Father knows me and I know the Father;
and I lay down my life for the sheep.

Collect

Almighty ever-living God,
who gather what is scattered
and keep together what you have gathered,
look kindly on the flock of your Son,
that those whom one Baptism has consecrated
may be joined together by integrity of faith
and united in the bond of charity.
Through our Lord Jesus Christ, your Son,
who lives and reigns with you in the unity of the Holy Spirit,
one God, for ever and ever.

Or:

We humbly ask you, Lord, lover of the human family,
to pour out more fully upon us the grace of your Spirit,
and grant that, walking worthily in the vocation
to which you have called us,
we may bear witness to the truth before others
and seek with confidence
the unity of all believers in the bond of peace.
Through our Lord Jesus Christ, your Son,
who lives and reigns with you in the unity of the Holy Spirit,
one God, for ever and ever.

Prayer over the Offerings

O Lord, who gained for yourself a people by adoption
through the one sacrifice offered once for all,
bestow graciously on us, we pray,
the gifts of unity and peace in your Church.
Through Christ our Lord.

FOR THE UNITY OF CHRISTIANS

children and filling and ruling the whole Church. And so, in company with the choirs of Angels, we praise you, and with joy we proclaim:

Holy, Holy, Holy Lord God of hosts . . .

Text without music:

V. **The Lord be with you.**
R. And with your spirit.

V. **Lift up your hearts.**
R. We lift them up to the Lord.

V. **Let us give thanks to the Lord our God.**
R. It is right and just.

It is truly right and just, our duty and our salvation,
always and everywhere to give you thanks,
Lord, holy Father, almighty and eternal God,
through Christ our Lord.

For through him you brought us
to the knowledge of your truth,
so that by the bond of one faith and one Baptism
we might become his Body.

Through him you poured out
your Holy Spirit among all the nations,
so that in a wondrous manner
he might prompt and engender unity
in the diversity of your gifts,
dwelling within your adopted children
and filling and ruling the whole Church.

And so, in company with the choirs of Angels,
we praise you, and with joy we proclaim:

Holy, Holy, Holy Lord God of hosts . . .

Communion Antiphon   Cf. 1 Cor 10:17

Though many, we are one bread, one body,
for we all partake of the one Bread and one Chalice.

Prayer after Communion

**As this reception of your Holy Communion, O Lord,
foreshadows the union of the faithful in you,
so may it bring about unity in your Church.
Through Christ our Lord.**

B

Entrance Antiphon   Ps 106 (105): 47

Save us, O Lord our God,
and gather us from the nations,
to give thanks to your holy name
and make it our glory to praise you.

Collect

**O God, who have united many nations in confessing your name,
grant us, we pray,
the grace to will and to do what you command,
that the people called to your Kingdom
may be one in the faith of their hearts
and the homage of their deeds.
Through our Lord Jesus Christ, your Son,
who lives and reigns with you in the unity of the Holy Spirit,
one God, for ever and ever.**

Or:

**Attend with favor to the prayers of your people,
we ask, O Lord,
and grant that the hearts of believers
may be united in your praise and in repentance together,
so that, with division among Christians overcome,
we may hasten with joy to your eternal Kingdom
in the perfect communion of the Church.
Through our Lord Jesus Christ, your Son,
who lives and reigns with you in the unity of the Holy Spirit,
one God, for ever and ever.**

Prayer over the Offerings

**Celebrating the memorial of our salvation,
we humbly beseech your mercy, O Lord,
that this Sacrament of your loving kindness
may be for us the sign of unity
and the bond of charity.
Through Christ our Lord.**

Proper Preface, pp. 1274-1275.

Communion Antiphon   Col 3: 14-15

And over all things put on love,
which is the bond of perfection.
And let the peace of Christ rule in your hearts,
the peace into which you were also called in one body.

Prayer after Communion

**Pour out on us, O Lord, the Spirit of your love
and, in your kindness,
make those who believe in you one in mind and heart
by the power of this sacrifice.
Through Christ our Lord.**

C

Entrance Antiphon   Eph 4: 4-6

One body and one Spirit,
as you were also called to the one hope of your call;
one Lord, one faith, one baptism;
one God and Father of all,
who is over all and through all and in us all.

Collect

**Look with favor on your people, Lord, we pray,
and pour out upon them the gifts of your Spirit,
that they may grow constantly in love of the truth
and devote themselves with zeal
to perfect unity among Christians.
Through our Lord Jesus Christ, your Son,
who lives and reigns with you in the unity of the Holy Spirit,
one God, for ever and ever.**

Or:

Make known in us, O Lord,
the abundance of your mercy
and, in the power of your Spirit,
remove the divisions between Christians,
that your Church may appear more clearly
as a sign raised high among the nations
and that the world, enlightened by your Spirit,
may believe in the Christ whom you have sent.
Who lives and reigns with you in the unity of the Holy Spirit,
one God, for ever and ever.

Prayer over the Offerings

May the sacrifice we offer you purify us, O Lord,
and make all who are joined in one Baptism
partakers at last of one and the same celebration
of these mysteries.
Through Christ our Lord.

Proper Preface, pp. 1274-1275.

Communion Antiphon
Jn 17: 21, 23

May all be one, as you, Father, are in me and I in you,
that they also may be one in us,
I in them and you in me,
that they may be brought to perfection as one.

Prayer after Communion

Receiving the Sacrament of your Christ,
we pray, O Lord, that you may renew in your Church
the sanctifying grace you have given
and that all who glory in the name of Christian
may come to serve you in unity of faith.
Through Christ our Lord.

18. FOR THE EVANGELIZATION OF PEOPLES

This Mass may be used even on Sundays of Ordinary Time, whenever there are special celebrations for the work of the missions, provided it does not occur on a Sunday of Advent, Lent or Easter, or on any Solemnity.

A

Entrance Antiphon
Cf. Ps 67 (66): 2-3

O God, be gracious and bless us,
and let your face shed its light upon us, and have mercy.
So will your ways be known upon earth
and all nations learn your salvation.

Collect

O God, whose will it is that all should be saved
and come to the knowledge of the truth,
look upon your abundant harvest
and be pleased to send workers to gather it,
that the Gospel may be preached to all creation
and that your people, gathered by the word of life
and sustained by the power of the Sacraments,
may advance in the path of salvation and love.
Through our Lord Jesus Christ, your Son,
who lives and reigns with you in the unity of the Holy Spirit,
one God, for ever and ever.

Or:

O God, who sent your Son into the world as the true light,
pour out, we pray, the Spirit he promised
to sow seeds of truth constantly in people's hearts
and to awaken in them obedience to the faith,
so that, being born to new life through Baptism,
all may become part of your one people.
Through our Lord Jesus Christ, your Son,
who lives and reigns with you in the unity of the Holy Spirit,
one God, for ever and ever.

Prayer over the Offerings

Look, O Lord, upon the face of your Christ,
who handed himself over as a ransom for all,
so that through him,
from the rising of the sun to its setting,
your name may be exalted among the nations
and in every place a single offering
may be presented to your majesty.
Through Christ our Lord.

Communion Antiphon Cf. Mt 28: 20

Teach all nations to keep whatever I have commanded you, says the Lord.
And behold, I am with you always, even to the end of the age.

Prayer after Communion

Nourished by these redeeming gifts,
we pray, O Lord,
that through this help to eternal salvation
true faith may ever increase.
Through Christ our Lord.

B

Entrance Antiphon Ps 96 (95): 3-4

Tell among the nations his glory,
and his wonders among all the peoples,
for the Lord is great and highly to be praised.

FOR THE EVANGELIZATION OF PEOPLES

Collect

O God, you have willed that your Church
be the sacrament of salvation for all nations,
so that Christ's saving work may continue to the end of the ages;
stir up, we pray, the hearts of your faithful
and grant that they may feel a more urgent call
to work for the salvation of every creature,
so that from all the peoples on earth
one family and one people of your own
may arise and increase.
Through our Lord Jesus Christ, your Son,
who lives and reigns with you in the unity of the Holy Spirit,
one God, for ever and ever.

Prayer over the Offerings

May the offerings and prayers of your Church, O Lord,
rise up in the sight of your majesty and gain acceptance,
just as the glorious Passion of your Son was pleasing to you
for the salvation of the whole world.
Through Christ our Lord.

Communion Antiphon   Ps 117 (116): 1-2

O praise the Lord, all you nations;
acclaim him, all you peoples!
For his merciful love has prevailed over us,
and the Lord's faithfulness endures for ever.

Or: Mk 16: 15

Go into all the world, and proclaim the Gospel, says the Lord.
I am with you always.

Prayer after Communion

May our participation at your table sanctify us,
O Lord, we pray,
and grant that through the Sacrament of your Church
all nations may receive in rejoicing
the salvation accomplished on the Cross
by your Only Begotten Son.
Who lives and reigns for ever and ever.

19. FOR PERSECUTED CHRISTIANS

Entrance Antiphon   Cf. Ps 74 (73): 20, 19, 22, 23

Look to your covenant, O Lord,
and do not forget the life of your poor ones for ever.
Arise, O Lord, and defend your cause,
and forget not the cries of those who seek you!

Or: Acts 12: 5

Peter thus was being kept in prison,
but prayer was made without ceasing
by the Church to God for him.

Collect

O God, who in your inscrutable providence
will that the Church be united to the sufferings of your Son,
grant, we pray, to your faithful who suffer for your name's sake
a spirit of patience and charity,
that they may be found true and faithful witnesses
to the promises you have made.
Through our Lord Jesus Christ, your Son,
who lives and reigns with you in the unity of the Holy Spirit,
one God, for ever and ever.

Prayer over the Offerings

Receive, we ask, O Lord,
the prayers and sacrificial gifts we offer in humility
and grant that those who suffer persecution
for their faithful service to you
may rejoice to be united to the sacrifice of Christ your Son
and may know that their names are written in heaven
among the company of the elect.
Through Christ our Lord.

Communion Antiphon
Mt 5: 11-12

> Blessed are you, when they insult you
> and persecute you because of me, says the Lord.
> Rejoice and be glad,
> for your reward will be great in heaven.

> Or:

Mt 10: 32

> Everyone who acknowledges me before others
> I will acknowledge before my heavenly Father, says the Lord.

Prayer after Communion

**By the power of this Sacrament, O Lord,
confirm your servants in the truth
and grant to your faithful who suffer tribulation
that, as they follow your Son in bearing their cross,
they may, in every trial, glory in the name of Christian.
Through Christ our Lord.**

20. FOR A SPIRITUAL OR PASTORAL GATHERING

Entrance Antiphon
Cf. Mt 18: 19, 20

Thus says the Lord:
Where two or three are gathered together in my name,
there am I in the midst of them.

Or:
Col 3: 14-15

And over all things put on love,
which is the bond of perfection.
And let the peace of Christ rule in your hearts,
the peace into which you were also called in one body.

Collect

Pour out on us, O Lord, we pray,
a spirit of truth, understanding and peace,
that we may know with all our hearts
what is pleasing to you
and, with one accord,
pursue what we have come to know.
Through our Lord Jesus Christ, your Son,
who lives and reigns with you in the unity of the Holy Spirit,
one God, for ever and ever.

Or:

O God, whose Son promised to all those gathered in his name
that he would be there in their midst,
grant, we pray,
that we may be aware of his presence among us
and, in truth and charity, experience in our hearts
an abundance of grace, mercy and peace.
Through our Lord Jesus Christ, your Son,
who lives and reigns with you in the unity of the Holy Spirit,
one God, for ever and ever.

Prayer over the Offerings

Look with gracious favor, O Lord, we pray,
on the offerings of your servants,
that they may truly understand and proclaim with confidence
what is right and wholesome in your sight.
Through Christ our Lord.

Preface II of the Holy Spirit, p. 1342.

Communion Antiphon

Where true charity is dwelling, God is present there.
By the love of Christ we have been brought together.

Prayer after Communion

Grant us, O merciful God,
that the holy gifts we have received
may confirm us in our resolve to do your will
and make us everywhere witnesses to your truth.
Through Christ our Lord.

II. FOR CIVIL NEEDS

21. FOR THE NATION OR STATE

Collect

O God, who arrange all things according to a wonderful design,
graciously receive the prayers
we pour out to you for our country (state),
that, through the wisdom of its leaders and the integrity of
    its citizens,
harmony and justice may be assured
and lasting prosperity come with peace.
Through our Lord Jesus Christ, your Son,
who lives and reigns with you in the unity of the Holy Spirit,
one God, for ever and ever.

22. FOR THOSE IN PUBLIC OFFICE

Collect

Almighty ever-living God,
in whose hand lies every human heart and the rights of peoples,
look with favor, we pray,
on those who govern with authority over us,
that throughout the whole world
the prosperity of peoples,
the assurance of peace,
and freedom of religion
may through your gift be made secure.
Through our Lord Jesus Christ, your Son,
who lives and reigns with you in the unity of the Holy Spirit,
one God, for ever and ever.

23. FOR A GOVERNING ASSEMBLY

Collect

O God, who arrange all things in wondrous order
and govern in marvelous ways,
look with favor on the assembled, for whom we now pray,
and mercifully pour out upon them the spirit of your wisdom,
that they may decide everything for the well-being and peace of all
and may never turn aside from your will.
Through our Lord Jesus Christ, your Son,
who lives and reigns with you in the unity of the Holy Spirit,
one God, for ever and ever.

24. FOR THE HEAD OF STATE OR RULER

Collect

O God, to whom every human power is subject,
grant to your servant (our president, sovereign) N.
success in the exercise of his (her) high office,
so that, always revering you and striving to please you,
he (she) may constantly secure and preserve
for the people entrusted to his (her) care
the freedom that comes from civil peace.
Through our Lord Jesus Christ, your Son,
who lives and reigns with you in the unity of the Holy Spirit,
one God, for ever and ever.

25. AT THE BEGINNING OF THE CIVIL YEAR

This Mass may not be used on the Solemnity of Mary, the Holy Mother of God, on January 1.

Entrance Antiphon — Cf. Ps 65 (64): 12

You crown the year with your bounty,
and abundance flows in your pathways.

Or: — Mt 28: 20

Behold, I am with you always, says the Lord,
even to the end of the age.

Collect

O God, who are without beginning or end,
the source of all creation,
grant us so to live this new year,
whose beginning we dedicate to you,
that we may abound in good things
and be resplendent with works of holiness.
Through our Lord Jesus Christ, your Son,
who lives and reigns with you in the unity of the Holy Spirit,
one God, for ever and ever.

Prayer over the Offerings

May the sacrificial gifts we offer you
be acceptable in your eyes, O Lord,
so that all of us, who celebrate with joy
the beginning of this year,
may for the rest of its course
be worthy to live in your love.
Through Christ our Lord.

Communion Antiphon — Heb 13: 8

Jesus Christ is the same yesterday, today, and for ever.

Prayer after Communion

O Lord, draw near to the peoples
who have known the sacred mysteries,
that throughout this year no dangers may afflict
those who always trust in your protection.
Through Christ our Lord.

26. FOR THE SANCTIFICATION OF HUMAN LABOR

A

Entrance Antiphon Gn 1: 1, 27, 31

In the beginning, when God created the heavens and the earth,
God created man in his image;
God looked at everything he had made, and he found it very good.

Or: Cf. Ps 90 (89): 17

May your favor, O Lord, be upon us,
and may you give success to the work of our hands.

Collect

O God, Creator of all things,
who have commanded the human race to bear the burden of labor,
grant that the work we are beginning
may bring progress in this life
and, by your favor,
advance the spread of the Kingdom of Christ.
Who lives and reigns with you in the unity of the Holy Spirit,
one God, for ever and ever.

Or:

O God, who through human labor
never cease to perfect and govern the vast work of creation,
listen to the supplications of your people
and grant that all men and women
may find work that befits their dignity,
joins them more closely to one another
and enables them to serve their neighbor.
Through our Lord Jesus Christ, your Son,
who lives and reigns with you in the unity of the Holy Spirit,
one God, for ever and ever.

Other prayers, p. 1291.

Prayer over the Offerings

O God, who in the offerings presented here
nourish the human race with food
and renew it with your Sacrament,
grant, we pray,
that the sustenance they provide
may not fail us in body or in spirit.
Through Christ our Lord.

Preface V of the Sundays in Ordinary Time, p. 580.

Communion Antiphon

Col 3: 17

Whatever you do in word or deed,
do everything in the name of the Lord Jesus Christ,
giving thanks to God the Father through him.

Prayer after Communion

Having been made partakers of this table of unity and charity,
we beseech your mercy, Lord,
that through the work you have given us to do
we may sustain our life on earth
and trustingly build up your Kingdom.
Through Christ our Lord.

B
Other Prayers

Collect

O God, who willed to subject
the forces of nature to human labor,
mercifully grant
that, undertaking in a Christian spirit what we are to do,
we may merit to join our brothers and sisters
in practicing sincere charity
and in advancing the fulfillment of your divine work of creation.
Through our Lord Jesus Christ, your Son,
who lives and reigns with you in the unity of the Holy Spirit,
one God, for ever and ever.

Prayer over the Offerings

Receive, O Lord, the offerings and supplications of your Church
and grant that, through the human labor we offer you,
we may have a part in the work of Christ the Redeemer.
Who lives and reigns for ever and ever.

Prayer after Communion

Govern with temporal assistance, we pray, O Lord,
those you graciously renew with these eternal mysteries.
Through Christ our Lord.

27. AT SEEDTIME

A

Entrance Antiphon   Cf. Ps 90 (89): 17

May your favor, O Lord, be upon us,
and may you give success to the work of our hands.

Collect

O God, by whose help we sow seeds in the earth
that will grow by the effect of your power,
grant that what we know to be lacking in our labors
may be supplied abundantly by you,
for you alone give increase.
Through our Lord Jesus Christ, your Son,
who lives and reigns with you in the unity of the Holy Spirit,
one God, for ever and ever.

Other prayers, p. 1293.

Prayer over the Offerings

O God, who are the true Creator of the earth's produce
and nurture carefully the fruits of the spirit,
give success to our labors, we pray,
so that we may gather the fruits of the earth in abundance
and that all things, owing their origin to a single providence,
may always work as one for your glory.
Through Christ our Lord.

Preface V of the Sundays in Ordinary Time, p. 580.

Communion Antiphon   Ps 85 (84): 13

The Lord will bestow his bounty,
and our earth shall yield its increase.

Prayer after Communion

O Lord, who renew us with your Sacraments,
assist, we pray, the work of our hands,
so that we, who live and move and have our being in you,
may, through your blessing of the seeds of the earth,
be fed by abundant crops.
Through Christ our Lord.

B
Other Prayers

Collect

Pour out your gracious blessing on your people, Lord God,
so that through your generosity
our land may yield its fruits
for us to enjoy with ever-grateful hearts,
to the honor of your holy name.
Through our Lord Jesus Christ, your Son,
who lives and reigns with you in the unity of the Holy Spirit,
one God, for ever and ever.

Prayer over the Offerings

Look with favor on our offerings, O Lord,
so that we, who bring you grains of wheat made into bread
to be changed into the Body of your Son,
may find joy in the blessing you bestow
on the seed to be sown in the earth.
Through Christ our Lord.

Prayer after Communion

Grant to your faithful, almighty God,
abundance of the earth's fruits,
that, nourished by these in the present age,
they may also grow in spiritual things
and so obtain the good things of eternity,
of which they have received a pledge in this Sacrament.
Through Christ our Lord.

28. AFTER THE HARVEST

Entrance Antiphon
Ps 67 (66): 7

The earth has yielded its fruit;
may God, our God, bless us.

Collect

O Lord, good Father, who in your providence
have entrusted the earth to the human race,
grant, we pray, that with the fruits harvested from it
we may be able to sustain life
and, with your help, always use them
to promote your praise and the well-being of all.
Through our Lord Jesus Christ, your Son,
who lives and reigns with you in the unity of the Holy Spirit,
one God, for ever and ever.

Or:

We give you thanks, O Lord,
for the fruits that earth has given to benefit the human family
and we pray
that, as the working of your supreme providence
    has produced them,
so you may cause the seed of justice and the fruits of charity
to spring up in our hearts.
Through our Lord Jesus Christ, your Son,
who lives and reigns with you in the unity of the Holy Spirit,
one God, for ever and ever.

Prayer over the Offerings

Sanctify, O Lord, the offerings
we bring to you with thanksgiving from the fertile earth
and, as you give us a rich harvest of the earth's produce,
so make our hearts abound with heavenly fruitfulness.
Through Christ our Lord.

Preface V of the Sundays in Ordinary Time, p. 580.

Communion Antiphon
Cf. Ps 104 (103): 13-15

The earth is replete with the fruits of your work, O Lord;
you bring forth bread from the earth,
and wine to cheer the heart.

Prayer after Communion

Grant, we pray, O Lord,
that, as we give you thanks in this saving mystery
for the crops harvested from the earth,
we may, through the same mystery working within us,
be worthy to receive still greater blessings.
Through Christ our Lord.

29. FOR THE PROGRESS OF PEOPLES

Entrance Antiphon
1 Jn 3: 17

When a person who has worldly means
sees a brother in need and refuses him compassion,
how can the love of God remain in him?

Collect

O God, who gave one origin to all peoples
and willed to gather from them one family for yourself,
fill all hearts, we pray, with the fire of your love
and kindle in them a desire
for the just advancement of their neighbor,
that, through the good things which you richly bestow upon all,
each human person may be brought to perfection,
every division may be removed,
and equity and justice may be established in human society.
Through our Lord Jesus Christ, your Son,
who lives and reigns with you in the unity of the Holy Spirit,
one God, for ever and ever.

Prayer over the Offerings

Hear, O Lord, in your mercy,
the prayers of those who cry to you
and, as you receive your Church's offering,
grant that all may be filled with the spirit of divine sonship,
so that, with inequalities overcome by charity,
one family of peoples may be formed in your peace.
Through Christ our Lord.

Communion Antiphon

Cf. Ps 104 (103): 13-15

The earth is replete with the fruits of your work, O Lord;
you bring forth bread from the earth,
and wine to cheer the heart.

Or:

Lk 11: 9

Ask, and it will be given to you, seek, and you will find,
knock, and the door will be opened to you, says the Lord.

Prayer after Communion

Having been fed with the one Bread
by which you constantly renew the human family,
we pray, O Lord,
that from participation in this Sacrament of unity
we may draw a love strong and pure
to help peoples in their development
and, prompted by charity, to fulfill what justice requires.
Through Christ our Lord.

30. FOR THE PRESERVATION OF PEACE AND JUSTICE

This Mass may not be used on the Solemnity of Mary, the Holy Mother of God, on January 1.

A

Entrance Antiphon
Cf. Sir 36: 18, 19

Give peace, O Lord, to those who wait for you;
hear the prayers of your servants
and guide us in the way of justice.

Collect

O God, who have revealed
that peacemakers are to be called your children,
grant, we pray,
that we may work without ceasing to establish that justice
which alone ensures true and lasting peace.
Through our Lord Jesus Christ, your Son,
who lives and reigns with you in the unity of the Holy Spirit,
one God, for ever and ever.

Or:

O God, who show a father's care for all,
grant, in your mercy,
that the members of the human race,
to whom you have given a single origin,
may form in peace a single family
and always be united by a fraternal spirit.
Through our Lord Jesus Christ, your Son,
who lives and reigns with you in the unity of the Holy Spirit,
one God, for ever and ever.

Other prayers, p. 1298.

Prayer over the Offerings

May the saving sacrifice of your Son, the King of peace,
offered under sacramental signs that signify peace and unity,
strengthen, we pray, O Lord,
concord among all your children.
Through Christ our Lord.

Communion Antiphon
Mt 5: 9

Blessed are the peacemakers, for they shall be called children of God.

Or: *Jn 14: 27*

Peace I leave with you,
my peace I give you, says the Lord.

Prayer after Communion

**Bestow on us, we pray, O Lord, the spirit of charity,
so that, sustained by the Body and Blood of your Only Begotten Son,
we may be effective in nurturing among all
the peace that he has left us.
Who lives and reigns for ever and ever.**

B

Other Prayers for Peace

Collect

O God, Creator of the world,
under whose governance the design for all the ages unfolds,
be attentive, we pray, to our petitions
and grant to our times tranquility and peace,
that we may exult with unceasing joy
in praise of your great mercy.
Through our Lord Jesus Christ, your Son,
who lives and reigns with you in the unity of the Holy Spirit,
one God, for ever and ever.

Or:

O God of peace, who are peace itself
and whom a spirit of discord cannot grasp,
nor a violent mind receive,
grant that those who are one in heart
may persevere in what is good
and that those in conflict
may forget evil and so be healed.
Through our Lord Jesus Christ, your Son,
who lives and reigns with you in the unity of the Holy Spirit,
one God, for ever and ever.

The Mass for Promoting Harmony, pp. 1268-1269, may also be used.

31. IN TIME OF WAR OR CIVIL DISTURBANCE

Entrance Antiphon

Jer 29: 11-12, 14

The Lord said: I think thoughts of peace and not of affliction.
You will call upon me, and I will answer you,
and I will lead back your captives from every place.

Or:

Cf. Ps 18 (17): 5-7

The waves of death rose about me;
the pains of the netherworld surrounded me.
In my anguish I called to the Lord,
and from his holy temple he heard my voice.

Collect

O God, merciful and strong,
who crush wars and cast down the proud,
be pleased to banish violence swiftly from our midst
and to wipe away all tears,
so that we may all truly deserve to be called your children.
Through our Lord Jesus Christ, your Son,
who lives and reigns with you in the unity of the Holy Spirit,
one God, for ever and ever.

Or:

O God, author and lover of peace,
to know you is to live, to serve you is to reign;
defend against every attack those who cry to you,
so that we, who trust in your protection,
may not fear the weapons of any foe.
Through our Lord Jesus Christ, your Son,
who lives and reigns with you in the unity of the Holy Spirit,
one God, for ever and ever.

Prayer over the Offerings

Be mindful, Lord, that your Son,
who himself is peace,
has destroyed our hatreds by his Blood;
look in mercy on our evil deeds
and grant that to those whom you love
this sacrifice may restore peace and tranquility.
Through Christ our Lord.

Communion Antiphon
Jn 14: 27

Peace I leave with you;
my peace I give to you, says the Lord.
Not as the world gives do I give it to you.
Do not let your hearts be troubled or afraid.

Prayer after Communion

Grant to us, O Lord,
that, nourished with the delights of the one Bread
that fortifies the human heart,
we may successfully overcome the fury of war
and resolutely keep your law of love and justice.
Through Christ our Lord.

32. FOR REFUGEES AND EXILES

Entrance Antiphon
Ps 91 (90): 11

For you has God commanded his angels
to keep you in all your ways.

Or:

Jer 29: 11-12, 14

The Lord said: I think thoughts of peace and not of affliction.
You will call upon me, and I will answer you,
and I will lead back your captives from every place.

Collect

O Lord, to whom no one is a stranger
and from whose help no one is ever distant,
look with compassion on refugees and exiles,
on segregated persons and on lost children;
restore them, we pray, to a homeland,
and give us a kind heart for the needy and for strangers.
Through our Lord Jesus Christ, your Son,
who lives and reigns with you in the unity of the Holy Spirit,
one God, for ever and ever.

Prayer over the Offerings

O Lord, who willed that your Son should lay down his life
to gather into one your scattered children,
grant that this sacrifice of your peace
may bring about a communion of minds and hearts
and an increase in fraternal charity.
Through Christ our Lord.

Communion Antiphon
Ps 91 (90): 2

My refuge and my stronghold,
my God, in whom I trust.

Prayer after Communion

O Lord, who have renewed us
with the one Bread and the one Chalice,
grant that in sincerity of heart
we may show true compassion
toward strangers and the abandoned
and that all of us may deserve to be gathered together at last
in the land of the living.
Through Christ our Lord.

33. IN TIME OF FAMINE
OR FOR THOSE SUFFERING HUNGER

A

Entrance Antiphon   Ps 74 (73): 20, 19

Look to your covenant, O Lord,
and forget not the life of your poor ones for ever.

Collect

O God, who, being both good and almighty,
provide for all creatures,
give us, we pray, an effective love
for our brothers and sisters who suffer hunger,
so that famine may be banished
and that they may have strength to serve you
with free and untroubled hearts.
Through our Lord Jesus Christ, your Son,
who lives and reigns with you in the unity of the Holy Spirit,
one God, for ever and ever.

Other prayers, to be said by those suffering from hunger, p. 1303.

Prayer over the Offerings

Look, O Lord, on the oblation we present to you
from among your wonderful gifts,
so that the offering which signifies abundance of divine life
and unity in charity
may impel us to share all things justly
and to care for one another as brothers and sisters.
Through Christ our Lord.

Communion Antiphon   Mt 11: 28

Come to me, all who labor and are burdened,
and I will refresh you, says the Lord.

IN TIME OF FAMINE OR FOR THOSE SUFFERING HUNGER

Prayer after Communion

O God, almighty Father,
we humbly ask you that the living Bread,
which has come down from heaven,
may give us strength
to relieve our brothers and sisters in their need.
Through Christ our Lord.

B
Other Prayers, to Be Said by Those Suffering Hunger

Collect

O God, who did not create death
and who provide food for all living things,
drive out, in your compassion,
the hunger of your servants,
that our hearts may serve you with greater readiness and joy.
Through our Lord Jesus Christ, your Son,
who lives and reigns with you in the unity of the Holy Spirit,
one God, for ever and ever.

Prayer over the Offerings

To you, O Lord, we gladly offer these gifts
from the little we have,
humbly imploring your kindness
that they may be for us the first fruits
of your life-giving generosity.
Through Christ our Lord.

Prayer after Communion

Having received the Bread of heaven
from your abundance, O Lord,
we pray that it may give us
such hope and strength for our labor,
that we may provide effectively for our own needs
and for those of our brothers and sisters.
Through Christ our Lord.

34. IN TIME OF EARTHQUAKE

Collect

O God, who set the earth on its firm foundation,
spare those who are fearful
and show favor to those who implore you,
so that, with all dangers of earthquake entirely gone,
we may continue to experience your mercy
and serve you in thankfulness,
safe under your protection.
Through our Lord Jesus Christ, your Son,
who lives and reigns with you in the unity of the Holy Spirit,
one God, for ever and ever.

35. FOR RAIN

Collect

O God, in whom we live and move and have our being,
grant us sufficient rain,
so that, being supplied with what sustains us in this present life,
we may seek more confidently what sustains us for eternity.
Through our Lord Jesus Christ, your Son,
who lives and reigns with you in the unity of the Holy Spirit,
one God, for ever and ever.

36. FOR FINE WEATHER

Collect

Almighty ever-living God,
who heal us through correction
and save us by your forgiveness,
grant to those who seek your favor
that we may rejoice at the good weather for which we hope
and always use what in your goodness you bestow
for the glory of your name and for our well-being.
Through our Lord Jesus Christ, your Son,
who lives and reigns with you in the unity of the Holy Spirit,
one God, for ever and ever.

37. FOR AN END TO STORMS

Collect

O God, to whose commands all the elements give obedience,
we humbly entreat you,
that the stilling of fearsome storms may turn a powerful menace
into an occasion for us to praise you.
Through our Lord Jesus Christ, your Son,
who lives and reigns with you in the unity of the Holy Spirit,
one God, for ever and ever.

III. FOR VARIOUS OCCASIONS
38. FOR THE FORGIVENESS OF SINS

A

Entrance Antiphon   Cf. Wis 11: 23, 24, 26

You have mercy on all, O Lord,
and despise nothing that you have made.
You overlook people's sins,
to bring them to repentance,
and you spare them, for you are the Lord our God.

Collect

Graciously hear the prayers of those who call upon you,
we ask, O Lord,
and forgive the sins of those who confess to you,
granting us in your kindness both pardon and peace.
Through our Lord Jesus Christ, your Son,
who lives and reigns with you in the unity of the Holy Spirit,
one God, for ever and ever.

Or:

Be merciful to your people, O Lord,
and absolve them from all sins,
so that what we deserve by our offenses
may be avoided by your pardon.
Through our Lord Jesus Christ, your Son,
who lives and reigns with you in the unity of the Holy Spirit,
one God, for ever and ever.

Other prayers, p. 1307.

Prayer over the Offerings

We offer you, O Lord,
the sacrifice of conciliation and praise,
that, being moved to compassion,
you may both pardon our offenses
and direct our wavering hearts.
Through Christ our Lord.

Preface IV of the Sundays in Ordinary Time, p. 578.

FOR THE FORGIVENESS OF SINS

Communion Antiphon
Lk 15: 10

There will be rejoicing among the angels of God
over one sinner who repents.

Prayer after Communion

Grant us, merciful God,
that, receiving in this gift the forgiveness of sins,
we may be able by your grace
to avoid sinning from now on
and to serve you in sincerity of heart.
Through Christ our Lord.

B
Other Prayers

Collect

Almighty and most gentle God,
who brought forth from the rock
a fountain of living water for your thirsty people,
bring forth, we pray,
from the hardness of our heart, tears of sorrow,
that we may lament our sins
and merit forgiveness from your mercy.
Through our Lord Jesus Christ, your Son,
who lives and reigns with you in the unity of the Holy Spirit,
one God, for ever and ever.

Prayer over the Offerings

Look mercifully, O Lord, upon this oblation,
which we offer to your majesty for our sins,
and grant, we pray, that the sacrifice
from which forgiveness springs forth for the human race
may bestow on us the grace of the Holy Spirit
to shed tears for our offenses.
Through Christ our Lord.

Prayer after Communion

May the reverent reception of your Sacrament, O Lord,
lead us to wash away the stains of our sins with sighs and tears,
and in your generosity
grant that the pardon we seek may have its effect on us.
Through Christ our Lord.

39. FOR CHASTITY

Collect

Purify our hearts, O Lord,
by the heavenly fire of the Holy Spirit,
that we may serve you with a chaste body
and please you with a pure heart.
Through our Lord Jesus Christ, your Son,
who lives and reigns with you in the unity of the Holy Spirit,
one God, for ever and ever.

Prayer over the Offerings

May our gifts be acceptable to you, O Lord,
that by your gift we may offer you the sacrifice of praise
in full freedom and with a pure mind,
for you have been pleased to save us by your grace.
Through Christ our Lord.

Prayer after Communion

Through the Sacraments we have received, O Lord,
may our heart and our body flourish anew
by a keen sense of modesty and renewed chastity,
so that what has passed our lips as food
we may possess in purity of heart.
Through Christ our Lord.

40. FOR CHARITY

Entrance Antiphon
  Ez 36: 26-28

  Thus says the Lord:
  I will take from your bodies your stony hearts
  and give you natural hearts.
  I will put my spirit within you.
  You will be my people, and I will be your God.

Collect

  Set our hearts aflame, O Lord,
  with the Spirit of your charity, we pray,
  that we may always think thoughts
  worthy and pleasing to your majesty
  and love you sincerely in our brothers and sisters.
  Through our Lord Jesus Christ, your Son,
  who lives and reigns with you in the unity of the Holy Spirit,
  one God, for ever and ever.

Prayer over the Offerings

  Sanctify these gifts in your mercy, O Lord,
  and, accepting the oblation of the spiritual sacrifice,
  grant, we pray, that we may extend your charity to all.
  Through Christ our Lord.

Communion Antiphon
  1 Cor 13: 13

  So faith, hope and charity remain, these three;
  but the greatest of these is charity.

Prayer after Communion

  Pour out the grace of the Holy Spirit, O Lord,
  on those you have replenished with the one Bread of heaven
  and refresh us, we pray,
  with the delights of perfect charity.
  Through Christ our Lord.

41. FOR RELATIVES AND FRIENDS

Entrance Antiphon
Cf. Ps 122 (121): 6, 8

For the peace of Jerusalem pray,
and may they prosper, those who love you.
For the sake of my family and friends,
I will say: Peace be upon you.

Collect

O God, who by the grace of the Holy Spirit
have filled the hearts of your faithful with gifts of charity,
grant health of mind and body to your servants,
for whom we beseech your mercy,
that they may love you with all their strength
and, with all their love, do what is pleasing to you.
Through our Lord Jesus Christ, your Son,
who lives and reigns with you in the unity of the Holy Spirit,
one God, for ever and ever.

Prayer over the Offerings

Have mercy, O Lord, on your servants,
for whom we offer your majesty this sacrifice of praise,
that through these holy gifts
they may obtain the grace of heavenly blessing
and the glory of eternal happiness.
Through Christ our Lord.

Communion Antiphon
Mt 12: 50

Whoever does the will of my heavenly Father
is my brother, and sister, and mother, says the Lord.

Prayer after Communion

We ask you, Lord, as we receive the divine mysteries:
grant your servants,
to whom you have given a love for us,
pardon for sins,
consolation in this life
and unfailing guidance,
that all of us, united in your service,
may rejoice together before your face.
Through Christ our Lord.

42. FOR OUR OPPRESSORS

Entrance Antiphon

Lk 6: 27-28

Love your enemies, says the Lord.
Do good to those who hate you,
bless those who curse you,
pray for those who mistreat you.

Collect

O God, who have laid down by your precept of charity
that we should sincerely love those who afflict us,
grant that we may follow the commands of the New Law,
striving to return good for evil
and bearing one another's burdens.
Through our Lord Jesus Christ, your Son,
who lives and reigns with you in the unity of the Holy Spirit,
one God, for ever and ever.

Prayer over the Offerings

In our longing to be at peace with everyone, O Lord,
we offer you this sacrifice for those who are against us
and we commemorate the Death of your Son,
through which, while still enemies,
we have been reconciled to you.
Through Christ our Lord.

Communion Antiphon

Mt 5: 9-10

Blessed are the peacemakers, for they shall be called children of God.
Blessed are they who are persecuted for the sake of righteousness,
for theirs is the Kingdom of Heaven.

Prayer after Communion

Through these mysteries of our peace,
grant, O God, that we may live in harmony with all
and bring those who are against us
to find favor with you and be reconciled to us.
Through Christ our Lord.

43. FOR THOSE HELD IN CAPTIVITY

Entrance Antiphon   Ps 88 (87): 2-3

O Lord and God of my salvation,
I have cried before you day and night.
Let my prayer come into your presence.
Incline your ear to my cry.

Collect

O God, whose Son humbled himself
and took the form of a slave
to redeem the human race from being captive to sin,
grant to your servants held in confinement
that they may obtain the freedom you destine to all,
for we are your sons and daughters.
Through our Lord Jesus Christ, your Son,
who lives and reigns with you in the unity of the Holy Spirit,
one God, for ever and ever.

Prayer over the Offerings

Through the saving Sacrament of human redemption
which we offer you, Lord,
grant that your servants may be released from captivity
and rejoice in lasting freedom of soul.
Through Christ our Lord.

Communion Antiphon   Ps 69 (68): 31, 34

I will praise God's name with a song,
and I will glorify him with thanksgiving.
For the Lord listens to the needy
and does not spurn his own in their chains.

Prayer after Communion

Mindful of the price paid for our deliverance,
we implore your mercy, O Lord,
upon our brothers and sisters,
that they may be released from captivity
and become servants of your justice.
Through Christ our Lord.

44. FOR THOSE IN PRISON

Collect

Almighty and merciful God,
to whom alone the secrets of the heart lie open,
who recognize the just and make righteous the guilty,
hear our prayers for your servants held in prison,
and grant that through patience and hope
they may find relief in their affliction
and soon return unhindered to their own.
Through our Lord Jesus Christ, your Son,
who lives and reigns with you in the unity of the Holy Spirit,
one God, for ever and ever.

For those imprisoned for the sake of the Gospel, the prayers For Persecuted Christians may be used, pp. 1282-1283.

45. FOR THE SICK

Entrance Antiphon
Ps 6: 3-4

Have mercy on me, Lord, for I languish;
Lord, heal me; my bones are trembling,
and my soul is greatly shaken.

Or:

Cf. Is 53: 4

Truly the Lord has borne our infirmities,
and he has carried our sorrows.

Collect

O God, who willed that our infirmities
be borne by your Only Begotten Son
to show the value of human suffering,
listen in kindness to our prayers
for our brothers and sisters who are sick;
grant that all who are oppressed by pain, distress or
   other afflictions
may know that they are chosen
among those proclaimed blessed
and are united to Christ
in his suffering for the salvation of the world.
Through our Lord Jesus Christ, your Son,
who lives and reigns with you in the unity of the Holy Spirit,
one God, for ever and ever.

Or:

Almighty ever-living God, eternal health of believers,
hear our prayers for your servants who are sick:
grant them, we implore you, your merciful help,
so that, with their health restored,
they may give you thanks in the midst of your Church.
Through our Lord Jesus Christ, your Son,
who lives and reigns with you in the unity of the Holy Spirit,
one God, for ever and ever.

Prayer over the Offerings

Since the moments of our life unfold, O God,
according to your good pleasure,
receive the prayers and sacrificial offerings
by which we implore your mercy
for our brothers and sisters who are ill,
that, having been anxious for them in their danger,
we may rejoice at their recovery of health.
Through Christ our Lord.

Communion Antiphon   Col 1: 24

In my flesh I am completing what is lacking in the afflictions of Christ
on behalf of his body, which is the Church.

Prayer after Communion

O God, only support of our human weakness,
show the power of your protection
over your servants who are sick,
that, sustained by your merciful help,
they may be restored to your holy Church in good health.
Through Christ our Lord.

46. FOR THE DYING

Entrance Antiphon   Rom 14: 7-8

No one lives for himself, and no one dies for himself.
For if we live, we live for the Lord,
and if we die, we die for the Lord;
so then, whether we live or die, we are the Lord's.

Or: Cf. Is 53: 4

Truly the Lord has borne our infirmities,
and he has carried our sorrows.

Collect

Almighty and merciful God,
who through the fact of death itself
have mercifully unlocked for the human race
the gate to eternal life,
look kindly on your servant in his (her) final struggle,
so that, united to your Son's Passion and sealed with his Blood,
he (she) may come without blemish into your presence.
Through our Lord Jesus Christ, your Son,
who lives and reigns with you in the unity of the Holy Spirit,
one God, for ever and ever.

Or, for those who will die today:

**Almighty and merciful God,
who show your love to all creatures everywhere,
hear graciously the prayers we make
for those who will die today,
that, redeemed by your Son's Precious Blood,
they may leave this world without stain of sin
and find eternal rest in the embrace of your mercy.
Through our Lord Jesus Christ, your Son,
who lives and reigns with you in the unity of the Holy Spirit,
one God, for ever and ever.**

Prayer over the Offerings

**Receive, O God, the sacrificial offering
we bring you with confidence
for your servant who has reached this life's end,
and grant, through this Sacrament,
the cleansing of all his (her) offenses,
that, though beset by the trials you ordain for us in this life,
he (she) may in the life to come know eternal rest.
Through Christ our Lord.**

Communion Antiphon
Col 1: 24

In my flesh I am completing what is lacking in the afflictions of Christ
on behalf of his body, which is the Church.

Or:
Jn 6: 54

Whoever eats my flesh and drinks my blood
has eternal life, says the Lord,
and I will raise him on the last day.

Prayer after Communion

**By the power of this Sacrament, O Lord,
be pleased to sustain your servant with your merciful grace,
that at the hour of death
he (she) may not see the enemy prevail against him (her)
but may be worthy to pass over to life eternal
in the company of your Angels.
Through Christ our Lord.**

47. FOR THE GRACE OF A HAPPY DEATH

Entrance Antiphon
Ps 23 (22): 4

Though I should walk in the valley of the shadow of death,
no evil will I fear, for you are with me, Lord, my God.
Your crook and your staff have given me comfort.

Collect

O God, who have created us in your image
and willed that your Son should undergo death for our sake,
grant that those who call upon you
may be watchful in prayer at all times,
so that we may leave this world without stain of sin
and may merit to rest with joy in your merciful embrace.
Through our Lord Jesus Christ, your Son,
who lives and reigns with you in the unity of the Holy Spirit,
one God, for ever and ever.

Prayer over the Offerings

As you have destroyed our death, O Lord,
by the Death of your Only Begotten Son,
grant, we pray, through the power of the same mystery,
that, obeying your will even until death,
we may go forth from this world in peace and trust
and by your gift be made sharers in his Resurrection.
Who lives and reigns for ever and ever.

Common Preface V, p. 618, or VI, p. 620.

Communion Antiphon
Rom 14: 7-8

No one lives for himself, and no one dies for himself.
For if we live, we live for the Lord,
and if we die, we die for the Lord;
so then, whether we live or die, we are the Lord's.

Or:
Lk 21: 36

Be vigilant at all times and pray
that you have the strength to stand before the Son of Man.

Prayer after Communion

Having received the pledge of immortality
through these mysteries, O Lord,
we humbly entreat your fatherly help
for the moment when we depart in death,
so that, overcoming the snares of the enemy,
we may be restored to life
in the embrace of your eternal glory.
Through Christ our Lord.

48. IN ANY NEED

A

Entrance Antiphon

I am the salvation of the people, says the Lord.
Should they cry to me in any distress,
I will hear them, and I will be their Lord for ever.

Collect

O God, our refuge in trials,
our strength in sickness, our comfort in sorrow,
spare your people, we pray,
that, though rightly chastised now by affliction,
they may find relief at last through your loving mercy.
Through our Lord Jesus Christ, your Son,
who lives and reigns with you in the unity of the Holy Spirit,
one God, for ever and ever.

Prayer over the Offerings

Accept in compassion, Lord, we pray,
the offerings of your family,
that under your protective care
they may never lose what they have received
but attain the gifts that are eternal.
Through Christ our Lord.

Communion Antiphon
Mt 11:28

    Come to me, all who labor and are burdened,
    and I will refresh you, says the Lord.

Prayer after Communion

**We pray, O Lord, that in receiving your Sacrament
we may experience help in mind and body,
so that, kept safe in both,
we may glory in the fullness of heavenly healing.
Through Christ our Lord.**

B

Entrance Antiphon
Ps 44 (43): 26

    Arise, O Lord, come to our help;
    redeem us with your merciful love.

Collect

**Almighty and merciful God,
look with compassion on our affliction,
and so lighten your children's burden and confirm their faith,
that they may always trust without hesitation
in your fatherly providence.
Through our Lord Jesus Christ, your Son,
who lives and reigns with you in the unity of the Holy Spirit,
one God, for ever and ever.**

Prayer over the Offerings

**Receive, O Lord, the offerings
we confidently bring before you,
and turn, we pray, the bitterness of the sorrow we bear
into a sweet and fragrant sacrifice before you.
Through Christ our Lord.**

Communion Antiphon
Jn 16: 23-24

    Whatever you ask the Father in my name, he will give you.
    Ask, and you will receive, so that your joy may be complete, says the Lord.

Prayer after Communion

We humbly entreat you, Lord,
that, nourished and fortified by this divine banquet,
we may have strength to face future trials with fortitude
and to lend more generous help
to our brothers and sisters in time of trouble.
Through Christ our Lord.

C
Other Prayers

Collect

O God, who know that because of human frailty
we cannot stand firm amid such great dangers,
grant us health of mind and body,
that what we suffer for our sins
we may overcome with your help.
Through our Lord Jesus Christ, your Son,
who lives and reigns with you in the unity of the Holy Spirit,
one God, for ever and ever.

Or:

Grant, we pray, O Lord,
that your people may avoid the contagion of the devil
and follow you, the only God, in purity of heart.
Through our Lord Jesus Christ, your Son,
who lives and reigns with you in the unity of the Holy Spirit,
one God, for ever and ever.

Prayer over the Offerings

Receive, we ask, our prayers and offerings, O Lord,
that, suffering from the scourge of our own sins,
we may find relief by the grace of your mercy.
Through Christ our Lord.

Prayer after Communion

Look with pity on our tribulation, O Lord, we pray,
and, though our sins deserve your anger,
mercifully turn it away from us
through the Passion of your Son.
Who lives and reigns for ever and ever.

[In the Dioceses of the United States]
48/1. FOR GIVING THANKS TO GOD FOR THE GIFT OF HUMAN LIFE

A

Entrance Antiphon   Cf. Ps 143 (142): 11

For the sake of your name, O Lord, give me life.

Collect

God our Creator,
we give thanks to you,
who alone have the power to impart the breath of life
as you form each of us in our mother's womb;
grant, we pray,
that we, whom you have made stewards of creation,
may remain faithful to this sacred trust
and constant in safeguarding the dignity of every human life.
Through our Lord Jesus Christ, your Son,
who lives and reigns with you in the unity of the Holy Spirit,
one God, for ever and ever.

Prayer over the Offerings

Accept our humble offerings,
O Lord of the living,
and unite us to the perfect sacrifice of your Son,
through whom you have made all creation new.
Who lives and reigns for ever and ever.

Communion Antiphon   Cf. Ps 36 (35): 10

With you, O Lord, is the fountain of life, and in your light, we see light.

Prayer after Communion

Increase your love within us, Lord God,
by the saving mysteries we have celebrated,
and bring people everywhere
to respect your gift of human life.
Through Christ our Lord.

B

Entrance Antiphon   Cf. Ps 31 (30): 15-16

I trust in you, O Lord; I say, you are my God. My life is in your hands.

Collect

O God, who adorn creation with splendor and beauty
and fashion human lives in your image and likeness,
awaken in every heart
reverence for the work of your hands,
and renew among your people
a readiness to nurture and sustain
your precious gift of human life.
Through our Lord Jesus Christ, your Son,
who lives and reigns with you in the unity of the Holy Spirit,
one God, for ever and ever.

Prayer over the Offerings

O God, who bring forth bread from the earth
to sustain our lives
and wine to gladden the heart,
be pleased to accept these gifts
and make them the Sacrament of our salvation.
Through Christ our Lord.

Communion Antiphon   Cf. Ps 36 (35): 10

With you, O Lord, is the fountain of life, and in your light, we see light.

Prayer after Communion

Confirm our resolve, O God,
by the life-giving Body and Blood of your Son,
that we may live always for others
and cherish your sacred gift of human life.
Through Christ our Lord.

49. FOR GIVING THANKS TO GOD

A

Entrance Antiphon   Eph 5: 19-20

    Sing and make music to the Lord in your hearts,
    always thanking God the Father for all things
    in the name of our Lord Jesus Christ.

Collect

    O God, who always listen mercifully
    to your servants in distress,
    we humbly beseech you,
    as we give thanks for your kindness,
    that, free from all evil,
    we may constantly serve you in gladness.
    Through our Lord Jesus Christ, your Son,
    who lives and reigns with you in the unity of the Holy Spirit,
    one God, for ever and ever.

    Other prayers, p. 1324.

Prayer over the Offerings

    O Lord, who gave us your Son
    to rescue us graciously from death and from every evil,
    accept, we pray, in mercy this sacrifice,
    which we offer you in thanksgiving
    for our deliverance from distress.
    Through Christ our Lord.

    Common Preface IV, p. 616.

Communion Antiphon   Ps 138 (137): 1

    I will thank you, Lord, with all my heart,
    for you have heard the words of my mouth.

    Or: Ps 116 (115): 12-13

    How can I repay the Lord for all his goodness to me?
    The chalice of salvation I will raise,
    and I will call on the name of the Lord.

Prayer after Communion

> Almighty God, who through this Bread of Life
> are pleased to free your servants from the bond of sin
> and in your compassion to restore their strength,
> grant us to advance without hindrance towards the hope of glory.
> Through Christ our Lord.

B
Other Prayers

Collect

> O God, the Father of every gift,
> we confess that all we have and are comes down from you;
> teach us to recognize the effects of your boundless care
> and to love you with a sincere heart and with all our strength.
> Through our Lord Jesus Christ, your Son,
> who lives and reigns with you in the unity of the Holy Spirit,
> one God, for ever and ever.

Prayer over the Offerings

> For the gifts you have bestowed, O Lord,
> we offer you the sacrifice of praise,
> humbly begging
> that what you have conferred upon us in our unworthiness
> we may give back, to the glory of your name.
> Through Christ our Lord.

Prayer after Communion

> O God, who have given to us as spiritual food
> the saving Sacrament of your Son,
> which we have offered you in thanksgiving,
> grant that, being strengthened by gifts of courage and joy,
> we may serve you more devotedly
> and be worthy of still further blessings.
> Through Christ our Lord.

VOTIVE MASSES

If some serious pastoral benefit is to be gained, an appropriately corresponding Votive Mass may be used, at the direction of the Ordinary, or with his permission, except on Solemnities, on the Sundays of Advent, Lent, and Easter, on days within the Octave of Easter, on the Commemoration of All the Faithful Departed (All Souls' Day), on Ash Wednesday, and on the weekdays of Holy Week.

Votive Masses are in principle forbidden on days on which there occurs an Obligatory Memorial, on a weekday of Advent up to and including December 16, on a weekday of Christmas Time from January 2, or on a weekday of Easter Time after the Octave of Easter. However, for pastoral reasons, as determined by the rector of the church or the Priest Celebrant himself, an appropriately corresponding Votive Mass may be used in celebration of Mass with the people.

On weekdays in Ordinary Time, even if an Optional Memorial occurs, a Votive Mass may be chosen by the Priest Celebrant for the sake of the devotion of the faithful.

1. THE MOST HOLY TRINITY

In this Mass, the color white is used.

Entrance Antiphon

Blest be God the Father, and the Only Begotten Son of God,
and also the Holy Spirit, for he has shown us his merciful love.

Collect

God our Father, who, by sending into the world
the Word of truth and the Spirit of sanctification,
made known to the human race your wondrous mystery,
grant us, we pray, that in professing the true faith
we may acknowledge the Trinity of eternal glory
and adore your Unity, powerful in majesty.
Through our Lord Jesus Christ, your Son,
who lives and reigns with you in the unity of the Holy Spirit,
one God, for ever and ever.

Prayer over the Offerings

Sanctify by the invocation of your name,
we pray, O Lord our God,
this oblation of our service,
and by it make of us an eternal offering to you.
Through Christ our Lord.

Preface: The mystery of the Most Holy Trinity.

V. **The Lord be with you.**
R. And with your spirit.

V. **Lift up your hearts.**
R. We lift them up to the Lord.

V. **Let us give thanks to the Lord our God.**
R. It is right and just.

It is truly right and just, our duty and our salvation,
always and everywhere to give you thanks,
Lord, holy Father, almighty and eternal God.

For with your Only Begotten Son and the Holy Spirit
you are one God, one Lord:
not in the unity of a single person,
but in a Trinity of one substance.

For what you have revealed to us of your glory
we believe equally of your Son
and of the Holy Spirit,
so that, in the confessing of the true and eternal Godhead,
you might be adored in what is proper to each Person,
their unity in substance,
and their equality in majesty.

For this is praised by Angels and Archangels,
Cherubim, too, and Seraphim,
who never cease to cry out each day,
as with one voice they acclaim:

Holy, Holy, Holy Lord God of hosts . . .

Text with music, pp. 496-497.

Communion Antiphon
Gal 4: 6

Since you are children of God,
God has sent into your hearts the Spirit of his Son,
the Spirit who cries out: Abba, Father.

Prayer after Communion

May receiving this Sacrament, O Lord our God,
bring us health of body and soul,
as we confess your eternal holy Trinity and undivided Unity.
Through Christ our Lord.

2. THE MERCY OF GOD

In this Mass, the color white is used. This Mass may not be said on the Second Sunday of Easter.

Entrance Antiphon
Cf. Jer 31: 3; 1 Jn 2: 2

God has loved us with an everlasting love;
he sent his Only Begotten Son as an expiation for our sins
and not for our sins alone, but for those of all the world.

Or:
Ps 89 (88): 2

I will sing for ever of your mercies, O Lord;
through all ages my mouth will proclaim your fidelity.

Collect

O God, whose mercies are without number
and whose treasure of goodness is infinite,
graciously increase the faith of the people consecrated to you,
that all may grasp and rightly understand
by whose love they have been created,
through whose Blood they have been redeemed,
and by whose Spirit they have been reborn.
Through our Lord Jesus Christ, your Son,
who lives and reigns with you in the unity of the Holy Spirit,
one God, for ever and ever.

Prayer over the Offerings

Receive our oblations in your mercy, O Lord,
and transform them into the Sacrament of redemption,
the memorial of your Son's Death and Resurrection,
so that, by the power of this sacrifice
and with constant trust in Christ,
we may come to eternal life.
Through Christ our Lord.

Communion Antiphon Ps 103 (102): 17
The mercy of the Lord is everlasting
upon those who hold him in fear.

Or: Jn 19: 34

One of the soldiers opened his side with a lance,
and at once there came forth blood and water.

Prayer after Communion
Grant to us, O merciful God,
that, nourished by the Body and Blood of your Son,
we may draw confidently from the wellsprings of mercy
and show ourselves ever more compassionate
towards our brothers and sisters.
Through Christ our Lord

3. OUR LORD JESUS CHRIST, THE ETERNAL HIGH PRIEST

In this Mass, the color white is used.

Entrance Antiphon Ps 110 (109): 4
The Lord has sworn an oath he will not change:
You are a priest for ever, according to the order of Melchizedek.

Collect
O God, who for your glory
and the salvation of the human race
willed to establish Christ as the eternal High Priest,
grant that the people he has gained for you by his Blood
may, through their participation in his memorial,
experience the power of his Cross and Resurrection.
Who lives and reigns with you in the unity of the Holy Spirit,
one God, for ever and ever.

Prayer over the Offerings
Grant us, O Lord, we pray,
that we may participate worthily in these mysteries,
for, whenever the memorial of this sacrifice is celebrated,
the work of our redemption is accomplished.
Through Christ our Lord.

THE MYSTERY OF THE HOLY CROSS

Preface of the Most Holy Eucharist, pp. 588-589.

Communion Antiphon
1 Cor 11: 24-25

This is the Body that will be given up for you;
this is the Chalice of the new covenant in my Blood, says the Lord;
do this, whenever you receive it in memory of me.

Prayer after Communion

We pray, O Lord, that through our partaking in this sacrifice,
which your Son commanded to be offered in his memory,
you may make us together with him
an everlasting oblation to you.
Through Christ our Lord.

4. THE MYSTERY OF THE HOLY CROSS

In this Mass, the color red is used.

Entrance Antiphon
Cf. Gal 6: 14

We should glory in the Cross of our Lord Jesus Christ,
in whom is our salvation, life and resurrection,
through whom we are saved and delivered.

Collect

O God, who willed that your Only Begotten Son
should undergo the Cross to save the human race,
grant, we pray,
that we, who have known his mystery on earth,
may merit the grace of his redemption in heaven.
Through our Lord Jesus Christ, your Son,
who lives and reigns with you in the unity of the Holy Spirit,
one God, for ever and ever.

Prayer over the Offerings

May this oblation, O Lord,
which on the altar of the Cross
canceled the offense of the whole world,
cleanse us, we pray, of all our sins.
Through Christ our Lord.

Preface: The victory of the glorious Cross.

 V. **The Lord be with you.**
 R. And with your spirit.

 V. **Lift up your hearts.**
 R. We lift them up to the Lord.

 V. **Let us give thanks to the Lord our God.**
 R. It is right and just.

It is truly right and just, our duty and our salvation,
always and everywhere to give you thanks,
Lord, holy Father, almighty and eternal God.

For you placed the salvation of the human race
on the wood of the Cross,
so that, where death arose,
life might again spring forth
and the evil one, who conquered on a tree,
might likewise on a tree be conquered,
through Christ our Lord.

Through him the Angels praise your majesty,
Dominions adore and Powers tremble before you.
Heaven and the Virtues of heaven and the blessed Seraphim
worship together with exultation.
May our voices, we pray, join with theirs
in humble praise, as we acclaim:

Holy, Holy, Holy Lord God of hosts . . .

Text with music, p. 946-947.

Preface I of the Passion of the Lord may also be used, p. 554.

Communion Antiphon   *Jn 12: 32*

When I am lifted up from the earth,
I will draw everyone to myself, says the Lord.

Prayer after Communion

Having been nourished by your holy banquet,
we beseech you, Lord Jesus Christ,
to bring those you have redeemed
by the wood of your life-giving Cross
to the glory of the resurrection.
Who live and reign for ever and ever.

5. THE MOST HOLY EUCHARIST

In this Mass, the color white is used.

Entrance Antiphon
Ps 78 (77): 23-25

The Lord opened the gates of heaven,
and rained down manna upon them to eat, and gave them bread from heaven:
man ate the bread of angels.

Collect

O God, who have accomplished the work of human redemption
through the Paschal Mystery of your Only Begotten Son,
graciously grant that we, who confidently proclaim,
under sacramental signs, the Death and Resurrection of Christ,
may experience continued increase of your saving grace.
Through our Lord Jesus Christ, your Son,
who lives and reigns with you in the unity of the Holy Spirit,
one God, for ever and ever.

Prayer over the Offerings

Celebrating the memorial of our salvation,
we humbly beseech your mercy, O Lord,
that this Sacrament of your loving kindness
may be for us the sign of unityand the bond of charity.
Through Christ our Lord.

Preface of the Most Holy Eucharist, pp. 588-589.

Communion Antiphon
Jn 6: 51-52

I am the living bread,
that came down from heaven, says the Lord.
Whoever eats of this bread will live for ever,
and the bread that I will give is my flesh for the life of the world.

Prayer after Communion

May sharing at the heavenly table
sanctify us, Lord, we pray,
so that through the Body and Blood of Christ
the whole family of believers may be bound together.
Through Christ our Lord.

As a Votive Mass of the Most Holy Eucharist, the Votive Mass of our Lord Jesus Christ, the Eternal High Priest may also be used, p. 1330; or the Mass of the Solemnity of the Most Holy Body and Blood of Christ, p. 499.

6. THE MOST HOLY NAME OF JESUS

In this Mass, the color white is used.

Entrance Antiphon
Phil 2: 10-11

At the name of Jesus every knee should bend,
of those in heaven and on earth and under the earth,
and every tongue confess
that Jesus Christ is Lord, to the glory of God the Father.

Collect

As we venerate the most holy Name of Jesus,
mercifully grant us, Lord,
that, savoring its sweetness in this life,
we may be filled with everlasting joy
in our heavenly homeland.
Through our Lord Jesus Christ, your Son,
who lives and reigns with you in the unity of the Holy Spirit,
one God, for ever and ever.

Prayer over the Offerings

Be pleased, almighty Father,
to accept our offerings in the Name of Jesus,
for we are confident that we shall receive
whatever we ask in your Son's Name,
as he himself, with such kindness, promises.
Who lives and reigns for ever and ever.

Communion Antiphon
Acts 4: 12

There is no other name under heaven given among the human race
by which we must be saved.

Prayer after Communion

Grant us in your mercy, O Lord, we pray,
that in these sacred mysteries
we may do worthy homage to the Lord Jesus,
for it is your will that at his Name
every knee should bend
and in him all people find salvation.
Who lives and reigns for ever and ever.

7. THE MOST PRECIOUS BLOOD OF OUR LORD JESUS CHRIST

In this Mass, the color red is used.

Entrance Antiphon
Cf. Rev 5: 9-10

You have redeemed us, Lord, by your Blood,
from every tribe and tongue and people and nation,
and have made us into a kingdom for our God.

Collect

O God, who by the Precious Blood of your Only Begotten Son
have redeemed the whole world,
preserve in us the work of your mercy,
so that, ever honoring the mystery of our salvation,
we may merit to obtain its fruits.
Through our Lord Jesus Christ, your Son,
who lives and reigns with you in the unity of the Holy Spirit,
one God, for ever and ever.

Prayer over the Offerings

As we offer our oblation to your majesty, O Lord,
may we draw near in these mysteries
to Jesus, the Mediator of the New Covenant,
and celebrate anew the sprinkling of his Blood,
in which lies all our salvation.
Through Christ our Lord.

Preface I of the Passion of the Lord, p. 554.

Communion Antiphon   Cf. 1 Cor 10: 16
The chalice of blessing that we bless
is a communion in the Blood of Christ;
and the bread that we break
is a sharing in the Body of the Lord.

Prayer after Communion

**Refreshed, O Lord, by this saving food and drink,
we pray that we may always be bathed
in the Blood of our Savior,
so that it may become for us
a spring of water welling up to eternal life.
Through Christ our Lord.**

Or:

**Restored with heavenly food and drink,
we beseech you, almighty God,
to protect from fear of their enemies
those you have redeemed by the Precious Blood of your Son.
Who lives and reigns for ever and ever.**

8. THE MOST SACRED HEART OF JESUS

In this Mass, the color white is used.

Entrance Antiphon   Ps 33 (32): 11, 19
The designs of his Heart are from age to age,
to rescue their souls from death
and to keep them alive in famine.

Collect

**Clothe us, Lord God,
with the virtues of the Heart of your Son
and set us aflame with his love,
that, conformed to his image,
we may merit a share in eternal redemption.
Through our Lord Jesus Christ, your Son,
who lives and reigns with you in the unity of the Holy Spirit,
one God, for ever and ever.**

Prayer over the Offerings

O God, Father of mercies,
who, because of the great love with which you loved us,
with untold goodness gave us your Only Begotten Son,
grant, we pray,
that, being perfectly united with him,
we may offer you worthy homage.
Through Christ our Lord.

Preface: The boundless charity of Christ.

V. **The Lord be with you.**
R. And with your spirit.

V. **Lift up your hearts.**
R. We lift them up to the Lord.

V. **Let us give thanks to the Lord our God.**
R. It is right and just.

It is truly right and just, our duty and our salvation,
always and everywhere to give you thanks,
Lord, holy Father, almighty and eternal God,
through Christ our Lord.

For raised up high on the Cross,
he gave himself up for us with a wonderful love
and poured out Blood and water from his pierced side,
the wellspring of the Church's Sacraments,
so that, won over to the open Heart of the Savior,
all might draw water joyfully from the springs of salvation.

And so, with all the Angels and Saints,
we praise you, as without end we acclaim:

Holy, Holy, Holy Lord God of hosts . . .

Text with music, p. 503.

Communion Antiphon
Cf. Jn 7: 37-38

Thus says the Lord:
Let whoever is thirsty come to me and drink.
Streams of living water will flow
from within the one who believes in me.

Or:
Jn 19: 34

One of the soldiers opened his side with a lance,
and at once there came forth blood and water.

Prayer after Communion

**Made partakers in your Sacrament of charity,
we humbly implore your mercy, Lord,
that we may be conformed to Christ on earth
and merit to be coheirs of his glory in heaven.
Who lives and reigns for ever and ever.**

As a Votive Mass, the Mass of the Solemnity of the Most Sacred Heart of Jesus may also be used, p. 502.

9. THE HOLY SPIRIT

In this Mass, the color red is used.

A

Entrance Antiphon
Rom 5: 5; cf. 8: 11

The love of God has been poured into our hearts
through the Spirit of God dwelling within us.

Collect

**O God, who have taught the hearts of the faithful
by the light of the Holy Spirit,
grant that in the same Spirit we may be truly wise
and ever rejoice in his consolation.
Through our Lord Jesus Christ, your Son,
who lives and reigns with you in the unity of the Holy Spirit,
one God, for ever and ever.**

Prayer over the Offerings

**Sanctify, we pray, O Lord, the offerings made here,
and cleanse our hearts by the light of the Holy Spirit.
Through Christ our Lord.**

Preface I of the Holy Spirit: The sending of the Spirit by the Lord upon the Church.

V. The Lord be with you.   R. And with your spir-it.

V. Lift up your hearts.   R. We lift them up to the Lord.

V. Let us give thanks to the Lord our God.   R. It is right and just.

It is truly right and just, our duty and our sal-va-tion, al-ways and everywhere to give you thanks, Lord, holy Father, almighty and e-ter-nal God, through Christ our Lord. As-cending above all the heavens and sitting at your right hand, he poured out the promised Ho-ly Spir-it on your a-dopt-ed chil-dren. There-fore, now and for ages unending, with all the host of An-gels, we sing to you with all our hearts, crying out as we ac-claim:

Holy, Holy, Holy Lord God of hosts . . .

Text without music:
V. The Lord be with you.
R. And with your spirit.

V. Lift up your hearts.
R. We lift them up to the Lord.

V. Let us give thanks to the Lord our God.
R. It is right and just.

It is truly right and just, our duty and our salvation,
always and everywhere to give you thanks,
Lord, holy Father, almighty and eternal God,
through Christ our Lord.

Ascending above all the heavens
and sitting at your right hand,
he poured out the promised Holy Spirit
on your adopted children.

Therefore, now and for ages unending,
with all the host of Angels,
we sing to you with all our hearts,
crying out as we acclaim:

Holy, Holy, Holy Lord God of hosts . . .

Communion Antiphon   Cf. Ps 68 (67): 29-30
Confirm, O God, what you have brought about in us,
from your holy temple, which is in Jerusalem.

Prayer after Communion
May the outpouring of the Holy Spirit
cleanse our hearts, O Lord,
and make them fruitful by the inner sprinkling of his dew.
Through Christ our Lord.

THE HOLY SPIRIT

B

Entrance Antiphon *Cf. Jn 14: 26; 15: 26*

When the Spirit of truth comes,
he will teach you all truth, says the Lord.

Collect

May the Paraclete who proceeds from you, we pray, O Lord,
enlighten our minds and lead us into all truth,
just as your Son has promised.
Who lives and reigns with you in the unity of the Holy Spirit,
one God, for ever and ever.

Or:

O God, to whom every heart lies open,
every desire speaks plainly
and from whom no secret is hidden,
cleanse, we pray, the thoughts of our heart
by the outpouring of the Holy Spirit,
that we may merit to love you perfectly
and offer you worthy praise.
Through our Lord Jesus Christ, your Son,
who lives and reigns with you in the unity of the Holy Spirit,
one God, for ever and ever.

Prayer over the Offerings

Look, we pray, O Lord, on the spiritual sacrifice
placed on your altar with loving devotion
and give your servants a right spirit,
so that their faith may make these gifts pleasing to you
and their humility commend them.
Through Christ our Lord.

Preface II of the Holy Spirit: The action of the Spirit in the Church.

V. The Lord be with you.   R. And with your spir-it.

V. Lift up your hearts.   R. We lift them up to the Lord.

V. Let us give thanks to the Lord our God.   R. It is right and just.

It is truly right and just, our duty and our sal-va-tion, al-ways and everywhere to give you thanks, Lord, holy Father, almighty and e-ter-nal God. For you bestow gifts suited to eve-ry sea-son and guide the governing of your Church in won-der-ful ways. By the power of the Holy Spirit you come unfailingly to her aid, so that with a heart always subject to you she may never fail to seek your help in time of trou-ble nor cease to give you thanks in time of joy, through Christ our Lord. And so, in company with the choirs of An-gels, we praise you, and with joy we pro-claim:

Holy, Holy, Holy Lord God of hosts . . .

THE HOLY SPIRIT

Text without music:

V. **The Lord be with you.**
R. And with your spirit.

V. **Lift up your hearts.**
R. We lift them up to the Lord.

V. **Let us give thanks to the Lord our God.**
R. It is right and just.

It is truly right and just, our duty and our salvation,
always and everywhere to give you thanks,
Lord, holy Father, almighty and eternal God.

For you bestow gifts suited to every season
and guide the governing of your Church in wonderful ways.

By the power of the Holy Spirit
you come unfailingly to her aid,
so that with a heart always subject to you
she may never fail to seek your help in time of trouble
nor cease to give you thanks in time of joy,
through Christ our Lord.

And so, in company with the choirs of Angels,
we praise you, and with joy we proclaim:

Holy, Holy, Holy Lord God of hosts . . .

Communion Antiphon
Jn 15: 26; 16: 14

The Spirit, whom I will send you from the Father,
will glorify me, says the Lord.

Prayer after Communion

Lord our God, who have been pleased
to nourish us with heavenly food,
pour, we pray, the delights of your Spirit
into the recesses of our heart,
that what we have devoutly received in time
we may possess as a gift for eternity.
Through Christ our Lord.

C

Entrance Antiphon   Cf. Lk 4: 18
The Spirit of the Lord is upon me,
he has sent me to preach the good news to the poor, says the Lord.

Collect
O God, who sanctify your universal Church
in every people and nation,
pour out, we pray, the gifts of your Spirit
across the face of the earth,
so that your divine grace, which was at work
when the Gospel was first proclaimed,
may now spread through the hearts of those who believe in you.
Through our Lord Jesus Christ, your Son,
who lives and reigns with you in the unity of the Holy Spirit,
one God, for ever and ever.

Or:

O God, by whose Spirit we are governed
and by whose protection we are kept safe,
extend over us your mercy
and give ear to our supplications,
that the faith of those who believe in you
may always be sustained by your gifts.
Through our Lord Jesus Christ, your Son,
who lives and reigns with you in the unity of the Holy Spirit,
one God, for ever and ever.

Prayer over the Offerings
May the fire of the Spirit, O Lord,
sanctify the sacrificial gifts offered in your sight,
just as it enkindled the hearts of the disciples of your Son.
Who lives and reigns for ever and ever.

Preface I of the Holy Spirit, p. 1339, or II, p. 1342.

Communion Antiphon

Cf. Ps 104 (103): 30

Send forth your Spirit, and they shall be created,
and you shall renew the face of the earth.

Prayer after Communion

May these gifts we have consumed
benefit us, O Lord,
that we may always be aflame with the same Spirit
whom you wondrously poured out on your Apostles.
Through Christ our Lord.

10. THE BLESSED VIRGIN MARY

In these Masses, the color white is used.

A

Any Mass from the Common of the Blessed Virgin Mary (pp. 1039-1051) is used, in accordance with the various times of the year.

B

Our Lady, Mother of the Church

Entrance Antiphon

Cf. Acts 1: 14

The disciples devoted themselves with one accord to prayer
with Mary, the Mother of Jesus.

Collect

O God, Father of mercies,
whose Only Begotten Son, as he hung upon the Cross,
chose the Blessed Virgin Mary, his Mother,
to be our Mother also,
grant, we pray, that with her loving help
your Church may be more fruitful day by day
and, exulting in the holiness of her children,
may draw to her embrace all the families of the peoples.
Through our Lord Jesus Christ, your Son,
who lives and reigns with you in the unity of the Holy Spirit,
one God, for ever and ever.

Prayer over the Offerings

Receive our offerings, O Lord,
and transform them into the mystery of salvation,
so that by its power we may be set aflame
with the charity of the Virgin Mary, Mother of the Church,
and with her may be united more closely
to the work of redemption.
Through Christ our Lord.

Preface: Mary, Model and Mother of the Church.

V. The Lord be with you. R. And with your spir-it.

V. Lift up your hearts. R. We lift them up to the Lord.

V. Let us give thanks to the Lord our God. R. It is right and just.

It is truly right and just, our duty and our sal-va-tion, al-ways and everywhere to give you thanks, Lord, holy Father, almighty and e-ter-nal God, and to proclaim your greatness with due praise, as we honor the Bless-ed Vir-gin Mar-y. Re-ceiving your Word in her Im-mac-u-late Heart, she was found worthy to conceive him in her vir-gin's womb and, giving birth to the Cre-a-tor, she nur-tured the be-gin-nings of the Church. Stand-ing beside the Cross,

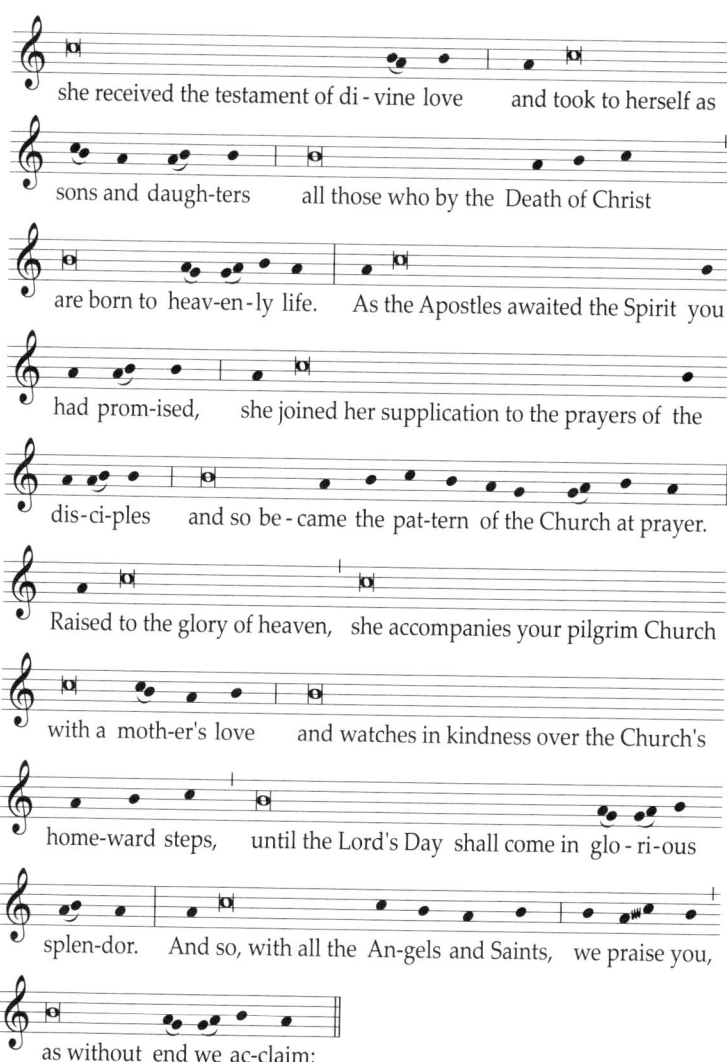

she received the testament of di-vine love and took to herself as sons and daugh-ters all those who by the Death of Christ are born to heav-en-ly life. As the Apostles awaited the Spirit you had prom-ised, she joined her supplication to the prayers of the dis-ci-ples and so be-came the pat-tern of the Church at prayer. Raised to the glory of heaven, she accompanies your pilgrim Church with a moth-er's love and watches in kindness over the Church's home-ward steps, until the Lord's Day shall come in glo-ri-ous splen-dor. And so, with all the An-gels and Saints, we praise you, as without end we ac-claim:

Holy, Holy, Holy Lord God of hosts . . .

Text without music:
V. **The Lord be with you.**
R. And with your spirit.

V. **Lift up your hearts.**
R. We lift them up to the Lord.

V. **Let us give thanks to the Lord our God.**
R. It is right and just.

It is truly right and just, our duty and our salvation,
always and everywhere to give you thanks,
Lord, holy Father, almighty and eternal God,
and to proclaim your greatness with due praise,
as we honor the Blessed Virgin Mary.

Receiving your Word in her Immaculate Heart,
she was found worthy to conceive him in her virgin's womb
and, giving birth to the Creator,
she nurtured the beginnings of the Church.

Standing beside the Cross,
she received the testament of divine love
and took to herself as sons and daughters
all those who by the Death of Christ
are born to heavenly life.

As the Apostles awaited the Spirit you had promised,
she joined her supplication to the prayers of the disciples
and so became the pattern of the Church at prayer.

Raised to the glory of heaven,
she accompanies your pilgrim Church with a mother's love
and watches in kindness over the Church's homeward steps,
until the Lord's Day shall come in glorious splendor.

And so, with all the Angels and Saints,
we praise you, as without end we acclaim:

Holy, Holy, Holy Lord God of hosts . . .

Communion Antiphon
Cf. Jn 2: 1, 11

A wedding was held in Cana of Galilee,
and the mother of Jesus was there;
then Jesus performed the first of his signs
and manifested his glory,
and his disciples believed in him.

Or:
Cf. Jn 19: 26-27

As he hung upon the cross,
Jesus said to the disciple whom he loved:
Behold your mother.

Prayer after Communion

Having received the pledge of redemption and of life,
we humbly pray, O Lord,
that, with the Blessed Virgin's motherly help,
your Church may teach all nations
by proclaiming the Gospel
and, through the grace of the outpouring of the Spirit,
fill the whole earth.
Through Christ our Lord.

C
The Most Holy Name of Mary

Entrance Antiphon
Cf. Jdt 13: 18-19

Blessed are you, O Virgin Mary, by the Lord God Most High,
above all women on the earth;
for he has so exalted your Name
that your praise shall be undying on our lips.

Collect

O God, who chose the Blessed Virgin Mary,
full of your grace, from among women
to become the Mother of your Son, our Redeemer,
mercifully grant that, venerating her holy name,
we may escape the dangers of this present age
and obtain with her life eternal.
Through our Lord Jesus Christ, your Son,
who lives and reigns with you in the unity of the Holy Spirit,
one God, for ever and ever.

Or:

O God, whose Son, dying on the altar of the Cross,
willed that the most Blessed Virgin Mary,
whom he had chosen as his Mother,
should be our Mother also,
graciously grant, we pray,
that we, who fly to her protection,
may find comfort by invoking our Mother's name.
Through our Lord Jesus Christ, your Son,
who lives and reigns with you in the unity of the Holy Spirit,
one God, for ever and ever.

Prayer over the Offerings

Look favorably on the offerings made here, O Lord,
that through the intercession of Blessed Mary ever-Virgin
our hearts, filled with the light of the Holy Spirit,
may constantly strive to cling to Christ, your Son.
Who lives and reigns for ever and ever.

Preface of the Blessed Virgin Mary, pp. 590-593.

Communion Antiphon
Cf. Lk 1: 26-27

The angel Gabriel was sent from God to a virgin,
and the virgin's Name was Mary.

Prayer after Communion

Grant us, we pray, O Lord,
whom you have strengthened at the table of word and Sacrament,
that, with Blessed Mary as our patron and guide,
we may reject whatever is contrary to the name of Christian
and follow whatever accords with it.
Through Christ our Lord.

D

Our Lady, Queen of Apostles

Entrance Antiphon
Cf. Acts 1: 14

The disciples devoted themselves with one accord to prayer
with Mary, the Mother of Jesus.

Collect

O God, who gave the Holy Spirit to your Apostles
as they prayed with Mary the Mother of Jesus,
grant that through her intercession
we may faithfully serve your majesty
and extend, by word and example, the glory of your name.
Through our Lord Jesus Christ, your Son,
who lives and reigns with you in the unity of the Holy Spirit,
one God, for ever and ever.

Prayer over the Offerings

By your favor, O Lord,
and through the intercession of Blessed Mary ever-Virgin,
may our offering obtain for your Church this grace,
that she may grow in the number of the faithful
and be ever radiant with an abundance of virtues.
Through Christ our Lord.

Preface of the Blessed Virgin Mary, pp. 590-593.

Communion Antiphon
Cf. Lk 11: 27-28

Blessed is the womb that bore Christ the Lord;
blessed, rather, are those who hear the word of God and keep it.

Prayer after Communion

Having partaken, O Lord, of these helps to our salvation
in our commemoration of the Blessed Virgin Mary,
Queen of Apostles,
we humbly beseech you,
that, persevering in your will
and in service of the human family,
your people may draw ever closer to salvation.
Through Christ our Lord.

11. THE HOLY ANGELS

In this Mass, the color white is used.

Entrance Antiphon
Cf. Ps 103 (102): 20

Bless the Lord, all you his angels, mighty in power,
fulfilling his word and heeding his voice.

Collect

O God, who dispose in marvelous order
ministries both angelic and human,
graciously grant
that our life on earth may be defended
by those who watch over us
as they minister perpetually to you in heaven.
Through our Lord Jesus Christ, your Son,
who lives and reigns with you in the unity of the Holy Spirit,
one God, for ever and ever.

Prayer over the Offerings

We offer you a sacrifice of praise, O Lord,
humbly entreating
that, as these gifts are borne by the ministry of Angels
into the presence of your majesty,
so you may receive them favorably
and make them profitable for our salvation.
Through Christ our Lord.

THE HOLY ANGELS

Preface of the Angels: God glorified through the Angels.

V. **The Lord be with you.**
R. And with your spirit.

V. **Lift up your hearts.**
R. We lift them up to the Lord.

V. **Let us give thanks to the Lord our God.**
R. It is right and just.

It is truly right and just, our duty and our salvation,
always and everywhere to give you thanks,
Lord, holy Father, almighty and eternal God,
and to praise you without end
in your Archangels and Angels.

For the honor we pay the angelic creatures
in whom you delight
redounds to your own surpassing glory,
and by their great dignity and splendor
you show how infinitely great you are,
to be exalted above all things,
through Christ our Lord.

Through him the multitude of Angels extols your majesty,
and we are united with them in exultant adoration,
as with one voice of praise we acclaim:

Holy, Holy, Holy Lord God of hosts . . .

Text with music, p. 960.

Communion Antiphon   Ps 138 (137): 1
In the presence of the Angels I will praise you, my God.

Prayer after Communion
Having been nourished with heavenly bread,
we beseech you humbly, O Lord,
that, drawing from it new strength,
under the faithful protection of your Angels,
we may advance boldly along the way of salvation.
Through Christ our Lord.

As a Votive Mass, the Mass of the Holy Guardian Angels may also be used, as on October 2 (pp. 964-965).

12. SAINT JOHN THE BAPTIST

In this Mass, the color white is used.

Entrance Antiphon
Lk 1: 15, 14

He will be great in the sight of the Lord
and will be filled with the Holy Spirit, even from his mother's womb;
and many will rejoice at his birth.

Collect

Grant, we pray, almighty God,
that your family may walk in the way of salvation,
and, attentive to what Saint John the Precursor urged,
may come safely to the One he foretold,
our Lord Jesus Christ.
Who lives and reigns with you in the unity of the Holy Spirit,
one God, for ever and ever.

Prayer over the Offerings

Look with favor, O Lord,
upon the offerings made by your people
in commemoration of Saint John the Baptist,
and grant that what we celebrate in mystery
we may pursue with deeds of devoted service.
Through Christ our Lord.

Preface: The mission of the Precursor.

V. **The Lord be with you.**
R. And with your spirit.

V. **Lift up your hearts.**
R. We lift them up to the Lord.

V. **Let us give thanks to the Lord our God.**
R. It is right and just.

It is truly right and just, our duty and our salvation,
always and everywhere to give you thanks,
Lord, holy Father, almighty and eternal God,
through Christ our Lord.

In his Precursor, Saint John the Baptist,
we praise your great glory,
for you consecrated him for a singular honor
among those born of women.

His birth brought great rejoicing;
even in the womb he leapt for joy
at the coming of human salvation.
He alone of all the prophets
pointed out the Lamb of redemption.

And to make holy the flowing waters,
he baptized the very author of Baptism
and was privileged to bear him supreme witness
by the shedding of his blood.

And so, with the Powers of heaven,
we worship you constantly on earth,
and before your majesty
without end we acclaim:

Holy, Holy, Holy Lord God of hosts . . .

Text with music, pp. 880-881.

Communion Antiphon
Lk 1: 68

Blessed be the Lord, the God of Israel!
He has visited his people and redeemed them.

Prayer after Communion

May the marvelous prayer of Saint John the Baptist
accompany us who have eaten our fill
at this sacrificial feast, O Lord,
and, since Saint John proclaimed your Son
to be the Lamb who would take away our sins,
may he now implore for us your favor.
Through Christ our Lord.

13. SAINT JOSEPH

In this Mass, the color white is used.

Entrance Antiphon   Cf. Lk 12: 42
Behold a faithful and prudent steward,
whom the Lord set over his household.

Collect
O God, who in your inexpressible providence
were pleased to choose Saint Joseph
as spouse of the most holy Mother of your Son,
grant, we pray,
that we, who revere him as our protector on earth,
may be worthy of his heavenly intercession.
Through our Lord Jesus Christ, your Son,
who lives and reigns with you in the unity of the Holy Spirit,
one God, for ever and ever.

Prayer over the Offerings
As we prepare to offer the sacrifice of praise, O holy Father,
we humbly ask to be sustained in our service
by the prayers of Saint Joseph,
whom you called to watch like a father on earth
over your Only Begotten Son.
Who lives and reigns for ever and ever.

Preface: The mission of Saint Joseph.

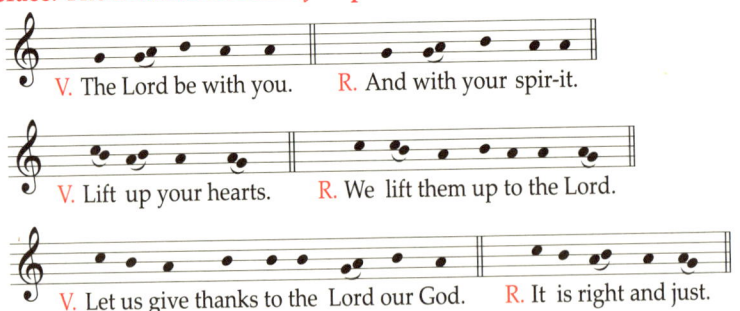

V. The Lord be with you.   R. And with your spir-it.

V. Lift up your hearts.   R. We lift them up to the Lord.

V. Let us give thanks to the Lord our God.   R. It is right and just.

SAINT JOSEPH

It is truly right and just, our duty and our sal-va-tion, al-ways and everywhere to give you thanks, Lord, holy Father, almighty and e- -ter-nal God, and in honor-ing Saint Jo-seph to give you fit-ting praise, to glori-fy you and bless you. For this just man was given by you as spouse to the Virgin Moth-er of God and set as a wise and faithful servant in charge of your house-hold to watch like a father over your Only Be-got-ten Son, who was conceived by the overshadowing of the Ho-ly Spir-it, our Lord Je-sus Christ. Through him the Angels praise your maj-es-ty, Domin-ions a-dore and Powers trem-ble be-fore you. Heav-en and the Virtues of heaven and the bless-ed Ser-a-phim worship to-geth-er with ex-ul-ta-tion. May our voices, we pray, join with theirs in hum-ble praise, as we ac-claim:

Holy, Holy, Holy Lord God of hosts . . .

Text without music:
V. **The Lord be with you.**
R. And with your spirit.

V. **Lift up your hearts.**
R. We lift them up to the Lord.

V. **Let us give thanks to the Lord our God.**
R. It is right and just.

It is truly right and just, our duty and our salvation,
always and everywhere to give you thanks,
Lord, holy Father, almighty and eternal God,
and in honoring Saint Joseph
to give you fitting praise,
to glorify you and bless you.

For this just man was given by you
as spouse to the Virgin Mother of God
and set as a wise and faithful servant
in charge of your household
to watch like a father over your Only Begotten Son,
who was conceived by the overshadowing of the Holy Spirit,
our Lord Jesus Christ.

Through him the Angels praise your majesty,
Dominions adore and Powers tremble before you.
Heaven and the Virtues of heaven and the blessed Seraphim
worship together with exultation.
May our voices, we pray, join with theirs
in humble praise, as we acclaim:

Holy, Holy, Holy Lord God of hosts . . .

Communion Antiphon — Mt 25: 21
Well done, good and faithful servant;
come, share your master's joy.

Prayer after Communion

Restored by these life-giving Sacraments, Lord,
may we live for you always in justice and holiness,
helped by the example and intercession of Saint Joseph,
who in carrying out your great mysteries
served you as a man just and obedient.
Through Christ our Lord.

If appropriate, the Mass of the Solemnity, as on March 19 (p. 835), or of Saint Joseph the Worker, as on May 1 (p. 854), may also be said.

14. ALL THE HOLY APOSTLES

In this Mass, the color red is used.

Entrance Antiphon
Jn 15: 16

It was not you who chose me, says the Lord,
but I who chose you and appointed you to go and bear fruit,
fruit that will last (E.T. alleluia).

Collect

May your Church always exult, O Lord,
in the honor given through the ages to the blessed Apostles,
that she may be guided by these protectors,
in whose teaching and merits she finds joy.
Through our Lord Jesus Christ, your Son,
who lives and reigns with you in the unity of the Holy Spirit,
one God, for ever and ever.

Prayer over the Offerings

Pour out on us, Lord, your Holy Spirit,
whom you poured in abundance upon the Apostles,
that we may recognize what you have given us through them
and duly offer the sacrifice of praise to your glory.
Through Christ our Lord.

Preface of the Apostles, pp. 594-597.

Communion Antiphon
Mt 19: 28

You who have followed me will sit on thrones,
judging the twelve tribes of Israel, says the Lord.

Prayer after Communion

Grant that we may persevere, O God,
with rejoicing and simplicity of heart
in the teaching of the Apostles,
in the breaking of the bread,
and in the prayers.
Through Christ our Lord.

15. SAINTS PETER AND PAUL, APOSTLES

In this Mass, the color red is used.

Entrance Antiphon

Peter the Apostle, and Paul the teacher of the Gentiles:
these have taught us your law, O Lord.

Collect

Grant, we pray, O Lord our God,
that we may be sustained by the intercession
of the blessed Apostles Peter and Paul,
that, as through them you gave your Church
the foundations of her heavenly office,
so through them you may help her to eternal salvation.
Through our Lord Jesus Christ, your Son,
who lives and reigns with you in the unity of the Holy Spirit,
one God, for ever and ever.

Prayer over the Offerings

We bring offerings to your altar, O Lord,
as we glory in the commemoration
of the blessed Apostles Peter and Paul,
so that the more we doubt our own merits,
the more we may rejoice that we are to be saved
by your loving kindness.
Through Christ our Lord.

Preface: The twofold mission of Peter and Paul in the Church.

V. **The Lord be with you.**
R. And with your spirit.

V. **Lift up your hearts.**
R. We lift them up to the Lord.

V. **Let us give thanks to the Lord our God.**
R. It is right and just.

It is truly right and just, our duty and our salvation,
always and everywhere to give you thanks,
Lord, holy Father, almighty and eternal God.

For by your providence
the blessed Apostles Peter and Paul bring us joy:
Peter, foremost in confessing the faith,
Paul, its outstanding preacher,
Peter, who established the early Church from the remnant of Israel,
Paul, master and teacher of the Gentiles that you call.

And so, each in a different way
gathered together the one family of Christ:
and revered together throughout the world,
they share one Martyr's crown.

And therefore, with all the Angels and Saints,
we praise you, as without end we acclaim:

Holy, Holy, Holy Lord God of hosts . . .

Text with music, pp. 887-888.

Communion Antiphon
Cf. Jn 21: 15, 17

Simon, Son of John, do you love me more than these?
Lord, you know everything; you know that I love you.

Prayer after Communion

By this heavenly Sacrament, O Lord, we pray,
strengthen your faithful,
whom you have enlightened with the teaching of the Apostles.
Through Christ our Lord.

16. SAINT PETER, APOSTLE

In this Mass, the color red is used.

Entrance Antiphon
Lk 22: 32

The Lord says to Simon Peter:
I have prayed for you that your faith may not fail,
and once you have turned back, strengthen your brothers.

Collect

O God, who gave the keys of the Kingdom of Heaven
to your blessed Apostle Peter
and handed over to him
the pontifical office of binding and loosing,
grant, we pray, that through the help of his intercession
we may be set free from the bonds of our sins.
Through our Lord Jesus Christ, your Son,
who lives and reigns with you in the unity of the Holy Spirit,
one God, for ever and ever.

Prayer over the Offerings

Receive with favor your people's oblation,
O Lord, we pray,
as we commemorate the blessed Apostle Peter,
for you taught him by a hidden revelation
to confess you, the living God, and the Christ your Son,
and led him to bear witness to his Master
by means of a glorious passion.
Through Christ our Lord.

Preface I of the Apostles, p. 594.

Communion Antiphon
Cf. Mt 16: 16, 18

Peter said to Jesus: You are the Christ, the Son of the living God.
And Jesus replied: You are Peter,
and upon this rock I will build my Church.

Prayer after Communion

Having been admitted, O Lord, to the banquet of salvation
as we venerate the memory of the blessed Apostle Peter,
we ask with gladness
that we may always hold fast to your Son,
who alone has the words of life,
so that, as faithful sheep of your flock,
we may be happily led to eternal pastures.
Through Christ our Lord.

17. SAINT PAUL, APOSTLE

In this Mass, the color red is used.

Entrance Antiphon
2 Tm 1: 12; 4: 8

I know the one in whom I have believed
and I am sure that he, the just judge, the mighty,
will keep safe what is my due until that day.

Collect

Lord God, who in a wondrous way
chose the blessed Apostle Paul to preach the Gospel,
grant, we pray, that the whole world
may be imbued with that faith
which he brought before rulers and nations,
for the unceasing growth of your Church.
Through our Lord Jesus Christ, your Son,
who lives and reigns with you in the unity of the Holy Spirit,
one God, for ever and ever.

Prayer over the Offerings

As we celebrate the divine mysteries, O Lord, we pray,
may the Spirit fill us with that light of faith
by which he constantly enlightened the blessed Apostle Paul
for the spreading of your glory.
Through Christ our Lord.

Preface I of the Apostles, p. 594.

Communion Antiphon   Gal 2: 20

I live by faith in the Son of God,
who has loved me and given himself up for me.

Prayer after Communion

Grant Lord, to those refreshed
by communion in the Body and Blood of your Son,
that Christ himself may be life to us,
that nothing may separate us from his love,
and that, attentive to the teaching of the blessed Apostle Paul,
we may walk in charity with our neighbor.
Through Christ our Lord.

18. ONE HOLY APOSTLE

In this Mass, the color red is used. The Mass of his Feast is said. But if he is honored together with another Apostle and the texts of the Mass are not appropriate for that Apostle, the following Mass is said with the color red.

Entrance Antiphon
Ps 96 (95): 2-3

Proclaim the salvation of God day by day;
tell among the nations his glory.

Collect

Strengthen in us, O Lord, the faith,
by which the blessed Apostle N.
clung wholeheartedly to your Son,
and grant that through the help of his prayers
your Church may become for all the nations
the sacrament of salvation.
Through our Lord Jesus Christ, your Son,
who lives and reigns with you in the unity of the Holy Spirit,
one God, for ever and ever.

Prayer over the Offerings

As we bring you these offerings
in commemoration of the blessed Apostle N.,
we pray, O Lord,
that, living by his example in a manner worthy of the
    Gospel of Christ,
we may work together for the faith it teaches.
Through Christ our Lord.

Preface II of the Apostles, p. 596.

Communion Antiphon
Lk 22: 29-30

I confer a kingdom on you,
just as my Father has conferred one on me,
that you may eat and drink
at my table in my kingdom, says the Lord.

Prayer after Communion

As we celebrate the memory of the blessed Apostle N.,
we have received the pledge of eternal salvation, O Lord,
and we pray that it may be of help to us,
both now and for the life to come.
Through Christ our Lord.

19. ALL SAINTS

In this Mass, the color white is used.

Entrance Antiphon

The souls of the Saints are rejoicing in heaven,
the Saints who followed the footsteps of Christ,
and so now exult with Christ for ever.

Collect

O God, fount of all holiness,
make us each walk worthily in our vocation,
through the intercession of your Saints,
on whom you bestowed
a great variety of graces on earth
and a single glorious reward in heaven.
Through our Lord Jesus Christ, your Son,
who lives and reigns with you in the unity of the Holy Spirit,
one God, for ever and ever.

Prayer over the Offerings

May these offerings we bring in honor of all the Saints
be pleasing to you, O Lord,
and grant that, just as we believe the Saints
to be already assured of immortality,
so we may experience their concern for our salvation.
Through Christ our Lord.

Preface of the Saints, pp. 598-601.

Communion Antiphon   Mt 5: 8-10

Blessed are the clean of heart, for they shall see God.
Blessed are the peacemakers, for they shall be called children of God.
Blessed are they who are persecuted for the sake of righteousness,
for theirs is the Kingdom of Heaven.

Prayer after Communion

O God, who refresh us with the one Bread
and sustain us with one hope,
strengthen us likewise, we pray, by your grace,
that, as we are one with your Saints,
one body and one spirit in Christ,
we may rise with him to glory.
Who lives and reigns for ever and ever.

MASSES FOR THE DEAD

1. Although for the sake of convenience, complete Masses with their own antiphons and prayers are given here, all the texts may be exchanged one for another, especially the prayers. In these latter, however, changes should be made, according to circumstances, in gender and number.
   Similarly, if the prayers given here for funerals and anniversaries are used in other circumstances, the phrasing that appears less suited should be omitted.

2. In Easter Time, the Alleluia at the end of the antiphons may, if appropriate, be omitted.

I. FOR THE FUNERAL

The Funeral Mass may be celebrated on any day, except on Solemnities that are Holydays of Obligation, on Thursday of Holy Week, during the Paschal Triduum, and on the Sundays of Advent, Lent and Easter Time.

A. Outside Easter Time

Entrance Antiphon   Cf. 4 Esdr 2: 34-35

Eternal rest grant unto them, O Lord,
and let perpetual light shine upon them.

Or:

Eternal rest grant unto him (her), O Lord,
and let perpetual light shine upon him (her).

Collect

O God, almighty Father,
our faith professes that your Son died and rose again;
mercifully grant, that through this mystery
your servant N., who has fallen asleep in Christ,
may rejoice to rise again through him.
Who lives and reigns with you in the unity of the Holy Spirit,
one God, for ever and ever.

Or:

O God, whose nature
is always to forgive and to show mercy,
we humbly implore you for your servant N.,
whom you have called (this day) to journey to you,
and, since he (she) hoped and believed in you,
grant that he (she) may be led to our true homeland
to delight in its everlasting joys.
Through our Lord Jesus Christ, your Son,
who lives and reigns with you in the unity of the Holy Spirit,
one God, for ever and ever.

Prayer over the Offerings

As we humbly present to you
these sacrificial offerings, O Lord,
for the salvation of your servant N.,
we beseech your mercy,
that he (she), who did not doubt your Son
to be a loving Savior,
may find in him a merciful Judge.
Who lives and reigns for ever and ever.

Preface for the Dead, pp. 622-631.

Communion Antiphon

Cf. 4 Esdr 2: 34-35

Let perpetual light shine upon them,
with your Saints for ever, for you are merciful.
Eternal rest grant unto them, O Lord,
and let perpetual light shine upon them,
with your Saints for ever, for you are merciful.

Or:

Let perpetual light shine upon him (her),
with your Saints for ever, for you are merciful.
Eternal rest grant unto him (her) O Lord,
and let perpetual light shine upon him (her),
with your Saints for ever, for you are merciful.

Prayer after Communion

Lord God, whose Son left us,
in the Sacrament of his Body,
food for the journey,
mercifully grant that, strengthened by it,
our brother (sister) N. may come
to the eternal table of Christ.
Who lives and reigns for ever and ever.

B. Outside Easter Time

Entrance Antiphon

May the Lord open to him (her) the gates of Paradise,
that he (she) may return to that homeland
where there is no death, where eternal joy endures.

Collect

O God, who are mercy for sinners
and the happiness of your Saints,
give, we pray, to your servant N.,
for whom (today) we perform the fraternal offices of burial,
a share with your chosen ones in the blessedness you give,
so that on the day of resurrection,
freed from the bonds of mortality,
he (she) may come before your face.
Through our Lord Jesus Christ, your Son,
who lives and reigns with you in the unity of the Holy Spirit,
one God, for ever and ever.

Or:

O God, who have set a limit to this present life,
so as to open up an entry into eternity,
we humbly beseech you,
that by the grace of your mercy
you may command the name of your servant N.
to be inscribed in the book of life.
Through our Lord Jesus Christ, your Son,
who lives and reigns with you in the unity of the Holy Spirit,
one God, for ever and ever.

Prayer over the Offerings

Be near, O Lord, we pray, to your servant **N.**,
on whose funeral day
we offer you this sacrifice of conciliation,
so that, should any stain of sin have clung to him **(her)**
or any human fault have affected him **(her)**,
it may, by your loving gift, be forgiven and wiped away.
Through Christ our Lord.

Preface for the Dead, pp. 622-631.

Communion Antiphon
Phil 3: 20-21

We await a savior, the Lord Jesus Christ,
who will change our mortal bodies,
to conform with his glorified body.

Prayer after Communion

Grant, we pray, almighty God,
that your servant **N.**,
who **(today)** has journeyed from this world,
may by this sacrifice be cleansed and freed from sin
and so receive the everlasting joys of the resurrection.
Through Christ our Lord.

C. During Easter Time

Entrance Antiphon
1 Thes 4: 14; 1 Cor 15: 22

Just as Jesus died and rose again,
so, through Jesus, God will bring with him
those who have fallen asleep;
and as in Adam all die,
so also in Christ will all be brought to life, alleluia.

Collect

Listen kindly to our prayers, O Lord:
as our faith in your Son,
raised from the dead, is deepened,
may our hope of resurrection for your departed servant N.,
also find new strength.
Through our Lord Jesus Christ, your Son,
who lives and reigns with you in the unity of the Holy Spirit,
one God, for ever and ever.

Or:

O God, who through the ending of present things
open up the beginning of things to come,
grant, we pray, that the soul of your servant N.
may be led by you
to attain the inheritance of eternal redemption.
Through our Lord Jesus Christ, your Son,
who lives and reigns with you in the unity of the Holy Spirit,
one God, for ever and ever.

Prayer over the Offerings

Look favorably on our offerings, O Lord,
so that your departed servant N.
may be taken up into glory with your Son,
in whose great mystery of love we are all united.
Through Christ our Lord.

Preface for the Dead, pp. 622-631.

Communion Antiphon   Jn 11: 25-26

I am the Resurrection and the Life, says the Lord.
Whoever believes in me, even though he dies, will live,
and everyone who lives and believes in me
will not die for ever, alleluia.

Prayer after Communion

Grant, we pray, O Lord, that your servant N.,
for whom we have celebrated this paschal Sacrament,
may pass over to a dwelling place of light and peace.
Through Christ our Lord.

D. Other Prayers for the Funeral Mass

Collect

O God, who alone are able to give life after death,
free your servant N. from all sins,
that he (she), who believed in the Resurrection of your Christ,
may, when the day of resurrection comes,
be united with you in glory.
Through our Lord Jesus Christ, your Son,
who lives and reigns with you in the unity of the Holy Spirit,
one God, for ever and ever.

Prayer over the Offerings

Almighty and merciful God,
by means of these sacrificial offerings,
wash away, we pray, in the Blood of Christ,
the sins of your departed servant N.,
and purify unceasingly by your merciful forgiveness
those you once cleansed in the waters of Baptism.
Through Christ our Lord.

Prayer after Communion

Having received the Sacrament of your Only Begotten Son,
who was sacrificed for us and rose in glory,
we humbly implore you, O Lord,
for your departed servant N.,
that, cleansed by the paschal mysteries,
he (she) may glory in the gift of the resurrection to come.
Through Christ our Lord.

E. For the Funeral of a Baptized Child

I

Entrance Antiphon
Mt 25: 34
Come, you blessed of my Father, says the Lord;
receive the kingdom prepared for you
from the foundation of the world (E.T. alleluia).

Collect
Most compassionate God,
who in the counsels of your wisdom
have called this little child to yourself
on the very threshold of life,
listen kindly to our prayers
and grant that one day we may inherit eternal life with him (her),
whom, by the grace of Baptism, you have adopted as your
   own child
and who we believe is dwelling even now in your Kingdom.
Through our Lord Jesus Christ, your Son,
who lives and reigns with you in the unity of the Holy Spirit,
one God, for ever and ever.

Prayer over the Offerings
Sanctify these offerings we bring you, O Lord,
that the parents, who now entrust to you
the child you gave to them,
may come to embrace him (her) with joy in your Kingdom.
Through Christ our Lord.

Preface for the Dead, pp. 622-631.

Communion Antiphon
Cf. Rom 6: 4, 8
Buried with Christ through baptism into death,
we believe that we shall also live with Christ (E.T. alleluia).

Prayer after Communion

Having received the Communion
of your Son's Body and Blood, O Lord,
we ask you faithfully
to comfort amid the sorrows of this life
those whom you have graciously nourished
by these sacred mysteries,
so as to strengthen their hope of life eternal.
Through Christ our Lord.

2
Other Prayers

Collect

O God, who know that our hearts
are weighed down by grief
at the death of this young child,
grant that, while we weep for him (her),
who at your bidding has departed this life so soon,
we may have faith that he (she) has gained
an eternal home in heaven.
Through our Lord Jesus Christ, your Son,
who lives and reigns with you in the unity of the Holy Spirit,
one God, for ever and ever.

Prayer over the Offerings

Graciously accept this offering, O God,
as a sign of our devotion,
so that, trusting in the designs of your providence,
we may be raised up by your gentle and fatherly care.
Through Christ our Lord.

Prayer after Communion

Nourished by your divine gifts,
we pray, O Lord,
that, just as you have given this little child
a place at the table in your heavenly Kingdom,
we, too, may find a place there.
Through Christ our Lord.

F. For the Funeral of a Child Who Died before Baptism

Should a child whom the parents wished to be baptized, die before Baptism, the Diocesan Bishop, taking into consideration pastoral circumstances, may permit the funeral to be celebrated in the home of the deceased child, or even according to the form of funeral rites otherwise customarily used in the region.

In funerals of this kind there should ordinarily be a Liturgy of the Word, as described in the Roman Ritual. Nevertheless, if at times the celebration of Mass is judged opportune, the following texts should be used.

In catechesis, however, proper care is to be taken that the doctrine of the necessity of Baptism is not obscured in the minds of the faithful.

Entrance Antiphon

Rev 21: 4

God will wipe every tear from their eyes,
and there shall be no more death
or mourning, crying or pain,
for former things have passed away.

Collect

**Receive the prayers of your faithful, Lord,
and grant that those you allow to be weighed down
by their longing for the child taken from them
may be raised up by faith to hope in your compassion.
Through our Lord Jesus Christ, your Son,
who lives and reigns with you in the unity of the Holy Spirit,
one God, for ever and ever.**

Or:

**O God, searcher of hearts and most loving consoler,
who know the faith of these parents,
grant that, as they mourn their child,
now departed from this life,
they may be assured
that he (she) has been entrusted to your divine compassion.
Through our Lord Jesus Christ, your Son,
who lives and reigns with you in the unity of the Holy Spirit,
one God, for ever and ever.**

Prayer over the Offerings

Graciously accept this offering, O God,
as a sign of our devotion,
so that, trusting in the designs of your providence,
we may be raised up by your gentle and fatherly care.
Through Christ our Lord.

Preface for the Dead, pp. 622-631.

Communion Antiphon   Is 25: 8

The Lord God will destroy death for ever.
He will wipe away the tears from every cheek.

Prayer after Communion

Having received the Communion
of your Son's Body and Blood, O Lord,
we ask you faithfully
to comfort amid the sorrows of this life
those whom you have graciously nourished
by these sacred mysteries,
so as to strengthen their hope of life eternal.
Through Christ our Lord.

II. ON THE ANNIVERSARY

This Mass may be celebrated on the first anniversary even on days within the Octave of the Nativity of the Lord, and on days when an Obligatory Memorial occurs and on weekdays, with the exception of Ash Wednesday and weekdays during Holy Week.

On other anniversaries, this Mass may be celebrated on weekdays in Ordinary Time even when an Optional Memorial occurs.

A. Outside Easter Time

Entrance Antiphon   Rev 21: 4

God will wipe every tear from their eyes,
and there shall be no more death
or mourning, crying or pain,
for former things have passed away.

Collect

O God, glory of the faithful and life of the just,
by the Death and Resurrection of whose Son
we have been redeemed,
look mercifully on your departed servant N.,
that, just as he (she) professed
the mystery of our resurrection,
so he (she) may merit to receive
the joys of eternal happiness.
Through our Lord Jesus Christ, your Son,
who lives and reigns with you in the unity of the Holy Spirit,
one God, for ever and ever.

Prayer over the Offerings

Look with favor, we pray, O Lord,
on the offerings we make for the soul of your servant N.,
that, being cleansed by heavenly remedies,
his (her) soul may be ever alive
and blessed in your glory.
Through Christ our Lord.

Preface for the Dead, pp. 622-631.

Communion Antiphon Jn 11: 25; 3: 36; 5: 24
   I am the Resurrection and the Life, says the Lord.
   Whoever believes in me has eternal life
   and does not come to condemnation,
   but has passed from death to life.

Prayer after Communion
   Restored by these sacred mysteries,
   we humbly beseech you, O Lord,
   that your servant N. may be cleansed from all offenses
   and merit for all eternity
   the precious gift of the resurrection.
   Through Christ our Lord.

B. Outside Easter Time

Entrance Antiphon
   Lord Jesus, grant eternal rest to those,
   for whom you poured out your precious Blood.

Collect
   Send down, we pray, O Lord,
   the lasting dew of your mercy on your servant N.,
   whose anniversary we commemorate,
   and be pleased to grant him (her)
   the company of your Saints.
   Through our Lord Jesus Christ, your Son,
   who lives and reigns with you in the unity of the Holy Spirit,
   one God, for ever and ever.

Prayer over the Offerings
   Be attentive, O Lord,
   to our prayers for your servant N.,
   whose anniversary we observe today,
   and through this sacrifice of conciliation and praise
   graciously add him (her) to the company of your Saints.
   Through Christ our Lord.

   Preface for the Dead, pp. 622-631.

Communion Antiphon
You are rest after toil, O Lord, life after death:
grant them eternal rest.

Prayer after Communion
Just as you have lovingly accepted, O Lord,
our prayers and sacrificial offerings
for the soul of your servant N.,
so, we humbly entreat you:
if any stain of sin has clung to him (her),
may it be wiped away by your merciful forgiveness.
Through Christ our Lord.

C. During Easter Time

Entrance Antiphon
Cf. Rom 8: 11

God, who raised Jesus from the dead,
will give life also to your mortal bodies,
through his Spirit that dwells in you, alleluia.

Collect
Almighty and merciful God,
whose Son, for our sake,
willingly underwent death in the flesh,
grant mercifully, we pray,
that your servant N. may have part
in the wondrous victory of Christ's Resurrection.
Who lives and reigns with you in the unity of the Holy Spirit,
one God, for ever and ever.

Prayer over the Offerings
Almighty and merciful God,
by means of these sacrificial offerings,
wash away, we pray, in the Blood of Christ,
the sins of your departed servant N.,
for you purify unceasingly by your merciful forgiveness
those you once cleansed in the waters of Baptism.
Through Christ our Lord.

Preface for the Dead, pp. 622-631.

Communion Antiphon
Jn 6: 51-52

I am the living bread, that came down from heaven, says the Lord.
Whoever eats of this bread will live for ever,
and the bread that I will give
is my flesh for the life of the world, alleluia.

Prayer after Communion

Having received the Sacrament of your Only Begotten Son,
who was sacrificed for us and rose in glory,
we humbly implore you, O Lord,
for your departed servant N.,
that, cleansed by the paschal mysteries,
he (she) may glory in the gift of the resurrection to come.
Through Christ our Lord.

D. Other Prayers on the Anniversary

Collect

Grant, we pray, O Lord,
through the blessed Passion of your Son,
that your servant N. may receive
the forgiveness for his (her) sins he (she) always desired,
so that, knowing you in truth,
he (she) may be worthy to rejoice
at being called to behold you for ever.
Through our Lord Jesus Christ, your Son,
who lives and reigns with you in the unity of the Holy Spirit,
one God, for ever and ever.

Prayer over the Offerings

We humbly offer you sacrifice, O Lord,
for N. your servant,
that he (she), who by your gift of the light of faith
already knew you,
may rejoice in holding fast to you for ever.
Through Christ our Lord.

Prayer after Communion

>Replenished by the food that renews and gives life,
>we pray, O Lord,
>that our brother (sister) N.,
>strengthened by it and cleansed from all sins,
>may pass over to the company of heaven.
>Through Christ our Lord.

E. Other Prayers on the Anniversary

Collect

>O God of all forgiveness,
>grant to the soul of your servant N.,
>whose anniversary we celebrate,
>a place of refreshment, of blessed rest and resplendent light.
>Through our Lord Jesus Christ, your Son,
>who lives and reigns with you in the unity of the Holy Spirit,
>one God, for ever and ever.

Prayer over the Offerings

>May both our prayer and our offering
>be pleasing to you, O Lord,
>that your servant N.,
>for whose salvation they are offered,
>may gain through them
>the fullness of your redemption
>Through Christ our Lord.

Prayer after Communion

>Grant, we pray, almighty God,
>that the soul of your servant N.,
>for whom we have offered
>this sacrifice to your majesty,
>may by the power of this Sacrament
>be cleansed of all sins
>and receive from your mercy
>the happiness of perpetual light.
>Through Christ our Lord.

III. VARIOUS COMMEMORATIONS

This Mass may be celebrated when the news of a death is first received or on the day of final burial, even on days within the Octave of the Nativity of the Lord, on days when an Obligatory Memorial occurs, and on weekdays, with the exception of Ash Wednesday and weekdays during Holy Week.

"Daily" Masses for the Dead may be celebrated on weekdays in Ordinary Time, even if an Optional Memorial occurs, provided such Masses are actually applied for the dead.

A. For One Deceased Person

1

Entrance Antiphon

May the Lord open to him (her) the gates of Paradise,
that he (she) may return to that homeland,
where there is no death, where eternal joy endures.

Collect

O God, almighty Father,
who have strengthened us by the mystery of the Cross
and promise us a share in the mystery of your Son's Resurrection,
mercifully grant, we pray,
that your departed servant N. may be gathered
into the company of your chosen ones.
Through our Lord Jesus Christ, your Son,
who lives and reigns with you in the unity of the Holy Spirit,
one God, for ever and ever.

Or:

Incline your ear, O Lord, to our prayers,
by which we humbly entreat your mercy,
that, as you graciously numbered your servant N.
among your people in this world,
you may now set him (her) in a place of peace and light
and grant him (her) a share in the company of your Saints.
Through our Lord Jesus Christ, your Son,
who lives and reigns with you in the unity of the Holy Spirit,
one God, for ever and ever.

FOR ONE DECEASED PERSON

Prayer over the Offerings
Look with favor, O Lord, on your servant N.,
for whom we offer you the sacrifice of praise,
humbly entreating
that, reconciled with you through these devoted offices,
he (she) may merit to rise again to life.
Through Christ our Lord.

Preface for the Dead, pp. 622-631.

Communion Antiphon
Jn 6: 37

Everything that the Father gives me will come to me, says the Lord,
and I will not reject anyone who comes to me.

Prayer after Communion
Renewed by this life-giving Sacrament,
we pray, O Lord,
that the soul of our brother (sister) N.,
to whom you gave a part in your covenant,
may be purified by the power of this mystery
and rejoice without end in the peace of Christ.
Who lives and reigns for ever and ever.

2

Entrance Antiphon
Job 19: 25, 26

I know that my Redeemer lives,
and that he will at last stand forth upon the dust;
and from my flesh I shall see God.

Collect
Free your servant N., we pray, O Lord,
from every bond of sin,
that he (she), who in this world
was found worthy to be conformed to Christ,
may be raised to the glory of the resurrection
and draw the breath of new life among your Saints.
Through our Lord Jesus Christ, your Son,
who lives and reigns with you in the unity of the Holy Spirit,
one God, for ever and ever.

Prayer over the Offerings

Grant our supplication, we pray, O Lord,
that this sacrifice may benefit your departed servant N.,
since through its offering
you have loosed the offenses of all the world.
Through Christ our Lord.

Preface for the Dead, pp. 622-631.

Communion Antiphon
Cf. Jn 6: 50

This is the bread that comes down from heaven, says the Lord;
so that one may eat it and not die.

Prayer after Communion

May the sacrifice of your Church, we pray, O Lord,
benefit the soul of your servant N.,
so that he (she), who received
the Sacrament of Christ's mercy,
may enter his company, together with your Saints.
Through Christ our Lord.

3
Other Prayers

Collect

O God, in whose presence the dead are alive
and in whom your Saints rejoice full of happiness,
grant our supplication, that your servant N.,
for whom the fleeting light of this world shines no more,
may enjoy the comfort of your light for all eternity.
Through our Lord Jesus Christ, your Son,
who lives and reigns with you in the unity of the Holy Spirit,
one God, for ever and ever.

Prayer over the Offerings

May the offering of this sacrifice
be pleasing to you, Lord,
so that the soul of your servant N.,
finding through your mercy
the pardon he (she) sought for his (her) sins,
may exult for ever with your Saints
and praise your glory for all eternity.
Through Christ our Lord.

Prayer after Communion

As we receive these heavenly gifts,
we give you thanks, O Lord,
and humbly pray that the soul of your servant N.,
freed through your Son's Passion from the bonds of sin,
may come happily into your presence.
Through Christ our Lord.

4
Other Prayers

Collect

May our prayers rise up to you, O Lord,
and may the soul of N. your servant
be welcomed into eternal joy;
for as you were pleased
to create him (her) in your own image
and adopt him (her) as your own,
so command, we pray,
that he (she) may have a share in your inheritance.
Through our Lord Jesus Christ, your Son,
who lives and reigns with you in the unity of the Holy Spirit,
one God, for ever and ever.

Prayer over the Offerings

Mercifully receive, we pray, O Lord,
the offering we trustingly present
for the soul of your servant N.,
that through this sacrifice,
which you ordained as the one true remedy for all,
you may grant him (her) everlasting salvation.
Through Christ our Lord.

Prayer after Communion

Renewed by the nourishment of this sacred gift,
we pray, O Lord,
that our brother (sister) N., freed from the bonds of death,
may rejoice to have a share in the Resurrection of your Son.
Who lives and reigns for ever and ever.

5

Other Prayers

Collect

Incline your merciful ear to our prayers, O Lord,
and grant to the soul of your servant N.
the remission of all his (her) sins,
that he (she) may have life on the day of resurrection
and may rest in the splendor of eternal light.
Through our Lord Jesus Christ, your Son,
who lives and reigns with you in the unity of the Holy Spirit,
one God, for ever and ever.

Prayer over the Offerings

Almighty ever-living God,
whose Son has given himself to us as the Bread of life
and has poured out his Blood as the Chalice of salvation,
have mercy, we pray, on your servant N.,
that the offering we make to you
may be for him (her) the source of salvation.
Through Christ our Lord.

Prayer after Communion

As we receive the pledge of eternal life,
we humbly implore you, O Lord,
for the soul of your servant N.,
that, freed from the bonds of mortality,
he (she) may join the company of the redeemed.
Through Christ our Lord.

B. For Several Deceased Persons or for All the Dead

1

Entrance Antiphon
Eternal rest grant unto them, O Lord,
and fill their souls with splendor.

Collect
O God, who willed that your Only Begotten Son,
having conquered death,
should pass over into the realm of heaven,
grant, we pray, to your departed servants (N. and N.)
that, with the mortality of this life overcome,
they may gaze eternally on you,
their Creator and Redeemer.
Through our Lord Jesus Christ, your Son,
who lives and reigns with you in the unity of the Holy Spirit,
one God, for ever and ever.

Prayer over the Offerings
Look with favor, we pray, O Lord,
on the sacrificial offerings
we present to you for the souls of your servants
and, just as you bestowed on them
the dignity of the Christian faith,
grant them also its reward.
Through Christ our Lord.

Preface for the Dead, pp. 622-631.

Communion Antiphon
1 Jn 4: 9

God sent his Only Begotten Son into the world,
so that we might have life through him.

Prayer after Communion
Through these sacrificial gifts,
which we have received, O Lord,
bestow on your departed servants your great mercy,
and, to those you have endowed with the grace of Baptism,
grant also the fullness of eternal joy.
Through Christ our Lord.

2

Entrance Antiphon
Jn 3: 16

> God so loved the world that he gave his Only Begotten Son,
> so that all who believe in him may not perish, but may have eternal life.

Collect

> Almighty ever-living God,
> life of all that is mortal and joy of the Saints,
> we humbly pray to you for your servants (N. and N.)
> that, freed from the bonds of mortality,
> they may possess your Kingdom in everlasting glory.
> Through our Lord Jesus Christ, your Son,
> who lives and reigns with you in the unity of the Holy Spirit,
> one God, for ever and ever.

Prayer over the Offerings

> Receive, O Lord, in your kindness
> the sacrificial offering we make
> for your departed servants (N. and N.)
> and for all who sleep in Christ,
> that, set free from the bonds of death
> by this singular sacrifice,
> they may merit eternal life.
> Through Christ our Lord.

Preface for the Dead, pp. 622-631.

Communion Antiphon
Phil 3: 20-21

> We await a savior, the Lord Jesus Christ,
> who will change our mortal bodies,
> to conform with his glorified body.

Prayer after Communion

> As we participate in the divine mysteries
> we pray, almighty God,
> that they may advance our salvation
> and bring pardon to the souls of your servants,
> for whom we implore your mercy.
> Through Christ our Lord.

3

Entrance Antiphon   Cf. Rev 14: 13

Blessed are the dead who die in the Lord.
Let them rest from their labors,
for their works accompany them.

Collect

O God, by whose mercy the souls of the faithful find rest,
graciously grant pardon for their sins
to your servants (N. and N.)
and to all who sleep in Christ,
so that, freed from all guilt,
they may have a share in the Resurrection of your Christ.
Who lives and reigns with you in the unity of the Holy Spirit,
one God, for ever and ever.

Prayer over the Offerings

Look with favor, Lord, we pray,
on the offerings we make
for the repose of the souls of your servants,
that through these helps to human salvation
they may be granted an unfailing portion
among the multitude of your redeemed.
Through Christ our Lord.

Preface for the Dead, pp. 622-631.

Communion Antiphon

Grant everlasting rest to them, O Lord,
for whose memory the Body and Blood of Christ are here received.

Prayer after Communion

We have received, O Lord, the Sacrament of redemption
and entreat your mercy, that in your compassion
you may give protection to us, the living,
and, to our departed brothers and sisters, everlasting pardon.
Through Christ our Lord.

4

Entrance Antiphon
Cf. Ps 31 (30): 2

In you, O Lord, I put my trust, let me never be put to shame;
in your justice, deliver me.

Collect

O God, Creator and Redeemer of all the faithful,
grant to your departed servants
the remission of all their sins,
so that through our devout supplications
they may obtain that pardon
which they have always desired.
Through our Lord Jesus Christ, your Son,
who lives and reigns with you in the unity of the Holy Spirit,
one God, for ever and ever.

Prayer over the Offerings

Be merciful, we pray, O Lord,
to your servants (N. and N.),
for whom we offer you the sacrifice of conciliation,
and, since in this life
they remained steadfast in the Catholic faith,
may they have their reward in the life to come.
Through Christ our Lord.

Preface for the Dead, pp. 622-631.

Communion Antiphon
Jn 8: 12

I am the light of the world, says the Lord;
whoever follows me will not walk in darkness,
but will have the light of life.

Prayer after Communion

May the prayer of those who plead before you
benefit the souls of your servants, we pray, O Lord,
so that through this sacrifice,
you may free them from all their sins
and make them sharers in eternal salvation.
Through Christ our Lord.

5

Entrance Antiphon   Cf. Ps 105 (104): 3-4

Let the hearts that seek the Lord rejoice;
turn to the Lord and his strength;
constantly seek his face.

Collect

Almighty ever-living God,
who rule both the living and the dead and are merciful to all,
we humbly beseech you,
that those for whom we pour out our prayers
may obtain pardon for their sins through your tender mercy,
rejoicing together, blessed in your sight,
and praising you without end.
Through our Lord Jesus Christ, your Son,
who lives and reigns with you in the unity of the Holy Spirit,
one God, for ever and ever.

Prayer over the Offerings

By your acceptance of this sacrificial offering, O God,
grant that your servants (N. and N.)
may be sharers in the abundant riches of Christ,
so that with him they may be raised again to life
and receive a place at his right hand.
Who lives and reigns for ever and ever.

Preface for the Dead, pp. 622-631.

Communion Antiphon   Cf. Ps 31 (30): 17-18

Let your face shine on your servant.
Save me in your merciful love.
O Lord, let me never be put to shame, for I call on you.

Prayer after Communion

Hear, O God, your children,
nourished now by the Sacrament of salvation,
and, as through the Holy Spirit,
you raised Christ, your Only Begotten Son, from the dead,
so grant to your faithful servants (N. and N.)
the joy of life and immortality.
Through Christ our Lord.

FOR SEVERAL DECEASED PERSONS OR FOR ALL THE DEAD

6

Entrance Antiphon
Ps 84 (83): 10-11

Look, O God, on the face of your anointed one;
one day within your courts is better than a thousand elsewhere.

Collect

Grant perpetual mercy to your departed servants,
we pray, O Lord,
that the hope and faith they had in you
may benefit them for all eternity.
Through our Lord Jesus Christ, your Son,
who lives and reigns with you in the unity of the Holy Spirit,
one God, for ever and ever.

Prayer over the Offerings

In this sacrifice, O Lord,
your Son, though innocent, was slain for us
and took away all the sins of the world;
grant, we pray,
that it may set your servants (N. and N.) free
from every failing of the human condition.
Through Christ our Lord.

Preface for the Dead, pp. 622-631.

Communion Antiphon
Cf. Ps 42 (41): 2-3

Like the deer that yearns for running streams,
so my soul is yearning for you, my God.

Prayer after Communion

May your departed servants
and all who sleep in Christ
inherit eternal light, we pray, O Lord,
for while still in this life
they received this, your holy Sacrament.
Through Christ our Lord.

7
Other Prayers

Collect

Be favorable, Lord, to your servants **(N. and N.)**,
whom you washed clean in the font of rebirth,
and bring them to the happiness of heavenly life.
Through our Lord Jesus Christ, your Son,
who lives and reigns with you in the unity of the Holy Spirit,
one God, for ever and ever.

Prayer over the Offerings

As we offer sacrifice to you, O Lord,
for your departed servants **(N. and N.)**,
we humbly entreat
that you may be pleased to answer our prayers
and confer on these your servants your perpetual mercy.
Through Christ our Lord.

Prayer after Communion

Having received your heavenly Sacrament, O Lord,
we humbly ask your mercy,
that your departed servants,
obtaining, through this gift, pardon for sins,
may be counted worthy to enter your Kingdom,
there to praise you for eternity.
Through Christ our Lord.

8
Other Prayers

Collect

To you, O Lord, we commend your servants (N. and N.)
that, having died to this world, they may live for you,
and we beseech you,
that whatever sins they committed
through the frailty of the flesh during their earthly lives
you may in your most tender mercy pardon and wipe away.
Through our Lord Jesus Christ, your Son,
who lives and reigns with you in the unity of the Holy Spirit,
one God, for ever and ever.

Prayer over the Offerings

Be merciful, we pray, O Lord,
to your servants (N. and N.),
for whom we offer you the sacrifice of conciliation,
and, since in this life they remained faithful to you,
may they have their reward in your presence.
Through Christ our Lord.

Prayer after Communion

Grant, we pray, almighty God,
that through the power of this Sacrament
your departed servants be made partakers of eternal happiness
in the gathering of the just.
Through Christ our Lord.

9
Other Prayers

Collect

Almighty ever-living God,
to whom we never pray without hope of your mercy,
be gracious to your servants (N. and N.),
who departed this life confessing your name,
and admit them to the company of your Saints.
Through our Lord Jesus Christ, your Son,
who lives and reigns with you in the unity of the Holy Spirit,
one God, for ever and ever.

Prayer over the Offerings

Lord God, whose Son offered himself to you as a living oblation,
accept, we pray, the sacrifice of your Church,
that your servants (N. and N.), freed from all sins,
may merit to attain the prize of immortality.
Through Christ our Lord.

Prayer after Communion

May the Sacrament we have received
purify us, almighty and merciful God,
and grant, we pray,
that this sacrifice may be for us
a plea for pardon,
strength for the weak,
a stronghold in all danger;
and may it be for the living and the dead
remission of all their sins
and the pledge of eternal redemption.
Through Christ our Lord.

IV. VARIOUS PRAYERS FOR THE DEAD

1. FOR A POPE

A

Collect

O God, faithful rewarder of souls,
grant that your departed servant Pope N.,
whom you made successor of Peter
and shepherd of your Church,
may happily enjoy for ever in your presence in heaven
the mysteries of your grace and compassion,
which he faithfully ministered on earth.
Through our Lord Jesus Christ, your Son,
who lives and reigns with you in the unity of the Holy Spirit,
one God, for ever and ever.

Prayer over the Offerings

We pray, O Lord,
that through these devoted offices of supplication
you may mercifully bestow a blessed reward
on the soul of your servant Pope N.
and on us, your gifts of grace.
Through Christ our Lord.

Prayer after Communion

Renewed by the Sacrament
of our communion with you, our God,
we pray, O Lord,
that your servant Pope N.,
who served by your will on earth
as the visible foundation of your Church's unity,
may be happily admitted to your blessed flock.
Through Christ our Lord.

B

Collect

O God, who in your wondrous providence
chose your servant Pope N. to preside over your Church,
grant, we pray,
that, having served as the Vicar of your Son on earth,
he may be welcomed by him into eternal glory.
Who lives and reigns with you in the unity of the Holy Spirit,
one God, for ever and ever.

Prayer over the Offerings

Look with favor on the offerings of your Church
as she calls on you, O Lord,
and by the power of this sacrifice
grant that, as you placed your servant Pope N.
as High Priest over your flock,
so you may set him among the number
of your chosen Priests in heaven.
Through Christ our Lord.

Prayer after Communion

As we receive sacred sustenance
from your charity, O Lord,
we pray that your servant Pope N.,
who was a faithful steward of your mysteries on earth,
may praise your mercy for ever in the glory of the Saints.
Through Christ our Lord.

C

Collect

O God, immortal shepherd of souls,
look on your people's prayers
and grant that your servant Pope **N.**,
who presided over your Church in charity,
may, with the flock entrusted to his care,
receive from your mercy
the reward of a faithful steward.
Through our Lord Jesus Christ, your Son,
who lives and reigns with you in the unity of the Holy Spirit,
one God, for ever and ever.

Prayer over the Offerings

Look with favor, we pray, O Lord,
on the peaceful offering of your people,
with which we confidently commit to your mercy
the soul of your servant Pope **N.**,
and grant, we pray, that,
having been, in the midst of the human family,
an instrument of your charity and peace,
he may merit to delight in the same,
for ever with all your Saints.
Through Christ our Lord.

Prayer after Communion

As we come to the table of your eternal banquet,
we humbly beg your mercy, Lord,
for the soul of your departed servant Pope **N.**,
that he may rejoice at last in possession of the truth
in which he faithfully confirmed your people.
Through Christ our Lord.

2. FOR A BISHOP
A. For a Diocesan Bishop

Collect

Grant, we pray, almighty God,
that the soul of your departed servant Bishop **N.**,
to whom you committed the care of your family,
may, with the manifold fruit of his labors,
enter into the eternal gladness of his Lord.
Who lives and reigns with you in the unity of the Holy Spirit,
one God, for ever and ever.

Prayer over the Offerings

We humbly beseech your boundless mercy, Lord,
that this sacrifice,
which your departed servant and Bishop **N.**,
while in the body, offered to your majesty
for the salvation of the faithful,
may now bring him, too, your pardon.
Through Christ our Lord.

Prayer after Communion

May your merciful kindness,
which we have implored, O Lord,
benefit the soul of your departed servant Bishop **N.**,
that, by these sacrificial gifts,
he may know the eternal company of Christ,
in whom he hoped and whom he preached.
Who lives and reigns for ever and ever.

B. For Another Bishop

Collect

O God, who chose your servant Bishop (Cardinal) N.
from among your Priests
and endowed him with pontifical dignity
in the apostolic priesthood,
grant, we pray,
that he may also be admitted to their company for ever.
Through our Lord Jesus Christ, your Son,
who lives and reigns with you in the unity of the Holy Spirit,
one God, for ever and ever.

Prayer over the Offerings

Accept, O Lord, we pray,
the sacrificial gifts we offer
for the soul of your servant Bishop (Cardinal) N.,
that, as you accorded him the pontifical dignity in this world,
so you may command him to be admitted
to the company of your Saints in the heavenly Kingdom.
Through Christ our Lord.

Prayer after Communion

We pray, almighty and merciful God,
that, as you made your servant Bishop (Cardinal) N.
an ambassador for Christ on earth,
so you may raise him, purified by this sacrifice,
to be seated with Christ in heaven.
Who lives and reigns for ever and ever.

3. FOR A PRIEST

A

Collect

Grant, we pray, O Lord,
that the soul of N., your servant and Priest,
whom you honored with sacred office
while he lived in this world,
may exult for ever in the glorious home of heaven.
Through our Lord Jesus Christ, your Son,
who lives and reigns with you in the unity of the Holy Spirit,
one God, for ever and ever.

Prayer over the Offerings

Grant, we pray, almighty God,
that through these holy mysteries
N., your servant and Priest,
may behold with clarity for ever
what he faithfully ministered here.
Through Christ our Lord.

Prayer after Communion

Having received the Sacrament of salvation,
we implore your kindness, O God,
for N., your servant and Priest,
that, as you made him a steward of your mysteries on earth,
so you may bring him to be nourished
by their truth and reality as unveiled in heaven.
Through Christ our Lord.

B

Collect

Hear with favor our prayers,
which we humbly offer, O Lord,
for the salvation of the soul of N., your servant and Priest,
that he, who devoted a faithful ministry to your name,
may rejoice in the perpetual company of your Saints.
Through our Lord Jesus Christ, your Son,
who lives and reigns with you in the unity of the Holy Spirit,
one God, for ever and ever.

Prayer over the Offerings

We ask your mercy, Lord,
that this sacrifice of our service,
offered for the soul of N., your servant and Priest,
may now bring pardon to him,
who devoutly offered sacrifice to you in the Church.
Through Christ our Lord.

Prayer after Communion

Renewed by food from your heavenly table,
we humbly beseech you, O Lord,
that by the power of this sacrifice
the soul of N., your servant and Priest,
who faithfully ministered in your Church,
may exult for ever in your sight.
Through Christ our Lord

4. FOR A DEACON

Collect

Grant, we pray, O merciful God,
a share in eternal happiness
to the soul of N., your servant and Deacon,
on whom you bestowed the gift of ministering in your Church.
Through our Lord Jesus Christ, your Son,
who lives and reigns with you in the unity of the Holy Spirit,
one God, for ever and ever.

Prayer over the Offerings

Be gracious, O Lord, to N., your servant and Deacon,
for whose salvation we offer you this sacrifice,
that, as in the flesh he ministered to Christ your Son,
so he may rise up with your faithful servants
to everlasting glory.
Through Christ our Lord.

Prayer after Communion

Replenished with these sacred gifts,
we humbly entreat you, O Lord,
graciously to grant through this sacrifice
that N., your servant and Deacon,
whom you called to be among those
who serve your Church,
once freed from the bonds of death,
may receive a share with those who have ministered well,
and enter into your joy.
Through Christ our Lord.

5. FOR A RELIGIOUS

Collect

Grant, we pray, almighty God,
that the soul of your servant N.,
who for love of Christ walked the way of perfect charity,
may rejoice in the coming of your glory
and together with his brothers (her sisters)
may delight in the everlasting happiness of your Kingdom.
Through our Lord Jesus Christ, your Son,
who lives and reigns with you in the unity of the Holy Spirit,
one God, for ever and ever.

6. FOR ONE WHO WORKED IN THE SERVICE OF THE GOSPEL

Collect

We humbly beseech your mercy, O Lord, for your servant N.,
that, having worked tirelessly for the spread of the Gospel,
he (she) may merit to enter into the rewards of the Kingdom.
Through our Lord Jesus Christ, your Son,
who lives and reigns with you in the unity of the Holy Spirit,
one God, for ever and ever.

7. FOR A YOUNG PERSON

Collect

O God, who direct our life in all its moments,
we humbly entrust to you this your servant N.,
whom we mourn as one whose life
was completed in so short a time;
grant that he (she) may flourish, for ever young,
in the happiness of your house.
Through our Lord Jesus Christ, your Son,
who lives and reigns with you in the unity of the Holy Spirit,
one God, for ever and ever.

8. FOR ONE WHO SUFFERED A LONG ILLNESS

Collect

O God, who called your servant **N.**
to serve you in affliction and sickness,
grant, we pray,
that he **(she)**, who followed your Son's example of suffering,
may also receive the reward of his glory.
Who lives and reigns with you in the unity of the Holy Spirit,
one God, for ever and ever.

9. FOR ONE WHO DIED SUDDENLY

Collect

Show us, Lord, the immense power of your goodness,
that, as we weep for our brother **(sister) N.**,
taken from us by a sudden death,
we may be confident that he **(she)** has passed over
into your eternal company.
Through our Lord Jesus Christ, your Son,
who lives and reigns with you in the unity of the Holy Spirit,
one God, for ever and ever.

10. FOR A MARRIED COUPLE

Collect

Grant merciful forgiveness, we pray, O Lord,
to your servants **N.** and **N.**,
that, just as faithful married love
bound them together in this life,
so the fullness of your charity
may unite them for all eternity.
Through our Lord Jesus Christ, your Son,
who lives and reigns with you in the unity of the Holy Spirit,
one God, for ever and ever.

Or, for one deceased spouse:

Grant merciful forgiveness, we pray, O Lord,
to your departed servant **N.**
and keep in your constant care your servant **N. (living spouse)**,
that, just as faithful married love
bound them together in this life,
so the fullness of your charity
may unite them for all eternity.
Through our Lord Jesus Christ, your Son,
who lives and reigns with you in the unity of the Holy Spirit,
one God, for ever and ever.

11. FOR THE PRIEST'S PARENTS

Collect

O God, who commanded us to honor father and mother,
have mercy in your compassion
on my father and mother (our parents),
forgive them their sins,
and bring me (us) to see them one day
in the gladness of eternal glory.
Through our Lord Jesus Christ, your Son,
who lives and reigns with you in the unity of the Holy Spirit,
one God, for ever and ever.

Prayer over the Offerings

Receive, O Lord, the sacrifice we offer you
for my father and mother (our parents);
grant them everlasting joy in the land of the living
and unite me (us) with them
in the happiness of the Saints.
Through Christ our Lord.

Prayer after Communion

May participation in this heavenly Sacrament
obtain perpetual light and rest
for my father and mother (our parents),
we pray, O Lord,
and bring me (us), along with them,
to the fullness of your everlasting glory.
Through Christ our Lord.

12. FOR RELATIVES, FRIENDS, AND BENEFACTORS

Collect

O God, giver of pardon and loving author of our salvation,
grant, we pray you, in your mercy,
that, through the intercession
of Blessed Mary, ever-Virgin, and all your Saints,
the members, friends, and benefactors of our community,
who have passed from this world,
may attain a share in eternal happiness.
Through our Lord Jesus Christ, your Son,
who lives and reigns with you in the unity of the Holy Spirit,
one God, for ever and ever.

Prayer over the Offerings

O God, whose mercy is beyond measure,
receive with favor our humble prayers
and through the Sacrament of our salvation
grant to the souls of our relatives, friends, and benefactors,
remission of all their sins.
Through Christ our Lord.

Prayer after Communion

Grant, we pray, almighty and merciful God,
that the souls of our relatives, friends, and benefactors,
for whom we have offered
this sacrifice of praise to your majesty,
may, through the power of this Sacrament,
be cleansed of all their sins,
and receive from your mercy
the happiness of perpetual light.
Through Christ our Lord.

APPENDICES

APPENDIX I
VARIOUS CHANTS FOR THE ORDER OF MASS

In choosing the simple or solemn tone (in place in the Order of Mass), it is desirable that the same tone for all parts of the Ordinary be used, in order to preserve the unity of the musical genre.

Penitential Act

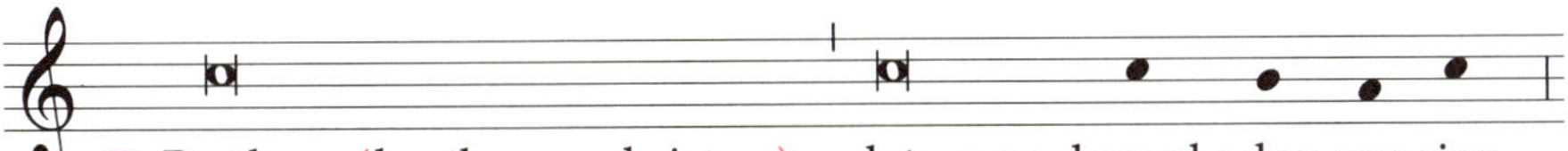

V. Brethren (brothers and sisters), let us ac-knowl-edge our sins,

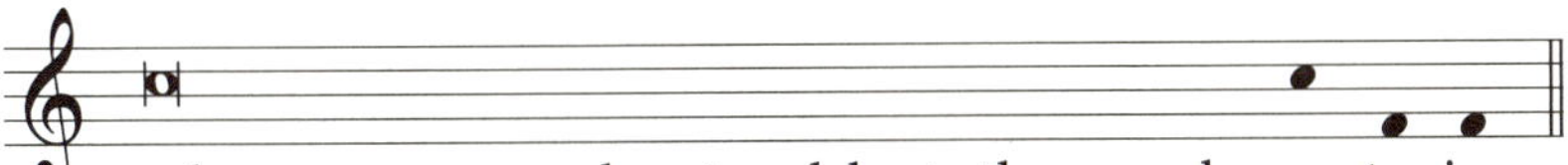

and so prepare ourselves to celebrate the sacred mys-ter-ies.

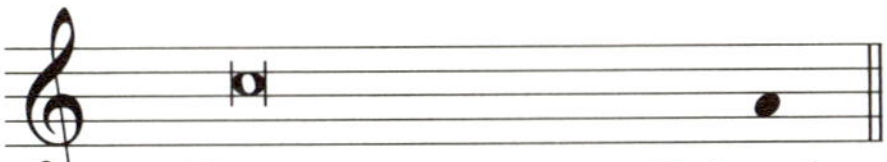

V. Have mercy on us, O Lord.

R. For we have sinned a-gainst you.

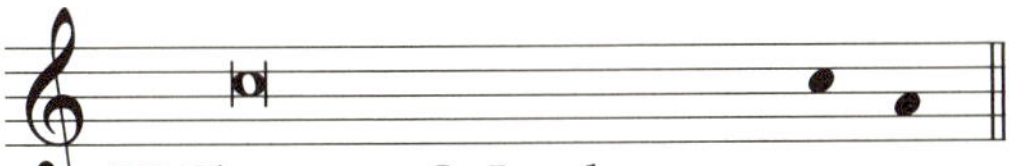

V. Show us, O Lord, your mer-cy.

R. And grant us your sal-va-tion.

V. May almighty God have mercy on us, for-give us our sins,

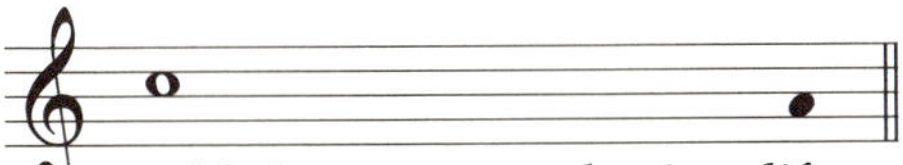

and bring us to everlasting life.

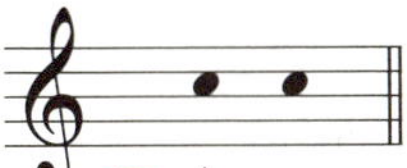

R. A-men.

Or:

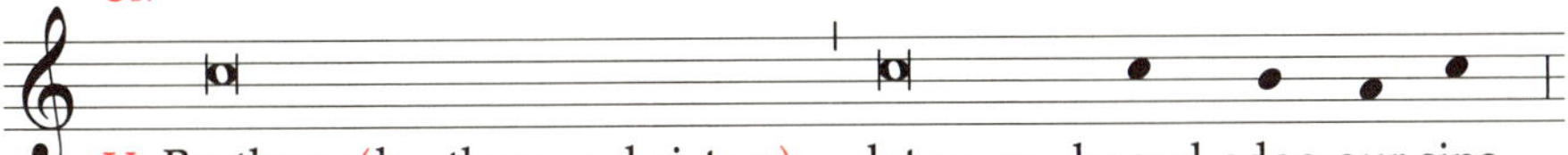

V. Brethren (brothers and sisters), let us ac-knowl-edge our sins,

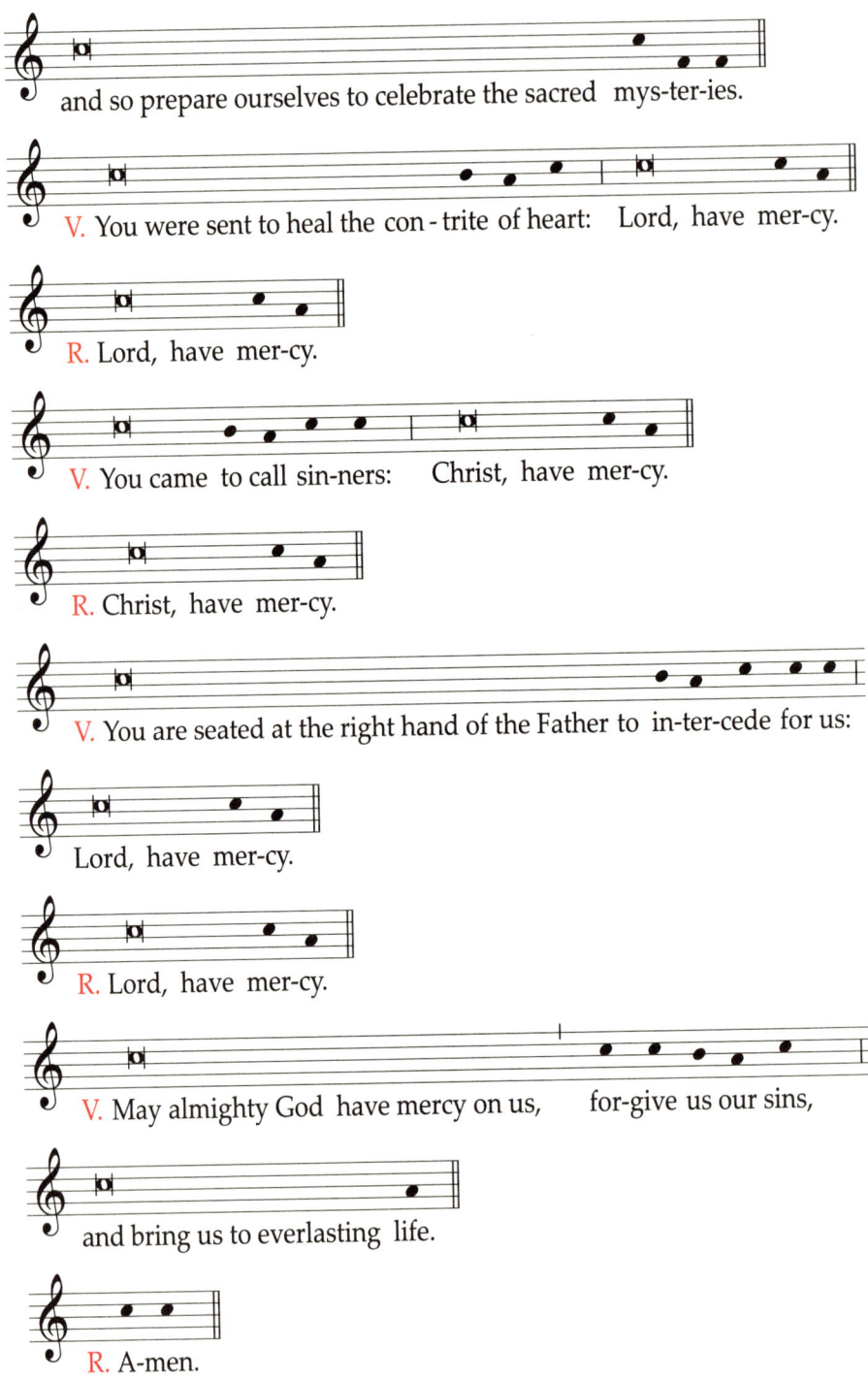

The Concluding Rites
Blessing

V. The Lord be with you.   R. And with your spir-it.

V. May al-might-y God bless you,   the Father, and the Son, ✠

and the Holy Spir-it.   R. A-men.

Episcopal Blessing

V. The Lord be with you.   R. And with your spir-it.

V. Blessed be the name of the Lord.   R. Now and for ev-er.

V. Our help is in the name of the Lord.   R. Who made heaven and earth.

V. May al-might-y God bless you,   the Father, ✠ and the Son, ✠

and the Holy ✠ Spir-it.   R. A-men.

Dismissal

V. Go forth, the Mass is end-ed.   R. Thanks be to God.

Or:

V. Go and an-nounce the Gos-pel of the Lord.   R. Thanks be to God.

Or:

V. Go in peace, glorifying the Lord by your life.   R. Thanks be to God.

Or:

V. Go in peace.   R. Thanks be to God.

Tones for the Presidential Prayers

Solemn Tone

All the presidential prayers in the Missal (Collects, Prayers over the Offerings, Prayers after Communion) may be pointed for use with the solemn tone according to the following formula. The reciting tone is preceded by one "G" (before ascending to "A"), including after the Flex. At every cadence, whether a Flex or a Full Stop, the grave (\) indicates where to descend to "G," and the acute (/) indicates where to ascend back to "A." The grave at the Flex may or may not fall on the the text accent, depending on the textual accent pattern. The grave at the Full Stop is always applied to the second to last syllable before the final accent, without respect to the accentuation of that syllable. When the Eucharistic Prayer is sung according to the tone in the Missal, the Prayer over the Offerings must be sung according to the solemn tone.

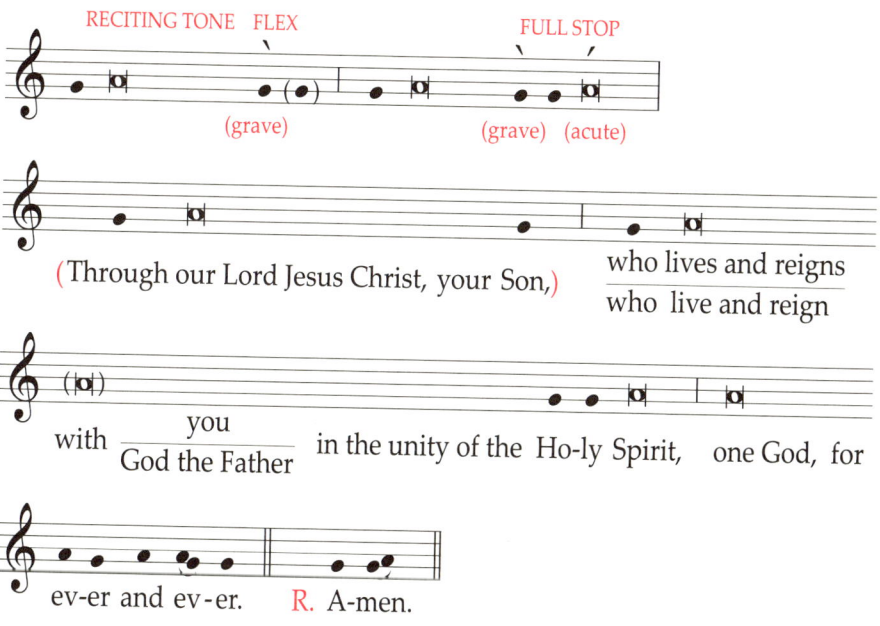

Or:

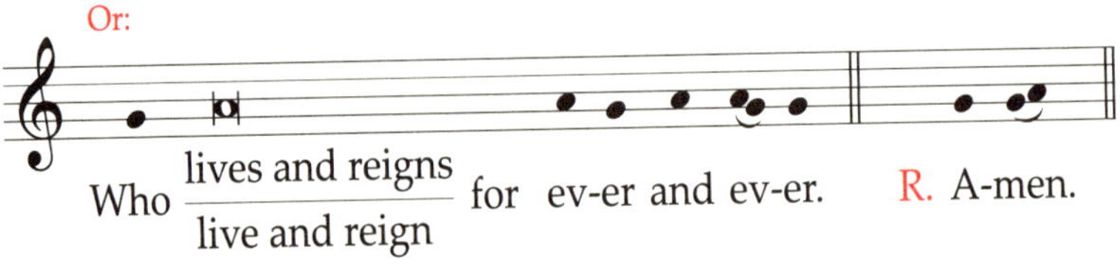

Who lives and reigns / live and reign for ev-er and ev-er. R. A-men.

Collect (First Sunday of Advent)

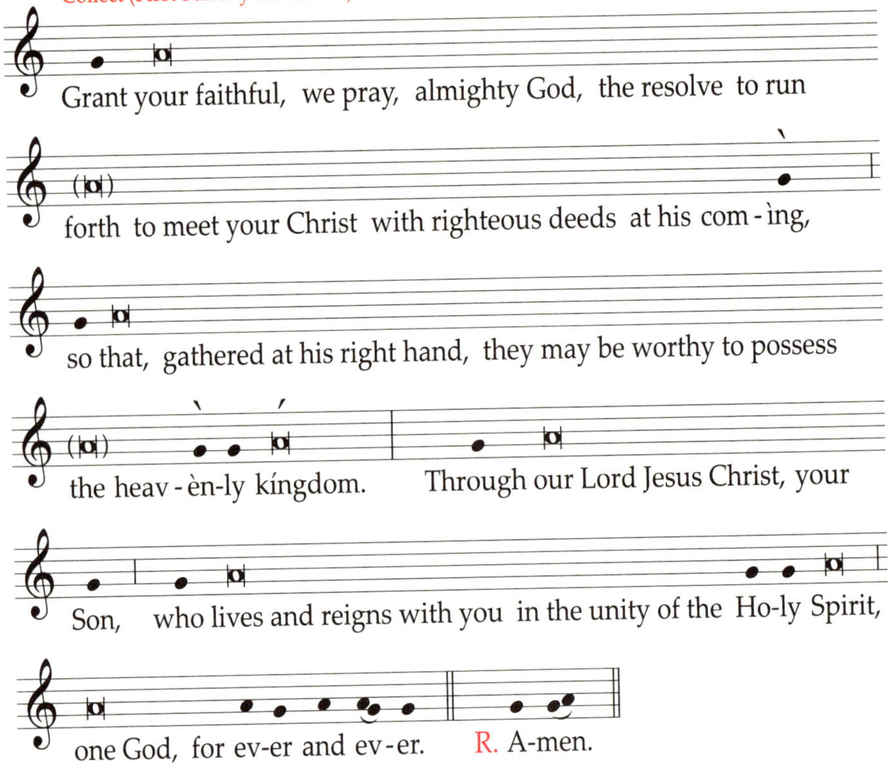

Grant your faithful, we pray, almighty God, the resolve to run

forth to meet your Christ with righteous deeds at his com-ing,

so that, gathered at his right hand, they may be worthy to possess

the heav-èn-ly kíngdom.   Through our Lord Jesus Christ, your

Son,   who lives and reigns with you in the unity of the Ho-ly Spirit,

one God, for ev-er and ev-er.   R. A-men.

Prayer over the Offerings (The Epiphany of the Lord, The Mass during the Day)

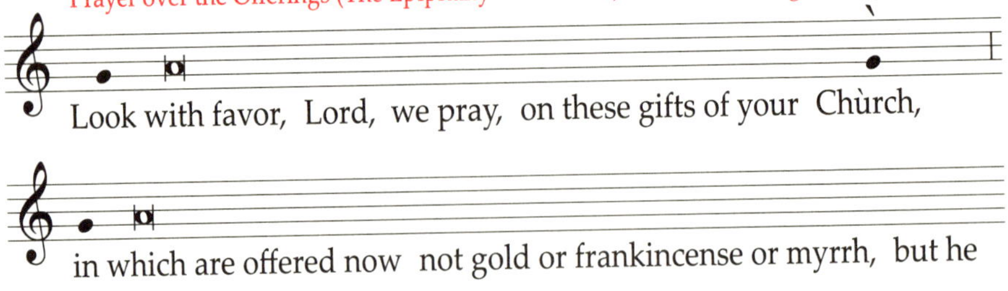

Look with favor, Lord, we pray, on these gifts of your Chùrch,

in which are offered now not gold or frankincense or myrrh, but he

APPENDIX I

Simple Tone

The presidential prayers (Collects, Prayers over the Offerings, Prayers after Communion) may also be sung according to the simple tone, which follows.

INVITATION
Let us pray.

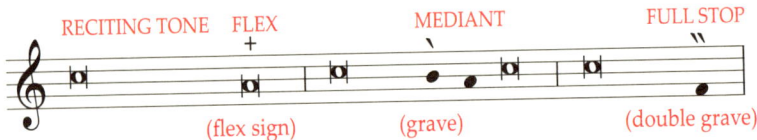

RECITING TONE — FLEX — MEDIANT — FULL STOP
(flex sign) — (grave) — (double grave)

For the Flex and Full Stop, the pointing depends upon where the accent falls. When the final syllable is accented, a flex (+) sign or double grave (⸝⸝) is to be given to it. When the final syllable is not accented, this syllable is sung on the Reciting Tone and the flex sign or double grave is to be placed so as to indicate where one descends for the non-accented syllable(s). Examples:

FLEX
...on the gifts of your CHURCH,
...from among your BLESS - ings

FULL STOP
...Jesus CHRIST
...reDEMP - tiòn.

For the Mediant cadence, the grave (`) is placed two syllables before the final accent, without respect to the accentuation of these two syllables.

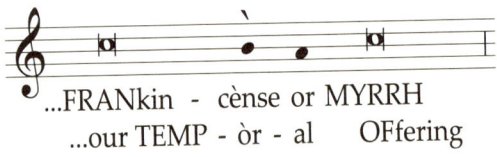

...FRANkin - cènse or MYRRH
...our TEMP - òr - al OFfering

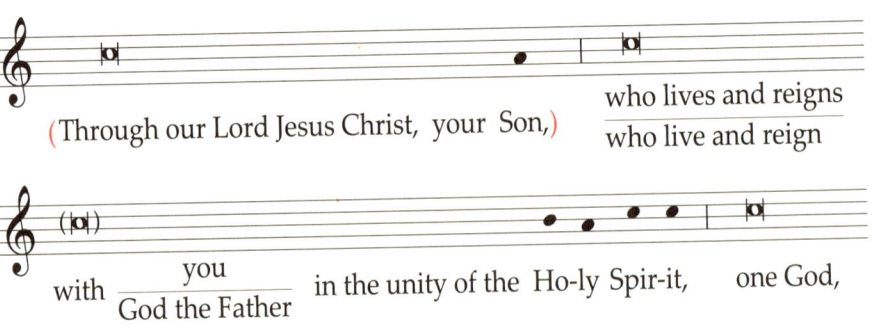

(Through our Lord Jesus Christ, your Son,) who lives and reigns / who live and reign
with you / God the Father in the unity of the Ho-ly Spir-it, one God,

VARIOUS CHANTS FOR THE ORDER OF MASS

for ever and ev-er.   ℟. A-men.

After the other Prayers

Through Christ our Lord.   ℟. A-men.

Or:

Who lives and reigns
Who live and reign   for ever and ev-er.   ℟. A-men.

Collect (First Sunday of Advent)

Grant your faithful, we pray, almighty God, the resolve to run forth to meet your Christ with righteous deeds àt his com-ing, so that, gathered at his right hand, they may be worthy to possess the heav--enly king-dòm.   Through our Lord Jesus Christ, your Son, who lives and reigns with you in the unity of the Ho-ly Spir-it, one God, for ever and ev-er.   ℟. A-men.

Tones for the Readings
I. Old Testament and Acts of the Apostles

INTRODUCTION

A reading from the Book of the Prophet I - sai - ah.
A reading from the Book of the Prophet E - zek - i - el.
A reading from the first Book of   Kings.
                    second
A reading from the Book of   Prov - erbs.
A reading from the Book of   Ex - o - dus.
A reading from the Book of   Wis - dom.
A reading from the Acts of the   A - pos - tles.

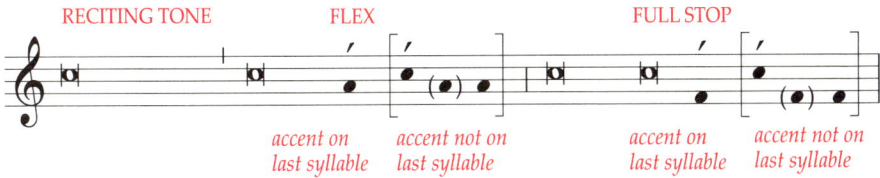

RECITING TONE   **FLEX**   **FULL STOP**

accent on   *accent not on*   *accent on*   *accent not on*
last syllable   *last syllable*   *last syllable*   *last syllable*

QUESTION

CONCLUSION

accent on   *accent not on*
last syllable   *last syllable*

ACCLAMATION

The word of the Lord.   Thanks be to God.

The flex is used at the end of major clauses within a sentence. In short sentences it may be omitted, and in long sentences it may be used more than once. For the flex, one leaves the reciting tone either on the last syllable or an earlier syllable, as the accentuation demands. The flex should not be used to introduce a question. The full stop is used at the end of every sentence. The question formula is used for all questions, except when the question occurs at the end of a reading. In the question formula, one leaves the reciting tone two syllables before the last accent. In long questions, the ending is used only for the last clause of the question, with the reciting tone for the first clause.

VARIOUS CHANTS FOR THE ORDER OF MASS

First Reading for the First Sunday of Advent, Year B (NAB)
Isaiah 63:16b-17, 19b; 64:2-7

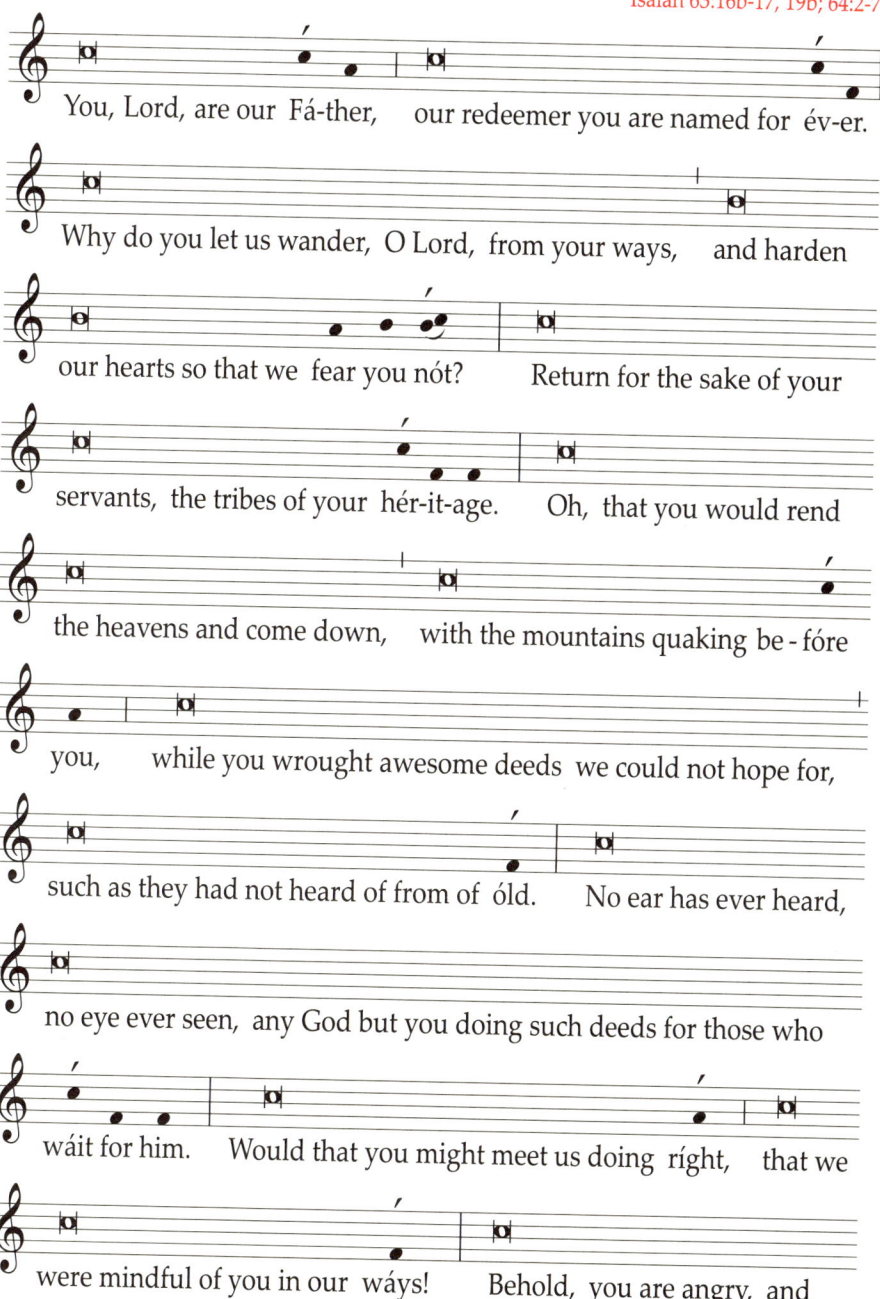

Tones for the Readings
II. The Epistle and the Book of Revelation

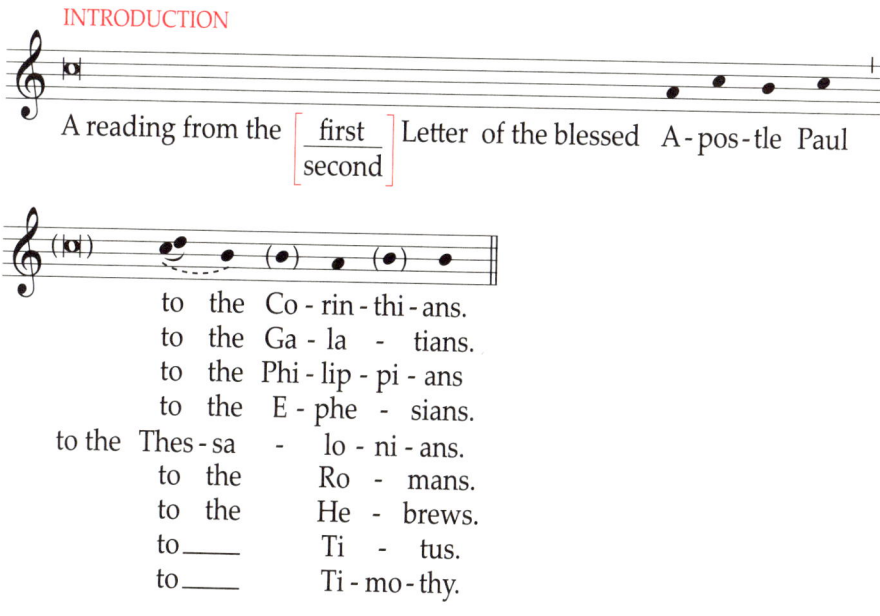

Or:

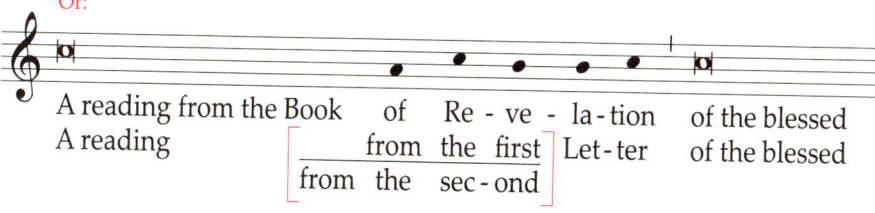

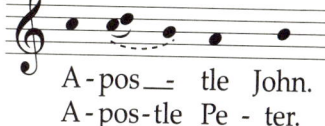

APPENDIX I

Each sentence (or group of phrases) in the body of the reading takes the following three elements:

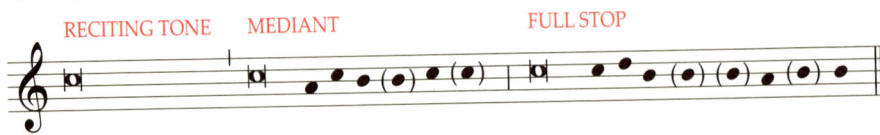

The mediant is used at the end of major clauses within a sentence. In short sentences it may be omitted, and in long sentences it may be used more than once. For the mediant, one always leaves the reciting tone three syllables before the last accent, and then completes the line as indicated for last accent on the final syllable or last accent not on the final syllable. The mediant should not be used to introduce a question. The full stop is used at the end of every sentence, with the formula applied as indicated for the various combinations and penultimate accent and last accent. The question formula is used for all questions, except when the question occurs at the end of a reading. In the question formula, one leaves the reciting tone two syllables before the last accent. In long questions, the ending is used only for the last clause of the question, with the reciting tone for the first clause. The conclusion with its two elements is used for the last two lines of the reading. For these two elements, one leaves the reciting tone one syllable before the last accent and then on the last accent.

The Mediant and the Full Stop are pointed according to the following accent patterns.

MEDIANT ACCENT PATTERNS

When the last accent is on the final syllable:

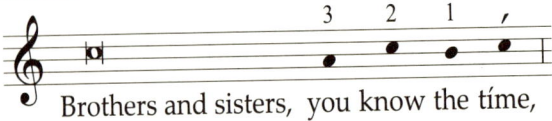

When the last accent does not fall on the final syllable:

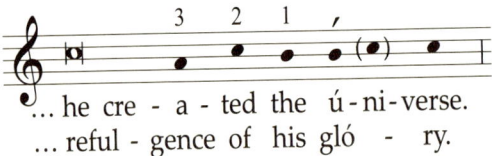

FULL STOP ACCENT PATTERNS When the last accent is on the final syllable:

Penultimate accent followed by one unaccented syllable: … ab-sólved ⎯ from sín.
Penultimate accent followed by two unaccented syllables: … the wón-ders   of Gód.
Penultimate accent followed by three unaccented syllables: … the wón-ders of his lóve.

VARIOUS CHANTS FOR THE ORDER OF MASS

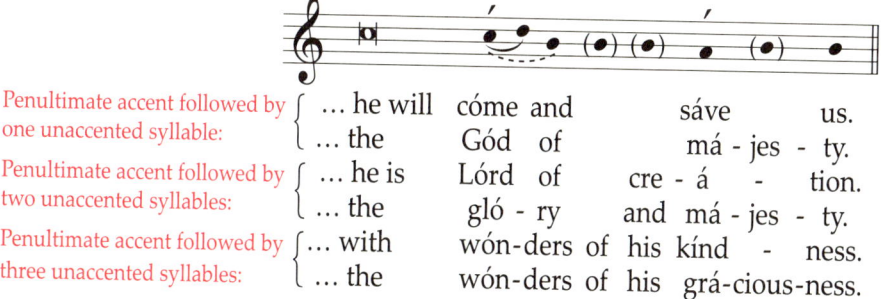

Penultimate accent followed by one unaccented syllable:	… he will … the	cóme and Gód of	sáve má - jes - ty.	us.
Penultimate accent followed by two unaccented syllables:	… he is … the	Lórd of gló - ry	cre - á - and má - jes -	tion. ty.
Penultimate accent followed by three unaccented syllables:	… with … the	wón-ders of his wón-ders of his	kínd - grá-cious-	ness. ness.

QUESTIONS

Questions are pointed with two syllables before the final accent:

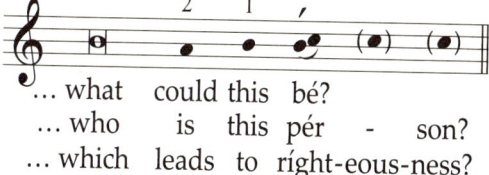

… what could this bé?
… who is this pér - son?
… which leads to ríght-eous-ness?

CONCLUSION

The end of the reading is pointed with two elements as follows.

Leave the reciting tone one syllable before the last accent: Leave the reciting tone on the last accent:

… no provisions for the flésh,   to gratify its de - síres.
… praise you among the Gén-tiles,   sing praises in your prés-ence.

ACCLAMATION

The word of the Lord.   Thanks be to God.

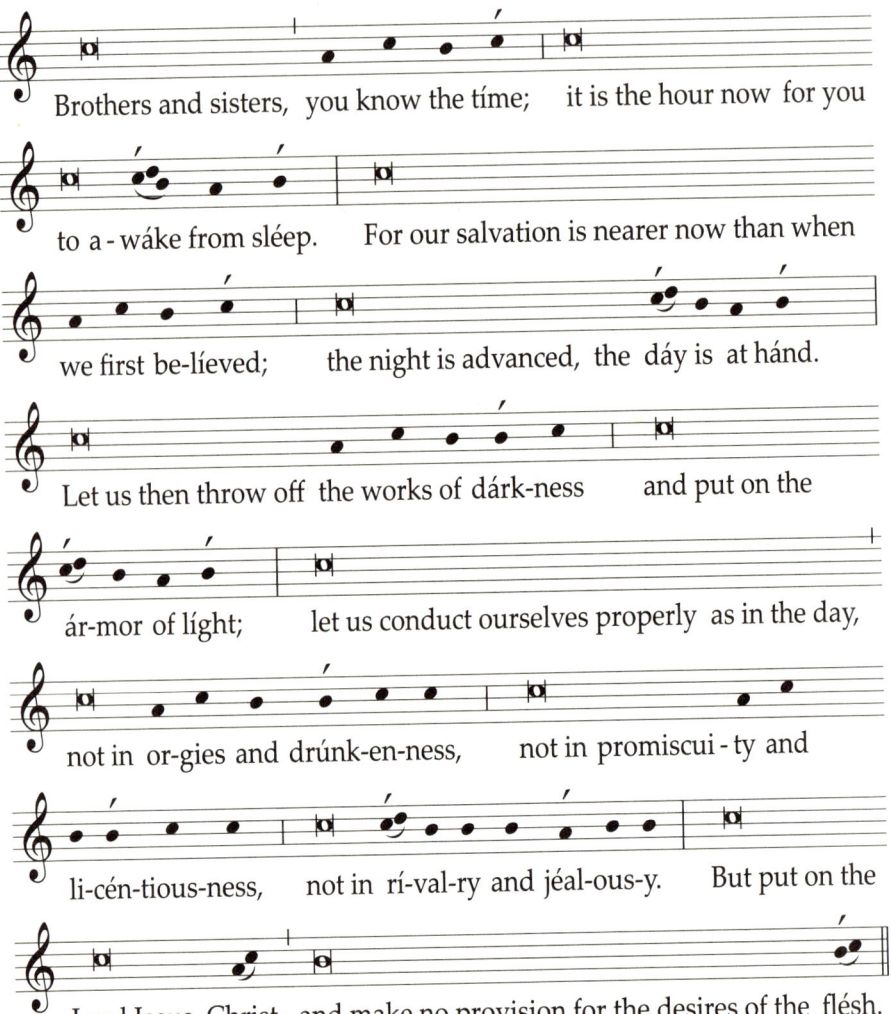

Tones for the Readings
III. The Gospel

The mediant is used at the end of major clauses within a sentence. In short sentences it may be omitted, and in long sentences it may be used more than once. It should not be used to introduce a question. The full stop is used at the end of every sentence. The question formula is used for all questions, except when the question occurs at the end of a Gospel reading. In the question formula, one leaves the reciting tone two syllables before the last accent. In long questions, the ending is used only for the last clause of the question, with the reciting tone for the first clause. The conclusion with its two elements is used for the last two lines of the reading. For each of these two elements, one leaves the reciting tone on the last accent.

VARIOUS CHANTS FOR THE ORDER OF MASS

Tones for the Readings
III. The Gospel
(Solemn Tone)

The mediant is used at the end of major clauses within a sentence. In short sentences it may be omitted, and in long sentences it may be used more than once. It should not be used to introduce a question. The full stop is used at the end of every sentence. The question formula is used for all questions, except when the question occurs at the end of a Gospel reading. In the question formula, one leaves the reciting tone two syllables before the last accent. In long questions, the ending is used only for the last clause of the question, with the reciting tone for the first clause. The conclusion with its two elements is used for the last two lines of the reading. For each of these two elements, one leaves the reciting tone on the last accent.

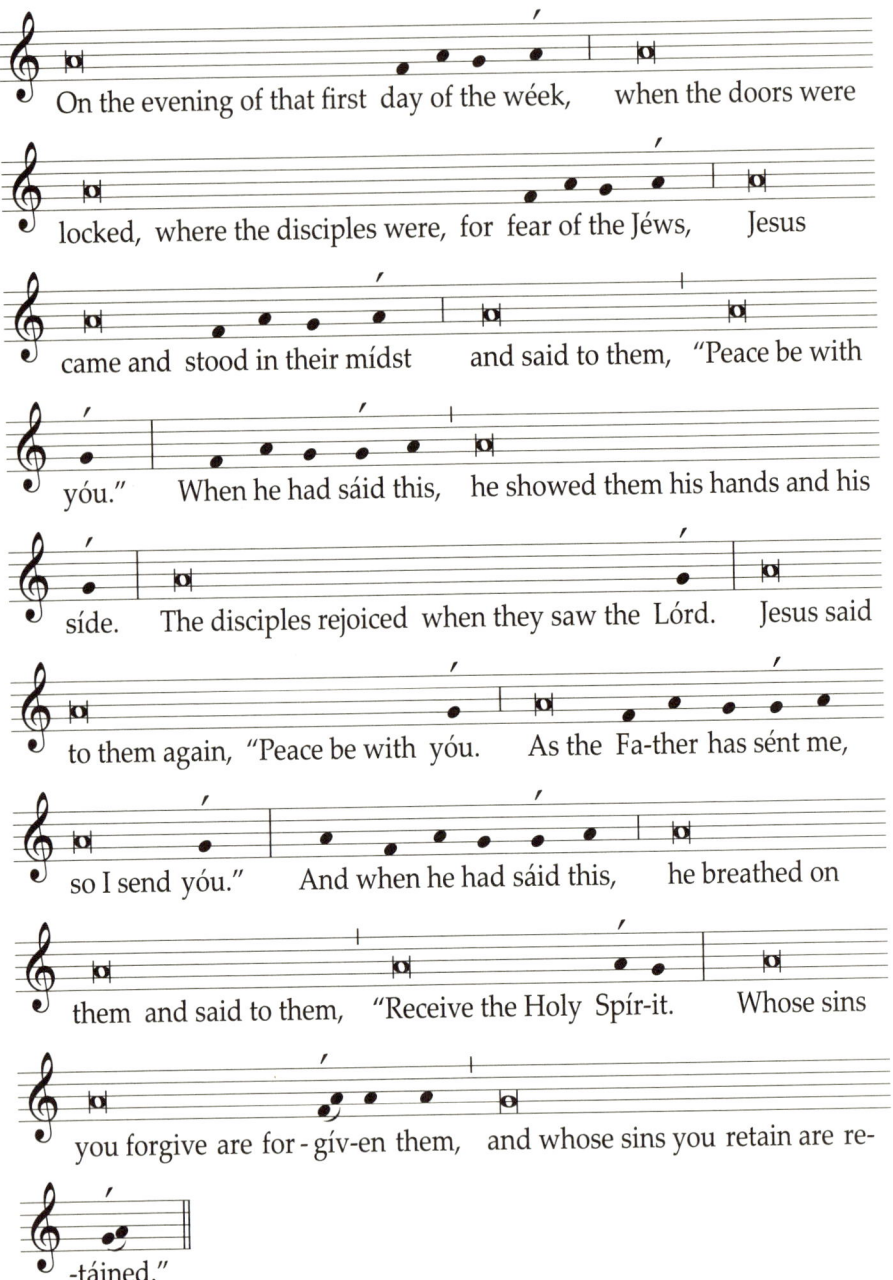

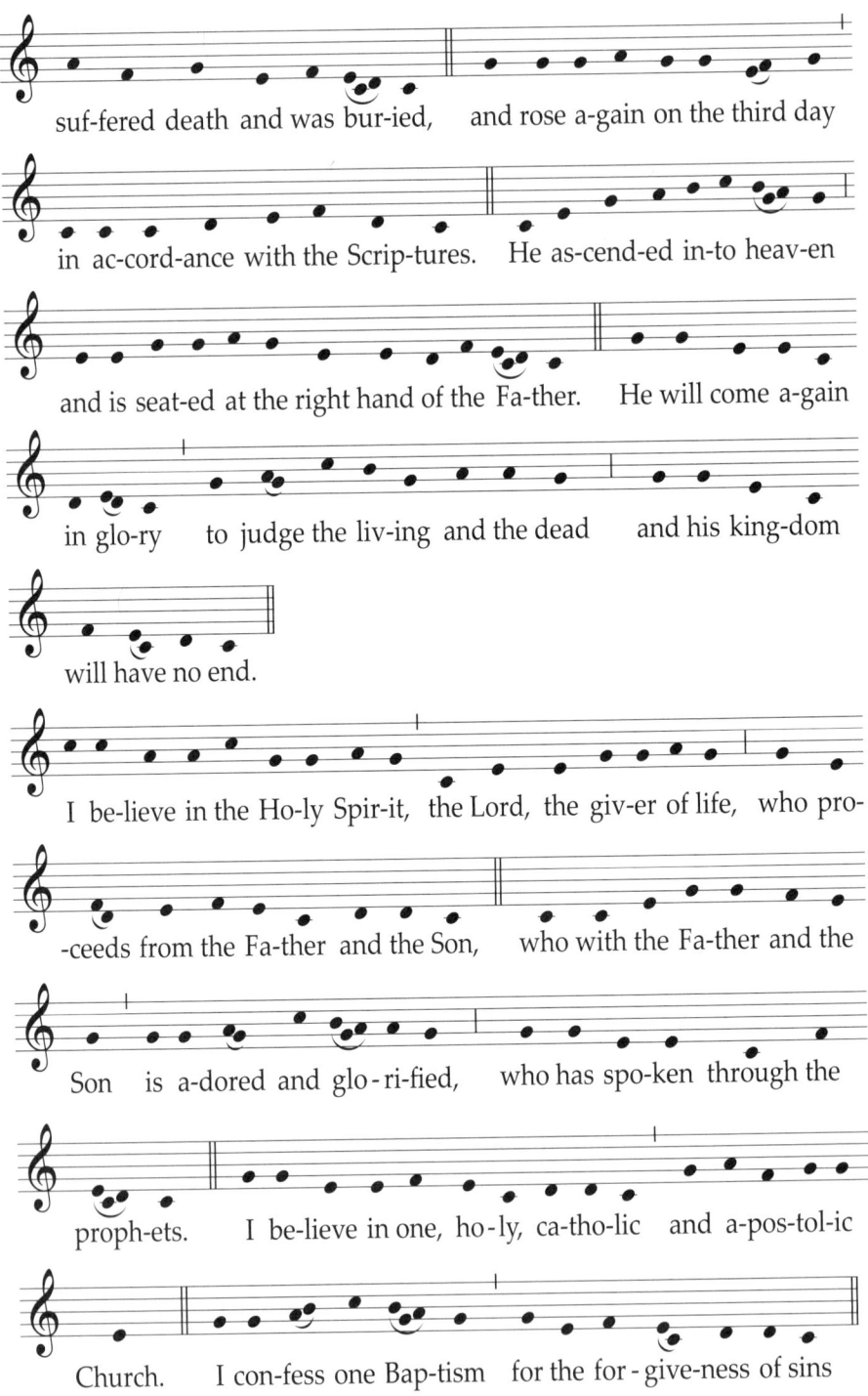

VARIOUS CHANTS FOR THE ORDER OF MASS

1441

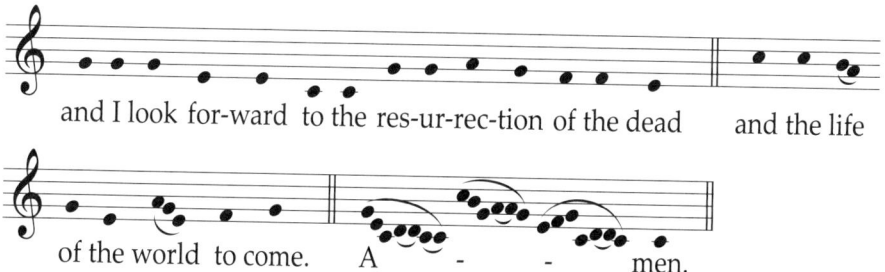

and I look for-ward to the res-ur-rec-tion of the dead   and the life of the world to come.   A - - men.

PRAYER OF THE FAITHFUL

The text that follows the dagger (†) in the invocations given below can also be used to conclude intentions that are not sung; alternatively, the final words of the individual intentions can take its place.

A

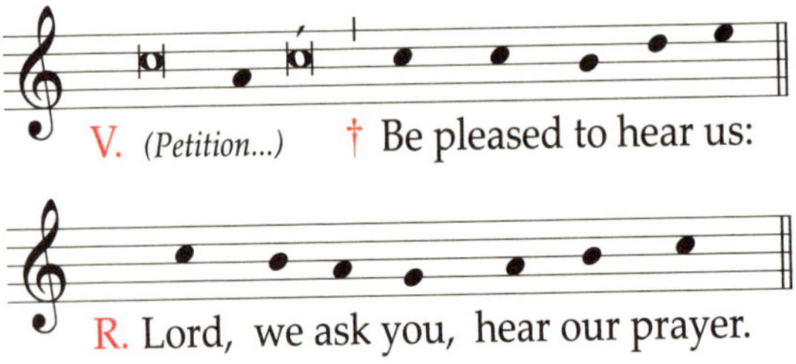

V. *(Petition...)* † Be pleased to hear us:

R. Lord, we ask you, hear our prayer.

B

V. *(Petition...)* † Let us call up-on the Lord: R. Hear us, O Christ.

C

V. *(Petition...)* † Let us pray to the Lord: R. Lord, hear our prayer.

Or:

R. Lord, have mer-cy.

D

V. *(Petition...)* † Let us im-plore the Lord: Ký-ri-e, e-lé-i-son.

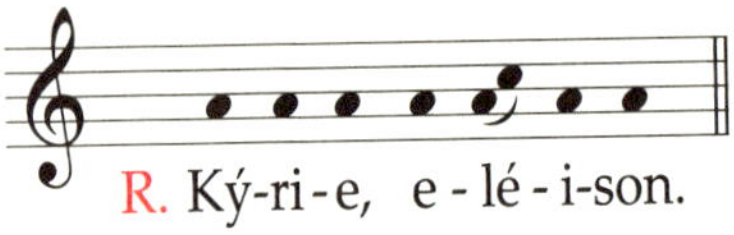

R. Ký-ri-e, e-lé-i-son.

The Lord's Prayer
Tone C (Solemn Anaphora Tone)

VARIOUS CHANTS FOR THE ORDER OF MASS

At the Solemn Blessing

Solemn Tone

The Deacon or, in his absence, the Priest himself, sings the invitation:

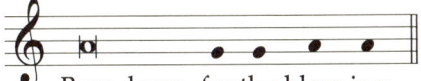
Bow down for the bless-ing.

Then the Priest, with hands extended over the people, sings the blessing:

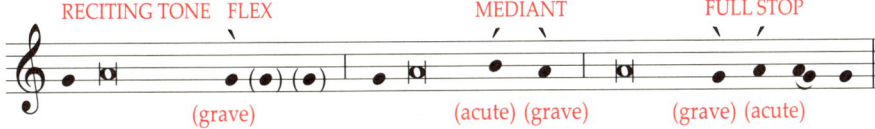

V. May the almighty and merciful God, by whose grace you have placed your faith in the First Coming of his Only Begotten Son and yearn for his coming a-gàin, sanc-tify you by the radiance of Christ's Ád-vènt and enrich you with hís bless-ing.

R. A-men.

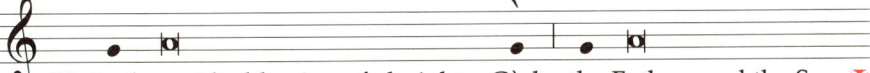
V. And may the blessing of almighty Gòd, the Father, and the Son, ✠

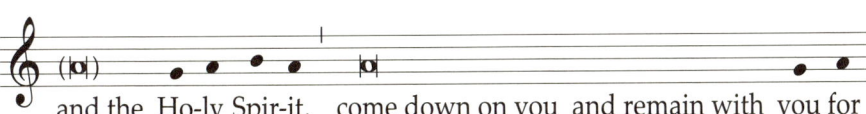
and the Ho-ly Spir-it, come down on you and remain with you for

ev-er.

R. A-men.

Or, in some Ritual Masses:

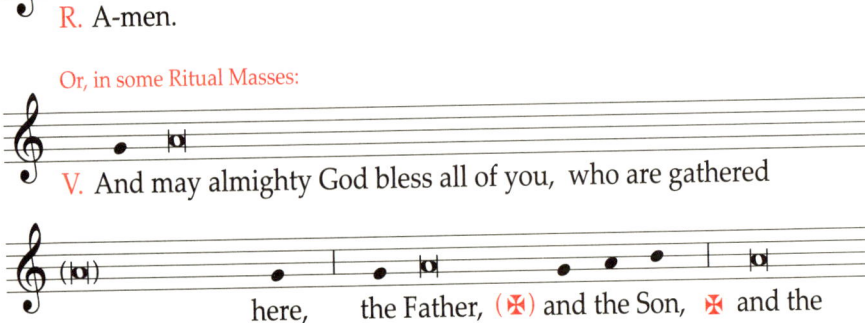
V. And may almighty God bless all of you, who are gathered here, for these sacred rites, the Father, (✠) and the Son, ✠ and the

Ho-ly (✠) Spir-it.

R. A-men.

Simple Tone

The Deacon or, in his absence, the Priest himself, sings the invitation:

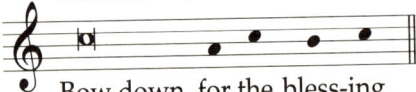
Bow down for the bless-ing.

Then the Priest, with hands extended over the people, sings the blessing:

RECITING TONE   FLEX   MEDIANT   FULL STOP
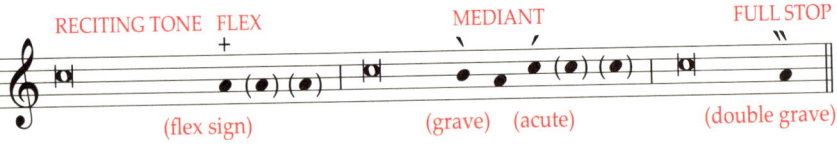
(flex sign)   (grave) (acute)   (double grave)

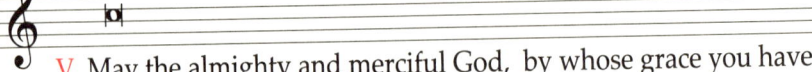
V. May the almighty and merciful God, by whose grace you have

placed your faith in the First Coming of his Only Begotten Son and

VARIOUS CHANTS FOR THE ORDER OF MASS

The Announcement of Easter and the Moveable Feasts

On the Epiphany of the Lord, after the singing of the Gospel, a Deacon or cantor, in keeping with an ancient practice of Holy Church, announces from the ambo the moveable feasts of the current year according to this formula:

Know, dear brethren, (broth-ers and sis-ters,) that, as we have re-joiced at the Nativity of our Lord Je-sus Christ, so by leave of God's mer-cy we announce to you al-so the joy of his Resur-rection, who is our Sav-ior. On the ... day of [February / March] will fall Ash Wednes-day, and the beginning of the fast of the most sacred Lent-en sea-son. On the ... day of [March / A-pril] you will celebrate with joy East-er Day, the Paschal feast of our Lord Je-sus Christ. On the ... day of [A-pril / May / June] will be the As-cen-sion of our Lord Je-sus Christ. On the ... day of [May, June,

VARIOUS CHANTS FOR THE ORDER OF MASS

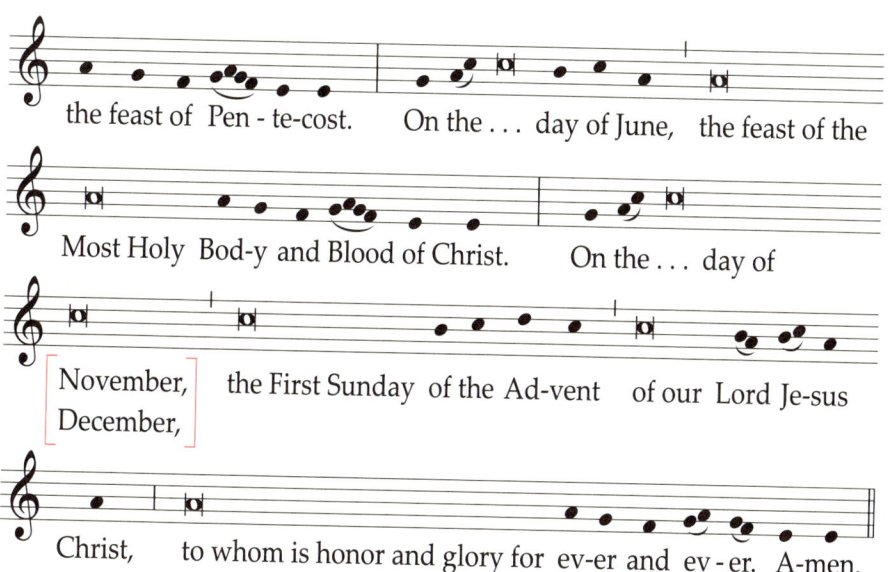

THE NATIVITY OF OUR LORD JESUS CHRIST
from the *Roman Martyrology*

The announcement of the Solemnity of the Nativity of the Lord from the *Roman Martyrology* draws upon Sacred Scripture to declare in a formal way the birth of Christ. It begins with creation and relates the birth of the Lord to the major events and personages of sacred and secular history. The particular events contained in the announcement help pastorally to situate the birth of Jesus in the context of salvation history.

This text, *The Nativity of our Lord Jesus Christ*, may be chanted or recited, most appropriately on December 24, during the celebration of the Liturgy of the Hours. It may also be chanted or recited before the beginning of Christmas Mass during the Night. It may not replace any part of the Mass.

The twenty-fifth day of De-cem-ber, when ages beyond number had run their course from the creation of the world, when God in the beginning created hea-ven and earth, and formed man in his own like-ness; when century upon century had passed since the Al--mighty set his bow in the clouds after the Great Flood, as a sign of covenant and peace; in the twenty-first century since Abraham, our father in faith, came out of the Ur of the Chal-dees; in the thirteenth century since the People of Israel were led by Moses in the

THE NATIVITY OF OUR LORD JESUS CHRIST

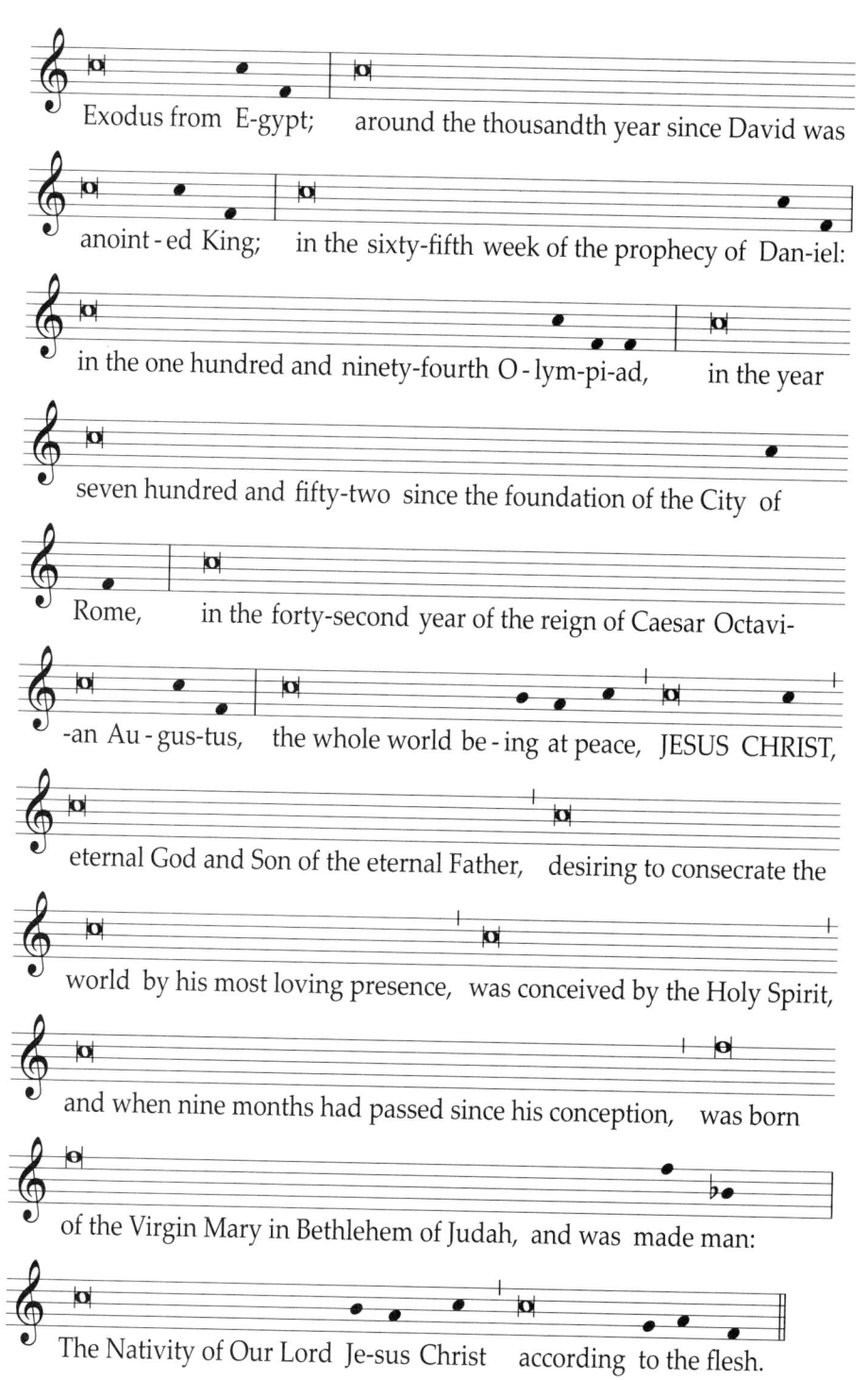

Exodus from E-gypt; around the thousandth year since David was anoint-ed King; in the sixty-fifth week of the prophecy of Dan-iel: in the one hundred and ninety-fourth O-lym-pi-ad, in the year seven hundred and fifty-two since the foundation of the City of Rome, in the forty-second year of the reign of Caesar Octavi--an Au-gus-tus, the whole world be-ing at peace, JESUS CHRIST, eternal God and Son of the eternal Father, desiring to consecrate the world by his most loving presence, was conceived by the Holy Spirit, and when nine months had passed since his conception, was born of the Virgin Mary in Bethlehem of Judah, and was made man: The Nativity of Our Lord Je-sus Christ according to the flesh.

Text without music:
The Twenty-fifth Day of December,
when ages beyond number had run their course
   from the creation of the world,
when God in the beginning created heaven and earth,
and formed man in his own likeness;
when century upon century had passed
since the Almighty set his bow in the clouds after the Great Flood,
as a sign of covenant and peace;
in the twenty-first century since Abraham, our father in faith,
came out of Ur of the Chaldees;
in the thirteenth century since the People of Israel were led
   by Moses
   in the Exodus from Egypt;
around the thousandth year since David was anointed King;
in the sixty-fifth week of the prophecy of Daniel;
in the one hundred and ninety-fourth Olympiad;
in the year seven hundred and fifty-two
   since the foundation of the City of Rome;
in the forty-second year of the reign of Caesar Octavian Augustus,
the whole world being at peace,

JESUS CHRIST, eternal God and Son of the eternal Father,
desiring to consecrate the world by his most loving presence,
was conceived by the Holy Spirit,
and when nine months had passed since his conception,
was born of the Virgin Mary in Bethlehem of Judah, and
   was made man:

The Nativity of Our Lord Jesus Christ according to the flesh.

APPENDIX II

RITE FOR THE BLESSING AND SPRINKLING OF WATER

1. On Sundays, especially in Easter Time, the blessing and sprinkling of water as a memorial of Baptism may take place from time to time in all churches and chapels, even in Masses anticipated on Saturday evenings.

    If this rite is celebrated during Mass, it takes the place of the usual Penitential Act at the beginning of Mass.

2. After the greeting, the Priest stands at his chair and faces the people. With a vessel containing the water to be blessed before him, he calls upon the people to pray in these or similar words:

    **Dear brethren (brothers and sisters),
    let us humbly beseech the Lord our God
    to bless this water he has created,
    which will be sprinkled on us
    as a memorial of our Baptism.
    May he help us by his grace
    to remain faithful to the Spirit we have received.**

    And after a brief pause for silence, he continues with hands joined:

    **Almighty ever-living God,
    who willed that through water,
    the fountain of life and the source of purification,
    even souls should be cleansed
    and receive the gift of eternal life;
    be pleased, we pray, to ✠ bless this water,
    by which we seek protection on this your day, O Lord.
    Renew the living spring of your grace within us
    and grant that by this water we may be defended
    from all ills of spirit and body,
    and so approach you with hearts made clean
    and worthily receive your salvation.
    Through Christ our Lord.**
    R. Amen.

    Or:

Almighty Lord and God,
who are the source and origin of all life,
whether of body or soul,
we ask you to ✠ bless this water,
which we use in confidence
to implore forgiveness for our sins
and to obtain the protection of your grace
against all illness and every snare of the enemy.
Grant, O Lord, in your mercy,
that living waters may always spring up for our salvation,
and so may we approach you with a pure heart
and avoid all danger to body and soul.
Through Christ our Lord.
R. Amen.

Or, during Easter Time:

Lord our God,
in your mercy be present to your people's prayers,
and, for us who recall the wondrous work of our creation
and the still greater work of our redemption,
graciously ✠ bless this water.
For you created water to make the fields fruitful
and to refresh and cleanse our bodies.
You also made water the instrument of your mercy:
for through water you freed your people from slavery
and quenched their thirst in the desert;
through water the Prophets proclaimed the new covenant
you were to enter upon with the human race;
and last of all,
through water, which Christ made holy in the Jordan,
you have renewed our corrupted nature
in the bath of regeneration.
Therefore, may this water be for us
a memorial of the Baptism we have received,
and grant that we may share
in the gladness of our brothers and sisters
who at Easter have received their Baptism.
Through Christ our Lord.
R. Amen.

RITE FOR THE BLESSING AND SPRINKLING OF WATER

3. Where the circumstances of the place or the custom of the people suggest that the mixing of salt be preserved in the blessing of water, the Priest may bless salt, saying:

We humbly ask you, almighty God:
be pleased in your faithful love to bless ✠ this salt
you have created,
for it was you who commanded the prophet Elisha
to cast salt into water,
that impure water might be purified.
Grant, O Lord, we pray,
that, wherever this mixture of salt and water is sprinkled,
every attack of the enemy may be repulsed
and your Holy Spirit may be present
to keep us safe at all times.
Through Christ our Lord.
R. Amen.

Then he pours the salt into the water, without saying anything.

4. Afterward, taking the aspergillum, the Priest sprinkles himself and the ministers, then the clergy and people, moving through the church, if appropriate.

Meanwhile, one of the following chants, or another appropriate chant is sung.

Outside Easter Time

Antiphon 1
Ps 51 (50): 9

Sprinkle me with hyssop, O Lord, and I shall be cleansed;
wash me and I shall be whiter than snow.

Antiphon 2
Ez 36: 25-26

I will pour clean water upon you,
and you will be made clean of all your impurities,
and I shall give you a new spirit, says the Lord.

Hymn

Cf. 1 Pt 1: 3-5

Blessed be the God and Father of our Lord Jesus Christ,
who in his great mercy has given us new birth into a living hope
through the Resurrection of Jesus Christ from the dead,
into an inheritance that will not perish,
preserved for us in heaven
for the salvation to be revealed in the last time!

During Easter Time

Antiphon 1   Cf. Ez 47: 1-2, 9

> I saw water flowing from the Temple,
> from its right-hand side, alleluia:
> and all to whom this water came
> were saved and shall say: Alleluia, alleluia.

Antiphon 2   Cf. Wis 3: 8; Ez 36: 25

> On the day of my resurrection, says the Lord, alleluia,
> I will gather the nations and assemble the kingdoms
> and I will pour clean water upon you, alleluia.

Antiphon 3   Cf. Dn 3: 77, 79

> You springs and all that moves in the waters,
> sing a hymn to God, alleluia.

Antiphon 4   1 Pt 2: 9

> O chosen race, royal priesthood, holy nation,
> proclaim the mighty works of him
> who called you out of darkness into his wonderful light, alleluia.

Antiphon 5

> From your side, O Christ,
> bursts forth a spring of water,
> by which the squalor of the world is washed away
> and life is made new again, alleluia.

5. When he returns to his chair and the singing is over, the Priest stands facing the people and, with hands joined, says:

> **May almighty God cleanse us of our sins,**
> **and through the celebration of this Eucharist**
> **make us worthy to share at the table of his Kingdom.**
> R. Amen.

6. Then, when it is prescribed, the hymn Gloria in excelsis (Glory to God in the highest) is sung or said.

APPENDIX III

RITE OF DEPUTING A MINISTER TO DISTRIBUTE HOLY COMMUNION ON A SINGLE OCCASION

1. The Diocesan Bishop has the faculty to permit individual Priests exercising sacred duties to depute a suitable member of the faithful to distribute Holy Communion with them on a single occasion, in cases of real necessity.

2. When one of the faithful is deputed to distribute Communion on a single occasion in such cases, it is fitting that a mandate to do so should be conferred according to the following rite.

3. After the Priest Celebrant himself has received the Sacrament in the usual way, the extraordinary minister comes to the altar and stands before the Celebrant, who blesses him or her with these words:

**May the Lord ✠ bless you,
so that at this Mass you may minister
the Body and Blood of Christ
to your brothers and sisters.**

And he or she replies:

Amen.

4. If the extraordinary minister is to receive the Most Holy Eucharist, the Priest gives Communion to the minister. Then the Priest gives him or her the ciborium or vessel with the hosts or the chalice and together they go to administer Communion to the faithful.

APPENDIX IV

RITE OF BLESSING A CHALICE AND A PATEN WITHIN MASS

1. Since the chalice and paten are used for the offering and consecration of the bread and wine and for communion, they are reserved exclusively and permanently for the celebration of the Eucharist, and so become "sacred vessels."

2. The intention of reserving these vessels exclusively for the celebration of the Eucharist is made manifest before the community of the faithful by a special blessing which is appropriate to impart during Mass.

3. Any Priest may bless a chalice and paten, provided these vessels have been made according to the norms indicated above in the *General Instruction of the Roman Missal*, nos. 327-332.

4. If only a chalice or only a paten is to be blessed, the texts should be suitably adapted.

5. After the reading of the word of God, a homily is given in which the Priest explains both the biblical readings and the meaning of the blessing of a chalice and paten that are used in the celebration of the Lord's Supper.

6. When the Universal Prayer is concluded, the ministers, or representatives of the community presenting the chalice and paten, place these latter on the altar. Then the Priest moves to the altar, while there is sung this antiphon:

Antiphon
The chalice of salvation I will raise,
and I will call on the name of the Lord.

Another appropriate chant may also be sung.

7. When the singing is over, the Priest says:

Let us pray.

RITE OF BLESSING A CHALICE AND A PATEN WITHIN MASS

And all pray in silence for a while. Then the Priest continues:

With joy, Lord God,
we place on your altar this chalice and paten
for the celebration of the sacrifice of the new covenant:
may the Body and Blood of your Son,
offered and received by means of these vessels,
make them holy.
Grant, we pray, O Lord,
that, celebrating the unblemished sacrifice,
we may be renewed by your Sacraments on earth
and endowed with your Spirit,
until with the Saints we come to delight in your banquet
in the Kingdom of Heaven.
Glory and honor to you for ever.

All reply:

Blessed be God for ever.

8. *The ministers then place the corporal on the altar. Some of the faithful carry forward bread, wine, and water for the celebration of the Lord's Sacrifice. The Priest puts the offerings on the newly blessed paten and in the newly blessed chalice and offers them in the usual way. Meanwhile, if appropriate, this antiphon with Psalm 115 is sung:*

Antiphon

The chalice of salvation I will raise,
and I will offer a sacrifice of praise (E.T. alleluia).

Psalm 116 (115)

I trusted, even when I said,
"I am sorely afflicted,"
and when I said in my alarm,
"These people are all liars."

(The antiphon is repeated)

How can I repay the Lord
for all his goodness to me?
The cup of salvation I will raise;
I will call on the name of the Lord.

(The antiphon is repeated)

My vows to the Lord I will fulfill
before all his people.
How precious in the eyes of the Lord
is the death of his faithful.

(The antiphon is repeated)

Your servant, Lord, your servant am I,
the son of your handmaid;
you have loosened my bonds.
A thanksgiving sacrifice I make;
I will call on the name of the Lord.

(The antiphon is repeated)

My vows to the Lord I will fulfill
before all his people,
in the courts of the house of the Lord,
in your midst, O Jerusalem.

(The antiphon is repeated)

Another appropriate chant may also be sung.

9. After the prayer **With humble spirit**, it is appropriate for the Priest to incense the gifts and the altar.

10. According to the circumstances of the celebration, it is fitting that the faithful receive the Blood of Christ from the newly blessed chalice.

APPENDIX V

EXAMPLES OF FORMULARIES FOR THE UNIVERSAL PRAYER

1. GENERAL FORMULA I

Priest's Introduction

To God the Father almighty,
dear brothers and sisters,
may every prayer of our heart be directed,
for his will it is that all humanity should be saved
and come to the knowledge of the truth.

Intentions

1. For the holy Church of God,
that the Lord may graciously watch over her and care for her,
let us pray to the Lord.
R. Grant this, almighty God.

2. For the peoples of all the world,
that the Lord may graciously preserve harmony among them,
let us pray to the Lord.
R. Grant this, almighty God.

3. For all who are oppressed by any kind of need,
that the Lord may graciously grant them relief,
let us pray to the Lord.
R. Grant this, almighty God.

4. For ourselves and our own community,
that the Lord may graciously receive us
as a sacrifice acceptable to himself,
let us pray to the Lord.
R. Grant this, almighty God.

Priest's Prayer

O God, our refuge and our strength,
hear the prayers of your Church,
for you yourself are the source of all devotion,
and grant, we pray, that what we ask in faith
we may truly obtain.
Through Christ our Lord.
R. Amen.

2. GENERAL FORMULA II

Priest's Introduction

Brothers and sisters,
as we now make our prayer
for our community and for the world,
let us all pray to Christ the Lord,
not only for ourselves and our own needs,
but for the entire people.

Intentions

1a. **For the whole Christian people,**
   let us beseech the abundance of divine goodness.
   R. Christ, hear us. or Christ, graciously hear us.

1b. **For all who do not yet believe,**
   let us implore the giver of all spiritual gifts.
   R. Christ, hear us.

2a. **For those who hold public office,**
   let us call upon the power of the Lord.
   R. Christ, hear us.

2b. **For favorable weather and abundant fruits from the earth,**
   let us entreat the Lord, the ruler of the world.
   R. Christ, hear us.

3a. **For our brothers and sisters**
   who cannot be present at this sacred assembly,
   let us beseech him who observes all things.
   R. Christ, hear us.

3b. **For the repose of the souls of the faithful departed,**
   let us call upon the judge of all humanity.
   R. Christ, hear us.

4a. **For all of us who pray in faith**
   and ask the mercy of the Lord,
   let us entreat the compassion of our Savior.
   R. Christ, hear us.

4b. **For ourselves and those close to us
who await the Lord's goodness,
let us call upon the mercy of Christ the Lord.**
R. Christ, hear us.

Priest's Prayer

**Incline your merciful ear to our prayers,
we ask, O Lord,
and listen in kindness to the supplications of those who call
  on you.
Through Christ our Lord.**
R. Amen.

3. ADVENT

Priest's Introduction

**As we await with longing
the coming of our Lord Jesus Christ,
dear brothers and sisters,
let us with renewed devotion beseech his mercy,
that, as he came into the world
to bring the good news to the poor
and heal the contrite of heart,
so in our own time, also,
he may bring salvation to all in need.**

Intentions

1a. **That Christ may visit his holy Church
and keep watch over her always,
let us pray to the Lord.**
R. Lord, have mercy. or Kyrie, eleison.

1b. **That Christ may fill the Pope,
our Bishop, and the whole Order of Bishops
with spiritual gifts and graces,
let us pray to the Lord.**
R. Lord, have mercy. or Kyrie, eleison.

2a. That under the protection of Christ
our times may be peaceful,
let us pray to the Lord.
℟. Lord, have mercy. or Kyrie, eleison.

2b. That Christ may guide the minds of those who govern us
to promote the common good according to his will,
let us pray to the Lord.
℟. Lord, have mercy. or Kyrie, eleison.

3a. That Christ may banish disease,
drive out hunger, and ward off every affliction,
let us pray to the Lord.
℟. Lord, have mercy. or Kyrie, eleison.

3b. That Christ in his mercy may free
all who suffer persecution,
let us pray to the Lord.
℟. Lord, have mercy. or Kyrie, eleison.

4a. That as witnesses to Christ's love before all
we may abide in the truth,
let us pray to the Lord.
℟. Lord, have mercy. or Kyrie, eleison.

4b. That Christ may find us watching when he comes,
let us pray to the Lord.
℟. Lord, have mercy. or Kyrie, eleison.

Priest's Prayer

Almighty ever-living God,
who bring salvation to all
and desire that no one should perish,
hear the prayers of your people
and grant that the course of our world
may be directed by your peaceful rule
and your Church rejoice in tranquility and devotion.
Through Christ our Lord.
℟. Amen.

4. CHRISTMAS TIME

Priest's Introduction

On this day (on this night, in this time)
when the goodness and kindness of God our Savior have
   appeared,
let us, dear brothers and sisters,
humbly pour forth to him our prayers,
trusting not in our own good works, but in his mercy.

Intentions

1. For the Church of God,
   that in integrity of faith she may await
   and may welcome with joy
   him whom the immaculate Virgin conceived by a word
   and wondrously brought to birth,
   let us pray to the Lord.
   R. Lord, have mercy.

2. For the progress and peace of the whole world,
   that what is given in time may become a reward in eternity,
   let us pray to the Lord.
   R. Lord, have mercy.

3. For those oppressed by hunger, sickness or loneliness,
   that through the mystery of the Nativity (Epiphany) of Christ
   they may find relief in both mind and body,
   let us pray to the Lord.
   R. Lord, have mercy.

4. For the families of our congregation,
   that, receiving Christ,
   they may learn also to welcome him in the poor,
   let us pray to the Lord.
   R. Lord, have mercy.

Priest's Prayer

We pray, O Lord our God,
that the Virgin Mary,
who merited to bear God and man in her chaste womb,
may commend the prayers of your faithful in your sight.
Through Christ our Lord.
R. Amen.

5. LENT I

Priest's Introduction

We should pour forth prayers at all times,
dear brothers and sisters,
but, above all, in these days of Lent
we ought to watch more intently with Christ
and direct our petitions more fervently to God.

Intentions

1. For the whole Christian people,
that in this sacred time they may be more abundantly nourished
by every word that comes from the mouth of God,
let us pray to the Lord.

2. For the whole world,
that in lasting tranquility and peace
our days may truly become
the acceptable time of grace and salvation,
let us pray to the Lord.

3. For sinners and the neglectful,
that in this time of reconciliation
they may return to Christ,
let us pray to the Lord.

4. For ourselves,
that God may at last stir up in our hearts
aversion for our sins,
let us pray to the Lord.

Priest's Prayer

> Grant, we pray, O Lord,
> that your people may turn to you with all their heart,
> so that whatever they dare to ask in fitting prayer
> they may receive by your mercy.
> Through Christ our Lord.
> R. Amen.

6. LENT II

Priest's Introduction

> As the Solemnity of Easter approaches, dear friends,
> let our prayer to the Lord be all the more insistent,
> that all of us, and the whole multitude of the baptized,
> together with the entire world,
> may come to share more abundantly in this sacred mystery.

Intentions

1. That God may be pleased to increase faith and understanding
   in the catechumens who are to be initiated by Holy Baptism
   in the coming Paschal Solemnity,
   let us pray to the Lord.

2. That peoples in need may find help
   and that peace and security may be firmly established everywhere,
   let us pray to the Lord.

3. That all who are afflicted or suffering temptation
   may be strengthened by his grace,
   let us pray to the Lord.

4. That all of us may learn to distribute the fruits of self-denial
   for the good of those in need,
   let us pray to the Lord.

Priest's Prayer

> Have mercy, O Lord, on the prayers of your Church
> and turn with compassion to the hearts that bow before you,
> that those you make sharers in the divine mystery
> may never be left without your assistance.
> Through Christ our Lord.
> R. Amen.

7. WEEKDAYS OF HOLY WEEK

Priest's Introduction

In this time of the Lord's Passion,
when Christ offered prayers and supplications to his Father
with loud cries and tears,
let us humbly beseech God,
that in answer to his Son's reverent submission
he may in mercy hear our prayers also.

Intentions

1. That the Church, the Bride of Christ,
   may be more fully cleansed by his Blood
   in this time of his Passion,
   let us pray to the Lord.

2. That through the Blood of Christ's Cross
   all things in the world
   may be brought to peace for the sake of salvation,
   let us pray to the Lord.

3. That God may grant fortitude and patience
   to all who through sickness or hardship
   have a share in Christ's Passion,
   let us pray to the Lord.

4. That we may all be led through the Lord's Passion and Cross
   to the glory of his Resurrection,
   let us pray to the Lord.

Priest's Prayer

Be present, O Lord, to your people at prayer,
so that what they do not have the confidence or presumption to ask
they may obtain by the merits of your Son's Passion.
Who lives and reigns for ever and ever.
R. Amen.

8. EASTER TIME

Priest's Introduction

Dear brothers and sisters,
filled with paschal joy,
let us pray more earnestly to God
that he, who graciously listened
to the prayers and supplications of his beloved Son,
may now be pleased to look upon us in our lowliness.

Intentions

1. For the shepherds of our souls,
   that they may have the strength to govern wisely
   the flock entrusted to them by the Good Shepherd,
   let us pray to the Lord.

2. For the whole world,
   that it may truly know the peace given by Christ,
   let us pray to the Lord.

3. For our brothers and sisters who suffer,
   that their sorrow may be turned to gladness
   which no one can take from them,
   let us pray to the Lord.

4. For our own community,
   that it may bear witness with great confidence
   to the Resurrection of Christ,
   let us pray to the Lord.

Priest's Prayer

O God, who know that our life in this present age
is subject to suffering and need,
hear the desires of those who cry to you
and receive the prayers of those who believe in you.
Through Christ our Lord.
R. Amen.

9. ORDINARY TIME I

Priest's Introduction

Dear brothers and sisters,
gathered as one to celebrate the good things
we have received from our God,
let us ask him to prompt in us
prayers that are worthy of his hearing.

Intentions

1. For N. our Pope and N. our Bishop
   and all the clergy,
   with the people entrusted to their charge,
   let us pray to the Lord.

2. For those who hold public office
   and those who assist them in promoting the common good,
   let us pray to the Lord.

3. For those who travel by sea, land or air,
   for captives and all held in prison,
   let us pray to the Lord.

4. For all of us gathered in this sacred place
   by faith and devotion
   and by love and reverence for God,
   let us pray to the Lord.

Priest's Prayer

May the petitions of your Church
be pleasing in your sight, O Lord,
so that we may receive from your mercy
what we cannot ask out of confidence in our own merits
Through Christ our Lord.
R. Amen.

10. ORDINARY TIME II

Priest's Introduction

We have all gathered here,
dear brothers and sisters,
to celebrate the mysteries of our redemption;
let us therefore ask almighty God
that the whole world may be watered
from these springs of all blessing and life.

Intentions

1. For all who have vowed themselves to God,
   that with his help they may faithfully keep to their resolve,
   let us pray to the Lord.

2. For peace among nations,
   that, delivered from all turmoil,
   the peoples may serve God in freedom of heart,
   let us pray to the Lord.

3. For the elderly who suffer from isolation or sickness,
   that they may be strengthened
   by our love of them as brothers and sisters,
   let us pray to the Lord.

4. For ourselves gathered here,
   that, as God does not cease to sustain us
   with the things of this life,
   we may know how to use them in such a way
   that we may hold even now
   to the things that endure for ever,
   let us pray to the Lord.

Priest's Prayer

May your mercy, we beseech you, O Lord,
be with your people who cry to you,
so that what they seek at your prompting
they may obtain by your ready generosity.
Through Christ our Lord.
R. Amen.

The General Formulas printed above, nos. 1-2, may also be used in Ordinary Time.

11. IN MASSES FOR THE DEAD

Priest's Introduction

Let us in faith call upon God the almighty Father,
who raised Christ his Son from the dead,
as we pray for the salvation of the living and the dead.

Intentions

1. That God may establish the Christian people in faith and unity,
   let us pray to the Lord.

2. That he may rescue the entire world from all the evils of war,
   let us pray to the Lord.

3. That he may be pleased to show himself a father
   to our brothers and sisters
   who lack work, food or housing,
   let us pray to the Lord.

4a. That he may be pleased
   to admit for ever to the company of the Saints
   his deceased servant N.,
   who once through Baptism received the seed of eternal life,
   let us pray to the Lord.

4b. That on the last day he may raise up N.,
   who fed on the Body of Christ,
   the Bread of eternal life,
   let us pray to the Lord.

   (Or for a Priest):

   That he may grant N. a share in the heavenly liturgy,
   for he exercised the priestly office in the Church,
   let us pray to the Lord.

4c. That he may grant to the souls
of our brothers and sisters, friends, and benefactors
the reward of their labors,
let us pray to the Lord.

4d. That he may welcome into the light of his face
all who have fallen asleep in the hope of the resurrection,
let us pray to the Lord.

4e. That he may graciously help and comfort
our brothers and sisters who are suffering affliction,
let us pray to the Lord.

4f. That he may be pleased to gather into his glorious Kingdom
all who have gathered here in faith and devotion,
let us pray to the Lord.

Priest's Prayer

May the prayer of those who cry to you
benefit the souls of your servants, O Lord:
free them, we pray, from all their sins
and make them sharers in your redemption.
Through Christ our Lord.
R. Amen.

APPENDIX VI

[In the Dioceses of the United States]
SAMPLE INVOCATIONS FOR THE PENITENTIAL ACT

Brethren (brothers and sisters), let us acknowledge our sins, and so prepare ourselves to celebrate the sacred mysteries.

A brief pause for silence follows.

The Priest, or a Deacon or another minister, then may use one of the following invocations with Kyrie, eleison (Lord, have mercy):

I

The Priest:
Lord Jesus, you came to gather the nations into the peace of God's kingdom:
Lord, have mercy.

The people reply:
Lord, have mercy.

The Priest:
Lord Jesus, you come in word and sacrament to strengthen us in holiness:
Christ, have mercy.

The people:
Christ, have mercy.

The Priest:
Lord Jesus, you will come in glory with salvation for your people:
Lord, have mercy.

The people:
Lord, have mercy.

The absolution by the Priest follows:
May almighty God have mercy on us,
forgive us our sins
and bring us to everlasting life.

The people reply:
Amen.

II

The Priest:

**Lord Jesus, you are mighty God and Prince of peace:
Lord, have mercy.**

The people reply:

Lord, have mercy.

The Priest:

**Lord Jesus, you are the Son of God and Son of Mary:
Christ, have mercy.**

The people:

Christ, have mercy.

The Priest:

**Lord Jesus, you are Word made flesh and splendor of the Father:
Lord, have mercy.**

The people:

Lord, have mercy.

The absolution by the Priest follows:

**May almighty God have mercy on us,
forgive us our sins
and bring us to everlasting life.**

The people reply:

Amen.

III

The Priest:
Lord Jesus, you came to reconcile us to one another and to the Father:
Lord, have mercy.

The people reply:
Lord, have mercy.

The Priest:
Lord Jesus, you heal the wounds of sin and division:
Christ, have mercy.

The people:
Christ, have mercy.

The Priest:
Lord Jesus, you intercede for us with your Father:
Lord, have mercy.

The people:
Lord, have mercy.

The absolution by the Priest follows:
May almighty God have mercy on us,
forgive us our sins
and bring us to everlasting life.

The people reply:
Amen.

IV

The Priest:
Lord Jesus, you raise the dead to life in the Spirit:
Lord, have mercy.

The people reply:
Lord, have mercy.

The Priest:
Lord Jesus, you bring pardon and peace to the sinner:
Christ, have mercy.

The people:
Christ, have mercy.

The Priest:
Lord Jesus, you bring light to those in darkness:
Lord, have mercy.

The people:
Lord, have mercy.

The absolution by the Priest follows:
May almighty God have mercy on us,
forgive us our sins
and bring us to everlasting life.

The people reply:
Amen.

V

The Priest:
Lord Jesus, you raise us to new life:
Lord, have mercy.

The people reply:
Lord, have mercy.

The Priest:
Lord Jesus, you forgive us our sins:
Christ, have mercy.

The people:
Christ, have mercy.

The Priest:
Lord Jesus, you feed us with your body and blood:
Lord, have mercy.

The people:
Lord, have mercy.

The absolution by the Priest follows:
May almighty God have mercy on us,
forgive us our sins
and bring us to everlasting life.

The people reply:
Amen.

VI

The Priest:
> Lord Jesus, you have shown us the way to the Father:
> **Lord, have mercy.**

The people reply:
> Lord, have mercy.

The Priest:
> **Lord Jesus, you have given us the consolation of the truth:**
> **Christ, have mercy.**

The people:
> Christ, have mercy.

The Priest:
> **Lord Jesus, you are the Good Shepherd, leading us into everlasting life:**
> **Lord, have mercy.**

The people:
> Lord, have mercy.

The absolution by the Priest follows:
> **May almighty God have mercy on us,**
> **forgive us our sins**
> **and bring us to everlasting life.**

The people reply:
> Amen.

VII

The Priest:
> **Lord Jesus, you healed the sick:**
> **Lord, have mercy.**

The people reply:
> Lord, have mercy.

The Priest:
> **Lord Jesus, you forgave sinners:**
> **Christ, have mercy.**

The people:
> Christ, have mercy.

The Priest:
> **Lord Jesus, you gave yourself to heal us and bring us strength:**
> **Lord, have mercy.**

The people:
> Lord, have mercy.

The absolution by the Priest follows:
> **May almighty God have mercy on us,**
> **forgive us our sins**
> **and bring us to everlasting life.**

The people reply:
> Amen.

PREPARATION FOR MASS

Prayer of Saint Ambrose

I draw near, loving Lord Jesus Christ,
to the table of your most delightful banquet
in fear and trembling,
a sinner, presuming not upon my own merits,
but trusting rather in your goodness and mercy.
I have a heart and body defiled by my many offenses,
a mind and tongue
over which I have kept no good watch.
Therefore, O loving God, O awesome Majesty,
I turn in my misery, caught in snares,
to you the fountain of mercy,
hastening to you for healing,
flying to you for protection;
and while I do not look forward to having you as Judge,
I long to have you as Savior.
To you, O Lord, I display my wounds,
to you I uncover my shame.
I am aware of my many and great sins,
for which I fear,
but I hope in your mercies,
which are without number.
Look upon me, then, with eyes of mercy,
Lord Jesus Christ, eternal King,
God and Man, crucified for mankind.
Listen to me, as I place my hope in you,
have pity on me, full of miseries and sins,
you, who will never cease
to let the fountain of compassion flow.
Hail, O Saving Victim,
offered for me and for the whole human race
on the wood of the Cross.
Hail, O noble and precious Blood,
flowing from the wounds
of Jesus Christ, my crucified Lord,
and washing away the sins of all the world.

Remember, Lord, your creature,
whom you redeemed by your Blood.
I am repentant of my sins,
I desire to put right what I have done.
Take from me, therefore, most merciful Father,
all my iniquities and sins,
so that, purified in mind and body,
I may worthily taste the Holy of Holies.
And grant that this sacred foretaste
of your Body and Blood
which I, though unworthy, intend to receive,
may be the remission of my sins,
the perfect cleansing of my faults,
the banishment of shameful thoughts,
and the rebirth of right sentiments;
and may it encourage
a wholesome and effective performance
of deeds pleasing to you
and be a most firm defense of body and soul
against the snares of my enemies.
Amen.

Prayer of Saint Thomas Aquinas

Almighty eternal God,
behold, I come to the Sacrament
of your Only Begotten Son,
our Lord Jesus Christ,
as one sick to the physician of life,
as one unclean to the fountain of mercy,
as one blind to the light of eternal brightness,
as one poor and needy to the Lord of heaven and earth.
I ask, therefore, for the abundance of your immense generosity,
that you may graciously cure my sickness,
wash away my defilement,
give light to my blindness,
enrich my poverty,
clothe my nakedness,
so that I may receive the bread of Angels,
the King of kings and Lord of lords,
with such reverence and humility,
such contrition and devotion,
such purity and faith,
such purpose and intention
as are conducive to the salvation of my soul.
Grant, I pray, that I may receive
not only the Sacrament of the Lord's Body and Blood,
but also the reality and power of that Sacrament.
O most gentle God,
grant that I may so receive
the Body of your Only Begotten Son our Lord Jesus Christ,
which he took from the Virgin Mary,
that I may be made worthy to be incorporated into his Mystical Body
and to be counted among its members.
O most loving Father,
grant that I may at last gaze for ever
upon the unveiled face of your beloved Son,
whom I, a wayfarer,
propose to receive now veiled under these species:
Who lives and reigns with you for ever and ever.
Amen.

Prayer to the Blessed Virgin Mary

O most blessed Virgin Mary,
Mother of tenderness and mercy,
I, a miserable and unworthy sinner,
fly to you with all the affection of my heart
and I beseech your motherly love,
that, as you stood by your most dear Son,
while he hung on the Cross,
so, in your kindness,
you may be pleased to stand by me, a poor sinner,
and all Priests who today are offering the Sacrifice
here and throughout the entire holy Church,
so that with your gracious help
we may offer a worthy and acceptable oblation
in the sight of the most high and undivided Trinity.
Amen.

Formula of Intent

My intention is to celebrate Mass
and to consecrate the Body and Blood of our Lord Jesus Christ
according to the Rite of Holy Roman Church,
to the praise of almighty God
and all the Church triumphant,
for my good
and that of all the Church militant,
for all who have commended themselves to my prayers
in general and in particular,
and for the welfare of Holy Roman Church.
Amen.

May the almighty and merciful Lord
grant us joy with peace,
amendment of life,
room for true repentance,
the grace and consolation of the Holy Spirit
and perseverance in good works.
Amen.

THANKSGIVING AFTER MASS

Prayer of Saint Thomas Aquinas

I give you thanks,
Lord, holy Father, almighty and eternal God,
who have been pleased to nourish me,
a sinner and your unworthy servant,
with the precious Body and Blood
of your Son, our Lord Jesus Christ:
this through no merits of mine,
but due solely to the graciousness of your mercy.

And I pray that this Holy Communion
may not be for me an offense to be punished,
but a saving plea for forgiveness.
May it be for me the armor of faith,
and the shield of good will.
May it cancel my faults,
destroy concupiscence and carnal passion,
increase charity and patience, humility and obedience
and all the virtues,
may it be a firm defense against the snares of all my enemies,
both visible and invisible,
the complete calming of my impulses,
both of the flesh and of the spirit,
a firm adherence to you, the one true God,
and the joyful completion of my life's course.

And I beseech you to lead me, a sinner,
to that banquet beyond all telling,
where with your Son and the Holy Spirit
you are the true light of your Saints,
fullness of satisfied desire, eternal gladness,
consummate delight and perfect happiness.
Through Christ our Lord.
Amen.

Prayer to the Most Holy Redeemer

Soul of Christ, sanctify me.
Body of Christ, save me.
Blood of Christ, embolden me.
Water from the side of Christ, wash me.
Passion of Christ, strengthen me.
O good Jesus, hear me.
Within your wounds hide me.
Never permit me to be parted from you.
From the evil Enemy defend me.
At the hour of my death call me
and bid me come to you,
that with your Saints I may praise you
for age upon age.
Amen.

Prayer of Self-Offering

Receive, Lord, my entire freedom.
Accept the whole of my memory,
my intellect and my will.
Whatever I have or possess,
it was you who gave it to me;
I restore it to you in full,
and I surrender it completely
to the guidance of your will.
Give me only love of you
together with your grace,
and I am rich enough
and ask for nothing more.
Amen.

Prayer to Our Lord Jesus Christ Crucified

Behold, O good and loving Jesus,
that I cast myself on my knees before you
and, with the greatest fervor of spirit,
I pray and beseech you to instill into my heart
ardent sentiments of faith, hope and charity,
with true repentance for my sins
and a most firm purpose of amendment.
With deep affection and sorrow
I ponder intimately
and contemplate in my mind your five wounds,
having before my eyes what the prophet David
had already put in your mouth about yourself, O good Jesus:
They have pierced my hands and my feet;
they have numbered all my bones (Ps 21: 17-18).

The Universal Prayer Attributed to Pope Clement XI

I believe, O Lord, but may I believe more firmly;
I hope, but may I hope more securely;
I love, but may I love more ardently;
I sorrow, but may I sorrow more deeply.

I adore you as my first beginning;
I long for you as my last end;
I praise you as my constant benefactor;
I invoke you as my gracious protector.

By your wisdom direct me,
by your righteousness restrain me,
by your indulgence console me,
by your power protect me.

I offer you, Lord, my thoughts to be directed to you,
my words, to be about you,
my deeds, to respect your will,
my trials, to be endured for you.

I will whatever you will,
I will it because you will it,
I will it in the way you will it,
I will it for as long as you will it.

Lord, enlighten my understanding, I pray:
arouse my will,
cleanse my heart,
sanctify my soul.

May I weep for past sins,
repel future temptations,
correct evil inclinations,
nurture appropriate virtues.

Give me, good God,
love for you, hatred for myself,
zeal for my neighbor,
contempt for the world.

May I strive to obey superiors,
to help those dependent on me,
to have care for my friends,

forgiveness for my enemies.

May I conquer sensuality by austerity,
avarice by generosity,
anger by gentleness,
lukewarmness by fervor.

Render me prudent in planning,
steadfast in dangers,
patient in adversity,
humble in prosperity.

Make me, O Lord, attentive at prayer,
moderate at meals,
diligent in work,
steadfast in intent.

May I be careful to maintain interior innocence,
outward modesty,
exemplary behavior,
a regular life.

May I be always watchful in subduing nature,
in nourishing grace,
in observing your law,
in winning salvation.

May I learn from you
how precarious are earthly things,
how great divine things,
how fleeting is time,
how lasting things eternal.

Grant that I may prepare for death,
fear judgment,
flee hell,
gain paradise.
Through Christ our Lord.
Amen.

Prayers to the Blessed Virgin Mary

O Mary, Virgin and Mother most holy,
behold, I have received your most dear Son,
whom you conceived in your immaculate womb,
brought forth, nursed and embraced most tenderly.
Behold him at whose sight
you used to rejoice and be filled with all delight;
him whom, humbly and lovingly,
once again I present
and offer him to you
to be clasped in your arms,
to be loved by your heart,
and to be offered up to the Most Holy Trinity
as the supreme worship of adoration,
for your own honor and glory
and for my needs and for those of the whole world.
I ask you therefore, most loving Mother:
entreat for me the forgiveness of all my sins
and, in abundant measure, the grace
of serving him in the future more faithfully,
and at the last, final grace,
so that with you I may praise him
for all the ages of ages.
Amen.

Hail, Mary, full of grace, the Lord is with you;
blessed are you among women,
and blessed is the fruit of your womb, Jesus.
Holy Mary, Mother of God,
pray for us sinners
now and at the hour of our death.
Amen.

INDEXES

ALPHABETICAL INDEX OF CELEBRATIONS

Achilleus and Nereus, Martyrs, May 12 859
Adalbert, Bishop and Martyr, April 23 849
Agatha, Virgin and Martyr, February 5 823
Agnes, Virgin and Martyr, January 21 809
Albert the Great, Bishop and Doctor of the Church, November 15 995
All Saints, November 1 979
All the Faithful Departed, Commemoration (All Souls' Day), November 2 982
Aloysius Gonzaga, Religious, June 21 876
Alphonsus Liguori, Bishop and Doctor of the Church, August 1 912
Ambrose, Bishop and Doctor of the Church, December 7 1009
André Bessette, Religious, January 6 [USA] 805
Andrew, Apostle, November 30 1003
Andrew Dũng-Lạc, Priest, and Companions, Martyrs, November 24 1001
Andrew Kim Tae-gŏn, Priest, and Paul Chŏng Ha-sang, and Companions,
    Martyrs, September 20 952
Angela Merici, Virgin, January 27 813
Angels, Guardian Angels, October 2 964
Anne and Joachim, Parents of the Blessed Virgin Mary, July 26 908
Anselm, Bishop and Doctor of the Church, April 21 848
Ansgar, Bishop, February 3 822
Anthony, Abbot, January 17 807
Anthony Mary Claret, Bishop, October 24 976
Anthony of Padua, Priest and Doctor of the Church, June 13 875
Anthony Zaccaria, Priest, July 5 899
Apollinaris, Bishop and Martyr, July 20 904
Archangels, Michael, Gabriel and Raphael, September 29 959
Athanasius, Bishop and Doctor of the Church, May 2 857
Augustine, Bishop and Doctor of the Church, August 28 938
Augustine of Canterbury, Bishop, May 27 866
Augustine Zhao Rong, Priest, and Companions, Martyrs, July 9 900

Barnabas, Apostle, June 11 874
Bartholomew, Apostle, August 24 935
Basil the Great and Gregory Nazianzen, Bishops and Doctors of the Church,
    January 2 801
Bede the Venerable, Priest and Doctor of the Church, May 25 864
Benedict, Abbot, July 11 901
Bernard, Abbot and Doctor of the Church, August 20 932
Bernardine of Siena, Priest, May 20 863
Blaise, Bishop and Martyr, February 3 822

Bonaventure, Bishop and Doctor of the Church, July 15 903
Boniface, Bishop and Martyr, June 5 872
Bridget, Religious, July 23.. 906
Bruno, Priest, October 6 967

Cajetan, Priest, August 7 920
Callistus I, Pope and Martyr, October 14.. 970
Camillus de Lellis, Priest, July 18 [USA] 904
Casimir, March 4 830
Catherine of Alexandria, Virgin and Martyr, November 25 1002
Catherine of Siena, Virgin and Doctor of the Church, April 29 852
Cecilia, Virgin and Martyr, November 22.. 999
Charles Borromeo, Bishop, November 4 986
Charles Lwanga and Companions, Martyrs, June 3 871
Christopher Magallanes, Priest, and Companions, Martyrs, May 21 863
Clare, Virgin, August 11 923
Clement I, Pope and Martyr, November 23 999
Columban, Abbot, November 23 1000
Commemoration of All the Faithful Departed, November 2 982
Cornelius, Pope, and Cyprian, Bishop, Martyrs, September 16.................................... 950
Cosmas and Damian, Martyrs, September 26.. 954
Cyprian, Bishop, and Cornelius, Pope, Martyrs, September 16.................................... 950
Cyril, Monk, and Methodius, Bishop, February 14... 826
Cyril of Alexandria, Bishop and Doctor of the Church, June 27 882
Cyril of Jerusalem, Bishop and Doctor of the Church, March 18................................. 833

Damasus I, Pope, December 11 1017
Damian and Cosmas, Martyrs, September 26... 954
Damien de Veuster, Priest, May 10 [USA] 859
Dedication of the Basilica of Saint Mary Major, August 5 914
Dedication of the Basilicas of Saints Peter and Paul, Apostles, November 18............. 997
Dedication of the Lateran Basilica, November 9 987
Denis, Bishop, and Companions, Martyrs, October 9 969
Dominic, Priest, August 8 921

Elizabeth Ann Seton, Religious, January 4 [USA] 803
Elizabeth of Hungary, Religious, November 17 996
Elizabeth of Portugal, July 5 [USA] 899
Ephrem, Deacon and Doctor of the Church, June 9 873
Eusebius of Vercelli, Bishop, August 2... 913

ALPHABETICAL INDEX OF CELEBRATIONS

Fabian, Pope and Martyr, January 20 808
Felicity and Perpetua, Martyrs, March 7 831
Fidelis of Sigmaringen, Priest and Martyr, April 24 849
First Martyrs of the Holy Roman Church, June 30 889
Founders of the Servite Order, February 17 827
Frances of Rome, Religious, March 9 832
Frances Xavier Cabrini, Virgin, November 13 [USA] 994
Francis de Sales, Bishop and Doctor of the Church, January 24 810
Francis of Assisi, October 4 966
Francis of Paola, Hermit, April 2 845
Francis Xavier, Priest, December 3 1007

Gabriel, Michael and Raphael, Archangels, September 29 959
George, Martyr, April 23 848
Gertrude, Virgin, November 16 996
Gregory Nazianzen, and Basil the Great, Bishops and Doctors of the Church,
   January 2 801
Gregory the Great, Pope and Doctor of the Church, September 3 941
Gregory VII, Pope, May 25 864
Guardian Angels, October 2 964

Hedwig, Religious, October 16 971
Henry, July 13 902
Hilary, Bishop and Doctor of the Church, January 13 806
Hippolytus, Priest, and Pontian, Pope, Martyrs, August 13 924
Holy Innocents, Martyrs, December 28 1025

Ignatius of Antioch, Bishop and Martyr, October 17 972
Ignatius of Loyola, Priest, July 31 911
Independence Day, July 4 [USA] 892
Innocents, Martyrs, December 28 1025
Irenaeus, Bishop and Martyr, June 28 883
Isaac Jogues and John de Brébeuf, Priests,
   and Companions, Martyrs, October 19 [USA] 974
Isidore, Bishop and Doctor of the Church, April 4 845
Isidore, May 15 [USA] 862

James, Apostle, July 25 907
James and Philip, Apostles, May 3 858
Jane Frances de Chantal, Religious, August 12 924
Januarius, Bishop and Martyr, September 19 951

Jerome, Priest and Doctor of the Church, September 30 962
Jerome Emiliani, February 8 824
Jesus Christ:
    Annunciation, March 25 841
    Ascension 429
    Baptism 202
    Corpus Christi 499
    Dedication of the Lateran Basilica, November 9 987
    Epiphany, January 6 185
    Exaltation of the Holy Cross, September 14 946
    Holy Family 176
    King of the Universe 505
    Most Holy Body and Blood of Christ 499
    Most Holy Name, January 3 802
    Nativity, December 25 169
    Presentation, February 2 815
    Resurrection 341
    Sacred Heart 502
    Transfiguration, August 6 917
Joachim and Anne, Parents of the Blessed Virgin Mary, July 26 908
John, Apostle and Evangelist, December 27 1024
John Baptist de la Salle, Priest, April 7 846
John Bosco, Priest, January 31 814
John Chrysostom, Bishop and Doctor of the Church, September 13 945
John Damascene, Priest and Doctor of the Church, December 4 1008
John de Brébeuf and Isaac Jogues, Priests,
    and Companions, Martyrs, October 19 [USA] 974
John Eudes, Priest, August 19 931
John Fisher, Bishop, and Thomas More, Martyrs, June 22 877
John I, Pope and Martyr, May 18 862
John Leonardi, Priest, October 9 969
John Neumann, Bishop, January 5 [USA] 804
John of Capistrano, Priest, October 23 976
John of God, Religious, March 8 832
John of Kanty, Priest, December 23 1022
John of the Cross, Priest and Doctor of the Church, December 14 1020
John the Baptist:
    Nativity, June 24 878
    Passion, August 29 939
John Vianney, Priest, August 4 914
Josaphat, Bishop and Martyr, November 12 993

ALPHABETICAL INDEX OF CELEBRATIONS

Joseph, Spouse of the Blessed Virgin Mary:
    Solemnity, March 19 835
    the Worker, May 1 854
Joseph Calasanz, Priest, August 25 937
Josephine Bakhita, Virgin, February 8 824
Juan Diego Cuauhtlatoatzin, December 9 1017
Jude and Simon, Apostles, October 28 977
Junípero Serra, Priest, July 1 [USA] 890
Justin, Martyr, June 1 870

Kateri Tekakwitha, Virgin, July 14 [USA] 902
Katharine Drexel, Virgin, March 3 [USA] 830

Lawrence, Deacon and Martyr, August 10 922
Lawrence of Brindisi, Priest and Doctor of the Church, July 21 905
Lawrence Ruiz and Companions, Martyrs, September 28 957
Legal Protection of Unborn Children, Day of Prayer, January 22 [USA] 809
Leo the Great, Pope and Doctor of the Church, November 10 991
Louis, August 25 936
Louis Grignion de Montfort, Priest, April 28 851
Lucy, Virgin and Martyr, December 13 1020
Luke, Evangelist, October 18 973

Marcellinus and Peter, Martyrs, June 2 871
Margaret Mary Alacoque, Virgin, October 16 972
Margaret of Scotland, November 16 995
Maria Goretti, Virgin and Martyr, July 6 900
Marie Rose Durocher, Virgin, October 6 [USA] 967
Mark, Evangelist, April 25 850
Martha, July 29 909
Martin de Porres, Religious, November 3 986
Martin I, Pope and Martyr, April 13 847
Martin of Tours, Bishop, November 11 992
Mary, Blessed Virgin:
    Assumption, August 15 927
    Dedication of the Basilica of Saint Mary Major, August 5 914
    Immaculate Conception, December 8 1011
    Immaculate Heart of the Blessed Virgin Mary,
        Saturday after the Second Sunday after Pentecost 869
    Most Holy Name, September 12 944
    Nativity, September 8 942

 Our Lady of Fatima, May 13 860
 Our Lady of Guadalupe, December 12 [USA] 1019
 Our Lady of Lourdes, February 11 825
 Our Lady of Mount Carmel, July 16 903
 Our Lady of Sorrows, September 15 949
 Our Lady of the Rosary, October 7 968
 Presentation, November 21 998
 Queenship, August 22 934
 Solemnity of Mary, the Holy Mother of God, January 1 182
 Visitation, May 31 867
Mary Magdalene, July 22 905
Mary Magdalene de' Pazzi, Virgin, May 25 865
Matthew, Apostle and Evangelist, September 21 953
Matthias, Apostle, May 14 861
Maximilian Mary Kolbe, Priest and Martyr, August 14 925
Methodius, Bishop, and Cyril, Monk, February 14 826
Michael, Gabriel and Raphael, Archangels, September 29 959
Miguel Austin Pro, Priest and Martyr, November 23 1000
Monica, August 27 937

Nereus and Achilleus, Martyrs, May 12 859
Nicholas, Bishop, December 6 1008
Norbert, Bishop, June 6 873

Pancras, Martyr, May 12 860
Patrick, Bishop, March 17 833
Paul, Apostle:
 Conversion, January 25 811
 Dedication of the Basilica, November 18 997
 Solemnity, June 29 885
Paul Chŏng Ha-sang, and Andrew Kim Tae-gŏn, Priest, and Companions,
 Martyrs, September 20 952
Paul Miki and Companions, Martyrs, February 6 823
Paul of the Cross, Priest, October 20 [USA] 975
Paulinus of Nola, Bishop, June 22 877
Perpetua and Felicity, Martyrs, March 7 831
Peter, Apostle:
 Chair, February 22 828
 Dedication of the Basilica, November 18 997
 Solemnity, June 29 885
Peter and Marcellinus, Martyrs, June 2 871

ALPHABETICAL INDEX OF CELEBRATIONS

Peter Canisius, Priest and Doctor of the Church, December 21 1022
Peter Chanel, Priest and Martyr, April 28 851
Peter Chrysologus, Bishop and Doctor of the Church, July 30 910
Peter Claver, Priest, September 9 [USA] 943
Peter Damian, Bishop and Doctor of the Church, February 21 827
Peter Julian Eymard, Priest, August 2 913
Philip and James, Apostles, May 3 858
Philip Neri, Priest, May 26 865
Pius of Pietrelcina, Priest, September 23 954
Pius V, Pope, April 30 853
Pius X, Pope, August 21 933
Polycarp, Bishop and Martyr, February 23 829
Pontian, Pope, and Hippolytus, Priest, Martyrs, August 13 924

Raphael, Michael and Gabriel, Archangels, September 29 959
Raymond of Penyafort, Priest, January 7 806
Rita of Cascia, Religious, May 22 864
Robert Bellarmine, Bishop and Doctor of the Church, September 17 951
Roman Church, First Martyrs, June 30 889
Romuald, Abbot, June 19 875
Rose of Lima, Virgin, August 23 935
Rose Philippine Duchesne, Virgin, November 18 [USA] 998

Scholastica, Virgin, February 10 825
Sebastian, Martyr, January 20 808
Servite Order, Seven Holy Founders, February 17 827
Seven Holy Founders of the Servite Order, February 17 827
Sharbel Makhlūf, Priest, July 24 907
Simon and Jude, Apostles, October 28 977
Sixtus II, Pope, and Companions, Martyrs, August 7 920
Stanislaus, Bishop and Martyr, April 11 847
Stephen, Martyr, December 26 1023
Stephen of Hungary, August 16 931
Sylvester I, Pope, December 31 1027

Teresa Benedicta of the Cross, Virgin and Martyr, August 9 922
Teresa of Jesus, Virgin and Doctor of the Church, October 15 970
Thanksgiving Day, Fourth Thursday in November [USA] 1004
Thérèse of the Child Jesus, Virgin and Doctor of the Church, October 1 963
Thomas, Apostle, July 3 890
Thomas Aquinas, Priest and Doctor of the Church, January 28 813

Thomas Becket, Bishop and Martyr, December 29 1026
Thomas More, and John Fisher, Bishop, Martyrs, June 22 877
Timothy and Titus, Bishops, January 26 812
Titus and Timothy, Bishops, January 26 812
Turibius of Mogrovejo, Bishop, March 23 839

Vincent, Deacon and Martyr, January 23 [USA] 809
Vincent de Paul, Priest, September 27 956
Vincent Ferrer, Priest, April 5 846

Wenceslaus, Martyr, September 28 957

INDEX OF PREFACES

A. Liturgical Times

1. Advent:
   - I. The two comings of Christ 534
   - II. The twofold expectation of Christ 536

2. The Nativity of the Lord:
   - I. Christ the Light 538
   - II. The restoration of all things in the Incarnation 540
   - III. The exchange in the Incarnation of the Word 542

3. The Epiphany of the Lord: Christ the light of the nations 544

4. Lent:
   - I. The spiritual meaning of Lent 546
   - II. Spiritual penance 548
   - III. The fruits of abstinence 550
   - IV. The fruits of fasting 552
   - V. The Temptation of the Lord (First Sunday) 216
   - VI. The Transfiguration of the Lord (Second Sunday) 226
   - VII. The Samaritan Woman (Third Sunday) 237
   - VIII. The Man Born Blind (Fourth Sunday) 247
   - IX. Lazarus (Fifth Sunday) 257

5. The Passion of the Lord:
   - I. The power of the Cross 554
   - II. The victory of the Passion 556
   - III. The Passion of the Lord (Palm Sunday) 285

6. Easter:
   - I. The Paschal Mystery 558
   - II. New life in Christ 560
   - III. Christ living and always interceding for us 562
   - IV. The restoration of the universe through the Paschal Mystery .. 564
   - V. Christ, Priest and Victim 566

7. The Ascension of the Lord:
   - I. The mystery of the Ascension 568
   - II. The mystery of the Ascension 570

8. Pentecost Sunday 454

9. Sundays in Ordinary Time
   - I. The Paschal Mystery and the People of God 572
   - II. The mystery of salvation 574
   - III. The salvation of man by a man 576
   - IV. The history of salvation 578
   - V. Creation 580
   - VI. The pledge of the eternal Passover 582
   - VII. Salvation through the obedience of Christ 584
   - VIII. The Church united by the unity of the Trinity 586

10. Common Prefaces:
    I. The renewal of all things in Christ 610
    II. Salvation through Christ..612
    III. Praise to God for the creation and restoration of the human race.....................614
    IV. Praise, the gift of God..616
    V. The proclamation of the mystery of Christ 618
    VI. The mystery of salvation in Christ 620

B. Feasts and Mysteries of the Lord

1. Most Holy Trinity...496
2. The mystery of the Incarnation (March 25) 842
3. The Baptism of the Lord...204
4. The Most Sacred Heart of Jesus 503
5. The victory of the glorious Cross (September 14). 946
6. Most Holy Eucharist:
    I. The Sacrifice and the Sacrament of Christ..588
    II. The fruits of the Most Holy Eucharist...589
7. The mystery of the Presentation of the Lord (February 2)......................................820
8. Our Lord Jesus Christ, King of the Universe 506
9. The mystery of the Transfiguration (August 6) 918
10. The Dedication of a Church:
    I. The mystery of the Temple of God, which is the Church 1033
    II. The mystery of the Church, the Bride of Christ
        and Temple of the Spirit..1037
11. The Holy Spirit:
    I. The sending of the Spirit by the Lord upon the Church 1339
    II. The action of the Spirit in the Church..1342

C. Feasts of the Saints

1. The Blessed Virgin Mary:
    I. The Motherhood of the Blessed Virgin Mary (Common I)................................590
    II. The Church praises God with the words of Mary (Common II) 592
    III. The mystery of Mary and the Church (December 8) 1014
    IV. The Glory of Mary assumed into heaven (August 15) 929
    V. Mary, Model and Mother of the Church (votive)...1346
2. The Angels: God glorified through the Angels (September 29; October 2) 960
3. The mission of the Precursor (June 24; August 29) 880
4. The mission of Saint Joseph (March 19; May 1)...836
5. The twofold mission of Peter and Paul in the Church (June 29).............................887

INDEX OF PREFACES

6. The Apostles:
   I. The Apostles, shepherds of God's people 594
   II. The apostolic foundation and witness..596

7. Saints:
   I. The glory of the Saints...598
   II. The action of the Saints 600
   III. The glory of Jerusalem, our mother (November 1)...................................980

8. Holy Martyrs:
   I. The sign and example of martyrdom..602
   II. The wonders of God in the victory of the Martyrs 604

9. Holy Pastors: The presence of holy Pastors in the Church 606

10. Holy Virgins and Religious: The sign of a life consecrated to God 608

D. In Ritual Masses

1. For the Conferral of Holy Orders:
   I. For the Ordination of a Bishop: The Priesthood of Christ and the ministry of Priests..1140
   II. For the Ordination of Priests: The Priesthood of Christ and the ministry of Priests..1153
   III. For the Ordination of Deacons: Christ, source of all ministry in the Church ..1162
   IV. For the Ordination of Deacons and Priests in the same Celebration: Christ, source of all ministry in the Church 1162

2. For the Celebration of Marriage:
   I. The dignity of the marriage covenant..1178
   II. The great Sacrament of Matrimony...1184
   III. Matrimony as a sign of divine love..1190

3. For Religious Profession: Religious life as service of God through the imitation of Christ 1210

4. For the Dedication of a Church:
   I. The mystery of God's Temple 1222
   II. The mystery of the Temple of God, which is the Church 1225

5. For the Dedication of an Altar: Christ himself is the altar 1230

E. In Various Celebrations

1. The Chrism Mass: The Priesthood of Christ and the ministry of Priests....................293

2. Eucharistic Prayer for use in Masses for Various Needs:
   I. The Church on the Path of Unity..774
   II. God Guides His Church along the Way of Salvation 780
   III. Jesus, the Way to the Father..786
   IV. Jesus, Who Went About Doing Good..792

3. In the Eucharistic Prayers for Reconciliation:
   I. Reconciliation with the Father in Christ 758
   II. The Gift of Mutual Reconciliation 766

4. For the Anniversary of the Dedication of a Church: The mystery of the Temple of God, which is the Church 1033

5. For the Unity of Christians: The unity of the Body of Christ, which is the Church 1274

6. For the Dead:
   I. The hope of resurrection in Christ 622
   II. Christ died so that we might live 624
   III. Christ, the salvation and the life 626
   IV. From earthly life to heavenly glory 628
   V. Our resurrection through the victory of Christ 630

7. Independence Day I [USA] 894
   Independence Day II [USA] 896

8. Thanksgiving Day [USA] 1005

GENERAL INDEX

Decree of the Sacred Congregation for Divine Worship 5
Concerning the Second Typical Edition 6
Concerning the Third Typical Edition 7
Decree of *Recognitio* [USA] 8
Decree of Publication [USA] 9
Apostolic Constitution of Pope Paul VI, *Missale Romanum* 11
General Instruction of the Roman Missal 17
Norms for the Distribution and Reception of Holy Communion
    Under Both Kinds in the Dioceses of the United States of America [USA] 89
Motu Proprio of Pope Paul VI, *Paschale Mysterium* 107
Universal Norms on the Liturgical Year and the Calendar 110
General Roman Calendar 121

PROPER OF TIME

Advent
    First Sunday and Week of Advent 139
    Second Sunday and Week of Advent 146
    Third Sunday and Week of Advent 153
    Fourth Sunday of Advent 159
    Weekdays from December 17 to 24 160

Christmas Time
    The Nativity of the Lord 169
    The Holy Family of Jesus, Mary and Joseph 176
    Days within the Octave of the Nativity of the Lord 176
    Solemnity of Mary, the Holy Mother of God 182
    Second Sunday after the Nativity 184
    The Epiphany of the Lord 185
    Weekdays of Christmas Time 190
    The Baptism of the Lord 202

Lent
    Ash Wednesday 209
    First Sunday and Week of Lent 216
    Second Sunday and Week of Lent 226
    Third Sunday and Week of Lent 236
    Fourth Sunday and Week of Lent 246
    Fifth Sunday and Week of Lent 256

Holy Week
    Palm Sunday of the Passion of the Lord 273
    Weekdays 287
    Thursday at the Chrism Mass 290

The Sacred Paschal Triduum
- Thursday of the Lord's Supper, At the Evening Mass 299
- Friday of the Passion of the Lord 314
- Holy Saturday 339
- Easter Sunday of the Resurrection of the Lord
  - The Easter Vigil in the Holy Night 343
  - At the Mass during the Day 387

Easter Time
- Days within the Octave of Easter 389
- Second Sunday and Week of Easter 395
- Third Sunday and Week of Easter 403
- Fourth Sunday and Week of Easter 411
- Fifth Sunday and Week of Easter 418
- Sixth Sunday and Week of Easter 425
- The Ascension of the Lord 429
- Seventh Sunday and Week of Easter 438
- Pentecost Sunday 445

Ordinary Time 459

Solemnities of the Lord during Ordinary Time
- The Most Holy Trinity 495
- The Most Holy Body and Blood of Christ 499
- The Most Sacred Heart of Jesus 502
- Our Lord Jesus Christ, King of the Universe 505

ORDER OF MASS

Order of Mass 511

Prefaces 534

Eucharistic Prayers
- Eucharistic Prayer I (Roman Canon) 635
- Eucharistic Prayer II 645
- Eucharistic Prayer III 650
- Eucharistic Prayer IV 656

The Communion Rite 663

The Concluding Rites 671

Blessings at the End of Mass and Prayers Over the People
- Solemn Blessings 674
- Prayers Over the People 685

Eucharistic Prayers with Musical Notation
- Eucharistic Prayer I 693
- Eucharistic Prayer II 721
- Eucharistic Prayer III 728

GENERAL INDEX

Eucharistic Prayer IV 736
Order of Mass, with the Participation of a Single Minister 745
Appendix to the Order of Mass
    Eucharistic Prayer for Reconciliation I 757
    Eucharistic Prayer for Reconciliation II 765
    Eucharistic Prayer for use in Masses for Various Needs
        Form I 774
        Form II 780
        Form III 786
        Form IV 792

PROPER OF SAINTS

January 801
February 815
March 830
April 845
May 854
June 870
July 890
August 912
September 941
October 963
November 979
December 1007

COMMONS

Common of the Dedication of a Church
    On the Anniversary of the Dedication 1032
      I. In the Church that was Dedicated 1032
     II. Outside the Church that was Dedicated 1036
Common of the Blessed Virgin Mary
      I. In Ordinary Time 1039
     II. In Advent 1048
   III. In Christmas Time 1049
   IV. In Easter Time 1051
Common of Martyrs
    I. Outside Easter Time
        A. For Several Martyrs 1052
        B. For One Martyr 1059
  II. During Easter Time
        A. For Several Martyrs 1062
        B. For One Martyr 1065

 III. For Missionary Martyrs
  A. For Several Missionary Martyrs 1066
  B. For One Missionary Martyr 1067
 IV. For a Virgin Martyr 1068
 V. For a Holy Woman Martyr 1069

Common of Pastors
 I. For a Pope or for a Bishop 1071
 II. For a Bishop 1074
 III. For Pastors
  A. For Several Pastors 1077
  B. For One Pastor 1078
 IV. For Founders of Churches
  A. For One Founder 1081
  B. For Several Founders 1082
 V. For Missionaries 1084

Common of Doctors of the Church 1088

Common of Virgins
 I. For Several Virgins 1091
 II. For One Virgin 1092

Common Of Holy Men and Women
 I. For All Categories of Saints
  A. For Several Saints 1097
  B. For One Saint 1101
 II. For Monks and Religious
  A. For an Abbot 1103
  B. For a Monk 1105
  C. For a Nun 1106
  D. For Religious 1107
 III. For Those Who Practiced Works of Mercy 1110
 IV. For Educators 1111
 V. For Holy Women 1113

RITUAL MASSES

I. For the Conferral of the Sacraments of Christian Initiation
  1. For the Election or Enrollment of Names 1119
  2. For the Celebration of the Scrutinies 1121
   For the First Scrutiny 1121
   For the Second Scrutiny 1124
   For the Third Scrutiny 1125
  3. For the Conferral of Baptism 1126
  4. For the Conferral of Confirmation 1130
II. For the Conferral of the Anointing of the Sick 1135
III. For the Administering of Viaticum 1136

IV.	For the Conferral of Holy Orders	
	1. For the Ordination of a Bishop	
	For the Ordination of One Bishop	1138
	For the Ordination of Several Bishops	1146
	2. For the Ordination of Priests	
	For the Ordination of Several Priests	1152
	For the Ordination of One Priest	1157
	3. For the Ordination of Deacons	
	For the Ordination of Several Deacons	1161
	For the Ordination of One Deacon	1168
	4. For the Ordination of Deacons and Priests in the Same Celebration	1172
V.	For the Celebration of Marriage	1177
VI.	For the Blessing of an Abbot or an Abbess	
	1. For the Blessing of an Abbot	1195
	2. For the Blessing of an Abbess	1199
VII.	For the Consecration of Virgins	1203
VIII.	For Religious Profession	
	1. For First Religious Profession	1207
	2. For Perpetual Profession	1209
	3. For the Renewal of Vows	1219
IX.	For the Institution of Lectors and Acolytes	1220
X.	For the Dedication of a Church and an Altar	
	1. For the Dedication of a Church	1221
	2. For the Dedication of an Altar	1228

MASSES AND PRAYERS
FOR VARIOUS NEEDS AND OCCASIONS

I. For Holy Church

1. For the Church 1237
2. For the Pope 1243
3. For the Bishop 1245
4. For the Election of a Pope or a Bishop 1247
5. For a Council or a Synod 1248
6. For Priests 1250
7. For the Priest Himself 1252
    On the Anniversary of His Ordination 1254
8. For Ministers of the Church 1255
9. For Vocations to Holy Orders 1256
10. For the Laity 1257
11. On the Anniversaries of Marriage
    On Any Anniversary 1259

  On the Twenty-Fifth Anniversary..1260
  On the Fiftieth Anniversary..1261
 12. For the Family..1262
 13. For Religious..1263
  On the Twenty-Fifth or Fiftieth Anniversary of Religious Profession.....1264
 14. For Vocations to Religious Life...1266
 15. For Promoting Harmony..1268
 16. For Reconciliation..1270
 17. For the Unity of Christians 1272
 18. For the Evangelization of Peoples..1279
 19. For Persecuted Christians 1282
 20. For a Spiritual or Pastoral Gathering 1284

II. For Civil Needs

 21. For the Nation or State..1286
 22. For Those in Public Office 1286
 23. For a Governing Assembly 1287
 24. For the Head of State or Ruler..1287
 25. At the Beginning of the Civil Year 1288
 26. For the Sanctification of Human Labor...1289
 27. At Seedtime...1292
 28. After the Harvest...1294
 29. For the Progress of Peoples 1295
 30. For the Preservation of Peace and Justice 1297
 31. In Time of War or Civil Disturbance...1299
 32. For Refugees and Exiles 1300
 33. In Time of Famine or for Those Suffering Hunger 1302
 34. In Time of Earthquake 1304
 35. For Rain..1304
 36. For Fine Weather 1305
 37. For an End to Storms 1305

III. For Various Intentions

 38. For the Forgiveness of Sins 1306
 39. For Chastity..1308
 40. For Charity...1309
 41. For Relatives and Friends...1310
 42. For Our Oppressors 1311
 43. For Those Held in Captivity 1312
 44. For Those in Prison 1313
 45. For the Sick..1313
 46. For the Dying 1315
 47. For the Grace of a Happy Death 1317
 48. In Any Need...1318
 48/1. For Giving Thanks to God for the Gift of Human Life [USA].................1321
 49. For Giving Thanks to God 1323

VOTIVE MASSES

1. The Most Holy Trinity 1327
2. The Mercy of God 1329
3. Our Lord Jesus Christ, the Eternal High Priest 1330
4. The Mystery of the Holy Cross 1331
5. The Most Holy Eucharist 1333
6. The Most Holy Name of Jesus 1334
7. The Most Precious Blood of Our Lord Jesus Christ 1335
8. The Most Sacred Heart of Jesus 1336
9. The Holy Spirit 1338
10. The Blessed Virgin Mary
    Our Lady, Mother of the Church 1345
    The Most Holy Name of Mary 1349
    Our Lady, Queen of Apostles 1351
11. The Holy Angels 1352
12. Saint John the Baptist 1354
13. Saint Joseph 1356
14. All the Holy Apostles 1359
15. Saints Peter and Paul, Apostles 1360
16. Saint Peter, Apostle 1362
17. Saint Paul, Apostle 1363
18. One Holy Apostle 1365
19. All Saints 1366

MASSES FOR THE DEAD

I. For the Funeral

    Outside Easter Time 1371
    During Easter Time 1374
    For the Funeral of a Baptized Child 1377
    For the Funeral of a Child Who Died before Baptism 1379

II. On the Anniversary

    Outside Easter Time 1381
    During Easter Time 1383
    Other Prayers on the Anniversary 1384

III. Various Commemorations

    For One Deceased Person 1386
    For Several Deceased Persons or for All the Dead 1392

IV. Various Prayers for the Dead

    1. For a Pope 1401

2. For a Bishop 1404
3. For a Priest 1406
4. For a Deacon 1408
5. For a Religious 1409
6. For One Who Worked in the Service of the Gospel 1409
7. For a Young Person 1409
8. For One Who Suffered a Long Illness 1410
9. For One Who Died Suddenly 1410
10. For a Married Couple 1411
11. For the Priest's Parents 1412
12. For Relatives, Friends, and Benefactors 1413

APPENDICES

I. Various Chants for the Order of Mass 1416

II. Rite for the Blessing and Sprinkling of Water 1453

III. Rite of Deputing a Minister to Distribute Holy Communion on a Single Occasion 1457

IV. Rite of Blessing a Chalice and a Paten Within Mass 1458

V. Examples of Formularies for the Universal Prayer 1461

VI. Sample invocations for the penitential act [USA] 1474

Preparation for Mass 1481

Thanksgiving After Mass 1485

INDEXES

Alphabetical Index of Celebrations 1495
Index of Prefaces 1503
General Index 1507

Cover illustration © 2011, United States Conference of Catholic Bishops.

p. 1, *The Good Shepherd*, detail from the Chapel of the Good Shepherd. Bancel La Farge and Ravenna Mosaic Company, 1926. Photograph courtesy of the Basilica of the National Shrine of the Immaculate Conception, Washington, DC, 2011. Photographer: Geraldine M. Rohling.

p. 138, "The Prophet Isaiah," detail from *The Birth of Jesus*, Chapel of the Joyful Mysteries of the Rosary. Joseph L. Young and Ravenna Mosaic Company, 1967. Photograph courtesy of the Basilica of the National Shrine of the Immaculate Conception, Washington, DC, 2011. Photographer: Geraldine M. Rohling.

p. 170, "The Incarnation" scene, *The Incarnation*. Knights of Columbus dome mosaic. Leandro Miguel Velasco and Travisanutto Mosaics, Italy, 2007. Photograph courtesy of the Basilica of the National Shrine of the Immaculate Conception, Washington, DC, 2007. Photographer: Geraldine M. Rohling.

p. 186, "Adoration of the Magi," detail from *The Birth of Jesus*. Chapel of the Joyful Mysteries of the Rosary. Joseph L. Young and Ravenna Mosaic Company, 1967. Photograph courtesy of the Basilica of the National Shrine of the Immaculate Conception, Washington, DC, 2011. Photographer: Geraldine M. Rohling.

p. 272, "Jesus' Entry into Jerusalem." Detail of stained glass window, South Bay 9, Cathedral of Mary our Queen, Baltimore, Maryland © 2009 Terry Ann Modica of Catholic Digital Resources, *catholicdr.com*. All rights reserved.

p. 302, *The Lord's Supper*, Chapel of the Blessed Sacrament. Millard Owen Sheets and Ravenna Mosaic Company, St. Louis, 1970. Photograph Courtesy of the Basilica of the National Shrine of the Immaculate Conception, Washington, DC, 2007. Photographer: Geraldine M. Rohling.

p. 342, *The Resurrection*. Chapel of the Glorious Mysteries of the Rosary. John de Rosen and Peter Recker, Germany, 1960. Photograph courtesy of the Basilica of the National Shrine of the Immaculate Conception, Washington, DC, 2011. Photographer: Geraldine M. Rohling.

p. 430, *The Ascension*. Detail from the Upper Sacristy fresco by Leandro Miguel Velasco, 1967. © Photograph courtesy of the Basilica of the National Shrine of the Immaculate Conception, Washington, DC, 2009. Photographer: Geraldine M. Rohling.

p. 446, *The Descent of the Holy Spirit*. Baldachin altar, interior dome, bronze and mosaic by George Snowden, 1960. Photograph courtesy of the Basilica of the National Shrine of the Immaculate Conception, Washington, DC, 2005. Photographer: Geraldine M. Rohling.

p. 512, *Fractio panis*. Mary Chase Stratton, 1927. Based on the fresco of the 2nd century in the Greek Chapel in the catacomb of Priscilla. Photograph courtesy of the Basilica of the National Shrine of the Immaculate Conception, Washington, DC, 2011. Photographer: Geraldine M. Rohling.

p. 634, "The Crucifixion" detail from the *Blessed Sacrament* mosaic by Millard Owen Sheets and the Ravenna Mosaic Company, 1970. Photograph courtesy of the Basilica of the National Shrine of the Immaculate Conception, Washington, DC, 2011. Photographer: Geraldine M. Rohling.

p. 644, "Jesus" detail from *The Ascension of Jesus*, Chapel of the Glorious Mysteries of the Rosary. John de Rosen and Peter Recker, Germany, 1960. Photograph courtesy of the Basilica of the National Shrine of the Immaculate Conception, Washington, DC, 2006. Photographer: Geraldine M. Rohling.

p. 834, *St. Joseph, the Defender of the Faith and the Patron of Workers*. Austin J. Purves, Jr. and Venetian Art Mosaics Studios, 1967. Photograph courtesy of the Basilica of the National Shrine of the Immaculate Conception, Washington, DC, 2007. Photographer: Robert Isacson.

p. 840, *The Annunciation*. Chapel of the Joyful Mysteries of the Rosary. Joseph L. Young and Ravenna Mosaic Company, 1967. Photograph courtesy of the Basilica of the National Shrine of the Immaculate Conception, Washington, DC, 2011. Photographer: Geraldine M. Rohling.

p. 884, *Petrus, Paulus*. Mary Chase Stratton, 1927. Photograph courtesy of the Basilica of the National Shrine of the Immaculate Conception, Washington, DC, 2010. Photographer: Geraldine M. Rohling.

p. 916, *The Transfiguration*. Luminous Mysteries, Chapel of Our Lady of Pompeii. Leandro Miguel Velasco and Travisanutto Mosaics, Italy, 2008. Photograph courtesy of the Basilica of the National Shrine of the Immaculate Conception, Washington, DC, 2011. Photographer: Geraldine M. Rohling.

p. 926, *The Assumption*. Chapel of the Glorious Mysteries of the Rosary. John de Rosen and Peter Recker, Germany, 1960. Photograph courtesy of the Basilica of the National Shrine of the Immaculate Conception, Washington, DC, 2011. Photographer: Geraldine M. Rohling.

p. 958, "Gabriel the Archangel" detail from "The Annunciation" scene, *The Incarnation*. Knights of Columbus dome mosaic. Leandro Miguel Velasco and Travisanutto Mosaics, Italy, 2007. Photograph courtesy of the Basilica of the National Shrine of the Immaculate Conception, Washington, DC, 2011. Photographer: Geraldine M. Rohling.

p. 978, "All Saints" detail from *The Last Judgment*. Mary Reardon and Ravenna Mosaic Company, 1973. Photograph courtesy of the Basilica of the National Shrine of the Immaculate Conception, Washington, DC, 2011. Photographer: Geraldine M. Rohling.

p. 1012, *The Immaculate Conception*. Mosaic reproduction of *La Purissma Bionda* by Bartolomé Estaban Murillo manufactured by the Reverenda Fabbrica di San Pietro di Vaticano (RFSPV), 1930. Photograph courtesy of the Basilica of the National Shrine of the Immaculate Conception, Washington, DC, 2009.

p. 1018, *Our Lady of Guadalupe*. Mary Reardon and Ravenna Mosaic Company, 1967. Photograph courtesy of the Basilica of the National Shrine of the Immaculate Conception, Washington, DC, 2004. Photographer: John Whitman.

p. 1368, "The Resurrection" scene detail, The Redemption. Leandro Miguel Velasco and Travisanutto Mosaics, Italy, 2006. Photograph courtesy of the Basilica of the National Shrine of the Immaculate Conception, Washington, DC, 2011. Photographer: Geraldine M. Rohling.